TRAVELGUIDES.COM

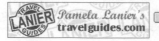

http://www.travelguides.com has been awarded the Yahoo! Gold Star and named **Best Bed and Breakfast Site** on the Internet.

Come visit us and get B&B tour itineries, thousands of blue-ribbon inn recipes and much more. *Travelguides* offers you the best in information on worldwide lodgings, golf courses, weather and reservations, all in one beautiful and fun-to-use site!

Wishing you
Sweet Dreams,

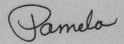

THE COMPLETE GUIDE TO

BED &

BREAKFASTS,

INNS & GUESTHOUSES

IN THE UNITED STATES, CANADA, & WORLDWIDE

PAMELA LANIER

YAHOO! **Internet Life's** **BEST** BED
Gold Star Sites: **& BREAKFAST**
GUIDE

PAMELA LANIER'S TRAVEL GUIDES ONLINE

❝Cozy and charming, a bed-and-breakfast inn can be a refreshing change of pace from staying in a hotel. Whatever your destination, Pamela Lanier's site covers small inns around the world with a personal touch. Besides searching by geography, you can specify whether you're looking for a family place or a romantic getaway, select such amenities as histoic locale or vegetarian food, and even limit your choice to B&Bs that you can book online. Most inn pages feature a photo and links to a map. Some even tell you which room is the best in the house, so you know what to ask for.❞

Visit our website: www.travelguides.com
Email: lanier@travelguides.com

A *Lanier* Guide

▲

Other Books By Pamela Lanier

All-Suite Hotel Guide
Elegant Small Hotels—U.S.A.
Elegant Hotels—Pacific Rim
Condo Vacations: The Complete Guide
Family Travel Guide Online
Golf Resorts: The Complete Guide
Golf Resorts International
22 Days in Alaska
Cinnamon Mornings
Bed & Breakfast Cookbook
Sweets & Treats

For further information, please contact:
 The Complete Guide to Bed & Breakfasts,
  Inns and Guesthouses
 Drawer D
 Petaluma, CA 94953

© 2000 by Lanier Publishing Int., Ltd.
All rights reserved. Published 2000

2000 edition. First printing

ISBN 1-58008-116-9

Distributed to the book trade by:
 Ten Speed Press
 P.O. Box 7123
 Berkeley, CA 94707
 website: www.tenspeed.com   tel. 1-800-841-2665

Cover by V. Ichioka, Laura Lamar

Design & Production by J.C. Wright

Typeset by John Richards

Printed in Canada on recycled paper

In a nationwide survey of innkeepers conducted by *Innsider Magazine*

Dear fellow travelers,

Those of you who have enjoyed my travel guides over the past years, share a common passion – a passion for the charms of the unique inns and bed and breakfasts of North America. As you know, these finds often provide a respite from the rigors of our everyday life, and put us back in touch with both nature and ourselves by providing a relaxing, comforting environment.

In my ongoing quest to make it as easy as possible to find and choose these getaways, I turned to the Internet for a partner that shared our collective passions and understood your needs.

inntopia.com is just such a company. Founded by web experts with innkeeping roots, inntopia.com is dedicated to making finding the best inns and bed and breakfasts as easy and effortless as possible. Through their Web site, travelers can find, research and book rooms for many of the locations in this book. You will be able to see pictures, read descriptions, and link to the web site of many of the inns identified in this guide. You can even post your own reviews on some of these fantastic vacation spots.

I encourage you to visit the site at inntopia.com and discover why I am so excited about this service.

And, as always, happy trails.

Pamela

Contents

2000 INN OF THE YEAR
ALBERGO ALLEGRIA
WINDHAM, NEW YORK

Albergo Allegria means "Inn of Happiness" in Italian. It's an apt name for a Bed & Breakfast that has been so lovingly restored and carefully maintained, and whose guests are always delighted with their stay. Innkeepers Lenore & Vito Radelich completed work on this Victorian haven in 1986. When their daughter and son-in-law, Marianna and Leslie Leman, joined them in 1993, Albergo Allegria became a two-generation operation.

Vito and Marianna are the inn chefs, and serve enticing breakfast entrees to their guests every morning. 16 guestrooms and 5 suites comprise the accommodations. Guestrooms feature antiques and period wallpapers together with modern amenities. Carriage House suites are located behind the main inn. 15-foot ceilings, skylights, king beds, double whirlpool tubs, marble-clad gas fireplaces, and private outdoor space create idyllic getaways for discerning travelers. Vito, Lenore, Marianna and Leslie have earned their kudos. We offer many congratulations to them as well as our warm wishes for continued success.

See their listing on page 346.

INNS OF THE YEAR	HONOR ROLL
1985 Joshua Grindle Inn, Mendocino, CA	1993 The Whalewalk Inn, Eastham, Cape Cod, MA
1986 Carter House, Eureka, CA	1994 The Captain Freeman Inn, Brewster, Cape Cod, MA
1987 Governor's Inn, Ludlow, VT	
1988 Seacrest Manor, Rockport, MA	1995 The Williamsburg Sampler B&B, Williamsburg, VA
1989 Wedgwood Inn, New Hope, PA	
1990 The Veranda, Senoia, GA	1996 Chicago Pike Inn B&B, Coldwater, MI
1991 Kedron Valley Inn, South Woodstock, VT	
	1997 The Legacy of Williamsburg B&B, Williamsburg, VA
1992 The Lamplight Inn, Lake Luzerne, NY	1998 Calico Inn, Sevierville, TN
	1999 Black Friar Inn, Bar Harbor, ME

Introduction

There was a time, and it wasn't so long ago, when bed and breakfast inns were a rarity in the United States. Travelers made do at a hotel or motel; there was no alternative. The few bed and breakfast inns were scattered across the rural areas of New England and California. They were little known to most travelers; often their only advertisement was by word of mouth.

But in a few short years that has changed, and changed in a way that could only be called dramatic. There has been an explosion in the number of bed and breakfast inns. Today, inns can be found in every state, and often in cities; they have become true alternatives to a chain motel room or the city hotel with its hundreds of cubicles.

This sudden increase in bed and breakfast inns started less than two decades ago when Americans, faced with higher costs for foreign travel, began to explore the backroads and hidden communities of their own country.

Other factors have influenced the growth and popularity of bed and breakfast inns. Among them, the desire to get away from the daily routine and sameness of city life; the desire to be pampered for a few days; and also the desire to stay in a place with time to make new friends among the other guests.

The restored older homes that have become bed and breakfast inns answer those desires. The setting most often is rural; the innkeepers provide the service—not a staff with name tags—and the parlor is a gathering place for the handful of guests. They are a home away from home.

The proliferation of these inns as an alternative lodging has created some confusion. It's been difficult to find—in one place—up-to-date and thorough information about the great variety of inns.

Some books published in the past five or six years have tried to provide this information. But those books focused on one region of the country or named too few inns. While some earlier books gave detailed descriptions of the inns, few bothered to provide information about the type of breakfast served, whether there are rooms for non-smokers, and such things as whether the inn offered free use of bicycles or whether it had a hot tub.

An effort to collect as much information about as many inns as possible in one book has been overdue. Now that has been remedied. You hold a copy of the result in your hands.

Richard Paoli,
Travel Editor
San Francisco Examiner

How to Use This Guide

Organization

This book is organized alphabetically by state and, within a state, alphabetically by city or town. The inns appear first. More inns are listed after the featured inns. At the end of the listings you will find the World Wide Listings by country and within the country by the city. At the back of the guide are listings of the reservation service organizations serving each state and inns with special characteristics.

Three Types of Accommodations

Inn: Webster's defines an inn as a "house built for the lodging and entertainment of travelers." All the inns in this book fulfill this description. Many also provide meals, at least breakfast, although a few do not. Most of these inns have under 30 guest rooms.

Bed and Breakfast: Can be anything from a home with three or more rooms to, more typically, a large house or mansion with eight or nine guest accommodations where breakfast is served in the morning.

Guest House: Private homes welcoming travelers, some of which may be contacted directly but most of which are reserved through a reservation service organization. A comprehensive list of RSOs appears toward the back of this guide.

Breakfasts

We define a **full breakfast** as one being along English lines, including eggs and/or meat as well as the usual breads, toast, juice and coffee.

Continental plus is a breakfast of coffee, juice, and choice of several breads and pastry and possibly more.

Continental means coffee, juice, bread or pastry

If there is a charge for breakfast, then we note it as (fee).

Meals

Bear in mind that inns that do not serve meals are usually located near a variety of restaurants.

Can We Get a Drink?

Those inns without a license will generally chill your bottles and provide you with set-ups upon request.

Prices

Price range at the top of the second column is for double room, double occupancy in U.S. dollars.

Appearing to the right of the price is a code indicating the type of food services available:

B&B: Breakfast included in quoted rate

EP (European Plan): No meals

MAP (Modified American Plan): Includes breakfast and dinner

AP (American Plan): Includes all three meals

Inns not in the U.S. and Canada are listed by their country's currency. Examples: Italian$ = Italian currency (lira), French$ = French currency (francs), etc.

All prices are subject to change. Please be sure to confirm rates and services when you make your reservations.

Credit Cards and Checks

If an establishment accepts credit cards, it will be listed as VISA, MC, AmEx, or Most CC. Most inns will accept your personal check with proper identification, but be sure to confirm when you book.

Ratings

One of the beauties of bed & breakfast travel is the individual nature of each inn. And innkeepers thrive on their independence! Some inns are members of their local, state or national inn association (most of which have membership requirements), and/or are members of or are rated by AAA, Mobil and others. Each of these rating systems relies upon different inspection protocol, membership and evaluative criteria. We use *Rated* in the listings to designate inns which have informed us that they have been rated by or are affiliated with any of these groups. If ratings are important to you, we suggest that you call and inquire of the specific inn for details. We continue to find, however, that some very good inns remain unrated, simply because of their size or idiosyncratic nature.

Reservations

Reservations are essential at most inns, particularly during busy seasons, and are appreciated at other times. Be sure to reserve, even if only a few hours in advance, to avoid disappointment. When you book, feel free to discuss your requirements and confirm prices, services and other details. We have found innkeepers to be delightfully helpful.

Most inns will hold your reservation until 6 p.m. If you plan to arrive later, please phone ahead to let them know.

A deposit or advance payment is required at some inns.

Children, Pets and Smoking

Children, pets, smoking and physical handicaps present special considerations for many inns. Whether or not they can be accommodated is generally noted as follows:

	Yes	Limited	No
Children	C-yes	C-ltd	C-no
Pets	P-yes	P-ltd	P-no
Smoking	S-yes	S-ltd	S-no
Handicapped	H-yes	H-ltd	H-no

However, many inns with limited facilities for children will often have one or two rooms set aside for families. Be sure to inquire when you book your room.

Accessibility for the Handicapped

Because many inns are housed in old buildings, access for handicapped persons in many cases is limited. Where this information is available, we have noted it as above. Be sure to confirm your exact requirements when you book.

Big Cities

In many big cities there are very few small, intimate accommodations. We have searched out as many as possible. We strongly advise you to investigate the guest house alternative, which can provide you with anything from a penthouse in New York to your own quiet quarters with a private entrance in the suburbs. See our RSO listings at the back of the book.

Farms

Many B&Bs are located in a rural environment, some on working farms. We have provided a partial list of farm vacation experiences. What a restorative for the city-weary. They can make a great family vacation—just be sure to keep a close eye on the kids around farm equipment.

Bathrooms

Though shared baths are the norm in Europe, this is sometimes a touchy subject in the U.S.A. We list the number of private baths available directly next to the number of rooms. Bear in mind that those inns with shared baths generally have more than one.

Manners

Please keep in mind when you go to an inn that innkeeping is a very hard job. It is amazing that innkeepers manage to maintain such a thoroughly cheerful and delightful presence despite long hours. Do feel free to ask your innkeepers for help or suggestions, but please don't expect them to be your personal servant. You may have to carry your own bags.

When in accommodations with shared baths, be sure to straighten the bathroom as a courtesy to your fellow guests. If you come in late, please do so on tiptoe, mindful of the other patrons visiting the inn for a little R&R.

Sample Bed & Breakfast Listing

Price and included meals
Numbers of rooms and private baths
Credit cards accepted
Name of inn   Travel agent commission •
Street address and zip code   Limitations:
Phone number   Children (C), Pets (P)
Name of innkeeper   Smoking (S), Handicapped Access (H)
Dates of operation   Foreign languages spoken

Name of city or town   Extra charge for breakfast

ANYPLACE ————————————————————————————————————
Any Bed & Breakfast   75-95-B&B   Full breakfast (fee)
Any Street, ZIP code   8 rooms, 6 pb   Lunch, dinner
555-555-5555   Visa, MC •   sitting room
Tom & Jane Innkeeper   C-yes/S-ltd/P-no/H-ltd library, bicycles
All year   French, Spanish   antiques

Large Victorian country house in historic village. Hiking, swimming and golf nearby. Old-fashioned comfort with modern conveniences.

Description given by the innkeeper about the   Meals and drinks
original characteristics of his establishment   Amenities

Ejemplo de una entrada para las posadas con cama & desayuno

Ciudad ó pueblo nombre

Nombre de la posada
Dirección
Teléfono
Fechas de temporada

Precio del alojamiento
Qué comidas van incluídas
Número de cuartos y número de cuartos
   con baño privado
Tarjetas de crédito aceptables
Agente de viaje comisión •
Limitaciones:
   niños (C); animales domésticos (P);
   prohibido fumar (S); entradas para
   minusválidos (H)
Se habla idiomas extranjeros

Comidas y bebidas

Entretenimientos

ANYPLACE ──
Any Bed & Breakfast   75-95-B&B   Full breakfast (fee)
Any Street, ZIP code   8 rooms, 6 pb   Lunch, dinner
555-555-5555   Visa, MC •   sitting room
Tom & Jane Innkeeper   C-yes /S-ltd/P-no/H-ltd   library, bicycles
All year   French, Spanish   antiques

*Large Victorian country house in historic village. Hiking, swimming and golf
nearby. Old-fashioned comfort with modern conveniences.*

Descripción proporcionada por el dueño de la
posada sobre las características especiales y
originales de establecimiento

Mode d'emploi

Nom de ville

Prix des chambres Repas inclus
   ou non
Nombre de chambres et
   chambres avec salle de bain
   privées
Cartes de crédit acceptées

Repas, boissons possibles

Commodités

ANYPLACE ──
Any Bed & Breakfast   75-95-B&B   Full breakfast (fee)
Any Street, ZIP code   8 rooms, 6 pb   Lunch, dinner
555-555-5555   Visa, MC •   sitting room
Tom & Jane Innkeeper   C-yes /S-ltd/P-no/H-ltd   library, bicycles
All year   French, Spanish   antiques

*Large Victorian country house in historic village. Hiking, swimming and golf
nearby. Old-fashioned comfort with modern conveniences.*

Nom de l'auberge
Addresse
Téléphone
Dates d'ouverture s'il n'y a
   pas de dates ouvert
   toute l'année

Restrictions—
   Enfants (C); Animaux (P);
   Fumeurs (S); Handicappés (H)
On parle les langues étrangères

L'aubergiste décrit ce qui rend
son auberge unique

Erläuterung der Eintragungen der Unterkunfsstätte

Name der Stadt oder
Ortschaft

Name der Unterkunft
Adresse
Telefon-Nummer
Zu welcher Jahreszeit
offen?

Preis für die Unterkunft, und welche
Mahlzeiten im Preis einbegriffen
sind
Reisebüro-Kommission •
Anzahl der Zimmer, und wieviel mit
eigenem
Badezimmer (=pb)
Beschränkungen in Bezug auf
Kinder, Haustiere, Rauchen, oder
für Behinderte geeignet (yes=ja;
ltd=beschränkt; no=nicht
zugelassen)
Man spricht Fremdsprachen

Was für ein Frühstück?
Andere Mahlzeiten und Bars

Was gibt's sonst noch?

ANYPLACE ───────────────────────

Any Bed & Breakfast
Any Street, ZIP code
555-555-5555
Tom & Jane Innkeeper
All year

75-95-B&B
8 rooms, 6 pb
Visa, MC •
C-yes /S-ltd/P-no/H-ltd
French, Spanish

Full breakfast (fee)
Lunch, dinner
sitting room
library, bicycles
antiques

Large Victorian country house in historic village. Hiking, swimming and golf nearby. Old-fashioned comfort with modern conveniences.

Beschreibung des Gastwirts, was an
diesem Gästehaus einmalig oder
besonders bemerkenswert ist

旅館名
住所
電話番号
利用期間。

朝食のタイプ
その他の設備
昼食、夕食、アルコールのサービス

都市又は町の名

ANYPLACE ───────────────────────

Any Bed & Breakfast
Any Street, ZIP code
555-555-5555
Tom & Jane Innkeeper
All year

75-95-B&B
8 rooms, 6 pb
Visa, MC •
C-yes /S-ltd/P-no/H-ltd
French, Spanish

Full breakfast (fee)
Lunch, dinner
sitting room
library, bicycles
antiques

Large Victorian country house in historic village. Hiking, swimming and golf nearby. Old-fashioned comfort with modern conveniences.

Wood Avenue Inn, Florence, AL

Alabama

ANNISTON

Victoria, A Country Inn
PO Box 2213, 36202
256 236 0503 Fax: 256-236-1138
800-260-8781
Fain & Beth Casey   All year

79-319-B&B
60 rooms, 60 pb
Most CC, *Rated*, •
C-yes/S-ltd/P-no/H-yes

Continental breakfast
Restaurant, bar service
Swimming pool, family
friendly facility, gardens,
gazebo

This Southern estate is located midway between Atlanta & Birmingham & offers Victorian amenities from the antiques within the main house to the reproductions in the annex.
E-mail: thevic@mindspring.com *Web site:* thevictoria.com

FLORENCE

Limestone Manor B&B
601 N Wood Ave, 35630
256-765-0314 Fax: 256-765-9920
888-709-6700
Bud & Lois Ellison
All year

72-95-B&B
3 rooms, 3 pb
Visa, MC, AmEx,
Rated, •
C-ltd/S-no/P-no/H-no

Full breakfast
Snacks
Sitting room, library,
bicycles, suites, cable TV,
video library, games

Henry Ford, Thomas Edison & Humphrey Bogart were entertained here. Perfect balance of antiques and modern conveniences. Impeccable service, candlelit gourmet breakfast. Stroll downtown or take a carriage ride.   E-mail: ellisons@hiwaay.net

Wood Avenue Inn
658 N Wood Ave, 35630
256-766-8441
Gene & Alvern Greeley
All year

64-99-B&B
5 rooms, 4 pb
Visa, MC, *Rated*, •
C-ltd/S-ltd/P-no/H-no

Full breakfast
Dinner available, tea, snacks
Sitting room, library,
bicycles, cable TV,
accommodate business
travelers

Elegant Victorian Mansion in the heart of historic Florience, the sister city of Florence Italy. Romantic garden for small weddings.   E-mail: woodaveinn@aol.com
Web site: woodavenueinn.com

GULF SHORES

Original Romar House, The
23500 Perdido Bch Blv, 36561
334-974-1625 Fax: 334-974-1163
800-487-6627
Darrell Finley   All year

79-129-B&B
7 rooms, 6 pb
Visa, MC,
C-ltd/S-ltd/P-no/H-no

Full breakfast
Complimentary wine and
cheese; Bar service, library,
sitting room, hot tubs,
bicycles, private beach

Quiet ambience, comfort, quaint surrounding, friendly service & white sandy beaches for romantic wkends. Restaurants, golf, sailing, fishing available. Now have Parrot House Cottage in addition to rooms.   E-mail: original@gulftel.com
Web site: bbonline.com/al/romarhouse/

LACEY'S SPRING

Apple Jack's Inn B&B
127 Double Creek Rd, 35754
256-778-7734 Fax: 256-778-9375
800-397-1506
Beverly Anne & Harley Fields
Closed 11/25, 12/25

75-85-B&B
3 rooms, 1 pb
Visa, MC, *Rated*, •
C-ltd/S-ltd/P-no

Full breakfast
Afternoon tea, snacks
Sitting room , library, bikes,
swimming pool, cable TV,
business travelers

Located on 27 acre semi-working farm in a country style ranch. Upon arrival enjoy home-baked delicacies. Enjoy the peace and tranquility as you take a stroll. Relax while fishing at the pond, bike ride, play croquet, board games, or read a book.

E-mail: AppleJ123@aol.com *Web site:* bbonline.com/al/applejacks

LEESBURG

Secret B&B Lodge, The
2356 Highway 68 W, 35983
256-523-3825
Diann Cruickshank All year

95-135-B&B
6 rooms, 6 pb
Visa, MC, *Rated*
S-no/P-no/H-no

Full breakfast
Sitting room, Jacuzzis, pool,
fireplace, VCR, private
balconies, views

Scenic mountain top lodge overlooks beautiful Weiss Lake and two states. Spectacular view by day, enchanting view by night. Romantic roof-top pool. Lodge area features fireplace, 22' vaulted ceiling. A treasure found—a memory made.
E-mail: secret@peop.tds.net *Web site:* bbonline.com/al/thesecret/

MENTONE

Mountain Laurel Inn
PO Box 443, 35984
256-634-4673 Fax: 256-634-4673
800-889-4244
Sarah Wilcox   All year

65-130-B&B
5 rooms, 5 pb
Visa, MC, Disc, *Rated*
C-yes/S-ltd/P-no/H-no

Full breakfast
Snacks
Sitting room, library, pool,
suites, can accommodate
business travelers

Country hideaway, seven acres on a bluff overlooking Little River. Hike to DeSoto Falls, relax on the porches. Full breakfast and coffee delivery.

MOBILE

Towle House
1104 Montauk Ave, 36604
334-432-6440 Fax: 334-433-4381
800-938-6953
Felix & Carolyn Vereen
All year

70-85-B&B
3 rooms, 3 pb
Visa, MC, Disc, *Rated*,
•
C-ltd/S-no/P-no/H-no

Full breakfast
Complimentary wine
Sitting room video, spa, sun
deck, library

Lovely home c.1874, located in the heart of Mobile's historic district. Gourmet breakfast and evening cocktails served with Southern hospitality.
E-mail: towlebb@aol.com *Web site:* towle-house.com

MONTGOMERY

Red Bluff Cottage
PO Box 1026, 36101
334-264-0056 Fax: 334-263-3054
888-551-CLAY   All year

75-B&B
4 rooms, 4 pb
Most CC, *Rated*, •
C-yes/S-no/P-no/H-no

Full breakfast
Deep porches, gardens,
gazebo, fenced play yard,
family suite

Two-story raised cottage in historic district. Panoramic view of river plain and state capitol. Family antiques, gazebo and gardens. Within blocks of I-65 & I-85
E-mail: redblufbnb@aol.com *Web site:* bbonline.com/al/redbluff

Alaska

ANCHORAGE ───────────────────────────────

Alaska Wilderness Inn
2910 West 31st Ave, 99517
907-243-3519 Fax: 907-243-1059
800-478-9657
Brian & Karrie Ringgisen
All year

95-179-B&B
8 rooms, 8 pb
Visa, MC, AmEx, •
C-yes/S-ltd/P-ltd/H-ltd

Continental plus breakfast
Snacks
Sitting room, Jacuzzis,
swimming pool, suites,
fireplaces, cable TV

*Formally a Southern style mansion, converted to warm & spacious inn. Over 10,000 sq.ft.
of living space, heated indoor pool, Jacuzzi & sauna-the ideal place to relax & play.*
E-mail: plantatn@alaska.net *Web site:* jakesalaska.com

Alaskan Frontier Gardens
PO Box 241881, 99524
907-345-6556 Fax: 907-562-2923
Rita Gittins
All year

75-195-B&B
3 rooms, 2 pb
Visa, MC, AmEx,
Rated, •
C-yes/S-no/P-no/H-no

Full gourmet breakfast
Sitting room, library, sauna,
laundry, Jacuzzi, fireplace, 6
person hot tub

*Elegant Alaska hillside estate on peaceful scenic acres by Chugach State Park. Spacious
luxury suites. Gourmet breakfast. Museum-like environment, Alaskan hospitality.*
E-mail: afg@alaska.net *Web site:* alaskaone.com/akfrontier

Camai B&B
3838 Westminster Way, 99508
907-333-2219 Fax: 907-337-3959
800-659-8763
Craig & Caroline Valentine
All year

55-95-B&B
2 rooms, 2 pb
Rated, •
C-yes/S-no/P-no/H-yes

Full breakfast
Suites kitchen & laundry
avail., suites have private
phone lines & dataports

*Old-fashioned hospitality in luxuriously decorated contemporary suites. Quiet Anchorage
neighborhood nestled on Chester Creek's green belt where moose are often seen.*
E-mail: camai@alaska.net *Web site:* camaibnb.com

Glacier Bear B&B
4814 Malibu Rd, 99517
907-243-8818 Fax: 907-248-4532
K. & G. Taton, M. Brown
All year

100-B&B
3 rooms, 3 pb
Visa, MC, *Rated*, •
C-ltd/S-ltd/P-no/H-no

Full breakfast
Snacks
Hiking & biking trails,
restaurants nearby, sitting
room, 8 person spa

*First-class accommodations at reasonable rates. Our location: 1.2 mi. from airport, 3 miles
to downtown. Airport pick-up. Bicycles available.   E-mail:* gbear@alaska.net
Web site: touristguide.com/b&b/alaska/glacierbear

K Street B&B
1443 "K" St, 99501
907-279-1443 Fax: 907-279-1443
888-KST-BANB
Kate Warrick   All year

55-105-B&B
3 rooms, 1 pb
•
C-ltd/S-no/P-no/H-no

Full breakfast
Aftn. tea
Sitting room, library,
conference facility, freezer

*This contemporary cedar-sided home features purple heart hardwood floors, tile, and
Alaskan Art. Located in a residential neighborhood with large spruce trees, garden and a
solarium.   E-mail:* kstbb@alaska.net

Lynn's Pine Point B&B
3333 Creekside Dr, 99504
907-333-2244 Fax: 907-333-2244
Lynn & Rich Stouff
All year

95-105-B&B
3 rooms, 3 pb
Visa, MC, *Rated*, •
C-yes/S-no/P-no/H-no

Full or continental plus
breakfast
Complimentary wine, snacks
Sitting room, VCR with
movies, robes, laundry,
family bedroom, 2 decks

*Lovely cedar retreat with all the comforts of home. Queen beds, priv. baths, VCRs. Compli-
mentary cocktails and hors d'oeuvres.   E-mail:* richs@gci.net *Web site:* home.gci.net/~richs

ANCHORAGE

Mahogany Manor
204 E 15th Ave, 99501
907-278-1111 Fax: 907-258-7877
888-777-0346
Mary Ernst, CTC/Russ
Campbell   All year

115-299-B&B
4 rooms, 4 pb
Most CC, *Rated*, •
C-ltd/S-no/P-no/H-ltd
Ltd. German & Spanish

Continental plus breakfast
Aftn tea, evening
snacks/dessert
Sitting room, library,
Jacuzzis, swimming pool,
suites, fireplaces, cable TV

Experience Alaska at Mahogany Manor. Enjoy warm hospitality in a lodge atmosphere in the midst of indoor waterfalls and gardens and crackling fireplaces, located 10 minutes from the airport in downtown Anchorage. E-mail: mahoganymanor@compuserve.com
Web site: mahoganymanor.com

Oscar Gill House, The
1344 W 10th Ave, 99501
907-258-1717 Fax: 907-258-6613
Mark & Susan Lutz
All year

85-95-B&B
3 rooms, 1 pb
Visa, MC, AmEx,
Rated, •
C-yes/S-ltd/P-ltd/H-no
French

Full breakfast
Sitting room, bikes,
accommodates business
travelers, tennis nearby

Superb downtown location with view of Denali and Alaska Range. Delicious breakfasts, relaxed ambiance, wonderful amenities and fantastic value. E-mail: togh@alaskabanb.com
Web site: alaskabandb.com/oscargillindex.html

Swan House South B&B
6840 Crooked Tree Dr, 99516
907-346-3033 Fax: 907-346-3535
800-921-1900
Judy & Jerry Swanson
May-Sept.

129-179-B&B
4 rooms, 4 pb
Most CC, *Rated*, •
C-ltd/S-no/P-ltd/H-no

Full American breakfast
Afternoon tea
Library, bikes, hiking, halibut
& salmon fishing charters,
suites available

Waterfront hideaway with never-ending views! Walking distance from airport, marina, & town. Fisherman's paradise, with King Salmon in sight from our deck.
E-mail: swan1@alaska.net *Web site:* alaskaswanhouse.com

Walkabout Town B&B
1610 "E" St, 99501
907-279-7808 Fax: 907-258-3657
Sandra J. Stimson
April-October

85-B&B
3 rooms
•
C-yes/S-no/P-no/H-no

Full breakfast
Deck, cable TV, freezer, free
laundry, parking, 4 in a room

Downtown convenience with beautiful park and coastal trail. Hearty Alaskan breakfast of sourdough waffles, reindeer sausage. Free bicycles available
E-mail: tstimson@compuserve.com *Web site:* travelguides.com/home/walkabout/

BIG LAKE

Sunset View B&B
PO Box 520373, 99652
907-892-8885 Fax: 907-892-8887
Kathy
All year

125-225-B&B
4 rooms, 4 pb
Visa, MC, •
C-yes/S-no/P-no/H-ltd

Full breakfast
Afternoon tea, snacks
Sitting room, Jacuzzis, suites,
fireplaces, cable TV

New three story b&b with a spectacular view of Mt. McKinley and beautiful Alaskan sunsets. Four exquisitely designed rooms featuring Jacuzzi tubs, satellite TV, phones.
E-mail: surratt@alaska.net *Web site:* alaska.net/~surratt

COOPER LANDING

Gwin's Lodge
14865 Sterling Hwy, 99572
907-595-1266 Fax: 907-595-1681
800-GWINS-44
Robert & Vicki Siter
All year

69-144-EP
11 rooms, 9 pb
Visa, MC, Disc, *Rated*,
•
C-yes/S-yes/P-ltd/H-yes

Restaurant, bar
Fishing tackle shop, parking,
embroidered clothing store

Alaska landmark log roadhouse lodge complex flanked by Kenai and Russian Rivers, the world's most productive sockeye salmon sport fishery. E-mail: gwins@arctic.net
Web site: www2.ool.com/gwins/index.html

DENALI NATIONAL PARK

EarthSong Lodge	105-125-B&B	Continental breakfast
PO Box 89, 99743	10 rooms, 10 pb	Tea
907-683-2863 Fax: 907-683-2868	Visa, MC, *Rated*, •	Sitting room, library, gift
Karin & Jon Nierenberg	C-yes/S-no/P-ltd/H-no	shop, eve. slide, show by
All year		staff

Located just above tree line, facing the Alaska Range. Spectacular vistas, wildlife viewing. 10 honey colored log cabins with priv. baths, hand-crafted decorations. E-mail: earthsong@mail.denali.k12.ak.us Web site: earthsonglodge.com

FAIRBANKS

7 Gables Inn	50-130-B&B	Full gourmet breakfast
PO Box 80488, 99708	11 rooms, 9 pb	Complimentary
907-479-0751 Fax: 907-479-2229	Visa, MC, *Rated*, •	refreshments
Paul & Leicha Welton	C-yes/S-ltd/P-ltd/H-yes	Sitting room, library, Cable
All year	Spanish, German	TV/VCR, phones, bikes,
		Jacuzzis, canoes

Spacious Tudor estate with solarium entrance & waterfall. Each rm. follows a stained-glass icon theme. 4 apartments, conference/reception room. E-mail: gables7@alaska.net Web site: alaska.net/~gables7

Alaska International House	65-95-B&B	Full breakfast
966 N Coppet, 99709	3 rooms, 1 pb	Snacks
907-474-0837 Fax: 907-479-4044	Visa, MC, *Rated*, •	Sitting room, small groups, 7
Tom & Keiko O'Brien	C-ltd/S-no/P-no/H-no	persons, bikes, Jacuzzis,
All year	Japanese	canoes

Great B&B for family or small group. Full kitchen, dining and living room available for guest use. Great Host! E-mail: obrien@ptialaska.net Web site: ptialaska.net/~obrien

All Seasons B&B	75-150-B&B	Full breakfast
763 7th Ave, Box 71131, 99701	8 rooms, 8 pb	Snacks
907-451-6649 Fax: 907-474-8448	Visa, MC, Disc, *Rated*,	Sitting rooms, cable TV,
888-451-6649	•	telephones, modem access
Mary Richards	C-yes/S-no/P-no/H-yes	
All year		

New, elegant, located downtown. Built, designed and decorated with guest comfort in mind. Great breakfasts and good conversation. E-mail: inn@alaska.net Web site: alaska.net/~inn

Crestmont Manor	75-115-B&B	Full breakfast
510 Crestmont Dr, 99709	5 rooms, 5 pb	In room coffee on request
907-456-3831 Fax: 907-456-3841	Visa, MC, AmEx,	Private bath, tv, telephone
888-283-3841	*Rated*, •	
Phil & Connie Horton	C-ltd/S-no/P-no/H-ltd	
All year		

Crestmont Manor serves as the guests second home. Located west of downtown near the university, airport, and fine restaurants. Offers spacious accomodations along with a gourmet breakfast. E-mail: crestmnt@mosquitonet.com Web site: mosquitonet.com/~crestmnt

Fox Creek B&B	68-98-B&B	Full breakfast
2498 Elliott Hwy, 99712	2 rooms, 1 pb	Sitting room, library,
907-457-5494 Fax: 907-457-5464	*Rated*, •	spacious rooms, family
Arna King-Fay & Jeff Fay	C-yes/S-ltd/P-yes/H-no	friendly facility
All year		

Quiet, secluded setting in historic Fox, Alaska. Modern Alaskan style home. Lifelong Alaskan proprietors. Frequent aurora/wildlife sightings. E-mail: foxcreek@ptialaska.net Web site: ptialaska.net/~foxcreek

GLACIER BAY

Gustavus Inn
PO Box 60, 99826
907-697-2254 Fax: 907-697-2255
800-649-5220
David & JoAnn Lesh
5/1-9/15

300-AP
13 rooms
Rated, •
C-yes/S-ltd/P-ltd/H-yes
French, Spanish

Full breakfast
All meals included in rate
Bar, tea, bicycles, van, fishing
poles, winter fax: 913-649-
5220

Original homestead, completely updated 1993. Garden & ocean harvest family-style dining. Glacier Bay boat tours, bicycling, charter & stream fishing, kayaking, whalewatching. E-mail: gustinn@ibm.net

HEALY •

Touch of Wilderness B&B
PO Box 397, 99743
907-683-2459 Fax: 907-683-2455
800-683-2459
Barbara M Claspill
All year

60-140-B&B
8 rooms, 6 pb
Most CC, *Rated*, •
C-yes/S-no/P-no/H-yes

Full or continental breakfast
Snacks, complimentary hot
beverages
Espresso bar, cable, sitting
room, fireplaces, fax, guest
cafe open til 8:30

Remote setting, cozy atmosphere. Enjoy the Alaskan range view both summer and winter from our great rooms. Enjoy a fire on chilly nites. View Northern lights when conditions are right. Phones, movies. Large deck with Jacuzzi hot tub. Small gift shop. E-mail: touchow@usibelli.com *Web site:* touchofwildernessbb.com

HOMER

Brigitte's Bavarian B&B
PO Box 2391, 99603
907-235-6620
Brigitte Suter
All year

105-B&B
3 rooms, 3 pb
Rated, •
C-yes/S-no/P-no/H-ltd
French/German/Swiss

Full hot breakfast
Complimentary wine
Library, bicycles

Brigitte's has an alpine flair—lovely gardens for walks with lots of flowers, short hiking trail starting right at the cottage door. E-mail: bbbb@xyz.net *Web site:* akms.com/brigitte

JUNEAU

1st Class Alaska Lodging
4541 Sawa Circle, 99801
907-789-3772 Fax: 907-789-6722
888-6-JUNEAU
Steve Pearson
All year

89-229-B&B
3 rooms, 3 pb
Most CC, *Rated*, •
C-ltd/S-no/P-ltd/H-ltd

Continental plus breakfast
Afternoon tea, wine, snacks
Sitting room, library, bikes,
Jacuzzis, suites, fireplaces,
cable TV

Renowned as a Best B&B of America and Alaska. Watch wildlife and glacier from your hot tub. Picturesque setting on peaceful pond. E-mail: pearsons.pond@juneau.com *Web site:* juneau.com/pearsons.pond

Mt. Juneau Inn B&B
1801 Old Glacier Hwy, 99801
907-463-5855 Fax: 907-463-5423
Karen & Phil Greeney
All year

85-120-B&B
8 rooms, 2 pb
Visa, MC, AmEx, Disc, •
C-yes/S-no/P-no/H-no
Spanish

Full breakfast
Afternoon tea, snacks
Snacks, guest kitchen,
library, bikes, robes,
slippers, hair dryers

Here you'll find comfort & hospitality that makes you feel right at home. From the warm, familiar feel of a plush robe, to the refreshments served in our parlor with native art, books & videos, you're assured that your stay will be relaxed & memorable. E-mail: mtjuneauinn@alaska.com *Web site:* mtjuneauinn.com

KENAI

Eldridge Haven B&B
2679 Bowpicker Ln, 99611
907-283-7152 Fax: 907-283-7152
Marta & Barry Eldridge
All year

80-B&B
2 rooms, 1 pb
Visa, MC, •
C-yes/S-ltd/P-ltd/H-no
Spanish

Full breakfast
Afternoon tea
Sitting room, library,
fireplaces, acommodate
business travelers

Hospitality at its best since 1988! Peaceful, friendly Christian home. Quiet wooded setting. Walk to beach. Extensive Alaskan library. Gourmet breakfasts. Baked pancakes, stuffed scones, gingered bananas, fritatas. Children welcome. E-mail: lridgebb@ptialaska.net

KETCHIKAN

Corner B&B
PO Box 5023, 99901
907-225-2655 Fax: 907-247-2655
Carolyn/Win Wilsie   All year

85-130-B&B
1 rooms, 1 pb
Rated, •
C-ltd/S-ltd/P-no/H-ltd

Continental breakfast
Sitting room, cable TV,
conference facilities

Clean, comfortable and private. Ground level and off street parking. One block from city bus. Fully equipped kitchen, cable TV/VCR. Convenient location.   E-mail: cjwilsie@ptialaska.net Web site: innsite.com/inns/A003828.html

D&W's "Almost Home" B&B
412 D-1 Loop Rd, 99901
907-225-3273 Fax: 907-247-5337
800-987-5337
Wanda & Darrell Vandergriff
All year

100-B&B
2 rooms, 2 pb
Visa, MC, AmEx,
Rated, •
C-yes/S-ltd/P-ltd/H-ltd

Continental breakfast
Outfitted kitchen, BBQ
Sitting room, suites, cable TV,
deck, family friendly facility,
conference

Privacy and comfort in your own outfitted two-bedroom apartment. Full kitchen stocked with all you need including staple foods and breakfast makings.   E-mail: krs@ktn.net Web site: ketchikan-lodging.com/bb15.html

KODIAK

Kodiak B&B
308 Cope St, 99615
907-486-5367 Fax: 907-486-6567
Mary Monroe
All year

74-88-B&B
2 rooms
Visa, MC, •
C-yes/S-no/P-yes/H-no

Full or continental plus
breakfast
Sitting room, library, can
accommodate business
travelers

Downtown, spectacular view of bustling boat harbor. Walk to museums, restaurants, bird rookery. Enjoy the magic of this fishing village with Russian heritage, beautiful beaches and cliffs. Abundant bird and animal life. Fresh fish often breakfast option
E-mail: monroe@ptialaska.net Web site: ptialaska.net/~monroe

PALMER

Iditarod House B&B
PO Box 3096, 99645
907-745-4348 Fax: 907-945-4348
Donna & Glenn Massay
All year

50-55-B&B
2 rooms, 2 pb
Visa, MC, *Rated*, •
C-ltd/S-no/P-ltd/H-yes

Continental plus breakfast
Afternoon tea, snacks
Sitting room

Private setting with mountain views only 1 mile from Palmer. B&B features a private entrance and sitting/dining room. Hostess is a retired sled dog musher.
E-mail: iditabed@matnet.com Web site: matnet.com/iditabed

Toller's Timbers Chalets
PO Box 872861, 99687
907-746-1438 Fax: 907-746-7470
800-795-1438
Doreen & Bob Toller
All year

95-125-B&B
5 rooms, 5 pb
Visa, MC, AmEx, •
C-yes/S-no/P-ltd/H-no

Continental breakfast
Sitting room, bikes, suites,
fireplaces, full kitchen,
washer/dryer, decks.

An Alaskan country retreat offering 5 private guesthouses of exceptional quality. Nestled on 14 peaceful acres with mountain views, wildflowers and songbirds.
E-mail: tollers@alaskantour.com Web site: alaskantour.com/homes

SELDOVIA

Seldovia Rowing Club B&B
PO Box 41, 99663
907-234-7614
Susan J. Mumma
All year

85-105-B&B
2 rooms, 2 pb
•
C-yes/S-yes/P-ltd/H-yes
Spanish, French

Full breakfast
Lunch, dinner by request
Bicycles, boating, sea kayaks,
skiffs

Private unit in historic home on Old Sedovia Boardwalk overlooks waterfront, can accommodate a family. Excellent service, cuisine; close to points of interest.
E-mail: rowing@ptialaska.net Web site: ptialaska.net/~rowing/

SEWARD

Falcon's Way B&B
PO Box 2089, 99664
907-224-5757 Fax: 907-224-5828
Clare & Mike Calhoon
All year

50-85-B&B
3 rooms, 1 pb
Visa, MC, Disc, *Rated*,
•
C-ltd/S-no/P-no/H-no

Full breakfast
Afternoon tea, snacks
Sitting room, phones, cable
all rooms, big screen
TV/VCR

In town bed & breakfast furnished with antiques & reproductions, charming Victorian home. Easy walk to all sites and activities. Web site: bnbweb.com/falconsway.html

SITKA

Alaska Ocean View B&B
1101 Edgecumbe Dr, 99835
907-747-8310 Fax: 907-747-3440
Carole & Bill Denkinger
All year

79-149-B&B
3 rooms, 3 pb
Visa, MC, AmEx,
Rated, •
C-yes/S-no/P-ltd/H-no

Full gourmet breakfast
Afternoon tea, snacks
Cable TV/VCR, phones,
microwaves, refrigerators,
luxurious robes/slippers

Western red cedar executive home in gorgeous setting. Walk to beach, wilderness trails, shopping, attractions and historic sites. Luxurious amenities, king/queen size beds.
E-mail: alaskaoceanview@gci.net *Web site:* sitka-alaska-lodging.com

SKAGWAY

Golden North Hotel
PO Box 343, 99840
907-983-2294 Fax: 907-983-2755
888-222-1898
Dennis & Nancy Corrington
April 1st to Oct. 1st

100-115-EP
31 rooms, 28 pb
Most CC, •
C-yes/S-no/P-no/H-yes

Restaurant
Bar service, sitt. room, family
friendly facility, brew pub,
tour bookings

Oldest hotel in Alaska. Located in historic district Brewery & Brew Pub on property. 31 unique rooms with antique furnishings. E-mail: corrington@msn.com
Web site: alaskan.com/goldenorth

Historic Skagway Inn
PO Box 500, 99840
907-983-2289
Suzanne Mullen
All year

95-115-B&B
14 rooms
Visa, MC,
C-yes/S-ltd/P-no/H-yes

Continental plus breakfast
Piano, sitting room, brew
pub, tour bookings

Operated as an inn since the 1920s—all rooms are decorated in period style. Right in historic district. E-mail: info@skagwayinn.com *Web site:* skagwayinn.com

VALDEZ

Downtown B&B Inn
PO Box 184, 99686
907-835-2791 Fax: 907-835-5406
800-478-2791
Glen and Sharron Mills
All year

45-100-B&B
31 rooms, 21 pb
Most CC, •
C-yes/S-no/P-ltd/H-yes
Spanish

Continental plus breakfast
Afternoon tea
Sitting room, cable TV,
accommodate business
travelers

Nestled within the Chugach Mountains, our Bavarian fashioned B&B Inn offers clean, comfortable rooms within walking distance of the boat harbor, ferry terminal & other attractions of Valdez. E-mail: onen2rs@alaska.net *Web site:* alaskan.com/downtowninn/index.html

Arizona

BISBEE

Bisbee Grand Hotel
PO Box 825, 85603
602-432-5900
800-421-1909
Bill Thomas
All year

55-175-B&B
11 rooms, 7 pb
Most CC, *Rated*, •
C-ltd/S-ltd/P-no/H-no

Full breakfast
Bar service
Sitting room, library coin
laundry, gift shop

Romantic Victorian decor, family heirlooms, turn-of-the-century rooming house. Old Western saloon, downtown historic Bisbee. Escape the modern world, relax.
Web site: travelguides.com/home/bisbeegrandhotel/

Hotel La More/Bisbee Inn
45 Ok St, 85603
520-432-5131 Fax: 520-432-5354
888-432-5131
Elissa Strati
All year

50-70-B&B
20 rooms, 16 pb
Most CC, *Rated*, •
C-yes/S-no/P-yes/H-no

Full breakfast
Sitting room, library, In
downtown historic, district

Restored 1917 miner's hotel furnished with antiques original to the building. Overlooking Brewery Gulch with many restaurants and attractions within walking distance. One and two bedroom suites with private garden area.   E-mail: bisbeeinn@aol.com

Vista Park Place
200 E Vista, 85603
520-432-3054
Fax: 520-459-7603
800-388-4388
Bob & Janet Watkins
All year

50-70-B&B
4 rooms, 2 pb
Visa, MC, *Rated*
C-ltd/S-ltd/P-no/H-no
Some Spanish

Full breakfast
Library, tennis court,
spacious bedrooms,
balconies, terraces

1920 vintage, 2 story Mediterranean style home with spacious bedrooms, balconies, library & sun room. 10 minutes to fascinating, quaint, Switzerland-like Bisbee District.
E-mail: parkplace@theriver.com

CAVE CREEK

Coyote Hills B&B
PO Box 393, 85327
602-488-1237
Faye Meador
All year

125-B&B
3 rooms, 3 pb
C-ltd/S-ltd/P-ltd/H-ltd

Continental plus breakfast
Sitting room, library,
fireplace, cable TV,
swimming pool

Southwestern Ranchito on ridge top view lot. Courtyard setting, comfy Mexican furnishings, cable TV, continental breakfast on porch, sunsets on the balcony. Close to hiking, horseback riding, golf.   E-mail: coytohills@aol.com *Web site:* coyotehills.com

FLAGSTAFF

Albers House B&B
705 N San Francisco St, 86001
520-779-0869
Fax: 520-779-9747
800-285-7664
Mary Rabe
All year

90-115-B&B
1 rooms, 1 pb
Most CC, *Rated*
C-ltd/S-no/P-no/H-yes
French

Full breakfast
Dinner (stay for 3 nights),
snacks
Sitting room, library,
bicycles, suite, conference

A 1932 Santa Fe Revival style home with a private suite, and an enclosed terraced garden. An afternoon repast, full gourmet breakfast, fresh fruits and chocolates will tempt your appetite.   E-mail: albershouse@aol.com *Web site:* travelguides.com/home/albers

FLAGSTAFF ——————————————————————————————

Birch Tree Inn	69-109-B&B	Full breakfast
824 W Birch Ave, 86001	5 rooms, 3 pb	Afternoon tea, snacks
520-774-1042 Fax: 520-774-8462	Visa, MC, *Rated*, •	Sitting room, piano, pool
888-774-1042	C-ltd/S-no/P-no/H-no	table, bicycles, tennis court
The Pettingers, The Znetkos		nearby
All year		

Comfortable, country charm; savory, down-home, hearty breakfasts. A four season retreat in the magnificent beauty of Northern Arizona. Outdoor hot tub, A/C upstairs.
E-mail: birch@flagstaff.az.us *Web site:* birchtreeinn.com

Comfi Cottages of Flagstaff	105-210-B&B	Full breakfast
1612 N Aztec St, 86001	6 rooms, 6 pb	Afternoon tea, snacks, comp.
520-774-0731 Fax: 520-779-2236	Most CC, *Rated*, •	wine
888-774-0731	C-yes/S-no/P-no/H-ltd	Sitting room, library, bikes,
Pat & Ed Wiebe	French	fireplaces, cable TV
All year		

Arizona Republic's choice "Best Weekend Getaway." 6 charming cottages, all located near the heart of downtown. Fully equipped with phones, cable TV, yard, fireplaces.
E-mail: pat@comficottages.com *Web site:* comficottages.com

Fall Inn to Nature	60-95-B&B	Continental plus breakfast
8080 N Colt Dr, 86004	3 rooms, 2 pb	Afternoon tea, snacks
520-714-0237	Most CC, *Rated*, •	Sitting room, fireplaces,
888-920-0237	S-ltd/P-ltd/H-no	cable TV, horseback
Ron Fallaha All year		riding/trails, outdoor hot tub

Away from city noise, 2.5 acres with views of San Francisco Peaks and Mt. Elden—Touch of nature decor. Continental plus breakfast, horseback riding, and walking trails close by. On the way to Grand Canyon and close to Sunset Crater/Wupatki.
E-mail: fallinn@infomagic.com *Web site:* bbonline.com/az/fallinn/

Inn at 410 B&B	125-175-B&B	Full breakfast
410 N Leroux St, 86001	9 rooms, 9 pb	Snacks
520-774-0088 Fax: 520-774-6354	Visa, MC, *Rated*, •	Sitting room, library, 8 rooms
800-774-2008	C-ltd/S-no/P-no/H-no	with fireplace, 3 rooms with
Howard & Sally Krueger		Jacuzzis
All year		

Experience award-winning hospitality at "The Place with the Personal Touch." Scrumptious, gourmet breakfasts, nine distinctive guest rooms, some with Jacuzzi or fireplace.
E-mail: info@inn410.com *Web site:* inn410.com

Jeanette's B&B	95-B&B	Full breakfast
3380 E Lockett Rd, 86004	4 rooms, 4 pb	Snacks
520-527-1912 Fax: 520-527-1713	Visa, MC, AmEx,	Sitting room, fireplaces, can
800-752-1912	*Rated*, •	accommodate business
Jeanette & Ray West	S-ltd/P-no/H-no	travelers.
All year		

Flagstaff's most romantic inn. This Victorian style bed and breakfast boasts antique-filled rooms, fresh flowers, private baths with clawfoot tubs, and a full gourmet breakfast.
E-mail: infomagic@jbb.com *Web site:* bbonline.com/az/jbb

Lake Mary B&B	80-110-B&B	Full breakfast
5470 S "J" Diamond Rd, 86001	4 rooms, 4 pb	Afternoon tea, snacks
520-779-7054 Fax: 520-779-7054	Visa, MC, *Rated*, •	Sitting room, library, family
888-244-9550	C-yes/S-ltd/P-no/H-no	friendly facility
Frank & Christine McCollum		
All year		

Small country style B&B with a big heart. Lots of antique furnishing, large guestrooms with private baths, gourmet breakfast. A great place to relax and unwind.

GLOBE

Cedar Hill B&B
175 E Cedar St, 85501
520-425-7530 Fax: 520-425-2888
Helen Elizabeth Gross
All year

40-50-B&B
2 rooms
C-yes/S-ltd/P-yes/H-no

Full breakfast
Snacks
Sitting room, library, cable
TV, accommodate business
travelers

Located in small, active mining town surrounded by mountains—antique furnishings— porch swings on the front porch—full breakfast your choice—cities, lakes, casino in area— feels like country home E-mail: 175cedar@GILA.net

GOLD CANYON

Sinelli's B&B
5605 S Sage Way, 85219
480-983-3650
Carl & Patricia Sinelli
All year

75-B&B
3 rooms, 1 pb
•
C-ltd/S-yes/P-no/H-no

Continental plus—wkdays
Full breakfast—wkends
Lunch & dinner by req.,
snacks, comp. wine, sitting
room

Two bedrm. apt., completely furnished, short or long stay. Casual southwest living in foothills of the Superstition Mtns. Outdoor recreation abundant.

GRAND CANYON

Mountain Country Lodge
437 W Rte 66, 86046
520-635-4341 Fax: 520-635-1450
800-973-6210
The Barnes
All year

54-99-B&B
9 rooms, 9 pb
Visa, MC, •
C-yes/S-no/P-ltd/H-
noSpanish

Continental plus breakfast
Snacks
Bicycles, cable TV, one
family suite, bikes, suites,
fireplace

Built as a mansion in 1909, the lodge boasts 9 uniquely decorated rooms. Located on Old Rte 66 & only 60 miles from the Grand Canyon, it's the ideal place for visiting in the southwest E-mail: DanD1245@aol.com Web site: thegrandcanyon.com/MCLodge/Index.htm

Red Garter Bed & Bakery
PO Box 95, 86046
520-635-1484
800-328-1484
John Holst
All year

65-105-B&B
4 rooms, 4 pb
Most CC, *Rated*, •
C-ltd/S-no/P-no/H-no

Continental plus breakfast
Afternoon tea, snacks
Bakery, coffee shop bikes,
suites, fireplace

Beautifully restored 1897 bordello in small mountain community next to Grand Canyon.
E-mail: redgarter@thegrandcanyon.com Web site: redgarter.com

Sled Dog Inn, The
10155 Mountainaire Rd, 86001
520-525-6212 Fax: 520-525-1855
800-754-0664
Wendy White & Jaime
Ballestero
All year

109-129-B&B
10 rooms, 10 pb
Most CC, •
C-ltd/S-no/P-no/H-ltd

Full breakfast
Dinner, lunch available
Sitting room, library, bikes,
Jacuzzis, suites, fireplaces,
sauna

Mountain lodge catering to outdoor recreationists. We offer adventures for beginners—rock climb, hike, bike, dogsled. Off the beaten path and surrounded by trees. Rock climbing wall. E-mail: sleddog@infomagic.com Web site: sleddoginn.com

JEROME

Ghost City Inn
995 S Page Springs Rd, 86325
520-634-4678 Fax: 520-634-4678
888-634-4678
Joy Beard
All year

75-95-B&B
5 rooms, 1 pb
Most CC, •
C-yes/S-no/P-no/H-no

Full American breakfast
Afternoon tea, snacks
Hot tubs, sitting room, family
friendly facility

Romantic get-a-way/pampered atmosphere. Experience the elegance of days gone by. Magnificent views that rival the Grand Canyon-unforgettable memories.
E-mail: ghostcityinn@yahoo.com Web site: ghostcityinn.com

KINGMAN

Hotel Brunswick	50-95-B&B	Continental plus breakfast
315 E Andy Devine Ave, 86401	24 rooms, 15 pb	Lunch/dinner available,
520-718-1800 Fax: 520-718-1801	Most CC, •	restaurant
All year	C-yes/S-ltd/P-ltd/H-yes	Sitting room, bar service,
	Fr., Ger., Sp., Flem.	suites, cable TV, massage,
		car rental service

An historical, boutique hotel on historic Route 66 in downtown Kingman. Features unique 24 rooms (suites available), an upscale restaurant and bar.
E-mail: rsvp@hotel-brunswick.com *Web site:* hotel-brunswick.com

PHOENIX

Honey House, The	69-89-B&B	Full breakfast
5150 N 36th St, 85018	3 rooms, 3 pb	Afternoon tea
602-956-5646 Fax: 602-224-9765	Visa, MC, •	Sitting room, library, bikes,
Jeanette Irwin	C-yes/S-ltd/P-yes/H-no	hot tub, conference facility
All year		

Historic homesteaded property (1895). Lush acre has citrus grove, antique roses, and arbored gardens. Centrally located near museums, shopping, and golfer's paradise.
E-mail: honeyhous@aol.com *Web site:* travelguides.com/home/honeyhouse/

Maricopa Manor	89-229-B&B	Continental plus breakfast
15 W Pasadena Ave, 85013	5 rooms, 5 pb	Complimentary wine
602-274-6302 Fax: 602-266-3904	*Rated*	Sitting room, library, pool
800-292-6403	C-yes/S-yes/H-yes	with fountains, hot tubs
Mary Ellen & Paul Kelley		
All year		

Old World charm, elegant urban setting. Central and Comeback, close to everything. Luxury suites, secluded, gardens, patios, and palm trees. E-mail: mmanor@getnet.com
Web site: maricopamanor.com

Villa on Alvarado	100-125-B&B	Continental plus breakfast
2031 N Alvarado Rd, 85004	3 rooms, 3 pb	Snacks
602-253-9352	Most CC,	Sitting room, swimming pool,
Kay & Chris King	C-yes/S-ltd/P-no/H-yes	family friendly facility
All year		

Centrally located in a quiet historic neighborhood, close to sports arenas, convention center, The Heard & art museum. 2 bdrm. guest cottage dec. in country charm, or an English tower with many antiques. E-mail: kingsvilla@uswest.net
Web site: azmasonryguild.org/castle

PINETOP

Pinetop Country B&B	85-95-B&B	Full breakfast
2444 Jan Lane, 85935	3 rooms, 3 pb	Snacks, complimentary wine
520-367-0479 Fax: 520-367-0479	Visa, MC,	Sitting room, library,
888-521-5044	C-ltd/S-no/P-no/H-no	bicycles, Jacuzzis, suites,
Karen & Steve Kraxberger		fireplace
All year		

5500 sq. ft. home nestled in the cool mountains in Arizona. We offer amenities that are too much to mention. Home made desserts every evening, large breakfasts.
E-mail: innkeepers@pinetopcountry.com *Web site:* pinetopcountry.com

PRESCOTT

Double D Guest Ranch	135-150-B&B	Full ranch breakfast
PO Box 334, 86334	2 rooms, 2 pb	Snacks, complimentary wine
520-636-0418	Most CC, *Rated*	Full kitchen, private patios,
Doug & Denise PiPietro	C-ltd/S-ltd/P-no/H-ltd	telescope, hot tub, suites,
All year		fireplaces

Authentic cowbowy hot tub, featherbeds, fresh flowers, private patios, exclusive use of main ranch living area, sandstone floors, leather furniture, lots of glass facing mountainous Black Mesa. E-mail: ddranch@goodnet.com *Web site:* virtualcities.com/ons/az/r/azr9601.htm

PRESCOTT

Hassayampa Inn	120-175-B&B	Full breakfast
122 E Gurley St, 86301	68 rooms, 68 pb	Lunch/dinner available (fee)
520-778-9434 Fax: 520-445-8590	Visa, MC, AmEx,	Restaurant, Bar service,
800-322-1927	*Rated*, •	tennis, suites, AAA 3
Bill & Georgia Teich	C-yes/S-ltd/P-no/H-yes	diamond, patio with Gazebo.
All year	Limited Spanish	

68-room, 3 diamond, historic hotel in mile-high Prescott; yesterday's charm gracefully restored, modern amenities; renowned 3-diamond restaurant. E-mail: inn@primenet.com Web site: hassayampainn.com

Lynx Creek Farm B&B	75-150-B&B	Full gourmet breakfast
PO Box 4301, 86303	6 rooms, 6 pb	Complimentary drinks,
520-778-9573	Most CC, *Rated*, •	appetizers
888-778-9573	C-yes/S-ltd/P-yes/H-ltd	Private decks & hot tubs,
Greg & Wendy Temple	Spanish	kitchenettes, BBQ, pool,
All year		wood stoves, croquet

Secluded, country setting on picturesque apple farm minutes from town. Coffee in rooms, quilts. Voted "Best B&B in Arizona" by The Arizona Republic 1994. Multi-night discounts. New cabins available. E-mail: lcf@vacation-lodging.com *Web site:* vacation-lodging.com/lcf/

Prescott Pines Inn	65-249-EP	Full breakfast available
901 White Spar Rd, 86303	14 rooms, 12 pb	BBQ, kitchenettes, lib., sitt.
520-445-7270 Fax: 520-778-3665	Visa, MC, *Rated*	rm., ceiling fan, games,
800-541-5374	C-ltd/S-no/P-no/H-ltd	gardens, porches
Jean, Mike, & Sue		
All year		

11 guestrooms in 3 guesthouses, 1-3 bedroom chalet for 4 couples, all on an acre with ponderosa pines & gardens. Some rooms with fireplaces & kitchenettes. Formerly the Haymore Dairy Farm. E-mail: info@prescottpinesinn.com *Web site:* prescottpinesinn.com

SCOTTSDALE

Bedlam B&B	75-105-B&B	Full breakfast
15253 N Skylark Circle, 85268	2 rooms, 2 pb	Snacks
602-837-9695 Fax: 480-836-1447	•	Sitting porch, Jacuzzis,
Pam & Tom Carlson	C-ltd/S-no/P-ltd/H-ltd	swimming pool, cable TV
All year	Some Spanish	

Our home is newly built next to desert wilderness. A 5,000 custom home on cul-de-sac acre. Designed for mountain views. Each suite has private entrance and private bath. You'll enjoy wildlife as you relax by our heated pool and spa & feed koi in the pond E-mail: pam.carlson@prodigy.net

Southwest Inn at Eagle Mtn.	99-395-B&B	Continental plus breakfast
9800 N Summer Hill Blvd,	42 rooms, 42 pb	Private decks and patios,
85268	•	great views, pool, spa,
480-816-3000 Fax: 480-846-3090		meeting rooms, golf
800-992-8083		
Joel & Sheila Gilgoff		
Season inquire		

Pampered is what you will be in this beautiful brand new Santa Fe style property on the Eagle Mountain Golf Course. This boutique resort hotel has 42 deluxe rooms and suites with fireplaces, refrigerators, coffee makers, and 2 person whirlpool tubs. E-mail: info@southwestinn.com *Web site:* southwestinn.com

Valley O' the Sun B&B	45-B&B	Continental plus breakfast
PO Box 2214, 85252	3 rooms, 1 pb	Full breakfast on weekends
480-941-1281 Fax: 800-689-1281	•	Sitting room, close to nearby,
800-689-1281		attractions
Kathleen Curtis		
All year		

Valley O' the Sun B&B is more than just a place to stay.

SEDONA

Adobe Village
140 Canyon Circle Dr, 86351
520-284-1425 Fax: 520-284-0767
800-228-1425
Roger & Carol Redenbaugh
All year

309-369-B&B
4 rooms, 4 pb
Most CC, *Rated*
C-yes/S-ltd/P-no/H-yes

Full breakfast
Afternoon tea, snacks
Sitting room, games, golf
nearby, TVs/VCRs, hot tub &
swimming pool

Bed and Breakfast as original art. Four luxury theme casitas with waterfall showers, bath fireplaces next to two-person Jacuzzi, and bread makers. E-mail: graham@sedona.net
Web site: sedonasfinest.com

Alma de Sedona Inn
50 Hozoni Dr, 86336
520-282-2737 Fax: 520-203-4141
800-923-2282
Ron & Lynn McCarroll
All year

149-225-B&B
12 rooms, 12 pb
Visa, MC, AmEx, •
C-ltd/S-no/P-no/H-yes

Full breakfast
Snacks
Sitting room, fireplaces,
swimming pool, cable TV,
conference facilities

Luxury, privacy, impeccable service. . .expect all this & much more. We offer beautiful accommodations with outstanding red rock views, gourmet food, heated pool, & a comfortable & inviting atmosphere. E-mail: innkeeper@almadesedona.com
Web site: almadesedona.com/

Apple Orchard Inn
656 Jordan Rd, 86336
520-282-5328 Fax: 520-204-0044
800-663-6968
Bob/Paula Glass,
Robin/Allison   All year

135-230-B&B
7 rooms, 7 pb
Visa, MC, AmEx,
Rated, •
C-ltd/S-no/P-no/H-yes
German

Full breakfast
Snacks
Sitting room, cable TV/VCRs,
Jacuzzis, fridge, fireplaces,
pool & spa

Sedona's newest AAA 4-Diamond. Romantic getaway in the heart of Sedona. Red rock, views, hiking, pool & spa. Theme rooms with all amenities, gourmet 3 course breakfast on red-rock patio. E-mail: appleorc@sedona.net *Web site:* appleorchardbb.com

Boots & Saddles Old West
65 Piki Dr, 86336
520-282-1944 Fax: 520-204-2230
800-201-1944
John & Linda Steele
All year

135-205-B&B
4 rooms, 4 pb
Most CC, •
C-ltd/S-ltd/P-no/H-no

Full breakfast
Snacks
Sitting room, bikes, hot tubs,
unique southwest decor

Rooms are decorated four casual western themes. Sidekick packages, horseback, jeep tours, & golf avail. Unique western cowboy headboards in each bedroom. 3 rooms with fireplace, whirlpool tub, private balcony on decks. E-mail: oldwest@sedona.net
Web site: oldwestbb.com/bsl.html

Briar Patch Inn
3190 N Highway 89 A, 86336
520-282-2342 Fax: 520-282-2399
888-809-3030
Rob Olson
All year

149-295-B&B
17 rooms, 17 pb
Visa, MC, AmEx,
Rated, •
C-yes/S-ltd/P-no/H-ltd
Spanish

Full breakfast by the creek
Homemade cookies, tea,
coffee
Sitting room, library,
fireplaces, kitchenettes,
massage, swimming hole

One of the most beautiful spots in Arizona. Cottages nestled on 9 spectacular acres on sparkling Oak Creek. Warm, generous hospitality. A real gem! Fishing, bird watching, massage in your room. E-mail: briarpatch@sedona.net *Web site:* sedona.net/bb/briarpch

Canyon Villa Inn
125 Canyon Circle Dr, 86351
520-284-1226 Fax: 520-284-2114
800-453-1166
Chuck & Marion Yadon
All year

145-225-B&B
11 rooms, 11 pb
Visa, MC, *Rated*, •
C-ltd/S-no/P-no/H-yes

Full breakfast
Snacks
Sitting room, library,
swimming pool, golf & tennis
nearby

Southwest-style inn offers unmatched red rock views, exceptional guest accommodations with private patio or balcony, full bath, television, telephone.
E-mail: canvilla@sedona.net *Web site:* canyonvilla.com

SEDONA

Canyon Wren—Cabins for 2
6425 N Hwy 89A, 86336
520-282-6900 Fax: 520-282-6978
800-437-9736
Mike & Milena Pfeifer Smith
Season Inquire

125-140-B&B
4 rooms, 4 pb
Most CC, •
S-no/P-no/H-ltd
Slovenian

Continental plus breakfast
Easy access to the creek,
hosts pleased to advise,
patios, hiking

In spectacular Oak Creek Canyon. Cabins have full kitchen, fireplaces, whirlpool bathtubs, decks. Gas grills on patios.   E-mail: cnynwren@sedona.net *Web site:* canyonwrencabins.com

---

Casa Sedona B&B Inn
55 Hozoni Dr, 86336
520-282-2938 Fax: 520-282-2259
800-525-3756
John & Nancy True
All year

125-205-B&B
16 rooms, 16 pb
Visa, MC, Disc, *Rated*,
•
C-ltd/S-no/P-no/H-yes

Full breakfast
Afternoon appetizers
Spa tubs, fireplaces, AAA 4-
diamond inn

Casa Sedona offers panoramic Red Rock views from a secluded acre. 16 individually decorated rooms with fireplaces, spa tubs, refrigerators. Outdoor spa. Smoke-free environment. A "TRUE" B&B.   E-mail: casa@sedona.net *Web site:* casasedona.com

---

Cozy Cactus B&B, The
80 Canyon Circle Dr, 86351
520-284-0082 Fax: 520-284-4210
800-788-2082
Linda Caldwell & Bruce Baillie
All year

105-125-B&B
5 rooms, 5 pb
Visa, MC, Disc, *Rated*,
•
C-yes/S-ltd/P-no/H-yes
Some Italian, Sign Lang.

Full breakfast
Snacks
Library, bicycles, tennis, golf
nearby, hiking nearby, sitting
room

Cozy home furnished in a comfortable Southwestern style. Patios border national forest and spectacular Red Rock views. Old-fashioned hospitality.
E-mail: cozycactus@sedona.net *Web site:* cozycactus.com

Creekside Inn at Sedona
PO Box 2161, 86339
520-282-4992 Fax: 520-282-0091
800-390-8621
The Jochim Family
All year

125-275-B&B
5 rooms, 5 pb
Most CC, *Rated*, •
C-ltd/S-no/P-no/H-yes

Full breakfast
Snacks, fresh baked goods
daily
Sitting room, library, suites,
fireplace, robes, chocolates
in room

Nestled on 2.8 acres of lush, secluded property on beautiful Oak Creek. Our inn is elegant, romantic, peaceful and furnished in authentic Victorian antiques. Views everywhere! Walking distance to town.   E-mail: creekinn@sedona.net *Web site:* bbhost.com/creeksideinn

---

Graham B&B Inn, The
150 Canyon Circle Dr, 86351
520-284-1425 Fax: 520-284-0767
800-228-1425
Roger & Carol Redenbaugh
All year

119-369-B&B
10 rooms, 10 pb
Most CC, *Rated*
C-yes/S-ltd/P-no/H-yes

Full breakfast
Afternoon tea, snacks
Sitting room, games, golf
nearby, TVs/VCRs, hot tub &
swimming pool

Find a special place in your heart. Award-winning inn. Private balconies with red rock views. Newly renovated common areas. All rooms & casitas have CD players.
E-mail: graham@sedona.net *Web site:* sedonasfinest.com

Inn on Oak Creek, The
556 Hwy 179, 86336
520-282-7896 Fax: 520-282-0696
800-499-7896
Rick Morris & Pam Harrison
All year

155-245-B&B
11 rooms, 11 pb
Most CC, *Rated*, •
C-ltd/S-no/P-no/H-yes

Full breakfast
Snacks
Jacuzzis, suites, fireplace,
cable TV, waterfront

Sedona's only AAA 4 diamond B&B on Oak Creek. Luxury, romance and culinary delights await you. Walk to Sedona's fine restaurants, shops and galleries from our inn.
E-mail: theinn@sedona.net *Web site:* sedona-inn.com

SEDONA

L'Auberge de Sedona Resort
PO Box B, 86336
520-282-1661 Fax: 520-282-2885
800-272-6777
Annika Chane
All year

160-425-EP/MAP
Most CC, *Rated*, •
C-yes/S-yes/P-no/H-yes
French, Spanish

Restaurant, bar, comp. coffee
MAP for cabins, sitting room,
library, sauna, swimming
pool

*A private paradise surrounded by a stunning display of natural beauty. Creekside cabins &
orchard-view rooms. Creekside French Gourmet restaurant and Orchards Seafood Grill.*
E-mail: info@lauberge.com *Web site:* lauberge.com

Lodge at Sedona, The
125 Kallof Place, 86336
520-204-1942 Fax: 520-204-2128
800-619-4467
Barb & Mark Dinunzio
All year

125-245-B&B
14 rooms, 14 pb
Visa, MC, Disc, *Rated*,
•
C-ltd/S-no/P-no/H-yes

Full gourmet breakfast
Afternoon refreshments
Sitting room, library, porch, 1
priv. hot tub, Jacuzzi
whirlpool tubs

*Voted "Arizona's best B&B,"–Arizona Republic newspaper, Sept. 93. Feel at home in our
elegant, secluded inn. Enjoy our gourmet breakfast, appetizers & desserts. Fireplaces,
labrynth garden on grounds. E-mail:* lodge@sedona.net *Web site:* lodgeatsedona.com

Rose Tree Inn
376 Cedar St, 86336
520-282-2065 Fax: 520-282-0083
888-282-2065
Gary, Gail, & Steve
All year

75-135-EP
5 rooms, 5 pb
Visa, MC, *Rated*, •
C-ltd/S-yes/P-no/H-no

In-room coffee & tea
Patios, library, Jacuzzi,
phones & TV/VCR in rms.,
bicycles, kitchenettes

*A quiet, cozy inn with five rooms, private baths, TV and VCR, kitchens. Two rooms with
fireplaces. Garden patio with spa, barbecue. E-mail:* rosetreeinn@verdenet.com
Web site: rosetreeinn.com

Southwest Inn at Sedona
3250 W Hwy 89A, 86336
520-282-3344 Fax: 520-282-0261
800-483-7422
Joel & Sheila Gilgoff
All year

99-219-B&B
28 rooms, 28 pb
Visa, MC, AmEx,
Rated, •
C-yes/S-no/P-no/H-yes
Spanish

Continental plus breakfast
Refreshments
Hot tubs, swimming pool,
phones, TVs, hiking,
fireplaces, mtn. biking

*Pampered is what you'll be when you are our guest at the beautiful Southwest Inn at
Sedona. Award winning southwest architecture and decor combined with great views
make our combination B&B/Small luxury inn unique. E-mail:* info@swinn.com
Web site: swinn.com

Territorial House B&B, A
65 Piki Dr, 86336
520-204-2737 Fax: 520-204-2230
800-801-2737
John & Linda Steele
All year

115-165-B&B
4 rooms, 4 pb
Visa, MC, *Rated*, •
C-yes/S-ltd/P-no/H-no

Full breakfast
Afternoon tea, snacks
Sitting room, bicycles,
whirlpool tub, fireplace,
deck, outdoor hot tub

Room decor depicts Sedona territorial days. Friendly, cozy, quiet, western hospitality
E-mail: oldwest@sedona.net *Web site:* oldwestbb.com/thl.html

Touch of Sedona B&B, A
595 Jordan Rd, 86336
520-282-6462 Fax: 520-282-1534
800-600-6462
Bill & Sharon Larsen
All year

99-159-B&B
5 rooms, 5 pb
Most CC, *Rated*, •
C-ltd/S-no/P-no/H-no

Full gourmet breakfast
Spec. diets welcomed
Deck & patio garden,
beautiful redrock views, near
art galleries

*Eclectic elegance. . .furnished with stained glass lamps, antiques, but with a mix of contem-
porary. Just walking distance to uptown. E-mail:* touch@sedona.net *Web site:* touchsedona.com

SEDONA

Wishing Well
995 N Hwy 89A, 86336
520-282-4914 Fax: 520-204-9766
800-728-9474
Valda & Esper Esau
All year

145-170-B&B
5 rooms, 5 pb
Most CC, *Rated*, •
C-ltd/S-no/P-no/H-no

Continental plus breakfast
Sitting room, library,
Jacuzzis, fireplaces, cable TV

5 room luxury B&B atop a hill nestled at forest edge, guests enjoy private baths, fireplaces, & hot tubs. Linger over breakfast served in your room or on your private deck.
E-mail: wishwell@sedona.net *Web site:* sedona.net/bb/wishwell

SONOITA

Sonoita Inn
PO Box 99, 85637
520-455-5935 Fax: 520-455-5069
Wystrach Family
All year

99-145-B&B
18 rooms, 18 pb
Most CC,
C-yes/S-no/P-no/H-yes

Continental breakfast
Sitting room, suites, cable TV

A one-of-a-kind country inn that features rustic western living and local history. Spacious rooms with spectacular views are named in honor of area ranches.
E-mail: info@sonoitainn.com *Web site:* sonoitainn.com

TUCSON

Agave Grove B&B Inn
800 W Panorama Rd, 85704
520-797-3400 Fax: 520-797-0980
888-822-4283
John & Denise Kiber
All year

65-165-B&B
5 rooms, 4 pb
Most CC, *Rated*, •
C-yes/S-ltd/P-no/H-yes

Full breakfast
Tea, snacks
Sitting room, library,
Jacuzzis, swimming pool,
suites, fireplace, cable TV

Romantic estate on 2.5 acres, majestic mountain views, private baths, gourmet breakfast, billiard table, courtyards with ramada, fountain.   E-mail: agavebb@azstarnet.com
Web site: bbonline.com/az/agave

Bienestar B&B
10490 E Escalante Rd, 85730
520-290-1048 Fax: 520-290-1367
800-293-0004
R. Scanlin & D. Strausser
All year

90-150-B&B
4 rooms, 4 pb
Most CC, *Rated*, •
C-ltd/S-no/P-no/H-ltd

Full breakfast
Evening refreshments
Sitting room, library, hot tub,
swimming pool, TV/VCRs in
each room

Lovely desert hacienda near national park featuring delicious breakfasts from whole natural foods. Solar pool, spa, fireplaces, complimentary horse facilities.
E-mail: bienestarbandb@hotmail.com *Web site:* bienestar.net

Cactus Cove B&B
10066 E Kleindale Rd, 85749
520-760-7730 Fax: 520-749-3304
888-466-0083
Sally and Ivan Gunderman
All year

145-195-B&B
3 rooms, 3 pb
Most CC, *Rated*
C-ltd/S-no/P-no/H-ltd

Full breakfast
Snacks
Sitting room, library,
Jacuzzis, swimming pool,
suites, cable TV

It is a peaceful oasis in the middle of the Sonoran Desert. Quiet is our most noticable quality.   E-mail: cactuscv@azstarnet.com *Web site:* azcactuscove.com

Cactus Quail B&B, The
14000 N Dust Devil Dr, 85739
520-825-6767
Marty & Sue Higbee
Season Inquire

E-mail: cactusq@si-systems.com *Web site:* bbonline.com/az/aabbi/tucson.html

TUCSON ————————————————————————————————————

Casa Alegre B&B Inn	80-125-B&B	Full breakfast
316 E Speedway Blvd, 85705	5 rooms, 5 pb	Afternoon tea, snacks
520-628-1800 Fax: 520-792-1880	Visa, MC, *Rated*, •	Sitting room, library,
800-628-5654	C-ltd/S-no/P-no/H-no	swimming pool, Jacuzzi,
Phyllis Florek		public tennis courts
All year		

Beautiful 1915 Craftsman bungalow near University of AZ, metropolitan Tucson, golf & mountain & desert attractions. Scrumptious breakfast, poolside refreshments. In-room television.   E-mail: alegre123@aol.com *Web site:* bbonline.com/az/alegre

Catalina Park Inn B&B	104-124-B&B	Full breakfast
309 E 1st St, 85705	6 rooms, 6 pb	Afternoon tea, snacks
520-792-4541	Visa, MC, Disc, *Rated*	Sitting room, lush gardens,
800-792-4885	C-ltd/S-no/P-no/H-no	many amenities
Mark Hall, Paul Richard		
All year		

Stylish inn featuring beautifully decorated guestrooms & full range of amenities. Enjoy our lush perennial garden. Just 5 blocks to University of Arizona.   E-mail: cpinn@flash.net *Web site:* catalinaparkinn.com

Crickethead Inn B&B	65-75-B&B	Full breakfast
9480 Picture Rocks Rd, 85743	3 rooms, 3 pb	
520-682-7126	C-ltd/S-ltd/H-no	
Michael Lord	Spanish	
Oct 1-May 31		

Secluded and quiet, beamed ceiling, fired adobe brick, Borders National Park, lots of birds, flowers, plants, mexican tile bathrooms, full breakfast, great coffee. Only 30 minutes to downtown Tucson.

El Adobe Ranch	110-175-B&B	Continental breakfast
4630 N El Adobe Ranch Rd,	5 rooms, 5 pb	Hot tubs, hiking, family
85745	Visa, MC, AmEx,	friendly facility, many
520-743-3525 Fax: 520-297-2080	C-yes/S-ltd/P-no/H-yes	amenities
J. Kranis, B.& E. Anastopoulos	Greek, Spanish	
All year		

Secluded desert retreat nestled in the Tucson mountains. Each room is a fully furnished casita. Decorated with traditional southwestern style and elegance. Fireplaces in bedroom and living room. Weekly and monthly guests welcome at discounted rates. E-mail: ellen@eladoberanch.com *Web site:* arizonaguide.com/el-adobe-ranch/

El Presidio B&B Inn	105-125-B&B	Full gourmet breakfast
297 N Main Ave, 85701	4 rooms, 4 pb	Afternoon tea, snacks
520-623-6151 Fax: 520-623-3860	*Rated*, •	Comp. wine, juice, soda,
800-349-6151	C-ltd/S-no/P-no/H-no	kitchenettes, phones, TV,
Patti Toci		nearby health club
All year except July		

Historic Victorian adobe with Old-Mexico ambiance, courtyards, gardens, fountains. Antique decor. Awarded "Best B&B in Southern Arizona" by Arizona Republic. *Awarded "Best B&B in Tucson" by* Tucson Weekly. *Zagat survey says "one of the best B&B's in USA."*

Hacienda Bed and Breakfast	120-190-B&B	Full breakfast
5704 East Grant Road, 85712	2 rooms, 2 pb	Afternoon tea
520-290-2224 Fax: 520-721-9066	Most CC, *Rated*, •	Solar pool, heated spa,
888-236-4421	C-yes/S-ltd/P-no/H-yes	exercise room, patio, dance
Barbara Shamseldin		floor, TV/VCR
All year		

A quiet place in the city, Hacienda Bed and Breakfast is centrally located on Grant Road in Tucson. We are eight miles east of I-10 and 20 minutes from the Tucson Airport E-mail: hacienda97@aol.com *Web site:* members.aol.com/hacienda97

TUCSON

Hacienda del Desierto
11770 E Rambling Trail, 85747
520-298-1764 Fax: 520-722-4558
800-982-1795
David and Rosemary Brown
All year

105-150-B&B
3 rooms, 3 pb
Visa, MC, *Rated*, •
C-yes/S-ltd/P-no/H-no

Continental plus breakfast
Kitchenettes
Sitt. rm., library, TV, VCR,
hydrotherapy spas, Spanish
courtyard

Old Spanish style Hacienda on 16 acres next to national park. Romantic hideaway. Nature lover's paradise: birding, hiking. Mountain views.   E-mail: oasis@tucson-bed-breakfast.com Web site: tucson-bed-breakfast.com

---

Jeremiah Inn B&B
10921 E Snyder Rd, 85749
520-749-3072
888-750-3072
Bob & Beth Miner
All year

80-110-B&B
5 rooms, 5 pb
Visa, MC, AmEx,
Rated, •
C-yes/S-no/P-no/H-ltd
Some French, Spanish

Full breakfast
Snacks
Sitting room, library,
Jacuzzis, swimming pool,
accommodate business
travel

Spectacular mountain views and desert acreage surround the quiet comfort of this 1995 inn. Bird, bike, hike or relax fueled by your satisfying full breakfast, inn-baked cookies and gracious hospitality.   E-mail: JeremiahInn@Juno.com Web site: bbonline.com/az/jeremiah

---

June's B&B
3212 W Holladay St, 85746
520-578-0857
June Henderson
All year

45-55-B&B
3 rooms

C-ltd/S-no/P-no/H-no

Continental plus breakfast
Sitting room, piano, heated
swimming pool, art studio,
exercise rm.

Mountainside home with pool. Majestic towering mountains. Hiking in the desert. Sparkling city lights. Beautiful backyard & patio. Owner's artwork for sale.

Mountain Views B&B
3160 N Bear Canyon Rd, 85749
520-749-1387 Fax: 520-749-1516
Roy & Miriam Kile
All year

75-B&B
2 rooms, 2 pb
Visa, MC, AmEx, •
C-ltd/S-no/P-no/H-ltd

Full breakfast
Complimentary wine
Sitting room, swimming pool,
cable TV, accommodate
business travelers

Mountain Views B&B is nestled in a vegetated desert setting, secluded on 3.3 acres on Tucson's far eastside with beautiful panoramic mountain views "Where guests become friends."   E-mail: Rkile85749@aol.com Web site: mtviewsbb.com

---

Peppertrees B&B Inn
724 E University Blvd, 85719
520-622-7167
800-348-5763
Marjorie G. Martin
All year

108-125-B&B
9 rooms, 3 pb
Rated, •
C-ltd/S-no/P-no/H-no

Full gourmet breakfast
Picnic lunch to go, afternoon
tea
Library, TV, VCR, walk to
restaurants

Warm, friendly territorial home. Antiques, gourmet breakfasts. Walk to U. of Arizona, downtown, shopping. Two 2-bedroom guesthouses.   E-mail: pepperinn@gci-net.com Web site: bbonline.com/az/peppertrees/

Quail's Vista B&B
826 E Palisades Dr, 85737
520-297-5980 Fax: 520-297-5980
Barbara & Richard Bauer
Oct. 1 - May 1

65-85-B&B
3 rooms, 1 pb
•
C-ltd/S-ltd/P-no/H-no

Continental plus breakfast
Snacks
Sitting room, Jacuzzis,
fireplace, cable TV, swim
stream spa outside

Passive solar rammed earth and adobe house has 27" thick walls and is located on two acres of desert with a panoramic view of the ever changing Catalina Mountains.
E-mail: quail-vista@juno.com *Web site: avicom.net/quails-vista*

TUCSON ————————————————————————————

Shadow Mountain Ranch B&B
8825 N Scenic Dr, 85743
520-744-7551
888-974-2369
Lyn Nelson
Closed in July

85-195-B&B
5 rooms, 3 pb
Rated, •
C-yes/S-ltd/P-ltd/H-no

Continental breakfast
Sitt. rm, piano, hot tub, pool,
queen rooms, hacienda &
guest house

Desert paradise located in Tucson Mts. (NW). Great location. 2 bedroom desert villa fully furnished, fireplace, full kitchen. E-mail: shadmtn@aol.com
Web site: members.aol.com/shadmtn

The Horse You Rode In On
PO Box 158, 85609
520-826-5410 Fax: 520-826-1078
Deborah and Will Scott
All year

70-75-B&B
4 rooms, 1 pb
C-ltd/S-no/P-no/H-yes
Spanish, French

Full breakfast
Snacks
Sitting room, library,
Jacuzzis, horse stalls

Furnished in southwestern style with amenities in each room including many items of Western art from the owners' personal collection, the inn reflects the mood of this historic western area. E-mail: horseinn@vtc.net

WILLIAMS ————————————————————————————

Terry Ranch B&B
701 Quarterhorse, 86046
520-635-4171 Fax: 520-635-2488
800-210-5908
Glenn & Leisa Watkins
All year

100-140-B&B
4 rooms, 4 pb
Most CC, *Rated*, •
C-ltd/S-no/P-no/H-yes
Spanish & Dutch

Full breakfast
Snacks
Sitting room, library,
fireplaces, cable TV, 2 person
jetted tub, gazebo

Our large log home offers country Victorian decor, spacious guest rooms with private baths and sitting areas, beautiful mountain scenery from a wraparound verandah and full family style country breakfasts. E-mail: terryranch@workmail.com *Web site:* grandcanyonlodging.net

Arkansas

BELLA VISTA ————————————————————————————

Inn at Bella Vista, The
1 Chelsea Rd, 72714
501-876-5645 Fax: 501-876-5662
877-876-5645
Bill & Beverly Williams
All year

110-140-B&B
5 rooms, 5 pb
Most CC, *Rated*, •
C-ltd/S-no/P-ltd/H-no

Full breakfast
Snacks
Sitting room, library, bikes,
pool, cable TV, fireplaces,
conference fac.

14 acres, 9,000 sq. ft., natural setting, breathtaking views, personal services, great food. Lots to do or nothing at all. Life as it's meant to be. E-mail: innkeeper@iabv.com *Web site:* iabv.com

EUREKA SPRINGS ————————————————————————————

11 Singleton House B&B
11 Singleton, 72632
501-253-9111
800-833-3394
Barbara Gavron
All year

69-135-B&B
5 rooms, 5 pb
Most CC, *Rated*, •
C-yes/S-no/P-no/H-no
Spanish (some)

Full breakfast
Guest ice-box, microwave
Cottage, swing, rockers,
INNternship program,
Jacuzzi w/private balcony

1894 Victorian, antiques, folk art; breakfast balcony overlooks magical garden & goldfish pond. Bird house collection. Historic district; scenic 1 block walk to shops. Cottage at a private wooded location with a swing and hammock. Jacuzzi/Fireplace.

EUREKA SPRINGS

1881 Crescent Cottage Inn	97-140-B&B	Full breakfast
211 Spring St, 72632	4 rooms, 4 pb	Coffee
501-253-6022 Fax: 501-253-6234	Visa, MC, Disc, *Rated*,	Historic district, all rooms
800-223-3246	•	have Jacuzzis, 2 rooms with
Ralph S. Becker	C-ltd/S-no/P-no/H-no	fireplaces
All year		

Famous 1881 landmark Victorian home on National Register. Porches, gardens, and superb mountain views. Antiques throughout, 2 rooms with fireplaces.   E-mail: raphael@ipa.net
Web site: 1881crescentcottageinn.com

5 Ojo Inn B&B	89-129-B&B	Full breakfast
5 Ojo St, 72632	10 rooms, 10 pb	Dietary attention, snack
501-253-6734 Fax: 501-253-8831	Visa, MC, Disc, *Rated*,	Library, hot tub, gazebo,
800-656-6734	•	Jacuzzis, fireplaces, deck,
Paula Kirby Adkins	C-yes/S-ltd/P-no/H-no	weddings, parking
All year		

Award winning restoration of Victorian home says "stay here and revive." Historic District; 8-min. walk to shops and galleries. Fireplaces and whirlpool tubs for 2 in six rooms. Library and games in common area perfect for family fun. Web site: eureka-usa.com/ojo

Arbour Glen B&B	85-135-B&B	Full breakfast
7 Lema, 72632	5 rooms, 5 pb	Afternoon tea, snacks
501-253-9010 Fax: 201-253-1264	Most CC, *Rated*, •	Sitting room, Jacuzzis, suites,
800-515-4536	C-ltd/S-ltd/P-ltd/H-no	fireplaces, cable TV
Jeffrey Beeler		
All year		

E-mail: arbglen@ipa.net *Web site:* abrourglen.com

Arsenic & Old Lace B&B Inn	106-160-B&B	Full gourmet breakfast
60 Hillside Ave, 72632	5 rooms, 5 pb	Snacks, complimentary wine
501-253-5454	Most CC, *Rated*, •	VCR library; TV/VCR,
Fax: 501-253-2246	C-ltd/S-no/P-no/H-ltd	fireplace, private balcony,
800-243-5223		Jacuzzi, all in-room
Gary & Phyllis Jones		
All year		

Historic-district Victorian mansion surrounded by wicker-filled verandas overlooking scenic wooded hills & gardens. Short walk to shops & restaurants.   E-mail: arseniclace@prodigy.net
Web site: eureka-usa.com/arsenic/

Bonnybrooke Farm/Misty Mtn	115-165-EP	Bread & fruit at arrival
72631	5 rooms, 5 pb	Books & games, fireplace,
501-253-6903	•	Jacuzzi, glass showers,
Bonny & Joshua	S-no/P-no/H-no	basketball court
All year		

Sweet quiet & serenity atop Misty Mountain. Fireplace, Jacuzzi (for 2), shower under the stars in glass shower. Web site: bonnybrooke.apexhosting.com

Candlestick Cottage Inn	65-120-B&B	Full breakfast
6 Douglas St, 72632	6 rooms, 6 pb	Reservations for local,
501-253-6813	Most CC, *Rated*, •	restaurants/attractions,
800-835-5184	C-ltd/S-no/P-no/H-no	Jacuzzi stes./queen beds
Bill & Patsy Brooks		
All year		

Located in historic district one block from downtown shops. Authentic Victorian-country setting. Breakfast served on treetop porch E-mail: candleci@ipa.net
Web site: candlestickcottageinn.com

EUREKA SPRINGS

Cliff Cottage, A
42 Armstrong St, 72632
501-253-7409
800-799-7409
Sandra CH Smith
All year

120-195-B&B
4 rooms, 4 pb
Visa, MC, *Rated*, •
C-ltd/S-no/P-no/H-no
French, Spanish,
German

Full breakfast served in room
Lunch/dinner avail.,
afternoon tea
Refrigerator in room, pool,
library, tennis, golf, boat,
picnics, Jacuzzis

Elegant Victorian suites/guestrooms in heart of Historic Downtown. Heirloom antiques, decadent breakfast, sunshine, laughter everywhere. Fireplace in Tennyson suite.
E-mail: cliffctg@aol.com *Web site:* cliffcottage.com

Enchanted Cottages
18 Nut St, 72632
501-253-6790
800-862-2788
Barbara Kellogg, David Pettit
All year

75-149-EP
3 rooms, 3 pb
•

These enchanted hideaways are located on a very peaceful historic district street complete-ly surrounded by fairy tale gardens and directly across from one of Eureka's picturesque springs. View of the surrounding Ozark Hills and downtown Eureka Spring.
Web site: websites2001.com/enchanted_cottages

Eureka Sunset
10 Dogwood Ridge, 72632
501-253-9565 Fax: 501-253-1265
888-253-9565
Jack & Ada Dozier
All year

100-125-B&B
2 rooms, 2 pb
Visa, MC, Disc, *Rated*,
•
S-no/P-ltd/H-no

Full breakfast
Snacks, complimentary wine
Jacuzzis, fireplaces, cable TV

For those of you too focused on the future to enjoy the present, we have the perfect remedy. Time runs backward at Eureka Sunset, where we take time to enjoy the past. Isn't it time you see for yourself? E-mail: esunset@ipa.net *Web site:* eureka-usa.com/sunset

---

Heart of the Hills Inn
RR2, Box 307, 65631
501-253-7468
800-253-7468
Jim & Kathy Vanzandt
All year

79-119-EP
3 rooms, 3 pb
Visa, MC, AmEx,
C-ltd/S-no/P-ltd/H-ltd

Sitting room, Jacuzzis, suites,
fireplaces, cable TV

The Inn features two Victorian suties and a country cottage. Private decks and porches. Heart of the Hills Inn offers its guests plenty of peace and relaxation.
Web site: usabest.com/heart

Heartstone Inn & Cottages
35 Kingshighway, 72632
501-253-8916 Fax: 501-253-6821
800-494-4921
Iris & Bill Simantel
February-mid December

73-129-B&B
12 rooms, 12 pb
Visa, MC, *Rated*, •
C-ltd/S-yes/P-no/H-no

Full gourmet breakfast
Complimentary beverages
Sitting room, cable TVs,
wedding gazebo, decks,
Jacuzzi suite

Award-winning. Antique furniture, private baths & entrances, king/queen beds. Historic district by attractions. "Best breakfast in the Ozarks"—NY Times 1989.
E-mail: heartinn@ipa.net *Web site:* heartstoneinn.com

Hidden Valley Guest Ranch
777 Hidden Vly. Ranch, 72632
501-253-9777 Fax: 501-253-5777
888-443-3368
Jordan & Tandy Maxfield
All year

129-189-EP
2 rooms, 2 pb
Visa, MC, Disc, *Rated*,
•
C-yes/S-no/P-no/H-no
Spanish

Sitting room, hot tubs,
TV/VCR, fireplaces,
whirlpool for 2

Country at its best! Secluded cabins high on an Ozark's mountainside. Full amenities. 5 minutes from Eureka Springs. Overnight horse boarding. E-mail: getaway@
hiddenvalleyguestranch.com *Web site:* hiddenvalleyguestranch.com

EUREKA SPRINGS

Palace Hotel & Bathhouse
135 Spring St, 72632
501-253-7474 Fax: 501-253-7494
Steve & Francie Miller
All year

135-155-B&B
8 rooms, 8 pb
Most CC, *Rated*, •
S-yes/P-no/H-no

Continental plus breakfast
Complimentary wine
Jacuzzis, suites, cable TV

Elegant hotel featuring 8 luxury suites, catering to those who want a little more in accommodations. Bathhouse featuring mineral baths, massage, eucalyptus steam treatment, and clay mask. Experience history.   E-mail: phbh@ipa.net Web site: palacehotelbathhouse.com

---

Piedmont House B&B Inn
165 Spring St, 72632
501-253-9258
800-253-9258
Vince & Kathy DiMayo
All year

79-135-B&B/MAP
10 rooms, 9 pb
Visa,
C-ltd/S-ltd/H-yes

Full breakfast
Dinner included on Friday
Wraparound porch, sitting
room, library

Over 100 years old with orig. guest book also over 100 years old. "Homey" atmosphere; comfortable rooms & beautiful views of the mountain & Christ of the Ozark Statue. Dinner included with price of room on Friday night with 2 night stay.   E-mail: piedmont@ipa.net Web site: eureka-usa.com/piedmont

---

Pond Mountain Lodge B&B
1218 Hwy 23 S, 72632
501-253-5877 Fax: 501-253-9087
800-583-8043
Judy Jones
All year

95-150-B&B
7 rooms, 7 pb
Visa, MC, Disc, *Rated*,
•
C-ltd/S-no/P-ltd/H-ltd

Full breakfast
Picnic lunch available
Sitting room, library, hot
tubs, swimming pool, fishing
ponds, horseback

Mountain-top breezes, panoramic views, casual elegance ... with fishing ponds, heated pool, riding stables, billiards, fireplace, and hearty breakfasts.
Web site: eureka-usa.com/pondmtn/

FORT SMITH

Beland Manor Inn
1320 S Albertpike, 72903
501-782-3300 Fax: 501-782-7674
800-334-5052
Mike & Suzy Smith
All year

75-150-B&B
8 rooms, 8 pb
Most CC, *Rated*, •
C-ltd/S-no/P-no/H-no
Spanish

Full breakfast
Weekend dinners
Snacks, bar service, sitting
room, Jacuzzis, fireplace,
cable TV

Comfortable beds, delectable breakfasts, memorable hospitality & superb location make Beland Manor 1st choice for the tourist as well as the business traveler. Faces a monastery with acres of grounds.   E-mail: belandbnb@ipa.net Web site: bbonline.com/ar/belandmanor

HARDY

Hideaway Inn B&B
84 W Firetower Rd, 72542
870-966-4770
888-966-4770
Julia Baldridge   All year

55-95-B&B
5 rooms, 3 pb
•
C-yes/S-ltd/H-no

Full breakfast
Snacks
Swimming pool, family
friendly facility, fireplace,
cable TV

Seeking solitude, this contemporary home or log cabin is an ideal place to hide away. Swimming pool, playground & gardens for guest enjoyment. Continental or gourmet breakfast.   Web site: bbonline.com/ar/hideaway

---

Olde Stonehouse B&B Inn
511 Main St, 72542
870-856-2983 Fax: 870-856-4036
800-514-2983
Peggy Volland
All year

69-125-B&B
9 rooms, 9 pb
Visa, MC, *Rated*, •
C-ltd/S-ltd/P-no/H-no

Full breakfast
Evening snacks
Sitting room, lib., A/C, ceiling
fans, TV, VCR, Jacuzzi tubs in
suites

Two-story native rock home with antiques. Two 2-room suites in separate building with Jacuzzis and fireplaces. Near quaint shops, Spring River, golf, water sports, antique auctions, fly fishing, conference rooms.   E-mail: oldestonehouse@centuryinter.net Web site: bbonline.com/ar/stonehouse/

Hideaway Inn B&B, Hardy, AR

HEBER SPRINGS

Anderson House Inn, The	65-84-B&B	Full breakfast
201 E Main St, 72543	16 rooms, 16 pb	Afternoon snacks
501-362-5266 Fax: 501-362-2326	Most CC, *Rated*	Sitting room, antiques, fly
800-264-5279	C-yes/S-no/P-no/H-no	tying bench, park, with
Terry, Amabilia & Ingrid	Fluent Spanish	tennis courts
All year		

Warm, comfortable country inn in the Ozark foothills; convenient to Grees Ferry Lake and world class fly fishing   E-mail: jhildebr@cswnet.com *Web site:* yourinn.com/

Azalea Cottage Inn B&B	·79-99-B&B	Full breakfast
320 Sunny Meadow, 72543	4 rooms, 4 pb	Snacks
501-362-1665 Fax: 501-362-2376	Visa, MC, *Rated*, ●	Sitting room, library, bikes,
888-233-7931	S-no/P-no/H-ltd	Jacuzzis, fireplace, cable TV
Betty & Sam Hazel		
All year		

Beautiful Colonial Revival inn on a peaceful, tree covered acre. Pampers guests with coffee service delivery, "Southern gourmet" breakfast on the patio, freshly baked cookies with bed turn-down service.   E-mail: azalea@arkansas.net *Web site:* AzaleaCottageInn.com

HELENA

Foxglove B&B	79-109-B&B	Full breakfast
229 Beech St, 72342	10 rooms, 10 pb	Complimentary wine
870-338-9391 Fax: 870-338-9391	Visa, MC, AmEx,	Whirlpool tubs, snack, sitting
800-863-1926	*Rated*, ●	room, antiques
John Butkiewicz	C-ltd/S-no/P-no/H-no	
All year		

Overlooks historic Helena and the Mississippi River. Stunning antiques, parquet floors, stained glass, complimented by marble baths and whirlpool tubs
Web site: bbonline.com/ar/foxglove

HOT SPRINGS

Williams House B&B	85-135-B&B	Full breakfast
420 Quapaw Ave, 71901	6 rooms, 5 pb	Spring water, iced tea
501-624-4275 Fax: 501-321-9466	Most CC, *Rated*, ●	Sitt. rm., piano, picnic
800-756-4635	C-ltd/S-ltd/P-no/H-no	tables, weddings, BBQ,
David & Karen Wiseman		hiking trail maps
All year		

Williams House shows Victorian flair for convenience and elegance. Your home away from home, nestled in Oachita Mountains. Romantic atmosphere. Mystery weekends. Free spring water, wine, & cookies. All rooms have TV/VCR. 3 rooms are 2 bedroom suites. E-mail: willmbnb@ipa.net *Web site:* bbonline.com/ar/williamshouse

LITTLE ROCK ───────────────────────

Empress of Little Rock	115-175-B&B	Full gourmet breakfast
2120 Louisiana, 72206	5 rooms, 5 pb	Snacks, comp. decanters of
501-374-7966 Fax: 501-375-4537	Visa, MC, AmEx,	liquor
Sharon Welch-Blair/Rbt. Blair	*Rated*, •	Sitting room, library, suites,
All year		fireplace, cable TV,
		dataports, feather beds

Experience the opulence of the 1880s in AAA 4-diamond luxury! Majestic double stairwell, secret card room in the turret, sensual featherbeds, candlelight gourmet breakfast, understated elegance, antique appointments, The Empress!!!   E-mail: hostess@theempress.com
Web site: TheEmpress.com

California

ALAMEDA ───────────────────────

Garratt Mansion	80-145-B&B	Full breakfast
900 Union St, 94501	7 rooms, 4 pb	Cookies, hot/cold drinks
510-521-4779 Fax: 510-521-6796	*Rated*	Sitting room, phones and,
Royce & Betty Gladden	C-ltd/S-no/P-no/H-no	private baths in most, rooms,
All year		TV available

An elegant Victorian in a quiet island community just 20 minutes from downtown San Francisco, offering personalized attention.   E-mail: garrattm@pacbell.net
Web site: garrattmansion.com

Krusi Mansion	100-130-B&B	Continental plus breakfast
2033 Central Ave, 94501	4 rooms, 4 pb	Snacks, complimentary wine
510-864-2300 Fax: 510-864-2336	Visa, MC, AmEx,	Sitting room, library, cable
Ty & Sonja Taylor	*Rated*, •	TV, accommodate business
All year	S-no/P-ltd/H-no	travelers, Newspapers

An elegant historic mansion, fully restored and decorated with authentic American antiques featuring four large guestrooms upstairs. All homemade, healthy vegetarian breakfast includes fresh fruit salad, muffins, custard, quiche, etc. . . . .   E-mail: kmansion@dnai.com
Web site: krusimansion.com

AMADOR CITY ───────────────────────

Imperial Hotel	80-110-B&B	Full breakfast
PO Box 195, 95601	6 rooms, 6 pb	Snacks, wine
209-267-9172 Fax: 209-267-9249	Visa, MC, AmEx,	Restaurant, bar, sitting room,
800-242-5594	*Rated*, •	library, family friendly,
Bruce Sherrill & Dale Martin	C-yes/S-ltd/P-no/H-no	heated towel bars
All year		

1879 restored hotel, six handsome guest rooms. Oasis bar and an elegant regionally acclaimed dining room with a courtyard.   E-mail: host@imperialamador.com
Web site: imperialamador.com

APTOS ───────────────────────

Inn at Manresa Beach	150-220-B&B	Full breakfast
1258 San Andreas Rd, 95076	8 rooms	Sitting room, library,
831-728-1000 Fax: 831-728-8294	Most CC, •	Jacuzzis, suites, bikes,
888-523-2244	C-yes/S-no/P-no/H-yes	adjustable massage beds
Susan Van Horn & Brian	French, German,	
Denny All year	Spanish	

An 1867 restored replica of Abraham Lincoln's Springfield home, located between Santa Cruz and Carmel on Monterey Bay. 8 elegant rooms and suites include fireplaces, TV/VCR, stereo, 2 phone lines, 2 person spa tubs & king or queen adjustable massage beds
E-mail: theinn@indevelopment.com Web site: indevelopment.com

Krusi Mansion, Alameda, CA

AUBURN

Power's Mansion Inn
PO Box 602076, 95603
530-885-1166 Fax: 530-885-1386
Arno & Jean Lejnieks All year

79-159-B&B
13 rooms, 13 pb •
C-ltd/S-no/P-no/H-yes
German, Latin

Full breakfast
Deluxe amenities, fireplaces,
patios/decks, terry robes

*1898 mansion built from gold-mining fortune. Has elegance of detailed restoration &
antique furnishings with queen beds & central air & heat.* E-mail: powerinn@westsierra.net
Web site: vfr.net/~powerinn

BASS LAKE

Jonnie's Inn at Bass Lake
PO Box 717, 93604
559-642-4966 Fax: 559-641-6043
Gene & Jonnie Baker
All year

95-135-B&B
2 rooms, 2 pb
C-ltd/S-no/P-no/H-no

Full breakfast
Afternoon tea, snacks
Cable TV, Lakeside
swimming

*Nestled in the pines with lake view. Within walking distance to shops, restaurants &
entertainment. 14 miles from Yosemite Park Gate. Gourmet breakfast served on front porch
with view of lake.* E-mail: jonnie@sierratel.com Web site: sierratel.com/jonnies/

BIG BEAR

Gold Mountain Manor B&B
PO Box 2027, 92314
909-585-6997 Fax: 909-585-0327
800-509-2604
Jose A. Tapia
All year

125-190-B&B
6 rooms, 6 pb
Rated, •
C-ltd/S-ltd/P-ltd/H-no
French

Full breakfast
Complimentary beverages,
snacks
Pool table, fireplaces,
veranda, hot tub, parlor with
large fireplace

*Magnificent, historic & romantic 1920s log mansion featured in Ralph Lauren ads. Gourmet
country breakfast. Near national forest and lake.* E-mail: goldmtn@bigbear.com
Web site: bigbear.com/goldmtn

BIG BEAR LAKE

Knickerbocker Mansion
PO Box 1907, 92315
909-878-9190 Fax: 909-878-4248
800-388-4179
S. Miller & T. Bicanic
All year

125-350-B&B
11 rooms, 11 pb
Most CC,
C-ltd/S-no/P-no/H-yes
German

Full breakfast
Afternoon tea, snacks
Sitting room, library, suites,
fireplaces, cable TV

*A magnificently restored unique historic log mansion and Carriage House built in 1920.
Rustic elegance on 2.5 private heavily treed acres with quite atmosphere and personal
attention.* E-mail: knickmail@aol.com Web site: knickerbockermansion.com

BISHOP

Chalfant House B&B, The
213 Academy St, 93514
760-872-1790
Fred & Sally Manecke
All year

60-100-B&B
8 rooms, 8 pb
Most CC, *Rated*
C-ltd/S-no/P-no/H-no

Full breakfast
Afternoon tea, snacks
Library, antiques, sitting
room, ice cream sundaes
every evening

Historical B&B furnished in antiques. In town, close to everything. Quiet; afternoon tea, ice cream sundaes every evening 8–9. We love to pamper you. The Victorian parlor has a fireplace, TV/VCR.   E-mail: chalfantbb@qnet.com Web site: thesierraweb.com/lodging/chalfant

BODEGA

Sonoma Coast Villa
PO Box 236, 94922
707-876-9818 Fax: 707-876-9856
888-404-2255
Cyrus Griffin
All year

225-295-B&B
12 rooms, 12 pb
Visa, MC, AmEx, •
C-ltd/S-no/P-no/H-yes
Polish, Spanish, French

Full breakfast
Restaurant, dinner
Sitting room, library,
complimentary wine,
Jacuzzis, swimming pool,
suites

Elegant country inn nestled within rolling hills. Private, quiet and secluded, only an hour north of San Francisco. Proximity to the coast, redwoods, and wine country.
E-mail: reservations@scvilla.com Web site: scvilla.com

BODEGA BAY

Bay Hill Mansion B&B Inn
3919 Bay Hill Rd, 94923
707-875-3577 Fax: 707-875-9456
800-526-5927
Fran Miller
All year

150-B&B
6 rooms, 3 pb
Most CC, *Rated*, •
C-ltd/S-no/P-no/H-no

Full breakfast
Afternoon tea, snacks, wine
Sitting room, library, hot
tubs, panoramic bay, &
ocean views

This magnificent inn is located in the quiet fishing village of Bodega Bay on the picturesque North Coast of California   E-mail: bayhill@mcn.org

BRIDGEPORT

Cain House, The
PO Box 428, 93517
760-932-7040 Fax: 760-932-7419
800-433-CAIN
Chris & Marachal Gohlich
May 1-Nov. 1

80-135-B&B
7 rooms, 7 pb
Most CC, *Rated*, •
C-ltd/S-no/P-no/H-no

Full breakfast
Complimentary wine and
cheese
Sitting room, tennis courts, 6
rooms A/C, 2 with private
entrance, phones.

The grandeur of the eastern Sierras is the perfect setting for evening wine and cheese. Quiet, romantic, peaceful getaway.   E-mail: cainhouse@qnet.com

CALISTOGA

Backyard Garden Oasis, The
24019 Hilderbrand, 95461
707-987-0505
Greta Zeit & James
Shackelford
All year

125-B&B
3 rooms, 3 pb
Visa, MC, Disc, *Rated*,
•
S-ltd/P-no/H-yes
Spanish

Full breakfast
Complimentary wine
Jacuzzis, Fireplaces, Cable
TV, Accommodate business
travelers

Rustic cottages, simple but elegant. Peace, serenity, privacy, king-sized beds, skylight, fireplace, A/C, TV, VCR, private bath, full country breakfast, lawns, gardens.
E-mail: bygoasis@jnb.com Web site: jnb.com/~bygoasis

Brannan Cottage Inn
PO Box 81, 94515
707-924-4200
Dieter & Ruth Back
All year

140-175-B&B
6 rooms, 6 pb
Visa, MC, *Rated*
C-ltd/S-no/P-no/H-no
Spanish, German

Full breakfast
Complimentary wine
Sitting room, A/C, library,
fireplace, refrig., TV in 2
rooms

Charming 1860 National Register cottage-style Victorian, original wildflower stencils, country furnishings, lovely grounds, close to famous spas, wineries.
Web site: bbinternet.com/brannan

CALISTOGA ————————————————————————————————

Calistoga Country Lodge
2883 Foothill Blvd, 94515
707-942-5555 Fax: 707-942-5864
Rae Ellen & Becky
February-Dec.

105-165-B&B
6 rooms, 4 pb
Most CC, *Rated*
C-ltd/S-no/P-no/H-no

Continental plus buffet
Snacks, complimentary wine
Sitting room, gardens,
Jacuzzi & new pool in
renovated patio area

1917 ranch house restored in Southwest style offering country solitude, spacious common area, views of valley & open land. 1 mile from Calistoga spas. Small parties to 35 people.
E-mail: bnbccl@napanet.net Web site: countrylodge.com

CasaLana
1316 South Oak St, 94515
707-942-0615
Fax: 707-942-0204
877-968-2665
Lana Richardson
All year

140-B&B
1 rooms, 1 pb
Visa, MC, AmEx,
Rated, •
C-ltd/S-no/P-no/H-ltd

Continental breakfast plus
In room coffee/tea
Cable TV, conference
facilities, private entrance

Luxurious privacy in the heart of Napa Valley in a tranquil river setting.
E-mail: lana@casalana.com Web site: casalana.com

Elms B&B, The
1300 Cedar St, 94515
707-942-9476 Fax: 707-942-9479
800-235-4316
Stephen & Karla Wyle
All year

115-210-B&B
7 rooms, 7 pb
Most CC, *Rated*
S-no/P-no/H-yes

Full gourmet breakfast
Snacks, complimentary wine
Sitting room, bicycles, Wine
& cheese in p.m., chocolates
at bedtime

Step into the past where life was quieter and the pace relaxed. Enjoy the romance and intimacy of this 1871 French Victorian. Web site: theelms.com

Foothill House B&B
3037 Foothill Blvd, 94515
707-942-6933
Fax: 707-942-5692
800-942-6933
Doris & Gus Beckert
All year

165-300-B&B
4 rooms, 4 pb
Visa, MC, AmEx,
Rated, •
C-ltd/S-no/P-no/H-no

Full breakfast
Complimentary wine &
cheese
Turndown service: sherry, 3
rooms with Jacuzzi tub,
sitting room, AC

In a country setting, Foothill House offers 3 spacious rooms individually decorated with antiques, each with private bath, entrance & fireplace. Web site: foothillhouse.com

Hideaway Cottages
1412 Fairway, 94515
707-942-4108 Fax: 707-942-6110
M. Wilkinson
All year

69-190-EP
17 rooms, 17 pb
Visa, MC, AmEx, •
S-no/P-no/H-yes
Spanish

Jacuzzis, swimming pool,
cable TV, conference
facilities

Situated amongst three tree filled acres, Hideaway Cottages is a perfect setting for complete relaxation. Offering a variety of accommodations—some including full kitchens, many taking on a wine country motif. Web site: hideawaycottages.com

Hillcrest Country B&B
3225 Lake Co Hwy, 94515
707-942-6334
Debbie O'Gorman
All year

60-165-B&B
6 rooms, 4 pb
•
C-ltd/S-ltd/P-ltd/H-ltd

Continental breakfast on
weekends
Sitting room, library,
Jacuzzis, pool, cable TV,
fireplaces, conference

Secluded hilltop home with million dollar valley view. Home is filled with antique silver, china, rugs, artwork, & furniture. Swim, hike, & fish on 40 acres. Outdoor Jacuzzi & large pool.

CALISTOGA ————————————————————————

Mount View Hotel	130-245-B&B	Continental breakfast
1457 Lincoln Ave, 94515	32 rooms, 32 pb	Lunch & dinner available,
707-942-6877 Fax: 707-942-6904	Most CC, *Rated*, •	bar
800-816-6877	C-yes/S-yes/P-no/H-yes	Jacuzzi, swimming pool,
Laurie Jordan		mesquite BBQ, golf, tennis,
All year		entertainment

An Art Deco dream in all its European elegance. The only full-service hotel in Calistoga.

Scarlett's Country Inn	115-175-B&B	Full breakfast
3918 Silverado Trail, 94515	3 rooms, 3 pb	Complimentary wine &
707-942-6669 Fax: 707-942-6669	•	cheese
Scarlett Dwyer	C-yes/S-no/P-no/H-no	Sitting room, A/C, TV's,
All year	Spanish	microwaves & refrig., coffee
		makers, pool

*Secluded French country farmhouse overlooking vineyards in famed Napa Valley. Break-
fast served by woodland swimming pool.   E-mail:* scarletts@aol.com
Web site: members.aol.com/scarletts

Trailside Inn	165-185-B&B	Continental plus breakfast
4201 Silverado Trail, 94515	3 rooms, 3 pb	Complimentary wine
707-942-4106 Fax: 707-942-4702	Most CC, •	Mineral water, fireplace,
Randy & Lani Gray	C-ltd/S-ltd/P-no/H-no	kitchens, library, A/C, spa,
All year		private deck

*1930s farmhouse comfortably decorated with quilts and antiques. Each suite has private
entrance, 3 rooms plus bath. Two suites sleep party of four. Family suite. Heated swimming
pool.   E-mail:* trailsideinn@worldnet.att.net *Web site:* trailsideinn.com

Zinfandel House	100-125-B&B	Full breakfast
1253 Summit Dr, 94515	3 rooms, 2 pb	Complimentary wine
707-942-0733 Fax: 707-942-4618	Visa, MC,	Library, sitting room, hot tub
Bette & George Starke	C-ltd/S-no/P-no/H-no	
All year		

*Beautiful home situated on wooded hillside overlooking vineyards and mountains. Lovely
breakfast served on outside deck or in dining room.   E-mail:* zinhouse@pon.net
Web site: geocities.com/napavalley/1510

CAMBRIA ————————————————————————

Cambria Landing Inn	95-250-B&B	Continental breakfast
6530 Moonstone Beach Dr,	26 rooms, 26 pb	Complimentary
93428	Visa, MC, Disc, *Rated*,	wine/champagne
805-927-1619	•	Hot tubs, Jacuzzis for 2,
800-549-6789	C-ltd/S-yes/P-no/H-yes	oceanfront Jacuzzi suites,
Joni Apathy		refrigerators, VCR
All year		

*Romantic country inn set on ocean bluff near rocky beaches. Oceanfront rooms with TV,
private decks with patios, fireplaces and "breakfast in bed."   Web site:* moonstonebeach.com

J. Patrick House B&B	125-180-B&B	Full breakfast
2990 Burton Dr, 93428	8 rooms, 8 pb	Comp. wine, gourmet hor'
805-927-3812 Fax: 805-927-6759	Most CC, *Rated*, •	douvres
800-341-5258	C-ltd/S-no/P-no/H-no	Sitting room, library, killer
Barbara & Mel Schwimmer		chocolate chip cookies and
All year		milk, loving dog.

*Log cabin in woods surrounded by country gardens. Woodburning fireplaces, private baths,
in-room massages. Ocean is minutes away.   E-mail:* jph@jpatrickhouse.com
Web site: jpatrickhouse.com

CAMBRIA

Olallieberry Inn, The
2476 Main St, 93428
805-927-3222 Fax: 805-927-0202
888-927-3222
Peter & Carol Ann Irsfeld
All year

90-185-B&B
9 rooms, 6 pb
Visa, MC, *Rated*, •
C-ltd/S-no/P-no/H-yes

Full gourmet breakfast
Complimentary wine &
appetizers
Parlor, gathering room,
antiques, special diets,
cookies and milk

Pamper yourself where time stands still. Full gourmet breakfast; complimentary afternoon wine & hors d'oeuvres; an endless supply of home baked cookies. 7 day cancellation notice. E-mail: olallieinn@olallieberry.com Web site: olallieberry.com

Pickford House B&B, The
2555 MacLeod Way, 93428
805-927-8619
Anna Larsen
All year

109-145-B&B
8 rooms, 8 pb
Visa, MC, *Rated*
C-ltd/S-ltd/P-no/H-yes

Full breakfast
Cookies, wine after 5
Homemade fruit breads,
sitting room, fireplaces, TV in
all rooms, antiques

All rooms named after silent film-era stars and furnished with genuine antiques. All rooms have showers, TV and tubs. 7 miles to Hearst Castle. Extra person, $20.

Squibb House, The
4063 Burton Dr, 93428
805-927-9600 Fax: 805-927-9606
Martha Gibson
All year

95-155-B&B
5 rooms, 5 pb
Visa, MC, *Rated*, •
C-ltd/S-no/P-no/H-no

Continental plus breakfast
Restaurant steps away
Comp. wine tasting, sitting
room, garden, gazebo for
small events

Restored 1877 Victorian in the heart of Cambria. Within steps of galleries, shops and fine restaurants.

CAPITOLA BY THE SEA

Inn at Depot Hill
250 Monterey Ave, 95010
831-462-3376 Fax: 831-462-3697
800-572-2632
Suzie Lankes & Dan Floyd
All year

190-275-B&B
12 rooms, 12 pb
Most CC, *Rated*, •
C-ltd/S-ltd/P-no/H-yes
German, Spanish, Italian

Full gourmet breakfast
Wine/appetizers/dessert
Private patios with hot tubs,
fireplace, TV/VCR, stereos,
phones/modem

Walk to beach, dining & shops. Santa Cruz County's only 4 star rated lodging. Voted one of top 10 Inns in the Country. Upscale rooms resemble different countries of the world. Room service. E-mail: lodging@innatdepothill.com Web site: innatdepothill.com/depot-frame.html

CARMEL

Carmel Country Inn
PO Box 3756, 93921
831-625-3263
All year

115-205-B&B
Visa, MC,
P-ltd

Continental breakfast
Comp. sherry, coffee, tea in-
suite
Fireplaces, cable TV,
telephones, wet bar with
refrigerator, concierge

Carmel Country Inn offers a great blend of convenience, comfort, and intimacy in a surrounding of natural beauty. A quaint and secluded B&B. The New York Times called it "The Best Bargain in Carmel." Off-street parking to accommodate 100% of your need E-mail: info@carmelcountryinn.com Web site: carmelcountryinn.com

Carmel River Inn
PO Box 221609, 93922
831-624-1575 Fax: 831-624-0290
800-882-8142
Matthew D'Attilio
All year

90-170-EP
43 rooms, 43 pb
Visa, MC, *Rated*, •
C-yes/S-yes/P-yes/H-yes

Kitchens
Heated swimming pool,
rooms & cottages, balconies,
fireplaces

Quaint woodsy cottages surrounded by lush meadow views make this a memorable get-away or ideal retreat for company and tour groups. Ask for Lucky Lanier Special. Meadow for outdoor weddings, receptions, meetings available for a fee. E-mail: carmelriverinn@hotmail.com Web site: carmelriverinn.com

CARMEL

Carriage House Inn	189-315-B&B	Continental plus breakfast
PO Box 101, 93921	13 rooms, 13 pb	Wine, hors d'oeuvres
831-625-2585 Fax: 831-624-0974	Most CC, *Rated*, •	Sitting room, library, some
800-433-4732	C-ltd/S-no/P-no/H-no	rooms with Jacuzzis, or
Cathy Lewis		whirlpools
All year		

Intimate, romantic. King-size beds, down comforters, fireplaces, some sunken tubs. Within walking distance of shops, galleries, restaurants, & white beaches.
E-mail: concierge@innsbythesea.com Web site: innsbythesea.com/innres.htm#ch

Cypress Inn	115-295-B&B	Continental breakfast
PO Box Y, 93921	34 rooms, 34 pb	Afternoon tea, bar service
831-624-3871 Fax: 831-624-8216	Most CC, *Rated*, •	Fruit basket, sherry, daily
800-443-7443	C-ltd/S-ltd/P-yes/H-ltd	paper, fresh flowers
Hollace Thompson		
All year		

Charming Spanish-Mediterranean style, built in 1929. In the heart of the village within walking distance to shops, restaurants and galleries. The Inn has recently undergone a major remodel.   E-mail: info@cypress-inn.com Web site: cypress-inn.com

Happy Landing Inn	90-170-B&B	Continental plus breakfast
PO Box 2619, 93921	7 rooms, 7 pb	Complimentary sherry
831-624-7917	Visa, MC, *Rated*	Sitting room, Gazebo,
Robert Ballard & Dick Stewart	C-ltd/S-no/P-no/H-yes	gardens, pond, Honeymoon
All year		cottage available

Hansel & Gretel cottages in the heart of Carmel, like something from a Beatrix Potter book. Surrounds a central flowering garden; breakfast is served in your room.
Web site: virtualcities.com/ons/ca/c/cac8501.htm

Homestead Inn, The	65-105-EP	Complimentary coffee in
PO Box 1285, 93921	12 rooms, 12 pb	rooms
831-624-4119 Fax: 831-624-7688	C-yes/S-yes	4 cottages with kitchens, 2
Betty Colletto		cottages with fireplaces
All year		

A unique inn nestled in the heart of Carmel. Rooms and cottages with private baths, some kitchens & fireplaces. Reasonably priced and close to town. Honeymoon cottage available.   Web site: travelguides.com/home/homestead/

Old Monterey Inn	200-350-B&B	Full breakfast
500 Martin St, 93940	10 rooms, 10 pb	Tea, snacks, wine
831-375-8284 Fax: 831-375-6730	Visa, MC, AmEx,	Sitting room, 2 double
800-350-2344	*Rated*, •	whirlpool tubs, TV & phone
Ann & Gene Swett	S-no/P-no/H-no	in room, suites, library
All year	French	

Classic English-style Tudor amid lush gardens. Exceptionally romantic. Service-oriented inn with privacy valued. Breakfasts in bed are not to be missed. Bikes, fireplaces, full-time concierge, robes, and hairdryers.   E-mail: omi@oldmontereyinn.com
Web site: oldmontereyinn.com

Sandpiper Inn by the Sea	104-260-B&B	Continental plus breakfast
2408 Bay View Ave, 93923	17 rooms, 17 pb	Coffee, tea, sherry
831-624-6433 Fax: 831-624-5964	Most CC, *Rated*, •	Library, flowers, bikes,
800-633-6433	C-ltd/S-ltd/P-no/H-no	fireplace, lounge, close, to
Audie Housman	Spanish, German	tennis, golf, hiking
All year		

One hundred yards from Carmel Beach. European-style country inn, with some antiques & fresh flowers. Ocean views, fireplaces, garden.   Web site: sandpiper-inn.com

CARMEL ————————————————————————

Stonehouse Inn	110-208-B&B	Continental plus breakfast
PO Box 2517, 93921	6 rooms	Comp. port & cookies
831-624-4569	Visa, MC, •	Sitting room, fireplace,
Cid Navailles	C-ltd/S-no/P-no/H-no	bicycles
All year		

Historic Carmel house built in 1906, traditional Bed & Breakfast. Within walking distance of shopping, restaurants, beach Web site: carmelstonehouse.com

Tally Ho Inn	125-250-B&B	Continental plus breakfast
PO Box 3726, 93921	12 rooms, 12 pb	Aft. tea, brandy
831-624-2232 Fax: 831-624-2661	Most CC, *Rated*, •	Floral garden, sun deck,
800-652-2632	C-yes/S-yes/P-no/H-no	fireplaces, ocean views,
John Wilson	some French	close to beach
All year		

This English country inn has bountiful gardens with sweeping ocean views from individually appointed rooms and sun decks. Former home of cartoonist Jimmy Hatlo.
E-mail: info@tallyho-inn.com Web site: tallyho-inn.com/

Vagabond's House Inn	95-185-B&B	Continental plus breakfast
PO Box 2747, 93921	11 rooms, 11 pb	Sitting room w/fireplace,
831-624-7738 Fax: 831-626-1243	Visa, MC, •	library, courtyard, 2 blocks
800-262-1262	C-ltd/S-yes/P-yes/H-no	to downtown
Sally Goss	French	
All year		

Antique clocks and pictures, quilted bedspreads, fresh flowers, plants, shelves filled with old books. Sherry by the fireplace; breakfast served in your room.
Web site: innbook.com/vagabond.html

CARMEL BY THE SEA ————————————————

Sea View Inn	90-160-B&B	Continental plus breakfast
PO Box 4138, 93921	8 rooms, 6 pb	Afternoon tea & coffee
831-624-8778 Fax: 831-625-5901	Visa, MC, *Rated*, •	Comp. evening wine, sitting
Marshall & Diane Hydorn	C-ltd/S-no/P-no/H-no	room, library, garden
All year		

Small, intimate, cozy Victorian near village and beach. Enjoy breakfast and evening wine served by the fireside, or relax in secluded garden

CARMEL VALLEY ————————————————————

Carmel Valley Lodge	129-299-B&B	Continental plus breakfast
PO Box 93, 93924	35 rooms, 35 pb	Library, hot tub, sauna, pool,
831-659-2261 Fax: 831-659-4558	Most CC, *Rated*, •	fitness center, TV,
800-641-4646	C-yes/S-yes/P-yes/H-yes	complimentary newspaper
Michael Cawdrey	French, Spanish	
All year		

Quiet, lovely spot. Romantic setting for lovers of privacy, nature, hiking, golf, tennis, swimming, riding & just plain lovers. Cozy fireplace cottages. Dogs welcome, $10/night. Conference facilities. E-mail: info@valleylodge.com Web site: valleylodge.com

CHESTER ——————————————————————————

Bidwell House	75-160-B&B	Full gourmet breakfast
PO Box 1790, 96020	14 rooms, 12 pb	Afternoon tea, snacks
530-258-3338	Visa, MC, *Rated*, •	Sitting room, library, hot tubs
Kim & Ian James	C-yes/S-ltd/P-no/H-yes	in rooms, Jacuzzis, fireplaces
All year		

Historical Inn on the edge of Lassen National Park, beautiful lake Almanor and next to the Feather River; gourmet breakfast; hikers, golfers, and skier of both kinds paradise! Full service gourmet dinners available. E-mail: bidwellhouse@thegrid.net
Web site: bidwellhouse.com

CLOVERDALE

Tea Garden Inn
119 West Third St, 95424
707-894-8557 Fax: 707-894-7548
800-996-8675
Hedley Cooper
Season Inquire

80-125-B&B
3 rooms, 3 pb
•
C-ltd/S-no/P-ltd/H-no

Full breakfast
Afternoon tea and cookies
Sitting room, library, suites

Beautifully restored 1870's Victorian two blocks from charming small town shops & restaurants. Sumptuous full breakfast. Suites with double whirlpool bath or clawfoot tub & large shower.

Vintage Towers Inn B&B
302 N Main St, 95425
707-894-4535
888-886-9377
Cindy & Gus Wolter
All year

75-165-B&B
8 rooms, 6 pb
Most CC, *Rated*, •
C-ltd/S-ltd/P-ltd/H-yes

Full breakfast
Afternoon snacks
3 sitting rms., piano, bicycles,
gazebo, TV, veranda &
gardens

A towered mansion on the national register, on a quiet tree-lined street in a wine country town. Walk to river, wineries and fine dining E-mail: gus@vintagetowers.com
Web site: vintagetowers.com

COFFEE CREEK

Coffee Creek Guest Ranch
HC 2 Box 4940, 96091
530-266-3343 Fax: 530-266-3597
800-624-4480
Ruth and Mark Hartman
All year

AP
15 rooms, 15 pb
Most CC, *Rated*, •
C-yes/S-ltd/P-no/H-yes
Dutch, German

Full breakfast
All meals included, comp.
wine
Restaurant, bar, bicycles,
Jacuzzis, swimming pool,
suites, fireplaces

Picture-postcare views await you on 127 acres within the Trinity Alps Wilderness of snow-capped mountains and sparkling lakes. Secluded cabins lie along Coffee Creek, meals, romantic weekends, horseback riding, and more! E-mail: ccranch@tds.net
Web site: coffeecreekranch.com

COLOMA

Coloma Country Inn, The
PO Box 502, 95613
530-622-6919
Alan & Cindi Ehrgott
All year

95-195-B&B
7 rooms, 3 pb
Rated, •
C-yes/S-no/P-no/H-no
Spanish, French

Full breakfast
Comp. wine, beverages
Sitting room, bicycles,
Victorian tea, rafting, 2 new
suites, canoeing

Country Victorian built in 1856, set among rose and flower gardens and pond on 5 acres. Half a block to Sutter's Mill and American River. Balloon flights nearby.
E-mail: info@colomacountryinn.com Web site: colomacountryinn.com

COLUMBIA

Blue Nile Inn
11250 Pacific St, 95310
209-532-8041
Ray & Anita Miller
All year

105-135-B&B
4 rooms, 4 pb
Most CC,
C-ltd/S-ltd/P-no/H-no

Full breakfast
Afternoon snacks
Sitting room, library,
Jacuzzis, fireplaces, phones,
TV/VCR-great rm.

Relaxing, romantic, fireplaces, 2-person Jacuzzi tubs, gourmet breakfast. Come stay with us & stroll to great restaurants, repertory theatre, shops, museums & stagecoach rides in Columbia State Park. E-mail: Innkeeper@Blue-Nile-Inn.com Web site: Blue-Nile-Inn.com

Columbia City Hotel
PO Box 1870, 95310
209-532-1479 Fax: 209-532-7027
800-532-1479
Tom Bender
All year

95-115-B&B
10 rooms, 10 pb
Visa, MC, AmEx,
Rated, •
C-yes/S-ltd/P-no/H-no

Continental plus breakfast
French restaurant
Sitting room, piano,
playhouse, beer on draft in
saloon

Historical location in a state-preserved Gold Rush town; 9 antique-appointed rooms; small elegant dining room and authentic saloon. Goldpanning nearby, wine tasting events.
E-mail: info@cityhotel.com Web site: cityhotel.com

COLUMBIA

Columbia Fallon Hotel
PO Box 1870, 95310
209-532-1470 Fax: 209-532-7027
800-532-1479
Tom Bender   All year

50-105-B&B
14 rooms, 14 pb
Visa, MC, *Rated*, •
C-yes/S-ltd/P-no/H-yes

Continental plus breakfast
Sitting room, rose garden,
live theater, gold panning
nearby, fishing

Restored Victorian hotel, full of antiques in state-preserved Gold Rush town. Elegant and intimate. Near Yosemite. Many historic family fun events throughout the year.
E-mail: info@cityhotel.com   Web site: cityhotel.com

CROWLEY LAKE

Rainbow Tarns B&B
HC79, Box 1053, 93546
760-935-4556
888-588-6269
Brock & Diane Thoman
Closed Dec 24/25, March

95-140-B&B
3 rooms, 3 pb
C-ltd/S-no/P-no/H-yes

Full country breakfast
Afternoon wine, snacks
Sitting room, library, 2 rooms
with Jacuzzis, vegy meals
arranged.

Secluded log cabin lodge in a beautiful, 7000 foot high, three acre Sierra mountain setting, among tall shade trees with stream and ponds, and a vast green meadow before you.
E-mail: info@rainbowtarns.com   Web site: rainbowtarns.com

DAVENPORT

Davenport B&B Inn
31 Davenport Ave, 95017
831-425-1818 Fax: 831-423-1160
800-870-1817
Bruce & Marcia McDougal
All year

75-125-B&B
12 rooms, 12 pb
Most CC, *Rated*, •
C-ltd/S-no/P-no/H-ltd

Full bkfst. (weekdays)
Cont. plus on weekends
Restaurant, gift shop, picnic
lunches, sitting room, gallery

Small coastal village half way between San Francisco & Carmel/Monterey. Ocean view rooms with antique & ethnic collections. Favorite destination restaurant and gallery gift shop   E-mail: inn@swanton.com   Web site: swanton.com/BnB

DAVIS

University Inn B&B
340 "A" St, 95616
530-756-8648 Fax: 530-753-6920
800-756-8648
Lynda & Ross Yancher
All year

55-75-B&B
4 rooms, 4 pb
Most CC, *Rated*, •
C-yes/S-no/P-yes/H-yes

Continental plus breakfast
Complimentary beverages
Microwave, bicycles, airport
shuttle

A great taste of Davis, ten steps from the University. Quiet location. Rooms with private phone, cable TV, refrigerator, microwave.   E-mail: yancher@aol.com

DUNSMUIR

Dunsmuir Inn
5423 Dunsmuir Ave, 96025
530-235-4543 Fax: 530-235-4154
888-386-7684
Julie & Jerry Iskra
All year

65-75-B&B
5 rooms, 5 pb
Most CC, •
C-yes/S-no/P-no/H-no

Full breakfast
Vegetarian bkfst. avail.
Lunch, snacks, sitting room,
BBQ, fishing close by

Year round recreation; skiing, fishing, golfing, hiking; northern California country inn; relax for one day or one week   E-mail: dunsinn@siskiyou.net   Web site: dunsmuirinn.com

EUREKA

Carter House Victorians
301 L St, 95501
707-444-8062 Fax: 707-444-8067
800-404-1390
Mark & Christi Carter
All year

125-495-B&B
8 rooms, 8 pb
Most CC,
C-yes/S-no/P-no/H-no

Full breakfast
Dinner (by reservation)
Whirlpools, fireplaces, sitt.
rms., Jacuzzis, TV,
VCR/CD/stereo, gardens

New Victorian. Enjoy wines & appetizers before dinner, cordials or teas & cookies at bedtime. Warm hospitality; award-winning bkfsts. Bell cottage. Restaurant 301 at Hotel Carter is one of 1998's four new recipients of Wine Spectator Magazine's Award.
E-mail: carter52@carterhouse.com   Web site: carterhouse.com

An Elegant Victorian Mansion, Eureka, CA

EUREKA

Cornelius Daly Inn
1125 H St, 95501
707-445-3638 Fax: 707-444-3636
800-321-9656
Sue & Gene Clinesmith
All year

85-150-B&B
5 rooms, 3 pb
Most CC, *Rated*, •
C-ltd/S-ltd/P-no/H-no

Full breakfast
Wine, hors d'oeuvres
Sitting room, library,
Victorian gardens, pond,
VCR/CD/stereo, gardens

A beautifully restored turn-of-the-century mansion, one of Eureka's finest. 1 room with twin beds, 4 rooms with queen beds. Victorian gardens, fish pond.   E-mail: dalyinn@ humboldt1.com Web site: humboldt1.com/~dalyinn

An Elegant Victorian Mansion
1406 "C" St, 95501
707-444-3144 Fax: 707-442-5594
Doug & Lily Vieyra
All year

85-225-B&B
4 rooms, 3 pb
Visa, MC, *Rated*, •
C-ltd/S-no/P-no/H-yes
French, Dutch, German

Full gourmet breakfast
Complimentary ice cream
sodas
Sauna, massage, croquet,
parlors, flower gardens,
antique autos, bay views

1888 National Historic Landmark "House-Museum" for the discriminating connoisseur of authentic Victorian decor, who has a passion for quality, service and the extra-ordinary. Web site: bbhost.com/eureka-california

Victorian Inn
PO Box 96, 95536
707-786-4949 Fax: 707-786-4558
888-589-1808
Lowell Daniels & Jenny Oaks
All year

85-150-B&B
12 rooms, 12 pb
Most CC,
C-yes/S-no/P-no/H-no

Full breakfast
Lunch/dinner available,
snacks
Restaurant, bar, sitting room,
suites, fireplace, cable TV

The Victorian Inn stands as a monument to luxurious comfort & exquisite craftsmanship. It embodies the elegance and romance of the timber boom era on the North Coast. E-mail: innkeeper@a-victorian-inn.com Web site: a-victorian-inn.com

Weaver's Inn, A
1440 "B" St, 95501
707-443-8119 Fax: 707-443-7923
800-992-8119
Lea L. Montgomery
All year

75-125-B&B
4 rooms, 3 pb
Most CC, *Rated*, •
C-ltd/S-ltd/P-ltd/H-no

Full gourmet breakfast
Afternoon tea or coffee
Sitting room, hot tub in one
room, Japanese garden

Stately Queen Anne Victorian (circa 1883). Quiet, genteel elegance, spacious lawn & flower gardens, gourmet breakfast, complimentary wine. Historic town in heart of Redwoods.   E-mail: weavrinn@humboldt1.com Web site: humboldt1.com/~weavrinn

FALLBROOK

Fallbrook Country Inn
1425 S Mission Rd, 92028
760-728-1114 Fax: 760-731-6754
Larry & Pam Lushanko
All year

70-90-B&B
28 rooms, 28 pb
Most CC, *Rated*, •
C-yes/S-ltd/P-no/H-ltd

Continental plus breakfast
Lunch/dinner available,
restaurant
Bar service, sitting rm.,
swimming pool, cable TV,
conference facilities

We won the Garden Award of the Year. We are close to 5 championship golf courses and the wine country in Temecula. We specialize in wedding accommodations.
E-mail: fallbrkinn@aol.com   Web site: fallbrookca.org/fbcoinn.htm

FERNDALE

Gingerbread Mansion Inn
PO Box 40, 95536
707-786-4000 Fax: 707-786-4381
800-952-4136
Ken Torbert   All year

140-375-B&B
10 rooms, 10 pb
Visa, MC, *Rated*, •
C-ltd/S-no/P-no/H-no
Port., Sp., Fr., Jap.

Full breakfast
Afternoon tea & cake
5 guest parlors, library with
fireplace, English gardens,
bikes

Northern California's most photographed inn! Perfect getaway in quiet Victorian village ("his & her bubble baths"). Turndown with chocolate.   E-mail: kenn@humboldt1.com
Web site: gingerbread-mansion.com

FORT BRAGG

Avalon House B&B
561 Stewart St, 95437
707-964-5555 Fax: 707-964-5555
800-964-5556
Anne Sorrells   All year

80-145-B&B
6 rooms, 6 pb
Most CC, *Rated*, •
C-yes/S-no/P-no/H-no

Full breakfast
Complimentary sherry/port
Fireplaces in rooms,
whirlpool tubs in rooms,
fishing, spas

1905 Craftsman house in a quiet neighborhood close to ocean and Skunk Train Depot. Fireplaces. Romantic Mendocino Coast retreat.   E-mail: anne@theavalonhouse.com
Web site: theavalonhouse.com

Cleone Gardens Inn
24600 N Hwy 1, 95437
707-964-2788
800-400-2189
Lar Krug   All year

80-150-EP
12 rooms, 12 pb
Most CC, *Rated*, •
C-ltd/S-ltd/P-ltd/H-ltd

Full breakfast available (fee)
Suites, fireplaces, cable TV,
Spa by reservation (extra
charge)

Quiet gardens amid trees on 5 acres near beach, lake, couples/families in rooms with fireplace, kitchen, suite or deck. Seperate beach house: 2 suites, 4 acres
E-mail: cleonegardensinn@mcn.org   Web site: cleonegardensinn.com

Grey Whale Inn
615 N Main St, 95437
707-964-0640 Fax: 707-964-4408
800-382-7244
John & Colette Bailey
All year

90-180-B&B
14 rooms, 14 pb
Most CC, *Rated*, •
C-ltd/S-no/P-no/H-yes

Full buffet breakfast
Tea, fresh fruit always
Parlor, TV-VCR, fireplace,
upgrades, gift shop, art
gallery

Mendocino coast landmark since 1915. Spacious rooms; ocean, town or garden views. Whale Watch with gas firepalce. Honeymoon suite with Jacuzzi & private sundeck.
E-mail: stay@greywhaleinn.com   Web site: greywhaleinn.com

Old Coast Hotel
19001 Springbrook Ln, 95070
707-961-4488 Fax: 707-961-4480
888-468-3550
Kathy Sauer   All year

95-125-B&B
16 rooms, 16 pb
Visa, MC, *Rated*, •
C-yes/S-no/P-no/H-yes
Spanish

Continental breakfast plus
Lunch, dinner, snacks,
restaurant
Comp. wine, bar service,
sitting room, library, bikes,
fireplaces, cable TV

The Old Coast Hotel is a meticulously restored c. 1892 landmark. Turn of the century lamps and fixtures, pressed tinwalls, and gleaming hardwood floors along with sundeck & flowering gardens make it Fort Bragg's destination of choice.

Avalon House B&B, Ft. Bragg, CA

FORT BRAGG

Weller House Inn
524 Stewart St, 95437
707-964-4415 Fax: 707-964-4198
877-8-WELLER
Ted & Eva Kidwell
All year

95-175-B&B
7 rooms, 7 pb
Most CC, •
C-ltd/S-no/P-ltd/H-ltd
Swedish

Full breakfast
Complimentary wine
Sitting room, library, cable,
Jacuzzis, fireplaces,
observation tower

Victorian beauty built in 1886. Lavish breakfast served in 900 square foot ballroom. Historic 4 story water tower with guest rooms, ceramic studio, hot tub & observation deck.   E-mail: innkeeper@wellerhouse.com *Web site:* wellerhouse.com

FREMONT

Lord Bradley's Inn
43344 Mission Blvd, 94539
510-490-0520 Fax: 510-490-3015
877-567-3272
Susie & Steve Wilson
All year

85-135-B&B
8 rooms, 8 pb
Visa, MC, *Rated*, •
C-yes/S-ltd/P-ltd/H-yes
Spanish

Continental plus breakfast
High tea by appointment
Sitting room, observation
tower

Adjacent to historic Mission San Jose de Guadalupe; nestled below Mission Peak. Kite fliers' paradise; Victorian antiques and decorations; gourmet breakfasts. New bridal suite with Jacuzzi tub.   E-mail: lbibandb@aol.com *Web site:* lordbradleysinn.com

GARBERVILLE

Benbow Inn
445 Lake Benbow Dr, 95542
707-923-2124 Fax: 707-923-2122
800-355-3301
Teresa & John Porter
Mid April- Jan. 2

99-135-EP
55 rooms, 55 pb
Most CC, *Rated*, •
C-ltd/S-no/P-no/H-no
German, Czech, Spanish

Lun./din.(fee), tea, snacks,
wine
Restaurant, bar service, sitt.
rm., lib., bikes, Jacuzzis,
pool, fireplaces

Tudor-Style Inn filled with antiques, objects D'art, whimsical touches. Voted most romantic getaway in Northern CA.   E-mail: benbow@benbowinn.com *Web site:* benbowinn.com

GILROY

Country Rose Inn B&B
PO Box 2500, 95021
408-842-0441 Fax: 408-842-6646
Rose Hernandez
All year

129-189-B&B
5 rooms, 5 pb
Visa, MC, *Rated*, •
C-ltd/S-no/P-no/H-no
Spanish

Full breakfast
Snacks
Library, sitting room, suite
with jet tub

A gracious farmhouse located in the heart of California's pastoral central coast. The coast is a scenic drive away. Unexpected. Serene. Debbie Reynolds has stayed here.
Web site: bbonline.com/ca/countryrose/

GLEN ELLEN ───────────────────────────────────────

Gaige House Inn, The	170-395-B&B	Full gourmet breakfast
13540 Arnold Dr, 95442	15 rooms, 15 pb	Afternoon tea, snacks
707-935-0237 Fax: 707-935-6411	Visa, MC, AmEx,	Comp. wine, sitt. rm., library,
800-935-0237	*Rated*, •	swimming pool, Jacuzzis,
Ken Burnett & Greg Nemrow	C-ltd/S-no/P-no/H-yes	cable TV, fireplace
All year		

*"One of the prettiest pools around." —*Travel & Leisure*. "The finest B&B in the wine country." —*Frommer's*. Restrained yet infinitely stylish with generous amenities.*
E-mail: gaige@sprynet.com Web site: gaige.com

GRASS VALLEY ─────────────────────────────────────

Murphy's Inn	110-165-B&B	Full breakfast
318 Neal St, 95945	8 rooms, 8 pb	Beverages, snacks
530-273-6873 Fax: 530-273-5157	Visa, MC, AmEx,	2 sitting rooms, 600 foot deck,
800-895-2488	*Rated*, •	house for families
Nancy & Ted Daus	C-ltd/S-no/P-no/H-no	
All year		

Victorian estate of gold baron. Walk to restaurants, historic district. Golf, ski, hike or pan for gold. Delicious breakfasts. E-mail: murphys@jps.net Web site: murphysinn.com

GROVELAND ──

Groveland Hotel, The	125-200-B&B	Continental plus breakfast
PO Box 289, 95321	17 rooms, 17 pb	Dinner served nightly
209-962-4000 Fax: 209-962-6674	Visa, MC, AmEx,	Conf. fac., comp. wine, bar
800-273-3314	*Rated*, •	service, sitting rm., lib., hot
Peggy A. Mosley	C-yes/S-ltd/P-ltd/H-yes	tubs, 3 suites
All year	AT&T interpreter service	

Beautiful, restored historic Gold Rush hotel. Gourmet dining in Victorian garden. Near Yosemite. Fly fishing and wilderness survival schools. E-mail: peggy@groveland.com
Web site: groveland.com

Inn at Sugar Pine Ranch	110-150-B&B	Full breakfast
21250 Hwy 120, 95321	12 rooms, 12 pb	Afternoon tea
209-962-7823 Fax: 209-962-7823	Visa, MC, *Rated*, •	Sitting room, library,
Elaine & Craig	S-no/P-no/H-no	swimming pool, whirlpool,
All year		tubs & fireplaces avail.

Situated on 60 acres, our home and cottages are a place for all seasons, just 22 miles from Yosemite's gate. Web site: bizware.com/sugarpine

GUALALA ──

North Coast Country Inn	150-175-B&B	Full breakfast to room
34591 S Highway 1, 95445	6 rooms, 6 pb	Wet bar in all rooms
707-884-4537	Visa, MC, AmEx,	Hot tub, library, gazebo,
800-959-4537	*Rated*, •	antique shop, fireplaces,
Loren & Nancy Flanagan	C-ltd/S-no/P-no/H-no	beach access, conference
All year		

A cluster of weathered redwood buildings on a forested hillside overlooking Pacific Ocean. Enjoy evening sherry/port. Close to golf, tennis & riding fac. 2 new deluxe guest rooms

Old Milano Hotel, The	80-210-B&B	Full breakfast
38300 Shoreline Hwy 1, 95445	9 rooms, 6 pb	Gourmet dining Wed-Sun
707-884-3256 Fax: 707-884-4249	Visa, MC,	Houseblend coffee & tea,
Leslie L. Linscheid	C-ltd/S-no/P-no/H-ltd	sitting room, hot tub, wine
All year		parlor

Lavishly refurbished inn on 3 acres. Breathtaking views of Mendocino coast. Near beaches & river, hiking, swimming, cycling. 4 new cottages with ocean views, queen beds, fireplaces, & private baths. E-mail: coast@oldmilanohotel.com Web site: oldmilanolhotel.com

GUERNEVILLE

Creekside Inn & Resort
PO Box 2185, 95446
707-869-3623 Fax: 707-869-1417
800-776-6586
Lynn & Mark Crescione
All year

70-225-B&B
6 rooms
Visa, MC, AmEx, •
C-yes/S-yes
Spanish

Full breakfast
Library, sitting room,
conference facilities, direct
phone

A relaxed and friendly atmosphere best describes this six-room bed & breakfast situated in the redwoods near the Russian River. E-mail: stay@creeksideinn.com
Web site: creeksideinn.com

Ridenhour Ranch House Inn
12850 River Rd, 95446
707-887-1033 Fax: 707-869-2967
888-877-4466
Meilani Naranjo & Chris Bell
Exc. Jan. & Feb.

105-160-B&B
8 rooms, 8 pb
Visa, MC, *Rated*, •
C-ltd/S-ltd/P-no/H-yes

Full gourmet breakfast
Complimentary port or
sherry
Picnic lunches, hot tub,
sitting room, fireplace

Country inn on the Russian River in the heart of the lush and lovely Sonoma wine country. Adjacent to historic Korbel Champagne Cellars. Fresh flowers. E-mail: ridenhourinn@earthlink.net Web site: ridenhourranchhouseinn.com

HALF MOON BAY

Goose & Turrets B&B
PO Box 370937, 94037
650-728-5451 Fax: 650-728-0141
Raymond & Emily Hoche-Mong
All year

100-150-B&B
5 rooms, 5 pb
Most CC, *Rated*, •
C-ltd/S-no/P-no
French

Full breakfast
Afternoon tea, snacks
Sitting room w/woodstove,
quiet garden, fireplaces, local
airport pickup

An historic inn catering to readers, nature lovers, pilots & enthusiastic eaters. Afternoon tea & 4-course breakfasts. E-mail: rhmgt@montara.com Web site: montara.com/goose.html/

Mill Rose Inn
615 Mill St, 94019
650-726-8750 Fax: 650-726-3031
800-900-7673
Eve & Terry Baldwin
All year

165-285-B&B
6 rooms, 6 pb
Most CC, *Rated*, •
C-ltd/S-no/P-no/H-no
Spanish, some French

Full breakfast
Comp. wine, aftn. tea,
desserts
Deluxe featherbeds, frplc.,
ceiling fans, spa, cable
TV/VCR, phones, robes

Exquisitely appointed flower-filled rooms & suites with private bath, entrance. English country gardens by the sea. Oriental rugs, European antiques, custom wallpaper. Horseback riding, bikes, hiking & golf. Nearby day spa, shops, galleries & restaurants
E-mail: tb@millroseinn.com Web site: millroseinn.com

Old Thyme Inn, The
779 Main St, 94019
650-726-1616 Fax: 650-726-6394
800-720-4277
Rick & Kathy Ellis   All year

100-255-B&B
7 rooms, 7 pb
Most CC, *Rated*, •
C-ltd/S-no/P-no/H-no
French

Full breakfast
Complimentary wine
Library, sitting room, herb
garden

The fully restored inn is furnished in antiques and the innkeepers' collection of fine art. Its 7 guest rooms take their names from herbs that grow in the garden-designed to help you slip effortlessly into the easy pace of the Coastside. E-mail: innkeeper@oldthymeinn.com
Web site: oldthymeinn.com

Rancho San Gregorio
Route 1, Box 54, 94074
650-747-0810 Fax: 650-747-0184
Bud & Lee Raynor
All year

95-160-B&B
4 rooms, 4 pb
Most CC, *Rated*, •
C-ltd/S-ltd

Full country breakfast
Complimentary beverages,
snacks
Sitting room, library,
antiques, gazebo, garden,
orchards, conferences

California Mission-style coastal retreat; serene; spectacular views of wooded hills; friendly hospitality; hearty breakfast; Near Ano Nuevo. E-mail: rsgleebud@aol.com Web site: san-gregorio-lodging.com

HEALDSBURG

Calderwood Inn	135-200-B&B	Full breakfast
25 W Grant St, 95448	Most CC,	woodstoves, fireplaces
707-431-1110	C-ltd/S-no/P-no/H-no	
800-600-5444		
Jennifer & Paul		
All year		

In the heart of the wine country. Web site: calderwoodinn.com

Camellia Inn	80-175-B&B	Full breakfast
211 North St, 95448	9 rooms, 9 pb	Complimentary beverage &
707-433-8182 Fax: 707-433-8130	Visa, MC, *Rated*, •	snacks
800-727-8182	C-ltd/S-ltd/P-no/H-ltd	Sitting room, swimming pool
Ray, Del & Lucy Lewand		in summer, 4 rooms with
All year		whirlpool tubs

Elegant Italianate Victorian built in 1869, near Sonoma's finest wineries—beautifully restored and furnished with antiques, Oriental rugs. E-mail: info@camelliainn.com
Web site: camelliainn.com

Grape Leaf Inn, The	115-185-B&B	Full country breakfast
539 Johnson St, 95448	7 rooms, 7 pb	Complimentary wine 5-8
707-433-8140 Fax: 707-433-3140	Visa, MC, *Rated*, •	Jacuzzi tub/showers for, two
Richard & Kae Rosenberg	C-ltd/S-no/P-no/H-no	in five guest rooms,
All year		fireplaces 2 rms.

Victorian elegance amidst Sonoma County's finest wineries. Generous full breakfast, complimentary premium wines, all private baths, and more! E-mail: grapeleaf@pacbell.net
Web site: grapeleafinn.com

Haydon Street Inn	95-175-B&B	Full breakfast
321 Haydon St, 95448	8 rooms, 8 pb	Afternoon tea, snacks
707-433-5228 Fax: 707-433-6637	Visa, MC, *Rated*, •	Sitting room, fireplaces,
800-528-3703	C-ltd/S-no/P-no/H-no	cable TV, Jacuzzis
Dick & Pat Bertapelle		
All year		

Historic wine country Queen Anne home in quaint, friendly Sonoma County town. Walk to historic town plaza with great restaurants, antique stores & boutiques.
E-mail: innkeeper@haydon.com Web site: haydon.com

Healdsburg Inn on the Plaza	115-265-B&B	Full healthy breakfast
110 Matheson St, 95448	10 rooms, 10 pb	Champagne brunch on
707-433-6991 Fax: 707-433-9513	Visa, MC, *Rated*	weekends
800-431-8663	C-ltd/S-no/P-no/H-yes	Gallery, gift shops, A/C,
Genny Jenkins		fireplaces, open balconies
All year		

Individually appointed Victorian rooms with antiques. Whirlpool tub for 2. Centrally located overlooking old town plaza. Enclosed solarium, TV/VCRs, video library, room phones. Web site: healdsburginn.com

Raford House	110-175-B&B	Full breakfast
10630 Wohler Rd, 95448	7 rooms, 5 pb	Complimentary wine
707-887-9573 Fax: 707-887-9597	Most CC, *Rated*, •	Porch, vineyards, patio,
800-887-9503	C-ltd/S-ltd/P-no/H-ltd	some fireplaces, roses
Carole & Jack Vore		
All year		

Victorian farmhouse overlooks vineyards of Sonoma County. Beautiful country setting is just 1 1/2 hours from San Francisco. County historical landmark. Web site: rafordhouse.com

HOLLYWOOD

Elaine's Hollywood B&B
1616 N Sierra Bonita Ave,
90046
323-850-0766 Fax: 323-851-6243
Elaine and Avik Gilboa
All year

60-80-B&B
2 rooms, 2 pb
•
C-yes/S-no/P-yes/H-no
Fr., Ger., Sp., It., Russ.

Continental
Cable TV

Our B&B is a very warm and friendly home. Our guests become part of our family and enjoy the full facilities available at the house. E-mail: Avikg@aol.com

HOPE VALLEY

Sorensen's Resort
14255 Hwy 88, 96120
530-694-2203
800-423-9949
John & Patty Brissenden
All year

65-EP/B&B
30 rooms, 30 pb
Most CC, *Rated*, •
C-yes/S-no/P-ltd/H-ltd
Some Spanish

Full breakfast (fee)
Snacks, restaurant, bar
service
Library, Jacuzzi in cabin, hot
springs nearby, fireplaces,
bikes/skis nearby

Cozy creekside cabins nestled in Alps of California. Close to Tahoe & Kirkwood, cross country skiing. Full-moon river rafting. Water color, fly tying & rod building courses.

HOPLAND

Thatcher Inn & Restaurant
PO Box 660, 95449
707-744-1890 Fax: 707-744-1219
800-266-1891
Don & Marlena Sacca
All year

130-B&B
20 rooms, 20 pb
Rated, •
C-ltd/S-no/P-no/H-no

Full breakfast
Full service restaurant
Library with fireplace,
swimming pool, lobby bar,
weddings, retreats

Historic, elegant 1890 Victorian Inn, completely refurbished & decorated with antiques, period furnishings, floral wallpaper & linens, large bathrooms. Lobby bar with single malts, brandies, wines. E-mail: info@thatcherinn.com Web site: thatcherinn.com

IDYLLWILD

Strawberry Creek Inn
PO Box 1818, 92549
909-659-3202
800-262-8969
Diana Dugan & Jim Goff
All year

75-150-B&B
9 rooms, 7 pb
Visa, MC, *Rated*
C-ltd/S-no/P-no/H-ltd

Full breakfast
Afternoon wine
Library, fireplaces, sitting
room, refrigerators

Country inn located in the pines where comfort mixes with nostalgia in a uniquely decorated home. Cottage with spas. Many hiking trails, quiet walks along the creek.
Web site: strawberrycreekinn.com

INVERNESS

Bayshore Cottage
PO Box 405, 94937
415-669-1148 Fax: 415-669-1148
Mare M. Hansen
All year

125-145-B&B
1 rooms, 1 pb
Rated
C-ltd/S-no/P-no/H-no

kitchen w/ provisions for
breakfast
Snacks, complimentary wine
Sitting room, library, hot tub,
cable TV, private deck,
barbecue pit

Bayshore Cottage. A quiet getaway for lovers Web site: innformation.com/ca/bayshore

Fairwinds Farm B&B
PO Box 581, 94937
415-663-9454 Fax: 415-663-1787
Joyce H. Goldfield
All year

91-135-B&B
2 rooms, 2 pb
Rated
C-yes/S-no/P-no/H-no
Sign language

Full breakfast in cottage
Continental plus (Dan's
room)
Full kitchen, library, TV, VCR
and movies, hot tubs,
fireplace

Large cottages sleep 6. Ridge-top cottage adjoins 68,000-acre National Seashore. Ocean view from hot tub. Garden with ponds & swing. Barnyard animals. Whale & bird watching. E-mail: fairwind@svn.net

INVERNESS ─────────────────────────

Hotel Inverness
PO Box 780, 94937
415-669-7393 Fax: 415-669-1702
Susan & Thomas Simms
All year

125-195-B&B
5 rooms, 5 pb
Visa, MC, *Rated*, •
C-yes/S-no/P-no/H-no

Continental plus breakfast
Picnics, croquet, lawn for
lounging

1906 shingle-style hotel in village's historical section. Upstairs rooms, queen beds, some private decks. Walk to shops, restaurants and bay.   E-mail: desk@hotelinverness.com
Web site: hotelinverness.com

Manka's Inverness Lodge
PO Box 110, 94937
415-669-1034 Fax: 415-669-1598
Margaret Grade
All year

185-345-B&B
12 rooms, 12 pb
Visa, MC,
C-ltd/S-no/P-no/H-no

Full breakfast
Dinner available, restaurant

1915 hunting & fishing lodge providing unique accommodations and acclaimed restaurant amidst the splendor of Tomales Bay and adjacent to the Pt. Reyes National Seashore. E-mail: mankas@best.com *Web site:* mankas.com

---

Rosemary Cottage
PO Box 273, 94937
415-663-9338
800-808-9338
Suzanne Storch
All year

160-200-B&B
1 rooms, 1 pb
Rated, •
C-yes/S-yes/P-yes/H-no

Full breakfast
Complimentary tea, coffee
Kitchen, fireplace, decks,
secluded, hot tub in garden

Charming, romantic French country cottage nestled in secluded garden with dramatic forest views. Close to beaches; families welcome.   E-mail: rosemarybb@aol.com
Web site: rosemarybb.com/rosemary.html

Ten Inverness Way
PO Box 63, 94937
415-669-1648 Fax: 415-669-7403
Teri Mattson Mowery
All year

145-180-B&B
4 rooms, 4 pb
Rated, •
C-ltd/S-ltd/P-no/H-no
French, Spanish

Full breakfast
Complimentary sherry
Sitting room, library, piano,
private hot tub

A classic bed and breakfast inn for lovers of handmade quilts, hearty breakfasts, great hikes and good books. Suites are equipped with a microwave and stereo.
E-mail: inn@teninvernessway.com *Web site:* teninvernessway.com

JAMESTOWN ─────────────────────────

Jamestown Hotel, The
PO Box 539, 95327
209-984-3902 Fax: 209-984-4149
800-205-4901
Jerry & Lucille Weisbrot
All year

70-135-B&B
11 rooms, 11 pb
Most CC, *Rated*, •
C-yes/S-ltd/P-no/H-no

Continental plus breakfast
Complimentary cocktails,
wine
Business center and TV
room with VCR, refrigerator
for guests

Gold rush town historic hotel-furnished in antiques with full service gourmet restaurant & saloon-near Yosemite, Railtown 1897, & antiques   E-mail: info@jamestownhotel.com
Web site: jamestownhotel.com

National Hotel Country Inn
PO Box 502, 95327
209-984-3446 Fax: 209-984-5620
800-894-3446
Stephen Willey
All year

80-120-B&B
9 rooms, 9 pb
Most CC, *Rated*, •
C-ltd/S-ltd/P-ltd/H-no
Spanish, French

Continental plus breakfast
Full restaurant, bar
Sitting room, library, live
entertainment, courtyard
dining

Victorian Hotel c.1859 in heart of Gold Rush area. Rms. restored to casual elegance of a simpler/romantic era. Near Yosemite. Warm/congenial staff. Gourmet restaurant, full bar & espresso. Can accept on-line reservations.   E-mail: info@national-hotel.com *Web site:* national-hotel.com

JAMESTOWN

Royal Hotel
PO Box 219, 95327
209-984-5271 Fax: 209-984-1675
888-523-6722
Richard & Cora Riddell
All year

55-100-B&B
19 rooms, 17 pb
Visa, MC, AmEx, •
C-ltd/S-no/P-no/H-ltd
Spanish, Filipino

Continental plus breakfast
Lost of good restaurants
Sitting room, library, suites,
balconies, patios

Lovely Victorian hotel with private, secluded cottage in the heart of Main Street! Fresh, homemade continental brakfast served in our oak-panelled parlor. Relax and enjoy our balconies with a view of Main Street and our back porches overlooking our garde E-mail: info@aRoyalHotel.com Web site: aRoyalHotel.com

JENNER

Jenner Inn & Cottages
PO Box 69, 95450
707-865-2377 Fax: 707-865-0829
800-732-2377
R. & S. Murphy, J. Carroll
All year

95-235-B&B
20 rooms, 20 pb
Visa, MC, AmEx,
Rated, •
C-yes/S-no/P-no/H-no

Continental plus breakfast
Complimentary teas &
aperitifs
Port & sherry available,
sitting room, private cottages

Coastal retreat inn—antiques, lots of character, peaceful, romantic, river & ocean views. Sunset weddings by the sea, wineries, redwoods nearby, 8 beautiful sandy beaches. Rooms with spas & fireplaces.   E-mail: innkeeper@jennerinn.com Web site: jennerinn.com

JOSHUA TREE

Rosebud Ruby Star
PO Box 1116, 92252
760-366-4676
877-887-7370
Sandy Rosen   All year

140-B&B
2 rooms, 2 pb
Visa, MC, •
C-ltd/S-no/P-no/H-no

Full breakfast
Afternoon tea, snacks
Complimentary wine,
evening food basket, spa on
premises, beverages

Intimate pueblo-style hideaway with panoramic views overlooking surreal Joshua Tree National Park west gateway. Artist-decorated rooms with private entryways from covered patio.   E-mail: sandy@rosebudrubystar.com Web site: rosebudrubystar.com

JULIAN

Julian Gold Rush Hotel
PO Box 1856, 92036
760-765-0201 Fax: 760-765-0327
800-734-5854
Steve & Gig Ballinger
All year

72-175-B&B
15 rooms, 15 pb
Visa, MC, AmEx,
Rated, •
C-yes/S-ltd/P-no/H-no

Full breakfast
Afternoon tea
Sitting room, library, piano,
cottage, family rates

Surviving 1897 hotel in southern Mother Lode of CA, restored to full glory with American antiques. National Register. "CA Point of Historical Interest."   E-mail: b&b@julianhotel.com Web site: julianhotel.com

KERNVILLE

Kern River Inn B&B
PO Box 1725, 93238
760-376-6750 Fax: 760-376-6643
800-986-4382
Carita Prestwich   All year

89-109-B&B
6 rooms, 6 pb
Most CC, *Rated*, •
C-yes/S-no/P-no/H-yes

Full breakfast
Afternoon tea
Riverviews, fireplaces,
whirlpool tubs, TV/VCR,
dinner theater (weekends)

New country inn on the Kern River. Fishing, golf, antique shops, giant redwoods. Outdoor activities, whitewater rafting, skiing. AAA 3-diamonds.   E-mail: kernriverinn@lightspeed.net Web site: virtualcities.com/ons/ca/s/cas3501.htm

**Whispering Pines Lodge
B&B**
Rt 1, Box 41, 93238
760-376-3733 Fax: 760-376-6513
877-241-4100
George Randall   All year

99-159-B&B
17 rooms, 17 pb
Most CC, *Rated*, •
C-yes/S-no/P-no/H-no

Full breakfast
Lunch, dinner
Afternoon tea, swimming
pool, Jacuzzi

Romantic country getaway featuring Roman Jacuzzis, fireplaces, gourmet breakfast on patio with view of Sequoia Forest & the wild and scenic Kern River, Decks and BBQs E-mail: thepines@kernvalley.com

KINGS CANYON NATIONAL PARK

Montecito-Sequoia Mtn. Inn	69-79-MAP	Full breakfast
8000 Generals Hwy box858,	36 rooms, 36 pb	Dinner, restaurant, bar
93633	Most CC, *Rated*, •	Outdoor spa, volleyball,
650-967-8612 Fax: 650-967-0540	C-yes/S-ltd/P-no/H-yes	tennis, hot tubs, pool, lake,
800-227-9900	Italian	canoeing
Virginia C. Barnes		
All year		

Charming alpine lodge at 7500 ft. on serene Lake Homavalo. Spectacular view of Sequoia National Park. E-mail: msreservations@montecitosequoia.com Web site: montecitosequoia.com

LAGUNA BEACH

Casa Laguna B&B Inn	79-249-B&B	Continental plus breakfast
2510 South Coast Hwy, 92651	20 rooms, 20 pb	Afternoon tea, snacks, comp.
949-494-2996 Fax: 949-494-5009	Most CC, *Rated*, •	wine
800-233-0449	C-yes/S-ltd/P-yes/H-no	Library, pool, suites,
Kathleen Flint	Spanish	fireplaces, cable TV,
All year		accommodate business
		travelers

In the scenic, seaside resort of Laguna Beach, nestled on a terraced hillside overlooking the Pacific Ocean. Queen palms & beautiful grounds frame the pool & sundeck. Offering sun, sand & sea.

LAKE TAHOE

Granny's Lake House	400-EP	Jacuzzis, fireplace, cable TV
PO Box 1-4444, 96151	3 rooms, 2½ pb	
530-543-1414 Fax: 530-543-1414	Visa, MC, *Rated*	
Mary Moline	C-yes/S-ltd/P-no/H-ltd	
All year		

This great home is neither rustic nor cozy. It is a new and spacious with an open winding staircase leading to three luxurious bedrooms of old European comfort, sleeps eight. The kitchen is a gourmet's delight. E-mail: marymoline@aol.com

Knotty Pine B&B, The	80-170-B&B	Full breakfast
PO Box 564, 96142	4 rooms, 2 pb	Snacks, wine,
530-525-1023 Fax: 530-525-1080	Visa, MC, Disc., •	complimentary soda
877-280-8915	C-ltd/S-no/P-no/H-no	Sitting room
Vaughn & Dan Hollingsworth		
All year		

A cozy, romantic getaway on the beautiful west shore of Lake Tahoe. A gourmet breakfast of homemade breads, fruit entree and a savory hot entree will start your day.
E-mail: vaughn@theknottypine.com Web site: theknottypine.com

Mayfield House	95-250-B&B	Full breakfast
PO Box 8529, 96145	6 rooms, 6 pb	Afternoon tea, snacks, wine
530-583-1001 Fax: 530-581-4104	Visa, MC, *Rated*, •	Sitting room, library, Jacuzzi,
888-518-8898	C-ltd/S-no/P-no/H-ltd	suites, fireplace, cable TV
Colleen McDevitt		
All year		

Romantic 1932 house with beautiful Old Tahoe architecture. The house boasts original stonework, hardwood floors, and comfortable mountain decor throughout.
E-mail: innkeeper@mayfieldhouse.com Web site: mayfieldhouse.com

Rockwood Lodge	100-200-B&B	Continental plus breakfast
PO Box 226, 96141	5 rooms, 5 pb	Complimentary cordials
530-525-5273 Fax: 530-525-5949	Visa, MC, •	Sitting room, game room,
800-LE-TAHOE	C-ltd/S-no/P-no/H-no	swimming pool, billiards
L. Reinkens & C. Stevens		
All year		

"Old Tahoe" estate nestled in pine forest; Lake Tahoe within 100 feet. Breakfast served in guest rooms. Many fine appointments. 20% rate increase for holidays and weekends.
E-mail: rockwood@inreach.com Web site: rockwoodlodge.com/

LAKE TAHOE

Shore House at Lake Tahoe	160-255-B&B	Full gourmet breakfast
PO Box 343, 96148	9 rooms, 9 pb	Afternoon tea, snacks, wine
530-546-7270 Fax: 530-546-7130	Visa, MC, *Rated*, •	All rooms with gas fireplaces,
800-207-5160	C-ltd/S-no/P-no/H-no	sitting room, skiing, hiking,
Marty & Barb Cohen All year		biking

Romantic lakefront hideaway, custom log beds, down comforters, feather beds. Gourmet breakfast in lakefront dining room or at lakefront lawns & gardens. Small weddings in lakefront garden. Hot tub.   E-mail: shorehouse@tahoeinn.com Web site: tahoeinn.com

LAKEPORT

Forbestown Inn	100-115-B&B	Full breakfast
825 Forbes St, 95453	5 rooms, 1 pb	Pool, spa, veranda, free ride
707-263-7858 Fax: 707-263-7878	Visa, MC, AmEx,	to airport, corporate rates
Wally & Pat Kelley	*Rated*, •	
All year	C-ltd/S-no/P-no/H-no	

1869 quaint Victorian inn. Country breakfast, refreshments, gardens, pool, spa, robes, bicycles, close to the lake, water sports, restaurants, wineries   E-mail: forbestowninn@zapcom.net Web site: innaccess.com/fti

LODI

Wine & Roses Country Inn	125-B&B	Full breakfast
2505 W. Turner Rd, 95242	10 rooms, 10 pb	Restaurant, lunch
209-334-6988 Fax: 209-334-6570	Visa, MC, AmEx, *Rated*	Dinner, snacks, comp. wine,
Del & Sherri Smith	C-yes/S-ltd/P-no/H-yes	bar service, sitting room,
All year		lake

Charming historical manor sequestered on 5 acres of towering trees & gardens. "Casually elegant" restaurant. Enjoyed by leisure & business travelers.   E-mail: info@winerose.com Web site: winerose.com

LONG BEACH

Kennebec Corner B&B	125-150-B&B	Full breakfast weekends
2305 E 2nd St, 90803	1 rooms, 1 pb	Continental plus weekdays,
562-439-2705 Fax: 562-433-7776	Visa, MC, AmEx, •	wine
Michael and Marty Gunhus	C-ltd/S-ltd/P-no/H-no	Sitt. rm., lib., bikes, Jacuzzis,
All year		suites, fireplace, CATV,
		business travel

From the moment you enter, you sense a spec. experience awaits you. Enjoy a priv. retreat in our circa 1920's California Craftsman home located in historic Bluff Park, just two blocks from the beach. In-room mini-ref. w/comp. soft drinks.   E-mail: kennebec@earthlink.net Web site: bbhost.com/kennebeccorner

Lord Mayor's B&B Inn	85-125-B&B	Full breakfast
435 Cedar Ave, 90802	12 rooms, 5 pb	Special luncheons/dinner
562-436-0324 Fax: 562-436-0324	Visa, MC, AmEx,	Library, sitting room,
Laura & Reuben Brasser	*Rated*, •	croquet, sundecks, IBM PC
All year	C-yes/S-no/P-no/H-no	on request
	Dutch, Danish	

Award-winning restored 1904 Edwardian home of Long Beach's first mayor. Spacious rooms with antiques, library, gardens, porches, parking. Guided walking tours, mystery nights.   E-mail: innkeepers@lordmayors.com Web site: lordmayors.com

Turret House	100-140-B&B	Full breakfast
556 Chestnut Ave, 90802	5 rooms, 5 pb	Afternoon tea, snacks
562-983-9812 Fax: 562-437-4082	Most CC,	Fireplaces, cable TV,
888-4TURRET	C-ltd/S-no/P-no/H-no	accommodate business
Nina & Lee Agee		travelers
All year		

Victorian hospitality and antique finery in elegantly restored 1906 home in historic downtown residential district, gourmet candlelit breakfasts of garden-fresh cuisine, stroll the beach, Aquarium, Convention Center, fine dining.   E-mail: innkeepers@turrethouse.com Web site: turrethouse.com

Turret House, Long Beach, CA

MAMMOTH LAKES

Cinnamon Bear Inn	79-159-B&B	Full breakfast
PO Box 3338, 93546	22 rooms, 22 pb	Snacks, Complimentary wine
760-934-2873 Fax: 760-934-2873	Most CC, *Rated*, •	Sitting room, Jacuzzis, Suites,
800-845-2873	C-yes/S-no/P-no/H-ltd	Fireplaces, Cable TV, Ski
Russ and Mary Ann Harrison		packages
All year		

"Who needs the Ritz?" Friendly folks feature full breakfasts, free hors d'oeuvres and fabulous ski packages. Forested view rooms with private baths; four-poster beds, kitchens, and fireplaces are available.   E-mail: cinnabear1@aol.com   Web site: cinnamonbearinn.com

Snow Goose Inn B&B	78-208-B&B	Full breakfast
PO Box 387, 93546	20 rooms, 20 pb	Complimentary wine,
760-934-2660 Fax: 760-934-5655	Visa, MC, AmEx,	appetizers
800-874-7368	*Rated*, •	Sitting room, bicycles, hot
Bob & Carol Roster	C-yes/S-yes/P-no/H-no	tubs, athletic club priveleges
All year		

Winter ski resort/Sierra's summer getaway. European-style deluxe mountain bed and breakfast. Offering special ski packages midweek. Whirlpool bathtubs in some rooms.
E-mail: snowgoose@qnet.com   Web site: snowgoose-inn.com/

MANCHESTER

Victorian Gardens	135-185-B&B	Full breakfast
14409 S Highway 1, 95459	4 rooms, 3 pb	Lunch/dinner available,
707-882-3606 Fax: 707-882-2128	Visa, MC, AmEx,	restaurant
Luciano & Pauline Zamboni	*Rated*, •	Aperitifs &, hors d'oeuvres 7-
All year	C-ltd/S-ltd/P-no/H-no	7:30pm, sitting room, library
	French, Italian	

An exquisitely appointed, fully restored gem of Victorian architecture offering total privacy & seclusion on 92 enchanted acres along the rugged Mendocino coast. Elegant Italian dinners served in evening.

MARINA DEL REY

Inn at Playa del Rey	125-275-B&B	Full breakfast
435 Culver Blvd, 90293	21 rooms	Afternoon tea, snacks, wine
310-574-1920 Fax: 310-574-9920	Visa, MC, AmEx,	Sitting room, library, bikes,
S. Zolla/L. Cresto/D. Donnely	*Rated*, •	romance suites, private
All year	C-yes/S-ltd/P-no/H-yes	garden with hot tub
	French, Japanese	

Overlooks sailboats and 200 acre bird sanctuary-3 blocks to beach. Decks, fireplaces, tubs, romance-a seaside hideaway. Conference facilities.   E-mail: playainn@aol.com
Web site: innatplayadelrey.com

MARIPOSA ────────────────────────────────

Highland House B&B	85-125-B&B	Full breakfast
3125 Wild Dove Lane, 95338	3 rooms, 3 pb	Afternoon tea, snacks
209-966-3737 Fax: 209-966-7277	Visa, MC, •	Sitting room, fireplaces,
888-477-5089	C-ltd/S-ltd/P-no/H-no	cable TV
Judith McLand		
All year		

Secluded country house on 10 acres of majestic cedars and pines. Three guest rooms created for your pleasure. Private baths, down comforters, fluffy robes. Your breakfast is our priority! E-mail: highland@sierratel.com Web site: moriah.com/highland

Oak Knoll Ranch	115-B&B	Snacks
5654 French Camp Rd, 95338	1 rooms, 1 pb	Jacuzzis
209-966-6946 Fax: 209-742-5493	Visa, MC, Disc, *Rated*	
Russ & Jeanie Bartholemew	C-ltd/S-ltd/P-no/H-no	
All year		

A unique guest stay in a country barn. Well furnished with local country finds and furniture. E-mail: jmb@yosemite.net Web site Web site: mariposa.yosemite.net/okranch

Rancho Bernardo B&B	85-100-B&B	Full gourmet breakfast
PMB-289, PO Box 5008, 95338	2 rooms, 2 pb	Afternoon tea, snacks
209-966-4511 Fax: 209-966-4511	C-ltd/S-ltd/P-no/H-no	Comp. wine for
877-930-1669		honeymooners, fireplaces,
Kathleen & Bernard Lozares		pool table, fax, videos,
All year		TV/VCR

Secluded 120 acre cattle ranch with views of rolling hills, dotted with oak trees, Chinese rock walls, springs and grazing livestock on your way to or from magnificent Yosemite National Park. E-mail: lozbnb@yosemite.net Web site: mariposa.yosemite.net/lozbnb/

Restful Nest B&B	85-105-B&B	Full gourmet breakfast
4274 Buckeye Creek Rd, 95338	3 rooms, 3 pb	Hot tubs, swimming pool
209-742-7127 Fax: 209-742-7127	Most CC,	
800-664-7127	C-ltd/S-ltd/H-no	
Lois Y Moroni	French	
All year		

We offer relaxation, old California hospitality & the flavor of Provence in the beautiful foothills of the Sierra Nevada mountains. E-mail: restful@yosemite.net
Web site: mariposa.yosemite.net/restful/

MENDOCINO ────────────────────────────────

Agate Cove Inn	109-269-B&B	Full country breakfast
PO Box 1150, 95460	10 rooms, 10 pb	Complimentary sherry in
707-937-0551 Fax: 707-937-0550	Visa, MC, AmEx, *Rated*	room
800-527-3111	C-ltd/S-ltd/P-no/H-ltd	Common room with
Dennis & Nancy Freeze		antiques, spectacular ocean
All year		views, whale watching Dec-Mar

Agate Cove's romantic cottages and 1860's farmhouse boast unparalleled ocean views and spectacular gardens. Rooms feature king or queen beds, fireplaces, CD players and TV/VCR's. All rooms have private baths, some with Jacuzzi or soaking tubs.
E-mail: agate@mcn.org Web site: agatecove.com

Albion River Inn	180-280-B&B	Full breakfast
Box 100, 95410	20 rooms, 20 pb	Din. (fee), comp. wine
707-937-1919 Fax: 707-937-2604	Visa, MC, AmEx, *Rated*	Bar service, Jacuzzis,
800-479-7944	S-no/P-no/H-yes	fireplaces, deck, priv.,
Peter Wells & Flurry Heal		cottages, restaurant
All year		

Ideal romantic getaway, cliff top inn & acclaimed restaurant on 10 headland acres. Magnificent ocean views, cottages, fireplaces, decks, spa tubs. E-mail: ari@mcn.org
Web site: albionriverinn.com

MENDOCINO ——————————————————————————————

C.O. Packard House B&B
PO Box 1065, 95460
707-937-2677 Fax: 707-937-1323
888-453-2677
Maria, Dan & Bette
All year

85-210-B&B
4 rooms, 4 pb
Visa, MC, Disc, *Rated*,
•
C-ltd/S-no/P-no/H-ltd
Portuguese

Full breakfast
Snacks, wine
Sitting room, bicycles,
fireplace, cable TV

Newly renovated Mendocino village Victorian. Antiques, art collections, jet tubs, fireplaces, gourmet breakfast. Everything in walking distance; Mendocino Headlands State Park, restaurants, ocean, etc. E-mail: info@packardhouse.com Web site: packardhouse.com

---

Cypress Cove at Mendocino
PO Box 303, 95460
707-937-1456 Fax: 707-937-0640
800-942-6300
Sue & Jim Hay
All year

190-225-EP
2 rooms, 2 pb
S-no/P-no/H-no

Kitchen, refrigerators
Fireplace, dramatic,
oceanfront, soft robes,
coffees, teas, brandy

Luxurious, private, romantic getaway for two! On the ocean bluff with spectacular view of Mendocino across the bay. Deluxe bathrooms with Jacuzzi for 2. E-mail: jimhay@ cypresscove.com Web site: cypresscove.com

---

Elk Cove Inn, The
PO Box 367, 95432
707-877-3321 Fax: 707-877-1808
800-275-2967
Elaine Bryant
All year

98-278-B&B
14 rooms, 14 pb
Visa, MC, AmEx,
Rated, •
C-ltd/S-no/P-no/H-yes
Spanish

Full gourmet breakfast
Cocktail Bar, complimentary
port
Kayaking, sitting room, deck,
VCR, library, stereo, fishing

1883 Victorian mansion on the Ocean. Dramatic views, private steps to beach, organic gardens, romantic gazebo. Cozy fireplace cottages and antique filled rooms
E-mail: elkcove@mcn.org Web site: elkcoveinn.com

Griffin House at Greenwood
PO Box 190, 95432
707-877-3422 Fax: 707-877-1853
Leslie Griffin Lawson
All year

95-225-B&B
7 rooms, 7 pb
•
C-ltd/S-no/P-no/H-no

Full breakfast
Complimentary juice, fruits
On the Ocean!

A snug and cozy inn with wood burning stoves, ocean views, flower gardens, sun decks. Breakfast served in your cottage. E-mail: griffinn@mcn.org Web site: griffinn.com

---

Harbor House Inn, The
PO Box 369, 95432
707-877-3203 Fax: 707-877-3452
800-720-7474
Sam & Elle Haynes
All year

195-350-MAP
10 rooms, 10 pb
Visa, MC, *Rated*
C-ltd/S-ltd/P-no/H-yes
French, Spanish

Full breakfast
4 course dinner included
Sitting room, piano, fireplace,
parlor stove, new gardens,
private beach

Spectacular north coast vistas of the sea. Renowned country gourmet cuisine. Wine lover's paradise. Rooms include original artwork, fireplaces or parlor stoves, and decks.
E-mail: harborhs@mcn.org Web site: theharborhouseinn.com

Hayloft, The
PO Box 303, 95460
707-937-1456 Fax: 707-937-0640
800-942-6300
Jim Hay
All year

145-165-B&B
1 rooms, 1 pb
Visa, MC,
S-ltd/P-no/H-no

Continental breakfast
Fireplaces, cable TV, hot tub

Just two miles from the center of Mendocino, The Hayloft is a cozy retreat. Warm and inviting, decorated with style and comfort in mind, The Hayloft suite is private, quiet and peaceful. E-mail: jimhay@mendocinopreferred.com
Web site: mendocinopreferred.com/accoms.htm#hayloft

MENDOCINO ───────────────────────────────

Inn at Schoolhouse Creek
PO Box 1637, 95460
707-937-5525 Fax: 707-937-2012
800-731-5525
Al & Penny Greenwood
All year

99-210-B&B
13 rooms, 13 pb
Most CC, *Rated*, •
C-yes/S-ltd/P-ltd/H-no

Continental plus breakfast
Complimentary wine, snacks
Common room with
antiques, VCR/TV & phone
in room, private beach
access

On the quiet side of Mendocino, relaxed country inn with romantic ocean view cottages, surounded by 8½ acres of gardens & meadows. Beach access, hot tub with panoramic ocean view, fireplaces. E-mail: innkeeper@binnb.com Web site: binnb.com

───

John Dougherty House
PO Box 817, 95460
707-937-5266
800-486-2104
David & Marion Wells
All year

95-229-B&B
6 rooms, 6 pb
Visa, MC, *Rated*, •
C-ltd/S-no/P-no/H-no

Full breakfast
Complimentary wine
Sitting room, verandas,
ocean views, near tennis,
antiques, English garden

Historic 1867 house in Village center. Large verandahs with ocean views; quiet peaceful nights; walk to shops & dining. Woodburning stoves in 5 rooms. E-mail: jdhbmw@mcn.org
Web site: jdhouse.com

───

Joshua Grindle Inn
PO Box 647, 95460
707-937-4143
800-GRINDLE
Arlene & Jim Moorehead
All year

105-195-B&B
10 rooms, 10 pb
Rated
C-ltd/S-no/P-no/H-ltd

Full gourmet breakfast
Aftn./eve. tea & goodies in
parlor
Sitting room, Parlor, ocean
views, fireplaces, 1985 Inn of
the Year

Historic country charm on 2 beautiful acres with gardens. 2 deep-soak tubs. Our best room has whirlpool tub with separate shower. New! E-mail: info@joshgrin.com
Web site: joshgrin.com

───

MacCallum House Inn
PO Box 206, 95460
707-937-0289 Fax: 707-937-3076
800-609-0492
Cheryl, Lauren
All year

100-190 B&B
19 rooms, 19 pb
Visa, MC, Disc, •
C-ltd/S-no/P-no/H-yes

Continental breakfast
Fine dining
Bar service, spa tubs,
fireplaces, cottages,
handicap access

An 1882 vintage Victorian with charming garden cottages in the heart of Mendocino village. Clawfoot tubs for two, fireplaces, ocean views, superb restaurant.
E-mail: machouse@mcn.org Web site: maccallumhouse.com

───

Sandpiper House Inn
PO Box 149, 95432
707-877-3587
800-894-9016
Claire Melrose
All year

135-225-B&B
5 rooms, 5 pb
Most CC, *Rated*
C-ltd/S-no/P-no/H-no

Full breakfast
Aftn. tea, snacks
Comp. sherry, breakfast in
dining rm., living room for
guests

Seaside country inn built in 1916. Rich redwood paneling, European charm, lush perennial gardens, stunning ocean views, private beach access. E-mail: eclaire@mcn.org
Web site: sandpiperhouse.com

───

Sea Rock B&B Inn
PO Box 906, 95460
707-937-0926
800-906-0926
Susie & Andy Plocher
All year

89-259-B&B
14 rooms, 14 pb
Most CC, *Rated*
C-yes/S-no/P-no/H-no

Continental plus breakfast
Sitting room, gardens, lawns,
ocean view, fireplace, king
bed

Country cottages on a hillside overlooking the ocean. Spectacular ocean views, fireplaces, featherbeds, TV/VCR, phones in all units, relaxing, private get-away. 4 new deluxe suites with king beds. E-mail: searock@mcn.org Web site: searock.com

MENDOCINO

Stanford Inn by the Sea	215-365-B&B	Full breakfast
PO Box 487, 95460	25 rooms, 25 pb	Wine, organic vegetables
707-937-5615 Fax: 707-937-0305	Most CC, *Rated*, •	Indoor pool, hot tub, decks,
800-331-8884	C-yes/S-yes/P-yes/H-yes	nurseries, llamas, bicycles,
Joan & Jeff Stanford	French, Spanish	canoe rentals
All year		

A truly elegant country inn in a pastoral setting. All accommodations with ocean views, fireplace, decks, antiques, four-posters and TVs. E-mail: stanford@stanfordinn.com
Web site: stanfordinn.com

Victorian Farmhouse, The	98-185-B&B	Full breakfast
PO Box 661, 95460	10 rooms, 10 pb	Complimentary wine
707-937-0697 Fax: 907-937-5238	Visa, MC, AmEx,	Sitting room, Jacuzzis,
800-264-4723	*Rated*, •	fireplaces, parks, tennis
Fred Cox & Jo Bradley	C-ltd/S-no/P-no/H-no	nearby
All year		

Built in 1877, immortalized by Thomas Kinkade, full of antiques, quality linens and comfort with you in mind. Enjoy deer, flower gardens and our creek. Quiet, serenity and a place to leave the work a day world behind. E-mail: prednjo@victorianfarmhouse.com
Web site: victorianfarmhouse.com

Whitegate Inn B&B	129-249-B&B	Full breakfast
PO Box 150, 95460	7 rooms, 7 pb	Complimentary wine
707-937-4892 Fax: 707-937-1131	Visa, MC, AmEx,	Sitting room, organ,
800-531-7282	*Rated*, •	fireplaces, TVs, gardens,
Carol & George Bechtloff	C-ltd/S-no/P-no/H-no	deck, gazebo, weddings
All year		

Located in historic Mendocino. All rooms decorated with French or Victorian antiques. Ocean views. English & herb gardens. Featured in "Country Inns" & "Bon Appetit."
E-mail: staff@whitegateinn.com Web site: whitegateinn.com

MILL VALLEY

Mountain Home Inn	143-269-B&B	Full breakfast
810 Panoramic Hwy, 94941	10 rooms, 10 pb	Lunch/dinner available (fee)
415-381-9000 Fax: 415-381-3615	Visa, MC, *Rated*, •	Jacuzzis, hiking trails,
Lynn M Saggese	C-ltd/S-yes/P-no/H-yes	telephones in rooms
All year		

Two-and-a-half-million-dollar restored classic California luxury inn. Adjacent to parklands, Muir Woods. Panoramic S.F. Bay views; Jacuzzis, fireplaces, terraces.
E-mail: mthomein@best.com Web site: mtnhomeinn.com

MONTE RIO

Village Inn	85-140-B&B	Continental breakfast
PO Box 850, 95462	10 rooms, 10 pb	Dinner, restaurant, bar
707-865-2304 Fax: 707-865-2332	Most CC, •	service
800-303-2303	C-ltd/S-ltd/P-no/H-yes	Sitting room, cable TV
Mike & Adel Rusanowski		
Feb-Dec		

Unsurpassed river and towering redwood views, fresh Sonoma wine country cuisine and outside dining. Renovated 1906 Country Inn with ten cozy rooms with antiques & private baths; some with riverside decks. E-mail: village@sonic.net Web site: village-inn.com

MONTEREY

Jabberwock B&B, The	110-220-B&B	Full breakfast
598 Laine St, 93940	7 rooms, 5 pb	Sherry & hors d'ouevres
831-372-4777 Fax: 831-655-2946	Visa, MC, *Rated*	Sitting room, sun porch, one
888-428-7253	C-ltd/S-ltd/P-no/H-no	room with Jacuzzi, suite
Joan & John Kiliany	Spanish	
All year		

Once a convent, this Craftsman home is above Cannery Row. Sherry on the sun porch overlooking Monterey Bay, gardens & waterfalls. Near Monterey Bay Aquarium.
Web site: Jabberwockinn.com

MORRO BAY

Baywood Inn B&B	80-140-B&B	Full breakfast
1370 Second St, 93402	15 rooms, 15 pb	Cafe, complimentary wine
805-528-8888 Fax: 805-528-8887	Visa, MC, *Rated*, •	Conferences for up to 14,
Suzanne McCollom	C-yes/S-no/P-no/H-yes	sitting room, fireplaces, 11
All year		suites w/amenities

Bayfront Inn on South Morro Bay. Each room has its own personality. Near Hearst Castle, San Luis Obispo, Montano De Oro State Park. 2 new bayfront homes available.
E-mail: innkeeper@baywoodinn.com Web site: baywoodinn.com

MOUNT SHASTA

Mount Shasta Ranch B&B	50-95-B&B	Full breakfast
1008 W.A. Barr Rd, 96067	10 rooms, 4 pb	Afternoon tea, wine, snacks
530-926-3870 Fax: 530-926-6882	Most CC, *Rated*, •	Sitting room, hot tub, library,
Mary & Bill Larsen	C-ltd/S-no/P-yes/H-no	Ping-Pong, TV & phone in
All year		room

Affordable elegance in historical setting; Main Lodge, Cottage and Carriage House. Nearby lake fishing, year-round golf and winter skiing. Pool tables, horseshoes.
E-mail: alpinere@snowcrest.net

MUIR BEACH

Pelican Inn	178-215-B&B	Full English breakfast
10 Pacific Way, 94965	7 rooms, 7 pb	Complimentary sherry
415-383-6000 Fax: 415-383-3424	Visa, MC, •	Sitting room, restaurant,
Katrinka McKay	C-yes/S-yes/P-no/H-ltd	British pub/bar, darts
Closed Christmas		

Romantic English inn capturing the spirit of the 16th century. Between ocean & redwoods, surrounded by countryside. Hiking, cycling trails. 20 minutes from Golden Gate Bridge.
E-mail: innkeeper@pelicaninn.com Web site: pelicaninn.com

MURPHYS

Dunbar House, 1880	135-195-B&B	Full country breakfast
271 Jones St, 95247	4 rooms, 4 pb	Complimentary bottle of
209-728-2897 Fax: 209-728-1451	Visa, MC, *Rated*, •	wine
800-692-6006	C-ltd/S-no/P-no/H-no	Sitting room, library, gas-
Barbara & Bob Costa		burning stoves, clawfoot
All year		tubs, TVs, VCRs

Restored 1880 home with historical designation located in Murphys, Queen of the Sierra. 2-room suite with double Jacuzzi, champagne, towel warmer.
E-mail: innkeep@dunbarhouse.com Web site: dunbarhouse.com

Redbud Inn, The	90-245-B&B	Full breakfast
402 Main St, 95247	14 rooms, 14 pb	Afternoon tea, snacks, wine
209-728-8533 Fax: 209-728-8132	Visa, MC, Disc, •	Restaurant, lunch, dinner,
800-4-REDBUD	C-ltd/S-no/P-no/H-yes	sitting rm., bikes, suites,
Pamela Hatch	Some Spanish	Jacuzzis, fireplaces
All year		

The Redbuds romance will engulf you & your loved one soaking in a spa while languishing the aroma from a glass of champagne & listening to the crackle of the radiant fireplace.
E-mail: innkeeper@redbudinn.com Web site: redbudinn.com

NAPA

1801 Inn, The	135-229-B&B	Full breakfast
1801 First St, 94559	5 rooms, 5 pb	Iced tea in shade garden
707-224-3739 Fax: 707-224-3932	*Rated*, •	Sitting & sun rooms,
800-518-0146	S-no/P-no/H-no	fountain, showers
Linda & Chris Craiker	Spanish	
All year		

A lovingly restored Queen Anne style Victorian home located at the gateway to the famous Napa Wine Country. King beds and fireplaces in rooms. E-mail: the1801inn@aol.com
Web site: napavalley.com/1801inn

NAPA

Arbor Guest House
1436 G St, 94559
707-252-8144
Fax: 707-252-7385
Gene & Andrea Chadwick
All year

145-200-B&B
5 rooms, 5 pb
Visa, MC, •
C-ltd/S-no/P-ltd/H-yes

Full breakfast
Afternoon tea, snacks
Quiet garden, sitting area,
winery passes and maps

Elegant rooms, private baths, spa tubs, hearty breakfasts served at garden patios or before fireplaces await guests celebrating special occasions. E-mail: arborgh@aol.com
Web site: arborguesthouse.com

Beazley House
1910 First St, 94559
707-257-1649 Fax: 707-257-1518
800-559-1649
Carol & Jim Beazley
All year

115-250-B&B
11 rooms, 11 pb
Visa, MC, *Rated*, •
C-ltd/S-ltd/P-no/H-yes

Full gourmet breakfast
Complimentary wine
Spas/fireplaces, gardens,
entertainment, sunroom,
sitting room, library

The Beazley House is a Napa landmark. Relax in old-fashioned comfort. Breakfast, complimentary sherry. Personal wine tour orientation E-mail: innkeeper@beazleyhouse.com
Web site: beazleyhouse.com

Blue Violet Mansion
443 Brown St, 94559
707-253-2583 Fax: 707-257-8205
800-959-2583
Bob & Kathy Morris
All year

179-339-B&B
17 rooms, 17 pb
Most CC, *Rated*, •
C-yes/S-no/P-no

Full breakfast
Dinner available, comp. wine
Sitting room, hot tubs,
swimming pool, deck,
bicycles, gazebo with swing

Theme floor; Camelot courtyard & rooms with deluxe amenities. 2 person whirlpool spas, French lighted mirror, silver goblets, port in crystal; hot & cold beverage service. French cuisine in Violette's. E-mail: bviolet@napanet.net Web site: bluevioletmansion.com

---

Candlelight Inn
1045 Easum Dr, 94558
707-254-3717 Fax: 707-257-3762
Johnanna & Wolfgang Brox
All year

125-255-B&B
10 rooms, 10 pb
Most CC, •
C-ltd/S-no/P-no/H-yes
German, French

Full breakfast
Aftn. tea, snacks, wine
Sitting room, Jacuzzis,
swimming pool, suites,
fireplaces, cable TV

The Candlelight Inn is a lovely English Tudor built in 1929 on a quiet park-like, 1 acre setting. E-mail: mail@candlelightinn.com Web site: candlelightinn.com

---

Cedar Gables Inn
486 Coombs St, 94559
707-224-7969 Fax: 707-224-4838
800-309-7969
Craig & Margaret Snasdell
All year

139-239-B&B
8 rooms, 8 pb
Most CC, *Rated*, •
C-no/S-no/P-no/H-no

Full breakfast
Wine, snacks, aftn. tea
Hot tubs, sitting room,
located in wine country,
romantic getaway

Built in 1892, this 10,000 sq. ft. mansion is styled after Shakespeare's time which makes it different from any other residence in the state. E-mail: info@cedargablesinn.com
Web site: cedargablesinn.com/

Hennessey House
1727 Main St, 94559
707-226-3774 Fax: 707-226-2975
Gilda & Alex Feit
All year

105-250-B&B
10 rooms, 10 pb
Most CC, *Rated*, •
C-ltd/S-no/P-no/H-no

Full sumptuous breakfast
Comp. wine, aftn. tea
Sitting room with TV,
whirlpool tubs, sauna,
fireplaces

Napa's 1889 Queen Anne Victorian B&B. "A Great Place to Relax." Walk to restaurants and shops. Share wine and conversation by the garden fountain.
E-mail: inn@hennesseyhouse.com Web site: hennesseyhouse.com

NAPA

La Belle Epoque B&B Inn
1386 Calistoga Ave, 94559
707-257-2161 Fax: 707-226-6314
800-238-8070
Georgia Jump
All year

169-219-B&B
6 rooms, 6 pb
Most CC, *Rated*, •
C-ltd/S-no/P-no/H-no

Full gourmet breakfast
Complimentary wine, snacks
Sitting room, fireplace, fully
A/C, TV/VCR

Historic Victorian bejeweled in stained glass, antique furnishings, gourmet breakfasts by the fireside. Walk to wine train depot, restaurant and shops. Wine tasting room and cellar.
E-mail: gerogia@labelleepoque.com   Web site: labelleepoque.com

---

La Residence
4066 St Helena Hwy, 94558
707-253-0337 Fax: 707-253-0382
David Jackson, Craig Claussen
All year

175-295-B&B
20 rooms, 18 pb
Visa, MC, *Rated*, •
C-yes/S-no/P-no

Full breakfast
Complimentary wine
CD players, hair dryers, new
veranda, Jacuzzi spa, garden
setting, vineyard

For the sophisticated traveler who enjoys elegant yet intimate style, La Residence is the only choice in Napa Valley. Two acres of landscaped grounds with ponds and fountains. Our "park-like" grounds create a beautiful, serene setting.   Web site: laresidence.com

---

Old World Inn, The
1301 Jefferson St, 94559
707-257-0112 Fax: 707-257-0118
800-966-6624
Sam van Hoeve
All year

125-225-B&B
8 rooms, 8 pb
Visa, MC, AmEx,
Rated, •
C-ltd/S-no/P-no/H-no

Full gourmet breakfast
Complimentary wine &
cheese
Afternoon tea, evening
dessert buffet, sitting room,
Jacuzzi

Run with Old World hospitality by its English innkeepers, this Victorian inn is uniquely decorated throughout in bright Scandinavian colors. Outdoor spa.
Web site: oldworldinn.com

Trubody Ranch B&B
5444 Trubody Lane, 94558
707-255-5907 Fax: 707-255-7254
Jeff & Mary Page
Exc Christmas & January

100-225-B&B
3 rooms, 3 pb
Visa, MC, *Rated*
S-no/P-no/H-no

Continental plus breakfast
Sitting room, fireplaces, air
conditioned rooms, cottage
w/two person tub

1872 Victorian home, water tower, & cottage nestled in 120 acres of family-owned vineyard. Stunning views. All rooms with phones, music system. Closed Sun/Mon excluding stay throughs.
E-mail: trubody@napanet.net Web site: napanet.net/~trubody/

NAPA VALLEY

Bylund House B&B
2000 Howell Mtn Rd, 94574
707-963-9073
Bill & Diane Bylund
All year

100-200-B&B
2 rooms, 2 pb
Rated, •
S-ltd/P-no/H-no

Continental plus breakfast
Wine & hors d'oeuvres
Sitting rm. w/fireplace, pool,
spa, near wineries,
restaurant, tennis, golf

Wine country villa designed by owner-architect in secluded valley with sweeping views. 2 private rooms with views, balconies and European feather beds.   *E-mail:* chrenblake@ aol.com

---

Crossroads Inn
6380 Silverado Trail, 94558
707-944-0646 Fax: 707-944-0650
Nancy & Sam Scott
All year

275-300-B&B
3 rooms, 3 pb
Visa, MC, •
C-ltd/S-no/P-no/H-no

Full breakfast
Complimentary wine, host
bar
Aftn. tea, eve. brandy,
library, game room, deck, hot
tubs, bikes, gardens

Sweeping Napa Valley views. Custom 2-person spas; complete privacy. King-sized beds, wine bars and full baths complement each suite. Hiking trails, swimming pool, and outdoor spa.   E-mail: infor@crossroadsnv.com Web site: crossroadsnv.com

Oak Knoll Inn, Napa Valley, CA

NAPA VALLEY

Oak Knoll Inn
2200 E Oak Knoll Ave, 94558
707-255-2200
Fax: 707-255-2296
Barbara Passino
All year

285-395-B&B
3 rooms, 3 pb
Visa, MC, *Rated*, •
C-ltd/S-no/P-no/H-no

Full breakfast
Afternoon tea, snacks
Complimentary wine, spa,
swimming pool, fireplaces in
all rooms

Romantic, elegant stone country inn surrounded by vineyards. Spacious rooms with fireplaces. Sip wine watching the sunset over the mountains. Winemaker special tasting in the evening. Web site: travelguides.com/home/oak_knoll

Tall Timber Chalets
1012 Darms Ln, 94558
707-252-7810
Mary Sandmann-Montes
All year

B&B
7 rooms, 7 pb
Visa, MC, AmEx, •
C-ltd/S-ltd/P-no/H-no

Continental breakfast
Cable TV, Accommodate
business travelers.

Tall Timbers Chalets is a two acre property with eight nicely dressed cottages (c.1940) reminiscent of places in Austria & Switzerland; squeaky clean with lace curtains, papered walls and carpets in light fresh colors. Web site: sirius.com/~hotelweb/TallTimbers

NEVADA CITY

Grandmere's Inn
449 Broad St, 95959
530-265-4660
Fax: 530-265-4416
Ruth Ann Riese
All year

110-170-B&B
6 rooms, 6 pb
Visa, MC, *Rated*, •
C-ltd/S-no/P-no/H-ltd

Full breakfast
Dinner by arrangement
Soft drinks, cookies, sitting
room, two in-room Jacuzzis

Historic landmark with country French decor in the heart of Nevada City. Lovely grounds suitable for weddings and private parties. E-mail: grandmere@nevadacityinns.com
Web site: nevadacityinn.com/grandmere.htm

NICE

Gingerbread Cottages B&B
PO Box 4004, 95464
707-274-0200
Buddy & Yvonne
Lipscomb
Feb-Nov

95-B&B
10 rooms, 10 pb
Most CC, •
C-ltd/S-ltd/P-no/H-no

Continental breakfast
Snacks
Bicycles, swimming pool,
suites, fireplaces, cable TV

Romantic, lakefront cottages on beautiful Clear Lake. Each is exquisitely decorated & themed.

NORTH LAKE TAHOE

Rainbow Lodge	79-119-B&B	Full breakfast
PO Box 1100, 95728	33 rooms, 10 pb	Restaurant, lunch
530-426-3871 Fax: 530-426-9221	Visa, MC, *Rated*, •	Dinner, snacks, bar service,
800-500-3871	C-yes/S-yes/P-no/H-yes	library, sitting room
Trudi Baer All year		

Cozy & romantic with Swiss-Italian cuisine. Enjoy a winter skiers paradise or summer serenity by the Yuba River. Hiking, biking, fishing areas.   E-mail: info@royalgorge.com Web site: royalgorge.com/rainbow.html

OAKHURST

Chateau du Sureau	325-525-B&B	Full breakfast
PO Box 577, 93644	10 rooms, 10 pb	Restaurant, complimentary
559-683-6860 Fax: 559-683-0800	Most CC, *Rated*, •	wine
Lucy Royse	S-no/P-no/H-yes	Bar service, sitting room,
All year	German, Spanish	library, pool, suites,
		fireplace, cable TV.

A 2,000 sq. ft. manor house located just below Chateau du Sureau's Nature Park. A tranquil haven sheltered by towering pine trees, surrounded by lovely scenery, fountains and private gardens.   E-mail: chateau@sierranet.net Web site: chateausureau.com

OLEMA

Roundstone Farm B&B	120-160-B&B	Full breakfast
PO Box 217, 94950	5 rooms, 5 pb	Afternoon tea
415-663-1020 Fax: 415-663-8056	Visa, MC, AmEx,	Sitting room, library,
800-881-9874	*Rated*, •	panoramic views of pond,
F. Borodic & K. Anderson	C-ltd/S-no/P-no/H-no	ridges, bay & meadow
All year		

The perfect place to refresh the spirit. Rooms have private bath, fireplace and magnificent views of bay, meadow or ridge. Hot tub. All rooms have fireplaces.   E-mail: refresh@ roundstonefarm.com Web site: roundstonefarm.com

OROVILLE

Jean's Riverside B&B	65-125 B&B	Full breakfast
1142 Middlehoff Ln, 95965	17 rooms, 17 pb	Complimentary wine
530-533-1413	Visa, MC, *Rated*, •	River waterfront with dock,
Jean Pratt	C-ltd/S-ltd/P-ltd/H-yes	deck overlooking river, lawn
All year		games, golf, pool

Romantic waterfront hideaway with private Jacuzzis, fishing, goldpanning, birdwatching, historical sites. Near hiking, Feather River Cyn, Oroville Dam. 6 acres of private waterfront, Oriental bridge overlooking Feather River with river rock walkways.   E-mail: jeansbandb@ yahoo.com Web site: oroville-city.com/jeans/

PACIFIC GROVE

Centrella Inn	109-219-B&B	Continental plus breakfast
612 Central Ave, 93950	26 rooms, 25 pb	Tea/wine/hors d'oeuvres
831-372-3372 Fax: 831-372-2036	Visa, MC, AmEx,	Parlor, dining room, beveled
800-433-4732	*Rated*, •	glass, gardens, weekly
Mark Arellano	C-ltd/S-no/P-no/H-yes	specials
All year	Italian	

Restored Victorian—award winner for interior design. Ocean, lovers' point and many attractions of the Monterey Peninsula. Fireplaces in suites.   E-mail: Concierge@innsbythesea.com Web site: innsbythesea.com/innres.htm#ct

Gatehouse Inn	110-165-B&B	Full breakfast
225 Central Ave, 93950	8 rooms, 8 pb	Afternoon tea
831-649-8436 Fax: 831-648-8044	Visa, MC, AmEx,	Comp. wine & cheese, sitting
800-753-1881	*Rated*, •	room, binoculars, near
Lois DeFord	C-ltd/S-no/P-no/H-yes	ocean and downtown
Season Inquire	Spanish	

Historic 1884 seaside Victorian home, distinctive rooms, stunning views, private baths, fireplaces, delicious breakfasts, afternoon wine and cheese. Centrally located E-mail: lew@redshift.com Web site: sueandlewinns.com/gatehouse/index.html

PACIFIC GROVE

Grand View Inn	165-285-B&B	Full breakfast
555 Ocean View Blvd, 93950	10 rooms, 10 pb	Afternoon tea
831-372-4341	Visa, MC, *Rated*, •	Very comfortable, very
831-372-4341	C-ltd/S-no/P-no/H-ltd	elegant in a more, subtle
Ed and Susan Flatley	German, Spanish	manner
All year		

Newly restored 1910 seaside Edwardian mansion overlooking Lover's Point and Monterey Bay. Elegant appointments, marble bathrooms, wraparound ocean views.
Web site: 7gables-grandview.com

Inn at 213- 17 Mile Dr	135-240-B&B	Full breakfast
213 Seventeen Mile Drive,	14 rooms, 14 pb	Snacks, complimentary wine
93950	Visa, MC, AmEx,	Sitting room, bicycles,
831-642-9514 Fax: 831-642-9546	*Rated*, •	Jacuzzis, cable TV,
800-526-5666	S-no/P-no/H-yes	accommodate business
Tony & Glynis Greening		travelers
All year		

A heritage award winning craftsman house set amongst monarch butterfly trees. Walk or bike to Victorian Pacific Grove town. E-mail: innat213@innat213-17miledr.com
Web site: innat213-17miledr.com

Martine Inn, The	155-300-B&B	Full breakfast
PO Box 232, 93950	23 rooms, 23 pb	Picnic lunches, wine
831-373-3388 Fax: 831-373-3896	Visa, MC, AmEx,	Hors d'oeuvres, sitting room,
800-852-5588	*Rated*, •	game room, bicycles, conf.
Don Martine	C-yes/S-yes/P-no/H-yes	room
All year	Italian, Russian, Spanish	

12,000-sq. ft. mansion on Monterey Bay. Elegant museum quality American antiques. Bkfst. served on old Sheffield silver, crystal, Victorian china, & lace. Rooms redecorated.
E-mail: innlight@radshift.com Web site: MARTINEINN.com

Old St. Angela Inn	100-195-B&B	Full breakfast
321 Central Ave, 93950	9 rooms, 9 pb	Complimentary wine/port,
831-372-3246 Fax: 831-372-8560	Visa, MC, AmEx,	cookies
800-748-6306	*Rated*, •	Solarium, gardens, hot tub in
Susan Kuslis & Lewis Shaefer	C-ltd/S-no/P-no/H-no	garden, rooms with
All year		fireplaces & Jacuzzis

Intimate Cape Cod elegance overlooking Monterey Bay; walking distance to ocean & beaches, aquarium, Cannery Row. Champagne breakfast. Restored church rectory. Ocean view rooms with fireplace or pot belly stoves.
E-mail: lew@redshift.com Web site: sueandlewinns.com/stangela/index.html

Seven Gables Inn	165-375-B&B	Full breakfast
555 Ocean View Blvd, 93950	14 rooms, 14 pb	High tea
831-372-4341	*Rated*, •	Grand Victorian parlor,
Ed and Susan Flatley	C-ltd/S-no/P-no/H-no	aquarium tickets, 2 bedroom
All year	French, Spanish	luxury suite

Elegant Victorian mansion at the very edge of Monterey Bay. Fine antique furnishings throughout. Incomparable ocean views from all rooms. Web site: 7gables-grandview.com

PALM DESERT

Tres Palmas B&B	80-185-B&B	Continental plus breakfast
PO Box 2115, 92261	4 rooms, 4 pb	Snacks
760-773-9858 Fax: 760-776-9159	Visa, MC, *Rated*, •	Library, sitting room, hot
800-770-9858	C-ltd/S-no/P-no/H-no	tubs, swimming pool
Karen & Terry Bennett		
All year		

Enjoy our casual, southwest elegance indoors or our warm desert sun outdoors. Walk to fabulous shopping & dining on El Paseo. Web site: innformation.com/ca/trespalmas

PALM SPRINGS

Casa Cody B&B Country Inn	89-349-B&B	Continental plus breakfast
175 S Cahuilla Rd, 92262	23 rooms, 24 pb	Hot tub, swimming pools,
760-320-9346 Fax: 760-325-8610	Most CC, *Rated*, •	hiking, bicycling
800-231-2639	C-ltd/S-ltd/P-ltd/H-yes	
Frank Tysen, Therese Hayes	French, Dutch, German	
All year		

Romantic hideaway in heart of Palm Springs Village. 1910 adobe house 2 bedrooms once owned by Metropolitan opera star Lawrence Tibbet and frequented by Charlie Chaplin.
E-mail: casacody@aol.com Web site: palmsprings.com/hotels/casacody

L'Horizon Garden Hotel	95-255-B&B	Continental breakfast
1050 E Palm Canyon Dr, 92264	22 rooms, 22 pb	Library, bicycles, hot tubs,
760-323-1858 Fax: 760-327-2933	Most CC, *Rated*, •	swimming pool
800-377-7855	C-ltd/S-no/P-no/H-no	
Sandi Howell		
Oct-June		

Secluded oasis with 22 private, luxurious rooms and suites decorated in beautiful desert pastels. Complimentary continental breakfast. Sparkling pool and Jacuzzi. Close to attractions.

Travellers Repose	65-85-B&B	Continental plus breakfast
PO Box 655, 92240	3 rooms, 3 pb	Afternoon tea
619-329-9584	*Rated*, •	Sitting room, Jacuzzis
Marian Relkoff	C-ltd/S-no/P-no/H-no	
Sept 1 - June 30		

Two-story Victorian, unique in the Desert. Quiet and private. Antiques and country furnishings, stained glass, oak floors, patio and garden. Heart motif predominates inside and out.

Villa Royale Inn	105-325-B&B	Continental plus breakfast
1620 Indian Trail, 92264	31 rooms, 31 pb	Restaurant, bar service
760-327-2314 Fax: 760-322-3794	Most CC, *Rated*, •	Full room service, spas, 2
800-245-2314	S-yes/P-no/H-yes	pools, in-room massage
Greg Purdy		
All year		

Rooms & villas decorated as different European countries on 3.5 acres of flowering gardens. Private patios, spas, fireplaces, poolside gourmet dinners. Villas, hotel rooms.
E-mail: info@villaroyale.com Web site: villaroyale.com

Willows Historic Inn, The	195-525-B&B	Full breakfast
412 W Tahquitz Cyn Way,	8 rooms, 8 pb	Rest., aftn. tea, snacks
92262	Most CC, *Rated*, •	Sitting room, library, pool,
760-320-0771 Fax: 760-320-0780	S-no/P-no/H-ltd	hot tubs, gardens, waterfall,
800-966-9597		mtn. views
Connie Stevens		
All year		

The Willows offers exquisite accommodations for discriminating guests in an historic home restored to recreate the ambience of Palm Springs in the 1930s.
E-mail: innkeeper@thewillowspalmsprings.com Web site: thewillowspalmsprings.com/

PALO ALTO

Victorian on Lytton	148-225-B&B	Continental breakfast
555 Lytton Ave, 94301	10 rooms, 10 pb	Complimentary appetizers,
650-322-8555 Fax: 650-322-6373	Visa, MC, *Rated*	port
Susan & Maxwell Hall	C-ltd/S-no/P-no/H-yes	Complimentary sherry,
All year		occasional entertainment,
		computer modem ports, TV

A lovely Victorian built in 1895 offering a combination of forgotten elegance with a touch of European grace. Near Stanford University, charming shops, cafes.

The Artists' Inn, Pasadena, CA

PASADENA

Artists' Inn	110-215-B&B	Full or cont. breakfast
1038 Magnolia St, 91030	9 rooms, 9 pb	Picnic lunch, aftn. tea
626-799-5668 Fax: 626-799-3678	Visa, MC, AmEx,	Snacks, sitt. rm., lib., Jacuzzi
888-799-5668	*Rated*, ●	tubs, suites, fireplaces, cable
Janet Marangi	C-yes/S-no/P-no/H-no	TV
All year		

Like Grandma's House. White wicker on big front porch, English Chintz, antiques, all cotton sheets, English towels, hair dryers, canopy & antique brass beds, fireplaces, Jacuzzis.
E-mail: artistsinn@artistsinns.com Web site: artistsinns.com

Bissell House B&B	100-150	Cont. plus bkfst. wkdays
201 Orange Grove Ave, 91030	3 rooms, 3 pb	Full breakfast weekends
818-441-3535 Fax: 818-441-3671	Visa, MC, AmEx,	Snacks, comp. wine, sitting
800-441-3530	*Rated*, ●	room, library, hot tubs,
Russell & Leonore Butcher	C-ltd/S-ltd/P-no/H-no	Jacuzzi tub
All year	Spanish	

1887 Victorian beautifully decorated with antiques. 12 min. & 100 years to downtown LA, received commendation from CABBI.   Web site: virtualcities.com/ons/ca/x/cax6602.htm

PETALUMA

Cavanagh Inn B&B	100-140-B&B	Full gourmet breakfast
10 Keller St, 94952	7 rooms, 5 pb	Afternoon wine
707-765-4657 Fax: 707-769-0466	Most CC, *Rated*, ●	Sitting room, parlor, library,
888-765-4658	C-ltd/S-no/P-no/H-no	evening turn-down, within
Ray & Jeanne Farris		historic downtown
All year		

Elegant 1902 Victorian & 1912 Craftsman cottage. 20 antique stores within walking distance. 32 miles N. of Golden Gate at the gateway to the wine country. Meetings.
E-mail: info@cavanaghinn.com Web site: cavanaghinn.com

PHILO

Philo Pottery Inn, The	95-115-B&B	Full breakfast
PO Box 166, 95466	5 rooms, 3 pb	Complimentary wine, tea,
707-895-3069	Visa, MC,	sherry
Jill & Drew Crane	C-ltd/S-ltd/P-no/H-ltd	Homemade cookies, library,
All year		sitting room, mountain bike
		trails

1888 redwood stagecoach stop—country antiques & English garden—near Anderson Valley Wineries & restaurants. Hendy Woods State Redwood Park. *E-mail:* philoinn@pacific.net
Web site: innaccess.com/PHI

PLACERVILLE

Chichester-McKee House	80-125-B&B	Special full breakfast
800 Spring St, 95667	4 rooms, 3 pb	Complimentary soft drinks,
530-626-1882 Fax: 530-626-7801	Most CC, *Rated*, •	mixes
800-831-4008	C-ltd/S-no/P-no/H-no	"Doreen's brownies", queen-
Doreen & Bill Thornhill		size beds, parlor, gardens,
All year		porches, lib.

Elegant 1892 grand Victorian home and gardens. Enjoy romance and relaxing hospitality. Find adventure in the Sierra foothills. E-mail: inn@innercite.com Web site: innercite.com/~inn/

River Rock Inn	80-100-B&B	Full breakfast
1756 Georgetown Dr, 95667	4 rooms, 2 pb	Complimentary sherry
530-622-7640	*Rated*, •	Sitting room, hot tub, TV
Dorothy Irvin	C-ltd/S-ltd/P-no/H-ltd	lounge, antiques
All year		

Relax on the 110-ft. deck overlooking the American River, fish and pan for gold in the front yard. Quiet and beautiful.

Shadowridge Ranch & Lodge	130-160-B&B	Full breakfast
3500 Fort Jim Road, 95667	4 rooms, 4 pb	Lunch available, snacks,
530-295-1000 Fax: 530-626-5613	Visa, MC, AmEx,	wine, bar
800-644-3498	*Rated*, •	Sitting room, library, suites,
Carlotta & James Davies	C-ltd/S-ltd/P-no/H-no	fireplaces, conference
April-Dec.	Spanish	facilities

Hand-Hewn Log Cabin B&B in the heart of California's Gold Country. Luxuriously furnished in lodge antiques, fireplaces, private baths and amenities.
E-mail: shadowridge@inforum.net Web site: shadowridgeranch.com

POINT ARENA

Coast Guard House	115-175-B&B	Full breakfast
695 Arena Cove, 95468	6 rooms, 6 pb	Fireplaces, whirlpools,
707-882-2442	Visa, MC,	views, patios and balconies
Kevin & Mia Gallagher	S-ltd/P-no	
All year		

Historic site of Coast Guard rescue operations at Point Arena. Arts and Crafts furnishings, oceanside location, exceptional breakfast. E-mail: coast@mcn.org
Web site: coastguardhouse.com

POINT REYES STATION

Cricket Cottage	135-155-B&B	Full breakfast
PO Box 627, 94956	1 rooms, 1 pb	Comp. sparkling juice
415-663-9139 Fax: 415-663-9090	*Rated*	Library, private hot tub,
P. Livingston, J. Stark	C-yes/P-ltd/H-yes	private garden, Franklin
All year		fireplace

A cozy, romantic cottage in an intimate garden overlooking a meadow, surrounded by cypress & eucalyptus trees. E-mail: pinc@nbn.com
Web site: permacultureinstitute.com/cottage.html

Ferrando's Hideaway B&B	150-250-B&B	Full breakfast
PO Box 688, 94956	5 rooms, 3 pb	Afternoon tea
415-663-1966 Fax: 415-663-1825	*Rated*, •	Sitting room, library, hot tub,
800-337-2636	C-yes/S-no/P-no/H-yes	Franklin fireplace
Greg & Doris Ferrando	German	
All year		

European hospitality. Elegant Alberti cottage. Cozy garden cottage. Rooms with private baths. TV-VCR, gardens E-mail: ferrando@nbn.com Web site: ferrando.com

POINT REYES STATION

Marsh Cottage B&B
PO Box 1121, 94956
415-669-7168
Wendy Schwartz
All year

120-140-B&B
1 rooms, 1 pb
C-yes/S-no/P-no/H-no

Full breakfast
Complimentary
coffee/tea/wine
Kitchen, library, sitting room,
fireplace, porch, sun deck

Cheerful, carefully appointed private cottage along bay. Kitchen, fireplace, queen bed, desk; extraordinary setting for romantics and naturalists. Web site: marshcottage.com

Neon Rose, A
PO Box 632, 94956
415-663-9143 Fax: 415-663-8060
800-358-8346
Sandy Fields
All year

135-175-B&B
1 rooms, 1 pb
C-ltd/S-no/P-no/H-no

Continental plus breakfast
Full kitchen
Jacuzzis, fireplaces, cable TV

A fully equipped guest cottage with Jacuzzi, bordered by the Pt. Reyes National Seashore, expansive view of Tomales Bay and the sunset. Easy access to San Francisco, Napa/Sonoma wine country. E-mail: neonrose@nbn.com Web site: neonrose.com

Point Reyes Country Inn
PO Box 501, 94956
415-663-9696 Fax: 415-663-8888
Thomas S. Evans
All year

105-270-B&B
6 rooms, 6 pb
Visa, MC, *Rated*, •
C-ltd/S-ltd/P-no/H-no

Full breakfast
Afternoon tea, snacks, wine
Sitting room, library, suites,
fireplace, overnight horse
boarding

The Country Inn is a spacious home on four sunny acres, furnished with antiques, down covered beds and welcoming reading chairs. Access to miles of trails and beaches. E-mail: prci@svn.net Web site: ptreyescountryinn.com

Thirty Nine Cypress
PO Box 176, 94956
415-663-1709 Fax: 415-663-9292
Julia Bartlett
All year

115-160-B&B
3 rooms, 3 pb
Rated, •
C-ltd/S-no/P-ltd/H-yes
French

Full breakfast
Hot tub with great view, 140
mi. of hiking trails, bicycles,
sitting room

Antiques, original art, oriental rugs, spectacular view! Close to beaches. Horseback riding arrangements available. Now have Redwing Cottage, 3 rooms with private gardens. E-mail: gartlett@svn.net Web site: point-reyes-inn.com

POINT RICHMOND

East Brother Light Station
117 Park Place, 94801
510-233-2385 Fax: 510-291-2243
Gary Herdlicka & Ann Selover
All year

290-370-MAP
4 rooms, 2 pb
Visa, MC, AmEx,
C-ltd/S-no/P-no/H-no

Full breakfast
Dinner included, lunch
available
Wine & hors d'oeuvres,
sitting room, library, fishing,
bird watching

Experience the panorama of San Francisco-Marin skylines from East Brother Island & lighthouse. Multi-course dinner with wine included. E-mail: ebls@ricochet.net
Web site: ebls.org

QUINCY

Feather Bed, The
PO Box 3200, 95971
530-283-0102 Fax: 530-283-0167
800-696-8624
Bob & Jan Janowski
All year

80-130-B&B
7 rooms, 7 pb
Visa, MC, AmEx,
Rated, •
C-ltd/S-no/P-no/H-yes

Full breakfast
Afternoon tea & cookies
Sitting room, porch,
Victorian garden, bikes,
fountain, frplcs., A/C

Country Victorian in forested surroundings, relaxing is our specialty, antiques in individually decorated rooms, located on Heritage Walk. E-mail: feathrbd@psln.com
Web site: innaccess.com/TFB

RED BLUFF

Faulkner House, The
1029 Jefferson St, 96080
530-529-0520 Fax: 530-527-4970
800-549-6171
Harvey & Mary Klingler
All year

65-90-B&B
4 rooms, 4 pb
Visa, MC, AmEx,
Rated, •
C-ltd/S-no/P-no/H-no

Full breakfast
Complimentary beverage
Sitting room, bicycles, all
rooms have private bath

1890s Queen Anne Victorian furnished in antiques. Screened porch on quiet street, hiking and skiing nearby. Visit Ide Adobe, Victorian Museum, Sacramento River.
E-mail: faulknerbb@snowcrest.net Web site: snowcrest.net/faulknerbb

REDDING

Palisades Paradise B&B
1200 Palisades Ave, 96003
530-223-5305 Fax: 530-223-1200
Gail Goetz
All year

70-100-B&B
2 rooms
Visa, MC, *Rated*, •
C-ltd/S-ltd/P-no/H-ltd

Continental plus breakfast
Full breakfast sometimes
Complimentary tea/coffee,
porch swing, garden spa,
cable TV, fireplace

Breathtaking view of Sacramento River, mtns., & city from secluded contemporary home in Redding. Gateway to Shasta-Cascade Wonderland. Excellent Bird-Watching.
E-mail: bnbno1@jett.net Web site: jett.net/~bnbno1

Tiffany House B&B Inn
1510 Barbara Rd, 96003
530-244-3225
Susan & Brady Stewart
All year

85-135-B&B
4 rooms, 4 pb
Visa, MC, AmEx,
Rated, •
C-yes/S-ltd/P-no/H-ltd

Full breakfast
Complimentary
refreshments
Sitting room, library, 1 room
with spa, gazebo, swimming
pool, parlor

Romantic Victorian within minutes of Sacramento River, beautiful lakes, water sports, championship golf. Elegant view of Lassen mountain range. Free champagne for honeymoons & anniversaries.   E-mail: tiffanyhse@aol.com Web site: sylvia.com/tiffany.htm

SACRAMENTO

Amber House B&B Inn
1315 22nd St, 95816
916-444-8085 Fax: 916-552-6529
800-755-6526
Michael Richardson   All year

125-259-B&B
14 rooms, 11 pb
Most CC, *Rated*, •
C-ltd/S-ltd/P-no/H-no

Full gourmet breakfast
Complimentary wine, tea,
coffee
Marble bathrooms, tandem
bicycle, phones

Luxury rooms offer ultimate comfort for the business traveler and perfect setting for a romantic escape. Phones, cable TV, breakfast in room. New historic 1895 Colonial revival home. 11 rooms have Jacuzzis for two.   E-mail: innkeeper@amberhouse.com
Web site: amberhouse.com

Hartley House B&B Inn
700 22nd St, 95816
916-447-7829 Fax: 916-447-1820
800-831-5806
Randy Hartley   All year

120-175-B&B
5 rooms, 5 pb
Rated, •
C-ltd/S-ltd/P-no/H-no
Spanish

Full gourmet breakfast
Complimentary beverages
Sitting room, piano, inroom
phones, modems, fax, A/C,
courtyard spa

A stunning turn-of-the-century mansion with the sophisticated elegance of a small European hotel in historic Boulevard Park in midtown.   E-mail: randy@hartleyhouse.com
Web site: hartleyhouse.com

Inn at Parkside
2116 6th St, 95818
916-658-1818 Fax: 916-658-1809
800-995-7275
Georgia McGreal, Weldon
Reeves
All year

95-225-B&B
7 rooms, 7 pb
Visa, MC, AmEx, •
C-ltd/S-no/H-ltd

Full breakfast
Sitting room, library, tennis
courts (at park), garden
courtyard, spa

Charming, elegant Mediterranean mansion in the heart of Sacramento's historic district. Historic renovation Award 1996, Best Front Entry Award 1997.   E-mail: gmcgreal@
innatparkside.com Web site: innatparkside.com

SACRAMENTO

On the Bluffs	80-95-B&B	Full breakfast
9735 Mira Del Rio, 95827	3 rooms, 2 pb	Snacks
916-363-9933	Visa, AmEx,	Sitting room, bicycles,
Penny & Mark Bingham	S-no/P-no/H-no	swimming pool, garden
All year		courtyard, spa & decks

Minutes from major freeway yet peaceful and serene. The river just yards away. The innkeeper prides herself on individual attention and strives to meet all your needs.
E-mail: otbluffs@aol.com Web site: usa-411.com/otbluffs.html

San Simeon Home Stay, The	59-62-B&B	Full breakfast
1222 San Simeon Dr, 95661	2 rooms, 2 pb	Bikes, swimming pool,
916-786-7021 Fax: 916-786-3530	Visa, MC, AmEx,	library, hot tub, office
Greg & Jan Huttula All year	S-no/P-no/H-no	equipment

The San Simeon has a French Country interior design with central heat and air as well as a fireplace and white parlor grand piano. Available in each room is a TV, computer, and/or telephone. Special breakfasts served each morning.

SALINAS

Barlocker's Rustling Oaks	90-150-B&B	Full breakfast
25252 Limekiln Rd, 93908	5 rooms, 4 pb	Snacks
831-675-9121 Fax: 831-675-2060	Visa, MC, *Rated*, •	Sitting room, library,
Margaret Barlocker	C-yes/S-ltd/P-yes	bicycles, swimming pool,
All year		horseback riding avail.

Country hideaway—couple, business traveler or a family, Barlocker's offers fun, nature, horses & ranch animals and down-home cooking!

SAN DIEGO

B&B Inn at La Jolla, The	109-299-B&B	Full breakfast
7753 Draper Ave, 92037	15 rooms, 15 pb	Complimentary wine &
858-456-2066 Fax: 858-456-1510	Visa, MC, AmEx,	cheese
800-582-2466	*Rated*, •	Library, sitting room,
Ron Shanks	C-ltd/S-no/P-no/H-ltd	complimentary bicycle
All year	Some Spanish	rentals, public tennis courts

Romantic getaway, 1 block from beach in heart of town. European ambiance, ocean/garden views, fireplaces.   E-mail: bed+breakfast@innlajolla.com Web site: innlajolla.com

Brookside Farm B&B Inn	85-120-B&B	Full breakfast
1373 Marron Valley Rd, 91917	11 rooms, 8 pb	4-course dinner by RSVP
619-468-3043 Fax: 619-468-9145	Visa, MC, *Rated*, •	Hot tub, piano, terraces,
Edd & Sally Guishard	C-ltd/S-ltd/P-no/H-ltd	gardens, cooking school,
All year		room w/2-sided fireplace

Quaint farmhouse nestled in mountain setting with stream. Handmade quilts and rugs, fireplace and farm animals. Gourmet dinners on weekends.

Butterfield B&B	115-160-B&B	Full breakfast
PO Box 1115, 92036	5 rooms, 5 pb	Dinner avail., tea, snacks
760-765-2179 Fax: 760-765-1229	Visa, MC, AmEx,	Sitting room, library, suites,
800-379-4262	*Rated*, •	fireplace, cable TV
Ed Glass	C-ltd/S-no/P-no/H-ltd	
All year		

Relax on our three-acre country garden setting in the quiet hills of Julian. Five unique rooms from country to formal decor. Full gourmet breakfast every morning.
E-mail: butterfield@abac.com Web site: butterfieldbandb.com

California Cruisin'	150 and up-EP	Full breakfast (fee)
1450 Harbor Island Dr, 92101	Visa, MC, AmEx, Disc, •	Restaurant, bar service,
619-296-8000	C-yes/S-ltd/P-ltd/H-ltd	snacks
800-44-YACHT		Swimming pool, jacuzzi,
All year		accommodate business
		travelers

Enjoy San Diego aboard your own luxurious private yacht. Web site: californiacruising.com

SAN DIEGO

Carole's B&B Inn
3227 Grim Ave, 92104
619-280-5258
800-975-5521
C. Dugdale & M. O'Brien
All year

69-159-B&B
8 rooms, 4 pb
Rated, •
C-ltd/S-yes/P-no/H-no

Continental plus breakfast
Cheese
Sitt. rm., conf. for 10,
swimming pool, spa, player
piano, cable TV

Historical house built in 1904, tastefully redecorated/antiques. Centrally located near zoo, Balboa Park. Friendly, congenial atmosphere. Our annex across the street has 2 garden studio apartments with private bath & kitchenette and a 2 bedroom apartment

Cottage, The
PO Box 3292, 92103
619-299-1564 Fax: 619-299-6213
Carol & Robert Emerick
All year

65-125-B&B
2 rooms, 2 pb
Visa, MC, *Rated*, •
C-yes/S-no/P-no/H-no

Continental breakfast
Herb garden, player piano,
cable TV

Relaxation in a garden setting with turn-of-the-century ambiance is offered in a residential downtown San Diego neighborhood.   E-mail: cemerick@sandiegobandb.com
Web site: sandiegobandb.com/cottage

Glorietta Bay Inn
1630 Glorietta Blvd, 92118
619-435-3103 Fax: 619-435-6182
800-283-9383
Lisa Reopelle
All year

130-195-B&B
100 rooms, 100 pb
Visa, MC, AmEx,
Rated, •
C-yes/S-ltd/P-no/H-yes
Spanish

Continental plus breakfast
Sitting room, library,
Jacuzzis, pool, suites, cable
TV

Overlooking Glorietta Bay and a block from the ocean, the Glorietta Bay Inn combines old-world charm with contemporary comfort including private baths, heating and air-conditioning.   E-mail: rooms@gloriettabayinn.com Web site: gloriettabayinn.com

Glory's Holiday House B&B
3330 Ingelow St, 92106
619-225-0784 Fax: 619-221-4420
Glory Giffin
All year

111-150-B&B
3 rooms, 2 pb
Most CC, •
C-yes/S-ltd/P-yes/H-no

Full breakfast
Complimentary wine
Snacks, sitting room,
swimming pool, hot tub

Incredible view of San Diego Bay, the city, Coronado, Mexico and ocean. Nautical decor. Queen-size Victorian bed, CATV/VCR, private phone line, private bathroom, full breakfast, pool, jacuzzi   E-mail: gloryanne@aol.com

Harbor Hill Guest House
2330 Albatross St, 92101
619-233-0638
Dorothy A. Milbourn
All year

75-95-B&B
6 rooms, 6 pb
Visa, MC, *Rated*, •
C-yes/S-ltd/P-no/H-no

Continental breakfast
Kitchens on each level
Large sun deck & garden,
barbecue, TV, phones,
rooms with harbor views

Charming circa 1920 home; private entrances. Near Balboa Park, zoo, museums, Sea World, Old Town, harbor, shopping, theater. Families welcome. Special rates for longer stays.   Web site: travelguides.com/home/harborhill

Heritage Park B&B Inn
2470 Heritage Park Row, 92110
619-299-6832 Fax: 619-299-9465
800-995-2470
Nancy & Charles Helsper
All year

100-235-B&B
12 rooms, 12 pb
Most CC, *Rated*, •
C-yes/S-no/P-no/H-yes
Spanish

Full breakfast
Afternoon tea, picnics
Sitting room, library,
bicycles, vintage films,
discount tickets to Zoo

San Diego's grand 1889 Queen Anne mansion, secluded in an historic Victorian village where we pamper guests with a sumptuous breakfast, aftn. tea on the veranda & eve. turndown chocolates   E-mail: innkeeper@heritageparkinn.com Web site: heritageparkinn.com

SAN DIEGO ────────────────

Prospect Park Inn	120-375-B&B	Continental breakfast
1110 Prospect St, 92037	25 rooms, 25 pb	Afternoon tea
858-454-0133 Fax: 858-454-2056	Visa, MC, AmEx,	Library, sun deck, color TV
800-433-1609	*Rated*, •	& A/C in rooms, small
John Heichman	C-yes/S-no/P-no/H-no	conference fac.
All year		

Contemporary furnishings face balconies with sweeping ocean views, yet the charm of Europe prevails. In the heart of La Jolla, "The Jewel" of So. California. AAA 2 stars.
Web site: tales.com/ca/prospectparkinn/

Seabreeze Inn B&B	75-150-B&B	Continental plus breakfast
121 N Vulcan Ave, 92024	5 rooms, 5 pb	Complimentary wine &
760-944-0318	*Rated*, •	cheese
Kirsten Richter	C-yes/S-yes/P-no/H-no	Wet bar, kitchenette, sitting
All year		room, near beach and tennis

N. San Diego quiet beach town. Contemporary B&B with ocean view. Penthouse Boudoir with private 8' hot tub. Intimate oceanview wedding grotto. Web site: seabreeze-inn.com

Villa Serena B&B	105-B&B	Full breakfast
2164 Rosecrans St, 92106	3 rooms, 2 pb	Snacks
619-224-1451 Fax: 619-224-2103	Visa, MC, Disc, •	Sitting room, library, hot
800-309-2778	C-yes/S-no/P-no/H-no	tubs, pool, children under 12-
Kae & Alex Schreiber	Spanish	free
All year		

A wonderful Mediterranean paradise, 5 minutes to Sea World. Comfortable rooms, spa, abundant breakfasts, friendly hosts can help with suggestions. Entire house available for $300 per day—sleeps 6. E-mail: kschrei468@aol.com Web site: inn-guide.com/villaserena

SAN FRANCISCO ────────────────

Alamo Square Inn	85-295-B&B	Full breakfast
719 Scott St, 94117	13 rooms, 13 pb	Complimentary tea, wine
415-922-2055 Fax: 415-931-1304	Visa, MC, AmEx,	Free off-st. parking, Jacuzzi
800-345-9888	*Rated*, •	suite, views, Near S.F.
K. May, B. Collins, D. Wong	C-ltd/S-ltd/P-no/H-no	attractions
All year	Ger., Fr., Mandarin	

Fine restoration of 2 magnificent mansions. Graced by European furnishings, Oriental rugs, flowers, fireplaces, Victorian conference center. E-mail: wcorn@alamoinn.com
Web site: alamoinn.com

Amsterdam Hotel, The	99-109-B&B	Continental breakfast
749 Taylor St, 94108	30 rooms, 22 pb	Sitting room, library, sunny
415-673-3277 Fax: 415-673-0453	Visa, MC, AmEx,	patio, color TV & phones in
800-637-3444	*Rated*, •	rms
Kenny Gopal	C-yes/S-yes/P-no/H-no	
All year		

Located on Nob Hill. Quality accommodations and friendly service provided at modest rates. A little bit of Europe in America. Near Union Square, Financial District, cable car.
E-mail: info@amsterdamhotel.com Web site: amsterdamhotel.com

Andrews Hotel, The	99-149-B&B	Continental plus breakfast
624 Post St, 94109	48 rooms, 48 pb	Restaurant, bar
415-563-6877 Fax: 415-928-6919	Most CC, *Rated*, •	Complimentary wine, coffee,
800-926-3739	C-yes/S-no/P-no/H-no	tea, small meetings, color TV
Barbara, Yvonne, Susan, Jessi	Spanish, some French	& phones in rooms
All year		

European-style charm in the heart of Union Square shopping and theater district. Features architectural bay windows. Just two blocks from cable cars. Breakfast and evening wine included in quoted rate. E-mail: res@andrewshotel.com

SAN FRANCISCO ———————————————————————————

Annie's Cottage	135-B&B	Continental breakfast
1255 Vallejo, 94109	1 rooms, 1 pb	Walk to wharf & downtown,
415-923-9990 Fax: 415-923-9911	•	phone/answering machine,
Annie Bone	S-no/P-no/H-no	TV/VCR, queen bed
All year		

Guest room with private entrance, sitting area & refrigerator/microwave. Country hide-away in the middle of San Francisco. Furnished with antiques. E-mail: abonesf@sirius.com
Web site: anniescottage.com

Archbishop's Mansion Inn	189-419-B&B	Continental plus breakfast
1000 Fulton St, 94117	15 rooms, 15 pb	Comp. wine, tea, coffee
415-563-7872 Fax: 415-885-3193	Visa, MC, AmEx,	Sitting room, piano,
800-543-5820	*Rated*, •	reception & conference,
Sondra Lender	C-yes/S-no/P-no/H-no	facilities, spa services
All year		

Luxury lodging in "Belle Epoque" style. "Arguably the most elegant, in-city small hotel on the West Coast if not the USA"–USA Today. Getaway packages. E-mail: abm@ jdvhospitality.com

Artists Inn	150-175-B&B	Continental breakfast
2231 Pine St, 94115	3 rooms, 3 pb	Complimentary wine
415-346-1919 Fax: 415-346-1904	Most CC,	Sitting room, fireplace in
800-854-5802	C-ltd/S-ltd/P-no/H-no	main living room of house
Denise & Bill Shields	Some French	
All year		

Artists Inn is a charming 19th century farm house and an artists studio building on either side of a secluded garden courtyard, located in Pacific Heights in the heart of SF. Less than a block away, Fillmore St. offfers shopping & dining. E-mail: shields@artistsinn.com
Web site. artistsinn.com

Bock's B&B	50-90-B&B	Continental plus breakfast
1448 Willard St, 94117	3 rooms, 1 pb	Coffee and tea service
415-664-6842 Fax: 415-664-1109	•	Sitting room, swimming pool
Laura J. Bock	C-yes/S-no/P-no/H-no	nearby, tennis court nearby
All year	Some French	

Restored 1906 Edwardian residence. Splendid view, decks, private phones, TVs in room. Golden Gate Park and excellent public transportation nearby

Carol's Cow Hollow Inn	125-250-B&B	Full breakfast
2821 Steiner St, 94123	3 rooms, 3 pb	Tea, complimentary wine
415-775-8295 Fax: 415-775-8296	Visa, MC, •	Sitting room, library, TV,
800-400-8295	C-yes/S-ltd/P-no/H-no	refrigerator, desks, phones,
Carol Blumenfeld	Rus., Ger., Fr., Sp.	superb location
All year		

Charm in the heart of Pacific Heights. Memorable views and cuisine, original art. Close to Victorian Union Street boutiques and restaurants. Fabulous views. E-mail: subtle@ ix.netcom.com Web site: subtleties.com/

Casa Arguello B&B	61-97-B&B	Continental plus breakfast
225 Arguello Blvd, 94118	5 rooms, 3 pb	Sitting room, TV, Suite w/one
415-752-9482 Fax: 415-681-1400	Visa, MC, AmEx, *Rated*	king & two, twin beds
Emma Baires, W. McKenzie	C-yes/S-no/P-no/H-no	available
All year	Spanish	

An elegant townhouse near Golden Gate Park, the Presidio, Golden Gate Bridge, 10 minutes to Union Square. Near restaurants and public transportation.
E-mail: 103221.3126@compuserve.com

SAN FRANCISCO ───

Chateau Tivoli
1057 Steiner St, 94115
415-776-5462 Fax: 415-776-0505
800-228-1647
Victoria, Soraya, Erica
All year

99-225-B&B
9 rooms, 5 pb
Visa, MC, AmEx,
Rated, •
C-yes/S-no/P-ltd/H-ltd
French, Spanish,
Swedish

Continental plus breakfast
Afternoon tea, snacks, wine
Sitting room, library, suites,
fireplace, wedding &
reception facilities

*An oppulent, colorful Victorian mansion; handcarved woodwork, antiques, period wallpa-
pers; afternoon wine & cheese, freshly baked breakfast pastries and weekend champagne
brunch; sincere friendliness makes you feel right at home.* E-mail: mail@chateautivoli.com
Web site: chateautivoli.com

Country Cottage B&B
PO Box 420009, 94110
415-899-0060 Fax: 415-899-9923
800-452-8249
Richard & Susan
Season Inquire

79-B&B
4 rooms, 4 pb

Full breakfast

*The Country Cottage B&B is a cozy country-style b&b in the heart of San Francisco. The
four guest rooms are comfortabely furnished in American country antiques and brass
beds.* E-mail: bbsf@linex.com Web site: bbsf.com/country.html

Dockside Boat & Bed
419 Water St, 94607
510-444-5858 Fax: 510-444-0420
800-436-2574
Rob & Molly Harris
All year

115-400-B&B
16 rooms, 16 pb
Most CC, *Rated*, •
C-ltd/S-no/P-no/H-no

Continental breakfast
Snacks, on board dinners
available
Restaurant, suites

*Intimate accommodations on private sail, motor yachts. Private charters & romantic can-
dlelight catered dinners available. Enjoy SF skyline from the deck of your own private
yacht.* E-mail: boatandbed@aol.com Web site: boatandbed.com

Gables Inn-Sausalito, The
62 Princess ST, 94965
415-289-1100 Fax: 415-339-0536
800-966-1554
Abraham & Patricia Chador
All year

155-300-B&B
9 rooms, 9 pb
Visa, MC, AmEx, •
C-yes/S-no/P-no/H-yes
Spanish, French

Continental breakfast
Wine, bar
Sitting room, bicycles, tennis,
Jacuzzis, fireplace, cable TV

*Originally built in 1869, the inn has recently been completely renovated into a cozy B&B
offering 9 distinctive suites artfully decorated. Just 5 minutes north of the Golden Gate.*
E-mail: gablesinns@aol.com Web site: gablesinnsausalito.com

Garden Studio, The
1387 Sixth Ave, 94122
415-753-3574 Fax: 415-753-5513
Alice & John Micklewright
All year

85-EP
1 rooms, 1 pb
C-yes/S-no/P-no/H-no
French

Coffee, Restaurants nby
Garden, private entrance,
fully equipped kitchen,
TV/VCR, telephone, radio

*On lower level of charming Edwardian home; 2 blocks from Golden Gate Park. Studio
opens to garden, has private entrance, private bath, queen-sized bed. 5 night minimum.*
E-mail: jamick@sirius.com

Golden Gate Hotel, The
775 Bush St, 94108
415-392-3702 Fax: 415-392-6202
800-835-1118
John & Renate Kenaston
All year

72-125-B&B
23 rooms, 14 pb
Most CC, *Rated*, •
C-yes/S-ltd/P-no/H-no
German, French

Continental breakfast
Afternoon tea
Sitting room, sightseeing
tours, TV/VCR, telephone,
radio

*Charming turn-of-the-century hotel. Friendly atmosphere. Antique furnishings, fresh flow-
ers. Ideal Nob Hill location. Corner Cable Car stop.* Web site: goldengatehotel.com

SAN FRANCISCO ─────────────────────────────────────

Grove Inn, The	100-145-B&B	Continental breakfast
890 Grove St, 94117	16 rooms, 9 pb	Sitting room, bicycles,
415-929-0780 Fax: 415-929-1037	Visa, MC, AmEx,	laundry
800-829-0780	*Rated*, •	
Klaus & Rosetta Zimmermann	C-yes/S-ltd/P-no/H-no	
All year	Italian, German	

Turn-of-the-century Victorian, fully restored, simply furnished. Community kitchen, refrigerator. Part of Alamo Square Historic District.   E-mail: grovinn@jps.net Web site: jps.net/grovinn/

Hotel Sausalito	135-295-EP	Continental breakfast
16 El Portal, 94965	16 rooms, 16 pb	Downstairs cafe
415-332-0700 Fax: 415-332-8788	Most CC, •	Sitting room, bikes, suites,
888-442-0700	C-ltd/S-no/P-no/H-yes	cable TV,terrace, modems,
Billy& Josephine Purdie	Dutch, Spanish, French	cafe, parking
All year		

Fabulous location. . .this historic boutique hotel has recently been redecorated in the French Riviera style and is just steps from the Sausalito Ferry.   E-mail: hotelsaus@aol.com Web site: hotelsausalito.com

Inn 1890	89-149-B&B	Continental plus breakfast
1890 Page St, 94117	10 rooms, 8 pb	Afternoon tea, snacks
415-386-0486 Fax: 415-386-3626	Visa, MC, *Rated*, •	Sitting room, library,
888-INN-1890	C-yes/S-no/P-ltd/H-no	bicycles, swimming pool,
All year		suites, fireplaces

Landmark Victorian Inn blending old elegance w/modern comforts. Centrally located, convenient to all SF destinations.   E-mail: inn1890@worldnet.att.net Web site: adamsnet.com/inn1890/

Inn at Union Square, The	250-EP	Continental breakfast (fee)
440 Post St, 94102	30 rooms, 30 pb	Complimentary wine,
415-397-3510 Fax: 415-989-0529	Visa, MC, AmEx,	afternoon tea
800-288-4346	*Rated*, •	Hors d'oeuvres,
Brooks Bayly	C-ltd/S-no/P-no/H-yes	complimentary shoe shine,
All year	French, Spanish	paper, turn-down service

Rooms are individually decorated with Georgian furniture and warm colorful fabrics by noted San Francisco interior designer Nan Rosenblatt. A non-tipping property. E-mail: inn@unionsquare.com Web site: unionsquare.com

Inn San Francisco, The	85-235-B&B	Full breakfast buffet
943 South Van Ness Ave, 94110	21 rooms, 19 pb	Complimentary fruit &
415-641-0188 Fax: 415-641-1701	Most CC, *Rated*, •	beverages
800-359-0913	C-yes/S-no/P-ltd/H-no	Sun deck, gazebo, garden,
Marty Neely		hot tub, phones, TVs, off-
All year		street parking

Authentic historic 1872 Italianate Victorian mansion. English garden with redwood hot tub in gazebo. Antiques, fresh flowers, Jacuzzi rooms, some with fireplaces. E-mail: innkeeper@innsf.com Web site: innsf.com

Moffatt House	41-91-B&B	Continental plus breakfast
431 Hugo St, 94122	4 rooms, 2 pb	Hot beverages, kitchen
415-661-6210 Fax: 415-564-2480	*Rated*, •	Tennis, bicycles nearby,
Ruth Moffatt	C-yes/S-yes/P-yes/H-no	Japanese Tea Garden,
All year	Spanish, French, Italian	runner's discount

Walk to Golden Gate Park's major attractions from our Edwardian home. Safe location for active, independent guests. Excellent public transportation   E-mail: moffattbb@cs.com Web site: travelguides.com/home/moffatthouse/

SAN FRANCISCO ───────────────────────────────────

Monte Cristo, The	73-118-B&B	Continental plus buffet
600 Presidio Ave, 94115	14 rooms, 12 pb	Complimentary tea, wine
415-931-1875 Fax: 415-931-6005	Visa, MC, AmEx, •	Parlor with fireplace,
All year	C-yes/S-yes/P-no/H-yes	phones, TV
	French, Spanish	

1875 hotel-saloon-bordello, furnished with antiques. Each room uniquely decorated: Georgian four-poster, Chinese wedding bed, spindle bed, etc.

Pensione International Htl	60-90-B&B	Continental breakfast
875 Post St, 94109	50 rooms, 15 pb	
415-775-3344 Fax: 415-775-3320	Visa, MC, AmEx, •	
Christian Kiyabu	C-yes/S-yes/P-no/H-no	
All year	Spanish	

A Victorian building with a contemporary setting, graced with contemporary art throughout it's public areas.   Web site: travelassist.com/reg/CA123s.html

Stanyan Park Hotel	125-325-B&B	Continental plus breakfast
750 Stanyan St, 94117	36 rooms, 36 pb	Afternoon tea
415-751-1000 Fax: 415-668-5454	Most CC, *Rated*, •	Sitting room, bikes, suites
John K. Brocklehurst	C-yes/S-no/P-no/H-yes	with kitchens, non-smoking
All year	Spanish, Russian	hotel

The Stanyan Park Hotel is an elegant, thoroughly restored Victorian Hotel that will take you back to a bygone era of style, grace, and comfort. All of their rooms have a color television with cable, direct dial telephone with a data port, and a full bath
E-mail: info@stanyanpark.com Web site: stanyanpark.com

Victorian Inn on the Park	124-174-B&B	Continental plus breakfast
301 Lyon St, 94117	12 rooms, 12 pb	Complimentary wine
415-931-1830 Fax: 415-931-1830	Most CC, *Rated*, •	Homemade breads, cheeses,
800-435-1967	C-yes/S-ltd/P-no/H-no	library, phones in rooms, TV
Lisa & William Benau		on request, parlor
All year		

1897 Queen Anne Victorian near Golden Gate Park, downtown. Each rm. has antiques, flowers, beautiful comforters, down pillows, phones. Historic landmark.
E-mail: vicinn@aol.com Web site: citysearch.com/sfo/victorianinn

Webster House B&B Inn	95-175-B&B	Full breakfast
1238 Versailles Ave, 94501	4 rooms, 3 pb	Restaurant, tea, snacks,
510-523-9697	AmEx, *Rated*, •	Sitting room, library,
Andrew & Susan McCormack	C-yes/S-ltd/P-no/H-no	bicycles, suites, fireplace,
All year		conference, waterfall

Oldest house on Island in San Francisco Bay, 22nd City Historical Monument built in New York and shipped around Cape Horn in 1854.   E-mail: websterhouse@netscape.net
Web site: sites.netscape.net/websterhouse/homepage

SAN FRANCISCO BAY AREA ──────────────────────

Hensley House, The	135-275-B&B	Full gourmet breakfast
456 N 3rd St, 95112	9 rooms, 9 pb	Afternoon tea, snacks
408-298-3537 Fax: 408-298-4676	Most CC, *Rated*, •	Sitting room, Jacuzzis, suites,
800-498-3537	C-ltd/S-no/P-no/H-no	fireplaces, cable TV,
Tonio, Ron, Gloria & Miguel	Spanish	conference facilities
All year		

The Hensley House is a 3 story Victorian and a two story craftsman style home. Each house is decorated in antiques relative to the period.   E-mail: henhouse@ix.netcom.com
Web site: hensleyhouse.com

SAN JOSE ─────────────

Briar Rose B&B Inn, The	100-140-B&B	Full breakfast
897 E Jackson St, 95112	5 rooms, 3 pb	Aftn. tea, sherry
408-279-5999 Fax: 408-279-4534	Visa, MC, AmEx, •	Porch, gardens, sitting room,
The Worthy's, J. Wolkenhauer	C-ltd/S-ltd/P-no/H-no	library, Period furnishings
All year		

An 1875 Victorian—once a flourishing walnut orchard—restored to its former grandeur. Rooms fabulously wallpapered with Bradbury & Bradbury papers   E-mail: worthy@briar-rose.com Web site: briar-rose.com

Inn at Saratoga	190-260-B&B	Continental breakfast
20645 Fourth St, 95070	45 rooms, 45 pb	Snacks, complimentary wine
408-867-5020 Fax: 408-741-0981	Visa, MC, AmEx,	Jacuzzis, suites, cable TV,
800-543-5020	*Rated*, •	free use of local health club
Jack Hickling	C-yes/S-no/P-no/H-yes	
All year	Spanish, German	

Beautifully furnished 45 room small hotel. All rooms have creekside view, most have private balconies. Walk to 24 fine restaurants. Convenient access to Silicon Valley, San Frnacisco, Monterey Peninsula.   Web site: innatsaratoga.com

SAN LUIS OBISPO ─────────────

Adobe Inn	59-118-B&B	Full homemade breakfast
1473 Monterey St, 93401	15 rooms, 15 pb	Coffeemaker, refrig.
805-549-0321 Fax: 805-549-0383	Visa, MC, AmEx,	Outdoor patio, cactus,
800-676-1588	*Rated*, •	garden, getaway packages,
Jim & Shari Towles	C-yes/S-ltd/P-no/H-yes	include spa, kayak, wine
All year		

Cozy, comfortable, southwestern-style inn, in the heart of charming town. Suite with fireplace & cozy sitting rm. Near Hearst Castle, beaches, restaurants   E-mail: jtowles@aol.com Web site: adobeinns.com/

Apple Farm Inn	129-249-EP	Afternoon tea/wine/cheese
2015 Monterey St, 93401	69 rooms, 69 pb	Swimming pool, spa, gift
805-544-2040 Fax: 805-544-2452	Most CC, *Rated*, •	shop, millhouse, with
800-374-3705	C-yes/S-ltd/P-no/H-yes	working waterwheel
Katy & Bob Davis All year		

A memorable experience; romantic rooms—canopy beds, fireplaces, cozy window seats. Breakfast in bed, box lunches, gardens, patio dining, carriage rides.
E-mail: res@applefarm.com Web site: applefarm.com

Arroyo Village Inn B&B	139-389-B&B	Full breakfast or brunch
407 El Camino Real, 93420	7 rooms, 7 pb	Weekend brunch
805-489-5926	Most CC, *Rated*, •	In-room spas, fireplaces,
800-563-7762	S-no/P-no/H-no	spacious suites, sitting room,
Gina Glass All year		parlor, Comp. wines

Half way between LA & SF on CA's central coast, 15 min. from San Luis Obispo. Elegant and romantic, award-winning Inn decorated with Laura Ashley prints, antiques, spas, fireplaces, window seats. Cable TV on request.   Web site: centralcoast.com/ArroyoVillageInn

SAN RAFAEL ─────────────

Gerstle Park Inn	159-250-B&B	Full breakfast
34 Grove St, 94901	10 rooms, 10 pb	Complimentary wine
415-721-7611 Fax: 415-721-7600	Visa, MC, AmEx,	Sitting room, library, tennis
800-726-7611	*Rated*, •	court, hot tubs, lush gardens,
Jim and Judy Dowling	C-yes/S-no/P-no/H-ltd	bicycles
All year		

Warm, elegant century old estate in Marin. Centrally located-30 minutes to San Francisco, wine country or the coast. Newly remodeled conference room invites meeting participants to enjoy the inn's elegance in Boardroom fashion.   E-mail: innkeeper@gerstleparkinn.com
Web site: gerstleparkinn.com

SAN RAFAEL

Glen Park House
PO Box 835, 94901
415-258-0714
All year

85-135-B&B
2 rooms, 2 pb
Rated, •
C-ltd/S-no/P-no/H-yes
Dutch, German

Full breakfast
Afternoon tea,
complimentary wine
Sitting room, library,
bicycles, fireplaces, beautiful
patios, gardens.

Gourmet meals, elegant sitting room, inner courtyard garden, modern architecture, well-appointed rooms. Spacious accommodations and warm hospitality.

Panama Hotel
4 Bayview St, 94901
415-457-3993 Fax: 415-457-6240
800-899-3993
Daniel Miller
All year

75-165-B&B
15 rooms, 9 pb
Most CC, *Rated*
C-yes/S-no/P-no/H-yes

Continental plus breakfast
Buffet brunch on Sunday
Dinner lush gardens,
bicycles

A landmark inn and restaurant for 60 years, between San Francisco and wine country. The Panama is celebrated for its eccentric charm   E-mail: innkeeper@panamahotel.com
Web site: panamahotel.com

SAN SIMEON

Blue Whale Inn, The
PO Box 403, 93428
805-927-4647
800-753-9000
Mary Lou & Richard
All year

190-250-B&B
6 rooms, 6 pb
Visa, MC, *Rated*
C-ltd/S-no/P-no/H-ltd

Full breakfast
Snacks, afternoon tea, compl.
wine
Sitting room, library,
fireplaces, cable TV,
romantic mini suites

Gracious hospitality. Luxurious and romantic ocean-view mini-suites. Gourmet breakfasts, wine, and hor d'oeuvres. All yours in an extraordinarily beautiful and romantic setting beside the sea. Web site: bluewhaleinn.com

SANTA BARBARA

Casa Del Mar Inn
18 Bath St, 93101
805-963-4418 Fax: 805-966-4240
800-433-3097
Yun Kim
All year

69-249-B&B
21 rooms, 21 pb
Most CC, •
C-yes/S-ltd/P-ltd/H-yes
Spanish & German

Continental plus breakfast
buffet
Evening wine/cheese buffet
Afternoon tea, sitting room,
hot tub, beach towels,
umbrellas

Spanish-style villa, quiet, charming. One block from beach. Courtyard Jacuzzi. Several units with fireplaces and kitchens. Golf and Day Spa Packages available.   E-mail: casadmar@silcom.com Web site: casadelmar.com

Cheshire Cat Inn
36 W Valerio St, 93101
805-569-1610 Fax: 805-682-1876
Amy Taylor, Christine Dunstan
All year

140-350-B&B
14 rooms, 14 pb
Visa, MC, *Rated*, •
C-ltd/S-no/P-no/H-no

Continental plus breakfast
Wine & hors d'oeuvres
Sitting room, library, library,
TV/VCR, bikes, 4 in-room
spas

Victorian elegance, uniquely decorated in Laura Ashley & English antiques; kitchenettes, private baths, Jacuzzis, balconies, fireplaces, gardens.   E-mail: cheshire@cheshirecat.com
Web site: cheshirecat.com

Glenborough Inn B&B
1327 Bath St, 93101
805-966-0589 Fax: 805-564-8610
800-962-0589
Michael Diaz, & Steve Ryan
All year

120-450-B&B
14 rooms, 14 pb
Most CC, *Rated*, •
C-ltd/S-ltd/P-no/H-no

Full gourmet breakfast
Wine & hors d'oeuvres
Bedtime snacks, Jacuzzi,
parlor with fireplace, 2
bedroom cottage avail.

Lovely grounds, elegant antique-filled rooms. Vegetarian dining only. Breakfast in bed, 9 rooms have fireplaces, 8 private entrances, 2 rooms have hot tubs, 5 with Jacuzzis.
E-mail: glenboro@silcom.com Web site: glenboroughinn.com

SANTA BARBARA

Long's Sea View B&B
317 Piedmont Rd, 93105
805-687-2947
LaVerne M. Long
All year

80-B&B
1 rooms, 1 pb
S-no/P-no/H-no

Full breakfast before 9:30 am
Continental breakfast after
9:30 am
King size bed, Gardens,
patio, 1.5 Miles from Hwy. 101

Home with a lovely view, furnished with antiques. Quiet neighborhood. Full breakfast served on the patio. Homemade jams and fresh fruits.

Old Yacht Club Inn, The
431 Corona Del Mar Dr, 93103
805-962-1277 Fax: 805-962-3989
800-676-1676
Nancy Donaldson & Sandy
Hunt
All year

110-195-B&B
12 rooms, 12 pb
Most CC, *Rated*, •
C-ltd/S-ltd/P-no/H-no
Spanish

Full breakfast
Dinner on Saturdays
Comp. evening beverage,
beach chairs & towels,
bicycles, whirlpool ltd.

1912 California classic. Beautifully decorated with antiques. Gourmet breakfast. Deluxe suites avail. Dinner on weekends. Close to beautiful beach   E-mail: oyci@aol.com
Web site: clia.com/members/OldYachtClubInn

Olive House Inn, The
1604 Olive St, 93101
805-962-4902 Fax: 805-962-9983
800-786-6422
Ellen Schaub
All year

110-180-B&B
6 rooms, 6 pb
Most CC, *Rated*, •
C-ltd

Full breakfast
Afternoon refreshments
Sitting room, library,
fireplace, fax, hot tubs,
telephones, TV

Quiet comfort & gracious hospitality in lovingly restored CA Craftsman home with bay windows, fireplaces, sundeck, ocean views, private decks & hot tubs.
E-mail: olivehse@aol.com Web site: sbinns.com/oliveinn/

Parsonage, The
1600 Olive St, 93101
805-962-9336 Fax: 805-962-2285
800-775-0352
Sibiha Pulley
All year

125-330-B&B
6 rooms, 6 pb
Rated, •
C-ltd/S-no/P-no/H-no
German

Full breakfast
Complimentary wine
Sitting room, sundeck, off-
season discounts, weekly
rates

A beautifully restored Queen Anne Victorian. An atmosphere of comfort, grace and elegance with ocean and mountain views. Close to shops, dining, sightseeing.
E-mail: parsonagel@aol.com Web site: parsonage.com

Prufrock's Garden Inn
5004 6th St, 93013
805-566-9696 Fax: 805-566-9404
888-778-3765
Judy & Jim Halvorsen
All year

110-230-B&B
4 rooms, 2 pb
Visa, MC, *Rated*, •
C-yes/S-ltd/P-no/H-no
Limited German,
Spanish

Full breakfast
Desserts, snacks, tea
Jacuzzis, fireplaces, in-room
flowers

Historic 1904 home, near beach, antique shops, eateries. 12 minutes to downtown Santa Barbara. Tremendous family hospitality and home cooking. Sunset hors d'oeuvres, chocolates on pillows.   Web site: prufrocks.com

---

Secret Garden Inn/Cottages
1908 Bath St, 93101
805-687-2300 Fax: 805-687-4576
Jack Greenwald
All year exc. Christmas

115-220-B&B
11 rooms, 11 pb
Visa, MC, AmEx,
Rated, •
C-ltd/S-ltd/P-no/H-no

Scrumptious Full breakfast
Cider, complimentary wine
Evening sweets, sitting room,
garden, brick patio, bicycles

Guest rooms, suites & private cottages filled with country charm in a delightfully quiet and relaxing country setting. 4 rooms with private patio with outdoor hot tubs.   E-mail: garden@secretgarden.com Web site: secretgarden.com

SANTA BARBARA

Simpson House Inn
121 E Arrellaga, 93101
805-963-7067 Fax: 805-564-4811
800-676-1280
G. & L. Davies, D. Budke
All year

200-450-B&B
14 rooms, 14 pb
Most CC, *Rated*, •
C-ltd/S-ltd/P-no/H-yes
Spanish

Full gourmet breakfast
Complimentary local wines
Sitt. rm., lib., patio, veranda,
garden, Jacuzzi, bikes,
fireplaces, VCRs

1874 Victorian estate secluded on acre of English garden. Cottages & barn suites. Full concierge service. Elegant antiques, art. Delicious leisurely breakfast on verandahs.
E-mail: simpsonhouseinn@simpsonhouseinn.com Web site: simpsonhouseinn.com

Tiffany Inn
1323 De La Vina, 93101
805-963-2283 Fax: 805-962-0994
800-999-5672
Janice Hawkins
All year

125-250-B&B
7 rooms, 7 pb
Visa, MC, AmEx,
Rated, •
C-ltd/S-no/P-no/H-no

Full breakfast
Complimentary wine
Spa in 2 rooms, fireplaces in
5 rooms, bikes, VCRs

Classic antiques & period furnishings welcome you throughout this lovely restored 1898 Victorian. Stroll to shops, restaurants, galleries, theaters, museums.
Web site: sbinns.com/tiffany

Upham Hotel & Cottages
1404 De La Vina St, 93101
805-962-0058 Fax: 805-962-0058
800-727-0876
Jan Martin Winn
All year

140-385-B&B
50 rooms, 50 pb
Most CC, *Rated*, •
C-yes/S-yes/P-no/H-no
Spanish

Continental plus breakfast
Complimentary wine, coffee,
tea
Newspaper, restaurant,
garden veranda, gardens,
valet laundry, phones

California's oldest Victorian hotel. Cottage rooms with patios and fireplaces, lawn, flowers. Restaurant on property. Complimentary wine and cheese by the lobby fireplace

SANTA CLARA

Madison Street Inn
1390 Madison St, 95050
408-249-5541 Fax: 408-249-6676
800-491-5541
Theresa Wigginton
All year

80-135-B&B
5 rooms, 3 pb
Visa, MC, AmEx,
Rated, •
C-yes/S-ltd/P-no/H-no
French

Full breakfast
Lunch, dinner w/notice
Comp. wine & beverages,
library, sitting room, hot tub,
bicycles, pool

Santa Clara's only inn! A beautiful Victorian with landscaped gardens near Winchester Mystery House. Eggs Benedict is a breakfast favorite. E-mail: madstinn@aol.com
Web site: santa-clara-inn.com

SANTA CRUZ

Babbling Brook Inn
1025 Laurel St, 95060
831-427-2437 Fax: 831-427-2457
800-866-1131
Dan Floyd & Suzie Lankes
All year

145-195-B&B
13 rooms, 13 pb
Most CC, *Rated*, •
C-ltd/S-ltd/P-no/H-ltd

Full buffet breakfast
Comp. wine, refreshments
Picnic baskets, phone & TV
in rooms, romantic garden
gazebo

Secluded among waterfalls, gardens, Laurel Creek, pines & redwoods. Country French decor; all rooms w/ fireplaces. Jet tubs in 4 rooms. Historic waterwheel. Garden gazebo weddings. E-mail: lodging@babblingbrookinn.com Web site: babblingbrookinn.com

Bayview Hotel, The
PO Box 1850, 95003
831-688-8654 Fax: 831-688-5128
800-422-9843
Dan Floyd, Suzie Lankes
All year

90-160-B&B
8 rooms, 8 pb
Visa, MC, *Rated*, •
C-yes/S-no/P-no/H-no
French, Italian

Continental plus breakfast
Lunch/dinner available
Sitting room, 2-room suite
available, TV's in all rooms

1878 California Victorian furnished with lovely antiques; near beaches, hiking trails, bicycle routes, golf, tennis, fishing, antique shops and restaurants. E-mail: lodging@ bayviewhotel.com Web site: bayviewhotel.com

SANTA CRUZ ——————

Blue Spruce Inn
2815 Main St, 95073
831-464-1137 Fax: 831-475-0608
800-559-1137
Pat & Tom O'Brien
All year

85-175-B&B
6 rooms, 6 pb
Visa, MC, AmEx, •
C-ltd/S-ltd/P-no/H-no
Spanish

Full breakfast
Snacks
Sitting room, conference,
library, spa tubs, gas
fireplaces

Award-winning inn as fresh as a sea breeze. Explore Monterey Bay! Enjoy Jacuzzis, fireplaces, original local art. Available for business meetings, retreats. Bay window/sitting area in the Summer Afternoon room. E-mail: innkeeper@bluespruce.com
Web site: bluespruce.com

Chateau Des Fleurs
7995 Hwy 9, 95005
831-336-8943
800-291-9966
Lee & Laura Jonas
All year

100-130-B&B
3 rooms, 3 pb
Most CC,
C-yes/S-no/P-no/H-yes
German

Full breakfast
Complimentary wine
Sitting room, library,
fireplaces, cable TV, A/C

A Victorian mansion once owned by the Barttlet (pear) family. This inn is special, spacious, sensational, historic, quiet, unforgettable, surrounded by evergreens and wineries.
E-mail: chateaubnb@aol.com Web site: chateaudesfleurs.com

Chateau Victorian-A B&B Inn
118 First St, 95060
831-458-9458
Alice June
All year

115-145-B&B
7 rooms, 7 pb
Visa, MC, *Rated*
S-no/P-no/H-no

Continental plus breakfast
Complimentary wine &
cheese
Sitting room, 2 decks, patio,
fireplaces in rooms

One block from the beach and the boardwalk, in the heart of the Santa Cruz fun area. All rooms have queen-size beds with private bathrooms.   Web site: chateauvictorian.com

Cypress Inn—Miramar Beach
PO Box 1850, 94019
650-726-6002 Fax: 650-712-0380
800-83-BEACH
Suzie Lankes & Dan Floyd
All year

170-275-B&B
12 rooms, 12 pb
Most CC, *Rated*, •
C-ltd/S-ltd/P-no/H-yes

Full gourmet breakfast
Afternoon tea
Wine & hors d'oeuvres',
unobstructed ocean views,
frplcs., Jacuzzis, decks

10 steps to the sand. Bay area's only oceanfront B&B located on 5 miles of sandy beach. Contemporary beach house with skylights, natural wicker & pine. In-house masseuse. Conference facilities, romance. Fresh paint inside and outside. TVs in all rooms.
E-mail: lodging@cypressinn.com Web site: cypressinn.com/cypress-frame.html

Darling House B&B, The
314 W Cliff Dr, 95060
831-458-1958
Darrell & Karen Darling
All year

95-260-B&B/MAP
8 rooms, 2 pb
Most CC, *Rated*, •
C-ltd/S-ltd/P-no/H-ltd

Continental plus breakfast
Complimentary beverages
Library, fireplaces, double
size bathtubs, fireplaces in
rooms

1910 ocean side mansion with beveled glass, Tiffany lamps, Chippendale antiques, open hearths and hardwood interiors. Walk to beach.   Web site: darlinghouse.com

Fairview Manor
PO Box 74, 95505
831-336-3355
800-553-8840
Nancy Glasson
Season Inquire

119-129-B&B
5 rooms, 5 pb
Visa, MC, *Rated*, •
C-ltd/S-yes/P-no/H-yes

Full breakfast
Complimentary wine/hors
d'ouevres
Sitting room, bordered by
river, weddings & meetings

Romantic country-styled redwood home, majestic stone fireplace, 2.5 wooded acres of Santa Cruz Mountains. Total privacy. Walk to town. E-mail: nancy@fairviewmanor.com
Web site: fairviewmanor.com

SANTA CRUZ ─────────────────────────────

Inn at Pasatiempo
555 Hwy 17, 95060
831-423-5000 Fax: 831-426-1737
800-834-2546
All year

81-165-EP
54 rooms, 54 pb
Most CC, *Rated*, •
C-yes/S-ltd/P-no/H-yes

Lunch & dinner available
Restaurant, bar service,
swimming pool, suites,
fireplaces, cable TV, danish

Return to relaxation and wooded seclusion. A lodge of warm, attractive settings and country charm nestled in the Santa Cruz mountains. E-mail: gcavall@innatpasatiempo.com
Web site: innatpasatiempo.com

Mangels House B&B
PO Box 302, 95001
831-688-7982
Jacqueline Fisher
All year

130-170-B&B
5 rooms, 5 pb
Visa, MC, •
C-ltd/S-ltd/P-no/H-no
French, Spanish

Full breakfast
Complimentary wine
Sitting room, fireplace, table
tennis and darts, English
garden, nursery

Casual elegance in country setting, 5 min. drive to Hwy 1. 4 acres of lawn and woodland on edge of Redwood State Park. 1 mi. from beach, golf, Monterey Bay. Ping pong table, croquet set. Web site: innaccess.com/mangels/

Marvista B&B
212 Martin Dr, 95003
831-684-9311 Fax: 831-684-0609
Amy Bowles
All year

135-225-B&B
2 rooms, 2 pb
Visa, MC, AmEx, •
C-ltd/S-ltd/P-no/H-ltd

Full breakfast
Snacks
Sitting room, library,
Jacuzzis, fireplaces, cable TV

Intimate luxury on an acre of lovely gardens with ocean views from all guest areas. Afternoon refreshments, in-room fridge with special treats. E-mail: innkeeper@2marvista.com
Web site: 2marvista.com/

Monarch Cove Inn
709 El Salto Dr, 95010
831-464-1295 Fax: 831-464-2812
877-EL-SALTO
Robin
All year

165-285-B&B
23 rooms, 23 pb
Most CC, •
C-yes/S-no/P-no/H-no

Continental breakfast
Complimentary wine

Enjoy a memorable stay overlooking picturesque Monterey Bay at Monarch Cove Inn. Our quaint Victorian guestrooms, cottages, and spacious deluxe apartments are a thoughtful blend of yesterday & today. Web site: monarch-cove-inn.com

---

Pleasure Point Inn
2-3665 East Cliff Dr, 95062
831-475-4657 Fax: 831-464-3045
800-872-3029
Sal & Margaret Margo
All year

130-155-B&B
3 rooms, 3 pb
Visa, MC, *Rated*, •
C-yes

Continental plus breakfast
Comp. wine & cheese
Frplcs., whirlpool tubs, 2
suites, TV, phones, day
cruises on yacht

On beach, overlooking beautiful Monterey Bay. Walk to beach & shopping village. Rooms include private bath, sitting room & deck. Motor yacht available for fishing or cruises.
Web site: innaccess.com/ppi/

Valley View B&B
PO Box 67438, 95067
650-321-5195 Fax: 650-325-5121
Tricia Young
All year

195-/house-B&B
2 rooms, 2 pb
Most CC, *Rated*, •
C-ltd/S-no/P-no/H-no
German, Spanish

Full breakfast
Aftn. tea, snacks, wine
Sitting room, library,
bicycles, hot tubs, 10 minutes
to beach

Secluded, romantic getaway! Un-hosted, self-catered contemporary glass & redwood house in forest overlooking 20,000 acre redwoods. Hot tub, fireplace, TV/VCR. Entire house to one party. E-mail: tricia@best.com Web site: valleyviewinn.com

SANTA MONICA

Channel Road Inn
219 W Channel Rd, 90402
310-459-1920 Fax: 310-454-9920
Heather Suskin, Susan Zolla
All year

145-315-B&B
14 rooms, 14 pb
Visa, MC, *Rated*, •
C-yes/S-yes/P-no/H-yes
Spanish, French,
German

Full breakfast
Afternoon tea,
complimentary wine
Sitting room, library, bikes,
hot tubs, spa, small suite
with fireplace

Elegant historic home converted to luxury inn. 1 block from sea & furnished in period antiques. Room with fireplace, deck & ocean view. Historic & intimate...so romantic. Jacuzzis in rooms. E-mail: channelinn@aol.com Web site: channelroadinn.com

SANTA ROSA

Gables Inn, The
4257 Petaluma Hill Rd, 95404
707-585-7777 Fax: 707-584-5634
800-GABLESN
Mike & Judy Ogne
All year

135-225-B&B
8 rooms, 8 pb
Visa, MC, AmEx,
Rated, •
C-ltd/S-no/P-no/H-yes

Full breakfast
Afternoon tea
TV/VCR, parking, fireplaces,
sitting room, piano, A/C,
hairdryers, irons

Built in 1877, on National Register of Historic Places. Museum-quality restoration, European-Victorian decor. Gateway to wine country; elegant, rural location. Cottage with Jacuzzi. E-mail: innkeeper@thegablesinn.com Web site: thegablesinn.com

Vintners Inn
4350 Barnes Rd, 95403
707-575-7350 Fax: 707-575-1426
800-421-2584
Cindy Duffy
All year

178-268-B&B
44 rooms, 44 pb
Most CC, *Rated*, •
C-yes/S-ltd/P-no/H-yes
Spanish

Continental plus breakfast
Restaurant, bar
Sitting room, hot tub, wine
touring, nearby tennis, pool,
safe, irons, robes

European-styled country inn surrounded by a 45-acre vineyard. Antique furniture, conference facilities. Home of John Ash & Co. Restaurant. AAA Four Diamond rating.
E-mail: info@vintnersinn.com Web site: vintnersinn.com

SEA RANCH

Sea Ranch Lodge, The
PO Box 44, 95497
707-785-2371
800-732-7262
Carol Hammerbeck   All year

165-325-EP
20 rooms, 20 pb
Visa, MC, AmEx, •
C-yes/S-yes/P-no/H-no

Room serv. for breakfast
All meals, bar (fee)
Hot tub, sauna, swimming
pool, tennis, fireside lounge,
piano

On the Sonoma coast 3 hours from San Francisco, Sea Ranch is famed for architecture and natural beauty. Hiking, golfing, tennis. E-mail: info@searanchlodge.com
Web site: searanchlodge.com

SEAL BEACH

Seal Beach Inn & Gardens
212 5th St, 90740
562-493-2416 Fax: 562-799-0483
800-HIDEAWAY
M. B. Schmaehl, H. Schmaehl
All year

165-345-B&B
23 rooms, 23 pb
Visa, MC, AmEx,
Rated, •
C-ltd/S-ltd/P-no/H-no

Lavish full breakfast
Complimentary wine and
cheese
Fruit, tea, coffee, sitting
rooms, library, pool,
Jacuzzis, fireplaces

Elegant historic So. CA Inn, 1 block from ocean beach in charming seaside town. Lush gardens, lovely estate appearance. Exquisite rooms & suites.
E-mail: hideaway@sealbeachinn.com Web site: sealbeachinn.com

SEQUOIA NATIONAL PARK

Mesa Verde Plantation B&B
33038 Sierra Hwy 198, 93244
559-597-2555 Fax: 559-597-2551
800-240-1466
Scott & Marie Munger
All year

69-159-B&B
8 rooms, 6 pb
Most CC, *Rated*, •
C-ltd/S-ltd/P-no/H-no

Gourmet vegie breakfast
Complimentary beverages &
snacks
Hot tub, gazebos, verandas,
courtyard, heated swimming
pool

Plantation home nestled in the foothills of the Sierra Nevada Mountains. Close to Sequoia National Park and beautiful mountain lake. E-mail: relax@plantationbnb.com
Web site: plantationbnb.com

SHASTA LAKE

O'Brien Mountain Inn	97-197-B&B	Full breakfast
PO Box 27, 96070	6 rooms, 6 pb	Snacks
530-238-8026 Fax: 530-238-2027	Most CC, *Rated*, •	Sitting room, library, suites,
888-799-8026	C-yes/S-ltd/P-no/H-ltd	fireplaces, accommodate
Greg & Teresa Ramsey		business travelers
All year		

If you're looking for fresh flowers, chocolates, private baths, patios with lush forest views. . . stay here. Activities include water sports, hiking, biking, or just relaxing! Featuring elaborate treehouse suites.   E-mail: info@obrienmtn.com Web site: obrienmtn.com

SONOMA

Bancroft House B&B	129-149-B&B	Full breakfast
786-790 Broadway, 95476	3 rooms, 3 pb	Sitting room, library,
707-996-4863 Fax: 707-935-0523	Visa, MC, *Rated*, •	fireplace parlor, garden
Diane & Michael Woods	C-yes/S-ltd/P-ltd/H-no	
All year	Fr., Sp., It., Ger.	

Victorian farmhouse three blocks from the historic Plaza in the heart of Sonoma's wine country. Friendly and comfortable. Weekend breakfasts include omelettes, quiche.
E-mail: mrwson@aol.com Web site: sonomabb.com/bancroft.htm

Rio Inn	99-149-B&B	Continental breakfast plus
4444 Wood Rd, 95446	12 rooms, 12 pb	Sitting room, library,
707-869-4444 Fax: 707-869-4443	Visa, MC, AmEx, •	Jacuzzis, swimming pool
800-344-7018	C-yes/S-no/P-yes/H-yes	
Dawson Church		
Season Inquire		

Epitomizing the grace, history and charm of the Russian River Wine Road, the 1890s vintage Rio Inn is nestled in the redwoods just 12 miles from Highway 101. Over 100 wineries and the superb Sonoma coast are within half an hour's drive.
E-mail: reservations@rioinn.com Web site: rioinn.com

Thistle Dew Inn	120-225-B&B	Full breakfast
171 W Spain St, 95476	6 rooms, 6 pb	Comp. wine & appetizers
707-938-2909 Fax: 707-996-8413	Most CC, *Rated*, •	Sitting room, spa, picnic
800-382-7895	C-ltd/S-ltd/P-no/H-ltd	baskets, bicycles, rare
Larry Barnett		plant/cactus coll.
All year		

Two Victorian homes near Sonoma's historic plaza. Collector pieces of Stickley furniture; fresh-cut flowers; extensive collection of rare plants and cactus.   E-mail: tdibandb@aol.com Web site: thistledew.com

Trojan Horse Inn	135-165-B&B	Full breakfast
19455 Sonoma Hwy, 95476	6 rooms, 6 pb	Complimentary wine
707-996-2430 Fax: 707-996-9185	Visa, MC, *Rated*, •	Hors d'oeuvres, outside
800-899-1925	C-ltd/S-no/P-no/H-yes	Jacuzzi, bikes, 2 night
Joe & Sandy Miccio		minimum
All year		

Beautifully decorated 1887 Victorian, 6 rooms, private baths, full breakfast. Spa, bicycles, complimentary hors d'ouvres with wine and wine country hospitality. 2 night minimum, weekends/holidays.   E-mail: trojaninn@aol.com Web site: trojanhorseinn.com

Victorian Garden Inn	99-185-B&B	Full breakfast
316 E Napa St, 95476	4 rooms, 3 pb	Therapeutic spa, full sized
707-996-5339 Fax: 707-996-1689	Visa, MC, AmEx,	swimming pool, gardens
800-543-5339	*Rated*, •	
Donna Lewis	C-ltd/S-ltd/P-no/H-no	
All year	Spanish, English	

Secluded, large 1870 Greek revival farmhouse. Antiques, private entrances, fireplaces, Victorian rose gardens, winding paths, near plaza. Breakfast served in room, dining room, patios. Gracious hospitality.   E-mail: vgardeninn@aol.com Web site: victoriangardeninn.com

SONORA ───────────────────────────

Lavender Hill B&B	65-95-B&B	Full breakfast
683 S Barretta St, 95370	4 rooms, 4 pb	Complimentary coffee or tea
209-532-9024	Most CC, *Rated*, •	Sitting room, porch swing,
800-446-1333	C-yes/S-ltd/P-no/H-no	phone & TV available, small
Jean & Charlie Marinelli	Italian	group events, patio
All year		

Restored Victorian in historic Gold Cntry. Antique furnishings, lovely grounds, porch swing, unmatched hospitality. Walk to town. Near Yosemite. Small conference facilities.
E-mail: lavender@sonnet.com   Web site: lavenderhill.com

Mountain View B&B	60-85-B&B	Full breakfast
12980 Mountain View Rd,	4 rooms, 3 pb	Snacks
95370	Visa, MC, Disc, •	Sitting room, pool, family
209-533-0628 Fax: 209-533-1461	C-yes/S-ltd/P-ltd/H-no	friendly facility
800-648-1334		
Carl & Doris Disbrow		
All year		

This country home B&B is on a quiet, winding road surrounded by gold rush history. Features a garden railroad, pool, and blue-ribbon winning breads & pastries.
E-mail: disbrow@mtvu.com   Web site: mtvu.com

SOUTH LAKE TAHOE ───────────────────────────

Inn at Heavenly	75-185-B&B	Continental plus breakfast
1261 Ski Run Blvd, 96150	14 rooms, 14 pb	Snacks, complimentary wine
530-544-4244 Fax: 530-544-5213	Most CC, •	Bikes, cable, Jacuzzis,
800-MY-CABIN	C-ltd/S-no/P-yes/H-ltd	fireplaces, VCRs, steam bath,
Paul Gardner & Sue Ogden	Some Spanish	sauna, fax
All year		

Cozy log cabin style rooms done in a "country mountain" decor with fireplaces, kitchenettes, and private baths.   E-mail: mycabin@sierra.net   Web site: 800mycabin.com

SPRINGVILLE ───────────────────────────

Annie's B&B	95-B&B	Full breakfast
33024 Globe Dr, 93265	3 rooms, 3 pb	Dinner, afternoon tea
559-539-3827 Fax: 559-539-2179	Most CC, *Rated*, •	Snacks, comp. wine, pool,
Annie & John Bozanich	C-ltd/S-no/P-no/H-no	sitting room, hot tubs,
All year		Cancellation policy

Quiet, beautifully furnished with antiques, on 5 acres in the Sierra foothills. Full breakfast cooked on a wood stove. Relax on deck overlooking pool/spa   E-mail: bozanich@ lightspeed.net   Web site: members.tripod.com/~anniesbandb

ST. HELENA ───────────────────────────

Ambrose Bierce House	169-209-B&B	Full gourmet breakfast
1515 Main St, 94574	3 rooms, 3 pb	Complimentary port & wines
707-963-3003 Fax: 707-963-9367	Visa, MC, •	Air conditioning, large sitting
John & Lisa Wild-Runnells	S-no/P-no/H-no	room, brass, beds, claw foot
All year		tubs

We offer unequaled hospitality, a historic, Victorian once the home of author Ambrose Bierce. Full gourmet champagne breakfasts and wines served each evening. Innkeepers are excellent concierge.   E-mail: ambrose@napanet.net   Web site: ambrosebiercehouse.com

Bartels Ranch Country Inn	185-425-B&B	Full breakfast
1200 Conn Valley Rd, 94574	4 rooms, 4 pb	In-room dinner service
707-963-4001 Fax: 707-963-5100	Most CC, *Rated*, •	Comp. wine/fruit/cheese,
Jami Bartels	C-ltd/S-yes/P-no/H-yes	library, sauna, Jacuzzi, darts,
All year	Spanish, German	horseshoes, BBQ

Elegant, secluded wine country estate; ideal for honeymoon. 10,000-acre view, fireplace, billiards, bicycles, TV/VCR & phones in all rooms.   E-mail: bartelsranch@webtv.net
Web site: bartelsranch.com

ST. HELENA ─────────────────────────────

Cinnamon Bear	125-190-B&B	Full breakfast
1407 Kearney St, 94574	3 rooms, 3 pb	Complimentary snacks
707-963-4653 Fax: 707-963-0251	Visa, MC, AmEx,	Sitting room, games,
888-963-4600	*Rated*, •	fireplace, piano, classical
Cathye Ranieri	C-ltd/S-no/P-no/H-no	music or swing
All year		

Homesick for a visit to your favorite aunt's house? Bring your teddy and come to the Napa Valley wine country.   E-mail: cinnamonbear@worldnet.att.net
Web site: bbchannel.com/bbc/p213930.asp

Deer Run Inn	140-195-B&B	Full breakfast
PO Box 311, 94574	3 rooms, 3 pb	Complimentary wine
707-963-3794 Fax: 707-963-9026	Most CC, *Rated*, •	Library, pool, Ping Pong,
800-843-3408	C-ltd/S-no/P-no/H-no	horseshoes, featherbeds,
Tom & Carol Wilson		frplcs., priv. entrances
All year		

Tucked away in the forest on Spring Mountain above valley vineyards. Affords the quiet serenity of a private hideaway. A truly secluded, peaceful, cozy mountain retreat. Full breakfast in dining area.   Web site: virtualcities.com/ons/ca/w/caw3602.htm

Erika's-Hillside	95-275-B&B	Continental plus breakfast
285 Fawn Park, 94574	3 rooms, 2 pb	Sparkling water
707-963-2887 Fax: 707-963-1558	*Rated*, •	Sitting room, fireplaces
Erika Cunningham	C-yes/S-ltd/P-no/H-no	
All year	German	

Enjoy a peaceful & romantic retreat nestled on a hillside overlooking the Silverado Trail with inspiring views of the Napa Valley and its vineyards.

Hilltop House B&B	135-195-B&B	Full breakfast
PO Box 726, 94574	3 rooms, 3 pb	Complimentary sherry after
707-944-0880 Fax: 707-571-0263	Visa, MC, *Rated*, •	dinner
Annette Gevarter	C-yes/S-no/P-no/H-yes	Guest refrigerator, sitting
All year		room, hot tub, hiking trails

Secluded mountain hideaway in romantic setting on 135 acres of unspoiled wilderness. A hang glider's view of Mayacamas Mountains. Hot tub on deck. Extra person $35, cancellation fee $15   Web site: virtualcities.com/ons/ca/w/caw3502.htm

Ink House B&B, The	100-200-B&B	Full gourmet breakfast
1575 St Helena Hwy, 94574	7 rooms, 5 pb	Sherry, brandy available
707-963-3890 Fax: 707-968-0739	•	Parlor, 3 sitting rooms,
Diane DeFilipi	C-ltd/S-no/P-no/H-no	concert grand piano,
All year		bicycles

Private, in beautiful St. Helena, antiques, fireplace, TV/VCRs. Rooftop observatory with views of vineyards and valley hills. Voted one of "Northern California's Best Places."
E-mail: inkhousebb@aol.com Web site: napavalley.com/inkhouse

La Fleur B&B	150-195-B&B	Continental plus breakfast
1475 Inglewood Ave, 94574	3 rooms, 3 pb	Snacks, sitting room
707-963-0233 Fax: 707-963-0233	*Rated*, •	Private tour of Villa, Helena
Kay Murphy	C-ltd/S-no/P-no/H-no	winery, bicycles
All year		

1882 Queen Ann Victorian in quiet rural setting, spectacular vineyard & rose garden views, gourmet breakfast served in beautiful solarium, located in heart of Napa Valley
Web site: lafleurinn.com

ST. HELENA

Shady Oaks Country Inn
399 Zinfandel Ln, 94574
707-963-1190 Fax: 707-963-9367
John & Lisa Wild-Runnells
All year

159-209-B&B
5 rooms, 5 pb
Rated, •
C-ltd/S-no/P-no/H-yes

Full gourmet with
champagne
Wine & cheese
Horseshoes, croquet,
sightseeing tips, garden,
balconies with view

Romantic, secluded on 2 acres among finest wineries in Napa Valley. Elegant ambiance; country comfort; antiques; fireplaces in guest rooms; warm hospitality. E-mail: shdyoaks@ napanet.net Web site: shadyoaksinn.com

Wine Country Inn, The
1152 Lodi Lane, 94574
707-963-7077 Fax: 707-963-7077
Jim Smith
All year

156-285-B&B
24 rooms, 24 pb
Rated, •
C-ltd/S-no/P-no/H-no

Full breakfast
Wine tasting seminar
Wine & appetizers daily,
fireplace, heated pool

Relax in this cozy cottage secluded in a private woodland setting of several acres. Victorian charm and beauty surround you. E-mail: romance@winecountryinn.com Web site: winecountryinn.com

Zinfandel Inn, The
800 Zinfandel Ln, 94574
707-963-3512 Fax: 707-963-5310
Jerry & Diane Payton
All year

175-330-B&B
3 rooms, 3 pb
Visa, MC,
C-ltd/S-no/P-no/H-no

Full breakfast
Complimentary wine
Sitting room, Jacuzzis, suites,
fireplace, cable TV, phones,
A/C

Zinfandel Inn "looks as if it were airlifted from the French countryside" as described by Bon Appetite Magazine. Web site: zinfandelinn.com

STINSON BEACH

Casa Del Mar
PO Box 238, 94970
415-868-2124 Fax: 415-868-2305
800-552-2124
Rick Klein
All year

150-260-B&B
5 rooms, 5 pb
Visa, MC, AmEx,
Rated, •
C-ltd/S-no/P-no/H-no

Full breakfast
Complimentary wine, juice
Hors d'oeuvres, sitting room,
library, garden, near ocean

Romantic ocean views, historic garden, delicious breakfasts, colorful artwork, and you can hear the waves break all day long. Hiking nearby, gardening. E-mail: inn@stinsonbeach.com Web site: stinsonbeach.com

SUMMERLAND

Inn on Summer Hill
PO Box 376, 93067
805-969-9998 Fax: 805-565-9946
800-845-5566
Denise LeBlanc
All year

215-325-B&B
16 rooms, 16 pb
Visa, MC, AmEx,
Rated, •
C-ltd/S-no/P-no/H-yes
Spanish

Full gourmet breakfast
Afternoon tea & wine
Sitting room, library, room
service, Jacuzzi, fireplaces,
canopy beds

Elegant, romantic European inn. Decks & balcony overlooking Pacific, spa, antiques. One of Country Inn magazine's top 12 inns for 1993. ABBA top rated inn. E-mail: innkeeper@ innonsummerhill.com Web site: innonsummerhill.com

SUTTER CREEK

Sutter Creek Inn
PO Box 385, 95685
209-267-5606 Fax: 209-267-9287
Jane Way
All year

95-175-B&B
18 rooms, 18 pb
Most CC, *Rated*, •
C-ltd/S-ltd/P-no/H-no

Full breakfast
Complimentary
refreshments
Sitt. rm., library, A/C, piano,
fishing, gardens, reflexology,
graphology

Lovely country inn known for swinging beds & fireplaces. Beautiful grounds with hammocks & chaise lounges. Professional massage & handwriting analysis. E-mail: info@ suttercreekinn.com Web site: suttercreekinn.com/

TAHOE

Hania's B&B
10098 High St, 96161
530-582-5775 Fax: 530-587-4424
888-600-3735
Hania
All year

110-135-B&B
4 rooms, 4 pb
Visa, MC, *Rated*, •
C-ltd/S-no/P-ltd/H-yes
Polish, German, Russian

Full breakfast
Afternoon tea,
complimentary wine
Sitting room, library,
Jacuzzis, fireplaces, cable TV

Southwestern, log style furnished bedrooms with private bath, cable TV/VCR, down pillows and comforters. Gourmet breakfast, afternoon wine in rustic bar by cozy woodstove and hot tub in beautiful garden with panoramic mountain view.
Web site: truckee.com/hania/index.htm

TAHOE CITY

Chaney House
PO Box 7852, 96145
530-525-7333 Fax: 530-525-4413
Gary & Lori Chaney
All year

110-195-B&B
4 rooms, 4 pb
Visa, MC, *Rated*, •
C-ltd/S-no/P-no/H-no

Full breakfast
Sitting room, bicycles,
private beach and pier,
reflexology, graphology

Unique stone lakefront home. Gourmet breakfast on patios overlooking the lake in season. Private beach and pier. Close to ski areas.   E-mail: gary@chaneyhouse.com
Web site: chaneyhouse.com

TEMECULA

Hearts Home Farm B&B
32643 Hwy 74, 92545
909-926-3343 Fax: 909-926-8814
800-965-1606
Ana & Larry Shurtz
All year

110-200-B&B
5 rooms, 3 pb
Visa, MC,
C-yes/S-ltd/P-no/H-no

Continental plus breakfast
Snacks, complimentary wine
Fireplace, cable TV, 2
cottages, 1 loft with kitchen

Romantic, 1930's restored cottages and loft suite on 4 acres with lush lawns, gardens and wedding pavillion. 1963 Cadillac limo tours of Temecula wine country available.
E-mail: heartshomefarm@yahoo.com Web site: heartshome.com

Loma Vista B&B
33350 La Serena Way, 92591
909-676-7047 Fax: 909-676-0077
Walt & Sheila Kurczynski
All year

125-185-B&B
6 rooms, 6 pb
Visa, MC, *Rated*
S-no/P-no/H-no
Spanish

Full champagne breakfast
Complimentary wine/snack
Sitting room, library, spa, hot
tubs, firepit

Mission style home, built as a B&B, located in the heart of the So. California wine country, surrounded by lush citrus groves and premium vineyards.

TIMBERCOVE

Timberhill Ranch
35755 Hauser Bridge Rd, 95421
800-847-3470 Fax: 707-847-3342
Tarran McDaid
All year

395-415-MAP
15 rooms, 15 pb
Visa, MC, *Rated*, •
C-ltd/S-ltd/P-no/H-yes

Continental plus breakfast
6-course dinner included
Bar, sitting room, hot tub,
heated swimming pool,
tennis courts, Jacuzzi

Romantic 80-acre resort featuring gourmet dining, 15 secluded cottages, fireplaces, private baths and decks. World-class tennis courts. Conference facility.   E-mail: timber@mcn.org
Web site: timberhillranch.com

TRINIDAD

Lost Whale Inn B&B
3452 Patrick's Point Dr, 95570
707-677-3425 Fax: 707-677-0284
800-677-7859
Susanne Lakin & Lee Miller
All year

136-186-B&B
9 rooms, 9 pb
Visa, MC, AmEx, Disc,
Rated, •
C-yes/S-no/P-no/H-ltd

Full gourmet breakfast
Afternoon tea, snacks
Farmhouse available, sitting
room, hot tubs, full
playground, garden

The only B&B in CA with a private beach. Spectacular ocean view, sea lions, greenhouse, gardens, decks, Jacuzzi, and huge breakfast. Newly remodeled. Rebuilt farmhouse on 5 acres.   E-mail: lmiller@lostwhaleinn.com Web site: lostwhaleinn.com

TRUCKEE

Richardson House B&B Inn
PO Box 2011, 96160
530-587-5388 Fax: 530-587-0927
888-229-0365
Lesley King & Juel Friedman
All year

100-200-B&B
8 rooms, 8 pb
Most CC, *Rated*, •
C-ltd/S-no/P-no/H-yes

Full breakfast
24 hr refreshment,afternoon
cookies
Parlor w/TV, VCR, CD player,
player piano, feather beds

Steeped in history and romance, surrounded by mountains, lakes, this recently restored Victorian offers 8 lovely guest rooms with private baths.   E-mail: innkeeper@ richardsonhouse.com Web site: richardsonhouse.com

TWAIN HARTE

Country Inn at Sugar Pine
PO Box 1235, 95383
209-586-4615
800-292-2093
Nancy Mulkey
All year

75-130-B&B
5 rooms, 5 pb
Visa, MC, *Rated*
C-yes/S-no/P-ltd

Full breakfast
Snacks
Sitting room, conference
facilities, TV/VCR in living
room

Situated just off Highway 108 on the edge of a ridge just above snowline, great view, tall trees, great sunsets! Full breakfast served in knotty pine paneled room, relaxing.
E-mail: nancy@goldrush.com Web site: mlode.com/~thcc/countryinn/

McCaffrey House B&B Inn
PO Box 67, 95383
209-586-0757 Fax: 209-586-3689
888-586-0757
M & S McCaffrey
All year

105-145-B&B
7 rooms, 7 pb
Visa, MC, AmEx,
Rated, •
C-yes/S-no/P-no

Full breakfast
Complimentary wine
Sitting room, library, outdoor
hot tub and sun deck

Artistically decorated inn nestled in the high country forest. Close to mountain lakes, fishing, golf, tennis, skiing. Gold country sightseeing and wine tasting.
E-mail: innkeeper@mccaffreyhouse.com Web site: mccaffreyhouse.com

UKIAH

Vichy Hot Springs Resort
2605 Vichy Springs Rd, 95482
707-462-9515 Fax: 707-462-9516
Gilbert & Marjorie Ashoff
All year

140-235-B&B
20 rooms, 20 pb
Most CC, *Rated*, •
C-yes/S-ltd/P-no/H-yes
Spanish

Full breakfast
Naturally wrm/carbonated,
mineral baths, hot pool,
Olympic size pool

An historic hot springs country inn—quiet, elegant and charming. The naturally warm and carbonated "Vichy" mineral baths are unique in North America.
E-mail: vichy@vichysprings.com Web site: vichysprings.com

VALLEY SPRINGS

10th Green Inn
14 St Andrews Rd, 95252
209-772-1084 Fax: 209-772-0267
888-727-8705
Jean & James Fox
All year

69-99-B&B
10 rooms, 10 pb
Most CC,
C-ltd/S-ltd/P-no/H-yes

Continental plus breakfast
Fireplaces, located on golf
course, next to club house

Beautiful English Tudor country inn nestled among majestic oak trees in heart of La Contenta, one of CA's finest golf courses.   E-mail: greeninn@goldrush.com
Web site: goldrush.com/~greeninn

VENTURA

La Mer B&B
411 Poli St, 93001
805-643-3600 Fax: 805-653-7329
888-223-0068
Gisela Baida
All year

95-185-B&B
5 rooms, 5 pb
Visa, MC, AmEx,
Rated, •
C-ltd/S-no/P-no/H-no
German, Spanish

Bavarian full breakfast
Complimentary wine or
champagne
Picnic baskets, library,
therapeutic massages,
antique carriage rides

Authentic European style in old Victorian. Ocean view, three blocks to beach. Private entrances. Special packages available.   Web site: vcol.net/lamer

Ben Maddox House, Visalia, CA

VISALIA

Ben Maddox House
601 N Encina St, 93291
559-739-0721 Fax: 559-625-0420
800-401-9800
Al & Diane Muro   All year

85-120-B&B
4 rooms, 4 pb
Most CC, *Rated*, •
C-ltd/S-no/P-no/H-ltd

Full breakfast
Tea and coffee upon request
Sitting room, swimming pool,
cable TV, accommodate
business travelers

Historic 1876 antique furnished home on ½ acre of gardens with decks and pool.
E-mail: dmuro@pacbell.net   Web site: benmaddoxhouse.com

Spalding House
631 E Encina, 93291
559-773-7877 Fax: 559-629-0902
Wayne Davidson
All year

85-B&B
3 rooms, 3 pb
Visa, MC, AmEx, *Rated*
C-ltd/S-no/P-ltd/H-no

Full breakfast
Library, Suites,
Accommodate business
travelers, All suites w/private
baths

Carefully restored Colonial Revival furnished with fine antiques, Persian rugs, Steinway player grand piano, large library, gourmet breakfast and more.

VOLCANO

St. George Hotel
PO Box 9, 95689
209-296-4458 Fax: 209-296-4458
Mark & Tracy Berkner
Wed-Sun, mid-Feb-Dec

65-80-B&B
20 rooms, 6 pb
C-ltd/S-no/P-ltd/H-ltd

Full breakfast (fee)
Dinner included, bar
Sitting room, pianos, new
porches & deck, fishing,
conferences

Elegant Mother Lode hotel built in 1862. Maintains a timeless quality. On Nat'l Registry of Historic Places. Back-to-1862 porches and balusters   E-mail: stgeorge@volcano.net
Web site: stgeorgehotel.com

WESTPORT

DeHaven Valley Farm
39247 N Hwy 1, 95488
707-961-1660 Fax: 707-961-1677
Christa Stapp
All year

85-140-B&B
8 rooms, 6 pb
Visa, MC, *Rated*, •
C-ltd/S-no/P-no
German

Full country breakfast
Restaurant
4-course dinner Wed-Sat,
meeting space, sitt. rm.,
library, hot tub, spa

1875 farmhouse & cottages on 20 acres of hills, meadows & streams, by beach. Horses, donkeys, sheep, goats. Lost Coast, wineries. Explore Mendocino, tide pools, redwood forest.   E-mail: dehavenval@aol.com   Web site: dehaven-valley-farm.com/

Howard Creek Ranch
PO Box 121, 95488
707-964-6725 Fax: 707-964-1603
Charles & Sally Grigg
All year

75-160-B&B
10 rooms, 8 pb
Visa, MC, AmEx,
Rated, •
C-ltd/S-ltd/P-ltd/H-ltd
German, Italian, Dutch

Full ranch breakfast
Complimentary tea
Piano, hot tub, cabins, sauna,
massage by res., heated
swimming pool

Historic farmhouse filled with collectibles, antiques & memorabilia, unique health spa with privacy and dramatic views adjoining a wide beach.   Web site: howardcreekranch.com

YOSEMITE

Hounds Tooth Inn
42071 Hwy 41, 93644
559-642-6600 Fax: 559-658-2946
888-642-6610
B&A Williams & R&L
Kiehlmeier
All year

105-225-B&B
13 rooms, 13 pb
Most CC, *Rated*, •
C-ltd/S-no/P-no/H-yes

Full breakfast
Afternoon tea, snacks
Library, Jacuzzis, suites,
fireplaces, cable TV, sitting
room

12 room Victorian style inn located 12 miles from Yosemite's Southern entrance in Oakhurst, 6 miles from Bass Lake, enjoy private rooms with fireplace and/or Jacuzzi and relax in our casual elegance.   E-mail: robray@sierratel.com *Web site:* sierranet.net/net/tooth

YOSEMITE NATIONAL PARK

Karen's Yosemite B&B
PO Box 8, 93623
559-683-4550 Fax: 559-683-8127
800-346-1443
Karen Bergh
All year

90-B&B
3 rooms, 3 pb
Rated, •
C-yes/S-ltd/P-no/H-no

Full breakfast
Afternoon tea, snacks
Sitting room, lib., private
baths, individual heating,
fireplace, cable TV

Only two miles from Yosemite National Park, Karen's, nestled in the towering pines and whispering cedars, offers a unique blend of contemporary country hospitality. E-mail: karenbnb@sierratel.com *Web site:* karensyosemitebnb.com

YOUNTVILLE

Burgundy House
PO Box 3156, 94599
707-944-0889
Deanna Roque
All year

145-165-B&B
5 rooms, 5 pb
Rated
C-ltd/S-no/P-no/H-no
French, German

Full breakfast
Complimentary wine
Air conditioned, Mobil 4-star
rated, view decks

1870 rustic country French stone house with Old World appeal. Furnished with country antiques. Perfect location in beautiful Napa Valley.   Web site: bbinternet.com/burgundy

Oleander House
7433 St Helena Hwy, 94599
707-944-8315 Fax: 707-944-4448
800-778-0357
Barbara and Jack Kasten
All year

145-180-B&B
4 rooms, 4 pb
Visa, MC, *Rated*, •
S-no/P-no/H-no
Spanish

Full breakfast
Comp. soft drinks
Sitting room, spa, patio, near
ballooning, tennis, golf,
dining, shops

Country French charm. Antiques. Spacious rooms with brass beds, private decks, fireplaces, central A/C, and Laura Ashley fabrics and wallpapers. Beautiful rose garden. E-mail: Innkeeper@Oleander.com *Web site:* oleander.com/

Colorado

ALAMOSA

Cottonwood Inn & Gallery
123 San Juan, 81101
719-589-3882 Fax: 719-589-6437
800-955-2623
Julie Mordecai
All year

72-99-B&B
9 rooms, 7 pb
Visa, MC, *Rated*, •
C-yes/S-ltd
Spanish

Full gourmet breakfast
Library, carriage house,
Neutrogena soaps/creams,
turn-down service

Lovely inn, rated as one of the best in Colorado, centrally located for exploring Souther Colorado and Northern New Mexico. Phenomenal, generous breakfasts. Arts and crafts/mission interior.   E-mail: julie@cottonwoodinn.com *Web site:* cottonwoodinn.com

ANTONITO ─────────────────────────────────────

Conejos River Guest Ranch	79-125-B&B	Full breakfast
PO Box 175, 81120	8 rooms, 8 pb	Snacks, restaurant
719-376-2464	Visa, MC, Disc, •	Bar service, sitting room,
Ms. Shorty Fry	C-yes/S-ltd/P-yes/H-yes	library, bikes, fishing, suites,
May-Nov.	Some Spanish	TV

The traveler's choice in south central Colorado; twelve park-like acres with mile of river frontage; fabulous food; hospitality extraordinaire; relax-revive-renew.
E-mail: info@conejosranch.com *Web site:* conejosranch.com

ASPEN ─────────────────────────────────────

Hotel Durant	79-309-B&B	Continental breakfast
233 W Main St, 81611		
970-925-8500 Fax: 970-925-8789		
877-438-7268		
Rhonda Ardis		
All year		

Welcome to the Hotel Durant where our extraordinary hospitality and special charm of our rooms brings our guests back. Superb location: two blocks from the gondola and all Aspen has to offer.   E-mail: durant@rof.net
Web site: webworks.tislink.com/webworks/state/co/durant/default.htm

Hotel Lenado	95-570-B&B	Full breakfast
200 S Aspen St, 81611	19 rooms, 19 pb	Appetizers, bar
970-925-6246 Fax: 970-925-3840	Visa, MC, AmEx,	Hot tub, library, screening
800-321-3457	*Rated*, •	room, meeting facilities
Kimberly	C-yes/S-ltd/P-no/H-no	
All year		

A new Aspen landmark—inventive architecture, romantic ambience, gracious service. Nineteen guestrooms and suites furnished in applewood, ironwood, willow.
E-mail: hotlsard@rof.net *Web site:* aspen.com/sardylenado

Innsbruck Inn	75-B&B	Continental plus breakfast
233 W Main St, 81611	30 rooms, 30 pb	Afternoon tea in the winter
970-925-2980 Fax: 970-925-6960	Most CC, *Rated*, •	Sitting room, hot tub, sauna
Marie Marx	C-yes/S-yes/P-no/H-no	
6/1-10/15, 11/23-4/15	German	

Warm hospitality and charm welcome you to this European style Inn. Offering a wonderful lobby, outdoor heated pool and Jacuzzi, this ski & sun lodge is ideally located a few blocks from the heart of town.   E-mail: innsbruk@rof.net *Web site:* aspenguide.com/innsbruk

L'Auberge d'Aspen	EP
233 W Main, 81611	
970-925-8297 Fax: 970-925-4164	
877-282-3743	
Kirstin Bundy	
Season Inquire	

Wonderful, warm cabins in the heart of one of the finest resorts in the world. Our cottages have peaked ceilings, fireplaces, kitchenettes, and down comforters. Romantic and charming.   E-mail: lauberge@rof.net *Web site:* aspenguide.com/lauberge

Sardy House Hotel	110-950-B&B	Full breakfast
128 E Main St, 81611	21 rooms, 21 pb	Restaurant dinner (fee)
970-920-2525 Fax: 970-920-4478	Visa, MC, AmEx, •	Bar, sitting room, library, hot
880-321-3457	C-yes/S-ltd/P-no/H-no	tub, sauna, swimming pool
Jun-Oct, Thksg-mid-Apr		

Beautifully restored 1892 Victorian with all the amenities of a small luxury hotel, on perfectly landscaped grounds in the heart of Aspen.   E-mail: hotlsard@rof.net
Web site: aspen.com/sardylenado

ASPEN

Snow Queen Victorian B&B
124 E Cooper St, 81611
970-925-8455 Fax: 970-925-7391
Norma Dolle & L. Ledingham
All year

85-135-B&B
7 rooms, 7 pb
Visa, MC, AmEx, •
C-yes/S-yes/P-no/H-no
Spanish

Continental plus breakfast
Weekly party in winter
Parlor with fireplace, TV,
outdoor hot tub, skiing, 2
kitchen units

Quaint, family-oriented Victorian lodge built in 1880s. Parlor with fireplace & color TV. Walk to restaurants, shops & ski area. Most rooms have TV & phone.   E-mail: sqlodge@rof.net *Web site:* destinationaspen.com/snowqueen

BASALT

Shenandoah Inn
PO Box 560, 81621
970-927-4991 Fax: 970-927-4990
Bob & Terri Ziets
All year

88-165-B&B
4 rooms, 4 pb
Rated, •
C-ltd/S-ltd/P-no/H-no
French, Spanish

Full breakfast
Snacks, wine
Sitting room, hot tub,
bicycles, skiing, rafts, golf,
tennis, fishing

Contemporary Colorado B&B, situated on 2 riverfront acres on premier gold-medal trout stream. 20 min. to Aspen. Friendly atmosphere, exceptional cuisine.
E-mail: shenando@sopris.net *Web site:* shenandoahinn.com

BOULDER

Alps Boulder Canyon Inn
38619 Boulder Canyon Rd,
80302
303-444-5445 Fax: 303-444-5522
800-414-2577
Jeannine & John Vanderhart
All year

108-225-B&B
12 rooms, 12 pb
Most CC, *Rated*, •
C-ltd/S-ltd/P-no/H-no
Spanish

Full breakfast
Afternoon tea, snacks
Lunch available, library,
Jacuzzis, fireplaces

Historic luxury country inn in scenic Boulder Canyon. Amenities include Jacuzzi tubs, fireplaces and antiques. Winner of many awards.   E-mail: alpsinn@aol.com
Web site: alpsinn.com

Briar Rose B&B
2151 Arapahoe, 80302
303-442-3007 Fax: 303-786-8440
Margaret & Bob Weisenbach
All year

129-169-B&B
9 rooms, 9 pb
Most CC, *Rated*, •
C-ltd/S-no/P-no/H-no
Spanish

Continental plus breakfast
Afternoon tea & cookies
Comp. sherry & lemonade,
bicycles, A/C, renovated,
AAA rated 3 diamonds

Entering the Briar Rose is like entering another time when hospitality was an art & the place for dreams was a feather bed. Three rooms with fireplaces.
E-mail: brbbx@aol.com *Web site:* globalmall.com/brose

Inn on Mapleton Hill, The
1001 Spruce St, 80302
303-449-6528 Fax: 303-415-0470
800-276-6528
Ray & Judi Schultze
All year

83-145-B&B
7 rooms, 5 pb
Visa, MC, AmEx,
Rated, •
C-ltd/S-no/P-no/H-no

Continental plus breakfast
Afternoon tea, snacks, wine
Sitting room, library, bikes,
fireplaces, A/C, phones,
cable TVs

1899 inn in quiet, historic neighborhood near downtown Boulder. Individually decorated rooms furnished with antiques. Warm welcome from resident innkeepers.
E-mail: maphillinn@aol.com *Web site:* innonmapletonhill.com

Pearl Street Inn
1820 Pearl St, 80302
303-444-5584
800-232-5949
Theresa Schuller
All year

119-179-B&B
7 rooms, 7 pb
Visa, MC, AmEx,
Rated, •
C-yes/S-yes/P-yes/H-no
French

Full breakfast
Complimentary
wine/cheese/tea
Sitting room, bar,
entertainment, TV/room,
Dinner served (fee)

A rare combination of a European inn and luxury hotel. Near Boulder's pedestrian mall. Refreshing breakfast and evening bar in garden courtyard.   E-mail: kate@pearlstreetinn.com
Web site: pearlstreetinn.com

BRECKENRIDGE

Allaire Timbers Inn	140-400-B&B	Full breakfast
PO Box 4653, 80424	10 rooms, 10 pb	Snacks, complimentary wine
970-453-7530 Fax: 970-453-8699	Visa, MC, AmEx,	Sitting room, fireplaces, hot
800-624-4904	*Rated*, •	tubs, in-room phones, TVs in
Jack & Kathy Gumph	C-ltd/S-no/P-no/H-yes	all rooms
All year		

Newly constructed log and stone Inn. Suites with private hot tub and fireplace. Spectacular mountain views; quiet luxury; personalized hospitality. E-mail: allairetimbers@worldnet.att.net *Web site:* allairetimbers.com

B&B's on N Main Street	85-289-B&B	Full breakfast
PO Box 2454, 80424	11 rooms, 11 pb	Afternoon tea, snacks
970-453-2975 Fax: 970-453-5258	Most CC, *Rated*, •	Sitting room, Jacuzzis,
800-795-2975	C-ltd/S-no/P-no/H-no	fireplaces, cable TV,
Fred Kinat & Diane Jaynes		accomodate business
All year		travelers.

Seeing the mountains from our historic western mining town evokes the feeling that inspired the word awesome. E-mail: bnb@imageline.com *Web site:* breckenridge-inn.com

Evans House B&B	63-140-B&B	Full breakfast
PO Box 387, 80424	5 rooms, 5 pb	Afternoon tea
970-453-5509	Most CC, *Rated*, •	Sitting room, library, meeting
Pete and Georgette Contos	C-yes/S-no/P-no/H-ltd	room, hot tub, TVs/phones
All year	Greek, French	in all rooms

Beautifully restored 1886 Victorian in heart of Breckenridge, all activities nearby. Known for our hospitality, service, and delicious breakfasts. Unique hot tub, true B&B experience. New suite and newly redecorated rooms. E-mail: evans@imageline.com *Web site:* colorado-bnb.com/evanshse

Hunt Placer Inn	99-235-B&B	Full breakfast
PO Box 4898, 80424	8 rooms, 8 pb	Afternoon tea
970-453-7573 Fax: 970-453-2335	Most CC, *Rated*, •	Sitting room, library, guest
800-472-1430	C-ltd/S-no/P-no/H-yes	area fireplaces, private
Carl & Gwen Ray	German	balconies available
All year		

New European-style chalet, surrounded by Spruce, Pine, & Aspen, with private balconies. In-town seclusion with marvelous breakfasts. Elevator for wheelchair access.
E-mail: hpi@colorado.net *Web site:* breck.net/lodging/huntplacer/

Lark Mountain Inn	70-170-B&B	Full breakfast
PO Box 1646, 80443	6 rooms, 4 pb	Lunch & dinner on requ.
970-668-5237 Fax: 970-668-1988	Visa, MC, *Rated*, •	Snacks, sitting room,
800-668-5275	C-ltd/S-no/P-no/H-no	bicycles, hot tub in yard,
Sheila Morgan		libary, fireplace, cable TV
All year		

The Lark is a log and timber inn with a view of Mount Royal. Cuddle up in front of the fireplace or use our bikes to tour the historic distict. Enjoy a full hot breakfast, and step into the hot tub any time. E-mail: smlark@oneimage.com *Web site:* toski.com/lark

Wellington Inn, The	139-299-B&B	Full breakfast
PO Box 5890, 80424	4 rooms, 4 pb	Lunch/dinner available (fee)
970-453-9464 Fax: 970-453-0149	Most CC, *Rated*, •	Restaurant & bar, snacks,
800-655-7557	C-ltd/S-no/P-no/H-no	complimentary wine, sitting
Hollie & Bill Vander Hoeven		room, balconies
All year		

The Inn's luxurious romantic mountain retreat sits on historical Main St., surrounded with breathtaking views providing every amenity & luxury available.
E-mail: welingtn@sni.net *Web site:* TheWellingtonInn.com

Black Forest B&B, Colorado Springs, CO

BUENA VISTA

Adobe Inn, The	59-89-B&B	Full breakfast
PO Box 1560, 81211	5 rooms, 5 pb	Complimentary beverages
719-395-6340	Visa, MC, *Rated*	Restaurant, sitting room,
888-343-6340	C-ltd/S-no/P-no/H-no	library, piano, solarium, 2
Paul, Marjorie & Michael	some Spanish	suites, Jacuzzi
Knox All year		

Santa Fe-style adobe hacienda. Indian, Mexican, antique, wicker & Mediterranean rooms. Indian fireplaces. Jacuzzi. Majestic mountains. Gourmet Mexican restaurant.
Web site: bbonline.com/co/adobe/

Meister House B&B	78-120-B&B	Full breakfast
PO Box 1221, 81211	7 rooms, 5 pb	Snacks
719-395-9220 Fax: 719-395-9455	Most CC, *Rated*	Sitting room, library, suites,
888-395-9220	C-ltd/S-no/P-no/H-ltd	fireplace, cable TV,
Linda & Skip Buhl		European dry sauna
All year		

Turn of the century hotel revitalized to comfortable unique lodging-freshly prepared gourmet breakfast and snacks.   E-mail: innkeeper@meisterhouse.com Web site: MeisterHouse.com

CARBONDALE

Mt. Sopris Inn	100-250-B&B	Full breakfast
Box 126, 81623	14 rooms, 14 pb	Sitting room, library, hot
970-963-2209 Fax: 970-963-8975	Visa, MC, *Rated*, •	tubs, swimming pool, adults
800-437-8675	S-no/P-no/H-yes	only
Barbara Fasching All year		

Treat yourself to the valley's best. If you value beauty, serenity and wish to renew yourselves, Mt. Sopris Inn is for you! Central to Aspen, Glenwood Springs and historic Redstone.   E-mail: mt.soprisinn@juno.com Web site: colorado-bnb.com/mtsopris

COLORADO SPRINGS

Black Forest B&B	75-200-B&B	Continental plus breakfast
11170 Black Forest Rd, 80908	5 rooms, 5 pb	Snacks
719-495-4208 Fax: 719-495-0688	Most CC, •	Sitting room, ibrary,
800-809-9901	C-yes/S-no/P-no/H-yes	weddings, retreats
Robert & Susan Putnam	Survival Spanish	
All year		

Rustic Romantic Retreat in a massive log home on 20 acres of pines overlooking the city lights and the Rocky Mountains.   E-mail: blackforestbandb@msn.com
Web site: blackforestbb.com

Cheyenne Canon Inn, The	95-200-B&B	Full breakfast
2030 W Cheyenne Rd, 80906	7 rooms, 7 pb	Snacks
719-633-0625 Fax: 719-633-8826	Most CC, *Rated*, •	Sitting rooms, hiking, hot
800-633-0625	C-ltd/S-no/P-no/H-no	tubs, great room, porch,
Steve & Nancy Stannard	French	library, Jacuzzi
All year		

Historic 10,000-sq.-ft. Arts & Crafts mansion secluded in Cheyenne Canyon.
E-mail: info@cheyennecanoninn.com *Web site:* cheyennecanoninn.com

Lennox House, Colorado Springs, CO

COLORADO SPRINGS

Crescent Lily Inn
6 Boulder Crescent St, 80903
719-442-2331 Fax: 719-442-6947
800-869-2721
Lin M. Moeller
All year

90-130-B&B
5 rooms, 5 pb
Visa, MC, AmEx,
Rated, •
C-ltd/S-no/P-no/H-ltd

Full breakfast
Comp. wine, snacks
Sitting room, suites, cable,
fireplaces, jetted tubs, conf.
room

This 100-year-old inn has beveled glass windows, interior woodwork and a vanbriggle fireplace. Amenities in guest rooms include private baths with jetted tubs, fireplaces and king/queen-size beds. E-mail: info@crescentlilyinn.com Web site: crescentlilyinn.com

Eastholme in the Rockies
PO Box 98, 80809
719-684-9901
800-672-9901
Terry Thompson
All year

69-140-B&B
8 rooms, 6 pb
Most CC, *Rated*, •
C-yes/S-no/P-no/H-ltd

Full gourmet breakfast
Snacks
Library, Jacuzzis, suites &
cottages, cable TV, fireplaces

Historic 1885 Victorian in gorgeous mountain setting. Close to all Pikes Peak area attractions. 15 min. to Colorado Springs. Beautifully decorated comfortable rooms. National Register of Historic Places. E-mail: eastholm@rmi.net Web site: eastholme.com

**Holden House-1902 B&B
Inn**
1102 W Pikes Peak Ave, 80904
719-471-3980 Fax: 719-471-4740
Sallie & Welling Clark
All year

120-140-B&B
5 rooms, 5 pb
Most CC, *Rated*, •
S-no/P-no/H-yes

Full gourmet breakfast
Complimentary coffee, tea,
snack
Parlor with TV, living room,
suite with disabled access,
veranda

Charming 1902 storybook Victorian home filled with antiques & family heirlooms near Historic District. Suites with fireplaces & phones. Conveniently located. Friendly resident cats. "Tubs for Two." E-mail: holdenhouse@worldnet.att.net Web site: bbonline.com/co/holden/

Lennox House B&B, The
1339 N Nevada Ave, 80903
719-471-9265 Fax: 719-471-0971
800-471-9282
Mark & Lisa Kolb
All year

75-110-B&B
3 rooms, 3 pb
Visa, MC, AmEx,
Rated, •
C-ltd/S-ltd/P-no/H-no

Full breakfast
Snacks
Sitting room, modem
connections, in room
phones, laundry, E-mail,
fireplaces

The Lennox House provides the atmosphere of a charming "Turn of the Century" Queen Anne Victorian. E-mail: info@lennoxhouse.com Web site: lennoxhouse.com

COLORADO SPRINGS ───────────────────────────────

Lion & Rose Castle, The	250-B&B	Continental plus breakfast
547 Douglas Fir Dr, 80863	2 rooms, 2 pb	Complimentary wine
719-687-9745 Fax: 719-687-1944	Most CC, •	Sitting room, period
888-536-4564	S-no/P-no/H-no	furnishings, stone castle
Eric & Nancy Glanzer	Limited German	
All year		

A Colorado mountain top stone castle, period furnishings, view, ambiance, a romantic retreat. The quintessential luxury B&B.   E-mail: lrcastle@ix.netcom.com
Web site: lionrosecastle.com

Old Town Guest House	95-160-B&B	Full breakfast
115 S 26th St, 80906	8 rooms, 8 pb	Afternoon tea, snacks
719-632-9194 Fax: 719-632-9026	Most CC, *Rated*, •	Sitting room, library,
888-375-4210	C-ltd/S-no/P-ltd/H-yes	Bicycles, hot tubs, adult
Kaye & David Caster		environment, voice/dataport
All year		

Experience historic Old Town in modern luxury. A guest house for discerning romantic & business travelers. Conference facilities, fully accessible. Voice/data ports all rooms. 4 Diamond award-AAA.   E-mail: oldtown@rmi.net *Web site:* colorado-springs-co.com/

Our Hearts Inn Old CO City	85-120-B&B	Full breakfast
2215 W Colorado Ave, 80904	4 rooms, 4 pb	Snacks, beverages
719-473-8684 Fax: 719-634-4954	Most CC, *Rated*, •	Sitting room, hot tubs, phone
800-533-7095	C-ltd/S-no/P-no/H-no	& TV in some rooms, rocking
Andy & Pat Fejedelem		chairs
All year		

Cozy, stenciled/antiques filled home plus western cottage with Jacuzzi. Two blocks east of Historic Old Colorado City shops and dining. Some rooms have fireplaces. Packages available with all rooms, all year: $15-$20 additional fee.   E-mail: hearts2@gateway.net
Web site: bbonline.com/ourhearts/

Outlook Lodge B&B	75-95-B&B	Full gourmet breakfast
PO Box 586, 80819	7 rooms, 7 pb	BBQ, Snacks
719-684-2303 Fax: 603-415-7811	Most CC, *Rated*, •	Piano, organ, sitt. rm., fishing,
877-684-7800	C-yes/S-no/P-no/H-ltd	tennis, hiking, horseback
Diane & Pat Drayton		ride, library
All year		

1889 Victorian lodge set in an alpine village at 7800 feet of clear Colorado altitude. Great hiking out the back door. 6-person Jacuzzi on the patio.   E-mail: goofy7@worldnet.att.net
Web site: outlooklodge.com

Painted Lady B&B Inn, The	95-150-B&B	Full breakfast
1318 W Colorado Ave, 80904	3 rooms, 3 pb	Complimentary coffee/tea,
719-473-3165 Fax: 719-635-1396	Most CC, *Rated*, •	snacks
800-370-3165	C-ltd/S-no/P-no/H-no	Parlor w/TV, tub for two,
Valerie Maslowski		wraparound porch, fireplace,
All year		outdoor hottub & deck

1894 Victorian home nestled in historic Old Colorado City. Guest rooms feature Victorian furnishings. Some with in-suite fireplaces. Phones, refrigerators, TV/VCR, CD, A/C. Hearty, healthy breakfasts begin your day. Friendly resident cat.   E-mail: innkeepers@
paintedladyinn.com *Web site:* paintedladyinn.com

Pikes Peak Paradise	195-240-B&B	Full breakfast
236 Pinecrest Rd, 80863	2 rooms	Picnic lunches avail.
719-687-6656 Fax: 719-687-9008	Most CC, •	Comp. sherry, cheese, fresh
800-728-8282	C-ltd	flowers, sitting room
Priscilla Arthur		
All year		

Relaxation was never better! A spectacular view of Pikes Peak, wildlife, birds. Fresh flowers. Breakfast buffet offered with a smile. Fireplaces, hot tubs in rooms
E-mail: pppbnb@bemail.com *Web site:* pikespeakmall.com/pppbandb

COLORADO SPRINGS

Red Crags B&B Inn
302 El Paso Blvd, 80829
719-685-1920 Fax: 719-685-1073
800-721-2248
Howard & Lynda Lerner
All year

80-180-B&B
8 rooms, 8 pb
Most CC, *Rated*, •
C-ltd/S-no/P-no/H-no

Full gourmet breakfast
Afternoon tea, wine, dessert
Parlor/sunroom, hot tub,
suites with jetted double
tubs

Historic 1870s Victorian mansion—a romantic hideaway. Lose yourself somewhere in time. Extensive herb & flower gardens. Sitting rooms. A favorite of Teddy Roosevelt.   E-mail: info@redcrags.com *Web site:* redcrags.com

Rockledge Country Inn
328 El Paso Blvd, 80829
719-685-4515 Fax: 719-685-1031
888-685-4515
Hartman and Nancy Smith
All year

195-250-B&B
4 rooms, 4 pb
Most CC, •
C-ltd/S-no/P-no/H-no

Full gourmet breakfast
Afternoon tea, snacks, wine
Sitting room, library,
swimming pool available,
murder mystery weekends

An elegant Bed & Breakfast on a 3.5 acre wooded estate. Offerings include 2 room suites, gourmet breakfast, feather beds, and spectacular views.   E-mail: rockinn@webcom.com *Web site:* rockledgeinn.com

Room at the Inn B&B
618 N Nevada Ave, 80903
719-442-1896 Fax: 719-442-6802
800-579-4621
Chick & Jan McCormick
All year

90-145-B&B
7 rooms, 7 pb
Most CC, *Rated*, •
C-ltd/S-no/P-no/H-yes

Full breakfast
Afternoon tea, snacks
Library, fireplaces, hot tubs,
phones, A/C, real antique
tubs for 2

Experience the charm, elegance and hospitality of an 1896 Victorian home. A romantic retreat in the heart of the city.   E-mail: roomatinn@pcisys.net *Web site:* roomattheinn.com

Serenity Pines Guesthouse
11910 Windmill Rd, 80908
719-495-7141 Fax: 719-495-7141
877-737-3674
Kathy & Bob
All year

69-129-B&B
2 rooms, 2 pb
Visa, MC, AmEx,
Rated, •
C-yes/S-ltd/P-ltd/H-yes

Continental breakfast plus
Snacks, dinner
Sitting room, suites,
fireplaces, cable TV, hottub,
suite with full kitchen

Experience a "True Colorado Getaway" amongst pristine acres of whispering pines under clear blue skies in clean crisp pine scented air. All within a short, scenic drive to area attractions.   E-mail: Serenpines@aol.com *Web site:* colorado-bnb.com/serenpines

Two Sisters Inn-a B&B
Ten Otoe Place, 80829
719-685-9684
800-2-SISINN
Sharon Smith, Wendy
Goldstein
All year

85-110-B&B
5 rooms, 3 pb
Visa, MC, *Rated*, •
C-ltd/S-no/P-no/H-no

Full healthy breakfast
Complimentary beverages
Manitou Mineral Water,
living room with fireplace,
parlor with 1896 piano

Award-winning gracious Victorian nestled at base of Pike's Peak in historic district. Garden honeymoon cottage. Mineral springs, hiking, art galleries, shops, restaurants. Web site: twosisinn.com

CRESTED BUTTE

Cristiana Guesthaus
PO Box 427, 81224
970-349-5326 Fax: 970-349-1962
800-824-7899
Rosemary & Martin Catmur
All year

70-91-B&B
21 rooms, 21 pb
Most CC, •
C-yes/S-no/P-no/H-no

Continental plus breakfast
Complimentary hot
beverages
Sitting room, hot tub, sauna

Close to historic downtown. Relaxed, friendly atmosphere. Enjoy the hot tub, sauna, sun deck, and homebaked breakfast served in our cozy lobby. Superb mountain views. E-mail: cristian@rmi.net *Web site:* crestedbuttechamber.com/cristiana

CRESTED BUTTE

Elk Mountain Lodge	75-133-B&B	Continental plus breakfast
PO Box 148, 81224	19 rooms, 19 pb	Afternoon tea, snacks, bar
970-349-7533 Fax: 970-349-5114	Most CC, •	Sitting room, library,
800-374-6521	C-ltd/S-no/P-no/H-no	Jacuzzis, suites, cable TV,
Lee Tauck & Mike Nolan	Little Spanish	conference facilities
Winter & Summer		

Crested Butte's historic Inn. Turn of the century miners hotel beautifully renovated. Located in town, walking distance to everything. Each room is decorated individually, some rooms with balconies overlooking the mountains.   E-mail: info@elkmountainlodge.net *Web site:* elkmountainlodge.net

DENVER

Adagio B&B, The	95-170-B&B	Full breakfast
1430 Race St, 80206	5 rooms, 5 pb	Aftn. tea, snacks
303-370-6911 Fax: 303-377-5968	Most CC, *Rated*, •	Sitting room, library, hot
800-533-3241	C-yes/S-no/P-no/H-no	tubs, family friendly facility,
Jim & Amy Cremmins		suites, fireplace
All year		

Beautiful Victorian mansion on Capitol Hill. Close to downtown, shopping, museums, parks, fabulous dining. Delicious European style breakfast served daily. E-mail: cremmins@sni.net *Web site:* sni.net/adagio

Capitol Hill Mansion	85-175-B&B	Full breakfast
1207 Pennsylvania St, 80205	8 rooms, 8 pb	Complimentary wine/snack,
303-839-5221 Fax: 303-839-9046	Most CC, *Rated*, •	refrig.
800-839-9329	C-ltd/S-no/P-no/H-yes	Sitting room, hot tub, A/C,
Wendy & Bill Pearson		cable TV, phones, heirlooms,
All year		original art

Colorado's most luxurious inn! Downtown Denver in historic mansion, perfect for business travelers but also designed for perfect romance. Historic Register. 2 rooms with king beds, 1 with king or 2 twins.   E-mail: info@capitolhillmansion.com *Web site:* capitolhillmansion.com/

Castle Marne—An Urban Inn	75-235-B&B	Full gourmet breakfast
1572 Race St, 80206	9 rooms, 9 pb	Afternoon tea 4:30-6:00
303-331-0621 Fax: 303-331-0623	Visa, MC, AmEx,	Library, gift shop, game room
800-92-MARNE	*Rated*, •	with pool table, computer,
Diane & Jim PeiKer	C-ltd/S-no/P-no/H-no	Fax, copier
All year	Spanish, Hungarian	

Luxury urban inn. Minutes from convention center, business district, shopping, fine dining. Nat'l Historic Structure. 3 rms. with priv. balconies, hot tubs for 2. Luncheons, candlelight dinners, ask.   E-mail: jim@castlemarne.com *Web site:* castlemarne.com

Dove Inn B&B, The	65-90-B&B	Full breakfast
711 14th St, 80401	6 rooms, 6 pb	Rooms have A/C, desks,
303-279-3283 Fax: 303-273-5272	Most CC, *Rated*, •	phones and TVs, Golden
888-278-2209	C-yes/S-no/P-no/H-no	West Shuttle
Connie & Tim Sheffield		
All year		

Built prior to 1873, lots of country charm in the West Denver foothills. All Denver attractions and Rocky Mountains are nearby. Suite that can sleep four comfortably. E-mail: innkeep@ix.netcom.com *Web site:* doveinn.com

Haus Berlin B&B	100-140-B&B	Full breakfast
1651 Emerson St, 80128	4 rooms, 4 pb	Complimentary beverage
303-837-9527 Fax: 303-837-9527	Most CC, *Rated*, •	Sitting room with cable TV,
800-659-0253	S-no/P-no/H-no	library, courtyard
Christiana & Dennis Brown	German	
All year		

Luxurious European, award winning, urban historic inn. Convenient for business traveler and tourist.   E-mail: haus.berlin@worldnet.att.net *Web site:* hausberlinbandb.com/

DENVER

Holiday Chalet A Victorian
1820 E Colfax Ave, 80218
303-321-9975 Fax: 303-377-6556
800-626-4497
Margot Crowe, owner
All year

94-155-B&B
10 rooms, 10 pb
Most CC, *Rated*, •
C-yes/S-no/P-ltd/H-no
Spanish, some French &
Ger

Continental plus breakfast
Library, fireplaces, beautiful
courtyard, accommodates
business travelers

We have offered warmth and comfort to travelers for over 47 years. Our luxury B&B is ideal for business travlers, vacationers and romantics. E-mail: holidaycha@aol.com
Web site: bbonline.com/co/holiday

Jameson House B&B Inn, The
1704 Illinois St, 80401
303-278-0200 Fax: 303-278-0200
888-880-4448
James & Carolyn Durgin
All year

80-120-B&B
4 rooms, 2 pb
Visa, MC, AmEx, •
C-ltd/S-ltd/P-no/H-no

Full breakfast
Snacks
Sitting rm., library, suites,
fireplace, cable TV, modem
jack, private phone

A charming, antique-filled turn of the century English country inn. A five minute walk from Coors Brewery and the shops, restaurants and museums of downtown historic Golden. E-mail: relax@jamesonhouse.com Web site: jamesonhouse.com

---

Merritt House B&B
941 E 17th Ave, 80218
303-861-5230 Fax: 303-861-9009
877-861-5230
Cathy Kuykendall
All year

100-160-B&B
10 rooms, 10 pb
Most CC, •
C-ltd/S-no/P-no/H-no

Full breakfast
Lunch & dinner available
Bar service, sitt. room,
Jacuzzis, suites, cable, TV,
conference facility

1889 Victorian Inn located in the heart of Denver. Extensive breakfast menu, cater to business and leisure traveler. E-mail: info@merritthouse.com Web site: merritthouse.com

---

Queen Anne B&B Inn
2147 Tremont Pl, 80205
303-296-6666 Fax: 303-296-2151
800-432-INNS
The King Family
All year

75-195-B&B
14 rooms, 14 pb
Most CC, *Rated*, •
C-ltd/S-no/P-no/H-ltd

Full breakfast
Afternoon wine
Fresh flowers, phone, A/C, 7
rooms with special tubs,
flower garden, patio

Award winning Victorian Inn. Facing downtown park. Walk to mall, shops, museums, convention center/business district. On National Historic Register. Airport shuttle. E-mail: queenanne@bedandbreakfastinns.org Web site: bedandbreakfastinns.org/queenanne

---

Victoria Oaks Inn
1575 Race St, 80206
303-355-1818 Fax: 303-331-1095
800-662-6257
Clyde & Ric
All year

70-95-B&B
9 rooms, 7 pb
Most CC, *Rated*, •
S-yes/P-no/H-no

Continental plus breakfast
Complimentary wine
Sitting room conference
facilities

Located 1 mile east of downtown Denver in the Wymans Historic District; convenient to restaurants, museums, shopping, zoo, parks, theater & sports E-mail: vicoaksinn@aol.com

DURANGO

Apple Orchard Inn
7758 Country Rd 203, 81301
970-247-0741 Fax: 970-385-6976
800-426-0751
Celeste & John Gardiner
All year

85-165-B&B
10 rooms, 10 pb
Most CC, *Rated*, •
C-yes/S-ltd/P-no/H-yes
Portuguese & Italian

Full breakfast
Afternoon tea,
complimentary wine
Lunch & dinner by
reservation, sitting room, hot
tub, Airport Shuttle

Charming, spacious rooms and cottages with featherbeds, fireplaces, Jacuzzi tubs, and private patios. Beautiful gardens. Convenient to town, golf, skiing. E-mail: apple@frontier.net
Web site: appleorchardinn.com

DURANGO

Blue Lake Ranch
16000 State Hwy 140, 81326
970-385-4537 Fax: 970-385-4088
888-BLUELAKE
Shirley & David Alford
All year

95-295-B&B
14 rooms, 14 pb
Rated, •
C-yes/S-no/P-no/H-ltd
German

Full European breakfast
Afternoon tea
Sitting room, hot tubs, lake,
family friendly facility

*Victorian farmhouse surrounded by gardens of flowers/vegetables/herbs. Spectacular lake
& mountain views, trout-stocked lake, meals of homegrown ingredients.*
E-mail: bluelake@frontier.net *Web site:* frontier.net/~bluelake/

Country Sunshine B&B
35130 US Hwy 550 N, 81301
970-247-2853 Fax: 970-247-1203
800-383-2853
Beanie & Gary Archie
All year

85-135-B&B
6 rooms, 6 pb
Most CC, *Rated*, •
C-ltd/S-no/P-no/H-yes

Full country breakfast
Aftn. tea, comp. wine/beer,
snacks
Sitting room, "secluded"
library, outdoor hot tub

*Spacious ranch-style house on 3 acres of Pine Oak Forest. Abundant wildlife, skiing,
fishing, golf, mountain biking, hot tub. Close to area attractions.*
E-mail: inn@countrysunshine.com *Web site:* countrysunshine.com/

Farmhouse Inn, The
3883 County Rd 207, 81301
970-259-9205 Fax: 970-382-0208
Tom Gorton & Kari Bouslaugh
All year

110-EP
4 rooms, 4 pb
Visa, MC, AmEx, Disc, •
C-yes/S-no/P-ltd/H-ltd

Bicycles trails, tennis court,
cable TV, playground

*Nestled in the pines, yet five miles from Durango. Furnished in a country decor, fully
equipped kitchens. Miles of hiking, mountain biking, cross country skiing, tennis courts and
excellent fly-fishing.*

Leland House B&B Suites
721 E Second Ave, 81301
970-385-1920 Fax: 970-385-1967
800-664-1920
Diane & Kirk Komick
All year

99-350-B&B
25 rooms, 25 pb
Most CC, *Rated*, •
C-ltd/S-no/P-ltd/H-yes
Spanish

Full gourmet breakfast
Afternoon tea, library
Sitting room, conference
space for 75, catering
available

*Historic downtown location-walk to unique shops, restaurants, Durango-Silverton RR Sta-
tion. Cowboy Victorianna decor inspired by movies made in this area.*
E-mail: leland@rochesterhotel.com *Web site:* rochesterhotel.com/history1.html

---

Lightner Creek Inn
999 CR 207, 81301
970-259-1226 Fax: 970-259-9526
800-268-9804
Suzy & Stan Savage
All year

75-185-B&B
10 rooms, 10 pb
Most CC, *Rated*, •
C-yes/S-no/P-no/H-ltd
Spanish, French,
German

Full breakfast
Afternoon tea, snacks
Sitting room, cross-country
skiing, hiking, mountain
biking, Grand piano

*Discover the romance of Lightner Creek Inn's country manor. Ten beautifully appointed
guestrooms, some with whirlpool tubs & fireplaces.   E-mail:* lci@frontier.net
Web site: lightnercreekinn.com

Rochester Hotel
721 E Second Ave, 81301
970-385-1920 Fax: 970-385-1967
800-664-1920
Diane & Kirk Komick
All year

99-350-B&B
25 rooms, 25 pb
Most CC, *Rated*, •
C-ltd/S-no/P-ltd/H-yes
Spanish

Full gourmet breakfast
Afternoon tea, library
Sitting room, conference
space for 75, catering
available

*Historic downtown location-walk to unique shops, restaurants, Durango-Silverton RR Sta-
tion. Cowboy Victorianna decor inspired by movies made in this area.   E-mail:* leland@
rochesterhotel.com *Web site:* rochesterhotel.com

DURANGO —————————————————————————————

Strater Hotel	99-215-B&B	Full breakfast
PO Drawer E, 81301	93 rooms, 93 pb	Restaurant, bar service
970-247-4431 Fax: 970-259-2208	Most CC, *Rated*, •	Sitting room, Jacuzzis, suites,
800-247-4431	C-yes/S-ltd/P-no/H-ltd	cable TV, meeting &
Rod Barker, Jim Bray	Spanish, French	conference facilities
All year		

"Colorado's finest Victorian hotel," the Strater is packed full of antiques, entertainment, history, quality and fun. Its full service features will pamper each visitor with a collection of amenities and services not found anywhere else in the country. E-mail: renate@strater.com *Web site:* strater.com

ESTES PARK ————————————————————————————

Anniversary Inn B&B, The	95-160-B&B	Full gourmet breakfast
1060 Mary's Lake Rd, 80517	4 rooms, 4 pb	Snacks
970-586-6200	Most CC, *Rated*, •	Sitting room, library,
Norma & Harry Menke	S-no/P-no/H-ltd	"Sweetheart" cottage, 3 rms
All year		with Jacuzzi tubs

Cozy, turn-of-the-century log home one mile from Rocky Mountain National Park. Come and be pampered. Member of BBIC and PAII. E-mail: estesharry@aol.com

Black Dog Inn B&B	90-160-B&B	Full gourmet breakfast
PO Box 4659, 80517	4 rooms, 4 pb	3 rms. w/Jacuzzi tubs, sitting
970-586-0374	Visa, MC, *Rated*, •	rooms, bungalow suites, and
Pete & Jane Princehorn	C-ltd/S-no/P-no/H-no	fireplaces
All year		

1910 mountain arts & crafts home snuggled among towering aspen & pine. View, antiques, cozy fireplace Library, 150+ movies, sitt. rooms. E-mail: blkdoginn@aol.com *Web site:* Blackdoginn.com

Eagle Cliff B&B	80-135-B&B	Full breakfast
Box 4312, 80517	3 rooms, 3 pb	Complimentary wine, snacks
970-586-5425 Fax: 970-577-0132	*Rated*, •	Hot tubs, golf, tennis,
800-414-0922	C-yes/S-no/P-no/H-no	horseback riding, hiking,
Nancy & Michael Conrin	Some Spanish	cross-country skiing, 2
All year		fireplaces

Enjoy our cozy and quaint B&B and join us for one of our favorite hikes. Jacuzzi tub & fireplace in cottage. Our backyard is the Rocky Mountain National Park! E-mail: m.conrin@worldnet.att.net

Mountain Home B&B	89-104-B&B	Full breakfast
663 Chapin Lane, 80517	2 rooms, 2 pb	Snacks
970-586-8676	Visa, MC, *Rated*, •	Sitting room, cable TV, front
888-686-4600	C-ltd/S-no/P-no/H-no	porch and deck in back
Johanna & Stan Gengler		
May-October		

Mountain Home B&B is nearly new but has old fashioned charm. You'll find the rooms decorated with antiques and stained glass & cozy places to relax. E-mail: mtnhomebnb@aol.com *Web site:* members.aol.com/mtnhomebnb/

Mountain Shadows B&B	185-B&B	Full breakfast
871 Riverside Dr, 80517	8 rooms, 8 pb	Snacks
970-577-0397 Fax: 970-577-1334	Visa, MC, Disc, *Rated*,	Jacuzzis, fireplaces, cable TV
Mark & Kelly Murray	•	
All year	S-ltd/P-no/H-yes	

Enjoy the personal touches of a B&B with the privacy and luxury of cabins. Each cabin includes: king sized bed, 2 person hot tub, fireplace, 2 person shower, TV and private deck. E-mail: mtnshadows@earthlink.net *Web site:* mountainshadowsbb.com

ESTES PARK

Quilt House B&B	55-65-B&B	Full breakfast
PO Box 339, 80517	4 rooms, 4 pb	Sitting room, library,
970-586-0427	*Rated*	handmade quilts on each,
Miriam & Hans Graetzer	C-ltd/S-no/P-no/H-ltd	bed
All year	German	

Clean, comfortable rms., hearty breakfast, free area maps, suggestions for hikes, scenic drives, rests., museums, shops, other activities. In gateway town to Rocky Mtn. Nat'l Park E-mail: hgraetzer@aol.com

Romantic RiverSong	145-275-B&B	Full breakfast
PO Box 1910, 80517	9 rooms, 9 pb	Afternoon tea, Dinner
970-586-4666 Fax: 970-577-0699	Visa, MC, *Rated*, •	available
Gary & Sue Mansfield, owners	C-ltd/S-no/P-no/H-yes	Sitting room, library, suites,
All year		fireplaces

Romantic RiverSong is Colorado's favorite romantic hideaway. Secluded on 27 wooded acres with ponds, trails and tree swings. E-mail: riversng@frii.com Web site: romanticriversong.com

Taharaa Mountain Lodge Inc	90-250-B&B	Full breakfast
PO Box 2586, 80517	12 rooms, 12 pb	Afternoon tea, wine, bar
970-577-0098 Fax: 970-577-0819	Most CC, *Rated*, •	Library, jacuzzis, suites,
800-597-0098	C-ltd/S-no/P-no/H-yes	fireplace, cable TV, indoor
Ken & Diane Harlan		sauna, sitting room
All year		

Taharra Mountain Lodge is A Luxury B&B offering unique accommodations of three suites & nine lodge rooms designed with the total comfort of our guests in mind. E-mail: info@taharaa.com Web site: taharaa.com/

EVERGREEN

Bears Inn B&B	90-160-B&B	Full breakfast
27425 Spruce Ln, 80439	11 rooms, 11 pb	Afternoon tea, snacks
303-670-1205 Fax: 303-670-8542	*Rated*	Sitting room, modem, fax,
800-863-1205	S-no/P-no/H-no	Use of executive office,
Darrell and Chris Jenkins		Murder mystery weekend
All year		

Historic 2-story mtn. lodge captures the charm of days-gone-by with hardwood floors & antiques throughout. E-mail: innkeepers@bearsinn.com Web site: bearsinn.com

Highland Haven Creekside	90-250-B&B	Full breakfast
4395 Independence Trail,	16 rooms, 16 pb	Afternoon tea, snacks
80439	Most CC, *Rated*	Sitting room, library,
303-674-3577 Fax: 303-674-9088	C-yes/S-no/P-no/H-no	bicycles, tennis courts, hot
800-459-2406		tubs, sauna, pool
Gail Riley & Tom Statzell		
All year		

Mountain hideaway with exquisite views of mountains, streams, towering pines and gardens. Stroll to quaint shops and fine dining on Main Street Evergreen. E-mail: thehaven@earthlink.net Web site: highlandhaven.com

Mountain View B&B	80-150-B&B	Full breakfast
PO Box 631, 80454	4 rooms, 4 pb	Afternoon tea
303-697-6896 Fax: 303-697-6896	Visa, MC, *Rated*, •	Sitting room, breathtaking
800-690-0434	C-ltd/S-no/P-no/H-no	view of Rockies
Graham & Ortrud Richardson	German	
All year		

Large 1920s mountain home with warm, homey atmosphere. Easy access to mountain parks. Elegant English tea and gourmet breakfast. E-mail: mtnviewbandb@juno.com Web site: fourcorners.com/co/inns/mtnview

FAIRPLAY

Hand Hotel B&B	60-B&B	Continental breakfast
PO Box 1059, 80440	11 rooms, 11 pb	Sitting room
719-836-3595 Fax: 719-836-1799	Most CC, •	
Dale & Kathy Fitting	C-yes/S-no/P-yes/H-no	
All year		

Genuine western hospitality high in the heart of the Rockies. Eleven rooms are each uniquely decorated, recalling the personalilties of the past.
E-mail: info@handhotel.com *Web site:* handhotel.com

FORT COLLINS

Porter House B&B Inn	79-115-B&B	Full breakfast
530 Main St, 80550	4 rooms, 4 pb	Lunch/dinner avail.,
970-686-5793 Fax: 970-686-7046	Visa, MC, AmEx,	afternoon tea
888-686-5793	*Rated*, •	Library, bicycles, conference
Tom & Marni Schmittling	C-ltd/S-no/P-no/H-no	center for 30, outdoor hot tub
All year		

Exquisite 1898 Queen Anne Victorian inn offering relaxation, comfort, beautiful surroundings & impeccable service. Many extra amenities and we serve gourmet meals including breakfast, lunch & dinner. E-mail: phbbinn@aol.com
Web site: travelguides.com/home/porterhouse/

FRISCO

Galena St. Mountain Inn	69-170-B&B	Full breakfast
PO Box 417, 80443	14 rooms, 14 pb	Afternoon snacks
970-668-9445 Fax: 970-668-1569	Most CC, *Rated*, •	Sitting room, library, hot
800-248-9138	C-yes/S-no/P-no/H-yes	tubs, sauna, meeting rooms
John & Sandra Gilfillan		
All year		

Striking Neo-mission-style furnishing, down comforters, windowseats, mountain views. Located minutes from Breckenridge, Keystone, Copper Mountain. E-mail: galenast@aol.com
Web site: colorado-bnb.com/galena

GLENWOOD SPRINGS

B&B on Mitchell Creek, The	90-B&B	Full breakfast
1686 Mitchell Creek Rd, 81601	1 rooms, 1 pb	Dinner, snacks
970-945-4002 Fax: 970-928-7842	Visa, *Rated*	Hiking trails, golf, horseback
Carole and Stan Rachesky	C-yes/S-no/P-ltd/H-no	riding, river rafting, massage
All year	Some Spanish	

Located in mountain setting, one private warm romantic suite; full breakfast served on deck overlooking rushing creek. Romantic dinners on request and vegetarian dining.
E-mail: carole@rof.net *Web site:* bbinternet.com/mitchell

GUNNISON

Mary Lawrence Inn, The	69-129-B&B	Full breakfast
601 N Taylor, 81230	7 rooms, 7 pb	Sack lunch (fee)
970-641-3343 Fax: 970-641-6719	Visa, MC, *Rated*, •	Three suites, many books,
B & D Parker/C & C Burback	C-yes/S-no/P-no/H-no	sitting room, hot tub in,
All year		gazebo, sunroom parlor

Our renovated home is inviting and comfortable; delectable breakfasts.
E-mail: marylinn@gunnison.com *Web site:* commerceteam.com/Mary.html

HOT SULPHUR SPRINGS

Casa Milagro B&B	120-160-B&B/MAP	Full breakfast
13628 County Rd 3, 80468	4 rooms, 4 pb	Homecooked dinners
970-725-3640 Fax: 970-725-3617	Most CC, •	available
888-632-8955	C-ltd/S-no/P-no/H-no	Overnight horse fac., hiking,
Lynn & Paul Schmaltz		skiing, golf, fly fishing
All year		instruction

Mountain getaway on the river- snowmobiling, snow shoeing, & only 18 mi. to hot springs! Vacation hemo dialysis facilities nearby for kidney patients. Ski rodeo & sleigh riding nearby. E-mail: casamilagro@rkymtnhi.com *Web site:* casamilagro.com

HOTCHKISS

Leroux Creek Inn, B&B	85-95-B&B	Full breakfast
PO Box 626, 81419	4 rooms, 4 pb	Snacks, complimentary wine
970-872-4746 Fax: 970-872-4746	Visa, MC, *Rated*	Sitting room, library,
Keith Hegarty	C-ltd/S-no/P-no/H-yes	bicycles, fly fishing
All year		instruction

Adobe house on 80 scenic acres; views of mountains, mesas, desert canyons; quiet for renewal of body and spirit. E-mail: leroux@tds.net

IDAHO SPRINGS

Brookside Inn	125-B&B	Full breakfast
2971 Fall River Rd, 80542	4 rooms, 4 pb	Afternoon tea
303-567-9610 Fax: 303-567-9611	Visa, MC, *Rated*, ●	Sitting room, library,
Dick & Sue Drummond	S-no/P-no/H-yes	Jacuzzis, fireplaces, cable
All year		TV, conference

Brookeside Inn was originally a hydro-electric plant built in 1910. Large great room with leather "fall asleep" furniture. Fireplace, right on river, picnic or barbeque on grounds. Each room has private entrance, bath, TV/VCR, coffee. Legendary breakfas E-mail: drummond@bewellnet.com *Web site:* brookside-inn.com

Miners Pick B&B	76-86-B&B	Full breakfast
PO Box 3156, 80452	3 rooms, 3 pb	Snacks
303-567-2975 Fax: 303-567-2975	Visa, MC, Disc, *Rated*,	Sitting room, fireplace, cable
800-567-2975	●	TV, fly fishing instruction
Deb & Ty Davies	C-ltd/S-no/P-no/H-no	
All year		

Centrally located in Colorado's Historic Mining country; built in 1895 and newly renovated; gourmet breakfast next to a cozy fire or while viewing big-horn sheep on our enclosed front porch.   E-mail: minerspik@bewellnet.com *Web site:* coloradovacation.com/bed/miners

LEADVILLE

Apple Blossom Inn, The	89-128-B&B	Full breakfast
120 W 4th St, 80461	5 rooms, 5 pb	Lunch/dinner available,
719-486-2141 Fax: 719-486-0994	Visa, MC, *Rated*, ●	snacks
800-982-9279	C-ltd/S-no/P-no/H-no	Homebaked brownies,
Maggie Senn		games provided, sitting room
All year		

Elegant & comfortable 1879 renovated banker's home. Beautiful & charming guest rooms in historic Leadville. Fabulous breakfast Fishing, golfing, hiking, biking, all in 1. E-mail: applebb@rmi.net *Web site:* colorado-bnb.com/abi

Delaware Hotel, The	70-130-B&B	Full breakfast
700 Harrison Ave, 80461	36 rooms, 36 pb	Continental plus breakfast
719-486-1418 Fax: 719-486-2214	Most CC, *Rated*, ●	Restaurant, bar service,
800-748-2004	S-ltd/P-no/H-ltd	lunch, dinner, library, sitting
Susan & Scott Brackett		room, hot tubs
All year		

"Award Winning" Historic Hotel. Period antiques, heirloom quilts, elegant Victorian lobby. Fine dining at Callaway's. Experience the charm of this 1860s Victorian mining town. E-mail: desk@delawarehotel.com *Web site:* delawarehotel.com

Ice Palace Inn B&B, The	79-139-B&B	Full breakfast
813 Spruce St, 80461	6 rooms, 6 pb	Afternoon tea, snacks
719-486-8272 Fax: 719-486-0345	Most CC, *Rated*, ●	Sitting room, library, biking,
800-754-2840	C-ltd/S-no/P-no/H-no	antiques, quilts, hiking,
Giles & Kami Kolakowski		tennis, fishing
All year		

This gracious Victorian inn was built in 1899 using the lumber from Leadville's famous Ice Palace.   E-mail: ipalace@sni.net *Web site:* icepalaceinn.com

Ice Palace Inn, Leadville, CO

LIMON

Midwest Country Inn
PO Box 550, 80828
719-775-2373
Harold & Vivian Lowe
All year

40-46-EP
32 rooms, 32 pb
Most CC, *Rated*, •
C-yes/S-yes/P-no/H-no

Restaurant—1 block
Sitting room, gift shop,
"listening" waterfall, and
"watching" fountain

*Beautiful rooms, oak antiques, stained glass, elegant wallpapered bathrooms. Quilts &
antiques in rooms. Near I-70, 1.5 hours from Denver and Colorado Springs. Train rides
available Saturday evenings.*

LONGMONT

Thompson House Inn
537 Terry St, 80501
303-651-6675 Fax: 303-682-5618
800-346-6675
Sheila Merrill   All year

89-124-B&B
8 rooms, 7 pb
Most CC, *Rated*, •
C-ltd/S-no/P-no/H-no

Full breakfast
Sitting room and "watching"
fountain

*Victorian elegance with modern amenities; furnished in period antiques. Gourmet break-
fast. Historic home located in heart of downtown. Quiet & serene.*

LOVELAND

Cattail Creek Inn B&B
2665 Abarr Dr, 80538
970-667-7600 Fax: 970-667-8968
800-572-2466
Sue & Harold Buchman
All year

95-155-B&B
8 rooms, 8 pb
Most CC, *Rated*, •
C-ltd/S-no/P-no/H-yes

Full breakfast
Complimentary wine
Sitting room, bicycles,
snacks, golf, trails, near art
galleries

*Designed and built to be a luxury inn, mountain views, golf course location, gourmet
breakfasts, bronze sculpture and original art work.   E-mail: ccinn@oneimage.com
Web site: colorado-bnb.com/cattailcreek*

Lovelander B&B Inn, The
217 W 4th St, 80537
970-669-0798 Fax: 970-669-0797
800-459-6694
Lauren and Gary Smith
All year

110-155-B&B
11 rooms, 11 pb
Most CC, *Rated*, •
C-ltd/S-no/P-no/H-ltd

Full gourmet breakfast
Comp. bev., champagne,
chocolates
Sitting room, library, meeting
& reception ctr., 3
whirlpool/deluxe rooms

*Victorian grace & old-fashioned hospitality from the heart of the Sweetheart City: a com-
munity of the arts. Gateway to the Rockies. Gardens with pond & waterfall. Complimentary
dessert.   E-mail: love@ezlink.com Web site: bbonline.com/co/lovelander*

LOVELAND ──────────────────────────────

Wild Lane B&B Inn	89-119-B&B	Full breakfast
5445 Wild Lane, 80538	5 rooms	In room tea and hot beverage
970-669-0303 Fax: 970-663-9100	Most CC,	Sitting room, library,
800-204-3320	C-ltd/S-no/P-no/H-ltd	fireplaces, accommodate
Steven & Lanette Wild		business travelers
All year		

Historic 1905 mansion with spacious rooms furnished in antiques. Full, gourmet breakfast. Extensively landscaped grounds with rose gardens. Unique gift shop and gallery. Nearby hiking trails.   E-mail: wildlane@info2000.net *Web site:* bbonline.com/co/wildlane

MANCOS ──────────────────────────────

Riversbend B&B	75-125-B&B	Full breakfast
42505 Hwy 160, 81328	5 rooms, 5 pb	Snacks, complimentary wine
970-533-7353 Fax: 970-533-1221	Most CC, *Rated*, •	Sitting room, hot tubs fishing,
800-699-8994	C-ltd/S-no/P-no/H-no	hiking, VCR
Gaye Curran		
All year		

Newly constructed log inn on banks of Mancos River. Located between Mesa Verde National Park and Durango Train. Sounds of river lull guests to sleep.
E-mail: riversbn@fone.net *Web site:* riversbend.com

Sundance Bear Lodge	80-160-B&B	Breakfast
Box 1045, 81328	5 rooms, 3 pb	Afternoon tea,
970-533-1504 Fax: 970-533-1507	C-yes/S-ltd/P-ltd/H-ltd	complimentary wine
Susan & Bob Scott		Snacks, sitting room,
All year		Jacuzzis, sauna, TV, office
		with computer

Enjoy Mesa Verde & mtn. views at sunset from decks or hot tub. 80+ acres to explore plus Nat'l Forest near.   E-mail: sue@sundancebear.com *Web site:* SundanceBear.com

OURAY ──────────────────────────────

China Clipper Inn	70-170-B&B	Delicious full breakfast
PO Box 801, 81427	11 rooms, 11 pb	Afternoon wine, snacks
970-325-0565 Fax: 970-325-4190	Visa, MC, *Rated*, •	Sitting room, library, hot
800-315-0565	C-ltd/S-no/P-no/H-yes	tubs, phones, TV,
Earl Yarbrough		champagne with 2 nights
All year		

Elegant, romantic, comfortable inn centrally located in Switzerland of America. In-room tubs for two, fireplaces, garden hot tub. Pampering, utter relaxation guaranteed.
E-mail: clipper@rmi.net *Web site:* colorado-bnb.com/clipper/

Chipeta Sun Lodge & Suites	75-205-B&B/EP	Full breakfast at Lodge
PO Box 2013, 81432	12 rooms, 12 pb	Afternoon tea, snacks
970-626-3737 Fax: 970-626-3715	Most CC, *Rated*, •	Rest. close by, hot tubs, sitt.
800-633-5868	C-ltd/S-no/P-no/H-ltd	rm., lib., pool, bikes, sauna
Lyle & Shari Braund		w/steam
All year		

CO- Top 10 Inns-Doris Kennedy '98. Central location for mtn. adventures, ski Telluride 1/2 price, disc't. golf pkgs., spa fac. with pool, hot springs nearby. Peaceful setting, enchanting mtn. views.   E-mail: info@chipeta.com *Web site:* chipeta.com

Christmas House B&B Inn	75-150-B&B	Full breakfast
PO Box 786, 81427	5 rooms, 5 pb	Afternoon tea, snacks
970-325-4992 Fax: 970-325-4992	Visa, MC, *Rated*, •	Sitting room, library,
888-325-XMAS	C-ltd/S-no/P-no/H-ltd	Jacuzzis, suites, fireplace,
George & Allyson Crosby		cable TV
All year		

Christmas is year round in this 1889 Ouray Victorian located in the heart of the 14,000 ft. San Juan Mountains. Enjoy all the amenities for a romantic getaway, anniversary or honeymoon!   E-mail: xmasbb@rmi.net *Web site:* ouraycolorado.com/xmasbb.html

The Manor B&B, Ouray, CO

OURAY

Manor B&B, The
PO Box 1165, 81427
970-325-4574
800-628-6946
John & Kay Gowins
All year

60-105-B&B
7 rooms, 7 pb
Visa, MC, *Rated*
C-ltd/S-no/P-no/H-no

Full breakfast
Aftn. tea, snacks, boxed
lunch-fee
Sitting room, Jacuzzis,
fireplaces, cable TV,
accommodate business
travelers

An elegant 1890 Victorian Inn, featuring peaceful places for rest, meditation, quiet reading or relaxed conversation amidst spectacular scenery; a step back in time with boutiful activities.　E-mail: themanor@ouraycolorado.net *Web site:* ouraycolorado.com/manor.html

St. Elmo Hotel
PO Box 751, 81427
970-325-4951
Fax: 970-325-0348
Dan & Sandy Lingenfelter
All year

69-110-B&B
9 rooms, 9 pb
Visa, MC, *Rated*, •
C-yes/S-ltd/P-no/H-no

Full breakfast
Restaurant
Comp. wine, coffee, tea,
piano, outdoor hot tub,
sauna, meeting room

Hotel & Bon Ton Restaurant surrounded by beautiful, rugged 14,000-ft. peaks. Furnished with antiques, stained glass & brass.　E-mail: steh@rmi.net *Web site:* stelmohotel.com

PAGOSA SPRINGS

Endaba Wilderness Retreat
1197A Perry Dr, 81147
970-731-4310
Fax: 970-731-4888
Bill & Lyn Gullette
All year

45-70-B&B
8 rooms, 2 pb
Visa, MC, *Rated*, •
C-yes/S-no/P-no/H-no
German, Spanish, Sign

Full breakfast
Some veg. dining
Sitting room, library, hot
tubs, barbeques, spa, game
rooms, lake fishing

Comfortable, secluded mountain lodge overlooking small lake, beautiful scenery and wildlife. Full breakfast.　E-mail: endaba@pagosa.net *Web site:* bbonline.com/co/endaba

PUEBLO

Abriendo Inn
300 W Abriendo Ave, 81004
719-544-2703 Fax: 719-542-6544
Kerrelyn Trent
All year

59-120-B&B
10 rooms, 10 pb
Most CC, *Rated*, •
C-ltd/S-no/P-no/H-no

Full breakfast
24 hr. snacks/beverages
All rooms have TV/phones,
rooms with double whirlpool

Distinctive lodging in park-like setting on national historic register. Voted first in Pueblo for "best weekend getaway." Walk to shops, restaurants and historic areas.
E-mail: abriendo@rmi.net *Web site:* bedandbreakfastinns.org/abriendo

PUEBLO

Baxter Inn, The	75-120-B&B	Full breakfast
325 W 15th St, 81003	5 rooms, 5 pb	Afternoon tea, snacks
719-542-7002	Most CC, *Rated*, •	Sitting room, library,
Dave & Lois Jones	C-yes/S-no/P-no/H-no	Whirlpool tubs, suites,
All year		fireplaces, CATV, bathrobes

Where your casual or business travel experience includes exceptional accommodations wrapped in the finest amenities and genuine hospitality.
E-mail: baxtrinn@rmi.net *Web site:* puebloonline.com/baxterinn

REDSTONE

Avalanche Ranch Cabins	70-175-EP	Bar service
12863 Hwy 133, 81623	12 rooms, 12 pb	Sitting room, library,
970-963-2846 Fax: 970-963-3141	Visa, MC, Disc, *Rated*,	bicycles, jacuzzi, snowshoes
877-963-9339	•	
Sharon Boucher	C-yes/S-no/P-yes/H-no	
All year		

Imagine a "Vermont picture postcard" in the heart of the Colorado Rockies; Cozy log cabins nestled on 45 acres.   E-mail: aranch@rof.net *Web site:* avalancheranch.com

McClure House B&B	75-195-B&B	Full breakfast
22995 Hwy 133, 81623	4 rooms, 4 pb	Afternoon tea
970-963-1020 Fax: 970-963-1020	Visa, MC, •	Sitting room, suites, satellite
800-303-3929	C-yes/S-no/P-no/H-no	TV & fireplaces in game
Wally & Judie Melby		room & Great Room.
All year		

Serenity surrounds you as you enjoy the sounds of the Crystal River. Beautiful mountain views at our romantic B&B. Fish, bike, hike, or just relax. Full breakfast. European antiques. Lovely decks.   E-mail: McClure@Sopris.net *Web site:* mcclurehouse.com

SALIDA

River Run Inn B&B	60-150-B&B	Full country breakfast
8495 Country Road 160, 81201	7 rooms, 3 pb	Complimentary tea, coffee,
719-539-3818	Visa, MC, *Rated*, •	cider
800-385-6925	C-ltd/S-ltd/P-no/H-no	Library, fishing, dorm room
Virginia Nemmers		available, reunions, stocked
All year		trout pond, view

Secluded area on Arkansas River. Turn of the century home, antiques. Special dinners for groups, meetings, events. Enjoy the four seasons.   E-mail: riverrun@amigo.net
Web site: riverruninn.com

Tudor Rose, The	50-145-B&B	Full breakfast
PO Box 89, 81201	6 rooms, 4 pb	Lunch (fee), afternoon
719-539-2002 Fax: 719-530-0345	Visa, MC, Disc, *Rated*,	refreshments
800-379-0889	•	Sitting room, library, hot
Jon & Terre' Terrell	C-yes/S-ltd/P-ltd/H-no	tubs, horse & dog facilities
All year		

Stately country manor on 37 acre mountain paradise. Elegant comfort. Min. from town, skiing, rafting. Horses welcome.   E-mail: tudorose@amigo.net
Web site: bbonline.com/co/tudorose/

SILVERTHORNE

Mountain Vista B&B	55-100-B&B	Full breakfast
PO Box 1398, 80498	3 rooms, 1 pb	Full breakfast, snacks
970-468-7700	Most CC,	Sitting room, recreation
800-333-5165	C-ltd/S-no/P-yes/H-no	center near, horse & dog
Sandy Ruggaber		facilities
All year		

Large, contemporary mountain home with guest kitchen. Winter and summer activities at Keystone, Breckenridge, Copper Mountain and Vail nearby.   E-mail: mtnvistabnb@juno.com
Web site: colorado-mtnvista.com

STEAMBOAT SPRINGS ───────────────────────────

Sky Valley Lodge	69-175-B&B	Full breakfast in winter
PO Box 3132, 80477	24 rooms, 24 pb	Continental plus breakfast-
970-879-7749 Fax: 970-879-7752	Visa, MC, AmEx,	summer
800-499-4759	*Rated*, •	Restaurant, bar, sitting room,
Jon Hardman and Beth	C-yes/S-no/P-no/H-no	library, hot tub, sauna.
Ziesenis		
All year		

Nestled in the side of the mountains, this English country manor-style lodge affords a sweeping view of the valley below. Nearby skiing, dining, shopping, hiking.
E-mail: info@steamboat-lodging.com *Web site:* steamboat-lodging.com/skyvalley.html

Steamboat Valley	85-158-B&B	Full breakfast
Guesthouse	4 rooms, 4 pb	Afternoon tea
PO Box 773815, 80477	Visa, MC, *Rated*, •	Library, Hot air balloon,
970-870-9017 Fax: 970-879-0361	C-ltd/S-no/P-no/H-no	swim, bike nearby, golf,
800-530-3866		public hot springs, ski
George & Alice Lund All year		

Hilltop log house. Scandinavian decor, charming wallpapers & antiques, spectacular views, fireplace, TV, piano. Homemade breakfasts.   E-mail: george@steamboatvalley.com
Web site: steamboatvalley.com

TELLURIDE ───────────────────────────

Alpine Inn B&B	80-230-B&B	Full breakfast
PO Box 2398, 81435	8 rooms	Afternoon tea, wine—winter
970-728-6282 Fax: 970-728-3424	Visa, MC, *Rated*, •	Sitting room with fireplace,
800-707-3344	C-ltd/S-no/P-no/H-no	hot tub, library
Denise & John Weaver		
All year		

Charming downtown Victorian. Enjoy a full breakfast in the sunroom. Relax in the hot tub with sunset views. Walk to slopes, gondola, and hiking trails.   E-mail: info@alpineinn.com
Web site: alpineinn.com

Bear Creek B&B	75-192-B&B	Full breakfast
PO Box 2369, 81435	9 rooms, 9 pb	Tea, snacks, wine
970-728-6681 Fax: 970-728-3636	Visa, MC, Disc, *Rated*,	Jacuzzi, fireplace, cable TV,
800-388-7064	•	cedar-lined sauna, steam
Colleen & Tom Whiteman	C-ltd/S-no/P-no/H-no	room.
All year		

European ambiance coupled with Old West Hospitality.   E-mail: info@bearcreektelluride.com
Web site: bearcreektelluride.com

Johnstone Inn	90-130-B&B	Full breakfast
PO Box 546, 81435	8 rooms, 8 pb	Ski season refreshments
970-728-3316 Fax: 970-728-0724	Visa, MC, AmEx,	Sitting room w/fireplace,
800-752-1901	*Rated*, •	games, outdoor hot tub,
Bill Schiffbauer	C-ltd/S-no/P-no/H-no	manicure on premises
Ski season & summer		

Restored historic Victorian boarding house in center of Telluride. Walk to lifts, shops, and everything else. A warm, comfortable inn in a friendly mountain town.   E-mail: bschiff@
rmii.com *Web site:* johnstoneinn.com

TWIN LAKES ───────────────────────────

Mount Elbert Lodge	65-95-B&B	Continental plus breakfast
PO Box 40, 81251	4 rooms, 4 pb	Sitting room, fishing, hiking,
719-486-0594 Fax: 719-486-2236	Most CC, *Rated*, •	snowshoeing, skiing
800-381-4433	C-yes/S-no/P-no/H-no	
Scott Body & Laura Downing		
All year		

Escape reality, surround yourself with mountain views, fish our stream or climb to the mountain's peak, whatever is your fancy   E-mail: mtelbert@amigo.net
Web site: colorado-bnb.com/mtelbert

VAIL ───

Alpine Hideaway B&B, The	125-165-B&B	Full gourmet breakfast
PO Box 788, 80444	3 rooms, 3 pb	Sitting room, Jacuzzis, suites,
303-569-2800	Visa, MC, *Rated*	fireplaces
800-490-9011	S-no/P-no/H-no	
Dawn Janov		
All year		

Mountain contemporary has a rock garden, pond. Above the lake in historic Georgetown, Colorado, each room has a fireplace and Jacuzzi tub. Spectacular views down the valley with steep mountains rising on either side.   E-mail: aahideaway@aol.com
Web site: entertain.com/wedgwood/hide.html

Black Bear Inn of Vail	105-225-B&B	Full breakfast
2405 Elliott Rd, 81657	12 rooms, 12 pb	Afternoon tea, snacks
970-476-1304 Fax: 970-476-0433	Visa, MC, Disc, *Rated*,	Sitting room, Jacuzzis,
David & Jessie Edeen	•	conference facilities
Closed end April-Mem.day	C-yes/S-no/P-no/H-yes	
	German	

Handcrafted log inn along Gore Creek. Spacious rooms, all with private baths, down comforters, log or brass beds. Outdoor hot tub. Game room with pool table. Hearty breakfasts. Afternoon snacks.   Web site: vail.net/blackbear

Eagle Street B&B	129-169-B&B	Full breakfast
PO Box 820, 81645	4 rooms, 4 pb •	Afternoon tea, snacks, wine
970-827-9647 Fax: 970-827-5590	Visa, MC, AmEx, •	Sitting room, Jacuzzis, suites,
888-646-8876	S-no/P-no/H-no	fireplace, cable TV
Tom & Cathy Sullivan		
All year		

Luxury accommodations located on the banks of the Eagle River in the old town of the Vail Valley only 5 miles to the Vail and Beaver Creek resorts. Each room features a large river rock fireplace, Jacuzzi tub for 2.   E-mail: eaglestbb@vail.net *Web site:* eaglestbb.com

Intermountain B&B	75-175-B&B	Continental plus breakfast
2754 Basingdale Blvd, 81657	2 rooms, 2 pb	Snacks
970-476-4935 Fax: 970-476-7926	*Rated*, •	Hot tubs, sitting room, cable
Kay & Sepp Cheney	C-ltd/S-no/P-no/H-no	TV
All year	German	

Contemporary home two miles from ski lifts on free bus route. Delicious home-baked pastries, fresh fruit and gourmet coffees.   E-mail: vailbb@compuserve.com
Web site: vail.net/vailbb

Lazy Ranch B&B, The	70-125-B&B	Full breakfast
PO Box 404, 81632	4 rooms, 1 pb	Afternoon tea, snacks
970-926-3876 Fax: 970-926-3876	Visa, MC, Disc, •	Horses-60 acres, library,
Buddy & Linda Calhoun	C-ltd/S-ltd/P-yes/H-yes	sitting room, lots of farm
All year		animals

Charming Victorian on 60 acres. Soft featherbeds, private trout stream, horseback rides, quiet, peaceful, romantic.   Web site: vail.net/lazyranch

West Beaver Creek Lodge	99-200-B&B	Full breakfast
PO Box 7626, 81620	9 rooms, 0 pb	Sitting room, Jacuzzis, suites,
940-949-9073 Fax: 970-949-9091	Visa, MC, *Rated*, •	cable TV, accommodate
888-795-1061	C-yes/S-no/P-no/H-ltd	business travelers
Theresa & Robert Borg		
All year		

E-mail: wbclodge@vail.net *Web site:* wbclodge.com

WINTER PARK

Alpen Rose B&B
PO Box 769, 80482
970-726-5039 Fax: 970-726-0993
800-531-1373
Robin & Rupert Sommerauer
Closed Oct.-Nov 15

65-145-B&B
8 rooms, 6 pb
Most CC, *Rated*, •
C-ltd/S-no/P-no/H-no
German

Full breakfast
Afternoon tea, snacks
Sitting room, library, outdoor
hot tub, beautiful mountain
view

Rocky Mountain hideaway with breathtaking views of The Continental Divide. Close to everything, but hidden away, with Austrian decor and hospitality. E-mail: robinann@rkymtnhi.com *Web site:* bbhost.com/alpenroasebb

Grand Victorian, The
PO Box 1045, 80482
970-726-5881 Fax: 970-725-5602
800-204-1170
Bonnie M. Warren
Closed May 1 - May 27

125-440-B&B
10 rooms, 10 pb
Most CC, *Rated*, •
S-no/P-no/H-yes

Full breakfast
Aftn. tea, snacks, wine,
dinner ₍
Sitt. rm., lib., Jacuzzi, suites,
fplcs., CATV, accom.
business travelers

Ultra luxurious B&B with on-site "Boutique Organics Spa" of Grand Neo-Victorian architectural style, distinguished as a CO "Top 10" B&B in 1998 by respected travel writer Doris Kennedy, noted for its impeccable housekeeping, value & service! Web site: winterpark-info.com/frame.html?target=507

Pines Inn, The
PO Box 15, 80482
970-726-5416 Fax: 970-726-1062
800-824-9127
Jan & Lee Reynolds
All year

85-130-B&B
8 rooms, 6 pb
Most CC, *Rated*, •
C-yes/S-no/P-no/H-ltd

Full breakfast
Afternoon tea, snacks
Library, bicycles, tennis
court, Jacuzzis, suites,
fireplaces, cable TV.

Comfortable, relaxed inn, close to slopes, but well-located for summer biking and golfing. We will recommend our favorite restaurants. E-mail: lee.reynolds@cwixmail.com *Web site:* winter-park-lodging.com

Whistle Stop B&B
PO Box 418, 80482
Fax: 970-726-0905
888-829-2632
Susan Stone
All year

65-155-B&B
3 rooms, 3 pb
Visa, MC,
C-ltd/S-no/P-no/H-no
Russian, Spanish

Full breakfast
Aftn. tea, snacks
Sun room, tennis court,
wood stove, cable TV,
hydrotherapy spa

Casual and inviting with downhome breakfasts, bottomless cookie jar, free shuttle, miles of ski/hike/bike trails, plus rejuvenating hydrotherapy spa. Hosts welcome guests from around the world. E-mail: whistle@rkymtnhi.com *Web site:* bestinns.net/usa/co/whistlestop.html

Connecticut

BARKHAMSTED

Rose & Thistle B&B
24 Woodland Acres, 06022
860-379-4744
Lorraine Longmoor
All year

115-B&B
4 rooms, 4 pb
Rated
C-ltd/S-ltd/P-ltd/H-yes

Full breakfast
10 acres, trout pond,
swimming, paddleboat,
skating, hikes, skiing

Breathe new life from garden & woods. Capture timelessness in a half-timbered English Cottage high on the edge of secluded valley. Gameroom with Inglenook fireplace and kitchen.

BRANFORD

Abigail's B&B
85 Cherry Hill Rd, 06405
203-483-1612
888-994-ABBY
Cathy & Lenny Pellegrino
All year

110-B&B
3 rooms, 3 pb
Visa, MC, Disc, •
C-ltd/S-no/P-ltd/H-no

Full breakfast on weekends
Continental breakfast on
weekdays
Sitting room, library, suites,
fireplace, cable TV, AC,
ceiling fans

1870's Center Hall Colonial, furnished with antiques and family heirlooms, large bedrooms with private baths, two bedrooms connect via sunporch as a suite. Full country breakfast on weekends, continental breakfast on weekdays.   E-mail: abigailsb-b@erols.com

BRISTOL

Chimney Crest Manor
5 Founders Dr, 06010
860-582-4219 Fax: 860-584-5903
Cynthia Cimadamore
All year

95-165-B&B
4 rooms, 4 pb
Visa, MC, *Rated*, •
C-ltd/S-no/P-no/H-no

Full breakfast
Sitting room, piano, 1 suite
with fireplace, 1 suite with
thermal spa

32-rm Tudor mansion on National Historic Register. 20 minutes from Hartford & Litchfield. Walking distance to Carousel Museum. Mobil 3-star rating. Small meetings and weddings E-mail: chimnycrst@aol.com

CHESTER

123 Main B&B
123 Main St, 06412
860-526-3456 Fax: 860-526-1003
Chris & Randy Allison
All year

85-125-B&B
5 rooms, 5 pb
Visa, MC, AmEx, Disc,
C-ltd/S-no/P-no/H-no

Full breakfast
Snacks

Chester has specialty shops and acclaimed restaurants for every taste from funky bistro to French with four stars   E-mail: rallinson@snet.net Web site: 123main.net

Inn at Chester
318 W Main St, 06417
860-526-9541 Fax: 860-526-4307
800-949-STAY
Deborah L. Moore
All year

105-215-B&B
48 rooms, 48 pb
Visa, MC, AmEx,
Rated, •
C-yes/S-yes/P-ltd/H-yes

Continental plus breakfast
Lunch/dinner available,
tavern
Bicycles, tennis, sauna,
sitting room, library, piano,
entertainment

The inn, on 15 acres centered around a 1776 farmhouse, abounds with fireplaces, antiques, and public areas for resting, reading, refreshment.   E-mail: innkeeper@innatchester.com Web site: innatchester.com/

CLINTON

Captain Dibbell House B&B
21 Commerce St, 06413
860-669-1646 Fax: 860-669-2300
888-889-6882
Helen & Ellis Adams
Closed Jan.-March (call)

79-109-B&B
4 rooms, 4 pb
Visa, MC, *Rated*, •
C-ltd/S-ltd/P-no/H-no

Full breakfast
Complimentary
refreshments & mug
Sitting room, gazebo,
bicycles, horseshoes, beach
chairs & towels

Our 1866 sea captain's Victorian offers comfortable lodging and home-baked savories to guests while they discover the charms of our coastal towns. A/C in summer months.

DEEP RIVER

Riverwind Inn
209 Main St, 06417
860-526-2014 Fax: 860-526-0875
Barbara Barlow, Bob Bucknall
All year

95-175-B&B
8 rooms, 8 pb
Visa, MC, *Rated*
C-ltd/S-yes/P-no/H-no

Full breakfast
Complimentary sherry
8 common rooms, piano,
classic British, limousine
service

Furnished in country antiques. Smithfield ham with breakfast, fireplace in dining room. New England charm and southern hospitality.   Web site: innformation.com/ct/riverwind

EAST HADDAM

Bishopsgate Inn
PO Box 290, 06423
860-873-1677 Fax: 860-873-3898
The Kagel Family
All year

100-150-B&B/MAP
6 rooms, 6 pb
Visa, MC, *Rated*
C-ltd/S-no/P-ltd/H-no

Full breakfast
Dinner available
Sitting room, library,
fireplaces

Circa 1818. This colonial house is furnished with period antiques and each floor of the Inn has a sitting area where guests often relax with a good book. Four of the guest rooms include a fireplace and the suite has a sauna. E-mail: ctkagel@bishopsgate.com
Web site: bishopsgate.com

ESSEX

Griswold Inn, The
36 Main St, 06426
860-767-1776 Fax: 860-767-0481
Douglas W. Paul
All year

120-195-B&B
28 rooms, 28 pb
Visa, MC, AmEx, *Rated*
C-yes/S-yes/P-ltd/H-yes

Continental breakfast
Restaurant, bar service
Lunch & dinner available,
sitting room, library, Suite
overlooking garden

Located in center of historic Essex. Renowned marine art collection. Entertainment nightly from Griswold Inn Banjo Band to Cliff Haslem's Sea Chantys. E-mail: griswoldinn@snet.net
Web site: griswoldinn.com

FARMINGTON

Farmington Inn, The
827 Farmington Ave, 06032
860-677-2821 Fax: 860-677-8332
800-648-9804
Elisa R. Aiello
All year

109-139-B&B
72 rooms, 72 pb
Most CC, *Rated*, •
C-yes/S-yes/P-yes/H-yes
Spanish, Polish

Continental plus breakfast
Lunch/dinner available,
snacks
Aftn. tea, comp. wine, rest.,
sitt. rm., lib., tennis, pool,
fireplaces

The Farmington Inn is a beautiful two story, 72 luxurious guest rm., elegant B&B. Decor of New England traditional. Furnished with antiques & unique local paintings, 4-star restaurant. E-mail: classic.htl@aol.com

GLASTONBURY

Butternut Farm
1654 Main St, 06033
860-633-7197 Fax: 860-659-1758
Don Reid
All year

79-99-B&B
5 rooms, 5 pb
AmEx, *Rated*
C-yes/S-ltd/P-no/H-no

Full breakfast
Complimentary wine,
chocolates
Piano, 8 fireplaces, sitting
rooms, library, bicycle

An 18th-century jewel furnished with period antiques. Attractive grounds with herb gardens and ancient trees, dairy goats and prize chickens. 10 minutes from Hartford.

IVORYTON

Copper Beech Inn, The
46 Main St, 06442
860-767-0330 Fax: 860-767-7840
888-809-2056
Sally & Eldon Senner
Closed Tuesdays Jan-Mar.

110-180-B&B
13 rooms, 13 pb
Most CC, *Rated*
C-ltd/S-no/P-no/H-ltd

Continental plus breakfast
French country dining
TV, Jacuzzi, meeting rm.,
lovely gardens & grounds,
Victorian conservatory

A hostelry where even a short visit is a celebration of good living. One of few 4-star restaurants in Connecticut. The feel of country elegance
Web site: copperbeechinn.com

KENT

Fife 'n Drum Rest. & Inn
PO Box 188, 06757
860-927-3509 Fax: 860-927-4595
Elissa Potts, Dolph Traymon
All year

85-110-EP
8 rooms, 7 pb
Visa, MC, AmEx, *Rated*
S-yes/P-ltd/H-ltd
Sp., It., Fr., Croatian

Restaurant
Bar, lunch, dinner,
telephones in rooms, newly
redecorated

Family owned and operated for 22 years and located in the center of rural Kent. "Excellent restaurant and wine list"—Wine Spectator.

Copper Beach Inn, Ivoryton, CT

KILLINGWORTH

Acorn Bed and Breakfast	95-105-B&B	Full breakfast
628 Rt 148, 06419	2 rooms, 2 pb	Complimentary wine
860-663-2214 Fax: 860-663-2214	Most CC,	Jacuzzis, swimming pool,
Carole & Richard Pleines	C-ltd/S-no/P-no/H-no	fireplace in living room,
All year		newly redecorated

Country setting, furnished in antiques, antique shop on premises. Our dining room features old hickory furniture.   E-mail: richard@acornbedandbreakfast.com
Web site: acornbedandbreakfast.com/

LEDYARD

Applewood Farms Inn B&B	125-290-B&B	Full country breakfast
528 Colonel Ledyard Hwy,	5 rooms, 5 pb	Coffee, tea, aperitifs
06339	Most CC, *Rated*, •	Fireplaces, Jacuzzi, USGA
860-536-2022 Fax: 860-536-6015	C-ltd/S-ltd/P-yes/H-no	designed putting green on
800-717-4262		property
Tom & Frankie Betz All year		

Historic farmhouse with rose & traditional gardens, quiet, serene with period & antique furniture. On 33 acres between Mystic & Casinos. Resident horse & Basset Hounds. E-mail: applewoodfarms@yahoo.com *Web site:* visitmystic.com/applewoodfarmsinn

Mare's Inn B&B, The	100-175-B&B	Full breakfast
333 Col Ledyard Hwy, 06339	5 rooms, 5 pb	pool, sauna, tennis courts,
860-572-7556 Fax: 860-572-2976	Most CC, *Rated*, •	common Jacuzzi
Marilyn Richard	C-ltd/S-ltd/P-ltd/H-ltd	
All year		

7 miles to Foxwoods & 3 miles to Mystic. Home away from home, great breakfasts & hospitality. Private baths, very comfortable. Lots of common space, 2.2 acres. Three rooms have fireplaces.   E-mail: maresinn@aol.com *Web site:* bestinns.net/usa/ct/maresinn.html

MADISON

Tidewater Inn	90-170-B&B	Full breakfast
949 Boston Post Rd, 06443	9 rooms, 9 pb	Complimentary wine
203-245-8457 Fax: 203-318-0265	Visa, MC, AmEx, *Rated*	Sitting room, Fireplaces,
Jean Foy & Rich Evans	C-ltd/S-no/P-no/H-no	antiques, Madison Beach
All year		passes

Explore coastal Connecticut. Elegant, cozy inn, circa 1880. Antiques and estate furnishings. Fireplaces, canopy beds, English garden. Beaches 1 mile.   Web site: madisonct.com/tidewater/

MIDDLEBURY

Tucker Hill Inn	85-135-B&B	Full breakfast
96 Tucker Hill Rd, 06762	4 rooms, 2 pb	Tea & coffee served
203-758-8334 Fax: 203-598-0652	Visa, MC, *Rated*, •	Sitt. room, library, A/C,
Susan & Richard Cebelenski	C-yes/S-no/P-no/H-no	TV/VCR with free movies,
All year		small conf. facilities

Large colonial-style inn near Village Green. Large, spacious period rooms. Hearty breakfast. Near sights & sports.   E-mail: tuckerhill@compuserve.com

MYSTIC

Adams House B&B	95-175-B&B	Full breakfast
382 Cow Hill Rd, 06355	7 rooms, 7 pb	Sitting room, fireplaces,
860-572-9551 Fax: 860-572-9552	Visa, MC, *Rated*	garden cottage
Gregory & Mary Lou Peck	C-ltd/S-no/P-no/H-no	
All year		

Historic 1750s home located 1 1/2 miles from downtown Mystic; close to seaport & aquarium. Surrounded by lush greenery and flower beds.   Web site: visitmystic.com/adamshouse

Comolli's Guest House	75-125-B&B	Continental breakfast
36 Bruggeman Place, 06355	2 rooms, 1 pb	Kitchen privileges
860-536-8723	C-ltd/S-no/P-no/H-no	TV in rooms, nearby many
Dorothy Comolli		activities, green on property
All year		

Immaculate home, situated on a quiet hill overlooking the Mystic Seaport complex; convenient to Olde Mystick Village & the Aquarium. Sightseeing & restaurant information provided.

Harbour Inne & Cottage	75-250-EP	Kitchen privileges
15 Edgemont St, 06355	5 rooms, 5 pb	Sitting room, A/C, canoe &
860-572-9253	•	boats, cable TV, fireplaces,
Charles Lecouras, Jr.	C-yes/S-yes/P-yes/H-no	hot tub
All year	Greek	

Small inn plus 3-room cottage on Mystic River. Walk to seaport & all attractions. Waterfront tables, canoeing and boating. Cottage with fireplace. Waterfront gazebo.
Web site: visitmystic.com/HarbourInne

Homespun Farm B&B	60-110-B&B	Full breakfast
306 Preston Rd, 06351	2 rooms, 1 pb	Snacks
860-376-5178 Fax: 860-376-5587	Visa, MC, Disc,	Sitting room, library, suites,
888-889-6673	C-yes/S-ltd/P-ltd/H-ltd	cable TV, conference, golf,
Kate Bauer		hiking
All year		

Homespun Farm bed and breakfast, a quintessential 1740 colonial farmhouse with beautifully kept grounds that include part of the 259 year old farm's apple orchard.
E-mail: innkeeper@homespunfarm.com Web site: homespunfarm.com

Inn at Harbor Hill Marina	85-165-B&B	Continental plus breakfast
60 Grand St, 06357	8 rooms, 8 pb	Complimentary wine
860-739-0331 Fax: 860-691-3078	Visa, MC, AmEx,	Sitting room, fireplaces,
Ed & Debbie Gottert	*Rated*, •	cable TV, kayaks, beach
All year	C-yes/S-no/P-no/H-no	passes, gardens
	French, Italian, Spanish	

The only thing we overlook is the water! Panoramic views of the Niantic River and/or views of Long Island Sound from our rooms or from wicker seating on wraparound porch or Adirondack chairs.   E-mail: info@innharborhill.com Web site: innharborhill.com

MYSTIC

Old Mystic Inn, The
PO Box 634, 06372
860-572-9422 Fax: 860-572-9954
Peter & Mary Knight
All year

95-165-B&B
8 rooms, 8 pb
Visa, MC, AmEx,
Rated, •
C-ltd/S-no/P-no/H-no

Full country breakfast
Afternoon tea
Sat. eve. wine & cheese,
sitting room, bicycles, comp.
wine on spec. occ.

Located minutes from Mystic Seaport and Aquarium, this charming inn offers a complete country breakfast to guests. New larger side porch in 1998 and two more fireplaces in 1999.   E-mail: oldmysticinn@aol.com Web site: visitmystic.com/oldmysticinn/

Pequot Hotel B&B
711 Cow Hill Rd, 06355
860-572-0390
Fax: 860-536-3380
Nancy Mitchell
All year

95-160-B&B
3 rooms, 3 pb
Visa, MC, *Rated*, •
C-ltd/S-no/P-no/H-no

Full country breakfast
Complimentary beverages
Picnic lunch, 2 sitting rooms,
library, A/C, whirlpool tubs

Authentically restored 1840s stagecoach stop; friendly, casual elegance amongst period antiques. Relaxing parlors, romantic fireplaces, & a welcoming screened porch. E-mail: pequothtl@aol.com Web site: visitmystic.com/pequothotel

Red Brook Inn
PO Box 237, 06372
860-572-0349
800-290-5619
Ruth Keyes
All year

95-189-B&B
9 rooms, 9 pb
Visa, MC, *Rated*
C-yes/S-no/P-no/H-no

Full country breakfast
Comp. wine, tea, cider
Sitting room, library,
bicycles, patio, A/C,
whirlpool, gardens

The inn strikes a nice balance between authentic handsome furnishings & comfort. Surrounded by wooded acres, convenient to old New England sights. National Historic Register   E-mail: redbrookin@aol.com Web site: virtualcities.com/ct/redbrookinn.htm

Six Broadway Inn
6 Broadway Ave, 06355
860-536-6010
Fax: 860-536-6010
888-44MYSTIC
Joan & Jerry Sullivan
All year

90-225-B&B
5 rooms, 5 pb
Most CC, *Rated*
C-ltd/S-no/P-no/H-no

Continental plus breakfast
Afternoon tea
Library, fireplace, A/C

The only B&B in historic downtown Mystic. Romantic, luxury, European elegance. Belgian and French antique bedrooms. Walk to Seaport Museum, shopping, river, dining and rail station.   E-mail: aprilanthony@compuserve.com Web site: visitmystic.com/sixbroadway

Steamboat Inn
73 Steamboat Wharf, 06355
860-536-8300 Fax: 860-536-9528
Diana Stadtmiller
All year

100-285-B&B
10 rooms, 10 pb
Most CC, *Rated*, •
C-ltd/S-no/P-no/H-yes

Continental plus breakfast
Restaurant
Sitting room, sailing trips,
A/C, whirlpool tubs

Elegant and intimate, on the waterfront in historic downtown Mystic. Shopping, restaurants and seaport within walking distance.   E-mail: sbwharf@aol.com Web site: visitmystic.com/steamboat/

Whitehall Mansion
42 Whitehall Ave., 06355
860-572-7280 Fax: 860-572-4724
800-572-3993
Waterford Hotel Group, Inc
All year

B&B
5 rooms, 5 pb
Visa, MC, AmEx,
Rated, •
S-no/P-no/H-yes

Continental breakfast
Complimentary wine
Sitting room, fireplaces,
cable TV, bathtub jets, wine
& cheese socials

All rooms are authentically decorated with antique furnishings, modern baths with Jacuzzi jet tubs, fireplaces.   E-mail: jzaske@connix.com Web site: wwitghutels.com

NEW MILFORD

Barton House, The	95-B&B	Full breakfast
34 E St, 06776	2 rooms, 2 pb	Snacks
860-354-3535 Fax: 860-350-0871	Visa, MC, AmEx,	Sitting room, library, piano,
Ray & Rachel Barton	C-ltd/S-no/P-no/H-no	fireplaces, cable TV, 3 acres
All year		with brook

Extra touches in room, fresh flowers, bottled water, fruits, romantic candlelight breakfast in formal/informal setting. Vegetable/cutting gardens. Each room tastefully decorated, A/C, ceiling fan, TV.   E-mail: BartonHou@aol.com

Heritage Inn Litchfield	95-105-B&B	Full breakfast
34 Bridge St, 06776	20 rooms, 20 pb	Cable TV, accommodate
860-354-8883 Fax: 860-350-5543	Most CC, *Rated*, •	business travelers
800-311-6294	C-yes/S-ltd/P-no/H-ltd	
Ray Barton		
All year		

A former tobaco warehouse, on national historic register, retains the charm of yesteryear, with all modern amenities. Walking distance to: New England's most beautiful village green, shops, restaurants, movie theater, churches, Housatonic River.

Homestead Inn, The	80-105-B&B	Continental plus breakfast
5 Elm St, 06776	15 rooms, 15 pb	Sitting room, front porch,
860-354-4080 Fax: 860-354-7046	Visa, MC, AmEx,	gardens, in village center
Rolf & Peggy Hammer	*Rated*, •	
All year	C-ltd/S-ltd/P-no/H-no	

Small country inn in picturesque New England town next to village green, near shops, churches, restaurants, antiques, galleries, hiking, crafts.   Web site: homesteadct.com

NEW PRESTON

Boulders Inn	225-345-B&B	Full breakfast
PO Box 2575, 06777	17 rooms, 17 pb	Restaurant, bar, dinner
860-868-0541 Fax: 860-868-1925	Visa, MC, AmEx,	Sitting room, bicycles, tennis,
800-552-6853	*Rated*, •	private beach, boats, hiking
Kees & Ulla Adema	C-ltd/S-yes/P-no/H-yes	trail
All year	German, Dutch, French	

Exquisitely furnished country inn in spectacular location, viewing Lake Waramaug. Lakeview dining inside or on terrace.   E-mail: boulders@bouldersinn.com *Web site:* bouldersinn.com/

NORFOLK

Blackberry River Inn	75-175-B&B	Full country breakfast
536 Greenwoods Rd W, 06058	19 rooms, 9 pb	Restaurant, bar
860-542-5100 Fax: 860-542-1763	Most CC, *Rated*, •	Sitt. rm., library, pool,
800-414-3636	C-yes/S-yes/P-no/H-ltd	Jacuzzi, 27 acres, lawns, 3
Jeanneth Angel		miles of hiking trails
All year		

A 225-year-old Colonial inn in rural northwest Connecticut serving fine continental country cuisine. 19 rooms, some with fireplaces. Hammocks, big old maple trees, A/C. A great country getaway!   E-mail: blackberry.river.inn@snet.net

Greenwoods Gate B&B Inn	175-250-B&B	Full gourmet breakfast
PO Box 491, 06058	4 rooms, 4 pb	Complimentary wine,
860-542-5439 Fax: 860-542-5897	•	afternoon tea
George E. Schumaker	C-ltd/S-no/P-no/H-no	Sitting room, library,
All year		fireplaces, antiques,
		tennis/swimming nearby

Warm hospitality greets you in this beautifully restored 1797 Colonial home. 4 exquisitely appointed guest suites (each with private bath), 1 with Jacuzzi. Sumptuous breakfasts.
Web site: greenwoodsgate.com

NORFOLK

Manor House	100-250-B&B	Full breakfast to rooms
69 Maple Ave, 06058	9 rooms, 9 pb	Complimentary tea, coffee,
860-542-5690 Fax: 860-542-5690	Visa, MC, *Rated*, •	cocoa
Hank & Diane Tremblay	C-ltd/S-ltd/P-no/H-ltd	Weddings, massages, piano,
All year	French	sun porch, gazebo, bicycles,
		gardens, lake

Historic Victorian mansion furnished with genuine antiques, on 5 acres. Romantic, elegant bedrooms. Deluxe room with gas fireplace/2 person Jacuzzi. Sleigh/carriage rides. Concert series.   E-mail: tremblay@esslink.com *Web site:* manorhouse-norfolk.com

NORTH STONINGTON

Antiques &	129-229-B&B	Full multi-course breakfast
Accommodations	6 rooms, 6 pb	Complimentary wine
32 Main St, 06359	Visa, MC, *Rated*, •	Sitting room, library, garden,
860-535-1736 Fax: 860-535-2613	C-ltd/S-no/P-no/H-no	edible flowers, bicycles,
800-554-7829	German	gardens, lake
Ann & Tom Gray		
All year		

Two historic homes in a quiet village setting, all furnished with period antiques. Multi-course breakfast. English gardens. Close to Mystic & Casinos
Web site: visitmystic.com/antiques

High Acres	110-145-B&B	Continental breakfast
222 Northwest Corner Rd,	4 rooms, 4 pb	Afternoon tea, snacks, comp.
06359	Visa, MC, •	wine
860-887-4355 Fax: 860-887-1433	C-yes/S-no/P-yes/H-no	Sitting room, library, trail
Peter & Liz Agnew		riding through the woods
All year		and meadows.

150 acre country estate. Private grounds with majestic views. 1743 Colonial furnished with antiques and family heirlooms. Miles of trails to walk or ride.   E-mail: hacre@aol.com
Web site: visitmystic.com/highacres

NORWALK

Silvermine Tavern	99-185-B&B	Continental breakfast
194 Perry Ave, 06850	11 rooms, 11 pb	Restaurant, bar
203-847-4558 Fax: 203-847-9171	Most CC, *Rated*, •	Lunch, dinner, live Jazz,
Frank & Marsha Whitman	C-yes/S-yes/P-no/H-no	sitting room, new suite,
All year		weddings and conferences

Charming 225-year-old country inn only an hour from New York City. Decorated with hundreds of antiques. Dixiland jazz on Thursday, Friday & Saturday nights. Outdoor dining in the summers. Overlooking the Tranquil Millpond. Twin, double & queen size beds.

OLD GREENWICH

Harbor House Inn	159-239-B&B	Continental breakfast
165 Shore Rd, 06870	23 rooms, 17 pb	Kitchen facilities
203-637-0145 Fax: 203-698-0943	Visa, MC, AmEx, Disc, •	Sitting room, piano
Dawn Browne & Dolly Stuttig	C-yes/S-no/P-no/H-no	
All year		

Beautiful Inn, close to beach, walking distance to lovely New England town, train 1 mile away. 45 minutes to NYC! E-mail: hhinn@aol.com *Web site:* hhinn.com

OLD LYME

Bee and Thistle Inn	99-159-EP	Lunch, dinner, bar
100 Lyme St, 06371	11 rooms, 9 pb	Bicycles, phone in room, 2
860-434-1667 Fax: 860-434-3402	Most CC, *Rated*, •	parlors, piano, harpist
800-622-4946	C-ltd/S-yes/P-no/H-no	Saturdays
Bob & Penny Nelson		
All year		

An inn on 5.5 acres in historic district. On the Lieutenant River set back amidst majestic trees. Sophisticated country cuisine   E-mail: info@beeandthistleinn.com
Web site: beeandthistle.com

OLD LYME

Old Lyme Inn	99-150-B&B	Continental plus breakfast
PO Box 787, 06371	13 rooms, 13 pb	Lunch/dinner available
860-434-2600 Fax: 860-434-5352	Most CC, *Rated*, •	Sitting room, TV, phones,
800-434-5352	C-yes/S-yes/P-ltd/H-yes	clock radios, porch, teddy
Diana Atwood-Johnson		bear in the rooms
All year		

An 1850 Victorian inn in Old Lyme's historic district. 3-star restaurant (New York Times, 3 times). Empire and Victorian furnishings. E-mail: olinn@aol.com *Web site:* oldlymeinn.com

OLD SAYBROOK

Deacon Timothy Pratt B&B	95-180-B&B	Full breakfast
325 Main St, 06475	3 rooms, 3 pb	Afternoon tea, snacks,
860-395-1229	Visa, MC, AmEx,	sherry
Shelley Nobile	*Rated*, •	Sitt. rm, library, swing, beach
All year	C-ltd/S-no/P-no/H-ltd	passes, gardens, hammock,
	A little Spanish	whirlpool, swing

Charming c.1746 center chimney colonial on pretty gas-lit main street walking distance to historic & shopping districts. E-mail: shelley.nobile@snet.net
Web site: topwebsite.com/pratthouse

PLYMOUTH

Shelton House B&B	70-95-B&B	Full breakfast
663 Main St Rt 6, 06782	4 rooms, 2 pb	Afternoon tea
860-283-4616 Fax: 860-283-4616	S-no/P-no/H-no	Large guest parlor with
Pat & Bill Doherty		fireplace, perennial garden
All year		

Historic 1825 Greek Revival in scenic Litchfield Hills. Beautiful grounds; fountain; antiques. Convenient to I-84 and Route 8. E-mail: sheltonhbb@prodigy.net

RIDGEFIELD

Elms Inn, The	130-185-B&B	Continental breakfast
500 Main St, 06877	20 rooms, 20 pb	Restaurant
203-438-2541 Fax: 203-438-2541	Most CC, *Rated*	Suites, cable TV, 4 poster
The Scala Family	C-yes/S-ltd/P-no/H-no	beds
All year	Spanish, German	

A 1799 Inn for the discriminating traveler located in beautiful Ridgefield, CT. Beautiful, peaceful New England charm, fun antique shopping, restaurants, boutiques, library, parks at your doorstep. E-mail: innkeeper@elmsinn.com *Web site:* elmsinn.com

West Lane Inn	125-185-B&B	Continental breakfast
22 West Ln, 06877	20 rooms, 20 pb	Full breakfast (fee)
203-438-7323 Fax: 203-438-7325	Most CC, *Rated*, •	Golf, tennis nearby, cable TV,
Deborah L. Prieger	C-yes/S-yes/P-no	voice mail
All year		

Colonial elegance framed by majestic old maples and flowering shrubs. Breakfast served on the verandah. Always a relaxing atmosphere. Newly decorated lobbies & rooms. E-mail: dlprieger@aol.com *Web site:* westlaneinn.com

RIVERTON

Old Riverton Inn	85-185-B&B	Full breakfast
PO Box 6, 06065	12 rooms, 12 pb	Lunch/dinner available, bar
860-379-8678 Fax: 860-379-1006	Most CC, *Rated*	Sitting room cable TV, voice
800-EST-1796	C-ltd/S-yes/P-no/H-yes	mail
Mark & Pauline Telford		
All year		

Hospitality for the hungry, thirsty and sleepy since 1796. Originally a stagecoach stop. Overlooks wild and scenic West Branch of Farmington River. Listed on National Register Historic Places. E-mail: mark.telford@snet.net
Web site: newenglandinns.com/inns/riverton/index.html

SIMSBURY

Simsbury 1820 House	155-225-B&B	Continental plus breakfast
731 Hopmeadow St, 06070	34 rooms, 34 pb	Dinner available Monday-
860-658-7658 Fax: 860-651-0724	Most CC, *Rated*, •	Thursday
800-879-1820	C-yes/S-yes/P-no/H-yes	Cafe (Mon-Thur), sitting
Diane Ropiak		room, 5 private dining
All year		rooms, weddings/meetings

A graciously restored 34-room, 19th-century mansion in period decor, with 20th-century amenities. Cafe open Monday-Thursday. Brochure available.

SOUTH WINDSOR

Watson House, The	95-125-B&B	Full breakfast weekends
1876 Main St, 06074	3 rooms, 3 pb	Continental breakfast
860-282-8888 Fax: 860-289-0530	Visa, MC, AmEx,	weekdays
Timothy Cameron	C-yes/S-no/P-no/H-yes	Comp. wine, sitting room,
All year		suites, all rms. w/cable, TV,
		phone, & fireplace

1788 palladian mansion located on historic Old Main Street, less than a mile from the Connecticut River. Each rooms features a private bath, private phone, cable TV and fireplace.

TOLLAND

English Lane B&B	C-ltd/S-no/P-no
816 Tolland Stage Rd., 06084	
860-871-6618 Fax: 860-871-0734	
Rick & Sheryl King	
Season Inquire	

Totally refurbished in 1994, English Lane iss decorated in a warm traditional English country theme.   E-mail: englishlane@compuserve.com *Web site:* travelassist.com/reg/ct907.html

Tolland Inn, The	80-140-B&B	Full breakfast
PO Box 717, 06084	7 rooms, 7 pb	Complimentary wine,
860-872-0800 Fax: 860-870-7958	Visa, MC, AmEx,	afternoon tea
Susan & Stephen Beeching	*Rated*, •	Winter/summer sunporch,
All year	C-ltd/S-no/P-no/H-no	sitting rm., bridal room, guest
		room with fireplace

Seven guest rooms, all with private baths. Two suites, one with kitchen, one with fireplace. All antique handmade furnishings. Excellent location, Brimfield antique shows. E-mail: tollinn@ntplx.net *Web site:* tollandinn.com

WATERTOWN

Addington's B&B	95-125-B&B	Continental plus breakfast
1002 Middlebury Rd, 06795	3 rooms, 1 pb	Afternoon tea, snacks
860-274-2647	Visa, MC, Disc,	Sitting room, library,
877-250-9711	C-ltd/S-no/P-ltd/H-no	fireplaces, cable TV,
Jan Lynn & Eric		Accommodates business
All year		travelers

Enjoy country charm in our 1840 dairy farmhouse with its widows walk and large wrap-around porch. The home is enhanced with antiques and crafts made and sold by the owner.   E-mail: jansbandb@aol.com

WESTBROOK

Westbrook Inn
976 Boston Post Rd, 06498
860-399-4777
Glenn DiMartino/Chris
Monroe
Season Inquire

E-mail: info@westbrookinn.com *Web site:* westbrookinn.com

WOODSTOCK ─────────────────────────────

Elias Child House B&B	95-120-B&B	Full breakfast
50 Perrin Rd, 06281	3 rooms; 3 pb	Sitting room, library,
860-974-9836 Fax: 860-974-1541	Visa, MC, Disc,	bicycles, pool, suites,
877-974-9836	C-ltd/S-ltd/P-ltd/H-no	fireplaces, cable TV
M. Gorke-Felice & T. Felice	Some Spanish	
All year		

Magnificent center hall colonial circa 1714 with fireplace in each room. All guest chambers have private baths & beautiful views. E-mail: tfelice@compuserve.com
Web site: eliaschildhouse.com

Taylor's Corner B&B	80-155-B&B	Cont. plus bkfst. wkdays
880 Route 171, 06281	4 rooms, 4 pb	Full bkfst. weekends
860-974-0490 Fax: 860-974-0498	Most CC,	Snacks, sitting room, suites,
888-503-9057	C-ltd/S-no/P-no/H-no	cable, robes
Peggy and Doug Tracy		
All year		

Romantic, antique-furnished, 18th century colonial in northeast Connecticut's "Quiet Corner" boasting 8 fireplaces; surrounded by herb gardens & towering trees; A/C; National Register. New England hospitality, colonial hearthside cooking. E-mail: taylors@neca.com
Web site: neguide.com/taylors

Delaware

LEWES ─────────────────────────────

Wild Swan Inn	85-150-B&B	Full breakfast
525 Kings Hwy, 19958	3 rooms, 3 pb	Afternoon tea, snacks
302-645-8550 Fax: 302-645-8550	S-no/P-no/H-no	Sitting room, library, bikes,
Mike & Hope Tyler		pool/patio area, gazebo
All year		overlooking garden

Queen Anne Victorian style, lovely antiques, swans, books, fresh flowers, gourmet award winning breakafst. Music is shared-player piano, Edison phonograph and a Victrola.
E-mail: wildswan@udel.edu

MILTON ─────────────────────────────

Victorian Jewel B&B	55-90-B&B	Full breakfast
411 Federal St, 19968	3 rooms, 3 pb	Afternoon tea, snacks
302-684-1960 Fax: 302-684-2776	Visa, MC,	Sitting room, bikes, Jacuzzis,
Marcell & Karen Cheplicki	C-ltd/S-no/P-no/H-ltd	pool, cable TV, VCR with
All year		video library

Relax in a small town within 10 minutes of Atlantic beaches E-mail: Victjewel@aol.com
Web site: miltonde.com

NEW CASTLE ─────────────────────────────

Armitage Inn	105-150-B&B	Full breakfast
2 The Strand, 19720	5 rooms, 5 pb	Sitting room, Jacuzzis, suites,
302-328-6618 Fax: 302-324-1163	Most CC, *Rated*, ●	cable TV, accommodate
Stephen Marks	C-ltd/S-no/P-no/H-no	business travelers
All year		

Beautifully historic 18th century house in historic New Castle, beautifully decorated rooms, each with cable TV, telephone, private bath & king or queen bed. Full gourmet breakfast.
E-mail: armitageinn@earthlink.net

NEW CASTLE ──

William Penn Guest House	70-95-B&B	Continental breakfast
206 Delaware St, 19720	4 rooms	Living room VCR with video
302-328-7736	Visa, MC, *Rated*	library
Irma & Richard Burwell	C-ltd/S-no/P-no/H-no	
All year	Italian	

This house was built about 1682, and William Penn stayed overnight! Restored and located in the center of the Square.

WILMINGTON ──

Darley Manor Inn B&B	95-150-B&B	Full breakfast
3701 Philadelphia Pike, 19703	6 rooms, 6 pb	Afternoon tea,
302-792-2127 Fax: 302-798-6143	Visa, MC, AmEx,	complimentary wine
800-824-4703	*Rated*, ●	Sitting room, TV/VCR,
Ray & Judith Hester	C-ltd/S-ltd/P-no/H-no	Jacuzzi, exercise room,
All year		frequent flyer miles

Historic register, c.1790 colonial manor house, offering southern hospitality, first class amenities, & easy access to all Brandywine Valley attractions.   E-mail: inn@focdarley.com
Web site: dca.net/darley

Hedgerow B&B Suites	135-170-B&B	Full breakfast
268 Kennett Pike, 19317	3 rooms, 3 pb	Afternoon tea, snacks
610-388-6080 Fax: 610-388-0194	Most CC, ●	Sitting room, library, Jacuzzi,
Barbara & John Haedrich	C-ltd/S-no/P-no/H-no	fireplaces, gardens, privacy,
All year		cable TV

Between Longwood/Winterthur. Beautifully restored Carriage House. Three luxurious, private suites with amenities plus A/C. Personal service.   E-mail: hedgerowbb@aol.com
Web site: bbonline.com/pa/hedgerow/

District of Columbia

WASHINGTON ──

Dupont at the Circle, The	130-225-B&B	Continental breakfast
1604 19th St NW, 20009	8 rooms, 8 pb	Sitting room, suite, cable TV
202-332-5251 Fax: 202-332-3244	Visa, MC, AmEx,	
Alan & Anexora Skvirsky	*Rated*, ●	
All year	C-ltd/S-no/P-no/H-no	
	Spanish	

Our charming Victorian inn with modern conveniences is in Washington DC's premier location. We are ½ block from Metrorail making all of Washington's tourist attractions and Business District easily accessible.   E-mail: dupontatthecircle@erols.com
Web site: dupontatthecircle.com

Embassy Inn, The	89-119-B&B	Continental plus breakfast
1627 16th St NW, 20009	38 rooms, 38 pb	Complimentary sherry
202-234-7800	Most CC, *Rated*, ●	Snacks, sitting room, cable
800-423-9111	C-yes/S-yes/P-no/H-no	TV & HBO, Near Metro &
J. Schroeder, S. Stiles	Spanish	White House
All year		

Near Metro, White House, restaurants and shops; knowledgeable and helpful staff. Colonial style, in renovated 1920s boarding house

WASHINGTON ─────────────────────

George Washington U Inn
824 New Hampshire, NW,
20037
202-337-6620 Fax: 202-337-2540
800-426-4455
All year

109-250-EP
95 rooms, 95 pb
Most CC, •
C-yes/S-yes/P-no/H-yes

All meals available
Restaurant, bar service,
swimming pool (off site),
Near Metro & White House

A quaint newly renovated inn, three blocks from downtown, one block from Metro and Watergate, historic Foggy Bottom, a short walk to Kennedy Center, Georgetown and the Potomac River. E-mail: info@gwuinn.com *Web site:* gwuinn.com

---

Kalorama Guest House
1854 Mintwood Place, NW,
20009
202-667-6369 Fax: 202-319-1262
Michael, Stephen, & Jessica
All year

50-135-B&B
29 rooms, 15 pb
Most CC, *Rated*, •
C-ltd/S-no/P-no/H-no

Continental plus breakfast
Comp. wine, lemonade
Parlor, sun room, fridge, 24-
hour message service, free
local phone calls

Victorian townhouse decorated in period furnishings. Antique-filled, spacious rooms. Beautiful sun room for your morning breakfast Charming, unique & inexpensive. Washer/dryer

---

Kalorama Guest House, The
2700 Cathedral Ave, NW, 20009
202-328-0860 Fax: 202-328-8730
Carlotta & Mary Ann
All year

45-105-B&B
19 rooms, 12 pb
Most CC, *Rated*, •
C-ltd/S-no/P-no/H-no

Continental breakfast
Complimentary wine,
lemonade
Sitting room, guest, fridge,
washer/dryer, 24 hr. message
service

Charming European-style bed & breakfast in 6 turn-of-the-century townhouses. Period art, furnishings, brass beds, plants, outdoor landscaped garden, and hospitality

---

McMillan House B&B
2417 First St, NW, 20001
202-986-8989 Fax: 202-986-9747
800-240-9355
Albert Ceccone
All year

60-90-B&B
10 rooms
Visa, MC, AmEx, •
C-yes/S-no/P-no/H-no
Italian & Spanish

Continental breakfast
Fireplace, cable TV,
conference facilities, 800
number extension 09

The McMillan House is a newly renovated turn of the century bed and breakfast with a fireplace, high ceilings and spacious rooms. E-mail: aceccone@aol.com
Web site: mcmillanhouse.net

Morrison-Clark Inn
Mass. Ave & 11th St NW, 20001
202-898-1200 Fax: 202-289-8576
800-332-7898
Bill Petrella
All year

89-B&B
54 rooms, 54 pb
Visa, MC, AmEx,
Rated, •
C-yes/S-yes/P-no/H-yes
Spanish

Continental plus breakfast
Award winning restaurant
Bar, sitting room, cable TV,
weddings, fitness center

The perfect urban oasis for visitors to downtown Washington. Victorian decor is alive in D.C.'s finest historic inn. All rooms have minibars, hairdryers, 2 phones & dataport

---

Reeds, The
PO Box 12011, 20005
202-328-3510 Fax: 202-332-3885
Charles & Jackie Reed
All year

60-150-B&B
6 rooms, 5 pb
Rated, •
C-yes/S-no/P-no/H-no
French, Spanish

Continental plus breakfast
Sitting room, gardens, library,
Victorian porch, piano,
antiques

Spacious rooms with wood-burning fireplaces and chandeliers bring a bit of the Nineteenth Century to historic downtown Washington. One bedroom apartment available.
E-mail: bnbaccom@aol.com *Web site:* bnbaccom.com/reeds.htm

WASHINGTON

Swann House	125-250-B&B	Continental plus breakfast
1808 New Hampshire Ave,	12 rooms, 12 pb	Tea, snacks
20009	Most CC, *Rated*	Sitt. room, Jacuzzis,
202-265-4414 Fax: 202-265-6755	C-ltd/S-no/P-no/H-no	swimming pool, suites,
Mary & Richard Ross	Amharic	fireplace, cable TV,
All year		conference

Grand Richardson Romanesque mansion in Dupont Circle, D.C.'s most vibrant neighborhood. Eat at local outdoor cafes, walk to museums or relax by the pool or on our roof deck. E-mail: stay@swannhouse.com *Web site:* swannhouse.com

Swiss Inn	68-108-EP	Kitchenettes in rooms
1204 Massachusetts NW, 20005	7 rooms, 7 pb	Television, air conditioning,
202-371-1816 Fax: 202-371-1138	Most CC, *Rated*, •	telephones
800-955-7947	C-yes/S-ltd/P-ltd/H-no	
Kelley Carpenter	French, German,	
All year	Spanish	

Within walking distance to White House, FBI, Convention Center, Smithsonian Museums, MCI Center, monuments, and the Mall. All rooms have private baths and fully equipped kitchenettes E-mail: swissinndc@aol.com *Web site:* theswissinn.com

Windsor Inn, The	B&B	Continental plus breakfast
1842 16th St NW, 20009	46 rooms, 46 pb	Complimentary sherry &
202-667-0300 Fax: 202-667-4503	Most CC, *Rated*, •	snacks
800-423-9111	C-yes/S-yes/P-no/H-no	Cable TV & HBO in rooms,
Susan Stiles	French, Spanish	renovated lobby, telephones
All year		

Relaxing and charming haven in heart of nation's capitol. Art deco flair. Close to Metro and many restaurants. 11 blocks north of White House. New carpeting, flagstone exterior landscaping, handpainted murals in stairwell.

Florida

AMELIA ISLAND

1857 Florida House Inn	70-175-B&B	Full breakfast
PO Box 688, 32034	15 rooms, 15 pb	Restaurant, bar
904-261-3300	Visa, MC, AmEx,	Sitting room, library,
800-258-3301	*Rated*, •	bicycles, near beaches, golf,
Bob & Karen Warner	C-ltd/S-no/P-ltd/H-yes	tennis, fishing
All year	some Spanish	

Florida's oldest continually operating hotel, c.1857, in 50-block historic district. Antiques, quilts, shady porches, Jacuzzis, fireplaces, courtyard with fountain & gazebo. 4 new rooms on "Tree Hous Row" all with king size bed, fireplaces, Jacuzzis. E-mail: innkeepers@ floridahouseinn.com *Web site:* floridahouseinn.com

Addison House	120-195-B&B	Full breakfast
614 Ash St, 32034	14 rooms, 14 pb	Snacks
904-277-1604	Visa, MC, AmEx,	Sitting room, library,
800-943-1604	*Rated*, •	Jacuzzis, cable TV,
John & Donna & Jennifer	C-ltd/S-no/P-no/H-yes	accommodate business
Gibson		travelers
All year		

Elegant Victorian home in the historic district; secret gardens and fountains; enjoy breakfast overlooking the gardens, private porches; restaurants and shops within walking distance. E-mail: AddisonHouse@Net-Magic.net *Web site:* addisonhousebb.com

AMELIA ISLAND

Amelia Is. Williams House
103 S 9th St, 32034
904-277-2328 Fax: 904-321-1325
800-414-9257
Richar Flitz & Chris Carter
All year

145-225-B&B
8 rooms, 8 pb
Visa, MC, *Rated*, •
C-ltd/S-no/P-no/H-yes
German

Full gourmet breakfast
Complimentary wine
Sitting room, bicycles, tennis
courts, hot tubs, frequent
flyer miles

"A top inn of the year," Country Inn magazine 1996. "One of the South's most exquisite B&B's." An 1856 Antebellum mansion.   E-mail: topinn@aol.com *Web site:* williamshouse.com

Bailey House
28 S 7th St, 32034
904-261-5390 Fax: 904-321-0103
800-251-5390
Tom & Jenny Bishop
All year

95-160-B&B
10 rooms, 10 pb
Most CC, *Rated*, •
C-ltd/S-no/P-no/H-yes

Full breakfast
Old pump organ, victrola,
authentic antiques, A/C,
heat, whirlpool tubs

Elegant 1895 Queen Anne Victorian on National Register, in historic district. Walk to shopping, restaurants, marina, dining. Near state park beach, large rooms. E-mail: bailey@net-magic.net *Web site:* bailey-house.com

Elizabeth Pointe Lodge
98 S Fletcher Ave, 32034
904-277-4851 Fax: 904-277-6500
888-757-1917
David & Susan Caples
All year

150-245-B&B
25 rooms, 25 pb
Most CC, *Rated*, •
C-yes/S-yes/P-no/H-yes

Full breakfast
Complimentary wine/snack
Sitting room, library, bikes,
oceanfront, kid friendly, 24
hr room service

Reminiscent of a turn-of-the-century lodge; oceanfront on a small Florida barrier island; bike to historic seaport village nearby.   E-mail: eliz.pt@worldnet.att.net *Web site:* elizabethpointelodge.com

Fairbanks House, The
227 S 7th St, 32034
904-277-0500 Fax: 904-277-3103
888-891-9897
Bill & Theresa Hamilton
All year

125-225-B&B
12 rooms, 12 pb
Most CC, *Rated*, •
C-ltd/S-no/P-no/H-no

Full breakfast
Complimentary social hour
Sitting room, bicycles, pool,
Jacuzzi, suites, conference
facility

1885 Italianate villa & historic cottages, landscaped grounds and swimming pool. Within walking distance of many shops & restaurants.   E-mail: fairbanks@net-magic.net *Web site:* fairbankshouse.com

Walnford Inn
102 S 7th St, 32034
904-277-4941 Fax: 904-277-4646
800-277-6660
Bob & Linda Waln
All year

75-145-B&B
9 rooms, 9 pb
Most CC, •
C-ltd/S-no/P-no/H-yes

Full breakfast
Sitting room, library, bikes,
by beaches, tennis, golf

Turn of the century home, located in historic district. Gourmet breakfast served on wrap around porch. Weddings, receptions   E-mail: waln@msn.com *Web site:* walnford.com

ANNA MARIA ISLAND

Harrington House B&B
5626 Gulf Dr, 34217
941-778-5444 Fax: 941-778-0527
Jo & Frank Davis
All year

129-239-B&B
8 rooms
Visa, MC, *Rated*, •
C-ltd/S-no/P-no

Full gourmet breakfast
Comp. iced tea, popcorn
Sitting room, bicycles,
swimming pool

Charming restored 1920s home directly on Gulf of Mexico reflects "casual elegance." E-mail: harhousebb@mail.pcsonline.com *Web site:* harringtonhouse.com

ANNA MARIE ISLAND

Duncan House B&B	79-129-B&B	Full breakfast
1703 Gulf Dr, 34217	4 rooms, 4 pb	Complimentary wine
941-778-6858 Fax: 941-778-2904	Visa, MC, AmEx,	Sitting room, sun deck,
Joe & Becky Garbus	*Rated*, •	swimming pool
All year	C-ltd/S-no/P-no/H-no	

Turn-of-the-century Victorian. Located on beautiful Anna Maria Island. Steps away from white sandy beaches   E-mail: duncanbb@aol.com *Web site:* duncanhousebb.com

APALACHICOLA

Brigittes Romantic Retreat	80-130-B&B	Full German breakfast
101 6th St, 32320	3 rooms, 3 pb	Complimentary wine
850-653-3270 Fax: 850-514-4386	Visa, MC, •	Sitting room, classic, rose
888-554-4376	S-no/P-no/H-no	garden, fountain, fish pond
Brigitte & Ken Schroeder	German	
All year		

European hospitality in a quaint Victorian setting. Wraparound porch with antique wicker to wile the hours and solve the worlds problems.
E-mail: ken@supernet.net *Web site:* romantic-retreat.com

BIG PINE KEY

Barnacle B&B	115-125-B&B	Full breakfast
1557 Long Beach Dr, 33043	4 rooms, 4 pb	Hot tub, bicycles,
305-872-3298 Fax: 305-872-3863	S-yes/P-no/H-no	refrigerators, weddings &
800-465-9100		receptions
Tim & Jane Marquis		
All year		

Barefoot living with panache. Secluded area on ocean in fabulous Florida Keys. Private cottage and efficiency unit   E-mail: barnacle@iamerica.net *Web site:* cust.iamerica.net/barnacle

Deer Run B&B	95-150-B&B	Full southern breakfast
PO Box 430431, 33043	3 rooms, 3 pb	Comp. bottle of wine
305-872-2015 Fax: 305-872-2842	*Rated*, •	Bicycles, beach, hot tubs,
Sue Abbott	S-no/P-no/H-yes	lib., hammocks, grill, king
All year		beds all rms

The house is 75 feet from the ocean- quiet, serene. Bkfst. is served on the verandah overlooking the ocean. Vegy dining by request. Adults only. 33 miles to Key West. All rms. with ocean view   E-mail: deerrunbb@aol.com *Web site:* travelguides.com/home/deer_run/

CLERMONT

Mulberry Inn, The	75-95-B&B	Continental plus breakfast
915 W Montrose St, 34711	5 rooms, 5 pb	Lunch avail., restaurant
352-242-0670 Fax: 352-242-9898	Most CC, *Rated*, •	Sitting room sitting & dining
800-641-0670	C-ltd/S-ltd/P-yes/H-no	room
Jeff & Rose Biddle		
All year		

Tucked back in a small town, you can walk to nearby parks and lakes or visit historic downtown.   E-mail: tfjeff@aol.com *Web site:* mulberryinn.com

DESTIN

Henderson Park Inn	B&B	Full breakfast
PO Box 30, 32541	35 rooms, 35 pb	Complimentary wine
850-654-0400 Fax: 850-654-0405	Most CC, *Rated*, •	Restaurant, bar service,
800-336-4853	S-yes/P-no/H-yes	Jacuzzis, pool, suites,
Susie Nunnelley		fireplaces, cable TV
All year		

Charming & romantic, this Queen Anne style inn celebrates a true Destin landmark. Its beachside elegance amid the pristine beauty of over a mile of untouched shoreline.
E-mail: innkeeper@hendersonparkinn.com *Web site:* hendersonparkinn.com

EVERGLADES CITY

Banks of the Everglades
PO Box 570, 34139
941-695-3151 Fax: 941-695-3335
888-431-1977
Patty Flick Richards
Oct. 1-July 6

75-130-B&B
11 rooms, 5 pb
Most CC, •
C-yes/S-no/P-ltd/H-yes

Full breakfast
Sitting room, library, suites,
cable TV, bicycles, tennis

Tranquility nestled, "On the Banks of the Everglades" is the bank of the everglades building; the first bank of Collier County, Florida, chartered in 1923. Breakfast is served in the walk-in VAULT! E-mail: patty@banksoftheeverglades.com *Web site:* banksoftheeverglades.com/

FORT LAUDERDALE

Caribbean Quarters
3012 Granada St, 33304
954-523-3226 Fax: 954-523-7541
888-414-3226
Steve McAllister
All year

110-220-B&B
12 rooms, 12 pb
Most CC, •
S-no/P-no/H-no

Continental plus breakfast
Tropical courtyard, bikes,
hot tubs, renovated in 1998

Superior, luxury B&B, half block from promenade, beach. Walk to restaurants, shopping and more. Caribbean motif of late '30s and many amenities. E-mail: bigbedsbnb@juno.com *Web site:* caribbeanquaters.com

Little Inn by the Sea, A
4546 El Mar Dr, 33308
954-772-2450 Fax: 954-938-9354
800-492-0311
U. & B. Brandt/C. & V. Lancry
All year

79-189-B&B
29 rooms, 29 pb
Most CC, *Rated*, •
C-yes/S-ltd/P-no/H-no
Dutch, French, Spanish

Continental plus breakfast
Sitting room, library, pool,
bicycles, tennis, family
friendly facility

European Mediterranean B&B on the beach, very tropical setting as if you are on an island, 3 natural reefs right in front of the beach, close to exciting places in S. Florida E-mail: alinn@icanect.net *Web site:* alittleinn.com

GAINESVILLE

Magnolia Plantation B&B
309 SE 7th St, 32601
352-375-6653 Fax: 352-338-0303
800-201-2379
Joe & Cindy Montalto
All year

85-175-B&B
5 rooms, 5 pb
Visa, MC, AmEx,
Rated, •
C-ltd/S-no/P-ltd/H-no

Full breakfast
Lunch by res., snacks
Comp. beverages, library,
sitting room, bicycles, 60-feet
pond, gazebo

Restored 1885 Victorian in downtown. Two miles from Univ. of Florida. Beautifully landscaped gardens, pond, waterfalls & gazebo. 1880s cottage 2 bedroom, 1 bath. E-mail: info@magnoliabnb.com *Web site:* magnoliabnb.com

Sweetwater Branch Inn
625 E University Ave, 32601
352-373-6760 Fax: 352-371-3771
800-595-7760
Cornelia Holbrook
All year

80-150-B&B
7 rooms, 7 pb
Visa, MC, AmEx,
Rated, •
S-no/P-no/H-yes
Spanish, Italian, French

Full breakfast
Dinner available, comp. wine
Afternoon tea, snacks, sitting
room, bicycles, airport/univ.
transport

Enjoy a piece of the past; restored 1880 Victorian with antiques, English garden/patio. Walk to historic district—fine dining, Hippodrome Theatre. 2 rooms with Jacuzzis. E-mail: reservations@sweetwaterinn.com *Web site:* sweetwaterinn.com

HOMESTEAD

Room at the Inn B&B
15830 SW 240 St, 33031
305-246-0492 Fax: 305-246-0590
Sally C. Robinson
All year

85-110-B&B
4 rooms, 3 pb
Rated
C-ltd/S-ltd/P-no/H-no

Full breakfast
Great room with fireplace,
swimming pool with, heated
spa, TV/VCR, flowers

Room at the Inn B&B is a charming, relaxing retreat on two acres in the agricultural/grove area five miles north of Homestead and two miles west of US1. From its convenient central location, you can, within minutes be visiting several hot spots.

INDIANTOWN

Seminole Country Inn
PO Box 1818, 34956
561-597-3777 Fax: 561-597-2883
888-394-3777
Jonnie Williams/Sheri
Hubbard
All year

75-95-AP
22 rooms, 22 pb
Most CC, *Rated*
C-yes/S-ltd/P-ltd/H-no

Continental breakfast
Lunch, dinner, snacks
Rest., sitt. rm., bikes, tennis,
pool, conference, fireplaces,
cable TV

Built in 1926, our Inn has the grandeur of an age gone by and outstanding southern food & hospitality. Pool & garden area.   E-mail: seminole@treco.net Web site: seminoleinn.com

JACKSONVILLE

House on Cherry Street
1844 Cherry St, 32205
904-384-1999 Fax: 904-384-5013
Carol Anderson
All year

79-105-B&B
4 rooms, 4 pb
Most CC, *Rated*, •
C-ltd/S-yes/P-no/H-no

Continental breakfast
Complimentary wine/snack
Sitting room, color TV, air
conditioned, porch, bicycles,
Fax

In historic Riverside, a restored colonial house filled with period antiques, decoys, four poster beds and country collectibles. On beautiful St. John's River.   E-mail: houseoncherry@compuserve.com

---

Plantation Manor Inn
1630 Copeland St, 32204
904-384-4630 Fax: 904-387-0960
Kathy & Jerry Ray
All year

120-160-B&B
9 rooms, 9 pb
Visa, MC, AmEx,
Rated, •
C-ltd/S-no/P-no/H-no

Full breakfast
Complimentary
refreshments
3rd night free wine, sitting
room, spa, swimming pool

Restored 1905 Southern Mansion with antique furnishings and oriental carpets. 2 blocks from river, restaurants, antique shops. Convenient to Cummer Art Museum, downtown. Rated 4 diamonds by AAA.   Web site: bbonline.com/fl/plantation/

St. Johns House B&B
1718 Osceola St, 32204
904-384-3724 Fax: 904-384-3724
Joan E. Moore
Closed July

70-B&B
3 rooms, 2 pb
C-yes/S-no/P-no/H-no

Full breakfast
Afternoon tea,
complimentary wine
Sitting room square along
river

A traditional B&B near downtown, the sports and convention centers and shopping. Just one block off the St. Johns River in a National Historic District. Carriage house available.

JACKSONVILLE BEACH

Pelican Path B&B by the Sea
11 N 19th Ave, 32250
904-249-1177 Fax: 904-346-5412
888-749-1177
Tom & Joan Hubbard
All year

80-175-B&B
4 rooms, 4 pb
Rated, •
S-no/P-no/H-no

Full breakfast
Sitt. rm., bikes, cable,
Jacuzzis, phones, TV/VCR,
refrigerators, spa tubs

Pelican Path enjoys a superb location-an oceanfront, residential neighborhood with easy access to beach, stores, & restaurants. Guest rooms feature ocean view, spa tub, VCRs & more.   E-mail: ppbandb@aol.com Web site: pelicanpath.com

KEY WEST

Andrews Inn
0 Whalton Lane, 33040
305-294-7730
888-263-7393
All year

115-175-B&B

Full breakfast
Evening cocktails
Swimming pool, tropical
gardens, bikes, vaulted
ceilings, private baths, a/c

To reach Andrews Inn, wander down a shady lane off Duval Street. Immediately, peace and tranquility reach out to you as you enter through a garden gate. Whether you prefer privacy or congeniality, Andrews Inn has it all.   E-mail: KWAndrews@aol.com Web site: andrewsinn.com

KEY WEST ─────────────────────────────────────

Blue Parrot Inn
916 Elizabeth St, 33040
305-296-0033
800-231-2473
Cleo, Frank & Larry
All year

70-179-B&B
10 rooms, 10 pb
Most CC, *Rated*, •
S-yes/P-no/H-ltd

Continental plus breakfast
Refrigerator, most rooms
Ceiling fan, cable TV, heated
pool, phones, A/C, private
bath, bikes

Classic 1884 historic restoration with charming gingerbread verandas. A quiet, secluded retreat in the heart of Old Town. Walk to beaches & all attractions. Sundeck. Resident cats. Web site: blueparrotinn.com

Center Court Historic Inn
916 Center St, 33040
305-296-9292 Fax: 305-294-4104
800-797-8787
Naomi Van Steelandt
All year

88-338-B&B
16 rooms, 16 pb
Most CC, *Rated*, •
C-ltd/S-ltd/P-ltd/H-ltd

Continental plus breakfast
Happy hour
Sitt. rm., library, pool, hot
tubs, exercise fac., A/C,
private bath, bikes

Located in the heart of the historic Old Town, 1/2 block from Duval on quiet lane. Winner 2 Historic Preservation awards. We'll pamper you with Caribbean charm.
E-mail: centerct@aol.com *Web site:* centercourtkw.com

Conch House Heritage Inn
625 Truman Ave, 33040
305-239-0020 Fax: 305-293-8447
800-207-5806
Sam Holland
All year

88-188-B&B
6 rooms, 6 pb
Most CC, *Rated*, •
C-ltd/S-yes/P-no/H-yes
Spanish

Continental plus breakfast
Swimming pool, phones,
bikes, porches, swimming
pool, garden

Victorian architecture with Bahama influences. Family owned & operated over 100 years. Extremely large rooms, tropical cottages by pool/garden; walk to everything
E-mail: conchinn@aol.com *Web site:* conchhouse.com

Curry Mansion Inn
511 Caroline St, 33040
305-294-5349 Fax: 305-294-4093
800-253-3466
Edith & Albert Amsterdam
All year

75-B&B
15 rooms, 15 pb
Visa, MC, AmEx,
Rated, •
C-yes/S-yes/P-yes/H-yes
Fr., Sp., Ger., It.

Continental plus breakfast
Full bar/snacks 5pm-7pm
Sitting room, library,
swimming pool, billiards,
private beach club

Landmark Victorian mansion with new poolside guest wing. Every amenity. Magnificent antiques, fabulous breakfast, daily cocktail party with music, beach club.
E-mail: frontdesk@currymansion.com *Web site:* currymansion.com

Cypress House
601 Caroline St, 33040
305-294-6969 Fax: 305-296-1174
800-525-2488
Dave Taylor
All year

99-300-B&B
16 rooms, 8 pb
Most CC, •
C-ltd/S-yes/P-no/H-no

Continental plus breakfast
Complimentary wine
Sitting room, library,
swimming pool, an adult
only inn

1888 Bahamian Conch mansion. Private, tropical. Large rooms with A/C and ceiling fans. Walk to all historic sites, shopping, restaurants. All rooms have color cable TV, phones with dataports and voice mail. E-mail: CypressKW@aol.com *Web site:* cypresshousekw.com

Douglas House
419 Amelia St, 33040
305-294-5269 Fax: 305-292-7665
800-833-0372
Robert Marrero
All year

98-B&B
15 rooms, 15 pb
Visa, MC, AmEx, •
C-ltd/S-yes/P-yes/H-no
Spanish, French,
German

Continental breakfast
Afternoon tea
Bikes, hot tub, swimming
pool, an adult only inn

Choose from 15 deluxe rooms & large suites. Imagine sitting on your own private porch as dusk turns into night and the warmth of the Caribbean Sea relaxes your entire body.
E-mail: doughous40@aol.com *Web site:* DouglasHouse.com

KEY WEST ——

Duval House
815 Duval St, 33040
305-294-1666 Fax: 305-292-1701
800-22-Duval
Renner James
All year

90-305-B&B
30 rooms, 30 pb
Most CC, *Rated*, •
S-yes/P-no/H-no
Spanish, German

Continental plus breakfast
3 stes. with kitchenette
Sitt. rm., sun deck, A/C,
phones, TV in rooms, gazebo
in gardens

"One of the 10 most affordable romantic inns in the U.S."—Vacations Magazine. *A romantic tropical inn with century-old Victorian houses surrounding a large jungle-like garden with pool.* E-mail: duvalhs@ibm.net Web site: kwflorida.com/duvalhse.html

---

Eden House
1015 Fleming St, 33040
305-296-6868 Fax: 305-294-1221
800-533-KEYS
Michael Eden
All year

60-275-EP
41 rooms, 41 pb
Visa, MC, AmEx,
C-yes/S-no/P-no/H-no
Spanish, French,
German

cold drink at check-in
Swimming pool, Jacuzzi,
snorkeling, scuba diving,
sailing & jet ski nearby

In old Key West. Ceiling fans, white wicker. Sip a cool drink under a poolside gazebo, lounge on verandah, dine in garden cafe. Hammock area, elevated sundeck. E-mail: mike@edenhouse.com Web site: edenhouse.com/

Heron House
512 Simonton St, 33040
305-294-9227 Fax: 305-294-5692
888-676-8648
Fred Geibelt/Robert Framarin
All year

170-329-B&B
23 rooms, 23 pb
Visa, MC, AmEx,
Rated, •
S-ltd/P-no/H-ltd

Continental plus breakfast
Breakfast bar
Orchid gardens, sun deck, in-
room safes, pool, robes,
concierge, phones

Old island charm situated in location central to all the main tourist attractions. Pool, sun deck, gardens. Daily newspapers. E-mail: heronkyw@aol.com Web site: fla-keys.com/heronhouse

---

Key West B&B/Popular House
415 William St, 33040
305-296-7274 Fax: 305-293-0306
800-438-6155
Jody Carlson
All year

59-265-B&B
8 rooms, 4 pb
Most CC, *Rated*, •
C-ltd/S-ltd

Continental plus breakfast
1 room with private deck,
hot tubs, sauna, Jacuzzi, sun
deck, sitting room

In heart of Historic District, restored 100-yr-old Victorian. Breakfast at your leisure. Classic Caribbean casual. E-mail: relax@keywestbandb.com Web site: keywestbandb.com

---

Knowles House, The
1004 Eaton St, 33040
305-296-8132 Fax: 305-296-2093
800-352-4414
Les Vollmert/Paul Masse
All year

70-200-B&B
8 rooms, 6 pb
Most CC, *Rated*, •
S-ltd/P-no/H-no

Continental plus breakfast
Complimentary wine
Jacuzzis, swimming pool,
cable TV

Romantic historic inn in the heart of the Old Town Historic District offering a relaxed, friendly atmosphere with exceptionally elegant decor, tropical pool. E-mail: knowleshse@aol.com Web site: knowleshouse.com

---

La Pensione Inn
809 Truman Ave, 33040
305-294-2361 Fax: 305-296-6509
800-893-1193
Carl Lopez-Porter
All year

98-168-B&B
7 rooms, 7 pb
Most CC, *Rated*
C-ltd/S-yes/P-no/H-yes
Spanish, French,
German

Continental plus breakfast
Swimming pool, mini-bar in
rooms, A/C

Old Victorian completely renovated with spacious, clean rooms simply furnished with private baths, A/C, pool, parking available. Close to all major attractions. Newly painted, recarpeted, new furniture. E-mail: lapensione@aol.com Web site: lapensione.com

KEY WEST ─────────────────────────────────────

Mermaid & Alligator, The
729 Truman Ave, 33040
305-294-1894 Fax: 305-295-9925
800-773-1894
Dean Carlson, Paul Hayes
All year

98-218-B&B
8 rooms, 5 pb
Visa, MC, AmEx, •
S-yes/P-no/H-no
German

Full breakfast
Off-street parking, swimming
pool, Wheelch. to priv. patio

An elegant Queen Anne house in a garden setting, with pool, off-street parking and a memorable breakfast, in the center of Key West's Old Town. E-mail: mermaid@joy.net
Web site: kwmermaid.com/

───

Nassau House
1016 Fleming St, 33040
305-296-8513 Fax: 305-293-8423
800-296-8513
Elizabeth & Joe Wells
All year

100 and up-B&B
6 rooms, 6 pb
Most CC, •
C-ltd/S-ltd/P-ltd/H-yes

Continental breakfast
Afternoon tea
Library, bicycles, Jacuzzis,
suites, cable TV

"From Baccarat to Sandals" we are just "chillin' in the Keys!" We are an upscale Inn and offer amenities that one should expect. E-mail: nassauh@aol.com *Web site:* noblinkin.com

───

New Orleans House
724 Duval St, 33040
305-295-2901 Fax: 305-294-9298
888-293-9893
Ed Cox
Season Inquire

70-250-B&B

Continental breakfast
free bottle of wine

All-male guestroom accommodations located above world-famous Bourbon Street Pub and across the street from the 801 Bourbon Bar. A taste of N'Awlins in a cruisy atmosphere guarantee a fantasy come true. Web site: neworleanshousekw.com

───

Pilot House
414 Simonton St, 33040
305-293-6600 Fax: 305-294-9298
800-648-3780
All year

100-250-EP
14 rooms, 14 pb
Visa, MC, AmEx, •
C-ltd/S-ltd/P-no/H-no

Fully equipped kitchens
Hot tubs, marble baths,
verandas, pool, garden

The 19th-century Victorian Guest House is conveniently located in the heart of Historic Old Town Key West. Suites have A/C, TV & phones. Spanish cabana guesthouse with in room Jacuzzis. Very gay friendly atmosphere. E-mail: pilotKW@aol.com *Web site:* travelbase.com

───

Seascape
420 Olivia St, 33040
305-296-7776 Fax: 305-296-6283
800-765-6438
Tom & Nancy Coward
All year

79-189-B&B
6 rooms, 6 pb
Visa, MC, AmEx, •
C-ltd/S-no/P-yes/H-no

Continental breakfast
Seasonal sunset wine hour
Heated pool-spa, sun decks,
wicker, A/C, TVs, Bahama
fans

Recommended by the NY Times, Seascape is ideally located in the heart of old town Key West. Relax poolside on our secluded sundecks and tropical gardens.
E-mail: seascape@kwest.net *Web site:* keywest.com/seascape

───

Weatherstation Inn
57 Front St, 33040
305-294-7277 Fax: 305-294-0544
800-815-2707
Walt Lee
All year

150-315-B&B
8 rooms, 8 pb
Visa, MC, AmEx,
Rated, •
C-ltd/S-no/P-no/H-yes

Continental breakfast
Sitting room, library,
swimming pool, full
concierge service

Secluded getaway nestled in the heart of old town. Exquisitely decorated rooms, private gated community, lush tropical landscaping, harbor views, walk to everything.
E-mail: weathersta@aol.com *Web site:* weatherstationinn.com

KEY WEST

Whispers B&B
409 William St, 33040
305-294-5969 Fax: 305-294-3899
800-856-7444
John W. Marburg
All year

85-175-B&B
7 rooms, 7 pb
Most CC, *Rated*, •
C-ltd/S-ltd/P-ltd/H-no

Full gourmet breakfast
Refrigerators in rooms
A/C, TV, health club, walk to
all activities, old town,
swimming, fans

Historic Register. Victorian old town inn. Gourmet breakfast in tropical garden. Antiques throughout. Jacuzzi on premise. Membership to private beach and health club. Quiet and romantic.   E-mail: Bbwhispers@aol.com *Web site:* whispersbb.com

White Street Inn
905 White St, 33040
305-295-9599 Fax: 305-295-9503
800-207-9767
Carla Biscardi
All year

85-220-B&B
7 rooms, 7 pb
Most CC, *Rated*, •
C-yes/S-yes/P-no/H-no
Italian, German

Continental plus breakfast
Swimming pool, microwave,
refrigerator, old town,
swimming, fans

Historic property surrounded by lush tropical garden & secluded pool. Newly renovated spacious rooms open out onto private deck/porches. Centrally located-marinas & beaches nearby.   E-mail: white_st_inn@juno.com *Web site:* whitestreetinn.com

William Anthony House
PO Box 107, 33041
305-294-2887 Fax: 305-294-9209
800-613-2276
Tony Minore & Bill Beck
All year

89-199-B&B
8 rooms, 8 pb
Most CC, *Rated*, •
C-ltd/S-no/P-no/H-yes
Spanish

Continental plus breakfast
Snacks, bar service
Hot tubs old town,
swimming, fans

Award winning historic inn with luxury suites and rooms. All with A/C, kitchenettes. Excellent quiet location. Complimentary breakfast & social hour.   E-mail: aminore@aol.com
Web site: wmanthonyhse.com

LAKE WALES

Chalet Suzanne Country Inn
3800 Chalet Suzanne Dr, 33853
941-676-6011 Fax: 941-676-1814
800-433-6011
Vita Hinshaw
All year

159-219-B&B
30 rooms, 30 pb
Most CC, *Rated*, •
C-yes/S-yes/P-no/H-yes
German, French

Full breakfast
Restaurant, lounge
Comp. sherry in room, pool
on lake, airstrip, some rooms
w/jet tub

*Unique country inn centrally located for Florida attractions. Gourmet meals; award-winning restaurant. Ranked one of 10 most romantic spots in Florida
E-mail:* info@chaletsuzanne.com *Web site:* chaletsuzanne.com

LAKE WORTH

Mango Inn B&B
128 N Lakeside Dr, 33460
561-533-6900 Fax: 561-533-6900
888-626-4619
Erin & Bo Allen
All year

75-200-B&B
8 rooms, 8 pb
•
C-ltd/H-no

Continental plus breakfast
Full breakfast weekends
Complimentary wine
weekends, bikes, swimming
pool

Lush, private pool with waterfall; walk to beach, golfing, parks, historic downtown "Arts & Antiques district" and fine restaurants.   E-mail: info@mangoinn.com *Web site:* mangoinn.com

LOXAHATCHEE

Southern Palm B&B
15130 Southern Palm Way,
33470
561-790-1413 Fax: 561-791-3035
Cheri Reed
All year

125-B&B
5 rooms, 5 pb
Most CC, •
C-ltd/S-no/P-no/H-yes

Continental plus breakfast
Library, basketball, court,
unique collection of animals

Tropical paradise with wildlife nestled on 20 acre wooded estate. Close to Palm Beach Polo Equestrian Club, Coral Sky Amphitheater, golf beaches, shopping & restaurants. French doors open to balcony.   E-mail: creen8569@aol.com *Web site:* computercoach.com/southernpalm/

MELBOURNE ─────────────────────────────

Wisteria Inn
1924 Catterton Dr, 32901
407-727-0717 Fax: 407-733-1854
888-787-0717
Valerie Bondy
All year

69-149-B&B
3 rooms, 3 pb
Visa, MC, AmEx, *Rated*
C-ltd/S-no/P-no/H-ltd

Full breakfast
Afternoon tea, lunch &
dinner
Sitting room, library, bikes,
Jacuzzis, suites, fireplaces,
cable TV, phones

Wisteria Inn, c. 1924 is tastefully furnished with antiques. It offers a tranquil setting but is convenient to all attractions, beach, golf, and shopping. E-mail: qhearts@bellsouth.net
Web site: wisteriainn.net

MIAMI ─────────────────────────────

Coconut Grove B&B
PO Box 331891, 33133
305-665-2274 Fax: 305-666-1186
800-339-9430
Annette Rawlings
All year

115-175-B&B
3 rooms, 3 pb
Visa, MC, AmEx,
Rated, •
C-yes/S-ltd/P-no/H-no

Full breakfast
Restaurant
Sitting room, tennis court,
Jacuzzis, swimming pool,
suites, cable TV

Enjoy country living in the city. A romantic getaway surrounded by lush tropical foliage located in a historic area among old family estates. Wake up to a full gourmet breakfast, relax amidst antiqes & original art. Sun bathe at the nearby beaches and pool
E-mail: CoCoBandB@aol.com *Web site:* kwflorida.com/coconut.html

MIAMI BEACH ─────────────────────────────

Bay Harbor Inn
9660 E Bay Harbor Dr, 33154
305-868-4141 Fax: 305-867-9094
Lior Dagan
All year

80-169-B&B
45 rooms, 45 pb
Visa, MC, AmEx,
Rated, •
C-yes/S-yes/P-no/H-ltd
Spanish

Continental plus breakfast
Lunch, dinner, snacks
Sitting room, pool, boat,
dock, bkfst. served on, yacht
the Celeste

Award-winning waterfront inn, adjacent to Bal Harbor shops. Beautiful tropical setting with world famous Palm Restaurant & Islands Cafe at Waterfront Tavern & London Pub
E-mail: bhi@aol.com *Web site:* bayharborinn.com

Brigham Gardens
1411 Collins Ave, 33139
305-531-1331 Fax: 305-538-9898
Erika & Hillary Brigham
All year

85-145-EP
18 rooms, 18 pb
Visa, MC, AmEx, •
C-yes/S-yes/P-yes/H-no
Spanish, German

Coffee service all rooms
Family friendly facility, close
to beach; in heart, of art
Deco district

Historical south beach guest house. Over 100 special plants and many tropical birds. Half a block to the beach. E-mail: brighamg@interpoint.net *Web site:* brighamgardens.com

Hotel Ocean
1230 Ocean Dr, 33139
305-672-2579 Fax: 305-672-7665
Xavier Lesmarie
All year

169-515-B&B
27 rooms, 27 pb
•
C-yes/P-yes

Full breakfast
Restaurant, bar
Valet, barber/beauty shop,
laundry, gift shop, TV
lounge, concierge

Beautiful elegant suites offering direct views of the ocean from every window. Sophistication in decor makes the perfect point of retreat. E-mail: ocean1230@aol.com
Web site: hotelocean.com

MICANOPY ─────────────────────────────

Herlong Mansion
PO Box 667, 32667
352-466-3322 Fax: 352-466-3322
800-HERLONG
H.C. (Sonny) Howard, Jr.
All year

70-175-B&B
12 rooms, 12 pb
Visa, MC, *Rated*, •
C-yes/S-no/P-no/H-yes

Full breakfast
Afternoon tea,
complimentary wine
Sitting room, library, Pump
House with Jacuzzi

Twenty antique and craft shops one block away. Historic Greek Revival house, c.1845. Moss draped oaks, pecans and dogwoods. E-mail: info@herlong.com *Web site:* herlong.com

MOUNT DORA

Darst Victorian Manor
495 Old Hwy 441, 32757
352-383-4050 Fax: 352-383-7653
888-53-DARST
Nanci & Jim Darst
All year

125-220-B&B
6 rooms, 6 pb
Most CC, *Rated*, •
C-ltd/S-no/P-no/H-ltd

Full gourmet breakfast
Afternoon tea, snacks
Sitting room, Jacuzzis, suites,
fireplaces, cable TV, game
area

3 story Queen Anne Victorian on three studded 2 acres overlooking Lake Dora, approximately 2 blocks west of historic downtown Mt. Dora. Perfect for romantic getaways as well as antique hunting. Web site: bbonline.com/fl/darstmanor

Mount Dora Historic Inn
221 E 4th Ave, 32757
352-735-1212 Fax: 352-735-9743
800-927-6344
Lindsay & Nancy Richards
All year

75-125-B&B
4 rooms, 4 pb
Most CC, *Rated*, •
C-ltd/S-ltd/P-no/H-no

Full breakfast
Afternoon tea,
complimentary wine
Sitting room, accommodate
business travelers

Relive the elegance of the past at the lovely Mount Dora Historic Inn. Only 25 minutes from Orlando. Escape to the gracious hospitality, authentic period antiques, and full gourmet breakfast. The Inn features beautifully appointed rooms. E-mail: info@
mountdorahistoricinn.com Web site: mountdorahistoricinn.com

NAPLES

Lemon Tree Inn
250 Ninth St South, 34102
941-262-1414 Fax: 941-262-2638
888-800-LEMON
All year

99-B&B
35 rooms, 35 pb
Most CC, *Rated*, •
C-yes/S-yes/P-no/H-yes
Spanish

Continental plus breakfast
Snacks
Bikes, tennis courts, pool,
steps from Old Naples, near
beach

A touch of Key West in the heart of Old Naples. Newly opened in 1997. Abundant gazebos, screened terraces & patios. Stroll to Old Naples & famed 5th Ave dining & boutiques. A very special B&B. E-mail: lt@aol.com Web site: lemontreeinn.com

NEW SMYRNA BEACH

Night Swan Int'coastal B&B
512 South Riverside Dr, 32168
904-423-4940 Fax: 904-427-2814
800-465-4261
Chuck & Martha Nighswonger
All year

80-175-B&B
15 rooms, 15 pb
Most CC, *Rated*, •
C-yes/S-no/P-no/H-yes

Full breakfast
Sitting room, 4 suites,
playground nearby, 140 foot
dock fishing

Located in the Historic District on the Intracoastal Waterway between Daytona Beach and Kennedy Space Center; just one mile from the beach. E-mail: nightswanb@aol.com
Web site: NightSwan.com

Somerset B&B
502 S Riverside Dr, 32168
904-423-3839 Fax: 904-423-2286
888-700-1440
Sammy & Susan Saglibene
All year

145-155-B&B
4 rooms, 4 pb
Visa, MC, AmEx, *Rated*
C-ltd/S-ltd/P-no/H-no

Continental plus breakfast
Complimentary wine
Sitting room, bicycles, suites,
fireplaces, cable TV, in-room
massages

Open, breezy southern verandahs. Great views! Guest rooms with French doors leading to verandah. E-mail: somerset@ucnsh.net Web site: somersetbb.com

NORTH HUTCHINSON ISLAND

Mellon Patch Inn, The
3601 N A-1-A, 34949
561-461-5231 Fax: 561-464-6463
800-656-7824
Andrea & Arthur Mellon
All year

85-120-B&B
4 rooms, 4 pb
Visa, MC, AmEx,
Rated, •
C-ltd/S-no/P-no/H-yes

Full breakfast
Afternoon tea
Sitting room, sailing, tennis
court, canoeing, fishing,
biking, spa

This new Florida-style B&B is across from a magnificent beach. All rooms have hand-painted furniture & water view. Enjoy a gourmet breakfast while your soul feasts on beauty. E-mail: mellon@sunet.net Web site: sunet.net/mlnptch

ORANGE PARK

Club Continental Suites
PO Box 7100, 32073
904-264-6070 Fax: 904-264-4044
800-877-6070
Caleb Massee & Karrie
Stevens   All year

70-160-B&B
22 rooms, 22 pb
Most CC, *Rated*, •
C-yes/S-yes/P-ltd/H-yes

Continental breakfast
Lunch/dinner (Tues-Fri)
Sunday Brunch, bar serv.,
restaurant, sitting room, 7
tennis courts, 2 pools

Florida riverfront inn with giant live oaks, gardens & fountains. Historical Palmolive Estate, superior suites, Jacuzzis, tennis.

ORLANDO

Clauser's Bed & Breakfast
201 E Kicklighter Rd, 32744
904-228-0310 Fax: 904-228-2337
800-220-0310
Tom & Marge Clauser All year

95-140-B&B
8 rooms, 8 pb
Most CC, *Rated*, •
C-ltd/S-no/P-no/H-yes

Full breakfast
Snacks, tea
Sitting room, verandas,
gardens, hot tub, bikes,
Sherlock's English Pub

1880s Victorian home in tranquil country setting. Magnificent trees, heirlooms, quilts, linens and lace. "Romance in the country." E-mail: clauserinn@totcon.com
Web site: clauserinn.com

Higgins House, The
420 S Oak Ave, 32771
407-324-9238 Fax: 407-324-9238
800-584-0014
Roberta & Walter Padgett
All year

95-150-B&B
3 rooms, 3 pb
Most CC, *Rated*, •
C-ltd/S-ltd/P-no/H-ltd

Continental plus breakfast
Snacks, wine
Sitting room, bicycles,
outdoor hot tub, deck,
gardens, tennis nearby

Romantic, elegant Victorian inn close to St. Johns River & Lake Monroe in Historic District. 3 rooms with private bath plus Cottage (handicap access) with 2 baths, living room, kitchen. Birding, hiking, canoeing. E-mail: reservations@higginshouse.com
Web site: higginshouse.com

Meadow Marsh B&B
940 Tildenville School, 34787
407-656-2064 Fax: 407-654-0656
888-656-2064
Cavelle & John Pawlack
All year

95-199-B&B
5 rooms, 5 pb
Visa, MC, *Rated*, •
C-ltd/S-no/P-no/H-ltd

Full 3 course breakfast
Refreshments always
available
Sitting room, piano, library, 3
suites with whirlpools,
Refreshments avail.

Experience romantic ol' Florida while exploring the "new attractions." Stroll under majestic oaks or through sunlit meadows to the 20 mile biking, blading, walking path adjacent our 12 acres. Special candlelight dinners and picnics available.   E-mail: JPawlack@aol.com
Web site: meadowmarsh.net

PerriHouse B&B Inn
10417 Centurion Court, 32836
407-876-4830 Fax: 407-876-0241
800-780-4830
Nick & Angi Perretti
All year

99-139-B&B
8 rooms, 8 pb
Most CC, *Rated*, •
C-yes/S-ltd/H-yes

Continental plus breakfast
All rooms private entrances,
pool, spa, A/C, TV, bird
sanctuary project

A private & secluded country estate on 16 acres conveniently nestled adjacent to the Walt Disney World complex. 3 min. to Downtown Disney; 5 min. to EPCOT; 20 min. to airport. Birdhouse Cottages, 3-5-7 day vacations offered. Double occupancy $225-399. E-mail: birds@perrihouse.com *Web site:* perrihouse.com/

Things Worth Remembering
7338 Cabor Court, 32818
407-291-2127 Fax: 407-291-2127
800-484-3585
Lindsey Cunningham
All year

65-B&B
1 rooms, 1 pb
•
C-ltd/S-no/P-no/H-ltd

Continental plus breakfast
Snacks, restaurant
Toll free number code 6908,
airport delivery/pickup, for
nominal charge

Awaken to baked goods & fresh brewed coffee after a peaceful nights sleep. Relax among the collectibles that are nestled in corners and hanging on walls E-mail: orlandob2b@aol.com

ORLANDO

Thurston House
851 Lake Ave, 32751
407-539-1911 Fax: 407-539-0365
800-843-2721
Carole M. Ballard
All year

120-140-B&B
4 rooms, 4 pb
Visa, MC, AmEx,
Rated, •
C-ltd/S-no/P-no/H-no

Continental plus breakfast
Comp. wine, snacks
Sitting room, screened
porches, lake front

Newly renovated 1885 Queen Anne Victorian home. Hidden away in a country setting but moments from downtown Orlando. Come experience the "old Florida."
E-mail: thurstonbb@aol.com *Web site:* thurstonhouse.com

Veranda B&B, The
115 N Summerlin Ave, 32801
407-849-0321 Fax: 407-849-0321
800-420-6822
Troy Benz
All year

99-199-B&B
9 rooms, 9 pb
Most CC,
C-yes/S-ltd/P-no/H-yes

Continental plus breakfast
Afternoon tea, snacks, comp.
wine
Jacuzzis, swimming pool,
suites, cable TV, conference
facilities

Classically elegant European style bed and breakfast. In historic Thronton Park near Lake Eola. Enjoy hors doeuvres and wine in our picturesque courtyard. Walk to casual or fine dining.   *E-mail:* verandabnb@aol.com *Web site:* theverandabandb.com

PALM BEACH

Royal Palm House, The
3215 Spruce Ave, 33407
561-863-9836 Fax: 561-848-7350
800-655-3196
Betty & Bob Faub
All year

75-155-B&B
5 rooms, 5 pb
Most CC, •
S-no/P-no/H-ltd

Full breakfast
Complimentary cocktails
and snacks
Sitting room, library,
Jacuzzis, pool, suites, cable
TV, adjoining rooms

The Royal Palm House is registered as an historic home, built in 1925, in the Old North-wood Historic District. Breakfast is served on the deck, by the pool or in our morning room. Not appropriate for children.   *E-mail:* faub1@juno.com *Web site:* bbhost.com/royalpalm

PALMETTO

Five Oaks Inn
1102 Riverside Dr, 34221
941-723-1236 Fax: 941-723-1236
800-658-4167
Frank & Pam Colorito
All year

75-110-B&B
4 rooms, 4 pb
Most CC, *Rated*, •
S-ltd/P-no/H-no

Full breakfast
Afternoon tea, snacks, comp.
wine
Bar service, sitting room,
library, bicycles, tanning
beach

Magnificent Southern estate. River setting, a taste of Florida elegance & grace. Antiques, history & hospitality. Near shops, restaurants, beach. Air/heat all rooms.

PENSACOLA

Schoolhouse Inn
Rt 6 Box 283, 32570
850-623-6197 Fax: 850-626-3124
800-239-6864
Evelyn & Bill Boswell
All year

89-109-B&B
8 rooms, 8 pb
Visa, MC, Disc, *Rated*,
•
C-yes/S-ltd/P-no/H-yes

Continental plus breakfast
Adventures Unlimited acnoe,
kayak and tub trips,
fireplaces

1926 country schoolhouse on Bubbling Creek. Rooms themed for American authors. 12' ceilings, antique furniture, homemade breakfast.   *E-mail:* aunlimited@aol.com
Web site: adventuresunlimited.com/bed.htm

Springhill Guesthouse
903 Spring St, 32501
850-438-6887 Fax: 850-438-9075
800-475-1956
Don & Wanda Laird
All year

79-139-B&B
2 rooms, 2 pb
•
C-yes/S-no/P-no/H-no

Full breakfast
Restaurant
Sitting room, suites, fireplace,
cable TV, conference

Charming and comfortable, this Queen Anne style home in Historic North Hill is the place to come home to. Conveniently located near downtown Pensacola.   *E-mail:* guesthouse@ pcola.gulf.net *Web site:* pcola.gulf.net/~guesthouse

QUINCY ————————————————————————

Allison House Inn
215 N Madison St, 32351
850-875-2511
888-904-2511
Stuart and Eileen Johnson
All year

75-95-B&B
5 rooms, 5 pb
Most CC, *Rated*, •
C-yes/S-no/P-ltd/H-yes

Continental plus breakfast
Bicycles, Sherry reception
in, the afternoon

Filled with antiques of the British Isles, the Inn is mindful of an English country manor in the heart of the historic district of Quincy, Florida. E-mail: innkeeper@tds.net
Web site: travelguides.com/bb/allison_house/

SEBRING ————————————————————————

Kenilworth Lodge
836 SE Lakeview Dr, 33870
941-385-0111 Fax: 941-385-4686
800-423-5939
Mark & Madge Stewart
All year

45-66-B&B
105 rooms, 105 pb
Most CC, •
C-yes/S-yes/P-no/H-no

Continental plus breakfast
Restaurant
Library, pool, suites,
fireplaces, cable TV, golf
packages, bike routes

Historic 100 room inn; overlooking Lake Jackson; 80 foot pool; large lobby to meet new friends; specializes in golf pkgs., bicycling, water sports. E-mail: mark@strato.net
Web site: kenlodge.com

SIESTA KEY ————————————————————————

Turtle Beach Resort
9049 Midnight Pass Rd, 34242
941-349-4554 Fax: 941-312-9034
Gail & David Rubinfeld
All year

125-295-EP
10 rooms, 10 pb
Most CC, *Rated*, •
C-yes/S-no/P-ltd

Restaurant
Hot tubs, swimming pool,
bicycles, honeymoons,
romantic getaways

Waterfront inn, island paradise. Private cottages with private hot tubs! Gourmet waterfront dining next door. Four boat docks. Secluded gulf beach, spectacular sunsets.
E-mail: turtlebch1@aol.com *Web site:* turtlebeachresort.com

SPRING HILL ————————————————————————

Verona House B&B
201 S Main St, 34601
352-796-4001 Fax: 352-799-0612
800-355-6717
Bob & Jan Boyd
All year

65-100-B&B
4 rooms, 4 pb
Most CC, *Rated*, •
C-ltd/S-ltd/P-no/H-ltd

Full breakfast
Aftn. tea, Comp. drinks & btl.
H20
Sitting room, bikes,
accommodates business
travelers

A Sears & Roebuck Catalog House on National Register furnished in collectibles.
E-mail: veronabb@gate.net *Web site:* bbhost.com/veronabb

ST. AUGUSTINE ————————————————————————

Alexander Homestead B&B
14 Sevilla St, 32084
904-826-4147 Fax: 904-823-9503
888-292-4147
Bonnie J. Alexander
All year

105-160-B&B
4 rooms, 4 pb
Most CC, *Rated*, •
C-ltd/S-no/P-no/H-no

Full breakfast
Afternoon tea
Sitting room, bikes, Jacuzzis,
fireplaces, cable TV

Elegant 1888 Victorian home, private baths, 1 with whirlpool Jacuzzi, woodburning fireplaces, private porches, authentic antique furnishings, TV, fresh flowers, chocolates, complimentary brandies. AAA 3 diamond rating. E-mail: bonnie@aug.com
Web site: alexanderhomestead.com

Carriage Way B&B
70 Cuna St, 32084
904-829-2467 Fax: 904-826-1461
800-908-9832
Bill & Larry Johnson
All year

69-175-B&B
9 rooms, 9 pb
Visa, MC, AmEx, Disc, •
C-ltd/S-no/P-no/H-no
French

Full breakfast
Snacks
Comp. wine & beverages,
picnics, whirlpool tub

1883 Victorian home in heart of historic district; antiques & reproductions, clawfoot tubs, bicycles available. Casual, friendly atmosphere E-mail: bjohnson@aug.com
Web site: Carriageway.com

Verona House B&B, Spring Hill, FL

ST. AUGUSTINE

Casa de La Paz Bayfront B&B 22 Avenida Menendez, 32084 904-829-2915 Fax: 904-824-6269 800-929-2915 Bob and Donna Marriott All year	125-230-B&B 6 rooms, 6 pb Most CC, *Rated* C-ltd/S-no/P-no/H-no	Full breakfast buffet Complimentary snacks/wine/sherry Sitting room, verandah, parking

On the Historic District's bayfront, this elegant Mediterranean-style home (1915) offers fine accommodations in a beautiful, central location. Spanish walled flower garden.
E-mail: delapaz@aug.com *Web site:* casadelapaz.com

Castle Garden B&B 15 Shenandoah St, 32084 904-829-3839 Fax: 904-829-9049 Bruce & Kimmy Kloecker All year	79-155-B&B 7 rooms, 7 pb Most CC, *Rated*, • C-ltd/S-ltd/P-no/H-no	Full breakfast Complimentary wine & champagne Picnic lunches, bicycles, fresh flowers, 3 bridal rooms with whirlpools

St. Augustine's only Moorish Revival dwelling, former Castle Warden Carriage House, built 1800s. Restored gardens. Quiet, country like setting.   E-mail: castleg@aug.com
Web site: castlegarden.com

Cedar House Inn-Victorian 79 Cedar St, 32084 904-829-0079 Fax: 904-825-0916 800-233-2746 Russ & Nina Thomas All year	84-164-B&B 6 rooms, 6 pb Visa, MC, Disc, *Rated*, • C-ltd/S-no/P-no/H-no	Full breakfast Dinner, afternoon tea, snacks Sitting room, library, piano, porches, bikes, free walking tour guide

Capture romantic moments at our beautiful 1893 Victorian home in the heart of historic St. Augustine. Enjoy hospitality at its finest.   E-mail: russ@aug.com *Web site:* cedarhouseinn.com

ST. AUGUSTINE ────────────────────────────────

Kenwood Inn, The	85-185-B&B	Continental plus breakfast
38 Marine St, 32084	15 rooms, 15 pb	Sitting room, piano,
904-824-2116 Fax: 904-824-1689	Visa, MC, Disc, *Rated*	swimming pool, walled in
800-824-8151	C-ltd/S-ltd/P-no/H-no	courtyard
Mark, Kerrianne, & Caitlan		
All year		

Lovely old 19th-century Victorian inn located in historic district of our nation's oldest city. Walk to attractions; beautiful beaches 5 minutes away.   Web site: oldcity.com/kenwood/

Southern Wind Inn	105-195-B&B	Full breakfast
18 Cordova St, 32084	10 rooms, 10 pb	Complimentary wine,
904-825-3623 Fax: 904-810-5212	Visa, MC, AmEx, *Rated*	lemonade
800-781-3338	C-ltd/S-no/P-no/H-no	Spacious verandas, large,
Alana & Bob Indelicato		parlor, wraparound porch,
All year		cable TV, bicycles

On the Carriage Trail through historic district, Southern Wind offers an elegant 1916 columned masonry home with exceptional buffet breakfast.   E-mail: swind@aug.com
Web site: southernwindinn.com

St. Francis Inn	95-199-B&B	Full breakfast
279 St George St, 32084	14 rooms, 14 pb	Iced tea & lemonade
904-824-6068 Fax: 904-810-5525	Most CC, *Rated*, •	Sunday afternoon music,
800-824-6062	C-ltd/S-no/P-no/H-no	swimming pool, bicycles,
Joe & Margaret Finnegan		private parking
All year		

Built in 1791, located in Historic District, one block west of the "Oldest House in USA." Sev. rooms with working fireplaces, telephones & Jacuzzi tubs. Recently renovated. AAA three diamonds.   E-mail: innceasd@aug.com *Web site:* stfrancisinn.com

ST. JOHN'S COUNTY ──────────────────────────

Penny Farthing Inn	95-150-B&B	Full breakfast
83 Cedar St, 32084	6 rooms, 6 pb	Snacks, wine
904-824-2100 Fax: 904-824-9074	Most CC, *Rated*, •	Sitting room, bicycles,
800-395-1890	C-ltd/S-no/P-no/H-no	Jacuzzis, suites, cable TV
Pam & Walt James		
All year		

1890 Victorian B&B in the heart of the olde city. 6 elegant bedchambers with an array of antiques, queen beds, veranders with swings or rockers. On-property parking, mid-weeks discounts & packages. . E-mail: penny@aug.com *Web site:* oldcity.com/pennyfarthing

ST. PETE BEACH ─────────────────────────────

Pasa Tiempo B&B	100-150-B&B	Continental plus breakfast
7141 Bay St, 33706	8 rooms, 8 pb	Snacks, complimentary wine
727-367-9907 Fax: 727-367-9906	Visa, MC, AmEx,	Sitting room, suites, cable TV,
P. Bishop, Sally McGuiness	*Rated*, •	accommodate business
All year	C-ltd/S-ltd/P-no/H-ltd	travelers

Forget about the everyday for a few days or longer. Pasa Tiempo is a B&B that makes it easy to recharge your batteries. From iced drinks on the balcony to the scent of just-cut flowers at every turn it's the kind of place that invites you to be yourself.
E-mail: info@pasa-tiempo.com *Web site:* pasa-tiempo.com

ST. PETERSBURG ─────────────────────────────

Bay Gables B&B	85-150-B&B	Continental breakfast
340 Rowland Court, 33701	9 rooms, 9 pb	Snacks, wine
727-822-8855 Fax: 727-824-7223	Most CC, *Rated*, •	Sitting room, Jacuzis, suites,
800-822-8803	C-ltd/S-no/P-no/H-ltd	cable TV, conference
David Lee		facilities
All year		

A beautifully restored Key West style Inn, downtown within walking distance to restaurants, museums, The Pier, Tropicana field-Devil Rays baseball, 9 beautifully decorated rooms & suites.   E-mail: solomio@msn.com *Web site:* baygablesbb.citysearch.com

ST. PETERSBURG

Bay Shore Manor
635 12th Ave NE, 33701
727-822-3438 Fax: 727-822-3438
Christa & Heiko Gross
All year

64-74-B&B
5 rooms, 5 pb
Visa, MC, AmEx, •
C-yes/S-ltd/P-no/H-no
German

Continental plus breakfast
Complimentary wine
Sitting room, library,
bicycles, tennis court, cable
TV

The Bay Shore Manor, built in 1928, is now hosted by the German Gross Family. Each suite is nicely furnished & has own bath, phone, TV, coffeemaker, microwave, and a refrigerator.   E-mail: baymanor@aol.com Web site: llc.net/~heiko/index.htm

Mansion House B&B
105 5th Ave NE, 33701
727-821-9391 Fax: 727-821-9391
800-274-7520
Robert & Rose Marie Ray
Jan-May, Jun-Dec

110-250-B&B
12 rooms, 12 pb
Visa, MC, AmEx,
Rated, •
C-ltd/S-no/P-no/H-no

Full American breakfast
Complimentary wine,
cheese, soda
Sitting room, 2 libraries,
patio, VCR, carriage room,
Jacuzzi, pool

12 deluxe rooms, cable TV, 2 Jacuzzi—one in outdoor swimming pool, 10 common area, courtyard garden, meeting/conference facilities, telephones with dataports. Weddings, receptions, family reunions on site, catering available.   E-mail: mansion1@ix.netcom.com Web site: mansionbandb.com

Sunset Bay Inn
635 Bay Street NE, 33701
727-896-6701 Fax: 727-898-5311
800-794-5133
Bob & Martha Bruce
All year

130-230-B&B
8 rooms, 8 pb
Most CC, *Rated*, •
C-ltd/S-ltd/P-no/H-ltd

Full breakfast
Comp. wine, soda, baked
goods
24 hour snack bar, library,
bicycles, cable TV/VCR,
Jacuzzis, ceiling fans

Beautifully restored historic 1911 colonial home located near bayfront and area attractions. As journaled by a guest, "The elegant but warm touches are surpassed only by your gracious hospitality." E-mail: wrbcom@aol.com Web site: sunsetbayinn.com

STUART

Harbor Front Inn B&B
310 Atlanta Ave, 34994
561-288-7289 Fax: 561-221-0474
JoAyne & John Elbert
All year

85-175-B&B
7 rooms, 7 pb
Most CC, *Rated*, •
C-ltd/S-ltd/P-no/H-no
Spanish

Full breakfast
Snacks, complimentary wine
Jacuzzis, suites, cable TV,
accommodate business
travelers

C. 1906, old Florida-style vernacular cottage built on 2 acres of breathtaking waterfront property. Private entrances to all accommodations.   Web site: harborfrontinn.com

TALLAHASSEE

McFarlin House
305 E King St, 32351
850-875-2526 Fax: 850-627-4703
Richard & Tina Fauble
All year

75-175-B&B
9 rooms, 9 pb
Rated
C-yes/S-no/P-no/H-ltd

Full breakfast
Snacks, Dinner upon
request/notice
Sitting room, Jacuzzis,
fireplaces, cable TV,
corporate rates

E-mail: inquiries@mcfarlinhouse.com Web site: mcfarlinhouse.com

**Simon Ridgeway House
B&B**
625 E Washington St, 32344
850-997-1376
James Roger & Carlotta Taylor
All year

85-125-B&B
5 rooms, 5 pb
Visa, MC, AmEx, •
C-ltd/S-ltd/P-ltd/H-no

Full breakfast
Lunch available (fee), snacks
Sitting room, Jacuzzis,
conference facilities

Opulently decorated B&B on the National Historic Register, circa 1880. Scrumptious breakfast served by candlelight. Located on historical tour of homes & churches built as early as 1840.   E-mail: srhbed@aol.com Web site: bbhost.com:8008/simonridgeway

TAMPA

Gram's Place B&B & Music
3109 N Ola Ave, 33603
813-221-0596
Mark Holland
All year

65-95-B&B
7 rooms, 4 pb
Visa, MC, AmEx, •
C-ltd/S-yes/P-no/H-no

Continental breakfast
Courtyard w/BYOB bar
Sitting room, Jacuzzi, 2
waterfalls, sun deck, artists
retreat, phone

European attitude. Music lovers paradise, shuttle serv. for 1/2 cab fare. If you like jazz, folk, country, blues, and/or rock, you'll love this place.   E-mail: gramspl@aol.com Web site: grams-inn-tampa.com/

Ruskin House B&B
120 Dickman Dr SW, 33570
813-645-3842
Mr. & Mrs. Arthur M. Miller
All year

75-B&B
3 rooms, 2 pb
Visa, MC, AmEx, •
C-yes/S-ltd/P-no/H-ltd
French, some Spanish

Continental plus breakfast
Full breakfast on weekends
Complimentary sherry and
tea, sitting room, library, 3
acres, bicycles

Gracious 1910 waterfront home with period (1860-1920) antiques, between Tampa & Sarasota on west coast. Three minutes from I-75.   E-mail: ruskinhouse@mindspring.com Web site: ruskinhouse.com

TARPON SPRINGS

Spring Bayou Inn
32 W Tarpon Ave, 34689
727-938-9333
Fax: 727-938-9333
Sharon A. Birk
All year

60-110-B&B
5 rooms, 3 pb
Rated
S-no/P-no/H-no

Full breakfast
Parlor, library, fireplace, front
porch, baby grand piano

Elegant Victorian with modern conveniences. Walk to shops, bayou, restaurants, sponge docks. Golf, beaches, tennis, and fishing nearby.

VENICE

Banyan House, The
519 S Harbor Dr, 34285
941-484-1385
Fax: 941-484-8032
Chuck and Susan McCormick
All year

89-129-B&B
9 rooms, 9 pb
Visa, MC, *Rated*
C-ltd/S-no/P-no

Continental plus breakfast
Sitting room, Jacuzzi,
bicycles, hot tubs, swimming
pool

Historic Mediterranean-style home. Enormous Banyan tree shades courtyard, pool and spa.   E-mail: relax@banyanhouse.com Web site: banyanhouse.com

Georgia

AMERICUS

1906 Pathway Inn
501 South Lee St, 31709
912-928-2078 Fax: 912-928-2078
800-889-1466
Chuck & Angela Nolan
All year

75-125-B&B
5 rooms, 5 pb
Most CC, *Rated*, •
C-yes/S-ltd/P-yes/H-no

Full breakfast
Snacks, complimentary wine
3 suites with whirlpools

Sumptuous candlelit breakfast, whirlpools, historic district. See Civil War Andersonville & former President Carter teach Sunday school. Stained glass. Romantic. Pampering. E-mail: pathway@sowega.net

AMERICUS ──────────────────────────────────

Rees Park Garden Inn	65-95-B&B	Full breakfast
504 Rees Park, 31709	6 rooms, 4 pb	Snacks
912-931-0122 Fax: 912-928-2934	Visa, MC, AmEx,	Sitting room, library, suites,
Don & Jodi Miles	C-yes/S-ltd/P-ltd/H-yes	cable TV, conferences
All year	Spanish	

We are a quiet comfortable inn located in a lovely historic district and furnished with all the guest amenities we could think of.   E-mail: reespark@americus.net
Web site: americus.net/~reespark

ATLANTA ──────────────────────────────────

Abbett Inn	79-149-B&B	Continental plus breakfast
1746 Virginia Ave, 30337	6 rooms, 4 pb	Dinner, tea, snacks, wine
404-767-3708 Fax: 404-767-1626	Most CC, *Rated*	Sitting room, suites, fireplace,
Donald Farmer & John Hoard	C-ltd/S-no/P-no/H-no	cable TV
All year		

Built in 1887, in Historic College Park, close to Hartsfield International Airport, 10 minutes from downtown Atlanta   E-mail: abbettinn@bellsouth.net *Web site:* abbettinn.com

Ansley Inn	109-169-B&B	Full breakfast
253 15th St NE, 30309	22 rooms, 22 pb	Afternoon refreshments
404-872-9000 Fax: 404-892-2318	Most CC, *Rated*, •	Sitting room, hot tubs, health
800-446-5416	C-yes/S-ltd/P-no/H-yes	club membership, Emory
Jan Partian	Spanish	University
All year		

Beautifully restored Tudor mansion in heart of Atlanta's business and art district. Full service luxury inn in the classic southern style. 24-hr. concierge. Close to Buckhead. E-mail: reservations@ansleyinn.com *Web site:* ansleyinn.com

Beverly Hills Inn	99-130-B&B	Continental plus breakfast
65 Sheridan Dr NE, 30305	18 rooms, 18 pb	Sitting room, library, piano,
404-233-8520 Fax: 404-233-8659	Most CC, *Rated*, •	health club, London taxi
800-331-8520	C-yes/S-yes/P-no/H-no	shuttle
Mit Amin		
All year		

Charming city retreat, fine residential neighborhood. Close to Lenox Square, Historical Society and many art galleries. 15 min. to downtown.   E-mail: info@beverlyhillsinn.com
Web site: beverlyhillsinn.com

Bonaventure, The	95-145-B&B	Full breakfast
650 Bonaventure Ave, 30306	4 rooms, 3 pb	Afternoon tea, snacks, wine
404-817-7024 Fax: 404-249-9988	Visa, MC, AmEx,	Sitting room, bicycles, suites,
Meredith Brooks	*Rated*, •	fireplace, cable TV, gardens,
All year	C-ltd/S-ltd/P-no/H-no	ponds
	French	

Nat'l Register property & winner of the GA Trust For Historic Preservations' 1998 Best Rehabilitation Project. A Victorian dream exuding old world charm with modern conveniences   E-mail: innkeeper@thebonaventure.com *Web site:* thebonaventure.com

Gaslight Inn B&B	95-195-B&B	Continental plus breakfast
1001 St Charles Ave NE, 30306	6 rooms, 6 pb	Snacks
404-875-1001 Fax: 404-876-1001	Most CC, *Rated*, •	Sitting room, library, grand
Jim Moss	C-ltd/S-no/P-no/H-ltd	piano, bike rental, walk to 35
All year		restaurants

Featured in Better Homes & Gardens and Southern Homes magazines. Single rooms, suites, fireplaces, Jacuzzi tubs, whirlpool baths, sauna & private gardens. E-mail: innkeeper@gaslightinn.com *Web site:* gaslightinn.com/

ATLANTA ─────────────────────────

Inmon Park B&B	90-110-B&B	Continental plus breakfast
100 Waverly Way, NE, 30307	3 rooms	Private garden
404-688-9498 Fax: 404-524-9939	Visa, MC, AmEx, •	Screened porch, fireplaces,
Eleanor Matthews	C ltd/S-no/P-no/H-no	secured parking
All year		

Totally restored Victorian located in historic Inman Park. 1 block to subway, close to restaurants. 12-ft ceilings, heart-pine woodwork, antiques. National Register of Historic Places. E-mail: Eleanor@bellsouth.net

King-Keith House B&B	75-175-B&B	Full gourmet breakfast
889 Edgewood Ave NE, 30307	5 rooms, 4 pb	Snacks
404-688-7330 Fax: 404-584-0730	Visa, MC, AmEx,	Sitting room, porch, cottage
800-728-3879	*Rated*, •	w/Jacuzzi/frplc., suite
Windell Keith	C-yes/S-no/P-no/H-no	w/kitchen sleeps 4
All year		

1890 Victorian loaded with charm. Period furnishings. Close to downtown. Shops & restaurants nearby. E-mail: kingkeith@mindspring.com *Web site:* kingkeith.com

Stonehurst B&B	90-110-B&B	Full breakfast
923 Piedmont Ave NE, 30309	3 rooms, 3 pb	Snacks
404-881-0722 Fax: 404-881-5324	Visa, MC, *Rated*, •	Sitting room, cable TV
Saundra Altekruse	C-ltd/S-no/P-no/H-no	
All year	French	

Built in 1896, this beautiful and historic B&B is located in historic Midtown Atlanta. E-mail: stonehurst@mindspring.com *Web site:* stonehurstbandb.com

Sugar Magnolia B&B	80-125-B&B	Continental plus breakfast
804 Edgewood Ave, NE, 30307	3 rooms, 3 pb	Afternoon tea, snacks
404-222-0226 Fax: 404-681-1067	Visa, MC, *Rated*, •	Bar service, sitting room,
Debi Starnes & Jim Emshoff	C-ltd/S-no/P-no/H-no	business center, roof deck,
All year		fireplaces, pool

Beautiful 1892 Queen Anne Victorian in historic in-town neighborhood near Atlanta's attractions. Garden room and cottage suite great for families. E-mail: sugmagbb@aol.com *Web site:* sugarmagnoliabb.com

Village Inn B&B	110-150-B&B	Full breakfast
992 Ridge Ave, 30083	6 rooms, 6 pb	Snacks
770-469-3459 Fax: 770-469-1051	Most CC, *Rated*, •	Library, Jacuzzis, suites,
800-214-8385	C-yes/S-ltd/P-no/H-ltd	fireplaces, cable TV, video
Earl & Christy Collins		library, VCRs
All year		

1820's Inn located in historic district, 1/2 mile from Stone Mountain Park. Whirlpool tubs, fireplaces, TV/VCR's, in-room telephones, verandas, full Southern breakfast. E-mail: villageinn@mindspring.com *Web site:* villageinnbb.com

AUGUSTA ─────────────────────────

Partridge Inn, The	85-150-B&B	Full breakfast
2110 Walton Way, 30904	156 rooms, 156 pb	Snacks, lunch/dinner
706-737-8888 Fax: 706-731-0826	Visa, MC, AmEx,	available
800-476-6888	*Rated*, •	Restaurant, bar service,
Thomas Haufe	C-yes/S-ltd/P-ltd/H-ltd	sitting room, library, pool,
All year		suites, cable TV

Historic 1890's Inn completely renovated and restored. Situated on the historic Summerville Hill. Easy access to downtown & area attractions. Award winning food & beverage. True southern hospitality.

BRUNSWICK ───────────────────────────────

Brunswick Manor
825 Egmont St, 31520
912-265-6889 Fax: 912-265-7879
Harry and Claudia Tzucanow
All year

80-95-B&B
9 rooms, 8 pb
Visa, MC, *Rated*, •
C-ltd/S-ltd/P-ltd/H-ltd
some Spanish

Full gourmet breakfast
Complimentary wine, high
tea
Sitting room, library,
bicycles, tennis courts, hot
tub, robes, veranda

Elegant historic 1886 inn near Golden Isles. Boat chartering avail. Gracious hospitality. All rooms with ceiling fans/refrigerators. Additions to antique & art collection.

CLARKESVILLE ───────────────────────────

Burns-Sutton Inn, The
855 Washington St, 30523
706-754-5565 Fax: 706-754-9698
Jaime G. Huffman
All year

85-125-B&B
7 rooms, 5 pb
Visa, MC, *Rated*
C-ltd/S-ltd/P-no

Full breakfast
Afternoon tea, snacks
Restaurant, sitting room, 1901
Queen Anne with antique
furnishings

Beautifully restored home built of heart pine & stained glass. Intimate inn with English gardens & wraparound front porch in historic district of NE Georgia mountains. Web site: georgiamagazine.com/burns-sutton

Glen-Ella Springs Inn
1789 Bear Gap Rd, 30523
706-754-7295 Fax: 706-754-1560
888-455-8893
Barrie & Bobby Aycock
All year

115-195-B&B
16 rooms, 16 pb
Visa, MC, AmEx,
Rated, •
C-ltd/S-yes/P-no/H-yes

Full breakfast
Rest., dinner only, BYOB
Conf. room, pool, gardens,
mountain creek, hiking trails

100-year-old inn on National Register, rustic rural setting near Tallulah Gorge, lovely views, genuine hospitality, outstanding food.   E-mail: info@glenella.com *Web site:* glenella.com

CLAYTON ─────────────────────────────────

English Manor Inns B&B
PO Box 1605, 30525
706-782-5780 Fax: 706-782-0079
800-782-5780
Susan & English Thornwell
May-November

119-199-B&B/AP
70 rooms, 70 pb
•
C-yes/S-yes/P-no
French, Spanish,
German

Full breakfast
Hors d'oeuvres,
lunch/dinner avail.
Complimentary wine, setups,
pool, hot tubs, croquet, golf,
tennis, croquet

8 inns furnished in exquisite antiques, reflecting charm of an earlier era with all of today's amenities. 10 Jacuzzis. White water rafting & skiing nearby. Wine bar and brown bag set up. Extensive libraries. Open January-April for groups only.

COMMERCE ───────────────────────────────

Magnolia Inn B&B
206 Cherry St, 30529
706-335-7257
800-989-5548
Annette & Jerry Potter
All year

60-70-B&B
4 rooms, 3 pb
Visa, MC, •
C-ltd/S-no/P-no/H-yes

Full breakfast
Afternoon tea
Sitting rm., rose garden,
wrap-around porch, theatre
weekend packages

Restored Victorian in downtown Historic Commerce. All guestrooms are furnished with antiques.

Pittman House, The
81 Homer Rd, 30529
706-335-3823
Tom & Dot Tomberlin
All year

60-75-B&B
4 rooms, 2 pb
Visa, MC, Disc, *Rated*,
•
C-ltd/S-no/P-no/H-no

Full breakfast
Snacks
Sitting room, library, tennis
court nearby, theatre
weekend packages

The Pittman House is a restored 1890 Colonial with wrap-around rocking porch. Completely furnished with antiques. Great sports & shopping nearby. 72 hr. cancellation notice required.

DAHLONEGA

Blueberry Inn, The
400 Blueberry Hill, 30533
706-219-4024 Fax: 706-219-4793
877-219-4024
Phyllis Charnley
All year

65-105-B&B
12 rooms, 12 pb
Visa, MC, •
C-ltd/S-ltd/P-no/H-yes

Full breakfast
Snacks, complimentary wine
Sitting room, library,
fireplaces, business
travelers, pleasure fishing

Country inn sits on top of a hill with wonderful views of the Blue Ridge Mountains, meadows & pond; large gourmet breakfast every morning; rooms furnished with antiques; close to Dahlonega & Helen.   E-mail: bluberrybb@aol.com *Web site:* blueberryinnandgardens.com

Lily Creek Lodge
2608 Auraria Road, 30533
706-864-6848 Fax: 706-864-6848
888-844-2694
Don & Sharon Bacek
All year

99-150-B&B
12 rooms, 12 pb
Visa, MC, AmEx,
Rated, •
C-yes/S-ltd/P-no/H-no
Some Spanish & French

Continental plus breakfast
Snacks, complimentary wine
Hot tub, pool, fireplace,
suites, cable TV, fax, copier,
laptop outlet

Furnished in European Royal Hunting Lodge style. Antiques, art, feather comforters & pillows, fine linens. Try breakfast in our treehouse!   E-mail: baceks@stc.net
Web site: lilycreeklodge.com

**Mtn. Top Lodge at
Dahlonega**
447 Mtn Top Lodge Rd, 30533
706-864-5257 Fax: 706-864-8265
800-526-9754
Karen A. Lewan
All year

70-145-B&B
13 rooms, 13 pb
Most CC,
C-ltd/S-ltd/P-no/H-ltd

Full breakfast
Sitting room, library, hot
tubs, horseshoe pit, suites,
cable TV

Classic country hideaway in the foothills of the North Georgia mountains. Atmosphere is relaxed and casual. Guest rooms are individually furnished with unique antiques & unusual flea mkt. finds.

DARIEN

Open Gates B&B
PO Box 1526, 31305
912-437-6985 Fax: 912-437-8211
Carolyn Hodges
All year

68-75-B&B
5 rooms, 3 pb
Rated
C-ltd/S-no/P-no/H-no

Full breakfast
Boxed lunch, complimentary
wine
Library, Steinway piano,
bicycles, pool, antiques,
sailing, boat tours

Timber baron's gracious home on oak-shaded historic square. Access to untrammeled Barrier Islands, including Sapelo and the Altamaha Delta rice culture.

GAINESVILLE

Dunlap House, The
635 Green St, 30501
770-536-0200 Fax: 770-503-7857
Dave & Karen Peters
All year

85-155-B&B
10 rooms, 10 pb
Most CC, *Rated*, •
C-yes/S-no/P-no/H-yes

Full American breakfast
Complimentary tea,
refreshments
Wedding facilities, no-
smoking inn, turndown
service

Luxurious historic accommodations. Breakfast in common area, bed or on verandah. Restaurant and lounge across the street. Lodging & dining excellence. AAA rating 3 diamonds.   E-mail: dunlaphouse@mindspring.com

HELEN

Alpine Hilltop Haus B&B
PO Box 154, 30545
706-878-2388
F. Allen & B. McNary
All year

89-110-B&B
4 rooms, 4 pb
C-yes/S-ltd/P-no/H-no

Full breakfast
Sitting rooms, with fireplaces

Tree-covered, secluded, hilltop location. Short walk to Alpine Village center. Deck overlooking Chattahoochee River.   Web site: georgiamagazine.com/hilltop/

HELEN

Dutch Cottage B&B	55-95-B&B	Buffet bkfst., weekends
PO Box 757, 30545	4 rooms, 4 pb	Full bkfst., weekdays
706-878-3135	•	Sitting room, hammock,
Chuck & Heidi Waldron	C-ltd/S-ltd/P-no/H-no	Jacuzzi/hot tub, walk to,
All year		town, bird watching

Tranquil waterfall. Ivy covered hillside. Idyllic wooded setting. Large rooms furnished with Dutch antiques. Also charming hillside chalet. Spring water E-mail: waldron@ngweb.net
Web site: community.ngweb.net/dutch

Lodge at Smithgall Woods	235-490-AP	Full breakfast
61 Tsalaki Trail, 30545	14 rooms, 14 pb	All meals included in rate
706-878-3087 Fax: 706-878-0301	Most CC, •	Snacks, comp. wine, sitting
800-318-5248	C-ltd/S-ltd/P-no/H-ltd	room, library, Jacuzzis,
John Erbele		suites, fireplaces
All year		

Our secluded setting is designated as a Heritage Preserve to conserve the area for future generations. Gracious accommodations and regional cuisine complement a host of outdoor activities. E-mail: sgwoods@stc.net Web site: smithgallwoods.com

HIAWASSEE

Creekside Hideaway B&B	65-85-B&B	Full breakfast or continental
PO Box 623, 30582	3 rooms, 3 pb	plus
706-379-1509 Fax: 706-379-1509	Visa, MC, Disc, •	Aftn. tea, snacks, fruit platter
888-CREEK	C-yes/S-ltd/P-ltd/H-ltd	Sitt. room, Jacuzzis, cable
Denise & Art Grassi		TV, lunch and dinner
All year		available

Treat yourself to a pleasurable stay in the beautiful NE Georgia Mountains. Enjoy your delectable meal in your privacy or our dining room with guests. E-mail: creeksidehideaway@ yahoo.com Web site: creeksidehideaway.com

HOGANSVILLE

Grand Hotel, The	100 150 B&B	Full breakfast
PO Box 249, 30230	10 rooms, 10 pb	Lunch, afternoon tea, comp.
706-637-8828 Fax: 706-637-4522	Visa, MC,	wine
800-324-7625	C-ltd/S-ltd/P-ltd/H-ltd	Bar service, sitting room,
Glenda M. Gorden		Jacuzzis, fireplaces, cable TV
All year		

Originally built in the late eighteen hundreds, the hotel has been completely remodeled and furnished throughout with period Antiques. E-mail: info@thegrandhotel.net
Web site: thegrandhotel.net

LAKEMONT

Lake Rabun Hotel	49-115-B&B	Dinner weekends
PO Box 10, 30552	16 rooms, 2 pb	Bar service, sitting room,
706-782-4946 Fax: 706-782-4946	•	library, bicycles, tennis
Roberta & Bill Pettys	C-yes/S-ltd/P-no/H-ltd	court, pool, fireplaces
April-Nov., weekends		

Unique, original mountain inn, built 1922, with homemade craftsman furniture, tastful, comfortable rooms, ambiance of yesteryear, overlooking beautiful, pristine Lake Rabun, one of the ten prettiest spots in the US.

LITTLE ST. SIMONS ISLAND

Little St. Simons Island	325-550-AP	Full breakfast
PO Box 21078, 31522	13 rooms, 13 pb	All meals included in rate
912-638-7472 Fax: 912-634-1811	Visa, MC, *Rated*, •	Pool, boats, shelling, canoes,
888-733-5774	C-ltd/S-ltd/P-no/H-ltd	wildlife, bikes, horses, hiking,
Maureen Ahern		birding
All year		

A 10,000-acre undeveloped barrier island with early 1900s lodge and guest cottages for up to 30 overnight guests. The Lodge serves regional southern cuisine. Meals & Activities included. E-mail: lssi@mindspring.com Web site: pactel.com.au/lssi

SAUTEE

Stovall House Country Inn	76-84-B&B	Continental plus breakfast
1526 Hwy 255 N, 30571	5 rooms, 5 pb	Restaurant
706-878-3355	*Rated*	Sitting room, A/C, central
Hamilton Schwartz	C-yes/S-no/P-no/H-ltd	heating, Historic Register
All year		

Award-winning restoration of 1837 country farmhouse on 28 serene acres with beautiful mountain views. One of the top 50 restaurants in Georgia.
Web site: georgiamagazine.com/stovall/index.html

SAVANNAH

118 West	115-150-B&B	Continental breakfast
118 W Gaston St, 31401	1 rooms, 1 pb	Fireplace, cable TV
912-234-8557 Fax: 912-232-4706	S-no/P-no/H-yes	
Andrea D. Walker		
All year		

One bedroom garden apartment with living room, fully equipped kitchen and full size bath, located in an 1850 townhouse in Savannah's historic district. E-mail: adwalker1@aol.com

Comer House	115-150-B&B	Continental breakfast
2 East Taylor St, 31401	3 rooms, 3 pb	Suites, cable TV
912-234-2923 Fax: 912-234-2923	C-ltd/S-no/P-no/H-no	
Comer House		
All year		

A very large and historic Victorian home located on the finest square offering self-catering guest quarters within a walled courtyard and garden. Private and non-commercial.
E-mail: comerhouse@bigfoot.com Web site: comerhouse.com

East Bay Inn	149-189-B&B	Continental plus breakfast
225 East Bay St, 31401	28 rooms, 28 pb	Wine & cheese reception
912-238-1225 Fax: 912-232-2709	Most CC, *Rated*, •	Restaurant, sitting room,
800-500-1225	C-ltd/S-ltd/P-ltd/H-no	cable TV, conference
Laura H. Guerard		facilities
All year		

Charming, romantic and exquisitely reminiscent of the 19th century, the East Bay Inn is located in the heart of historic Savannah. Just steps away from the bustling waterfront.
E-mail: saveb@mastersinns.com Web site: eastbayinn.com

Eliza Thompson House	119-229-B&B	Full breakfast
5 West Jones St, 31401	25 rooms, 25 pb	Sherry on arrival
912-236-3620 Fax: 912-238-1920	Visa, MC, AmEx,	Evening cordials/sweets,
800-348-9378	*Rated*, •	small conference room,
Carol Day	C-yes/S-ltd/P-no/H-yes	imported wine, concierge
All year		

Regally refurbished home in the heart of the Historic District. Elegant parlor, updated furnishings, beautifully landscaped courtyard with splashing fountains.
E-mail: elizath@aol.com Web site: elizathompsonhouse.com

Foley House Inn, The	165-275-B&B	Continental plus breakfast
14 W Hull St, 31401	20 rooms, 20 pb	Complimentary port, sherry,
912-232-6622 Fax: 912-231-1218	Visa, MC, AmEx,	tea
800-647-3708	*Rated*, •	Hot tub, newspaper, shoes
Inge & Mark Moore	C-yes/S-yes/P-no/H-no	shined on request, VCR &
All year		film lib. in rooms

A restored antebellum mansion, furnished with antiques, 5 Jacuzzi rooms. Turndown service, fireplace rooms. Truly the best of two worlds. E-mail: foleyinn@aol.com
Web site: foleyinn.com

SAVANNAH ─────────────────────────────────────

Forsyth Park Inn, The
102 W Hall St, 31401
912-233-6800
Hal & Virginia Sullivan
All year

145-225-B&B
10 rooms, 10 pb
Visa, MC, AmEx, *Rated*
C-yes/S-yes
Some French

Continental breakfast
Complimentary wine
Sitting room, park near,
tennis courts, hot tubs, piano
music nightly

An elegantly restored Victorian mansion in the historic district. Rooms feature fireplaces, whirlpool tubs, antiques and 16-foot ceilings. Same owners have been operating the inn for 11 years.

───

Hamilton-Turner Inn
330 Abercorn St, 31401
912-233-1833 Fax: 219-233-0291
888-448-8849
Charlie & Sue Strickland
All year

160-275-B&B
14 rooms, 14 pb
Most CC, *Rated*, •
C-yes/S-no/P-ltd/H-yes
Spanish & French

Full breakfast
Afternoon tea
Sitting room, bicycles,
Jacuzzis, suites, fireplaces,
cable TV

Located in the heart of the historic district overlooking Lafayette Square, the entire inn is furnished with Empire, Eastlake and Renaissance Revival antique and features a full Southern breakfast and afternoon tea.   E-mail: homemaid@attworldnet.net
Web site: hamilton-turnerinn.com

───

Joan's on Jones B&B
17 West Jones St, 31401
912-234-3863 Fax: 912-234-1455
800-407-3863
Joan & Gary Levy
All year

135-150-B&B
2 rooms, 2 pb
Rated
C-yes/S-no/P-ltd/H-yes

Continental breakfast
Complimentary wine
Sitting room, tennis nearby,
golf, fishing by nearby

Victorian townhouse with private entrance to each suite, secluded garden. Here are location, comfort and southern hospitality . . . amid period antiques.
Web site: bbonline.com/ga/savannah/

───

Kehoe House, The
123 Habersham St, 31401
912-232-1020 Fax: 912-231-1587
800-820-1020
Martha Geiger
All year

195-250-B&B
15 rooms, 15 pb
Most CC, *Rated*, •
C-yes/S-no/P-no/H-yes

Full breakfast
Aftn. tea, comp. wine
Snacks, bar service, sitting
room, free off-street parking

Located in historic Savannah on Columbia Square. Each luxurious guest room is uniquely decorated with antiques. Evening hors d'oeuvres, 24 hr concierge, nightly turndown
E-mail: bshotels@mindspring.com *Web site:* travelguides.com/home/kehoe_house

───

Magnolia Place Inn
503 Whitaker St, 30075
912-236-7674 Fax: 912-236-1145
800-238-7674
R. & J. Sales, K. Medlock
All year

135-250-B&B
15 rooms, 15 pb
Most CC, *Rated*, •
C-ltd/S-no/P-no/H-no

Continental plus breakfast
Afternoon tea & wine
Verandas, courtyard,
Jacuzzis, 2 suites in adjacent
property

In the heart of Savannah's famed historic district, circa 1878. Several rooms offer luxuries, baths and fireplaces. All rooms furnished in English antiques. 2 new suites with fireplaces.   E-mail: b.b.magnolia@cwix.com *Web site:* magnoliaplaceinn.com

───

Olde Harbour Inn
508 E Factor's Walk, 31401
912-234-4100 Fax: 912-233-5979
800-553-6533
Russ Mitchell
All year

149-249-B&B
24 rooms, 24 pb
Most CC, *Rated*, •
C-yes/S-ltd/P-ltd/H-no

Continental plus breakfast
Wine & cheese reception
Suites, cable TV, conference
facilities, turn down service

Above the colorful cobblestones of River Street awaits an historic hideaway. Elegant, romantic, and exquisitely reminiscent of the 19th century. Built in 1892, the Olde Harbour Inn is a three story bluff side warehouse that has been richly restored.
E-mail: savoh@mastersinns.com *Web site:* oldeharbourinn.com

SAVANNAH

Planters Inn
29 Abercorn St, 31401
912-232-5678 Fax: 912-232-8893
800-554-1187
Natalie Almon
All year

120-175-B&B
56 rooms, 56 pb
Visa, MC, AmEx,
Rated, •
C-yes/S-yes/P-no/H-yes

Continental plus breakfast
Complimentary wine
Athletic club, pool, parking
garage, family friendly facility

This award-winning property blends the warmth and charm of a small inn with the services of a grand hotel.   E-mail: plantinn@aol.com Web site: plantersinnsavannah.com

President's Quarters, The
225 E President St, 31401
912-233-1600 Fax: 912-238-0849
800-233-1600
Hank Smalling, Stacy Stephens
All year

137-250-B&B
19 rooms, 19 pb
Most CC, *Rated*, •
C-yes/S-ltd/P-no/H-yes

Continental plus breakfast
Complimentary wine,
afternoon tea
Limited bar, lite menu, sitting
room, courtyard, free
parking

Newly restored 1855 home in heart of Historic District: Jacuzzi bathtubs, gas log fireplaces, antiques & period furniture. Spacious rooms. Honeymoon & mid-week specials. E-mail: pqinn@aol.com Web site: presidentsquarters.com

Sarah's Garden
402 E Gaston St, 31401
912-234-7716 Fax: 912-234-7716
Jane & Rocky Reed
All year
E-mail: sjrreed@www.com

140-220-B&B
5 rooms, 5 pb
Visa, MC, •
C-yes/S-ltd/P-no/H-yes

Full breakfast
Snacks, complimentary wine
Sitting room, swimming pool,
suites, fireplace, cable TV

Timmons House
407 E Charlton St, 31401
912-233-4456
Gloria Stover
All year

130-B&B
1 rooms, 1 pb
C-ltd/S-no/P-ltd/H-no

Continental breakfast
Sitting room, fireplaces,
cable TV

Be a guest in the historic district and enjoy our 1876 restored townhouse garden apartment which has a bedroom, private bath, sitting room and kitchen.   E-mail: glorias@sepconn.com

SENOIA

Culpepper House B&B
35 Broad St, 30276
770-599-8182 Fax: 770-559-8182
Maggie & Barb
All year

85-B&B
3 rooms, 3 pb
Visa, MC, *Rated*, •
C-ltd/S-ltd/P-yes/H-no

Full gourmet breakfast
Complimentary wine
Sitting room, porch, tandem
bicycles

Enjoy romance as you step back 120 years to casual Victorian elegance. Share a special evening in a four-poster canopy bed next to a fireplace-wake to a gourmet breakfast.

ST. MARYS

Goodbread House
209 Osborne St, 31558
912-882-7490   888-236-6482
Michele Becnel
All year

75-85-B&B
5 rooms, 5 pb
C-ltd/S-ltd/H-no

Full breakfast
Afternoon wine and brandy
Sitting room tennis, fishing
nearby

Victorian hideaway in quaint fishing village off I-95. Ferry to Cumberland National Seashore. Seated breakfast in cozy dining room.

THOMASVILLE

Evans House Christian B&B
725 S Hansel St, 31799
912-226-1343 Fax: 912-226-0653
800-344-4717
Gladys Deese
All year

105-182-B&B
4 rooms, 4 pb
Rated, •
C-ltd/S-no/P-ltd/H-yes

Full breakfast
Snacks
Bicycles porch

Restored Victorian home located in Parkfront historical district across from Paradise Park. Walking distance of historic downtown, tours, antique shops and restaurants.
Web site: innsite.com/inns/A002296.html

THOMASVILLE

Melhanna Plantation	200-450-B&B	Full breakfast
301 Showboat Lane, 31792	30 rooms, 30 pb	Lunch & dinner (fee)
912-226-2290 Fax: 912-226-4585	Most CC, *Rated*, •	Restaurant, bar, sitting room,
888-920-3030	C-yes/S-no/P-no/H-yes	library, tennis, suites, bikes
Rich Graham		
All year		

Moss laden oaks & fragrant magnolias line the entrance to historic Melhana Plantation. Guests are pampered in our elegantly appointed suites. Luxury, comfort and grand style characterize your stay.

Serendipity Cottage B&B	85-110-B&B	Full breakfast
339 E Jefferson St, 31792	4 rooms, 4 pb	Snacks, complimentary wine
912-226-8111 Fax: 912-226-2656	Most CC, *Rated*, •	Sitting room, bikes, Exercise
800-383-7377	C-ltd/S-no/P-no/H-no	equipment & golf, at private
Kathy & Ed Middleton		country club
All year		

Lovely old house, welcoming porches, gourmet breakfast, caring accommodations, Southern hospitality, all located in a charming Victorian town.   E-mail: goodnite@rose.net
Web site: bbhost.com/serendipity

THOMSON

1810 West Inn	65-105-B&B	Continental plus breakfast
254 N Seymour Dr, 30824	10 rooms, 10 pb	Afternoon tea, snacks
706-595-3156	Most CC, *Rated*, •	Sitting room, library, jogging
Fax: 706-595-3155	C-ltd/S-no/P-no/H-no	trail, pond, peacocks, 11
800-515-1810		acres
Virginia White		
All year		

Country charm, city amenities-restored historic plantation house c.1810 and adjoining folk houses on 14 landscaped acres. Convenient to I-20 and Augusta.
Web site: bbonline.com/ga/1810west

Hawaii

BIG ISLAND, CAPTAIN COOK

Affordable Hawaii Pomaikai	50-65-B&B	Full breakfast
83-5465 Mamalahoa Hwy,	5 rooms, 4 pb	Snacks from farm
96704	*Rated*, •	Large lanai, BBQ available,
808-328-2112 Fax: 808-328-2255	C-yes/S-ltd/P-yes/H-ltd	game room, TV, VCR, golf,
800-325-6427	French	tennis available
Nita Isherwood		
All year		

Experience living on an old Hawaii kona coffee and macadamia nut farm.
E-mail: nitabnb@kona.net

Rainbow Plantation B&B	75-95-B&B	Continental plus breakfast
PO Box 122, 96704	5 rooms, 5 pb	Sitting room, kayak, rentals
808-323-2393 Fax: 808-323-9445	Visa, MC, *Rated*, •	on premises, free snorkeling
800-494-2828	C-ltd/S-ltd/P-yes/H-no	gear
Marianna & Reiner Schrepfer	German, French	
All year		

A tropical island hideaway on a macadamia & coffee plantation. Private baths & entrance. Delicious breakfasts on oceanview lanai above Kealakekua Bay.   E-mail: sunshine@
aloha.net   *Web site:* wwte.com/hawaii/rainbow.htm

BIG ISLAND, HILO

Butterfly Inn for Women
PO Box 6010, 96760
808-966-7936
800-54-MAGIC
Patti & Kay
All year

55-65-B&B	Continental plus breakfast
2 rooms	Sitting room, library, bikes,
Visa, MC, Disc, •	Jacuzzis, TV
S-ltd/P-no/H-no	

A women's B&B on the Big Island near Hilo, beaches and Volcano. Cozy haven nestled in luscious emerald landscape.   E-mail: The.Butterfly.Inn@prodigy.net *Web site:* thebutterfyinn.com

Inn at Kulaniapia, The
PO Box 11338, 96721
808-966-6373 Fax: 808-968-7580
888-838-6373
Len & Jane Sutton
All year

99-119-B&B	Full breakfast
4 rooms, 4 pb	Sitting room, fireplaces,
Visa, MC, *Rated*, •	cable TV, accommodate
C-yes/S-no/P-no/H-no	business travelers, pond

Have a close encounter with our 120' waterfall, or walk over 2 miles of trails along our river. Have lunch at our Botanical Garden where 3 more waterfalls cascade.
E-mail: waterfalls@prodigy.net *Web site:* waterfall.net

Ironwood House B&B
2262 Kalanianaole Ave, 96721
808-934-8855 Fax: 808-934-8855
888-334-8855
Doug & Piper McKern
All year

55-85-B&B	Continental plus breakfast
3 rooms, 1 pb	Sitting room, ocean just 300
Visa, MC, *Rated*, •	feet away
C-ltd/S-ltd/P-no/H-ltd	

We are located 4 miles south of Hilo and a 4 minute walk to Richardson Beach Park. Our 1939 Manor style house offers a relaxed island atmosphere.   E-mail: ironwd@aloha.net
Web site: ironwoodhouse.com

Shipman House B&B Inn
131 Kaiulani St, 96720
808-934-8002 Fax: 808-934-8002
800-627-8447
Barbara & Gary Andersen
All year

140-160-B&B	Continental plus breakfast
5 rooms, 5 pb	Snacks
Visa, MC, *Rated*, •	Sitting room, library, 2 units-
C-ltd/S-no/P-no/H-no	1910 house, 1 unit-big house,
A little French	Grand piano

Hospitality so real you'll want to stay longer. Exotic flowers & fruits, garden-fresh.
E-mail: bighouse@bigisland.com *Web site:* hilo-hawaii.com

BIG ISLAND, KAILUA-KONA

Hale Maluhia Country Inn
76-770 Hualalai Rd, 96740
808-329-1123 Fax: 808-326-5487
800-559-6627
Ken & Sue Smith
All year

90-150-B&B	Full breakfast buffet
5 rooms, 5 pb	Island fruit, fresh daily bread
Most CC, *Rated*	Music room, piano, art
C-ltd/S-ltd/P-no/H-ltd	gallery, library/game room
Some Japanese	w/pool table, Japanese spa

(House of Peace) Tropical shaded estate. All private baths, stone/tile Japanese spa, Full buffet breakfast.   E-mail: hawaii-inns@aloha.net *Web site:* hawaii-bnb.com/halemal.html

Kailua Plantation House
75-5948 Alii Dr, 96740
808-329-3727 Fax: 808-326-7323
Donna Stonerock & John
Strach
All year

160-235-B&B	Continental plus breakfast
5 rooms, 5 pb	Restaurants nearby
Visa, MC, AmEx, •	Sitting room, dipping pool,
C-ltd/S-no/P-no/H-no	hot tubs, private baths &
	lanais

Hawaii's most elegant oceanfront B&B. Situated atop a promontory of black lava rocks under 1 mile from the quaint town of Kailua-Kona.   E-mail: kphbnb@ilhawaii.net
Web site: tales.com/KPH

BIG ISLAND, KAILUA-KONA

Kokoke Lani B&B Inn
PO Box 2728, 96745
808-329-2226 Fax: 808-329-2226
Terry & Meredith Neumann
All year

125-225-B&B
5 rooms, 5 pb
Visa, MC, •
C-ltd/S-no/P-no/H-no

Full breakfast
Afternoon tea, snacks
Sitting room, hot tubs,
swimming pool, studio with
kitchenette

Private estate with breathtaking views overlooking the Pacific. Sparkling full sized pool & hot tub. Gourmet breakfast served daily on our lanai. E-mail: terry@ilhawaii.net
Web site: kokokelani.com

BIG ISLAND, VOLCANO

Guesthouse at Volcano, The
PO Box 6, 96785
808-967-7775 Fax: 808-967-8295
Bonnie Goodell
All year

60-B&B
1 rooms, 1 pb
•
C-yes/S-yes
Spanish, Greek,
Mandarin

Continental plus breakfast
TV, telephone, children
bicycles, extensive library

Cozy cottage with kitchen on 6 acres of orchards and pristine native forest, next to National Park and Volcano Golf Course. Cottage with kitchen. E-mail: cmaplan@interpac.net
Web site: volcanoguesthouse.com

Kilauea Lodge & Restaurant
PO Box 116, 96785
808-967-7366 Fax: 808-967-7367
Lorna & Albert Jeyte
All year

120-160-B&B
13 rooms, 13 pb
Visa, MC, *Rated*
C-yes/S-ltd/P-no/H-ltd
German, Spanish

Full breakfast
Restaurant, bar, dinner
available
Sitting room, garden gazebo,
two bedroom cottage,
Volcanoes National Park

Mountain lodge with full service restaurant. 6 rooms with fireplace. One mile from spectacular Volcanoes National Park. E-mail: stay@kilauea-lodge.com *Web site:* kilauea-lodge.com

Volcano Heart Chalet
PO Box 404, 96713
808-248-7725 Fax: 808-248-7725
John & JoLoyce Kaia
All year

75-B&B
2 rooms, 2 pb
•
S-no/P-no/H-no

Continental breakfast
Shared kitchenette
Sitting room with gas
fireplace, queen & twin beds,
laundry room facilities

Explore Volcano National Park, exotic gardens, macadamia nut farms, Hilo's zoo and great restaurants! Then relax in the cool mountain air of Volcano. There is a 10% tax on the rates. No alcohol allowed E-mail: volcanoheartchal@aol.com

BIG ISLAND, VOLCANO VILLAGE

Chalet Kilauea Collection
PO Box 998, 96785
808-967-7786 Fax: 808-967-8660
800-937-7786
Brian & Lisha Crawford
All year

45-395-B&B
6 rooms, 6 pb
Most CC, *Rated*, •
C-ltd/S-ltd/P-no/H-no
French, Dutch, Jap., Sp.

Full breakfast
Afternoon tea
Sitting room, library, hot
tubs, 6 vacation homes-1
with Jacuzzi, massages

The collection offers a selection of fine accommodations set outside Hawaii's Volcanoes National Park. This signature property is the Inn at Volcano, a luxurious boutique Inn with theme suites richly decorated with treasures from around the world. E-mail: reservations@volcano-hawaii.com *Web site:* volcano-hawaii.com/Accommodations.htm

Hale Ohia Cottages
PO Box 758, 96785
808-967-7986 Fax: 808-967-8610
800-455-3803
Michael Tuttle
All year

95-145-B&B
6 rooms, 6 pb
Most CC, *Rated*, •
C-yes/S-no/P-no/H-ltd

Continental breakfast
Hot tubs, lush fern forests,
active volcano nearby

A popular retreat for local residents, historic estate. Beautiful grounds, private, romantic and quiet. *Web site:* haleohia.com

CAPTAIN COOK, KONA

Merryman's B&B	80-125-B&B	Full Hawaiian breakfast
PO Box 489, 96704	4 rooms, 2 pb	Aftn. tea, snacks
808-323-2276 Fax: 808-323-3749	*Rated*, •	Jacuzzi, sunset view in Lanai.
800-545-4390	C-yes/S-ltd/P-no/H-no	
Janice & Steve Glass		
All year		

The Areca Palms Estate / Merryman's B&B is a tropical country estate beautifully furnished and fresh flowers.   E-mail: merryman@ilhawaii.net   Web site: konabedandbreakfast.com

HILO

Na'ali'i Plantation	55-100-B&B	Continental plus breakfast
2939A Pulima Dr., 96720	2 rooms, 1 pb	Full kitchen, BBQ, Lanai
808-935-2109 Fax: 808-935-2109	•	Croquet, badminton, VCR
Anne & Michael Maguire	C-yes/S-ltd/P-no/H-ltd	and videos
All year	Spanish	

Very homey, country hideaway Hawaiian style—mauka—up the mountain.
E-mail: naaliiplantation@prodigy.net   Web site: pages.prodigy.net/naaliiplantation/aloha.html

Our Place Papaikou's B&B	50-85-B&B	Continental plus breakfast
PO Box 469, 96781	3 rooms, 1 pb	Sitting room, library, cable
808-964-5250	Visa, MC, *Rated*, •	TV
800-245-5250	C-ltd/S-ltd/P-no/H-no	
Ouida Trahan & Sharon Miller		
All year		

Located near Hilo on beautiful Hamakua Coast overlooking Kapua stream and tropical gardens.   E-mail: rplace@aloha.net   Web site: best.com/~ourplace

KAUAI

Hale Kua Guests	90-99-EP	Suites, cable TV, guest units
PO Box 649, 96765	5 rooms, 5 pb	with full kitchens, full baths,
808-332-8570	*Rated*, •	washer/dryer
800-440-4353	C-yes/S-ltd/H-no	
Bill & Cathy Cowern		
All year		

Our secluded hillside retreat located on Kauai's sunny south side offers peace and serenity in one of our five choice accomodations.   E-mail: halekua@aloha.net   Web site: planet-hawaii.com/halekua

Ole Kamaole's Beach House	99-185-B&B	Full "self-serve" breakfast
2299-C Kaupakalua Rd, 96708	2 rooms, 2 pb	Restaurant
808-573-2865	*Rated*, •	Restaurant, tennis court,
800-528-2465	C-ltd/S-ltd/P-no/H-no	cable TV, ocean front
Richard "Ole" & Eileen Olson	Some Hawaiian	
All year		

80 feet from the ocean on Kauai's sunny Leeward side, at the foot of Mark Twain's "Grand Canyon of the Pacific", Waimea Canyon.   Web site: virtualcities.com/vacation/hi/k/hik17v2.htm

KAUAI, HANALEI

Bed, Breakfast & Beach	65-115-B&B	Continental plus breakfast
PO Box 748, 96714	4 rooms, 4 pb	Restaurant nearby
808-826-6111	•	Sitting room, library,
Carolyn Barnes	C-ltd/S-no/P-no/H-no	television, coolers &, snorkel
All year		equipment available

Beach on famous Hanalei Bay is 125 yards away. View of 1000-foot waterfalls. Antiques & rattan. Hike Na Pali, snorkel, golf, kayak, windsurf, fish & sail. Cottage with kitchen available.   E-mail: hanaleibay@aol.com   Web site: bestofhawaii.com/hanalei

KAUAI, HANALEI

River Estate
PO Box 169, 96714
808-826-5118 Fax: 808-826-4616
800-484-6030
Mark Barbanell
All year

145 and up-B&B
2 rooms, 2 pb
•
C-yes/S-ltd/P-no/H-no

Continental breakfast
Barbeque
River, beach chairs, snorkel
gear, fishing, toll free pin #
2468

River Estate is a deluxe destination on a river a block up from a secluded beach that's perfect for honeymooners, wedding parties, families, & large groups. E-mail: markbar@aloha.net *Web site:* riverestate.com

KAUAI, KAPAA

Plantation Retreat
6538 Kahuna Rd, 96746
808-822-7832
Jim & Becky Brawner
All year

85-B&B
3 rooms, 3 pb
Rated, •
C-yes/S-ltd/P-no/H-no
Spanish, French,
Chinese

Continental plus breakfast
Sauna, hot tubs, river, rope
swing over swimming hole,
family friendly

On a beautiful 10 acre plantation nestled in Kauai's Makaheha Mountains, 6 miles from beach. 3 rental cottages are completely private. Gorgeous views. E-mail: bananas@aloha.net *Web site:* plantationretreat.com

KAUAI, PRINCEVILLE

An Angel Inn
PO Box 3597, 96722
360-456-4040 Fax: 360-826-6678
Gail Spicuzza
All year

85-95-B&B
3 rooms, 3 pb
•
C-yes/S-no/P-no/H-no

Breakfast basket in suite
Snacks, rest. nearby
Library, bikes, boogie,
boards, golf clubs, snorkel
gear, suites, cable TV

Enjoy, relax, renew! Tastefully-appointed, spacious vacation rentals with lush tropical panoramic views of Kauai's mountains and/or ocean. Located on the 2nd. hole of the world famous Princeville Makai Golf Course. E-mail: therock@aloha.net *Web site:* travelkauai.com

Hale 'Aha at Princeville
PO Box 3370, 96722
808-826-6733 Fax: 808-826-9052
800-826-6733 ,
Ruth Bockelman
All year

110-275-B&B
2 rooms, 2 pb
Visa, MC, *Rated*
C-ltd/S-no/P-no/H-no

Continental plus breakfast
Many restaurants nearby
Hot tubs, 480 feet of,
Princeville golf course,
tennis/health spa nearby

On the golf course. Walk to our hidden beach or enjoy 10 miles of sand beaches plus rivers to kayak. E-mail: kauai@pixi.com *Web site:* pixi.com/~kauai

LAHAINA

Garden Gate B&B
67 Kaniau Rd, 96761
808-661-8800 Fax: 808-661-0209
800-939-3217
Jaime & Bill Mosley
All year

65-95-B&B
4 rooms, 4 pb
Visa, MC, AmEx, •
C-yes/S-ltd/P-no/H-no
Spanish, little Japanese

Continental breakfast plus
Snacks
Bicycles, Jacuzzis, cable TV,
conference facilities

We are a lovely Bed & Breakfast minutes from Lahaina and walking distance to Ka'anapali beaches. We are in a tropical garden atmosphere on the Valley Isle of Maui. E-mail: garden@mauigateway.com *Web site:* gardengatebb.com

MAUI, HAIKU

Haikuleana B&B Plantation
555 Haiku Rd, 96708
808-575-2890 Fax: 808-575-9177
Ralph & Jeanne Elizabeth
Blum
All year

100-150-B&B
3 rooms, 3 pb
•
C-ltd/S-ltd/P-no/H-no
Rus., Fr., Ger., It., Sp

Full breakfast
Sitting room, library, hot
tubs, swimming pool, snorkel
gear

Hawaiian country life with waterfalls, beaches and quiet relaxation, built amongst pineapple fields and pine trees in the time of King Kamehameha. Therapeutic jet hot tubs seats 10. Exotic gardens with pond and statues. E-mail: blumblum@maui.net

---

MAUI, HAIKU ───────────────────────────────

Lanikai Farm B&B	70-120-B&B	Continental breakfast
P.O. Box 797, 96708	3 rooms, 1 pb	Comp. tea and coffee
808-572-1111 Fax: 808-723-3498	Visa, MC, •	Sitting room, Squash court,
Margaret & Achim Koebke	C-yes/S-ltd/P-no/H-no	Jacuzzi, German library
All year	German	

Peaceful, tropical setting off the beaten path; far from the maddening crowd in European private home charm, near the Hana & Haleakala Crater E-mail: lanibb@maui.net
Web site: maui.net/~lanibb/

Maui Dream Cottage	490 / week-EP	
265 W Kuiaha Rd, 96708	2 rooms	
808-575-9079 Fax: 808-575-9477	Visa, MC, AmEx, •	
Gregg Blue	C-yes/S-ltd/P-no/H-no	
All year	French, Spanish	

Two acres of tropical fruits and flowers with ocean and mountain views. Full kitchens, washer/dryer and very private. E-mail: gblue@aloha.net *Web site:* planet-hawaii.com/haiku

MAUI, HANA ───────────────────────────────

Hana Hou B&B	175-300-B&B	Continental breakfast
PO Box 940, 96713	2 rooms, 2 pb	Sitting room, Jacuzzis
808-661-1095 Fax: 808-661-5254	•	
H. Jon Applegate	C-ltd/S-no/P-no/H-no	
All year		

The Hana Hou Farm B&B is a spacious 2 bedroom plantation style home with high, open beam ceilings, large covered lanais, and capacious living areas. The 2 bedrooms feature king size beds, private entries, TV and entertainment centers. E-mail: Ukuhame@aol.com

---

Kaia Ranch B&B	75-100-B&B	Continental in refrigerator
PO Box 404, 96713	2 rooms, 2 pb	Coffee, tea, cocoa, juice,
808-248-7725 Fax: 808-248-7725	•	muffins
John & JoLoyce Kaia	S-no/P-no/H-no	Private kitchens, fresh fruit
All year		picking, queen-size beds, no
		alcohol

Located in a tropical botanical garden/ranch—the real Hawaii that few visitors see. Experience gardens, animals & friends you'll never forget. Hana is a unique experience! E-mail: kaiaranch@aol.com

MAUI, KIHEI ───────────────────────────────

Aloha Pualani	79-129-B&B	Continental plus breakfast
15 Wailana Place, 96753	5 rooms, 5 pb	Sitting room, swimming pool,
808-874-9265 Fax: 808-874-9127	Visa, MC, AmEx, •	beach, snorkel, sailing trips
800-782-5264	C-yes/S-no/P-no/H-ltd	
Keith & Marina Dinsmoor		
All year		

Cozy suites with full kitchens face pool and tropically landscaped courtyard only 100 feet from Maui's longest sandy beach. 4 cozy suites. E-mail: pualani@mauigateway.com
Web site: alohapualani.com

MAUI, KULA ───────────────────────────────

Kula Cottage	85-B&B	Continental breakfast
206 Puakea Place, 96790	1 rooms, 1 pb	Stylish retreat, gardens,
808-878-2043 Fax: 808-871-9187	•	woodburning stove, patio,
Cecilia Gilbert	H-no	washer, dryer, color TV
All year	Spanish	

Fully equipped luxury one bedroom cottage with private driveway. Fireplace, patio and much more. A quiet, romantic and cozy hideaway. E-mail: ceci@gilbertadvertising.com
Web site: gilbertadvertising.com/kulacottage

MAUI, LAHAINA

Old Lahaina House
PO Box 10355, 96761
808-667-4663 Fax: 808-667-5615
800-847-0761
John & Sherry Barbier
All year

69-95-B&B
4 rooms, 4 pb
Visa, MC, AmEx,
Rated, •
C-yes/S-no/P-no

Continental breakfast
No breakfast on Sundays
Swimming pool, bikes, TVs,
phones, A/C, beach across
street, laundry fac.

Air-conditioned privacy, tropical courtyard. Walk to historic Lahaina town with museums, shops, restaurants & harbor. Your own bit of paradise. E-mail: olh@oldlahaina.com
Web site: mauiweb.com/maui/olhouse/

OAHU, HAWAII KAI

Aloha B&B
909 Kahauloa Place, 96825
808-395-6694
All year

60-B&B
2 rooms

Continental plus breakfast
Library, swimming pool,
cable TV, large deck with
patio table & chairs

Hawaii Kai home in executive community with partial ocean and marina view. Minutes from famed snorkeling beach, Hanauma Bay. Homemade muffins, bread, fresh fruit, cereals & homemade granola. Will customize breakfast for special needs. E-mail: phyllis@ aloha.net

OAHU, HONOLULU

At Home in Honolulu
2442 Kuhio Ave #902, 96815
808-538-7179 Fax: 808-949-2928
Gary L. Smith
All year

35-90-B&B
3 rooms, 3 pb
Visa, MC,
C-yes/S-ltd/P-no/H-no

Full breakfast
Cable TV

Luxurious private room and bath with separate bath. Spectacular views.
E-mail: glsmith@lava.net Web site: athomeinhonolulu.com/Honolulu.htm

Hale Hoffman
2914 Lauoha Pl, 96813
808-526-0393 Fax: 808-545-3577
Kay Hoffman
All year

80-110-B&B
1 room, 1 pb
C-ltd/S-ltd/P-no/H-no

Continental breakfast
Complimentary wine
Sitting room, Jacuzzis, cable
television, spectacular view

This is actually a one bedroom, one bath apartment with living room, kitchen, lanai, hot tub, private entrance, orchids and fruit trees on the hill above Honolulu.
E-mail: kayhoff@lava.net

VOLCANO

Volcano Inn
19-3820 Old Volcano Hwy,
96785
808-967-7293 Fax: 808-985-7349
800-997-2292
E Lighter & J Prescott-Lighter
All year

75-135-B&B
10 rooms, 10 pb
Most CC, *Rated*, •
C-yes/S-no/P-ltd/H-ltd
French

Full breakfast
Aftn. tea, comp. wine,
lunch,dinner
Sitting room, library, bikes,
suites, fireplaces, cable TV

Spacious inn and fully equipped cedar cottages tucked into native giant tree ferns. Most unique accommodations adjacent to Hawaii Volcanoes National Park offering true "Aloha" hospitality! E-mail: volcano@volcanoinn.com Web site: volcanoinn.com

WAIOHINU

Macadamia Meadows B&B
PO Box 756, 96772
808-929-8097 Fax: 808-929-8097
888-929-8118
Charlene and Cortney Cowan
All year

65-99-B&B
3 rooms, 3 pb
Visa, MC, AmEx,
Rated, •
C-yes/S-ltd/P-no/H-ltd

Continental breakfast
Snacks
Tennis, swimmingpool,
suites, cable TV, conference,
compl. orchard tours

For those seeking the "real" non-commercialized Hawaii. Located on an 8 acre working Macadamia nut farm estate in the historic Kau area, tennis court, pool, sumptuous tropical breakfasts. E-mail: kaleena@aloha.net Web site: stayhawaii.com/macmed/macmed.html

Idaho

BOISE

Maples B&B, The
PO Box 1, 83669
208-286-7419
877-286-7419
Mary and Don Wertman
All year

60-125-B&B
3 rooms, 3 pb
Visa, MC, *Rated*, •
C-ltd/S-no/P-no/H-no

Full breakfast
Lunch/dinner available (fee)
Snacks, comp. wine, sitting
room, cable TV, custom
packages available

Like a trip to Grandma's only better! Beautifully restored 1888 farmhouse features antiques, quilts, air-conditioning & wood stove. Fabulous breakfast is served on an antique table. E-mail: maplesbb@micron.net *Web site:* netnow.micron.net/~maplesbb/

COEUR D'ALENE

Berry Patch Inn B&B
1150 N Four Winds Rd, 83814
208-765-4994 Fax: 208-667-7336
Ann M Caggiano
All year

125-150-B&B
3 rooms, 3 pb
Visa, MC, *Rated*, •
S-no/P-no/H-no

Full breakfast
Snacks, complimentary night
cap
Afternoon tea, sitting room,
Indian teepee, library

Secluded mountain chalet, low fat cookery-homemade conserves. Near lake, downtown, golf, skiing. Honeymoons-Pampering. Private road, peaceful. Nordstroms recognition. National Geographic Traveler acclaimed. Web site: bbhost.com/berrypatchinn

HARRISON

Hidden Creek Ranch
7600 E Blue Lake Rd, 83833
208-689-3209 Fax: 208-689-9115
Iris Behr & John Muir
All year

1481-2068-AP
C-ltd

Full breakfast
Dinner & Lunch
Your own horse, log cabins,
fitness center, hot tubs,
gourmet meals, bikes

At Hidden Creek Ranch, we want to share our love for horseback riding and the great outdoors in an unspoiled environment surrounded by the beauty of nature. E-mail: hiddencreek@hiddencreek.com *Web site:* nidlink.com/~hiddencreek

RIGBY

BlackSmith Inn B&B
227 N 3900 E, 83442
208-745-6208 Fax: 208-745-0602
888-745-6208
Mike & Karla Black
All year

65-75-B&B
6 rooms, 6 pb
Visa, MC, Disc, *Rated*,
•
C-yes/S-no/P-ltd/H-yes

Full breakfast
Afternoon tea, snacks
Sitting room, Jacuzzis, Cable
TV, Accommodate business
travelers

The BlackSmith Inn is a contemporary round "Eagle's Nest" home. Hand-painted murals adorn each room, our decks and patio allow a comfortable way to enjoy our pleasant evenings and beautiful sunsets. E-mail: theinn@blacksmithinn.com *Web site:* blacksmithinn.com

SALMON

Greyhouse Inn B&B
HC 61, Box 16, 83467
208-756-3968
800-348-8097
Sharon & David Osgood
All year

65-90-B&B
4 rooms, 2 pb
Visa, MC, Disc, *Rated*,
•
C-ltd/S-ltd/H-no

Full gourmet breakfast
Lunch, dinner, afternoon tea
Snacks, sitting room, library,
bikes, cable, hot tub, tours of
Lewis & Clark

Charming Victorian with comfortable beds, park-like setting, clean air. Wildlife abounds, bring your camera. Antiques in every room, very relaxing, walk to Salmon River. You'll love it. E-mail: osgoodd@dmi.net *Web site:* greyhouseinn.com

SANDPOINT

Paradise Valley Inn
PO Box 689, 83805
208-267-4180 Fax: 208-267-3673
888-447-4180
Gene & Arlene Sloan
All year

105-160-B&B
5 rooms, 5 pb
Visa, MC, AmEx,
Rated, •
C-ltd/S-ltd/P-ltd/H-ltd

Full breakfast
Aftn. tea, snacks, dinner
available
Sitting room, library,
Jacuzzis, suites, fireplaces

Experience one of the most dramatic vistas in North Idaho while you relax in casual luxury in a new elegant Northwest Lodge Inn on 64 acres. Majestic & serene getaway.
E-mail: info@paradisevalleyinn.com *Web site:* paradisevalleyinn.com

STANLEY

Idaho Rocky Mtn. Ranch
HC 64, Box 9934, 83278
208-774-3544 Fax: 208-774-3477
Bill Leavell/Sandra Beckwith
June-Sept, Dec-Mar

148-248-MAP
21 rooms, 21 pb
Visa, MC, Disc, *Rated*
C-yes/S-no/P-no/H-ltd
Spanish

Full breakfast
Dinner included in price
Dining room, beer & wine,
library, horses, bikes, natural
hot springs pool

Historic log lodge and cabins; spectacular mountain scenery; gourmet dining in rustic atmosphere; extensive outdoor activities. Live entertainment. Weekly rates.
E-mail: idrocky@ruralnetwork.net *Web site:* ruralnetwork.net/~idrocky

SUN VALLEY

River Street Inn B&B, The
PO Box 182, 83340
208-726-3611 Fax: 208-726-2439
888-726-3611
Sigrun & Daemion Glantz
All year

135-165-B&B
8 rooms, 8 pb
Visa, MC, AmEx,
Rated, •
C-yes/S-no/P-yes/H-no

Full breakfast
Full catering
Apres-ski refreshments,
sitting room, fireplace, skiing,
fax/copier

Located on Trail Creek. Mtn. views, spacious rooms with shower and Japanese soaking tub. E-mail: riverstreetinn@micron.net *Web site:* riverstreetinn.com

Illinois

ALTON

Beall Mansion B&B
407 12th St, 62002
618-474-9100 Fax: 618-474-9090
800-990-2325
Jim & Sandy Belote
All year

119-179-B&B
5 rooms, 5 pb
Most CC, *Rated*, •
S-no/P-no/H-no

Full breakfast
Complimentary champagne
Sitting room, Jacuzzis,
fireplace, cable TV,
conference facilities

Let us pamper you with champagne, chocolates, nightly turn down service, plush robes and gourmet breakfasts. Guest rooms feature private baths with whirlpool for two or clawfoot tub, marble floors and chandeliers. E-mail: bepampered@beallmansion.com
Web site: beallmansion.com

BELLEVILLE

Swans Court B&B
421 Court St, 62220
618-233-0779 Fax: 618-277-3150
800-840-1058
Monty Dixon
All year

65-90-B&B
4 rooms, 2 pb
Most CC, *Rated*, •
C-ltd/S-no/P-no/H-ltd
Spanish

Full breakfast
Snacks
Sitting room, cable TV, libary,
accommodate business
travelers

National Register home furnished in antiques. Walk the town's three historic districts, screened porch for rocking and reading, special diets accommodated, restaurants and activities recommended. E-mail: mdixon@isbe.accessus.net
Web site: bbonline.com/il/swanscourt

152   Illinois

BELLEVILLE ─────────────────────

Victory Inn
712 S Jackson St, 62220
618-277-1538 Fax: 618-277-1576
888-277-8586
Tom & Jo Brannan
All year

60-125-B&B
3 rooms, 3 pb
Visa, MC, AmEx,
Rated, •
C-yes/S-ltd/P-no/H-no

Continental plus breakfast
Sitting room, Jacuzzis, suites,
cable TV/VCR with movies

Victorian charm with modern comforts, this house has a warmth that is inviting. Hosts welcome you with true hospitality, offering comforts of home without the intrusions of the world. E-mail: jo@victoryinn.com Web site: victoryinn.com

CARBONDALE ─────────────────────

Hidden Lake B&B
PO Box 593, 62952
618-833-5252 Fax: 618-833-5252
John & Mary Jo Smith
All year

80-115-B&B
5 rooms, 5 pb
Visa, MC, AmEx, *Rated*
C-ltd/S-no/P-no/H-no

Full breakfast
Sitting room, bicycles,
Jacuzzis, suites, fireplace,
conference facilities

Captivating theme rooms welcome you to first class treatment and quiet, country elegance. Gourmet breakfast as you watch the wildlife. Use our paddleboat on the lake; rent bikes to tour the historic areas. E-mail: HidenLk@aol.com

Sassafras Ridge B&B
382 Fawn Trail, 62901
618-529-5261 Fax: 618-529-5261
Frances & Myers Walker
All year

65-80-B&B
3 rooms, 3 pb
Most CC, *Rated*, •
C-ltd/S-no/H-no

Full breakfast
Snacks
Sitting room, library, pet
kennel nearby, cable TV,
VCR with movies

*Quiet, privacy, and informal hospitality in a modern country home, at the end of a lane near Shawnee National Forest. E-mail: sassybb@go-illinois.com
Web site: bbonline.com/il/sassafras*

CHAMPAIGN ─────────────────────

Golds B&B
2065 County Rd 525 E, 61822
217-586-4345
Rita & Bob Gold
All year

50-B&B
3 rooms, 1 pb
Rated, •
C-yes/S-no/P-no/H-no

Continental plus breakfast
cable TV, VCR w/movies

Country charm & hospitality in 1874 farmhouse. Handy to interstate & university attractions. Furnished with antiques. Quiet & peaceful.

CHICAGO ─────────────────────

Chateau des Fleurs
552 Ridge Rd, 60093
847-256-7272 Fax: 847-256-7272
Sally H. Ward
All year

130-B&B
3 rooms, 3 pb
Rated
C-ltd/S-no/P-no/H-no

Full breakfast
Afternoon tea, snacks
Grand piano, 50" TV, VCR
with movies, bikes, Jacuzzis
in 2 rooms, pool

Beautiful French country home furnished in rare antiques. Lovely views of magnificent trees, English gardens. Near train & private road for walking/jogging. 2 night minimum. Private phones in rooms.

City Scene B&B
2101 North Clifton Ave, 60614
773-549-1743
Fax: 773-529-4711
Mary A. Newman
All year

90-190-B&B
2 rooms, 2 pb
Rated
C-ltd/S-no/P-no/H-no

Continental breakfast
Sitting room each unit has
cable TV

*A comfortable suite on a residential street in the Sheffield historic District; close to dining, shopping, museums, parks, theatres, transportation. E-mail: cityscene@aol.com
Web site: cityscenebb.com*

CHICAGO

Gold Coast Guest House B&B 113 West Elm St, 60610 312-337-0361 Fax: 312-337-0362 Sally Baker All year	129-229-B&B 4 rooms, 4 pb Most CC, *Rated*, • C-ltd/S-no/P-no/H-no	Continental breakfast Afternoon tea, snacks Comp. wine, sitting room, Jacuzzis, each unit has cable TV

This 1873 Victorian hides a contemporary secret inside. . .a 20 foot high window-wall lets the garden in while you enjoy breakfast. E-mail: sally@bbchicago.com *Web site:* bbchicago.com

Homestead, The 1625 Hinman Ave, 60201 847-475-3300 Fax: 847-570-8100 Lynn Killinger All year	95-160-B&B 35 rooms, 35 pb Visa, MC, AmEx, C-ltd/S-yes/P-no/H-ltd	Continental plus breakfast French restaurant Facilities for meetings of up to 15 people, on Mississippi River

Historic residential neighborhood; two blocks from Lake Michigan & Northwestern Univ.; 30 minutes from downtown Chicago. Award winning restaurant. E-mail: office@ homesteader.com *Web site:* homesteader.com

House of Two Urns, The 1239 N Greenview Ave, 60622 773-235-1408 Fax: 713-235-1410 Kapra Fleming All year	79-160-B&B 5 rooms, 1 pb Visa, MC, AmEx, Disc, Most CC, *Rated*, • C-yes/S-no/P-no/H-no German, Spanish, French	Continental plus breakfast Comp. drinks Sitting room, cable TV, 3-night minimum, phone, answering machine

Charming urban inn complete with antiques & original art. Near downtown, public transportation, art galleries, nightlife & restaurants. E-mail: twourns@earthlink.net *Web site:* twourns.com

Margarita European Inn 1566 Oak Ave, 60201 847-869-2273 Barbara & Tim Gorham All year	80-145-B&B 32 rooms, 16 pb Most CC, *Rated*, • C-yes/S-yes/P-no/H-yes Spanish, some French	Continental bkfst. (fee) Restaurant—lunch/dinner Afternoon tea, sitting room, library, on Mississippi River

Relax to afternoon tea in our Georgian parlor room; snuggle up to a book in our wood-panelled English library.

Rodgers Park House 2909 W Fargo Ave, 60645 773-262-5757 Fax: 773-262-4018 Dr. Jerry Porzemsky All year	100-B&B 2 rooms, 2 pb • C-ltd/S-no/P-ltd/H-yes German, Spanish	Continental breakfast Sitting room, fireplace.

Fantastic home—1,000 house plants, gardens, exotic decor, patio, fireplace, kitchen facilities. Near transportation, Lake Michigan, bike trails, tennis courts, expressways. Host has travelled to 70 countries and knows Chicago well. E-mail: DrJerry4@hotmail.com

Windy City B&B Inn 607 W Deming Place, 60614 773-248-7058 Fax: 773-248-7090 800-375-7084 Mary & Andy Shaw All year	115-285-B&B 8 rooms, 8 pb Most CC, • C-ltd/S-no/P-no/H-no Spanish, Italian	Continental plus breakfast Snacks, comp. wine Sitting room, Jacuzzis, fireplaces, cable TV, surrounds

Victorian mansion offers choice of rooms within the elegant main house or in the more cottage-like coach house. Between the two lies a garden surrounded by ivy covered walls. E-mail: stay@chicago-inn.com *Web site:* chicago-inn.com

CHICAGO

Wooded Isle Suites
5750 S Stony Island Ave, 60637
773-288-5578 Fax: 773-288-8972
800-290-6844
Charlie Havens & Sara Pitcher
All year

139-195-EP
13 rooms, 13 pb
Most CC, *Rated*, •
C-yes/S-no/P-no/H-no

Family friendly facility,
equipped kitchens

Near Lake Michigan & Museum of Science & Industry. Guests flats in diverse, dynamic neighborhood south of McCormick Convention Center. Across from park with playground   E-mail: chavenswi@aol.com   Web site: woodedisle.com/

DU QUOIN

Francie's Inn On-Line B&B
104 S Line St, 62832
618-542-6686 Fax: 618-542-4834
877-877-2657
Catherine & Benny
Trowbridge
All year

60-100-B&B
5 rooms, 3 pb
Most CC, *Rated*
C-yes/S-ltd/P-ltd/H-no

Full breakfast
Snacks, complimentary
beverages
Sitting room, bikes, suites,
cable TV, accommodate
business travelers

The place for a getaway vacation, romantic escape or business retreat. Walking distance to restaurants, shops or relax on one of our big decks. Clean, comfortable, room and great food too!   E-mail: bbinn@midwest.net   Web site: midwest.net/bbinn

GALENA

Captain Gear Guest House
PO Box 328, 61036
815-777-0222 Fax: 815-777-3210
800-794-5656
Susan Pettey
All year

155-195-B&B
3 rooms, 3 pb
Visa, MC, Disc, *Rated*
S-no/P-no/H-no

Full formal breakfast
Historic house tour, garden
patio, whirlpool, tub,
VCR/TV in rooms

1855 Mansion, eight fireplaces, American antique furniture, on four secluded acres in the Galena National Register Historic District. Walking distance to downtown shops and restaurants.   E-mail: gearhouse@galenalink.com   Web site: captaingearguesthouse.com

DeZoya House B&B
1203 Third St, 61036
815-777-1203 Fax: 815-777-8645
F.G. Tuttle and J.J. Zalewski
All year

100-205-B&B
6 rooms, 4 pb
Most CC,
C-ltd/S-no/P-no/H-yes

Full breakfast
Sitting room, library

Exceptional 3-story Federal-style mansion, constructed by Virginia steamboat captain circa 1830 of native limestone and oak, split by hand.   Web site: dezoya.com

Park Avenue Guest House
208 Park Ave, 61036
815-777-1075 Fax: 815-777-1097
800-359-0743
Sharon & John Fallbacher
All year

95-125-B&B
4 rooms, 4 pb
Visa, MC, Disc, *Rated*
C-ltd/S-no/P-no/H-no

Full breakfast
Afternoon tea, snacks
Sitting room with TV, 2
parlours, gazebo, A/C,
fireplaces in rooms

Elegant yet comfortable, in quiet residential area. Short walk to beautiful Grant Park, Galena River and Main St. shopping and restaurants.   E-mail: parkave@galenalink.com   Web site: galena.com/parkave

Percival's Country Inn
1030 S Percival St, 53811
608-854-2881
David J. Wezzer
All year

79-109-B&B
5 rooms, 5 pb
Visa, MC, AmEx,
C-ltd/S-ltd/P-ltd/H-ltd

Full breakfast
Snacks, complimentary wine
Sitting room, Jacuzzis, suites,
cable TV, outdoor &
screened decks

1870's country Victorian brick home nestled on 1 acre in the village of Hazel Green, Wisconsin. Furnished in antiques, surrounded by flower gardens, just 8 minutes to historic Galena, Illinois.

GALENA ─────────────────────────────

Pine Hollow Inn	75-125-B&B	Continental plus breakfast
4700 N Council Hill Rd, 61036	5 rooms, 5 pb	Complimentary wine, snacks
815-777-1071	Visa, MC, *Rated*, •	Afternoon tea, hiking,
Larry & Sally Priske	C-ltd/S-no/P-no/H-no	streams, whirlpool bath
All year		

A secluded country inn located on 120 acres, surrounded by one hundred and twenty acres of woods. Nestle in front of your own cozy fireplace.   E-mail: pinehollowinn@ pinehollowinn.com *Web site:* pinehollowinn.com

Stillman's Country Inn	80-160-B&B	Continental breakfast
513 Bouthillier, 61036	7 rooms, 7 pb	Whirlpool rooms, cable TV
815-777-0557	Visa, MC, *Rated*	in rooms, fireplaces
Bill & Pamela Lozeau	C-ltd/P-no/H-no	
All year		

Stillmans Country Inn is an 1858 Victorian Mansion, high on a hill, on Galena's east side across from President Grant's home.

KEWANEE ─────────────────────────────

Aunt Daisy's B&B	95-B&B	Full breakfast
223 W Central Blvd, 61443	4 rooms, 4 pb	Snacks, comp. dessert in
309-853-3300 Fax: 309-853-4148	Most CC, *Rated*, •	evenings
888-422-4148	C-ltd/S-no/P-no/H-no	Library, suites
Glen & Michele Schwarm		
All year		

Gothic Victorian 1890 home. Many stained glass windows await the opportunity to charm you. Music parlor with a 1929 Aeolian player piano & a baby grand.   E-mail: antdaisy@ inw.net *Web site:* members.aol.com/dschwarz/index3.html

LEBANON ─────────────────────────────

Landmark on Madison B&B	75-95-B&B	Full breakfast
118 S Madison St, 62254	3 rooms, 3 pb	Afternoon tea, snacks
618-537-9532	Most CC, *Rated*, •	Sitting room, library, cable
John and Betty Carter	C-ltd/S-ltd/P-no/H-no	TV, accommodate business
All year		travelers

Historic landmark mansion, elegantly furnished in antiques, rich colors, cozy comfortable atmosphere, gourmet breakfasts, complementary beverages, snacks and desserts in our Magnolia Room. Flowers or sparkling wine for special occasions.
Web site: bbonline.com/il/landmark/

METROPOLIS ─────────────────────────────

Isle of View B&B	65-125-B&B	Full gourmet breakfast
205 Metropolis, 62960	5 rooms, 5 pb	Sitting room, whirlpools,
618-524-5838	Most CC, *Rated*, •	near antique/specialty,
800-566-7491	C-ltd/S-ltd/P-ltd/H-no	shops, cable TV
Kim & Gerald Offenburger		
All year		

1889 Victorian mansion, 1 block from Riverboat Casino. Spacious, antique-appointed rooms; lots of romance. Romance packages.   E-mail: kimoff@hcis.net
Web site: bbonline.com/il/isleofview

MORRISON ─────────────────────────────

Hillendale B&B	60-160-B&B	Full breakfast
600 W Lincolnway, 61270	10 rooms, 10 pb	Sitting room, fireplaces,
815-772-3454 Fax: 815-772-7023	Visa, MC, *Rated*, •	billiard & fitness rooms,
Barb Winandy	C-ltd/S-no/P-no/H-no	whirlpools for two
All year		

Travel the world from rural America in our international theme rooms. Relax in the Japanese Teahouse & enjoy fish in the water gardens.   E-mail: hillend@clinton.net
Web site: hillend.com

MOUNT CARMEL

Poor Farm B&B, The
Poor Farm Rd, 62863
618-262-4663 Fax: 618-263-4618
800-646-3276
Liz & John Stelzer
All year

45-85-B&B
5 rooms, 5 pb
Most CC, *Rated*, •
C-yes/S-ltd/P-no/H-yes

Full country breakfast
Lunch & dinner by res.
Sitt. room, bike built for 2,
player piano, antique juke
box, 4000 movies

A gracious glimpse of yesteryear. Old-time charm just minutes from golf, swimming, fishing, boating, parks. Full country breakfasts—private baths   E-mail: poorfarm@midwest.net Web site: travelassist.com/reg/il102s.html

PEORIA

Glory Hill B&B
18427 N Old Galena Rd, 61523
309-274-4228 Fax: 309-274-3266
Bonnie Russell
All year

75-95-B&B
2 rooms, 2 pb
Visa, MC, Disc, *Rated*
C-ltd/S-ltd/P-no/H-no

Full breakfast
Afternoon tea, snacks
Sitting room, library,
swimming pool, color TV, 1
room has whirlpool

1841 country estate, antique furnishings, verandah, porch, fireplace, gourmet breakfasts, elegant, relaxed, comfortable, romantic, scenic, warm, friendly, quiet seclusion.

PRINCETON

Chestnut Street Inn
PO Box 25, 61361
815-454-2419
800-537-1304
Gail Bruntjen
All year

85-165-B&B
4 rooms, 4 pb
Visa, MC, *Rated*, •
C-ltd/S-no/P-no/H-no

Full breakfast
Afternoon tea, snacks
Morning wake up tray

Historic landmark offering gracious accommodations in the English tradition-inviting, serene, sophisticated, lavishly elegant. Exquisite candlelight breakfasts. Antiquing, biking, golf.   E-mail: gail@chestnut-inn.com   Web site: chestnut-inn.com

ROCK ISLAND

Victorian Inn B&B
702 20 St, 61201
309-788-7068 Fax: 309-788-7086
800-728-7068
David & Barbara Parker
All year

65-85-B&B
6 rooms, 6 pb
Visa, MC, AmEx, *Rated*
C-ltd/S-no/P-no/H-no

Full gourmet breakfast
Afternoon beverages, snacks
Sitting room, 2 rooms with
working fireplaces

20 room mansion furnished with genuine antiques. Gourmet breakfast served on fine china, crystal and sterling silver. Welcome to our home. Web site: bbonline.com/il/victorianinn/

ROCKFORD

River House B&B
11052 Ventura Blvd, 61115
815-636-1884 Fax: 815-636-1884
Patty Rinehart
All year

95-135-B&B
2 rooms, 2 pb
Visa, MC, *Rated*, •
C-ltd/S-ltd/P-no/H-no

Full breakfast
Snacks
Sitting room, swimming pool,
hot tubs

Wooded river setting with spacious theme suites just outside Rockford, Illinois. E-mail: riverhous@aol.com   Web site: members.aol.com/rivrhousbb/index.htm

SESSER

Gretchen's Country Home
14186 Cherry St, 62884
618-625-6067
877-495-2372
Gretchen & Roger Cook
All year

50-59-B&B
4 rooms, 2 pb
Visa, MC, *Rated*
C-ltd/S-no/P-no/H-no

Full breakfast
Sitting room shop, live
entertainment

Country hideaway with private lake. Minutes away are Rend Lake, golf, boating, swimming, horseback riding, The National Coal Museum, & Shawnee National Forest. Paddleboat, gazebo, & gardens.   E-mail: rcook@midwest.net

SPRINGFIELD

Country Dreams B&B	75-165-B&B	Full breakfast on weekends
3410 Park Lane, 62563	*Rated*, •	Cont. plus breakfast
217-498-9210 Fax: 217-498-8178	C-ltd/S-no/P-no/H-yes	weekdays
Ralph & Kay Muhs		Snacks, sitting room, library,
All year		bicycles, fireplaces, cable TV

Newly built country hideaway. Perfect for anniversary weekends, short getaways & honeymooners. Located on 16 acres of grass with flowers, fruit trees, gardens, & a small lake E-mail: host@countrydreams.com *Web site:* countrydreams.com

Inn at 835	98-195-B&B	Full breakfast
835 South 2nd St, 62704	7 rooms, 7 pb	Snacks, complimentary wine
217-523-4466 Fax: 217-523-4468	Visa, MC, AmEx,	Sitting room, bicycles,
888-217-4835	*Rated*, •	fireplace & Jacuzzi, rooms
Court and Karen Conn	C-ltd/S-no/P-no/H-yes	available
All year		

National register. Luxurious rooms with fireplaces, Jacuzzis and gorgeous antiques. Walking distance to historic sites. Gourmet breakfast, wine and cheese. Web site: innat835.com

Inn On Edwards	65-75-B&B	Snacks, complimentary wine
107 W Cook St, 62704	4 rooms, 4 pb	Cable TV, accommodate
217-528-0420 Fax: 217-747-0025	*Rated*, •	business travelers
Charles Kirchner	C-yes/S-no/P-no/H-no	
All year		

A charming, antiques filled Inn located adjacent to the Lincoln Home National Historic Site and within walking distance to many other historic tourist attractions. E-mail: inn1@ juno.com *Web site:* bbonline.com/il/edwards

Indiana

ANGOLA

Hartman House Inn	75-155	Full breakfast
417 E Maumee St, 46703	4 rooms, 4 pb	Restaurant
219-665-9080 Fax: 219-668-7083	Visa, MC, AmEx,	Sitting room, suites, fireplace,
800-909-9080	*Rated*, •	cable TV, jacuzzi, business
Linda & Jerry Fejedelem	C-yes/S-ltd/P-no/H-no	travelers.
All year		

Located west of historic downtown. Lovingly restored to much of its original grandeur. E-mail: hartmanhouse@hotmail.com *Web site:* locl.net/homes/hartman/

BEVERLY SHORES

Dunes Shore Inn	60-B&B	Continental plus breakfast
PO Box 807, 46301	8-12 rooms, 4 pb	Fruit, cider & cookies
219-879-9029	*Rated*	Library, sitting room,
Rosemary & Fred Braun	C-ltd/S-ltd/P-no/H-no	outdoor grill, tables
April-November	German	

Located one block from Lake Michigan and surrounded by the National Lakeshore and Dunes State Parks, this inn is a casual oasis for nature lovers. One hour from Chicago.

BLOOMINGTON

Grant Street Inn	90-160-B&B	Full breakfast buffet
310 N Grant St, 47408	24 rooms, 24 pb	Snacks
812-334-2353 Fax: 812-331-8673	Most CC,	Sitting room, TV's & phones
800-328-4350	S-ltd/P-no/H-yes	in rooms
Bob Bohler All year		

Suites have fireplaces and whirlpool Jacuzzis. Walk to downtown or Indiana University. Web site: grantstinn.com/

Prairie Manor B&B, Goshen, IN

CHESTERTON

Gray Goose Inn
350 Indian Boundary Rd,
46304
219-926-5781 Fax: 219-926-4845
800-521-5127
Tim Wilk, Charles Ramsey
All year

80-165-B&B
8 rooms, 8 pb
Most CC, *Rated*, •
C-ltd/S-ltd/P-no/H-no

Full gourmet breakfast
Complimentary beverages,
snacks
Sitting & meeting rooms,
telephones in rooms,
bicycles, boats

In Dunes Country. English country house on priv. wooded lake. Charming guest rooms, private baths, fireplaces, Jacuzzis, sun porch. Jogging/hiking trails.   E-mail: graygoose@niia.net *Web site:* graygooseinn.com

EVANSVILLE

Cool Breeze Estate B&B
1240 SE Second St, 47713
812-422-9635
Katelin & David Hills
All year

85-B&B
4 rooms, 4 pb
AmEx, Disc, *Rated*
C-yes/S-no/H-no

Full breakfast
Sitting room, library, family
friendly facility, meetings for
small groups

Historic Graham-Ingleheart 1906 home near river, 1½ shady acres. Spacious rooms. Dining room mural also in White House. Home-made breads.   E-mail: coolbreeze27@juno.com *Web site:* coolbreezebb.com

---

Historic Newborgh B&B
224 State St, 47630
812-858-3590 Fax: 812-858-3591
888-448-3590
Cecil M. Lasher
All year

79-99-B&B
3 rooms, 3 pb
Visa, MC, *Rated*
C-ltd/S-no/P-no/H-no

Full breakfast
Afternoon tea, snacks
Complimentary wine, sitting
room, fireplaces, library,
cable TV

Old world charm & modern conveniences join together to give this 2-story home, located 2 blocks from the Ohio River, an aura of elegance that is sure to comfort the weary traveler or business guest.   E-mail: nbrgbnb@aol.com

GOSHEN

Prairie Manor B&B
66398 US 33 S, 46526
219-642-4761 Fax: 219-642-4762
800-791-3952
Jean & Hesston Lauver
All year

69-95-B&B
4 rooms, 4 pb
Visa, MC, Disc, *Rated*
C-yes/S-no/P-no/H-no

Full breakfast
Snacks
Library, swimming pool,
cable TV, Accommodate
business travelers

Come visit Indiana Amish country. Relax in our spacious historic English country manor home, enjoy our bountiful breakfast, find your treasure in Grandma's Attic, and explore many attractions in the area.   E-mail: jeston@npcc.net *Web site:* prairiemanor.com

GOSHEN

Red Rooster Inn
61168 SR 15, 46528
219-534-3121 Fax: 219-537-0186
Milton & Kirsten Miller
All year

59 and up-B&B
4 rooms, 4 pb
Most CC,
C-yes/S-no/P-no/H-no

Continental breakfast

The perfect place to stay in the heart of Indiana's Amish Country. Close to Notre Dame, South Bend, Shipshewana, Middlebury, Nappanee and Elkhart. E-mail: redrooster@ redroosterinnbb.com *Web site:* redroosterinnbb.com

GOSHEN, ELKHART

Rust Hollar B&B
55238 CR 31, 46507
219-825-1111 Fax: 219-825-4614
800-313-7800
Tim & Janine Rust
All year

79-89-B&B
4 rooms, 4 pb
Visa, MC, AmEx, Disc,
Rated
C-yes/S-ltd/P-no/H-ltd

Full breakfast
Sitting room, cable TV,
conferences.

Rustic log home situated in a secluded "hollar." E-mail: tim@rusthollar.com *Web site:* rusthollar.com/RHBB/index.html

GRANDVIEW

River Belle B&B
PO Box 669, 47615
812-649-2500 Fax: 812-649-2530
800-877-5165
Pat and Don Phillips
All year

65-75-B&B
5 rooms, 3 pb
Visa, MC, *Rated*
C-yes/S-no/P-no/H-no

Continental breakfast plus
Sitting room, library,
fireplaces, cable TV, fax and
copy machine

A little bit of southern charm in southern Indiana. Stay in a beautifully restored 1860 Steamboat style home, an 1880 Italianate, or an 1860's cottage. Located on the Ohio River. *Web site:* bbonline.com/in/riverbelle

INDIANAPOLIS

Speedway B&B
1829 Cunningham Rd, 46224
317-487-6531 Fax: 317-481-1825
800-975-3412
Robert & Pauline Grothe
All year

75-135-B&B
5 rooms, 5 pb
Most CC, *Rated*
C-ltd/S-ltd/P-no/H-no

Full breakfast
Bicycles, suites, fireplaces,
cable TV, accommodate
business travelers

Located in the little town of Speedway. Surrounded by the city of Indianapolis, you'll find a feeling of home. When May rolls around, everything is exciting and alive as the town is jump started to life with people from all corners of the world. E-mail: speedwaybb@msn.com *Web site:* innsites.com/inns/A003249.html

Tranquil Cherub B&B, The
2164 N Capitol Ave, 46202
317-923-9036 Fax: 317-923-8676
Barbara & Thom Feit
All year

65-95-B&B
4 rooms, 4 pb
Visa, MC, AmEx, *Rated*
C-ltd/S-ltd/P-no/H-no

Full gourmet breakfast
Snacks
Airport pickup, library,
sitting room, transportation
downtown

This lovingly restored, antique filed, 100 year old b&b is located minutes from downtown in a safe culturally diverse urban neighborhood. E-mail: tcherubbnb@aol.com *Web site:* members.aol.com/tcherubbnb/cherub.html

JASPER

Powers Inn B&B
325 W 6th St, 47546
812-482-3018
Larry & Alice Garland
All year

60-B&B
3 rooms, 3 pb
Visa, MC, *Rated*
C-ltd/S-no/P-no/H-no

Full breakfast
Sitting room, cable TV,
accommodate business
travelers

Renovated Second Empire home from 1880's. Original wood floors, pleasant mix of antiques. Three cozy guest rooms with private baths. Enjoy a full breakfast in spacious dining room. Tour the flower gardens and relax on the shady brick patio.

KNIGHTSTOWN

Main Street Victorian B&B	70-B&B	Full breakfast
130 W Main St, 46148	3 rooms, 3 pb	Evening dessert
765-345-2299	S-ltd/P-no/H-no	Gardens, sitting room, swing,
800-817-8210		bikes, golf, TV, loft
Don & Ginny Warnick		
All year		

1850 restored Victorian on Antique Alley, coppersmith, train trip, historical homes, covered bridges. 2 resident dogs. Business traveler friendly. Plush robes, romantic setting.

Old Hoosier House B&B	70-80-B&B	Full gourmet breakfast
7601 S Greensboro Pike, 46148	4 rooms, 3 pb	Cheese, snacks, dessert
765-345-2969	*Rated*, •	Sitting room, library,
800-775-5315	C-yes/S-ltd/P-no/H-no	bicycles, special golf rates
Jean & Tom Lewis		
All year		

1840 country home near Indianapolis in antique area. Comfortable homey atmosphere; delicious breakfast on patio with view of Royal Golf Club

LAPORTE

Arbor Hill Inn	71-189-B&B	Full breakfast
263 W Johnson Rd, 46350	7 rooms, 7 pb	Lunch/dinner available (fee)
219-362-9200 Fax: 219-326-1778	Most CC, *Rated*	Sitting room, Jacuzzis, suites,
L. Kobat/M. Wedow/K.	C-yes/S-no/P-no/H-yes	fireplaces, cable TV
Demoret		
All year		

Historic 1910 Greek Revival Structure. Elegant, peaceful surroundings create a haven for business and leisure travelers. Breakfast is served in your room or one of our 2 porches. Private dining available.   E-mail: arborh@netnitco.net

LEAVENWORTH

Leavenworth Inn	59 and up-B&B	Full breakfast
PO Box 9, 47137	10 rooms, 10 pb	Afternoon tea, snacks
812-739-2120 Fax: 812-739-2012	Most CC, *Rated*	Sitting room, library,
888-739-2120	C-ltd/S-no/P-no/H-yes	bicycles, tennis court, suites,
Amy Valentine		fireplaces, cable TV.
Feb 1-Dec 31		

Country hideaway overlooking the Ohio River, beautifully landscaped grounds with gazebo, tennis courts and walking trails. Great for family vacations, romantic weekends or business retreats. Hospitality is our specialty.   Web site: leavenworthinn.com

LOGANSPORT

Inntiquity, A Country Inn
1075 St Rd 25 N, 46947
219-722-2398
George & Lee Nafzger
Season Inquire

E-mail: inntiquity@cqc.com *Web site:* innsite.com/inns/A003919.html

MADISON

Schussler House B&B	99-B&B	Full breakfast
514 Jefferson St, 47250	3 rooms, 3 pb	Snacks
812-273-2068	Most CC, *Rated*, •	Sitting room wicker porches,
800-392-1931	C-ltd/S-no/P-no/H-no	private parking, AC, gift
Judy & Bill Gilbert		certificates avail.
All year		

Gracious accommodations in the heart of the historic district; a sumptuous breakfast served in the formal dining room. Breakfast includes fresh fruit, coffee cakes & muffings & features treats such as apple flan or caramel glased frnch toast.

McCORDSVILLE

Round Barn Inn B&B
6794 N CR 600 W, 46055
317-335-7023
888-743-9819
Dean & Dana Ice
All year

72-96-B&B
3 rooms, 2 pb
Visa, MC, *Rated*
C-yes/S-ltd/P-no/H-no

Full breakfast
Sitting room, library, suites,
fireplaces, game room with
pool table

1916 Historic Round Barn, furnished in antiques, large country breakfast. The Barn is 7,000 square feet. We're 25 minutes from downtown Indianapolis, IN. Rural, unique, historic. Web site: bbonline.com/in/roundbarn

MICHIGAN CITY

Hutchinson Mansion Inn, The
220 W 10th St, 46360
219-879-1700
Mary DuVal
All year

85-140-B&B
10 rooms, 10 pb
Visa, MC, AmEx,
Rated, •
C-ltd/S-ltd/P-no/H-ltd

Full breakfast
Snacks
Sitting room, piano,
whirlpools, Fax, tennis & golf
nearby

Elegant Victorian mansion filled with antiques, stained glass, friezes. Near National Lakeshore, dunes, beaches, antique stores, shopping, orchards, wineries.

MIDDLEBURY

Bee Hive B&B
Box 1191, 46540
219-825-5023
Herb & Treva Swarm
All year

55-75-B&B
3 rooms, 1 pb
Visa, MC, *Rated*
C-yes/S-no/P-no

Full breakfast
Complimentary
refreshments
Sitting room, restaurant
nearby, guest cottage
available

A country home in a relaxing atmosphere. Located in Amish Country with plenty of local attractions. Ski trails nearby. Easy access to Indiana Toll Road.

Essenhaus Country Inn
PO Box 2608, 46540
219-825-9471
800-455-9471
Wilbur & Rosalie Bontrager
All year

73-145-B&B
40 rooms, 40 pb
Most CC, *Rated*
C-yes/S-no/P-no/H-yes

Continental breakfast
Afternoon tea, snacks,
restaurant
Suites, cable TV

40 unique guest rooms, 1100 seat family style restaurant featuring Amish food, 7 village shops, petting farm, miniture golf and seasonal carriage rides on our 110 acre property. E-mail: jlsauder@essenhouse.com *Web site:* essenhaus.com

Patchwork Quilt Cntry. Inn
11748 CR 2, 46540
219-825-2417 Fax: 219-825-5172
Ray & Rosetta Miller
All year

70-110-B&B
15 rooms, 15 pb
Rated
C-ltd/S-no/P-no/H-no

Full breakfast
Lunch, dinner available
Sitting room, piano, Amish
tours, gift shop, buggy rides

Prepare to be pampered in gracious country home. In Amish country. Near Shipshewana Flea Auction. Closed Sundays. Conference facilities.   E-mail: rgminn@aol.com
Web site: patchworkquiltinn.com

MIDDLETOWN

Cornerstone Guest House
705 High St, 47356
765-354-6004
800-792-6004
Dave & Debbie Lively
All year

75-95-B&B
3 rooms, 3 pb
Visa, MC,
C-ltd/S-ltd/P-no/H-no

Full breakfast
Snacks
Sitting room, library,
bicycles, computer & fax, for
business travelers

*Experience Hoosier hospitality with a touch of elegance in this 1909 home. Close to Indianapolis, outlet shopping, golf & horse racing. New cottage suite
Web site:* ourcornerstone.com

NASHVILLE ───────────────────────────────────

Allison House Inn	95-B&B	Full breakfast
PO Box 1625, 47448	5 rooms, 5 pb	Library, sitting room, art
812-988-0814	*Rated*	gallery, gift shop
Tammy Galm	C-ltd/S-no/P-no/H-no	
All year		

In the heart of Brown County, the center for the arts and craft colony. Coziness, comfort and charm.   E-mail: tammy@kiva.net   Web site: nashvilleindiana.com/lodging/allison/allison.html

Story Inn	88-126-B&B	Full country breakfast
PO Box 847, 47448	12 rooms, 12 pb	Lunch, dinner, aftn. tea
812-988-2273 Fax: 812-988-6516	Visa, MC, *Rated*, ●	Restaurant, bar, sitting room,
800-881-1183	C-ltd/S-no/P-ltd/H-no	larger units available, for 2-6
Frank Mueller	German	persons
All year		

Located on the southern edge of Brown County State Park, this 1850's General Store has been restored into a B&B Inn featuring a gourmet restaurant.   E-mail: reservations@ storyinn.com *Web site:* storyinn.com

NEW CASTLE ───────────────────────────────────

La Casa di' Maroni	60-90-B&B	Full breakfast
5835 W County Rd 200 S, 47362	3 rooms	Sitting room, bicycles,
765-785-2810	●	fireplaces; private, reading
Sandra Maroney	S-no/P-no/H-no	parlor
Closed Dec-Feb		

Our inn offers a warm & friendly atmosphere in a country setting. We feature nicely decorated & spacious bedrooms with antiques. Family gathering area with gas log fireplace.   E-mail: cmaroney@modelaircraft.org

ROCKVILLE ───────────────────────────────────

"Suits Us" B&B	55-125-B&B	Full breakfast
514 N College St, 47872	4 rooms, 4 pb	Afternoon tea, snacks
765-569-5660	*Rated*	Sitting room, library, color
888-4SUITSUS	C-ltd/S-no/P-no/H-no	TVs, books in rms, bicycles,
Andy & Lianna Willhite		tennis court
All year		

Golf, antique shops, see 32 covered bridges, hiking at Turkey Run Park, movie library for guests and complimentary refreshments. Working farm guest house with 4 bedrooms available.

SOUTH BEND ───────────────────────────────────

Book Inn B&B, The	85-130-B&B	Full breakfast
508 W Washington, 46601	5 rooms, 5 pb	Library, sitting room, quality
219-288-1990 Fax: 219-234-2338	Visa, MC, AmEx,	used bookstore, located
Peggy & John Livingston	*Rated*, ●	downstairs
All year	C-ltd/S-no/P-no/H-no	

Designers Showcase Second Empire urban home. Twelve-foot ceilings, irreplaceable butternut woodwork, comfortable antiques & fresh flowers welcome you E-mail: bookinn@aol.com *Web site:* members.aol.com/bookinn/

Oliver Inn B&B, The	85-192-B&B	Full breakfast
630 W Washington St, 46601	9 rooms, 7 pb	Snacks, aftn. tea, wine
219-232-4545 Fax: 219-288-9788	Most CC, *Rated*, ●	Sitting room, library,
888-697-4466	C-yes/S-no/P-ltd/H-ltd	fireplaces, cable TV
Richard & Venera Monahan		
All year		

Magnificent 1886 Victorian mansion, one-acre estate with Carriage House and c. 1920 Playhouse. Jacuzzi, 7 fireplaces, computerized baby grand.   E-mail: oliver@michiana.org *Web site:* lodging-south-bend.com

TERRE HAUTE

Farrington B&B
931 South 7th St, 47807
812-238-0524 Fax: 812-242-8335
Mike & Connie Mutterspaugh
All year

85-B&B
5 rooms, 3 pb
Visa, MC, *Rated*
C-yes/S-yes/P-no/H-no

Full breakfast
Snacks
Sitting room, fireplaces,
covered porches in rooms,
family friendly facility

A Colonial Revival home adapted to Queen Anne style. Built in 1898. Located in the heart of Terre Haute's historical district. E-mail: abednbkfst@aol.com
Web site: members.aol.com/abednbkfst

VALPARAISO

Inn at Aberdeen, Ltd.
1758 Clifty Creek Ct, 46385
219-465-3753 Fax: 219-465-9227
Bill Simon
All year

94-173-B&B
11 rooms, 11 pb
Most CC, *Rated*
C-yes/S-no/P-no/H-yes

Full gourmet breakfast
Evening dessert, snacks
Sitting room, library, bikes,
hot tubs, pool, conference
center, tennis

Travel back to the 1800s while enjoying your own Jacuzzi, balcony, cozy fire and truly regal service and amenities. 18 hole champion golf course. E-mail: innaberd@netnitco.net
Web site: innataberdeen.com

Iowa

ADAIR

Lalley House B&B
1205 Ridgewood Ave, 50010
515-742-5541
Fax: 515-742-3901
Linda Faga
All year

65-150-B&B
5 rooms, 5 pb
Visa, MC, Disc, *Rated*,
•
C-ltd/S-no/P-no/H-ltd

Full breakfast
Afternoon tea, snacks
Sitting room, suites, fireplace,
cable TV, conference
facilities

This romantic turn of the century painted lady with whirlpools, fireplaces, candlelit breakfasts, and a full cookie jar are just waiting for you. It is wonderful for a honeymoon or an anniversary gift for that special person. E-mail: dakyfg@aol.com *Web site:* lalleyhouse.com

ALGONA

Heartland B&B
400 E Nebraska St, 50511
515-295-9445
Vickie Woods & Randy Roeber
All year

65-120-B&B
4 rooms, 4 pb
Rated
C-ltd/S-no/P-no/H-no

Full breakfast
Sitting room, bicycles,
Jacuzzis, fireplaces, cable
TV, massage next door

Constructed 1913 restored 1990's, heirlooms, oak floors, trim, window seats, marble fireplace, central air, breakfast in dining room or wrap around porches, walk to downtown boutiques, theaters, antique shops and parks. Softball and basketball nearby.

ATLANTIC

Chestnut Charm B&B
1409 Chestnut St, 50022
712-243-5652
Barbara Stensvad
All year

70-250-B&B
9 rooms, 9 pb
Visa, MC, *Rated*, •
S-no/P-no/H-ltd

Full breakfast
Sitt. room, piano, sauna, sun
rooms, A/C, antiques,
fountained patio, gazebo

Enchanting 1898 Victorian mansion on large estate. Just a short drive to the famous bridges of Madison County. Gourmet dining. Experience beauty & fantasy with someone special. Fireplaces and Jacuzzi brand name tubs for two. E-mail: chestnut@netins.net
Web site: chestnutcharm.org

BURLINGTON

Mississippi Manor B&B Inn
809 N 4th, 52601
309-753-2218
Francesca Harris
All year

55-75-B&B
4 rooms, 4 pb
Visa, MC, •
C-ltd/S-no/P-no/H-no

Continental breakfast
Full breakfast available
Lunch, dinner (fee), sitting
room, porch, bicycles

Enjoy peace & quiet, elegance & hospitality at this handsome Victorian Italianate home (circa 1877) located in a charming river town. *E-mail:* fhdjd@aol.com

Schramm House B&B, The
616 Columbia St, 52601
319-754-0373
Fax: 319-754-0373
800-683-7117
Sandy & Bruce Morrison
All year

75-95-B&B
4 rooms, 4 pb
Most CC, *Rated*, •
S-no/P-no/H-no

Full breakfast
Complimentary wine, snacks
Sitting room, library bicycles

Charming Victorian in historic district. Furnished with antiques throughout. Walk to downtown, Mississippi River, antique district, restaurants and more. *E-mail:* visit@schramm.com
Web site: visit.schramm.com

CEDAR RAPIDS

2325 Grande Avenue Homestay
2325 Grande Ave SE, 52403
319-363-5389 Fax: 319-362-8391
George & Kay Henry
Sept 15-June 15

50-65-B&B
3 rooms, 1 pb
Visa, MC,
C-yes/S-no/P-no/H-no

Full breakfast
Snacks
Sitting room, Jacuzzis, cable
TV, accommodate business
travelers

We would like to have you stay with us in our 1918 Prairie style home, conveniently located to downtown. Amenities include a full breakfast and cable TV. Exercise equipment and a hot tub are in our common room. *E-mail:* kshiveh326@aol.com

Belmont Hill Victorian B&B
1525 Cherokee Dr NW, 52405
319-366-1343 Fax: 319-366-1351
Ken & Shelley Sullens
All year

99-152-B&B
3 rooms, 3 pb
Visa, MC,
C-ltd/S-no/P-no/H-yes

Full breakfast
Afternoon tea
Suites, firplace,
accommodate business
travelers, wooded grounds,
gardens

Experience a unique level of pampering and privacy. Restored 1882 National Register home and carriage house. Immaculate accommodations, private baths. Lovely secluded grounds, terrace and gardens. Gourmet breakfast, corporate amenities. *E-mail:* belmonthil@aol.com *Web site:* belmonthill.com

COON RAPIDS

Garst Farm Resorts
1390 Hwy 141, 50058
712-684-2964 Fax: 712-684-2887
Liz Garst
All year

75-120-B&B
8 rooms, 6 pb
Visa, MC, AmEx,
C-yes/S-ltd/P-ltd/H-ltd
Spanish

Full breakfast
Catered meals for groups-6
or more
Sitting room, library, bikes,
Jacuzzis, suites, cable TV

Beautiful 4500 acre property features a comfortable b&b farmhouse which Soviet Premier Khruschchev visited in 1959. Also, cottages, campsites, horesback riding, canoes, farm and nature tours, hiking, astronomy and fishing. *E-mail:* gresort@pionet.net
Web site: farmresort.com

DES MOINES

Be-Bop Inn
50021
515-964-3138 Fax: 515-964-3161
800-758-1539
Linda Brown
All year

85-B&B
1 rooms, 1 pb
C-ltd/S-no/P-no/H-ltd

Full breakfast
Snacks, complimentary wine
Sitting room, library, bikes,
cable TV, hot tub, private
patio

Rural community 12 minutes from Des Moines. 1200 sq. ft. of privacy.
E-mail: BeBopInn@aol.com

The Carlson House, Swedesburg, IA

DUBUQUE

Mandolin Inn, The
199 Loras Blvd, 52001
319-556-0069 Fax: 319-556-0587
800-524-7996
Amy Boynton
All year

75-135-B&B
7 rooms, 5 pb
Most CC,
C-ltd/S-no/P-no/H-no
Some Spanish & French

Full breakfast
Sitting room, parlor, music
room, suites, cable TV,
resident cat

1908 Edwardian mansion dedicated to sharing elegance & comfort. Perfect for kindling romance as well as exploring the upper Mississippi river. Gourmet breakfast, queen size beds & beautiful rooms.   E-mail: innkeeper@mandolininn.com *Web site:* mandolininn.com

Richards House, The
1492 Locust St, 52001
319-557-1492
Michelle A. Delaney
All year

45-95-B&B
5 rooms, 4 pb
Most CC, *Rated*, •
C-yes/S-ltd/P-ltd/H-no

Full breakfast
Snacks
Sitting room, antiques,
concealed TVs, phones,
fireplaces

1883 Stick-style Victorian mansion with over 80 stained-glass windows. Seven varieties of woodwork and period furnishings.   Web site: the-richards-house.com/

FORT MADISON

Kingsley Inn
707 Ave H, 52627
319-372-7074 Fax: 319-372-7096
800-441-2327
Alida Willis
All year

70-150-B&B
14 rooms, 14 pb
Most CC, *Rated*, •
C-ltd/S-no/P-no/H-yes

Continental plus breakfast
Snacks, restaurant
Sitting room, hot tubs,
Thomas Jefferson suite, w/2
bedrooms, kitchen

Historic inn on Mississippi River. Antique furnishings, all modern conveniences, museums, shops, riverboat, fifteen miles to Nauvoo, Illinois. New gift shop   E-mail: kingsley@interl.net
Web site: KingsleyInn.com

GRINNELL

Carriage House B&B
1133 Broad St, 50112
515-236-7520 Fax: 515-236-5085
Ray & Dorothy Spriggs
All year

55-70-B&B
5 rooms, 5 pb
Visa, MC, *Rated*, •
C-ltd/S-no/P-no/H-no

Full breakfast
Afternoon tea, snacks
Sitting room, library,
Jacuzzis, fireplaces,
accommodate business
travelers

Victorian home restored with your comfort in mind; gourmet breakfast, afternoon tea available. Enjoy the wicker on the porch or read by the fire; good restaurants nearby. E-mail: irishbnb@pcpartner.net

The Lion & The Lamb B&B, Vinton, IA

LANSING

Suzanne's Inn, B&B
PO Box 128, 52151
319-538-3040 Fax: 608-788-7779
Suzanne Cansler
Closed January

60-75-B&B
4 rooms, 2 pb
Rated
C-ltd/S-ltd/P-no/H-no

Full breakfast
Afternoon tea
Sitting room, suites,
fireplaces, sauna in the root
cellar

Antique-filled gothic revival perched on the bluffs of the Mississippi River.
E-mail: suzanneinn@aol.com *Web site:* bestinn.net/usa/ia/suzanne.htmlm

MAQUOKETA

Squiers Manor B&B
122 McKinsey Dr, 52060
319-652-6961 Fax: 319-652-5995
Virl & Kathy Banowetz
All year

80-195-B&B
8 rooms, 8 pb
Visa, MC, AmEx, *Rated*
C-yes/S-no/P-no/H-no

Full gourmet breakfast
Sitting room, library, bridal
suite available, fireplaces,
whirlpool

Experience Victorian elegance, ambiance & hospitality at its finest. Private whirlpool
baths, fireplaces, antiques. Candlelight evening dessert. 1100 square foot suite available.
E-mail: banowetz@caves.net *Web site:* squiersmanor.com

MCGREGOR

McGregor Manor
320 4th St, 52157
319-873-2600 Fax: 319-873-2218
Carolyn & David Scott
All year

68-78-B&B
4 rooms, 4 pb
Visa, MC, *Rated*, •
C-ltd/S-no/P-no/H-no

Full breakfast
Snacks, dinner (fee)
Sitting room, bicycles
fireplaces, whirlpool

Come share the warmth and hospitality of our home, one that will transport you back to an
era of Victorian elegance and charm E-mail: mmanor@mhtc.net

NEWTON

LaCorsette Maison Inn
629 First Ave E, 50208
515-792-6833
Kay Owen
All year

75-190-B&B
7 rooms, 7 pb
Visa, MC, AmEx,
Rated, •
C-ltd/S-no/P-ltd/H-no

Full breakfast
Gourmet dinner, Restaurant
Whirlpools, fireplaces, sitting
room. Near I-35., Near Des
Moines on I-80

Turn-of-the-century mission-style mansion. Charming French bedchambers, beckoning
hearths. Gourmet Dining 4½ star rating. One suite has double whirlpool. Vegetarian dining
by pre-arrangement. Web site: innbrook.com/inns/LaCor

SWEDESBURG

Carlson House, The
PO Box 8, 52652
319-254-2451 Fax: 319-254-8809
888-841-7199
Ruth & Ned Ratekin   All year

50-B&B
2 rooms, 2 pb
Rated
C-ltd/S-no/P-no/H-no

Full breakfast
Afternoon tea, snacks
Lunch/dinner available (fee),
sitting room, library, Jacuzzi
on private deck

The stately Carlson House provides a Swedish accent in decor, foods & ambiance. Comfortable lounging in sitting rooms & porches. A rich supply of browsing materials, A/C & gracious hosts. Full office.   E-mail: r2009@se-iowa.net

VINTON

Lion & The Lamb B&B, The
913 2nd Ave, 52349
319-472-5086 Fax: 319-472-9115
888-390-5262
Richard & Rachel Waterbury
All year

85-185-B&B
6 rooms, 3 pb
Visa, MC, •
C-yes/S-no/P-no/H-no

Full breakfast
Evening dessert
Sitting room, bicycles, year
round boutique, many
attractions nearby

1892 Victorian mansion with seven fireplaces. Each guest room has a queen size bed, air conditioning, ceiling fan and TV.   E-mail: lionlamb@lionlamb.com *Web site:* lionlamb.com

Kansas

COUNCIL GROVE

Cottage House-Hotel, The
25 N Neosho, 66846
316-767-6828 Fax: 316-767-6414
800-727-7903
Connie Essington
All year

62-140-B&B
26 rooms
Most CC, *Rated*, •
C-yes/S-yes/P-ltd/H-yes

Continental plus breakfast
Restaurant nearby
Sitting room, sauna room, 6
rms. w/whirlpool tubs, next
to Neosho Riverwalk

Beautifully renovated Victorian hotel with modern comforts & lovely antique furnishings in historic "Birthplace of the Santa Fe Trail." Honeymoon cottage   E-mail: essin@midusa.net *Web site:* travelguides.com/home/cottagehouse/

HUMBOLDT

Bailey Hotel B&B, The
822 Bridge St, 66748
316-473-3322 Fax: 316-473-2016
Gertie Miles
All year

55-99-B&B
6 rooms, 6 pb
Most CC, •
C-ltd/S-no/P-no/H-no
German

Full breakfast
Lunch, dinner, tea, snacks
(fee)
Restaurant, sitting room,
bicycles on request, tennis,
family-friendly

Elegant turn-of-the-century restored hotel, situated on the town square of the 7th-oldest city in Kansas. Restaurant fetures home cooking and upscale cuisine.

LAWRENCE

Circle S Guest Ranch
3325 Circle S Lane, 66044
785-843-4124 Fax: 785-843-4474
800-625-2839
Mary Beth/Mitchell Stevenson
All year

149-205-B&B
12 rooms, 12 pb
Visa, MC, AmEx, •
C-yes/S-ltd/P-no/H-yes

Full breakfast
Dinner (fee), snacks, bar
service
Sitting room, bikes, Jacuzzis,
fireplaces, hiking trails,
birdwatching.

12 spacious guest rooms each with elegant country decor, private bath and beautiful views. Full breakfast, rustic fancy dinners.   E-mail: msteven103@aol.com *Web site:* CircleSRanch.com

WICHITA ——————————

Castle Inn Riverside, The
1155 N River Blvd, 67203
316-263-9300
Paula & Terry Lowry
All year

125-295-B&B
14 rooms, 14 pb
Most CC, *Rated*, •
C-ltd/S-no/P-no/H-ltd

Full breakfast
Complimentary wine
Sitting room, library, 6 in-
room hot tubs

The one hundred nine year old Scottish Castle has fourteen uniquely appointed rooms. European antiques grace the Castle's common areas and guest rooms.
E-mail: lcastle@gte.net *Web site:* castleinnriverside.com

Kentucky

BARDSTOWN ——————————

Arbor Rose
209 E Stephen Foster Ave,
40004
502-349-0014 Fax: 502-349-7322
888-828-3330
Judy & Derrick Melzer
All year

89-114-B&B
5 rooms, 5 pb
Most CC, *Rated*, •
C-yes/S-no/P-no/H-ltd

Full breakfast
Snacks
Sitting room, tennis court,
fireplaces, cable TV, garden
terrace

Late Victorian style home within walking distance of shopping and antiques. Area has 5 golf courses. Our full "country gourmet" breakfast is served on garden terrace overlooking rose gardens and fountain.   *E-mail:* arborrose@bardstown.com
Web site: bardstown.com/~arborrose

Beautiful Dreamer B&B
440 E Stephen Foster Ave,
40004
502-348-4004
800-811-8312
Lynell & Dan Ginter
All year

99-119-B&B
4 rooms, 4 pb
Most CC, *Rated*, •
S-no/P-no/H-no

Full breakfast
Snacks
Sitting room, Jacuzzis,
fireplaces, cable TV,
conference facilities

Federal design home in historic district complemented with antiques and cherry furniture. Striking view of My Old Kentucky Home from double front porches. Hearty homemade breakfast. Fully A/C, Jacuzzis.   *Web site:* bbonline.com/ky/dreamer

---

Jailer's Inn
111 W Stephen Foster, 40004
502-348-5551 Fax: 502-349-1852
800-948-5551
C. Paul McCoy
March-Dec.

65-105-B&B
6 rooms, 6 pb
Visa, MC, *Rated*, •
C-yes/S-ltd/H-yes

Full breakfast
Complimentary wine &
cheese
Sitting room, gazebo,
landscaped courtyard, roses,
2 rooms w/Jacuzzi

Jailer's Inn is a place of wonderful, thought provoking contrasts. Each of our six guest rooms are beautifully decorated with antiques and heirlooms, all located in the renovated front jail, and all rooms with private baths two with double Jacuzzis.   *E-mail:* cpaul@
jailersinn.com *Web site:* Jailersinn.com

Mansion B&B, The
1003 N Third St, 40004
502-348-2586 Fax: 502-349-6098
800-399-2586
Charmaine & Dennis Downs
All year

85-125-B&B
8 rooms, 8 pb
Most CC, *Rated*, •
S-ltd/P-no/H-no

Continental plus breakfast
Sitting room, piano, mimosa
trees, roses, 2 rm. w/Jacuzzi

Bardstown's most elegant B&B. Greek revival mansion with beautiful period antiques. Seated breakfast using our silver, crystal and china   *E-mail:* ddowns@bardstown.com
Web site: bbonline.com/ky/mansion

BELLEVUE

Christopher's B&B
604 Poplar St, 41073
606-491-9354 Fax: 513-853-1360
888-585-7085
Brenda Guidugli
All year

75-140-B&B
3 rooms, 3 pb
Visa, MC, *Rated*
C-yes/S-ltd/P-no/H-ltd

Continental plus breakfast
Snacks
Sitting room, suites, cable TV,
roses, 2 rooms with Jacuzzis

This late 1800s church was transformed into Christopher's B&B in 1997. A unique establishment in Bellevue's historic district. Guest rooms have stained-glass windows, private baths with whirlpools.   E-mail: christbb@fuse.net   Web site: bbonline.com/ky/christophers/

BEREA

Berea Shady Lane B&B
123 Mt Vernon Rd, 40403
606-986-9851 Fax: 606-986-9851
Clarine & Les Webber
All year

55-70-B&B
2 rooms, 2 pb
Rated, •
C-ltd/P-ltd/H-no

Full breakfast
Afternoon tea, snacks
Sitting room, bar service,
bicycles, hot tub, fireplaces,
cable TV

We are a small B&B, catering to your personal needs, whether it be shopping, vacationing or business. Our afternoon tea is our special way of greeting you.   E-mail: lrwebber@aol.com   Web site: bbonline.com/ky/shadylane

CINCINNATI AREA

First Farm Inn
2510 Stevens Rd, 41080
606-586-0199 Fax: 606-586-0299
800-277-9527
Jen Warner & Dana Kisor
All year

90-110-B&B
2 rooms, 2 pb
Visa, MC, •
C-yes/S-no/P-ltd/H-ltd

Full breakfast
Snacks
Sitting room, library,
Jacuzzis, fireplaces,
massages

Elegant 1870's farmhouse on 20 rolling acres. Horseback riding, massages, spa, ski packages, fishing, meeting rooms, office space, mid-week, multi-day discounts. Beautiful homemade breakfast. 20 minutes outside Cincinnati.   E-mail: firstfarm@goodnews.net   Web site: bbonline.com/ky/firstfarm

GEORGETOWN

Jordan Farm B&B
4091 Newtown Pike, 40324
502-863-1944
Harold & Rebecca Jordan
All year

85-100-B&B
4 rooms, 4 pb
C-yes/S-no/P-no/H-yes

Full breakfast
Afternoon tea, snacks
Family friendly facility near
shops, restaurants

Jordan Farm offers a unique opportunity to stay on a beautiful 100 acre working Bluegrass thoroughbred farm. Mares & foals romp outside the charming carriage house in manicured paddocks.   E-mail: hjordan@mis.net   Web site: jordanfarmbandb.com

Pineapple Inn B&B
645 S Broadway, 40324
502-868-5453 Fax: 502-868-5453
Muriel & Les
All year

65-90-B&B
4 rooms, 4 pb
Visa, MC, *Rated*, •
C-ltd/S-ltd/P-no/H-no

Full breakfast
Snacks, complimentary wine
Sitting room, bar service,
Heart of Bluegrass, horse
country, spa available

Built in 1876—on historical register—gourmet breakfast in country French dining room. Furnished with antiques. Close to many activities.

GHENT

Ghent House
PO Box 478, 41045
502-347-5807
Wayne G. & Diane J. Young
All year

70-150-B&B
4 rooms, 4 pb
Most CC, *Rated*, •
C-yes/S-no/P-no/H-no

Full breakfast
Snacks, restaurants
Sitting room, library,
Jacuzzis, suites, fireplaces

Historic 1833 Federal-style brick, featuring crystal chandeliers. 4 rooms with Jacuzzis & fireplaces. Walk the rose garden & English walking garden, relax in the hot tub. Come as a guest, leave as a friend!   Web site: bbonline.com/ky/ghent

Ghent House B&B, Ghent, KY

HARRODSBURG

Shaker Village Pleas. Hill
3501 Lexington Rd, 40330
606-734-5411 Fax: 606-734-5411
800-734-5611
James C. Thomas
All year

66-80-EP
80 rooms, 80 pb
Visa, MC, *Rated*, •
C-yes/S-yes/P-no/H-ltd

Full breakfast (fee)
Lunch, dinner
Afternoon tea in Winter,
meeting facilities, sitt. rm.,
hiking trails

America's largest restored Shaker Village. National Historic Landmark. 30 restored buildings amid 2700 acres of bluegrass farmland. E-mail: diana@shakervillageky.org
Web site: shakervillageky.org/

LEXINGTON

1823 Historic Rose Hill Inn
233 Rose Hill, 40383
606-873-5957
Fax: 606-873-1813
800-307-0460
Sharon & Marianne Amberg
All year

95-135-B&B
6 rooms, 6 pb
Most CC, *Rated*, •
C-ltd/S-ltd/P-ltd/H-ltd

Full breakfast
Snacks
Sitting room, library, bikes,
suites, fireplaces

Victorian home with estate-like yard in historic district. Easy walk for antiquing and dining. Lovingly restored with original stained glass windows, hardwood floors.
E-mail: Innkeepers@rosehillinn.com *Web site:* rosehillinn.com

B&B at Sills Inn
270 Montgomery Ave, 40383
606-873-4478
Fax: 606-873-7099
800-526-9801
Tony Sills and Glenn Blind
All year

79-179-B&B
12 rooms, 12 pb
Most CC, *Rated*, •
C-ltd/S-no/P-no/H-no
Spanish

Full gourmet breakfast
Snacks
Sitting room, library,
Jacuzzis, suites, cable TV,
conference facilities

Enjoy the ambiance of Southern Hospitality as you step into the 1911, three-storied restored Victorian Inn. E-mail: blindbo@aol.com *Web site:* sillsinn.com

Sandusky House
1626 Delaney Ferry Rd, 40356
606-223-4730
Jim & Linda Humphrey
All year

85-120-B&B
5 rooms, 5 pb
Visa, MC, *Rated*
H-no

Full breakfast
Snacks
Sitting room

Surrounded by small agriculture and horse farms only 6 miles SW of Lexington. Private baths. Furnished in period type furnishing. Full country breakfast. Close to all central Kentucky attractions. E-mail: humphlin@aol.com

Sandusky House, Lexington, KY

LOUISVILLE

Inn at the Park
1332 S Fourth St, 40208
502-637-6930
Fax: 502-637-2796
800-700-PARK
John and Sandra Mullins
All year

89-179-B&B
7 rooms, 7 pb
Visa, MC, AmEx, ●
S-ltd/P-no/H-no
German

Full breakfast
Afternoon tea, snacks
Complimentary wine, sitting
room, library, tennis court

Southern charm & hospitality await you at Inn at the Park. Located adjacent to Louisville Central Park in the midst of largest remaining collection of Victorian homes in the nation! E-mail: innatpark@aol.com *Web site:* bbonline.com/ky/innatpark/

Inn at Woodhaven, The
401 S Hubbards Ln, 40207
502-895-1011
Fax: 502-895-1011
888-895-1011
Marsha Burton
All year

75-175-B&B
7 rooms, 7 pb
Visa, MC, AmEx,
Rated, ●
C-ltd/S-no/P-ltd/H-ltd

Full breakfast
Snacks
Sitting room, library,
Jacuzzis, suites, fireplaces,
cable TV

Elegant and comfortable inn in beautiful suburb 8 minutes from downtown and close to attractions, fine dining, and shopping. Furnished in antiques. Full gourmet breakfast served from 7:30-9:30. E-mail: woodhavenb@aol.com *Web site:* bbonline.com/ky/woodhaven/

Old Louisville Inn
1359 S Third St, 40208
502-635-1574
Fax: 502-637-5892
Marianne Lesher
All year

95-195-B&B
10 rooms, 10 pb
Visa, MC, *Rated*, ●
C-yes/S-ltd/P-no/H-no

Full breakfast
Afternoon tea
Sitting room, library,
bicycles, tennis, piano, hot
tub, exercise room

"Your home away from home." Wake up to the aroma of freshly baked breads and muffins and Southern hospitality. Children under 12 free   E-mail: oldlouinn@aol.com
Web site: oldlouinn.com

LOUISVILLE ──────────────────────────

Pinecrest Cottage B&B
2806 Newburg Rd, 40205
502-454-3800 Fax: 502-452-9791
Nancy Morris
All year

125-155-B&B
1 rooms, 1 pb
Visa, MC, AmEx,
C-yes/S-no/P-no/H-yes

Continental plus breakfast
Snacks
Sitting room, fireplaces,
tennis court, cable TV,
swimming pool

Pinecrest Cottage is a separate, well-appointed guest house, affording guests complete privacy. It offers a king-size bedroom, full bath, living room with 2 sofas, TV/VCR, fireplace, & fully stocked kitchen. Web site: bbonline.com/ky/pinecrest/

───────────────────────────────────

Sulphur Trace B&B
PO Box 127, 40070
502-743-5956
Fax: 502-743-5464
K.P. Sanders & F.C. Thiemann
March 1-October 31

65-B&B
2 rooms, 2 pb
C-yes/S-ltd/P-ltd/H-yes

Full breakfast
Afternoon tea, snacks
Sitting room

A lovely, spacious, contemporary B&B nestled in the trees with a feeling of the great outdoors. Breakfast is served in the great room with sheep and goats not far from the door. E-mail: sulphtrace@aol.com

MURRAY ──────────────────────────────

Diuguid House B&B
603 Main St, 42071
502-753-5470
888-261-3028
Karen & George Chapman
All year

40-45-B&B
3 rooms
Visa, MC, *Rated*, •
C-yes/S-no/P-no/H-no

Full breakfast
Afternoon tea, snacks
Sitting room, porch, piano,
TV, laundry, children
welcome

Historic Queen Anne centrally located in beautiful university town; close to Kentucky Lake and many antique shops. Nice retirement area. E-mail: gachap@hotmail.com

Louisiana

ALEXANDRIA ──────────────────────────

Loyd Hall Plantation B&B
292 Loyd Bridge Rd, 71325
318-776-5641 Fax: 318-776-5886
800-240-8135
Melinda F. Anderson   All year

95-165-B&B
6 rooms, 6 pb
Visa, MC, AmEx,
Rated, •
C-yes/S-ltd/P-no

Continental plus breakfast
Snacks, complimentary wine
Bicycles, Jacuzzi, pool,
fireplace, cable TV

Six suites with private kitchens/baths. Pool, biking, fireplaces, 640 acre working plantation. Civil War history and ghosts. AAA-3 Diamond Award. E-mail: mande10032@aol.com
Web site: louisianatravel.com/loyd_hall

───────────────────────────────────

Matt's Cabin/Inglewood
PO Box 5443, 71307
318-487-8340 Fax: 318-448-0441
888-575-6288
S.J. Peyton
All year

100-125-B&B
2 rooms, 2 pb
C-yes/H-no
French, Japanese

Full breakfast
Tennis court, pool, family
friendly facility, tour of
plantation home

Escape to sample the unique flavor of central Louisiana in our secluded, elegant 1900s retreat with all the amenities from a time gone by. Queen 4-poster and trundle bed. Main plantation now available for weddings, house parties, etc. E-mail: susan@
inglewoodplantation.com *Web site:* bbchannel.com/bbc/p240900.asp

BATON ROUGE

Tree House in the Park	110-175-B&B	Full breakfast
16520 Airport Dr, 70769	4 rooms, 3 pb	Dinner included 1st nite
225-622-3885 Fax: 225-622-2850	Visa, MC, •	Gazebo, pool table, ping,
800-532-2246	S-no/P-no/H-no	pong, kayak & pirogues,
Vic & Vikki Hotopp		heated swimming pool
All year		

Cajun cabin in the swamp. Rooms have private entrance, queen waterbed, TV/VCR, hot tub on deck under stars. Comp. first supper. Cypress trees, moss, ponds. Satellite TV
E-mail: vichotopp@eatel.net

FRANKLIN

Hanson House	125-B&B	Full breakfast
114 E Main St, 70538	4 rooms, 3 pb	Snacks, wine
318-828-3271 Fax: 318-828-0497	Most CC, *Rated*	Sitting room, library, the
800-256-2931	C-ltd/S-ltd/P-ltd/H-no	house has been in, the family
Bette & Caunse Kemper	Limited French &	since 1860
All year	German	

In the heart of Franklin's historic district, this 10,000 sq foot antebellum cottage sits on 4.5 acres on the banks of Bayou Teche some 50 miles from the Evangeline Oak.
E-mail: caunse@aol.com *Web site:* hansonhouse.bigdogz.com

LAFAYETTE

La Maison de Campagne	105-135-B&B	Full breakfast
825 Kidder Rd, 70520	4 rooms, 4 pb	Snacks, lunch available with
318-896-6529 Fax: 318-896-1494	Visa, MC, *Rated*, •	notice
800-895-0235	C-ltd/S-no/P-no/H-no	Sitting room, library,
Joeann & Fred McLemore	French	swimming pool, antiques,
All year		biking, jogging trail

Beautiful, quiet countryside. Great music, food, festivals & attractions nearby. Full country gourmet breakfasts. Newly refurbished. "Love, laughter & romance in a box"—ABC News. Fresh paint throughout, covered back deck. Added king bed. F-mail: fmclemore@the-fish.net
Web site: cajuncountryhouse.com

La Maison de Repos	65-85-B&B	Full southern breakfast
218 Vincent Rd, 70508	3 rooms, 1 pb	Happy hour with mint juleps
318-856-6958 Fax: 318-857-8113	Most CC, *Rated*, •	Airport pickup, custom,
Mildred & Roland Doucet	C-yes/S-yes/P-no/H-yes	tours & dinner by arr.,
All year	French	business travelers 10% off

Come experience true Cajun hospitality with French, Cajun hosts. Learn all about the history & culture of Cajun Country and its people. Located in the beautiful, quiet countryside of Lafayette. E-mail: mrdoucet@aol.com

LAKE CHARLES

Reid-Toerner House, The	125-B&B	Full breakfast
820 S Division St, 70601	4 rooms, 4 pb	Snacks, comp. wine
318-439-6165 Fax: 318-439-6187	Visa, MC,	Sitting room, sporting
All year	S-ltd/P-ltd/H-no	packages, from riverboat
	German	casinos

This romantic revival home was built in 1903. Located in the Charpentier District which contains nearly 20 blocks of historic homes and architecture. Web site: reid-toerner.com

Walter's Attic	65-110-B&B	Continental breakfast
618 Ford, 70601	1 rooms, 1 pb	Snacks
318-439-3210	Visa, MC, AmEx,	Bikes, hot tub
Tanis Robinson Teague	S-no/P-no/H-no	
All year		

Total privacy, catering to the honeymoon couple. 1130 square ft. suite, 16 ft. ceiling, outside private hot tub, private entrance. Close to the Riverboat Casino. E-mail: walteratt@aol.com
Web site: travelguides.com/home/waltersattic/

LAROSE

Gautreaux Couche et Dejeune	85-B&B	Continental plus breakfast
PO Box 1030, 70373	1 rooms, 1 pb	Sitting room, library, cable
504-693-4316 Fax: 504-693-4369	C-yes/S-no/P-no/H-no	TV, complete
Gilbert & Ethel Gautreux	French	cottage,business travelers
All year		welcome

Country cottage nested among trees and flowers; continental breakfast, complete bath with amenities, full enclosed laundry, spacious grounds, fishing ponds. Experience Cajun life among the people of South Louisiana. Web site: angelfire.com/biz2/gautreauxbb

NAPOLEONVILLE

Madewood Plantation House	225-MAP	Full breakfast
4250 Hwy 308, 70390	8 rooms, 8 pb	Dinner included
504-369-7151 Fax: 504-369-9848	*Rated*, •	Wine & cheese included,
800-375-7151	C-yes/S-ltd/P-ltd/H-no	sitting room, piano, canopied
Millie Marshall All year	Some French	beds

Greek Revival mansion. Canopied beds, antiques, fresh flowers, wine and cheese, dinner by candlelight in formal family dining room. Cover story in Country Inns.
E-mail: info@madewood.com Web site: madewood.com

NEW ORLEANS

1870 Banana Courtyard B&B	75-265-B&B	Continental plus breakfast
Box 70556, 70172	8 rooms, 7 pb	Afternoon tea
504-947-4475 Fax: 504-949-5689	*Rated*, •	Sitting room, library, suites,
800-842-4748	C-ltd/S-ltd/P-ltd/H-ltd	cable TV, accommodate
Mary Brock All year		business travelers

Enchanting Creole/Victorian. Bourbon St. 3-block walk under century-old live-oaks.
E-mail: bananacour@aol.com Web site: lodging-new-orleans.com

1895 St Charles Guest House	55-150-B&B	Continental breakfast
1748 Prytania St, 70130	26 rooms, 26 pb	Bakery
504-523-6556 Fax: 504-522-6340	Visa, MC, AmEx,	Swimming pool, library,
Dennis & Joanne Hilton	C-ltd/S-ltd/P-no	ample reading material
All year	Spanish	(books/magazines)

Historic Garden District, sweet, unpretentious, inexpensive, like Grandma's! Family owned business for 50 years, on streetcar line, minutes to Quarta, Convention Center, major attractions; swimming pool, bakery, breakfast. E-mail: dhilton111@aol.com
Web site: stcharleguesthouse.com

A Quarter Esplanade	75-150-B&B	Continental breakfast
719 Esplanade Ave, 70116	5 rooms, 5 pb	Bicycles, jacuzzi, suites,
504-948-9328 Fax: 504-940-6190	Visa, MC, AmEx, Disc, •	fireplace, cable TV,
800-546-0076	C-yes/S-ltd/P-ltd/H-ltd	conferences
Andrea Kudelich All year	German	

We offer spacious, well appointed accommodations in a charming old mansion with an excellent French Quarter location (on picturesque Esplanade Ave. between Royal and Bourbon St.). All this at very resonable rates! E-mail: info@quarteresplanade.com
Web site: quarteresplanade.com

Annabelle's House B&B	85-150-B&B	Continental breakfast
1716 Milan St, 70115	5 rooms, 5 pb	Complimentary wine
504-899-0701 Fax: 504-899-0095	Visa, MC, •	Sitting room, family friendly
Grey Rayburn	C-yes/S-no/P-yes/H-no	facility, canopied beds
All year		

Experience peaceful antique atmosphere with the luxury of every modern amenity. Elegant 1840s Greek Revival mansion in uptown. One block to street car. Open since 1984.

NEW ORLEANS

Ashton's Mechling B&B
2023 Esplanade Ave, 70116
504-942-7048 Fax: 504-947-9382
800-725-4131
Karma & Patrick Ashton
All year

125-255-B&B
4 rooms, 4 pb
Visa, MC, AmEx, •
C-yes/S-ltd/P-no/H-no

Full breakfast
Afternoon tea, snacks, wine
Sitting room, cable TV,
conference facilities, voice
mail, modem ports

Personal service and southern hospitality that only a small B&B can offer. Restored 1860's Greek Revival mansion, just a few blocks from French Quarter. Convenient to all attractions. E-mail: pashton@bellsouth.net Web site: ashtonsbb.com

---

Bougainvillea House
841 Bourbon St, 70116
504-525-3983 Fax: 504-522-5000
Flo Cairo & Pat Kahn
All year

125-B&B
2 rooms, 2 pb
AmEx, •
C-ltd/P-no/H-no

Continental breakfast
Or continental plus breakfast
All rooms have A/C, TV, and
phones, courtyard, patio,
jogger's guide

In the heart of the French Quarter, antique ambiance with all of the modern conveniences. Off street parking for cars. Private phone, cable TV, central A/C. Tropical patio, balcony, antique furniture.

Bywater Bed & Breakfast
1026 Clouet St, 70117
504-944-8438 Fax: 504-947-2795
Betty-Carol & Martha
All year

65 and up-B&B
3 rooms, 1 pb
Visa, MC,
C-ltd/S-no/P-ltd/H-no

Continental plus breakfast
Sitting room, library, cable
TV, conference

Completely renovated "double shotgun" house in National Historic District. Easy access (1 mile) to the French Quarter, but out of the usual tourist path. Cool, comfortable, and home-like. E-mail: bywaterbnb@juno.com

---

Chateau du Louisiane
1216 Louisiana Ave, 70115
504-269-2600 Fax: 504-269-2603
800-734-0137
Jeff O'Hara
All year

79-159-B&B
5 rooms, 5 pb
Most CC, *Rated*, •
C-yes/S-no/P-no/H-no

Continental breakfast
Complimentary wine
Bar service, sitting room,
bicycles, suites, cable TV

Historic B&B, circa 1885, featuring antique furnishings, high ceilings and hardwood floors. Located in historic Garden District. Can accommodate business travelers. E-mail: chateau@ neworleans.com Web site: neworleans.com/chateau

---

Chimes B&B plus RSO, The
PO Box 52257, 70152
504-488-4640 Fax: 504-488-4639
800-729-4640
Jill Abbyad and Hazell Boyce
All year

85-140-B&B
5 rooms, 5 pb
Most CC, *Rated*, •
C-yes/S-ltd/P-ltd/H-no
French, Arabic

Continental Plus
Suites, cable TV,
accommodate business
travelers, data ports, private
phones

A special place. . .cherished by many returning guests for comfort, charm and location. The Kretchmers have enjoyed 12 anniversaries here! And, the Shapiro family has visited often to see their son at Tulane University. E-mail: Info@HistoricLodging.com Web site: HistoricLodging.com/ChimesRS

Cornstalk Hotel, The
915 Royal St, 70116
504-523-1515 Fax: 504-522-5558
Debi & David Spencer
All year

75-185-B&B
14 rooms, 14 pb
Visa, MC, AmEx,
C-yes/S-yes/P-no/H-no
French, German

Continental plus breakfast
Complimentary tea, wine,
paper
Stained-glass windows,
oriental rugs, fireplaces

Small, elegant hotel in heart of French Quarter. All antique furnishings. Recent renovation Web site: travelguides.com/home/cornstalk/

NEW ORLEANS ──────────────────────────────────

Creole House, A
1013 St Ann, 70116
504-524-8076
Fax: 504-581-3277
800-535-7858
Brenda Kovach
Season Inquire

49-150-B&B
Rated, •

Continental breakfast
canopied beds

E-mail: Ach5555@aol.com   *Web site:* big-easy.org

Dauphine House
1830 Dauphine St, 70116
504-940-0943
Karen Jeffries
All year

65-85-B&B
3 rooms, 3 pb
•
S-no

Continental breakfast
Host lives on property,
fireplaces

Built in 1860 & located 1½ blocks from the enchanting French Quarter near Bourbon & Esplanade, Dauphine House offers cozy rooms with hardwood floors & 12' ceilings. Walk to restaurants & entertainment.   E-mail: dauphinehouse@worldnet.att.net
Web site: bbhost.com/dauphinehouse

Depot House at Mme Julia's
748 O'Keefe, 70113
504-529-2952
Fax: 521-529-1908
Joanne Hilton
All year

65-100-B&B
15 rooms, 0 pb
C-ltd/S-ltd/P-no

Continental breakfast
Snacks

Most unique accommodations downtown—Old Railroad Boarding House, circa 1900, in business district, near French Quarter, convention center, street car, all attractions.
E-mail: dhilton111@aol.com   *Web site:* mmejuliadepothouse.com

---

Dusty Mansion, The
2231 Gen Pershing, 70115
504-895-4576
Fax: 504-891-0049
Cynthia Riggs
All year

60-90-B&B
4 rooms, 2 pb
Most CC, •
C-yes/S-yes/P-no/H-no
Spanish, French

Continental plus breakfast
Sunday champagne brunch
Complimentary wine,
beverages, sitting room, hot
tub, pool table, sun deck

Charming turn-of-the-century home, spacious, comfortable. Near St. Charles Street Car; easy access to French Quarter. Southern hospitality

---

Fairchild House
1518 Prytania St, 70130
504-524-0154 Fax: 504-568-0063
800-256-8096
Rita Olmo & Beatriz
Aprigliano
All year

75-145-B&B
18 rooms, 18 pb
Visa, MC, AmEx,
Rated, •
C-yes/S-no/P-no/H-no
Spanish, Portuguese

Continental breakfast plus
Afternoon tea, wine
Sitting room, suites,
accommodate business
travelers

Classic, comfortable B&B in antique setting, located in the lower Garden District, one block from streetcar line, 15 blocks to the French Quarter.   E-mail: fairchildhou@earthlink.net
Web site: fairchildhouse.com

Frenchmen Hotel
417 Frenchmen, 70116
504-948-2166 Fax: 504-948-2258
800-831-1781
Brent Kovach
All year

59-175-B&B
25 rooms, 25 pb
Visa, MC, AmEx,
Rated, •
C-yes/S-yes/P-no/H-yes

Continental breakfast
Lunch, snacks
Bar, sitting room, hot tubs,
swimming pool, sun deck,
books

Each of the rooms is decorated with period furniture, ceiling fan & high ceiling.
E-mail: fm5678@aol.com   *Web site:* french-quarter.org

NEW ORLEANS ─────────────────────────────────

Girod House, The	175-275-B&B	Continental
937 Esplanade Ave, 70116	6 rooms, 6 pb	Suites, cable TV,
504-944-2255 Fax: 504-945-1794	Visa, MC, AmEx, •	accommodate business
800-650-3323	C-ltd/S-no/P-no/H-no	travelers, balcony-2 suites
The Torres Family		
Season Inquire		

Girod House is a typical Creole house located on Esplanade Avenue. It features six suites, each with a living room, bedroom, bath and kitchen.   E-mail: melrosemansion@ worldnett.att.net *Web site:* girodhouse.com

Glimmer Inn, The	65-85-B&B	Continental plus breakfast
1631 Seventh St, 70115	6 rooms, 1 pb	Sitting room, cable TV,
504-897-1895	*Rated*, •	accommodate business
Sharon Agiewich & Cathy	C-yes/S-yes/P-ltd/H-no	travelers, VCR, movies, CDs
Andros		
All year		

Relaxed New Orleans atmosphere in a grand 1891 Queen Ann with a 7-color, "painted lady" exterior. One block to St. Charles streetcar. Centrally located between French Quarter and Uptown attractions.   Web site: bbonline.com/la/glimmer

Inn the Quarter	55-165-EP	Cable TV, French Quarter,
935 Dumaine St, 70116	4 rooms, 4 pb	courtyard and balcony
888-523-5235	•	
Robin Kaplan	C-ltd/S-ltd/P-no/H-ltd	
All year		

The perfect location in historic 1840s townhouse. A rooftop view or real street site balcony and a cool plant filled courtyard

Jana's B&B	125-375-B&B	Continental breakfast
638 Royal St, 70113	4 rooms, 3 pb	Snacks
504-524-6473 Fax: 504-524-6473	Visa, MC, AmEx, •	Sitting room, library,
888-751-3273	C-yes/S-ltd/P-ltd/H-no	Jacuzzis, suites, fireplace,
Jane Napoli	Spanish, Italian, French	cable TV, restaurant
All year		

Urban getaway in historic 1840's townhouse which also houses two art galleries. Furnished with antiques and unique art. Numerous services available on request.   E-mail: jananaps@ earthlink.net *Web site:* 628baronne.com

La Dauphine	85-150-B&B	Continental breakfast
2316 Dauphine St, 70117	4 rooms, 4 pb	Sitting room, library,
504-948-2217 Fax: 504-948-3420	Visa, MC, Disc,	bicycles, bath robes
Ray Ruiz	S-no/P-no/H-no	
All year	French	

Located in the bohemian, artsy and gay Faubourg Marigny. A non-smoking European style guest house for the budget-minded.   E-mail: ladauphine@aol.com *Web site:* ladauphine.com

Lafitte Guest House	109-199-B&B	Continental plus breakfast
1003 Bourbon St, 70116	14 rooms, 14 pb	Wine & hors d'oeuvres
504-581-2678 Fax: 504-581-2677	Visa, MC, AmEx,	Sitt. rm., clock radios,
800-331-7971	*Rated*, •	balconies, courtyard, queen
Andrew Crocchiolo/Edward	C-ltd/S-ltd/P-no/H-ltd	& king-size beds
Dore		
All year		

This fine French manor building greets you with elegance & tradition. Fine antique pieces & reproductions. In the heart of the French Quarter & liveliness of Bourbon St. Down comforters/pillows, TVs.   E-mail: lafitteguesthouse@travelbase.com *Web site:* lafitteguesthouse.com

NEW ORLEANS ───

Lamothe House	59-275-B&B	Continental breakfast
621 Esplanade Ave, 70116	20 rooms, 20 pb	Pralines, complimentary
504-947-1161 Fax: 504-943-6536	Visa, MC, AmEx,	beverage
800-367-5858	*Rated*, •	Sitting room, courtyard,
Brent Kovach	C-yes/S-yes/P-no/H-no	newspaper, parking, AAA 4-
All year		Diamond rating

An elegantly restored historic old mansion located on the eastern boundary of the French Quarter.   E-mail: lam567842@aol.com   *Web site:* new-orleans.org

Macarty Park Guest House	59-115-B&B	Continental plus breakfast
3820 Burgundy St, 70117	8 rooms, 8 pb	Pool, suites, accommodate
504-943-4994 Fax: 504-943-4999	Most CC, •	business travelers
800-521-2790	C-ltd/S-yes/P-no/H-no	
John Maher		
All year		

Go for a splash in our in-ground heated pool. Cottages and rooms beautifully furnished primarily in antiques. All have private baths, color cable TV and phone. Free parking. Expanded continental breakfast.   E-mail: macpar@aol.com   *Web site:* macartypark.com

Maison Esplanade	79-189-B&B	Continental breakfast
1244 Esplanade Ave, 70116	10 rooms, 10 pb	Sitting room, suites, cable TV,
504-523-8080 Fax: 504-527-0040	Most CC, *Rated*, •	accommodate business
800-892-5529	S-ltd/P-ltd/H-ltd	travelers
Jarret Marshall		
All year		

This 1846 Greek Revival mansion, located on the beautifully oak lined Esplanade Ave., is just 2 short blocks from the French Quarter. Maison Esplanade boasts 10 guest rooms with 2 suites. All accommodations have 1 or 2 queen size beds with private baths. E-mail: maison@neworleans.com   *Web site:* neworleans.com/maison

Mandevilla B&B	125-155-B&B	Continental plus breakfast
7716 St Charles Ave, 70118	6 rooms, 6 pb	Afternoon tea,
504-862-6396 Fax: 504-866-4104	Visa, MC, Disc, *Rated*,	complimentary wine
800-288-0484	•	Sitting room, library,
Marnie & Allen Borne	C-yes/S-ltd/P-no/H-ltd	bicycles, Jacuzzi, suites,
All year		fireplaces, cable TV

On streetcar line near universities. Beautifully restored 19th century mansion, fine antiques, safe area.   E-mail: mandevla@bellsouth.net   *Web site:* mandevilla.com

Melrose Mansion	225-425-B&B	Continental plus breakfast
937 Esplanade Ave, 70116	10 rooms, 10 pb	Complimentary wine (5-7),
504-944-2255 Fax: 504-945-1794	Most CC, *Rated*, •	honor bar
800-650-3323	C-ltd/S-ltd/P-no/H-no	Sitting room, swimming pool,
The Torres Family		exercise room
Season Inquire		

Ultimate full service luxury located in the residential district of the historic French Quarter. Romance abounds.   E-mail: melrosemansion@worldnet.att.net   *Web site:* melrosemansion.com

Muses, The	85-B&B	Full breakfast
1455 Magazine St, 70130	3 rooms, 3 pb	Snacks, wine
504-522-7976 Fax: 504-524-4466	•	Sitting room, library, suites,
Georgia Ross	C-ltd/S-yes/P-yes/H-no	fireplace, cable TV
All year		

A classic Greek Revival style home built in 1858 and furnished with period antiques, Oriental rugs, and artworks including those of artist/owner, Georgia Ross. Elegant but understated, The Muses is a prime example of New Orleans antebellum architecture. E-mail: themuses@gs.verio.net   *Web site:* members.tripod.com/~themuses

NEW ORLEANS

New Orleans First B&B
PO Box 8163, 70182
504-947-3401 Fax: 504-838-0140
888-240-0070
Sarah Margaret Brown
All year

65-95-B&B
4 rooms, 3 pb
Visa, MC, AmEx, *Rated*
C-ltd/S-no/P-ltd
French & German

Continental breakfast
Sitting room, library, New
Orleans first B&B, Near zoo,
aquarium, park

All who enter pause to look around at the high ceilings, hardwood floors, marble mantle, comfortable furnishings and pleasant, homey atmosphere. Their comment: "What a lovely home." There is safety, comfort and convenience. E-mail: smb@ neworleansbedandbreakfast.com Web site: neworleansbandb.com/gentilly.htm

Nine-O-Five Royal Hotel
905 Rue Royal St, 70116
504-523-0219
J.M.
All year

85-185-EP
14 rooms, 14 pb
Rated
C-yes/S-yes/P-no/H-no

Kitchens in all rooms
Daily maid service, three
suites, Near zoo, aquarium,
park

Quaint hotel located in the heart of the French Quarter. Built in the 1800s, period furnishings, daily maid service, kitchenettes, private baths. Suites overlooking Royal Street. Please call for special events rates. Web site: travelguides.com/home/nineofive/

Old World Inn
1330 Prytania St, 70130
504-566-1330
Jean & Charlie Matkin
All year

75-100-B&B
20 rooms, 10 pb
Visa, MC, •
C-ltd/S-yes/P-no/H-no
French, Spanish, Arabic

Continental plus breakfast
Comp. wine, juice
Sitting room, library,
common rm w/piano, chess,
fireplaces, A/C

French cafe style with unique ambiance, excellent concierge. Hosts are professional broadcasters/musicians. Int'l clientele. Location, comfort, personality E-mail: trips@angelfire.com Web site: angelfire.com/biz/oldworldinn

Parkview Marigny B&B
726 Frenchmen St, 70116
504-945-7876 Fax: 504-945-7886
877-645-8617
Chris Liddy & Larry Molaison
All year

95-115-B&B
5 rooms, 5 pb
•
S ltd/P-no/H-no

Continental plus breakfast
Sitting room, Next to French
Quarter, Summer rates
available

130-year-old Creole townhouse on Washington Square Park. Two blocks from the French Quarter and one block from the many restaurants and music clubs of Frenchmen St. E-mail: pmarigny@aol.com Web site: neworleansbb.com

Pecan Tree Inn
2525 N Rampart St, 70117
504-944-4841 Fax: 504-943-6388
800-460-3667
Michael & William Thomas
All year

200-300-B&B
5 rooms, 5 pb
•
C-yes/S-ltd/P-ltd/H-no
Spanish

Continental plus breakfast
Snacks, wine
Sitting room, suites,
fireplaces, cable TV, 2 & 3
bedroom houses

A row of 3 19th century Creole houses built in the late 1800s. In the heart of the Old Bernard de Marigny Plantation. Furnished with fine antiques & reproductions E-mail: MWT952@aol.com

Place D'Alyce
1106 Treme St, 70116
504-523-1625 Fax: 504-524-0003
Alvino Jackson, Beverly Smith
All year

75-125-B&B
6 rooms, 6 pb
•
C-ltd/S-ltd/P-no/H-no
Sp., Ger., Fr., It.

Continental breakfast
Wine
Cable TV, tours, sailing, 2 & 3
bedroom houses

Best kept secret in town. Two blocks from French Quarter. Use our bikes to tour our historic district. Take a romantic sunset sailing adventure. E-mail: Placedalyce@webtv.net

NEW ORLEANS ──────────────────────────────

Prytania Inns, The
1415 Prytania St, 70130
504-566-1515 Fax: 504-566-1518
Peter Schrieber
All year

29-49-B&B
50 rooms, 44 pb
Most CC, •
C-yes/S-yes/P-ltd/H-yes
German, Spanish,
French

Full breakfast
Sitting room, Jacuzzis, suites,
courtyard, balconies

In 3 historic Antebellum mansions in the majestic Garden District, The Prytania Inns provide guests with old world charm at unbeatable prices. Rooms are simply comfortably furnished and feature high ceilings and original architectural moldings.
E-mail: PeterSchreiber@compuserve.com *Web site:* prytaniainns.com

St. Peter Guest House
1005 St Peter, 70116
504-524-9232 Fax: 504-523-5198
800-535-7815
Brenda Kovach
Season Inquire

59-275-B&B
Rated, •

Continental breakfast
on street car line, cozy

E-mail: sptl5678@aol.com *Web site:* crescent-city.org

St. Vincents Guest House
1507 Magazine St, 70130
504-566-1515 Fax: 504-566-1518
Peter & Sally Schreiber
All year

59-79-B&B
75 rooms, 75 pb
Most CC, •
C-yes/S-ltd/P-ltd/H-yes
German, French,
Spanish

Full breakfast
Lunch, aftn. tea, rest.
Sitting room, swimming pool,
suites, free on site parking lot

Romantic, historic old south inn furnished in wicker, chintz, antiques; wraparound balconies, patio, pool; gourmet breakfast & traditional English aftn. tea served tearoom
E-mail: peterschreiber@compuserve.com *Web site:* bcity.com/prytaniainns

Sully Mansion, The
2631 Prytania St, 70130
504-891-0457 Fax: 504-899-7237
Maralee Prigmore
All year

125-275-B&B
7 rooms, 7 pb
Most CC, •
S-no/P-no/H-no

Continental plus breakfast
sitting room, library

Circa 1890. Only inn nestled in the renowned Garden District. Well appointed rooms, antiques and today's furnishings. Minutes to main attractions. *Web site:* sullymansion.com/

Victoria Inn & Gardens
Hwy 45, Box 545 B, 70067
504-689-4757 Fax: 504-689-3399
800-689-4797
Dale & Roy Ross
All year

89-139-B&B
14 rooms, 14 pb
Visa, MC, AmEx,
Rated, •
C-yes/S-no/P-ltd/H-no
Spanish (with notice)

Full breakfast
Comp. refreshments
Sea-water pool, hot tub, full
concierge service, for area
tours & trips

Experience Cajun living near bayous once haunted by the pirate, Jean Lafitte. A raised cottage on 9 acres of gardens overlooking lake, only 22 miles from New Orleans
E-mail: info@victoriainn.com *Web site:* victoriainn.com

Wisteria Inn, The
200 Carondelet ste 2005, 70130
504-558-0181 Fax: 504-558-0319
888-246-4183
Zennette Austin & Mark
Thomas
All year

B&B
6 rooms, 5 pb
AmEx, •
C-yes/S-ltd/P-no/H-no

Continental breakfast
Sitting room, cable TV,
conference facilities, rooms
with kitchenette

The Wisteria Inn located in the historic Esplanade Ridge District, minutes away from the French Quarter, Fairgrounds & New Orleans Museum of Art. *E-mail:* nowisteria@aol.com
Web site: wisteriainn.com

SHREVEPORT

2439 Fairfield, A B&B
2439 Fairfield Ave, 71104
318-424-2424
Jimmy & Vicki Harris
All year

125-200-B&B
4 rooms, 4 pb
Most CC, *Rated*, •
S-no/P-no/H-no

Full breakfast
Whirlpools, private garden,
gazebo, sitting room, library

1905 Victorian with balconies overlook English gardens featuring gazebo, fountain, Victorian swing. Full English breakfast served. E-mail: 2439fair@bellsouth.com

Columns on Jordan, The
615 Jordan, 71101
318-222-5912 Fax: 318-459-1155
800-801-4950
Judith & Edwin Simonton
All year

125-250-B&B
5 rooms, 4 pb
Visa, MC, AmEx, •
S-yes/P-ltd/H-no
Spanish

Full breakfast
Complimentary wine, snacks
Afternoon tea, sitting room,
library, bicycles, spa, pool

Sleep in the splendor and comfort of an antique bed and have a leisurely breakfast in the morning room. Enjoy the elegance of Southern living. E-mail: bnb615@aol.com
Web site: bbonline.com/la/columns/

Fairfield Place B&B Inn
2221 Fairfield Ave, 71104
318-222-0048 Fax: 318-226-0631
Jane Lipscomb
All year

145-250-B&B
9 rooms, 9 pb
Visa, MC, AmEx,
Rated, •
C-ltd/S-ltd/P-ltd/H-no

Full breakfast
Dining room
Sitting room, whirlpools,
suites, library, acre of,
gardens, weddings

Casually elegant 1900s inn. European and American antiques, gourmet breakfast. Ideal for business travelers and tourists. E-mail: fairfldpl@aol.com *Web site:* fairfieldbandb.com

SLIDELL

Salmen-Fritchie House B&B
127 Cleveland Ave, 70458
504-643-1405 Fax: 504-643-2251
800-235-4168
Sharon & Homer Fritchie
All year

95-150-B&B
6 rooms, 6 pb
Visa, MC, AmEx,
Rated, •
C-ltd/S-ltd/P-no/H-ltd

Full breakfast
Afternoon tea
greenhouse

elegance of the Old South, c.1895 National Register, dressed in period antiques. Just 25 miles from the French Quarter on the North Shore of Lake Pontchartrain and from the MS Gulf Coast. E-mail: sfritbb@communique.net *Web site:* salmen-fritchie.com

ST. FRANCISVILLE

Barrow House Inn
PO Box 1461, 70775
225-635-4791 Fax: 225-635-1863
Shirley Dittloff, Chris Dennis
All year

95-150-B&B
7 rooms, 5 pb
Rated, •
C-ltd/S-yes/P-no/H-no

Continental breakfast
Full breakfast (fee)
Dinner (res), comp. wine,
sitting room, bicycles,
cassette walking tours

Circa 1809, located in historic district. Balconies & period antiques. Cassette walking tours. Honeymoon packages. Arnold Palmer golf course nearby. E-mail: staff@topteninn.com
Web site: topteninn.com

Butler Greenwood
8345 US Highway 61, 70775
225-635-6312 Fax: 225-635-6370
Anne Butler
All year

100-110-B&B
6 rooms, 6 pb
Visa, MC, *Rated*, •
C-yes/S-ltd/P-ltd/H-no
Some French

Continental plus breakfast
Meeting facilities, library,
balloon trips, nature walk,
pool, bikes

6 private cottages with plenty of historic charm, scattered across peaceful landscaped plantation grounds. All cottages have Jacuzzis. On National Register of Historic Places. Antebellum House tour included. E-mail: butlergree@aol.com *Web site:* butlergreenwood.com

ST. FRANCISVILLE ───────────────────────────────

Green Springs Inn
7463 Tunica Trace, 70775
225-635-4232 Fax: 225-635-3355
800-457-4978
Madeline Nevil
Season Inquire

95-160-B&B
7 rooms, 7 pb
Visa, MC, AmEx,
Rated, •
C-yes/S-ltd/P-ltd/H-ltd

Full breakfast
Sitting room, library,
Jacuzzis, suites, fireplaces,
cable TV, hiking trails

Gracious country estate in Tunica Hills. Peacefull garden setting with hiking trails. Spacious rooms and cottages with antique furnishings, king- or queen-size beds, private baths, some Jacuzzis. Plantation breakfast. Web site: greensprings-inn.com

Shadetree Inn
PO Box 1818, 70775
225-635-6116
Fax: 225-635-0072
K. W. Kennon
All year

99-195-B&B
3 rooms, 3 pb
Visa, MC, Disc, •
C-ltd/S-ltd/P-ltd/H-ltd

Continental plus breakfast
Snacks, comp. wine
Cocktails, appetizers,
Jacuzzis, bicycles, cable TV

Three unique romantic suites on wooded hilltop in historic district. Each has king size bed, private phone, stereo, cable TV, private bath, wet bar with fridge, microwave, & coffee maker E-mail: shadetreeinn@bsf.net

THIBODAUX ───────────────────────────────

Lovell House B&B
221 W 7th St, 70301
504-446-2750
Charlene Elmore
All year

60-B&B
2 rooms, 2 pb
C-ltd/S-no/P-no/H-no
Little German

Full breakfast
Cable TV, accommodate
business travelers

A small, intimate B&B offering Cajun Bayouland hospitality in the heart of town. Decor is an eclectic mixture of antiques and collectibles from abroad. Birds and squirrels abound in the backyard.

WHITE CASTLE ───────────────────────────────

Nottoway Plantation Inn
PO Box 160, 70788
225-545-2409 Fax: 225-545-8632
Cindy A. Hidalgo
All year exc. Christmas

125-250-B&B
13 rooms, 13 pb
Visa, MC, *Rated*, •
C-yes/S-no/P-no/H-ltd
French

Full or continental breakfast
Restaurant serving
lunch/dinner
Swimming pool, meeting,
space, sitting room, piano,
tennis nearby

Fresh flowers in your room, chilled champagne or sherry, a wake-up call consisting of hot sweet potato muffins, coffee and juice delivered to your room. Also a guided tour of mansion. E-mail: nottoway@worldnet.att.net Web site: nottoway.com

Maine

ACADIA SCHOODIC ───────────────────────────────

Acadia Oceanside Meadows
PO Box 90, 04669
207-963-5557 Fax: 207-963-5928
Sonja Sundaram, Ben Walter
All year

85-145-B&B
14 rooms, 14 pb
Most CC,
C-yes/S-no/P-yes/H-yes

Full gourmet breakfast
Afternoon tea
Sitting room, library,
fireplace, lawn games,
flowers, private beach

Historic sea captain's with magnificent ocean views on 100+ acres with private sand beach, Acadia National Park, great hiking, biking, swimming, sea kayaking, canoeing. E-mail: oceaninn@oceaninn.com Web site: oceaninn.com

AUGUSTA

Maple Hill Farm B&B
RR1 Box 1145, 04347
207-622-2708 Fax: 207-622-0655
800-622-2708
Scott Cowger & Vince Hannan
All year

55-140-B&B
7 rooms, 4 pb
Most CC, *Rated*, •
C-ltd/S-no/P-no/H-yes

Full country breakfast
Afternoon tea, snacks
Lunch (fee), bar service,
sitting room/art gallery,
swimming hole, trails

"Best of Maine, hands down" (Maine Times). Immaculate, spacious Victorian farmhouse, 130 serene acres of hayfields and woods, farm animal menagerie. E-mail: stay@
maplebb.com *Web site:* maplebb.com

BAILEY ISLAND

Captain York House B&B
PO Box 298, 04003
207-833-6224
Alan & Jean Thornton
All year

70-110-B&B
5 rooms, 3 pb
Visa, MC, *Rated*, •
C-ltd/S-no/P-no/H-no

Full breakfast
flowers, private beach

A restored Captain's home located on a small, quiet island in mid-coast Maine. Close to Freeport and Brunswick, Maine. E-mail: athorn7286@aol.com *Web site:* iwws.com/captainyork

Log Cabin Lodging
PO Box 41, 04003
207-833-5546 Fax: 207-833-7858
Sue Favreau
Mid-March thru mid-Oct

95-210-B&B
8 rooms, 8 pb
Most CC, *Rated*
C-ltd/S-no/P-no/H-yes

Full breakfast
Dinner, restaurant, bar
Hot tubs, flowers, private
beach, swimming pool

Rooms with panoramic ocean views and private decks. Located on a quiet Maine island. Restaurant, gift shop, & bar. Great sunsets! E-mail: info@logcabin-maine.com
Web site: logcabin-maine.com

BAR HARBOR

Acadia Hotel
20 Mt Desert St, 04609
207-288-5721 Fax: 207-288-5789
Monika & Brandan McCallion
Season Inquire

45-145-EP
10 rooms, 10 pb
Visa, MC,
C-yes/S-ltd/P-no/H-no
German

Full breakfast (fee)
Jacuzzis, cable TV, porch &
balcony, AC &, queen/king
beds all rms.

Tastefully restored Victorian home on historic corridor in heart of picturesque village of Bar Harbor. E-mail: acadiahotel@acadia.net *Web site:* acadiahotel.com

Anne's White Columns Inn
57 Mt Desert St, 04609
207-288-5357 Fax: 207-288-5357
800-321-6379
Anne & Robert Bahr
May-November

80-120-B&B
10 rooms, 10 pb
Visa, MC, AmEx, *Rated*
C-ltd/S-no/P-no/H-ltd

Continental plus breakfast
Afternoon tea,
complimentary wine
Sitting room, cable TV, in
rooms, queen beds, covered
porch, gardens

Impressive Georgain structure located in the historical corridor in downtown Bar Harbor. "As contemporary a Victorian B&B as you can find"—Weedending in New Enland. E-mail: anneswci@aol.com *Web site:* anneswhitecolumns.com

Balance Rock Inn
21 Albert Meadow, 04609
207-288-2610
800-753-0494
Nancy Cloud
May—October 27

95-525-B&B
14 rooms, 14 pb
Most CC, *Rated*, •
C-ltd/S-ltd/P-no/H-no
French

Continental breakfast
Full breakfast (fee)
Aftn. tea, sitting room, hot
tubs, fireplaces, oceanside
heated pool

Turn-of-the-century oceanfront mansion with lovely rooms & spectacular views. Ideal spot for romantic vacations. Walk to downtown E-mail: barhbrinns@aol.com
Web site: barharborvacations.com/welcomebrl.htm

BAR HARBOR

Bar Harbor Tides	150-325-B&B	Full breakfast
119 West St, 04609	3 rooms, 3 pb	Sitting room, 2nd floor guest
207-288-4968 Fax: 207-288-2997	Visa, MC, Disc, *Rated*	living room with gas
Joe & Judy Losquadro	C-ltd/S-no/P-no/H-no	fireplace
All year		

Magnificent water views from every bed chamber. Private but walk to town. Sumptuous full breakfast on the verandah with sweeping views of Frenchman's Bay. 3 suites.
E-mail: info@barharbortides.com *Web site:* barharbortides.com/

Black Friar Inn	90-145-B&B	Full gourmet breakfast
10 Summer St, 04609	7 rooms, 7 pb	Afternoon tea &
207-288-5091 Fax: 207-288-4197	Visa, MC, Disc, *Rated*	refreshments
Perry & Sharon Risley, Falke	C-ltd/S-no/P-no/H-no	Sitting room, fishing guide
All year		available, Sea Kayak School-June

Rebuilt in 1981 with antiques & architectural finds from Mt. Desert Island. Victorian & country flavor. Near Acadia National Park, shops, restaurants.   E-mail: blackfriar@blackfriar.com *Web site:* blackfriar.com

Canterbury Cottage B&B	B&B	Full breakfast
12 Roberts Ave, 04609	4 rooms, 4 pb	Afternoon tea, snacks
207-288-2112 Fax: 207-288-5681	Visa, MC, Disc, *Rated*	Sitting room, fireplace, cable
Armando & Maria Ribeiro	C-ltd/S-no/P-no/H-no	TV
All year	Portuguese	

Cozy and comfortable accommodations just minutes away from Acadia National Park and within walking distance to downtown Bar Harbor.   E-mail: canterbury@gwi.net
Web site: canterburycottage.com

Castlemaine Inn	50-195-B&B	Continental plus breakfast
39 Holland Ave, 04609	12 rooms, 12 pb	All A/C, all cable TV, Main
207-288-4563 Fax: 207-288-4525	Visa, MC, *Rated*	street 3 blocks, water 2
800-338-4563	C-ltd/S-ltd/P-no	blocks, Fax, VCR
T. O'Connell & N. O'Brien		
All year		

The inn is nestled on a quiet side street in Bar Harbor Village, surrounded by the magnificent Acadia National Park.   Web site: acadia.net/castle/

Chiltern Inn	205-295-B&B	Full breakfast
3 Cromwell Harbor Rd, 04609	4 rooms, 4 pb	Snacks
207-288-0114 Fax: 207-288-0124	Most CC,	Sitting room, library,
800-404-0114	S-no/P-no	Jacuzzis, indoor pool,
Pat & John Shaw		fireplaces, cable TV, sauna
All year		

Complete luxury in a 1905 Edwardian Carriage House furnished with period antiques, fine art and luxurious linens. Enjoy your Jacuzzi and fireplace in your own suite, as well as the indoor lap pool, spa and sauna.   E-mail: chiltern@acadia.net *Web site:* chilterninn.com

Cleftstone Manor	70-200-B&B	3 course breakfast
92 Eden St, 04609	16 rooms, 16 pb	Afternoon & evening
207-288-4951 Fax: 207-288-2089	Visa, MC, *Rated*	refreshments
888-288-4951	C-ltd/S-no/P-no/H-no	Sitting room, library, games,
Kelly & Steve Hellmann		all rooms: A/C, some with
Mid-May-mid-Oct.		fireplaces, balconys

Historic Victorian mansion, beautiful antiques, set on a terraced hillside. Near Acadia National Park.   E-mail: cleftstone@acadia.net *Web site:* cleftstone.com

BAR HARBOR ────────────────────────────

Graycote Inn	65-155-B&B	Full breakfast
40 Holland Ave, 04609	12 rooms, 12 pb	Afternoon refreshments
207-288-3044 Fax: 207-288-2719	Most CC, *Rated*	Some rooms w/sitt. rm.,
Pat & Roger Samuel	C-ltd/S-ltd/P-no/H-no	fireplaces, balcony., king or
All year		queen size beds

Restored Country Victorian inn located on quiet in-town street. Near Acadia National Park. E-mail: graycote@acadia.net *Web site:* graycoteinn.com

Hatfield B&B	75-115-B&B	Full breakfast
20 Roberts Ave, 04609	6 rooms, 4 pb	Afternoon tea
207-288-9655	Most CC, *Rated*	Living room, dining room,
Jeff & Sandy Miller	C-ltd/S-ltd/P-no/H-no	porch, 3rd floor sun deck,
All year		outdoor smoking area

"Country comfort" in downtown Bar Harbor, fantastic breakfast, short walk to the water front, 5 minutes to Acadia National Park. 3rd floor sun deck   E-mail: hatfield@hatfieldinn.com *Web site:* hatfieldinn.com

Hearthside B&B	95-145-B&B	Full breakfast
7 High St, 04609	9 rooms, 9 pb	Afternoon tea & cookies
207-288-4533 Fax: 207-285-9818	Visa, MC, *Rated*	All rooms have A/C, 3 rooms
Susan & Barry Schwartz	C-ltd/S-no/P-no/H-no	w/fireplaces, 3 bath
All year		w/whirlpool jets

Small, gracious hostelry in quiet in-town location; elegant & comfortable; blend of antiques & traditional furniture.   E-mail: hearth@acadia.net *Web site:* hearthsideinn.com

Holbrook House	70-145-B&B	Full breakfast
74 Mt Desert St, 04609	12 rooms, 12 pb	Afternoon refreshments
207-288-4970	Visa, MC, *Rated*	Old fashion porch-parlor,
800-860-7430	C-ltd/S-no/P-no/H-no	library, inn rooms, beautiful
Bill & Carol Deike		furnishings
May-Oct.		

An elegantly restored 1876 Victorian offering gracious hospitality and gourmet breakfasts. E-mail: info@holbrookhouse.com *Web site:* holbrookhouse.com

Holland Inn	65-145-B&B	Full breakfast
35 Holland Ave, 04609	5 rooms, 5 pb	Sitting room, library, suites,
207-288-4804	Visa, MC, *Rated*	fireplace, cable TV
Evin & Tom Hulbert	C-ltd/S-no/P-no/H-no	
All year		

Short stroll to center of town, minutes from the park   E-mail: evintom@downeast.net *Web site:* hollandinn.com

Inn at Bay Ledge, The	170-300-B&B	Full breakfast
1385 Sand Point Rd, 04609	10 rooms, 10 pb	Heated pool, fireplaces,
207-288-4204 Fax: 207-288-5573	*Rated*	sauna, steam rooms,
Jack & Jeani Ochtera	S-no/P-no	Jacuzzis, meeting rroom
May-Oct/June 15-Oct. 1		

Amidst towering pines, the inn literally clings to the cliffs of Mt. Desert Island. Many tiered decks overlook spectacular coastline. Priv. beach. All rooms with ocean views. Breakfast served in sunroom overlooking Fisherman's Bay.   E-mail: bayledge@downeast.net *Web site:* maineguide.com/barharbor/bayledge

Ledgelawn Inn, The	65-225-B&B	Continental plus breakfast
66 Mount Desert St, 04609	33 rooms, 33 pb	Bar service, comp. tea
207-288-2610	Visa, MC, AmEx,	Sitting room, library, piano,
800-274-5334	*Rated*, ●	pool, sauna, modern
Nancy Cloud	C-yes/S-yes/P-no/H-no	exercise room
April–November		

A graceful turn-of-the-century mansion with antiques, sitting areas, fireplaces, hot tub; in a quiet location, 5-min. walk to downtown   Web site: barharborvacations.com/welcomelli.htm

BAR HARBOR ───

Manor House Inn
106 West St, 04609
207-288-3759 Fax: 207-288-2974
800-437-0088
Mac Noyes
May-mid-Oct.

65-185-B&B
14 rooms, 14 pb
Visa, MC, AmEx,
Rated, •
C-ltd/S-no/P-no/H-no

Full breakfast
Afternoon tea
Sitting room, fireplaces,
swimming pool, piano,
gardens, tennis courts

Many special touches. Restored Victorian, National Register, antique furniture. Bedrooms include parlor, bath. Near Acadia National Park.   E-mail: manor@acadia.net Web site: acadia.net/manorhouse

Mansion at the Oakes
PO Box 3, 04609
207-288-5801 Fax: 207-288-8402
800-33-MAINE
The Cough Family
May to mid-October

73-252-B&B
9 rooms, 9 pb
Visa, MC, AmEx, •
C-ltd/S-no/P-no/H-ltd

Continental plus breakfast
Sitting room, tennis court,
indoor swimming pool,
suites, cable TV

Restored Bar Harbor summer "cottage" built on the ocean in 1913. Gardens and stone walls recall Bar Harbor's "Cottage Era." An additional 144 hotel rooms are available separate from the B&B.   E-mail: oakes@barharbor.com Web site: barharbor.com/mansion.html

Maples Inn, The
16 Roberts Ave, 04609
207-288-3443 Fax: 207-288-0356
Tom & Sue Palumbo
All year

60-150-B&B
6 rooms, 6 pb
Visa, MC, Disc, *Rated*
C-ltd/S-no/P-no/H-no
Some Spanish

Full gourmet breakfast
Afternoon tea
Sitting room, library, suites,
fireplaces

Experience classic tranquility in our 1903 Victorian B&B. Located on a residential side street, just a five-minute walk to restaurants, shops and activities. Join us for a truly personalized visit.   E-mail: maplesinn@acadia.net Web site: maplesinn.com

Mira Monte Inn & Suites
69 Mt Desert St, 04609
207-288-4263 Fax: 207-288-3115
800-553-5109
Marian Burns
Early May-late Oct.

140-210-B&B
16 rooms, 16 pb
Visa, MC, AmEx,
Rated, •
C-ltd/S-ltd/P-no/H-yes

Full breakfast buffet
Complimentary wine &
cheese
Juice, snacks, piano, sitting &
meeting rooms, all rms:
phones, A/C, TV

Renovated Victorian estate; period furnishings, fireplaces; quiet, in-town location, walk to waterfront.   E-mail: mburns@acadia.net Web site: miramonteinn.com

Moseley Cottage Inn
399 Main St, 04609
207-288-5548 Fax: 207-288-9406
800-458-8644
Joe & Paulette Paluga
May-Oct.

95-155-B&B
9 rooms, 9 pb
Visa, MC, AmEx, Disc,
Rated, •
C-yes/S-no/P-no/H-ltd

Continental plus breakfast
Sitting room, courtesy
phone, free calls, fax

Queen Anne Victorian furnished with antiques, also modern conveniences. E-mail: paluga@acadia.net Web site: mainesunshine.com/townmotl

Primrose Inn
73 Mt Desert St, 04609
877-846-3424
877-TIME-4BH
Pamela & Bryan
May-Oct.

90-155-B&B
15 rooms, 15 pb
Most CC, *Rated*, •
C-yes/S-ltd/P-no

Continental buffet breakfast
Afternoon tea with
homemade treats
Spacious living room with
fireplace, large front porch,
on-site parking

1878 Victorian guest house on "Historic Corridor." Antique furnishings, some rooms with whirlpool, porch, fireplace. Near Acadia and downtown. 10 rooms and 5 suites. E-mail: primrose@acadia.net Web site: primroseinn.com

BAR HARBOR

Sunset on West
115 West Street, 04609
207-288-4242 Fax: 207-278-4545
Nancy & Mel Johnson
May 1-October 31

175-275-B&B
4 rooms, 4 pb
Visa, MC,
C-ltd/S-no/P-no/H-no
French

Full breakfast
Tea, snacks, wine
Sitting room, library, suites,
fireplace, conference, ocean
views

Ideally situated in the historic district overlooking Frenchman Bay. Magnificent, landmark Bar Harbor Cottage built in 1910. Ocean views in well appointed suites overlooking the ocean. E-mail: sunsetonwest@gwi.net Web site: sunsetonwest.com

BASS HARBOR

Pointy Head Inn
HCR 33, Box 2A, 04653
207-244-7261
Doris & Warren Townsend
Late May-mid Oct.

70-110-B&B
6 rooms, 3 pb
Rated
C-ltd/S-no/P-no/H-no

Full breakfast
Sitting room with TV, porch
& deck, overlook harbor

Old sea captain's home on the ocean in Bass Harbor. 1 mile from Bass Harbor Headlight in Acadia National Park. Web site: acadia.net/pointyheadinn/

BATH

Benjamin F. Packard House
45 Pearl St, 04530
207-443-6069
800-516-4578
Debby & Bill Hayden
All year

75-100-B&B
3 rooms, 3 pb
Most CC,
C-ltd/S-no/P-no/H-no
French

Full breakfast
Sitting room, library

The Benjamin F. Packard House is a treasure in historic Bath, a perfect place in which to return to the mid 19th century. Our rooms are spacious, inviting and quiet. E-mail: packardhouse@clinic.net Web site: mainecoast.com/packardhouse

Fairhaven Inn
118 N. Bath Road, 04530
207-443-4391 Fax: 207-443-6412
888-443-4391
Susie & Dave Reed
All year

80-125-B&B
8 rooms, 6 pb
Rated, •
C-ltd/S-no/P-no/H-no

Full breakfast
Tea, soda
Piano, library, bicycles,
hiking trail

Quiet country inn on 16 acres of woods, meadows, lawns. Antique & country furnishings. Occasional baking lessons from pastry chef/owner E-mail: fairhvn@gwi.net Web site: mainecoast.com/fairhaveninn

Galen C Moses House B&B
1009 Washington St., 04530
207-442-8771
800-442-8771
Jim Haught & Larry Kieft
All year

89-129-B&B
5 rooms, 4 pb
Visa, MC, *Rated*
C-ltd/S-no/P-no/H-no

Afternoon tea, wine

Built in 1874, the Galen C. Moses House is reminiscent of the 19th century grand Victorian style. Selected for the National Register of Historic Homes, the home has been opened to the public for the first time. E-mail: galenmoses@clinic.net Web site: galenmoses.com

Inn at Bath, The
969 Washington St, 04530
207-443-4294 Fax: 207-443-4295
Nick Bayard
All year

85-185-B&B
9 rooms, 9 pb
Most CC, •
C-ltd/S-no/P-ltd/H-yes
Some French

Full breakfast
Complimentary tea, coffee
2 rooms with Jacuzzis and/or
fireplaces, cable TV, VCRs,
phones, A/C

Elegant, comfortable, romantic 1810 Greek Revival b&b inn in heart of Historic District. Short walk to shops & restaurants. Near ocean beaches, Maritime Museum, Bowdoin College, L.L. Bean, outlets. E-mail: innkeeper@innatbath.com Web site: innatbath.com

BATH

Kennebec Inn B&B
1024 Washington St, 04530
207-443-5202 Fax: 207-443-1411
800-822-9393
Ronald Lutz & Blanche Sefton
All year

100-165-B&B
7 rooms, 7 pb
Most CC, •
C-ltd/S-no/P-no/H-no

Full breakfast
Sitting room, library,
Jacuzzis, fireplaces, cable
TV, A/C, fax machine

Luxurious historic mansion featuring marble fireplaces, crystal chandeliers, antiques, parqueted hardwood floors.   E-mail: kennebecinn@clinic.net *Web site:* kennebecinn.com

Rock Gardens Inn
PO Box 178, 04565
207-389-1339 Fax: 207-389-9112
Ona Barnet
June-Sept

200-250-MAP
13 rooms, 13 pb
C-yes/S-ltd/P-no/H-ltd

Full breakfast
Picnic lunch, dinner
Sitting room, library, tennis
court and bicycles nearby,
swimming pool

Maine style cottages on private penninsula facing Casco Bay. New England breakfast and dinner daily, lobster cookouts weekly. Pool, dock with kayaks.
Web site: rockgardensinn.com

BELFAST

Belfast Bay Meadows Inn
192 Northport Ave, 04915
207-338-5715
800-335-2370
John Lebowitz
All year

85-145-B&B
12 rooms, 12 pb
Most CC, *Rated*, •
C-yes/S-no/P-yes/H-ltd

Full gourmet breakfast
Lunch, dinner available
Dedicated conference rm.,
boat & train tour rides,
antique shops/auctions

The Country Inn by the Sea. Penobscot Bay view. Antique decor; A/C, phone, TV. Bay view dining deck, enclosed porch.   E-mail: bbmii@ctel.net *Web site:* baymeadowsinn.com

Brass Lantern Inn
81 W Main St, 04974
207-548-0150 Fax: 207-548-0304
800-691-0150
Maggie & Dick Zieg
All year

85-100-B&B
5 rooms, 5 pb
Visa, MC, Disc, *Rated*,
•
C-ltd/S-no/P-no/H-ltd
German, some Swedish

Full breakfast
Tea and snacks
Family friendly & conference
facilities, Sitting room, cable
TV, library

Elegant, yet warm and friendly. Sea captain's home centrally located for sightseeing day trips to national parks, lighthouses, museums, antiques, tec. Gourmet breakfasts by candlelight. Walk to harbor, restaurants and shops.   E-mail: stay@brasslanternmaine.com
Web site: brasslanternmaine.com

Jeweled Turret Inn, The
40 Pearl St, 04915
207-338-2304
800-696-2304
Carl & Cathy Heffentrager
All year

85-135-B&B
7 rooms, 7 pb
Rated, •
C-ltd/S-ltd/P-no/H-no

Full breakfast
Afternoon tea by
reservation, ltd
Sitting rooms, parlors,
antiques, tennis & pool
nearby

Intimate & charming. Unique architectural features; turrets, verandahs, beautiful woodwork. Walk to town, shops & harbor. On National Register
Web site: bbonline.com/me/jeweledturret/

BLUE HILL

Oakland House's-Shore Oaks
RR 1, Box 400, 04617
207-359-8521 Fax: 207-359-9865
800-359-7352
Jim & Sally Littlefield
All year

85-209-B&B/MAP
10 rooms, 7 pb
•
C-ltd/S-ltd/P-no/H-no

Continental breakfast
Full breakfast/dinner (MAP)
Snacks, children 14+ OK, sitt.
rm., lib., beaches, gazebo,
boating, hikes

Beautiful, turn-of-the-century coastal summer home. Dock, trails, rowboats, magnificent views in a simple setting. Special getaways, schooner trips, lobster dinners. Honeymoons. Smoking outside only.   E-mail: jim@oaklandhouse.com *Web site:* oaklandhouse.com

BOOTHBAY HARBOR

1830 Admiral's Quarters Inn	85-155-B&B	Full breakfast
71 Commercial St, 04538	7 rooms, 7 pb	Complimentary coffee
207-633-2474 Fax: 207-633-5904	Visa, MC, *Rated*	Unsurpassed harbor view,
Les and Deb Hallstrom	C-ltd/S-yes/P-no/H-ltd	decks, sea views, landscaped
All year		garden, cable TV

Commanding a view of the Harbor unsurpassed by all, this large old sea captain's house & newly-bought adjacent house have pretty rooms, private baths and decks for viewing. E-mail: loon@admiralsquartersinn.com *Web site:* admiralsquartersinn.com/

Anchor Watch B&B	80-150-B&B	Full breakfast
9 Eames Rd, 04538	5 rooms, 5 pb	4 rooms with ocean views,
207-633-7565	*Rated*, •	whirlpool, fireplace, fishing
Diane Campbell, Kathy Reed	C-ltd/S-no/P-no/H-no	and boating
All year		

Scenic shore; winter ducks feed near the rocks; flashing lighthouses; lobstermen hauling traps, walk to restaurants, shops, boats. Shorefront patio and pier for lounging, swimming or fishing.   E-mail: diane@lincoln.midcoast.com   *Web site:* anchorwatch.com

Atlantic Ark Inn	95-169-B&B	Full gourmet breakfast
64 Atlantic Ave, 04538	7 rooms, 7 pb	Complimentary afternoon
207-633-5690	*Rated*	beverage
Donna	C-ltd/S-ltd/P-no/H-no	Sitt. rm., wrap around,
May-Oct.		veranda with arbor, fresh
		flowers, walk to town

Quaint & intimate, this small inn offers lovely harbor views, balconies, Oriental rugs, mahogany furnishings, flowers. Luxurious suite/special occasion room available with Jacuzzi, balcony, panoramic views.   E-mail: donnz@atlanticarkinn.com *Web site:* atlanticarkinn.com/

Five Gables Inn	100-170-B&B	Full breakfast
PO Box 335, 04544	15 rooms, 15 pb	Fireplaces, games,
207-633-4551	*Rated*, •	wraparound veranda, pool &
800-451-5048	C-ltd/S-no/P-no	boating nearby
Mike & De Kennedy		
Season Inquire		

Charm & elegance of old Victorian decor, the convenience of spotless facilities. E-mail: info@fivegablesinn.com *Web site:* fivegablesinn.com

Harbour Towne Inn	69-259-B&B	Continental plus breakfast
71 Townsend Avenue, 04538	6 rooms, 3 pb	Walking distance to
207-633-4300	•	waterfront, kitchen, suites
800-722-4240	C-yes/S-no/P-no/H-no	available
The Thomas Family		
All year		

Sits atop McKown Hill overlooking town & harbor; walk to all activities. Parking in our lot.   E-mail: mainco@gwi.net *Web site:* acadia.net/harbourtowneinn

Lawnmeer Inn & Restaurant	80-195-EP	Breakfast/dinner available
Box 505, 04575	32 rooms	Restaurant, bar, sitting room,
207-633-2544	Visa, MC, *Rated*, •	library, complimentary
800-633-7645	S-ltd/P-yes/H-no	coffee
Lee & Jim Metzger		
May-Oct.		

Handsome 1898 Maine Country Inn & modern annex located on 3 attractive acres of lawn descending to oceanfront. Oldest continuously operating inn in Boothbay region. Fireplaces in common rooms.   E-mail: cooncat@lawnmeerinn.com *Web site:* lawnmeerinn.com

BOOTHBAY HARBOR

Lion d' Or B&B
106 Townsend Ave, 04538
207-633-7367
800-887-7367
Fern Robicaud
All year

60-90-B&B
5 rooms, 5 pb
Visa, MC, *Rated*
C-yes/S-no/P-ltd/H-ltd
A little French

Full breakfast
Afternoon tea, snacks
Sitting room, cable TV

*A cozy, intimate (c.1857) Victorian home where every guest is a special guest. A full gourmet breakfast and homemade afternoon treats served.   E-mail: liondor@gwi.net
Web site: gwi.net/liondor*

Ocean Gate
PO Box 240, 04576
207-633-3321 Fax: 207-633-7332
800-221-5924
Ted & Judith Kolva
Memorial Day-Columbus

100-160-B&B
66 rooms, 66 pb
Visa, MC, *Rated*, ●
C-yes/S-ltd/P-no/H-ltd

Full breakfast
Free tennis courts, children's
playground, heated pool,
fitness center

Escape to 85 wooded waterfront acres on scenic Southport Island just five miles across the bridge from Boothbay Harbor. Enjoy free full breakfast. Cottages and two bedroom units available.   E-mail: ogate@oceangateinn.com Web site: oceangateinn.com

Ocean Point Inn
PO Box 409, 04544
207-633-4200
800-552-5554
Dave & Beth Dudley
All year

104-165-EP/B&B
61 rooms, 61 pb
Most CC, *Rated*, ●
C-yes/S-ltd/P-no/H-no

Continental breakfast off
season
Restaurant, bar service
Dinner available, swimming
pool, family friendly facility,
game room

Traditional seacoast inn on beautiful Ocean Point. A natural, unspoiled oceanfront setting in a relaxed atmosphere with a spectacular open ocean view. Living room with fireplace, game room in main inn.   E-mail: opi@oceanpointinn.com Web site: oceanpointinn.com/

Welch House Inn
56 McKown St, 04538
207-633-3431
800-279-7313
Closed winter

60-145-B&B
16 rooms, 16 pb
Visa, MC, AmEx,
Rated, ●
C-ltd/S-ltd/P-ltd/H-ltd

Continental plus buffet
Afternoon tea
Sitting room, cable TV

*Unsurpassed views from atop McKown hill. 60 second walk to center of harbor. Most rooms have harbor and Atlantic Ocean views.   E-mail: welchhouse@wiscasset.net
Web site: wiscasset.net/welchhouse*

BRIDGTON

Noble House B&B
PO Box 180, 04009
207-647-3733 Fax: 207-647-3733
Jane Starets
May-Oct.

80-130-B&B
9 rooms, 6 pb
●
C-ltd/S-ltd/P-no/H-no

Full breakfast
Private lake frontage, baby
grand piano, organ, free
canoe, pedal boat

Majestic Queen Anne set on a hillcrest looking across to Highland Lake and the White Mountains.

BRUNSWICK

Brunswick B&B
165 Park Row, 04011
207-729-4914
800-299-4914
Steve & Mercie Normand
Closed January

90-130-B&B
8 rooms, 8 pb
Visa, MC,
C-ltd/S-no/P-no/H-no

Full breakfast
Snacks
Sitting room, suites,
fireplaces, cable TV,
accommodate business
travelers

Gracious lodging in Greek Revival home decorated with quilts and antiques. Easy walk to restaurants, shops, museums, Bowdoin College. Wake to the aroma of coffee brewing, enjoy a full breakfast.   E-mail: innkeeper@brunswickbnb.com Web site: brunswickbnb.com

CALAIS

Brewer House	60-85-B&B	Full breakfast
PO Box 94, 04671	5 rooms, 3 pb	Snacks
207-454-2385	Visa, MC, AmEx,	Sitting room, library,
800-821-2028	C-ltd/S-no/P-ltd/H-no	fireplaces, business travelers
Estelle & David Holloway		welcome, outdoor porch
All year		

Historic sea captain's mansion. 6-acre country estate. Casual, elegant interiors with ornate antique furnishings. Spectacular water views. Sumptous 3-course gourmet breakfast. National Register of Historic Places. 12 miles from International border. Web site: mainerec.com/brewer.html

CAMDEN

Abigail's B&B by the Sea	110-175-B&B	Full breakfast
8 High St, 04843	4 rooms, 4 pb	Afternoon tea,
207-236-2501 Fax: 207-230-0657	Visa, MC, *Rated*	complimentary wine
800-292-2501	C-ltd/S-no/P-no/H-no	Sitting room, library, jacuzzi,
Ed & Donna Misner		suites, fireplace, cable TV,
All year		A/C, business.

Let yourself be pampered; cozy four-poster bed, tempting breakfast, jacuzzi, fireplaces, afternoon tea, and just a short walk to Camden harbor and village. E-mail: abigails@midcoast.com Web site: midcoast.com/~abigails

Blackberry Inn	110-135-B&B	Full breakfast
82 Elm St, 04843	10 rooms, 10 pb	Afternoon tea, snacks
207-236-6060 Fax: 207-236-9032	Visa, MC, Disc, ●	Sitting room, library,
800-388-6000	C-yes/S-no/P-no/H-no	Jacuzzis, fireplace, cable TV
Jim & Cyndi Ostrowski		
All year		

Maine's only "painted lady" Victorian, just a 3 block stroll to windjammer harbor, shops and restaurants. Gracious parlors, original tin ceilings, beautiful parquet floors. E-mail: blkherry@midcoast.com Web site: blackberryinn.com

Camden Windward House	105-185-B&B	Full gourmet breakfast
B&B	8 rooms, 8 pb	Complimentary port and
6 High St, 04843	Visa, MC,	sherry
207-236-9656 Fax: 207-230-0433	C-ltd/S-no/P-no/H-no	Sitting rooms, library, garden
Del & Charlotte Lawrence		room, walk to village &
All year		harbor

Historic 1854 home. Rooms offer canopied beds, clawfoot soak tubs, fireplaces, romantic music. 1 block from village, harbor, shops, and restaurants. Indulge in our candlelight, full service breakfast. E-mail: bnb@windwardhouse.com Web site: windwardhouse.com

Castleview by the Sea	75-195-B&B	Full breakfast
59 High St, 04841	3 rooms, 3 pb	Balconies, decks, A/C, cable
207-236-2344		TV, ocean views
800-272-8439		
Bill Butler		
April-October		

Only inn on the ocean side of the bay-view section of Camden's historic district. Web site: castleviewinn.com

Elms B&B, The	75-105-B&B	Full breakfast
84 Elm St, 04843	6 rooms, 6 pb	Afternoon tea, restaurants
207-236-6250 Fax: 207-236-7330	Visa, MC, *Rated*, ●	Cottage gardens, frplcs.,
800-755-ELMS	C-ltd/S-no/P-no/H-ltd	period furniture, lib.,
Ted & Jo Panayotoff		phone/data ports in rooms
All year		

Experience the casual warmth of this restored 1806 Colonial, with a lighthouse theme. Enjoy collection of lighthouse artwork, books & collectibles. Walk to harbor and shops. E-mail: theelms@midcoast.com Web site: midcoast.com/~theelms/

CAMDEN

Featherbed
705 Commercial St, 04856
207-596-7230 Fax: 207-596-7657
Michelle Painchaud
All year

125-B&B
2 rooms, 2 pb
Visa, MC, •
C-ltd/S-ltd/P-no/H-ltd

Full breakfast
Dinner available, afternoon
tea
Sitting room, fireplace, cable
TV, conference facilities, art
gallery

Indulge your senses! Romantic rooms, stenciled ceilings, decadent feather beds. Private baths with handmade soaps and scented toiletries. Breakfasts lavishly served featuring lobster omelets. Water access. Gift shop. E-mail: chelted@midcoast.com
Web site: midcoast.com/~chelted/featherB.html

Hartstone Inn
41 Elm St, 04843
207-236-4259 Fax: 207-236-9575
800-788-4823
Mary Jo & Michael Salmon
All year

95-140-B&B
10 rooms, 10 pb
Most CC, *Rated*, •
C-ltd/S-no/P-ltd/H-no

Full breakfast
Dinner, picnic sails
Comp. tea, cookies, sitting
room, fireplaces, library, TV
room, phones

Come fall under the spell of one of Camden's grandest historic homes located in the heart of the village. Elegant china, fine crystal, and our internationally award winning chef make breakfast and dinner a truly memorable experience. E-mail: info@hartstoneinn.com
Web site: hartstoneinn.com

Hawthorn Inn
9 High St, 04843
207-236-8842 Fax: 207-236-6181
Nick & Patty Wharton
All year

100-205-B&B
10 rooms, 10 pb
Visa, MC, *Rated*, •
C-ltd/S-no/P-no/H-no

Full breakfast
2 sitting rooms, double
Jacuzzi tubs, fireplaces,
decks

Stately Victorian mansion with light, airy rooms. Views of Camden Harbor and mountains. E-mail: hawthorn@midcoast.com *Web site:* camdeninn.com

---

Lord Camden Inn
24 Main St, 04843
207-236-4325
800-336-4325
Bill Hughes
All year

128-178-B&B
31 rooms, 28 pb
Visa, MC, AmEx,
Rated, •
C-yes/S-yes/P-no/H-ltd

Continental breakfast
Tennis available, bicycles
next door, All rooms A/C

Restored 1893 Main Street building has 31 Colonial furnished rooms with private baths, TVs and phones. E-mail: lordcam@midcoast.com *Web site:* lordcamdeninn.com

---

Maine Stay
22 High St, 04843
207-236-9636 Fax: 207-236-0621
Peter Smith, Donny, Diana
All year

100-145-B&B
8 rooms, 8 pb
Visa, MC, *Rated*, •
C-ltd/S-no/P-no/H-no

Full breakfast
2 parlors with fireplaces, TV
room, 4 rooms with fireplace,
deck

Built in 1802, the inn is situated in the high street historic district on two acres of lovely grounds only two blocks from the harbor and village center. E-mail: innkeeper@
mainstay.com *Web site:* mainestay.com/

Swan House
49 Mountain St (Rt 52), 04843
207-236-8275 Fax: 207-236-0906
800-207-8275
Lyn & Ken Kohl
All year

85-130-B&B
6 rooms, 6 pb
Visa, MC,
C-ltd/S-no/P-no/H-ltd

Full country breakfast
Sitting rooms, gazebo,
enclosed sunporch,
mountain hiking trail

Located in a quiet neighborhood, away from busy Route 1. Short walk to Camden's beautiful harbor, or hike backyard trail to Mt. Battie summit for spectacular views. Antiques. E-mail: hikeinn@swanhouse.com *Web site:* swanhouse.com

The Swan House, Camden, ME

CENTER LOVELL

Pleasant Point Inn
PO Box 218, 04016
207-925-3008 Fax: 207-925-3328
Susan Perry
All year

95-250-EP
Visa, MC, •
C-yes/P-no/H-yes

Continental breakfast (fee)
Restaurant, bar service
Dinner available, snacks,
sitting room, library, tennis
courts

Leave your cares behind—relax on Keyzar Lake and enjoy our view of the picturesque White Mountains. E-mail: ppi@pleasantpoint.com *Web site:* pleasantpoint.com

COREA

Black Duck on Corea Harbor
Crowley Island Rd, 04624
207-963-2689 Fax: 207-963-7495
Barry Canner & Bob Travers
All year

80-155-B&B
5 rooms, 3 pb
Visa, MC, *Rated*, •
C-ltd/S-no/P-no/H-no
Danish, ltd. French

Full breakfast
Special diets catered
Sitting room, library,
bicycles, hiking trails

Casual elegance, antiques and art. Overlooking working lobster harbor. Village charm with rural atmosphere. Near national park and bird sanctuary. Off-season rates Oct 15-May 15. Weekly rates cottages. E-mail: bduck@acadia.net *Web site:* blackduck.com

DAMARISCOTTA

Brannon-Bunker Inn
349 State Route 129, 04573
207-563-5941
800-563-9225
Jeanne & Joe Hovance
All year

65-75-B&B
9 rooms, 4 pb
Visa, MC, *Rated*, •
C-yes/S-no/P-no/H-ltd

Continental plus breakfast
Kitchen facilities
Sitting room, porch, antique
shop, 3 room suite for family

Country B&B; charming rooms furnished with antiques; close to all mid-coast recreational facilities including ocean, beach, boating, golf, antiquing E-mail: brbnkinn@
lincoln.midcoast.com

Newcastle Inn, The
60 River Rd, 04553
207-563-5685 Fax: 207-563-6877
800-832-8669
Howard & Rebecca Levitan
All year

95-250-B&B/MAP
15 rooms, 15 pb
Visa, MC, AmEx,
Rated, •
C-ltd/S-no/P-no/H-ltd
French, Spanish

Full breakfast
Evening reception bar
Dinner, aftn. beverages,
sitting room w/fireplace,
screened-in porch, deck

Fine dining and a pampering environment in an intimate, full-service, country inn on the Damariscotta River. Briar Patch Pub; fireside dining. Fireplaces in rooms.   E-mail: innkeep@
newcastleinn.com *Web site:* newcastleinn.com

EASTPORT ─────────────────────────────────

Milliken House, The	50-65-B&B	Full breakfast
29 Washington St, 04631	5 rooms, 3 pb	Complimentary wine
207-853-2955	Visa, MC, AmEx, •	Sitting room, library, family
Joyce & Paul Weber	C-yes/S-no/P-yes/H-no	friendly facility
All year		

Elegant accommodations in large, gracious 1846 home furnished with ornately carved Victorian marble-topped furniture. Noted for our sumptuous breakfasts.
E-mail: millikenhouse@eastport-inn.com *Web site:* eastport-inn.com

Todd House	45-80-B&B	Continental plus breakfast
1 Capen Ave, 04631	7 rooms, 3 pb	Bbq deck with a view
207-853-2328	C-yes/S-ltd/P-yes/H-yes	Library, fireplace, yard with
Ruth M. McInnis		barbecue, picnic facilities
All year		

Step into the past in our revolutionary-era Cape with wide panorama of Passamaquoddy Bay.

ELIOT ─────────────────────────────────

High Meadows B&B	80-90-B&B	Full breakfast
2 Brixham Rd, Rt 101, 03903	5 rooms, 5 pb	Afternoon wine, tea
207-439-0590 Fax: 207-439-6343	*Rated*	Sitting room, Barn available
Elaine Raymond	S-ltd/P-no/H-no	for parties and weddings
April-November		

1736 colonial house in the country. Walking & cross-country ski trails. *E-mail:* hymedobb@aol.com

FREEPORT ─────────────────────────────────

Bagley House, The	85-150-B&B	Full breakfast
1290 Royalsborough Rd, 04222	8 rooms, 5 pb	Complimentary beverages,
207-865-6566 Fax: 207-353-5878	Most CC, *Rated*, •	cookies
800-765-1772	C-yes/S-no/P-no/H-yes	Sitting room, library, cross
S. O'Connor & S. Backhouse		country skiing, 6-acre yard,
All year		BBQ

Peace, tranquillity & history abound in this magnificent 1772 country home. A warm welcome awaits you from us & resident dog & cat. *E-mail:* bglyhse@aol.com
Web site: members.aol.com/bedandbrk/bagley

Brewster House B&B	85-120-B&B	Full breakfast
180 Main St, 04032	7 rooms, 7 pb	Snacks
207-865-4121 Fax: 207-865-4221	Most CC, *Rated*	Sitting room, suites, discount
800-865-0822	C-ltd/S-no/P-no/H-ltd	coupons to some area
Matt & Amy Cartmell		restaurants
All year		

Newly renovated 1888 Queen Anne. Tastefully decorated with antiques. Family suites, full-size private bathrooms, delicious full breakfast with a variety of choice.
Web site: brewsterhouse.com

Captain Briggs House B&B	62-120-B&B	Full homemade breakfast
8 Maple Ave, 04032	5 rooms, 5 pb	Sitting room with cable TV,
207-865-1868 Fax: 207-865-1868	Visa, MC, *Rated*	VCR, books, games or,
800-217-2477	C-yes/S-no/P-no/H-no	conversation
The Frank Family	German	
All year		

Quaint village on the sea coast of Maine. 1853 Federal house with cozy and cheerful guestrooms. Beautiful gardens, quiet side street. Private baths. Walk to village and L.L. Bean. *Web site:* bbhost.com/freeportmaine

FREEPORT

Harraseeket Inn
162 Main St, 04032
207-865-9377 Fax: 207-865-1684
800-342-6423
The Gray Family
All year

140-235-B&B
84 rooms, 84 pb
Visa, MC, AmEx,
Rated, •
C-yes/S-ltd/P-no/H-yes

Full breakfast buffet
2 restaurants, aftn. tea
Indoor pool, 23 fireplaces,
ballroom, Tavern w/open
kitchen, 7 meeting rooms

Luxury Country Inn. Private baths (Jacuzzi), cable TV, elegant Maine buffet country breakfast. E-mail: harraseeke@aol.com Web site: stayfreeport.com

---

Maple Hill B&B
18 Maple Ave, 04032
207-865-3730 Fax: 207-865-9859
800-867-0478
Susie Vietor, Lloyd Lawrence
All year

85-150-B&B
3 rooms, 3 pb
Most CC,
C-yes/S-no/P-yes/H-no

Full breakfast
Snacks
Sitt. rm., bikes, tennis, stes.,
cable, fireplaces, hiking,
shopping, beach

Historic home built in 1831. Quiet, peaceful, romantic, 2 blocks from LL Bean, scrumptious breakfasts, beautiful gardens, cozy fireplace, your home away from home. E-mail: mplhll@ aol.com Web site: web-knowledge.com/maplehill

---

White Cedar Inn
7 Merganser Way, 04032
207-865-9099
800-853-1269
Carla & Phil Kerber
All year

85-135-B&B
7 rooms, 7 pb
Most CC, *Rated*
C-ltd/S-no/P-no/H-no

Full breakfast
Sitting room, picnic table,
patio, all rooms have A/C

Recently restored 100-year-old home with large uncluttered antique-furnished rooms. Located just 2 blocks from L.L. Bean. E-mail: capandphil@aol.com Web site: members.aol.com/bedandbrk/cedar

FRYEBURG

Acres of Austria
RR #1 Box #177, 04037
207-925-6547 Fax: 207-925-6547
800-988-4391
Franz & Candice Redl
All year

79-165-B&B
6 rooms, 6 pb
Visa, MC, *Rated*, •
C-yes/S-no/P-ltd/H-yes
German

Full breakfast
Dinner available
Libary, sitting rm., fireplaces,
suites, billiards, canoe,
TV/VCR, A/C

Peaceful retreat set on 65 acres along the Old Saco River near the Mount Washington Valley. Spot moose, heron, etc. on our 5+ miles of nature trails. E-mail: info@ acresofaustria.com Web site: acresofaustria.com

---

Admiral Peary House B&B
9 Elm St, 04037
207-935-3365 Fax: 207-935-3365
800-237-8080
Nancy & Ed Greenberg
All year

65-128-B&B
6 rooms, 6 pb
Visa, MC, AmEx,
Rated, •
C-ltd/S-no/P-no/H-no
French

Full breakfast
Complimentary beverage
Sitting room, library,
bicycles, tennis court, hot
tub, billiards, A/C

Charming historical home in a picturesque White Mountain village. Clay tennis court, skiing, canoeing, hiking, spacious grounds, perennial gardens. E-mail: admpeary@uxi.com Web site: mountwashingtonvalley.com/admiralpearyhouse

---

Oxford House Inn, The
105 Main St, 04037
207-935-3442 Fax: 207-935-7046
800-261-7206
John & Phyllis Morris
All year

95-125-B&B
4 rooms, 4 pb
Most CC, *Rated*
C-yes/S-no/P-no/H-no

Full breakfast
Dinner available, snacks
Restaurant, bar, sitting room,
cable TV, conference
facilities

Charming country inn/bed and breakfast with a gourmet restaurant with spectacular mountain views. Famous for the area's best dining. Nearby hiking, canoeing, antiquing, cycling, fishing, golf and outlet shopping galore! E-mail: innkeeper@oxfordhouseinn.com Web site: oxfordhouseinn.com

The Grey Havens, Georgetown, ME

GEORGETOWN

Coveside B&B
HC 33 Box 462, 04548
207-371-2807
800-232-5490
Carolyn & Tom Church
May-Oct.

95-145-B&B
4 rooms, 4 pb
Visa, MC, Disc, *Rated*,
●
C-ltd/S-no/P-no/H-no
French (limited)

Full breakfast
Box lunch
Sitting room, bicycles,
Jacuzzis, fireplaces, canoe

Turn-of-century seaside cottage on secluded rocky cove in mid-coast Maine. Explore scenic Georgetown. Beaches, hiking, bird-watching, & fishing nearby. E-mail: coveside@gwi.net *Web site:* gwi.net/coveside

Grey Havens, The
PO Box 308, 04548
207-371-2616 Fax: 207-371-2274
Bill & Haley Eberhart
Mid-April through Nov.

100-205-B&B
13 rooms, 13 pb
Visa, MC,
C-ltd/S-ltd/P-no/H-no

Continental plus breakfast
Snacks, bar service
Sitting room, library,
bicycles, canoe, rowboat,
canoe

Maine's most breathtaking view can be seen from most of the windows in this casual, friendly, historic, summer "hotel." E-mail: greyhavens@clinic.net *Web site:* greyhavens.com

GOULDSBORO

Sunset House B&B
HCR 60, Rt 186, 04607
207-963-7156 Fax: 207-963-5859
800-233-7156
Carl & Kathy Johnson
All year

79-99-B&B
8 rooms, 8 pb
Most CC, *Rated*
C-yes/S-ltd/P-no/H-no

Full breakfast
Restaurant features BYOB
Sitting room, canoes,
conference facilities up to 30
persons, kayak

A quiet, serene, beautiful setting nestled among whispering pines atop a 200-foot bluff. Overlooking Frenchman Bay and its islands. Large decks with million dollar view. E-mail: lodging@sunsethousebnb.com *Web site:* sunsethousebnb.com

GREENVILLE

Evergreen Lodge B&B
HC 76, Box 58, 04441
207-695-3241 Fax: 207-695-3084
888-624-3993
Sonda & Bruce Hamilton
All year

95-135-B&B
6 rooms, 6 pb
Visa, MC, AmEx,
Rated, ●
C-ltd/S-no/P-no/H-no

Full breakfast
Dinner (Dec-March only)
Snacks, sitting room,
bicycles, moose safaris,
snowmobile rentals

Private setting on 30 wooded acres, moose frequent grounds. Rustic but elegant accommodation with 2 common areas with fireplaces. Boat tours on Moosehead twice daily for moose watching. Hot tub on outdoor deck, luxury cottage for up to 12 people. E-mail: evergreen@moosehead.net *Web site:* mainelodge.com

GREENVILLE

Greenville Inn
PO Box 1194, 04441
207-695-2206 Fax: 207-695-0335
888-695-6000
Elfi, Susie, Michael Schnetzer
May-Oct, Dec 15-Mar 15

105-225-B&B
12 rooms, 12 pb
Visa, MC, Disc, *Rated*,
•
C-ltd/S-yes/P-ltd/H-ltd
German

Continental plus breakfast
Dinner, restaurant, bar
Sitting room, queen beds, 4
new cottages, suite, common
rooms redecorated

Restored lumber baron's mansion with many unique features on a hill in town overlooking Moosehead Lake and Squaw Mountain. E-mail: gvlinn@moosehead.net
Web site: greenvilleinn.com

Lodge at Moosehead Lake
Box 1167, 04441
207-695-4400 Fax: 207-695-2281
Roger & Jennifer Cauchi
All year

145-395-B&B
8 rooms, 8 pb
Visa, MC, Disc, *Rated*
C-ltd/S-no/P-no/H-ltd

Full breakfast
Dinner available, snacks, bar
Sitting room, library, bikes,
Jacuzzis, suites, fireplace,
cable TV

Outdoor persons paradise in pampered luxury. Spectacular panoramic views of lake and mountains. The Lodge marries the amenities of a luxury hotel with the casual intimacy of a country inn. E-mail: innkeeper@lodgeatmooseheadlake.com *Web site:* lodgeatmooseheadlake.com

ISLE AU HAUT

Keeper's House, The
PO 26, 04645
207-367-2261
Jeff & Judi Burke
May-Oct.

257-297-AP
4 rooms
C-yes/S-no/P-no/H-no
Spanish

Full breakfast
All meals included in rate
Vegetarian dining, snacks,
hiking, bicycles, ocean
swimming

Operating lighthouse station on island in Acadia National Park. Tiny fishing village, spectacular natural surroundings. No electricity or telephone. Web site: keepershouse.com

KENNEBUNK

Alewife House B&B, The
756 Alewive Rd, Rt #35, 04043
207-985-2118
Maryellen & Tom Foley
All year

95-99-B&B
3 rooms, 2 pb
Visa, MC, •
C-ltd/S-no/P-no/H-no

Continental plus breakfast
Perked coffee served on sun
porch
Antique shop on premises,
sun porch, ocean swimming

A 1756 restored Colonial farmhouse located in the horse-country area of Kennebunk and Kennebunkport, about 10 minutes from the area's beaches & quaint village centers. E-mail: alewifehouse@mainecoast.net *Web site:* virtualcities.com/ons/me/k/mek9502.htm

Arundel Meadows Inn
PO Box 1129, 04043
207-985-3770 Fax: 207-967-4704
Mark Bachelder, Murray
Yaeger   All year

75-135-B&B
7 rooms, 7 pb
Visa, MC, *Rated*, •
C-ltd/S-no/P-no/H-ltd

Full gourmet breakfast
Afternoon tea
Set-ups, library, sitting room,
ocean swimming, Barney the
cat.

Rooms individually decorated with art, antiques. Some with fireplaces; all with private baths. E-mail: docmy@aol.com *Web site:* gwi.net/arundel_meadows_inn

Kennebunk Inn
45 Main St, 04043
207-985-3351 Fax: 207-985-8865
John & Kristen Martin
All year

75-135-B&B
33 rooms, 27 pb
Most CC,
C-yes/S-yes/P-yes/H-yes
French, Italian

Continental breakfast
Full service dining room
Sitting room, piano,
entertainment, A/C, great
restaurant

Village inn, beautifully restored. Acclaimed dining room, recommended by Travel and Leisure (Sept. '84).

KENNEBUNK BEACH

Ocean View, The
171 Beach Ave, 04043
207-967-2750 Fax: 207-967-5418
Carole & Bob Arena
April-mid Dec.

125-275-B&B
9 rooms, 9 pb
Most CC, *Rated*
S-no/P-no/H-no
French

Full breakfast
Late afternoon refreshments
Living room, library, TV
room, exclusive boutique,
concierge service

"The closest you'll find to a bed on the beach." An intimate oceanfront Inn. Whimsical and colorful. E-mail: arena@theoceanview.com *Web site:* theoceanview.com

Captain Fairfield Inn, Kennebunkport, ME

KENNEBUNKPORT

Captain Fairfield Inn PO Box 2690, 04046 207-967-4454 Fax: 207-967-8537 800-322-1928 Janet & Rick Wolf Season Inquire	110-250-B&B 9 rooms, 9 pb Visa, MC, *Rated* C-yes/S-no/P-no/H-no some French	Full gourmet breakfast Afternoon tea Sitting room, library, gardens, beach, boats

Gracious 1813 Federal Sea Captain's mansion beautifully appointed. Romantic, spacious bedrooms. Some with fireplaces. E-mail: jrw@captainfairfield.com *Web site:* captainfairfield.com

Captain Jefferds Inn, The PO Box 691, 04046 207-967-2311 Fax: 207-967-0721 800-839-6844 Pat & Dick Bartholomew April-Dec.	135-285-B&B 16 rooms, 16 pb Visa, MC, *Rated*, • C-ltd/S-no/P-yes/H-yes	Full breakfast Afternoon tea Library, garden, breakfast on terrace, 3 suites, sitting room

Especially beautiful, quiet, private. In "House Beautiful" and "Country Living" 12/92. Completely newly decorated. E-mail: captjeff@captainjefferdsinn.com *Web site:* captainjefferdsinn.com

Captain Lord Mansion PO Box 800, 04046 207-967-3141 Fax: 207-967-3172 Bev Davis & Rick Litchfield All year	175-400-B&B 16 rooms, 16 pb Most CC, *Rated*, • C-ltd/S-ltd/P-no/H-no	Full breakfast Afternoon tea, sweets Accessories in bathrooms, sitting room, piano, A/C, beach towels, umbrellas

Situated at the head of a sloping village green, overlooking the Kennebunk River. E-mail: captain@biddeford.com *Web site:* captainlord.com

Chetwynd House Inn, The PO Box 130, 04046 207-967-2235 Fax: 207-967-5406 800-833-3351 Susan Knowles Chetwynd All year	99-169-B&B 4 rooms, 4 pb • C-ltd/S-ltd/P-no/H-no French, Italian	Full multi-course breakfast Complimentary tea Sitting room, library, 2 room suite, all rooms have cable TV & A/C

Pristine rooms. Handsome, lovely furnishings. Rich mahogany & cherry wood antique pieces. King & queen poster beds; tea tables. E-mail: chetwynd@gwi.net *Web site:* gwi.net/chetwynd

Crosstrees PO Box 1333, 04046 207-967-2780 Fax: 209-967-2610 800-564-1527 Dennis Rafferty, Keith Henley May 1-mid Dec.	100-215-B&B 4 rooms, 4 pb Visa, MC, *Rated* C-ltd/S-no/P-no/H-no	Full gourmet breakfast Complimentary wine, beverages Sitting room, porch, lawn, A/C, 3 room with fireplaces, warm, inviting rooms

Charming Federal inn located in historic area, a short walk to shops & beach. Traditional hospitality & "down east" comfort. E-mail: info@crosstree.com *Web site:* crosstrees.com

KENNEBUNKPORT

Inn at Goose Rocks	65-175-EP	Dinner, restaurant
71 Dyke Rd, 04046	32 rooms, 32 pb	Bar service, sitting room,
207-967-5425 Fax: 207-967-0204	Visa, MC, AmEx,	library, hot tubs, pool, cable
800-457-7688	*Rated*, •	TV
Skip and Gerry Magan	C-yes/S-ltd/P-no/H-yes	
All year		

Nestled in a wooded landscape near the sea and bordering salt marshes, we offer quiet surroundings, gracious accommodations and fine dining you would expect of a New England country inn. E-mail: innatgrb@innatgooserocks.com Web site: innatgooserocks.com

Inn at Harbor Head	130-315-B&B	Full gourmet breakfast
41 Pier Rd, 04046	4 rooms, 4 pb	Afternoon tea, wine
207-967-5564 Fax: 207-967-1294	Visa, MC, *Rated*	Sitting room, library,
Eve & Dick Roesler	C-ltd/S-no/P-no/H-no	bicycles, Jacuzzis, suites,
February-December		fireplace

Nestled on a rocky knoll on Cape Porpoise Harbor, this rambling, romantic inn is a base for your visit to historic Kennebunkport and surrounding area. E-mail: info@harborhead.com Web site: harborhead.com

Kennebunkport Inn, The	79-279-EP	Continental breakfast (Nov-
PO Box 111, 04046	34 rooms, 34 pb	Apr)fee
207-967-2621 Fax: 207-967-3705	Visa, MC, AmEx,	Cont. plus breakfast May-Oct-
800-248-2621	*Rated*, •	fee
Rick & Martha Griffin	C-yes/P-no/H-yes	Pub, restaurant, pool, color
All year	French	TV, phones, golf, tennis,
		whirlpools, fireplace

Country inn in old sea captain's home. All rooms with private baths. Gourmet patio dining, turn-of-the-century bar, piano bar. Web site: kennebunkportinn.com

King's Port Inn, A B&B Inn	65-185-B&B	Continental plus breakfast
PO Box 1070, 04046	32 rooms, 32 pb	Complimenteray hot
207-967-4340 Fax: 207-967-4810	Most CC, •	beverages
800-286-5767	C-yes/S-ltd/P-no/H-yes	Fireside parlor, in-room
Bill and Rosita Greer	French	Jacuzzis and fireplaces,
All year		surround sound theater

This New England coastal inn, nestled near the quaint, historical seacoast village of Kennebunkport, offers affordable, comfortable, gracious hospitality. E-mail: info@kingsportinn.com Web site: kingsportinn.com

Lake Brook B&B	90-130-B&B	Full breakfast
PO Box 762, 04046	4 rooms, 4 pb	Golf, tennis nearby, just $1/2$
207-967-4069	Visa, MC, •	mile from, downtown
Carolyn A. McAdams	C-ltd/S-no/P-no/H-no	Kennebunkport
Late April thru Feb.	Spanish	

Nestled at the edge of a salt marsh & tidal brook, Lake Brook offers charming rooms with antiques & paddle fans, great breakfasts, extensive gardens & rockers on the porch. New paint and wallpaper. E-mail: carolyn@lakebrookbb.com Web site: lakebrookbb.com

Maine Stay Inn & Cottages	95-250-B&B	Full breakfast
PO Box 500 A, 04046	17 rooms, 17 pb	Afternoon tea, snacks
207-967-2117 Fax: 207-967-8757	Most CC, *Rated*, •	Sitting room, swing set,
800-950-2117	C-yes/S-no/P-no/H-no	garden, porch, 9 rooms with
Lindsay & Carol Copeland		fireplaces
All year		

Victorian inn known for exceptional warmth, hospitality and great breakfasts. E-mail: innkeeper@mainestayinn.com Web site: mainestayinn.com

KENNEBUNKPORT

Old Fort Inn
PO Box M, 04046
207-967-5353 Fax: 207-967-4547
David & Sheila Aldrich
Season Inquire

145-310-B&B
16 rooms, 16 pb
Visa, MC, AmEx,
Rated, •
C-ltd/S-no/P-no/H-no

Full breakfast
Cable TV, phone in room,
tennis, pool, Jacuzzis, A/C,
some fireplaces

A luxurious resort in a secluded charming setting. The inn has yesterday's charm with today's conveniences. Within walking distance to the ocean. E-mail: oldfort@cybertours.com
Web site: oldfortinn.com

Sundial Inn, The
PO Box 500B, 04046
207-967-3850 Fax: 207-967-4719
Laurie
All year

190-295-B&B
34 rooms, 34 pb
Visa, MC, AmEx,
Rated, •
C-ltd/S-no/P-no/H-yes
French

Continental plus breakfast
Afternoon tea (winter)
Sitting room, whirlpool tubs,
beach & ocean views

On Kennebunkport beach. Country Victorian antiques, beautiful ocean views. An elevator for your convenience. Near hiking, beach, swimming, shopping, dining, fishing.
E-mail: sundial@lamere.net

Welby Inn, The
PO Box 774, 04046
207-967-4655
Fax: 207-967-8654
A. Rowley & M. Weston
All year

95-120-B&B
7 rooms, 7 pb
Visa, MC, Disc, *Rated*,
•
C-ltd/S-no/P-no/H-no

Full breakfast
Eve. homemade Amaretto
Guest pantry, large,
welcoming living room, 5
queen, 2 full beds

Gracious turn-of-the-century home in historic Kennebunkport. Walk to beach, marina and shops. Deep-sea fishing and harbor cruises available E-mail: welbyinn@gwi.net
Web site: welbyinn.com

White Barn Inn, The
PO Box 560 C, 04046
207-967-2321
Fax: 207-967-1100
Laurie Bingiorno
All year

320-475-B&B
24 rooms, 24 pb
Visa, MC, AmEx,
Rated, •
C-ltd/S-ltd/P-no/H-ltd

Continental plus breakfast
Dinner prix fix (fee)
Swimming pool, landscape,
steam shower, Jacuzzi,
renovated cottage, VCR

Elegant farmhouse Inn-5-diamond restaurant. Set in the original, architecturally preserved barn. E-mail: innkeeper@whitebarninn.com Web site: whitebarninn.com/

KITTERY

Enchanted Nights B&B
29 Wentworth St, 03904
207-439-1489
Peter Lamardia
All year

48-202-B&B
8 rooms, 7 pb
Most CC, •
C-yes/S-ltd/P-yes/H-yes

Full breakfast
Sitting room, family friendly
facility, bikes, tennis, sauna

Victorian/Country French. Whimsical, colorful, fanciful. Whirlpool for 2, elegant breakfasts. E-mail: info@enchanted-nights-bandb.com Web site: enchanted-nights-bandb.com

Inn at Portsmouth Harbor
6 Water St, 03904
207-439-4040 Fax: 207-438-9286
Kim & Terry O'Mahoney
All year

110-150-B&B
6 rooms, 6 pb
Visa, MC, •
C-ltd/S-no/P-no/H-ltd
some French, Slovak

Full breakfast
Complimentary wine
Sitting room, piano, games,
porch, patio, garden

Comfortable brick Victorian with beautifully appointed rooms, water views, stroll to historic Portsmouth. Near beaches, outlets. Recommended by NY Times.
E-mail: info@innatportsmouth.com Web site: innatportsmouth.com

MONHEGAN ISLAND

Island Inn
PO Box 128, 04852
207-596-0371 Fax: 207-594-5177
Philip L. Truelove
May 25-Oct 14

98-185-B&B
36 rooms, 7 pb
Visa, MC, •
C-yes/S-no/P-yes/H-no

Full breakfast
Afternoon tea, restaurant
Lunch, dinner (fee),
Barnacle coffee house, sitting
room, library

A turn of the century summer hotel overlooking Monhegan Harbor and the ocean. Relax on the porch & admire the setting sun as it displays its glorious colors in front of you. Game room, babysitting. E-mail: islandin@midcoast.com *Web site:* islandinnmonhegan.com

Monhegan House
PO Box 345, 04852
207-594-7983 Fax: 207-596-6472
800-599-7983
Zoe Zanidakis
Mid-May thru mid Oct.

95-EP
33 rooms
Most CC, *Rated*
C-yes/S-no/P-no/H-no

Restaurant, all meals
available
Sitting room, library

Enjoy the friendly relaxed atmosphere, inviting front porch and cozy fireplace of our 1870s island inn. Long a haven for artists, birdwatchers, and nature lovers. We will do our best to make your stay a pleasant and memorable one.

NAPLES

Augustus Bove House
RR 1, Box 501, 04055
207-693-6365
David & Arlene Stetson
All year

59-175-B&B
11 rooms, 7 pb
Visa, MC, AmEx,
Rated, •
C-yes/S-ltd/P-yes/H-ltd

Full breakfast
Honeymoon/Anniversary
tray
Complimentary coffee, tea,
sitting room, veranda, lawn

Recently restored, offers authentic colonial accommodations in a relaxing atmosphere. Between 2 lakes, 20 minutes from mountain skiing. E-mail: augbovehouse@pivot.net
Web site: maineguide.com/naples/augustus/

Inn at Long Lake
PO Box 806, 04055
207-693-6226
800-437-0328
Maynard and Irene Hincks
All year

55-159-B&B
16 rooms, 16 pb
Most CC, *Rated*, •
C-yes/S-no/P-no/H-no
Some French, Spanish

Continental plus breakfast
Complimentary
coffee/tea/hot cocoa
Sitting room, library, great
room with fireplace

Restored 16 room inn nestled by Sebago Lake, year-round activities, shopping, fine dining. Romantic elegance, Maine hospitality, Murder Mystery Weekends. New carpeting throughout. E-mail: innatll@megalink.net *Web site:* travelguides.com/home/long_lake/

NEW HARBOR

Gosnold Arms
145 State Route 32, 04554
207-677-3727 Fax: 207-677-2662
The Phinney Family
Mid-May-Oct.

79-144-B&B
26 rooms, 19 pb
Visa, MC, *Rated*
C-yes/S-ltd/P-no/H-ltd

Full breakfast
Dinner, cocktails, restaurant
Sitting room, small wharf,
cable TV available in some
rooms & cottages

Charming country inn and cottages. All-weather dining porch overlooking harbor. Web site: gosnold.com

OCEAN PARK

Nautilus Guest House, The
PO Box 7276, 04063
207-934-2021 Fax: 207-934-2022
800-981-7018
Dick & Patte Kessler
May-Oct.

50-95-B&B
13 rooms, 5 pb
Visa, MC, Disc, •
C-yes/S-yes/P-no/H-no

Continental plus breakfast
Sitting room, library,
fireplace, cable TV, close to
beach

Facing directly on the ocean, this Victorian summer mansion offers large, airy rooms with dramatic views, and enclosed porch overlooking the dunes and bay plus a very continental breakfast daily. E-mail: nautilus@cybertours.com *Web site:* NautilusByTheSea.com

OGUNQUIT ───

Blue Shutters Inn	65-B&B	Full breakfast
PO Box 655, 03907	12 rooms, 12 pb	Sitting room, library,
207-646-2163 Fax: 207-646-7225	Most CC,	bicycles, cable TV
800-633-9550	C-yes/S-no/P-no/H-no	
Phyllis & Dick Norton	Italian	
All year		

Share the peacefulness and ocean view of this special guest house with color coordinated rooms. Web site: blueshutters.com

Clipper Ship B&B	40-135-B&B	Continental breakfast
PO Box 236, 03907	28 rooms, 20 pb	Sitting room, library, suites,
207-646-9735	Visa, MC,	cable TV
Lois & Kaye Siegel	C-yes/S-no/P-ltd/H-no	
May-Columbus Weekend	Some French	

A Charming, non-smoking Inn with wonderfully decorated rooms, beautiful gardens & efficiencies. Some with porches or decks, private & shared baths, TV, A/C and the best of in-town locations. Pets Welcome.

Gorges Grant Hotel	78-181-B&B/MAP	Full breakfast
PO Box 2240 239 Route 1,	81 rooms, 81 pb	Restaurant, bar, dinner
03907	*Rated*	Hot tub, fitness room, indoor
207-646-7003 Fax: 207-646-0660	C-yes/S-no/P-no/H-yes	& outdoor pool
800-646-5001		
Karen and Bob Hanson		
Season Inquire		

Elegant, small, modern hotel operated with an inn flavor. Located in Ogunquit near (within short trolley ride) one of the world's best beaches   E-mail: gorgesgrant@ogunquit.com
Web site: ogunquit.com/gorgesgrant/index.html

Hartwell House Inn	90-190-B&B	Full gourmet breakfast
PO Box 393, 03907	16 rooms, 16 pb	Afternoon tea daily
207-646-7210	Most CC, *Rated*, ●	Swimming, tennis, A/C,
Fax: 207-646-6032	C-ltd/S-no/P-no/H-yes	banquet/conference fac., golf
800-235-8883		privileges, fishing
J & T Hartwell/Tracy		
Anderson		
All year		

This elegant, antique-filled country inn is perfectly located. Set amid 2 acres of sculpted gardens, perfect for relaxing.   E-mail: hartwell@cybertours.com
Web site: innbook.com/hartwell.html

Pine Hill Inn, The	95-150-B&B	Full breakfast
PO Box 2336, 03907	5 rooms, 5 pb	Afternoon tea, snacks, wine
207-361-1004 Fax: 207-361-1815	Most CC, *Rated*	Sitting room, library off,
Frank & Lou-Ann Agnelli	C-ltd/S-no/P-no/H-no	suites, fireplace, cable TV
All year		

100-year old Victorian furnished with fine antiques. Quite and secluded & just 5 minute walk to Perkins Cove which abounds with lobster boats, shops, restaurants, and the rocky coast of Maine. A scenic 1 mile path along the ocean.   E-mail: pinehill@cybertours.com
Web site: pinehillinn.com

Puffin Inn B&B	70-135-B&B	Full breakfast
PO Box 2232, 03907	10 rooms, 10 pb	Conference facilities
207-646-5496 Fax: 207-641-8746	Visa, MC, AmEx, *Rated*	
Lee & Maurice Williams	C-ltd/S-ltd/P-no/H-no	
April-October 25	French	

A charming country inn by the sea, offering a peaceful and relaxed atmosphere.
E-mail: puffin@cybertours.com *Web site:* puffininn.com

OGUNQUIT

Rockmere Lodge	75-175-B&B	Continental plus breakfast
PO Box 278, 03907	8 rooms, 8 pb	Afternoon tea,
207-646-2985 Fax: 207-646-6947	Visa, MC,	complimentary wine
Andy Antoniuk & Bob Brown	C-ltd/S-no/P-no/H-no	Sitting room, library, beach
All year		chairs, cool drinks for beach

Seaside, shingled cottage in out-of-the-way location. Very quiet. Listen to the ocean and relax. Walking distance to everything. Cable TV in all rooms. E-mail: rockmere@ cybertours.com *Web site:* chickadee.com/rockmere/

Trellis House	100-150-B&B	Full breakfast
PO Box 2229, 03907	8 rooms, 8 pb	Afternoon beverages
207-646-7909	Visa, MC,	Sitting room, porches, ocean
Pat & Jerry Houlihan	C-ltd/S-no/P-no/H-no	views, trolley stop
All year		

A year-round inn close to all that is special to Ogunquit. Furnished with an eclectic blend of antiques, coupled with some ocean views and quiet surroundings. E-mail: trellishouse@ cybertours.com *Web site:* trellishouse.com

OQUINQUIT

Woodland Gardens B&B	120-140-B&B	Full breakfast
150 Josiah Norton Rd, 03902	3 rooms, 3 pb	Snacks
207-361-1310	C-yes/S-no/P-no/H-no	Cable TV, Accommodate
Paulette & Peter O'Connor		business travelers
All year		

Resident hens provide huge jumbo eggs daily and vegetable garden provides blueberries, raspberries, herbs, cantaloupe and vegies for our recipes. E-mail: woodland@cybertours.com *Web site:* woodlandgardens.com

PORTLAND

Inn at St. John	45-145-B&B	Continental breakfast
939 Congress St, 04102	31 rooms, 20 pb	Family friendly facility deck,
207-773-6481 Fax: 207-756-7639	Most CC, *Rated*, •	solarium
800-636-9127	C-yes/S-yes/P-yes/H-yes	
Paul Hood		
All year		

A most unique 100 year old Inn noted for its European charm and quiet gentility. Tastefully decorated with traditional and antique furnishings. E-mail: info@innatstjohn.com *Web site:* innatstjohn.com

Inn On Carleton B&B	99-199-B&B	Full breakfast
46 Carleton St, 04102	6 rooms, 6 pb	Afternoon tea
207-775-1910 Fax: 207-761-0956	Visa, MC, Disc, *Rated*	Sitting room, resident cats,
800-639-1779	C-ltd/S-no/P-no/H-no	deck, solarium, conference
Phil & Sue Cox		
All year		

1869 Victorian Bed and Breakfast located in Portland, Maine's prestigious, historic Western Promenade neighborhood. E-mail: innkeeper@innoncarleton.com *Web site:* innoncarleton.com

Pine Crest B&B	69-109-B&B	Continental breakfast
91 South St, 04038	3 rooms, 3 pb	canoe
207-839-5843	Visa, MC, *Rated*	
Jane & Joe Carlozzi	C-ltd/S-no/P-no/H-no	
All year		

Maine's best location near Portland, minutes to galleries, beaches, lakes, golf, skiing and fine dining. Spacious rooms with sitting areas and coffee stations. E-mail: pinecrst@aol.com *Web site:* ccsme.com/pinecrest

PORTLAND ──────────────────────────────
West End Inn
PO Box 4612, 04112
207-772-1377 Fax: 207-828-0984
800-338-1377
Kelly Gillespie
All year

129-189-B&B
6 rooms, 6 pb
Most CC, *Rated*, •
C-yes/S-no/P-no/H-no

Full breakfast
Afternoon tea, snacks
Cable TV, remodeled &
redecorated, old port, dining,
museum

Very comfortable, relaxing home atmosphere in the heart of the city in historical district.
Art Museum, theaters and Old Port within walking distance

RANGELEY ──────────────────────────────
Rangeley Inn
PO Box 160, 04970
207-864-3341 Fax: 207-864-3634
800-MOMENTS
David & Rebecca Schinas
All year

69-120-EP
50 rooms, 50 pb
Most CC, *Rated*, •
C-yes/S-yes/P-no/H-yes

Restaurant—dinner
Bar service, library, hot tubs,
sitting room

Old-fashioned country inn 1500 ft. above sea level, in the lakes and mountain resort area
of western Maine. Come visit. AAA rated 3 diamonds; Mobil 3 star. Tavern now serving
dinners nightly. The menu includes pub fare as well as fine dining entrees.
E-mail: rangeinn@rangeley.org *Web site:* rangeleyinn.com

ROCKLAND ──────────────────────────────
Lakeshore Inn
184 Lakeview Dr, 04841
207-594-4204 Fax: 207-596-6407
877-783-7371
Joseph McCluskey &
Paula Nicols   All year

105-125-B&B
4 rooms, 4 pb
Visa, MC, *Rated*, •
C-ltd/S-no/P-no/H-no
Greek

Full gourmet breakfast
Refreshments
Sitting room, library, close to
boat rentals, fishing,
parasailing

Elegant c.1767 New England farmhouse. Special soaps, gels, robes. Ladies spa weekends.
Close to Rockland, Schooner-lobster capital, home of Wyeth Art. Shop Camden. Relax in
our hot tub/spa in its own teahouse.   E-mail: lakshore@midcoast.com
Web site: midcoast.com/~lakshore

Old Granite Inn
546 Main St, 04841
207-594-9036
Ragan & John Cary
All year

100-150-B&B
11 rooms, 8 pb
Visa, MC, •
C-ltd/S-no/P-no/H-yes

Bountiful breakfast
sitting room, library, garden,
piano

Comfortable, historic inn, overlooking a busy harbor filled with boats.   E-mail: ogi@
midcoast.com *Web site:* oldgraniteinn.com

SACO ──────────────────────────────
Crown 'N' Anchor Inn
PO Box 228, 04072
207-282-3829 Fax: 207-282-7495
800-561-8865
John Barclay/ Martha Forester
All year

65-120-B&B
6 rooms, 6 pb
Visa, MC, AmEx,
Rated, •
C-ltd/S-no/P-ltd/H-ltd
Some French

Full breakfast
Afternoon tea
Sitting room, library,
fireplaces, cable TV,
conference facilities

The Inn is a National Historic Register House situated on 3 acres in the heart of Saco
Historic District. Rooms are antique furnished and the Inn is close to many beaches. Barn
are recently converted to library and function room.   E-mail: cna@gwi.net

SEARSPORT ──────────────────────────────
Homeport Inn
PO Box 647, 04974
207-548-2259 Fax: 978-443-6682
800-742-5814
George & Edith Johnson
All year

55-100-B&B
11 rooms, 7 pb
Most CC, *Rated*, •
C-ltd/S-ltd/P-no/H-yes

Full breakfast
Soda fountain, garden,
antique shop, ocean view,
bicycles, golf, tennis

On Historic Register. Ideal mid-coast location for an extended stay on coast of Maine.
Victorian cottage available by the week.   E-mail: hportinn@acadia.net
Web site: bnbcity.com/inns/20015

SEARSPORT

Watchtide "B&B by the Sea"	95-145-B&B	Full gourmet breakfast
190 W Main St, 04974	4 rooms, 4 pb	Afternoon tea
207-548-6575	Visa, MC, Disc, •	Turndown, sitting room,
800-698-6575	C-ltd/S-no/P-no/H-no	library, barn
Nancy-Linn & Jack Elliott	Some French	antiques/giftshop, 60'
All year		sunporch

18th century inn features all season sunporch where breakfast is served overlooking Penobscot Bay. Serene and romantic with never ending seascape, flowers and birds on 3.5 panoramic oceanside acres.   E-mail: info@watchtide.com *Web site:* watchtide.com

SORRENTO

Bass Cove Farm B&B	50-80-B&B	Full breakfast
312 Eastside Rd, 04677	3 rooms, 1 pb	Library, porch, gardens,
207-422-3564 Fax: 207-422-3564	Visa, MC,	sitting room
Mary Solet & Michael Tansey	C-ltd/S-no/P-ltd	
All year		

Coastal Maine farmhouse in active summer colony. Convenient to Acadia National Park. Comfortable beds, delicious breakfast. Explore, shop, relax.   E-mail: basscove@downeast.net *Web site:* downeast.net/com/basscove

SOUTH WATERFORD

Bear Mountain Inn	90-250
Rt 35/37, 04081	10 rooms, 6 pb
207-583-4404 Fax: 207-583-4404	
Lorraine Blais	
All year	

Bear Mountain Inn is nestled on 52 acres of country charm. It's location is in Western Maine between the lakes and the mountains. Bear Mountain Inn's property includes 3 acres of private beachfront on Bear Lake.   E-mail: bearmtin@megalink.net *Web site:* bearmtninn.com

SOUTHWEST HARBOR

Harbour Cottage Inn	60-145-B&B	Full and continental
PO Box 258, 04679	8 rooms, 8 pb	breakfasts
207-244-5738 Fax: 207-244-7003	Most CC, *Rated*, •	Afternoon snacks
Glenda Sekulich	C-ltd/S no/P-no/H-no	Sitting room, piano,
All year		whirlpools, steam shower,
		breakfast also on deck

Harbour Cottage Inn is a quiet and elegant, but informal bed & breakfast, welcoming vicitors year-round. Renovations blend modern conveniences with historical architecture. E-mail: harbour@downeast.net *Web site:* downeast.net/com/harbour

Island House, The	60-145-B&B	Full breakfast
PO Box 1006, 04679	5 rooms, 5 pb	Breakfast for vegetarians
207-244-5180	*Rated*	Sitting room/fireplace,
Ann & Charlie Bradford	C-ltd/S-no/P-no	library, large garden, fishing
All year		docks, harbor

A gracious, restful, seacoast home on the quiet side of Mt. Desert Island. An efficiency apartment available. Near wharves; 5 min. to Acadia National Park.   E-mail: islandab@acadia.net *Web site:* acadia.net/island_house/

Kingsleigh Inn 1904, The	60-190-B&B	Full candlelight breakfast
PO Box 1426, 04679	8 rooms, 8 pb	Afternoon refreshments
207-244-5302 Fax: 207-244-7691	Visa, MC, *Rated*	Living room with fireplace,
Ken & Cyd Collins	C-ltd/S-no/P-no/H-no	library, wraparound porch
All year		

Cozy intimate inn overlooking the harbor. Filled with many antiques. Rooms with harbor views, 3 room suite with fireplace.   E-mail: info@kingsleighinn.com *Web site:* kingsleighinn.com

SOUTHWEST HARBOR

Lambs Ear Inn, The	85-175-B&B	Full breakfast
PO Box 30, 04679	6 rooms, 6 pb	Peace & quiet, sitting room,
207-244-9828 Fax: 207-244-9924	Visa, MC, *Rated*, •	room with priv. balcony
Elizabeth Hoke	C-ltd/S-no/P-no/H-ltd	
May 1-Oct. 1		

This comfortable and serene inn was built in 1857 in the village overlooking South West Harbor and surrounded by Acadia National Park.   E-mail: lambsear@acadia.net
Web site: acadia.net/lambsear

Penury Hall	85-B&B	Full breakfast
PO Box 68, 04679	3 rooms, 3 pb	Complimentary wine, coffee,
207-244-7102 Fax: 207-244-5651	C-ltd/S-no/P-no/H-no	tea
Toby & Gretchen Strong		Sitting room, sauna, picnic
All year		day sails, canoeing

Comfortable rambling Maine home for us and our guests. Decor reflects hosts' interests in art, antiques, books, gardening, sailing.   E-mail: tstrong@acadia.net
Web site: acadia.net/penury_n

SPRUCE HEAD

Craignair Inn	83-125-B&B	Continental plus breakfast
533 Clark Island Rd, 04859	16 rooms	Restaurant, coffee, tea
207-594-7644 Fax: 207-596-7124	Visa, MC, AmEx,	Full liquor service, library,
800-320-9997	*Rated*, •	flower garden, coastal
Neva & Steve Joseph	C-yes/S-no/P-yes/H-no	activities
All year		

Area alive with history of quarrying days. Extensive hiking. Delightful swimming in abandoned granite quarry.   E-mail: craignar@midcoast.com *Web site:* midcoast.com/~craignar/

TENANTS HARBOR

East Wind Inn, The	98-285-B&B	Full breakfast
PO Box 149, 04860	26 rooms, 12 pb	All meals, sitting room,
207-372-6366 Fax: 207-372-6320	Visa, MC, AmEx,	entertainment, piano,
800-241-VIEW	*Rated*, •	conference room for 30
Tim Watts & Jay Taylor	C-ltd/S-yes/P-ltd/H-ltd	
Closed Jan-March		

Resting at water's edge, The East Wind Inn offers spectacular views of the harbor & the island-studded waters beyond.   E-mail: info@eastwindinn.com *Web site:* eastwindinn.com

VINALHAVEN

Payne Homestead	75-100-B&B	Full breakfast
PO Box 216, 04863	4 rooms	Sitting room, cable TV, game
207-863-9963 Fax: 207-863-2295	C-yes/S-ltd/P-no/H-yes	room with video collection
888-863-9963		for children.
Lee & Donna Payne		
All year		

Step back in time and experience life as it ought to be...non-commercial and uncluttered. A wonderful combination of Victorianna and family comfort.   E-mail: payne@foxislands.net
Web site: bbonline.com/me/payne

WALDOBORO

Broad Bay Inn & Gallery	75-85-B&B	Full gourmet breakfast
PO Box 607, 04572	5 rooms, 3 pb	Wine
207-832-6668	Visa, MC, •	Library, cable TV,
800-736-6769	C-ltd/S-no/P-no/H-no	conference facilities
Libby Hopkins	French	
All year		

Center of small quiet village midcoast gives easy access to most of the interesting areas of Maine.   E-mail: brdbayin@midcoast.com *Web site:* obs-us.com/chesler/broadbayinn

YORK

Cape Neddick House, The	95-120-B&B	Full breakfast
PO Box 70, 03902	6 rooms, 6 pb	Complimentary wine, tea,
207-363-2500	*Rated*	coffee
Fax: 207-363-4499	C-ltd/S-ltd/P-no/H-no	Parlor & living room,
Dianne & John Goodwin		bicycles, guitar, trails,
All year		horseshoes, picnic area

Coastal country 4th-gen. Victorian home. Close to beach, antiques, outlets, boutiques.
E-mail: Jgood4499@aol.com *Web site:* capeneddickhouse.com

YORK HARBOR

Dockside Guest Quarters	130-185-EP	Continental plus (fee)
PO Box 205, 03909	21 rooms, 19 pb	Lunch, dinner, bar room
207-363-2868	Visa, MC, *Rated*, •	Restaurant, sitting room,
Fax: 207-363-1977	C-yes/S-no/P-no/H-ltd	porches, lawn games,
800-270-1977		marina, boat rentals, phones
The Lusty Family		
Weekends, Nov-May		

Unsurpassed location along edge of harbor. Tranquil, beautiful scenery abounds.
E-mail: info@docksidegq.com *Web site:* docksidegq.com

Inn at Harmon Park	79-109-B&B	Full breakfast
415 York St, 03911	5 rooms, 5 pb	Afternoon tea
207-363-2031 Fax: 207-351-2948	*Rated*, •	Sitting room, bicycles, suite
Sue Antal	C-ltd/S-no/P-no/H-no	with fireplace
All year		

Charming Victorian home close to harbor, beach & cliffwalk. Creative breakfasts, fresh
flowers, fireplaces & a warm, friendly atmosphere *E-mail:* santal@gwi.net
Web site: yorkme.org/inns/harmonpark.html

York Harbor Inn	89-249-B&B	Continental plus breakfast
PO Box 573, 03911	33 rooms, 33 pb	Lunch/dinner available, bar
207-363-5119 Fax: 207-363-7151	Most CC, *Rated*, •	Comp. soft drinks, rest.,
800-343 3869	C-yes/S-ltd/P-no/H-ltd	ocean swimming, sitt. rm,
Garry & Nancy Dominguez		outdoor hot tub, gazebo
All year		

Quiet, authentic country inn (c.1637) listed in National Register. Overlooks ocean & York
Harbor Beach. Oceanview rooms with decks. *E-mail:* garyinkeep@aol.com
Web site: yorkharborinn.com

Maryland

ANNAPOLIS

Barn on Howard's Cove, The	95-110-B&B	Full breakfast
500 Wilson Rd, 21401	2 rooms, 2 pb	Snacks
410-266-6840	*Rated*, •	Sitting room, near pool,
Graham & Libbie Gutsche	C-yes/S-no/P-no/H-no	tennis, dock, deep water
All year		docking avail

Minutes from Annapolis. 1850 restored horsebarn on Severn River; antiques, quilts, deep-
water docking, guestrooms overlooking water. *E-mail:* gdgutsche5@aol.com
Web site: bnbweb.com/howards-cove.html

ANNAPOLIS ─────────────────────────────

Chesapeake Waterfront B&B	99 and up-B&B	Continental plus breakfast
101 Swan Cove Ln, 21619	5 rooms, 5 pb	Snacks
410-757-0248 Fax: 410-757-0248	Visa, MC, *Rated*, •	300-foot pier, TV and game
Bill & Janice Costello	C-ltd/S-no/P-no/H-no	room, pool table, fishing
All year		

Located on the eastern shore of Maryland, the land of pleasant living. 15 miles from annapolis across the Chesapeake Bay Bridge, boat rentals for fishing or pleasure, walking distance to casual or formal restaurants.

Chez Amis B&B	105-130-B&B	Full breakfast
85 East St, 21401	4 rooms, 2 pb	Snacks
410-263-6631 Fax: 410-295-7889	Visa, MC, •	Complimentary wine, sitting
888-224-6455	C-ltd/S-no/P-no/H-no	room, "European-country"
Don & Mickie Deline		decor
All year		

Former circa 1900 grocery store, transformed into a B&B in 1989. Perfect location for enjoying historic area, harbor & Academy.　Web site: chezamis.com

Dolls' House B&B, The	115-125-B&B	Full breakfast
161 Green St, 21401	3 rooms, 3 pb	Parlor, flower garden, all
410-626-2028 Fax: 410-626-9884	*Rated*	bedrooms have private baths
Barbara & John Dugan	C-ltd/S-ltd/P-ltd	
Season Inquire		

Decorated in Victorian whimsy with furniture & decor true to that nostalgic time. The tiger oak woodwork, Georgia pine floors, brass & tile fireplaces, large windows reflect the Victorian period. TV.　E-mail: dugan@annapolis.net *Web site:* annapolis.net/dollshouse

Jonas Green House	105-140-B&B	Continental plus breakfast
124 Charles St, 21401	3 rooms, 1 pb	Complimentary wine
410-263-5892 Fax: 410-263-5892	Most CC, •	Sitting room, library library
Randy & Dede Brown	C-yes/S-no/P-yes/H-no	
All year	Danish	

Lovingly restored 1690s-1740s home; in innkeeper's family since 1738; genuine antiques; in center of historic district; off-street parking.　E-mail: jghouse@erols.com *Web site:* bbhost.com/jghouse

Mary Rob B&B	95-125-B&B	Full breakfast to order
243 Prince George St, 21401	2 rooms, 2 pb	Special diet requests, snacks
410-268-5438 Fax: 410-268-9623	Visa, MC, AmEx,	A/C, off street parking, fax,
Mary Stuart, Bob Carlson	C-ltd/S-no/P-no/H-no	copy mach., modem hookup,
All year		piano, bicycles, TV

Circa 1864 Victorian Italinate villa with tower. Furnished in antiques and in the heart of the Historic District. Walk to many fine restaurants, antique and decorator shops. Beds are queen size.

Scotlaur Inn	80-99-B&B	Full breakfast
165 Main St, 21401	10 rooms, 10 pb	Snacks, restaurant,
410-268-5665 Fax: 410-269-6738	Visa, MC, •	lunch/dinner
Ted & Beth Levitt	C-yes/S-no/P-ltd/H-no	Suites, accommodate
All year		business travelers.

The Scotlaur Inn is family owned. Our 10 beautifully decorated guest rooms are set in the heart of historic Annapolis with the look and feel of the early 1900s.　E-mail: tclmagic@ aol.com *Web site:* scotlaurinn.com

Two-O-One B&B	120-170-B&B	Full breakfast
201 Prince George St, 21401	4 rooms, 4 pb	Sitting room, library,
410-268-8053 Fax: 410-263-3007	Most CC,	Jacuzzis, suites, fireplace,
G. Gardner & R. Bryant	C-ltd/S-no/P-no/H-no	cable TV
All year		

English country house style, with fine period antiques, in the heart of Historic Annapolis. E-mail: BBat201@aol.com *Web site:* 201BB.com

William Page B&B Inn, Annapolis, MD

ANNAPOLIS

William Page B&B Inn	105-200-B&B	Full breakfast
8 Martin St, 21401	5 rooms, 3 pb	Afternoon tea
410-626-1506 Fax: 410-263-4841	Visa, MC, *Rated*, •	Sitting room, suites, Jacuzzis,
800-364-4160	C-ltd/S-no/P-no/H-no	cable TV
Robert L. Zuchelli		
All year		

1908 Historic District 5 guestroom Inn. Furnished in antiques and family collectibles. Quiet elegance within walking distance to historic sites. Off-street parking. Full breakfast. AAA & Mobil approved.   E-mail: wmpageinn@aol.com *Web site:* williampageinn

BALTIMORE

Abacromble Badger B&B	105-145-B&B	Continental plus breakfast
58 W Biddle St, 21201	12 rooms, 12 pb	Restaurant
410-244-7227 Fax: 410-244-8415	Most CC, *Rated*, •	Bar, sitting room, A/C,
Paul Bragaw	C-ltd/S-no/P-no/H-no	private phones, parlor, cable
All year	German, Dutch, French	TV

1880 house in the heart of Baltimore's Cultural Center. Walk to symphony, opera, museums, Antique Row. Near Inner Harbor. Streetcar line one block away.   E-mail: ABadger722@ aol.com *Web site:* badger-inn.com

Celie's Waterfront B&B	120-220-B&B	Continental plus breakfast
1714 Thames St, 21231	7 rooms, 7 pb	Refrigerators
410-522-2323 Fax: 410-522-2324	Most CC, *Rated*, •	Private phones/answering,
800-432-0184	C-ltd/S-no/P-no/H-yes	machines, cable TV, A/C,
Celie Ives		whirlpools, fireplaces
All year		

Urban inn in Fell's Point historic maritime community. Near Harbor Place, business district & Orioles Park by water taxi.   E-mail: celies@aol.com *Web site:* bbonline.com/md/celies/

Mr. Mole B&B	105-135-B&B	Continental plus breakfast
1601 Bolton St, 21217	5 rooms, 5 pb	Sitting room, A/C, garage
410-728-1179 Fax: 410-728-3379	Most CC, *Rated*, •	parking, parlor, phones,
Collin Clarke & Paul Bragaw	C-ltd/S-no/P-no/H-no	modem connection
All year		

Elegant and spacious 1870 Baltimore row house on historic Bolton Hill. "... decorated like a designer's showcase home ..." (The Discerning Traveler).   E-mail: MrMoleBB@aol.com

Merry Sherwood Plantation, Berlin, MD

BERLIN

Merry Sherwood Plantation	150-175-B&B	Full breakfast
108 Williams St, 21811	8 rooms, 5 pb	Afternoon tea
410-641-2112 Fax: 410-641-9528	Visa, *Rated*, •	Sitting room, library, bikes,
800-660-0358	C-ltd/S-no/P-no/H-no	Jacuzzi, suite, fireplace,
W. Kirk Burgabe		cable TV
All year		

An elegant c.1859 Victorian home restored to its former grandeur with gothic Italianate architectural additives. Relax on the wraparound verandah and view the lush gardens.
E-mail: info@merrysherwood.com *Web site:* merrysherwood.com

BETTERTON

Lantern Inn B&B	75-90-B&B	Continental plus breakfast
PO Box 29, 21610	13 rooms, 4 pb	Complimentary wine
410-348-5809 Fax: 410-348-2323	Visa, MC,	Beach & tennis, 2 blocks,
800-499-7265	C-ltd/S-no/P-no/H-no	sitting room, library
Ray & Sandi Sparks All year		

Small quiet town on Chesapeake Bay. One and one half hours from Philadelphia, Baltimore, D.C. Sandy beaches, great cycling, seafood, wildlife preserves, antiquing, tennis
E-mail: lanterninn@dmv.com

CHESAPEAKE CITY

Blue Max Inn B&B, The	80-130-B&B	Full breakfast
PO Box 30, 21915	7 rooms, 7 pb	Tea, snacks
410-885-2781 Fax: 410-885-2809	Most CC, *Rated*, •	Sitting room, library,
Wayne & Wendy Mercer	C-ltd/S-ltd/P-no/H-yes	Jacuzzis, fireplace, cable TV,
All year		conference

Located in the heart of town this elegant historic Inn offers charm and Southern hospitality. Seven luxurious rooms, private baths.   E-mail: bluemax@crosslink.net
Web site: bluemaxinn.com

Inn at the Canal	80-130-B&B	Full breakfast
PO Box 187, 21915	6 rooms, 6 pb	Complimentary iced tea,
410-885-5995 Fax: 410-885-3585	Most CC, *Rated*, •	cider
Mary & Al Ioppolo	C-ltd/S-no/P-no/H-no	Sitting room, porch, guests
All year		receive 10% discount our
		antique shop

Elegant waterside Victorian in quaint historic district on banks of Chesapeake and Delaware Canal. Fine shops and restaurants all within walking distance.
Web site: chesapeakecity.com/innatthecanal/inn.htm

CHESTERTOWN

Brampton Inn	125-195-B&B	Full breakfast
25227 Chestertown Rd, 21620	10 rooms, 10 pb	Complimentary wine,
410-778-1860 Fax: 410-778-1805	Visa, MC, *Rated*	afternoon tea
Michael & Danielle Hanscom	C-ltd/S-no/P-no/H-ltd	Sitting room, library,
All year	French, German	bicycles, one suite, one room
		sleeps 4

1860 National Register manor house. 35-acre estate one mile south of historic Chestertown. Luxurious rooms, furnished in antiques and with woodburning fireplaces.
E-mail: innkeeper@bramptoninn.com *Web site:* bramptoninn.com

Great Oak Manor B&B	75-175-B&B	Continental plus breakfast
10568 Cliff Rd, 21620	11 rooms, 11 pb	Afternoon tea, snacks
410-778-5943 Fax: 410-778-5943	Visa, MC, •	Sitting room, library,
800-504-3098	S-ltd/P-no/H-no	bicycles, tennis, swimming
Don & Dianne Cantor		pool
April 1-Feb.15		

Historic manor house set on 12 acres at the water's edge of the Chesapeake Bay on Maryland's eastern shore. Executive 9 hole golf course next door. *E-mail:* innkeeper@ greatoak.com *Web site:* greatoak.com

White Swan Tavern, The	110-185-B&B	Continental plus breakfast
231 High St, 21620	5 rooms, 5 pb	Complimentary wine,
410-778-2300 Fax: 410-778-4543	Visa, MC, *Rated*	evening sherry
Mary Susan Maisel	C-yes/S-yes/P-no/H-ltd	Comp. fruit basket, sitting
All year		room, bicycles, terrace,
		garden, tea room

18th-century inn nestled in Maryland's historic eastern shore. Genuine antiques, home-made continental breakfast, tea, complimentary wine & fruit. *Web site:* chestertown.com

CUMBERLAND

Inn at Walnut Bottom, The	81-125-B&B	Full breakfast
120 Greene St, 21502	12 rooms, 10 pb	Full service restaurant
301-777-0003 Fax: 301-777-8288	Most CC, *Rated*, •	Afternoon refreshments,
800-286-9718	C-yes/S-no/P-no/H-ltd	sitting room, in-room TV,
Kirsten Hansen & Grant Irvin		telephones, bicycles
All year		

Charming traditional country inn. Beautiful mtn. town with scenic railroad, historic district, extraordinary hiking, sight-seeing. Fine restaurant. *E-mail:* iwb@hereintown.net
Web site: iwbinfo.com

DEEP CREEK LAKE

Carmel Cove Inn	100-160-B&B	Full breakfast
PO Box 644, 21550	10 rooms, 10 pb	Snacks, complimentary wine
301-387-0067	Most CC, •	Sitting room, bikes, tennis,
Ed Spak	C-ltd/S-ltd/P-no/H-no	hot tubs, skiing, fireplaces,
All year	Some French & German	dock, canoes

Deep Creek Lake's premier country inn. Tranquil wooded setting. Canoe, fish, swim from our dock. *E-mail:* carmelcove@aol.com *Web site:* carmelcoveinn.com

EASTON

Bishop's House B&B, The	110-120-B&B	Full breakfast
PO Box 2217, 21601	6 rooms, 5 pb	Complimentary wine &
410-820-7290 Fax: 410-820-7290	*Rated*, •	beverages
800-223-7290	C-ltd/S-no/P-no/H-no	Sitting rooms, bikes, A/C,
Diane Laird & John Ippolito		whirlpool tubs, fireplaces,
All year		parking

Historic District c.1880 in town Victorian. Romantically furnished in period style. An excellent location for visiting all points of interest. 2 night minimum stay. *E-mail:* bishopshouse@ skipjack.bluecrab.org

FREDERICK ────────────────────────────────

Middle Plantation Inn	90-110-B&B	Continental plus breakfast
9549 Liberty Rd, 21701	4 rooms, 4 pb	Afternoon tea (Tues-Thur),
301-898-7128	Visa, MC, *Rated*, •	fee
Shirley & Dwight Mullican	C-ltd/S-no/P-no/H-no	Sitting room, garden, hen
All year		house, brook, four golf
		courses nearby

A charming stone and log B&B, furnished with antiques, television and A/C. In room phones avail. Near Gettysburg, Antietam, Harper's Ferry, Washington D.C., and Baltimore. E-mail: bandb@mpinn.com *Web site:* mpinn.com

Spring Bank—A B&B Inn	85-100-B&B	Continental plus breakfast
7945 Worman's Mill Rd, 21701	5 rooms, 1 pb	Double parlors, library, view
301-694-0440	Most CC, *Rated*, •	from observatory, 10 acres
800-400-INNS	C-ltd/S-no/P-no/H-no	for roaming
Beverly & Ray Compton		
All year		

On National Register of Historic Places. Antiques. Near Baltimore, Washington, D.C., and Civil War battlefields. Exceptional dining in Frederick Historic District 2 mi. away. E-mail: rcomp1880@aol.com *Web site:* bbonline.com/md/springbank

Stone Manor	150-275-B&B	Continental plus breakfast
5820 Carroll Boyer Rd, 21769	6 rooms, 6 pb	Lunch/dinner available
301-473-5454 Fax: 301-371-5622	Most CC, *Rated*	Snacks, restaurant, sitting
Judith V. Harne	C-ltd/S-no/P-no/H-yes	room, library, fireplaces,
All year		whirlpools

Savor the magic of exceptional cuisine, luxurious suites, and 18th-century charm in this 114-acre country estate. E-mail: themanor@stonemanor.com *Web site:* stonemanor.com

GRANTSVILLE ────────────────────────────────

Walnut Ridge B&B	75-125-B&B	Full breakfast
PO Box 368, 21536	4 rooms, 4 pb	Snacks
301-895-4248 Fax: 301-895-4054	Visa, MC, *Rated*, •	Hot tub, Sitting room, Videos,
888-419-2568	C-ltd/S-no/P-yes/H-ltd	Fireplaces, Cable TV, Suites
Tim & Candace Fetterly		
All year		

Find refuge and romance in western Maryland. Quiet charm and grace will greet you! Wrap up in comfort. E-mail: walnutridge@usa.net *Web site:* walnutridge.net

HAGERSTOWN ────────────────────────────────

Beaver Creek House B&B	75-95-B&B	Full breakfast
20432 Beaver Creek Rd, 21740	5 rooms, 5 pb	Afternoon tea, snacks
301-797-4764 Fax: 301-797-4976	Visa, MC, AmEx,	Hiking, antiquing, sitting
888-942-9966	*Rated*, •	room, library, restaurants
Don & Shirley Day	C-ltd/S-no/P-no/H-no	nearby
All year		

Country Victorian home filled with family antiques & memorabilia. Full country breakfast served on screened porch. Hiking, Civil War battlefields nearby. Web site: bbonline.com/md/beavercreek

HAVRE DE GRACE ────────────────────────────────

Vandiver Inn	85-150-B&B	Full breakfast
301 S Union Ave, 21078	9 rooms, 9 pb	2 rooms private porch &
410-939-5200 Fax: 410-939-5202	Most CC, *Rated*, •	entrance, gazebo, large front
Suzanne T. Mottek	C-ltd/S-ltd/P-no/H-yes	porch, phones in room
All year		

1886 Victorian mansion. Surrounded by historic sites, antiquing, museums, marinas. Dinner served on Friday & Saturday evenings. 2 blocks from Chesapeake Bay. E-mail: innkeeper@vandiverinn.com *Web site:* vandiverinn.com

KEEDYSVILLE

Antietam Overlook Farm	115-165-B&B	Full breakfast
PO Box 30, 21756	5 rooms, 5 pb	Complimentary wine,
301-432-4200 Fax: 301-432-5230	Most CC, *Rated*	chocolates
800-878-4241	C-ltd/S-no/P-no/H-no	After dinner drinks, sitting
John & Barbara Dreisch		room, library, large front
All year		porch

Extraordinary 95-acre mountaintop farm with four-state view at Antietam National Battle-field. Yesterday's architecture—today's comfort. Sumptuous breakfast.
E-mail: antietamoverlookfarm@erols.com

OCEAN CITY

Atlantic House B&B	75-225-B&B	Full breakfast
501 N Baltimore Ave, 21842	12 rooms, 8 pb	Snacks, afternoon tea
410-289-2333 Fax: 410-289-2430	Most CC, •	Sitting room, bicycles,
Paul Cook & Debi Thompson	C-ltd/S-ltd/P-no/H-no	swimming pool, suites, cable
Presidents'-Columbus day		TV

Comfort convenience, and service provided by knowledgeable life long resident with a breakfast to excite and ocean sunsets to remember. Atlantic House is "your house at the beach." E-mail: ocbnb@Atlantichouse.com *Web site:* atlantichouse.com

Inn on the Ocean, An	150-300-B&B	Continental plus breakfast
1001 Atlantic Ave, 21842	6 rooms, 6 pb	Snacks, comp. wine
410-289-8894 Fax: 410-289-8215	Most CC, *Rated*	Sitting room, bicycles,
888-226-6223	S-no/P-no/H-no	Jacuzzis, fireplaces, cable,
The Barrett's		children over 16 only
All year		

A deluxe, romantic, magnificently restored oceanfront B&B/Inn. Oceanfront wraparound verandah. Fireplace in winter. Jacuzzis. Romantic getaways, weddings, special occasions, corporate meetings. E-mail: innonoc@aol.com *Web site:* innontheocean.com

OXFORD

Robert Morris Inn	110-240-EP	All meals available
PO Box 70, 21654	35 rooms, 35 pb	Restaurant, bar service, non-
410-226-5111 Fax: 410-226-5744	Visa, MC, AmEx,	smoking inn, private beach
Jay Gibson	*Rated*, •	
April-November	C-ltd/S-no/P-no/H-ltd	

Historic Chesapeake Bay romantic inn. Featuring the best crab cakes on the eastern shore. Tennis, fishing, boating, golfing nearby. Web site: robertmorrisinn.com

PRINCE FREDERICK

Cliff House B&B, The	95-120-B&B	Full breakfast
PO Box 2085, 20678	1 rooms	Afternoon tea
410-535-4839	C-ltd/S-no/P-no/H-no	Sitting room, Jacuzzis, Suites,
C. J. Ferrandino	German	Cable TV, Accommodate
All year		business travelers

A home away from home. The Cliff House is an intimate private house high on a cliff with a spectacular view of the Chesapeake Bay. The comfortable and cozy air-conditioned suite overlooks the water. E-mail: cferrand@chesapeake.net *Web site:* bbonline.com/md/cliffhouse

SALISBURY

Waterloo Country Inn	125-225-B&B	Full gourmet breakfast
28822 Mt Vernon Blvd, 21853	5 rooms, 5 pb	Restaurant on premises,
410-651-0883 Fax: 410-651-5592	Visa, MC, AmEx,	snacks
Erwin & Theresa Kraemer	*Rated*, •	A/C, bikes, golf nearby,
March-Dec.	C-ltd/S-no/P-ltd/H-yes	outdoor pool, lounge, canoes
	German, French, Italian	on property

Beautiful, historic, breathtaking, relaxing & fulfilling Eastern Shore 1750s waterfront estate with elegant & comfortable rooms. Canoes, bikes. Nestled close to beach. Golfer's paradise. Restaurant on premises. E-mail: innkeeper@waterloocountryinn.com
Web site: waterloocountryinn.com

SHARPSBURG

Inn at Antietam
PO Box 119, 21782
301-432-6601
Charles Van Metre, Bob
LeBlanc
Exc. Dec 20-Jan 2

55-B&B
5 rooms, 5 pb
AmEx, •
C-ltd/S-ltd/P-no/H-no

Continental plus breakfast
Afternoon tea
Sitting room, piano, bicycles

Lovely 1908 Victorian fully restored and furnished in antiques, on Antietam Battlefield in Civil War historic area. Special hospitality. Web site: bbonline.com/md/mbba/sharpsburg.html

SNOW HILL

River House Inn
201 E Market St, 21863
410-632-2722 Fax: 410-632-2866
Larry & Susanne Knudsen
All year

120-205-B&B
8 rooms, 8 pb
Most CC, *Rated*, •
C-yes/S-no/P-ltd/H-yes

Full breakfast
Lunch/dinner available,
snacks
Comp. wine/tea, porches,
A/C, fishing, boating, country
club golf, bikes

*Come relax at our elegant 1860s riverfront country home in historic Snow Hill. Canoe or bike inn-to-inn. Enjoy Maryland's eastern shore, beaches, bayou, AARP.
E-mail:* innkeeper@riverhouseinn.com *Web site:* riverhouseinn.com

SOLOMONS

Solomons Victorian Inn
PO Box 759, 20688
410-326-4811 Fax: 410-326-0133
Helen & Richard Bauer
All year

90-175-B&B
8 rooms, 8 pb
Rated
C-ltd/S-no/P-no/H-no

Full breakfast
Boating, shops, hiking, 3
rooms w/whirlpool tubs,
restaurants nearby

Let the Chesapeake romance you from the porch of this charming Queen Anne Victorian. Convenient to Washington, Baltimore, and Richmond. Wonderful water views from most rooms   E-mail: solvictinn@chesapeake.net *Web site:* chesapeake.net/solomonsvictorianinn

ST. MICHAELS

Barrett's B&B Inn
PO Box 279, 21663
410-745-3322 Fax: 410-745-3888
Jim & Lin Barrett
All year

180-250-B&B
7 rooms, 7 pb
Most CC, *Rated*, •
S-no/P-no/H-ltd

Full gourmet breakfast
Snacks
Tea Room, Jacuzzis,
fireplaces, cable TV, gift
shop, espresso bar

Double Jacuzzi tub in front of fireplace, priv. bathroom, candles, fresh flowers, hand-made quilts, cable TV, central air, queen beds, shopping, boating, golf, biking, espresso bar, snacks, tea room   E-mail: JWBarrett@yahoo.com *Web site:* barrettbb.com

Chesapeake Wood Duck Inn
PO Box 202, 21671
410-886-2070 Fax: 410-886-2263
800-956-2070
Stephanie & Dave Feith
All year

139-219-B&B
7 rooms, 7 pb
Visa, MC, *Rated*, •
S-no/P-no/H-no

Full gourmet breakfast
Afternoon tea, snacks
Sitting rooms, frplcs., sun
rm., bikes, kayaking, nearby
restaurants

*Award winning waterfront B&B. "It's hard to imagine a more perfect place for a romantic rendezvous."—New York Post. "Unforgetable"—Innspots.
E-mail:* wooduck@bluecrab.org *Web site:* wooduckinn.com

Kemp House Inn
PO Box 638, 21663
410-745-2243
Steve & Diane Cooper
All year

85-115-B&B
8 rooms, 6 pb
Visa, MC, *Rated*, •
C-yes/S-yes/P-yes/H-no

Continental plus breakfast
Bicycles, queen-sized beds,
private cottage available

1805 Georgian house with four-poster beds and working fireplaces in historic eastern shore village; close to restaurants, museums, harbor.

ST. MICHAELS

Parsonage Inn	100-185-B&B	Full gourmet breakfast
210 N Talbot (Rt 33), 21663	8 rooms, 8 pb	Afternoon tea at 4pm
410-745-5519 Fax: 410-745-6869	Visa, MC, *Rated*, •	Parlor with books & menus,
800-394-5519	C-ltd/S-no/H-yes	spec. order wine/cheese, or
Walt & Jane Johnson		flower arrangements
All year		

Unique brick Victorian, part of historic district. Walking distance to maritime museums. Bikes available. Cable TV in parlor, rooms #6 & #8. Laura Ashley linens. 8% sales tax added to room rates. E-mail: parsinn@dmv.com Web site: parsonage-inn.com

TAKOMA PARK

Davis Warner Inn, The	75-125-B&B	Full breakfast
8114 Carroll Ave, 20912	4 rooms, 1 pb	Afternoon tea
301-408-3989 Fax: 301-408-4840	Visa, MC,	Sitting room, library,
Robert Patenaude	C-yes/S-ltd/P-ltd/H-no	Jacuzzis, fireplace,
All year		bikes/golf/tennis/trails

An elegant and fully restored Victorian mansion, the Davis Warner Inn is widely known for its gourmet breakfasts, featherbeds and hospitality. E-mail: davisinn@ibm.net Web site: bbonline.com/md/daviswarner

TANEYTOWN

Glenburn B&B	85-110-B&B	Full breakfast
3515 Runnymede Rd, 21787	3 rooms, 2 pb	Refrigerator, kitchen
410-751-1187	•	2 bedroom cottage with
Robert & Elizabeth Neal	C-yes/S-ltd/P-no/H-no	kitchen, swimming pool,
All year		porches, golf, A/C

Georgian house with Victorian addition, antique furnishings, featured in Maryland House & Garden Pilgrimage. Historic rural area close to Gettysburg.

TILGHMAN ISLAND

Black Walnut Point Inn	135-175-B&B	Continental plus breakfast
PO Box 308, 21671	7 rooms, 7 pb	Screened porches with rock
410-886-2452 Fax: 410-886-2053	*Rated*	rocking chairs, 57-acre
Brenda and Tom Ward	S-ltd/P-no/H-yes	wildlife reserve
All year		

The inn at the end of the road. Key West sunsets. Hammocks by the bay. Quiet and peaceful. Fishing. E-mail: mward@shore.intercom.net Web site: tilghmanisland.com/blackwalnut

VIENNA

Tavern House, The	70-75-B&B	Full breakfast
PO Box 98, 21869	3 rooms	Afternoon tea,
410-376-3347	Visa, MC, •	complimentary wine
Harvey & Elise Altergott	C-ltd/S-yes	Sitting room, tennis courts
All year	Spanish, German	nearby, 1830s grand piano

Restored Colonial tavern on Nanticoke River. Simple elegance; stark whites, detailed woodwork. Looking out over river and marshes. Great for bicycling and bird-watching.

WHITEHAVEN

Whitehaven B&B	75-100-B&B	Full breakfast
23844 River St, 21856	5 rooms, 3 pb	Complimentary wine, snacks
410-873-3294 Fax: 410-873-2162	Most CC,	Sitting rooms, library, cable
888-205-5921	C-ltd/S-ltd/P-no/H-ltd	TV, 1830s grand piano
Maryen, Carlton, Mark Herrett		
All year		

19th century charm in tiny, historic village, scenic, all rooms water view, lovely country Victorian furnishings with luxurious linens and baths, delicious food. Come be pampered. E-mail: whavenbb@dmv.com Web site: whitehaven.com/

WITTMAN ————————————————————————

Inn at Christmas Farm	110-205-B&B	Full farm breakfast
8873 Tilghman Isl. Rd, 21676	6 rooms, 6 pb	Golf/tennis/bicycling,
410-745-5312 Fax: 410-745-5618	*Rated*, •	catering/cookouts,
800-987-8436		magnificent birding, AC,
Beatrice & David Lee		Jacuzzis
Season Inquire		

50 acre waterfront farm with restored farmhouse and St. James chapel near St. Michaels. Enjoy our "toy farm," stroll along Cummings Creek, enjoy sitting beside our spring fed pond. New trail along shoreline for walking, jogging, bridwatching.
Web site: innatchristmasfarm.com

Massachusetts

AMHERST ————————————————————————

Allen House Victorian Inn	55-135-B&B	Full breakfast
599 Main St, 01002	7 rooms, 7 pb	Afternoon tea
413-253-5000	*Rated*	Evening refreshments, sitting
Alan & Ann Zieminski	C-ltd/S-no/P-no/H-no	room, library, veranda,
All year		gardens, A/C

Authentic 1886 stick-style Victorian on 3 acres. Spacious bed chambers, personal phones with modems, ceiling fans and central air conditioning.   E-mail: allenhouse@webtv.net
Web site: allenhouse.com

Lord Jeffery Inn, The	69-158-B&B	no
30 Boltwood Ave, 01002	48 rooms, 48 pb	Restaurant (lunch/dinner)
413-253-2576 Fax: 413-256-6152	Most CC, *Rated*, •	bar serv.
800-742-0358	C-yes/S-yes/P-yes/H-yes	Sitting room, suites,
Michael Maderia		fireplaces, cable TV,
All year		accommodate business
		travelers.

The perfect setting for a romantic getaway, casual lunch, Sunday jazz brunch, intimate dining, family reunion, garden party, or business function.
Web site: pinnacle-inns.com/lordjefferyinn/

BELCHERTOWN ————————————————————————

B&B at Ingate Farms	60-90-B&B	Continental plus breakfast
60 Lamson Ave, 01007	5 rooms, 3 pb	Afternoon tea, snacks
413-253-0440 Fax: 413-253-0440	Visa, MC, AmEx,	Sitting rooms, library,
888-INGATEBB	*Rated*, •	swimming pool, antique
V. Keir & B. McCormick	C-yes/S-no/P-no/H-no	rocking chairs
All year		

250 yr-old converted bobbin factory in secluded valley on 500 acres; Olympic-sized pool. Indoor equestrian center, riding lessons. 5 major colleges nearby. Whole house/business/extended stay discounts.

BERKSHIRES ————————————————————————

Chambery Inn	75-275-B&B	Continental plus breakfast
199 Main St, 01238	9 rooms, 9 pb	Adjacent restaurant
413-243-2221 Fax: 413-243-0039	Most CC, *Rated*	Adjacent bar, TV, spa,
800-537-4321	S-no/P-no/H-yes	fireplace, refrigerator,
Lynn Toole All year		Jacuzzi for two

1885 restoration masterpiece with 500 sq. ft. suites, king canopy beds, fireplaces whirlpool baths. Sumptuous breakfast, impeccable facilities. 1997 Editor's Pick Travel Guide to New England.   E-mail: chambery@javanet.com *Web site:* berkshireinns.com

BERKSHIRES

Devonfield
85 Stockbridge Rd, 01238
413-243-3298 Fax: 413-243-1360
800-664-0880
Sally & Ben Schenck
All year

100-260-B&B
10 rooms, 10 pb
Visa, MC, AmEx,
Rated, •
C-ltd/S-ltd/P-no/H-no

Full breakfast
Guest pantry
Heated pool, tennis, bicycles,
lawn sports, sitting room, ski
area

Historic Revolutionary setting, heated pool, golf, tennis, luxury, comfort, local fine restaurants. Comp. breakfast. Relax in Old World charm   E-mail: innkeeper@devonfield.com
Web site: devonfield.com

Ramblewood Inn
PO Box 729, 01257
413-229-3363 Fax: 413-229-3363
800-854-1862
June & Martin Ederer
All year

95-145-B&B
7 rooms, 5 pb
Visa, MC, *Rated*
C-ltd/S-no/P-no/H-ltd

Full breakfast
Afternoon tea
Sitting room, bicycles, tennis
court, suites, fireplaces,
cable TV

A country inn with style, Ramblewood is nestled among the pines, the mountain, and a serene, spring-fed lake, yet convenient to all the scenic and cultural attractions which make the Berkshires famous.   E-mail: info@ramblewoodinn.com *Web site:* ramblewoodinn.com

Weathervane Inn
PO Box 388, 01258
413-528-9580 Fax: 413-528-1713
800-528-9580
Maxine & Jeffrey Lome
All year

135-245-B&B/MAP
10 rooms, 10 pb
Visa, MC, AmEx, *Rated*
C-yes/S-no/P-no/H-ltd

Full breakfast
Afternoon tea, bar service
Sitting room, library, pool, 2
suites, fireplaces, cable TV

The Inn began in 1785 as a farmhouse and today sits on 10 beautifully landscaped acres of gardens and trees. Featuring 10 period-appointed bedrooms all with private baths. E-mail: innkeeper@weathervaneinn.com *Web site:* weathervaneinn.com

BLANDFORD

Baird Tavern B&B
2 Old Chester Rd, 01008
413-848-2096
Carolyn Taylor
All year

60-75-B&B
3 rooms
C-yes/S-no/P-no/H-no

Full breakfast
Snacks
Sitting room, fireplaces,
accommodate business
travelers, woodstove

Historic country home built in 1768 and originally a tavern. Flower gardens, home grown blueberries, fireplaces, antiques.   Web site: hamphillsbandb.com/bairdtavern

BOSTON

Anthony's Town House
1085 Beacon St, 02446
617-566-3972 Fax: 617-232-1085
Barbara A. Anthony
All year

75-95-EP
14 rooms
Rated, •
C-yes/S-yes/P-no/H-no

Restaurant/stores nearby
Near major league sports, all
hospitals, sitt. rm., historical
sites, TV

Turn-of-the-century Brownstone townhouse; spacious rooms in Victorian atmosphere; family-operated for over 50 years; on trolley line, 10 min. to Boston

B&B in Cambridge, A
1657 Cambridge St #3, 02138
617-868-7082 Fax: 617-876-8991
800-795-7122
Doane Perry & Family
All year

125-180-B&B
3 rooms
Visa, MC, AmEx, •
C-ltd/S-no/P-no/H-no
Fr.,Ger., Greek, Swahili

Continental plus breakfast
Aftn. tea, snacks, wine
Sitting room, library,
swimming pool, cable TV

1897 Colonial Revival home, close to Harvard Square, affordable elegance near museums, theaters, restaurants. Fresh flowers, antiques, great beds, afternoon tea, homebaked specialties, rocking chairs.   E-mail: doaneperry@compuserve.com *Web site:* cambridgebnb.com

BOSTON

Beacon Hill B&B
27 Brimmer St, 02108
617-523-7376
Susan Butterworth
All year

160-250-B&B
3 rooms, 3 pb
•
C-ltd/S-no/P-no/H-no
French

Full breakfast
Restaurants nearby
Sitting room, garage nearby,
two rooms with queen beds

1869 Victorian townhouse. Fireplaces, riverview. Gas-lit, historically preserved downtown neighborhood. Boston Common, "Cheers" bar, Freedom Trail, Convention Center easy walk. All rooms have double or queen sofabeds. E-mail: BHillBB@aol.com

Beech Tree Inn
83 Longwood Ave, 02446
617-277-1620 Fax: 617-277-0657
800-544-9660
All year

135-155-B&B
11 rooms, 7 pb
Visa, MC, AmEx, •
C-yes/S-no/P-yes/H-no

Continental breakfast
Snacks
Sitting room, cable TV, tennis
courts nearby, historical
sites, TV

Victorian style b&b boasts individually decorated guest rooms, all with phones and A/C. Enjoy downtown Boston via nearby trolley. A pleasant interlude at affordable prices E-mail: btinn83ave@aol.com

Bertram Inn, The
92 Sewall Avenue, 02446
617-566-2234 Fax: 617-277-1887
800-295-3822
Bryan Austin
All year

104-249-B&B
14 rooms, 14 pb
Most CC, *Rated*, •
C-ltd/S-no/P-yes/H-no
Spanish, German, Fr., It.

Continental plus breakfast
Afternoon tea, snacks
Iron & board, hairdryers in
all rooms, A/C, fax on
premises

Come home to Victorian elegance. Ten minutes to Boston by trolley. Furnished with period antiques. Hearty continental breakfast. Parking included. E-mail: bertraminn@msn.com *Web site:* bertraminn.com

Cambridge House, B&B Inn, A
2218 Massachusetts Ave, 02140
617-491-6300 Fax: 617-868-2848
800-232-9989
Ellen Riley
All year

129-275-B&B
16 rooms, 14 pb
Most CC, *Rated*, •
C-ltd/S-no/P-no/H-no
Italian

Full breakfast
Comp. hors d'oeuvres
Lemonade, coffee, tea,
cookies & brownies, sitt. rm,
voice mail/fax

Urban inn close to Harvard Square in Cambridge. "Boston's finest gem"—Country Inns Magazine; "Boston's premier B&B"—BBC; "Our vote goes to Cambridge House"—L.A. Times E-mail: innach@aol.com *Web site:* acambridgehouse.com

Diamond District Inn
142 Ocean St, 01902
781-599-4470 Fax: 781-599-2200
800-666-3076
Sandra & Jerry Caron
All year

120-250-B&B
11 rooms, 7 pb
Most CC, *Rated*, •
C-ltd/S-no/P-ltd

Full breakfast
Afternoon tea, snacks
Overlooks garden & ocean,
library, home-cooked low fat,
vegetarian food

1911 clapboard mansion. Gracious foyer, grand staircase winding up three floors. Firepalce living room. E-mail: diamonddistrict@msn.com *Web site:* diamonddistrictinn.com

Golden Slipper B&B
PO Box 251, 02055
781-545-2845
Gretchen & Jack Stephenson
May 1-October 31

145-B&B
1 rooms, 1 pb
•
C-yes/S-ltd/P-no/H-no

Continental breakfast

Golden Slipper, Boston's afloat is a 1960 40' Chris Craft located in the heart of historical Boston accommodating up to 4 people. The boat stays at Lewis Wharf, a very secure dock, and you are within walking distance of many attractions.

BOSTON ─────────────────────────────────

Harding House
288 Harvard St, 02139
617-876-2888 Fax: 617-497-0953
Rachael Solem/Jane Jones
All year

99-219-B&B
14 rooms, 14 pb
Visa, MC, AmEx,
C-yes/S-no/P-no/H-yes

Continental plus breakfast
Afternoon tea
Sitting room, voice mail, fax

Located within an easy walk of Harvard Square, Harding House offers quiet, friendly charm in its 14 rooms on a tree-lined residential street.   Web site: irvinghouse.com

Irving House
24 Irving St, 02138
617-547-4600
Fax: 617-576-2814
877-547-4600
Patsy Yike
All year

70-250-B&B
29 rooms, 15 pb
Visa, MC, AmEx,
Rated, •
C-yes/S-no/P-ltd/H-yes
Swahili, Hindi

Continental plus breakfast
Sitting room, library, cribs,
central A/C, fax, laundry,
conference room

Friendly accommodations in the heart of Cambridge. Off-street parking. 10 min. walk to Harvard Square. Children under 7 free. I. Harding House opens in 98.   E-mail: reserve@ irvinghouse.com Web site: irvinghouse.com

Joan's B&B
210R Lynn St, 01960
978-532-0191
Joan Hetherington
All year

65-85-B&B
3 rooms, 1 pb
C-ltd/S-no/P-no/H-no

Continental plus breakfast
Afternoon tea, snacks
Sitting room, patio,
swimming pool, laundry, use
of whole house

Located 10 min. from historic Salem, 25 min. from Boston, and 25 min. from picturesque Gloucester and Rockport. All the rooms have A/C. Small basement apartment available for longer stays.

Mary Prentiss Inn, The
6 Prentiss St, 02472
617-661-2929 Fax: 617-661-5989
Nicholas & Jennifer Fandetti
Season Inquire

109-229-B&B
18 rooms, 18 pb
Visa, MC, AmEx, •
C-yes/S-no/P-no/H-yes

Full breakfast
Afternoon tea, snacks
Sitting room, large, outdoor
deck, laundry, conference
room

Historic house in neoclassical Greek Revival style. Rooms furnished with genuine antiques. Complimentary cookies every afternoon; homemade jams. Near Harvard Square. E-mail: njfandetti@aol.com Web site: maryprentissinn.com

Oasis Guest House
22 Edgerly Rd, 02115
617-267-2262 Fax: 617-267-1920
All year

89-119-B&B
16 rooms, 10 pb
Visa, MC, AmEx, •
C-ltd/S-ltd/P-no/H-no

Continental breakfast
Snacks
Sitting room, cable TV, fax
capabilities

Two townhouses in the heart of Boston. Telephone, televisions, central air, outdoor decks, parking on a quiet residential street. Just a few steps to everything Boston has to offer. E-mail: oasisgh@tiac.net Web site: oasisgh.com

Park Lane B&B
11 Park Lane, 02459
617-964-1666 Fax: 617-964-8588
800-772-6759
Pat & Jim
All year

60-95-B&B
3 rooms, 1 pb
Visa, MC, AmEx, •
C-yes/S-ltd/P-no/H-no

Continental breakfast
Fresh bread
Sitting room, bikes, Jacuzzi,
cable TV, room seats 20
people

A 10 minute walk to Newton Centre T Station (high speed light rail) in a quiet tree-lined neighborhood.   E-mail: pranpran@juno.com Web site: bostonapts.com/parklane

BOSTON

Taylor House B&B	89-155-B&B	Continental plus breakfast
50 Burroughs St, 02130	3 rooms, 3 pb	Snacks
617-983-9334 Fax: 617-522-3852	Most CC,	TV/VCR in room, tape,
888-228-2956	C-ltd/S-no/P-yes/H-no	library, common room,
Dave Elliott		modem access, phones
All year		

Italiante Victorian home with spacious rooms, high ceilings, private baths, near public transportation, restaurants & shopping. E-mail: dave@taylorhouse.com *Web site:* taylorhouse.com

Vine & Ivy	100-150-B&B	Full breakfast
212 Hart St, 01915	3 rooms, 2 pb	Tea, snacks
978-927-2917 Fax: 978-927-4610	Most CC, •	Sitting room, pool, suites,
800-975-5516	C-ltd/S-ltd/P-no/H-no	fireplace, cable TV,
James Cletus Glesener	French, Greek	courtyard
All year		

Turn of the century equestrian estate turned into a Bed and Breakfast. True New England charm with many extras such as swimming pool. Near Boston on the North Shore. Complimentary port wine in room. E-mail: antoniou@compuserve.com *Web site:* vineandivy.com

Well-Feathered Nest B&B	70-125-B&B	Full breakfast
119 Kent St, 02066	4 rooms, 4 pb	Sitting room, library
781-545-5591	Visa, MC, AmEx,	
Terry Stephens	C-ltd/S-ltd/P-no/H-no	
All year		

Our 1872 home features a wrap-around porch. Featherbeds offer a sound night's sleep. Breakfast in the chandeliered dining room is a highlight of the day.

BREWSTER

Beechcroft Inn	85-105-B&B	Full breakfast
1360 Main St, 02631	10 rooms, 10 pb	Restaurant
508-896-9534 Fax: 508-896-8812	Most CC, *Rated*, •	Bar service, sitting room,
877-233-2446	C-yes/S-no/P-no/H-no	bicycles, fireplaces, cable TV
Bob & Celeste Hunt		
All year		

Nestled among stately beech trees and surrounded by the traditional privet hedge, Beechcroft Inn offers the hospitality and warmth that reflects over a 140 year tradition so much admired in the small New England Inn. Web site: beechcroftinn.com

BROOKLINE

Beacon Inn	79-B&B	Continental breakfast
665 Salem St, 02146	25 rooms, 6 pb	Lobby fireplaces, original
617-566-0088 Fax: 617-278-9736	Visa, MC,	woodwork, one room with
888-575-0088	C-yes/S-no/P-no/H-no	queen bed
David Walsh		
All year		

Large, comfortably furnished, sunny rooms provide pleasant accommodations at a surprisingly affordable price. Near subway line.

CAPE COD

Academy Place B&B	75-100-B&B	Continental plus breakfast
PO Box 1407, 02653	5 rooms, 3 pb	Afternoon tea
508-255-3181 Fax: 508-247-9812	Visa, MC,	Sitting room, swimming &
Sandy & Charles Terrell	C-ltd/S-no/P-no/H-no	fishing close
Late May-Mid October		

Antique Cape Cod sea captain's home on Village Green. Walk to restaurants & shops. Nationall seashore 10 minutes away. Bike path 1/4 mile. E-mail: academyplace@mindspring.com

CAPE COD

Acworth Inn, The
PO Box 256, 02637
508-362-3330 Fax: 508-375-0304
800-362-6363
Cheryl & Jack Ferrell
All year

95-185-B&B
5 rooms, 5 pb
Visa, MC, AmEx,
Rated, •
C-ltd/S-no/P-no/H-no
German

Full breakfast
Afternoon tea, snacks
Sitting room, bicycles, flower
and herb gardens

Cape Cod charm in the center of the historic district; especially noted for the hand painted furnishings; easy access to islands. E-mail: hosts@acworthinn.com *Web site:* acworthinn.com

---

Ashley Manor
PO Box 856, 02630
508-362-8044 Fax: 508-362-9927
888-535-2246
Donald Bain
All year

135-195-B&B
6 rooms, 6 pb
Visa, MC, Disc, *Rated*,
•
C-ltd/S-no/P-no/H-no

Full gourmet breakfast
Complimentary wine, sherry,
port
Flowers, fruit, snacks, sitting
rm, croquet, A/C, bikes,
tennis, garden

1699 mansion in the historic district; rooms & suites have antiques, fireplaces, & private baths; walk to beach, village & harbor. E-mail: ashleymn@capecod.net
Web site: capecod.net/ashleymn

Augustus Snow House
528 Main St, 02646
508-430-0528 Fax: 508-432-6638
800-320-0528
Joyce & Steve Roth
All year

145-180-B&B
5 rooms, 5 pb
Most CC, *Rated*, •
C-ltd/S-no/P-no/H-no

Full breakfast
Afternoon tea
Gazebo and verandah, close
to quaint shops of Chatham

Romantic Victorian mansion. Exquisite bedrooms, PB (some with Jacuzzis), fireplaces all rooms, TVs. Gourmet breakfast, afternoon tea. Walk to private beach.
E-mail: snowhouse1@aol.com *Web site:* augustussnow.com

Beach House B&B, The
429 Center Hill Rd, 02360
508-224-3517 Fax: 508-224-3517
888-262-2543
Denise & Jack Kedian
All year

80-B&B
3 rooms, 3 pb
Visa, MC,
C-ltd/S-ltd/P-ltd/H-no

Sitting room, bicycles, suites,
fireplace, cable TV,
conferences, beach

Direct oceanfront, charmingly decorated, light, airy, 20' from Cape Cod Bay. Waterfront sundeck, screen porch, fireplaced living/dining room. E-mail: denise@beachhousebandb.com
Web site: beachhousebandb.com

Beechwood Inn
2839 Main St (Rt 6A), 02630
508-362-6618 Fax: 508-362-0298
800-609-6618
Ken & Debbie Traugot
All year

140-175-B&B
6 rooms, 6 pb
Most CC, *Rated*, •
C-ltd/S-no/P-no/H-no

Full gourmet breakfast
Afternoon snacks & bev.
Parlor, veranda, croquet,
bikes, garden, all rooms have
A/C

Award winning romantic Victorian inn along the historic "Old King's Way." Spacious antique-filled guest rooms offer fireplaces and views of Cape Cod Bay. Walk to shops, beaches E-mail: info@beechwoodinn.com *Web site:* beechwoodinn.com

---

Bradford of Chatham, The
PO Box 750, 02633
508-945-1030 Fax: 508-945-9652
800-562-4667
Sharon Loeffler
All year

95-375-B&B
35 rooms, 29 pb
Most CC, *Rated*, •
C-ltd/S-ltd/P-no/H-no

Continental breakfast
Sitt. rm., lib., TV/VCR, heated
pool, hair dryers, tennis
nearby, phones

Set like a jewel in the center of town, this lovely two acre retreat is a "village within a village," offering a variety of accommodations in its collection of restored historic houses.
E-mail: info@bradfordinn.com *Web site:* bradfordinn.com

CAPE COD ————————————————————————————————

Bradford-Carver House
70 Bradford St, 02657
508-487-4966 Fax: 508-487-7213
800-826-9083
Ken "Bill" Nelson
All year

49-169-B&B
5 rooms, 5 pb
Most CC, *Rated*, •
S-no/P-no/H-no
English

Continental breakfast
Sitting room, fireplace, cable
TV, fridge, A/C, VCR,
CD/AM/FM, clock radio

Your home away from home, where there are no strangers, only friends you haven't met!
"Highly-Recommended"-Out & About Newsletter. E-mail: bradcarver@capecod.net
Web site: capecod.net/bradfordcarver

Candleberry Inn
1882 Main St, 02631
508-896-3300 Fax: 508-896-4763
800-573-4769
Gini & David Donnelly
All year

85-195-B&B
9 rooms, 9 pb
Most CC, *Rated*
C-ltd/S-no/P-no/H-no

Full breakfast
Afternoon tea, snacks, wine
Sitting room, library,
Jacuzzis, fireplaces, suites,
cable TV

Elegant 250 yr. old inn. 2 acres priv. gardens. Rooms furnished with antiques; some with fireplaces or Jacuzzi. Guests pampered with robes, sherry, full gourmet breakfast E-mail: candle@cape.com *Web site:* candleberryinn.com

Cape Cod Claddagh Inn
77 Rt 28 PO 667, 02671
508-432-9628 Fax: 508-432-6039
800-356-9628
Eileen & Jack Connell
All year

95-125-B&B
8 rooms, 8 pb
Visa, MC, *Rated*
C-ltd/S-ltd/P-ltd/H-ltd

Full breakfast
Lunch/dinner available,
restaurant
Afternoon tea, bar service,
sitting room, library, pool,
fireplace, cable TV

Irish hospitality in a Victorian ambiance. Just what you would expect on your visit to Grandma's. E-mail: claddagh@capecod.net *Web site:* capecodcladdaghinn.com

Capt. Tom Lawrence House
75 Locust St, 02540
508-540-1445 Fax: 508-457-1790
800-266-8139
Barbara Sabo-Feller
All year

95-165-B&B
6 rooms, 6 pb
Visa, MC, *Rated*
C-ltd/S-yes/P-no/H-no
German

Full gourmet breakfast
Complimentary tea
Sitting room, library, piano,
A/C, porch, cable TV in each
room

Redecorated Victorian captain's home close to village ctr, beaches, golf, island ferries. Breakfast with homemade, organic bread. E-mail: capttom@capecod.net
Web site: sunsol.com/captaintom/

Captain Freeman Inn
15 Breakwater Rd, 02631
508-896-7481 Fax: 508-896-5618
800-843-4664
Carol & Tom Edmondson
All year

125-250-B&B
12 rooms, 12 pb
Most CC, *Rated*, •
C-ltd/S-no/P-no/H-no

Full breakfast
Afternoon tea, al fresco
dining
Sitting room, Jacuzzi,
bicycles, badminton, A/C,
swimming pool, croquet

Charming, quiet inn in a sea captain's mansion. Canopy beds, romantic porch. 3 luxury suites with fireplaces. Weekend cooking school, Innkeeping seminars. 4 new luxury rooms. Gardens, wrap around porch. OUR 1994 INN OF THE YEAR! E-mail: visitus@capecod.net *Web site:* captainfreemaninn.com

Captain Isaiah's House
33 Pleasant St, 02664
508-394-1739
Marge & Alden Fallows
Late June-early Sept.

50-75-B&B
6 rooms, 2 pb
C-ltd/S-no/P-no/H-no

Continental plus breakfast
With home-baked goodies
Sitting room, fireplaces, 2
studio apartments, whale
watching nearby

Charming, restored old sea captain's house in historic Bass River area. Most rooms have fireplaces. Studios have kitchens, TV and A/C.

CAPE COD ——————————————————————————————

Captain's House Inn
371 Old Harbor Rd, 02650
508-945-0127 Fax: 508-945-0866
800-315-0728
David & Janet McMaster
All year

165-350-B&B
19 rooms, 16 pb
Visa, MC, AmEx,
Rated, •
C-ltd/S-ltd/P-no/H-no

Full gourmet breakfast
Comp. afternoon tea
Sitting room, bikes, lawn
croquet, 3 new suites
w/frplcs.

Antiques and Williamsburg wallpapers. Charming guest rooms have four-poster beds, fireplaces. Private 2-acre estate of lawns and gardens. Quiet and elegant. AAA 4-Diamond (1987). E-mail: info@captainshouseinn.com *Web site:* captainshouseinn.com

Captains Choice B&B
PO Box 78, 02647
508-775-0101 Fax: 508-778-4235
Jack & Carol Cummiskey
All year

90-110-B&B
3 rooms, 2 pb
Visa, MC, *Rated*, •
S-no/P-no/H-ltd

Full breakfast
Snacks, wine
Sitting room, swimming pool,
fireplace, cable TV

Award winning B&B. Completely rebuilt home is immaculate and welcoming with friendly hosts who great every guest. E-mail: bandb@captchoice.com *Web site:* Captchoice.com

Chatham Town House Inn
11 Library Ln, 02633
508-945-2180 Fax: 508-945-3990
800-242-2180
Russell & Svea Peterson
All year

165-335-B&B
30 rooms, 30 pb
Most CC, *Rated*, •
C-ltd/S-no/P-no/H-ltd
Swedish, German

Full gourmet breakfast
Restaurant, bar service
Sitting room, library, tennis,
Jacuzzis, pool, suites,
fireplace

Captain's 2 acre estate, c.1881. Complex of 4 bldgs. including a culinary restaurant called Two Turtles. E-mail: chathamthi@capecod.net *Web site:* chathamtownhouse.com

Chatham Wayside Inn, The
PO 685, 02633
508-945-5550 Fax: 508-945-3407
800-391-5734
Jennifer Butler
Season Inquire

95-375-EP
Rated, •
C-yes

Suites, fireplace

Quiet comfortable elegance in the heart of the village. Warm hospitality, year 'round, lovely rooms, private baths, many balconies. Full service restaurant, heated outdoor pool. Children welcomed. E-mail: info@waysideinn.com *Web site:* waysideinn.com/

Cobb's Cove Inn
PO Box 208, 02630
508-362-9356 Fax: 508-362-9356
Evelyn Chester & Henri-Jean
All year

149-189-B&B
6 rooms, 6 pb
•
S-ltd/P-no/H-no
French

Full breakfast
Dinner, complimentary wine,
tea
Whirlpool tubs, robes,
toiletries, piano, sitting room,
library

Secluded getaway inn for couples. Two fabulous honeymoon suites with water views. Located on Cape Cod's unspoiled North Shore overlooking Cape Cod Bay.

Colonial House Inn
277 Main St, Rt 6A, 02675
508-362-4348 Fax: 508-362-8034
800-999-3416
Malcolm J. Perna
All year

70-95-B&B
21 rooms, 21 pb
Most CC, *Rated*, •
C-yes/S-yes/P-yes/H-yes

Continental plus breakfast
Dinner available (fee)
Game room, bar, pool,
cribs/high chair, TV/VCR,
Jacuzzi, fitness center

Decorated guest rooms furnished with antiques, canopy beds. Charming grounds by historic homes. Indoor heated pool, conference center. Victorian sitt. room, lovely outdoor deck. E-mail: colhseinn@capecod.net *Web site:* capecod.net/colonialhseinn

CAPE COD ──────────────────────────────────

Cyrus Kent House Inn
63 Cross St, 02633
508-945-9104 Fax: 508-945-9104
800-338-5368
Sharon Mitchell Swan
All year

95-250-B&B
11 rooms, 10 pb
Visa, MC, AmEx,
Rated, •
C-ltd/S-yes/P-no/H-no

Continental plus breakfast
Porch, deck, gardens, ample
parking, phones, art &
antique gallery

Sea captain's house reborn in heart of the quaint seaside village of Chatham. Picturesque stroll to Main St. shops, beaches, restaurants. Re-decorated.   E-mail: swan@cape.com
Web site: capecodtravel.com/cyruskent

Dunscroft By-the-Sea
24 Pilgrim Rd, 02646
508-432-0810 Fax: 508-432-5134
800-432-4345
Alyce & Wally Cunningham
All year

95-250-B&B
9 rooms, 9 pb
Rated, •
C-ltd/S-no/P-no/H-yes

Full breakfast
Juices
Piano, terrace, canopied 4-
posters, Jacuzzis, A/C, king
suite with fireplace

Breathtaking, private mile-long beach! Quiet & romantic. In-town to restaurants, shops. King/queen canopies & 4 posters.   E-mail: dunscroft@capecod.net
Web site: dunscroftbythesea.com

Farmhouse at Nauset, The
163 Beach Rd, 02653
508-255-6654
Dot Standish & children
All year

52-110-B&B
8 rooms, 8 pb
Visa, MC, •
C-ltd/S-ltd/P-no/H-no

Continental plus breakfast
Afternoon tea
Picnic tables, toys, sitting
room, massage with notice

1.6 quiet & peaceful acres. Bright, airy rooms with ocean breeze. Firm mattress for restful sleep. Old fashioned American warm hospitality. 1/2 mile to Atlantic Ocean. Helpful hostess. Seniors welcomed.

Grafton Inn
261 Grand Ave South, 02540
508-540-8688 Fax: 508-540-1861
800-642-4069
Liz & Rudy Cvitan
Feb.-Dec

95-189-B&B
11 rooms, 11 pb
Visa, MC, *Rated*, •
C-ltd/S-no/P-no/H-yes
Croatian

Full gourmet breakfast
Complimentary wine/cheese
Sitting room, porch, bicycles,
all rooms have phones, A/C,
cable TV

Oceanfront Victorian; panoramic view; delectable croissants from France. Convenient to ferry, shops, restaurants. Gallery throughout.   Web site: graftoninn.com

Harbor Walk
6 Freeman St, 02646
508-432-1675
Marilyn & Preston Barry
May-Oct.

75-B&B
6 rooms, 4 pb
Rated
C-yes/S-no/P-ltd/H-no
some French

Continental plus breakfast
Canopy beds, library, sitting
room, tennis & ocean nearby

Victorian charmer, featuring antiques, homemade quilts and queen canopy beds. Walk to beach and most photographed harbor on Cape Cod. Summer sports paradise.
Web site: obs-europa.de/obs/english/books/chesler/ne/05/bnb/maeb/42.htm

Hewins House B&B
20 Hewins St, 02540
508-457-4363 Fax: 508-540-5891
877-4-HEWINS
Virginia Price
All year

100-115-B&B
3 rooms, 3 pb
Disc, •
C-yes/S-no/P-no/H-no

Full breakfast
Kitchen facility
Sitting room, porch, walk to
free shuttle for Martha's
Vineyard ferry

Your home on Olde Cape Cod-National Register Historic District. Gardens, porch, breakfast in dining room. Convenient location for all Cape attractions.

Honeysuckle Hill, Cape Cod, MA

CAPE COD

Honeysuckle Hill
591 Old Kings Hwy, 02668
508-362-8418 Fax: 508-362-8386
800-441-8418
Bill & Mary Kilburn
All year

95-185-B&B
5 rooms, 4 pb
Most CC, *Rated*
C-ltd/S-ltd/P-no/H-no

Full gourmet breakfast
Chocolates & sherry
A/C, screened porch, near
beaches, fresh, flowers, am
coffee

On National Register, c.1810, this enchanting cottage offers comfortably elegant rooms & graciously served breakfasts. Rooms furnished in antiques and white wicker, featherbeds and Battenburg lace. E-mail: stay@honeysucklehill.com Web site: honeysucklehill.com

Inn at One Main, The
One Main St, 02540
508-540-7469
888-281-6246
Jeanne Dahl & Llona
Cleveland
All year

105-150-B&B
6 rooms, 6 pb
Visa, MC, AmEx,
Rated, •
C-ltd/S-no/P-no/H-ltd

Full breakfast
Snacks
Sitting room, A/C, cable TV,
Martha's Vineyard ferry

This light and airy 1892 Victorian welcomes guests year-round. Walk to shops, beaches, everything. Full breakfast, private baths. Close to Green & Logan airports. E-mail: innat1main@aol.com Web site: bbonline.com/ma/onemain

Inn on Sea Street, The
358 Sea St, 02601
508-775-8030 Fax: 508-771-0878
Slvia & Fred LaSelva
May-Nov.

90-140-B&B
9 rooms, 7 pb
Visa, MC, AmEx, *Rated*
C-ltd/S-no/P-no/H-no

Full gourmet breakfast
Fruit & cheese
Library, sitting room, small
weddings, 4-room cottage for
two

Elegant Victorian inn, steps from beach & Kennedy Compound. Antiques, canopy beds, goose down pillows, radios, fireplace, home-baked delights, most rooms with A/C, many with TV. A favorite with travel writers. E-mail: innonsea@capecod.net Web site: capecod.net/innonsea/

Inn on the Sound
313 Grand Ave S, 02540
508-457-9666 Fax: 508-457-9631
800-564-9668
Renee Ross & David Ross
All year

60-195-B&B
10 rooms, 10 pb
Visa, MC, *Rated*, •
C-ltd/S-no/P-no/H-no

Full breakfast
Upscale casual beach,
house, walk to MA V., ferry,
golf, tennis

Spacious rooms with spectacular ocean views, short walk to vineyard ferry; beach just outside the door; new private decks; call for info on exciting winter packages. E-mail: innontheso@aol.com Web site: innonthesound.com

CAPE COD

Isaiah Hall B&B Inn
PO Box 1007, 02638
508-385-9928 Fax: 508-385-5879
800-736-0160
Marie Brophy
April-mid October

97-163-B&B
10 rooms, 10 pb
Visa, MC, AmEx,
Rated, •
C-ltd/S-no/P-no/H-ltd

Continental plus breakfast
Complimentary tea, coffee
Library, gift shop, TVs, 2
sitting rooms, gardens, A/C

Enjoy our relaxing quiet country ambiance and hospitality in the heart of Cape Cod. Walk to beach, village, Playhouse and restaurants. E-mail: isaiah@isaiahhallinn.com *Web site:* isaiahhallinn.com

Liberty Hill Inn, Cape Cod
77 Main St, 02675
508-362-3976 Fax: 508-362-6485
800-821-3977
Jack & Beth Flanagan
All year

85-185-B&B
9 rooms, 9 pb
Visa, MC, AmEx,
Rated, •
C-yes/S-yes/P-no/H-yes

Full gourmet breakfast
Free soft drinks, juice
Cable TV in all rooms,
whirlpool, court phone, maid
& concierge service

Elegant inn in gracious Greek Revival Manor house, c.1825. A romantic hideaway, fireplaces, canopy beds, shoppers paradise, antique furnishings. A/C & cable TV in all rooms. E-mail: libertyh@capecod.net *Web site:* capecod.net/libertyhillinn

Mary Rockwell Stuart House
314 Main St, 02633
508-945-4634 Fax: 508-945-8012
Ron & Deborah McClelland
All year

195-275-B&B
6 rooms, 6 pb
Visa, MC, AmEx,
C-ltd/S-no/P-no/H-yes

Full breakfast
Suites, fireplaces

Elegant restored Victorian home. Six spacious quiet rooms, fireplaces, queen size beds, private baths, full breakfast, walk to town and beach. Web site: axs.com/mrshouse

Morgan's Way B&B
Nine Morgan's Way, 02653
508-255-0831 Fax: 508-255-0831
Page McMahan & Will Joy
All year

95-125-B&B
3 rooms, 3 pb
•
C-ltd/S-no/P-no/H-no

Full gourmet breakfast
Guest refrigerators
Sitting room, library, fresh
flowers, chocolate, firm beds,
heated pool

Romantic and elegant contemporary hideaway. Five acres of gardens and woodlands, heated pool; a birdwatcher's paradise. E-mail: morgnway@capecod.net *Web site:* capecodaccess.com/morgansway/

Moses Nickerson House Inn
364 Old Harbor Rd, 02633
508-945-5859 Fax: 508-945-7087
800-628-6972
Linda & George Watts
All year

139-189-B&B
7 rooms, 7 pb
Most CC, *Rated*, •
C-ltd/S-no/P-no/H-no

Full breakfast
In room phones, fresh
flowers, antiques, turndown
service, TV A/C

Elegant sea captain's home built 1839. Canopy beds, fireplaces, romantic, quiet. Walk to village & beaches. Glass-enclosed breakfast room overlooking garden E-mail: tmnhi@capecod.net *Web site:* capecodtravel.com/mosenickersonhouse

Mostly Hall B&B Inn
27 Main St, 02540
508-548-3786 Fax: 508-457-1572
800-682-0565
Caroline & Jim Lloyd
Feb.-Dec.

105-145-B&B
6 rooms, 6 pb
Most CC, *Rated*
S-no/P-no/H-no
German

Full gourmet breakfast
Coffee, tea, sherry
Sitting room, piano, gazebo,
veranda, porch, bicycles,
gardens

Majestically set back from the road surrounded by beautiful gardens, this 1849 Captain's home is a quiet oasis in the historic district. Canopy beds. Walk to beaches, shops, ferries. E-mail: mostlyhl@cape.com *Web site:* mostlyhall.com

Mostly Hall, Cape Cod, MA

CAPE COD

Nauset House Inn
PO Box 774, 02643
508-255-2195 Fax: 508-240-6276
D & A Johnson, C & J Vessella
April-October

75-135-B&B
14 rooms, 8 pb
Most CC, *Rated*
C-ltd/S-no/P-no/H-no

Full breakfast
Wine & hors d'oeuvre
Commons room,
conservatory, dining room

Intimate 1810 inn, unique turn-of-the-century conservatory, warm ambiance, only 1/2 mile to the beautiful Nauset Beach. Near biking, hiking, golf, shopping.   E-mail: jvessell@ capecod.net Web site: nausethouseinn.com

---

Old Harbor Inn, The
22 Old Harbor Rd, 02633
508-945-4434 Fax: 508-945-7665
800-942-4434
Judy & Ray Braz
All year

99-219-B&B
8 rooms, 8 pb
Visa, MC, *Rated*, •
C-ltd/S-no/P-no/H-no

Continental plus breakfast
Restaurants nearby
Sitting rm. w/fireplace, sun
room, deck, A/C, near golf,
boating

English country decor. King/Queen/Twin beds. Delectable buffet breakfast. Walk to quaint seaside village attractions.   E-mail: brazohi@capecod.net Web site: capecod.net/oldharborinn

---

Old Manse Inn & Rest., The
PO Box 745, 02631
508-896-3149 Fax: 508-896-1546
David & Suzanne Plum
March-Dec.

105-125-B&B
9 rooms, 9 pb
Visa, MC, AmEx, *Rated*
C-ltd/S-yes/P-no/H-yes

Full breakfast
Gourmet dinner, bar,
afternoon tea
Coffee, library, patio, garden,
A/C, 6 room have cable TV

Enjoy salt air from room in antique sea captain's home. Walk to Cape Cod's attractions. Gourmet dining by reservation; award-winning food.   E-mail: oldmanse@cape.com Web site: oldmanseinn.comm

---

Old Sea Pines Inn
PO Box 1026, 02631
508-896-6114 Fax: 508-896-7387
Stephen & Michele Rowan
April-Dec. 22

65-125-B&B
23 rooms, 14 pb
Most CC, *Rated*, •
C-ltd/S-no/P-no/H-ltd
Italian, German

Full breakfast
Beverage on arrival
Restaurant, parlor with,
fireplace, deck, Sunday,
dinner theatre summers

Turn-of-the-century mansion furnished with antiques. Near beaches, bicycle trails, quality restaurants & shops. Nightly dinner, July & August   E-mail: seapines@c4.net Web site: oldseapinesinn.com

CAPE COD ————————————————————————————————————

Olde Captain's Inn
101 Main St, Rt 6A, 02675
508-362-4496 Fax: 508-362-4496
888-407-7161
Sven Tilly & Betsy O'Connor
All year

60-120-B&B
5 rooms, 3 pb
C-ltd/S-no/P-no/H-no

Continental plus breakfast
maid & concierge service

A charming Greek Revival c.1812 former sea Captain's house located in the historic district. Walk to fine restaurants, craft shops and antique shops. Beaches, golf & tennis nearby.
E-mail: general@oldecaptainsinn.com Web site: oldecaptainsinn.com

One Centre Street Inn
1 Centre St, 02675
508-362-8910 Fax: 508-362-0195
888-407-1653
Karen Iannello
All year

95-155-B&B
6 rooms, 4 pb
Visa, MC, *Rated*, •
C-ltd/S-no/P-no/H-no

Full gourmet breakfast
Piano, bicycles, flower &
herb gardens, whale
watching close by

Vintage antique-furnished parsonage, 1 mile to Cape Cod Bay or village. Fireplace available. Delicious breakfasts in formal dining room or shady screened porch.

Over Look Inn, The
PO Box 771, 02642
508-255-1886 Fax: 508-240-0345
Ian & Nan Aitchison
All year

95-165-B&B
14 rooms, 14 pb
Rated, •
C-ltd/S-ltd/P-no/H-ltd
Fr., Sp., It., Port.

Full breakfast
Dinner occ., Afternoon tea
Sitting room, library, bikes,
tours, packages, 3 suites for
families

Victorian country inn & cottage within walking distance of Cape Cod National Seashore. Bike paths & nature trails. Tranquil wooded setting. Children welcome in suite.
E-mail: stay@overlookinn.com Web site: overlookinn.com

Sea Breeze Inn
397 Sea St, 02601
508-771-7213 Fax: 508-862-0663
Patricia Gibney
All year

80-150-B&B
15 rooms, 13 pb
Disc, *Rated*, •
C-yes/S-yes/P-no/H-no

Continental plus breakfast
Kitchen privileges
Sitting room, cable TV,
bicycles, canopy beds, 3
cottages, A/C

Quaint, nautical atmosphere, private setting, beach & Hyannisport Harbor 900 ft., near center of Hyannis. E-mail: seabreeze@capecod.net Web site: seabreezeinn.com

Simmons Homestead Inn
288 Scudder Ave, 02647
508-778-4999 Fax: 508-790-1342
800-637-1649
Bill Putman
All year

150-200-B&B
14 rooms, 14 pb
Visa, MC, AmEx,
Rated, •
C-yes/S-ltd/P-ltd/H-no

Full breakfast
Complimentary wine and
cheese
Sitting room, library, wraparound porch, bikes, huge
yard, beaches

Beautifully restored 1820 sea captain's home abounds in art, priceless antiques, canopy beds. Lovely grounds. New billiard room, two bedroom suite, 2 common rooms.
E-mail: simmonsinn@aol.com Web site: capecodtravel.com/simmonsinn

Village Green Inn
40 Main St, 02540
508-548-5621 Fax: 508-457-5051
800-237-1119
Don & Diane Crosby
All year

85-165-B&B
5 rooms, 5 pb
Rated, •
C-ltd/S-no/P-no/H-no

Full gourmet breakfast
Seasonal beverages
Parlor, piano, A/C, fireplaces,
open porches, bikes, colored
cable TV

Old Victorian ideally located on Falmouth's historic green. 19th-c. charm & warm hospitality in lovely spacious rooms. Walk to shops, restaurants, complimentary shuttle to ferry for M.V. Telephones in rooms. E-mail: vgi40@aol.com Web site: villagegreeninn.com

The Whalewalk Inn, Cape Cod, MA

CAPE COD

Wedgewood Inn
83 Main St, 02675
508-362-5157 Fax: 508-362-5851
Milt & Gerrie Graham
All year

105-195-B&B
9 rooms, 9 pb
Most CC, *Rated*, •
C-ltd/S-ltd/P-no/H-ltd

Full breakfast
Afternoon tea, fruit
Common room, fireplaces,
private porches,
gardens/gazebo, A/C

Romantic inn in historic area of Cape Cod. Near beaches & restaurants. Antiques, wood-burning fireplaces, plank floors, canopy beds, private sitting rooms. We have restored an old barn and added 3 deluxe suites along with a dramatic central area. E-mail: info@wedgewood-inn.com *Web site:* wedgewood-inn.com

---

Whalewalk Inn, The
220 Bridge Rd, 02642
508-255-0617 Fax: 508-240-0017
Richard & Carolyn Smith
April-November

155-260-B&B
16 rooms, 16 pb
Rated, •
C-ltd/S-ltd/P-no/H-no

Full gourmet breakfast
Comp. hors d'ouevres
Bar, sitting room, patio, all
rooms are A/C, all suites
with fireplaces

Restored 1830s whaling master's home. Elegance, hospitality. Uniquely decorated. On quiet road by bay, ocean. E-mail: whalewak@capecod.net *Web site:* whalewalkinn.com

---

Wildflower Inn, The
167 Palmer Ave, 02540
508-548-9524 Fax: 508-548-9524
800-294-5459
Phil & Donna Stone   All year

85-195-B&B
6 rooms, 6 pb
Most CC, *Rated*, •
C-ltd/S-no/P-no/H-no

Full gourmet breakfast
Tea, snacks, comp. wine
Sitt. rm., library, A/C, bikes,
whirlpool tubs, fish, golf,
tennis near

Restored Victorian in historic district close to shops, rest., & Island Ferry. Dine in fireplaced gathering rm., wraparound porch. As seen on PBS: Country Inn Cooking with Gail Greco E-mail: wldflr167@aol.com *Web site:* wildflower-inn.com

CONCORD

Col. Roger Brown House
1694 Main St, 01742
978-369-9119 Fax: 978-369-1305
800-292-1369
Mrs. Lauri Berlied
All year

80-165-B&B
5 rooms, 5 pb
Most CC, •
C-ltd/S-no/P-no/H-no

Continental plus breakfast
Snacks
Sitting room, library, sauna &
swimming pool, next door to
health club

National historic register 1775 Colonial; private baths; hearty breakfast; cozy, relaxed atmosphere; near historic areas. E-mail: innkeeper@colrogerbrown.com *Web site:* colrogerbrown.com

---

Hawthorne Inn
462 Lexington Rd, 01742
978-369-5610 Fax: 978-287-4949
G. Burch & M. Mudry
All year

150-235-B&B
7 rooms, 7 pb
Most CC, *Rated*, •
C-yes/S-ltd/P-no/H-no

Continental plus breakfast
Tea & coffee at check-in
Sitting room, garden, yard,
small pond, swings, bicycles,
tree house

On the "Battle Road" of 1775, furnished with antiques, quilts and artwork with the accent on New England comfort and charm. Extensive gardens, canopy queen bed. E-mail: hawthorneinn@concordmass.com *Web site:* concordmass.com

Yellow Gabled House, Deerfield, MA

CUMMINGTON

Cumworth Farm	80-B&B	Full breakfast
472 W Cummington Rd, 01026	6 rooms	Afternoon tea, snacks, wine
413-634-5529 Fax: 413-634-5411	*Rated*	Sitting room, piano, hot tub,
Edward McColgan	C-yes/S-ltd	bicycles
Closed Nov 1-May 1		

Big, 200-year-old farmhouse; sugarhouse on premises; sheep; berries—pick your own in season. Close to cross-country skiing, hiking trails. Quiet getaway, sweeping views.

DEERFIELD

Deerfield Inn	141-207-B&B	Full breakfast
81 Old Main St, 01342	23 rooms	Afternoon tea
413-774-5587 Fax: 413-773-8712	Most CC, *Rated*, ●	Restaurant, bar service,
800-926-3865	C-yes/S-no/P-no/H-yes	lunch, dinner (fee), sitting
Karl & Jane Sabo		room
Closed Christmas		

Located in an historic village surrounded by 14 museum houses, our 1884 inn & award-winning restaurant invite you into a gracious past. E-mail: frontdesk@deerfieldinn.com *Web site:* deerfieldinn.com

Yellow Gabled House	75-135-B&B	Full breakfast
111 N Main St, 01373	3 rooms, 1 pb	Antiques, gardens, tennis
413-665-4922	*Rated*, ●	nearby, library, carriage
Edna Julia Stahelek	C-ltd/S-no/P-no/H-no	rides arranged
All year	Lithuanian	

Old country house in the heart of historical and cultural area. 1.5 miles from crossroads of I-91, Rt. 116, Rt. 5 & 10. 4 miles to Historical Deerfield. Near 5-college area.

DENNIS

Rose Petal B&B, The	59-99-B&B	Full breakfast
PO Box 974, 02639	3 rooms, 2 pb	Complimentary beverages
508-398-8470	Most CC, *Rated*, ●	Sitting rm., TV, gardens,
Gayle Kelly	C-yes/S-no/P-no/H-no	brass beds, piano, A/C,
All year	some French	handstitched quilts

Excellence & sophistication. 1872 Seafarer's home in a delightful seaside resort neighborhood. E-mail: rosepetl@capecod.net *Web site:* rosepetalofdennis.com/

DUXBURY

Winsor House Inn
390 Washington St, 02332
781-934-0991 Fax: 781-934-5955
Mr. & Mrs. David M. O'Connell
All year

130-210-B&B
4 rooms, 4 pb
Most CC, *Rated*
C-yes/S-yes/P-no/H-no

Full breakfast
Lunch seasonal (fee)
Sitting room, Plymouth- 10
minutes, handstitched quilts

Charming 19th-Century sea captain's home located in quaint seaside village of Duxbury, 35 miles S. of Boston, 10 miles from historic Plymouth. Walk to beach and shopping.
E-mail: winsordhouse@dreamcom.net

EAST ORLEANS

Ship's Knees Inn
PO Box 756, 02643
508-255-1312 Fax: 508-240-1351
Jean & Ken Pitchford
All year

50-130-B&B
25 rooms, 11 pb
Rated, •
C-ltd/S-yes/P-no/H-no

Continental breakfast
Sitting room, pool, tennis,
additional beach cottages 3
miles away

170-year-old restored sea captain's home. 3 minute walk to Nauset Beach. 3 miles away, Cove House offers 3 rooms, 1-bedroom apartment & 2 heated cottages.
Web site: capecodtravel.com/shipskneesinn

EAST SANDWICH

Wingscorton Farm Inn
Olde Kings Hwy, Rt #6A, 02537
508-888-0534
All year

135-185-B&B
4 rooms, 4 pb
Visa, MC, AmEx, •
C-yes/S-yes/P-yes/H-yes

Full breakfast
Picnic basket lunch
Dinner, comp. wine, library,
bicycles, private ocean
beach

A special retreat for couples seeking a private, intimate getaway. Eclectic mix of antiquity and modern conveniences in a setting of a working New England farm. Private beach.

EASTHAM

Penny House Inn
PO Box 238, 02651
508-255-6632 Fax: 508-255-4893
800-554-1751
Margaret Keith
All year

135-250-B&B
12 rooms, 12 pb
Visa, MC, *Rated*, •
C-ltd/S-yes/P-no/H-no
French

Full breakfast
Comp. wine, aftn. tea
Sitting room, gazebo, brick
patio, gardens, great room
w/fireplace

Experience original Cape Cod charm & serenity in this 1751 bow-roof rambling Cape conveniently near all Nat'l Seashore Park activities. E-mail: pennyhouse@aol.com
Web site: virtualcapecod.com/pennyhouseinn/

EGREMONT

Baldwin Hill Farm B&B
121 Baldwin Hill Rd N/S, 01230
413-528-4092 Fax: 413-528-6365
888-504-2092
Richard & Priscilla Burdsall
All year

B&B
6 rooms, 5 pb
Visa, MC, AmEx,
Rated, •
C-ltd/S-no/P-no/H-no

Full country breakfast
Afternoon tea, snacks
2 sitting rooms, library,
screened porch, pool,
fireplace, cross country ski

Spacious Victorian farmhouse. Mountain views, nature hikes. Restaurants nearby. Hiking, tennis, golf, boating, fishing. Friendly and elegant. 2 queen rooms, 2 king or twin rooms.
E-mail: rpburds@aol.com

Egremont Inn, The
PO Box 418, 01258
413-528-2111 Fax: 413-528-3284
800-859-1780
Steve & Karen Waller
All year

90-185-B&B/MAP
19 rooms, 19 pb
Most CC, •
C-yes/S-ltd/P-no/H-no

Full breakfast, weekends
Continental breakfast,
weekdays
Sitting room, fireplaces,
tennis courts, pool,
wraparound porch

Wonderful Colonial inn offering charm & comfort. Tavern, restaurant. Close to antiquing, cycling, hiking, skiing & Tanglewood-Come join us. E-mail: egremontinn@taconic.net
Web site: egremontinn.com

FAIRHAVEN

Edgewater B&B	75-100-B&B	Continental plus breakfast
2 Oxford St, 02719	5 rooms, 5 pb	Complimentary tea, coffee
508-997-5512 Fax: 508-997-5784	*Rated*	Sitting room, library,
Kathy Reed	C-ltd/S-no/P-no/H-no	spacious lawns, cable TV in
All year		all rooms

Gracious waterfront mansion overlooking Bedford Harbor. Spacious accommodations; 2 suites with fireplaces. 5 min. from I-195. Close to historic areas, beaches, factory outlets. New stone seawall. E-mail: kprof@aol.com Web site: rixsan.com/edgewater/

FALL RIVER

Lizzie Borden B&B/Museum	150-200-B&B	Full breakfast
92 Second St, 02721	8 rooms, 1 pb	Snacks
508-675-7333 Fax: 508-675-7333	Most CC, •	Sitting room, library, cable
Ron Evans & Martha McGinn	C-ltd/S-no/P-no/H-no	TV in all rooms
All year		

Fully restored Victorian Home. Infamous world-wide as the scene of the unsolved double-homicide of Andrew and Abby Borden in 1892. Overnight guests receive a full tour of the mansion. E-mail: lizziebnb@lizzie-borden.com Web site: lizzie-borden.com

FALMOUTH

Old Silver Beach B&B	65-70-B&B	Continental breakfast
PO Box 642, 02574	2 rooms, 0 pb	Afternoon tea
508-540-5446	*Rated*	Sitting room, fireplace, cable
Beverly A. Kane	C-ltd/S-ltd/P-no/H-no	TV, free parking
All year		

Charming 1/2 cape decorated with country and antiques. 1/2 mile walk to beautiful, warm, sandy beach. Relax on all glass porch or deck surrounded by beautiful gardens and birds.

Woods Hole Passage B&B	125-145-B&B	Full breakfast
186 Woods Hole Rd, 02540	5 rooms, 5 pb	Dinner (off season)
508-548-9575 Fax: 508-540-4771	Most CC, *Rated*, •	Bicycles, library, spacious
800-790-8976	C-ltd/S-no/P-no/H-no	grounds, flower & herb
Deb Pruitt		gardens, outdoor shower
All year		

Graceful, 100 year old carriage house and renovated barn providing a magical retreat year round. Bike paths, nature trails, beaches and ferry minutes away. E-mail: inn@woodsholepassage.com Web site: woodsholepassage.com

FALMOUTH HEIGHTS

Moorings Lodge, The	95-145-B&B	Full breakfast
207 Grand Ave, 02540	8 rooms, 8 pb	Afternoon tea
508-540-2370 Fax: 508-457-6074	Visa, MC, *Rated*, •	Sitting room, fireplace, cable
800-398-4007	C-yes/S-no/P-no/H-no	TV, across from, ocean &
Ernie & Shirley Benard		public beach
May 15-October 15		

Sun, sand, & surf- We've got it all! Lovely Victorian with large glassed in porch for your full homemade breakfast enjoyment with ocean views. Call us home while you tour Cape Cod. Web site: bbonline.com/ma/moorings/

GREAT BARRINGTON

1898 House, The	60-120-B&B	Full breakfast
89 Taconic Ave, 01230	3 rooms, 3 pb	Afternoon tea, snacks
413-528-1315 Fax: 413-528-2631	Visa, MC,	Complimentary wine,
Wayne & Carol Deming	C-ltd/S-no/P-no/H-no	fireplaces, cable TV, library,
All year		sitting room

Lovely Victorian on The Hill. Withing walking distance of Main Street, Great Barrington centrally located to the Berkshires' major attractions including Tanglewood, the Norman Rockwell Museum, Stockbridge's historic sites and more. E-mail: the1898house@eudoramail.com

GREAT BARRINGTON

Old Inn on the Green	175-350-B&B	Continental plus breakfast
Star Route 70, 01230	21 rooms, 17 pb	Restaurant, bar
413-229-3131 Fax: 413-229-8236	Visa, MC, •	Dinner (Fri-Sun), five public
800-286-3139	C-yes/S-yes/P-no/H-yes	rooms, whirlpools, pool
B. Wagstaff & L. Miller	French, German,	
All year	Spanish	

1760 colonial inn on historic landmark register. 3 public rooms downstairs. Parlor, dining room, old tavern.   E-mail: brad@oldinn.com *Web site:* oldinn.com

Windflower Inn	100-200-B&B	Full breakfast
684 S Egremont Rd, 01230	13 rooms, 13 pb	Afternoon tea, snacks
413-528-2720 Fax: 413-528-5147	*Rated*, •	Sitting room, library,
800-992-1993	C-yes/S-ltd/P-no/H-ltd	swimming pool
C. & J. Ryan, B. & G. Liebert		
All year		

Elegant small country Inn. Beautiful rooms, some with fireplaces. Produce from our organic garden. Relax on our porch with beautiful wicker furniture.   E-mail: wndflowr@windflowerinn.com *Web site:* windflowerinn.com

GREENFIELD

Brandt House B&B Inn, The	100-195-B&B	Continental plus breakfast
29 Highland Ave, 01301	8 rooms, 6 pb	Afternoon tea,
413-774-3329 Fax: 413-772-2908	Most CC, *Rated*, •	complimentary wine
800-235-3329	C-ltd/S-ltd/P-ltd/H-no	Snacks, sitting room, library,
Phoebe Compton		tennis, Jacuzzis, cable,
All year		frplcs., fax, phones

An elegant turn-of-the-century Colonial Revival mansion. Has original beautiful woodwork & personally selected furnishings & decor. Relax in the comfort of spacious, light-filled rooms. Covered porches.   E-mail: info@brandthouse.com *Web site:* brandthouse.com

HAMILTON

Miles River Country Inn	110-165-B&B	Full breakfast
PO Box 149, 01936	8 rooms, 5 pb	Afternoon tea
978-468-7206 Fax: 978-468-3999	*Rated*	Library, gardens, paths in
Gretel & Peter Clark	C-yes/S-no/P-no/H-no	woods, field, wildlife,
All year	Spanish, French,	beaches
	German	

200-year-old country Colonial on large estate. Summer breakfast on shaded garden terraces. Winter evenings by your bedroom's fireplace. Outdoor weddings. Apartment available with 2 queen beds and a pull out couch.   E-mail: milesriver@mediaone.net *Web site:* milesriver.com

IPSWICH

Town Hill B&B	85-160-B&B	Full breakfast
16 N Main Street, 01938	11 rooms, 9 pb	Sitting room, suites,
978-356-8000 Fax: 978-356-8000	Visa, MC, AmEx, •	fireplaces, cable TV, huge
800-457-7799	C-ltd/S-ltd/P-no/H-no	yard, beaches
Robert and Chere Statho		
Closed part of Feb.		

1850 Greek Revival property located in historic district with 11 individually decorated rooms. Walk to restaurants, Boston train, crane beach, canoeing, kayaking, golf, antiquing and great shopping.   E-mail: reserve@townhill.com *Web site:* townhill.com

LENOX

Cornell Inn	89-249-B&B	Continental plus breakfast
203 Main St, 01240	30 rooms, 30 pb	Health spa with whirlpool,
413-637-0562 Fax: 413-637-0927	Most CC,	sauna, exercise, Japanese
800-637-0562	C-ltd/S-no/P-no/H-yes	style garden
Doug McLaughlin All year		

A full service country inn. Choose a cozy bdrm., a fully equipped suite with fireplace and kitchen or a four poster fireplace & Jacuzzi in our newly renovated 200 year old MacDonald House. Web site: cornellinn.com

LENOX ──────────────────────────────────────

Gables Inn, The	90-225-B&B	Full breakfast
81 Walker St, 01240	17 rooms, 17 pb	Complimentary wine, dinner
413-637-3416 Fax: 413-637-3416	Most CC, *Rated*	packages
800-382-9401	C-ltd/S-yes/P-no/H-no	Sitting room, library, tennis
Frank Newton	Spanish	courts, swimming pool
All year		

Built in 1885, this gracious "cottage" was home of Edith Wharton at turn of the century. Lovingly furnished in period style. 2 new suites: Teddy & Edith Wharton suites. Dinner packages in Winter. Web site: gableslenox.com

Garden Gables Inn	90-225-B&B	Full breakfast
PO Box 52, 01240	18 rooms, 18 pb	Complimentary port and
413-637-0193 Fax: 413-637-4554	Visa, MC, *Rated*	sherry
Mario & Lynn Mekinda	C-ltd/S-ltd/P-no/H-no	Library, fireplace,
All year	German, French	whirlpools, porches, largest
		pool in the USA

220-year-old gabled inn located in center of Lenox on five wooded acres. Furnished with antiques. E-mail: gardeninn@aol.com *Web site:* lenoxinn.com

Gateways Inn	125-400-B&B	Full breakfast
51 Walker St, 01240	12 rooms, 12 pb	Restaurant, bar, dinner
413-637-2532 Fax: 413-637-1432	Most CC, *Rated*	available
888-492-9466	S-no/P-no/H-no	Sitting room with TV,
Fabrizio/Rosemary Chiariello	Italian, Spanish	telephones in room, A/C,
All year		fireplaces, tennis

Victorian Inn located in the center of city with turn-of-the-century elegance. Famous for magnificent staircase & restaurant where Fiedler & Rockwell used to indulge. Recently renovated with all new bathrooms, 9 rooms with fireplaces. E-mail: gateways@berkshire.net *Web site:* gatewaysinn.com

Kemble Inn, The	85-275-B&B	Continental breakfast
2 Kemble St, 01240	15 rooms, 15 pb	A/C, fireplaces, tennis
413-637-4113	Visa, MC, AmEx, *Rated*	
800-353-4113	S-no/P-no/H-yes	
All year		

Elegant 1881 Georgian mansion, magnificent mountain views, spacious rooms with private baths, fireplaces, A/C, TV, and one and a half miles to Tanglewood. Web site: kembleinn.com

Rookwood Inn, The	100-300-B&B	Full breakfast
PO Box 1717, 01240	20 rooms, 20 pb	Afternoon tea
413-637-9750 Fax: 413-637-1352	Most CC, *Rated*, •	Sitting room, suites,
800-223-9750	C-yes/S-no/P-no/H-ltd	fireplaces, cable TV, tennis
Amy & Stephen Lesser	Spanish, some German	
All year		

Comfortable Queen Anne Victorian serving bountiful, heart healthy breakfasts. Near the town center and cultural attractions. E-mail: stay@rookwoodinn.com *Web site:* rookwoodinn.com

Summer Hill Farm	90-165-B&B	Full breakfast
950 East St, 01240	7 rooms, 7 pb	Sitting room, fireplaces, 3
413-442-2057 Fax: 413-448-6106	Visa, MC, AmEx, *Rated*	bedroom farmhouse, 2-room
800-442-2059	C-ltd/S-no/P-no/H-yes	guest cottage
Michael & Sonya Wessel		
All year		

200 year old Colonial with small horse farm. Elegantly & comfortably furnished with English antiques and oriental rugs. Rural setting, close to all local amenities. E-mail: innkeeper@summerhillfarm.com *Web site:* summerhillfarm.com

LENOX ————————————————————————————

Village Inn, The	50-250-B&B	Continental breakfast
PO Box 1810, 01240	32 rooms, 32 pb	Dinner
413-637-0020 Fax: 413-637-9756	Most CC, *Rated*, •	Sitt. rm., lib., TV/VCRs in
800-253-0917	C-ltd/S-yes/P-no/H-yes	each room, movie lib., voice
Clifford Rudisill, Ray Wilson	Spanish, French,	mail, hair dryers
All year	German	

Historic 1771 inn reflecting charm & warmth of colonial New England. Rooms furnished in country antiques. Afternoon tea with homemade scones, dinner served July-October E-mail: villinn@vgernet.net Web site: villageinn-lenox.com

Walker House	80-210-B&B	Continental plus breakfast
64 Walker St, 01240	8 rooms, 8 pb	Complimentary wine,
413-637-1271 Fax: 413-637-2387	*Rated*	afternoon tea
800-235-3098	C-ltd/S-no/P-ltd/H-ltd	Sitting room, piano, library
Peggy & Richard Houdek	Spanish, French	video theatre, opera/film
All year		weekends

Our guests feel like special pampered friends. Lovely country atmosphere on 3 acres. E-mail: phoudek@vgernet.net Web site: walkerhouse.com

MARBLEHEAD ————————————————————————

Harbor Light Inn	125-275-B&B	Continental plus breakfast
58 Washington St, 01945	20 rooms, 20 pb	Aftn. tea, coffee/cookies
781-631-2186 Fax: 781-631-2216	Visa, MC, AmEx,	Sitting rm., conf. room, hot
Peter C. Conway	*Rated*, •	tubs, courtyard, heated
All year	C-ltd/S-yes/P-no/H-no	swimming pool

The north shore's premier inn. Elegant 18th-century Federalist mansion. Jacuzzis, sundecks, in heart of historic Harbor District. Conference facilities   E-mail: hli@shell2.shore.net Web site: harborlightinn.com

Harborside House	75-90-B&B	Continental plus breakfast
23 Gregory St, 01945	2 rooms	Harbor Sweets candy
781-631-1032	•	Living room with fireplace,
Susan Livingston	C-ltd/S-no/P-no/H-no	deck, period dining room,
All year		bicycles available

C. 1850 colonial home offers antiques/modern amenities. Homemade baked goods. Sunny porch, flower gardens. Walk to historic sites, shops, beach, restaurants   E-mail: swliving@ shore.net Web site: shore.net/~swliving/

Oceanwatch	180-280-B&B	Continental breakfast
8 Fort Sewall Lane, 01945	3 rooms, 3 pb	Sitting room, fireplaces,
781-639-8660 Fax: 781-639-4034	Visa, MC, AmEx, •	cable TV, beach, ocean-front
Diane & Paul Jolicoeur	C-ltd/S-no/P-no/H-no	park, deck
All year	French	

Victorian-era home in Old Marblehead, overlooking harbor entrance, next to pre-Revolutionary fort. Ocean harbor views from all rooms. Walk to shops, restaurants, and historic sites.   E-mail: oceanwatch@mediaone.net Web site: people.ne.mediaone.net/oceanwatch/

Pheasant Hill Inn	105-160-B&B	Continental plus breakfast
71 Bubier Rd, 01945	3 rooms, 3 pb	Snacks
781-639-4799 Fax: 781-639-4799	Visa, MC, AmEx, •	Sitting room, library, phones,
Bill & Nancy Coolidge	C-ltd/S-ltd/P-no/H-no	TV, A/C, suite with fireplace
All year		

Charming 1920 summer estate. Private all-suites, getaway. Country-like setting and views to water. Memorable!   Web site: pheasanthill.com

MARTHA'S VINEYARD

Arbor Inn, The
PO Box 1228, 02539
508-627-8137
Peggy Hall
May-Oct.

95-175-B&B
8 rooms, 8 pb
Visa, MC, *Rated*, •
C-ltd/S-ltd/P-no/H-no

Continental breakfast
Complimentary wine,
beverages
Parlor, fresh flowers, garden,
courtyard, A/C, antique shop
in yard

Turn-of-the-century home in historic Edgartown. Walk to town & harbor. Rooms are delightfully and typically New England. Enchanting 3 room cottage available by the week.
Web site: mvy.com/arborinn

Captain Dexter House
PO Box 2457, 02568
508-693-6564 Fax: 508-693-8448
Mike and Laura
All year

95-275-B&B
8 rooms, 8 pb
Most CC, *Rated*, •
C-yes/S-yes/P-no/H-no

Continental plus breakfast
Complimentary sherry,
afternoon tea
Library, fireplaces, use of
beach towels, fresh flowers,
sitting room

Beautifully restored 1843 sea captain's home. Furnished with fine antiques. Some rooms have fireplaces and canopied beds. Walk to beach   Web site: mvy.com/captdexter

Captain Dexter House
PO Box 2798, 02539
508-627-7289 Fax: 508-627-3328
Pam and Greg
April 15-Nov. 15

95-300-B&B
11 rooms, 11 pb
Visa, MC, AmEx,
Rated, •
C-yes/S-yes/P-no/H-no

Continental plus breakfast
Complimentary wine
Hot cider, lemonade,
landscaped garden, sitt. rm.,
beach towels

Lovely 1840s home; romantic antique-filled guest rooms with canopied beds and working fireplaces. Landscaped gardens. Near harbor, shops and restaurants
Web site: mvy.com/captdexter

Chadwick Inn
PO Box 1035, 02539
508-627-4435 Fax: 508-627-5656
Peter & Jurate Antioco
All year

149-499-B&B
21 rooms, 21 pb
Visa, MC, AmEx, •
C-ltd/S-yes/P-no/H-yes
French

Continental breakfast
Complimentary sherry
Sitting room, library, beach
towels

In stately Edgartown Historic District, 1840s Greek Revival buildings, gardens, brick courtyard. Rooms furnished with antiques, canopy beds, fireplaces and terraces.
E-mail: chedwickinn@capecod.com *Web site:* chadwickinn.com

Colonial Inn Martha's Vyd
PO Box 68, 02539
508-627-4711 Fax: 508-627-5904
800-627-4701
Linda Malcouronne
April 1-December 1

100-300-B&B
43 rooms, 43 pb
Visa, MC, AmEx,
Rated, •
C-yes/S-yes/P-no/H-yes
Portuguese

Continental plus breakfast
Restaurant, bar
Sitting room, library, by
tennis, riding, golf, sailing,
fishing, beach

Charming, lovingly refurbished inn with brass beds offers affordable luxury. Packages: Happy Haunting Weekend and home for the Holidays. 2 suites with kitchens. Near museums, galleries, shops. 1/3 of rooms refurbished annually.   Web site: colonialinnmvy.com

Dockside Inn, The
PO Box 1206, 02557
508-693-2966 Fax: 508-696-7293
800-245-5979
Patrick Mullin, Siobhan Casey
Mid May-Mid October

75-B&B
20 rooms, 20 pb
Visa, MC, Disc, *Rated*,
•
C-ltd/S-yes/P-no/H-yes

Continental plus breakfast
Bicycles, A/C, sitting, room,
TV, Kitchen suites, Garden
area w/BBQ grill

A romantic Victorian Inn on the harbor. Built in 1989 with all the charm of the 1800s and all the amenities of today. Hairdryers have been added to all bathrooms.
E-mail: Inns@vineyard.net

MARTHA'S VINEYARD

Greenwood House B&B
PO Box 2734, 02568
508-693-6150 Fax: 508-696-8113
800-525-9466
Larry Gomez & Kathy Stinson
All year

179-269-B&B
Most CC, *Rated*, •
S-no/P-no/H-no
Hungarian

Full breakfast
Sitting room, library, suites,
cable TV, telephones, A/C

This island B&B is uniquely nestled in a quiet neighborhood for that romantic getaway near ferry, shops, restaurants and the beach.   E-mail: innkeeper@greenwoodhouse.com
Web site: greenwoodhouse.com

Hob Knob Inn
PO Box 239, 02539
508-627-9510 Fax: 508-627-4560
800-696-2723
Margaret H. White
All year

125-375-B&B
16 rooms, 16 pb
Visa, MC, AmEx,
Rated, •
C-ltd/S-no/P-no/H-yes

Full breakfast
Picnic lunches
Aftn. tea, snacks, comp. port,
sitting room, library,
bicycles, cable

16 luxurious rooms. Large, airy bedrooms with king size beds and down comforters and pillows.   E-mail: hobknob@vineyard.net *Web site:* hobknob.com/

Martha's Place B&B
PO Box 1182, 02568
508-693-0253
Martin Hicks & Richard Alcott
All year

125-395-B&B
6 rooms
Visa, MC, *Rated*, •
C-ltd/S-ltd/P-no/H-ltd

Continental or cont. plus
breakfast
Sitting room, bikes, tennis
court, Jacuzzis, fireplaces,
cable TV

Built in 1840 and renovated in 1987, Martha's Place offers beautifully deocrated rooms adorned with crystal chandeliers, antiques, water views, Jacuzzi tubs, fireplaces, Egyptian cotton linens, and down comforters.   E-mail: marthas@vineyard.net *Web site:* marthasplace.com

---

Martha's Vineyard Resort
117 New York Ave, 02557
508-693-5411 Fax: 508-693-2609
800-874-4403
Claudette & Jack Robinson
All year

60-125-B&B
10 rooms, 10 pb
Visa, MC, AmEx, Disc, •
C-yes/S-ltd/P-no/H-ltd

Continental breakfast
Comp. wine, aftn. tea
Sitting room, library, tennis,
suites, cable TV

*This modern B&B provides modern conveniences, while preserving the quiet idyllic aura of a bygone era. This B&B is a country hideaway in a pristine setting.
E-mail:* jackerobin@aol.com *Web site:* marthasvineyardresort.com

---

Oak House, The
PO Box 299CG, 02557
508-693-4187
Betsi Convery-Luce
May-mid-October

75-B&B
10 rooms, 10 pb
Visa, MC, *Rated*, •
C-ltd/S-yes/P-no/H-no

Continental plus breakfast
Afternoon tea
Sitting room, piano, sun
porch, bicycles, near town,
ferry, beach

*Romantic Victorian Inn on the beach. Richly restored 1872 Governor's home. Oak paneling, wide porches, balconies, leaded windows, water views.
E-mail:* Inns@vineyard.net *Web site:* triple1.com/usa/ma/usma003.htm

---

Shiverick Inn, The
5 Pease Point Way, 02539
508-627-3797
Denny and Marty Turmelle
All year

120-325-B&B
10 rooms, 10 pb
Visa, MC, AmEx, •
C-ltd/S-ltd

Continental plus breakfast
Complimentary tea or coffee
Sitting room, library, dining
room, parlor, formal garden,
bicycles

Exquisitely restored 19th-century mansion offering one-of-a-kind suites and guest rooms with fireplaces, library, formal parlor and garden.   E-mail: shiverickinn@vineyard.net
Web site: mvweb.com/shiv

MARTHA'S VINEYARD

Thorncroft Inn
PO Box 1022, 02568
508-693-3333 Fax: 508-693-5419
800-332-1236
Karl & Lynn Buder
All year

180-475-B&B
14 rooms, 14 pb
Rated, •
C-ltd/S-ltd/P-no/H-no

Full breakfast in dining room
Continental breakfast in
room
Afternoon tea, TV, evening
turndown service, 3.5 acres,
morning paper

Romantic country inn. AAA 4 diamond; Mobil 4 stars. Fireplaces; central A/C; luxury suites with Jacuzzi or private hot tub, balconies; canopied 4-poster beds.   E-mail: innkeeper@ thorncroft.com *Web site:* thorncroft.com

NANTUCKET

Carriage House, The
5 Rays Court, 02554
508-228-0326
Jeanne McHugh & son, Haziel
All year

70-170-B&B
7 rooms, 7 pb
Rated, •
C-yes/S-no/P-no/H-no
Fr., Ger., Sp., Japanese

Continental plus breakfast
Guest refrigerator
Sitting room, library, patio,
beach towels, discount rates,
ask

Converted carriage house on the prettiest country lane; beautifully quiet, yet right in town. B&B and more, since 1974. Tennis, boating and unspoiled beaches nearby.

Century House, The
10 Cliff Rd, 02554
508-228-0530
Gerry Connick & Jeane Heron
All year

95-225-B&B
9 rooms, 9 pb
Rated, •
C-ltd/S-ltd/P-no/H-no
Fr., Rus., Ger., Jap.

Gerry's buffet breakfast
Happy hour setups
Afternoon tea, munchies,
sitting room, veranda, H.
Miller player piano

Historic sea captain's B&B inn in operation since the mid-1800s. Minutes to beaches, restaurants, galleries, shops.   E-mail: centurybnb@aol.com *Web site:* centuryhouse.com

Four Chimneys Inn
38 Orange St, 02554
508-228-1912 Fax: 508-325-4864
Bernadette & Michael Feeney
May-late December

150-275-B&B
10 rooms, 10 pb
Most CC, *Rated*
C-ltd/S-yes/P-no/H-no

Continental plus breakfast
Complimentary hors
d'oeuvres
Sitting room, antiques,
secluded garden, porches

Distinctively Nantucket. Be a guest in a 1835 sea captain's mansion, the largest on this faraway island. Return to gracious living and hospitality.   E-mail: fourchim@nantucket.net *Web site:* 4chimneys.com

Hawthorn House
2 Chestnut Street, 02554
508-228-1468 Fax: 508-228-1468
Diane and Mitchell Carl
All year

70-180-B&B
9 rooms, 7 pb
Visa, MC, •
C-ltd/S-no/P-no/H-no

Full breakfast
Sitting room porches

Charming home located in the center of Nantucket's historic core district. Filled with work of local artisans. Breakfast is provided at either one of two excellent restaurants. E-mail: hhguests@nantucket.net

House of the Seven Gables
32 Cliff Road, 02554
508-228-9446
Sue Walton
April-December

85-175-B&B
10 rooms, 8 pb
Visa, MC, AmEx,
C-ltd/S-no/P-no/H-no

Continental plus breakfast
Sitting room porches

A quiet Victorian in the Old Historic District. Walk to Main Street, beaches, museums and restaurants. A continental breakfast is served to your room each morning.

Inn at Captain's Corners
PO Box 628, 02554
508-228-1692 Fax: 508-228-4186
800-319-9990
B. Bowman
April-October

99-175-B&B
15 rooms, 11 pb
Visa, MC, AmEx, •
C-yes/S-no/P-no/H-no
Spanish (seasonally)

Continental plus breakfast
Sitting room, suites, cable TV,
complementary wine

An elegant captain's home with friendly service and spotless accommodations. Enjoy breakfast on our porch with your fellow guests, or an afternoon of relaxation in our shaded backyard.   E-mail: captainscorners@nii.net *Web site:* captainscorners.com

NANTUCKET

La Petite Maison	165-395-B&B	Continental plus breakfast
132 Main St, 02554	4 rooms, 1 pb	Afternoon tea
508-228-9242	Visa, MC, *Rated*	Sitting room, dining room
Holli Martin	C-ltd/S-yes/H-ltd	w/fireplace,
April 15-January 15	French	Cottage/apt./studio

Located on upper Main St., a 6 minute walk to town center is our owner managed European guesthouse. Breakfast on the sunporch amid international clientele as you enjoy the ambiance & friendliness.

Martin House Inn	80-275-B&B	Continental plus breakfast
61 Centre St, 02554	14 rooms, 10 pb	Complimentary sherry
508-228-0678 Fax: 508-325-4798	Visa, MC, AmEx, *Rated*	Sitting room, fireplace,
Debbie Wasil	C-ltd/S-no/P-no/H-no	veranda, beach towels
All year		

Stately 1803 Mariner's home in Nantucket's historic district. Four-poster canopy beds, 13 airy rooms. Spacious living room, dining room, veranda. 4 rooms with fireplaces. E-mail: martinn@nantucket.net *Web site:* nantucket.net/lodging/martinn/

Nantucket Whale	225-550-EP	Complimentary coffe &
Guesthouse	10 rooms, 10 pb	bottled water
PO Box 1337, 02554	Visa, MC, AmEx,	Suites, remote contol cable
508-228-6597 Fax: 508-228-6291	C-ltd/S-no/P-no/H-no	TV, cooking facilities in each
800-462-6882		room, stereo/CD
Calliope K. Ligelis/Randi Ott		
April-November		

Small, luxury 1850 guest house with private entrances and decks. Equipped to allow simple preparation of your own breakfast, lunch or cocktails. Luxurious linens, down comforters, bathrobes. Steps to finest beaches, restaurants, museums and shops. E-mail: nanwhaler@ aol.com *Web site:* nantucketwhaler.com

Pineapple Inn, The	110-275-B&B	Continental plus breakfast
10 Hussey St, 02554	12 rooms, 12 pb	Sitting room, cable TV,
508-228-9992 Fax: 508-325-6051	Visa, MC, AmEx,	conference facility
Bob & Caroline Taylor	*Rated*, •	
Spring/Summer/Fall	S-no/P-no/H-no	

Centrally located 1838 whaling captain's house with 12 elegantly furnished rooms (Ralph Lauren bedding, Oriental carpets, marble baths, antiques), serving a truly gourmet conti-nental breakfast (espessos, fresh fruits, OJ and baked breakfast treats). E-mail: info@pineappleinn.com *Web site:* pineappleinn.com

Stumble Inne	95-210-B&B	Continental plus breakfast
109 Orange St, 02554	9 rooms	Afternoon tea,
508-228-4482 Fax: 508-228-4752	Visa, MC, AmEx,	complimentary wine
800-649-4482	*Rated*, •	Sitting room, parking,
Jeanne and George Todor	C-ltd/S-no/P-no/H-no	spacious grounds, Voted #1-
April-December		Cape Cod Life

Nantucket's friendliest bed & breakfast. Delightful Laura Ashley decor. Hearty breakfast in a gracious dining room. Near activities & sites. E-mail: romance@nantucket.net *Web site:* stumbleinne.com

Tuckernuck Inn	80-180-B&B	Continental plus bkfst.-low
60 Union St, 02554	18 rooms, 17 pb	season
508-228-4886 Fax: 508-228-4890	Visa, MC, AmEx,	April-Oct: restaurant open
800-228-4886	*Rated*, •	Complimentary wine/snack,
Ken & Phyllis Parker	C-ltd/S-no/P-no/H-yes	sitting room, library, full
All year		service dining-Apr-Oct

Wonderful in-town location; panoramic harbor view from our widow's walk; spacious lawn with recreational facilities; Colonial ambiance. Rooms include TV/VCR, phones with voice mail, more. E-mail: tuckinn@nantucket.net *Web site:* nantucket.net/lodging/tuckinn

NANTUCKET

Woodbox Inn, The	165-285-EP	Continental breakfast
29 Fair St, 02554	9 rooms, 9 pb	Gourmet dinner available
508-228-0587 Fax: 508-228-7527	*Rated*	Restaurant, suites
Dexter Tutein	C-ltd/S-no/P-no/H-no	w/fireplaces, canopy, high-
May-December	French, German,	poster beds
	Spanish	

Nantucket's oldest inn (c.1709). 9 units, queen beds, 1 and 2 bedroom suites with working fireplaces. Just 1½ blocks from historic Main St. Award-winning dining room
E-mail: woodbox@nantucket.net   *Web site:* woodboxinn.com

NANTUCKET ISLAND

Wade Guest House	125-250-B&B	Continental breakfast
PO Box 211, 02564	7 rooms, 4 pb	Sitting room, suites, private
508-257-6308 Fax: 508-257-4602	Visa, MC, AmEx,	beach
Susanne & Wade Greene	C-yes/S-yes/P-no/H-ltd	
Late May-mid-October	French	

The Wade Cottages are a traditional Nantucket-style cluster of houses near the center of the historic village of Siasconset, on a bluff overlooking the open Atlantic. One of lovelier settings, on an island known for its sites and vistas.   E-mail: wgreene@aol.com

NEWBURYPORT

Windsor House, The	135-B&B	Full English breakfast
38 Federal St, 01950	4 rooms, 4 pb	Afternoon tea
978-462-3778 Fax: 978-465-3443	Most CC, *Rated*, •	Common room, organ, and
888-TRELAWNY	C-ltd/S-no/P-yes/H-no	meeting room seats 20
Judith & John Harris		people, shops, museums
All year		

Federalist mansion/ship's chandlery in restored historic seaport furnished in period antiques. The Inn offers four spacious rooms each with a memory of its original use.
E-mail: tintagel@greennet.net   *Web site:* bbhost.com/windsorhouse

NORTHAMPTON

Knoll, The	55-65-B&B	Full breakfast
230 N Main St, 01062	3 rooms	Ocean & public beach
413-584-8164	*Rated*	
Lee (Leona) Lesko	C-ltd/S-no/P-no/H-no	
All year		

Large Tudor house in quiet rural setting on 16 acres. Near 5 colleges: Smith, Amherst, Mt. Holyoke, University of Massachusetts, Hampshire.   E-mail: theknoll@crocker.com
Web site: crocker.com/~theknoll

NORWELL

1810 House B&B	75-85-B&B	Full breakfast
147 Old Oaken Bucket Rd,	3 rooms, 2 pb	Sitting room, family suite,
02061	•	antique 1915 Model T
781-659-1810 Fax: 781-659-1810	C-ltd/S-no/P-no/H-no	
888-833-1810		
Susanne & Harold Tuttle		
All year		

Enjoy a memorable stay in an antique home with great beds, good food and friendly hosts. Wonderful location near Boston and Plymouth. 2 night minimum weekends May thru October.   E-mail: tuttle1810@aol.com

PETERSHAM

Winterwood at Petersham	90-B&B	Continental plus breakfast
PO Box 176, 01366	8 rooms, 8 pb	Restaurant
978-724-8885	Visa, MC, AmEx, •	Bar service, sitting room,
Jean & Robert Day	C-yes/S-ltd/P-no/H-no	library, working fireplaces
All year		

Sixteen-room Greek revival mansion—built as private summer home—on National Register of Historic Homes. Beautifully appointed and professionally decorated. One suite available.

Another Place Inn, Plymouth, MA

PLYMOUTH

1831 Zachariah Eddy B&B
51 S Main St, 02346
508-946-0016 Fax: 508-947-2603
Cheryl & Bradford Leonard
All year

75-129-B&B
3 rooms, 1 pb
Most CC, •
C-ltd/S-no/P-no/H-no

Full breakfast
Dinner available, snacks, wine
Sitting room, library, bicycles, fireplace, cable TV, conference

This 1831 historic home offers quiet, comfortable elegance and sumptous breakfasts. Conveniently located within 35 miles of Boston, Providence, Plymouth, Newport and Cape Cod. E-mail: ZachEddy@aol.com *Web site:* bbhost.com/zacheddyhouse

---

Another Place Inn
240 Sandwich St, 02360
508-746-0126
800-583-0126
Carol Barnes
March-November

85-100-B&B
3 rooms, 3 pb
Rated
C-ltd/S-no/P-no/H-no

Full breakfast
Afternoon tea
Sitting room, suites, fireplaces, cable TV, accommodate business travelers

Only at "Another Place" can you experience the reality of another time in Plymouth. In this 200 year old half-cape family home, an experienced gourmet inn-keeper will surprise your palate with authentic 1620 fare or hearty New England cuisine.

Foxglove Cottage
101 Sandwich Road, 02360
508-747-6576 Fax: 508-747-7622
800-479-4746
Mr. & Mrs. Charles K. Cowan
All year

80-95-B&B
3 rooms, 3 pb
Most CC, *Rated*, •

Full breakfast
Afternoon tea
Sitting room, video library, bicycles, breakfast on deck

Charming, romantic restored 1800 Cape in pastoral setting. Furnished with Victorian antiques. Full breakfast on deck. Minutes from plantation, beaches & town.
E-mail: tranquility@foxglove-cottage.com *Web site:* foxglove-cottage.com

---

Plymouth Bay Manor B&B
259 Court St, 02360
508-830-0426 Fax: 508-747-3382
800-492-1828
Larry & Cindi Hamlin
All year

85-110-B&B
3 rooms, 3 pb
Visa, MC, •
C-ltd/S-no/P-no/H-no

Full breakfast
Afternoon tea
Sitting room, library, fireplace, cable TV, ocean views from all rooms.

Plymouth Bay Manor B&B is a grand 1903 three story shingle style Colonial with water views of Plymouth Bay from each guest room. Near historic sites and Plymouth Rock.
E-mail: info@plymouthbaymanor.com *Web site:* plymouthbaymanor.com

PROVINCETOWN

Cape Codder Guest House
570 Commercial St, 02657
508-487-0131
Deborah Dionne
Mid-April-October

45-65-B&B/EP
14 rooms, 1 pb
Visa, MC,
C-yes/S-ltd/P-ltd/H-ltd

Continental breakfast
Private sandy beach, sun
deck, seaside garden, 1 apt.
with private bath

Old-fashioned comfort in quiet area; private beach, sun deck; whale-watching and bicycling nearby; informal friendly atmosphere; resident marine biologists! Daily maid.
E-mail: ddionne@capecod.net

Gabriel's
104 Bradford St, 02657
508-487-3232 Fax: 508-487-1605
800-969-2643
Gabriel Brooks   All year

65-200-B&B
20 rooms, 20 pb
Most CC, *Rated*, •
C-yes/S-ltd/P-ltd/H-no
Spanish, French

Continental plus breakfast
Sitting room, library,
conference fac., bikes,
Jacuzzis, suites, cable TV

2 beautiful homes graced by antique furnishings, patios & gardens. Each guest room & apartment is distinguished by its own personality.   E-mail: gabrielsma@aol.com
Web site: gabriels.com

Lands End Inn
22 Commercial St, 02657
508-487-0706
800-276-7088
Anthony Arakelian   All year

87-285-B&B
14 rooms, 14 pb
C-ltd/S-no/P-no/H-no

Continental breakfast
Restaurants
Sitting room, near shops,
panoramic views, some
queen-size beds

Victorian summer house set high on a hill overlooking Provincetown with panoramic views of Cape Cod and the marshes.

Revere House
14 Court St, 02657
508-487-2292
800-487-2292
Gary Palochko   May-October

35-145-B&B
8 rooms, 2 pb
Most CC, •
S-ltd/P-no/H-no

Continental breakfast
Sitting room, fireplaces,
cable TV

Revere House is listed as an historic home built in 1830. In 1998, the historical commission awarded the Revere House for being maintained in an authentic manner. We are centrally located to all attractions. Enjoy the gardens or the new common room.   E-mail: reveregh@ tiac.net *Web site:* provincetown.com/revere

REHOBOTH

Gilbert's Tree Farm B&B
30 Spring St, 02769
508-252-6416
Jeanne D. Gilbert
All year

60-80-B&B
4 rooms, 1 pb
•
C-yes/S-no/P-no/H-no

Full breakfast
Afternoon tea
Sitting room, swimming pool,
fireplaces, accommodate
business travelers

New England Cape was built in 1830s. Features original floors, windows & hardward. Has a fireplace, in-ground pool & hiking trails. Surrounded by trees. Peaceful. Hearty country breakfast.   E-mail: jeanneg47@aol.com

Perryville Inn B&B
157 Perryville Rd, 02769
508-252-9239 Fax: 508-252-9054
800-439-9239
Tom & Betsy Charnecki
All year

65-95-B&B
5 rooms, 4 pb
Visa, MC, AmEx,
Rated, •
C-yes/S-ltd/P-no/H-no

Continental plus breakfast
Complimentary wine, tea,
coffee
2 sitting rooms, piano,
balloon rides, bicycles,
central A/C

Newly renovated 19th-century spacious farmhouse in quiet country setting. Located between Boston, Newport, Providence. On National Register of Historic Homes.
E-mail: pvinn@hotmail.com *Web site:* perryvilleinn.com

RICHMOND

B&B in the Berkshires, A
1666 Dublin Rd, 01254
413-698-2817 Fax: 413-698-3158
800-795-7122
Doane Perry & Family
All year

95-200-B&B
3 rooms, 3 pb
Visa, MC, AmEx, •
C-yes/S-no/P-ltd/H-ltd
Fr.,Ger., Greek, Swahili

Continental plus breakfast
Afternoon tea, snacks
Sitting room, library,
bicycles, comp. wine, cable
TV

Serene valley views, 3½ miles to Tanglewood and Hancock Shaker Village. Gracious hosts offer great beds and breakfasts, private baths, hammock in the orchard, rolling lawns and meadows. E-mail: doaneperry@compuserve.com *Web site:* berkshirelodgings.com/abed.html

ROCKPORT

Emerson Inn by the Sea
PO Box 2369, 01966
978-546-6321 Fax: 508-546-7043
800-964-5550
Bruce & Michele Coates
April-December

95-245-B&B
36 rooms, 36 pb
Most CC, *Rated*, •
C-yes/S-no/P-no/H-ltd

Full or continental breakfast
Restaurant
Sitting room, hot tubs, sauna,
swimming pool, family
friendly facility

Come to Cape Ann's oldest Country Inn on the rocky shores of the Atlantic. Ralph Waldo Emerson called it "thy proper summer home." E-mail: info@emersoninnbythesea.com
Web site: emersoninnbythesea.com

Inn on Cove Hill, The
37 Mt Pleasant St, 01966
978-546-2701
888-546-2701
John & Marjorie Pratt
Mid Apr.-Mid Oct.

50-125-B&B
11 rooms, 9 pb
Visa, MC, *Rated*
C-ltd/S-no/P-no/H-no

Continental breakfast
Afternoon tea
Canopy beds, garden,
panoramic view, porch, all
rooms A/C, sitting room

Friendly innkeepers with 20 years experience. Lovingly restored Bicentennial home featured in "Country Living" decorating magazine. Views of ocean from porch.
Web site: cape-ann.com/covehill

Linden Tree Inn
26 King St, 01966
978-546-2494 Fax: 978-546-3297
800-865-2122
Jon & Dawn Cunningham
Open mid-April-end Oct.

70-119-B&B
18 rooms, 18 pb
Visa, MC, AmEx,
Rated, •
C-yes/S-yes/P-no/H-no

Continental plus breakfast
Afternoon tea, cookies
Lemonade, sitting room,
guest living room

Easy access by train, romantic inn. Short walk to beach, shops, restaurants, galleries. Widow's walk views of ocean & mill pond. Local art collection & flower gardens
E-mail: ltree@shore.net *Web site:* linden-tree.com

Rocky Shores Inn/Cottages
65 Eden Rd, 01966
978-546-2823
800-348-4003
Renate & Gunter Kostka
May-Oct.

90-135-B&B
20 rooms, 20 pb
Rated, •
C-ltd/S-ltd/P-no/H-no
German

Continental plus (inn)
Sitting room, rooms with
ocean views, walk to
beaches

Inn & cottages with unforgettable view of Thatcher Island lights & open sea. Inn has 7 firepalces and beautiful woodwork. Complimentary breakfast incl. for inn guests.
Web site: rockportusa.com/rockyshores

Sally Webster Inn
34 Mt Pleasant St, 01966
978-546-9251
877-546-9251
Rick & Carolyn Steere
All year

80-94-B&B
8 rooms, 8 pb
Visa, MC, *Rated*
C-ltd/S-no/P-no/H-no

Continental plus breakfast
Complimentary wine-special
occ.
Sitting room, piano

Historic, colonial home built in 1832. Antique decor. Walk to village and sea. Welcome to the charm of yesteryear. E-mail: sallywebsterinn@hotmail.com
Web site: rockportusa.com/sallywebster/index.html

ROCKPORT

Seacrest Manor	108-148-B&B	Full breakfast
99 Marmion Way, 01966	8 rooms, 6 pb	Afternoon tea
978-546-2211	*Rated*	Library, sitting room,
L. Saville, D. MacCormack, Jr	C-ltd/S-no/P-no/H-no	gardens, sun deck, bicycles,
April-November	some French	cable TV

Decidedly small, intentionally quiet inn. Prizewinning gardens overlook woods & sea. Across street from John Kieran Nature Preserve. E-mail: seacrestmanor@rockportusa.com *Web site:* rockportusa.com/seacrestmanor/

Tuck Inn B&B, The	59-129-B&B	Continental plus breakfast
17 High St, 01966	11 rooms, 11 pb	Snacks
978-546-7260	Visa, MC, *Rated*	Sitting room, A/C, swimming
800-789-7260	C-yes/S-no/P-no/H-no	pool, bicycles, scenic walks,
Liz & Scott Wood		beach
All year		

Lovely 1790 Colonial with a quiet & homey atmosphere. A few minutes' walk to everything. Antiques, gardens, special home-baked breakfast buffet. E-mail: tuckinn@shore.net *Web site:* rockportusa.com/tuckinn/

SALEM

Amelia Payson House	75-130-B&B	Continental plus breakfast
16 Winter St, 01970	4 rooms, 4 pb	Restaurant nearby
978-744-8304	Most CC, *Rated*	beach equipment
Ada May & Donald Roberts	C-ltd/S-no	
All year		

Celebrating 16 years of innkeeping in 2000. Elegantly restored 1845 Greek Revival-style home. Five minute stroll finds restaurants, museums, shopping & train station. E-mail: bbamelia@aol.com *Web site:* salemweb.com/biz/ameliapayson/

Coach House Inn	85-145-B&B	Continental breakfast
284 Lafayette St, 01970	11 rooms, 10 pb	Non-smoking Inn, completely
978-744-4092 Fax: 978-745-8031	Visa, MC, AmEx,	restored and, redecorated
800-688-8689	*Rated*, •	rooms
Patricia Kessler	C-yes/S-no/P-no/H-no	
All year		

Return to elegance. Enjoy the intimacy of a small European-type inn. Victorian fireplaces highlight the charming decor of each room. E-mail: coachhse@star.net *Web site:* salemweb.com/biz/coachhouse

Salem Inn, The	129-290-B&B	Continental breakfast
7 Summer St, 01970	39 rooms, 39 pb	Complimentary sherry,
978-741-0680 Fax: 978-744-8924	Most CC, *Rated*, •	restaurant
800-446-2995	C-yes/S-ltd/P-no/H-no	Private garden, phones, TV,
Richard & Diane Pabich		A/C, canopy beds, fireplaces,
All year		Jacuzzi baths

Spacious, luxuriously appointed rooms in elegantly restored Federal mansion. Some, Jacuzzis, fireplaces & family suites. In the heart of historic district. E-mail: saleminn@ earthlink.net *Web site:* saleminnMA.com

Stephen Daniels House	95-120-B&B	Continental breakfast
One Daniels St, 01970	5 rooms, 3 pb	Complimentary tea
978-744-5709	*Rated*, •	Sitting rooms, walk-in
Mrs. Kay Gill	C-yes/S-yes/P-yes/H-no	fireplaces, private garden,
All year		bicycles

300-year-old house furnished with canopy beds, antiques throughout, fireplaces in every room. Lovely flower-filled English garden, private for guests. Do not charge tax

SALEM

Stepping Stone Inn
19 Washington Square N, 01970
978-741-8900
800-338-3022
John W. Brick
All year

85-130-B&B
8 rooms, 8 pb
Visa, MC, AmEx,
C-ltd/S-no/P-no

Continental breakfast
Sitting room, available for
private, functions

Step into the past at our elegant inn located in Heritage Trail. Continental breakfast in a candlelit dining room. 8 unique guest rooms. Rated "best" by The Washington Post.

Suzannah Flint House
98 Essex St, 01970
978-744-5281
800-893-9973
Scott Eklind
All year

80-110-B&B
3 rooms, 3 pb
Most CC,
C-yes/S-no/P-no/H-no

Continental plus breakfast

1808 Federalist Architecture, in historic Salem, walk to attractions, waterfront, shops and restaurants. Spacious rooms, antiques, decorative fireplaces, cable color TV/VCR. Web site: salemweb.com/biz/suzannahflint

SANDWICH

Bay Beach B&B
PO Box 151, 02563
508-888-8813 Fax: 508-888-5416
800-475-6398
Emily & Reale Lemieux
May 1-November 15

175-345-B&B
6 rooms, 6 pb
Visa, MC, *Rated*
C-ltd/S-no/P-no/H-ltd
French

Full breakfast
Afternoon tea,
complimentary wine
Sitting room, CD player,
bicycles, phones, A/C,
exercise room, fireplaces

Located on secluded & private Bay Beach, offering relaxation & privacy. Complimentary fruit, wine & cheese/crackers welcomes your arrival. Jacuzzis in rooms. Boardwalk to private beach. E-mail: info@baybeach.com Web site: baybeach.com/

Belfry Inn & Bistro
PO Box 2211, 02563
508-888-8550 Fax: 508-888-3923
800-844-4542
Christopher Wilson
All year

95-165-B&B
14 rooms, 14 pb
Visa, MC, AmEx, •
C-yes/S-no/P-no/H-no

Full breakfast
Dinner (fee), afternoon tea
Restaurant, bar service,
Jacuzzis, fireplaces,
conference facilities

Fourteen suites, some featuring whirlpools, fireplace, A/C, TV, balconies. Two buildings: The Drew House is a Victorian Painted Lady; The Abbey was formerly a church and has six suites and a bistro on the first floor. E-mail: info@belfryinn.com Web site: belfryinn.com

Captain Ezra Nye House
152 Main St, 02563
508-888-6142 Fax: 508-833-2897
800-388-2278
Elaine & Harry Dickson
All year

85-110-B&B
6 rooms, 6 pb
Most CC, *Rated*, •
C-ltd/S-no/P-no/H-no
Spanish

Full breakfast
Complimentary wine
Sitting room, library, 3
canopy beds, working,
fireplaces, TV in suite

1829 Federal home; near museums, antique shops, ocean and Heritage Plantation. Voted Reader's Choice-Upper Cape 1993-1998, Cape Cod Life Magazine. Rooms redecorated. E-mail: captnye@aol.com Web site: captaineezranyehouse.com

Isaiah Jones Homestead
165 Main St, 02563
508-888-9115 Fax: 508-888-9648
800-526-1625
Jan & Doug Klapper
All year

85-165-B&B
5 rooms, 5 pb
Visa, MC, AmEx,
Rated, •
C-ltd/S-no/P-no/H-no

Full breakfast
Aftn. tea, lemonade
Phone, TV, fax available, 3
rooms with fireplace, 2 with
whirlpool tub

Elegant Victorian B&B, 5 guestrooms, all with private baths & queen-sized beds. Furnished with museum-quality antiques. E-mail: info@isaiahjones.com Web site: isaiahjones.com

SANDWICH

Summer House, The
158 Main St, 02563
508-888-4991
800-241-3609
Erik Suby & Phyllis Burg
All year

65-110-B&B
5 rooms, 5 pb
Most CC,
C-ltd/S-no/P-no/H-no

Full breakfast
Afternoon tea
Sitting room, library,
common room w/color TV,
books & board games

Exquisite 1835 Greek Revival in historic Sandwich Village. Large, airy rooms with fireplaces, antiques, hand-stitched quilts, and beautiful English gardens. Special diets accommodated, bikes. E-mail: sumhouse@capecod.net *Web site:* capecod.net/summerhouse

Village Inn at Sandwich
PO Box 951, 02563
508-833-0363 Fax: 508-833-2063
800-922-9989
Susan Fehlinger
April-Dec. 23

105-125-B&B
6 rooms, 6 pb
Visa, MC, AmEx,
Rated, •
C-ltd/S-no/P-no/H-no
German

Continental plus wkdays
Full breakfast wkends
Feather comforters, painting
workshops, art studio,
antiques

*1830s Federal-style home in the heart of the village. Wraparound porch surrounded by fragrance of roses. Walking distance to boardwalk, beach and restaurants.
E-mail:* capecodinn@aol.com *Web site:* capecodinn.com

SCITUATE

Allen House, The
18 Allen Place, 02066
781-545-8221 Fax: 781-545-8221
Christine & Iain Gilmour
All year

69-209-B&B
6 rooms, 6 pb
Most CC, *Rated*, •
C-ltd/S-no/P-no/H-yes
French, German,
Spanish

Full gourmet breakfast
Complimentary afternoon
tea
Sitting room, library/music
center, whirlpool bath

Gourmet cook-owner serves "Fantasy Breakfast" on Victorian porch overlooking harbor in unpretentious fishing town 25 miles south of Boston. E-mail: allenhousebnb@worldnet.att.net
Web site: allenhousebnb.com

SHELBURNE FALLS

Bear Haven B&B
22 Mechanic St, 01370
413-625-9281 Fax: 413-625-8474
D. Merrill & C. Merrill-Morben
All year

69-99-B&B
3 rooms, 1 pb
Visa, MC, AmEx,
C-ltd/S-ltd/P-no/H-no
French, German,
Russian

Continental breakfast
Sitting room, cable TV,
feather beds, family cats,
ceiling fans, A/C

"A Rest Home for Teddy Bears." Moses W. Merrill Homestead, 1852. Cozy Victorian ambiance. Five minute walk to restaurants, antique and gift shops, famous Bridge of flowers, unique glacial potholes. E-mail: info@bearhaven.com *Web site:* bearhaven.com

SOUTH DENNIS

Captain Nickerson Inn
333 Main St, 02660
508-398-5966 Fax: 508-398-5966
800-282-1619
Pat & Dave York
March-Dec.

84-105-B&B
5 rooms, 5 pb
Visa, MC, Disc, *Rated*,
•
C-yes/S-ltd/P-no/H-no

Full breakfast
Sitting room, bicycles, Board
games, magazines, ocean
view, beach pool

*Comfortable and pretty Victorian home on bike path in Historic District of Mid-Cape area.
Close to beaches, golf courses and all points of interest E-mail:* captnick@capecod.net
Web site: virtualcities.com/ons/ma/c/mac2601.htm

STERLING

Sterling Inn
PO Box 609, 01564
978-422-6592 Fax: 978-422-3127
Mark & Patricia Roy
All year

68-75-B&B
6 rooms, 6 pb
Most CC, *Rated*
C-ltd/S-ltd/P-no/H-ltd

Continental breakfast
Lunch/dinner available, bar
Afternoon cheese & fruit,
sitt. room, meeting rooms,
fireplaced dining rooms

Turn-of-the-century setting, unique to the area. Rooms have TVs and phones. Dine outside by our landscaped rock garden. E-mail: markeyroy@sprintmail.com

STOCKBRIDGE

Arbor Rose B&B	85-175-B&B	Full breakfast
8 Yale Hill Rd, 01262	6 rooms, 6 pb	Afternoon tea
413-298-4744 Fax: 413-298-4235	Visa, MC, AmEx,	Sitting room, family friendly
877-298-4744	*Rated*, •	facility, fireplaced dining
Christina Alsop and family	C-yes/S-no/P-no/H-no	rooms
All year	Some French	

Charming 1810 farmhouse & mill with flowing pond, gardens, antiques, home-baking, & rural paintings by family of artists/hosts. Tranquil, private, yet close to all attractions.
E-mail: innkeeper@arborrose.com *Web site:* arborrose.com

Historic Merrell Inn	85-215-B&B	Full breakfast
1565 Pleasant St, 01260	10 rooms, 9 pb	Afternoon refreshments
413-243-1794 Fax: 413-243-2669	Visa, MC, *Rated*	Fireplace rooms, antiques,
800-243-1794	C-ltd/S-no/P-no/H-no	telephones, A/C
Faith & Charles Reynolds		
All year		

One of New England's most historic stage coach inns, a few miles from Norman Rockwell Museum, Stockbridge. Full country breakfast of your choice. Most rooms have televisions.
E-mail: merey@bcn.net *Web site:* Merrell-Inn.com

Inn at Stockbridge	115-275-B&B	Full breakfast
PO Box 618 Rt 7, 01262	12 rooms, 12 pb	Complimentary wine
413-298-3337 Fax: 413-298-3406	Visa, MC, AmEx,	Sitting room, library,
888-466-7865	*Rated*, •	antiques, phones, A/C, pool,
Alice & Len Schiller	C-ltd/S-no/H-no	fireplace
All year		

Consummate hospitality distinguishes this Georgian estate. In the heart of the Berkshires, close to Norman Rockwell museum, Tanglewood, summer theaters, winter skiing.
E-mail: innkeeper@stockbridgeinn.com *Web site:* stockbridgeinn.com

Seasons on Main B&B	125-175-B&B	Full breakfast
PO Box 634, 01262	4 rooms, 4 pb	Afternoon tea, snacks, comp.
413-298-5419 Fax: 413-298-0092	Visa, MC, AmEx,	wine
Greg and Pat O'Neill	*Rated*, •	Sitting room, cable TV, tennis
All year	S-no/P-no/H-no	court, fireplaces

1860 Greek Revival home in the heart of the village. "Norman Rockwells' Main Street", beautiful gardens, large front porch furnished with fine heirloom antiques—fireplace & TV in front parlor.

STURBRIDGE

Sturbridge Country Inn	59-B&B	Continental plus breakfast
PO Box 60, 01566	9 rooms, 9 pb	Restaurant, bar
508-347-5503 Fax: 508-347-5319	Visa, MC, AmEx,	Lunch & dinner in tavern,
Ms. Affenito	*Rated*, •	complimentary champagne,
All year	C-ltd/S-yes/P-no/H-yes	hot tubs

Close to Old Sturbridge Village lies our grand Greek Revival structure. Each room has period reproductions, fireplaces, and whirlpool tubs.

TRURO

Parker House B&B	55-B&B	Continental breakfast
PO Box 1111, 02666	2 rooms	Ocean and bay beaches,
508-349-3358	S-no/P-no/H-no	national park, tennis
Stephen Williams		
All year		

A warmly classic 1850 Cape house with many antiques. Close to beaches and charm of Wellfleet and Provincetown.

WARE

Wildwood Inn B&B
121 Church St, 01082
413-967-7798
800-860-8098
F. Fenster & R. Watson
All year

50-90-B&B
9 rooms, 7 pb
Visa, MC, AmEx,
Rated, •
C-ltd/S-no/P-no/H-yes

Full breakfast
Lemonade, cider
Sitting room, tennis courts,
swimming, canoeing, hiking,
games

Relax! Enjoy American antiques & heirloom quilts. Near Sturbridge, Deerfield, Amherst. Canoe, swim, bike, hike. We'll spoil you.

WAREHAM

Mulberry B&B
257 High St, 02571
508-295-0684 Fax: 508-291-2909
Frances A. Murphy
All year

55-70-B&B
3 rooms
Visa, MC, •
C-yes/S-no/P-no/H-no

Full breakfast
Afternoon tea, snacks
Sitting room, library, bicycle
routes with maps, restaurant
discounts

Charming 1840s Cape Cod style home built by blacksmith. Used as a general store by B&B owner's grandfather. Restful location, close to Boston.
Web site: innsandouts.com/property/mulberry_bed_and_breakfast.html

WEST STOCKBRIDGE

Williamsville Inn, The
Rt 41, 01266
413-274-6118
Fax: 413-274-3539
Gail & Kathleen Ryan
All year

120-185-B&B
16 rooms, 16 pb
Visa, MC, AmEx,
Rated, •
C-ltd/S-ltd/P-no/H-no

Full breakfast
Restaurant, bar service
Sitting room, library, tennis
court, pool, candlelight
dining

1797 farmhouse on ten beautiful acres on a quiet country road in the heart of the Berkshires. Gourmet candlelit dining. E-mail: williamsville@taconic.net
Web site: williamsvilleinn.com

WEST TISBURY

Bayberry Inn, The
PO Box 654, 02575
508-693-1984
800-693-9960
Rosalie H. Powell
All year

125-175-B&B
5 rooms, 3 pb
Visa, MC, •
C-ltd/S-no/P-no/H-ltd

Full gourmet breakfast
Complimentary tea, wine
Sitting room, gardens, piano,
croquet, hammock, beach
pass and towels

Gourmet breakfast served by fireplace in charming country home on historic Martha's Vineyard. E-mail: mvbayberry@aol.com *Web site:* vineyard.net/biz/bayberry

WILLIAMSTOWN

House On Main Street, The
1120 Main St, 01267
413-458-3031 Fax: 413-458-2254
Henry Poses
All year

75-100-B&B
6 rooms, 3 pb
Visa, MC, •
C-yes/S-no/P-ltd/H-ltd

Full breakfast
Sitting room, fireplace in
living room, cable TV in 1
bedroom & living room

An 1850 Victorian home in walking distance to theatre, shops, Williams campus and Museum and the Clark Art Institute. Three rooms with private bath, 3 rooms with shared bath. Healthful breakfast served each morning. E-mail: thoms@vgernet.net
Web site: houseonmainst.com

Steep Acres Farm B&B
520 White Oaks Rd, 01267
413-458-3774
Mary & Marvin Gangemi
All year

85-B&B
4 rooms
Rated
C-ltd/S-no/P-no/H-no

Full gourmet breakfast
Complimentary wine
Sitting room, swimming, 1½
acre pond, fishing, hiking
trails, boating

Country home on a high knoll—spectacular views of Berkshire Hills & Vermont's Green Mts. Furnished in country antiques. Trout & swimming pond, 50 acres of woods & pastures.

WORCESTER ———————————————————————————

Rose Cottage	79.95-B&B	Full breakfast
24 Worcester St, 01583	5 rooms, 2 pb	Welcoming beverage
508-835-4034	C-yes/S-no/P-no/H-ltd	Sitting room, suites,
Michael & Loretta Kittredge	Little Italian	fireplaces, cable TV,
All year		accommodate business
		travelers

Gracious 1850 Gothic Revival cottage situated on 4 acres of lawn overlooking Wachusett Reservoir. Cool in summer with high ceilings, window & ceiling fans; warm in winter w/each room setting their own temperature.   Web site: obs-us.com/chesler/rosecottage

YARMOUTH ———————————————————————————

Manor House, The	75-128-B&B	Full breakfast
57 Maine Ave, 02673	7 rooms, 6 pb	Afternoon tea at 4:00
508-771-3433 Fax: 508-790-1186	Visa, MC, AmEx,	Sitting room, views of the
800-962-6679	*Rated*, •	Bay, turn-down service,
Rick & Liz Latshaw	C-ltd/S-no/P-no/H-no	beach chairs & towels
All year		

Lovely Dutch colonial a block from the water and minutes to Hyannis, the ferries to the islands, and fine dining. Canopy beds.   E-mail: manorhse@capecod.net
Web site: capecod.net/manorhouse

Michigan

ANN ARBOR ———————————————————————————

Dundee Guest House, The	65-135-B&B	Continental Plus
522 Tecumseh (M-50), 48131	5 rooms, 5 pb	Sitting room, Jacuzzis, suites,
734-529-5706	Visa, MC, Disc, *Rated*,	fireplaces, Victorian gazebo
800-501-4455	•	in garden
Karen & Jerry Glover	C-ltd/S-no/P-no/H-no	
All year		

A 19th century historic home graced with a beautiful Victorian gazebo with a panoramic view of our formal garden. Choose between our elegant Bridal Suite, Garden View, Rustic or Jacuzzi Room.   E-mail: raglover@umich.edu *Web site:* dundeeguesthouse.com

Urban Retreat B&B, The	65-70-B&B	Full breakfast
2759 Canterbury Rd, 48104	2 rooms, 1 pb	Sitting room, gardens, patio,
734-971-8110	Visa, MC, *Rated*	air conditioning
Andre Rosalik & Gloria Krys	C-ltd/S-ltd/P-no/H-no	
All year		

Comfortable 1950s ranch home on quiet tree-lined street; furnished with antiques; adjacent to 127-acre meadowland park & wildlife preserve; minutes from major universities. Resident house cats.

AUTRAIN ———————————————————————————

Pinewood Lodge	95-110-B&B	Full breakfast
Box 176, M-28-W, 49806	8 rooms, 4 pb	Snacks
906-892-8300 Fax: 906-892-8510	Visa, MC, Disc, *Rated*,	Library, sitting room, hot tub,
Jerry & Jenny Krieg	•	sauna, beach on Lake
All year	C-ltd/S-no/P-no/H-ltd	Superior

Enjoy our log home & breakfast overlooking our sand beach, Lake Superior & AuTrain Island. Hike, swim or relax in our sauna, hot tub, or warm up at fireside in 2 great rooms. E-mail: pinewood@mail.tds.net

BEULAH

Brookside Inn
115 US 31, 49617
231-882-9688 Fax: 231-882-4600
Pamela & Kirk Lorenz
All year

220-300-MAP
40 rooms, 40 pb
Most CC, *Rated*, •
S-yes/P-no/H-yes
German, French

Full breakfast
Dinner included,
complimentary wine
Restaurant, bar service,
sitting room, bikes, hot, tubs,
sauna, steambaths

Created for romantics, couples only rooms, hot tubs, waterbeds, perhaps steam bath, sauna. King canopy waterbeds, log stoves. Dinner & breakfast included. Wine cellar, gift shop E-mail: brooksideinn@brooksideinn.com *Web site:* brooksideinn.com/

BIG BAY

Big Bay Lighthouse B&B
PO Box 3, 49808
906-345-9957 Fax: 906-345-9418
Jeff & Linda Gamble
All year

95-175-B&B
7 rooms, 7 pb
Rated, •
C-ltd/S-no/P-no/H-no

Full breakfast
Afternoon tea, snacks
Sitting room, library,
Jacuzzis, fireplaces, sauna

Escape the ordinary, high on cliff overlooking Lake Superior the lighthouse beckons you to experience a secluded retreat from modern life with quiet nights and northern lights. E-mail: keepers@lighthousebandb.com *Web site:* LighthouseBandB.com

BOYNE CITY

Deer Lake B&B
00631 E Deer Lake Rd, 49712
231-582-9039
Shirley & Glenn Piepenburg
All year

80-105-B&B
5 rooms, 5 pb
Most CC, *Rated*, •
C-ltd/S-no/P-no/H-no

Full breakfast
Sitting room, bikes,
pond/lake, boats, all rooms
air condition

Modern comfort in quiet country setting on lake and pond in an all season resort area. Jewelry class available. E-mail: info@deerlakebb.com *Web site:* deerlakebb.com

BROOKLYN

Dewey Lake Manor B&B
11811 Lair Rd, 49230
517-467-7122 Fax: 517-467-2356
Joe & Barb Phillips
All year

60-125-B&B
4 rooms, 4 pb
Visa, MC, *Rated*, •
C-ltd/S-ltd/P-ltd/H-no
Some Japanese

Full breakfast
Picnic lun., snacks, tea
Sitting room with piano,
croquet, bonfires, ice skating

Sitting atop a knoll overlooking Dewey Lake, a "country retreat" awaits Manor guests in the Irish hills of S. Michigan. Century-old, Italianate-style home furnished with antiques, original kerosene lamps. Web site: getaway2smi.com/dewey/

CANTON

Kathy's Country Retreat
5925 Beck Rd, 48111
734-480-1577
888-831-8925
Kathy Bush
All year

90-100-B&B
2 rooms, 2 pb
Visa, MC, AmEx,
Rated, •
C-ltd/S-ltd/P-no/H-no

Full breakfast
Snacks, complimentary wine
Sitting room, bikes, suites,
fireplaces, conference
facilities, hot tub

Turn of the century farmhouse with garden pond (Koi fish) and flower gardens. Ten acres with walking nature trails. E-mail: joebushlll@aol.com *Web site:* laketolake.com/retreat

Willow Brook Inn B&B
44255 Warren Rd, 48187
734-454-0019 Fax: 734-451-1126
888-454-1919
B & M Van Lenten
All year

95-125-B&B
3 rooms, 3 pb
Most CC, *Rated*, •
C-ltd/S-no/P-yes/H-no
French

Full breakfast
Lunch/dinner(fee)
Aftn. tea, snacks, comp.,
wine, sitt. rm., library,
bicycles, fitness center

Childhood memories. . .pampering pleasures. Brookside Gazebo for weddings or intimate candlelight dinners (fee). Complimentary afternoon tea, snacks, beverages. E-mail: wbibnb@earthlink.net

DEARBORN

Dearborn B&B	95-165-B&B	Continental plus breakfast
22331 Morley, 48124	4 rooms, 4 pb	Snacks, complimentary wine
313-563-2200 Fax: 313-277-2962	Most CC, •	Swimming pool, cable TV,
888-959-0900	C-ltd/S-no/P-no/H-no	accommodate business
Nancy Siwik & Rick Harder		travelers
All year		

Unique, antique filled home, located in quiet, charming neighborhood. Just a short walk to shopping, museums, and fine dining. Perfect place for romantic getaways or business travelers. E-mail: nancyswork@aol.com Web site: dearbornbb.com

FLINT

Avon House B&B	55-B&B	Full breakfast
518 Avon St, 48503	3 rooms	Formal dining room
810-232-6861 Fax: 810-233-7437	C-yes/S-no/P-no/H-no	Sitting room, A/C, play yard,
888-832-0627		grand piano, extended stay
Arletta E. Minore		rates
All year		

Enchanting Victorian home close to College & Cultural Center with art & entertainment. Driving distance to Manufacturer's Marketplace. Children's play yard. E-mail: avonhsebed@ aol.com Web site: accessflint.com/~avonhouse

GLEN ARBOR

Sylvan Inn	65-135-B&B	Continental plus breakfast
PO Box 648, 49636	14 rooms, 7 pb	Sitting room, whirlpool &
231-334-4333	Visa, MC, *Rated*, •	sauna room, extended stay
Jenny & Bill Olson	C-ltd/S-no/P-no/H-yes	rates
May-February		

Luxuriously renovated 1885 historic inn situated in the heart of Sleeping Bear National Lakeshore. Easy access to fine dining, shopping, swimming, biking, skiing.

HARBOR SPRINGS

Veranda at Harbor Springs	140-225-B&B	Full breakfast
403 E Main St, 49740	6 rooms	Snacks, complimentary wine
616-526-7782 Fax: 616-526-8278	Visa, MC,	Jacuzzis, cable TV
Susan Howard	C-ltd/S-no/P-no/H-no	
All year		

The Veranda welcomes you with a sunny porch and candlelit evenings. Walk downtown to unique shops and wonderful restaurants. E-mail: showard@netonecom.net Web site: harborspringsveranda.com

HARRISON

Serendipity B&B	65-125-B&B	Full breakfast
PO Box 377, 48625	3 rooms, 3 pb	Afternoon tea, snacks
517-539-6602	Most CC, *Rated*, •	Sitting room, library,
Bill & Lori Schuh	S-no/P-no/H-ltd	Jacuzzis, fireplaces, gardens,
All year		walking trails

Romantic escape or solitary respite. Nested on 16 acres of woodland with walking trails, perennial and herb gardens. Three unique guest rooms. Distinctive full country breakfast served by the fireplace. E-mail: serendipitybbin@webtv.net Web site: laketolake.com/serendipity/index.htm

HOLLAND

Dutch Colonial Inn	80-150-B&B	Full breakfast
560 Central Ave, 49423	4 rooms, 4 pb	Afternoon tea, snacks
616-396-3664 Fax: 616-396-0461	Most CC, *Rated*	In-room phone with data-
Bob & Pat Elenbaas	S-no/P-no/H-no	port, in-room TV, double
All year		whirlpool tubs

Lovely 1928 Dutch Colonial home. Touches of elegance and antiques. Lovely common areas. Whirlpool tubs for 2 in private baths; fireplaces; honeymoon suites. E-mail: dutchcolonialinn@juno.com Web site: bbonline.com/mi/dutch

—The Munro House, Jonesville, MI

HOLLAND

North Shore Inn of Holland
686 N Shore Dr, 49424
616-394-9050 Fax: 616-392-1389
Beverly & Kurt Van Genderen
March 15-December 15

95-110-B&B
3 rooms, 2 pb
C-ltd/S-no/P-no/H-no

Full breakfast
Complimentary soft drinks
Sitting room, bicycles

Quiet lakeside location with gardens and woods, yet close to public beaches and historic downtown Holland. Gourmet breakfasts are a specialty.

JONESVILLE

Horse & Carriage B&B
7020 Brown Rd, 49250
517-849-2732 Fax: 517-849-2732
Keith Brown & Family
All year

85-100-B&B
3 rooms, 2 pb
Rated
C-yes/S-no/P-no/H-no
Limited Portuguese

Full breakfast
Picnic lunch, snacks
Sitting room, library, Family
friendly facility, carriage ride
by request

Horse drawn carriage ride and picnic awaits you at our quaint 1898 schoolhouse nestled on our peaceful sesquicentennial dairy farm. Hearty breakfast served.

Munro House, The
202 Maumee, 49250
517-849-9292 800-320-3792
Joyce A. Yarde   All year

80-150-B&B
7 rooms, 7 pb
Visa, MC, *Rated*, •
C-yes/S-no/P-no/H-ltd

Full breakfast
Evening dessert
Sitting room, library, 2 rooms
with Jacuzzis, 5 rooms with
fireplaces

This 1840 Greek Revival home (once a station on the underground railroad) is filled with history and the charm of a bygone era.   Web site: getaway2smi.com/munro

KALAMAZOO

Hall House B&B
106 Thompson St, 49006
616-343-2500 Fax: 616-343-1374
888-761-2525
Jerry & Joanne Hofferth
All year

75-150-B&B
6 rooms, 6 pb
Visa, MC, AmEx,
Rated, •
C-ltd/S-no/P-no/H-no

Full breakfast on weekends
Continental plus on
weekdays
Goodies always available,
sitting room, sun porch,
cable TV/VCRs in rooms

Stately 1920s Georgian Colonial home, minutes from downtown, on the edge of the Kalamazoo College campus.   E-mail: hofferth@hallhouse.com *Web site:* hallhouse.com

LELAND

Whaleback Inn
PO Box 1125, 49654
616-256-9090 Fax: 616-256-2255
800-942-5322
Ron Koehler   All year

59-169-B&B
17 rooms, 17 pb
Visa, MC,
C-yes/S-ltd/P-no/H-yes

Continental breakfast
Sitting room, hot tubs, sauna,
hiking, lake, swimming,
basketball

Relaxing getaway. Beautiful scenic area. All accommodations new or recently remodeled with private baths and ground floor entry. Volleyball.   E-mail: wbi@wfn.net
Web site: leelanau.com/whaleback

LEWISTON, GAYLORD

LakeView Hills B&B Resort
PO Box 365, 49756
517-786-2000 Fax: 517-786-3445
S. Chapoton & J. Coudneys
All year

98-149-B&B
15 rooms, 15 pb
Visa, MC, Disc, *Rated*,
•
C-ltd/S-no/P-no/H-yes

Full breakfast
Lunch, dinner, tea, snacks,
wine
Sitting room, library,
bicycles, jacuzzi, suites,
fireplace, cable TV

Located on one of the highest elevations in the state of Michigan. This is also SPA Resort with all services available. E-mail: info@lakeviewhills.net *Web site:* lakeviewhills.net

LOWELL

McGee Homestead B&B
2534 Alden Nash NE, 49331
616-897-8142
Bill & Ardie Barber
March 1-December 31

42-62-B&B
4 rooms, 4 pb
Most CC, *Rated*
C-yes/S-ltd/P-ltd/H-no

Full breakfast
Afternoon tea, snacks
Sitting room, library, guest
kitchen with microwave &
fridge

Wake up to the rooster crowing. Our 1880's farmhouse is filled with antiques but it very comfy. Walk our five acres and surrounding orchards, visit the barn full of animals or just relax in the hammock.

LUDINGTON

Inn at Ludington, The
701 E Ludington Ave, 49431
213-845-7055 Fax: 213-845-0794
800-845-9170
Diane & David Nemitz
All year

75-100-B&B
6 rooms, 6 pb
Most CC, *Rated*, •
C-ltd/S-no/P-no/H-no

Full buffet breakfast
Picnic lunches (fee)
Sitting room, library, murder
mystery weekends, family
country suite

This 1890 Queen Anne painted lady combines the charm of the past with the comforts of today. Conveniently located on the avenue, walk to shops, restaurants, marina & car ferry. Fireplace rooms. *Web site:* inn-ludington.com

Ludington House
501 E Ludington Ave, 49431
231 845-7769
800-827-7869
Virginia Boegner
All year

80-135-B&B
8 rooms, 8 pb
Visa, MC, *Rated*, •
C-yes/S-no/P-ltd/H-no

Full breakfast
Sitting room, library,
Jacuzzis, fireplaces, cable
TV, parlor games, fridge

1878 Lumber Baron home. Romantic interlude, vacation, or family reunions. House capacity 20. Queen beds. Hearty gourmet breakfast; special diets available. Murder Mysteries. Gift certificates. Quiet season/weekday discounts. *Web site:* bbonline.com/mi/tlh

Snyder's Shoreline Inn
PO Box 667, 49431
213-845-1261 Fax: 213-843-4441
Angie Snyder & Kate Whitaker
Open May-Oct.

59-289-B&B
44 rooms, 44 pb
Most CC, *Rated*
S-no/P-no/H-yes

Continental breakfast
Box lunches available
Library, hot tub, swimming
pool, in room spas

Country inn with private balconies facing Lake Michigan. In-room spas. Near shopping, restaurants, golf & bike paths. On the beach E-mail: sharon@snydersshoreinn.com
Web site: snydersshoreinn.com

NEW BUFFALO

Sans Souci Euro Inn
19265 S Lakeside Rd, 49117
616-756-3141 Fax: 616-756-5511
The Siewerts
All year

110-195-B&B
9 rooms, 9 pb
Most CC, *Rated*, •
C-ltd/S-ltd/P-no/H-yes
German, Spanish

Full breakfast/suites
Full kitchens/houses
TV/VCR, phones, skate,
private lake/beach/fish,
birdwatching, CD, WP, FP

Choose your destination to be "without a care." Our Euro vacation home, honeymoon suite, or family cottage come with luxury amenities. Near Lake Michigan.
E-mail: sans-souci@worldnet.att.net *Web site:* sans-souci.com

PENTWATER

Candlewyck House B&B, The
PO Box 392, 49449
231-869-5967 Fax: 231-869-5968
John & Mary Jo Meidow
All year

79-110-B&B
6 rooms, 6 pb
Visa, MC, •
C-yes/S-ltd/P-no/H-no

Full breakfast
Snacks
Sitting room, library, bikes,
suites, fireplaces, cable TV

Built in the 1870s, the Candlewyck House was restored to its original character and opened to guests in 1989. For the comfort and convenience of our guests, all rooms have private baths, air-conditioning and color cable TV. Web site: bbonline.com/mi/candlewyck/index.html

Pentwater "Victorian" Inn
PO Box 98, 49449
616-869-5909 Fax: 616-869-7002
Donna & Quintus Renshaw
All year

85-150-B&B
5 rooms, 5 pb
Visa, MC, *Rated*
C-yes/S-no/P-no/H-no
German, French

Full breakfast
Evening beverage & snack
Sitting room, antiques,
Jacuzzi suite, bicycles—near,
snowmobile

1869 Victorian Inn in quiet residential area. Within walking distance of Lake Michigan Beach, village shops & fine dining. Web site: pentwaterinn.com

PETOSKEY

Serenity, A B&B
504 Rush St, 49770
231-347-6171 Fax: 231-439-0337
877-347-6171
Ralph and Sherry Gillet
All year

75-92-B&B
3 rooms, 3 pb
Visa, MC, *Rated*
C-ltd/S-no/P-no/H-no

Full breakfast
Afternoon tea, snacks
Sitting room, air-conditioned
rooms

1890's Victorian B&B close to downtown Petoskey. Serenity offers casual elegance, soft music & lace. Air-conditioned rooms and private baths. E-mail: serenitybb@mail.unnet.com Web site: serenitybb.com

Terrace Inn
PO Box 266, 49770
231-347-2410 Fax: 231-347-2407
800-530-9898
Tom & Denise Erhart
All year

75-B&B
43 rooms, 43 pb
Visa, MC, AmEx,
Rated, •
C-yes/S-no/P-no/H-yes

Continental plus breakfast
Rest. serves dinner(fee)
Sitting room, bicycles, tennis,
private beach, Jacuzzi suite
$129

1910 furnishings are at home in this Victorian inn among 400 Victorian cottages, each room having own decor. E-mail: info@theterraceinn.com Web site: theterraceinn.com

PORT HURON

Victorian Inn, The
1229 7th St, 48060
810-984-1437 Fax: 810-984-5777
Marvin & Susan Burke
All year

95-135-B&B
4 rooms, 2 pb
Most CC, *Rated*, •
C-ltd/S-yes/P-no/H-no

Full breakfast
Restaurant, pub
Lunch, dinner, near
museum, downtown, civic
center, marina

The Victorian Inn features fine dining with creative cuisine and guest rooms presenting a timeless ambiance in authentically restored Victorian elegance.
E-mail: marv-sue@victorianinn-mi.com

PORT SANILAC

Raymond House Inn, The
PO Box 438, 48469
810-622-8800 Fax: 810-622-9587
800-622-7229
Gary & Chris Bobofchek
April-November

75-115-B&B
7 rooms, 7 pb
Visa, MC, Disc, *Rated*,
•
C-ltd/S-no/P-no/H-no

Full breakfast
Comp. sherry, snacks
A/C, TV, phones, sitting
room, deck, fitness salon

127-year-old Victorian home on Michigan's Historic Register, furnished in antiques. On Lake Huron—marina, boating, shipwreck, scuba diving, fishing, swimming. Pamper room.
E-mail: rayhouse@greatlakes.net Web site: bbonline.com/mi/raymond

SAGINAW

Montague Inn	65-160-B&B	Continental plus breakfast
1581 S Washington, 48602	18 rooms, 16 pb	Restaurant, bar service
517-752-3939 Fax: 517-752-3159	Visa, MC, AmEx, *Rated*	Lunch, dinner (fee), library,
Janet Hoffmann	C-yes/S-ltd/P-no/H-yes	Jacuzzi suite
All year		

Georgian mansion restored to its original splendor. Surrounded by spacious lawns with flower & herb gardens. The Inn provides a peaceful & elegant oasis in the heart of the city. E-mail: montaguein@aol.com Web site: montagueinn.com

SAUGATUCK

Bayside Inn	80-235-B&B	Continental plus breakfast
PO Box 186, 49453	10 rooms, 10 pb	Snacks
616-857-4321 Fax: 616-857-1870	Most CC, *Rated*	Converted boathouse,
Kathy and Frank Wilson	C-yes/S-no/P-no/H-ltd	private bath/deck ea.rm.,
All year		cable TV, phones

Bayside is an old boathouse converted to a B&B on the water, near downtown Saugatuck. Inground, outdoor hot tub situated 4 feet from the waters edge. Web site: bbonline.com/mi/bayside

Beachway Resort	75-145-EP	Snacks
PO Box 186, 49453	28 rooms, 28 pb	Swimming pool, cable TV,
616-857-3331	Visa, MC, AmEx, *Rated*	video library
Fax: 616-857-3912	C-yes/S-no/P-no/H-yes	
Frank & Kathy Wilson		
May-end of Oct.		

Overlooking the harbor on the banks of the Kalamazoo River, just a 100-foot ferry ride to downtown. Web site: macatawa.org/~beachway

Hidden Pond B&B	64-110-B&B	Full breakfast
PO Box 461, 49408	2 rooms, 2 pb	Snacks, complimentary
616-561-2491	*Rated*, •	sherry
Priscilla & Larry Fuerst	C-ltd/S-no/P-no/H-no	Sitting room, library, guest
All year		use of home, A/C, bicycles,
		fresh flowers

28 acres of wooded, ravined land for your relaxation. Full gourmet breakfast. Beaches, Saugatuck, Holland & Fennville 10 minutes away. Lovely quiet retreat. Hiking, fireplace.

Kingsley House, The	80-175-B&B	Full breakfast
626 W Main St, 49408	9 rooms, 9 pb	Continental plus weekdays
616-561-6425	Most CC, *Rated*, •	Sitting rooms, fireplace,
Fax: 616-561-2593	C-ltd/S-no/H-yes	bicycles, porch swing
Gary And Kari King		
All year		

Turreted, elegant, Queen Anne Victorian built 1886. Just min. from Saugatuck and Holland, & the sandy beaches of Lake Michigan. Top 50 inn by "Inn Times." E-mail: garyking@accn.org Web site: kingsleyhouse.com

Park House, The	95-165-B&B	Full breakfast
888 Holland St, 49453	8 rooms, 8 pb	Soft drinks, juice
616-857-4535 Fax: 616-857-1065	Visa, MC, *Rated*, •	Sitting room, TV, 3rd floor
800-321-4535	C-ltd/S-yes/P-no/H-yes	game loft, suites with jet tub,
Lynda & Joe Petty		fireplace
All year		

Country home with New England charm; built in 1857. National Historic Register Home. Near town, beaches, paddleboat rides, dinner cruises, cross country skiing, golf. 2 rooms/2 cottages with hot tubs. E-mail: parkhouse@softhouse.com Web site: bbonline.com/mi/parkhouse/

SAUGATUCK ──────────────────────────────

Sherwood Forest B&B	85-165-B&B	Full breakfast
PO Box 315, 49453	5 rooms, 5 pb	Afternoon tea, snacks
616-857-1246 Fax: 616-857-1996	Visa, MC, *Rated*, •	Sitting room, bicycles, heated
800-838-1246	C-ltd/S-no/P-no/H-no	pool, skiing, Jacuzzi, cottage
Susan & Keith Charak		
All year		

Surrounded by woods, this beautiful Victorian-style home offers fireplace-Jacuzzi suites, heated pool, bicycles and wrap-around porch. E-mail: sf@sherwoodforestbandb.com Web site: sherwoodforestbandb.com

Twin Gables Inn	70-160-B&B	Full breakfast
PO Box 1150, 49453	17 rooms, 17 pb	Refreshments
616-857-4346 Fax: 616-857-3482	Most CC, *Rated*, •	Whirlpool/hot tub, pool, A/C,
800-231-2185	C-ltd/S-ltd/P-no/H-yes	bicycles, pond, garden park
B. Lawrence & S. Schwaderer		
All year		

Relaxing and romantic overlooking Kalamazoo Lake. Quaint guestrooms, some with fireplaces. Short walk to downtown. 3 comfortable cottages. E-mail: relax@twingablesinn.com Web site: twingablesinn.com

Twin Oaks Inn	75-125-B&B	Full breakfast
227 Griffith St, 49453	10 rooms, 10 pb	Afternoon tea, snacks
616-857-1600	Most CC, *Rated*, •	Hot tubs, bicycles, TVs, VCRs
800-788-6188	C-yes/S-no/P-no	with movie library
Nancy & Jerry Horney		
All year		

Relax in the warmth and charm of antiques and modern amenities. Six guest rooms with queen/king size beds, Jacuzzi suite. Cottage with fireplace and hot tub. All have private baths, A/C, and TV/VCR. 700 movies and full breakfasts. Web site: bbonline.com/mi/twinoaks/

Will O'Glenn Irish B&B	99-145-B&B	Full breakfast
PO Box 288, 49416	4 rooms, 4 pb	Tea, snacks, wine
616-227-3045 Fax: 616-227-3045	Visa, MC, *Rated*, •	Sitting room, library,
888-237-3009	C-ltd/S-no/P-no/H-ltd	Jacuzzis, fireplace,
Shelley & Ward Gahan	Some French	conference facilities
All year		

Tranquility & serenity are the order of the day in these peaceful surroundings. Unwind in the country at our Irish Country Manor House on 17 acres with Saugatuck & South Haven minutes away E-mail: shamrock@irish-inn.com Web site: irish-inn.com

SOUTH HAVEN ──────────────────────────

Carriage House at Harbor	95-185-B&B	Full breakfast
118 Woodman Ave, 49090	11 rooms, 11 pb	Evening hors d'oeuvres
616-639-1776 Fax: 616-639-2308	Visa, MC, AmEx, *Rated*	Sitting room, library, adult
Jay & Joyce Yelton	S-no/P-no/H-yes	get-away, 2 people per room
All year		only, screend porch

Three story elegant Victorian home overlooking harbor & marina. Decks, sun porch, luxurious rooms with fireplaces & whirlpools- 19 fireplace rooms, 14 whirlpool rooms, and 8 with decks. Web site: theinnplace.com

Old Harbor Inn	75-230-EP	Comp. paper, Jacuzzis, near
515 Williams St, 49090	44 rooms, 44 pb	fishing/boats/golf,
616-637-8480 Fax: 616-637-9496	Most CC, *Rated*, •	tennis/beaches/sailing
800-433-9210	C-yes/S-yes/P-no/H-yes	
Gwen DeBruyn		
All year		

Nestled on banks of the Black River, Old Harbor Inn offers guests the charm & grace of a quaint coastal village. Luxury suites, fireplaces, kitchenettes, indoor pool E-mail: Robin@oldharborinn.com Web site: oldharborinn.com

SOUTH HAVEN

Sand Castle Inn	85-195-B&B	Full breakfast
203 Dyckman Ave, 49090	9 rooms, 9 pb	Afternoon tea, snacks
616-639-1110 Fax: 616-637-1050	Most CC, *Rated*	Sitting room, library, bikes,
Mary Jane & Charles Kindred	S-no/P-no/H-yes	suites, fireplaces, private
All year		balconies.

Beautifully restored historic Lake Michigan Resort Hotel. One block to beach, three blocks to downtown. Walk to shops, restaurants. Designer decorated.   E-mail: sandcasinn@aol.com Web site: yesmichigan.com/sandcastleinn

Seymour House, The	95-145-B&B	Full breakfast
1248 Blue Star Hwy, 49090	7 rooms, 6 pb	Lunch (fee), afternoon tea
616-227-3918 Fax: 616-227-3010	Visa, MC, *Rated*, •	Snacks, Jacuzzis, sitting
Tom & Gwen Paton	C-ltd/S-no/P-no/H-no	room, library, pond to swim
All year		in

Historic 1862 mansion in picturesque wooded setting near Lake Michigan's sandy beaches. Pamper yourself with decadent breakfasts, Jacuzzis, and fireplaces. 2 of 7 rooms in log cabin.   E-mail: seymour@cybersol.com   Web site: seymourhouse.com

Yelton Manor B&B	95-260-B&B	Full or Continental plus
140 North Shore Dr, 49090	17 rooms, 17 pb	breakfast
616-637-5220 Fax: 616-637-4957	Visa, MC, AmEx, *Rated*	Evening hors d'oeuvres
Elaine Herbert, Rob Kripaitis	C-ltd/S-no/P-no/H-no	Library, porch, Jacuzzis in, 11
All year		rooms, fireplaces in 8 rooms

Fabulous lakeside Victorian mansion. Elegant fireplace and Jacuzzi rooms and lake views. Porches, parlors, antiques, award winning gardens with tours, great food.   E-mail: elaine@ yeltonmanor.com Web site: yeltonmanor.com

ST. JOSEPH

South Cliff Inn B&B	75-169-B&B	Continental plus breakfast
1900 Lakeshore Dr, 49085	7 rooms, 7 pb	Sunday brunch, snacks
616-983-4881 Fax: 616-983-4881	Most CC, *Rated*, •	Sitting room, library, formal
Bill Swisher	C-ltd/S-no/P-no/H-no	gardens, fireplaces
All year		

South Cliff Inn is perched on a bluff overlooking Lake Michigan. Each guest room is beautifully appointed. Homemade breakfasts beyond compare. Web site: laketolake.com/southcliffinn

TRAVERSE CITY

Linden Lea On Long Lake	85-110-B&B	Full breakfast
279 S Long Lake Rd, 49684	2 rooms, 2 pb	Complimentary wine, snacks
231-943-9182	*Rated*, •	Sitting room, whirlpool, tub,
Jim & Vicky McDonnell	C-ltd/S-no	lake frontage, sandy beach,
All year	Spanish	boating

Wooded lakeside retreat with private sandy beach, fishing, swimming, rowboat & raft. Comfortable country furnishings, window seats, antiques & beveled glass throughout. Heavily wooded. Peaceful.   E-mail: lindenlea@aol.com

UNION PIER

Inn at Union Pier, The	135-205-B&B	Full breakfast
PO Box 222, 49129	16 rooms, 16 pb	Snacks & beverages
616-469-4700	Most CC, *Rated*	Great room, library, bikes,
Fax: 616-469-4720	C-ltd/S-no/P-no/H-yes	outdoor hot tub, Lake
Mark & Joyce Erickson Pitts		Michigan beach
All year		

Elegantly refurbished inn blending barefoot informality with gracious hospitality. In "Harbor Country", known for Lake Michigan beaches, antiques, galleries, and wineries. Host corporate retreats.   Web site: innatunionpier.com

UNION PIER —————————————————————————————

Rivers Edge B&B
9902 Community Hall Rd,
49129
616-469-6860 Fax: 616-469-6890
800-742-0592
Gretchen & Mark Robbins
All year

89-155-B&B
8 rooms, 8 pb
Visa, MC, AmEx,
Rated, •
C-ltd/S-no/P-no/H-yes

Full breakfast
Snacks, wine
Sitting room, library, bikes,
Jacuzzis, suites, fireplaces,
canoes

A pine lodge located on 30 acres of land with close to a mile of frontage on the Galein River. All rooms have fireplaces, double Jacuzzis, TVs. E-mail: zigzag@enteract.com
Web site: riversedgebandb.com

YPSILANTI ————————————————————————————

Parish House Inn
103 S Huron St, 48197
734-480-4800 Fax: 734-480-7472
800-480-4866
Mrs. Chris Mason   All year

89-134-B&B
9 rooms, 9 pb
Most CC, *Rated*, •
C-ltd/S-no/P-no/H-yes

Full breakfast
Afternoon tea, snacks

Victorian charm, modern amenities, hearty breakfasts, great for corporate travel, romantic getaways. Near golf, restaurants, historic interests. Easy highway access. E-mail: parishinn@ aol.com Web site: bbonline.com/mi/parish

Minnesota

AFTON ——————————————————————————————————

Afton House Inn
PO Box 326, 55001
651-436-8883 Fax: 651-436-6859
877-436-8883
Gordy & Kathy Jarvis
All year

60-175-B&B
16 rooms, 16 pb
Rated
C-ltd/S-ltd/P-no/H-yes

Continental plus breakfast
Lunch/dinner available,
restaurant
Bar service, Jacuzzis,
fireplaces, cable TV,
accommodate business
travelers

Historic country inn furnished with unique antique decor, modern conveniences, private baths and televisions. E-mail: info@aftonhouseinn.com Web site: aftonhouseinn.com

ALBUQUERQUE ————————————————————————————

Hacienda de Colores
1113 Montoya NW, 87104
505-247-0013 Fax: 505-242-7063
877-265-6737
Rey & Kim Vejih   All year

100-185-B&B
3 rooms, 3 pb
Visa, MC, AmEx, •
C-ltd/S-ltd/P-ltd/H-ltd
Spanish

Full breakfast
Afternoon tea, snacks, comp.
wine
Sitting room, library,
bicycles, Jacuzzis, fireplaces,
cable TV

Spanish hacienda a heartbeat away from Old Town Plaza and downtown Albuquerque with an inviting covered portal for refreshments nestled among ageless native trees shading a six-acre pastoral setting. Wedding chapel. E-mail: hdecolores@aol.com
Web site: haciendadecolores.com

ALEXANDRIA ——————————————————————————————

Cedar Rose Inn
422 7th Ave West, 56308
320-762-8430 Fax: 320-762-8044
888-203-5333
Aggie & Florian Ledermann
All year

75-125-B&B
5 rooms, 4 pb
Visa, MC, *Rated*, •
C-ltd/S-no/P-no/H-no

Full breakfast
Snacks, complimentary wine
Sitting room, library,
bicycles, hot tubs,
swimming, fishing

Cozy 1903 Tudor-Revival style home, walking distance to downtown, many beautiful roses, located in heart of Minnesota lake country. Complimentary infrared sauna.
E-mail: cedarose@gctel.com Web site: echopress.com/cedarose

COOK

Ludlow's Island Lodge
PO Box 1146, 55723
218-666-5407 Fax: 218-666-2488
877-583-5697
Mark and Sally Ludlow
May-Oct.

165-195-EP
56 rooms, 56 pb
Most CC, *Rated*, •
C-yes/S-yes/P-no/H-no

Breakfast by request (fee)
Dinner by request
Sitting room, library, tennis
court, sauna, family friendly
facility

Our private land with cottages is situated under a canopy of pine and birch, on the water's edge. Explore our wilderness. E-mail: info@ludlowsresort.com *Web site:* ludlowsresort.com

CROSBY-DEERWOOD

Hallet House B&B
12131 Hwy 6 N, 56444
218-546-5433 Fax: 218-546-5933
877-546-5433
Bob Novak, Scott Berg
All year

65-105-B&B
5 rooms, 5 pb
Most CC,
C-ltd/S-ltd/P-no/H-ltd
German, Russian

Full breakfast
Wine
Sitting room, library,
Jacuzzis, suites, fireplace,
cable TV, conference

An elegant countryside, 1920's deco-style mansion nestled in mature pines. Exceptional rooms and suites; antiques about; fireplaces; Jacuzzi; sumptuous breakfasts. Literary theme stems from a fabulous sunken library. E-mail: hallett@emily.net
Web site: halletthouse.com

DETROIT LAKES

Log House and Homestead
PO Box 130, 56587
218-342-2318 Fax: 218-342-3294
800-342-2318
Suzanne Tweten & Patrice
Allen
All year

100-175-B&B
5 rooms, 5 pb
Visa, MC, *Rated*
S-ltd/P-no/H-no
French

Full breakfast
Private candlelit dinners
available
Sitting room, hike, bike,
whirlpool, skiing, boats, large
suite w/balconies

Romantic, elegant retreat in restored 1889 loghouse & turn-of-the-century homestead with in-room fireplaces. Tranquillity & pampered comfort with charm of a bygone era. E-mail: loghouse@tekstar.com *Web site:* loghousebb.com

DULUTH

Charles Weiss Inn, A
1615 E Superior St, 55812
218-724-7016
800-525-5243
Dave & Peg Lee
All year

77-135 B&B
5 rooms, 5 pb
Visa, MC, Disc, *Rated*
C-ltd/S-no/P-ltd/H-no

Full breakfast
Complimentary wine
Sitting room, library,
Jacuzzis, suites, fireplaces,
cable TV

Historic 1895 Victorian colonial with 5 fireplaces and whirlpool room. Located 3 blocks from Lake Superior, Lakewalk, quick access to Canal Park, skiing and 3 golf courses. E-mail: dglee@uslink.net *Web site:* duluth.com/acweissinn

Firelight Inn on Oregon Ck
2211 E Third St, 55812
218-724-0272 Fax: 218-724-0304
888-724-0273
Jim & Joy Fischer   All year

129-229-B&B
6 rooms, 6 pb
Most CC, *Rated*
C-ltd/S-no/P-no/H-no

Full breakfast
Snacks
Sitting room, Jacuzzis, suites,
fireplaces, cable TV,
bathrobes, hair dryers

The Inn is located next to a wooded ravine adjacent to the babbling creek as it flows to Lake Superior. A full breakfast in a basket is delivered each morning. E-mail: firelight@duluth.com *Web site:* duluth.com/firelightinn

FERGUS FALLS

Bakketopp Hus B&B
RR 2, Box 187A, 56537
218-739-2915
800-739-2915
Dennis & Judy Nims   All year

70-105-B&B
3 rooms, 3 pb
Visa, MC, Disc, *Rated*
C-ltd/S-no/P-no/H-no

Full special breakfast
Afternoon tea, snacks
Sitting room, antiques,
fishing, golf, hot tubs, decks
on the lakeside

Wooded hillside lake view. A scenic lake setting. Listen to loons at dusk, enjoy flowers in tiered gardens or relax in spa. Golf, antiques & restaurants nearby. Group meetings, fishing. E-mail: ddn@prtel.com *Web site:* bbonline.com/mn/bakketopp

GRAND MARAIS

Dream Catcher B&B
2614 Country Rd #7, 55604
218-387-2876 Fax: 218-387-2870
800-682-3119
Jack & Sue McDonnell
All year

93-102-B&B
3 rooms, 3 pb
Visa, MC, Disc, *Rated*
C-ltd/S-no/P-no/H-no

Full breakfast
Afternoon tea, snacks
Trail lunch available, sitting
room, library, sauna

Quiet, comfortable seclusion, nestled in the northwoods overlooking Lake Superior. Numerous hiking, mountain biking, skiing trails nearby; canoeing.
E-mail: info@dreamcatcherbb.com *Web site:* dreamcatcherbb.com

Gunflint Lodge
143 S Gunflint Lake, 55604
218-388-2294 Fax: 218-388-9429
800-328-3325
Bruce & Susan Kerfoot
All year

99-320-EP/MAP/AP
25 rooms, 25 pb
Visa, MC, AmEx,
Rated, •
C-yes/S-yes/P-yes/H-yes

Full breakfast
Lunch, dinner, restaurant,
bar
Sauna, outdoor hot tubs,
sitting room, sauna, fireplace,
suites

Upscale family, fishing and riding resort in northern Minnesota, gourmet chef, guides, family activities, honeymoon packages, women's retreats, canoeing, hiking, winter cross-country skiing, dog sledding and snowshoeing. *E-mail:* gunflint@gunflint.com
Web site: gunflint.com

Old Shore Beach B&B
1434 Old Shore Rd, 55604
218-387-9707 Fax: 218-387-9811
888-387-9707
Paulette Anholm
All year

115-145-B&B
4 rooms, 4 pb
Visa, MC,
C-ltd/S-no/P-no/H-no

Full breakfast
Snacks
Sitting room, on Lake
Superior, snowshoe rental,
mountain bike rental

Situated on a cobblestone beach on Lake Superior. Enjoy a sauna, stroll the beach, lounge on the redwood deck or at the fireside while wrapped in our deluxe terry robes *E-mail:* visit@oldshorebeach.com

LITTLE MARAIS

Stone Hearth Inn
6598 Lakeside Estates Rd,
55614
218-226-3020 Fax: 218-226-3966
888-206-3020
Charlie & Susan Michels
All year

90-150-B&B
8 rooms, 8 pb
Visa, MC, Disc, *Rated*
C-ltd/S-no/P-no/H-no

Full or continental breakfast
Jacuzzis, suites, fireplaces

Enjoy refined comforts of a classic B&B on the shore of Lake Superior. Private baths, whirlpool tubs and fireplaces, continental and full gourmet breakfast. A warmth without pretence that makes you feel entirely at home. *E-mail:* michels@lakenet.com
Web site: stonehearthinn.com

LUTSEN

Lindgren's B&B
PO Box 56, 55612
218-663-7450 Fax: 218-663-7450
Shirley Lindgren
All year

90-135-B&B
4 rooms, 4 pb
Visa, MC, *Rated*, •
C-ltd/S-no/P-no/H-no

Full gourmet breakfast
Tea, snacks, soda, cocoa
Whirlpool/sauna,
horseshoes, hike, kayak, fall
colors, golf, bike, ski

1920s Northwoods rustic lodge log home in Superior National Forest on Lake Superior's walkable shoreline. Baby grand piano. Bonfires, swing & hammock on water's edge. Hearty breakfast served lakeside or fireside. Fireplaces in some rooms.

MANKATO

Butler House B&B, The
704 S Broad St, 56001
507-387-5055
Sharalyn & Ron Tschida
All year

69-119-B&B
5 rooms, 5 pb
Visa, MC, AmEx, *Rated*
C-ltd/S-no/P-no/H-no

Full breakfast
Sitting room, bikes, suites,
fireplaces, cable TV

Beautiful fresco paintings in dining room, entrance, and stairway to second floor.
E-mail: butler@mnic.net *Web site:* butlerhouse.com

MINNEAPOLIS

1900 Dupont Guest House	85-139-B&B	Full breakfast
1900 Dupont Ave S, 55403	3 rooms, 3 pb	Library, convention center
612-374-1973	Visa, MC, AmEx, •	nearby, fall colors, golf, bike
Chris Viken	C-ltd/S-no/P-no/H-no	
All year		

Enjoy Minneapolis' finest: walk to downtown, uptown, convention center, Guthrie Theatre, Walker Art Center, & Sculpture Garden, the Lakes, Riverwalk, restaurants. Gracious 1896 home with three story staircase, library, and solarium.

Elmwood House	75-105-B&B	Continental plus breakfast
1 East Elmwood Pl, 55419	3 rooms, 1 pb	Sitting room, 3rd-floor 2-
612-822-4558	Visa, MC, *Rated*, •	bedroom suite, with private
888-822-4558	C-yes/S-no/P-no/H-no	bath
Barbara & Robert Schlosser		
All year		

1887 Norman chateau. Historical home on National Register. 3 miles from downtown. 10 miles from Mall of America and airport. Near walks and nature trails.
E-mail: elmwood@iaxs.net *Web site:* iaxs.net/~elmwood/

Evelo's B&B	60-B&B	Continental plus breakfast
2301 Bryant Ave S, 55405	3 rooms	TV, refrigerator, coffee
612-374-9656	Most CC,	maker, air conditioning
David & Sheryl Evelo	C-yes/S-no/P-no/H-no	
All year		

1897 Victorian, period furnishings. Located on bus line, walk to Guthrie Theater, Minneapolis Art Institute, children's theater. Near historic Lake District. *E-mail:* sevelo@ mpls.k12.mn.us

Nan's B&B	50-60-B&B	Full breakfast
2304 Fremont Ave S, 55405	3 rooms	Beautiful porch, antique
612-377-5118	Visa, MC, AmEx,	furnishings, near many
800-214-5118	C-yes/S-ltd/P-no/H-no	restaurants
Nan & Jim Zosel		
All year		

Comfortable urban 1890s Victorian family home, near best theaters, galleries, restaurants, Minneapolis. Friendly, informative hosts. *E-mail:* zosel@mn.mcad.edu
Web site: virtualcities.com/ons/mn/m/mnm2601.htm

Rand House, The	95-145-B&B	Full breakfast
1 Old Territorial Rd, 55362	4 rooms, 4 pb	Afternoon tea, snacks
612-295-6037 Fax: 612-295-6037	Visa, MC, Disc, *Rated*,	Complimentary wine, sitting
Duffy & Merrill Busch	•	room, library, bicycles,
All year	C-ltd/S-no/P-no/H-ltd	tennis court, fireplace

One of the last remaining great Victorian country estates established by one of Minneapolis' most prominent families, the Rand House at 'Random' offers country elegance and seclusion, just 40 minutes from downtown Minneapolis & St. Paul. *E-mail:* randhaus@ aol.com *Web site:* randhouse.com

NEW PRAGUE

Schumachers' Hotel	165-275-EP	Breakfast (fee)
212 W Main St, 56071	11 rooms, 11 pb	Lunch, dinner, bar
612-758-2133 Fax: 612-758-2400	Most CC, *Rated*, •	Comp. wine, piano, seven
John & Kathleen Schumacher	S-yes/P-no/H-ltd	rooms with TV's, whirlpools,
All year		fireplaces

National and regional award-winning country inn and restaurant. Central European theme. Restaurant & gift shop. Front porch. *E-mail:* snph@email.msn.com
Web site: schumachershotel.com

The Rand House, Minneapolis, MN

NORTHFIELD

Archer House
212 Division St, 55057
507-645-5661
Fax: 507-645-4295
800-247-2235
Dallas Haas
All year

40-140-EP
36 rooms, 36 pb
Visa, MC, AmEx,
Rated, •
C-yes/S-yes/P-no/H-no

Full service restaurant
Sitting room, near golf, ski,
bike, hike trails &, whirlpool
suites

Built in 1877, 36 room historic inn located downtown. Within walking distance to numerous shops, restaurants and colleges. Three restaurants and five shops in the hotel. Located along the river with a riverwalk. Close to arboretum. Web site: archerhouse.com

RED WING

Candlelight Inn, The
818 W 3rd St, 55066
651-388-8034
800-254-9194
Lynette and Zig Gudrais
All year

99-169-B&B
5 rooms, 5 pb
Visa, MC, AmEx, *Rated*
C-ltd/S-no/P-no/H-no

Full
Snacks
Sitting room, Library,
Jacuzzis, Fireplaces

Beautiful appointed Victorian home with fireplaces in every room. Three blocks to historic and beautiful downtown Red Wing. Be pampered with coffee in room followed by sumptuous gourmet breakfast. E-mail: candlerw@rconnect.com Web site: candlelightinn-redwing.com

ST. PAUL

Chatsworth B&B
984 Ashland Ave, 55104
612-227-4288 Fax: 612-665-0388
Neelie Forrester
All year

70-135-B&B
5 rooms, 3 pb
Most CC, *Rated*
C-ltd

Continental plus breakfast
Tea, coffee, cocoa
Sitting room, library, 2 rooms
with whirlpools

Peaceful retreat in city near Governor's Mansion. Down comforters, lace curtains. Excellent restaurants & unique shops within walking distance
E-mail: chats@isd.net Web site: chatsworth-bb.com

STILLWATER

Aurora Staples Inn
303 N Fourth St, 55082
651-351-1187
C. Hendrickson & J. Roesler
All year

125-180-B&B
5 rooms, 5 pb
Visa, MC, AmEx, *Rated*
C-ltd/S-no/P-no/H-no

Full breakfast
Sitting room, library,
Jacuzzis, suites, fireplaces

Queen Anne Victorian close to downtown shopping and restaurants. Wraparound porch, formal gardens with a fountain. Riverview. Historic landmark built by local lumber baron families. Beautiful woodwork and parquet floors. Web site: aurorastaplesinn.com

STILLWATER ───────────────────────────────────

Elephant Walk Inc, The	159-249-B&B	Full 4 course breakfast
801 W Pine St, 55082	4 rooms, 4 pb	Comp. wine, snacks
651-430-0359 Fax: 651-351-9080	Visa, MC, *Rated*	Sitting room, hot tubs, Int'l
888-430-0359	C-ltd/S-no/P-no/H-no	flavor, 2 room, ste. w/priv.
Rita Graybil	Thai	garden
All year		

Walk to historic Stillwater. Flower gardens. Tour the world, one room at a time. A bit of the tropics in Minnesota! E-mail: info@elephantwalkbb.com Web site: elephantwalkbb.com

James A. Mulvey Inn	99-199-B&B	Full breakfast
622 W. Churchill St, 55082	7 rooms, 7 pb	Tea, outside eating
651-430-8008 Fax: 651-430-2801	Most CC, *Rated*, •	Sitting room, bicycles,
800-820-8008	C-ltd/S-no/P-no/H-no	Jacuzzi, swimming pool,
Truett and Jill Lawson		suites, conference
All year		

This is an enchanting place. Built by lumberman James Mulvey in 1878, the Italinate residence and stone carriage house grace the most visited historic river town in the upper midwest. E-mail: Truettldem@aol.com Web site: jamesmulveyinn.com

Rivertown Inn, The	89-169-B&B	Full breakfast
306 W Olive St, 55082	8 rooms, 8 pb	Complimentary wine on
651-430-2955 Fax: 651-430-0034	Visa, MC, *Rated*, •	weekends
800-562-3632	C-yes/S-ltd/P-no/H-no	Sitting areas, A/C, screen
Judy & Chuck Dougherty		porch, gazebo, whirlpool
All year		bath, bicycles

Beautifully restored 1882 3-story lumberman's mansion. Individually decorated rooms with Victorian antiques. 4 blocks from Historic Main St. Stillwater's oldest B&B.
E-mail: rivertn@aol.com Web site: rivertowninn.com

The Cover Park Manor	99-179-B&B	Full breakfast
15330 58th St., North, 55082	4 rooms, 4 pb	P.M. tea, snacks, compl. wine
651-430-9292 Fax: 651-430-0034	Most CC, *Rated*, •	Sitting room, Jacuzzis, suites,
811-430-9292	C-ltd/S-no/P-no/H-yes	fireplaces, cable TV,
Chuck & Judy Dougherty	Spanish, German	business travelers
All year		

This romantic 1890's home is situated on six city lots and borders Cover Park.
E-mail: coverpark@coverpark.com Web site: coverpark.com

WABASHA ───────────────────────────────────

Anderson House, The	50-149-EP/MAP	Breakfast avail. (Fee)
333 W Main St, 55981	26 rooms, 24 pb	Lunch & dinner available
651-565-4524 Fax: 651-565-4003	Visa, MC, Disc, •	(fee)
800-535-5467	C-yes/S-yes/P-yes/H-yes	Restaurant, bar service,
John Hall		sitting room, hot tub, large
All year		suite with balconies

Enjoy our country inn, Dutch kitchen & homemade breads. Antique filled rooms overlooking the Mississippi River come with our without a cat! E-mail: andtours@wabasha.net
Web site: theandersonhouse.com

WINONA ───────────────────────────────────

Windom Park B&B	84-155-B&B	Full or continental plus
369 W Broadway, 55987	4 rooms, 4 pb	breakfast
507-457-9515	Most CC, *Rated*	Snacks
Craig and Karen Groth	C-ltd/S-ltd/P-no/H-no	Sitting room, Library, Suites,
All year	Polish	Fireplaces, Cable TV,
		Business travelers

Enjoy the quiet charm of our 1900 Colonial Revival home located in the historic rivertown of Winona, Minnesota. An American bed and breakfast with an English accent.
Web site: windompark.com

Mississippi

BILOXI

Green Oaks B&B	88-155-B&B	Full breakfast
580 Beach Blvd, 39530	8 rooms, 8 pb	Afternoon tea, snacks
228-436-6257 Fax: 228-436-6225	Most CC, *Rated*, •	Sitting room, library,
888-436-6257	C-yes/S-ltd/P-no/H-yes	bicycles, located on the, Gulf
Oliver & Jennifer Diaz		of Mexico on beach
All year		

Mississippi's oldest beachfront mansion. Circa 1826 National Historic Register 2 acres with 28 live oaks overlooking white sand beachs and Gulf of Mexico.
E-mail: greenoaks4@aol.com *Web site:* gcww.com/greenoaks

Old Santini House B&B Inn	100-160-B&B	Full gourmet breakfast
964 Beach Blvd, 39530	4 rooms, 4 pb	Tea, wine
228-436-4078 Fax: 228-436-4078	Visa, MC, AmEx,	Sitting room, library, bikes,
800-686-1146	*Rated*, •	Jacuzzis, suites, fireplace,
James & Patricia Dunay	C-ltd/S-ltd/P-no/H-no	cable TV
All year		

Relive the quaint charm of the early 1800s in our 160 year old "American Cottage." Antiques & fine furnishings, located downtown across from beach.
E-mail: JDunay9900@aol.com *Web site:* waidsoft.com/santinibnb

Red Creek Inn	54-147-B&B	Continental plus breakfast
Vinyrd/Stable	7 rooms, 5 pb	Full breakfast upon request
7416 Red Creek Rd, 39560	*Rated*, •	Coffee, afternoon tea, hot
228-452-3080	C-yes/S-ltd/P-ltd	tub, Racing Stable
Fax: 228-452-4450	Spanish	
800-729-9670		
Karl & Toni Mertz		
All year		

Three-story "raised French cottage" with 6 fireplaces, 64-foot porch, and antiques. Amid 11 acres of live oaks & magnolias near beaches. *E-mail:* info@redcreekinn.com
Web site: redcreekinn.com

JACKSON

Fairview Inn	115-165-B&B	Full breakfast
734 Fairview St, 39202	8 rooms, 8 pb	Snacks, complimentary wine
601-948-3429 Fax: 601-948-1203	Most CC, *Rated*, •	Dinner (fee), dataports,
888-948-1908	C-ltd/S-no/P-no/H-yes	sitting room, library, special
Carol & Bill Simmons	French	occasion facilities
All year		

Colonial Revival mansion on National Register of Historic Places. Luxury accommodations. Fine dining for groups. AAA Four Diamond Award.
E-mail: fairview@fairviewinn.com *Web site:* fairviewinn.com

LORMAN

Rosswood Plantation	115-135-B&B	Full breakfast
Rt 1, Box 6, 39096	4 rooms, 4 pb	Sitting room, library, hot
601-437-4215 Fax: 601-437-6888	Most CC, *Rated*, •	tubs, nature trails, swimming
800-533-5889	C-yes/S-ltd/P-no/H-ltd	pool
Jean & Walt Hylander		
March-Dec.		

Authentic columned mansion on working plantation near Natchez, Vicksburg. Heirloom antiques, canopied beds, Civil War history, slave quarters. *E-mail:* whylander@aol.com
Web site: rosswood.net

Red Creek Inn, Bixoli, MS

NATCHEZ

Briars Inn, The	145-160-B&B	Continental plus breakfast
PO Box 1245, 39120	14 rooms, 14 pb	Bar service, snacks
601-446-9654 Fax: 601-445-6037	Visa, MC, AmEx, •	Sitting room, library,
800-634-1818	C-ltd/S-ltd/P-no/H-yes	swimming pool, porch,
Newt Wilds & R.E. Canon		gardens
All year		

Circa 1812, retreat into unique 19th century splendor with modern amenities. National Register. 19 acres of gardens overlooking Mississippi River. Entirely antique-furnished. E-mail: thebriarsinn@bkbank.com   *Web site:* thebriarsinn.com

Glenfield Plantation B&B	80-135-B&B	Full southern breakfast
6 Providence Rd, 39120	4 rooms, 4 pb	Complimentary wine
601-442-1002 Fax: 601-422-1002	*Rated*, •	Sitting room, All rooms with
888-388-1002	C-yes/S-ltd/P-no/H-yes	private bath, banquet
Marjorie & Lester Meng		facilities
All year		

Family owned-5th generation c.1778 Spanish and 1840 English Gothic architecture. On the National Register of Historic Places. Antiques throughout. Located 1 1/2 miles from downtown Natchez. Bullet hole in front door from Civil War skirmish.   E-mail: Glnfield@ lamerica.net *Web site:* travelguides.com/home/glenfieldplantation/

Linden B&B	90-125-B&B	Full Southern breakfast
1 Linden Place, 39120	7 rooms, 7 pb	Early morning coffee
601-445-5472 Fax: 601-445-5472	*Rated*, •	Sitting room, piano, banquet
800-2-LINDEN	C-ltd/S-yes/P-no/H-yes	facilities
Jeanette Feltus All year		

Antebellum home furnished with family heirlooms. Park-like setting of mossy live oaks. Occupied by same family since 1849.   Web site: natchezms.com/linden

Monmouth Plantation	145-375-B&B	Full breakfast
36 Melrose Avenue, 39120	31 rooms, 31 pb	Dinner, bar
601-442-5852 Fax: 601-446-7762	Most CC, *Rated*, •	Sitting room, library, suites,
800-828-4531	C-ltd/S-no/P-no/H-ltd	fireplaces, cable TV, conf.
Ron & Lani Riches	French (on request)	fac.
High season-Mar-May, Oct		

Glorious return to the Antebellum South. Monmouth is listed as a National Historic Landmark. Situated on 26 beautifully landscaped acres. Every modern comfort in these elegantly appointed rooms.   E-mail: luxury@monmouthplantation.com
Web site: monmouthplantation.com

OLIVE BRANCH

Country Goose Inn
350 Hwy 305, 38654
662-895-3098
Fax: 622-895-3098
877-895-3098
Jeanette Martin
All year

89-135-AP
15 rooms, 5 pb
Most CC, •
C-yes/S-yes/P-no/H-no
French

Full breakfast
All meals included,
afternoon tea
Snacks, complimentary
wine, sitting room, hot tubs,
swimming pool

Small convention facility, lakeside cottages with picturesque surroundings. Fishing & pedal boating, horseback riding, playground, suitable for leisure or business travel.
Web site: brigadoonfarms.com

PORT GIBSON

Oak Square Plantation
1207 Church St, 39150
601-437-4350
Fax: 601-437-5768
800-729-0240
Mrs. William D. Lum
All year

85-125-B&B
11 rooms, 11 pb
Most CC, *Rated*, •
C-ltd/S-ltd/P-no/H-ltd

Full breakfast
Complimentary wine & tea
Victorian parlor, piano, TV,
courtyard, fountain, gazebo

Antebellum mansion in the town General Ulysses S. Grant said was "too beautiful to burn." Heirloom antiques. Canopied beds. National Register. AAA 4-diamond rated. E-mail: kajunmade@aol.com

VICKSBURG

Anchuca
1010 First East St, 39180
601-661-0111
Fax: 601-661-0420
888-686-0111
Loveta Byrne
All year

80-140-B&B
9 rooms, 9 pb
Most CC, *Rated*, •
C-ltd/S-ltd/P-ltd/H-no

Full breakfast
Complimentary evening
drinks
Phones in all rooms,
swimming pool, hot tub,
sitting room, piano

Rooms furnished in beautiful antiques; sumptuous swimming pool, hot tub, breakfast served in magnificent dining room. Turndown service; mint juleps; honor bar.
E-mail: anchuca@anchuca.zzn.com   *Web site:* anchuca.cjb.net

Annabelle B&B
501 Speed St, 39180
601-638-2000
Fax: 601-636-5054
800-791-2000
George & Carolyn Mayer
All year

93-125-B&B
7 rooms, 7 pb
Most CC, *Rated*, •
C-ltd/S-no/P-ltd/H-no
Ger., Sp., Portuguese

Full breakfast
Afternoon tea
Sitting room, library,
Jacuzzis, swimming pool,
fireplaces, cable TV

Find refuge and romance in George and Carolyn Mayer's historic Annabelle built in 1868, where true grace and charm will greet you, then gently settle into luxurious comfort
E-mail: annabelle@vicksburg.com   *Web site:* annabellebnb.com

Cedar Grove Mansion Inn
2200 Oak St, 39180
601-636-1000
Fax: 601-634-6126
800-862-1300
Ted Mackey
All year

85-165-B&B
29 rooms, 29 pb
Most CC, *Rated*, •
C-yes/S-ltd/P-ltd/H-yes

Full breakfast
Dinner (fee), afternoon tea
Restaurant, bar service,
bikes, tennis court, Jacuzzis,
pool, suites

Experience Vicksburg in style. Cedar Grove Mansion offers a warm southern welcome to all travelers to Vicksburg. With 29 rooms and suites, tours of the mansion, Andre's Restaurant and Mansion Bar, Cedar Grove is the place to visit. E-mail: info@cedargroveinn.com
Web site: cedargroveinn.com

Missouri

BONNE TERRE

Victorian Veranda B&B
207 E School St, 63628
573-358-1134
800-343-1134
Galen & Karen Forney
All year

70-95-B&B
4 rooms, 4 pb
Visa, MC, Disc, *Rated*,
•
C-ltd/P-no/H-no

Full breakfast
Snacks, afternoon tea
Sitting room, Jacuzzis, suites,
fireplaces, cable TV,
accomm. bus. travelers

Our historic home was built circa 1880 as a boarding house for St. Joe Lead Co. With its 17 rooms, it has been fully restored to capture its timeless beauty and charm.   E-mail: victoriaveranda@1dd.net Web site: bbim.org/vicveranda.html

BONNOTS MILL

Dauphine Hotel B&B Inn
PO Box 36, 65016
573-897-4144
Fax: 573-897-9822
Sandra & Scott Holder
All year

50-60-B&B
6 rooms, 4 pb
Visa, MC, Disc, *Rated*
C-ltd/S-ltd/P-no/H-no

Full breakfast
Restaurant
Sitting room, boat ramp

Authentic river town lodging establishment serving guests since 1875. Located in national historic district along the banks of the Osage River.   E-mail: info@dauphinehotel.com Web site: dauphinehotel.com

BRANSON

Branson Hotel B&B Inn
214 W Main, 65616
417-335-6104
Opal Kelly & Teri Murguia
All year

85-105-B&B
8 rooms, 8 pb
Visa, MC, *Rated*, •
C-ltd/S-ltd/P-no/H-no

Full gourmet breakfast
Complimentary wine,
afternoon tea
Sitting room, two large
verandas, guest refrigerator,
cable TV

Branson's elegant little hotel built in 1903 is aso a B&B inn. Beautifully restored in 1992. Perfectly located in historic downtown Branson. Eight distinctive guestrooms offer history and romance.

**Branson House B&B Inn,
The**
120 N Fourth St, 65616
417-334-0959
Sylvia Voyce
March-Dec.

65-90-B&B
7 rooms, 7 pb
Rated, •
C-ltd/S-ltd/P-no/H-no

Full gourmet breakfast
Complimentary wine,
cookies
Sitting room, yard, central
A/C, guest refrigerator

Old home furnished with antiques. Breakfast served in the dining room or on the front porch. Overlooking downtown Branson and beautiful lake. Quaint, romantic surroundings.   Web site: bbonline.com/mo/bransonhouse

Brass Swan B&B, The
202 River Bend Rd, 65616
417-336-3669
Fax: 417-334-6873
800-280-6873
Dick & Gigi House
All year

70-85-B&B
4 rooms, 4 pb
Visa, MC, Disc, *Rated*,
•
C-ltd/S-no/P-no/H-no

Full breakfast
Snacks
Sitting room, hot tubs;
phones and, VCRs in all
rooms

Prepare to be pampered in an elegant, contemporary with quiet surroundings yet only minutes away from shows, attractions and shopping.   E-mail: dhouse202@aol.com Web site: virtualcities.com/ons/mo/m/mom7601.htm

BRANSON ───────────────────────────────────

Cameron's Crag	85-105-B&B	Full hearty breakfast
PO Box 295, 65615	3 rooms, 3 pb	Video lib., area sites, private
417-335-8134 Fax: 417-335-8134	Visa, •	entrance & tubs, hot tubs,
800-933-8529	C-ltd/S-no/P-no/H-no	cable TV/VCR
Kay & Glen Cameron		
All year		

Contemporary hideaway on bluff overlooking Lake Taneycomo. Fantastic views! Three separate guest areas, delightful accommodations. One suite with kitchen.
E-mail: mgcameron@aol.com *Web site:* travelguides.com/home/camerons_crag

Emory Creek B&B & Gift	85-125-B&B	Full breakfast
Shop	6 rooms	Afternoon tea, snacks
143 Arizona Dr, 65616	Visa, MC, •	Sitting room, library,
417-334-3805 Fax: 417-337-7045	C-ltd/S-no/P-no/H-no	Jacuzzis, suites, fireplaces
800-362-7404		
Sammy & Beverly Gray Pagna		
All year		

A magnificent Victorian Inn with refinement and grandeur, yet a welcome home feeling of the country. 18th century antiques, elegant bathrooms, oversized Jacuzzis & fireplaces. 4 course gourmet breakfasts. *E-mail:* emorycreekbnb@pcis.net *Web site:* emorycreekbnb.com

Fall Creek B&B	79.50-B&B	Full breakfast
4988 Fall Creek Rd, 65616	19 rooms, 15 pb	Free morning coffee
417-334-3939 Fax: 417-332-2439	Visa, MC, AmEx, •	Sitting room, library,
800-482-1090	C-yes/S-ltd/P-ltd/H-yes	whirlpool Jacuzzis, pool,
Bob Doyle & Sheila Learn		cable TV
All year		

Pamper yourselves at the Victorian B&B Inn. Full country buffet breakfast. Double queen beds, walkout wooden decks! Relax in whirlpool or swimming pool. Located near many attractions. Conference facilities. *Web site:* usrc.net/fallcreekbedandbreakfast

Historic Kite House B&B	85-95-B&B	Full breakfast
PO Box 1504, 65615	5 rooms, 3 pb	Jacuzzis, suites, fireplaces,
417-334-7341	Visa, MC,	cable TV, hot tubs,
Mark & Donel McCauley	C-yes/S-ltd/P-no/H-no	telephones
All year		

Branson B&B Kite House-A grand century old home close to all Branson attractions yet private and secluded. *E-mail:* Kitemanor@aol.com *Web site:* Kitehouse.com

Leisure Wood B&B	40-60-B&B	Full breakfast
PO Box 281, 65624	3 rooms, 3 pb	Sitting room, hot tubs, family
417-538-2143	Most CC,	friendly facility
800-619-5727	C-yes/S-no/P-ltd/H-yes	
Virginia-Richard Smallwood		
March 15 - Dec. 31		

Park-like setting in the heart of the Ozarks at Table Rock Lake. Short drive to Branson and other attractions.

Red Bud Cove B&B Suites	79-115-B&B	Full breakfast
162 Lakewood Dr, 65672	8 rooms, 8 pb	Sitting room, hot tubs,
417-334-7144 Fax: 417-337-8823	Visa, MC, Disc, *Rated*,	seminars
800-677-5525	•	
Carol & Rick Carpenter	C-ltd/S-no/P-no/H-yes	
All year		

On beautiful Table Rock Lake only 15 minutes from Branson. Spacious lakefront suites, some with spa and fireplace. *E-mail:* redbudcove@aol.com *Web site:* redbudcove.com

CAPE GIRARDEAU

Bellevue B&B	70-105-B&B	Full breakfast
312 Bellevue, 63701	4 rooms, 4 pb	Complimentary beverages,
573-335-3302	Most CC, *Rated*, •	snacks
800-768-6822	C-yes/S-ltd/P-no/H-no	Sitt. rm. w/large-screen TV,
Marsha Toll		business facility, massage by
All year		app't., mtg. rms.

1891 Queen Anne Victorian faithfully restored, furnished with period antiques and modern amenities. E-mail: BellevueBb@compuserv.com Web site: flinthills.com/~atway/mo/bellevue.html

COLUMBIA

Gathering Place, The	85-130-B&B	Full breakfast
606 S College, 65201	5 rooms, 5 pb	Snacks
573-815-0606 Fax: 573-817-1653	Visa, MC, AmEx,	Sitting room, library, tennis
877-731-6888	*Rated*, •	court, exercise fac. nearby
R. & S. Duff/J. & K. Steelman	C-ltd/S-no/P-no/H-yes	
All year		

College town B&B. University of Missouri is our front yard. Bountiful Missouri breakfasts. Jacuzzis. King & queen suites. Business & leisure guests welcome. E-mail: rossduff@aol.com

DIXON

Rock Eddy Bluff Farm	70-95-B&B	Full breakfast
10245 Maries Rd 511, 65459	4 rooms, 2 pb	Snacks
573-759-6081	Visa, MC, Disc, *Rated*	Sitting room, library, hot tub,
800-335-5921	C-yes/S-ltd/P-ltd/H-no	fireplaces, fishing, bird
Kathy & Tom Corey		watching
All year		

Scenic, country B&B rooms, cottage, and cabin overlooking Ozark river valley. Come back to nature. Hike, canoe, fish, relax. Country antique decor. E-mail: welcome@rockeddy.com Web site: rockeddy.com

FULTON

Loganberry Inn	55-105-B&B	Full gourmet breakfast
310 W 7th St, 65251	4 rooms, 4 pb	Afternoon tea, snacks
573-642-9229	Visa, MC, AmEx, Disc,	Sitting room, library,
888-866-6661	*Rated*	fireplace, cable TV, Murder
Carl & Cathy McGeorge	C-ltd/S-no/P-ltd/H-no	Mystery weekends, Spa Day
All year		

Top rated Inn in the heart of historic Fulton, this inviting 1899 Victorian hosted Margaret Thatcher and Scotland Yard. Minutes from I-70 between St. Louis and Kansas City, MO. E-mail: stay@loganberryinn.com Web site: loganberryinn.com

Romancing the Past	80-150-B&B	Full breakfast
830 Court St, 65251	3 rooms, 3 pb	Afternoon tea, snacks, comp.
573-592-1996	Visa, MC, AmEx, *Rated*	wine
Jim & ReNee Yeager	C-ltd/S-ltd/P-ltd/H-ltd	Sitting room, bicycles,
All year		Jacuzzis, suites, fireplaces,
		cable TV

Enchanting Victorian in beautiful historic neighborhood surrounded by trees and gardens. Grand hall with magnificent arch and staircase. E-mail: innkeeper@sockets.net Web site: romancingthepast.com

HANNIBAL

Garth Woodside Mansion	69-110-B&B	Full breakfast
11069 New London Rd, 63401	8 rooms, 8 pb	Complimentary tea or hot
573-221-2789	Visa, MC, *Rated*	cider
Diane & Irv Feinberg	C-ltd/S-ltd	Library, tour planning,
All year		turndown service, guest
		nightshirts

Mark Twain was a guest at this 39-acre country estate. Original Victorian furnishings, double Jacuzzi. Elegance, privacy, hospitality. E-mail: garth@nemonet.com Web site: hannable-missouri.com

HANNIBAL

LulaBelle's	60-90-B&B	Full breakfast
111 Bird, 63401	6 rooms, 6 pb	Lunch & dinner (fee)
573-221-6662 Fax: 573-221-5155	Most CC, *Rated*	Snacks, restaurant, sitting
800-882-4890	C-yes/S-yes/P-no/H-no	room, hot tubs, family
Mike & Pam Ginsberg		friendly facility
All year		

Originally built as a bordello in 1917. Newly renovated fine dining restaurant with 6 charming rooms overlooking the Mississippi River E-mail: 24dinr@nemonet.com
Web site: hanmo.com/lulabelles

HERMANN

Hermann Hill Vineyard &	120-200-B&B	Full breakfast
Inn	5 rooms, 5 pb	Sitting room, library, cable,
PO Box 555, 65041	Most CC, *Rated*	Jacuzzis, fireplaces, gym,
573-486-4455 Fax: 573-486-5373	S-no/P-no/H-yes	modems/data ports
Terry & Peggy Hammer		
All year		

Sited on a bluff overlooking the town, vineyard & river; upscale decor enhanced with antiques; lavishly appointed guest rooms; private & quiet; we specialize in romantic getaways.

INDEPENDENCE

Woodstock Inn B&B	65-159-B&B	Full breakfast
1212 W Lexington, 64050	11 rooms, 11 pb	Complimentary coffee, tea,
816-833-2233	Most CC, *Rated*, •	etc.
800-276-5202	C-yes/S-no/P-no/H-yes	Sitting room, National
Todd & Patricia Justice	Spanish	Frontier Trails, Center 6
All year		blocks away

Enjoy comfort, privacy and tastefully appointed rooms in this century-old renovated bed and breakfast. Individualized breakfasts. Truman, Missouri history sites nearby.
Web site: independence-missouri.com

JOPLIN

Grand Avenue B&B	69-89-B&B	Full breakfast
1615 Grand Ave, 64836	4 rooms, 4 pb	Lunch & dinner, tea, snacks
417-358-7265 Fax: 417-358-7265	Most CC, •	Sitting room, library,
888-380-6786	C-yes/S-no/P-no/H-no	swimming pool, Jacuzzi,
Jeanne & Michael Goolsby	French	suites, cable TV, conferences
All year		

Beautiful 100 year old Victorian home near Precious Moments Chapel, antique Shopping, Civil War Museum. Stained glass windows. Private baths in rooms. E-mail: reservation@grand-avenue.com *Web site:* grand-avenue.com

KANSAS CITY

Brookside House	105-B&B	Continental plus breakfast
6315 Walnut, 64113	3 rooms, 2 pb	Complimentary wine
913-491-8950 Fax: 913-381-6256	C-yes/S-no/P-no/H-no	2nd & 3rd bedrooms are, $35
Vern & Brenda Otte		each., yard, airport shuttle
All year		

Guests have entire house: 3 bedroom, 2 bath, kitchen, living room, fireplace, dining room, piano, cable TV, stereo. Walk to shopping district. Two miles to Plaza E-mail: murphyotte@aol.com

Cedarcroft Farm	80-200-B&B	Full breakfast
431 SE County Rd Y, 64093	2 rooms, 2 pb	Comp. evening snack
660-747-5728	Most CC, *Rated*	Sitting room, library,
800-368-4944	C-ltd/S-ltd/P-no/H-no	Jacuzzis, suites, fireplace,
Sandra & Bill Wayne		cable TV
All year		

Romantic cottage for two or whole-house family suite at 1867 National Register farm. Farmhouse has turn-of-century antiques. Explore our 80 acres of woods & meadows, visit local Amish. E-mail: ltg@cedarcroft.com *Web site:* cedarcroft.com

KANSAS CITY

Doanleigh Inn, The
217 E 37th St, 64111
816-753-2667 Fax: 816-531-5185
Cynthia Brogdon & Terry
Maturo
All year

105-160-B&B
5 rooms, 5 pb
Most CC, *Rated*
C-ltd/S-no/P-no/H-no

Full gourmet breakfast
Snacks in pantry
Facilities for meetings,
weddings, TV, Jacuzzis,
phone & dataports in rms

Located between the Plaza & Crown Center. Georgian mansion with European & American antiques. Comfortable elegance in the heart of the city.   E-mail: doanleigh@aol.com
Web site: doanleigh.com

Inn on Crescent Lake, The
1261 St. Louis Ave, 64024
Anne & Bruce Libowitz
All year

125-175-B&B
8 rooms, 8 pb
Visa, MC, *Rated*, •
C-ltd/S-ltd/P-no/H-ltd

Full breakfast
Dinner, bar service available
color TV, inner tubes

1915 mansion on 22 acres surrounded by two ponds. Boats, swimming pool and walking path. Innkeepers are graduates of the French Culinary Institute. Extensively renovated in 1997.   E-mail: info@crescentinn.com *Web site:* crescentinn.com

---

Kelley's B&B
321 N Van Brunt Blvd, 64123
816-483-8126
Mary Jo Kelley
All year

50-60-B&B
3 rooms
•
C-yes/S-no/P-no/H-no

Full family-style bkfst.
Cont. bkfst. if pref.
Highchair, crib, babysitting
arranged, phone, cable TV

Large home located minutes from sports, culture, parks, convention centers, riverboat casinos. Comfortable rooms with decor handcrafted like Grandma's place. Refrigerator, cable TV

MARIONVILLE

White Squirrel Hollow
203 Mill St
PO Box 416, 65705
417-463-7626
Clint Wise
All year

40-65-B&B
2 rooms, 2 pb
Rated, •
C-yes/S-ltd/P-ltd/H-ltd

Full breakfast
Sitting room, library,
bicycles, fireplaces, cable TV

We have white squirrels, 2 acres landscaped yard, 42 miles from Branson

SPRINGFIELD

Virginia Rose B&B
317 E Glenwood, 65807
417-883-0693 Fax: 417-883-0693
800-345-1412
Jack & Virginia Buck
All year

60-100-B&B
5 rooms, 4 pb
Most CC, *Rated*, •
C-ltd/S-no/P-no/H-ltd

Full breakfast
Afternoon tea, snacks
Sitting room, accommodate
business travelers, large
parking area

Lovely country-Victorian hideaway on tree-covered acre right in town. Private yet close to walking trail, antique & mall shopping and restaurants. Hospitality & your comfort is our business! E-mail: vrosebb@mocom.net *Web site:* bbonline.com/mo/virginiarose

---

Walnut Street Inn
900 E Walnut St, 65806
417-864-6346 Fax: 417-864-6184
800-593-6346
Gary & Paula Blankenship
All year

84-159-B&B
12 rooms, 12 pb
Most CC, *Rated*, •
C-yes/S-no/P-no/H-yes

Full breakfast
Beer & wine available
Sitting room, hot tubs, tennis
nearby

1894 Victorian showcase inn in Historic District. Gourmet breakfast; walking distance to shops, theater, live music E-mail: walnutstinn@pcis.net *Web site:* pcis.net/walnutstinn/

Virginia Rose B&B, Springfield, MO

ST. CHARLES

Boone's Lick Trail Inn
1000 So Main St, 63301
636-947-7000 Fax: 636-946-2637
800-366-2427
V'Anne & Paul Mydler
All year

95-175-B&B
6 rooms, 6 pb
Most CC, *Rated*, •
C-yes/S-no/P-no/H-ltd

Full breakfast
Hiking/biking, sitting room,
conference, folk art,
rollaways available

Escape to restored 1840 Inn. Flower gardens, regional antiques, duck decoys in historic river settlement. Duck hunting. Walk to restaurants, gift/antique shops, museums, and "Katy Trail." E-mail: innkeeper@booneslick.com Web site: booneslick.com

ST. LOUIS

Eastlake Inn B&B
703 N Kirkwood Rd, 63122
314-965-0066 Fax: 314-966-8615
Lori & Dean Murray
All year

65-100-B&B
3 rooms, 3 pb
Visa, MC, *Rated*, •
C-yes/S-no/P-no/H-no

Full gourmet breakfast
Outdoor patios, porch,
perennial gardens, large
suite avail.

1920 colonial decorated with Eastlake Victorian furniture. 20 minutes from St. Louis. Walk to antique shops E-mail: info@eastlakeinn.com Web site: eastlakeinn.com/

Lafayette House B&B
2156 Lafayette Ave, 63104
314-772-4429 Fax: 314-664-2156
800-641-8965
N.Hammersmith & A. Millet
All year

65-150-B&B
6 rooms, 3 pb
Most CC, *Rated*, •
C-ltd/S-ltd/P-ltd/H-no

Full gourmet breakfast
Afternoon tea, snacks
Sitting room, library, cable
TV, VCR, A/C, Jacuzzi

Old world charm overlooking historic Lafayette Park. In the center of things to do! Delightful gourmet breakfast. Web site: bbonline.com/mo/lafayette

Napoleon's Retreat B&B
1815 Lafayette Ave, 63104
314-772-6979 Fax: 314-772-7675
800-700-9980
J. Archuleta & M Lance
All year

80-125-B&B
5 rooms, 5 pb
Most CC, •
C-ltd/S-no/P-no/H-no

Full breakfast
Snacks, afternoon tea
Sitting room, Jacuzzis, suites,
fireplaces, cable TV

Exquisite 1880 French second empire Victorian set in the heart of Victorian Lafayette Square, 1 mile to downtown. Stunning accommodations, queen-size bed, private baths. Walk to restaurants. Web site: bbonline.com/mo/napoleons

ST. LOUIS

Winter House B&B, The	90-110-B&B	Full breakfast
3522 Arsenal St, 63118	3 rooms, 3 pb	Complimentary
314-664-4399	Most CC, *Rated*, •	refreshments
Kendall Winter	C-yes/S-ltd/P-no/H-no	Sitt. rm. w/gas logs and,
All year exc. Chritsmas		piano, 24 hr Kinko nrby, near
		shops & restaurants

1897 Victorian 9-room house with turret. Hand-squeezed O.J. and live piano at breakfast by reservation. Near Missouri Botanical Gardens & fine restaurants. Cut flowers, fruit bowl, & candy in each room.   E-mail: kmwinter@swbell.net

STE. GENEVIEVE

Inn St. Gemme Beauvais	89-185-B&B	Full breakfast
78 N Main, Box 231, 63670	8 rooms, 8 pb	Tea, hors d' oeuvres
573-883-5744 Fax: 573-883-3899	MC, *Rated*, •	Beer and wine garden,
800-818-5744	C-yes/S-yes/P-no/H-no	special packages avail., free
Janet Joggerst		bicycles, Jacuzzis
All year		

Charming little Victorian inn located just one hour from St. Louis in small historic French town. Within walking distance of all restored French homes
E-mail: Buffin@msn.com   *Web site:* bbhost.com/innstgemme

Southern Hotel B&B	83-128-B&B	Full breakfast
146 S Third St, 63670	8 rooms, 8 pb	Complimentary wine
573-883-3493 Fax: 573-883-9612	Visa, MC, *Rated*	Sitting room, pool room,
800-275-1412	C-ltd/S-no/P-no/H-no	parlors, free bicycles,
Mike & Barbara Hankins		Jacuzzis, gift shop
All year		

Step gently into the time when Riverboats plied the mighty Mississippi and weary travelers looked forward to the hospitality of this famous 1800s hotel.
E-mail: mike@southernhotelbb.com   *Web site:* southernhotelbb.com

TRENTON

Hyde Mansion B&B Inn	65-85-B&B	Full breakfast
418 E 7th St, 64683	5 rooms, 5 pb	Complimentary beverages,
660-359-5631 Fax: 660-359-5632	Visa, MC, AmEx,	snacks
Robert & Carolyn Brown	C-ltd/S-ltd/P-no/H-no	Sitting room, library, Baby
All year		grand piano, patio, screened
		porch, bicycles

Inviting hideaway in rural America, 1949 mansion refurbished for your convenience. Close to Amish country, serves full breakfast.

WASHINGTON

De Bourge House B&B	90-B&B	Full breakfast on weekends
119 Johnson St, 63090	3 rooms, 2 pb	Continental breakfast on
314-390-4898 Fax: 314-390-4898	Visa, MC, *Rated*, •	weekdays
Gail L. De Bourge	C-ltd/S-no/P-no/H-no	Sitting room, bikes, 2 blocks
All year		from public pool

My 1928 home has been carefully decorated with antiques, quilts, family heirlooms for your comfort and to reflect the feel of graciousness and charm. Gourmet breakfast. Strolling distance to restaurants, shops, etc.

La Dolce Vita	90-B&B	Full breakfast
72 Forest Hills Dr, 63090	2 rooms, 2 pb	Snacks, complimentary wine
636-239-0399 Fax: 636-239-7279	Most CC,	Sitting room, accommodate
Wayne & Marcy Halbert	S-no/P-no/H-no	business travelers
All year		

La Dolce Vita offers a unique overnight stay by combining antiques and contemporary style. The 2 bedrooms overlook the vineyard. Tour the boutique winery. Come enjoy the sweet life!   E-mail: marcey@ladolcevitawinery.com   *Web site:* ladolcevitawinery.com

WASHINGTON

Schwegmann House B&B Inn	85-150-B&B	Full breakfast served in
438 W. Front St, 63069	9 rooms, 9 pb	parlor
636-239-5025 Fax: 636-239-3920	Visa, MC, AmEx, *Rated*	Or on patio
800-949-2262	C-ltd/S-no/P-no/H-yes	Private baths and direct dial
Cathy & Bill Nagel		phones, patios, parlors, and
All year		porch

Missouri Wine Country with 11 wineries & historic communities. Rekindles local flour miller's hospitality of more than 100 years ago. Business meetings.
E-mail: cathy@schwegmannhouse.com *Web site:* schwegmannhouse.com

Washington House	85-B&B	Full or continental breakfast
100 W Front St, 63090	2 rooms, 2 pb	Tea, coffees
636-742-4360 Fax: 636-451-0737	Most CC,	Private, romantic getaway
Terry and Susan Black	C-yes/H-yes	
All year		

Our historic 1837 inn on the Missouri River features antique furnishings and decor, queen-sized canopy beds, river views, country breakfasts. Balcony and terrace on riverside.

Montana

BIG TIMBER

Burnt Out Lodge	78-88-B&B	Lunch & Dinner available
HC 88 Box 3620, 59011	5 rooms, 5 pb	Sitting room, library
406-932-6601	Visa, MC, AmEx,	
888-873-7943	C-yes/S-ltd/P-ltd/H-yes	
Marlyn & Ruth Drange		
May-Nov		

Log Lodge on a working ranch. Our spacious rooms with private entrances and baths, large main lodge, delicious meals, stone patio and flower garden invite you to relax and enjoy.
E-mail: burntout@ttc-cmc.net *Web site:* burntoutlodge.com

BIGFORK

Burggraf's Countrylane B&B	100-140-B&B	Full breakfast
Rainbow Dr on Swan Lake, 59911	5 rooms, 5 pb	Complimentary
	Visa, MC, *Rated*, •	wine/cheese/fruit
406-837-4608 Fax: 406-837-2468	C-ltd/S-ltd/P-no/H-yes	Picnic baskets, fishing, lake,
800-525-3344		snowmobiles, boating,
Natalie & R.J. Burggraf		canoes, Jacuzzi
May-Sept.		

True log home nestled in heart of Rocky Mountains; 7 acres on the shores of Swan Lake; panoramic view; country breakfast. Lawn croquet & putting green, paddle boats
E-mail: burggraf@digisys.net

O'Duachain Country Inn	110-180-B&B	Full gourmet breakfast
675 Ferndale Dr, 59911	5 rooms, 4 pb	Sitting room, hot tubs, water
406-837-6851 Fax: 406-837-0778	Visa, MC, AmEx, Disc,	sports, will help w/tours,
800-837-7460	*Rated*, •	dinner plans
William & Mary Corcoran Knoll	C-yes/S-ltd/P-ltd/H-ltd	
All year		

Elegant, rustic log home nestled in the woods and mountain meadows, antique furniture, original artwork, two huge stone fireplaces and manicured grounds. Books, bird watching.
South of Kalispell. E-mail: knollmc@aol.com *Web site:* Montanainn.com

BILLINGS

Josephine B&B, The
514 North 29th St, 59101
406-248-5898
800-552-5898
Douglas & Becky Taylor
All year

68-140-B&B
6 rooms, 4 pb
Most CC, *Rated*, •
C-ltd/S-no/P-no/H-no

Full breakfast
Afternoon tea, comp. liqueur
Snacks, sitting room, library,
tennis/pool/, hot tubs/sauna
nearby

Lovely historic home within walking distance to downtown. Comfortably elegant, delicious gourmet breakfasts—a refreshing alternative. E-mail: josephine@imt.net
Web site: thejosephine.com

BOZEMAN

Cottonwood Inn B&B
13515 Cottonwood Cyn Rd,
59718
406-763-5452 Fax: 406-763-5639
888-TRY-INNS
Joe and Debbie Velli
All year

69-129-B&B
5 rooms, 5 pb
Visa, MC, *Rated*, •
C-ltd/S-no/P-no/H-no
Italian

Full breakfast
Snacks, comp. beverages
Hot tubs, sitting room,
library, nightly turndown
service

Mountain hideaway, built in 1996. 10 minutes from Bozeman. Enjoy gourmet breakfasts, skiing, biking, and hiking steps away. E-mail: info@cottonwood-inn.com Web site: cottonwood-inn.com

Fox Hollow B&B
545 Mary Rd, 59718
406-582-8440 Fax: 406-582-9752
800-431-5010
Nancy & Michael Dawson
All year

79-120-B&B
5 rooms, 5 pb
Most CC, *Rated*, •
C-ltd/S-no/P-no/H-no

Full breakfast
Dinner (fee), snacks
Sitting room, hot tubs, art
gallery

"Without equal-by far the best B&B we have ever stayed in." Jay & Sue, Boca Raton, FL.
E-mail: foxholow@bozeman-MT.com Web site: bozeman-MT.com

Howlers Inn
3185 Jackson Creek Rd, 59715
406-586-0304
888-HOWLERS
Dan & Janice Astrom
All year

80-100-B&B
3 rooms, 3 pb
Visa, MC, *Rated*, •
C-yes/S-no/P-no/H-no

Full breakfast
Sitting room, Jacuzzis,
fireplace, sauna, game room,
exercise facilities

North America's only B&B and wolf sanctuary. This impressive log and stone home on 84 acres has spacious rooms, private baths and sweeping views. E-mail: howlers@theglobal.net
Web site: howlersinn.com

Lehrkind Mansion B&B
719 N Wallace Ave, 59715
406-585-6932
800-992-6932
Jon Gerster/Christopher
Nixon
All year

78-158-B&B
5 rooms, 3 pb
Visa, MC, AmEx,
Rated, •
C-ltd/S-no/P-no/H-no
German

Full breakfast
Afternoon tea
Sitting room, library, bikes,
hot tubs, large yard &
mountain views

Queen Anne Victorian mansion furnished in 1890s antiques. Tea served in our music parlor to Montana's largest music box, 7 feet tall! E-mail: lehrkindmansion@imt.net
Web site: bozemanbedandbreakfast.com

Silver Forest Inn
15325 Bridger Canyon Rd,
59715
406-586-1882 Fax: 406-582-0492
888-835-5970
Chris & Ashley Jackson
All year

75-250-B&B
6 rooms, 4 pb
Visa, MC, AmEx, •
C-yes/S-ltd/P-ltd/H-no
Spanish

Full breakfast
Lunch, snacks, bar
2 hot tubs, massage, TV,
Sitting room, Skiing.

Historic 1932 log home nestled in the pines at the base of the Bridger Mountains.
E-mail: jackson@silverforestinn.com Web site: silverforestinn.com

BOZEMAN

Torch & Toes B&B
309 S 3rd Ave, 59715
406-586-7285 Fax: 406-585-2749
800-446-2138
Judith Hess
All year

70-130-B&B
4 rooms, 4 pb
Visa, MC, *Rated*, •
C-yes/S-no/P-no/H-no

Full breakfast
Complimentary sherry
Sitting room, library, bikes,
porch swing, hot tub, 6
person carriage house

Friendly cat, gourmet breakfast & unique collections of dolls, mouse traps, & brass rub-
bings make for a pleasant stay. Nearby skating, concerts, & market. Badminton, croquet.
E-mail: tntbb@avicom.net *Web site:* avicom.net/torchntoes/

Voss Inn
319 S Willson Ave, 59715
406-587-0982 Fax: 406-585-2964
Bruce & Frankee Muller
All year

95-110-B&B
6 rooms, 6 pb
Most CC, *Rated*, •
C-ltd/S-ltd/P-no/H-no

Full breakfast in parlor
Or guest room, afternoon tea
Sitt. rm, parlour, piano,
fax/comp machines avail.,
frequent stay discounts

Warm, elegant historic Victorian mansion beautifully decorated with period wallpaper &
furniture. Walk to university, museums, restaurants, shopping.
E-mail: vossinn@imt.net *Web site:* bozeman-vossinn.com

EMIGRANT

Johnstad's B&B Guesthouse
PO Box 981, 59027
406-333-9003 Fax: 406-333-9003
800-340-4993
Ron & Mary Ellen Johnstad
All year

85-110-B&B
6 rooms, 4 pb
Most CC, •
C-ltd/S-no/P-ltd/H-yes
Spanish, Norwegian, Ger.

Full breakfast
Afternoon tea, snacks
Sitting room, library,
fireplace, conference,
facilities

Classic Montana hospitality in the heart of Paradise Valley just north of Yellowstone Park.
Stay in our B&B with spacious rooms and majestic views or in our log guest house.
E-mail: rjohnstad@aol.com *Web site:* wtp.net/go/johnstad

Yellowstone Riverview B&B
186 East River Road, 59027
406-848-2156
888-848-2550
Steve Koester, Bill Wagner
All year

75-120-B&B
4 rooms, 2 pb
Visa, MC, *Rated*
C-yes/S-no/P-ltd/H-no

Full breakfast
Lunch & dinner (fee), snacks
Sitting room, library,
recreational planning, hiking
guide service

Beautiful hand-hewn log home overlooking the Yellowstone River. Spectacular views, blue
ribbon fly fishing, endless outdoor activities.   E-mail: riverview@imt.net
Web site: wtp.net/go/riverview

GLACIER NATIONAL PARK

Bad Rock Country B&B
480 Bad Rock Dr, 59912
406-892-2829 Fax: 406-892-2930
888-892-2829
Jon & Sue Alper
All year

120-169-B&B
7 rooms, 7 pb
Most CC, *Rated*, •
C-yes/S-no/P-no/H-no

Full breakfast
Complimentary wine/snack
Afternoon tea, hot tubs,
sitting room, library, small
groups facility

Four stunning rooms made of hand-hewn square logs, with fireplaces, three beautiful
rooms in the home, Old West antiques. Twenty minutes to Glacier National Park.
E-mail: stay@badrock.com *Web site:* badrock.com

GLENDIVE

Hostetler House B&B, The
113 N Douglas St, 59330
406-377-4505 Fax: 406-377-8456
800-965-8456
Craig & Dea Hostetler
All year

50-B&B
2 rooms
Visa, MC, Disc, *Rated*,
•
C-ltd/S-no/P-no/H-no
Basic German

Full gourmet breakfast
Sitting room/library, hot
tub/gazebo, tandem
mountain bike

Charming 1912 historic home with two comfortable guest rooms in casual country. Hot tub,
sitting room, sun porch, full breakfast. E-mail: hostetler@mcn.net

The Hostetler House B&B, Glendive, MT

HAMILTON

Deer Crossing B&B
396 Hayes Creek Rd, 59840
406-363-2232 Fax: 406-375-0771
800-763-2232
Mary Lynch
All year

80-115-B&B
5 rooms, 4 pb
Visa, MC, AmEx,
Rated, •
C-yes/S-ltd/P-ltd/H-no

Full country breakfast
Afternoon tea, snacks
Fishing guide, shuttle,
horseback riding, Bunk
house with full bath

Experience Old West charm & hospitality. 25 acres of pines/pasture. Incredible views. Hearty ranch breakfast. Luxury suites with double Jacuzzi tub. Private deck with Morning Star Room.   E-mail: deercros@bitterroot.net   Web site: wtp.net/go/deercrossing

HELENA

Birdseye B&B
6890 Raven Rd, 59601
406-449-4380 Fax: 406-449-4380
888-449-4380
BJ Block   All year

75-95-B&B
5 rooms, 1 pb
Visa, MC, *Rated*, •
C-ltd/S-ltd/P-yes/H-no

Full breakfast
Snacks, dinner available
Sitting room, library

Once upon a mountain in Montana, we decided to share our 5 bedrooms, our goat & llama ranch with visitors.   E-mail: rooms@birdseyebb.com   Web site: birdseyebb.com

LIVINGSTON

River Inn on Yellowstone
4950 Hwy 89 S, 59047
406-222-2429 Fax: 406-222-2625
DeeDee VanZyl & Ursula
Neese
May 1-Oct. 31

60-100-B&B
5 rooms, 3 pb
Visa, MC, •
C-ltd/S-no/P-ltd/H-no
Some Spanish

Full gourmet breakfast
Aftn. tea, comp. liquor
Lunch & dinner (fee), sitting
room, library, bikes

Secluded, historic farmhouse on the banks of the Yellowstone River. Superb mountain and river views. Excellent dining. Guided trips.   E-mail: riverinn@wtp.net Web site: wtp.net/go/riverinn

NOXON

Bighorn Lodge B&B
2 Bighorn Lane, 59853
406-847-4676 Fax: 406-847-4676
888-347-8477
Dave & Cindy Nye   All year

105-B&B
5 rooms, 5 pb
Visa, MC,
C-yes/S-no/P-no

Full breakfast
Fireplaces, bicycles, cable
TV, accommodate business
travelers

For a little luxury with your wilderness.... Enjoy hiking, mountain biking, canoeing, rafting, horseback riding, skiing & spectacular fishing or just relax and enjoy breath-taking views.   E-mail: bullriver@bighornlodgemontana.com   Web site: bighornlodgemontana.com

POLSON

Hawthorne House B&B	40-EP	Full breakfast (fee)
304 Third Ave E, 59860	4 rooms, 0 pb	Sitting room, cable TV
406-883-2723 800-290-1345	C-ltd/S-no/P-no/H-no	
Karen & Gerry Lenz		
All year		

Hawthorne House is a two story English Tudor house with seven gables. It expresses a diversity of cultures. There are local Indian artifacts, antique furnishings and various collections.

RED LODGE

Willows Inn	55-80-B&B	Continental plus breakfast
PO Box 886, 59068	6 rooms, 4 pb	Gourmet picnics available
406-446-3913	Visa, MC, •	TV/VCR parlor with movies,
Kerry, Carolyn, Elven Boggio	C-yes/S-no/P-no/H-no	games/books, local menus,
All year	Finnish, Spanish	ski racks, sun decks

Charming Victorian. Delicious homebaked pastries. Spectacular mountain scenery.
E-mail: willowinn@earthlink.net *Web site:* bbhost.com/willowsinn

SEELEY LAKE

Emily A. B&B, The	95-150-B&B	Full breakfast
PO Box 350, 59868	5 rooms, 2 pb	Snacks, complimentary wine
406-677-3474 Fax: 406-677-3474	Visa, MC, *Rated*, •	Bar service, sitting room,
800-977-4639	C-yes/P-ltd	library, bicycles, fireplaces,
Marilyn & Keith Peterson	Spanish	conference
All year		

The lodge, named for Marilyn's grandmother, is the perfect place for adventure and relaxation. Whether you want to hike, hunt or read in peace, Emily A. is an ideal location.
E-mail: slk3340@montana.com *Web site:* theemilya.com

ST. IGNATIUS

Mandorla Ranch B&B	125-B&B	Continental plus breakfast
327 Main St SW Ronan MT,	•	
59865		
406-676-2255 Fax: 406-676-8524		
Cappuccino Cowboy		
Season Inquire		

Mandorla Ranch, an exculsive B&B, featuring upmarket accommodations. Designer log home, beautiful furnishings, spectacular and secluded mountain setting. Terrific amenities and great ambiance in the foothills of the Mission Mountains. *E-mail:* tlc@ronan.net

THREE FORKS

Sacajawea Hotel	60-105-B&B	Continental breakfast
PO Box 648, 59752	34 rooms	Restaurant, bar service
406-285-6515 Fax: 406-285-4210	Most CC, *Rated*, •	All meals in dining room,
800-821-7326	C-yes/S-ltd/P-ltd/H-ltd	library, hot tub, conference
Jane & Smith Roedel	Spanish, French	facilities
All year		

Casual elegance of a bygone era in this 1910 National Historic Landmark. Excellent fishing, hunting, biking. Between Glacier & Yellowstone Parks. *E-mail:* sac3forks@aol.com
Web site: sacajaweahotel.com

WHITE FISH

Gasthaus Wendlingen B&B	70-125-B&B	Full breakfast
700 Monegan Rd, 59937	4 rooms, 3 pb	Afternoon tea, snacks, comp.
406-862-4886 Fax: 406-862-4886	Visa, MC, *Rated*, •	wine
800-811-8002	C-ltd/S-no/P-no/H-ltd	Sitting room, library,
Barbara & Bill Klein	German	fireplaces, cable TV,
All year		accommodate business
		travelers

German-Western hospitality. Private 8 acre setting. A real Montana feeling. Home baked specialties. Relax on patio, front porch or around our fieldstone fireplace.
Web site: whitefishmt.com/gasthaus

WHITE FISH ———————————————

Good Medicine Lodge
537 Wisconsin Ave, 59937
406-862-5488 Fax: 406-862-5489
800-860-5488
Christopher & Susan Ridder
All year

85-125-B&B
9 rooms, 9 pb
Visa, MC, *Rated*, •
C-yes/S-no/P-no/H-yes
German, French

Full breakfast
Guest bar, no alcohol
Ski boot & glove dryers, hot
tubs, library, sitting room,
guest laundry

A classic Montana getaway. Built of solid cedar; has balconies with stunning views, crackling fireplaces, outdoor spa, and loads of western hospitality, plus new honeymoon suite. A/C in all rooms.   E-mail: goodrx@digisys.net   Web site: wtp.net/go/goodrx

Nebraska

LINCOLN ———————————————

Atwood House B&B, The
740 S 17th St, 68508
402-438-4567 Fax: 402-477-8314
800-884-6554
Ruth & Larry Stoll
All year

78-165-B&B
3 rooms, 3 pb
Most CC, *Rated*
C-ltd/S-no/P-no/H-no

Full breakfast
Snacks, complimentary soft
drinks
Sitting room, library,
Jacuzzis, suites, fireplace,
cable TV

"Experience the Elegance" of a suite in this 7,500-plus square foot 1894 Neoclassical Georgian Revival mansion. Suites have queen/king beds, sitting areas with TV/VCR's and private baths.   E-mail: lstoll2@unl.edu   Web site: atwoodhouse.com

OMAHA ———————————————

Offutt House B&B
140 North 39th St, 68131
402-553-0951 Fax: 402-553-0704
Janet & Paul Koenig
All year

65-105-B&B
6 rooms, 6 pb
Visa, MC, AmEx, *Rated*
C-ltd/S no/P-ltd/H-no

Full breakfast on weekends
Continental plus breakfast
weekdays
Sitting room, library, deep
claw-foot tubs

Mansion built in 1894 furnished with antiques. Centrally located near historic "Old Market" area of shops, restaurants. Sun porch, bar on 1st floor. Sodas and tea available at check-in.   Web site: virtualcities.com/ons/ne/m/nem27020.htm

SCOTTSBLUFF ———————————————

Barn Anew B&B
170549 County Rd L, 69357
308-632-8647 Fax: 308-632-5518
Dick & Jane Snell
All year

75-80-B&B
4 rooms, 4 pb
Visa, MC, AmEx, *Rated*
C-ltd/S-ltd/P-no/H-no

Full breakfast
Snacks
Sitting room, library, satellite
TV, accommodate business
travelers

Historical setting on Oregon Trail. . . next to ScottsBluff National Monument. Renovated 90 year old barn. Quiet, peaceful country location.   E-mail: barnagin@richochet.net Web site: prairieweb.com/barnagain

Nevada

CARSON CITY

Deer Run Ranch B&B
5440 Eastlake Blvd, 89704
775-882-3643
David & Muffy Vhay
All year

85-110-B&B
2 rooms, 2 pb
Most CC,
C-ltd/S-no/P-no/H-ltd

Full breakfast
Complimentary wine,
beverages
Snacks, refrigerator, sitting
room, library, TV, VCR,
private entry

Western ambiance in a unique architect-designed & built ranch house between Reno & Carson City overlooking Washoe Lake. Nature/wildlife watching. Pottery, pond, swimming pool, privacy, great breakfast *Web site:* virtualcities.com/nv/deerrun.htm

ELY

Steptoe Valley Inn
PO Box 150100, 89315
775-289-8687
Jane & Norman Lindley
June-Sept.

84-90-B&B
5 rooms, 5 pb
Visa, MC, AmEx,
Rated, •
C-ltd/S-no/P-no/H-no
Spanish

Full breakfast
Afternoon snack
Sitting room, library, rose
garden, back porch, private
balconies, TVs

Romantic, historic structure near railroad museum, reconstructed in 1990. Elegant dining room/library. Rooms have country-cottage decor. *Web site:* nevadaweb.com/steptoe

INCLINE VILLAGE

Haus Bavaria B&B
PO Box 9079, 89452
775-831-6122 Fax: 775-831-1238
800-731-6222
Bick Hewitt   All year

95-249-B&B
5 rooms, 5 pb
Most CC, *Rated*, •
C-ltd/S-no/P-no/H-no

Full breakfast
Large family room, TV, frplc.,
ski packages, horse
accommodations

There's much to do and see in this area, from gambling casinos to all water sports and golf, hiking, tennis and skiing at 12 nearby sites. *E-mail:* info@hausbavaria.com
Web site: hausbavaria.com

New Hampshire

ASHLAND

Glynn House Inn
PO Box 719, 03217
603-968-3775 Fax: 603-968-3129
800-637-9599
Betsy & Karol Paterman
All year

99-165-B&B
9 rooms, 9 pb
Rated, •
C-ltd/S-no/P-no/H-no
Polish, Russian

Full gourmet breakfast
Complimentary wine, snacks
Sitting room, VCR, A/C,
tennis, lake, golf nrby.,
canopy beds, cable TV

In the heart of New Hampshire among lakes & the White Mountains. Boston 2 hours, Manchester 1 hour away. *E-mail:* glynnhse@lr.net *Web site:* new-hampshire-lodging.com

BARTLETT

Country Inn at Bartlett
PO Box 327, 03812
603-374-2353 Fax: 603-374-2547
800-292-2353
Mark Dindorf   All year

79-144-B&B
17 rooms, 17 pb
Visa, MC, AmEx,
Rated, •
C-yes/S-ltd/P-ltd

Full breakfast
Comp. tea/coffee, snacks
Sitting room, outdoor hot
tub, cross-country ski trails

A B&B inn for hikers, skiers & outdoors enthusiasts in the White Mountains. New addition of 2-rm. cottage with fireplace Expert hiking & trail advice, mtn. bike from door
E-mail: stay@bartlettinn.com *Web site:* bartlettinn.com

Candlelite Inn B&B, Bradford, NH

BETHLEHEM

Mulburn Inn at Bethlehem
2370 Main St, 03574
603-869-3389
800-457-9440
C. Ferraro & A. Loveless
All year

65-120-B&B
7 rooms, 7 pb
Most CC, *Rated*, •
C-yes/S-no/P-no/H-no

Full breakfast
Afternoon tea, snacks
Library, ski & golf packages,
wraparound porches, hot
tub, exercise equip.

Sprawling summer cottage built 1913 as family retreat known as the Ivy House on the Woolworth Estate. Warm, fireside dining, hot country breakfast. Total renovations throughout. Expanded guest areas. E-mail: info@mulburninn.com Web site: mulburninn.com

Wayside Inn, The
3738 Main St, 03574
603-869-3364 Fax: 603-869-5765
800-448-9557
Victor & Kathe Hofmann
May-Oct. & Dec.-March

74-99-B&B/EP/MAP
26 rooms, 26 pb
Most CC,
C-yes/S-ltd/P-ltd/H-yes
French & German

Full breakfast
Dinner avail.
Restaurant, bar, sitting room,
library, tennis, cable TV,
frplc.

New England Country Inn with a European flavour where the whole family is welcome. 14 newly renovated guestrooms in the Inn, 12 additional rooms. Wonderful meals, Swiss specialties, overlook gardens. E-mail: info@thewaysideinn.com Web site: thewaysideinn.com

BRADFORD

Candlelite Inn B&B
5 Greenhouse Lane, 03221
603-938-5571 Fax: 603-938-2564
888-812-5571
Marilyn & Les Gordon
All year

70-95-B&B
6 rooms, 6 pb
Most CC, *Rated*
C-ltd/S-no/P-no/H-no

Full gourmet breakfast
Snacks
Fireplace in parlor, gazebo
porch, woodstove, sun
rooms, games

A lovely country Victorian Inn with handmade cross stitch, tole painting & quilts. Breakfast served in the sun-room overlooking pond & 3 acres of countryside. Justice of the Peace available. E-mail: candlelite@conknet.com Web site: virtualcities.com/nh/candleliteinn.htm

Mountain Lake Inn
PO Box 443, 03221
603-938-2136 Fax: 603-938-5622
800-662-6005
Bob & Tracy Foor
All year

80-85-B&B
9 rooms, 9 pb
Most CC,
C-yes/S-no/P-ltd/H-no
A little Spanish

Full country breakfast
Afternoon tea
Sitting room, library, full
porch, beach, piano

An 18th century inn overlooking lovely Lake Massasecum and the splendid mountain peaks. E-mail: rfoor@conknet.com Web site: mountainlakeinn.amtg.com

BRADFORD

Thistle & Shamrock Inn	75-120-B&B	Full breakfast
11 W Main St, 03221	11 rooms, 11 pb	Restaurant, bar service
603-938-5553 Fax: 603-938-5554	Most CC, •	Dinner (fee), Sitting room,
888-938-5553	C-yes/S-no/P-no/H-yes	library, family friendly
Jim & Lynn Horigan		facility
All year		

Discover the quiet corner of New Hampshire in our historic 1898 Inn. B&B accommodations, great breakfasts, and casual gourmet dining E-mail: stay@thistleandshamrock.com
Web site: thistleandshamrock.com

BRETTON WOODS

Bretton Arms Country Inn	99-219-EP	Restaurant, all meals
Route 302, 03575	34 rooms, 34 pb	available
603-278-1000 Fax: 603-278-8828	Most CC, *Rated*, •	Bar service, sitting room,
800-258-0330	C-yes/S-yes/P-no/H-yes	library, bikes, golf, tennis
Eleanor Imrie All year		court, sauna/pool

Lovingly restored 1896 Inn nestled on picturesque grounds of the historic Mt. Washington Hotel. Cozy country atmosphere, carriage & sleigh rides, skiing. Supervised kids camp May-Oct. Alpine and cross country skiing. National Historic Landmark. E-mail: hotelinfo@ mtwashington.com *Web site:* mtwashington.com/other/brettonarms.html

CAMPTON

Mountain Fare Inn	75-125-B&B	Full breakfast
PO Box 553, 03223	9 rooms, 9 pb	Tea, snacks, wine
603-726-4283 Fax: 603-726-4285	Visa, MC, Disc, *Rated*,	Sitting room, suites, fireplace,
Susan & Nick Preston	•	cable TV, conference, sauna,
All year	C-yes/S-no/P-ltd/H-ltd	soccer field
	A little French	

Lovely 1830's village farmhouse. Summer gardens, foliage in fall, a skiers lodge in winter. E-mail: mtnfareinn@cyberportal.net *Web site:* mountainfareinn.com

CENTRE HARBOR

Red Hill Inn	105-175-B&B	Full breakfast
RFD 1, Box 99M, 03226	26 rooms, 26 pb	Lunch (summer), dinner
603-279-7001 Fax: 603-279-7003	Visa, MC, AmEx,	Bar, Sunday brunch, lake
800-5-REDHIL	*Rated*, •	swimming, small conference
R Miller/B McKenna/G Strobel	C-ltd/S-yes/P-no/H-no	center
All year		

Lovely restored mansion on fifty private acres overlooking Squam Lake (Golden Pond) and White Mountains. E-mail: info@redhillinn.com *Web site:* redhillinn.com

CHARLESTOWN

Maple Hedge B&B Inn	90-105-B&B	Full 3-course breakfast
PO Box 638, 03603	5 rooms, 5 pb	Afternoon tea,
603-826-5237 Fax: 603-826-5237	Visa, MC, *Rated*, •	complimentary wine
800-9-MAPLE9	C-ltd/S-ltd/P-no/H-no	Sitting room, library, with
Joan & Dick DeBrine		fireplace, biking, golf,
Closed January-March		horseshoes, antiquing

Luxurious accommodations in elegant home set among lovely gardens & 200 year old maples. Part of longest National District in New Hampshire. Memorable 3 course breakfast. Located in CT River Valley. Complimentary California wine with New Hampshire cheese E-mail: debrine@fmis.net *Web site:* maplehedge.com

CLAREMONT

Goddard Mansion B&B	65-125-B&B	Full breakfast
25 Hillstead Rd, 03743	10 rooms, 3 pb	Snacks
603-543-0603 Fax: 603-543-0001	Visa, MC, AmEx, *Rated*	Sitting room, library,
800-736-0603	C-yes/S-no/P-no/H-ltd	bicycles, 1 king-size room,
Debbie Albee All year	Some French	golf & tennis nearby

Delightful, c.1902, 18 room English Manor style mansion, acres of lawns, gardens, easy elegance yet comfortable/homey atmosphere. A romantic Victorian getaway. E-mail: deb@ goddardmansion.com *Web site:* goddardmansion.com

CONWAY

Darby Field Inn, The	110-250-B&B/MAP	Full breakfast
PO Box D, 03818	15 rooms, 15 pb	Dinner, bar, MAP avail.
603-447-2181 Fax: 603-447-5726	Visa, MC, AmEx,	Sitting room, piano, outdoor
800-426-4147	*Rated*, •	hot tub, hiking,
Marc & Maria Donaldson	C-ltd/S-ltd/P-no/H-no	entertainment, birding
All year	Spanish	

Cozy country inn overlooking Mt. Washington Valley & Presidential Mountains, rivers.
E-mail: marc@darbyfield.com *Web site:* darbyfield.com

Foothills Farm B&B	50-60-B&B	Full breakfast
PO Box 1368, 03818	5 rooms, 1 pb	Dinner (fee)
207-935-3799 Fax: 603-356-2763	Visa, MC, AmEx, •	Sitting room, bikes, stables
Theresa & Kevin Early	C-yes/S-no/P-ltd/H-no	for guests with, horses
All year		

1850s farmhouse furnished in period antiques. 50 acre country hideaway has stables, trout stream & trails for cross-country skiing, hiking & mountain biking. E-mail: foothillsbb@ landmark.net.com *Web site:* virtualcities.com/ons/nh/n/nhn5801.htm

DURHAM

Three Chimneys Inn	149-189-B&B	Full breakfast
17 Newmarker Rd, 03824	24 rooms, 24 pb	Lunch, dinner, aftn. tea
603-868-7800 Fax: 603-868-2964	Most CC, •	Snacks, rest., bar serv., sitt.
888-399-9777	C-ltd/S-no/P-no/H-yes	rm., lib., cable, Jacuzzis,
Jim Roy		fireplaces
All year		

A newly restored 1649 Homestead & Carriage House, overlooks formal gardens, the Oyster River, & offers 24 guestrooms, Georgian furnishings, fine dining, casual "Tavern" fare, & outdoor dining. E-mail: chimney3@threechimneysinn.com *Web site:* threechimneysinn.com

EAST ANDOVER

Highland Lake Inn	85-125-B&B	Full country breakfast
PO Box 164, 03231	10 rooms, 10 pb	Setups, snacks
603-735-6426 Fax: 603-735-5355	Most CC, *Rated*	Cable TV, VCR, library,
Mary & Peter Petras	C-ltd/S-no/P-no/H-no	antiques, private beach,
All year		fireplace

A 1767 classic building set on 12 acres in a Currier & Ives setting with lake & mountain views. Secluded beach, fishing, hiking, cross country skiing, antiquing.
Web site: highlandlakeinn.com

EXETER

Curtis Field House, The	75-B&B	Full breakfast
735 Exeter Rd, 03842	3 rooms, 2 pb	Dinner (on request)
603-929-0082	Visa, MC, *Rated*	Afternoon tea, sundeck,
Mary Folsom Houston	C-ltd/S-ltd/P-no	sitting room, library, tennis
Open May-Oct.		courts, pool, A/C

Royal Bairy Wills Cape-country setting. Near Phillips Exeter, antiques, historical area, ocean. Breakfast served on terrace. Lobster dinners on request. E-mail: gadabout@ttlc.net

FRANCONIA

Franconia Inn	98-158-B&B	Full breakfast
1300 Easton Rd, 03580	35 rooms, 34 pb	Restaurant, full bar
603-823-5542 Fax: 603-823-8078	Most CC, *Rated*, •	Lounge with movies, library,
800-473-5299	C-yes/S-yes/P-no/H-no	bicycles, heated pool
The Morris Family		
Mem. Day—Oct; 12/15-4/1		

Located in the Easton Valley—Mt. Lafayette & Sugar Hill. Riding stable, ski center. Rooms beautifully decorated. E-mail: info@franconiainn.com *Web site:* franconiainn.com

FRANCONIA

Inn at Forest Hills, The
PO Box 783, 03580
603-823-9550 Fax: 603-823-8701
800-280-9550
Gordon & Joanne Haym
All year

95-165-B&B
7 rooms, 7 pb
Most CC, *Rated*
C-ltd/S-no/P-no/H-no

Full breakfast
Three large living rooms,
Innkpr. is Justice of, Peace &
will marry

*Charming, historic 18 rm. Tudor Manor among majestic scenery of the White Mountains.
Enjoy tennis, golf, hiking trails, cross-country/downhill skiing.   E-mail:* lanier@innfhills.com
Web site: innatforesthills.com

Sugar Hill Inn
Route 117, 03580
603-823-5621
Jim & Barbara Quinn
All year exc. April

85-225-B&B/MAP
17 rooms, 17 pb
Visa, MC, AmEx,
C-ltd/S-no/P-no/H-no

Full 3-course breakfast
Dinner, bar
Queen Anne living room,
antique player piano, Peace
& will marry

*We are furnished with lovely antiques, located in the heart of skiing, antiquing, hiking,
fishing, swimming & golfing.   E-mail:* info@sugarhillinn.com *Web site:* sugarhillinn.com

GILFORD

Inn at Smith Cove, The
19 Roberts Rd, 03246
603-293-1111 Fax: 603-293-1111
Bob & Maria Ruggiero
All year

85 and up-B&B
11 rooms, 11 pb
Most CC, *Rated*
C-ltd/S-no/P-no/H-no

Full breakfast
Sitting room, Jacuzzis,
private beach, gazebo, boat
slips, antiques

*Circa 1898 Victorian on Lake Winnepesaukee. Close to Gunstock ski area, outlet shopping,
golf courses, health club, fishing, hiking. Breakfast in dining room or outside patio. Restaurant discounts.   Web site:* inatsmithcove.com

GLEN

Bernerhof Inn
PO Box 240, 03838
603-383-9132 Fax: 603-383-0809
800-548-8007
Sharon & Ted Wroblewski
All year

75-150-B&B
9 rooms, 9 pb
Most CC, *Rated*
C-ltd/S-no/P-no/H-no

Full breakfast
Lunch (limited), dinner
Restaurant, pub, sitting
room, cooking school, pool,
cable TV, phones, A/C

*An elegant small hotel featuring antique rooms, many with private spa tubs and one with a
fireplace.   E-mail:* stay@bernerhofinn.com *Web site:* bernerhofinn.com

GORHAM

Libby House B&B, The
PO Box 267, 03581
603-466-2271
800-453-0023
Margaret, Paul, & Lily Kuliga
All year

59-90-B&B
3 rooms, 3 pb
Visa, MC, Disc, •
C-yes/S-ltd/P-yes

Full breakfast
Hot or iced tea, snacks
Sitting room, library, all
rooms have mountain views,
skiing/weekly rentals

*1891 Victorian on town common. Closest B&B to White Mtn. Nat'l Forest & Mount Washington. Fine restaurants, golf, hiking, skiing, sightseeing nrby. Newly renovated rms. 2 rm.
suite   E-mail:* libbyhouse@worldnet.att.net

GREENFIELD

Greenfield B&B Inn
PO Box 400, 03047
603-547-6327 Fax: 603-547-2418
800-678-4144
Barbara & Vic Mangini
All year

49-139-B&B
13 rooms, 10 pb
Visa, MC, *Rated*, •
C-yes/S-ltd/P-no/H-no

Full breakfast
Lunch (for groups to 12)
Comp. wine, tea, coffee,
Jacuzzis, hayloft suite, conf.,
cottage, phones

*Play hooky. Make it together. 90 minutes from Boston. Mountain village Victorian rooms-
$49-$79, suites-$119, house-$139.   E-mail:* innkeeper@greenfieldinn.com
Web site: greenfieldinn.com

HAMPSTEAD

Stillmeadow B&B
PO Box 565, 03841
603-329-8381 Fax: 603-329-0137
Lori Offord
All year

65-100-B&B
4 rooms, 4 pb
Most CC, *Rated*
C-ltd/S-no/P-no/H-no
Some French, Ger., Sp.

Continental plus breakfast
Comp. wine and cookies
Croquet, gardens, bikes, near
lake & cross-country skiing,
conf., cottage, phones

Discover Southern New Hampshire's best kept secret. Memorable, charming getaway. Inviting Greek Revival Colonial with 5 chimneys and 3 staircases. Wedding brunches. Established 1987. E-mail: stillmeadowb@yahoo.com

HAMPTON

D.W.'s Oceanside Inn
365 Ocean Blvd, 03842
603-926-3542 Fax: 603-926-3549
Skip & Debbie Windemiller
Mid-May-Mid-October

105-150-B&B
10 rooms, 10 pb
Most CC, *Rated*, •

Continental plus breakfast
Bar service, sitting room,
library, beach chair & towels

Directly across from sandy beach; beautiful ocean views. Active, resort-type atmosphere during mid-summer. Recent renovations, many antiques. Not appropriate for children. E-mail: oceansid@nh.ultranet.com *Web site:* nh.ultranet.com/~oceansid

HANCOCK

John Hancock Inn
PO Box 96, 03449
603-525-3318 Fax: 603-525-9301
800-525-1789
Christopher, Linda & Joseph
All year

125-250-B&B
15 rooms, 15 pb
Most CC, *Rated*, •
C-ltd/S-no/P-no/H-yes
German

Restaurant, dinner, snacks,
tea
All meals available
Sitting room, library, tennis,
Jacuzzis, suites, fireplace,
cable TV, bar

Since 1789, the first year of George Washington's presidency, the Hancock Inn has been in continuous operation, hosting thousands of visitors, from cattle drovers and rum runners to aristocracy and a U.S. president. E-mail: innkeeper@hancockinn.com *Web site:* hancockinn.com

HANOVER

Alden Country Inn
PO Box 60, 03768
603-795-2222 Fax: 603-795-9436
800-794-2296
Mickey Dowd & Kelly White
All year

115-165-B&B
15 rooms, 15 pb
Most CC, *Rated*
C-yes/S-no/P-no/H-ltd

Full breakfast
Lunch/dinner available,
restaurant
Afternoon tea, bar service,
bicycles, tennis court,
fireplaces

A dependable inn & tavern for almost 200 years; built in 1809. Enjoy hearty portions of victuals, a jug of ale and a clean room to rest the body. E-mail: info@aldencountryinn.com *Web site:* aldencountryinn.com

HENNIKER

Colby Hill Inn
PO Box 779, 03242
603-428-3281 Fax: 603-428-9218
Ellie, John & Laurel Day
All year

85-185-B&B
16 rooms, 16 pb
Visa, MC, AmEx,
Rated, •
C-ltd/S-ltd/P-no/H-ltd

Full breakfast
Dinner, complimentary
beverages
Bar, cookies, sitting room,
library, A/C, croquet, pool,
badminton, pool

1800 country inn on 5 acres in a quiet village. Antique-filled rooms, smiling hosts, fine dining. E-mail: info@colbyhillinn.com *Web site:* colbyhillinn.com

HOLDERNESS

Inn on Golden Pond, The
PO Box 680, 03245
603-968-7269 Fax: 603-968-9226
Bill & Bonnie Webb
All year

120-150-B&B
8 rooms, 8 pb
Visa, MC, *Rated*, •
C-ltd/S-no/P-no/H-no

Full breakfast
Piano, air conditioned
rooms, full service
restaurant

*Located on 55 wooded acres across the street from Squam Lake, setting for "On Golden Pond." Close to major attractions, skiing.
E-mail:* innongp@lr.net *Web site:* newhampshirebandb.com

The Country Porch B&B, Hopkinton, NH

HOPKINTON

Country Porch B&B, The	70-80-B&B	Full breakfast
281 Moran Road, 03229	3 rooms, 3 pb	Snacks
603-746-6391 Fax: 603-746-6391	Visa, MC, •	Sitting room, swimming,
Tom & Wendy Solomon	C-ltd/S-no/P-no/H-no	fireplaces, cable TV,
All year		conference facilities

The Country Porch is situated on 15 peaceful acres of lawn, pasture and forest. It is an authentic reproduction of an 18th century colonial featuring wide pine floors, a rumford fireplace and a wraparound porch.

JACKSON

Christmas Farm Inn, The	150-270-B&B	Full breakfast
PO Box #CC, 03846	34 rooms, 34 pb	Snacks
603-383-4313 Fax: 603-383-6495	Visa, MC, AmEx,	Restaurant, dinner, bar,
800-HI-ELVES	*Rated*, •	sitting room, library,
Bill & Sydna Zeliff	C-yes/S-ltd/P-no/H-no	Jacuzzis, pool, suites
All year		

The spirit of Christmas lives year round at this classic inn. From hillside setting to hearty meals, the hosts' warm hospitality lives up to their motto, "we make memories."
E-mail: info@christmasfarminn.com *Web site:* christmasfarminn.com

Dana Place Inn	95-175-B&B/MAP	Full breakfast in season
PO Box L, 03846	35 rooms, 31 pb	Dinner, pub
603-383-6822 Fax: 603-383-6022	Visa, MC, AmEx,	Piano, river swimming,
800-537-9276	*Rated*, •	indoor pool, tennis courts,
The Levine Family	C-yes/S-yes/P-yes/H-no	Jacuzzi
All year	French	

Historic country inn at base of Mt. Washington. Cozy rooms, fine dining, afternoon tea. Three 2-room family suites. *E-mail:* dpi@ncia.net *Web site:* danaplace.com

Ellis River House	89-289-B&B	Full country breakfast
PO Box 656, 03846	18 rooms, 18 pb	Tea, coffee, cookies
603-383-9339 Fax: 603-383-4142	Most CC, *Rated*, •	Tavern with billiards, darts,
800-233-8309	C-ltd/S-no/P-ltd/H-ltd	cable, fishing, atrium with
Barry & Barbara Lubao	Polish	Jacuzzi, sauna
All year		

Romantic 20 room Inn located at the base of Mt. Washington in the White Mountains region. *E-mail:* innkeeper@erhinn.com *Web site:* erhinn.com

JACKSON

Inn at Jackson	98-198-B&B	Continental plus breakfast
PO Box 807, 03846	14 rooms, 14 pb	Library, sitting room,
603-383-4321 Fax: 603-383-4085	Most CC, *Rated*, •	fireplaces, A/C, TVs, outdoor
800-289-8600	C-ltd/S-ltd/P-no/H-no	hot tub Jacuzzi
Lori Tradewell		
All year		

Stanford White mansion in the heart of the White Mountains. Adjacent to Jackson ski touring trails. Spacious rooms, common rooms, porch dining room, fireplace rooms.
E-mail: innjack@ncia.net *Web site:* innatjackson.com

Nestlenook Farm Resort	125-320-B&B	Full breakfast
PO Box Q, 03846	7 rooms, 7 pb	Social hour wine/snacks
603-383-9443 Fax: 603-383-4515	Visa, MC, Disc, *Rated*,	Sitting room, bikes, pool,
800-659-9443	•	skating, snowshoeing,
Robert Cyr	C-ltd/S-no/P-no/H-no	Austrian sleigh rides
All year		

Escape into a Victorian fantasy. Seven elegant rooms with canopy beds, 19th century parlor stoves & fireplaces available.   E-mail: vacations@nestlenook.com
Web site: luxurymountaingetaways.com/nnmain.html

Whitneys' 1842 Inn	79-199-B&B	Continental plus breakfast
PO Box 822, 03846	30 rooms, 30 pb	Restaurant, dinner available
603-383-8916 Fax: 603-383-6886	Most CC, *Rated*, •	(fee)
800-677-5737	C-yes/S-ltd/P-ltd/H-no	Afternoon tea, bar service,
Bob & Barb Bowman		sitting room, tennis, hot tub,
All year		heated pool

Just up a country road, nestled at the base of the mountains our 14 private acres await you. Gourmet dining & cozy lodging in a casual, family friendly classic country inn.   E-mail: whitneyinn@aol.com *Web site:* whitneysinn.com

JAFFREY

Benjamin Prescott Inn	75-140-B&B	Full breakfast
Route 124 W, 03452	12 rooms, 9 pb	Complimentary tea, coffee
603-532-6637 Fax: 603-532-6637	Visa, MC, *Rated*, •	Sitting room, bicycles, Air
Jan & Barry Miller	C-ltd/S-ltd/P-no/H-no	conditioned suites
All year		

Relax...Indulge...Less than two hours from Boston, the inn offers the opportunity to reset your pace and explore the Monadnock region

JEFFERSON

Applebrook B&B	55-90-B&B	Full breakfast
Route 115A, 03583	12 rooms, 4 pb	Dinner by reservation
603-586-7713	Visa, MC, Disc, *Rated*,	Sitting room, library, hot tub
800-545-6504	•	under the stars, family suite
Sandra Conley & Martin Kelly	C-yes/S-no/P-yes/H-no	
All year		

Hike, golf, ski from comfortable Victorian farmhouse. Taste mid-summer raspberries & enjoy mountain views. Stained glass & goldfish pool   E-mail: vacation@applebrook.com
Web site: applebrook.com

KEENE

Post and Beam B&B	55-95-B&B	Full breakfast
HCR 33, Box 380, 03445	7 rooms, 2 pb	Afternoon tea, snacks
603-847-3330 Fax: 603-847-3306	Most CC, *Rated*, •	Sitting room, library, suites,
888-3ROMANCE	C-ltd/S-no/P-no/H-yes	frplcs, hot tub, cable TV
Darcy Bacal & Priscilla Hardy	French	
All year		

1791 New England farmstead with 7 lovely bedrooms decorated with colonial antiques. View the hand-hewn beams, wide pine floors, fireplaces.   E-mail: postandbeam@monad.net
Web site: postandbeambb.com

LACONIA

Rest Assured
47 Laighton Ave S, 03246
603-524-9021 Fax: 603-528-9000
Maurice & Helene Gouin
All year

75-100-B&B
3 rooms, 1 pb
•
S-no/P-no/H-no
French

Full breakfast
Complimentary wine &
cheese
2 TV rooms, solarium,
seasonal activities, golf,
make maple syrup

Come and share with us a piece of heaven. The serenity of the lake, mountains & woodlands lift one's spirit.

LINCOLN

Red Sleigh Inn B&B, The
PO Box 562, 03251
603-745-8517
Bill & Loretta Deppe
All year

65-85-B&B
6 rooms, 2 pb
Visa, MC, *Rated*
C-ltd/S-no/P-no/H-no

Full hearty breakfast
Complimentary tea
Sitting room, library

Mountains surrounding us abound in ski touring trails. Bedrooms are tastefully decorated with many antiques. E-mail: redsleigh@linwoodnet.com

LITTLETON

Beal House Inn
2 W Main St, 03561
603-444-2661 Fax: 603-444-6224
888-616-BEAL
Pat and Michael McGuinn
All year

65-150-B&B
7 rooms, 7 pb
Visa, MC, AmEx,
Rated, •
C-yes/S-no/P-no/H-no

Full breakfast
Dinner, comp. wine, snacks,
bar
Restaurant, sitting room,
fishing, canoeing, books,
suites, fireplace, cable

Cozy historic 1833 Inn on Main Street in the quaint town of Littleton, furnished with antiques, suites available with fireplaces. E-mail: beal.house.inn@connriver.net
Web site: bealhouseinn.com

MANCHESTER

Breezy Hill B&B
119 Adams Rd, 03053
603-432-0122 Fax: 603-432-0511
Emily & Ron Foley
All year

75-100-B&B
4 rooms, 2 pb
Visa, MC,
C-yes/S-ltd/P-no/H-no

Full breakfast
Sitting room, cable TV,
swimming pool, fishing,
canoeing, books

An 1850's New England farmhouse, wonderful farm fresh breakfasts. Guests enjoy beautiful views of acres of orchardland; seasonal pool. Close to Manchester Airport, New England's hassle free gateway. E-mail: breezyhill@worldnet.att.net Web site: breezyhill.com

Stepping Stones B&B
6 Bennington Battle Tr, 03086
603-654-9048 Fax: 603-654-6821
888-654-9048
D. Ann Carlsmith
All year

60-65-B&B
3 rooms, 3 pb
Rated, •
C-yes/S-ltd/P-ltd/H-no

Full breakfast
Complimentary tea, wine
Stereo, color TV, looms,
library, sitting room,
breakfast room, gardens

Quiet country setting in Monadnock hills, near picture-book village. Summer theater & music. Antiquing, hiking, civilized atmosphere.

MARLBOROUGH

Peep-Willow Farm
51 Bixby St, 03455
603-876-3807
Noel Aderer
All year

75-B&B
3 rooms, 1 pb
•
C-yes/S-no/P-yes/H-no

Full breakfast
Complimentary wine
Snacks, sitting room, trails,
cross country skiing

I raise thoroughbred horses—you can help with chores (no riding), watch the colts play and enjoy the view all the way to Vermont's Green Mountains. Web site: peepwillowfarm.com

MEREDITH ─────────────────────────

Inns at Mill Falls, The
312 Daniel Webster Hwy28,
03253
603-279-7006 Fax: 603-279-6797
800-622-6455
Rusty McLear   All year

69-259-EP
101 rooms, 101 pb
Most CC, *Rated*, •
C-yes/S-ltd/P-no/H-yes

Lunch, dinner, restaurant,
snacks
Jacuzzis, swimming pool,
suites, fireplaces, cable TV,
fitness room

Country Elegance on Lake Winnipesaukee. 101 designer decorated rooms, many with fireplaces and views of the lake. Five wonderful restaurants, a 40 foot waterfall and 15 shops/galleries. Simply superb! E-mail: info@millfalls-baypoint.com *Web site:* millfalls-baypoint.com

MOULTONBORO ─────────────────────

Olde Orchard Inn
RR Box 256, 03254
603-476-5004 Fax: 603-476-5419
800-598-5845
Jim & Mary Senner   All year

70-140-B&B
9 rooms, 6 pb
Visa, *Rated*, •
C-yes/S-no/P-ltd/H-ltd
French, Finnish

Full breakfast
Sitting room, fishing, library,
bicycles, spa, sauna,
conferences

C.1790 Federal nestled in twelve acre apple orchard. Furnished with antiques collected by former diplomat owners. Near large lake. 2 rooms with queen bed, fireplace, Jacuzzi. E-mail: innkeep@oldeorchardinn.com *Web site:* oldeorchardinn.com

MOUNT SUNAPEE ────────────────────

Blue Goose Inn
PO Box 2117, 03255
603-763-5519 Fax: 603-763-8720
Meryl & Ronald Caldwell
All year

65-75-B&B
5 rooms, 3 pb
Visa, MC, *Rated*, •
C-yes/S-no/P-no/H-yes

Full breakfast
Dinner on request
Sitting room, bicycles, lake,
downhill skiing, picnicking,
lawn games, A/C

Adjacent to Mt. Sunapee State Park; 19th-century farmhouse on 3.5 acres. Picnicking, grill, bikes available. Mystery weekends. Non-smoking policy. E-mail: brire2@kear.tdsnet.com

NEW LONDON ──────────────────────

Follansbee Inn
PO Box 92, 03260
603-927-4221 Fax: 603-754-6353
800-626-4221
Sandy & Dick Rellein
Except Mar., Apr., Nov.

90-120-B&B
23 rooms, 11 pb
Visa, MC, *Rated*
C-ltd/S-no/P-no/H-no

Full breakfast
Snacks, bar
Sitting room, bicycles, lake

You will find our Inn nestled in a quiet rural village with porch views of the town green and peaceful Kezar Lake. You may feel as if you have walked into a quaint farmhouse, which is, in fact, the origin of this c. 1840 landmark. E-mail: follansbeeinn@conknet.com *Web site:* follansbeeinn.com

Inn at Pleasant Lake, The
PO Box 1030, 03257
603-526-6271 Fax: 603-526-4111
800-626-4907
Linda & Brian MacKenzie
All year

110-165-B&B
12 rooms, 12 pb
Visa, MC, Disc, *Rated*,
•
C-yes/S-no/P-no/H-ltd

Full breakfast
Continental breakfast
Dinner, aftn. tea, rest., Bar
service, sitting rm., Lake,
conference

Gracious 1790 lakeside inn. Twelve well-appointed guest rooms all with private bath & A/C. E-mail: bmackenz@kear.tds.net *Web site:* innatpleasantlake.com

NEWFOUND LAKE ────────────────────

Inn on Newfound Lake, The
1030 Mayhew Pike, Rt 3A,
03222
603-744-9111 Fax: 603-744-3894
800-745-7990
Larry Delangis & Phelps
Boyce   All year

105-265-B&B
31 rooms, 23 pb
Most CC, *Rated*, •
C-ltd/S-no/P-no/H-yes

Continental breakfast
Restaurant, bar service
Snacks, fishing in lake, sitting
room, library, private beach
& dock

One of the few remaining true country inns. We have a 260-ft. private beach and private dock on one of the cleanest lakes in the country. Exercise/Jacuzzi room. E-mail: inonlk@cyberportal.net *Web site:* newfoundlake.com

NORTH CONWAY ————————————————————

1785 Inn & Restaurant, The	69-239-B&B	Full country breakfast
PO Box 1785, 03860	13 rooms, 8 pb	Restaurant, lounge
603-356-9025 Fax: 603-356-6081	Visa, MC, AmEx,	2 sitting rooms, piano,
800-421-1785	*Rated*, •	classical guitar Sat-Sun,
Becky & Charlie Mallar	C-yes/S-ltd/P-ltd/H-ltd	ski/honeymoon pkgs, pool
All year	French	

Newly redecorated historic inn at The Scenic Vista overlooking the Saco River Valley.
E-mail: the1785inn@aol.com *Web site:* the1785inn.com

Buttonwood Inn, The	95-250-B&B	Full breakfast
PO Box 1817, 03860	10 rooms, 10 pb	Sitting room, library, 40-foot
603-356-2625	Most CC, *Rated*, •	swimming pool, TV, lawn
Fax: 603-356-3140	C-ltd/S-ltd/P-no/H-no	sports, skiing
800-258-2625		
Peter & Claudia Needham		
All year		

Tucked away on Mt. Surprise. Quiet, secluded yet only 2 mi. to town-excellent dining,
shopping. Near all outdoor activities. Apres-ski gameroom with fireplace 2 rooms with gas
fireplace. *E-mail:* button_w@moose.ncia.net *Web site:* buttonwoodinn.com

Cabernet Inn	75-189-B&B	Full breakfast
PO Box 489, 03860	11 rooms, 11 pb	Aftn. tea, comp. wine on
603-356-4704 Fax: 603-356-5399	Most CC, *Rated*, •	Spec. occasion, sitt. rm, 2
800-866-4704	C-ltd/S-ltd/P-no/H-ltd	common rms. w/frplcs.,
Debbie & Rich Howard		upper deck for breakfast
All year		

Nestled in the heart of the spectacular White Mountains, the Cabernet is the perfect
romantic getaway. Guest rooms with Jacuzzi tubs or gas fireplaces, gorgeous views
E-mail: info@cabernetinn.com *Web site:* cabernetinn.com

Locust Hill B&B	80-B&B	Full breakfast
PO Box 427, 03860	1 rooms, 1 pb	Sitting room, library,
603-356-6135	Visa, MC, •	swimming pool, suites, cable
Cynthia & Conrad Briggs	C-yes/S-no/P-no/H-no	TV.
All year		

In the English tradition of vacation accommodations in a private home, the Briggs wel-
come a limited number of guests to their home. *E-mail:* locusthill@landmarknet.net
Web site: pts.placestostay.com/gen_prop.asp?hotel_id=1892&N=1907

Nereledge Inn	59-139-B&B	Full breakfast
PO Box 547, 03860	11 rooms, 5 pb	Dinner for groups
603-356-2831 Fax: 603-356-7085	Visa, MC, AmEx,	Fireplace room with, darts &
Valerie & Dave Halpin	C-yes/S-no/P-no/H-no	games, 2 sittup, rooms, 1
All year		w/woodstove

Cozy 1787 inn, 5 minute walk to village, close to skiing areas, fishing, golf, climbing,
canoeing. Home-cooked meals including country-style breakfast
E-mail: info@nereledgeinn.com *Web site:* nereledgeinn.com

Old Red Inn & Cottages	59-175-B&B	Full breakfast
PO Box 467, 03860	17 rooms, 15 pb	Kitchenettes
603-356-2642 Fax: 603-356-6626	Most CC, *Rated*	Living room w/woodstove,
800-338-1356	C-yes/S-ltd/P-no/H-no	piano, herb garden, gardens,
Terry & Dick Potochniak	French	park, cable TV, pool
All year		

Enjoy warm hospitality in our four-season circa 1810 country inn and individually decorat-
ed cottages, featuring gas log fireplaces. *E-mail:* oldredin@nxi.com *Web site:* oldredinn.com

NORTH CONWAY

Scottish Lion Inn & Rest.	65-120-B&B	Full breakfast
PO Box 1527, 03860	8 rooms, 8 pb	Lunch/dinner available, bar
603-356-6381 Fax: 603-356-4802	Most CC, •	Sitting room, library, hot tub,
800-356-4945	C-yes/S-yes/P-no/H-no	bicycles, A/C, hiking
Michael & Janet Procopio	It., Phil., Hawaiian	
All year exc. Christmas		

Traditional Scottish country inn. Over 60 scotches & an American Scottish Highland menu. Skiing out backdoor. E-mail: info@scottishlioninn.com Web site: ScottishLionInn.com

Stonehurst Manor	96-196-MAP	Full breakfast
PO Box 1937, 03860	25 rooms, 23 pb	Dinner included, tea/coffee
603-356-3113 Fax: 603-356-3217	Visa, MC, AmEx, *Rated*	Library, piano, bar,
800-525-9100	C-yes/S-yes/P-no/H-yes	swimming pool, hot tub,
Peter Rattay	German	tennis, fireplaces
All year		

Turn-of-the-century mansion with old oak and stained glass. Relax by our fireplace in the library. Guided walking and hiking tours. Mount Washington Valley. E-mail: smanor@aol.com Web site: stonehurstmanor.com

Victorian Harvest Inn, The	80-150-B&B	Full breakfast
28 Locust Ln, Box 1763, 03860	6 rooms, 6 pb	Afternoon tea
603-356-3548 Fax: 603-356-8430	Visa, MC, *Rated*	Sitting room, library,
800-642-0749	C-ltd/S-no/P-no/H-no	swimming pool, suites,
David & Judy Wooster		fireplaces, cable TV
All year		

1850s restored Victorian on quiet side street close to village, outlet shopping, restaurants, hiking trails. All private baths, pool, antiques and gardens, full gourmet breakfasts. E-mail: info@victorianharvestinn.com Web site: victorianharvestinn.com

NORTH WOODSTOCK

Three Rivers House	60-170-B&B	Full breakfast
RR#1 Box 72, 03262	18 rooms, 18 pb	Dinner
603-745-2711 Fax: 603-745-2773	Most CC, *Rated*, •	Porches with rockers,
800-241-2711	C-yes/S-no/P-no/H-no	fireplace sitting room, hot
Brian Crete & Diane Brisson		tub in winter
All year		

Warm hospitality since 1875, full country breakfast, in-rm TVs. Located on edge of village near trails, skiing, & attractions. Some rooms with 2 person Jacuzzi, gas fireplace. Web site: threerivershouse.com

Wilderness Inn B&B	50-120-B&B	Full gourmet breakfast
RFD 1, Box 69, 03262	8 rooms, 6 pb	Dinner with reservation
603-745-3890 Fax: 603-745-6367	Visa, MC, AmEx,	Aftn. tea, cider, cocoa,
800-200-WILD	*Rated*, •	swimming hole, 3 porches,
Michael & Rosanna Yarnell	C-yes/S-no/P-no/H-no	fireplace in cottage
All year	Fr., It., Hindi, Amharic	

"The quintessential country inn." Circa 1912, located in quaint New England town. Inn & rooms furnished with antiques & Oriental carpets. 3 miles to Loon Mt. & downhill skiing. Central air upstairs. Non-Smoking Inn. E-mail: wildernessinn@juno.com Web site: musar.com/wildernessinn

NORTHWOOD

Meadow Farm B&B	65-70-B&B	Full breakfast
454 Jenness Pond Rd, 03261	3 rooms	Private beach, canoeing,
603-942-8619 Fax: 603-942-5731	C-ltd/S-ltd/P-ltd/H-no	sitting room, antiquing,
Janet & Douglas Briggs		cottage on lake for rent
All year		

Restored charming 1770 colonial home—50 acres of fields, woods. Private beach on lake.

PORTSMOUTH

Inn at Strawbery Banke	85-120-B&B	Full breakfast
314 Court St, 03801	7 rooms, 7 pb	Sitting room, outdoor garden,
603-436-7242	Visa, MC, AmEx, *Rated*	bikes, all guest rooms have
800-428-3933	C-ltd/S-no/P-no/H-ltd	A/C
Sarah Glover O'Donnell		
All year		

This colonial inn charms travelers with its beautiful rooms & outdoor garden. Located in heart of old Portsmouth with its quaint shops, working port, parks, historical homes.

Martin Hill Inn	80-120-B&B	Full breakfast
404 Islington St, 03801	7 rooms, 7 pb	All rooms have writing,
603-436-2287	Visa, MC, *Rated*	tables and sofas or, separate
Jane & Paul Harnden	C-ltd/S-no/P-no/H-no	sitting areas
All year		

1810 colonial has beautifully appointed rooms with period antiques. Elegant yet comfortable.   Web site: portsmouthnh.com/martinhillinn

Rock Ledge Manor B&B	100-135-B&B	Full breakfast
1413 Ocean Blvd, 03870	4 rooms, 4 pb	Afternoon tea, snacks
603-431-1413	*Rated*	Sitting room
Stella & Stanley Smith	C-ltd/S-no/P-no/H-no	
All year		

From our porch, enjoy the panoramic Atlantic views, watch the lobster men haul in their catch and the sail boats cruise to Portsmouth Harbor. All rooms have ocean views, queen size beds, paddle fans and include a full gourmet style breakfast.
E-mail: rlmbb@mediaone.net   Web site: people.ne.mediaone.net/rlmbb

SUGAR HILL

Homestead Inn, The	60-115-B&B	Full country breakfast
Route 117 Box 619, 03585	18 rooms, 9 pb	Afternoon tea
603-823-5564 Fax: 603-823-9599	Most CC, *Rated*, •	Music rm., frplc, museum,
800-823-5564	C-yes/S-ltd/P-yes/H-no	cable TV, gift shop, pets ltd.
Paul & Melody Hayward		to certain rms
All year		

The Homestead was the home of the area's first permanent settler in 1780. Hand hewn beams, hand sewn boards and hand cut brick make evident the work of our great, great, great, great grandfather.   E-mail: homested@together.net   Web site: thehomestead1802.com

WEARE

Weare House B&B	65-85-B&B	Full breakfast
76 Quaker St, 03281	4 rooms, 2 pb	Sitting room
603-529-2660	Visa, MC, Disc,	
Ellen & Curt Goldsberry	C-yes/S-no/P-ltd/H-no	
All year		

Colonial farmhouse built in 1819, situated on 12 rural acres. Four unique guestrooms with down comforters. Sitting area with fireplace; huge barn with animals. Children welcome.
E-mail: info@thewearehouse.com   Web site: thewearehouse.com

WHITE MOUNTAINS

Fieldstone Country Inn	65-85-B&B	Full breakfast
PO Box 456, 03595	7 rooms, 3 pb	Afternoon tea, snacks, wine
603-846-5646 Fax: 603-846-5646	Visa, MC,	Sitting room, library, cable
Susan & Mark Clark	C-yes/S-no/P-yes/H-no	TV
All year		

Country setting, quiet and relaxing. Our own farm fresh bacon and eggs. Views of the White Mountains.   E-mail: fieldstone.ctry.inn@worldsurfer.net   Web site: musar.com/fieldstonecountryinn

WOLFEBORO ───

Tuc'Me Inn B&B	90-100-B&B	Full country breakfast
PO Box 657, 03894	7 rooms, 3 pb	Parlor w/TV/VCR, phone,
603-569-5702	Visa, MC, *Rated*, ●	library, music room, 2
Terrille S. Foutz	C-ltd/S-no/P-no/H-no	screened porches
All year		

1850 Colonial/Federal Inn. Homey atmosphere, tastefully furnished in family antiques. "Cook's whims" breakfast 2-block walk to downtown & beautiful Lake Winnipesaukee.
E-mail: tucmeinn@worldpath.net *Web site:* worldpath.net/~tucmeinn/

New Jersey

ATLANTIC CITY ─────────────────────────────────────

Dr. Jonathan Pitney House	99-225-B&B	Full breakfast
57 North Shore Road, 08201	11 rooms, 11 pb	Afternoon tea
609-569-1799 Fax: 609-569-9224	Visa, MC, *Rated*, ●	Sitting room, library, Jacuzzi,
888-7-PITNEY	S-no/P-no/H-yes	fireplaces, cable, suites, sm.
Don Kelly & Vonnie Clark		conf.
All year		

The home of the "Father of Atlantic City." Built in 1799 and restored and renovated in 1997. Furnished with antiques from both Colonial and Victorian eras. Gourmet breakfast and afternoon tea.   *E-mail:* drpitney@pitneyhouse.com *Web site:* pitneyhouse.com

AVON BY THE SEA ───────────────────────────────────

Atlantic View Inn	89-179-B&B	Full breakfast
20 Woodland Ave, 07717	Visa, MC, AmEx, *Rated*	Afternoon tea, snacks
732-774-8505 Fax: 732-869-0187	C-ltd/S-no/P-no/H-no	Sitting room, library, bikes,
Bill & Cathy Dey		suites, fireplaces, badges for
All year		beach access

The charm of an English seashore home overlooking the ocean. Scrumptious breakfasts served on an open porch. Featherbeds, fireplaces, candlelight breakfasts & intimate classical performances provide a warm, relaxed atmosphere in our quiet season.   *E-mail:* wdey@ atlanticviewinn.com *Web site:* atlanticviewinn.com

Avon Manor Inn, The	130-B&B	Full breakfast
109 Sylvania Ave, 07717	9 rooms, 9 pb	Aftn. tea, comp. wine
732-776-7770 Fax: 732-776-7476	Most CC, *Rated*, ●	Restaurant, sitting room,
Greg Dietrich	C-ltd/S-no/P-no/H-no	library, tennis court, A/C,
All year		cottage available

Romantic seaside inn furnished with antiques & wicker. Hearty breakfast. Fireplace in parlor for cozy winter nights. Central New Jersey; 1 hour to NY & Phily
E-mail: gregmar@aol.com *Web site:* avonmanor.com

Cashelmara Inn	83-276-B&B	Full breakfast
22 Lakeside Ave, 07717	14 rooms, 14 pb	Wine, ice machine
732-776-8727 Fax: 732-988-5819	Visa, MC, AmEx, *Rated*	Beach chairs, umbreallas,
800-821-2976	C-ltd/S-no/P-no/H-no	wind breaks, resident
Mary E. Wiernasz		retrievers: Cody & Lucy
All year		

European antiques, water views complemented by designer fabrics & window treatments. In-season complimentary beach badges. In-home "theater." Hearty breakfast served on oceanside verandah. Two suites with Jacuzzis.   *E-mail:* cashelmara@monmouth.com
Web site: avonbythesea.com/cashelmara

Connover's Bay Head Inn, Bay Head, NJ

BAY HEAD

Bay Head Gables
200 Main Ave, 08742
732-892-9844 Fax: 732-295-2196
800-984-9536
Don Haurie & Ed Laubusch
Wkends only in Winter

95-195-B&B
11 rooms, 11 pb
Most CC, *Rated*, •
C-ltd/S-no/P-no/H-no

Full breakfast
Snacks, complimentary wine
Sitting room, 75 yds. to
ocean, in room phones &
A/C

A 3-story Georgian Colonial overlooking ocean. Elegant Victorian to ultra contemporary—to please the most discriminating guest. Memorable breakfasts. AAA rates 3 diamonds. E-mail: bhgables@monmouth.com Web site: bayheadgables.com

Conover's Bay Head Inn
646 Main Ave, 08742
732-892-4664 Fax: 732-892-8748
800-956-9099
Beverly, Carl, & Tim Conover
All year

140-250-B&B
12 rooms, 12 pb
Visa, MC, AmEx,
Rated, •
S-no/P-no/H-no

Full breakfast
Complimentary tea
Sitting room, dining room,
library, parlor, porch, sm.
conf. room, gardens

Romantic hideaway on ocean furnished with antiques, handmade pillows, bedcovers, family pictures. Fireplaces in 2 bedrooms. 1996 Waverly Hon. Cut stone fireplace. Jacuzzi spa in the south garden. E-mail: beverly@conovers.com Web site: conovers.com

BELMAR

Down the Shore B&B
201 7th Ave, 07719
732-681-9023
Annette & Al Bergins
All year

75-100-B&B
3 rooms, 2 pb
Visa, MC, *Rated*, •
C-ltd/S-no/P-no/H-no

Full breakfast
Snacks
Sitting room, library, cable
TV, accommodate business
travelers

Cozy, comfortable but only six years old. One block to boardwalk and beach, attentive, not intrusive service provided by friendly well-informed hosts. Breakfasts are healthful and substantial. Off-street parking, beach passes and towels provided. E-mail: lodging@ monmouth.com Web site: belmar.com/downtheshore

Inn at the Shore, The
301 Fourth Ave, 07719
732-681-3762 Fax: 732-280-1914
Tom & Rosemary Volker
All year

95-125-B&B
12 rooms, 3 pb
Visa, MC, AmEx,
Rated, •
C-yes/S-ltd/P-no/H-no

Continental plus breakfast
Sitt. rm., lib., bikes,
aquarium, phones, TV/VCR,
patio & gas grill, A/C

Let us pamper you at our Victorian country inn while rocking away & enjoying sea & lake breezes on a wraparound porch. Rates include beach badges. Guest pantry with fridge & microwave. Amenities include bath robes and slippers. E-mail: tomvolker@aol.com Web site: bbianj.com/innattheshore

CAPE MAY ────────────────────────────────────

7th Sister Guesthouse, The
10 Jackson St, 08204
609-884-2280 Fax: 609-898-9899
Bob & JoAnne Echevarria-
Myers
All year

75-175-EP
6 rooms, 1 pb
C-ltd/S-no/P-no/H-no
Spanish, French,
German

Guest refrigerator
Piano, library, sunporch,
rooms 100 ft. from beach,
restaurants, sitt. room

Ocean view, wicker-filled rooms with a hint of eccentricity. Paintings by the owner/inn-keeper, JoAnne Echevarria Myers, hang throughout. Private bath available occasionally, A/C

Abbey B&B, The
34 Gurney St, 08204
609-884-4506 Fax: 609-884-2379
Jay & Marianne Schatz
Easter-Dec.

100-275-B&B
14 rooms, 14 pb
Visa, MC, *Rated*
C-ltd/S-ltd/P-no/H-no

Full breakfast buffet on
veranda
Complimentary wine, snacks
2 parlors, piano, harp, off-
street parking, fax

Elegantly restored villa, with period antiques. Genuine merriment in a warm atmosphere. A/C available. One block from Atlantic Ocean.   E-mail: theabbey@bellatlantic.net
Web site: abbeybedandbreakfast.com

Albert Stevens Inn
127 Myrtle Ave, 08204
609-884-4717 Fax: 609-884-8320
800-890-CATS
Diane & Curt Diviney-Rangen
All year

120-195-B&B/MAP
6 rooms, 6 pb
Visa, MC, AmEx,
Rated, •
C-ltd/S-no/P-ltd/H-no
French

Full 3-course breakfast
Comp. Dinner (Nov-Mar)
Evening tea, sherry, Stress-
Reduction Center, large,
lighted Jacuzzi

1889 country Queen Anne Victorian on Cape May's quiet side. Antiques, crystal & porce-lain. Home of Cat's Garden Tea & Tour. Hot tub open from Sept-Apr
Web site: beachcomber.com/Capemay/Bbs/stevens.html

Angel of the Sea B&B
5 Trenton Ave, 08204
609-884-3369 Fax: 609-884-3331
800-848-3369
Lorie & Greg Whissill
All year

95-285-B&B
27 rooms, 27 pb
Visa, MC, AmEx,
Rated, •
C-ltd/S-no/P-no/H-no

Full breakfast
Wine, tea, sitting room,
oceanfront porch, fireplaces,
bicycles

Cape May's most luxurious B&B mansion; fabulous ocean views. Rooms have private baths, ceiling fans, ocean views, clawfoot tubs. Free use of bicycles and all beach equip-ment.   Web site: angelofthesea.com

Barnard Good House
238 Perry St, 08204
609-884-5381
Nan & Tom Hawkins
April 1-Nov 1

95-160-B&B
5 rooms, 5 pb
Visa, MC, *Rated*
C-ltd/S-ltd/P-no/H-no

Full 4-course breakfast
Wine, snacks (sometimes)
Sitting room, antique, organ,
private baths, A/C in rooms

Victorian splendor in landmark-dotted town. Breakfast is a taste thrill...sumptuous & lovingly created for you. Awarded best breakfast in N.J. Vegetarian & special diet with advance notice.

Bedford Inn
805 Stockton Ave, 08204
609-884-4158 Fax: 609-884-6320
Cindy & James Schmucker
March-Dec.

85-195-B&B
11 rooms, 11 pb
Visa, MC, *Rated*, •
C-ltd/S-no/P-no/H-no

Full breakfast
Afternoon tea
Sitting room, parlor, A/C, sun
porch, color TVs, limited on-
site parking

Elegant 1880 Italianate seaside inn with unusual double staircase; lovely, antique-filled rooms, suites. Near beach & historic shopping district. Afternoon tea.   E-mail: lucindo2@
bellatlantic.net *Web site:* bedfordinn.com

Canterbury Cottage Inn, Cape May, NJ

CAPE MAY

Canterbury Cottage Inn
725 Kearney Ave, 08204
609-884-1724
Fax: 609-884-2477
Liz & Niels Favre
Closed January

120-170-B&B
7 rooms, 7 pb
Visa, MC,
C-ltd/S-no/P-no/H-no

Full breakfast
Afternoon tea
Sitting room, on-site parking,
beach tags, A/C

A delightful seaside cottage built for a member of the J.B. Stetson hat family of Philadelphia. Tastefully decorated & air conditioned rooms. Breakfast served in the dining room or on one of the large porches with ocean views.   E-mail: innkeeper@canterburycottageinn.com
Web site: canterburycottageinn.com

Captain Mey's Inn
202 Ocean St, 08204
609-884-7793 Fax: 609-884-7793
800-981-3702
George & Kathleen Blinn
All year

85-225-B&B
7 rooms, 7 pb
Visa, MC, *Rated*, ●
C-ltd/S-no/P-no/H-no

Full country breakfast
Complimentary wine,
refreshments
A/C, on-site parking, 1 block
to beach, shops, restaurants,
verandah

Victorian 1890 inn with wraparound verandah. Period antiques. Fireplace in dining room. Victorian parlor. 2 bedroom suite. Have only brassfooted, Victorian whirlpool tub in Cape May.   Web site: captainmeys.com

---

Carroll Villa Hotel
19 Jackson St, 08204
609-884-9619 Fax: 609-884-0264
Mark Kulkowitz & Pamela
Huber
Feb. 14-Dec. 31

88-175-B&B
22 rooms, 22 pb
Visa, MC, *Rated*, ●
C-ltd/S-no/P-no/H-no

Full breakfast
Restaurant w/fireplace,
sitting room, conf. fac.,
garden terrace, A/C, heat

Restored 1881 Victorian hotel. Mid-block between ocean and Victorian Mall. Porch and garden dining. European ambiance.   E-mail: mbatter@cyberenet.net *Web site:* carrolvilla.com

---

Chalfonte Hotel, The
301 Howard St, 08204
609-884-8409 Fax: 609-884-4588
Anne LeDuc
Memorial Day-Colum. Day

100-230-MAP
80 rooms, 11 pb
Visa, MC, AmEx,
Rated, ●
C-yes/S-no/P-no/H-no

Dinner, afternoon tea, snacks
Restaurant, bar service,
sitting room, library,
children's workshops

Cape May's oldest Victorian hotel, since 1876. Relaxing atmosphere, antiques, verandas & rockers, southern cuisine/hospitality. Children, weddings, groups, welcome
E-mail: chalfontnj@aol.com *Web site:* chalfonte.com

Captain Mey's Inn, Cape May, NJ

CAPE MAY

Cliveden Inn & Cottage
709 Columbia Ave, 08204
609-884-4516 800-884-2420
Susan & Al DeRosa
All year

110-170-B&B
10 rooms, 10 pb
Visa, MC, AmEx,
C-ltd/S-ltd/P-no/H-no

Full breakfast buffet
Afternoon tea, snacks
Library, veranda, rocking
chairs, Victorian cottage
available

Fine accommodations, delicious breakfasts and gracious hospitality have made the Cliveden one of the popular inns of Cape May. Web site: clivedeninn.com

Dormer House, The
800 Columbia Ave, 08204
609-884-7446 Fax: 609-884-7446
800-884-5052
Lucille & Dennis Doherty
All year

80-210-B&B
10 rooms, 10 pb
Visa, MC, AmEx,
Rated, •
C-ltd/S-no/P-no/H-no

Full breakfast
Afternoon tea
Sitting room, glass enclosed
breakfast porch, bikes,
Jacuzzi room

One of the great summer houses of the 1890s. Long porches, enjoy full breakfast/tea. An inn for all seasons. "Come for the tea, stay for the night." Web site: dormer-house.com

Duke of Windsor Inn, The
817 Washington St, 08204
609-884-1355 Fax: 609-884-1887
800-826-8973
Patricia Joyce
All year

85-200-B&B
10 rooms, 10 pb
Visa, MC, *Rated*
C-ltd/S-no/P-no/H-no

Full breakfast
Afternoon tea
Sitting rooms, cable TV, on-
site parking, suites, veranda

Grand & elegant home built in 1896. Dramatic 45 foot tower provides for 2 unique guest rooms. Original oak woodwork and wainscotting, 9 foot sliding doors, and Tiffany stained glass window. All rooms have private baths and A/C.
E-mail: innkeeper@dukeofwindsorinn.com Web site: dukeofwindsorinn.com

Fairthorne B&B
PO Box 2381, 08204
609-884-8791 Fax: 609-884-1902
800-438-8742
Ed & Diana Hutchinson
All year

120-220-B&B
7 rooms, 7 pb
Visa, MC, *Rated*, •
C-ltd/S-no/P-no/H-no

Full breakfast
Afternoon tea
Public library across street,
bicycles, sitting room, near
ocean

Light & airy, pastel pinks, lace curtains & antique furnishings. Sumptuous breakfasts are served outside on verandah during warm weather. 3 new rooms with fireplaces.
E-mail: wehfair@aol.com Web site: bbianj.com/fairthorne

Inn at 22 Jackson, Cape May, NJ

CAPE MAY

Frog Hollow Inn
819 Kearney Ave, 08204
609-884-1426 Fax: 609-884-1638
Jane & Carl Buck   All year

90-160-B&B
5 rooms, 5 pb
Visa, MC, AmEx, •
C-ltd/S-no/P-no/H-no

Full breakfast
Afternoon tea, snacks, wine
Sitting room

We are a comfortable inn located in a secondary historic district. Close to beaches and our famous pedestrian mall. We offer a respite from the noise of life in an oasis of relaxation.

Gingerbread House
28 Gurney St, 08204
609-884-0211
Fred & Joan Echevarria
All year

98-260-B&B
6 rooms, 3 pb
Rated
C-ltd/S-yes/P-no/H-no

Full breakfast
Afternoon tea with baked
goods
Wicker-filled porch, parlor
with fireplace, Victorian
antiques, A/C

The G.B.H. offers period furnished rooms—comfortable accommodations within walking distance to major sights. Half block from the beach.   Web site: gingerbreadinn.com

Humphrey Hughes House, The
29 Ocean St, 08204
609-884-4428 Fax: 609-898-1845
800-582-3634
Lorraine & Terry Schmidt
Mid-April-Oct.

125-265-B&B
10 rooms, 10 pb
Visa, MC, AmEx, *Rated*
S-ltd/P-no/H-no

Full buffet breakfast
Afternoon tea & treats
Library, veranda, beach,
tags, rocking chairs,
Victorian cottage

Enjoy buffet breakfast & afternoon tea & treats on our large, wraparound verandah. Cozy Victorian cottage. Center of Historic District. All rooms have TV. Rated 3 diamonds by AAA.   Web site: bbhost.com/humphreyhugheshouse

Inn at 22 Jackson
22 Jackson St, 08204
609-884-2226 Fax: 609-884-0055
800-452-8177
Chip Masemore   All year

95-375-B&B
7 rooms, 7 pb
Visa, MC, AmEx,
C-ltd/S-no/P-no/H-no

Full breakfast
Afternoon tea, snacks, wine
Sitting room, bicycles near
beach/ocean's edge

Whimsical, yet romantic Victorian; center of historic district; collections of majolica, toys and bawdy women; a nine iron to the beach. Central air and TV.   E-mail: innat22@ algorithms.com Web site: bbianj.com/innat22jackson

CAPE MAY ——————————————————————————

Inn On Ocean, The	129-259-B&B	Full breakfast
25 Ocean St, 08204	5 rooms, 5 pb	Golf, tennis, antiques,
609-884-7070 Fax: 609-884-1384	Most CC, *Rated*, •	birdwatching, fishing, near
800-304-4477	C-ltd/S-no/P-no/H-no	beach/ocean's edge
Jack & Katha Davis		
All seasons		

Intimate, elegant restored Victorian. Steps to beach. Romantic ocean view porches. Victorian Billiard Room. Luxurious Honeymoon Suite. C/A and TV. On site parking.
E-mail: innocean@bellatlantic.net *Web site:* theinnonocean.com

John F. Craig House, The	85-180-B&B	Full gourmet breakfast
609 Columbia Ave, 08204	8 rooms, 8 pb	Afternoon tea, snacks
609-884-0100 Fax: 609-898-1307	Visa, MC, Disc, *Rated*, •	Parlor with fireplace, library,
Frank & Connie Felicetti	C-ltd/S-ltd/P-no/H-no	beach tags, A/C in all rooms
March-December	Some French	

1866 Victorian inn, period furnishings & decor. Wraparound veranda with a swing, enclosed sunporches. Delicious breakfast & tea served in elegant dining room. English cottage, perennial garden. *E-mail:* fe6119@bellatlantic.net *Web site:* johncraig.com

John Wesley Inn	125-170-B&B	Continental plus breakfast
30 Gurney St, 08204	6 rooms, 4 pb	Sitting room, library, beach
609-884-1012	•	tags, beach chairs, parking
Rita Tice & Capt John	C-ltd/S-no/P-no/H-no	
All year		

Elegant Victorian interior designed for relaxation & romance. Centrally located in Historic District, 1/2 block from beach. On-site parking. A/C all rooms and apartments.

Leith Hall Seashore Inn	85-280-B&B	Full breakfast
22 Ocean St, 08204	7 rooms, 7 pb	Afternoon English tea
609-884-1934	C-ltd/S-no/P-no/H-no	Whirlpool tubs, fireplaces,
Susan & Elan Zingman-Leith	French, Yiddish	cable TV, A/C in all rooms,
All year		ocean views

Elegantly restored 1880s home in the heart of the Victorian district. Only half block from the beach, with ocean views. 6 rooms have queen beds.
Web site: capenet.com/capemay/leith

Linda Lee B&B	80-160-B&B	Full breakfast
725 Columbia Ave, 08204	5 rooms, 5 pb	Afternoon tea
609-884-1240 Fax: 609-884-6762	Visa, MC, *Rated*, •	Sitting room, fireplaces,
Lynda and Corbin Cogswell	C-ltd/S-no/P-no/H-no	Victorian suite, A/C
2nd week Feb-Jan 1		

One of three Cape May Victorians featured in America's Painted Ladies. 1872 Carpenter Gothic in historic district furnished in period antiques. Delicious hot breakfast and elegant afternoon tea. *E-mail:* lindale@bellatlantic.net

Mainstay Inn, The	95-275-B&B	Full breakfast (spring/fall)
635 Columbia Ave, 08204	16 rooms, 9 pb	Continental breakfast
609-884-8690	*Rated*	(summer)
Tom & Sue Carroll	C-ltd/S-no/P-no/H-no	Afternoon tea, 10 A/C rooms,
April-November		piano, 3 sitting rooms

Two wealthy 19th-century gamblers spared no expense to build this luxurious villa. Sumptuous Victorian furnishings, garden. New "Officers' Quarters" building. Suites with whirlpools available. *Web site:* mainstayinn.com

Mason Cottage, The	95-285-B&B	Full gourmet breakfast
625 Columbia Ave, 08204	9 rooms, 9 pb	Afternoon tea
609-884-3358	Visa, MC, AmEx,	Sitting room, veranda, parlor,
800-716-2766	*Rated*, •	fireplaces, A/C, whirlpool,
Dave & Joan Mason	C-ltd/S-no/P-no/H-no	beach towels
Open Feb.-Dec.		

An elegant seaside inn located on a quiet, tree-lined street in the center of historic district, 1 block to beach & close to other attractions.

CAPE MAY ──────────────────────────────────

Mooring, The
801 Stockton Ave, 08204
609-884-5425 Fax: 609-884-1357
Leslie Valenza
April 3-Dec. 30

75-165-B&B
12 rooms, 12 pb
Visa, MC, •
C-ltd/S-no/P-no/H-no

Full breakfast
Afternoon tea
Sitting room

Victorian mansard structure furnished in original period antiques. One block to ocean and easy walking distance to five different restaurants.   E-mail: info@themooring.com
Web site: themooring.com

Perry Street Inn
29 Perry St, 08204
609-884-4590 Fax: 609-884-8444
800-29-PERRY
John & Cynthia Curtis
April-November

75-135-B&B
20 rooms, 13 pb
Visa, MC, *Rated*, •
C-ltd/S-yes/H-yes

Full breakfast
Afternoon tea, snacks
Sitting room, bicycles, in-
room phones, Mystery!,
oceanfront porch, phones

National historic landmark city. Victorian guest house & modern efficiency suites. Beach block; close to unique shopping, fine restaurants. Meeting space for up to 20 people. Millennium tour and party of the century.   E-mail: perryinn@bellatlantic.net
Web site: perrystinn.com/

Poor Richard's Inn
17 Jackson St, 08204
609-884-3536
Richard Samuelson
Valentines-New Year's

50-145-B&B
9 rooms, 4 pb
•
C-ltd/S-yes/P-no/H-no

Continental breakfast
Sitting room, oriental rock
garden, near beach

Classic gingerbread guest house offers accommodations with eclectic Victorian & country decor; friendly, unpretentious atmosphere.   Web site: poorrichardsinn.com

---

Queen Victoria, The
102 Ocean St, 08204
609-884-8702
Dane & Joan Wells
All year

90-300-B&B
21 rooms, 21 pb
Visa, MC, *Rated*
C-ltd/S-ltd/P-no/H-ltd
French

Full buffet breakfast
Afternoon tea, comp.
beverages
Bikes, evening turn-down,
refrigerators in all rooms, 2
luxury suites

A B&B located in the center of the nation's oldest seaside resort; specialty is comfort & service. Morning and evening room cleanings. A/C in rooms.   E-mail: qvinn@bellatlantic.net
Web site: queenvictoria.com

Queen's Hotel
102 Ocean Street, 08204
609-884-1613 Fax: 609-884-1666
Joan & Dane Wells
All year

75-260-EP
11 rooms, 11 pb
Visa, MC, *Rated*
C-ltd/S-no/P-no/H-no

Continental breakfast (fee)
Bikes, whirlpools, suites,
fireplaces, cable TV, A/C,
phones, some parking

The Queen's Hotel is an elegant, historic hotel in the center of Cape May's Historic District, one block from the ocean.   E-mail: reservation@queenshotel.com *Web site:* queenshotel.com

---

Rhythm of the Sea
1123 Beach Dr, 08204
609-884-7788 Fax: 609-884-7799
800-498-6888
Robyn & Wolfgang Wendt
All year

99-255-B&B
8 rooms, 8 pb
Most CC, •
C-ltd/S-no/P-no/H-no
German

Multi-course breakfast
Afternoon refreshments
Eve. meals upon request,
gathering rooms, library,
bikes, beach towels

With the ocean as our front yard, we provide fragrant breezes & a wealth of seaside activities. We invite you to come savor our scrumptious meals, peaceful privacy & ge-muetlichkeit   E-mail: rhythm@algorithms.com *Web site:* rhythmofthesea.com

CAPE MAY ─────────────────────────────────

Summer Cottage Inn, The	85-275-B&B	Full breakfast
613 Columbia Ave, 08204	9 rooms, 9 pb	Snacks, afternoon tea
609-884-4948	Visa, MC, *Rated*	Sitting room, bicycles,
Skip & Linda Loughlin	C-yes/S-no/P-no/H-no	garden, queen size beds
All year	French (a little)	

Enjoy beautiful Cape May, the nation's oldest seashore resort while vacationing in an authentic Victorian summer cottage with gracious hospitality. Victorian decor yet casual and relaxing. E-mail: sumcot@bellatlantic.net *Web site:* summercottageinn.com

Victorian Lace Inn	85-220-B&B	Full breakfast
901 Stockton Ave, 08204	5 rooms, 5 pb	Sitting room, library,
609-884-1772 Fax: 609-884-0983	*Rated*, ●	Jacuzzis, suites, cable TV
Carri & Andy O'Sullivan	C-yes/S-no/P-no/H-no	
Mid-February-New Years		

Beautiful all suite colonial revival inn with ocean views and fireplaces. Cottage with fireplace and Jacuzzi. Enjoy warm hospitality in our nation's oldest seashore resort.

White Dove Cottage	80-215-B&B	Full breakfast
619 Hughes St, 08204	6 rooms, 6 pb	Afternoon tea,
609-884-0613	*Rated*, ●	complimentary wine
800-321-DOVE	C-ltd/S-no/P-no/H-no	Sitting room, two block from
Frank and Sue Smith		ocean, queen size beds
All year		

Elegant 1866 B&B located in center of Historic District on tree-lined, gas-lit street. A memorable occasion—a delightful retreat. AAA 3 star rating.
Web site: whitedovecottage.com

Windward House	90-187-B&B	Full breakfast
24 Jackson St, 08204	8 rooms, 8 pb	Afternoon tea, sherry
609-884-3368 Fax: 609-884-1575	Visa, MC, *Rated*, ●	Sitting room, library, A/C,
Sandy & Owen Miller	C-ltd/S-ltd/P-no/H-no	ocean view sundeck, TV,
All year		beach passes

Elegant Edwardian seaside inn, spacious antique-filled guest rooms; massive oak doors with stained & leaded glass. Sun/shade porches. Parking. 1/2 block to beach.
Web site: windwardhouseinn.com/

Wooden Rabbit, The	90-260-B&B	Full breakfast
609 Hughes St, 08204	4 rooms, 4 pb	A/C rooms, garden room,
609-884-7293 Fax: 609-898-6081	Visa, MC,	guest phone, suite w/1 king,
Nancy & Dave McGonigle	C-ltd/S-no/P-no/H-no	2 twins, whirlpool tubs
All year		

Circa 1838 Federal home. Horse-drawn carriages roll through our quiet, shaded neighborhood. Victorian homes; fine restaurants; antiques. 2 rooms and 2—2 bedroom suites. All with private baths. E-mail: wrabbit@bellatlantic.net *Web site:* woodenrabbit.com

Woodleigh House	95-145-B&B	Full breakfast
808 Washington St, 08204	5 rooms, 5 pb	Afternoon refreshments
609-884-7123 Fax: 609-884-8065	Visa, MC,	Sitting room, queen beds,
Joe & Jo Anne Tornambe	C-ltd/S-no/P-no/H-no	gardens, guest phone, A/C,
All year		romantic suite

Nestled in Cape May's historic district, surrounded by porches and courtyards. This attractive example of "Country Victorian" is charmingly hosted. Queen beds. 2 family suites available. Front porch with rockers. *Web site:* beachcomber.com/Capemay/Bbs/woodle.html

Woodleigh House, Cape May, NJ

CHATHAM

Parrot Mill Inn
47 Main St, 07928
973-635-7722 Fax: 973-701-0620
Betsy Kennedy
All year

105-115-B&B
11 rooms, 10 pb
Visa, MC, AmEx,
Rated, •
C-yes/S-no/P-no/H-no

Continental breakfast
Afternoon tea
Sitting room, wedding
facilities, romantic packages,
suite

English country elegance. Tastefully decorated bedrooms with private baths, situated ideally near major corporate offices and universities
E-mail: parrotmillinn@yahoo.com *Web site:* parrotmillinn.com

CHESTER

Neighbor House, The
143 W Mill Rd, 07853
908-876-3519
Rafi & Iris Kadosh
All year

75-90-B&B
4 rooms, 2 pb
Visa, MC,
C-ltd/S-no/P-no/H-no
Hebrew

Full breakfast
Afternoon tea
Sitting room, bicycles,
fireplaces, cable TV, hiking,
antique shops

Our guests are enjoying elegantly furnished rooms, an enchanting, pastoral setting (we're surrounded by 800 beautiful green acres). *E-mail:* rkadosh@worldnet.att.net
Web site: bbonline.com/nj/neighbour

CLINTON

Seven Springs Farm B&B
14 Perryville Rd, 08867
908-735-7675
Dina W. Bowers All year

85-175-B&B
4 rooms, 4 pb
Rated
C-yes/S-ltd/P-no/H-no

Full breakfast; Snacks
Sitting room, library,
Jacuzzis, suite, fireplaces,
cable TV, gardens, farm

DENNISVILLE

Henry Ludlam Inn, The
1336 Rt 47, 08214
609-861-5847
Chuck & Pat DeArros
All year

85-120-B&B
5 rooms, 5 pb
Most CC, *Rated*, •
C-ltd/S-no/P-no/H-no

Full country breakfast
Picnic baskets, wine
Sm. receptions, showers,
sitting room, fireplaces,
gazebo, lake

Historic B&B (c. 1740) situated on 56-acre lake. 3 wood-burning fireplace rms. Mecca for birders. Listed on Nat'l Historic Register. "We know the hot spots." Fishing, hiking, bike paths *Web site:* bbianj.com/henryludlam/index.html

FLEMINGTON

Jerica Hill, A B&B Inn
96 Broad St, 08822
908-782-8234 Fax: 908-237-0587
888-650-8499
V. Eugene Refalvy All year

85-125-B&B
5 rooms, 5 pb
Visa, MC, AmEx,
Rated, •
C-ltd/S-no/P-no/H-no

Full breakfast
Sherry, refreshments
Picnic & wine tours, guest
pantry, refrig., fax on
premises

Gracious Victorian in heart of historic Flemington. Spacious, sunny guest rooms with A/C. Phones/TV by request. Antiques, living room with fireplace, wicker-filled screened porch. Home made baked goods, coffee, tea, sherry. *E-mail:* glneinn@ptd.net
Web site: bbianj.com/jericahill

FLEMINGTON

Main Street Manor B&B	85-135-B&B	Full breakfast on weekends
194 Main St, 08822	5 rooms, 5 pb	Continental breakfast
908-782-4928	Visa, MC, AmEx,	(weekdays)
Elinor & Dennis Lengle	*Rated*, •	Snacks, complimentary
All year	C-ltd/S-no/P-no/H-no	wine, sitting room, cable TV

Historic home restored to elegance. Period antiques, two parlors, satellite TV, paneled dining room. Five guest rooms, each with private bath, queen-size beds, sitting area, air conditioning, phone. Steps away from shopping, antiques, & fine dining.
E-mail: innkeeper@mainstreetmanor.com   *Web site:* mainstreetmanor.com

FRENCHTOWN

Widow McCrea House	115-135-B&B	Full breakfast
53 Kingwood Ave, 08825	3 rooms, 3 pb	Afternoon tea,
908-996-4999 Fax: 908-806-4496	Visa, MC, AmEx, *Rated*	complimentary wine
Burt Patalane, Lynn Marad	C-ltd/S-no/P-no/H-no	Sitting room, bicycles,
All year		fireplaces, cable TV,
		accommodate business
		travelers

Charming 1878 Italinate Victorian Home located in a splendid riverside village. Three elegant guestrooms featuring queen-size feather beds, fireplace mantels, private baths, a complimentary bottle of wine.   E-mail: bpatalane@sprintmail.com
Web site: frenchtown.com/widowmccrea

GLENWOOD

Apple Valley Inn	80-120-B&B	Full breakfast
PO Box 302, 07418	6 rooms, 1 pb	Picnic lunch avail., afternoon
973-764-3735 Fax: 973-764-1050	*Rated*, •	tea
Mitzi Durham	C-ltd/S-ltd/P-no/H-no	Complimentary wine, sitting
All year		room, library, pool, tennis
		court, porches

Historic 1831 mansion located in Skylands Region, adjacent to Appalachian Trail. Close to ski area, trout stream, water park. Genuine rural refreshment.   Web site: applevalleyinn.com

HIGHLANDS

SeaScape Manor B&B	90-160-B&B	Full breakfast
3 Grand Tour, 07732	4 rooms, 4 pb	Complimentary wine
732-291-8467 Fax: 732-872-7932	Visa, MC, AmEx, *Rated*	Sitting room, library, bikes,
Sherry Ruby, Gloria Miller	C-ltd/S-no/P-no/H-no	ocean swimming, fireplace,
All year		fish

Secluded manor nestled in the tree covered hills overlooking the blue Atlantic and Sandy Hook Nationall Recreation area. 45 minutes from NYC. Spacious antique filled rooms, private decks, sailing. All rooms have cable TV/VCR.   Web site: bbianj.com/seascape

JOBSTOWN

Belle Springs Farm	70-B&B	Full breakfast
RD 1, Box 420, 08041	3 rooms	Piano and fireplace, living
609-723-5364	C-yes/S-yes/P-no/H-no	room
Lydia Sudler All year		

This spacious contemporary farmhouse is comfortably furnished with unusual family antiques. The Steinway piano stays tuned for the musical guest who wants to play by the fire. Breakfast served year round by the fire or on the porch overlooking pastures.

LAMBERTVILLE

Chimney Hill Farm Estate	95-289-B&B	Full breakfast
207 Goat Hill Rd, 08530	12 rooms, 12 pb	Afternoon tea, snacks, wine
609-397-1516 Fax: 609-397-9353	Visa, MC, AmEx,	Sitting room, library, pool,
800-211-4667	*Rated*, •	nature trails, Jacuzzis, suites,
Terry Ann & Richard	C-ltd/S-no/P-no/H-ltd	cable TV
Anderson All year		

A unique country estate—the perfect setting for a rejuvenating getaway. Romantic with a touch of elegance.   E-mail: chbb@erols.com *Web site:* chimneyhillinn.com

LAMBERTVILLE

Lambertville House	165-300-B&B	Continental plus breakfast
32 Bridge St, 08530	26 rooms, 26 pb	Bar service, cable TV, suites,
609-397-0200 Fax: 609-397-0511	Most CC, *Rated*, •	Jacuzzis, fireplaces, bike
888-867-8859	C-ltd/S-no/P-no/H-yes	path
Brad Michael		
All year		

26-room National Historic Inn, jetted tubs, balconies, fireplaces, conference facilities, AAA Four Diamond Award, Left Bank Libations Lounge, one hour from Philadelphia E-mail: innkeeper@lambertvillehouse.com *Web site:* lambertvillehouse.com

York Street House	95-185-B&B	Full gourmet breakfast
42 York Street, 08530	5 rooms, 5 pb	Sitting room, piano,
609-397-3007 Fax: 609-397-9677	Visa, MC, AmEx,	fireplaces, gardens, baths
888-398-3199	*Rated*, •	
N. Ferguson & B. Wetterskog	S-no/P-no/H-no	
All year		

House & Gardens Home of the Year (1911). Winding staircase, Waterford chandelier, mercer tile fireplaces, leaded glass. Gardens. Gourmet breakfast. In-town. E-mail: yorksthse@aol.com *Web site:* yorkstreethouse.com

LONG BEACH ISLAND

Amber Street Inn	105-170-B&B	Full breakfast-weekdays
118 Amber St, 08008	6 rooms, 6 pb	Afternoon tea/lemonade
609-492-1611 Fax: 609-492-9165	*Rated*	Fireplace in parlor & dining
Joan & Michael Fitzsimmons	C-ltd/S-no/P-no/H-no	room, beach tags/chairs,
Mid February-Nov.	Spanish	bicycles

Victorian seaside B&B ½ block away from the beach. Antiques, great breakfasts, 2 fireplaces, English garden. Close to shops, restaurants, bay cruises, Barnegat lighthouse. Fans and A/C in all rooms. Web site: bbianj.com/amber

MANASQUAN

Nathaniel Morris Inn	85-200-B&B	Full breakfast
117 Marcellus Ave, 08736	6 rooms, 6 pb	Snacks, wine
732-223-7826 Fax: 732-223-7827	*Rated*, •	Sitting room, library,
Joe and Barbara Jackson	C-ltd/S-ltd/P-no/H-no	bicycles, suites, cable TV,
All year	Spanish, French	beach chairs

1882 Victorian Inn with six romantic, antique filled rooms, all with private baths, three with private porches. Close to Spring Lake/Bay Head area, beaches, shopping/antiquing, great restaurants and more. E-mail: joej@monmouth.com *Web site:* nathanielmorris.com

NORTH WILDWOOD

Candlelight Inn	100-275-B&B	Full breakfast
2310 Central Ave, 08260	10 rooms, 10 pb	Refreshments
609-522-6200 Fax: 609-522-6125	Most CC, *Rated*, •	Sitting room, piano, hot tub,
800-992-2632	S-no/P-no/H-no	sun deck, TV, 3 suites,
Bill & Nancy Moncrief	French	Jacuzzi, A/C
All year exc. Jan.		

Seashore B&B with genuine antiques, fireplace, wide verandah. Getaway specials & murder mystery parties available. Close to beach & boardwalk. 2 new suites with fireplace, Jacuzzi, TV, wet bar. E-mail: info@candlelight-inn.com *Web site:* candlelight-inn.com

OCEAN CITY

Barnagate B&B	85-160-B&B	Full breakfast (winter)
637 Wesley Ave, 08226	5 rooms, 1 pb	Continental breakfast
609-391-9366	Visa, MC, AmEx,	(summer)
Frank & Lois Barna	*Rated*, •	Afternoon tea, Sitting room,
All year	C-ltd/S-ltd/P-no/H-no	library, tennis court, cable
		TV, suites

A Seashore Country Victorian that returns guests to an era when hospitality was a matter of pride. Awaken in one of five quaint air-conditioned rooms to the aroma of homemade goodies. E-mail: bblois@aol.com *Web site:* barnagate.com

OCEAN CITY ──

Castle by the Sea	95-239-B&B	Full breakfast
701 Ocean Ave, 08226	9 rooms, 9 pb	Lunch, afternoon tea, snacks
609-398-3555 Fax: 609-398-8742	Visa, MC, AmEx,	Sitting room, Jacuzzis, suites,
800-622-4894	*Rated*, •	fireplace, cable TV
Renee & Jack Krutsick	C-ltd/S-ltd/P-no/H-no	
All year		

Experience a truly rare discovery, exquisite accommodations, spectacular cuisine, bedside chocolates, delectable afternoon tea & sweets, lavish bed linens, indulgent amenities, romantic fireplaces and the warmest of hospitality. E-mail: castle701@aol.com
Web site: bbianj.com/castlebythesea/

Koo-Koo's Nest B&B, The	60-135-B&B	Continental plus breakfast
615 Wesley Ave, 08226	4 rooms, 4 pb	Afternoon tea
609-814-9032	Visa, MC, AmEx,	Jacuzzis, suites, cable TV,
Tom, Anna and KooKoo	C-ltd/S-no/P-no/H-no	wrap around porch, terrace,
Closed winter		VCRs, massage

Beautiful Victorian seaside B&B in the heart of Ocean City's historic district. Two blocks to beach and boardwalk. One of the Ocean City's classics. Come enjoy the sun and surf. E-mail: bnbkookoo@aol.com *Web site:* kookoosnest.com

Northwood Inn B&B	90-210-B&B	Full breakfast on weekends
401 Wesley Ave, 08226	8 rooms, 8 pb	Cont. plus breakfast on
609-399-6071	Visa, MC, *Rated*	weekdays
Marj & John Loeper	C-ltd/S-no/P-no/H-no	Snacks, roof-top deck with
All year		yearround whirlpool, bikes,
		game room, pool table

Elegantly restored 1894 Victorian with 20th-century comforts. 3 blocks to beach & boardwalk. Between Atlantic City & Cape May. 4 person whirlpool spa on starlit rooftop deck. New Tower Suite with luxury bath/Jacuzzi. E-mail: info@northwoodinn.com
Web site: northwoodinn.com

Scarborough Inn	90-180-B&B	Full breakfast weekdays
720 Ocean Ave, 08226	23 rooms, 23 pb	Continental plus breakfast
609-399-1558 Fax: 609-399-4472	Most CC, *Rated*, •	weekends
800-258-1558	C-ltd/S-no/P-no/H-no	Afternoon refreshments,
Gus & Carol Bruno	Italian	wraparound porch, lib., patio
May-Oct		garden w/fountain

The Scarborough Inn is reminiscent of a European-style inn, small enough to be intimate, yet large enough for privacy. E-mail: cgbruno@earthlink.net *Web site:* scarboroinn.com

Sea Cottage Inn B&B	65-135-B&B	Full breakfast on weekends
1136 Ocean Avenue, 08226	8 rooms, 8 pb	Continental plus weekdays
609-399-3356 Fax: 609-399-3004	Visa, MC, Disc, *Rated*	Dinner by arrangement,
Pamela Green Manganelli	C-ltd/S-no/P-ltd/H-ltd	sitting room, library, patio
All year		garden with fountain

A romantic Victorian seaside cottage. Steps away to beach and boardwalk attractions. Enjoy ocean breezes, bountiful breakfasts and treats, and our warm hospitality. E-mail: seacottinn@aol.com *Web site:* travelguides.com/home/seacottage

Serendipity B&B	95-159-B&B	Full breakfast
712 Ninth St, 08226	6 rooms, 4 pb	Afternoon tea, snacks
609-399-1554 Fax: 609-399-1527	Most CC, *Rated*, •	Dinner (fee), sitt. rm., beach
800-842-8544	C-ltd/S-no/P-no/H-no	passes, color TV, off-street
Clara & Bill Plowfield		parking
All year		

Air-conditioned seashore inn decorated in wicker & pastels; 1/2 block to beach & boardwalk; healthy & delicious food. Anniversary & birthday packages. E-mail: serendipitynj@prodigy.net *Web site:* serendipitynj.com

OCEAN GROVE

Cordova B&B Inn, The	50 and up-B&B	Continental plus breakfast
531 Main St #1013, 07756	20 rooms, 7 pb	Guest kitchen
732-774-3084 Fax: 212-751-4720	•	Sat. night wine & cheese,
Doris Chernik	C-yes/S-no/P-no/H-no	sitting room, bikes, BBQ,
All year	Spanish	garden, picnic tables

Century-old Victorian inn with antiques, in lovely historic beach community. Feel like one of the family—experience Old World charm! Great for family gatherings, weddings, showers and retreats. Many amenities. 15 rooms, 3 suites and 2 cottages.

Pine Tree Inn	70-129-B&B	Continental plus breakfast
10 Main Ave, 07756	13 rooms, 3 pb	Reflexology, jinshin, fresh
732-775-3264 Fax: 732-775-2439	*Rated*	flowers, TV lounge, pillow
Karen Mason	C-ltd/S-no/P-no/H-no	mints, bicycles
All year		

Small inn furnished with Victorian antiques & collectibles. Room & porch ocean views. Homemade muffins. Near boardwalk & beach. Historic seaside town.
Web site: pinetreeinn.com

PLAINFIELD

Pillars of Plainfield B&B	90-150-B&B	Full breakfast
922 Central Ave, 07060	7 rooms, 7 pb	Evening sherry, cookies,
908-753-0922	Visa, MC, AmEx, •	chocolates
888-PILLARS	C-ltd/S-no/P-ltd/H-no	Swedish home baking, sitting
Chuck & Tom Hale	Some Swedish	room, library, woodburning
All year		fireplaces, turndown

Victorian mansion on secluded acre of trees & gardens in the Van Wyck Brooks Historic District. "Sylvan Seclusion with Urban Access." Enjoy stained glass windows, music room. Private phone/modem/voice mail, coffee service. E-mail: pillars2@juno.com
Web site: pillars2.com

PRINCETON

Red Maple Farm	65-85-B&B	Full country breakfast
211 Raymond Rd, 08540	3 rooms, 3 pb	Self service beverages and
732-329-3821 Fax: 732-329-3821	*Rated*	snacks
Roberta & Lindsey Churchill	C-ltd/S-no/P-no/H-no	Sitting room, library, tennis,
All year	Some French	lawn games, swimming pool,
		bicycles

Charming, gracious 1740 Historic Register Colonial farm. A 2-acre country retreat minutes from Princeton University & Rt 1 business. Handgrown organic produce, fresh eggs.

SPRING LAKE

Ashling Cottage	95-189-B&B	Full breakfast
106 Sussex Ave, 07762	10 rooms, 8 pb	Complimentary wine
732-449-3553 Fax: 732-974-0831	*Rated*	AAA rated 3 diamonds, TV,
888-ASHLING	S-ltd/P-no/H-no	VCR, sitting room, library,
Goodi & Jack Stewart	German	games, bicycles
March-Dec.		

Victorian gem furnished with oak antiques & solarium breakfast room, a block from ocean, in storybook setting. Rowboating on Spring Lake. Economy suite- 2 rooms with one bath, sleeps four. E-mail: ashling@lonekeep.com *Web site:* bbianj.com/ashling

La Maison-A B&B & Gallery	185-325-B&B	Full breakfast
404 Jersey Ave, 07762	8 rooms, 8 pb	Snacks, complimentary wine
732-449-0969 Fax: 732-449-4860	Visa, MC, AmEx, Disc,	Sitting room, bicycles,
800-276-2088	*Rated*, •	Jacuzzis, suites, cable TV,
Julie Corrigan	C-ltd/S-ltd/P-no/H-ltd	free access to club.
All year	Some french	

La Maison is a getaway for the soul — it is like a private European residence, filled with art, done by owners and staff. Breakfast is delicious and varied and was written up in gourmet magazine. We are dedicated to exceeding our guests requests. E-mail: lamaisonnj@aol.com
Web site: lamaisoninn.com

SPRING LAKE

Normandy Inn, The	112-205-B&B	Full breakfast
21 Tuttle Ave, 07762	17 rooms, 17 pb	Complimentary wine
732-449-7172 Fax: 732-449-1070	*Rated*, •	Sitting/meeting room,
800-449-1888	C-yes/S-ltd/P-no/H-no	bicycles, front porch, newly
Michael and Susan Ingino		built suite
All year		

A country inn at the shore, decorated with lovely Victorian antiques, painted with 5 different Victorian colors. Conference facilities E-mail: normandy@bellatlantic.net
Web site: normandyinn.com

Sea Crest by The Sea	165-265-B&B	Full breakfast
19 Tuttle Ave, 07762	11 rooms, 11 pb	Afternoon tea
732-449-9031 Fax: 732-974-0403	Visa, MC, AmEx,	Bicycles, beach chairs,
800-803-9031	*Rated*, •	beach towels, beach
J & C Kirby and A & T	S-no/P-no/H-no	umbrellas, croquet
Thomson		
All year		

A Spring Lake B&B just for the two of you. A lovingly restored 1885 Queen Anne Victorian with beautiful antiques, ocean views, fireplaces, Carol's famous buttermilk scones. E-mail: jk@seacrestbythesea.com *Web site:* seacrestbythesea.com

Spring Lake Inn	125-200-B&B	Continental breakfast
104 Salem Avenue, 07762	15 rooms, 15 pb	Sitting room, library croquet,
732-449-2010	Visa, MC, *Rated*	beach towels
The Gatens Family	C-ltd/S-no/P-no/H-no	
All year		

A private place for one, a romantic place for two. Full breakfast in quiet time, continental in season. Circa 1888, 80-foot Victorian porch. E-mail: sprnglkinn@aol.com
Web site: springlakeinn.com

Victoria House B&B	115-245-B&B	Full breakfast
214 Monmouth Ave, 07762	9 rooms, 7 pb	Snacks, afternoon beverage
732-974-1882 Fax: 732-974-2132	Most CC,	Sitting room, TV, VCR,
888-249-6252	S-no/P-no/H-no	bicycles, tennis pass, beach
Louise & Robert Goodall		towels & chairs
All year		

An 1882 quiet seashore Victorian which will charm you with stained glass, antiques, wraparound porch, and old-world hospitality. Featured on Spring Lake Historical Tour. B&B for all seasons. E-mail: victoriahousebb@worldnet.att.net *Web site:* victoriahouse.net

Villa Park House	100-125-B&B	Full breakfast
417 Ocean Rd, 97762	8 rooms, 4 pb	Sitting room, bicycles, cable
732-449-3642 Fax: 732-449-0966	C-yes/S-no/P-no/H-no	TV
Alice & David Bramhall		
Spring/Summer/Fall		

Our Seashore Inn has a breezy wicker furnished wrap-around front porch. We serve a full breakfast with fresh fruit, home baked bread and golden french toast. E-mail: VilaParkSL@ aol.com *Web site:* villaparkhouse.com

STANHOPE

Whistling Swan Inn	95-150-B&B	Full breakfast buffet
110 Main St, 07874	10 rooms, 10 pb	Complimentary sherry,
973-347-6369 Fax: 973-347-3391	Most CC, *Rated*, •	snacks
Joe & Paula Williams Mulay	C-ltd/S-no/P-no/H-no	2 sitting rooms, TV/VCRs,
All year		phones in rm., dataports,
		irons/boards, hair dryer

Northwestern NJ's finest Victorian B&B. 2.5 miles from historic Waterloo Village, International Trade Center (we cater to business travelers), 25 miles from the Delaware Water Gap E-mail: wswan@worldnet.att.net *Web site:* bbianj.com/whistlingswan

STOCKTON ——————————————————————————

Woolverton Inn
6 Woolverton Rd, 08559
609-397-0802 Fax: 609-397-0987
888-AN-INN4U
C. McGavin,M. Lovette,M.
Smith
All year exc. Dec 20-26

80-190-B&B
10 rooms, 10 pb
Visa, MC, AmEx, •
C-ltd/S-no/P-no/H-ltd
Some Spanish and
German

Full country breakfast
Snacks
Sitting room, suites,
fireplaces, Jacuzzis, gardens,
meeting facilities

A 1792 stone manor house on 10 acres of lawns and gardens, surrounded by 400 acres of rolling farmland. So close to everything, but a world away. Elegant hearty breakfasts.
E-mail: woolinn@voicenet.com *Web site:* woolvertoninn.com

TUCKERTON ——————————————————————————

J.D. Thompson Inn
149 E Main, 08087
609-294-1331 Fax: 609-294-2091
888-393-5723
Joe & Gloria Gartner
All year

75-145-B&B
7 rooms, 7 pb
Visa, MC, AmEx,
Rated, •
C-ltd/S-no/P-no/H-ltd

Full breakfast
Afternoon tea, snacks, comp.
wine
Sitting room, bikes, suites,
cable TV, outdoor spa and
gazebo

Romantic, c.1823, fully restored Gothic Revival located in historic seaport town. Beautifully furnished in period antiques. *E-mail:* jdthompsoninn@worldnet.att.net
Web site: tuckerton.com/JDT.htm

New Mexico

ABIQUIU ——————————————————————————

Casa Del Rio
PO Box 702, 87510
505-753-2035 Fax: 505-753-2035
800-920-1459
Eileen Sopanen- Mel Vigil
All year

100-125-B&B
2 rooms, 2 pb
Most CC, *Rated*, •
C-ltd/S-no/P-ltd/H-no
Spanish

Full breakfast
Wakeup tray to room,
refrigerators in rooms,
handmade crafts & rugs

A Gold Medallion certified B&B that offers intimate luxury in a country setting. Situated halfway between Taos and Santa Fe. 3 Diamond AAA rating, member New Mexico B&B Association. *E-mail:* casadelr@roadrunner.com *Web site:* bbonline.com/nm/casadelrio/

ALBUQUERQUE ——————————————————————————

Bottger-Koch Mansion B&B
110 San Felipe NW, 87104
505-243-3639 Fax: 505-243-4378
800-758-3639
Yvonne & Ron Koch
All year

99-179-B&B
8 rooms, 8 pb
Visa, MC, AmEx, Disc,
C-ltd/S-ltd/P-no/H-ltd

Full breakfast
Aftn. tea, snacks, wine
Sitting room, library, cable
TV, handmade crafts & rugs

Award winning, elegant, luxurious. Victorian decor. 1st B&B in New Mexico to be awarded Inn of the Year NMM. *E-mail:* BottgerK@aol.com *Web site:* bottger.com/

Brittania & W.E. Mauger
701 Roma Ave NW, 87102
505-242-8755 Fax: 505-842-8835
800-719-9189
Mark Brown & Keith Lewis
All year

89-179-B&B
8 rooms, 8 pb
Visa, MC, AmEx,
Rated, •
C-yes/S-no/P-yes/H-no

Full breakfast
Snacks, complimentary wine
Sitting room, family friendly
facility, handmade crafts &
rugs

Wonderful Queen Anne Victorian on the National Register. Within walking distance of old town, downtown, convention center and many restaurants. *E-mail:* maugerbb@aol.com
Web site: maugerbb.com

ALBUQUERQUE

Casita Chamisa B&B
850 Chamisal Rd NW, 87107
505-897-4644
Kit & Arnold Sargeant
Exc. Oct. 15-Nov. 1

95-B&B
3 rooms, 2 pb
Visa, MC, AmEx, •
C-yes/S-no/P-ltd/H-no

Continental plus breakfast
Homemade coffee cakes
Sitting room, patio, decks,
indoor pool, near tennis,
horses

2 Bedroom country guesthouse and 19th century adobe house 15 minutes to downtown. Near museums, art galleries, aerial tram, Indian petroglyphs, skiing. Archaeologist-owner.   Web site: southwesterninns.com/chamisa.htm

---

Chocolate Turtle B&B
1098 W Meadowlark, 87048
505-898-1800 Fax: 505-898-5328
800-898-1842
Carole Morgan
All year

75-100-B&B
4 rooms, 4 pb
Most CC, *Rated*, •
C-ltd/S-no/P-no

Full & Cont. plus bkfsts
Handmade chocolates
TV/videos, dining room, spa,
Romantic packages

*Relax in historic Corrales. Located on the northern boundary of Albuquerque, yet in a country-like setting with incredible mountain views, horses, and great golfing.
E-mail:* turtlebb@aol.com   *Web site:* collectorsguide.com/chocturtle

---

Hacienda Antigua B&B
6708 Tierra Dr NW, 87107
505-345-5399 Fax: 505-345-3855
800-201-2986
Ann Dunlap & Melinda Moffitt
All year

95-179-B&B
5 rooms, 5 pb
Most CC, *Rated*, •
C-ltd/S-ltd

Full breakfast
Sitting room, library, hot
tubs, swimming pool, great
for small reunions

Peaceful gardens, kiva fireplaces, antique furnishings, warm hospitality fill this 200 year old hacienda. Featured on TLC's "Great Country Inns" 1996. AAA 3 Diamonds, Mobil 3 Stars   E-mail: innkeeper@haciendantigua.com   *Web site:* haciendantigua.com

---

Nora Dixon Place B&B
312 Dixon Rd, 87048
505-898-3662 Fax: 505-898-6430
888-667-2349
Norris & Cynthia C. Tidwell
All year

65-125 B&B
3 rooms, 3 pb
Most CC, *Rated*, •
C-yes/S-no/P-ltd/H-ltd

Continental breakfast
weekdays
Full breakfast on weekends
Sitting room, suites,
fireplaces, conference
facilities, TV, phones

Quiet New Mexico Territorial Style B&B, facing Sandia Mountain in Corrales. Located Northside Albuquerque where historic sites are easily visited on day excursions. All units open onto an enclosed Courtyard with great views of the Mountain.   E-mail: noradixon@aol.com   *Web site:* noradixon.com

---

Old Town B&B
707 17th St NW, 87104
505-764-9144
888-900-9144
Nancy Hoffman
All year

70-85-B&B
2 rooms, 1 pb
Rated, •
C-ltd/S-no/P-no/H-no

Continental plus breakfast
Refreshment in room
Sitting room, library,
Jacuzzis, fireplaces, garden

Old Town B&B provides the comforts of home in a quiet, secluded garden setting with a wealth of interesting activities just minutes away from its doorstep.

ARTESIA

Heritage Inn B&B
1211 W Main St, 88210
505-748-2552 Fax: 505-746-3407
James & Wanda Maupin
All year

50-65-B&B
9 rooms, 9 pb
Most CC, *Rated*
C-ltd/S-no/P-no/H-no

Continental
Accommodate business
travelers

Located downtown, convenient to shops and restaurants, 2nd story property, nice and quiet, very clean & comfortable. Preferred by business travelers, "Best kept secret in New Mexico."

Casa del Gavilan, Cimarron, NM

BERNALILLO

La Hacienda Grande
21 Baros Ln, 87004
505-867-1887 Fax: 505-771-1436
800-353-1887
Shoshana Zimmerman
All year

99-139-B&B
6 rooms, 6 pb
Visa, MC, Disc, •
C-ltd/S-ltd/P-no/H-no

Full breakfast
Lunch, dinner by
arrangement
Weddings, retreats, Jacuzzi
for 2, hot tubs, business
meetings, library

*250 year old authentic hacienda. 2 ft. thick walls, wood ceilings, fireplaces, private baths,
A/C. Near Santa Fe, Albuquerque & minutes to most New Mexico sites.*
E-mail: lhg@swcp.com *Web site:* lahaciendagrande.com

CEDAR CREST

Angels' Ascent B&B/Retreat
PO Box 4, 87008
505-286-1588 Fax: 505-286-1588
All year

70-150-B&B
3 rooms, 3 pb
Most CC, *Rated*, •
C-yes/S-ltd/P-yes/H-ltd
Spanish

Full breakfast
Lun./din. (fee), snacks
Sitting room, library,
Jacuzzis, suites, cable, video
lib., spec. pkgs.

*A little bit of heaven in the heart of the Sandias with magnificent views on the Turquoise
Trail. The decor is English country with antiques, outdoor Jacuzzi, waterfall & fishpond*
E-mail: angelsasc1@aol.com *Web site:* showemall.com/showmall/angels/

CIMARRON

Casa del Gavilan
PO Box 518, 87714
505-376-2246 Fax: 505-376-2247
800-GAVILAN
Isabel Lloyd
All year

75-105-B&B
7 rooms, 6 pb
Visa, MC, AmEx,
Rated, •
C-yes/S-no/P-no/H-yes
Spanish

Full breakfast
Lunch, dinner by arrangment
Afternoon tea, comp. wine,
sitting room, library, hiking,
skiing, fishing

*Casa del Gavilan, the perfect retreat, overlooking the Santa Fe trail. Service, view, gardens
and quiet will delight you.* *Web site:* casadelgavilan.com

FARMINGTON

Casa Blanca Inn
505 E La Plata St, 87401
505-327-6503 Fax: 505-326-5680
800-550-6503
Jim & Mary Fabian
All year

68-128-B&B
6 rooms, 6 pb
Most CC, *Rated*, •
C-ltd/S-no/P-no/H-yes

Full breakfast
Afternoon tea, snacks
Lunch & dinner available,
sitting room, library,
Jacuzzis, suites

*Beautiful mission style home in town yet near ancient Anazasi sites, world class fly fishing
& golf. Luxurious rooms. Gourmet breakfasts and other meals. Ideal for business and
recreational traveler.* *E-mail:* fabian@cyberport.com *Web site:* cyberport.com/casablanca/

FARMINGTON

Silver River Adobe Inn B&B
PO Box 3411, 87499
505-325-8219 Fax: 505-325-5074
800-382-9251
Diana Ohlson & David Beers
All year

75-125-B&B
3 rooms, 3 pb
Visa, MC, •
C-ltd/S-no/P-no/H-yes

Full gourmet breakfast
Dinner, ask
River walk, wildlife, 5 star
golfing, weddings,
workshops

New Mexico adobe with large timbers. Day trips to Chaco Canyon, Mesa Verde, Aztec ruins, Salmon ruins, Canyon de Chelly. Conferences for up to 12 people.
E-mail: sribb@cyberport.com *Web site:* cyberport.com/silveradobe

JEMEZ SPRINGS

Desert Willow B&B
PO Box 255, 87025
505-829-3410
Leone Wilson
All year

95-135-B&B
2 rooms, 2 pb
Most CC, •
C-ltd/S-no/P-no/H-ltd

Full breakfast
Snacks
Sitting room, library, cable
TV, 2 bedroom cottage with
fireplace

Charming northern New Mexico style home on the Jemez River, nestled between red rock cliffs. Furnished with an eclectic mix of antiques and contemporary artwork. Tasty breakfast, elegantly served. E-mail: wilsons@desertwillowbandb.com *Web site:* desertwillowbandb.com

LAS CRUCES

Happy Trails Ranch B&B
1857 Paisano Rd, 88005
505-527-8471 Fax: 505-532-1937
Barry & Sylvia Byrnes
All year

85-100-B&B
3 rooms, 1 pb
Visa, MC, AmEx, •
C-yes/S-ltd/P-yes
Spanish

Full breakfast
Snacks
Sitting room, library, bikes,
Jacuzzis, cable TV

Hideaway, magnificent views of 4 mountain ranges, swimming pool, Jazuzzi in season. Children and pets welcome. Bikes to tour Mesillla, Rio Rande. E-mail: htralls@zianet.com
Web site: las-cruces-new-mexico.com

Hilltop Hacienda B&B
PO Box 2534, 88004
505-382-3556 Fax: 505-382-3556
Bob & Teddi Peters
All year

75-85-B&B
3 rooms, 3 pb
Most CC, *Rated*, •
C-ltd/S-ltd/P-ltd/H-yes
Spanish, Portuguese

Full breakfast
Sitting room, library,
fireplace, cable TV, 20 acres
of peace and quiet

Secluded, peaceful, romantic retreat with spectacular views and skies. 360 degree vistas atop 20 acres. E-mail: teddipeters@juno.com *Web site:* travelassist.com/reg/nm102.html

LAS VEGAS

Plaza Hotel
230 Old Town Plaza, 87701
505-425-3591
800-328-1882
Wid & Kak Slick
All year

72-140-EP
37 rooms, 37 pb
Most CC, *Rated*, •
C-yes/S-yes/P-yes/H-yes
Spanish

Meals available (fee)
Sitting room, personalized
meeting, planner service

Center of activity on old-town plaza. Turn-of-the-century furnishings. Glass-enclosed brick conservatory for performers. Children under 12 free with parents E-mail: plazahotel@
worldplaces.com *Web site:* lasvegasnewmexico.com/plaza

LOS ALAMOS

Adobe Pines B&B
2101 Loma Linda Dr, 87544
505-662-6761 Fax: 505-661-8829
Dan Partin
All year

71-78-B&B
5 rooms, 3 pb
Most CC, •
C-ltd/S-no/P-no/H-no

Continental plus breakfast
Sitting room, tennis court,
cable TV, Accomodate
business travelers

Nestled among the tall Ponderosa Pines, Adobe Pines is just minutes away from the Los Alamos National Laboratory. Our gracious home is for the discriminating traveler who wants quiet luxury. E-mail: Adobepines@losalamos.com *Web site:* losalamos.com/adobepines/

LOS ALAMOS

Bud's B&B
1981 C/B North Road, 87544
505-662-4239 Fax: 505-661-6904
800-581-BUDS
Jim "Bud" Farley
All year

65-75-B&B
6 rooms, 2 pb
Visa, MC, *Rated*, •
C-ltd/S-no/P-no/H-no
French, Spanish

Full homecooked breakfast
Sitt. rm., library, pool, bikes,
tennis, hot tub, sauna

Nestled in the arms of the Santa Fe National Forest. Bud's offers a hearty vegy cuisine including French roast coffee & in season fresh vegetables from the Inn's own organic gardens. E-mail: budsbb@aol.com Web site: VLA.com/Buds

---

Canyon Inn
12 Timber Ridge, 87544
505-662-9595
800-662-2565
Rich Kraemer
All year

55-B&B
4 rooms, 4 pb
Visa, MC, AmEx,
C-ltd/S-no/P-no/H-no

Continental plus breakfast
Laundry and kitchen,
facilities available, close to
downtown

Convenient to town and national lab. Guests have use of entire house including kitchen and laundry facilities. Ideal for long stays. Web site: los.alamos/canyon

---

Casa del Rey B&B
305 Rover Blvd, 87544
505-672-9401
Virginia King
All year

45-B&B
2 rooms, 1 pb
C-ltd/S-no/P-no/H-no

Continental plus breakfast
Homemade breads, granola
Sitting room, patio, sun
porch, garden, tennis courts
nearby

Quiet residential area, friendly atmosphere, beautiful mountain views from patios. Excellent library, restaurants and recreational facilities nearby. 2 resident cats.
E-mail: vlking@aol.com

SANTA FE

Adobe Abode
202 Chapelle St, 87501
505-983-3133 Fax: 505-424-3027
Pat Harbour
All year

110-160-B&B
6 rooms, 6 pb
Visa, MC, Disc, *Rated*,
•
C-ltd/S-ltd/P-no/H-yes
Spanish

Full gourmet breakfast
Complimentary cookies &
sherry
Sitting room with fireplace,
private phones, TVs, off-
street parking

Restored, historic adobe 3 blocks from the Plaza, with a sophisticated mix of Southwest decor and European touches. E-mail: adobebnb@sprynet.com Web site: adobeabode.com

---

Alexander's Inn
529 E Palace Ave, 87501
505-986-1431 Fax: 505-982-8572
888-321-5123
Kerry Lindsay
All year

80-160-B&B
9 rooms, 7 pb
Visa, MC, *Rated*, •
C-ltd/S-no/P-yes/H-no
French

Continental plus breakfast
Afternoon tea, beverages
Sitting room w/fireplace, hot
tub in back garden, dbl.
Jacuzzi in cottage

Cozy, quiet & romantic, yet just minutes from the Plaza. Full continental breakfast served by fireside or on terrace. Free use of mountain bikes. Private casita available. Peaceful and quiet E-mail: alexandinn@aol.com Web site: collectorsguide.com/alexandinn

---

Casa De La Cuma B&B
105 Paseo de la Cuma, 87501
505-983-1717 Fax: 505-983-2241
888-366-1717
Dona Hufton
All year

70-145-B&B
4 rooms, 2 pb
Rated, •
C-ltd/S-ltd/P-no/H-no

Continental plus breakfast
Complimentary beverages
TV, solarium, garden, patio
w/barbecue, A/C, avail. as
rental house

Mountain views! Walking distance to downtown Plaza, shopping, restaurants, galleries, library, museums, banks. Hot tubs and gardens. City sports facilities across street
E-mail: casacuma@swcp.com Web site: casacuma.com/bb

Dunshee's B&B, Santa Fe, NM

SANTA FE

Casa Escondida B&B
PO Box 142, 87522
505-351-4805 Fax: 505-351-2575
800-643-7201
Irenka Taurek
All year

80-140-B&B
8 rooms
Visa, MC, AmEx,
Rated, •
C-yes/S-no/P-ltd/H-ltd
German, French, Polish

Full breakfast
Afternoon tea, snacks, comp.
wine
Jacuzzis, suites, fireplaces

Casa Escondida, the Hidden House, nestled on six acres of secluded land is an intimate and serene inn built in the Spanish Colonial adobe style, typical of northern New Mexico. It is a place to come to find your inspiration. Web site: bbhost.com/casaescondida

Casitas de las Palomas
511 Douglas St, 87501
505-984-2270
Fax: 505-474-5675
Wendy & Willy Kapp
All year

85-EP
3 rooms, 3 pb
C-yes/S-ltd/P ltd/H-ltd

Fireplaces, cable TV

Old Authentic Adobe casitas located on one of Santa Fe's most charming streets. One block from Canyon Rd gallery district on the historic eastside. Full kitchenettes, tastefully decorated in southwest style. Private bathrooms. E-mail: twocasitas@aol.com

Dos Casas Viejas
610 Agua Fria, 87501
505-983-2000
Fax: 505-983-1749
Susan & Michael Strijek
All year

185-265-B&B
8 rooms, 8 pb
Visa, MC, •
C-yes/S-ltd/P-no/H-yes

Continental plus breakfast
Snacks, complimentary wine
Lib., pool, stes., fireplaces,
cable TV, accommodate
business travelers.

A unique, intimate, & sophisticated collection of charming adobe buildings housed w/in a walled & gated half acre adobe compound in heart of Santa Fe. Aspens, native grasses & flowering plants abound. Dining room w/French doors to pool, lobby & library.
E-mail: doscasas@rt66.com Web site: doscasasviejas.com

Dunshee's B&B
986 Acequia Madre, 87501
505-982-0988
Susan Dunshee
All year

125-B&B
2 rooms, 2 pb
Visa, MC,
C-yes/S-no/P-no/H-no

Full breakfast in suite
Continental plus in casita
Sitting room, refrigerator,
homemade cookies, TV,
private patio & gardens

Romantic hideaway in adobe compound in historic zone. Choice of 2-room suite or 2-bedroom guesthouse furnished with antiques, folk art, fresh flowers, fireplaces.
E-mail: sdunshee@aol.com Web site: bbhost.com/dunshee

SANTA FE

El Farolito B&B Inn
514 Galisteo St, 87501
505-988-1631 Fax: 505-988-4589
888-634-8782
Walt Wyss   All year

95-165-B&B
7 rooms, 7 pb
Most CC, *Rated*, •
C-yes/S-no/P-no/H-no

Continental plus breakfast
Sitting room, A/C, family
friendly facility, private
entrances, fireplaces

In the city's historic district, just a short walk to the plaza, El Farolito offers 7 romantic casitas. All accoms. feature patios, authentic southwestern decor & art. Gardens, outdoor sitting areas. 1999 winner of "Best Small Property of the Year."   E-mail: innkeeper@ farolito.com *Web site:* farolito.com

El Paradero
220 W Manhattan, 87505
505-988-1177 Fax: 505-988-3511
Ouida MacGregor & Thom
Allen
All year

65-140-B&B
14 rooms, 8 pb
Visa, MC, *Rated*, •
C-ltd/S-ltd/P-ltd/H-ltd
Spanish

Full gourmet breakfast
TV rm., liv. rm., piano,
central cooling in rooms, 2
suites available

180-year-old adobe in quiet downtown location near plaza. Gourmet breakfasts, warm atmosphere, detailed visitor information. True Southwestern hospitality. E-mail: elpara@trail.com *Web site:* elparadero.com

Four Kachinas Inn
512 Webber St, 87501
505-982-2550 Fax: 505-989-1323
800-397-2564
John Daw & Andrew
Beckerman
All year

70-149-B&B
6 rooms, 6 pb
Visa, MC, Disc, *Rated*,
•
C-ltd/S-no/P-no/H-yes
Spanish, French

Continental plus breakfast
Afternoon tea
Sitting room, breakfasts are
vegetarian, 2 suites available

Only 4 blocks from historic Plaza; furnished with handcrafted furniture, Navajo rugs & Indian art; breakfast, award-winning baked goods served in your room. E-mail: info@fourkachinas.com *Web site:* fourkachina.com

Galisteo Inn, The
HC 75-Box 4, 87540
505-466-4000 Fax: 505-466-4008
Joanna & Wayne Aarniokoski
Feb.-Dec.

115-190-B&B
12 rooms, 9 pb
Visa, MC, Disc, *Rated*,
•
C-ltd/S-ltd/P-no/H-yes
Spanish

Full breakfast
Lunch, dinner, tea
Rest., bar, lib., bikes, hot
tubs, sauna, massage, spa,
horseback riding

Magical 250 year old Spanish hacienda on eight country acres, half hour from Santa Fe. Romantic dinners & buffet breakfasts, serene and retreat like.   E-mail: galisteoin@aol.com *Web site:* galisteoinn.com

Grant Corner Inn
122 Grant Ave, 87501
505-983-6678 Fax: 505-983-1526
800-964-9003
Louise Stewart
All year

80-165-B&B
14 rooms, 8 pb
Visa, MC, *Rated*, •
C-ltd/S-yes/P-no/H-yes
Spanish

Full breakfast
Complimentary wine &
cheese
Gourmet picnic lunches,
private club access, (pool,
sauna, tennis)

Elegant colonial home located in the heart of downtown Santa Fe, nine charming rooms furnished with antiques; friendly, warm atmosphere.   E-mail: info@grantcornerinn.com *Web site:* grantcornerinn.com

Hacienda Vargas B&B Inn
PO Box 307, 87001
505-867-9115 Fax: 505-867-1902
800-261-0006
Paul Vargas
All year

69-149-B&B
7 rooms, 7 pb
Visa, MC, *Rated*, •
C-ltd/S-no/P-no/H-ltd
Spanish, German

Full country breakfast
Complimentary wine
Hot tubs, sitting room,
library, golf courses, nearby,
private Jacuzzis

Hacienda Vargas has 2 bedrooms & 5 suites with private entrances, bathrooms & fireplaces 4 suites have Jacuzzi tubs. Large BBQ area also available. Romance packages available.   E-mail: hacvar@swcp.com *Web site:* swcp.com/hacvar/

SANTA FE ―――――――――――――――――

Heart Seed B&B & Spa
PO Box 6019, 87502
505-471-7026
Judith Polich, Gayle Price
All year

79-89-B&B
6 rooms, 6 pb
Visa, MC, *Rated*, •
C-ltd/S-ltd/P-no/H-no

Full gourmet breakfast
Afternoon tea, snacks
Day spa on premises, 1 room
50s cowboy/cowgirl motif
and camp kitchen

Spectacular mountain setting on historic Turquoise Trail, day spa, massage, hot tub, 100 acres, full gourmet breakfast, rooms with kitchenettes. Two new rooms. Casita vacation rental available. E-mail: hrtseed@nets.com Web site: nets.com/heartseed/

Inn of the Turquoise Bear
342 E Buena Vista St, 87501
505-983-0798 Fax: 505-988-4225
800-396-4104
Ralph Bolton and Robert Frost
All year

95-290-B&B
10 rooms, 8 pb
Most CC, •
C-ltd/S-no/P-ltd/H-ltd
Sp., Fr., Ger., Nor.

Continental plus breakfast
Complimentary wine
Sitting room, library, cable
TV

Authentic adobe villa in a garden setting close to the Plaza. Walled estate on the National Register of Historic Places. E-mail: bluebear@roadrunner.com Web site: turquoisebear.com

La Tienda Inn
445-447 W San Francisco,
87501
505-989-8259 Fax: 505-820-6931
800-889-7611
Leighton & Barbara Watson
All year

100-160-B&B
7 rooms, 7 pb
Visa, MC, *Rated*, •
C-ltd/S-ltd/P-no/H-yes

Continental plus breakfast
Afternoon tea
Sitting room, library, bottled
water and fresh flowers in
room

A romantic adobe compound just 4 blocks from the Plaza. Private entrances; private baths; fireplaces. Breakfast in your room or in the garden in summer. E-mail: info@latiendabb.com Web site: latiendabb.com

Madeleine, The
106 Faithway St, 87501
505-986-1431 Fax: 505-982-8572
888-321-5123
Carolyn Lee
All year

70-165-B&B
8 rooms, 6 pb
Visa, MC, *Rated*, •
C-ltd/S-ltd/P-no/H-no

Full breakfast
Afternoon tea & dessert
Sitting room, lawn, quiet
location, 3 blocks, from Plaza

Historic 100-year-old Queen Anne house on Nat'l Register with fireplaces & antiques. Sensational English garden with hot tub for relaxing under the stars. E-mail: alexandinn@aol.com Web site: madeleine.com

Pueblo Bonito B&B Inn
138 W Manhattan Ave, 87501
505-984-8001 Fax: 505-984-3155
800-461-4599
Herb & Amy Behm
All year

70-150-B&B
14 rooms, 14 pb
Most CC, •
C-yes/S-ltd/P-no/H-ltd

Continental plus to room
Afternoon tea, snacks
Laundry, cable TV, A/C,
tours, sightseeing arr., airport
pickup, hot tub

Secluded historic adobe; 5-minute walk from Santa Fe Plaza. Traditional New Mexico living and decor. 15 guest rooms with private bath & fireplace. Landscaped grounds. Inside hot tub facility. E-mail: pueblo@roadrunner.com Web site: travelbase.com/destinations/santa-fe/pueblo

Spencer House B&B Inn
222 McKenzie St, 87501
505-988-3024
800-647-0530
Jan McConnell & John Pitlak
All year

99-160-B&B
5 rooms, 5 pb
Visa, MC, AmEx,
Rated, •
C-ltd/S-no/P-no/H-no

Full breakfast
Snacks
Sitting room, airport pickup,
hot tub

Cozy cottage-like charm around corner from the new Georgia O'Keefe Museum. Outstanding close-in location, queen size beds, antique furnishings, gourmet breakfasts. E-mail: jan@spencerhse-santafe.com Web site: spencerhse-santafe.com

TAOS

Adobe & Stars B&B Inn
PO Box 2285, 87571
505-776-2776 Fax: 505-776-2872
800-211-7076
Judy Salathiel
All year

75-180-B&B
8 rooms, 8 pb
Most CC, *Rated*, •
C-yes/S-no/P-ltd/H-yes
Spanish

Full breakfast
Afternoon tea, snacks
Comp. wine, sitting room,
library, Jacuzzi tubs, starry
skies

Brand new southwestern style inn with beamed ceilings, kiva fireplaces, Jacuzzi tubs, sweeping mountain views. Mountain biking/hiking trails accessible
E-mail: stars@taos.newmex.com *Web site:* taosadobe.com

Alma del Monte B&B
PO Box 1434, 87571
505-776-2721 Fax: 505-776-8888
800-273-7203
Suzanne S. Head
All year

125-250-B&B
5 rooms, 5 pb
Visa, MC, AmEx,
Rated, •
C-ltd/S-ltd/P-no/H-ltd

Full breakfast
Afternoon tea, snacks, wine
Sitting room, library,
Jacuzzis, fireplaces, suites,
conference facilities

Quality built for romance & luxury with magnificent views. Each intimate but spacious guestroom has a kiva fireplace, down comforter, heated tile floors, antiques & large bath with whirlpool.   E-mail: suzanneh@newmex.com *Web site:* AlmaDelMonteB-B.com/spirit/

American Artists B&B
PO Box 584, 87571
505-758-4446 Fax: 505-758-0497
800-532-2041
LeAn & Charles Clamurro
All year

78-185-B&B
10 rooms, 10 pb
Visa, MC, AmEx,
Rated, •
C-ltd/S-no/P-no/H-ltd
Spanish

Full breakfast
Afternoon snacks/goodies
Hot tub, sitting room, skiing,
hiking, kayaking, art gallery,
kiva fireplace

One of Taos' most romantic bed and breakfast inns. Fireplaces, outdoor hot tub and gourmet breakfasts. Discover the magic of Taos at this delightful southwest hacienda.
E-mail: aagh@taosnm.com *Web site:* taosbedandbreakfast.com

Brooks Street Inn
PO Box 4954, 87571
505-758-1489
800-758-1489
Carol Frank & Randy Hed
All year

80-115-B&B
7 rooms, 5 pb
Visa, MC, *Rated*, •
C-ltd/H-yes
Spanish

Full breakfast
Complimentary espresso bar
Snacks, sitting room, library,
shaded patio, hammock

Rambling adobe with charming guest house. Fireplaces & cozy alcoves. Quiet, tree-shaded garden. Short walk to historic plaza & galleries. Vegetarian breakfasts available. All rooms have refrigerators, robes provided, in room coffee.   E-mail: brooks@taos.newmex.com
Web site: brooksstreetinn

Casa Encantada
6460 NDCBU, 87571
505-758-7477 Fax: 505-737-5085
800-223-TAOS
Sharon Nicholson
All year

95-140-B&B
9 rooms, 9 pb
Visa, MC, AmEx,
Rated, •
C-yes/S-no/P-yes/H-no

Full breakfast
Snacks
Sitting room, suites, fireplace,
cable TV, conference
facilites, hammocks

Welcome home to our peaceful, "enchanted" hacienda with its soft adobe walls, gardens and kivas.   E-mail: encantada@newmex.com *Web site:* casaencantada.com

Casa Europa Inn & Gallery
HC 68, Box 3F, 87571
505-758-9798
888-758-9798
Rudi & Marcia Zwicker
All year

95-165-B&B
6 rooms, 6 pb
Visa, MC, *Rated*, •
C-yes/S-no/P-no/H-no
German

Full breakfast
Wine, snacks, afternoon tea
Hot tub in one room, art
gallery, shaded patio,
hammock

Luxury country inn-historical Southwest estate; horses, views, ambiance. Romantic rooms/suites; marble baths (hot tubs), fireplaces. Pamper yourself with the best!
E-mail: casa-europa@travelbase.com *Web site:* travelbase.com/destinations/taos/casa-europa/

Cottonwood Inn B&B, Taos, NM

TAOS ─────────────────────────────

Cottonwood Inn B&B
HCR 74 Box 24609, 87529
505-776-5826 Fax: 505-776-1141
800-324-7120
Bill & Kit Owen
All year

95-175-B&B
7 rooms, 7 pb
Visa, MC, Disc, *Rated*,
●
C-yes/S-ltd/P-no/H-yes
Spanish, German

Full breakfast
Afternoon tea, snacks
Concierge service, sitting
room, library, hot tubs,
sauna

Exceptional views. Extensive gardens. Distinctive rooms with fireplaces, whirlpools Southwestern art display & gallery. Outdoor hot tub. Convenient to town, ski slopes and other outdoor activities. Guided fly-fishing. E-mail: cottonbb@newmex.com
Web site: taos-cottonwood.com

Dreamcatcher B&B
PO Box 2069, 87571
505-758-0613 Fax: 505-751-0115
888-758-0613
Bob & Jill Purtee
All year

79-104-B&B
7 rooms, 7 pb
Most CC, ●
C ltd/S-ltd/P-no/H-yes
Some Spanish

Full breakfast
Afternoon tea, snacks
Sitting room, library,
Jacuzzis, fireplaces, hot tubs,
sauna

A unique NM adobe inn situated in a secluded wooded setting a short 10 minute walk to Historic Taos Plaza. E-mail: dream@taosnm.com Web site: taoswebb.com/hotel/dreamcatcher

Hacienda Del Sol
PO Box 177, 87571
505-758-0287 Fax: 505-758-5895
Dennis Sheehan
All year

85-165-B&B
11 rooms, 11 pb
Visa, MC, *Rated*, ●
C-yes/S-no/P-no/H-ltd

Full breakfast
Complimentary snacks
Library, fireplaces, gallery,
outdoor hot tub, robes, golf
nearby, gardens

180-yr-old large adobe hideaway purchased by Mabel Dodge for Indian husband, Tony. Adjoins vast Indian lands yet close to Plaza. Tranquillity, mountain views.
E-mail: sunehouse@newmex.com Web site: taoshaciendadelsol.com

Inn on La Loma Plaza, An
Box 4159, 87571
505-758-1717 Fax: 505-751-0155
800-530-3040
Jerry & Peggy Davis
All year

95-235-B&B
7 rooms, 7 pb
Most CC, *Rated*, ●
C-yes/S-ltd/P-ltd/H-ltd
French & Spanish

Full breakfast
Afternoon tea, snacks
Sitting room, library,
Jacuzzis, swimming pool,
suites, fireplaces, cable TV

An elegant historic Inn, featuring exceptional hospitality, Southwestern ambiance, romantic rooms with fireplaces, mountain views, patios, and outdoor hot tub.
E-mail: laloma@taoswebb.com Web site: taoswebb.com/laloma

TAOS

La Posada de Taos
PO Box 1118, 87571
505-758-8164 Fax: 505-751-3294
800-645-4803
Bill Swan & Nancy Brooks
All year

95-145-B&B
6 rooms, 6 pb
Rated, •
C-ltd/S-yes/P-no/H-yes

Full breakfast
Large dining room
Sitting room, patios, sun
room, portals, fireplaces,
courtyards

We have a new large dining room with 13' high beamed ceiling overlooking the garden & Taos Mountain. Also added private patios for 2 rooms. Host meetings & classes.
E-mail: laposada@newmex.com *Web site:* taosnet.com/laposada/

Laughing Horse Inn
PO Box 4889, 87571
505-758-8350 Fax: 505-751-1123
800-776-0161
Bob Bodenhamer
All year

58-130-B&B
13 rooms, 3 pb
Most CC, •
C-yes/S-no/P-yes/H-no
Spanish

Full breakfast
Guest kitchen
Fireplaces, 500 videos, free
mountain bikes, hot tub, pets
welcome

An eclectic 1887 adobe that was once home to the publisher of The Laughing Horse magazine and his guests, D.H. Lawrence and Georgia O'Keeffe. Jerry Garcia shrine.
E-mail: laughinghorse@laughinghorseinn.com *Web site:* laughinghorseinn.com

Orinda B&B
PO Box 4451, 87571
505-758-8581
Fax: 505-751-4895
800-847-1837
Adrian & Sheila Percival
All year

80-145-B&B
5 rooms, 5 pb
Visa, MC, Disc, •
C-ltd/S-no/P-no/H-no

Full breakfast
Snacks
Sitting room w/kiva fireplace,
library, tennis ct, hottubs,
sauna/pool, golf

Quiet, pastoral setting on 2 acres, southwest adobe home close to town, shops, galleries and skiing (16 miles). Free pass to health spa and tennis. *E-mail:* orinda@newmex.com
Web site: taosnet.com/orinda

Stewart House B&B, The
PO Box 3020, 87571
505-776-2557
Fax: 505-776-2557
888-505-2557
Carl & Sharon Fritz
All year

65-115-B&B
4 rooms, 4 pb
Visa, MC, •
C-yes/S-no/P-no/H-yes
German, Spanish

Full breakfast
Afternoon tea
Sitting room, library, hot
tubs, weddings, conference
& retreat facility

Unique country inn; magical view of spectacular Taos Mountain; warm, friendly old west ambiance; hot tub; fireplaces; gourmet breakfast. *E-mail:* stewarthouse@laplaza.org
Web site: laplaza.org/~stwrths/

New York

ALBANY

Greenville Arms 1889 Inn
PO Box 659, 12083
518-966-5219 Fax: 518-966-8754
Eliot & Letitia Dalton
Closed Dec.

125-165-B&B
14 rooms, 14 pb
Visa, MC, *Rated*, •
C-ltd/S-no/P-no/H-no

Full breakfast from menu
Elegant country dining
Library, secluded 50' pool,
living/sitting rooms, art
workshops, croquet

Historic Victorian country inn on 6 acres, with established shade trees, gardens, outdoor pool. Hudson Valley mansions, hiking, biking, & relaxing. Expanded conference rooms. All rooms air-conditioned. *E-mail:* ny1889inn@sprintmail.com
Web site: artworkshops.com/page5html

River Hill II, Albany, NY

ALBANY

Pine Haven B&B
531 Western Ave, 12203
518-482-1574
Janice Tricarico
All year

59-99-B&B
5 rooms, 2 pb
Most CC, *Rated*, •
C-ltd/S-no/P-no/H-no

Continental plus breakfast
Living room, TV, books,
board games, antiques,
original oak woodwork

Victorian ambience in the heart of the city. Century-old Victorian in a beautiful residential
area of the state's capital. Features iron & brass beds, feather mattresses
Web site: travelguides.com/home/pinehaven/

River Hill II
PO Box 253, 12124
518-756-3313
Julia Coryell
All year

75-80-B&B
2.5 rooms, 2 pb
Visa, MC,
C-yes/S-yes/P-ltd/H-no
Some Spanish

Full breakfast
Aftn. tea, comp. wine
Sitting room, library, family
friendly facility, one
bedroom has a/c.

Charming, Victorian overlooking Hudson River; antiques, four poster beds, grand piano;
bountiful breakfast served on terrace or by fire. Nearby marina.

AMENIA

Troutbeck
Leedsville Rd, 12501
914-373-9681 Fax: 914-373-7080
800-978-7688
Garret Corcoran
All year

650-1050-AP
42 rooms, 37 pb
AmEx, *Rated*, •
C-ltd/S-yes/P-no/H-no
Spanish, Port., It., Fr.

Full breakfast excluding
Sunday
All meals & open bar
included
Pub. rooms, piano, library,
tennis courts, ballroom, 2
pools, exercise room

Historic English country estate on 422 acres, with indoor & outdoor pools, fine chefs,
12,000 books, lovely grounds, gazebo brookside for weddings. A quiet retreat.
E-mail: innkeeper@troutbeck.com *Web site:* troutbeck.com

BELMONT

Pollywogg Holler EcoLodge
6242 South Rd, 14813
716-268-5819 Fax: 716-268-5819
800-291-9668
Bill & Barbara Castle
All year

260-1000-B&B
3 rooms, 1 pb
Visa, MC,
C-yes/S-ltd/P-yes/H-no

Full breakfast
Dinner & lunch (fee)
Sitting room, Finnish style
sauna, non-electric cooking

Established in 1987 as an alternative EcoLodge Bed & Breakfast nestled amid 46,000 acres of New York State Forest in Allegany County. E-mail: stay@pollywoggholler.com
Web site: pollywoggholler.com

BERLIN

Sedgwick Inn
Route 22, 12022
518-658-2334 Fax: 518-658-3998
Diane Niedzwiecki
All year

95-165-B&B
11 rooms, 11 pb
Most CC, *Rated*, •
C-ltd/S-ltd/P-ltd/H-no
Polish, Russian

Full breakfast
Lunch/dinner, restaurant
Bar service, sitt. room,
library, tennis nearby,
swimming lakes, spa, pool

1791 "quintessential country inn"—old-world charm, casual elegance, fine food. In tri-state corner near excellent theater, music, hiking, skiing. E-mail: sedgwickin@aol.com
Web site: Regionnet.com/colberk/sedgwickinn.html

BOLTON LANDING

Hilltop Cottage B&B
4825 Lakeshore Drive, 12814
518-644-2492
Anita Richards
May-Nov.

65-85-B&B
3 rooms, 3 pb
Visa, MC, *Rated*
C-ltd/S-no/P-no/H-no
German

Full breakfast
in-room phones & TV's

Summer resort area in Northern N.Y.S.- Adirondack Park- Lake George. Walk to beach, restaurants and shops. Clean, comfortable, renovated farmhouse. Helpful hosts.

BROCKPORT

Victorian B&B, The
320 Main St, 14420
716-637-7519 Fax: 716-637-7519
800-836-1929
Sharon M. Kehoe
All year

66-94-B&B
7 rooms, 7 pb
Rated, •
C-yes/S-no/P-no/H-no

Full breakfast
Afternoon tea
Sitting room, library, bikes,
Jacuzzis, fireplaces, fax,
cable TV

Late 19th-century Queen Anne home with pleasing blend of antiques and modern furnishings. Short walk from historic Erie Canal. E-mail: skehoe@po.brockport.edu
Web site: victorianbandb.com

BUFFALO, SALAMANCA

Jefferson Inn, The
PO Box 1566, 14731
716-699-5869 Fax: 716-699-5758
800-577-8451
Donna Gushue & Jim
Buchanan
All year

65-175-B&B
7 rooms, 7 pb
Most CC, *Rated*
C-ltd/S-no/P-ltd/H-yes

Full breakfast
Sitting room, library, suites,
fireplace, cable TV, catering

Romantic, quiet location, historic four-season resort village. Get away from Cleveland, Toronto, Rochester and Pittsburgh. Stroll to excellent restaurants. E-mail: jeffinn@eznet.net
Web site: thejeffersoninn.com

BURDETT

Red House Country Inn, The
4586 Picnic Area Rd, 14818
607-546-8566 Fax: 607-546-4105
Sandy Schmanke & Joan
Martin
All year

69-89-B&B
5 rooms
Most CC, *Rated*, •
C-ltd/S-no/P-no

Full breakfast
Complimentary tea, coffee
Large in-ground pool, sitting
room, nature trails

Within national forest; 28 miles of trails. Beautiful rooms in gorgeous setting. Near famous Watkins Glen, Eastside Seneca Lake. E-mail: redhsinn@aol.com
Web site: fingerlakes.net/redhouse

CANANDAIGUA

Acorn Inn	95-195-B&B	Full gourmet breakfast
4508 State Rt 64 S, 14424	4 rooms, 4 pb	Snacks, complimentary
716-229-2834 Fax: 716-229-5046	Most CC, *Rated*, •	beverages
Louis & Joan Clark	C-ltd/S-no/P-no/H-no	Sitting room, library, hot
All year		tubs, wineries,
		golf/skiing/tennis nearby

Charming 1795 inn furnished with period antiques, canopy beds, luxury baths, colonial fireplace in book-lined gathering room. Beautiful gardens with spa.
Web site: acorninnbb.com

Greenwoods B&B Inn, The	90-145-B&B	Full breakfast
8136 Quayle Rd, 14471	6 rooms, 6 pb	Snacks, picnic basket,
716-229-2111 Fax: 716-229-2111	Visa, MC, AmEx,	dinner/Sat.
800-914-3559	*Rated*, •	Sitting room, library,
Mike Ligon & Lisa Bortolotto	C-ltd/S-ltd/P-no/H-no	Jacuzzis, suites, fireplaces,
All year		cable TV

Country log inn displaying influences from the Great Adirondack camps of yesterday. Hilltop setting provides panoramic lake/valley views.   Web site: Greenwoodsinn.com

Sutherland House B&B Inn	95-175-B&B	Full country breakfast
3179 State Rte 21 South, 14424	5 rooms, 5 pb	Afternoon tea
716-396-0375 Fax: 716-396-9281	Most CC, *Rated*, •	Snacks, sitting room, hot
800-396-0375	C-ltd/S-no/P-no/H-no	tubs, skiing nearby
Cor & Diane Van Der Woude	Dutch	
All year		

Warmth and hospitality await you at Sutherland House. "Tyson" our boxer, willingly entertains! A country setting close to everything. Welcome. Breakfast served outdoors in the summer.   E-mail: goodnite@frontiernet.net *Web site:* sutherlandhouse.com

CANTON

White Pillars B&B	50-75-B&B	Full breakfast
PO Box 185, 13617	4 rooms, 2 pb	Afternoon tea, snacks, comp.
315-386-2353	Most CC, •	wine
800-261-6292	C-yes/S-no/P-no/H-ltd	Sitting room, tennis court,
Donna & John Clark		Jacuzzis, cable TV
All year		

Country homestead on 165 acres of meadows and pines. Fully renovated home has unique combination of luxury and antiquity. Hosts' private recreational facilities on Trout Lake for guests' use.   Web site: whitepillars.com

CATSKILL MOUNTAINS

Palenville House B&B	85-150-B&B	Full breakfast
PO Box 465, 12463	5 rooms, 5 pb	Comp. snacks, tea, cider
518-678-5649 Fax: 518-678-9038	Most CC, •	10 person hot tub, sitting
877-689-5101	C-ltd/S-ltd/P-no/H-no	room, fireplace, cable TV,
Jim Forster		conference, Jacuzzis.
All year		

Magnificent Victorian guest house located in the heart of the Catskill Mountains—only 2 hours north of NYC. Easily accessible by bus.   E-mail: palenville@aol.com
Web site: catskillsbb.com

CHAPPAQUA

Crabtree's Kittle House	108-138-B&B	Continental breakfast
11 Kittle Rd, 10514	12 rooms, 12 pb	Lunch, dinner
914-666-8044 Fax: 914-666-2684	Most CC,	Restaurant, bar, gift shop,
800-235-6186	C-yes/S-ltd/P-ltd/H-ltd	cable TV, accommodates
Judith Kissel	Spanish	business travelers
All year		

Built in 1790, country charm, historic character, world class American cuisine. New York Times rated excellent. Grand Award wine cellar.   E-mail: kittlemimi@aol.com
Web site: kittlehouse.com

CHAUTAUQUA

Plumbush B&B
PO Box 864, 14722
716-789-5309 Fax: 716-357-9727
Gary & Mary Doebler
All year

85-130-B&B
5 rooms, 5 pb
Visa, MC, AmEx, •
S-no/P-no/H-no

Continental breakfast plus
Sitting room, library, cable
TV, conference facilities,
hiking/skiing trails

Plumbush is a gracious circa 1865 Italianate villa restored to its original grandeur.
E-mail: plumbush@yahoo.com *Web site:* chautauquainfo.com

St. Elmo Accommodations
1 Pratt Ave, 14722
716-357-3566
Fax: 716-357-3317
Joreta & Richard Speck
All year

65-175-EP
35 rooms, 35 pb
Visa, MC, *Rated*, •
C-ltd/S-ltd/H-yes

Lunch, dinner, snacks
Restaurant
Sitting room, bicycles, hot
tubs, swimming pool,
meeting rooms, Fax

New Victorian-style hotel located in the center of world-renowned Chautauqua Institution.
Business groups welcome. Meeting facilities E-mail: careelmo@chautauquaarea.com
Web site: ChautauquaArea.com/stelmo/stelmo.html

CHESTERTOWN

Friends Lake Inn
963 Friends Lake Rd, 12817
518-494-4751 Fax: 518-494-4616
Sharon Taylor
All year

135-335-B&B
17 rooms, 17 pb
Visa, MC, *Rated*, •
C-ltd/S-ltd/P-no/H-no

Full country breakfast
Restaurant, bar service
Library, swimming,
Adirondack suites with view,
outdoor sauna

Fully restored 19th century inn with lake view. Award-winning rest. & wine list. 2 rooms
with working fireplaces. Cross country skiing & mountain biking. Private beach & canoes
on Friends Lake. E-mail: friends@netheaven.com *Web site:* friendslake.com/

Landon Hill B&B
10 Landon Hill Rd, 12817
518-494-2599
888-244-2599
All year

80-120-B&B
5 rooms, 4 pb
Visa, MC, *Rated*, •
C-yes/S-ltd/P-ltd/H-yes

Full breakfast
Sitting room, fireplaces,
cable TV, canoe, snowshoe
rental

Landon Hill is an historic house built in the 1860s. There are 5, large distinctive guestrooms
with queen or king beds. E-mail: landon@bedbreakfast.net *Web site:* bedbreakfast.net

CLINTON

The Artful Lodger,
7 E Park Row, 13323
315-853-3672 Fax: 315-853-1489
888-LODGERS
Susan & Claire Ostinett
All year

65-115-B&B
5 rooms, 5 pb
Most CC, *Rated*, •
C-yes/S-no/P-no/H-ltd
Some French

Full breakfast on weekends
Continental breakfast on
weekdays
Sitting room, library, art
gallery, piano, family friendly
facility

Located on a historic Village Green, this 1835 federal-style inn showcases the work of
regional artists. You'll appreciate the artful blending of old world charm with modern
convenience.

COLDEN

Back of the Beyond
7233 Lower E Hill Rd, 14033
716-652-0427
Shash Georgi
All year

65-B&B
3 rooms
C-yes/S-no/P-no/H-no

Full country breakfast
Complimentary beverages &
snacks
Kitchen, fireplace, pool table,
gift shop, swimming pond

Charming mini-estate 50 mi. from Niagara Falls. Organic herb, flower & vegetable gardens.
Breakfast served on deck or in living room. Hiking. E-mail: shashibotb@aol.com

COOPERSTOWN

Adalaide Country Inn
RR 3, Box 304K, 13326
607-547-1215 Fax: 607-547-1215
Neal & Gail McManus
All year

80-165-B&B
4 rooms, 3 pb
C-yes/S-no/P-no/H-no

Full breakfast
Snacks
Sitting room, open meadows,
trails, verandah, hammock

Close to Cooperstown yet offering a retreat into nature. Treat yourself to serenity, hospitality and a good night's sleep. Efficiency cabins in wooded settings.   E-mail: nmc777@juno.com

Angelholm B&B
PO Box 705, 13326
607-547-2483 Fax: 607-547-2309
Jan & Fred Reynolds
All year

80-110-B&B
5 rooms, 5 pb
Visa, MC, *Rated*, •
C-ltd/S-no/P-no/H-no

Full breakfast
Deluxe & afternoon tea
Sitting room, library, porch,
piano, TV room, specialty
diets, A/C

*Historic 1805 Federal Colonial with off-street parking. Walking distance to shops, restaurants and Hall of Fame Museum. Comfortably elegant   E-mail: anglholm@telenet.net
Web site: angelholmbb.com*

Chestnut Street GuestHouse
79 Chestnut St, 13326
607-547-5624
John & Pam Miller
All year

100-175-B&B
4 rooms, 4 pb
AmEx,
C-ltd/S-no/P-no/H-no

Continental plus breakfast
Restaurants nearby
Sitting room, walk to 3
museums, tennis nearby

Park your car and enjoy the beauty of our delightful village. Warm hospitality and a lovely home await you. Please come share it with us.

Cooper Inn, The
PO Box 311, 13326
607-547-2567 Fax: 607-547-1271
800-348-6222
Steven C. Walker
All year

99-160-B&B
15 rooms, 15 pb
•
C-yes/S-no/P-no/H-no

Continental breakfast
Facilities of Otesaga Resort
Hotel available to inn guests
during season

Classic Federal brick landmark Inn built in 1812 & located on its stately grounds in the heart of Cooperstown.   E-mail: reservations@cooperinn.com   Web site: cooperinn.com

Edgefield
PO Box 152, 13459
518-284-3339
Daniel Marshall Wood
All year

95-160-B&B
5 rooms, 5 pb
C-ltd/S-no/P-no/H-no

Full breakfast
Afternoon tea,
complimentary wine
Living room, queen & twin
beds, friendly host & cat

A well-appointed Edwardian home in quaint village. Comfortable, elegant English country-house decoration, antiques, fireplace.   Web site: members.tripod.com/~edgefield

Inn at Cooperstown, The
16 Chestnut St, 13326
607-547-5756 Fax: 607-547-8779
Michael Jerome
All year

85-150-B&B
18 rooms, 18 pb
Most CC, *Rated*, •
C-ltd/S-yes/P-no/H-yes

Continental breakfast
1986 NY State Historic
Preservation award winner,
conf. facilities

*Restored Victorian inn providing genuine hospitality; close to Baseball Hall of Fame, Fenimore House and Farmer's Museum.   E-mail: theinn@telenet.net
Web site: cooperstown.net/theinn*

Litco Farms B&B
PO Box 1048, 13326
607-547-2501 Fax: 607-547-7079
Jim & Margaret Wolff
All year

79-129-B&B
4 rooms, 2 pb
Most CC, *Rated*, •
C-yes/S-no/P-no/H-no

Full breakfast
Sitting room, swimming,
library, pool, hikes, cross-
country ski trails,ponds

*Families & couples enjoy 20'x40' pool, 70 acres, nature trails, & a pond. Handmade quilts by resident quilter. Warm hospitality; marvelous breakfasts   E-mail: wolffj@wpe.com
Web site: heartworksquilts.com*

COOPERSTOWN

Main Street B&B	85-115-B&B	Full breakfast
202 Main St, 13326	3 rooms, 3 pb	Family friendly facility, sitting
607-547-9755 Fax: 607-547-9755	C-yes/S-ltd/P-no/H-no	room, TV, A/C, ponds
800-867-9755		
Ron & Susan Streek		
All year		

A Victorian B&B within walking distance to Baseball Hall of Fame and highlights of Cooperstown. Lovely front porch for relaxation.
Web site: cooperstownchamber.org/mainstreetbb

Sunrise Farm	60-B&B	Full breakfast
331 County Hwy 17, 13411	1 rooms, 1 pb	Complimentary wine
607-847-9380	C-yes/S-no/P-no/H-no	
Janet Schmelzer		
All year		

Quiet, hill farm on paved road. Scottish Highland cattle. Lake swimming, hiking at nearby State Parks. Private bathroom. Full breakfast. Small enough for hosts to be flexible. Cooperstown 20 miles.

Thistlebrook B&B	120-145-B&B	Full breakfast
RD1 Box 28, 13326	5 rooms, 5 pb	Complimentary port &
607-547-6093	•	sherry
800-596-9305	C-ltd/S-no/P-no/H-yes	Sitting room, library,
Paula & Jim Bugonian		oversized guest rooms, pool,
Open May-Nov.		4 private acres

Voted as a "Top Twelve Inn" in 1992 by Country Inns magazine. Circa 1866 barn with European, American, antique furnishings. Beautiful valley views. Natural pond-wildlife-birds.

CORNING

Addison Rose B&B	85-105-B&B	Full breakfast
37 Maple St, 14801	3 rooms, 3 pb	Afternoon tea
607-359-4650	*Rated*	Antiques, near golf, hiking,
Bill & Mary Ann Peters	S-no/P-no/H-no	skiing, lakes & streams
All year		

Discover "Victorian elegance in the heart of the country" in this restored, period-furnished "painted lady." Minutes from Corning and Finger Lakes Wineries.

CORNWALL

Cromwell Manor Inn	135-275-B&B	Full breakfast
174 Angola Rd, 12518	13 rooms, 13 pb	Afternoon tea, picnic basket
914-534-7136	Visa, MC, *Rated*, •	Sitting room, fireplaces, hot
Dale & Barbara Ohara	C-ltd/S-no/P-no/H-ltd	tubs, 7 acres garden, hiking,
All year		biking, wineries

Historic 1820 Greek revival mansion on a seven-acre estate. Formal mountain setting, fully restored inn. 5 miles to West Point, 1 hour north of New York City.
Web site: bbonline.com/ny/cromwell

CROWN POINT

Crown Point B&B	60-130-B&B	Continental plus breakfast
PO Box 490, 12928	6 rooms, 5 pb	Afternoon tea, wine, snacks
518-597-3651 Fax: 518-597-4451	Visa, MC, *Rated*, •	Sitting room, gift shop,
Hugh and Sandy Johnson	C-ltd/S-no/P-no/H-yes	bicycles, Jacuzzi,
All year	Spanish	robes/slippers, croquet

Victorian manor house rich in raised paneled woodwork, decorated with antiques & customized linens. Home baking done daily. New game rm. Shower massages, make-up mirrors E-mail: *mail@crownpointbandb.com* Web site: *crownpointbandb.com*

DE BRUCE

De Bruce Country Inn	180-250-MAP	Full breakfast
De Bruce Rd #286-A, 12758	15 rooms, 15 pb	Dinner included, bar
914-439-3900	*Rated*, •	Library, sauna, pool, private
All year	C-yes/S-yes/P-yes/H-no	forest preserve, trout pond,
	French	art gallery

Within the Catskill Forest Preserve with its trails, wildlife, famous trout stream, our turn-of-the-century inn offers superb dining overlooking the valley. Whirlpool.
Web site: debrucecountryinn.com

DEPOSIT

Alexander's Inn	79-109-B&B	Full breakfast
770 Oquaga Lake Rd, 13754	5 rooms, 5 pb	Dinner by appointment
607-467-6023 Fax: 607-467-5355	Most CC, *Rated*, •	Boats, bicycles, hiking,
Alexander Meyer	C-yes/S-ltd/P-yes/H-ltd	sauna, hot tub, pool
All year	German, French	

Beautiful lake, elegant & relaxing meeting place for world travelers. Golf, fishing. Day trips to Catskills, Finger Lakes, Niagara Falls   E-mail: alexinn@aol.com
Web site: tempotek.com/alexinn

EAST HAMPTON

1848 House	115-135-B&B	Continental breakfast
100 Pantigo Rd, 11937	5 rooms, 2 pb	Beach passes
516-324-4622	Visa, MC,	
Lois Brown & John Kelman	C-no/S-no/P-no/H-no	
Spring, Summer, Fall		

A historic house in the village of East Hampton, NY, on an acre and a half of grounds.
E-mail: blois@aol.com   Web site: peconic.net/1848house

Mill House Inn	275-425-B&B	Full gourmet breakfast
33 N Main St, 11937	8 rooms, 8 pb	Cooking workshops
631-324-9766 Fax: 631-324-9793	Most CC,	Air conditioning, spa, in-
877-324-9753	C-yes/S-no/P-no/H-yes	room fireplaces, whirlpool
Katherine & Dan Hartnett	Spanish	tubs
All year		

Magnificently restored 1790 B&B located across from historic Windmill. Delicious buffet breakfasts. Experience the charm, luxury, hospitality. Families/children welcome. "Tasting the Hamptons Cookbook and Area Guide" available.   E-mail: millhouseinn@worldnet.att.net
Web site: millhouseinn.com

Pink House, The	275-345-B&B	Full breakfast
26 James Ln, 11937	5 rooms, 5 pb	Sitting room, porch,
631-324-3400 Fax: 631-324-5254	Most CC,	swimming pool
Ron Steinhilber	C-ltd/S-no/P-no/H-no	
All year	Spanish	

A distinctive B&B located in the historic district of East Hampton. Newly renovated with marble bathrooms, lush bathrobes & special emphasis on personal service.   E-mail: roso@hamptons.com   Web site: thepinkhouse.net

EAST MARION

Quintessentials B&B	135-170-B&B	Full breakfast
8985 Main Rd, Rt 25A, 11939	3 rooms, 3 pb	Afternoon beverage, snacks
516-477-9400	Visa, MC, AmEx, •	Sitting room, library,
Sylvia M. Daley	C-ltd/S-ltd/P-no/H-ltd	fireplaces, cable TV,
All year	German, Portuguese, Sp.	massage, bikes

An 1840's, newly renovated, 14-room Victorian set in beautiful gardens. Guest rooms are spacious with private baths, great mattresses and reading lamps.   E-mail: Sylvia@QuintessentialsInc.com   Web site: QuintessentialsInc.com/bed&brk.htm

ELMIRA

Rufus Tanner House B&B
60 Sagetown Rd, 14871
607-732-0213
Donna & Rick Powell
All year

60-105-B&B
3 rooms, 3 pb
Visa, MC, •
C-yes/S-no/P-no/H-ltd

Full breakfast
Dinner available, afternoon
tea
Snacks, sitting room,
bicycles, Jacuzzi, fireplace,
AC

1864 Greek Revival farmhouse, full breakfast, great antiques. One room with Jacuzzi, one room with fireplace. Rooms are air-conditioned. E-mail: rufustan@servtech.com
Web site: rufustanner.com

ESSEX

Champlain Vistas B&B
183 Lake Shore Rd, 12996
518-963-8029
Barbara and Bob Hatch
All year

85-105-B&B
5 rooms, 3 pb
Visa, MC,
C-ltd/S-no/P-no/H-no

Full breakfast
Snacks, afternoon tea
Sitting room, trails for, hiking
& biking nearby, near golf

Lake & mountain views with antiques thruout; wraparound porch & stone fireplace; spec. wedding site; artists' paradise. E-mail: rdhatch@willex.com
Web site: virtualcities.com/ons/ny/z/nyz5701.htm

FAIR HAVEN

Black Creek Farm B&B
PO Box 390, 13064
315-947-5282 Fax: 315-947-5282
Bob & Kathy Sarber
All year

60-125-B&B
4 rooms, 2 pb
Visa, MC, AmEx,
Rated, •
C-ltd/S-ltd/P-no/H-no

Full breakfast
Snacks
Sitting room, bicycles, cable
TV

Lovingly restored 1888 Victorian farmhouse surrounded by peaceful countryside. Quiet, full of antiques. Newly built guesthouse overlooks a 2-acre stocked pond with pedal boat in a quiet meadow, secret and private. E-mail: ksarber@redcreek.net
Web site: fairhavenny.com/bcf

FINGER LAKES

Silver Strand At Sheldrake
7398 Wyers Point Rd, 14521
607-532-4972 Fax: 607-532-9597
800-283-5253
Maura Donnelly   All year

99-195-B&B
5 rooms, 5 pb
Visa, MC, •
C-ltd/S-ltd/P-no/H-yes

Full breakfast
Snacks
Bar, sitting room, bicycles,
Jacuzzis, swimming pool,
fireplace, cable TV

Waterfront Victorian in the heart of the Finger Lakes Wine Region. Walk to find dining and neighborhood vineyard. Swim in crystal clear glacier lake. E-mail: skipstam@epix.net
Web site: silverstrand.net

FLEISCHMANNS

River Run B&B Inn
Main St, 12430
914-254-4884
Larry Miller
All year

60-115-B&B
9 rooms, 6 pb
Visa, MC, AmEx,
Rated, •
C-yes/S-ltd/P-yes/H-no

Full breakfast
Fireplace, stained glass,
beautiful grounds, piano,
front porch/trout stream

Exquisite country village Victorian, at the edge of the Catskill Forest. Enjoy hiking trails, superb skiing, antiquing, auction, fishing, golf & tennis. Voted the 1998 "Catskill Service Award" for best accommodations in the region. E-mail: riverrun@catskill.net
Web site: bbonline.com/ny/riverrun

FREDONIA

Brookside Manor B&B
3728 Rt 83, 14063
716-672-7721
800-929-7599
Andrea Andrews & Dale Mirth
All year

75-B&B
3 rooms, 3 pb
Visa, MC,
C-yes/S-no/P-yes/H-no

Full breakfast
Sitting room, cable TV,
accommodate business
travelers, garden, patio,
brook

Enchanting Victorian manor on beautiful grounds near Historic Fredonia, Lake Erie, Lily Dale; spacious, comfortable, tastefully appointed non-smoking guest rooms with private bathrooms and A/C; gourmet breakfast included. Web site: bbonline.com/ny/brookside/

GARRISON

Bird & Bottle Inn, The	220-260-MAP	Full breakfast
1123 Old Albany Post Rd,	4 rooms, 4 pb	Dinner included, bar
10524	Visa, MC, AmEx,	Gazebo near brook, cedar
914-424-3000 Fax: 914-424-3283	*Rated*, •	shake roof, special diets
800-782-6837	C-ltd/S-ltd/P-no/H-no	available
Ira Boyar All year		

Established in 1761, the inn's history predates the Revolutionary War. Each room has period furniture, a working fireplace & four-poster or canopy bed.
E-mail: info@birdbottle.com *Web site:* birdbottle.com

GREENPORT

Bartlett House Inn, B&B	95-125-B&B	Continental plus breakfast
503 Front St, 11944	10 rooms, 10 pb	Fireplace, conferences, In
516-477-0371	Most CC, *Rated*	house massage, phones
Diane & Bill May All year	C-ltd/S-ltd/P-no/H-no	w/data ports & voicemail.

Stately Victorian home furnished with brass beds & period antiques. Conveniently located near North Fork Wineries, beaches, Greenport Village and Shelter Island.
Web site: greenport.com/bartlett/

HADLEY

Saratoga Rose Inn & Rest.	85-175-B&B	Full gourmet breakfast
4274 Rockwell St, 12835	4 rooms, 4 pb	Restaurant, bar, dinner
518-696-2861 Fax: 518-696-5319	Visa, MC, AmEx, •	Library, some in-room,
800-942-5025	C-ltd/S-ltd/P-no/H-no	fireplace &/or Jacuzzi, gift
Chef Anthony & Nancy		shop, garden/gazebo
Merlino All year		

Romantic Victorian inn and restaurant. Near Saratoga, Lake George, skiing, recreation. Carriage House with spa & fireplace. Gourmet meals, complimentary wine.
E-mail: sararose@capital.net *Web site:* saratogarose.com

HAMLIN

Sandy Creek Manor House	70-100-B&B	Full breakfast
1960 Redman Rd, 14464	4 rooms, 1 pb	Afternoon tea, snacks
716-964-7528 Fax: 716-964-9244	Visa, MC, AmEx,	Sitting room, library,
800-594-0400	*Rated*, •	Jacuzzis, fireplaces,
S. Hollink & J. Krempasky	C-ltd/S-no/P-yes/H-ltd	accommodates business
All year		travelers

Luxurious hot tub spa soothes away your stress while the king-size beds and sounds of nature enfold you in comfort. Waken to tantalizing gourmet breakfasts, browse the gift shop...and return home much too soon. E-mail: agreatbnb@aol.com
Web site: sandycreekbnb.com

HAMMONDSPORT

Amity Rose B&B	85-125-B&B	Full breakfast
8264 Main St, 14840	4 rooms, 4 pb	Afternoon tea
607-569-3408 Fax: 607-569-2483	*Rated*	Sitting room, Jacuzzis, tennis
877-230-5761	C-ltd/S-ltd/P-no/H-ltd	court, suites, fireplaces,
Ellen & Frank Laufersweiler		conference
May 1-Dec 31		

A 1900 country house. 2 rooms have 6 foot whirlpool soaking tubs, one a 2 room suite. Nice large living room with fireplace. Dinner boat nearby, walk to historic village square & shops. Wineries galore! Web site: amityroseinn.com

Another Tyme B&B	70-80-B&B	Full gourmet breakfast
PO Box 134, 14840	3 rooms, 1 pb	Afternoon tea & snacks
607-569-2747	Visa, MC, *Rated*, •	Sitting room, complimentary
Carolyn Clark	C-ltd/S-no/P-no/H-no	wine at local restaurants
All year		

3 guest rooms recapture the grace and charm of another time. Close to wineries, Watkins Glen racetrack, museums. Lake nearby. E-mail: clrkmark@infoblvd.net

Blushing Rose B&B, Hammondsport, NY

HAMMONDSPORT

Blushing Rose B&B
PO Box 201, 14840
607-569-3402 Fax: 607-569-2504
800-982-8818
April 15-Dec. 15

85-105-B&B
4 rooms, 4 pb
Rated
C-ltd/S-no/P-no/H-no

Full breakfast
In-room coffee
Afternoon refreshment,
bicycles, sitting room, lake
nearby

An 1843 Victorian Italianate located in heart of a historic village. Enjoy museums, wineries, Corning, swimming, fishing, boating or just strolling.   Web site: blushingroseinn.com

HARLEM

Urban Jem Guest House, The
2005 Fifth Ave, 10035
212-831-6029
Fax: 212-831-6940
Jane & Alex Mendelson
All year

105-200-B&B
4 rooms, 2 pb
Visa, MC, AmEx, ●
C-yes/S-ltd/P-no/H-no

Continental
Sitting room, suites, cable TV,
conference, a/c, in-room
phones

Renovated 1878 brownstone, just steps from the Marcus Garvey Memorial Park in the historic community of Mount Morris Park, Harlem, New York.
E-mail: JMendel760@aol.com *Web site:* urbanjem.com

HARTSDALE

Krogh's Nest B&B
4 Hillcrest Rd, 10530
914-946-3479
Claudia & Paul Krogh
All year

75-B&B
2 rooms, 2 pb
AmEx,
C-yes/S-ltd/P-no/H-ltd

Full breakfast
Sitting room, hammock, lawn
swing, picnic table

100 year old home on hillside acre with country atmosphere. Walk to 10 restaurants and train. 21 rail miles to NY City.

HIGHLAND

Highland Manor B&B
PO Box 1305, 12528
914-691-9080 Fax: 914-691-9080
Joan Garcia & Anthony Garcia
All year

85-115-B&B
4 rooms, 4 pb
Most CC, ●
C-ltd/S-ltd/P-no/H-yes
Spanish

Full breakfast
Snacks
Sitting room, library,
Jacuzzis, swimming pool,
suites, fireplace, cable TV

Quiet, pleasant, comfortable accommodations. Located on 3.5 acres of woodlands. Warm & friendly atmosphere, where gracious hospitality awaits you.
E-mail: ajg1305@aol.com *Web site:* bbonline.com/ny/highland/

HILLSDALE

Swiss Hutte Country Inn
PO Box 357, 12529
518-325-3333
Mr.& Mrs. Gert, Cindy Alper
April 15-March

110-200-EP/MAP
16 rooms, 16 pb
Visa, MC, *Rated*
C-yes/S-yes/P-yes/H-yes
German

Full breakfast with MAP plan
Restaurant, bar service
Vegetarian dishes, in-room
phones, parlor room, tennis,
pool, skiing

Swiss chef & owner. Nestled in hidden wooded valley. French continental decor. Indoor/outdoor garden dining, banquets, conference facilities. Restaurant renovated.
E-mail: 8057@msn.com *Web site:* swisshutte.com

HUNTER

Greene Mountain View Inn
S Main Street, 12485
518-589-9886 Fax: 518-589-5886
Glenn & Donna Weyant
All year

75-150-B&B
12 rooms, 12 pb
Most CC,
C-yes/S-yes/P-no/H-no

Continental plus breakfast
Restaurant, bar
Sitting room, fireplace, cable
TV, game room, Newly
renovated 3rd flr.

Quaint B&B nestled on 7 acres; mountainous views & immaculate accommodations. Relaxing atmosphere. Each cozy room is beautifully decorated with special amenities, priv. baths *E-mail:* gweyant@ix.netcom.com *Web site:* greenemountainviewinn.com

Washington Irvin Lodge
Rt 23A Box 675, 12442
518-589-5560 Fax: 518-589-5775
Stefania Jozic
All year

90-145-B&B
20 rooms, 7 pb
Visa, MC, AmEx, •
C-yes/S-yes/P-no/H-no
Serbo-Croatian

Full breakfast
Restaurant on premises
Sitting room, TV, tennis
courts, pool, near slopes,
cross country skiing

A classic Catskills country inn built in 1890. Accommodations are homey and comfortable. A warm, informal atmosphere makes every guest feel welcome.
Web site: washingtonirving.com

HYDE PARK

Costello's Guest House
21 Main St, 12538
914-229-2559
Patsy Newman Costello
All year

45-65-EP
2 rooms
C-yes/S-no/P-no/H-no

Close to F.D. Roosevelt,
home & library, Culinary
Institute of America

Home built in 1867. Listed on National Register of Historic Places. Comfortable, A/C guest rooms. *E-mail:* patsyc97@aol.com *Web site:* members.aol.com/patsyc97/index.html

Saltbox B&B, The
255 Ruskey Ln, 12538
914-266-3196
Sue De Lorenzo
April thru Dec.

75-100-B&B
2 rooms, 1 pb
C-ltd/S-no/P-no/H-no

Full breakfast
Snacks
Inground swimming pool,
sitting room,
colleges/wineries nearby

Featuring hospitality & quaint country charm in an 1840 "Saltbox"; low beamed ceilings, fireplaces, high post beds, period antiques. Convenient to historic mansions, antique shops.

Willows B&B, The
53 Travis Rd, 12538
914-471-6115
Lisa & Lee Fraitag
All year

80-90-B&B
2 rooms
C-ltd/S-ltd/P-no/H-no

Full breakfast
Snacks
Sitting room, library,
fireplace, cable TV

Country farmhouse from 1765 where you will be indulged by a Culinary Institute of America graduate who makes homemade products such as jams, breads, sausages, soaps, honey. Even the flour is homeground. *E-mail:* willowsbandb@compuserve.com
Web site: pojonews.com/willows

ITHACA ─────────────────────────────────

Edge of Thyme B&B, The	70-135-B&B	Full breakfast
PO Box 48, 13743	Most CC, *Rated*, •	High tea by appointment
607-659-5155 Fax: 607-659-5155	C-yes/S-no/P-no/H-no	Sitting rms w/fireplaces,
800-722-7365		piano, indoor games, lawn
Frank and Eva Mae Musgrave		games, gift shoppe
All year		

Gracious Georgian home, antiques, gardens, arbor, leaded glass windowed porch. Finger Lakes, Cornell, Ithaca College, Watkins Glen, Corning, wineries nearby.
Web site: edgeofthyme.baka.com

Hound & Hare B&B, The	85-125-B&B	Full gourmet breakfast
1031 Hanshaw Rd, 14850	5 rooms, 4 pb	Afternoon tea, snacks
607-257-2821 Fax: 607-257-3121	Most CC, *Rated*	Sitting room, library,
800-652-2821	C-yes/S-no/P-no/H-no	bicycles, Jacuzzi, cable,
Zetta Sprole		suites, fireplaces,
All year		

White brick Colonial built on land given to my forbears by General George Washington for service in Revolutionary War. A romantic fantasy filled with antiques & heirlooms
E-mail: ZSprole@clarityconnect.com Web site: wordpro.com/hound&hare/

Log Country Inn B&B	55-85-B&B	Full breakfast
PO Box 581, 14851	5 rooms, 3 pb	Afternoon tea
607-589-4771 Fax: 607-589-6151	Most CC, *Rated*, •	Sitting room, library, sauna,
800-274-4771	C-yes/S-no/P-yes/H-no	family friendly facility
Wanda Grunberg	Polish, Russian	
All year		

Enjoy Wanda's blintzes & Russian pancakes. Rest in cozy rooms furnished with custom made furniture. Relax in a double Jacuzzi in your private suite or at the fireplace in the living room. E-mail: wanda@logtv.com Web site: logtv.com/inn

Rose Inn	120-180-B&B	Full breakfast
PO Box 6576, 14851	16 rooms, 16 pb	Gourmet dinner by
607-533-7905 Fax: 607-533-7908	AmEx, *Rated*, •	reservation
Charles & Sherry Rosemann	C-ltd/S-no/P-no/H-no	Antique shop, parlor, piano,
All year	German, Spanish	bikes, Jacuzzis, garden
		w/wedding chapel

The inn has a non-smoking Jazz Club with a-la-carte dinner on Fri. & Sat. night April-Dec. Conference facility in restored 1850s Carriage House for 60 people. E-mail: roseinn@ clarityconnect.com Web site: roseinn.com/

JAY ─────────────────────────────────

Book & Blanket B&B	55-75-B&B	Full breakfast
PO Box 164, 12941	3 rooms, 1 pb	Afternoon tea—request
518-946-8323	C-yes/S-no/P-no/H-no	Sitting room, library,
Kathy/Fred/Sam &		fireplace, porch swing,
Daisy(Hound) All year		piano, village green

1850s Greek Revival near Lake Placid. Picturesque Adirondack hamlet with village green & swimming hole. Bedrooms honor famous authors. Resident Basset Hound
Web site: theadirondacks.com/bookandblanket/

KEENE VALLEY ─────────────────────────────────

Trail's End Inn	75-200-B&B	Full breakfast
HCI Box 103, 12943	12 rooms, 8 pb	Snacks, lunch
518-576-9860 Fax: 518-576-9235	Visa, MC, AmEx, •	Sitting room, library,
800-281-9860	C-yes/S-no/P-ltd/H-no	Jacuzzis, suites, fireplaces,
Jenny & Curt Borchardt		cable TV
All year		

Secluded 1902 lodge & cottages in the Adirondack mountains; clawfoot tubs, patchwork quilts, wood floors, fireplaces; hike, bike ski; visit Lake Pacid Olympic sites. Ask us to recommend a hike. E-mail: borchardt@kvvi.net Web site: trailsendinn.com

KINGSTON

Rondout B&B	85-115-B&B	Full breakfast
88 W Chester St, 12401	4 rooms, 2 pb	Snacks
914-331-8144 Fax: 914-331-9049	Visa, MC, AmEx, •	Sitting room, piano, library,
Adele & Ralph Calcavecchio	C-yes/S-ltd	in-room A/C, glassed-in
All year	Some Italian & French	porch, garden

Art, antiques, and light-filled 1906 spacious house near the Hudson River with gardens and woods. Near buses, trains, airports. Glassed in porch with rattan.   E-mail: calcave@ibm.net
Web site: pojonews.com/rondout

LAKE GEORGE

Lamplight Inn, The	95-225-B&B	Full breakfast
PO Box 70, 12846	10 rooms, 10 pb	Complimentary tea & coffee
518-696-5294 Fax: 518-696-5256	Visa, MC, AmEx,	Sitting rm. w/fireplaces,
800-262-4668	*Rated*, •	porch with swing, gardens,
Gene & Linda Merlino	C-ltd/S-ltd/P-no/H-ltd	lake swimming, Jacuzzi
All year		

Romantic 1890 Victorian, 5 fireplaced bedrooms, antiques, comfortable atmosphere. Spacious sun porch breakfast room. Jacuzzi/fireplace bedrooms. Honeymoon packages. New chef for dinner. OUR 1992 INN OF THE YEAR!   E-mail: lamp@netheaven.com
Web site: lamplightinn.com

LAKE PLACID

Interlaken Inn	140-210-MAP	Full breakfast
15 Interlaken Ave, 12946	11 rooms, 11 pb	Dinner incl, rest., bar
518-523-3180 Fax: 518-523-0117	Visa, MC, *Rated*, •	Comp. wine, high tea, sitting
800-428-4369	C-ltd/S-yes/P-no/H-no	room, croquet, lake
Roy & Carol Johnson		swimming, Jacuzzi
Exc. April & November		

Adirondack inn; heart of Olympic country; quiet setting-half block from Main St. between Mirror Lake & Lake Placid. Balconies. Great food!   E-mail: interlkn@northnet.org
Web site: Innbook.com/inns/inter/index.html

South Meadow Farm Lodge	70-90-B&B	Full breakfast
HCR 1, Box 44 Cascade, 12946	5 rooms	Trail lunch, farm dinner
518-523-9369 Fax: 515-523-8749	Visa, MC,	Comp. hot cider (winter),
800-523-9369	C-yes/S-yes/P-no/H-no	sitting room, piano,
Tony & Nancy Corwin		swimming pond
All year		

Enjoy the Olympic cross-country ski trails that cross our small farm, the view, our fireplace, and home-grown meals.   E-mail: tcorwin@aol.com *Web site:* southmeadow.com

LOCKPORT

Hambleton B&B	50-85-B&B	Continental breakfast
130 Pine St, 14094	3 rooms, 3 pb	Snacks
716-439-9507	Visa, MC, •	Sitting room, private baths all
716-634-3650	C-ltd/S-ltd/P-no/H-no	rooms, air conditioning
Hambleton Family		
All year		

Gracious, historic city home where Lockport carriage maker resided in the 1850s. Each room a delicate blending of the past and present. Walk to city's main street.

LOCKPORT/NIAGARA FALLS

Maplehurst B&B	60-75-B&B	Full breakfast
4427 Ridge Rd, 14094	4 rooms, 3 pb	Afternoon tea, snacks
716-434-3502	*Rated*, •	Sitting room, cable TV,
Mark & Peggy Herbst	C-ltd/S-ltd/P-no/H-no	accommodate business
All year	Some German	travelers

Historic, spacious, antique filled country bed & breakfast located minutes from world famous scenic and historic sites. Large comfortable guest rooms tastefully decorated. Superb breakfasts. Warmth and serenity exude this place. E-mail: maplehurst@webtv.net

Centerport Harbor B&B, Long Island, NY

LONG EDDY

Rolling Marble Guest House
PO Box 33, 12760
914-887-6016
Karen Gibbons & Peter Reich
Memorial Day-Labor Day

75-80-B&B
5 rooms, 0 pb
Visa, MC,
C-yes/S-ltd/P-no/H-no

Full breakfast
Snacks
Sitting room, bicycles, use of
canoes

Enjoy a magical atmosphere where each room is special, breakfasts bountiful, and beauty abounds. Our sundappled paths lead to a stone beach and the pristine waters of the Delaware River. Web site: obs-us.com/obs/english/books/chesler/babima/bnb/nyb271.htm

LONG ISLAND

Centerport Harbor B&B
129 Centershore Rd, 11721
516-754-1730
Fax: 516-754-6241
Jean & Jim Vavrina
All year

179-195-B&B
1 rooms, 1 pb
Visa, MC, •
C-yes/S-no/P-no/H-no

Full breakfast
In-room tea kettle, beverages
Cable TV, waterfront, private
beach, private balcony

Romantic accommodation overlooking scenic harbor, private beach and dock. Gourmet breakfast served in-room or on poolside patio. Many excellent restaurants & shops within three mile radius. E-mail: centerport.hrbr.bnb@eudoramail.com

MILLBROOK

Parc Brook Farms
RR1 Box 99, 12545
914-677-5950
Fax: 914-677-5528
M. Heidi Otto
All year

110-375-B&B
21 rooms, 17 pb
Visa, MC, *Rated*, •
C-ltd/S-ltd/P-yes/H-ltd
Spanish, French

Full breakfast
Aftn. tea, snacks, wine
Library, sitting room, tennis,
bicycles, suites, VCRs

European style country estate located 1½ hours from NYC. Open for weddings, private parties, corporate events, wellness spa. E-mail: parcbrook@cybermax.net
Web site: parcbrook.com

MUMFORD

Genesee Country Inn, C1833
PO Box 340, 14511
716-538-2500 Fax: 716-538-4565
800-NY-STAYS
Glenda Barcklow
All year

85-145-B&B
12 rooms, 12 pb
Most CC, *Rated*, •
C-ltd/S-no/P-no/H-ltd

Full breakfast
Afternoon tea, snacks
Common rooms, fireplaces,
canopy beds, gift shop, A/C,
fly fishing, TVs

17-room 1833 stone mill specializing in hospitality and quiet, comfortable retreats. Unique natural setting—woods, gardens, waterfalls. E-mail: gbarcklow@aol.com
Web site: geneseecountryinn.com

NEW BERLIN

Preferred Manor, The
45 S Main St, 13411
607-847-6238 Fax: 607-847-9414
Julia A. King
All year

54-65-B&B
5 rooms, 1 pb
Visa, MC,
C-yes/S-no/P-no/H-no

Continental plus breakfast
Sitting room, fireplaces,
cable TV, accommodate
business travelers

Built in 1831, this spacious stone house was entered in 1974 on the National Register of Historic Places. The Manor offers you the opportunity to enjoy overnight relaxation and comfort in elegant surroundings.   E-mail: john.frisch@pminsco.com
Web site: preferredmanor.com

NEW PALTZ

Whispering Pines B&B
60 Cedar Hill Rd, 12440
914-687-2419
Celia & HD Seupel
All year

99-119-B&B
3 rooms, 3 pb
Visa, MC, Disc, •
C-ltd/S-no/P-no/H-no
German, French

Full breakfast
Afternoon tea
Sitting room, library, babysitting available, VCR, 2
rooms with Jacuzzis

Light filled B&B on 50 acres of woods; historic sightseeing, crafts, woodland-walking, fine dining, antiquing, biking, sun & snow fun.   E-mail: seupel@aol.com
Web site: whisperingpinesbandb.com

NEW YORK

Chelsea Pines Inn
317 W 14th St, 10014
212-929-1013 Fax: 212-620-5645
Jay Lesiger & Al Ridolfo
All year

89-149-B&B
23 rooms, 15 pb
Visa, MC, AmEx, Most
CC, •
S-yes/P-no/H-no
Spanish

Continental plus breakfast
Outdoor patio, greenhse., all
rms. have A/C, color, cable
TV, phone, refrig.

One of the most popular gay & lesbian inns in the city. Chelsea Pines is charmingly decorated with original vintage film posters from the Golden Age of Hollywood.
E-mail: cpiny@aol.com *Web site:* q-net.com/chelseapines

Cooper Mansion, The
396 Van Duzer St, 10304
718-273-1869 Fax: 718-273-1869
Susan Cooper
All year

50-150-B&B
8 rooms, 3 pb
Visa, MC, AmEx, •
C-yes/S-ltd/P-ltd/H-no
Spanish

Continental breakfast
Sitting room, fireplace, cable
TV, conference facilities

The Inn is a comfortable home built in 1875 in the artist community of Stapleton, Staten Island. The inn has easy access to Manhattan and all New York airports. The rooms are appointed with antiques and four of our guest rooms have working fireplaces.

Gorham Hotel, The
136 W 55th St, 10019
212-245-1800 Fax: 212-582-8332
800-735-0710
Mr. David Sabo
All year

215-475-EP
139 rooms, 139 pb
Visa, MC, AmEx,
C-yes/S-yes/P-no/H-yes

Bar & restaurant serves all
meals
Sittng room, Jacuzzis, suites,
cable TV, fitness room

Charming European boutique hotel near Rockefeller Center, 5th Ave and theater district. Large, newly decorated rooms, 3rd-floor breakfast room, and fitness center.   E-mail: reservations@gorhamhotel.com *Web site:* gorhamhotel.com/corp/index.html

Ranney-Crawford House
B&B
1097 Westminster W Rd, 05346
802-387-4150
800-731-5502
Arnie & Diane Glim
All year

100-120-B&B
4 rooms
Visa, MC, AmEx,
C-ltd/S-no/P-no/H-no

Full breakfast
Fireplace

An elegant c.1810 Federal brick colonial bed and breakfast, near Putney, Vermont, located on a scenic country road, offering full breakfast and beautifully appointed accommodations. Excellent cycling, skiing and cultural activities.   E-mail: arnyglim@zdnetmail.com
Web site: ranney-crawford.com

NEW YORK

Rose Hill Guest House
44 Rose Hill Ave, 10804
914-632-6464
Marilou Mayetta
All year

75-105-B&B
2 rooms
Rated, •
C-yes/S-yes/P-ltd/H-no

Continental plus breakfast
Complimentary wine, tea
Sitting room, library, VCR,
cable TV, bicycles

Beautiful Norman Rockwell home 20 min. from Manhattan or Greenwich. Enjoy "Big Apple" & country living in one. Horseback riding, golfing, sailing, etc
E-mail: rosehillguests@webtv.net

Westfield House
PO Box 505, 14787
716-326-6262
Betty & Jud Wilson
All year

75-85-B&B
7 rooms, 7 pb
Visa, MC, *Rated*, •
C-yes/S-no/P-no/H-yes

Full breakfast
Complimentary wine, snacks
Sitting room, bicycles,
needlework shop, small
meeting facilities

Elegant red brick Gothic Revival inn amid maples overlooking vineyards. Near antique shops, recreational & cultural activities

NEW YORK CITY

English B&B at the Manor
126 Vanderbilt Ave, 10304
718-273-7365 Fax: 718-273-7365
Karen T. Stanbrook
All year

55-65-B&B/AP
4 rooms, 4 pb
Visa, MC, •
C-yes/S-ltd/P-yes/H-no

Continental breakfast
Afternoon tea, snacks
Sitting room, library,
bicycles, fireplaces, cable
TV, conference facilities

The Stanbrook Manor is an 18th Century Gothic Tudor home. It was built by the legendary Cornelius Vanderbilt II for his family & friends. E-mail: ke396@aol.com *Web site:* nycbnb.com

---

Harbor House B&B, The
1 Hylan Blvd, 10305
718-876-0056 Fax: 718-983-7768
800-626-8096
Mervyn Rampaul
All year

79-150-B&B
11 rooms, 5 pb
Visa, MC, Disc, *Rated*,
•
C-ltd/S-no/P-ltd/H-ltd

Continental plus breakfast
Complimentary wine,
afternoon tea
Sitting room, suites,
fireplaces, accommodate
business travelers

This 110 year old Victorian mansion on the New York Harbor commands an unobstructed panorama of the New York City skyline including the Statue of Liberty; quiet country-like atmosphere. E-mail: skyline@erols.com *Web site:* nyharborhouse.com

---

Inn on 23rd, The
131 W 23rd St, 10011
212-463-0330 Fax: 212-463-0302
877-387-2323
Annette Fisherman
All year

150-250-B&B
4 rooms, 4 pb
Visa, MC, AmEx, *Rated*
C-yes/S-no/P-no/H-ltd

Continental plus breakfast
Sitting room, library, cable
TV, suites, fax, copy
machine, hair dryers

The Inn on 23rd is a classic 5 story 19th century townhouse which has been renovated into a B&B and the home of your host Annette Fisherman. Modern conveniences such as private bathrooms, televisions, two line room phones, and a 5 story elevator.
E-mail: InnOn23rd@aol.com

NEWBURGH

Morgan House B&B
12 Powelton Rd, 12550
914-561-0326
Pat & Richard Morgan
All year

85-B&B
2 rooms
Visa, MC, AmEx, •
C-ltd/S-ltd/P-ltd/H-no

Full breakfast
Snacks, complimentary wine
Sitting room, library, bikes,
cable TV

We serve a lovely candlelight breakfast featuring gourmet dishes, coffees & teas. Beds are turned down and little sleep notes are tucked near pillows. E-mail: morganhouse@ibm.net
Web site: hudval.com/morgan

NIAGARA FALLS

Asa Ransom House
10529 Main St, 14031
716-759-2315 Fax: 716-759-2791
Robert Lenz, Judy Lenz
All year exc. Jan.

95-155-B&B
9 rooms, 9 pb
Visa, MC, Disc, *Rated*,
•
C-ltd/S-ltd/P-no/H-ltd

Full breakfast
Dinner (except Mon), bar,
snacks
Sitting room, library, most
rooms with fireplaces, herb
garden, bicycles

Village inn furnished with antiques, period reproductions; gift shop, herb garden, regional dishes, homemade breads & desserts. Rehearsal dinners, herb lecture/luncheons. E-mail: innfo@asaransom.com Web site: asaransom.com

Cameo Inn & Cameo Manor
3881 Lower River Rd, 14174
716-745-3034 Fax: 716-745-7444
Greg & Carolyn Fisher
All year

65-130-B&B
8 rooms, 4 pb
Visa, MC, Disc, *Rated*,
•
C-ltd/S-no/P-no/H-no

Full breakfast
Antiquing, fishing, bicycling,
cross-country ski, relax by
river, library

Choose Victorian elegance in a romantic river setting or a secluded English manor, both just minutes from Niagara Falls. A/C in guestrooms E-mail: cameoinn@juno.com Web site: cameoinn.com

Country Club Inn, The
5170 Lewiston Road, 14092
716-285-4869 Fax: 716-285-5614
Barbara Ann Oliver
All year

80-110-B&B
3 rooms, 3 pb
•
C-ltd/S-no/P-ltd/H-no

Full breakfast
Library, sitting room,
fireplaces, cable TV, self-
service ice cream parlor

Three beautifully furnished rooms. Great room with pool table, games and wood-burning fireplace. Patio overlooks golf course. Built in 1976, lovingly updated in 1991. Breakfast at guests convenience. E-mail: ctyclubinn@ccnn.net Web site: countryclubinn.com

Manchester House
653 Main St, 14301
716-285-5717 Fax: 716-282-2144
800-489-3009
Lis & Carl Slenk   All year

70-100-B&B
3 rooms, 3 pb
Visa, MC, *Rated*
C-yes/S-no/P-no/H-no
German

Full breakfast
Sitting room, Health club
membership, during stay
available

Award-winning renovated former doctor's office and residence provides a comfortable, convenient home for your visit. Conf. facilities across street. Ample off-street parking E-mail: carl@manchesterhouse.com Web site: manchesterhouse.com

Red Coach Inn, The
2 Buffalo Ave, 14303
716-282-1459 Fax: 716-282-2650
800-282-1459
Thomas Reese   All year

69-199-B&B
10 rooms, 10 pb
Most CC, *Rated*, •
C-ltd/S-no/P-no/H-ltd

Continental plus breakfast
Lunch, dinner (fee), snacks
Restuarant, bar service,
sitting room, library,
Jacuzzis, suites

Chosen as a Top Ten Weekend Getaway Destination by Fortune magazine. Overlooking the breathtaking Upper Rapids and just steps away from the American Falls, the Inn is Niagara's most distinctive historic structure with its English Tudor exterior. E-mail: redcoach@wnyip.net Web site: redcoach.com

NORTH RIVER

Highwinds Inn
Barton Mines Rd, 12856
518-251-3760 Fax: 518-251-5701
800-241-1923
Holly Currier
All year

75-184-B&B/MAP
4 rooms, 4 pb
Visa, MC, Disc, •
C-ltd/S-no/H-no
French

Full breakfast
Dinner available (fee)
Snacks, restaurant, sitting
room, library, bicycles,
tennis court

An intimate country inn on 1600 private acres. Spectacular views from all rooms and glassed-in dining porch. Four season destination. Winter, 20k cross country trails connect with Garnet Hill's 54k. E-mail: highwinds@barton.com Web site: highwindsinn.com

NORTHVILLE

Inn at the Bridge	75-90-B&B	Full breakfast
PO Box 450, 12134	6 rooms, 6 pb	Dinner
518-863-2240 Fax: 518-863-2717	Most CC,	Sitting room, bicycles, boat
888-245-8220	C-yes/S-no/P-no/H-yes	docks, beach, lake swimming
Lee & Dot Brenn All year		

A turn of the century Victorian home with wraparound porch overlooking the Great Sacandaga Lake and Adirondack Mountains. We serve a full country breakfast and also have dinner available. E-mail: innbridg@klink.net *Web site:* innbridge.klink.net

OLD CHATHAM

Old Chatham Sheep Inn	185-550-B&B	Full breakfast
99 Shaker Museum Rd, 12136	14 rooms, 14 pb	Afternoon tea, Sunday
518-794-9774 Fax: 518-794-9779	Most CC, *Rated*, •	brunch
George Shattuck III	C-yes/S-no/P-no/H-no	Sitting rooms, bikes, tennis
All year		courts, business facilities

The Old Chatham Sheepherding Company Inn is an antique filled 1790 manor house on 500 acres dotted with sheep. Luxurious lodging and exquisite dining. Two and a half hours from NYC and Boston. Three new suites. E-mail: inn@oldsheepinn.com *Web site:* oldsheepinn.com

OLD FORGE

Big Moose Inn	88-160-B&B	Cont'l. breakfast weekdays
1510 Big Moose Rd, 13331	16 rooms, 12 pb	All meals available
315-357-2042 Fax: 315-357-3423	Most CC, *Rated*	(weekends), bar
The Bennett Family	C-yes/S-yes/P-no/H-ltd	Sitting room, floating gazebo,
Exc. April, Nov-Dec 26		canoes, some rooms with
		fireplace

Casually elegant resort country in with award winning epicurean dining delights. Spectacular wine list. Complimentary lakeside deck dining. Floating gazebo. Canoes, paddle boat, kayak available to guests. E-mail: bigmoose@telenet.net *Web site:* bigmooseinn.com

OLIVEREA

Slide Mt. Forest House	50-90-B&B	Full breakfast
805 Oliverea Rd, 12410	21 rooms, 17 pb	Lunch & dinner avail. (fee)
914-254-5365	Visa, MC, Disc,	Restaurant, bar, pool, sitting
Ralph & Ursula Combe	C-yes/S-yes/P-no/H-no	room, hiking, tennis courts,
All year	German	fishing

Fresh air, nature & a touch of Old World charm await you at our German/American Catskill Mountains Inn. Congenial family atmosphere. E-mail: combe1@ibm.net

PINE BUSH

Milton Bull House, The	75-85-B&B	Full breakfast
1065 Route 302, 12566	2 rooms, 1 pb	Afternoon tea
914-361-4770	Visa, MC, *Rated*	Sitting room, swimming pool,
Graham & Ellen Jamison	C-ltd/S-no/P-no/H-no	fireplaces, accommodate
All year	French	business travelers

Come to a traditional bed and breakfast. Breakfast served in our elegant dining room; swimming in our pool; enjoy our historic home located near wineries, antique shops, golf courses, hiking trails and major highways. Web site: new-york-inns.com/bed-breakfast-new-york/milton/default.htm

PINE HILL

Birchcreek Inn	85-145-B&B	Full breakfast
Route 28, Box 323, 12465	7 rooms, 7 pb	Snacks, complimentary wine
914-254-5222 Fax: 914-254-5812	*Rated*, •	Sitting room, library, bikes,
Julie & Ron Odato	C-yes/S-ltd/P-ltd/H-no	tennis court, frplcs., cable TV
All year	Some Spanish	

A turn of the century country estate on 23 secluded acres in the heart of the Catskill Mountain Forest. Beautiful guest rooms, all with private baths. "A gem of an Inn"

Tumblin' Falls House B&B, Purling, NY

PITTSFORD

Oliver Loud's Inn
1474 Marsh Rd, 14534
716-248-5200
Fax: 716-248-9970
Vivienne Tellier
All year

135-175-B&B
8 rooms, 8 pb
Most CC, *Rated*, •
C-ltd/S-ltd/P-no/H-yes
French, Spanish

Continental plus breakfast
Restaurant, welcome tray
Comp. cocktails/dessert,
snacks, sitting room, jogging

English country-house charm & service in restored c.1810 stagecoach inn on banks of Historic Eric Canal. 12 minutes from downtown Rochester. E-mail: rchi@frontiernet.net *Web site:* frontiernet.net/~rchi

POUGHKEEPSIE

Inn at the Falls
50 Red Oaks Mill Rd, 12603
914-462-5770
Fax: 914-462-5943
800-344-1466
Arnold Sheer
All year

150-185-B&B
36 rooms, 36 pb
Rated, •
C-yes/S-yes/P-no/H-yes

Continental plus breakfast
Complimentary evening
snacks/port
Hiking, whirlpool tubs in all
suites, landscaped grounds,
swimming pool

Quiet country inn, well off the main highway. Glass-enclosed common area with fireplace. E-mail: innatfalls@aol.com *Web site:* innatthefalls.com

PRATTSBURGH

Feather Tick 'N Thyme
7661 Tuttle Rd, 14873
607-522-4113
Fax: 607-522-4651
Ruth and Deb Cody
All year

75-100-B&B
4 rooms, 2 pb
C-ltd/S-ltd/P-no/H-no

Full breakfast
Afternoon tea,
complimentary wine
Sitting room

An "unforgetable stop in Thyme." Country Victorian offers romantic getaway, luxurious furnishings, antiques, quiescent sleep, gracious hospitality, hiking, campfires and lawn games.

PURLING

Tumblin' Falls House B&B	75-150-B&B	Full breakfast
PO Box 281, 12473	5 rooms, 2 pb	Complimentary wine
518-622-3981 Fax: 518-622-3981	C-ltd/S-no/P-yes	Sitting room, bikes,
800-473-0519		fishing/swimming @ falls,
Linda and Hugh Curry		hiking/skiing/antiquing
All year		

Nestled in the hamlet of Purling, the clear cool waters of Shinglekill Falls have drawn visitors since the early 1800's. Hidden among the trees is Tumblin' Falls House, with an incomparable view.   E-mail: tfallsbb@francomm.com *Web site:* tumblinfalls.com

RENSSELAER

Tibbitt's House Inn	58-95-EP	Breakfast menu (fee)
100 Columbia Turnpike, 12144	5 rooms, 1 pb	Enclosed porch, garden,
518-472-1348	C-yes/S-yes/P-no/H-ltd	patio, maid service, one
Claire & Herbert Rufleth		apartment available
All year		

Comfortable, 135-year-old, antique-furnished farmhouse, 2 miles from Albany, State Museum, Hudson River, hiking/biking, old Dutch fort.

RHINEBECK

Lakehouse Inn	125-650-B&B	Full gourmet breakfast
Shelley Hill Rd, 12581	8 rooms, 8 pb	Afternoon appetizers
914-266-8093 Fax: 914-266-4051	Visa, MC, AmEx,	7-acre private lake,
Judy Kohler	*Rated*, •	swimming, boating, bass
All year	C-ltd/S-no/P-no/H-no	fishing

Circa 1898 country farmhouse on 6 separate and rolling acres with 2 fireplaces, Jacuzzi, ktichen and in ground pool for seasonal rental or weekend rental.   E-mail: judy@lakehouseinn.com *Web site:* lakehouseinn.com

Mansakenning Carriage	125-375-B&B	Full gourmet breakfast
House	7 rooms, 7 pb	Sitting room, library, Jacuzzi,
29 Ackert Hook Rd, 12572	C-ltd/S-ltd/P-ltd/H-yes	fireplaces, private satellite
914-876-3500 Fax: 914-876-6179		TV, phones
Michelle Dremann		
All year		

Historic hideaway featuring luxurious guest rooms filled with many amenities. Full gourmet breakfast delivered to your room. Close to area attractions. Private balconies, air conditioning.

Veranda House B&B	90-130-B&B	Full gourmet breakfast
82 Montgomery St, 12572	4 rooms, 4 pb	Breakfast on terrace
914-876-4133 Fax: 914-876-4133	C-yes/S-no/P-no/H-no	Sitting room, library, A/C,
Linda & Ward Stanley		concierge service, veranda
All year		with wicker

Charming 1845 Federal house located in historic Hudson Valley. Restaurants, fairs, antiques. Gourmet breakfasts, complimentary wine & cheese Saturday evenings. Phones in rooms.   E-mail: veranda82@aol.com *Web site:* verandahouse.com

ROCHESTER

428 Mt. Vernon—A B&B Inn	90-110-B&B	Full breakfast from menu
428 Mt Vernon Ave, 14620	7 rooms, 7 pb	Afternoon tea
716-271-0792 Fax: 716-271-0946	Most CC, *Rated*, •	Sitting room, library TV,
800-836-3159	C-yes/S-ltd/P-no	games, refrigerator
Philip & Claire Lanzatella		
All year		

Elegant estate home on two wooded acres at the entrance to historic Highland Park. All seven antique-filled rooms have phones, cable TV, and private baths.

ROCHESTER

Country Corner, The	716-964-9935
317 Redman Rd, 14464	All year

65-80-B&B	Full breakfast
4 rooms, 2 pb	Snacks
Visa, MC,	Sitting room, library, antique
C-ltd/S-no/P-no/H-ltd	shop onsite in season

Located in a serene country setting convenient to Lake Ontario beaches and Rochester. Perfect environment for relaxing and reading.   E-mail: linda@thecountrycorner.com
Web site: thecountrycorner.com

Dartmouth House B&B Inn	95-110-B&B	Full candlelit breakfast
215 Dartmouth St, 14607	4 rooms, 4 pb	Bottomless cookie jar
716-271-7872	Most CC, *Rated*, •	Library, porches, organ,
Fax: 716-473-0778	C-ltd/S-no/P-no/H-no	grand piano, A/C, movies,
Ellie & Bill Klein		TV/VCRs & phones in rooms
All year		

Quiet, spacious Tudor in city's cultural district. Architecturally-fascinating, residential neighborhood. Hosts are well traveled & love people. Great breakfasts! Antiques. Walk to museums.   E-mail: stay@dartmouthhouse.com Web site: dartmouthhouse.com

---

Rosewood B&B	69-89-B&B	Full gourmet breakfast
68 Geddes St, 14470	4 rooms, 1 pb	Snacks
716-638-6186	Most CC, •	Sitt. rm., lib., bikes,
Fax: 716-638-7568	S-no/P-no/H-no	fireplaces, cable TV, antique
Karen Cook & Roy Nichols		& gift shop
All year		

Rosewood offers Victorian elegance for business or pleasure. Beautiful antique furnishings mingled with modern amenities, lovely gardens, just blocks from historic Erie Canal
E-mail: rosewdbnb@aol.com

Serenity, A B&B	70-225-B&B	Full breakfast
2284 Dutch Hollow Rd, 14414	5 rooms, 3 pb	Afternoon tea, snacks
716-226-9252	Most CC, *Rated*, •	Sitting room, Jacuzzis, suites,
Fax: 716-226-6274	S-no/P-no/H-no	fireplaces, outdoor spa
Steve & Kimberle Miller		
All year		

"Comfortably Posh", This newly renovated 1823 7000 sq ft manor is splended for a romantic getaway or relaxing retreat. 10 acres with walking trails, video library, outdoor spa, careful attention to detail.   E-mail: serenity1@prodigy.net Web site: Serenitybandb.com

---

Woods Edge	75-125-B&B	Full breakfast
PO Box 444, 14450	•	Fireplace, AC
716-223-8877 Fax: 716-223-5508	C-ltd/S-no/P-no/H-no	
Betty Kinsman		
All year		

You will find a warm welcome at Woods Edge B&B. We share our secluded site with white-tailed deer, red foxes, raccoons, wood thrushes and a forest of fragrant pines.   E-mail:
bkinsman1@aol.com Web site: home.eznet.net/~ekinsman/bb/woodsedge.htm

---

ROME

Maplecrest B&B	70-75-B&B	Full gourmet breakfast
6480 Williams Rd, 13440	3 rooms, 1 pb	Beverage on arrival
315-337-0070	*Rated*, •	Refrig. use, central A/C,
Diane Saladino	C-ltd/S-no/P-no/H-no	sitting room, grill, picnic
All year	Italian	facilities

Modern split-level home. Close to historic locations. Adirondack foliage, lakes, & skiing. Near Griffis Business Park. Complimentary beverage at restaurant.

SARATOGA

Agape Farm B&B	65-150-B&B	Full breakfast
4894 Rt 9 N, 12822	6 rooms, 6 pb	Snacks
518-654-7777 Fax: 518-654-7777	Visa, MC, Disc,	Gardens, trout stream, farm
Fred & Sigrid Koch	C-yes/S-no/P-no/H-yes	animals, dogs, cats, family
All year		friendly facility

Enjoy an old farm atmosphere in our large country home. Six guest rooms, one handicapped equipped. Convenient to area attractions
Web site: travelguides.com/home/agape_farm/

Country Life B&B	75-175-B&B	Full breakfast on weekends
67 Tabor Rd, 12834	3 rooms, 1 pb	Continental plus breakfast
518-692-7203 Fax: 518-692-9203	*Rated*, •	weekdays
888-692-7203	C-yes/S-no/P-no/H-no	Complimentary wine, Patio,
Richard & Wendy Duvall	Spanish, German,	118 acres, color TV
All year	French	

Beautifully restored 1829 farmhouse near Saratoga, skiing, fishing, hiking museums, shopping. Seasonal rates apply. We have a beautiful location for weddings & fireworks available too. E-mail: R_WDUVALL@hotmail.com *Web site:* bbonline.com/ny/countrylife/

SARATOGA SPRINGS

Adelphi Hotel	110-340-B&B	Continental breakfast
365 Broadway, 12866	20 rooms, 20 pb	Summer dinners, bar
518-587-4688 Fax: 518-587-0851	Visa, MC, AmEx,	Entertainment, sitting room,
Gregg Siefker, Sheila Parkert	*Rated*, •	library, piano, swimming
May-Nov.	C-yes/S-yes/P-no/H-no	pool

Charming accommodations. Opulently restored high Victorian hotel located in the historic district of the renowned resort and spa of Saratoga Springs. Web site: adelphihotel.com

Apple Tree B&B	75-199-B&B	Full breakfast
49 West High St, 12020	4 rooms, 4 pb	Sitting room, TV/VCR, tennis
518-885-1113 Fax: 518-885-9758	Visa, MC, AmEx,	court, whirlpool tub
Dolores & James Taisey	*Rated*, •	
All year	C-ltd/S-no/P-no/H-no	

Second Empire Victorian with romantic ambience. Close to SPAC, Spa Park & Saratoga attractions. Delightful breakfast, private baths with whirlpool. E-mail: mail@appletreebb.com *Web site:* appletreebb.com

Chestnut Tree Inn	85-110/up-B&B	Continental plus breakfast
9 Whitney Pl, 12866	10 rooms, 7 pb	Afternoon tea, lemonade
518-587-8681	Visa, MC, •	Comp. wine, snacks, sitting
888-CHES-NUT	C-ltd/S-no/P-no/H-no	room, antiques, porch, spas
Cathleen & Bruce DeLuke		
Mid-April-Nov.		

Restored turn-of-the-century guest house. Walk to racetrack & downtown. Furnished with antiques; large wicker porch. Soft drinks, coffee, fruit always available
Web site: travelguides.com/home/chestnut_tree/

Lombardi Farm B&B	100-150-B&B	4-course breakfast
41 Locust Grove Rd, 12866	4 rooms, 4 pb	Afternoon tea, snacks
518-587-2074	*Rated*, •	Sitting room, hot tubs,
Dr. & Mrs. Vincent Lombardi	C-yes/S-yes/P-no/H-yes	exercise machine, national
All year		museum

Informal friendly gentleman's farm with beauty, warmth, privacy, peace. Four-course heart-smart gourmet breakfast. Near famous mineral baths/massage. Hot tub/Jacuzzi in Florida Room.

SARATOGA SPRINGS

Mansion, The	95-250-B&B	Full gourmet breakfast
801 Rd 29 Box 77, 12863	7 rooms, 7 pb	Aftnernoon tea, snacks, wine
518-885-1607 Fax: 518-885-6753	*Rated*	Bar service, sitting room,
Louise V. Brown	C-ltd/S-no/P-no/H-no	library, tennis courts, hot
All year		tubs, sauna, pool

Elegant, romantic 1866 Victorian Italianate mansion. Gracious guest rooms with private baths gourmet breakfast. Spacious grounds, gardens & porches. 7 miles west of Saratoga Springs on Route 29. Web site: thesaratogamansion.com

Six Sisters B&B	85-300-B&B	Full gourmet breakfast
149 Union Ave, 12866	4 rooms, 4 pb	Complimentary beverages
518-583-1173 Fax: 518-587-2470	Visa, MC, AmEx,	Sitting room, porch, A/C,
Kate Benton & Steve Ramirez	*Rated*, •	rooms have TV & refrig.,
All year	C-ltd/S-no/P-no	mineral bath/massage

Beautifully appointed 1880 Victorian, recommended by Gourmet, NY Times, & McCall's.
E-mail: stay@sixsistersbandb.com *Web site:* sixsistersbandb.com

Union Gables B&B	110-290-B&B	Continental plus breakfast
55 Union Ave, 12866	12 rooms, 12 pb	Hot tub outdoors, tennis,
518-584-1558 Fax: 518-583-0649	Visa, MC, AmEx, *Rated*	telephones, TVs, A/C, sitting
800-398-1558	C-yes/S-ltd/P-yes/H-no	room, bicycles
Jody Roohan		
All year		

Restored turn of the century Queen Ann Victorian. Gigantic front porch. Great downtown location; walk to everything. Small meetings welcome. *E-mail:* information@uniongables.com
Web site: uniongables.com

Westchester House B&B, The	90-275-B&B	Continental breakfast
102 Lincoln Ave, 12866	7 rooms, 7 pb	Complimentary beverages
518-587-7613	Visa, MC, AmEx,	Sitting room, library,
800-581-7613	*Rated*, •	wraparound porch, piano,
Bob & Stephanie Melvin	C-ltd/S-ltd/P-no/H-no	A/C, games
All year	French, German	

Gracious Queen Anne Victorian Inn surrounded by old fashioned gardens. Elegant bedrooms combine old world ambiance with up to date comforts. Web site: westchester-bb.saratoga.ny.us

SAUGERTIES

Bluestone Country Manor B&B	79-125-B&B	Full breakfast
PO Box 144, 12490	4 rooms, 2 pb	Afternoon tea
914-246-3060	Visa, MC, •	Sitting room, library, one
John. K. Lynch	C-ltd/S-no/P-ltd/H-no	room with Jacuzzi
All year	Spanish, Portuguese	

Brick "Manor House" on a hilltop where the Catskills meet the Hudson has large comfortable rooms and magnificent mountain views. *E-mail:* b&bblue@netstep.net
Web site: ulster.net/~bnbblue

SKANEATELES

Arbour House Inn	95-160-B&B	Continental plus breakfast
24 East St, 13152	5 rooms, 5 pb	Snacks
315-685-8966 Fax: 315-685-6104	Visa, MC, •	Sitting room, Jacuzzis, suites,
888-234-4558	C-ltd/S-no/P-no/H-ltd	fireplace, cable TV
Renee Valentine & Nancy Shaver		
All year		

In the heart of historic Skaneateles Village. C.1850 Inn elegantly furnished in antiques.
E-mail: arborh5632@aol.com *Web site:* arborhouseinn.com

SODUS BAY

Bonnie Castle Farm B&B	85-160-B&B	Full breakfast
PO Box 188, 14590	8 rooms, 8 pb	Hot tubs, sitting room,
315-587-2273 Fax: 315-587-4003	Most CC, *Rated*, •	library, A/C, swimming,
800-587-4006	C-yes/S-no/P-no/H-no	fishing, boating
Eric & Georgia Pendleton		
All year		

"Turn of the Century" waterfront home on Sodus Bay, Northern Finger Lakes, between Rochester & Syracuse. Waterfront location. Near Renaissance Festival. Call for update on prices. Web site: virtualcities.com/ons/ny/r/nyr9701.htm

SOUTHAMPTON

Mainstay Bed & Breakfast	125-395-B&B	Continental breakfast
579 Hill St, 11968	8 rooms, 5 pb	Restaurant nearby
516-283-4375 Fax: 516-287-6240	Most CC, *Rated*	Sitting room, bikes, tennis
Elizabeth Main	C-ltd/S-no/P-no/H-no	court, swimming pool
All year		

1870s Colonial guest house, all antique iron beds & country pine furniture. Minutes to ocean beaches, town and shopping. E-mail: elizmain@hamptons.com
Web site: hamptons.com/mainstay

SOUTHOLD

Goose Creek Guesthouse	95-100-B&B	Full country breakfast
Box 377, 11971	3 rooms, 1 pb	Tea, snacks
516-765-3356	•	Homegrown vegetables &,
Mary Mooney-Getoff	C-yes/S-no/P-ltd/H-no	fruit, sitting room, library
All year	Spanish	

Pre-Civil War farmhouse, secluded in 7 acres of woods, near golf, beaches and ferries. Gourmet country breakfasts, garden-fresh food Web site: northfork.com/goosecreek/

ST. JOHNSVILLE

INn by the Mill	70-125-B&B	Continental plus breakfast
1679 Mill Rd, 13452	5 rooms, 4 pb	Afternoon tea, snacks
518-568-2388 Fax: 518-568-2388	Visa, MC, Disc, *Rated*	Sitting room, library,
Ron and Judith Hezel	C-ltd/S-no/P-no/H-no	fireplaces, bicycles, waterfall,
5/1-11/1;winter holidays		gardens

Historical 1835 stone grist mill and miller's home, flower & watergardens. Elegant rooms, private baths. 1888 cottage overlooking gorge and waterfalls, museum-like emporium ice cream parlor. E-mail: inbymill@telenet.net Web site: innbythemill.com

SUGAR LOAF

Sugar Loaf Village B&B	120-130-B&B	Continental plus breakfast
PO Box 23, 10981	2 rooms, 2 pb	Snacks, complimentary wine
914-469-2717	*Rated*	Jet tubs, cable TV, central
Maxine Charles	C-ltd/S-no/P-no/H-no	A/C, walk to shops and fine
All year		restaurants

Quientessential romantic getaway, charming accommodations, quaint craft village, hearty country fare, clean fresh air, flowers, birds, cheery fireplaces, sunny skylights, cozy down comforters. You won't believe you're just 53 miles from New York City!

SYRACUSE

B&B Wellington	75-125-B&B	Full breakfast weekends
707 Danforth St, 13208	5 rooms, 5 pb	Continental plus wkdays
315-474-3641 Fax: 315-474-2557	Most CC, •	Aftn. tea, sitting room, suites,
800-724-5006	C-ltd/S-no/P-no/H-no	frplcs., cable, fax, copier,
Wendy Wilber & Ray Borg		porches
All year		

Nationally recognized historic 1914 brick & stucco Tudor-style home. Contains rich wood interiors, tiled fireplaces, & cozy porches. E-mail: bbw@ix.netcom.com
Web site: flbba.com/wellington

SYRACUSE

Dickenson House on James
1504 James St, 13203
315-423-4777 Fax: 315-425-1965
888-423-4777
Pam & Ed Kopiel
All year

95-350-B&B
5 rooms, 5 pb
Most CC, *Rated*, •
C-ltd/S-no/P-no/H-ltd

Full breakfast
Afternoon tea, snacks, comp.
wine
Sitting room, library,
bicycles, tennis court,
Jacuzzi, fireplaces, cable TV

Retreat to a haven of old world elegance & hospitality with all the modern conveniences.
Breakfast will delight your senses. Guest kitchen filled with your favorites, included in
lodging. Web site: dreamscape.com/dickensonhouse

Hobbit Hollow B&B
3061 West Lake Rd, 13152
315-685-2791 Fax: 315-685-3426
Richard Flynn
All year

110-270-B&B
5 rooms, 4 pb
Visa, MC, AmEx, *Rated*
C-ltd/S-no/P-no/H-no

Full breakfast
Afternoon tea, snacks, wine
Sitting room, library,
Jacuzzis, fireplace, cable TV

Restored turn of the centruy. Elegantly refurbished in a quiet country setting on 320 acres.
Equestrian stables nearby. Elegant dining within 2 miles. E-mail: innkeeper@
hobbithollow.com *Web site:* hobbithollow.com

Pandora's Getaway
83 Oswego St, 13027
315-635-9571
888-638-8668
Sandra Wheeler
All year

60-80-B&B
4 rooms, 3 pb
Visa, MC, Disc, *Rated*,
•
S-ltd/P-no

Full breakfast
Sitting room, swimming &
beaver ponds

Historic Greek Revival, minutes from all locations in Syracuse. Decorated with antiques,
collectibles with country charm. Fireplace in one bedroom. E-mail: pgetaway@att.net

TANNERSVILLE

Eggery Inn, The
County Rd 16, 12485
518-589-5363 Fax: 518-589-5774
800-785-5364
Abraham Abramczyk
All year

85-125-B&B
15 rooms, 15 pb
Visa, MC, AmEx, *Rated*
C-yes/S-ltd/P-no/H-ltd

Full breakfast from menu
Group dinners, wine list,
cable TV in rooms, Newly
renovated 3rd flr.

Majestic setting, panoramic views, dining in a garden setting, fireplaces, atmosphere &
individualized attention. Near Hunter Mountain ski slopes. E-mail: eggeryinn@aol.com
Web site: eggeryinn.com

TARRYTOWN

Alexander Hamilton House
49 Van Wyck St, 10520
914-271-6737 Fax: 914-271-3927
Barbara Notarius, Maggie
Moore
All year

95-250-B&B
7 rooms, 7 pb
Visa, MC, AmEx,
Rated, •
C-yes/S-no/P-no/H-no
French

Full gourmet breakfast
Snacks
Sitting room, bicycles,
Jacuzzis, swimming pool,
suites, fireplace, cable TV

We are a romantic, Victorian Inn close to all the attractions of the lower Hudson Valley, 48
minutes from the heart of NYC, river view, village setting, with pool. E-mail: alexhouse@
bestweb.net *Web site:* alexanderhamiltonhouse.com

THOUSAND ISLANDS

Thousand Islands Inn
PO Box 69, 13624
315-686-3030
800-544-4241
Susan & Allen Benas
Memorial Day-late Sept

63-80-EP
14 rooms, 14 pb
Most CC, *Rated*
C-yes/S-yes/P-no/H-no

Full breakfast (fee)
lunch & dinner available
Piano, fishing nearby, near
public tennis, courts and
pool

The last full-service inn in the Islands. 1000 Islands salad dressing originated here in the
early 1900s. E-mail: tiinn@1000-islands.com *Web site:* 1000-islands.com

UTICA

Adam Bowman Manor	50-75-B&B	Full breakfast
197 Riverside Dr, 13502	4 rooms, 2 pb	Snacks
315-738-0276 Fax: 315-738-0276	Visa, MC, *Rated*, •	Afternoon tea—weekends,
Marion & Barry Goodwin	C-yes/S-no/P-no/H-no	sitting room/lib., A/C,
All year	Some Italian & German	fountain, spec. lighting

Nestled in the foothills of the Adirondacks, this historic 1823 brick Federal Manor offers the elegance once enjoyed by the Duke & Duchess of Windsor. E-mail: bargood@msn.com

Iris Stonehouse B&B, The	50-80-B&B	Full breakfast
16 Derbyshire Place, 13501	4 rooms, 2 pb	Snacks
315-732-6720 Fax: 315-732-6854	Most CC, •	Sitting room, central A/C,
800-446-1456	C-ltd/S-no/P-no/H-no	fountain, special lighting
Jim & Nellie Chanatry		
All year		

City charm, close to everything. Full breakfast served from menu. Central A/C for hot days; blazing fireplace for cold days. Easy access to I-90, exit 31 and route 5, 8 & 12. E-mail: irisbnb@borg.com

WARRENSBURG

Country Road Lodge B&B	55-65-B&B	Full breakfast
115 Hickory Hill Rd, 12885	4 rooms, 2 pb	Sitting room, library,
518-623-2207 Fax: 518-623-4363	•	birdwatching, hiking
Steve & Sandi Parisi	S-no/P-no/H-no	
All year		

Quiet, idyllic setting along Hudson River at the end of a country road. Discreetly sociable host. No traffic or TV. Southern Adirondack Mountains, near Lake George. Celebrating our 25th year! E-mail: parisibb@netheaven.com *Web site:* countryroadlodge.com

White House Lodge	85-B&B	Continental breakfast
3760 Main St, 12885	3 rooms, 2 pb	Complimentary wine,
518-623-3640	Visa, MC,	cookies
Ruth & Jim Gibson	C-ltd/S-ltd/P-no/H-no	Homemade cakes, pies,
All year		sitting room, television, front
		porch

An 1847 Victorian in the heart of the Adirondacks. The home is furnished with many antiques. Enjoy the comfort of the air conditioned TV lounge.

WARWICK

Glenwood House B&B	110-250-B&B	Full breakfast
49 Glenwood Road, 10969	7 rooms, 5 pb	Library, fireplaces, whirlpool
914-258-5066 Fax: 914-258-4226	Most CC,	tubs for two, bkfst. in bed,
Andrea & Kevin Colman	C-yes/S-ltd/P-no/H-no	modem hookup
All year	Italian, German	

Restored Victorian Farmhouse overlooking the beautiful Pochuck Valley. Canopy beds, feather beds, fireplaces, antiques, whirlpool for 2 and candles! What better way to generate romance? Only an hour from NYC! E-mail: glenwood@warwick.net
Web site: glenwoodhouse.com

Warwick Valley B&B	100-125-B&B	Full breakfast
24 Maple Ave, 10990	5 rooms, 5 pb	Sitting room, bicycles,
914-987-7255 Fax: 914-988-5318	•	fireplaces, cable TV, covered
888-280-1671	C-ltd/S-ltd/P-no/H-no	porch, back lawn
Loretta Breedveld		
All year		

Come to my completely restored 1900 Colonial Revival & enjoy a high standard of cleanliness & landscaping that is both pleasing to the eye and comforting to the soul! E-mail: loretta@warwick.net *Web site:* wvbedandbreakfast.com

WATKINS GLEN

Rock Stream B&B	95-165-B&B	Full breakfast
524 Rock Stream Rd, 14878	5 rooms, 5 pb	Snacks
607-243-5898	Visa, MC, AmEx,	Sitting room, tennis, suites,
Carleton and Pauline Dailey	C-ltd/S-ltd/P-no/H-no	cable TV, conference
Spring, Summer, Fall		facilities

An upscale, elegantly restored, twenty three room country estate on five acres. Gazebo, grass tennis court, patios. Spacious guest room furnished to provide luxurious sleeping comfort. Web site: bbhost.com/rockstreambb

WEST POINT

Empty Nest B&B	85-100-B&B	Full breakfast
423 Lake Rd, 12553	3 rooms	Cable TV, screened porch
914-496-9263	*Rated*	overlooking countryside.
Pat & Dick Coleman	C-ltd/S-no/P-no/H-no	
Jan 15-Nov 15		

Country home; pretty florals and prints, cozy quilts, family antiques and dolls. Breakfast served on porch overlooking countryside. Hospitality that you would only expect to find in the South.

WESTHAMPTON

Westhampton Country	99-225-B&B	Full breakfast
Manor	5 rooms, 5 pb	Sitting room, library, tennis
28 Jagger Lane, 11977	Visa, MC, AmEx,	court, pool, fireplace,
516-288-9000 Fax: 516-288-3292	C-ltd/S-no/P-no/H-no	guesthouse
888-288-5540		
Susan & Bill Dalton All year		

Simple elegance. Quiet, romantic getaway in historic (c.1865) home decorated with many antiques. Frplc., piano & a gourmet breakfast. Har-tru tennis court & heated pool in season. Business services. E-mail: innkeeper@hamptonsbb.com Web site: hamptonsbb.com

WESTHAMPTON BEACH

1880 House B&B	100-200-B&B	Full breakfast
PO Box 648, 11978	3 rooms, 3 pb	Complimentary sherry &
516-288-1559 Fax: 516-288-7696	*Rated*, ●	muffins
800-346-3290	C-yes/S-no/P-no/H-no	Sitting room, piano, tennis
Elsie Pardee Collins		court, library, pool
All year		

Country hideaway with 3 suites furnished in antiques. Gourmet breakfast served in lovely decorated dining room or enclosed porch overlooking pool. Web site: 1880-House.com

WESTPORT

All Tucked Inn	65-110-B&B	Full breakfast
PO Box 324, 12993	9 rooms, 9 pb	Dinner, snacks, wine
518-962-4400 Fax: 518-962-4400	*Rated*, ●	Championship golf, beach,
888-ALL-TUCK	C-ltd/S-no/P-no/H-no	marina close by, sitting room
Claudia Ryan & Tom Haley		
All year		

Four season inn overlooking Lake Champlain. Cozy rooms, fireplaces. Enjoy championship golf and the year round activities of the Adirondacks. Web site: alltuckedinn.com

Inn on the Library Lawn	69-115-B&B	Full breakfast
PO Box 390, 12993	10 rooms, 10 pb	Beer, wine & dinner
518-962-8666 Fax: 518-962-2007	Most CC, *Rated*	available
888-577-7748	C-ltd/S-no/P-no/H-no	Lunch served on weekends,
Donald & Susann Thompson		May-Oct. library, sitting
All year		room, snacks

Elegant Victorian inn with period decor & furnishings. Spectacular Lake Champlain views. Walk to restaurants, marina, beach, golf, theater & shopping. Conference facilities. E-mail: innthompson@msn.com Web site: theinnonthelibrarylawn.com

Inn on the Library Lawn, Westport, NY

WHITEFACE MOUNTAIN

Willkommen Hof B&B
PO Box 240, 12997
518-946-7669 Fax: 518-946-7626
800-541-9119
Heike & Burt Yost
Closed Nov.

58-115-B&B
8 rooms, 3 pb
Visa, MC, •
C-yes/S-no/P-yes/H-no
German

Full breakfast
Afternoon tea, bar service
Dinner available (fee), hot
tubs, sauna, near golf, cross-
country skiing

European tradition in the heart of the Adirondack Mountains with indoor sauna & outdoor hot tub. *E-mail:* willkommenhof@whiteface.net *Web site:* lakeplacid.net/willkommenhof

WINDHAM

Albergo Allegria
PO Box 267, 12496
518-734-5560 Fax: 518-734-5570
Vito & Lenore Radelich
All year

73-233-B&B
21 rooms, 21 pb
Visa, MC, *Rated*
C-yes/S-no/P-no/H-yes
Croatian, Italian

Full gourmet breakfast
Dinner available (fee)
Sitting room, fireplaces,
cable TV/VCR, videos, bikes
& tennis (fee)

1876 Victorian mansion nestled in the Catskill Mountain Forest Preserve.
E-mail: mail@albergousa.com *Web site:* AlbergoUSA.com

WOODSTOCK

Twin Gables of Woodstock
73 Tinker St, 12498
914-679-9479 Fax: 914-679-5638
914-679-5638
Albert & JoAnne Hoffman
All year

60-85-EP
9 rooms, 3 pb
Most CC, *Rated*
C-yes/S-no/P-no/H-no

State parks close by,
swimming, fishing and, skiing
nearby

1930s ambiance revives the easy living of the time. Woodstock "Colony of the Arts," world-wide reputation for art, literature and music. *Web site:* twingableswoodstockny.com

WOODSTOCK

Woodstock Country Inn	90-165-B&B	Full breakfast
PO Box 704, 12498	5 rooms, 2 pb	Sitting room, swimming pool,
914-679-9380	Visa, MC,	suites, fireplace, cable TV
Carol Wandrey	C-ltd/S-no/P-no/H-ltd	
All year		

A turn-of-the centruy artist's home set in a peaceful idyllic country setting only minutes from the village of Woodstock, New York. Swimming, hiking, close to gourmet restaurants. E-mail: inn@ulster.net Web site: woodstockcountryinn.com

North Carolina

ALBERMARLE

Pines Plantation Inn, The	60-85-B&B	Full breakfast
1570 Lilly's Bridge Rd, 27306	5 rooms, 5 pb	Snacks
910-439-1894 Fax: 910-439-1894	Visa, MC, *Rated*	Sitting room, library,
800-711-1134	C-ltd/S-no/P-no/H-no	fireplaces, cable TV,
Carol and Don Day		accommodate business
All year		travelers

A beautiful country inn nestled on 10 acres near Lake Tillery and the Uwharrie National Forest. Working fireplaces, library, sun porch, high ceilings, antiques, calm, quiet, great breakfasts. E-mail: pinesinn@aol.com Web site: bbonline.com/nc/pinesinn

ANDREWS

Cover House B&B Inn, The	80-120-B&B	Full breakfast
173 Wilson St, 28901	5 rooms, 3 pb	Whitewater rafting, fish, train
828-321-5302 Fax: 828-321-2145	Most CC, *Rated*, •	rides, hiking, biking, antique
800-354-7642	C-yes/S-no/P-no/H-ltd	shops
Philip & Gayle Horton		
All year		

Charming historic home furnished with antiques & beautiful artwork where you can "sit a spell" & enjoy mountain views from the valley town. E-mail: cover@grove.net Web site: bbonline.com/nc/coverhouse

Hawkesdene House B&B	70-185-B&B	Full breakfast
PO Box 670, 28901	5 rooms, 5 pb	No breakfast in cottages
828-321-6027 Fax: 828-321-5007	Most CC, *Rated*, •	Sitting room, library, suites,
800-447-9549	C-ltd/S-no/P-no/H-yes	fireplaces, cable TV
Roy & Daphne Sargent		
All year		

Romantic English country inn & family cottages nestled in the Great Smoky Mountains. Hiking or llama treks from the inn. Nearby whitewater rafting, biking, trout fishing, tours. E-mail: hawke@dnet.net Web site: hawkbb.com

APEX

B&B's Country Garden Inn	100-110-B&B	Continental breakfast
1041 Kelly Rd, 27502	4 rooms, 4 pb	Afternoon tea, snacks
919-303-8003 Fax: 919-851-3494	Visa, MC, AmEx,	Sitting room, Jacuzzis, suites,
800-251-3171	C-yes/S-no/P-no/H-no	cable, hammock, gazebo,
Bud & Beth		swing, fishing
All year		

Our secluded, cozy inn is perfect for a romantic weekend getaway, or convenient to Research Triangle Park and the Triangle area for harried business travelers who like to relax in the off time. E-mail: budnbeth@aol.com Web site: b-and-b-country-inn.com

ASHEVILLE

Abbington Green B&B Inn	125-225-B&B	Full breakfast
46 Cumberland Cir, 28801	7 rooms, 6 pb	Afternoon tea
828-251-2454 Fax: 828-251-2872	Visa, MC, AmEx,	Sitting room & library with
800-251-2454	*Rated*, •	piano, chess, etc., bicycles,
V., J. & G. Larrea	C-ltd/S-no/P-no	A/C
All year		

Elegant, light-filled, historic home—English garden theme with antiques throughout & 6 working fireplaces. Sumptuous, full breakfast. E-mail: abbington@msn.com
Web site: abbingtongreen.com

Albemarle Inn	110-300-B&B	Full breakfast
86 Edgemont Rd, 28801	11 rooms, 11 pb	Afternoon tea, snacks
828-255-0027 Fax: 828-236-3397	Visa, MC, Disc, *Rated*,	Sitting room, suites,
800-621-7435	•	fireplaces, gardens, private
Kathy and Larry Sklar	C-ltd/S-no/P-no/H-no	balcony, private sunporch
All year		

Greek Revival Mansion on landscaped grounds. Spacious period guest rooms feature high ceilings, thick mattresses, fine European linens, private baths with clawfoot tubs.
E-mail: info@albemarleinn.com *Web site:* albemarleinn.com

AppleWood Manor Inn	95-115-B&B	Full gourmet breakfast
62 Cumberland Circle, 28801	4 rooms, 4 pb	Complimentary beverages
828-254-2244 Fax: 828-254-0899	Visa, MC, Disc, *Rated*,	Sitting room, library, free
800-442-2197	•	fitness club, bikes,
Johan & Coby Verhey	C-ltd/S-no/P-no/H-no	badminton, croquet
All year		

Balconies, fireplaces, private baths, delicious breakfasts & aftn. tea-just to mention a few pleasures. Come romance yourselves with a stay. Cottage for 4 available.
E-mail: johan.verheij@gte.net *Web site:* comscape.com/apple

At Cumberland Falls	100-200-B&B	Organic full breakfast
254 Cumberland Ave, 28801	5 rooms, 5 pb	Afternoon tea, snacks, comp.
828-253-4085 Fax: 828-253-5566	Visa, MC, Disc, *Rated*,	wine
888-743-2557	•	Jacuzzis, fireplaces, cable
Denise & Mike Greenfield	C-ltd/S-no/P-no/H-no	TV, accommodate business
All year		travelers

We are a turn-of-the-century home located in historic Asheville. Our home features water-falls and gardens, Jacuzzis and fireplaces. At Cumberland Falls, you'll discover that Bed & Breakfast has been elevated to a new level. E-mail: fallsinn@aol.com
Web site: cumberlandfalls.com/

Beaufort House Victorian	65-195-B&B	Full breakfast
61 N Liberty St, 28801	10 rooms, 10 pb	Afternoon tea
828-254-8334 Fax: 828-251-2082	Visa, MC, *Rated*, •	Sitting room, bicycles, hot
800-261-2221	C-yes/S-no/P-no/H-no	tubs
Jacqueline & Robert Glasgow		
All year		

National Historic property. Lovely tea garden & manicured lawns. All homemade baked goods. VCR & cable in each room. Free movies E-mail: info@beauforthouse.com
Web site: beauforthouse.com

Black Walnut B&B Inn	95-200-B&B	Full gourmet breakfast
288 Montford Ave, 28801	7 rooms, 7 pb	Vegetarian dining available
828-254-3878 Fax: 828-236-9393	Most CC, *Rated*, •	Sitting room, fireplace, tennis
800-381-3878	C-yes/S-ltd/P-no/H-no	& golf nearby, cottage,
Sandra & Randy Glasgow	Italian, French	carriage house
All year		

Turn-of-the-Century shingle-style home in heart of historic district. Minutes from downtown & Biltmore Estate. Welcoming refreshments. E-mail: info@blackwalnut.com
Web site: blackwalnut.com

Chestnut Street, Asheville, NC

ASHEVILLE

Bridle Path Inn
30 Lookout Rd, 28804
828-252-0035 Fax: 828-252-0035
Carol & Fred Halton
All year

85-110-B&B
8 rooms, 8 pb
Visa, MC, AmEx,
Rated, •
C-yes/S-ltd/P-no/H-yes

Full breakfast
Dinner by great cooks
Sitting room, verandah,
picnic baskets, hiking trails

Comfortable and secluded on mountain overlooking downtown Asheville. Full breakfast served on verandah. Ten minutes to Biltmore Estate E-mail: fjhalton3@aol.com
Web site: travelguides.com/bb/bridle_path/

Cedar Crest Victorian Inn
674 Biltmore Ave, 28803
828-252-1389 Fax: 828-253-7667
800-252-0310
Jack & Barbara McEwan
All year

145-210-B&B
11 rooms, 11 pb
Visa, MC, *Rated*, •
C-ltd/S-ltd/P-no/H-no

Full breakfast
Afternoon refreshments
Evening beverages/sweets,
sitting room, piano, A/C,
phones, desks

The essence of Victoriana—carved woodwork, beveled glass, period antiques, fireplaces. Breakfast & tea on verandah. E-mail: jack@cedarcrestvictorianinn.com
Web site: cedarcrestvictorianinn.com

Chestnut Street
176 E Chestnut St, 28801
828-285-0705
800-894-2955
Paulette & Gene Dugger
All year

125-225-B&B
6 rooms, 6 pb
Most CC, *Rated*, •
S-ltd/P-no
Little Turkish

Full breakfast
Afternoon tea
Sitting room, library,
Jacuzzis, suites, fireplaces,
cable TV

Beautifully restored colonial revival c. 1905 in historic district. Features antique furnishings, private baths, large porches and antique/gift shop. Enjoy sumptuous breakfasts, afternoon tea, and five-minute walk to downtown. Web site: chestnutstreetinn.com

Colby House, The
230 Pearson Dr, 28801
828-253-5644 Fax: 828-259-9479
800-982-2118
Peter & Bonnie Marsh
All year

115-165-B&B
4 rooms, 4 pb
Rated, •
C-ltd/S-no/P-no/H-no

Full breakfast
Refreshments all day
Library, fireplaces, lovely
gardens, A/C, phones, desks

Historic Dutch Tudor home of charm and elegance. Full gourmet breakfast varies daily. Hosts' personal attention to every guest's needs. Web site: colbyhouse.com

ASHEVILLE ───────────────────────────────────

Corner Oak Manor
53 St. Dunstans Rd, 28803
828-253-3525
888-633-3525
Karen & Andy Spradley
All year

100-175-B&B
4 rooms, 4 pb
Most CC, *Rated*
C-yes/S-no/P-no/H-no

Full breakfast
Picnic baskets, snacks
Sitting room, A/C, fireplace,
hot tub, cottage has TV &
fireplace

Elegant & comfortable; full gourmet breakfast; queen-size beds; outdoor deck with Jacuzzi; flowers/chocolates. Minutes from Biltmore Estate & Blue Ridge Parkway.
E-mail: vineguy@aol.com *Web site:* bbonline.com/nc/corneroak/

Dogwood Cottage Inn
40 Canterbury Rd N, 28801
828-258-9725
Joan & Don Tracy
All year

100-120-B&B
4 rooms, 4 pb
Visa, MC, AmEx,
Rated, •
C-yes/S-ltd/P-yes/H-yes

Full breakfast
Afternoon tea, snacks, wine
Sitting room, library,
swimming pool, veranda,
Blue Ridge views

Historical, rustic brown shingled lodge, wood floors, French doors, wood-burning fireplaces, beamed ceilings, 40 foot porch, stunning views, great location, pool.

Dry Ridge Inn
26 Brown St, 28787
828-658-3899
800-839-3899
Paul & Mary Lou Gibson
All year

95-135-B&B
7 rooms, 7 pb
Visa, MC, *Rated*, •
C-ltd/S-ltd

Full breakfast
Sitting room, A/C, outdoor
spa, gift shop, art gallery,
antiques

Close to Asheville & Blue Ridge Parkway with small town charm. Large comfortable guest rooms; antiques & homemade quilts. Small conference facility. Patio dining next to koi water garden with waterfall. *E-mail:* dryridgeinn@msn.com *Web site:* bbonline.com/nc/dryridge

Inn at Old Fort, The
PO Box 1116, 28762
828-668-9384
800-471-0637
Debbie & Chuck Aldridge
All year

60-80-B&B
4 rooms, 4 pb
•
C-yes/S-ltd/P-no/H-no

Continental plus breakfast
Snacks
Parlor and library, cable TV,
large porch, pin for #800 is
1709

1880s Victorian cottage furnished with antiques, library, large porch for rocking, lawn and many special gardens with sitting areas set on 3.5 acres overlooking Blue Ridge town near Asheville, Lake Lure. Toll free line extension 1709.

Inn on Main Street
88 S Main St, 28787
828-645-4935
877-873-6074
Dan & Nancy Ward
All year

85-125-B&B
7 rooms, 7 pb
Visa, MC, Disc, •
C-ltd/S-no/P-no/H-no
Spanish, some Ger. & Fr.

Full breakfast
Complimentary evening
refreshments
Sitting room, bicycles, picnic
lunches/dinners by request
for extra $$

Victorian escape midway between Asheville & mtn. recreation- golf, rafting, hiking, skiing & exploring the Blue Ridge Parkway. Make us your base camp for active days, relaxed evenings. *E-mail:* relax@innonmain.com *Web site:* innonmain.com

Inn on Montford, The
296 Montford Ave, 28801
828-254-9569 Fax: 828-254-9518
800-254-9569
Lynn & Ron Carlson
All year

145-195-B&B
4 rooms, 4 pb
Visa, MC, AmEx,
Rated, •
S-no/P-no/H-no
French

Full breakfast
Comp. evening refreshments
Sitting room, library,
fireplaces in all rooms, 3 rms.
w/whirlpool baths

Arts and crafts style home in historic district. Perfect setting for the owner's collection of porcelains, antiques, oriental rugs *E-mail:* info@innonmontford.com
Web site: innonmontford.com

ASHEVILLE

Lion & the Rose B&B, The
276 Montford Ave, 28801
828-255-7673 Fax: 828-285-9810
800-546-6988
Rice & Lisa Yordy
All year

135-225-B&B
5 rooms, 5 pb
Visa, MC, AmEx, Disc,
Rated, •
C-ltd/S-no/P-no/H-no

Full breakfast
Afternoon tea, snacks
Sitting room, Jacuzzis, suites,
fireplace, cable TV, water
fountain garden

This 1895 Mansion furnished in period antiques is notable for its historic, architectural and literary significance. Located in National Historic District, minutes to downtown and Biltmore Estate.   E-mail: info@lion-rose.com *Web site:* lion-rose.com

---

North Lodge on Oakland
84 Oakland Rd, 28801
828-252-6433 Fax: 828-252-3034
800-282-3602
Herb & Lois Marsh
All year

95-130-B&B
4 rooms, 4 pb
Most CC, *Rated*, •
C-ltd/S-no/P-no/H-no

Full breakfast
Afternoon tea, snacks
Sitting room, library,
enclosed porch, front parlor,
TV, phones

Warm, friendly environment. English antiques and contemporary decor. Deluxe breakfasts! Can satisfy special dietary needs. Centrally located; quiet shady street. E-mail: stay@northlodge.com *Web site:* northlodge.com

---

Old Reynolds Mansion, The
100 Reynolds Heights, 28804
828-254-0496
800-709-0496
Fred & Helen Faber
Exc. weekdays Dec-Mar

65-135-B&B
10 rooms, 7 pb
Rated
C-ltd/S-yes/P-no/H-no

Continental plus breakfast
Complimentary wine
Afternoon beverages, sitting
room, verandahs, pool, A/C,
guest cottage

A restored 1850 Antebellum mansion in a country setting. Wide verandahs, mountain views, woodburning fireplaces, huge old swimming pool. On the National Register.
Web site: oldreynoldsmansion.com

Owls Nest Inn at Engadine
2630 Smokey Park Hwy, 28715
828-665-8325 Fax: 828-667-2539
800-665-8868
Marg Dente & Gail Kinney
All year

105-165-B&B
5 rooms, 5 pb
Most CC, *Rated*, •
S-no/P-no/H-no

Full breakfast
Afternoon tea, snacks, comp.
wine
Sitting room, Jacuzzis, suites,
fireplaces, cable TV, accom.
bus. travelers

Historic Victorian Inn built in 1885; mountain views; fireplaces; Jacuzzi suite; situated on over four acres, yet just 15 minutes from downtown Asheville and Biltmor Estate; full breakfast, evening reception.   E-mail: owlsnest@circle.net *Web site:* circle.net/owlsnest

---

Richmond Hill Inn
87 Richmond Hill Dr, 28806
828-252-7313 Fax: 828-252-8726
800-545-9238
Michael Schmidt
All year

145-450-B&B
36 rooms, 36 pb
Visa, MC, AmEx,
Rated, •
C-yes/S-no/P-no/H-ltd

Full gourmet breakfast
2 gourmet restaurants
Library, garden rooms, turndown, phone, TV, conference
facilities

Historic 1889 Victorian inn, magnificently renovated, with gracious service and fine dining. Elegant setting for meetings & small weddings.   Web site: richmondhillinn com

---

Secret Garden B&B
PO Box 2226, 28787
828-658-9317 Fax: 828-645-6420
800-797-8211
Karen & Jack Hultin
All year

110-130-B&B
3 rooms, 3 pb
Visa, MC, •
C-ltd/S-no/P-no/H-no

Full breakfast
Afternoon tea, snacks, wine
Library by request for extra
$$

Elegant c.1904 home located near many amenities in the Asheville area. Known for our gracious hospitality and sumptuous breakfasts.   E-mail: garden56@aol.com
Web site: bbonline.com/nc/secretgarden/

ASHEVILLE ────────────────────────────

Wright Inn & Carriage House
235 Pearson Dr, 28801
828-251-0789 Fax: 828-251-0929
800-552-5724
Carol & Art Wenczel   All year

115-250-B&B
12 rooms, 11 pb
Visa, MC, Disc, *Rated*
C-ltd/S-no/P-no/H-no

Full breakfast in inn
Afternoon tea, snacks
TVs, phones, hairdryers, in
all rooms—Carriage, House
sleeps 8, bikes

This elegantly restored Queen Anne Victorian allows you to step back to the peaceful and gracious time at the turn of the century. Wraparound porch and lovely gardens
Web site: wrightinn.com

BALD HEAD ISLAND ────────────────────────

Theodosia's B&B
PO Box 3130, 28461
910-457-6563 Fax: 910-457-6055
800-656-1812
Donna and Gary Albertson
All year

175-265-B&B
13 rooms, 10 pb
Most CC, *Rated*
C-ltd/S-no/P-no

Full breakfast
Comp. wine, Dinner by
reserv.
Sitting room, snacks,
bicycles, tennis court,
swimming pool, fireplace

Stay in the most beautiful & romantic inn on an incredible island. Modern Victorian structure, named after the daughter of vice president Aaron Burr, perished in East coast shipwreck. Rooms beautifully decorated, bikes for riding and golf carts
E-mail: garrett.albertson@worldnet.att.net *Web site:* theodosias.com

BALSAM ─────────────────────────────

Balsam Mountain Inn
PO Box 40, 28707
828-456-9498 Fax: 828-456-9298
800-224-9498
M. Teasley, I. Baldwin, F. Ray
All year

100-175-B&B
50 rooms, 50 pb
Visa, MC, Disc, *Rated*,
•
C-ltd/S-ltd/P-no/H-yes
French

Full breakfast
Restaurant
Game room, porches, 26
acres, springs,
rhododendron forest

Rest, read, ramble, romp and revel in the easy going hospitality of our southern mountains. Magical enchantment awaits at our historic inn. Library, mountain views.
E-mail: merrily@dnet.net *Web site:* balsaminn.com

Hickory Haven Inn
PO Box 88, 28707
704-452-1106
800-684-2836
C. Nicholson & J. Eukers
Closed January

85-150-B&B
6 rooms, 6 pb
Visa, MC, •
C-ltd/S-no/P-no/H-yes

Full breakfast
Afternoon tea, snacks, wine
Sitting room, library, hot
tubs, adjacent to, Blue Ridge
Parkway

Romantic mountain hideaway. Elegant yet casual. King beds, whirlpools, fireplaces, wraparound verandah. Peaceful woodland setting E-mail: smkymtbb@primeline.com
Web site: hickoryhaven.com

BANNER ELK ───────────────────────────

Archers Mountain Inn
2489 Beech Mtn Parkway,
28604
828-898-9004 Fax: 828-898-9004
888-827-6155
Candi McClamm   All year

90-200-B&B
15 rooms, 14 pb
Visa, MC, *Rated*, •
C-yes/S-yes/P-no/H-ltd

Full breakfast
Dinner available
Library, sitting room, large
hot tub for guests, Jacuzzi
and king suites

Quaint country inn with long-range view and fireplaces in most rooms. Two miles from the ski slopes. Hiking trail on premises E-mail: tony@archersinn.com *Web site:* archersinn.com

Azalea Inn
PO 1151, 28604
828-898-8195 Fax: 828-898-3482
888-898-2743
Karen Wimbush   All year

99-125-B&B
7 rooms, 7 pb
Visa, MC, AmEx,
Rated, •
C-ltd/S-no/P-no/H-yes

Full breakfast
Afternoon tea, snacks
Sitting room, antiques, tennis
court, in town, newly
refurbished

The secret is never the inn, it's the innkeepers. The b&b you'll want to keep a secret. Privacy & personal attention are the hallmarks of the inn. Close to shopping/restaurants. ADA facilities available. Cottage available. E-mail: azaleainn@skybest.com
Web site: azalea-inn.com

BEAUFORT

Cedars Inn by the Sea, The	85-165-B&B	Full breakfast
305 Front St, 28516	12 rooms, 12 pb	Wine bar
252-728-7036 Fax: 252-728-1685	Most CC, *Rated*, •	Private Cottage, Jacuzzi,
Linda & Sam Dark	C-ltd/S-ltd/P-no/H-no	Cooking classes, TV, A/C,
All year		priv. sitt. rms, bikes

Selected as one of North Carolina's 10 best inns. Perfect for romantic and intimate getaways. Waterfront setting, shopping, restaurants, tours, and golfing. Web site: cedarsinn.com

Delamar Inn	78-116-B&B	Continental plus breakfast
217 Turner St, 28516	4 rooms, 4 pb	Complimentary wine, ltd.
252-728-4300 Fax: 252-728-1471	Visa, MC, *Rated*, •	Snacks, sitting room, library,
800-349-5823	C-ltd/S-ltd/P-no/H-no	bicycles, tennis, beach
Tom & Mabel Steepy		furniture
All year		

Authentically furnished guestrooms in charming Civil War home. Enjoy a lavish breakfast. Historic homes tour, 2nd yr Web site: bbonline.com/nc/delamarinn/index.html

Langdon House B&B	75-135-B&B	Full breakfast
135 Craven St, 28516	4 rooms, 4 pb	Dinner reservations
252-728-5499 Fax: 252-728-1717	*Rated*	Refreshments, sitting room,
Jimm Prest	C-ltd/S-ltd/P-no/H-no	bicycles, fishing & beach
All year		supplies

Friends who help you make the most of your visit. Restored 18th-century home in historic seaside hamlet on the outer banks. Wonderful waffle breakfasts! E-mail: innkeeper@ coastainet.com

Pecan Tree Inn	75-140-B&B	Continental plus breakfast
116 Queen St, 28516	7 rooms, 7 pb	Soda & juices
252-728-6733	Visa, MC, Disc, *Rated*,	Jacuzzi in 1 room, sitting
Susan & Joe Johnson	•	room, library, bicycles,
All year	C-ltd/S-no/P-no/H-no	beach chairs

Antique-filled 1866 Victorian home in the heart of Beaufort's Historic District. Half a block from waterfront. E-mail: pecantreeinn@coastalnet.com *Web site:* pecantree.com

BLACK MOUNTAIN

Guesthouse Over Yonder	70-B&B	Full breakfast
433 N Fork Rd, 28711	5 rooms, 5 pb	Comp. wine (occ.),snacks
828-669-6762	*Rated*, •	Sitting room, library,
Wilhelmina K. Headley	C-ltd/S-no/P-no/H-no	wildflower gardens, near
May–November		tennis, pool, golf

Secluded & comfortable on wooded hillside. Breakfast of mountain trout served on rock terraces surrounded by flowers, views of highest peaks in eastern U.S.

BLOWING ROCK

Inn at Ragged Gardens, The	125-200-B&B	Full breakfast
PO Box 1927, 28605	12 rooms, 12 pb	Complimentary
828-295-9703	Visa, MC, *Rated*, •	champagne/newlywed
Lee & Jana Hyett	C-ltd/S-no/P-no/H-no	Completely renovated '96,
All year		beautiful walled garden,
		whirlpool baths, library

Near Blue Ridge Parkway and majestic Grandfather Mountain. People come here for the fantastic cool summers and the scenery. Every room has fireplace, 9 rooms with whirlpool tubs. Children over 12 welcome. E-mail: Innkeeper@ragged-gardens.com *Web site:* ragged-gardens.com/

BLOWING ROCK

Maple Lodge
PO Box 1236, 28605
828-295-3331
Marilyn Bateman
Mar-Dec, wkends Jan-Feb

100-170-B&B
11 rooms, 11 pb
Most CC, *Rated*, •
C-ltd/S-no/P-no/H-no

Full breakfast
Complimentary sherry,
afteroon tea
Parlors, fireplace, canopy
beds, quilts, splendor
packages

*Perennial gardens. Gracious charm in the heart of village, offering privacy, personal
attention & understated elegance. Blue Ridge Parkway one mile. Near golf, fishing &
hiking. E-mail:* innkeeper@maplclodge.net *Web site:* maplelodge.net

BOONE

Prospect Hill B&B Inn
801 W Main St, 37683
423-727-0139 Fax: 423-727-6979
800-339-5084
Robert & Judy Hotchkiss
All year

99-250-B&B
5 rooms, 5 pb
Visa, MC, •
C-yes/S-no/P-no/H-ltd

Full breakfast
Snacks, complimentary wine
Sitt. rm., lib., fireplaces,
bikes, tennis, Jacuzzis, cable
TV, gardens, spa

*A rare Victorian mansion near an unspoiled small town. Tranquility, mountain views, and
nature. E-mail:* host@prospect-hill.com *Web site:* prospect-hill.com

BREVARD

Key Falls Inn
151 Everett Rd, 28768
828-884-7559 Fax: 828-885-8342
C & P Grosvenor & J
Fogleman
All year

60-105-B&B
5 rooms, 5 pb
Visa, MC, AmEx,
C-ltd/S-ltd/P-no/H-no
Spanish

Full breakfast
Afternoon tea, lemonade
Sitting room, cable TV, VCR,
trail to waterfall, tennis ct.,
fishing pond

*Charming, restored Victorian farmhouse furnished with antiques on 28 acres near Brevard.
Porches, mountain view, waterfall, wooded setting & sumptuous breakfasts.*

Red House Inn B&B, The
412 Probart St, 28712
828-884-9349
M. O. Ong
All year

59-99-B&B
5 rooms, 3 pb
•
C-ltd/S-ltd/P-no/H-no

Full breakfast
Complimentary wine
Sitting room, porches, air
conditioned, off-street
parking

*Lovingly restored antebellum home. Former trading post, courthouse, school and more.
Near park, outlets, theater and sights. Completely furnished in antiques.*

Womble Inn
301 W Main St, 28712
828-884-4770
Beth & Steve Womble
All year

62-72-B&B
6 rooms, 6 pb
C-yes/S-yes/P-no/H-yes

Continental plus breakfast
Lunch available, Mon-Fri
Sitting room, piano, off-street
parking

*Gracious atmosphere of antiquity, private baths, near town and Brevard Music Center,
wonderful Christmas shop. E-mail:* wombleinn@citcom.net *Web site:* thewombleinn.com

BRYSON CITY

Chalet Inn, The
285 Lone Oak Dr, 28789
828-586-0251
800-789-8024
George & Hanneke Ware
March-Dec.

86-110-B&B
6 rooms, 6 pb
Visa, MC, *Rated*, •
C-ltd/S-no/P-no/H-ltd
German, Dutch, French

Full breakfast
Snacks, comp. wine
Great room w/fireplace,
private balconies/views,
brook, hiking trails

*Authentic Alpine Chalet nestled in mountain cove of Blue Ridge Mtns. Secluded with
spectacular views, 12 minutes to Great Smoky Mtn. National Park & convenient to attractions. Picnic area, lawn games. E-mail:* paradisefound@chaletinn.com *Web site:* chaletinn.com

BRYSON CITY

Charleston Inn, The
208 Arlington Ave, 28713
828-488-4644
Rollon & Sherry Smith
March-December

69-149-B&B
18 rooms, 18 pb
Most CC, •
C-yes/S-no/P-no/H-no

Full breakfast
Afternoon tea, snacks
Sitting room, library, bikes,
Jacuzzis, outdoor, hot tub,
gardens

Southern hospitality abounds in our 1920s house & inn. Enjoy mountain scenery and activities or rest & relax. After a full gourmet breakfast, raft, hike, mountain bike, fish E-mail: chasinn@daet.net Web site: charlestoninn.com

Euchella Sport Lodge
PO Box 177, 28702
828-488-8835
800-446-1603
Gary & Esther
All year

60-80-EP
8 rooms, 8 pb
Visa, MC,
C-yes/S-no/P-no/H-ltd

Full breakfast (fee)
Restaurant
Library, bicycles, fireplace,
cable TV, conferences

A beautiful and charming lodge located on the southern boundary of the Great Smoky Mountains National Park & Lake Fontana. E-mail: euchella@main.nc.us Web site: main.nc.us/Euchella

Folkestone Inn B&B
101 Folkestone Rd, 28713
828-488-2730 Fax: 828-488-0722
888-812-3385
Ellen & Charles Snodgrass
All year

69-108-B&B
10 rooms, 10 pb
Most CC, *Rated*, •
C-ltd/S-ltd/P-no/H-no

Full gourmet breakfast
Complimentary snacks, wine
Sitting room, library, porch,
rocking chairs, balconies,
antiques

Comfortable country farmhouse, beside mountain brook. Walk to 3 waterfalls in the Smokies. Hiking, fishing, birding, scenic railway, whitewater rafting. E-mail: innkeeper@ folkestone.com Web site: folkestone.com

Fryemont Inn
PO Box 459, 28713
828-488-2159
800-845-4879
Sue/George/Monica/George
Jr.
April-November

75-225-MAP
44 rooms, 44 pb
Visa, MC, Disc, *Rated*
C-yes/S-no/P-no/H-no

Full breakfast menu
Full dinner included
Full service lounge, library,
sitting room, swimming pool

Price includes breakfast and dinner! Located on a mountain shelf overlooking the Great Smoky Mountains National Park. A tradition in mountain hospitality since 1923. E-mail: fryemont@dnet.net Web site: fryemontinn.com

Randolph House Country Inn
PO Box 816, 28713
828-488-3472
800-480-3472
Bill & Ruth Randolph Adams
April–November

120-160-B&B
6 rooms, 3 pb
Most CC, *Rated*, •
C-ltd/S-yes/P-no/H-yes

Full country breakfast
Dinner, tea on request
Wine, set-ups, sitting room,
library, piano

Sitting on a mountian shelf overlooking the quaint town of Bryson City, the Inn contains many original furnishings, some dating back to the 1850's. Each bedroom is coordinated in a different color with some containing two double beds.

BURNSVILLE

Wray House B&B
PO Box 546, 28714
828-682-0445 Fax: 828-682-3750
877-258-8222
Ron & Julia Thompson
All year

95-110-B&B
5 rooms, 5 pb
Most CC, *Rated*, •
C-ltd/S-ltd/P-no/H-yes

Full breakfast
Afternoon tea, snacks
Sitting room, library,
fireplaces, cable TV,
accommodate business
travelers

E-mail: wrayhouse@mindspring.com Web site: wrayhouse.net

CAPE CARTERET ————————————————————————

Harborlight Guest House B&B	75-200-B&B	Full breakfast
332 Live Oak Dr, 28584	9 rooms, 9 pb	Snacks
252-393-6868 Fax: 252-393-6868	Most CC,	Sitting room, fireplaces, 2
800-624-VIEW	P-no/H-yes	person, whirlpools in rooms
Anita & Bobby Gill		
All year		

Romantic, coastal inn. Every suite is waterfront, secluded & private inn. Luxury suites feature two-person whirlpools, fireplaces & in-suite breakfast. 7 luxury suites and 2 water-view rooms typical of hotel rooms in size & amenities. Stunning water views
Web site: bbhost.com/harborlightgh

CASHIERS ————————————————————————

River Lodge B&B, The	95-135-B&B	Full breakfast
619 Roy Tritt Rd, 28723	5 rooms, 5 pb	Afternoon tea, snacks, comp.
828-293-5431	Visa, MC,	wine
877-384-4400	C-ltd/S-no/P-no/H-no	Sitting room, 1923 antique
Cathy & Anthony Sgambato		Brunswick Billiard table
All year		

Experience rustic elegance...experience The River Lodge. A mountain hideaway with river frontage. Greatroom with massive stone fireplace. Unique guestrooms, mountain made log beds, private baths. Full breakfast.

CHAPEL HILL ————————————————————————

Fearrington House Inn, The	175-350-B&B	Full breakfast
2000 Fearrington, 27312	31 rooms, 31 pb	Lunch/dinner available (fee)
919-542-2121 Fax: 919-542-4202	Most CC, *Rated*, •	Afternoon tea, weddings,
The Fitch Family	C-ltd/S-ltd/P-no/H-yes	sitting room, pool/bikes,
All year		meeting facilities

Classic countryside elegance in suites furnished with English antiques. Charming courtyard and gardens. Delicately prepared regional cuisine. E-mail: fhouse@fearrington.com
Web site: fearrington.com

Inn at Bingham School	75-120-B&B	Full breakfast
PO Box 267, 27514	5 rooms, 5 pb	Snacks, complimentary wine
919-563-5583 Fax: 919-563-9826	Visa, MC, AmEx,	Sitting room, library, small
800-566-5583	*Rated*, •	meetings, wedding facilities
Francois & Christina Deprez	C-yes/S-no/P-no/H-no	
All year	French, Spanish	

Step back to a slower time, a slower pace. Rock by the fire with your wine or stroll the surrounding woodlands, four rooms have fireplaces. E-mail: fdeprez@aol.com
Web site: bbhost.com/binghamschool

CHARLOTTE ————————————————————————

Homeleigh B&B	100-125-B&B	Continental breakfast
PO Box 426, 28012	5 rooms, 5 pb	Complimentary wine
704-829-6264 Fax: 704-829-6677	Visa, MC,	Sitting room, cable TV, golf,
Greg and Donna Schramek	C-ltd/S-no/P-no/H-no	tennis & swimming nearby
All year	French	

Spacious Renaissance Revival style home furnished in period furniture. Enjoy the garden surrounding the house. E-mail: homleigh@aol.com *Web site:* members.aol.com/homleigh

Morehead Inn, The	120-190-B&B	Continental plus breakfast
1122 E. Morehead St, 28204	11 rooms, 11 pb	Complimentary wine, tea
704-376-3357 Fax: 704-335-1110	Most CC, *Rated*, •	Meeting/social functions,
Bill Armstrong	C-yes/S-ltd/P-no/H-ltd	piano, whirlpool, bikes,
All year	Sp., Fr., It., Port.	YMCA fitness privileges

Restored estate in historic district; furnished with American & English art; quiet elegance. Churchill Galleries on-site: exclusive antiques. E-mail: morehead@charlotte.infi.net
Web site: moreheadinn.com

CHARLOTTE

Still Waters
6221 Amos Smith Rd, 28214
704-399-6299
Janet & Rob Dyer
All year

65-100-B&B
4 rooms, 4 pb
Visa, MC, *Rated*
C-ltd/S-no/P-no/H-no

Full breakfast
Sport court, tennis,
basketball, volleyball, boat
ramp, dock, gazebo

Log resort home on two wooded acres overlooking Lake Wylie. Near Charlotte downtown & airport. E-mail: rdyer399@aol.com Web site: members.aol.com/bbdyer399/homepage/index.html

CHIMNEY ROCK

Dogwood Inn, The
PO Box 159, 28720
828-625-4403 Fax: 828-625-8825
800-992-5557
Marsha Reynolds, Robert
Brooks
March-Dec.

80-130-B&B
11 rooms, 7 pb
Most CC, *Rated*, •
C-ltd/S-no/P-no/H-no

Full breakfast
Afternoon tea,
complimentary wine
Sitting room, boat ramp,
dock, gazebo

Riverfront inn nestled in Hickory Nut Gorge at the base of Chimney Rock Park. Gourmet breakfast served on outside porch. E-mail: dogwoodinn@blueridge.net
Web site: blueridge.net/~dogwoodinn

CHIMNEY ROCK VILLAGE

Wicklow Inn, The
PO Box 246, 28720
828-625-4038 Fax: 828-325-0435
877-625-4038
Sharon & Jack Ryan
All year

75-115-B&B
7 rooms, 5 pb
Visa, MC, *Rated*, •
C-ltd/S-ltd/P-no/H-no

Full breakfast
Afternoon tea
Sitting room, library, cable
TV, on rushing Mtn. River

Country inn on banks of Rocky Broad River in Blue Ridge Mountains. Rustic furniture, antiques, contemporary mountain crafts. Breakfast served on deck overlooking river. 2 blocks from Chimney Rock Park. E-mail: wicklowinn@blueridge.net Web site: chimney-rock.com/wicklow-inn.htm

CLINTON

Ashford Inn, The
615 College Ave, 28328
910-596-0961 Fax: 910-596-0961
888-ATTHEINN
C.H. Parrish & A.M. Carberry
All year

75-130-B&B
4 rooms, 4 pb
Visa, MC, AmEx,
C-ltd/S-no/P-ltd/H-no

Full breakfast

Historic inn for the selective traveler. E-mail: annec97757@aol.com
Web site: travelguides.com/home/ashford

**Shield House/Courthouse
Inn**
216 Sampson St, 28328
910-592-2634 Fax: 910-592-2634
800-462-9817
Anita Green
All year

65-150-B&B
15 rooms, 15 pb
Most CC, •
C-yes/S-ltd/P-no/H-yes

Continental breakfast inn
Full breakfast main house
Sitting room, porches, tennis
& golf nearby, 2-bedroom
bungalow avail

Reminiscent of Gone With The Wind. Elegant furnishings; outstanding architectural features. 2 estates listed in National Register Web site: clintonlodging.com

DAVIDSON

Davidson Village Inn
PO Box 1463, 28036
704-892-8044 Fax: 704-896-2184
800-892-0796
Gordon & Rebecca Clark
All year

100-175-B&B
18 rooms, 18 pb
Most CC, *Rated*, •
C-yes/S-ltd/P-no/H-yes

Continental plus breakfast
Afternoon tea, snacks
Library, sitting room,
lakefront recreation, 4 new
"executive rooms"

Warm relaxed inn, located in quaint college town serving a unique blend of historic & contemporary southern pleasures. VCRs, coffee makers, hairdryers in some rooms. E-mail: info@davidsoninn.com Web site: davidsoninn.com

DILLSBORO

Freeze House, The
71 Sylvan Heights, 28779
828-586-8161 Fax: 828-631-0379
Patrick & Mary Ellen
Montague
All year

65-100-B&B
4 rooms, 4 pb
Rated, •
C-ltd/S-no/P-no/H-no
French, German

Full breakfast
Sitting room, library, tennis
court, swimming pool, cable
TV, health club.

On a tree-shaded knoll overlooking the village, we offer excellent accommodations in the middle of a varied vactionland. National parks, Cherokee Indian Reservation, tourist attractions, water sports, wonderful breakfasts.   E-mail: freezeh@dnet.net *Web site:* cruising-america.com/freezehouse

Mountain Brook
208 Mountain Brook Rd, 28779
828-586-4329
Gus & Michele McMahon
All year

80-200-EP
12 rooms, 12 pb
Rated, •
C-yes/S-yes/P-no/H-ltd
Some French

Jacuzzis, fireplaces, all
cottages equipped for
homemaking

Quaint c.1930s cottages with fireplaces & porch swings. Nestled on a brook filled wooded mountainside in Smokies. Near historic Dillsboro. No phones or TVs to disturb your tranquility.   E-mail: memories@mountainbrook.com *Web site:* mountainbrook.com

DUCK

Advice 5 Cents, a B&B
PO Box 8278, 27949
252-255-1050
800-238-4235
Donna Black/Nancy Caviness
February-November

95-175-B&B
5 rooms, 5 pb
Visa, MC, *Rated*
C-ltd/S-no/P-no/H-no

Continental plus breakfast
Afternoon tea
Sitting rm., library, tennis,
cable TV, beach
chairs/towels, outdoor
showers

E-mail: advice5@theouterbanks.com *Web site:* theouterbanks.com/advice5

DURHAM

Blooming Garden Inn, The
513 Holloway St, 27701
919-687-0801 Fax: 919-688-1401
Frank & Dolly Pokrass
All year

100-195-B&B
5 rooms, 5 pb
Most CC, *Rated*, •
C-yes/S-no/P-no/H-no

Full gourmet breakfast
Comp. wine, tea, snacks
Sitting rooms, library, 145
foot porch, antiques, 2 rm.
suite w/footed tub

Vibrant colors transform this restored Victorian into a cozy, memorable retreat in downtown historic Durham. Abundant flower gardens. Antiques.

EDENTON

Lords Proprietors' Inn
300 N Broad St, 27932
252-482-3641 Fax: 252-482-2432
800-348-8933
Arch & Jane Edwards
All year

155-275-B&B/MAP
20 rooms, 20 pb
Rated, •
C-ltd/S-ltd/P-no/H-ltd

Full breakfast
4 course dinner included
with MAP
Tea, homemade cookies,
sitting room, bicycles,
private pool privileges

Edenton's oldest and most elegant inn offering the finest dining in eastern North Carolina. E-mail: reserv@lordspropedenton.com *Web site:* lordspropedenton.com

Trestle House Inn
632 Soundside Rd, 27932
252-482-2282 Fax: 252-482-7003
800-645-8466
Peter L. Bogus
All year

65-100-B&B
5 rooms, 5 pb
Most CC, *Rated*, •
C-ltd/S-ltd/P-no/H-no

Full breakfast
BYOB
Sitting room, billiards, steam,
exercise room, TV,
shuffleboard, hiking

Immaculate accommodations. Tranquil setting overlooking private 15-acre fishing lake and 60 acres of trees. Canoeing, bird watching. E-mail: thinn@coastalnet.com
Web site: edenton.com/trestlehouse

EMERALD ISLE

Emerald Isle Inn and B&B	75-160-B&B	Continental breakfast
502 Ocean Dr, 28594	4 rooms, 4 pb	Sitting room, library, direct
252-354-3222 Fax: 252-354-3222	*Rated*, •	ocean access, beach chairs,
Marilyn & AK Detwiller	C-yes/S-ltd/P-no/H-ltd	umbrellas
All year		

Enjoy a warm, relaxing getaway at the beach. Ocean/bay views. Our new Josephine suite with oceanview provides all the charm to bring you back in time.   E-mail: adetwiller@ coastalnet.com *Web site:* www4.coastalnet.com/emeraldisleinn

FLAT ROCK

Highland Lake Inn	79-150-EP	Continental bkfst. (Sun)
PO Box 1026, 28731	58 rooms, 56 pb	Restaurant, lunch, dinner
828-693-6812 Fax: 828-696-8951	Most CC, •	Tennis court, hot tubs, pool,
800-762-1376	C-yes/S-no/P-no/H-ltd	organic gardens, hiking, spa,
Pola Laughlin		paddleboats
All year		

Voted best B&B in Western NC, 1999. We combine the up-to-date with the gentle elements of a time gone by. Luxury inn, cozy rustic cabins, award-winning restaurant, organic gardens, lake, canoes, massage.   E-mail: judith@highlandlake.com *Web site:* highlandlake.com

FRANKLIN

Buttonwood Inn	55-90-B&B	Full breakfast
50 Admiral Dr, 28734	4 rooms, 4 pb	Sitting room, TV, golf nearby,
828-369-8985	*Rated*, •	entertainment
888-368-8985	C-ltd/S-ltd/P-no/H-no	
Liz Oehser		
All year		

Completely surrounded by tall pines, small and cozy Buttonwood will appeal to the person who prefers simplicity and natural rustic beauty.

Franklin Terrace	52-69-B&B	Full breakfast
159 Harrison Ave, 28734	9 rooms, 9 pb	Complimentary
828-524-7907	Visa, MC, •	refreshments
800-633-2431	C-ltd/S-ltd/P-no/H-no	2 beautiful sitting rooms,
Ed & Helen Henson		color/cable TV, A/C, 2
May-Oct.		porches with rockers

All rooms furnished with antiques. First floor houses dessert shop with cheesecakes, homemade pies & cakes—also antique shop. In town. Beautiful views. E-mail: stay@franklinterrace.com *Web site:* franklinterrace.com

Heritage Inn	75-95-B&B	Full breakfast
43 Heritage Hollow Dr, 28734	5 rooms, 5 pb	Snacks, complimentary
828-524-4150	Visa, MC, AmEx,	beverages
888-524-4150	*Rated*, •	Sitting room with cable TV,
Tina & Jim Bottomley	C-ltd/S-ltd/P-no/H-no	reading materials, games,
All year		videos

Rock on the verandah. Enjoy the beauty of the Smoky Mountains. Near rafting, hiking, gem mining. In downtown Franklin, just off Business Rt. 441.   E-mail: heritage@smnet.net *Web site:* intertekweb.com/heritage

Hummingbird Lodge B&B	85-95-B&B	Full breakfast
1101 Hickory Knoll Rd, 28734	3 rooms, 3 pb	Aftn. tea, comp. wine
828-369-0430	Visa, MC,	Sitting room, Jacuzzis,
Rota & Harvey Krape	C-ltd/S-ltd/P-no/H-ltd	fireplaces, cable TV, eve.
All year	Latvian	hors d'oeuvres

Country log home provides peace and quiet but close to all adventures surrounding mountains have to offer. Large gourmet breakfast, heart healthy breakfast available with 24 hour notice. Rooms decorated with Appalachian themes; great restaurants in town. E-mail: krape@dnet.net *Web site:* bbonline.com/nc/hummingbird

FRANKLIN

Mulberry Mountain	85-95-B&B	Full breakfast
444 Mulberry Gap Rd, 28763	4 rooms, 4 pb	Afternoon tea, snacks, comp.
828-524-8519 Fax: 828-524-8519	Visa, MC, *Rated*	wine
Gail & Hal Chapman	C-ltd/S-ltd/P-no/H-ltd	Sitting room, library, suites,
All year		fireplace

High in the mountains in the heart of the Nantahala Forest. Coffee or tea on the upper veranda; gourmet breakfast; absorbing the peace and quiet of Mulberry Mountain.
E-mail: HChap62@aol.com *Web site:* mulberrymountain.com

GREENSBORO

Biltmore Greensboro Hotel	85-110-B&B	Continental plus breakfast
111 W Washington St, 27401	26 rooms, 26 pb	Lunch/dinner available,
336-272-3474	Most CC, *Rated*, •	snacks
Fax: 336-275-2523	C-ltd/S-ltd/P-ltd/H-ltd	Complimentary wine, sitting
800-332-0303	German, Spanish	room, suites, cable TV, 6
Karl and Mary Lack		restaurants nearby.
All year		

Historic section of town, secure, garage parking, Victorian style furniture.
E-mail: thebiltmore@juno.com *Web site:* members.aol.com/biltmoreNC/index.html

Troy-Bumpas Inn B&B, The	95-175-B&B	Full, cont. plus bkfst.
114 S Mendenhall St, 27403	4 rooms, 4 pb	Snacks
336-370-1660 Fax: 336-274-3939	Most CC, •	Sitting room, central YMCA
800-370-9070	C-ltd/S-ltd/P-no/H-no	next door-, facilities available
Charles and Gwen Brown		
All year		

Wander through the rooms and hallways where union and confederates alike walked more than a century ago *E-mail:* ggbrowntbi@aol.com *Web site:* troy-bumpasinn.com

HATTERAS

Seaside Inn at Hatteras	85-B&B	Full breakfast
Box 688, 91998	10 rooms, 10 pb	Sitting room, library,
252-986-2700	Visa, MC,	spacious porches, small,
Sharon & Jeff Kennedy	C-yes/S-no/P-yes/H-yes	gatherings, Jacuzzis
All year		

Established in 1928, the inn has been refurbished as one of the most unique, comfortable, convenient places to stay on Hatteras Island. *E-mail:* SeasideBB@aol.com
Web site: hometown.aol.com/seasidebb/website/seasidin.html

HERTFORD

1812 on the Perquimans
Box 10, 27983
919-426-1812
Peter & Nancy Rascoe
Season Inquire

HIGH POINT

Bouldin House B&B, The	90-120-B&B	Full breakfast
4332 Archdale Rd, 27263	4 rooms, 4 pb	Evening beverage, snacks
336-431-4909	Most CC, *Rated*, •	Sitting room, large verandah,
Fax: 336-431-4914	C-ltd/S-ltd/P-no/H-no	board games, TV
800-739-1816		
Larry & Ann Miller		
All year		

Fine lodging and hospitality amidst America's finest home furnishings showrooms. Historic home; relaxed and casual, yet elegant. Wonderful gourmet breakfasts. *E-mail:* lmiller582@ aol.com *Web site:* bbonline.com/nc/bouldin/

HIGHLANDS

Colonial Pines Inn
541 Hickory St, 28741
828-526-2060
Chris & Donna Alley
All year

85-145-B&B
9 rooms, 9 pb
Visa, MC,
C-ltd/S-ltd/P-no/H-no

Full breakfast
Afternoon refreshments
Sitting room, kitchen, grand
piano, picnic area, 2 new
suites, cool summ.

Two acres of lawn and trees. Mountain view from verandah. Antique furnishings and country charm. Guest house with fireplace, sleeps up to six. Close to waterfalls, great shopping. E-mail: sleeptight@colonialpinesinn.com Web site: colonialpinesinn.com

Highlands Inn, The
PO Box 1030, 28741
828-526-9380
800-964-6955
Rip & Pat Benton
April-November

99-125-B&B
30 rooms, 30 pb
Visa, MC, AmEx, *Rated*
C-ltd/S-ltd/P-no/H-yes

Continental plus breakfast
Restaurant, lunch
Dinner, complimentary
snacks, sitting room, library,
meeting rooms available

Located in heart of historic Highlands. Near all outdoor activities. Breathtaking mountain views, waterfalls, shops. On National Registry of Historic Places. E-mail: hlinn@dnet.net

Kelsey & Hutchinson Lodge
PO Box 2129, 28741
828-526-4746 Fax: 828-526-4921
888-245-9058
Nancy Plate
All year

99-219-B&B
33 rooms, 33 pb
Visa, MC, AmEx,
C-yes/S-no/P-ltd/H-yes

Continental plus breakfast
Snacks, complimentary wine
Sitting room, library,
bicycles, Jacuzzis, fireplace,
cable TV

Quiet deluxe mountain rustic lodge overlooking downtown Highlands. Known for friendly, personalized service. 2 blocks from the boutiques and fine dining restaurants of Main Street. E-mail: innkeeper@k-hlodge.com Web site: k-hlodge.com

Yc Olde Stone House B&B
1337 S 4th St, 28741
828-526-5911
888-526-5911
Jim & Rene Ramsdell
All year

95-125-B&B
4 rooms, 4 pb
Visa, MC,
C-ltd/S-no/P-no/H-no

Full breakfast
Snacks
Sitting room, families
welcome in, guest houses

Hidden in a vale, enjoy a touch of yesterday. Savor a delicious country breakfast and true Southern hospitality you'll long remember. Two guest cottages ($95-170) Web site: yeoldestonehouse.com

HILLSBOROUGH

Hillsborough House Inn
PO Box 880, 27278
919-644-1600 Fax: 919-644-1308
800-616-1660
Lauri & Kirk Michel
Closed Xmas - New Years

95-200-B&B
6 rooms, 6 pb
Visa, MC, AmEx,
Rated, •
C-ltd/S-no/P-no/H-no

Continental breakfast
Snacks
Library, swimming pool, 7
acres nature paths, separate
suite with kitchen.

Italianate mansion with dream of a front porch (80 ft.) on 7 acres in the Historic District. Eclectic, gracious & convenient. Extensive gardens. E-mail: lmmichel@msn.com Web site: hillsboroughinn.citysearch.com

KENANSVILLE

Graham House Inn
PO Box 613, 28349
910-296-1032 Fax: 910-296-1147
800-767-9397
Phyllis Brown & Nick
Halbrook
All year

95-135-B&B
4 rooms, 2 pb
Most CC,
C-ltd/S-no/P-no/H-no

Full breakfast
Snacks
Sitting room, library, tennis,
suites, fireplace, conference
facilities

A landmark mid 1850s Greek Revival Southern Aristocratic home gorgeously furnished & decorated. Delicious complete freshly cooked breakfast. Beautiful grounds with azaleas, camelias, forsythia and more. Cordless phones & computer connections in each room E-mail: innkeeper@grahamhouseinn.com Web site: grahamhouseinn.com

KILL DEVIL HILLS

Cypress House B&B	75-120-B&B	Full breakfast
500 N Virginia Dare Tr, 27948	6 rooms, 6 pb	Afternoon tea
252-441-6127 Fax: 252-441-2009	Most CC, *Rated*, •	Wrap around porches,
800-554-2764	C-ltd/S-no/P-no/H-no	overhead fans, bikes, Senior
Karen Roos All year		Citizen discount

Romantic Seaside Inn ideally located on the outer banks of North Carolina. Only 200 yards from the Atlantic Ocean. Enjoy our quiet, relaxing home and delicious breakfast. Near historic sites, shops and restaurants. E-mail: cypresshse@aol.com
Web site: cypresshouseinn.com

KURE BEACH

Ocean Princess B&B Inn	99-179-B&B	Full breakfast
824 Ft Fisher Blvd S, 28449	9 rooms, 9 pb	Complimentary wine, bar
910-458-6712 Fax: 910-458-7788	Most CC, *Rated*, •	service
800-762-4863	S-no/P-no/H-yes	Sitting room, bikes, tennis,
K. Brimmer & J. Youngblood		courts, hot tubs, swimming
All year		pool

400 ft. to the beautiful beach of the Atlantic Ocean. 3 Diamond amenities in modern beach house, all rooms with private entrances. Evening social hour. 2 night minimum on weekends. E-mail: queensrest@aol.com Web site: lookingup.com/oceanprincessb&b

LAKE LURE

Lodge on Lake Lure	99-155-B&B	Full breakfast
Box 519, 28746	11 rooms, 11 pb	complimentary wine
828-625-2789 Fax: 828-625-2421	Visa, MC, AmEx,	Sitt. rm., lib., piano, lake
800-733-2785	*Rated*, •	swimming, 2 docks, tennis,
Robin Stanier April-November	C-ltd/S-no/P-no/H-no	golf nearby

Adult getaway in the Blue Ridge Mountains. Giant stone fireplace, breathtaking view of Mtns. & lake. Only public facility actually on Lake Lure. Frplcs. in 2 rooms, A/C. Fishing boats, eve. lake cruises. E-mail: info@lodgeonlakelure.com Web site: lodgeonlakelure.com

LAWSONVILLE

Southwyck Farm B&B	90-130-B&B/MAP/AP	Full breakfast
1070 Southwyck Farm Rd,	6 rooms, 3 pb	Lunch, dinner, afternoon tea
27022	Visa, MC,	Snacks, comp. wine, library,
336-593-8006 Fax: 336-593-8006	C-ltd/S-no/H-no	sitting room, fishing pond,
Diana, Carl & David Hoskins		walking trails
All year		

Blue Ridge Foothills, fully stocked bass pond, "Murder Mystery" weekends, canoeing on Dan River, gourmet meals at Southwyck, antiques, American & Oriental art throughout house. E-mail: SouthwyckFarm@mindspring.com Web site: southwyckfarm.com

LENOIR

Summer Hill B&B	75-105-B&B	Full breakfast
1248 Harrisburg Dr, 28645	3 rooms, 3 pb	Snacks
828-757-0204	Most CC, •	Sitting room, library, tennis,
800-757-0204	C-ltd/S-ltd/P-no/H-no	sauna, swimming pool
Mary Pegram All year		nearby

Surrounded by mtn. vistas, old fashioned porches welcome visitors. Romantic English atmosphere on 35 acres of woodlands. Hiking, biking, skiing, golf. 7 day cancellation policy. E-mail: mcpegram@twave.net Web site: travelguides.com/home/summer_hill/

LITTLE SWITZERLAND

Big Lynn Lodge	83-125-MAP	Full breakfast
PO Box 459, 28749	40 rooms, 40 pb	Dinner included, fruit
828-765-4257 Fax: 828-765-0301	Visa, MC, Disc, *Rated*,	Sitting room, library, player
800-654-5232	•	piano lounge, TV, billiards,
Gale & Carol Armstrong	C-ltd/S-yes/P-no/H-ltd	shuffleboard
April 15-Oct.	German	

Old-fashioned country inn. Cool mountain air; elevation 3200 ft. Breathtaking view. Rocking chairs on porches. Main lodge remodeled & A/C. Some rooms with A/C and TVs. Now serve beer/wine with dinner.

MURPHY

Huntington Hall B&B	65-125-B&B	Full breakfast
272 Valley River Ave, 28906	5 rooms, 5 pb	Complimentary beverages
828-837-9567 Fax: 828-837-2527	Visa, MC, AmEx,	Sitting room, library, public
800-824-6189	*Rated*, •	pool & tennis, white water
Curt and Nancy Harris	C-yes/S-no/P-no/H-ltd	rafting package
All year		

A Bed & Breakfast well done! Circa 1881, former mayor's home, delightful country Victorian. Sumptuous breakfast, cool mountain breezes await you! Murder Mystery weekend package.   E-mail: huntington@grove.net *Web site:* bed-breakfast-inn.com

NAGS HEAD

First Colony Inn, The	165-300-B&B	Continental plus buffet
6720 S Virginia Dare Tr, 27959	26 rooms, 26 pb	Afternoon tea,
252-441-2343 Fax: 252-441-9234	Visa, MC, Disc, *Rated*,	complimentary wine
800-368-9390	•	Sitting room, library,
The Lawrences	C-yes/S-ltd/P-no/H-yes	verandas, pool, croquet,
All year		ocean, fishing, weddings

With verandahs along all four sides; antiques, wonderful big beds. Ocean views on 2nd & 3rd floors. Access to uncrowded private beach   E-mail: innkeeper@firstcolonyinn.com *Web site:* firstcolonyinn.com

NEW BERN

Aerie Inn B&B, The	89-99-B&B	Full gourmet breakfast
509 Pollock St, 28562	7 rooms, 7 pb	Afternoon tea, scones, tarts
252-636-5555 Fax: 252-514-2157	Visa, MC, AmEx,	Private baths, cable TV,
800-849-5553	*Rated*, •	antiques & reproductions,
Doug & Donna Bennetts	C-yes/S-ltd/P-no/H-no	player piano, phones
All year		

Relax and share the warmth and charm of this turn-of-the-century Victorian home, one block from the Tyron Palace in the heart of the historic district.   E-mail: aeriebb@coastalnet.com

Harmony House Inn	109-150-B&B	Full breakfast
215 Pollock St, 28560	10 rooms, 10 pb	Comp. drinks/wine/sherry
252-636-3810 Fax: 252-636-3810	Visa, MC, AmEx,	Victorian pump organ, 1
800-636-3113	*Rated*, •	suite, parlor, porch,
Ed & Sooki Kirkpatrick	C-yes/S-no/P-no/H-no	w/swings, rocking chairs
All year		

Unusually spacious c.1850 home, rocking chairs on porch, lovely yard. In historic district, near Tryon Palace; shops, fine restaurants.   E-mail: harmony@cconnect.net *Web site:* harmonyhouseinn.com/

OCEAN ISLE BEACH

Winds Oceanfront Clarion	57-164-B&B	Full breakfast
310 E First Street, 28469	73 rooms	Comp. wine, snacks
910-579-6275 Fax: 910-579-2884	Visa, MC, AmEx,	Library, bar service, pool,
800-334-3581	*Rated*, •	tennis, cable TV, suites,
Gary & Debra Pope-Chadwick	C-yes/S-ltd/P-no/H-ltd	Jacuzzis, bikes
All year		

Oceanfront rooms and 1, 2 & 3 bedroom suites with kitchens overlooking palm trees, lush sub-tropical gardens and island beach. Also four bedroom spa houses available   E-mail: info@thewinds.com *Web site:* thewinds.com

PINEHURST

Knollwood House	115-175-B&B	Full breakfast buffet
1495 W Connecticut Ave, 28387	6 rooms, 6 pb	Golf packages includes,
910-692-9390 Fax: 910-692-0609	Visa, MC, *Rated*, •	breakfast, lodgings, dinner
Dick Beatty	C-ltd/S-ltd/P-no/H-no	and greens fee
All year		

A luxurious English manor house with 18th century antiques & contemporary comforts in the heart of golf country.   E-mail: knollwood@pinehurst.net *Web site:* knollwoodhouse.com

The Oakwood Inn B&B, Raleigh, NC

PISGAH FOREST

Pines Country Inn, The
719 Hart Rd, 28768
828-877-3131
Mary McEntire
Memorial Day-end of Oct.

65-B&B
22 rooms, 19 pb
C-yes/S-yes/P-no/H-ltd

Full breakfast
Sitting room, piano, children
play yard, great biking &
hiking

Quiet, homey country inn. Fantastic view. Accommodations in the Inn or the 4 cabins and cottages. Where guests are treated like family at Grandma's house.

RALEIGH

Oakwood Inn B&B, The
411 N Bloodworth St, 27604
919-832-9712 Fax: 919-836-9263
800-267-9712
B & D Smith/C & D Collinet
All year

85-135-B&B
6 rooms, 6 pb
Visa, MC, *Rated*, •
C-ltd/S-no/P-no/H-no

Full breakfast
Complimentary wine,
afternoon tea
Bedside treat, snacks, sitting
room, piano, parlor, porch

Victorian retreat nestled in the heart of Raleigh's Historic Oakwood District. 6 guest rms, each with PB, remote control fireplaces, priv. phone lines, & richly furnished with period antiques & accessories.   E-mail: oakwoodbb@aol.com   Web site: members.aol.com/oakwoodbb/

ROBBINSVILLE

Blue Boar Inn
200 Santeetlah Rd, 28771
828-479-8126 Fax: 828-479-2415
Kathy & Roy Wilson
April-December

95-165-MAP
9 rooms, 9 pb
Visa, MC,
C-yes/S-yes/P-no/H-no

Full breakfast
Dinner included
Sitting room, game room,
lake swimming, boat rental,
fishing

Secluded hideaway in the Smoky Mountains, near beautiful hiking trails and lake activities. Family-style meals.   E-mail: innkeeper@blueboarinn.com   Web site: blueboarinn.com

Snowbird Mountain Lodge
275 Santeetlah Rd, 28771
828-479-3433 Fax: 828-479-3473
800-941-9290
Robert Rankin   April 15-Nov. 6

130-275-AP
21 rooms, 21 pb
Most CC, *Rated*
C-ltd/S-ltd/P-no/H-ltd

Full breakfast
Lunch & dinner included
Sitting room, piano,
vegetarian meals, wildflower
hikes

Located in the heart of the National Forest. Fishing, hiking, mountain stream swimming, canoeing, whitewater rafting, shuffleboard, and horseback riding.
E-mail: innkeeper@snowbirdlodge.com   Web site: snowbirdlodge.com

RUTHERFORDTON

Pinebrae Manor B&B
1286 NC 108 Hwy, 28139
828-286-1543 Fax: 828-288-1161
Allen & Charlotte Perry
March 15-November 30

59-69-B&B
4 rooms, 4 pb
Visa, MC, AmEx, •
C-yes/S-ltd/P-no/H-yes

Full breakfast
Snacks
Sitting room, library,
firepalces, accommodate
business travelers, VCR

A large Georgian style home located in an area steeped in Revolutionary and Civil war history. Our guest rooms are spacious clean, fine furniture & renovated to insure comfort.
E-mail: pinebrae@blueridge.com

SALUDA

Oaks, The
339 Greenville St, 28773
828-749-9613
800-893-6091
Crowley & Terry Murphy
All year

85-150-B&B
5 rooms, 5 pb
Most CC, *Rated*, •
C-ltd/S-ltd/P-no/H-no

Full breakfast
Sitting room, library, decks,
porches, Jacuzzi tub in one
room

Charming Victorian with wrap-around porch furnished with American and Oriental antiques. In small town in western North Carolina mountains. Cable TV/HBO in all rooms.
E-mail: oaks@saluda.tds.net

SAPPHIRE

Woodlands Inn of Sapphire
1305 US 64W, 28774
828-966-4709 Fax: 828-966-4544
Sherry & Bill Coy
Mar-Nov

65-125-B&B
16 rooms, 16 pb
Most CC, •
C-yes/S-ltd/P-ltd/H-ltd

Cont. plus (weekdays)
Restaurant
Sitting room, Jacuzzis,
swimming pool, suites,
fireplaces, cable TV

Privacy and price of a motel with all the niceties of a B&B. Many themed rooms: "Lisa's Garden", "Pap's Tackle Room." Back to nature cypress and glass breakfast room
E-mail: woodlandsinn@citcom.net *Web site:* woodlandsinn.net

SILER CITY

B&B at Laurel Ridge
3188 SC-Snow Camp Rd, 27344
919-742-6049
800-742-6049
David Simmons
All year

70-125-B&B
3 rooms, 3 pb
Visa, MC, AmEx, *Rated*
C-yes/S-no/P-no/H-no

Full breakfast
Aftn. tea, snacks
Sitting room, large deck,
tennis court, screened,
porch, 2 person Jacuzzi

Located in heart of North Carolina, post-and-beam country home on 26 acres, overlooks Rocky River. Gourmet breakfast by award-winning chef/owner. *E-mail:* davids@nc.webtel.net
Web site: bbonline.com/nc/laurelridge/

SPRUCE PINE

Richmond Inn B&B
51 Pine Ave, 28777
877-765-6993
Carmen Mazzagatti
All year

65-110-B&B
8 rooms, 8 pb
Visa, MC, Disc, *Rated*,
•
C-yes/S-ltd/P-no/H-no

Full breakfast
includes breads and gourmet
entree
Sitting room, library, dinner
and greens fee

A rambling country estate located in a serene mountain setting. The half-century old Inn is shaded by towering white pines and landscaped with native dogwood trees, mountain lavender and rhododendrons. *E-mail:* innkeeper@richmond-inn.com *Web site:* richmond-inn.com

TARBORO

Little Warren B&B
304 E Park Ave, 27886
252-823-1314 Fax: 252-823-1314
800-309-1314
Patsy & Tom Miller
All year

58-65-B&B
3 rooms, 3 pb
Most CC, *Rated*, •
C-ltd/S-yes/P-no/H-no
Spanish

Continental plus breakfast
Complimentary beverage
Sitting room, tennis courts,
sitting room, library

Gracious, Edwardian home full of antiques & collectibles. In quiet neighborhood, historic district. Special attention to newlyweds, anniversary couples, business guests.
E-mail: lwarrenbb@aol.com

TRYON

Pine Crest Inn
200 Pine Crest Ln, 28782
828-859-9135 Fax: 828-859-9135
800-633-3001
Jennifer & Jeremy Wainwright
All year

160-380-B&B
35 rooms, 32 pb
Visa, MC, AmEx,
Rated, •
C-yes/S-ltd/P-no/H-ltd
French

Continental plus breakfast
Restaurant & bar (fee)
Sitting room, library, frplc.,
putting green, volleyball,
Country Club

Elegant country inn located in foothills of North Carolina. Near the Blue Ridge Parkway. Gourmet restaurant, library, bar and wide verandahs add to the casual elegance. E-mail: info@pinecrestinn.com *Web site:* pinecrestinn.com

Stone Hedge Inn
PO Box 366, 28782
828-859-9114 Fax: 828-859-5928
800-859-1974
Tom and Shaula Dinsmore
All year

100-125-B&B
6 rooms, 6 pb
Visa, MC, *Rated*
C-ltd/S-no/P-no/H-ltd

Full breakfast
Restaurant, dinner available
Swimming pool, hiking in
wooded meadows,
receptions & reunions,
weddings

Restaurant and lodge on peaceful 28-acre estate. Small meetings, conferences, weddings. Contemporary fine dining. E-mail: stonehedgeinn@alltel.net *Web site:* stone-hedge-inn.comj

WARRENTON

Ivy B&B, The
331 N Main St, 27589
252-257-9300 Fax: 252-257-1960
800-919-9886
Pat & Marney Bowlds
All year

75-110-B&B
4 rooms, 3 pb
Visa, MC, AmEx,
Rated, •
C-ltd/S-ltd/P-no/H-no

Full breakfast
Comp. wine, 5 course dinner
avail.
Sitting room, library, bikes,
Jacuzzis, fireplaces, cable TV

A luxury Queen Anne, beautifully decorated and furnished with antiques. Located in a charming small town in the triangle arch near I-85. Gourmet cooking, art lessons, golf and theater packages. E-mail: drpat@compuserve.com *Web site:* bbonline.com/nc/theivy

WASHINGTON

Acadian House B&B
129 Van Norden St, 27889
252-975-3967 Fax: 252-975-1148
Leonard & Johanna Huber
February 1-Dec. 15

60-70-B&B
4 rooms, 4 pb
Rated, •
C-ltd/S-no/P-no/H-no

Full breakfast
Afternoon tea
Sitting room, library, bikes,
small meetings, wedding
reception

Located in the historic downtown district. Southern Louisiana's delicacies such as beignets, cafe au lait, and pain perdu often served at breakfast

Pamlico House
400 E Main St, 27889
252-946-7184 Fax: 252-946-9944
800-948-8507
George & Jane Fields
All year

75-95-B&B
4 rooms, 4 pb
Most CC, *Rated*, •
C-ltd/S-ltd/P-no/H-no

Full breakfast
Sitting room, color TV in
room, tennis nearby

Turn-of-the-century home in historic district, three blocks from waterfront. Antique furnishings, elegant guest rooms, wraparound porch. E-mail: pamlicohouse@coastalnet.com *Web site:* bbonline.com/nc/pamlico/

WAYNESVILLE

Brookside B&B
213 Walnut Dr, 28751
828-926-0708
800-754-1288
Betty Flynn & Armand
Favreau
All year

90-155-B&B
4 rooms, 2 pb
Visa, MC, AmEx, •
C-ltd/S-ltd/P-no/H-no

Full breakfast
Tea, snacks, wine
Lunch & dinner available,
sitting room, library,
Jacuzzis, fireplace

Visit Maggie Valley and the Great Smoky Mountains. Close to Cherokee and the Blue Ridge Parkway. Let yourself be cared for in the friendly atmosphere of Brookside B&B. E-mail: getaway@brookside-maggievalley.com *Web site:* brookside-maggievalley.com

WAYNESVILLE ───────────────────────────────

Grandview Lodge
466 Lickstone Rd, 28786
828-456-5212 Fax: 828-452-5432
800-255-7826
Stan & Linda Arnold
All year

105-115-MAP
9 rooms, 9 pb
Visa, MC, *Rated*, •
C-yes/S-no
Polish, Russian, German

Full breakfast
Dinner included, lunch
available
Restaurant (reservations),
fax, library, piano, golf,
tennis, shuffleboard

Inn located on rolling land, with an orchard & arbor. Breakfast features homemade jams & jellies. Dinner includes fresh vegetables, baked breads & desserts. All rooms with AC.
E-mail: innkeeper@grandviewlodgenc.com   *Web site:* bbonline.com/nc/grandview

Haywood House
675 S Haywood St, 28786
828-456-9831 Fax: 828-456-4400
Lynn & Chris Sylvester
All year

75-95-B&B
4 rooms, 2 pb
Visa, MC, AmEx, •
C-ltd/S-no/P-no/H-no

Full breakfast
Comp. beverage, snacks
Sitting room, library, laundry
fac., Fax, veranda & picnic
areas

Rock, relax, view the mountains and enjoy small town charm. Comfortable, beautifully furnished historic home.   E-mail: info@haywoodhouse.com   *Web site:* haywoodhouse.com

Herren House B&B
94 E Street, 28786
828-452-7837 Fax: 828-452-7706
800-284-1932
Jackie & Frank Blevins
All year

85-140-B&B
6 rooms, 6 pb
Most CC, *Rated*, •
C-ltd/S-no/P-no/H-yes

Full breakfast
Afternoon tea, snacks, wine
Lunch available (fee), sitting
room, library, cable TV

A special place filled with Victorian charm and casual elegance. Unique 19th century boardinghouse, completely and exquisitely restored. Gourmet breakfast by candlelight. Romantic weekend packages.   E-mail: herren1@mindspring.com   *Web site:* circle.net/~herren

Mountain Creek B&B
146 Chestnut Walk Dr, 28786
828-456-5509
800-557-9766
Hylah & Guy Smalley
All year

99-125-B&B
6 rooms, 6 pb
Visa, MC, *Rated*, •
C-ltd/S-no/P-no/H-no

Full breakfast
Complimentary wine
Sitting room, 1600 sq foot
deck, cable TV

Nestled on 6 acres with 2 creeks, a pond & millwheel, this ex-corporate retreat has a rustic but contemporary lodge feeling. Surrounded by woods & mountains creating a relaxing environment.   E-mail: guylah@aol.com   *Web site:* bbonline.com/nc/mcbb

Old Stone Inn
109 Dolan Rd, 28786
828-456-3333
800-432-8499
Robert & Cindy Zinser
Easter-Jan. 1

94-164-B&B
22 rooms, 22 pb
Rated
S-yes/P-no/H-ltd
Spanish

Full breakfast
Fireside dining
Sitting room, library, outdoor
deck, gift shop, color TV in
rm, 2 pianos

On a wooded hillside—mountain inn with beamed ceilings & country furnishings. Golf, train ride, whitewater pkgs. Celebrating 50 years. Not appropriate for children
Web site: bbonline.com/nc/oldstone

Swag Country Inn, The
2300 Swag Rd, 28786
828-926-0430 Fax: 828-926-2036
800-789-7672
Deener Matthews
May 2-November 21

250-550-AP
18 rooms, 18 pb
Most CC, *Rated*, •
C-ltd/S-ltd/P-no/H-ltd

Full breakfast
All meals included in rate
Library, piano, sauna,
racquetball, hiking, croquet
field above pond

At 5,000 feet, hand-hewn log lodge. Elegant, intimate hideaway. Fifteen unique bedrooms, excellent cuisine, breathtaking views. Executive retreat, honeymoon haven. Mobil 4-Star rating for the past 5 years and has been in business 18 years.   E-mail: letters@theswag.com
Web site: theswag.com/

The Old Stone Inn, Waynesville, NC

WAYNESVILLE

WindDancers Lodging	115-135-B&B	Continental plus breakfast
1966 Martins Creek Rd, 28721	9 rooms, 9 pb	Snacks
828-627-6986 Fax: 828-627-0754	Visa, MC, *Rated*	Sitting room, library, suites,
Donna & Gale Livengood,	C-yes/S-no/P-no/H-no	fireplace, llama dinner, lunch
family All year		hikes

Our contemporary log lodging is nestled in a peaceful mountain cove of woodlands, stream & llama-scaped pastures. The 9 bright, spacious guest accommodations offer a choice of exotic, ethnic decors.   E-mail: info@winddancersnc.com   Web site: winddancersnc.com

Yellow House, The	125-240-B&B	Full breakfast
89 Oakview Dr, 28786	6 rooms, 6 pb	Hors d'oeuvres hour
828-452-0991 Fax: 828-452-1140	Visa, MC, •	Sitting room, library, bikes,
800-563-1236	C-ltd/S-no/P-no/H-no	tennis court, hot tubs,
Ron & Sharon Smith		swimming pool
All year		

Western NC's most romantic inn; gourmet breakfast may be served in your room. Every quarter has fireplace, coffee service, robes, & music. 2.5 acres of lawn, lily pond and gardens   E-mail: yelhouse@asap-com.com   Web site: theyellowhouse.com

WILMINGTON

Anderson Guest House	90-B&B	Full breakfast
520 Orange St, 28401	2 rooms, 2 pb	Complimentary wine, mixed
910-343-8128	C-ltd/S-yes/P-yes/H-no	drinks
888-265-1216		Afternoon tea, fireplace,
Connie Anderson		restaurant nearby, baby-
All year		sitting service

1851 Italianate townhouse; separate guest quarters overlooking private garden. Furnished with antiques, ceiling fans, fireplaces. Drinks upon arrival. Delightful breakfasts.

Catherine's Inn	80-115-B&B	Full breakfast
410 S Front St, 28401	3 rooms, 3 pb	Complimentary wine,
910-251-0863 Fax: 910-772-9550	Visa, MC, AmEx,	snacks, tea
800-476-0723	*Rated*, •	Bar service, sitting room,
Catherine & Walter AcKiss	C-yes/S-yes/P-no/H-no	library, baby-sitting service
All year		

In heart of the historical district. Experience warm gracious hospitality, tasty breakfasts. E-mail: catherin@wilmington.net   Web site: catherinesinn.com

WILMINGTON

Curran House, The
312 S 3rd St, 28401
910-763-6603 Fax: 910-763-5116
800-763-6603
Vickie & Greg Stringer
All year

80-129-B&B
3 rooms, 3 pb
Visa, MC, AmEx,
Rated, •
C-ltd/S-ltd/P-no/H-no

Full breakfast
Afternoon tea, snacks
Sitting room, library, cable
TV, accommodate business
travelers

Three large guest rooms, two with king beds, 1 with queen bed. Central air, cable/VCR, guest robes, telephone, ceiling fans in each room. 3 diamond AAA rated in Historic Downtown Wilmington Web site: bbonline.com/nc/curran

Darlings by the Sea
PO Box 373, 28449
910-458-8887 Fax: 910-458-6468
800-383-8111
Kip & Maureen Darling
All year

109-229-B&B
5 rooms, 5 pb
Most CC, *Rated*, •
S-yes/P-no/H-no
Spanish

Continental plus breakfast
Bicycles, Jacuzzis, suites,
cable TV, fitness center,
beach

Fabulously appointed oceanfront whirlpool suites. King beds, down comforters. Satellite TV, music, VCR, dbl. whirlpools. Oceanfront fitness center, lush ctyard, sun deck & lighthouse E-mail: reservations@darlingsbythesea.com *Web site:* darlingsbythesea.com

Docksider Oceanfront Inn
PO Box 373, 28449
910-458-4200 Fax: 910-458-6468
800-815-8636
Kip & Maureen Darling
All year

60-160-EP
34 rooms, 34 pb
Most CC, *Rated*, •
C-yes/S-yes/P-no/H-yes

Swimming pool, family
friendly facility, fitness
center, beach

"Captains Cabins," our most luxurious oceanfront accommodations, come complete with gourmet breakfast in bed, midnight snacks, wine & cheese, all prestocked in your cabin prior to your arrival. E-mail: reservations@docksiderinn.com *Web site:* docksiderinn.com

Front Street Inn
215 S Front St, 28401
910-762-6442 Fax: 910-762-8991
Jay & Stefany Rhodes
All year

95-165-B&B
9 rooms, 9 pb
Most CC,
C-ltd/S-ltd/P-no/H-no
Spanish, French

Continental plus breakfast
Snacks, bar service
Hot tub, bikes, sitting, room,
phones TVs-modems, in all
rooms & suites

Intimate, European style inn. Privacy and charm. One block from river in historic downtown. Abundant healthful breakfast served all morning. E-mail: jay@frontstreetinn.com *Web site:* frontstreetinn.com

Graystone Inn
100 S Third St, 28401
910-763-2000 Fax: 910-763-5555
888-763-4773
Paul & Yolanda Bolda
All year

159-289-B&B
7 rooms, 7 pb
Most CC, *Rated*, •
C-ltd/S-yes/P-no/H-no

Full breakfast
Complimentary sherry &
fruit
Sitt. rm., piano, robes,
library, fitness center,
phones with voice mail

Magnificently restored limestone mansion in historic district; large formal ballroom, perhaps most beautiful home in North Carolina. On Cape Rear River. E-mail: paulb@ graystoneinn.com *Web site:* graystoneinn.com

Inn at St. Thomas Court
101 S Second St, 28401
910-343-1800 Fax: 910-251-1149
800-525-0909
Mike Compton & Tom Scott
All year

145 and up-B&B
40 rooms, 40 pb
Visa, MC, AmEx,
Rated, •
C-ltd/S-yes/H-yes

Continental plus breakfast
In suites—kitchen included
Concierge, conservatory,
billiard room, courtyard, in-
house pub, conference

Elegant accommodations for discriminating travelers, located in romantic Historic District. Walk along Cape Fear River paths to fine restaurants, museums and specialty shops. E-mail: innatstthomascourt@juno.com *Web site:* innatstthomascourt.com

WILMINGTON

Rosehill Inn B&B	149-229-B&B	Full or continental plus
114 S Third St, 28401	6 rooms, 6 pb	breakfast
910-815-0250 Fax: 910-815-0350	Most CC, *Rated*, •	Complimentary wine
800-815-0250	C-ltd/S-no/P-no/H-no	Sitting room, library, phones
Laurel Jones & Dennis Fietsch		with fax/modem jacks
All year		

Rosehill is a beautifully restored Victorian/neo-classical home in the heart of Wilmington's historic district. E-mail: rosehill@rosehill.com Web site: rosehill.com

Verandas, The	130-180-B&B	Full breakfast
202 Nun Street, 28401	8 rooms, 8 pb	Complimentary wine
910-251-2212 Fax: 910-251-8932	Most CC, *Rated*, •	Sitting room, cable TV, piano
D. Madsen & C. Pennington	C-ltd/S-no/P-no/H-no	
All year	American Sign Language	

Grand yet affordable luxury on a quiet street two blocks from riverwalk, restaurants, shopping. Large rooms with marble baths, phone & modem jacks. E-mail: verandas4@aol.com Web site: verandas.com/

Worth House, The	80-125-B&B	Full breakfast
412 S Third St, 28401	7 rooms, 7 pb	Complimentary beverages
910-762-8562	Visa, MC, AmEx,	3 sitting rooms, fax, laundry,
800-340-8559	*Rated*, •	modem, porches, gardens,
All year	C-ltd/S-no/P-no/H-no	fireplaces

1893 Queen Anne in historic district. A/C, period art and furnishings. With our 7 guest rms. and 4 common rms., we are ideal for reunions & retreats. 5 min. walk downtown, 15 min. drive to beach. Web site: bbonline.com/nc/worth/

WILSON

Miss Betty's B&B Inn	60-90-B&B	Full breakfast
600 W Nash St, 27893	14 rooms, 14 pb	3 parlors, antique shop, A/C,
252-243-4447 Fax: 252-243-4447	Most CC, *Rated*	golf, swimming pool, games,
800-258-2058	S-yes/P-no/H-yes	executive suites
Betty & Fred Spitz		
All year		

Selected as one of "best places to stay in the South." A touch of Victorian elegance & beauty. Executive suites for long-term business guests. Close to main North-South Route I-95. Phones in rooms.

WINSTON-SALEM

Augustus T. Zevely Inn	80-205-B&B	Continental plus-weekdays
803 S Main St, 27101	12 rooms, 12 pb	Full breakfast on weekends
336-748-9299 Fax: 336-721-2211	Visa, MC, AmEx,	Afternoon tea, snacks, wine,
800-928-9294	*Rated*, •	sitting room, library, bikes,
Linda Anderson	C-yes/S-yes/P-no/H-yes	sauna, pool
All year		

Moravian-style B&B restored to museum quality, overlooking historic Old Salem. Formal dining room & parlor, spacious covered porch. Period garden and orchard. Health facility. Web site: travelguides.com/home/zevely

Brookstown Inn B&B	90-155-B&B	Continental plus breakfast
200 Brookstown Ave, 27101	71 rooms, 71 pb	Snacks, complimentary wine
336-725-1120 Fax: 336-773-0147	Most CC, •	Sitting room, suites, cable TV,
888-845-4262	C-yes/S-yes/P-no/H-ltd	restaurant on site
Gary Colbert		
All year		

This historic Brookstown Inn was originally built in 1837 as a textile mill. The conversion carefully preserved the handmade bricks and exposed wooden beams visual throughout the Inn today. Guests enjoy a complimentary European breakfast each morning. E-mail: broj6@aol.com

WINSTON-SALEM ──────────────────────────────

Colonel Ludlow Inn	159-209-B&B	Full breakfast
434 Summit at W 5th, 27101	12 rooms, 12 pb	King bed, some frplcs., in-
336-777-1887 Fax: 336-777-0518	Visa, MC, AmEx,	room CDs/tapes/VCR,
800-301-1887	*Rated*, •	gardens, fountains
Constance Creasman	C-ltd/S-yes/P-no/H-no	
All year		

Two adjacent beautifully restored 1887 & 1890 National Register homes. Exercise room, antiques. Deluxe rooms with private 2-person Jacuzzi in romantic alcove. Near downtown, shops, fine restaurants. E-mail: inkeeper@bbinn.com *Web site:* bbinn.com

North Dakota

COOPERSTOWN ──────────────────────────────

Volden Farm B&B	60-95-B&B	Full breakfast
11943 County Rd 26, 58056	4 rooms, 1 pb	Lunch, dinner, snacks, wine
701-769-2275 Fax: 701-769-2610	*Rated*, •	Canoeing, sitt. rm., hammock
Jim & JoAnne Wold	C-yes/S-ltd/P-ltd/H-no	swing, bikes, billiard, library,
All year	Russian, Norwegian	fireplaces

An unexpected old world atmosphere on the wide prairie of eastern North Dakota. We have collected things Russian and Norwegian which reflect our years in Moscow and family heritage. E-mail: voldenfarm_bb@broadvu.com *Web site:* broadvu.com/voldenfarm

Ohio

BERLIN ──────────────────────────────

Barn Inn B&B	69-159-B&B	Full breakfast
6838 CR 203, 44654	7 rooms, 7 pb	Snacks
330-674-7600 Fax: 330-674-0761	Visa, MC, AmEx, Disc,	Fireplaces, satellite TV
877-674-7600	C-ltd/S-ltd/P-no/H-yes	
Paul & Loretta Coblentz		
All year		

The charm of this barn is enhanced by original beams which contrast with Victorian elegance. VIP and standard rooms, whirlpools, fireplaces, TV, full country breakfast, large common area, resident innkeepers. Web site: bbonline/oh/thebarn/

Fields of Home Guest House	65-125-B&B	Continental plus breakfast
7278 CR 201, 44654	5 rooms, 5 pb	Snacks, complimentary
330-674-7152	Visa, MC, Disc, *Rated*	sodas
Mervin & Ruth Yoder	C-yes/S-no/P-no/H-ltd	Suites, firepalces,
All year	Limited German	accommodate business
		travelers

Our log cabin B&B invites you to relax and enjoy the peace and quiet of rural Amish Country. Enjoy the perennial gardens, fish pond and paddle boat. Relax by your own personal fireplace or luxuriate in a whirlpool bath.

BUCYRUS

Hide Away B&B	97-195-B&B	5 course breakfast
1601 State Route 4, 44820	6 rooms, 6 pb	Candlelight dinner available
419-562-3013 Fax: 419-562-3003	Visa, MC, *Rated*, •	Sitting room, library, 3 rooms
800-570-8233	C-yes/S-ltd/P-no/H-no	with Jacuzzi, frplcs., priv.
Debbie & Steve Miller		garden
All year		

Elegant country manor nestled among majestic century-old oak trees. Gracious guest-rooms, gourmet breakfasts, antiques, golf, Jacuzzi, pool E-mail: hideaway@cybrtown.com
Web site: hideawayinn.com

CINCINNATI

Ohio River House	65-125-B&B	Full breakfast
PO Box 188, 45131	8 rooms, 8 pb	Snacks, complimentary wine
937-375-4395 Fax: 937-375-4394	Visa, MC,	Sitting room, bikes, pool,
Andy & Judy Lloyd	C-yes/S-no/P-yes/H-no	family friendly
All year		

1830 Federal Colonial situated on river. Fully furnished with comfortable antiques. Lovely terrace and veranda at river's edge. Antique shop on premises for browsing pleasure. E-mail: fdsinc@bright.net *Web site:* OhioRiverHouse.com

CLEVELAND

Crest B&B	75-95-B&B	Continental plus breakfast
1489 Crest Rd, 44121	2 rooms, 1 pb	Afternoon tea,
216-382-5801	•	complimentary wine
Clark & Phyllis Gerber	C-yes/S-no/P-no/H-no	Sitting room, accommodate
All year	Some German	business travelers, tennis
		nearby

Affordable housing near cultural activities and excellent restaurants. Continental plus breakfast served in dining room. Hosts knowledgable about Cleveland & surrounding area. Located on a quiet residental street. E-mail: crest@dellnet.com

Spitzer house B&B	70-110-B&B	Full breakfast
504 West Liberty St, 44256	4 rooms, 4 pb	Snacks
330-725-7289 Fax: 330-725-7289	Visa, MC, Disc., •	Sitting room, Jacuzzis,
888-777-1379	C-ltd/S-no/P-no/H-no	fireplace, cable TV, rose
Dale and Janet Rogers		garden
All year		

Beautifully restored 1890 Queen Anne filled with warm antiques, lacey linens and Victori-an charm. Walking distance to candle outlet, antique shops, specialty stores and restau-rants. E-mail: innkeepers@spitzerhouse.com *Web site:* spitzerhouse.com

COLUMBUS

Candlelite Lane B&B	85-B&B	Continental plus breakfast
1466 Candlelite Ln, 43035	2 rooms, 1 pb	Snacks
614-885-8165 Fax: 614-885-7451	Most CC, •	Sitting room, library,
877-604-1075	C-ltd/S-ltd/P-ltd/H-no	fireplace, cable TV,
Shirley & Jerry Young		accommodate business
All year		travelers

Classic Cape Cod-style home on one acre in Southern Delaware County, catering to busi-ness travelers in the Polaris Parkway, Worthington and North Columbus area. Convenient to restaurants, shopping, businesses, yet sits on a quiet country acre. E-mail: 105400.131@compuserve.com *Web site:* bbonline.com/oh/candlelite

Penguin Crossing B&B	100-225-B&B	Full breakfast on weekends
3291 State Rt 56 W, 43113	5 rooms, 5 pb	Continental plus breakfast
740-477-6222 Fax: 740-420-6060	Most CC, *Rated*, •	midweek
800-PENGUIN	C-yes/S-ltd/P-no/H-yes	Sitting room, hot tubs,
Ross & Tracey Irvin		stargazing, hiking, kennel
All year		nearby, snacks

Central Ohio romantic getaway, 1820s farmhouse, heart-shaped Jacuzzis, fireplaces, an-tiques, historical country inn. State Parks and downtown Columbus nearby. New room added. E-mail: innkeepers@penguin.cc *Web site:* penguin.cc

DANVILLE

White Oak Inn, The
29683 Walhonding Rd, 43014
740-599-6107
Ian & Yvonne Martin
All year

85-140-B&B
10 rooms, 10 pb
Most CC, *Rated*, •
C-ltd/S-no/P-no/H-no

Full breakfast
Dinner with notice
Afternoon snacks, common
room, porch, screen house,
lawn games

Large country home nestled in wooded area. Outdoor enthusiasts' paradise. Comfortable antique decor; 3 fireplace rooms. Near Amish country/antiques. E-mail: yvonne@ecr.net
Web site: whiteoakinn.com

DAYTON

English Manor
505 E Linden Ave, 45342
937-866-2288
800-676-9456
Ken & Jeannette Huelsman
All year

65-95-B&B
5 rooms, 3 pb
Visa, MC, AmEx, *Rated*
C-ltd/S-no

Full breakfast
Afternoon tea
Sitting room, Just 10 miles
south of Dayton

A Tudor style mansion. Tranquility in a setting of elegance—Hand-rubbed wood, leaded glass windows and antique furnishings. Step back in time
Web site: bbdirectory.com/Inn/1493.html

DOVER

Olde World B&B
2982 State Rt 516 NW, 44622
330-343-1333 Fax: 330-364-8022
800-447-1273
Jonna Sigrist
All year

55-100-B&B
5 rooms, 5 pb
Visa, MC, Disc, *Rated*,
•
C-ltd/S-no/P-no/H-no

Full breakfast
Lunch/dinner avail.,
afternoon tea
Hot tubs, flower gardens,
sitting room, outdoor
verandah with grill

Stately 1881 Victorian home furnished with antiques; suites include Victorian, Oriental, Parisian, Mediterranean & Alpine. E-mail: owbb@tusco.net *Web site:* oldeworldbb.com

GRANVILLE

Willowbrooke B&B
4459 Morse Rd, 43001
740-924-6161 Fax: 740-924-0224
800-772-6372
Sandra Gilson
All year

85-125-B&B
5 rooms, 4 pb
Most CC,
C-ltd/S-no/P-no/H-ltd

Full breakfast
Snacks
Sitting room, Jacuzzis, suites,
fireplaces, cable TV

Secluded in 34 acres of woods. Candlelight, fireplaces, featherbeds & Jacuzzi tubs add to romantic atmosphere of the large elegant English Tudor Manor House and separate Guest House E-mail: wilbrk@aol.com

HANOVERTON

Spread Eagle Inn
PO Box 44, 44423
330-223-1583 Fax: 330-223-1445
Pete & Jean Johnson
All year

100-225-B&B
5 rooms, 5 pb
Most CC,
C-yes/S-no/P-no/H-ltd

Full breakfast
Restaurant, bar service
Sitting room, fireplaces,
cable TV

The Spread Eagle Tavern is an artfully restored Federal style historic brick Inn that features a gourmet restaurant, unique rathskeller, seven dining rooms and five overnight guest rooms furnished with antiques. E-mail: jsweat@summitville.com

HURON

Captain Montague's B&B
229 Center St, 44839
419-433-4756
800-276-4756
Judy and Mike Tann
April-October

95-175-B&B
6 rooms, 6 pb
S-no/P-no/H-no
English

Continental plus breakfast
Lunch (picnic basket)
Afternoon tea, snacks,
swimming pool, parlor,
garden and gazebo

Captain Montague's Guest House is near a summer theater, waterfront parks, a boat harbor and Cedar Point. E-mail: judytann@aol.com *Web site:* bbhost.com/captainmontagues

KELLEYS ISLAND

Water's Edge Retreat
PO Box 839, 43438
419-746-2455 Fax: 419-746-2242
Elizabeth Hermes
All year

169-300-B&B
6 rooms, 6 pb
•
C-ltd/S-no/P-no/H-no
Some French, ASL

Full breakfast
Snacks, comp. wine
Sitting room, library, bridal
suite, fireplaces, Jacuzzis,
beach, bikes

Waterfront, elegant Queen Anne Victorian style. Travel & Leisure rated "... best of the Great Lakes." E-mail: watersedge@mindspring.com *Web site:* WatersEdgeRetreat.com

LISBON

Inn at Willow Pond
41932 St Rt 517, 44432
330-424-4660 Fax: 330-424-4661
888-345-2809
Bea & Chuck Delpapa
Closed January

95-110-B&B
3 rooms, 3 pb
Visa, MC, Disc, *Rated*
C-ltd/S-no/P-no/H-ltd
Some Spanish

Full breakfast
Snacks, complimentary wine
Sitting room, Jacuzzis

Restored 1860s farmhouse on 11 secluded acres; pond and gardens. Gourmet breakfasts— Mexican breakfast on request. Exquisite collection of Mexican and SW folk art. E-mail: wilopond@raex.com *Web site:* virtualcities.com/oh/willowpond.htm

LOGAN

Inn at Cedar Falls, The
21190 St Rt 374, 43138
740-385-7489 Fax: 740-385-0820
800-65-FALLS
Ellen Grinsfelder
Cabins closed on X-mas

85-220-B&B
13 rooms, 13 pb
Visa, MC, *Rated*, •

Full breakfast
Lunch/dinner available (fee)
Restaurant, bar service,
sitting room, library, Call for
winter rates

1840s log cabin houses-open kitchen. Gourmet meals prepared from inn's organic garden. Antique furnished rooms (9) & log cabins (6) surrounded by Hocking State Parks. E-mail: innatcedarfalls@hockinghills.com *Web site:* innatcedarfalls.com

MILLSERBURG

Port Washington Inn B&B
4667 TR 312, 44654
330-674-7704 Fax: 216-521-6869
888-674-7704
Lois Stutzman, Yamileth Ulrich
All year

59-225-B&B
8 rooms, 8 pb
Visa, MC, Disc, *Rated*
C-yes/S-no/P-no/H-no

Full breakfast
Snacks
Sitting room, Jacuzzis,
swimming pool, suites,
fireplace, cable TV, hot tub

Secluded in the heart of Amish Country, 45 acre county estate provides something for everyone.   E-mail: portwinn@aol.com *Web site:* members.aol.com/portwinn

NAPOLEON

Augusta Rose B&B, The
345 W Main St, 43545
419-592-5852
877-590-1960
Ed & Mary Hoeffel
All year

60-75-B&B
4 rooms, 4 pb
Visa, MC, AmEx,
C-yes/S-no/P-no/H-no

Full breakfast
2 sitting rooms, 1 w/TV
recreational assistance

Stately Victorian with wrap-around porch located one block from scenic Maumee River. Tranquil small town. Wonderful antique shops. Central air-conditioning. E-mail: augrose@bright.net

NEW PLYMOUTH

Ravenwood Castle
65666 Bethel Rd, 45654
740-596-2606 Fax: 740-596-5818
800-477-1541
Sue & Jim Maxwell
All year

95-175-B&B
16 rooms, 16 pb
Visa, MC, Disc, •
C-yes/S-no/P-no/H-yes

Full breakfast
Lunch & dinner available
Afternoon tea, snacks, suites,
fireplaces, Jacuzzis, library

Re-creation of a 12th century Medieval Castle with two "villages" of cottages, shops, tearoom, etc. Many special "Medieval" or "British" events. E-mail: ravenwood@ohiohills.com *Web site:* Ravenwoodcastle.com

SANDUSKY ————

Wagner's 1844 Inn
230 E Washington St, 44870
419-626-1726 Fax: 419-626-8465
Walt & Barbara Wagner
All year

70-100-B&B
3 rooms, 3 pb
Visa, MC,
S-no/P-yes/H-ltd

Continental plus breakfast
Complimentary wine,
chocolates
Billiard room with TV, air-
conditioning, weddings,
receptions

Elegantly restored Victorian home. Listed on National Register of Historic Places. Near Lake Erie attractions. Air-conditioned rooms.   E-mail: wagnersinn@sanduskyohio.com
Web site: lrbcg.com/wagnersinn

SANDUSKY, NORWALK ————

Georgian Manor Inn
123 W Main St, 44857
419-663-8132 Fax: 419-668-3542
800-668-1644
Judy & Gene Denney
Closed Christmas

95-165-B&B
4 rooms, 4 pb
Visa, MC, AmEx, *Rated*
C-ltd/S-no/P-no/H-no

Full breakfast
Afternoon tea, snacks, comp.
wine
Sitting room, library,
Jacuzzis, fireplaces, cable
TV, in room phones

Stately mansion on historic, architecturally rich West Main. Well appointed, plush surroundings. First Class personal service. 600 book library, living room—oak mantled fireplace. Pathed gardens & pond.   E-mail: GeorgianManorInn@nwonline.net
Web site: bbhost.com/georgianmanorinn/

YOUNGSTOWN ————

Inn At The Green
500 S Main St, 44514
330-757-4688
Ginny & Steve Meloy
All year

60-B&B
5 rooms, 4 pb
Visa, MC, *Rated*, •
C-ltd/S-no/P-no/H-no

Continental plus breakfast
Complimentary wine
Oriental rugs, deck, patio,
antiques, garden, sitting
room, fireplaces

Authentically restored Victorian townhouse in preserved Western Reserve Village near Youngstown. Convenient to Turnpike and I-80. Poland is 7 mi. S.E. of Youngstown.

ZOAR ————

Cowger House #9
PO Box 527, 44697
330-874-3542 Fax: 330-874-4172
800-874-3542
Ed & Mary Cowger
All year

65-150-B&B
10 rooms, 10 pb
Rated
C-ltd/S-yes/P-no/H-no

Full country breakfast
Lunch & dinner by RSVP
Entertainment, honeymoon
suite with fireplace & Jacuzzi

A little bit of Williamsburg. 1817 log cabin with 2-acre flower garden maintained by the Ohio Historic Society. 1865 re-enactment dinners.   E-mail: cowgerhous@aol.com
Web site: zoarvillage.com

Oklahoma

CHECOTAH ————

Sharpe House
301 NW Second St, 74426
918-473-2832
Kay Kindt
All year

50-B&B
3 rooms, 3 pb
•
C-yes/S-ltd/P-yes/H-no
Some Spanish

Full breakfast
Snacks, complimentary wine
Sitting room, library, cable
TV

Elegant turn-of-the-century home furnished with period furniture. It is a two-story home with "Tara" type columns in front and a large screened porch in back. Innkeeper is retired college instructor.

EDMOND ─────────────────────────────────

Arcadian Inn B&B
328 East First, 73034
405-348-6347 Fax: 405-348-8100
800-299-6347
Martha & Gary Hall
All year

95-170-B&B
5 rooms, 5 pb
Visa, MC, AmEx,
Rated, •
C-ltd/S-no/P-no/H-no

Full breakfast
Dinner by reservation
Sitting room, hot tubs, family
friendly facility

Luxurious, romantic setting, sumptuous homemade breakfast. Intimate getaway for couples, perfect for the business traveler. Specializing in preferential treatment.
E-mail: arcadianinn@juno.com *Web site:* bbonline.com/ok/arcadian

NORMAN ─────────────────────────────────

Holmberg House B&B
766 De Barr, 73069
405-321-6221 Fax: 405-321-6221
800-646-6221
Jo Meacham & Michael Cobb
All year

65-120-B&B
4 rooms, 4 pb
Most CC, *Rated*
C-ltd/S-no/P-no/H-no

Full breakfast
Restaurants close by
Near historic shopping,
sitting room & library, herb
& flower gardens

Historic home across the St. from the U of O. Built in 1914, National Register. Entirely furnished with antiques. Shopping nearby. Facilities for weddings & receptions
E-mail: holmberg@telepath.com

Montford Inn
322 W Tonhawa, 73069
405-321-2200 Fax: 405-321-8347
800-321-8969
Phyllis, Ron & William Murray
All year

90-200-B&B
16 rooms, 16 pb
Most CC, *Rated*, •
C-yes/S-no/P-no/H-yes

Full breakfast
Afternoon tea, wine
Sitting room, library,
fireplaces in rooms, 2
outdoor/private hot tubs

New urban inn with antiques & gift shop. Restaurants, shops, parks, Oklahoma University nearby. Off-street parking. 2 suite cottage with 2 person Jacuzzi.
E-mail: montford@telepath.com *Web site:* montfordinn.com/

Oregon

ASHLAND ─────────────────────────────────

Country Willows B&B Inn
1313 Clay St, 97520
541-488-1590 Fax: 541-488-1611
800-WILLOWS
Dan Durant
All year

95-195-B&B
9 rooms, 9 pb
Visa, MC, *Rated*, •
C-ltd/S-ltd/P-no/H-yes

Full breakfast
Sitting room, hot tubs,
library, outdoor Jacuzzi,
heated swimming pool

Romantic, peaceful, rural setting. 1896 farmhouse, 5 acres. Rooms in house, cottage & barn with mountain views. Hiking, porches, duck pond, bikes, in-room phones.
E-mail: willows@willowsinn.com *Web site:* willowsinn.com

Neil Creek House
341 Mowetza Dr, 97520
541-482-6443 Fax: 541-482-1074
800-460-7860
Paul & Gayle Nego
All year

85-115-B&B
2 rooms, 2 pb
Rated, •
C-ltd/S-no/P-no/H-no

Full breakfast
Library, swimming pool,
suites, fireplace

Enjoy the ambiance of this country hideaway with all the luxury of a fine hotel. Breakfast is served al fresco at this intimate, pristine setting that is home to wildlife and many waterfowl. E-mail: neilcrk@mind.net *Web site:* mind.net/neilcrk

ASHLAND ―――――――――――――――――――――――――――――

Wolfe Manor Inn	109-139-B&B	Full breakfast
586 B St, 97520	5 rooms, 5 pb	Snacks
541-488-3676 Fax: 541-488-4567	Most CC, *Rated*, •	Sitting room, library in room
800-801-3676	C-ltd/S-no/P-no/H-no	phones, music
Sybil Maddox		
February-Oct.		

Lovingly restored 1910 Craftsman home in quiet neighborhood surrounded by beautiful garden. A short walk to theatres and fine restaurants. Room with mountain views.
E-mail: wolfebandb@aol.com *Web site:* wolfemanor.com

ASTORIA ―――――――――――――――――――――――――――――

Grandview B&B	59-98-B&B	Full breakfast
1574 Grand Ave, 97103	9 rooms, 7 pb	Snacks
503-325-5555 Fax: 707-982-8790	Most CC, *Rated*, •	Sitt. rm., canopy beds, books,
800-488-3250	C-ltd	games, binoculars, liquor not
Charleen Maxwell		permitted
All year		

Light, airy, cheerful Victorian close to superb Maritime Museum, Lightship, churches, golf, clam-digging, fishing, beaches and rivers. Sleeps 21.   E-mail: grandviewbedandbreakfast@ usa.net *Web site:* travelguides.com/home/grand_view/

Rose River Inn	85-125-B&B	Full breakfast
1510 Franklin Ave, 97103	4 rooms, 4 pb	Afternoon tea
503-325-7175 Fax: 503-325-7188	Visa, MC, *Rated*, •	Sitting room, suites,
888-876-0028	C-ltd/S-no/P-ltd/H-no	fireplaces, cable TV, sauna-
Kati & Jaakko Tuominen	Finnish, Swedish,	bath/massage
All year	German	

Rose River Inn B&B is an old Victorian house with Finnish owners. The inn specializes in Finnish sauna and massage. Our rose garden is well known in Astoria as well as the art and antiques.   E-mail: jaska@pacifier.com *Web site:* moriah.com/roseriver

BANDON ―――――――――――――――――――――――――――――

Lighthouse B&B	105-175-B&B	Full breakfast
PO Box 24, 97411	5 rooms, 5 pb	Complimentary teas, hot
541-347-9316	Visa, MC, *Rated*	cocoa
Shirley Chalupa	C-ltd/S-no/P-no/H-no	Sitting room, bicycles, hot
All year		tub in one room, on the
		beach

Located on the beach across from historic lighthouse. Panoramic views, quiet location. Walk to fine restaurants. 2 rooms with whirlpool and fireplace. A non-smoking inn.
E-mail: lthousbb@harborside.com *Web site:* moriah.com/lighthouse

BEAVERTON ―――――――――――――――――――――――――――

Aloha Junction Inn B&B	60-B&B	Full breakfast
5085 SW 170th Ave, 97007	4 rooms, 1 pb	Snacks
503-642-7236 Fax: 503-642-7236	Visa, MC, *Rated*	Sitting room, library, hot
Sandra Elmers	C-ltd/S-ltd/P-no/H-yes	tubs, gardens and farm goats
All year		

Unique country setting in the heart of high tech metropolis, with Intel, Nike & Tex campuses nearby. Gourmet breakfast served in the garden room or on a tray in your room. Oregon wine country

BEND ―――――――――――――――――――――――――――――――

Cricketwood Country B&B	60-90-B&B	Full breakfast
63520 Cricketwood Rd, 97701	3 rooms, 1 pb	Snacks
541-330-0747 Fax: 541-330-0747	Visa, MC, Disc,	Library, Jacuzzis, fireplace,
877-330-0747	C-yes/S-ltd/P-ltd/H-no	cable TV, gardens and farm
Lindy Knight		animals
All year		

Spacious country home, front yard "park" setting, back area mini farm with planted field & assorted farm animals. Full country breakfast served in our dining room our outdoors
E-mail: cricket@bendnet.com

BEND

Lara House B&B
640 NW Congress, 97701
503-388-4064 Fax: 541-388-4064
800-766-4064
Doug & Bobbye Boger
All year

85-135-B&B
5 rooms, 5 pb
Visa, MC, *Rated*, •
C-yes/S-ltd/P-no/H-no

Full breakfast
Snacks
Sitting room w/fireplace, sun
room, flower gardens,
bicycles, hot tub

A magnificent 1910 historical home overlooking Drake Park and Sechutes River. Cozy living room with fireplace, sunroom with view of park & manicured grounds. 6 suites with sitting areas and private bath. E-mail: larahousebnb@webtv.net Web site: moriah.com/larahouse

BROOKINGS

Chetco River Inn
21202 High Prairie Rd, 97415
541-670-1645
800-327-2688
Sandra Brugger
Exc. Thanksgiving & Xmas

115-B&B
3 rooms, 3 pb
Visa, MC, *Rated*, •
C-ltd/S-ltd/P-no/H-no

Full breakfast
Lunch, dinner with res.
Beverages & cookies, sitting
room, library, games, hiking,
river

Relax in peaceful seclusion of our private 35-acre forest, bordered on 3 sides by the Chetco River. Enjoy "Old World" hospitality & "New World" comfort Web site: chetcoriverinn.com

South Coast Inn
516 Redwood Street, 97415
503-469-5557 Fax: 541-469-6615
800-525-9273
Ken Raith & Keith Pepper
All year

84-94-B&B
5 rooms, 5 pb
Most CC, *Rated*
C-ltd/S-no/P-no/H-no

Full breakfast
Sitting room, library, Jacuzzi,
fireplace, cable TV

Centrally located, Maybeck Craftman home furnished in antiques. Enjoy coffee in front of the stone fireplace. Wake up to a gourmet breakfast and a beautiful ocean view.
E-mail: scoastin@wave.net Web site: virtualcities.com/ons/or/y/ory9501.htm

CORVALLIS

Harrison House B&B
2310 NW Harrison Blvd, 97330
541-752-6248 Fax: 541-754-1353
800-233-6248
Charlie & Maria Tomlinson
All year

70-80-B&B
4 rooms, 2 pb
Most CC, *Rated*, •
C-ltd/S-no/P-no/H-no

Full breakfast
Afternoon tea, snacks, wine
Sitting room, cable TV,
telephones, data ports, deck
with heated spa

Harrison House is a lovely restored Dutch Colonial style historic home. Elegant furnishings, delicious full breakfast and gracious hospitality await your stay.
E-mail: stay@corvallis-lodging.com Web site: corvallis-lodging.com

ELMIRA

McGillivray's Log Home B&B
88680 Evers Rd, 97437
541-935-3564
Evelyn R. McGillivray
All year

70-80-B&B
2 rooms, 2 pb
Visa, MC,
C-ltd/S-no/P-no/H-yes

Full breakfast
whale watching, fishing

Enjoy hearty breakfasts in this secluded country home. Rooms feature king beds, private baths, and air-conditioning. 14 miles west of Eugene, Oregon.

EUGENE

Campbell House, a City Inn
252 Pearl St, 97401
541-343-1119 Fax: 541-343-2258
800-264-2519
Myra Plant
All year

85-349-B&B
18 rooms, 18 pb
Visa, MC, AmEx,
Rated, •
C-yes/S-no/P-no/H-yes

Full breakfast
Lunch & dinner arranged
Jetted tubs, beer & wine for
sale, sitting room, library

Built in 1892 and restored in the tradition of a small European hotel. "Classic elegance, exquisite decor and impeccable service." E-mail: campbellhouse@campbellhouse.com
Web site: campbellhouse.com/

EUGENE

Oval Door B&B Inn, The
988 Lawrence St, 97401
541-683-3160 Fax: 541-485-0260
800-882-3160
N. Wergeland & M. Coray
All year

75-115-B&B
4 rooms, 4 pb
Visa, MC, AmEx,
Rated, •
C-ltd/S-no/P-no/H-no

Full breakfast
Tea, soft drinks, cookies
Sitting room, library, Jacuzzi,
sitting room, wrap-around
porch

Offering warm hospitality in the heart of Eugene. Private baths, bountiful breakfast, home-baked treats, walk to restaurants.   E-mail: ovaldoor@ovaldoor.com *Web site:* ovaldoor.com

---

Pookie's B&B College Hill
2013 Charnelton St, 97405
541-343-0383 Fax: 541-431-0967
800-558-0383
Pookie & Doug Walling
All year

70-95-B&B
3 rooms, 2 pb
C-ltd/S-ltd/P-no/H-no

Full breakfast
Snacks
Sitting room, library, shade
trees, antiques, gas BBQ in
back

Our restored craftsman home built in 1918 is in a quiet, older neighborhood. Sitting room & bedroom are done in a mixture of antiques. Bartolette Suite for three available.
Web site: pookiesbandblodging.com

FLORENCE

Johnson House B&B Inn, The
PO Box 1892, 97439
541-997-8000 Fax: 541-997-2364
800-768-9488
Jayne & Ron Fracse
All year

95-125-B&B
6 rooms, 4 pb
Visa, MC, Disc, *Rated*,
•
S-no/P-no/H-no
French

Full breakfast
Afternoon tea
Sitting room, 3 deluxe rooms
w/private baths, library

Beautifully restored 1892 Victorian; down comforters; genuine antiques throughout; turn-of-the-century charm; in Old Town one block from bayfront   E-mail: fraese@presys.com
Web site: touroregon.com/thejohnsonhouse

GRANTS PASS

Flery Manor
2000 Jumpoff Joe Cr Rd, 97526
541-476-3591 Fax: 541-471-2303
Marla & John Vidrinskas
All year

75-140-B&B
4 rooms, 3 pb
Visa, MC, *Rated*, •
C-ltd/S-no/P-no/H-no
Lithuanian, Russian

Full 3 course breakfast
Afternoon tea, snacks, wine
Sitting room, library, frplc.,
piano, gazebo with waterfall,
stream, pond

Elegant country manor on 7 acres of mountain-side. Healthy gourmet breakfast. Access to private health club. Romantic suite with Jacuzzi, private balcony.   E-mail: flery@
flerymanor.com *Web site:* flerymanor.com

Ivy House, The
139 SW I St, 97526
541-474-7363
All year

60-75-B&B
5 rooms, 1 pb
Visa, MC, Disc,
C-yes/S-no/P-ltd/H-no

Full English Breakfast
Tea & biscuits are offered in
bed prior to breakfast upon
request

Step down from the busy street into the quiet green lawn and rose edged path of The Ivy House and you immediately feel that you've entered a quieter, more genteel era. Comfortable cozy beds with Eiderdown quilts and lace curtains.

Lawnridge House B&B
1304 NW Lawnridge, 97526
541-476-8518 Fax: 541-476-8518
Barbara Head
All year

65-85-B&B
2 rooms, 2 pb
Rated, •
C-yes/S-ltd
Spanish, some French

Full breakfast
Room refrig w/beverages
Alfresco dining, secluded
deck & porch, filled
bookshelves, VCP

1909 historic home with antique furnishings, canopy beds, fireplace, beamed ceilings, wood floors, oriental rugs, cable TV, phone, A/C. Regional NW breakfast Honeymoon & Family suites

GRANTS PASS

Weasku Inn Historic Resort	85-295-B&B	Continental plus breakfast
5560 Rogue River Hwy, 97527	17 rooms, 17 pb	Snacks, comp. wine
541-471-8000 Fax: 541-471-7038	Visa, MC, AmEx,	Sitting room, Jacuzzis, suites,
800-4-WEASKU	*Rated*, •	fireplaces, cable TV, conf.
Dayle Sedgmore	C-yes/S-no/P-no	fac.
All year		

A cozy, riverfront inn, built around a colorful historical fishing lodge. Decorated with locally hand-crafted furniture, one of a kind lamps, hand-quilted bed covers, chairs and fishing memorabilia. Available are 5 Lodge Rooms, 9 River Cabins.
E-mail: info@weasku.com *Web site:* weasku.com

HOOD RIVER

Avalon B&B	65-75-B&B	Full breakfast
3444 Avalon, 97031	2 rooms	Sitting room, cable TV, hot
541-386-2560	Visa, MC, Disc, *Rated*,	tub (limited), family friendly
888-386-3941	•	facility
Jim & Dorothy Tollen	C-yes/S-ltd/P-ltd/H-no	
All year		

Country get-a-way that caters to your need. Close to shopping, skiing, hiking, and water sports. A must for newlyweds. A place to relax. Special packages. *E-mail:* jtollen@gorge.net
Web site: moriah.com/avalon

Hood River Hotel	69-155-B&B	Continental breakfast
102 Oak Ave, 97031	41 rooms, 41 pb	Pasquale's Ristorante
541-386-1900 Fax: 541-386-6090	Most CC, •	Bar service, snacks, tea,
800-386-1859	C-yes/S-ltd/P-ltd/H-yes	sitting room, hot tubs, sauna,
Jacque & Pasquale Barone	Italian, some Jap. & Sp.	exercise facility
All year		

National Historic Landmark evoking warm European charm in the center of the Columbia River Gorge. Romantic riverview rooms. Historic downtown location.
E-mail: hrhotel@gorge.net *Web site:* HoodRiverHotel.com

JACKSONVILLE

Jacksonville Inn	119-250-B&B	Full breakfast
PO Box 359, 97530	11 rooms, 11 pb	Restaurant, lounge
541-899-1900 Fax: 541-899-1373	Most CC, *Rated*, •	Lunch & dinner (fee),
800-321-9344	C-yes/S-no/P-no/H-no	luxurious cottages with
Jerry & Linda Evans	Greek, Danish, Italian	many amenities avail.
All year		

The Inn offers its guests elegance in an historic setting with gourmet dining, a connoisseur's wine cellear, luxurious hotel accommodations, and 3 honeymoon cottages that are "suites extraordinaire." *E-mail:* jvinn@mind.net *Web site:* jacksonvilleinn.com

McCully House Inn	85-115-B&B	Full breakfast
PO Box 13, 97530	4 rooms, 4 pb	Restaurant, complimentary
541-899-1942	C-ltd/S-no/P-no/H-no	wine
800-367-1942		Lunch, dinner, sitting room,
Mary Ann & Dennis Ramsden		many amenities available
All year		

Charming 1861 Classical Revival home on National Registry. Located in heart of Historic Jacksonville near Ashland's Shakespearean Festival, Rogue River.
E-mail: mccully@wave.net *Web site:* mccullyhouseinn.com

LINCOLN CITY

Brey House Ocean View Inn	80-145-B&B	Full breakfast
3725 NW Keel, 97367	4 rooms, 4 pb	Sitting room, hot tub, ocean
541-994-7123 Fax: 541-994-5941	Visa, MC, Disc, •	view deck, landscaped yard
Milt & Shirley Brey	C-yes/S-ltd/P-no/H-no	
All year		

The ocean awaits you just across the street. We are located within the city limits of Lincoln City. Fireplace in some rooms. Casino 2 blocks away. *Web site:* moriah.com/breyhouse

LINCOLN CITY

Pacific Rest B&B
1611 Northeast 11th St, 97367
541-994-2337
888-405-7378
R. & J. Waetjen, B. Beard
All year

90-95-B&B
2 rooms, 2 pb
C-yes/S-ltd/P-no/H-yes

Full gourmet breakfast
Snacks, coffee, tea
Family friendly facility, suites
for families, landscaped yard

Newer home especially designed with the "B&B" guest in mind. Relaxed, restful atmosphere just 4 blocks to beach. E-mail: jwaetjen@wcn.net *Web site:* pacificrestbb.hypermart.net/

Salmon River B&B
5622 Salmon River Hwy 18,
97368
541-994-2639
Marvin & Pawnee Pegg
All year

55-70-B&B
4 rooms, 2 pb
Visa, MC, Disc, •
C-yes/S-no/P-no/H-no

Full breakfast
Private entry, sitting room,
fireplace, reservation

Near ocean and 5-mile lake; warm winters, cool summers; huckleberry hotcakes and homemade fruit syrups; quiet wooded setting. E-mail: mpezz@wcn.net
Web site: lincolncity.com/salmonriverb&b

MT. HOOD

**Brightwood Guesthouse
B&B**
PO Box 189, 97011
503-622-5783 Fax: 503-622-5783
888-503-5783
Jan Estep
All year

100-125-B&B
1 rooms, 1 pb
•
C-ltd/S-ltd/P-no/H-no
Some German

Full gourmet breakfast
Snacks, occasional comp.
wine
Living room, library, bikes,
washer & dryer, TV, VCR,
games, flowers

Peaceful, private, romantic mountain house of your own; Japanese watergarden; Oriental antiquities; fantastic breakfasts; bikes provided. For fun, beauty, joy.

Falcon's Crest Inn
PO Box 185, 97028
503-272-3403 Fax: 503-272-3454
800-624-7384
B.J. & Melody Johnson
All year

99-179-B&B
5 rooms, 5 pb
Most CC, *Rated*, •
C-ltd/S-no/P-no/H-no

Full breakfast
Gourmet restaurant
Dinner, VCR, fishing,
Alcoholic beverages, hot
tubs, golf, hiking

*Elegance in heart of Mt. Hood Nationall Forest. Conference facilities. Inn special events, movie collection, outdoor recreation, ski packages, Christmas Holiday Specialists.
E-mail:* falconcrest@earthlink.net *Web site:* falconscrest.com

NEWPORT

Oar House B&B
520 SW 2nd St, 97365
541-265-9571
800-252-2358
Jan LeBrun
All year

100-130-B&B
5 rooms, 5 pb
Visa, MC, *Rated*
S-no/P-no/H-no
Spanish

Full breakfast
Snacks, tea
Sitting room with fireplace,
libraries, art, music,
lighthouse tower

*Lincoln Country historic landmark built 1900. Renovated, expanded 1993. Lighthouse tower with widow's walk-panoramic views. Spacious, elegant guest areas.
E-mail:* oarhouse@newportnet.com *Web site:* newportnet.com/oarhouse/

Ocean House
4920 NW Woody Way, 97365
541-265-6158
800-562-2632
Marie & Bob Garrard
All year

65-165-B&B
5 rooms, 5 pb
Visa, MC, *Rated*
S-no/P-no/H-no

Full breakfast
Snacks, coffee, tea
Sitting room, library, 3 rms.
w/spas, 5 w/decks, All rooms
w/ocean views

*Near center of coastal activities & fun. Large comfortable home with beautiful surroundings, expanded garden with ocean decks. Near Yaquina Head Lt. House. King/queen beds.
Rms. with frplcs E-mail:* garrard@oceanhouse.com *Web site:* oceanhouse.com

NEWPORT

Solace by the Sea B&B
9602 South Coast Hwy 101,
97366
541-867-3566 Fax: 541-867-3599
888-4-SOLACE
Todd and Lisa Whear
All year

110-175-B&B
3 rooms, 3 pb
Most CC, *Rated*
C-ltd/S-no/P-ltd/H-no

4-course full breakfast
Soda, coffee, tea
Sitting room, library,
bicycles, Jacuzzis, fireplaces,
cable TV

A romantic retreat located 3.5 miles south of Newport off Hwy 101. A new 3 story contemporary home nestled amongst shore pines and overlooking the mighty Pacific Ocean. E-mail: solace@newportnet.com *Web site:* solacebythesea.com

---

Tyee Lodge-Oceanfront B&B
4925 NW Woody Way, 97365
541-265-8953 Fax: 541-265-3901
888-553-8933
Mark & Cindy McConnell
All year

90-125-B&B
5 rooms, 5 pb
Visa, MC, AmEx,
Rated, •
C-ltd/S-ltd/P-no/H-no
Spanish, French,
German

Full breakfast
Convenience bar
Private trail to beach, sitting
room, fireplace, accom.
special diets

Our park-like setting is unequaled on the Oregon Coast. Sit by your window, or by the fire, and watch the waves. Complimentary beverages. Convenient, on-site parking E-mail: mcconn@teleport.com *Web site:* tyeelodge.com

PORT ORFORD

Home by the Sea B&B
PO Box 606, 97465
541-332-2855
Alan & Brenda Mitchell
All year

95-105-B&B
2 rooms, 2 pb
Visa, MC, *Rated*
C-ltd/S-no/P-no/H-no

Full breakfast
Refrigerator
Laundry, sitting room, beach
access, ocean view, cable TV,
phones, spa

Enjoy dramatic views of the Oregon Coast, direct beach access and miles of unspoiled public beaches in this quiet fishing village. E-mail: stay@homebythesea.com *Web site:* homebythesea.com

PORTLAND

General Hooker's B&B
125 SW Hooker St, 97201
503-222-4435 Fax: 503-295-6410
800-745-4135
Lori Hall
All year

85-125-B&B
4 rooms, 2 pb
Visa, MC, AmEx,
Rated, •
C-ltd/S-no/P-no/H-no

Continental plus—veg.
Comp. wine & beverages
Sitting room, library, A/C,
roof deck, cat, TV, VCR,
phones in rooms

Casually elegant Victorian in quiet, historic neighborhood; walking distance of City Center. Classical music throughout E-mail: lori@generalhookers.com *Web site:* generalhookers.com

---

Georgian House B&B
1828 NE Siskiyou, 97212
503-281-2250 Fax: 503-281-3301
888-282-2250
Willie Jean Ackley
Season Inquire

65-125-B&B
4 rooms, 2 pb
Visa, MC, *Rated*
C-ltd/S-ltd/P-no/H-no

Full breakfast
Afternoon tea, restaurant
Sitting room, library, tennis
court, TV, VCR, phones in
rooms

Take a romantic step back to "Olde England." Enjoy gazebo, gardens, tree lined historic streets. Quiet, convenient to shops, cafes, lightrail. Web site: travelguides.com/home/georgianhouse/

MacMaster House, c1895
1041 SW Vista Ave, 97205
503-223-7362 Fax: 503-224-8808
800-774-9523
Cecilia Murphy
All year

85-130-B&B
8 rooms, 2 pb
Most CC,
C-ltd/S-no/P-no/H-no

Very full breakfast
Complimentary wine & local
ale
Sitting room, library, tennis
court nearby

Historic Colonial mansion near Washington Park. Convenient to rose & Japanese gardens, cafes, galleries, boutiques, theater and commercial districts. E-mail: cmurphy656@aol.com *Web site:* macmaster.com

PORTLAND

Portland Guest House	70-100-B&B	Full breakfast
1720 NE 15th, 97212	7 rooms, 5 pb	Complimentary beverages
503-282-1402	Visa, MC, AmEx, *Rated*	Room phones, antiques,
Susan Gisvold	C-yes/S-no/P-no	jogging routes, crtyard, bus
All year		& light rail tickets

1890 Victorian in historic Irvington neighborhood. All rooms have phones, antiques, heirloom linens, great beds. Luscious breakfasts. Family suite with 3 beds. Walk to restaurants, movies, coffee shops. E-mail: pgh@teleport.com Web site: teleport.com/~pgh/

Terwilliger Vista B&B	85-150-B&B	Full breakfast
515 SW Westwood Dr, 97201	5 rooms, 5 pb	Complimentary wine
503-244-0602 Fax: 503-293-8042	Visa, MC, •	Sitting room, library, suites,
888-244-0602	C-ltd/S-no/P-no/H-ltd	fireplaces, cable TV
Dick & Jan Vatert		
All year		

Terwilliger Vista B&B is situated on over a half acre of gardens featuring mature trees, manicured lawns, camellias, rhododendron and fruit trees. Fabulous views of the Willamette River, Mt. Hood and city lights. This 1940 home was recently refurbished. Web site: terwilligervista.com

PORTLAND, SALEM

Hunter Creek Farm	100-150-B&B	Full breakfast
14441 SW Wilsonville Rd,	5 rooms, 5 pb	Snacks, wine
97070	Visa, MC, *Rated*, •	Sitting room, library,
503-625-3424 Fax: 503-625-7581	C-yes/S-ltd/P-no/H-no	Jacuzzis, swimming pool,
Lar Algatt		suites, fireplace, cable TV
All year		

Hunter Creek Farm is located on a beautiful 120 acre Equestrian Park on the Willamette river. The interior of the B&B resembles an old English fox hunting lodge, decorated in Ralph Lauren fabric. Lounge with computer and fax. Fresh flowers & wine in room E-mail: Huntercrkf@aol.com Web site: bbhost.com:8008/huntercreekfarm/

SALEM

Cottonwood Cottage B&B	60-65-B&B	Full breakfast
960 E Street NE, 97301	2 rooms, 0 pb	Sitting room, cable TV,
503-362-3979	Visa, MC, Disc, •	accommodate business
800-349-3979	S-ltd/P-no/H-no	travelers
Bill & Donna Wickman		
All year		

1924 home within walking distance of the state capitol, downtown & Willamette University. Gourmet breakfast on china, 2 cats, well traveled innkeepers located in the gateway to the Oregon Garden. E-mail: ctnwdctg@open.org Web site: open.org/ctnwdctg

Creekside Inn, Marquee Hse	65-90-B&B	Full breakfast
333 Wyatt Ct NE, 97301	5 rooms, 3 pb	Snacks
503-391-0837 Fax: 503-391-1713	Visa, MC, *Rated*, •	Sitting room, movies,
800-949-0837	C-ltd/S-no/P-no/H-no	comports for business,
Rickie Hart All year		traveler, hammock chairs

Mt. Vernon Colonial; has antiques, fireplace. Nightly film showing with "bottomless" popcorn bowl. Walk to the capitol. Pillow talk room (private bath) now has queen & twin bed. E-mail: rickiemh@open.org Web site: marqueehouse.com/rickiemh

SEASIDE

Sea Side Inn Oceanfront B&B	115-255-B&B	Full breakfast
581 S Promenade, 97138	14 rooms, 14 pb	Afternoon tea, snacks,
503-738-6403 Fax: 503-738-6634	Visa, MC, Disc, *Rated*, •	restaurant
800-772-7766	C-yes/S-no/P-no/H-yes	Sitting room, library,
Susan Peters All year	Spanish, Phillipino	Jacuzzis, suites, fireplaces, cable TV, bar service

384   Oregon

SHERIDAN

Middle Creek Run B&B
25400 Harmony Rd, 97378
503-843-7606
John & Marc
All year

85-115-B&B
3 rooms, 2 pb
Rated
C-ltd/S-ltd/P-no/H-no

Full breakfast
Afternoon tea, snacks
Sitting room, library,
Jacuzzis, suites, fireplaces

Historic Victorian offers quietude & old world comfort. The proprietors designed their home around their collection of art, antiques, asian and ethnic treasures. Three course breakfast, flowers and truffles await you.   Web site: moriah.com/middlecreek

SISTERS

Conklin's Guest House
69013 Camp Polk Rd, 97759
541-549-0123
Fax: 541-549-4481
800-549-4262
Frank & Marie Conklin
All year

90-140-B&B
5 rooms, 5 pb
Rated, •
C-ltd/S-ltd/P-ltd/H-yes
Spanish

Full breakfast
Snacks, complimentary wine
Sitting room, heated
swimming pool, trout ponds

A spectacular country paradise of spacious grounds, ponds, & mountain vistas. Tasteful country decor & gourmet breakfasts complete the setting.
Web site: informat.com/bz/conklins/

WALDPORT

Cliff House
PO Box 436, 97394
541-563-2506
Fax: 541-563-4393
Gabrielle Duvall
All year

115-245-B&B
4 rooms, 4 pb
Visa, MC, Disc, *Rated*
S-ltd/P-no/H-ltd
Spanish

Full breakfast
Aftn. tea, comp. wine
Restaurant, sitting room,
library, hot tubs, sauna,
ocean

Pampered elegance by the sea. Perched high on a cliff, we offer gourmet breakfasts, spa, sauna, gazebo for massage (by appointment) and luxury rooms.   E-mail: clifhos@pioneer.net

WHEELER

Wheeler On The Bay Lodge
PO Box 580, 97147
503-368-5858 Fax: 503-368-4204
800-469-3204
Juana Del Handy, Dana Zia
All year

75-115-EP
10 rooms, 10 pb
Visa, MC, Disc, •
C-ltd/S-ltd/P-ltd/H-ltd

Complimentary wine
Kayaks, Jacuzzis, fireplaces,
cable TV, massages

Rare find on Oregon Coast. Bay watch, soak in private spas. Enjoy ambience of Nehalem Bay & Neahkahnie Mt. Moat moorage for boating or fishing. Services are massages, movies, kayaks, boat space.   E-mail: handypdx@oneworld.com *Web site:* mkt-place.com/wheeler/

YAMHILL

Flying M Ranch
23029 NW Flying M Rd, 97148
503-662-3222 Fax: 503-662-3202
B & B Mithell & Beth Belanger
All year exc. Dec 24-25

60-200-EP
28 rooms, 28 pb
Visa, MC, AmEx, •
C-yes/S-ltd/P-ltd/H-yes

Restaurant, bar, Sunday
buffet
Private airstrip, horses,
tennis court, piano,
honeymoon cabin, fishing

Rustic & warm log lodge offers dining, dancing, mountain trail rides, camping, fishing, swimming pond, airstrip & wineries nearby.   E-mail: flyingm@bigplanet.com
Web site: Flying-M-Ranch.com

Pennsylvania

ABBOTTSTOWN

Altland House, The
PO Box 448, 17301
717-259-9535 Fax: 717-259-9956
Kim Billinger
All year

89-125-B&B
10 rooms
Most CC, *Rated*, •
C-yes/S-ltd/P-ltd/H-yes

Continental plus breakfast
Restaurant, bar service
Tennis & pool nearby,
Jacuzzis, suites, fireplaces,
cable TV

A country inn with exquisite cuisine and gracious hospitality in a cozy historic atmosphere. Web site: altlandhouse.com

ADAMSTOWN

Barnyard Inn, The
2145 Old Lancaster Pike, 17569
717-484-1111 Fax: 717-484-0722
888-738-6624
Pam & Jerry Pozniak
All year

75-150-B&B
5 rooms, 5 pb
Most CC, *Rated*, •
C-yes/S-no/P-no/H-no

Full gourmet breakfast
Complimentary beverages &
snacks
Sitting room, bikes, pool &
golf nearby, antiquing

A 150-year-old restored German schoolhouse on 2.5 wooded acres overlooking countryside. Located in the Antique Capital of USA & minutes from outlet shopping and Pennsylvania Dutch attractions. E-mail: jerry@barnyardinn.com Web site: barnyardinn.com

Living Spring Farm B&B
2614 RR#2, 19540
610-775-8525
Fax: 610-775-1399
Debra Cazille
All year

75-150-B&B
4 rooms, 4 pb
C-ltd/S-no/P-no/H-no

Full breakfast
Snacks, wine
Sitting room, fireplace, cable
TV

A 200 year old, 32 acres gentlemans farm decorated with antiques. Enjoy breakfast or a snack outside on the veranda overlooking beauitful farmland or do some bird watching. Lots of attractions. Hiking trails on property. F-mail: DebCaz@worldnet.att.net Web site: readingberkspa.com/living.html

AKRON

Bella Vista B&B
1216 Main St, 17501
717-859-4227
Fax: 717-859-4071
888-948-9726
J. & S. Shirk, D. & M. Wallace
All year

75-85-B&B
6 rooms, 5 pb
Visa, MC,
C-ltd/S-no/P-no/H-no

Full breakfast
Afternoon tea, snacks
Sitting room, bikes, tennis,
cable TV, conference
facilities

Quite, country setting et within 15 minutes of all Lancaster County attractions (antiquing, outlets, Amish). We have a 50 acre park less than a block away with tennis, frezbee golf. Family style breakfast can be served on our large porches. E-mail: jshirk@epix.net Web site: cookee.com/bellavista/index.html

Springhouse Inn B&B
806 New St, 17501
717-859-4202
Ray & Shirley Smith
All year

65-105-B&B
4 rooms, 2 pb
Visa, MC,
C-ltd/S-no/P-no/H-no

Full breakfast
Snacks
Sitting room, library,
perennial & herb gardens,
public tennis and pool

18th-Century farmhouse in historic Lancaster County. Breakfast by the fireplace. Cozy stenciled rooms with queen beds. Spacious grounds with spring house Web site: obs-us.com/obs/english/books/chesler/babima/bnb/pab402.htm

BEDFORD

Bedford House
203 W Pitt St, 15522
814-623-7171
Lyn & Linda Lyon
All year

75-125-B&B
11 rooms, 11 pb
Most CC, •
C-ltd/S-no/P-no/H-yes

Full breakfast
Afternoon tea
Sitting rm, library nook,
Frplc. in 5 guestrooms,
tennis, golf nearby

The in-town B&B. C.1800 brick Federal near shops, restaurants, churches. A path through the flower garden leads to the guest house. Located halfway btwn Pittsburgh & Harrisburg, PA Turnpike exit 11. E-mail: bedhouse@bedford.net *Web site:* bedfordcounty.net/bedhouse.htm

BELLEFONTE

Reynolds Mansion
101 W Linn St, 16823
814-353-8407 Fax: 814-353-1530
800-899-3929
Joseph & Charlotte Heidt
All year

95-175-B&B
3 rooms, 3 pb
Visa, MC, *Rated*, •
C-ltd/S-ltd/P-no/H-no

Full breakfast
Complimentary brandy
Sitting room, library, bikes,
billiards room, Jacuzzi,
fireplaces

Beautiful Victorian mansion—perfect for romantic getaways! Rooms with Jacuzzis and fireplaces; billiards room. E-mail: innkeeper@reynoldsmansion.com
Web site: reynoldsmansion.com

BIRD IN HAND

Mill Creek Homestead B&B
2578 Old Philadelphia, 17505
717-291-6419 Fax: 717-291-2171
800-771-2578
Vicki & Frank Alfone
All year

99-125-B&B
3 rooms, 3 pb
Most CC, *Rated*, •
C-ltd/S-no/P-no/H-no

Full breakfast
Sitting room, library,
swimming pool, Jacuzzi,
fireplaces

Country hideaway in restored stone farmhouse amidst Amish farmland. Decorated with family heirlooms & quilts. Hearty breakfast & pampering abound.
E-mail: valfone@concentric.net *Web site:* bbhost.com/millcreekhomestead

Village Inn Bird-in-Hand
PO Box 253, 17505
717-293-8369 Fax: 717-768-1117
800-914-2473
Rick Meshey
All year

79-149-B&B
11 rooms, 11 pb
Most CC, *Rated*
C-yes/S-ltd/P-no/H-no

Continental plus breakfast
Evening snacks
Sitting room, Dutch Country
bus tour, hot tubs in 2 suites

Beautifully restored historic inn located in Pennsylvania Dutch Country. Country setting. Victorian-style architecture and furnishings. Individually decorated deluxe rooms.
E-mail: lodging@bird-in-hand.com *Web site:* bird-in-hand.com/villageinn

BLOOMSBURG

Inn at Turkey Hill, The
991 Central Rd, 17815
570-387-1500 Fax: 570-784-3718
Andrew B. Pruden
All year

88-190-B&B
23 rooms, 23 pb
Most CC, *Rated*, •
C-yes/S-yes/P-yes/H-yes

Full continental breakfast
Dinner every evening
Bar, vegetarian also, fax
machine, golf & tennis
nearby

Nestled amid PA's rolling hills & farmlands. Inn extends warmth, comfort, charm and hospitality. E-mail: info@innatturkeyhill.com *Web site:* innatturkeyhill.com

BRANDYWINE VALLEY

Folke Stone B&B
777 Copeland School Rd,
19380
610-429-0310 Fax: 610-918-9228
800-884-4666
Marcy & Walter Schmoll
All year

75-100-B&B
3 rooms, 3 pb
Most CC, *Rated*
C-ltd/S-no/P-no/H-no

Full breakfast
Snacks
Sitting room, fireplaces,
cable TV, accommodate
business travelers

Enjoy the ambience of yesteryear in this charming beautifully furnished 1732 William Penn land grant manor house. Read by one of the huge fireplaces, play the Steinway piano or relax on the veranda overlooking the idyllic pond. E-mail: folkbandb@aol.com
Web site: bbonline.com/pa/folkestone

BRANDYWINE VALLEY

Scarlett House B&B
503 W State St, 19348
610-444-9592 Fax: 610-925-0373
800-820-9592
Jane & Sam Snyder
All year

85-135-B&B
4 rooms, 2 pb
Rated
C-ltd/S-no/P-no/H-no

Full gourmet breakfast
Afternoon tea, snacks
Sitting room, library,
Victorian parlor, piano, A/C,
fireplaces, porch

Elegantly restored Victorian minutes from Longwood Gardens, Winterthur & Brandywine Valley attractions. Old-fashioned hospitality, gracious atmosphere, antiques, gardens E-mail: janes10575@aol.com   Web site: traveldata.com/inns/data/scarlett.html

CANADENSIS

Brookview Manor B&B Inn
RR 1 Box 365, 18325
570-595-2451 Fax: 570-595-5065
800-585-7974
Maryanne Buckley
All year

100-150-B&B
10 rooms, 10 pb
Most CC, *Rated*, •
C-ltd/S-ltd/P-no/H-no

Full breakfast
Afternoon tea, snacks
Sitting room, library, pool
table, Ping-Pong, lawn games,
waterfall

On 400 picturesque acres, wrap-around porch, panoramic view of the forest. Hiking trails, golf, skiing, excellent dining nearby. 2 rooms with Jacuzzi tubs and 1 room with fireplace.

Hillside Lodge
PO Box 268, 18325
570-595-7551 Fax: 570-595-3050
800-666-4455
Dave and Sandy Kline
All year

145-250-B&B/EP/MAP
33 rooms, 33 pb
Visa, MC, Disc, *Rated*,
•
C-yes/S-yes/P-no/H-yes

Full breakfast
Dinner available
Restaurant, pool, bar
service, sitting room, tennis
court, hot tubs

A mountain adventure with a touch of class. Enchanted suite, & luxury suites with 2-person Jacuzzi tubs, fireplaces, king beds and more.   E-mail: dkline@ptdprolog.net Web site: hillsidelodge.com

CARLISLE

Jacob's Resting Place B&B
1007 Harrisburg Pike, 17013
717-243-1766 Fax: 717-241-5010
Terry & Marie Hegglin
All year

70-85-B&B
5 rooms, 2 pb
Visa, MC, AmEx, Disc, •
C-ltd/S-ltd/P-no/H-no

Full breakfast
Snacks
Hot tubs, swimming pool
swimming pool, hiking

Historical Inn from 1790. Antique decor, working fireplaces, trout stream, pool, hot tub, air conditioning & gourmet breakfasts for your enjoyment.   E-mail: jacobsrest@pa.net

Pheasant Field B&B
150 Hickorytown Rd, 17013
717-258-0717 Fax: 717-258-1352
877-258-0717
Dee Fegan & Chuck DeMarco
All year

85-120-B&B
4 rooms, 4 pb
Visa, MC, AmEx,
Rated, •
C-ltd/S-ltd/P-ltd/H-no

Full breakfast
Snacks
Sitting room, tennis courts,
horse boarding available

Lovely 200-year-old brick farmhouse. History, antiques, fly fishing, car shows. Appalachian trail nearby. Easy drive to Gettysburg, Hershey.   E-mail: pheasant@pa.net Web site: pa.net/pheasant

CLEARFIELD

Christopher Kratzer B&B
101 E Cherry St, 16830
814-765-5024
888-252-2632
Bruce & Ginny Baggett
All year

55-70-B&B
3 rooms, 1 pb
Visa, MC, Disc, *Rated*,
•
C-yes/S-ltd/P-no/H-no

Full breakfast
Afternoon tea,
complimentary wine
Snacks, sitting room, library,
attic flea market for browsing

1840 historic house overlooking river & park. 2 bedroom suite; shared bath. Honeymoon suite with breakfast in room; complimentary champagne.   E-mail: bbaggette@mail.csrlink.net Web site: travelguides.com/home/kratzerhouse/

COOKSBURG

Gateway Lodge & Restaurant
Route 36 Box 125, 16217
814-744-8017 Fax: 814-744-8017
800-843-6862
Joseph & Linda Burney
All year

85-275-B&B
18 rooms, 18 pb
Rated
C-ltd/S-yes/P-ltd/H-ltd

Full breakfast
Snacks, lunch/dinner
available
Piano, buggy rides, sitting
room, hot tubs, heated pool,
sauna

18 king size square logged fireside Jacuzzi suites, new common room with cathedral ceiling and stone fireplace for inn guests only. Exercise room, library, gift shop featuring pewter, bathrobes, and other Gateway signature gift items. E-mail: info@gatewaylodge.com *Web site:* gatewaylodge.com

DANVILLE

Pine Barn Inn
#1 Pine Barn Pl, 17821
570-275-2071 Fax: 570-275-3248
800-627-2276
Martin Walzer
All year

52-98-EP
102 rooms, 102 pb
Most CC, *Rated*, •
C-yes/S-yes/P-yes/H-ltd
Spanish

Full breakfast (fee)
Lunch, dinner, bar
Dining patio, hiking, fitness
room, all rooms have A/C

Main inn is 19th-century barn; guest rooms located in new lodge building. Located in residential part of community. Especially popular locally for fine food. Six suites with king size beds. E-mail: innkeeper@pinebarninn.com *Web site:* pinebarninn.com

DOYLESTOWN

Sign of The Sorrel Horse
4424 Old Easton Rd, 18901
215-230-9999 Fax: 215-230-8053
Monique Gaumont
All year

85-175-B&B/EP
5 rooms, 5 pb
Visa, MC, AmEx, *Rated*
C-ltd/S-no/P-yes/H-no
French, German

Continental breakfast
Restaurant, bar, dinner
Comp. sherry & fruits, sitting
room, bicycles, meeting
room for parties

Built in 1714 as a gristmill, in the heart of Bucks County—now a gracious historic inn. Fine gourmet dining. Garden weddings a specialty E-mail: mgaumont@aol.com *Web site:* sorrelhorse.com

DUSHORE

Cherry Mills Lodge
RR4, Box 4231, 18614
570-928-8978
Florence & Julio
All year

55-75-B&B
8 rooms, 1 pb
Disc, •
C-yes/S-ltd/P-no/H-no

Full breakfast
Packed lunches for hikes
Wine w/dinner, fishing,
fireplaces, porches, sauna,
ponds, streams

Historic 1865 country hotel, antique furnished. Secluded 27 acres, mountain trout stream, hiking, biking. Nearby Victorian Eagles Mere, 2 state parks. Web site: endlessmountains.org/ads/cherrymiles.htm

EAGLES MERE

Crestmont Inn
Crestmont Dr, 17731
570-525-3519 Fax: 570-525-3534
800-522-8767
Kathleen Oliver & Doug Rider
All year

99-178-B&B
15 rooms, 15 pb
Visa, MC, *Rated*, •
C-ltd/S-ltd/P-no/H-yes

Full breakfast
Dinner, restaurant, bar
service
Sitting room, library,
bicycles, tennis court,
Jacuzzis, pool, cable TV

Crestmont Inn is a hidden treasure nestled in the endless mountains in "the town that time forgot, Eagles Mere, PA." Award winning cuisine, gracious hospitality, and beautifully decorated suites await you. E-mail: crestmnt@epix.net *Web site:* crestmont-inn.com

Eagles Mere Inn
PO Box 356, 17731
717-525-3273
800-426-3273
Susan & Peter Glaubitz
All year

139-225-MAP
18 rooms, 18 pb
Visa, MC, *Rated*, •
C-yes/S-ltd/P-no/H-ltd

Full breakfast
5-course dinner included
Bar, sitting room, tennis,
swimming, golf, skiing,
hunting

Charming country inn in quiet Victorian town high in the Endless Mountains. Superb food/wine list. Food & wine seminars. E-mail: eminn@epix.net *Web site:* eaglesmereinn.com

Cherry Mills Lodge, Dushore, PA

EAGLES MERE

Shady Lane B&B
PO Box 314, 17731
570-525-3394
800-524-1248
Pat & Dennis Dougherty
All year

95-B&B
8 rooms, 8 pb
Rated, •
C-ltd/S-no/P-no/H-yes

Full breakfast
Comp. wine, aftn. tea
Two sitting rooms, tennis
court, lake, golf, skiing, ice
skate

Picturesque mountaintop resort near hiking, swimming, fishing, skiing & tobogganing. Eagles Mere: "the town time forgot." Summer craft & antique shops.
Web site: atrois.com/shady-lane/

EASTON

Lafayette Inn, The
525 W Monroe St,
18042
610-253-4500
Fax: 610-253-4635
Scott & Marilyn Bushnell
All year

95-175-B&B
16 rooms, 16 pb
Most CC, *Rated*
C-yes/S-no/P-no/H-ltd

Continental plus breakfast
Snacks
Sitting room, Jacuzzis, suites,
fireplaces, cable TV, VCRs,
fax, dataports

Our 16 antique filled rooms and landscaped grounds offer distinctive accommodations in Pennsylvania's historic Lehigh Valley. Our lounge, sunroom, garden patio, and wrap around porch are ideal for a memorable visit!   E-mail: lafayinn@fast.net
Web site: lafayetteinn.coml

EPHRATA

Clearview Farm B&B
355 Clearview Rd, 17522
717-733-6333
Glenn & Mildred Wissler
All year

95-140-B&B
5 rooms, 5 pb
Most CC, *Rated*
C-ltd/S-no/P-no/H-no

Full breakfast
Tastefully decorated rooms
with antiques, tennis court

Located on 200 acres of peaceful farmland-old limestone restored house, manicured lawn, lots of flowers, pond graced with swans. 4 excellent restaurants within 5 minutes.
Web site: 800padutch.com/clearvw.html

EPHRATA

Historic Smithton Inn	75-155-B&B	Full breakfast
900 W Main St, 17522	9 rooms, 9 pb	Comp. tea, snacks
717-733-6094	Visa, MC, *Rated*	Sitting room, fireplaces,
Dorothy R. Graybill	C-ltd/S-no/P-ltd/H-ltd	whirlpool baths, gardens,
All year		library, canopy beds

Picturesque 1763 Penn. Dutch Country Inn. Fireplaces in parlor, dining and guest rooms. Chamber music; canopy four-poster beds, refrigerator, quilts and candles in each room.

Jacob Keller House	75-95-B&B	Full breakfast
990 Rettew Mill Rd, 17522	4 rooms, 2 pb	Sitting room, library, prefer
717-733-4954	Visa, MC, •	adults
Richard Bennett	C-ltd/S-no/P-no/H-no	
All year		

1814 stone house in Ephrata. Near antique alley. On the Nat'l Historic Register. Minutes from the Ephrata Cloister. 17 miles from Hershey. Near Landis Museum. In the heart of the Amish country.

EQUINUNK

Hills Twin Spruce Lodge	55-B&B	Full breakfast
RR 1 Box 212, 18417	11 rooms, 11 pb	Sitting room, suites,
570-224-4845	Visa, MC,	fireplaces, cable TV,
M. Adam Hill	C-yes/S-yes/P-ltd/H-yes	swimming pool
All year		

Nestled near the Delaware River, this spacious and quiet Victorian Inn (established in 1885) is near many golf courses, fishing, hiking, biking, antique shops. Many historic sites.   Web site: twinsprucelodge.com

ERWINNA

Evermay on-the-Delaware	135-350-B&B	Continental plus breakfast
PO Box 60, 18920	16 rooms, 16 pb	Complimentary sherry in
610-294-9100 Fax: 610-294-8249	Visa, MC, *Rated*, •	parlor
877-864-2365	C-ltd/S-ltd/P-no/H-yes	Cordial in rm., bar, tea,
Bill & Danielle Moffly		restaurant (weekends),
All year exc. Christmas		sitting room, piano

Romantic Victorian inn on 25 acres of gardens, woodlawn paths and pastures. Elegant dinner served Friday-Sunday & holidays. Rooms face the picturesque Delaware River E-mail: moffly@evermay.com Web site: evermay.com

Golden Pheasant Inn	95-195-B&B	Continental plus breakfast
763 River Rd, 18920	6 rooms, 6 pb	Dinner (Tues.–Sun.)
610-294-9595 Fax: 610-294-9882	Visa, MC, *Rated*, •	Restaurant, bar, canoes,
800-830-4474	C-ltd/S-ltd/P-ltd	Delaware Canal & River,
Barbara Faure	French, Spanish, Italian	wine in rm., hiking/bike
All year		

1857 fieldstone inn situated between river and canal. Six rooms furnished with incredible blend of antiques.   E-mail: barbara@goldenspeasant.com Web site: goldenpheasant.com

EXTON

Duling-Kurtz House & Inn	55-B&B	Continental breakfast
146 S Whitford Rd, 19341	15 rooms, 15 pb	Restaurant, bar
610-524-1830	Most CC, *Rated*	Lunch, dinner, sitting room,
Tish Morescalchi	C-ltd/S-yes/P-no/H-yes	golf courses
All year	Ger., Fr., Sp., It.	

Charming 1830s stone house and stable, elegantly furnished with period reproductions furniture. Landscaped grounds with covered gazebo and flowing stream.

FOGELSVILLE

Glasbern
2141 Pack House Rd, 18051
610-285-4723 Fax: 610-285-2862
Erik Sheetz
All year

145-355-B&B
25 rooms, 25 pb
Visa, MC, AmEx, *Rated*
C-ltd/S-ltd/P-no/H-yes

Full breakfast
Dinner, restaurant
Bar service, pool, bikes,
walking paths, whirlpools,
fireplaces

At Glasbern, guests feel comfortably removed from civilization. Here, one can savor views of fish ponds, a sparkling stream and flourishing gardens on the gently rolling terrain.
E-mail: innkeeper@glasbern.com *Web site:* glasbern.com

FRANKLIN

Quo Vadis B&B
1501 Liberty St, 16323
814-432-4208
800-360-6598
Mark & Samantha
All year

60-95-B&B
6 rooms, 6 pb
Visa, MC, AmEx,
Rated, •
C-yes/S-no/P-no/H-no

Full breakfast weekends
Cont. bkfst. weekdays
Sitting room, library, near
hiking, canoeing, museums,
restaurants

Victorian elegance, heritage antiques located in historic district on Federal Register. Cultural and recreational activities. 200 years of history, beauty of mtn. foothills

GETTYSBURG

Appleford Inn, The
218 Carlisle St, 17325
717-337-1711 Fax: 717-334-6228
800-275-3373
John & Jane Wiley
All year

95-140-B&B
10 rooms, 10 pb
Most CC, *Rated*, •
C-ltd/S-no/P-no/H-ltd

Full breakfast
Afternoon tea, snacks, wine
Sitting room, library, grand
piano, library

1867 elegant Victorian mansion/antiques. 2 blocks from town square, 1 block from college; delicious full breakfast; fireplaces, candlelight, canopies E-mail: jwiley@cvn.net
Web site: bbonline.com/pa/appleford

Baladerry Inn
40 Hospital Rd, 17325
717-337-1342
Tom & Caryl O'Gara
All year

98-118-B&B
8 rooms, 8 pb
Most CC, *Rated*, •
C-ltd/S-no/P-no/H-no

Full breakfast
Snacks
Sitting room, library, tennis,
fireplace, conferences, in-
room phones.

Private, quiet, historic and spacious, country location at the edge of the Gettysburg National Historic Park. E-mail: baladerry@mail.wideopen.net *Web site:* baladerryinn.com

Baltimore Street B&B
449 Baltimore St, 17325
717-334-2454 Fax: 717-334-6890
888-667-8266
Jan & George Newton
All year

90-155-B&B
10 rooms, 10 pb
Visa, MC, *Rated*
C-ltd/S-no/P-no/H-no

Full breakfast
Complimentary evening
beverage
Sitting room, library, rocking
chairs on, front porch, golf
nearby

Built in 1868 Gothic structure, Baltimore St. B&B (formerly The Tannery B&B) is within walking distance of historical sites, museums, restaurants. E-mail: tannery@cvn.net
Web site: bestinns.net/usa/pa/tannery.html

Bechtel Mansion Inn
PO Box 688, 17316
717-259-7760
800-331-1108
Carol & Richard Carlson
All year

90-150-B&B
9 rooms, 9 pb
Visa, MC, AmEx,
Rated, •
C-yes/S-ltd/P-no/H-no

Full breakfast
Complimentary tea
Sitting room, library, A/C,
meeting rm, garden

Restored Victorian mansion with fine antiques, in Pennsylvania German Nat'l Historical District. Popular with honeymooners, Civil War and architecture buffs
E-mail: please_phone@bbinternet.com *Web site:* bbonline.com/pa/bechtel/rooms.html

GETTYSBURG

Brafferton Inn, The
44 York St, 17325
717-337-3423
Bill and Maggie Ward
All year

95-160-B&B
10 rooms, 10 pb
Most CC, *Rated*, •
C-ltd/S-no/P-no/H-yes

Full breakfast
Coffee, tea
Library, atrium, piano, hat
collection, old mags,
primitive mural

Stone and clapboard inn circa 1786 near the center square of Gettysburg. The rooms have stenciled designs, antiques. Walk to battlefield and restaurants.
Web site: bbhost.com/braffertoninn

Brickhouse Inn
452 Baltimore St, 17325
717-338-9338 Fax: 717-338-9265
800-864-3464
Craig & Marion Schmitz
All year

85-140-B&B
7 rooms, 7 pb
Visa, MC, •
C-yes/S-no/P-no/H-no

Full breakfast
Snacks
Sitting room, walk to,
restaurants, shops and
battlefield

1898 brick Victorian nestled in the historic district. Walk to battlefields, great restaurants, antique and gift shops.   *E-mail:* stay@brickhouseinn.com   *Web site:* brickhouseinn.com

---

Country Escape
PO Box 195, 17343
717-338-0611 Fax: 717-334-5227
800-484-3244
Merry V. Bush
All year

65-80-B&B
3 rooms, 1 pb
Most CC, •
C-yes/S-no/P-no/H-no

Full breakfast
Snacks
Hot tub, family friendly,
facility, crib available, code
for 800# is 4371

Laid back country decor, peaceful and quiet. Extensive garden. Located near Gettysburg.
E-mail: merry@innernet.net

Doubleday Inn, The
104 Doubleday Ave, 17325
717-334-9119 Fax: 717-334-7907
Charles E. & Ruth Anne
Wilcox
All year

89-109-B&B
9 rooms, 5 pb
Visa, MC, Disc, *Rated*,
•
C-ltd/S-no/P-no/H-no

Full breakfast
Afternoon tea, snacks
Sitting room, battlefield
guide, presentations

The only inn directly on Gettysburg Battlefield. Cozy antiques, Civil War accents and splendid views. Discussion of Battle of Gettysburg with knowledgeable battlefield histori-ans on selected days.   *E-mail:* doubledayinn@wideopen.net *Web site:* bbonline.com/pa/doubleday/

Gaslight Inn, The
33 East Middle Street, 17325
717-337-9100 Fax: 717-337-9616
Denis and Roberta Sullivan
All year

110-165-B&B
9 rooms, 9 pb
Most CC, *Rated*, •
C-ltd/S-ltd/P-no/H-yes

Full breakfast
Snacks, restaurant
(reservations)
Sitting room, library, Jacuzzi,
fireplaces, cable, conference
room

Luxury touches, wonderful outdoor living spaces & gardens, & the best food in town are complemented by hosts' pampering & concierge service. Walk to attractions, shops & restaurants.   *E-mail:* gaslight@cvn.net

---

Hickory Bridge Farm
96 Hickory Bridge Rd, 17353
717-642-5261 Fax: 717-642-6419
Robert & Mary Lynn Martin
All year

50-225-B&B
9 rooms, 8 pb
Visa, MC, *Rated*
C-ltd/S-yes/P-no/H-no

Full breakfast
Dinner available Friday-
Sunday
Sitting room, fireplaces,
bicycles, fishing, 8 miles from
Gettysburg

Relax in the country by enjoying a cozy cottage by the stream, a hearty breakfast at the farmhouse, and dine in restored PA barn during the weekends.   *E-mail:* hickory@
innbook.com *Web site:* hickorybridgefarm.com

GETTYSBURG

Historic Farnsworth House	95-150-B&B	Full breakfast
415 Baltimore St, 17325	9 rooms, 9 pb	Restaurant, bar, tea
717-334-8838 Fax: 717-334-5862	Visa, MC, AmEx, Disc,	Treats, sitt. rm., lib., garden,
Loring Shultz	*Rated*	gallery, cable, fireplaces,
All year	C-yes/S-ltd/P-no/H-ltd	whirlpools

Surround yourself with the enchanting blend of intimate atmosphere and Victorian elegance. E-mail: farnhaus@mail.cvn.net *Web site:* gettysburgaddress.com

James Gettys Hotel	115-135-B&B	Continental breakfast
27 Chambersburg St, 17325	11 rooms, 11 pb	Sitting room, suites, cable TV
717-337-1334 Fax: 717-334-2103	Most CC, *Rated*	
Stephanie McSherry	C-yes/S-no/P-no/H-yes	
All year	French	

Restored in 1996, this 195 year old hotel, located in downtown Gettysburg, offers 11 tastefully appointed suites with sitting room, bedroom & private bath. E-mail: jghotel@ mail.cvn.net *Web site:* jamesgettyshotel.com

Keystone Inn B&B	69-109-B&B	Full breakfast from menu
231 Hanover St, 17325	5 rooms, 5 pb	Lemonade, coffee, tea
717-337-3888	Visa, MC, *Rated*	Sitting room, library, suite
Doris & Wilmer Martin	C-yes/S-ltd/P-no	with TV, microwave &, frige
All year		tennis nearby

Unique decor, antiques and lots of natural chestnut and oak; comfort our priority. Area rich in history; antique lover's paradise. Country breakfast.   Web site: bbonline.com/pa/keystone

Old Barn, The	75-120-B&B	Full breakfast
1 Main Trail, 17320	12 rooms, 12 pb	Lunch & dinner available
717-642-5711	Most CC, *Rated*, •	Afternoon tea, swimming
800-640-BARN	C-yes/S-no/P-no/H-ltd	pool, sitting room, library,
John & Janet Malpeli		suites, cable TV
All year		

1853 barn renovated into most unique b&b w/lovely guestrooms and suites. Great patio and pool. Walk to PGA Championship golf course, wild game park and covered bridge. Web site: gettysburg.com/gcvb/oldbarn.htm

Shultz Victorian Mansion	66-115-B&B	Full breakfast
756 Philadelphia Ave, 17201	10 rooms, 10 pb	Sitting room, large lawn, fly
717-263-3371	Visa, MC, *Rated*, •	fishing/skiing nearby,
Joe & Doris Shultz	C-ltd/S-no/P-no/H-no	Victorian gardens
All year		

Charming 1880 historic home, elaborate wood carving throughout; furnished with antiques, A/C, beautiful gardens and lawn, near Gettysburg and ski slope

GROVE CITY

As Thyme Goes By	55-75-B&B	Full breakfast
PO Box 493, 16038	3 rooms, 3 pb	Afternoon tea, snacks
724-735-4003	*Rated*	Sitting room, Library,
Susan M. Haas	C-ltd/S-ltd/P-no/H-no	fireplaces, cable TV, classical
All year		music, picnics

We do for our guests what they don't take time to do for themselves, come prepared to be pampered during your stay at As Thyme Goes By. Candlelit breakfasts, homemade baked goods/jams E-mail: asthymegoesby@pathway.net *Web site:* asthymegoesby.com/

HANOVER

Beechmont Inn	80-135-B&B	Full breakfast
315 Broadway, 17331	7 rooms, 7 pb	Snacks, afternoon tea
717-632-3013 800-553-7009	Most CC, *Rated*, •	Sitting room, library,
William/Susan Day All year	C-ltd/S-no/P-no/H-no	honeymoon/golf packages

Federal period elegance; echoes of Civil War memories; a refuge from the 20th century rush—a bridge across time. Near Gettysburg, antiquing. Whirlpool tub, fireplace available. Web site: virtualcities.com/ons/pa/y/paya801.htm

HARRISBURG

Farm Fortune B&B
204 Lime Kiln Rd, 17070
717-774-2683 Fax: 717-774-5089
Phyllis Combs
All year

85-95-B&B
3 rooms, 3 pb
Visa, MC, AmEx, •
C-ltd

Full breakfast
Lunch & dinner nearby
Sitting room, library, tennis
courts, fishing, & skiing
nearby

Believed to be part of the underground railroad in the 1790s, this limestone home is furnished in antiques. E-mail: FrmFortune@aol.com Web site: members.aol.com/FrmFortune/

HAWLEY

Falls Port Inn & Restaurant
330 Main Ave, 18428
570-226-2600 Fax: 570-226-6409
Dorothy S. Fenn
All year

75-120-B&B
9 rooms, 5 pb
Visa, MC, AmEx, *Rated*
C-yes/S-ltd/P-ltd/H-ltd

Continental breakfast
Lunch, dinner, restaurant
Bar service, sitting room,
cable TV, brunch on Sunday

Restored Victorian Inn. Guest rooms & dining rooms filled with antiques & elegant decor. Restaurant creates an oasis of both elegant & casual affordable dining with superior cuisine, quality service & congenial hospitality.

Settlers Inn, The
4 Main Ave, 18428
717-226-2993 Fax: 717-226-1874
800-833-8527
Grant & Jeanne Genzlinger
All year

95-160-B&B
20 rooms, 18 pb
Most CC, *Rated*, •
C-yes/S-yes/P-ltd/H-no

Full breakfast
Lunch, dinner, bar
Sitting room, library, phones
in rooms, bikes, tennis,
piano, gift shop

Delightful country inn of Tudor architecture, with gift shops and art gallery. Lake Wallenpaupack and shopping are nearby. Air conditioned rooms E-mail: settler@ptdprolog.net *Web site:* thesettlersinn.com

HUNTINGDON

Inn at Solvang, The
RR4, Box 301-A, 16652
814-643-3035 Fax: 814-641-7306
888-814-3035
Pamela & J. J. Henry
All year

95-135-B&B
6 rooms, 4 pb
Visa, MC, AmEx, *Rated*
C-ltd/S-no/P-no/H-ltd

Full breakfast
Sitt. rm., lib., deck, cable TV,
music room, 3rd floor
terrace, conf.

The Inn at Solvang is a gracious, secluded, southern colonial style house noted for exceptional gourmet breakfasts. E-mail: solvang@rnrnow.com Web site: solvang.com

INTERCOURSE

C.1766 Osceola Mill B&B
313 Osceola Mill Rd, 17529
717-768-3758 Fax: 717-768-7539
800-878-7719
Elaine & John Lahr
All year

85-135-B&B
5 rooms, 5 pb
Visa, MC, *Rated*
C-ltd/S-no/P-no/H-no

Afternoon tea, snacks
Sitting room, fireplace, cable
TV, air conditioning

Beautiful stone Georgian Colonial c.1766 set amongst Old Order Amish farms. Fireplaces, antiques, canopy beds, quilts adds to the charm of the tranquil setting. E-mail: elalahr@epix.net Web site: lancaster-inn.com

Carriage Corner B&B
PO Box 371, 17534
717-768-3059 Fax: 717-768-0691
800-209-3059
Gordon & Gwen Schuit
All year

68-90-B&B
5 rooms, 5 pb
Visa, MC, *Rated*, •
C-ltd/S-no/P-no/H-no

Full breakfast
Afternoon tea, use of
refrigerator
Sitting room, central AC,
cable TV in rooms, free
attractions coupons

At the hub of the Amish area, our B&B offers a relaxing country atmosphere. Dinner with an Amish family arranged. Special diets will be accommodated. Web site: bbonline.com/pa/carriagecorner/

Carriage Corner B&B, Intercourse, PA

INTERCOURSE

Intercourse Village B&B	89-199-B&B	Gourmet breakfast
Rt 340 Main St, Box 340, 17534	9 rooms, 9 pb	Snacks
717-768-2626	Visa, MC, AmEx,	Sitting room, Jacuzzis, suites,
800-664-0949	*Rated*, ●	fireplaces, cable TV, steam
Ruthann Thomas All year	S-no/P-no/H-no	showers

A romantic inn for couples in an Amish country village. Jacuzzis, Fireplaces, Private baths, Antiques, walk to the craft shoppes.   E-mail: ivbbs@aol.com *Web site:* amishcountryinns.com

JIM THORPE

Harry Packer Mansion, The	85-495-B&B	Full breakfast
PO Box 458, 18229	13 rooms, 11 pb	Sitting room, library, tennis,
570-325-8566	Visa, MC, *Rated*, ●	small meetings, murder
Robert & Patricia Handwerk	C-ltd/S-ltd/P-no/H-no	mystery weekends
All year		

Magnificent Victorian mansion in historic district with period furnishings, original woodwork and stained glass. Small weddings, Victorian balls in June & Dec. 4 diamond rating. E-mail: mystery@murdermansion.com *Web site:* murdermansion.com

Inn at Jim Thorpe, The	65-250-B&B	Continental plus breakfast
24 Broadway, 18229	37 rooms, 37 pb	Snacks, lunch/dinner
570-325-2599 Fax: 570-325-9145	Most CC, *Rated*, ●	available
800-329-2599	C-yes/S-ltd/P-no/H-yes	Restaurant, bar, sitting room,
David Drury All year		game room, suites

Historic New Orleans style inn, combine Victorian splendor with 21st century comforts. Located in village known as "America's Little Switzerland." E-mail: innjt@ptd.net *Web site:* innjt.com

KENNETT SQUARE

B&B at Walnut Hill	75-95-B&B	Full breakfast
541 Chandler's Mill Rd, 19311	2 rooms	Afternoon tea, snacks
610-444-3703 Fax: 610-444-6889	*Rated*	Sitting room, Jacuzzis, tennis,
Sandy & Tom Mills	C-yes/S-ltd/P-no/H-no	court, fireplaces, canoeing,
All year	Ltd. Spanish & French	cable TV

Warm, cozy, antique filled B&B, bucolic setting, minutes to major attractions. Creative all natural full country breakfast Guests report, "came as strangers, left as friends." E-mail: millsjt@magpage.com

LANCASTER

Alden House, The	85-120-B&B	Full breakfast
62 E Main St, 17543	5 rooms, 5 pb	Dinner with Amish arranged
717-627-3363 800-584-0753	Visa, MC, *Rated*	Sitting room, suites with
Tom & Lillian Vasquez	C-ltd/S-no/P-no/H-no	fireplaces, route maps, bike
All year		storage

1850 brick Victorian home in the heart of Pennsylvania Dutch Country. Walk to all local attractions and fine dining.   E-mail: inn@aldenhouse.com *Web site:* aldenhouse.com/

LANCASTER ───────────────────────────────

Apple Bin Inn B&B, The
2835 Willow Sreet Pike, 17584
717-464-5881 Fax: 717-464-1818
800-338-4296
Debbie & Barry Hershey
All year

95-135-B&B
5 rooms, 5 pb
Visa, MC, *Rated*
C-ltd/S-no/P-no/H-no

Full breakfast
Afternoon tea, snacks
Sitting room, patios, 2 story
Carriage House, w/frplc.,
living room

Warm colonial charm with country flavor. Antiques, reproductions. Near Amish community, antique & craft shops, excellent restaurants & historical sites. A/C, phone, & cable TV in rooms. E-mail: bininn@aol.com Web site: applebininn.com/

Australian Walkabout Inn
PO Box 294, 17537
717-464-0707 Fax: 717-464-2501
Richard & Margaret Mason
All year

99-199-B&B
3 rooms, 3 pb
Visa, MC, AmEx,
Rated, •
C-ltd/S-no/P-no/H-no

Full Aussie breakfast
Goldfish pond & fountain, in-
room whirlpools/hot tubs,
cable TV, fireplaces

Victorian restored 1925 Mennonite house, landscaped, in a quaint village setting. Dinner and tour with Amish family can be arranged. Extensive gardens. Restaurant coupons. Honeymoon & anniversary suites. Web site: bbonline.com/pa/walkabout/index.html

B&B—The Manor
830 Village Rd, 17602
717-464-9564
MaryLou Paolini
All year

79-99-B&B
6 rooms, 4 pb
Visa, MC, *Rated*
C-yes/S-no/P-no/H-yes

Full buffet breakfast
Lunch, dinner, tea
Snacks, sitting room, A/C,
swimming pool, winter &
group discounts

On 4½ acres with 20' x 40' inground pool. Breakfast served on Victorian sunporch. Web site: bbdirectory.com/Inn/0817.html

B.F. Hiestand House
722 E Market St, 17547
717-426-1924
Jan Beitzer
All year

85-105-B&B
4 rooms, 4 pb
Visa, MC,
C-ltd/S-no/P-yes/H-no

Full breakfast
Snacks
Sitting room, suites, cable TV

Historic 1887 High Queen Anne Victorian Home. Come experience the elegance of a bygone era. Enjoy a full breakfast in our spectacular dining room. Relax on the verandah or walk the trails of the Susquehanna River. Web site: authenticbandb.org/hiestand/index.htm

Candlelight Inn B&B
2574 Lincoln Hwy E, 17572
717-299-6005 Fax: 717-299-6397
800-77CANDLE
Tim & Heidi Soberick
All year

79-139-B&B
7 rooms, 7 pb
Most CC, *Rated*, •
C-ltd/S-no/P-no/H-no
French, Italian

Full candlelit breakfast
Afternoon tea & snacks
Sitting room, antiques &
oriental rugs, Victorian style

Large country home, elegantly decorated with Victorian antiques & oriental rugs. Surrounded by Amish farms in the heart of PA Dutch country. Convenient location E-mail: candleinn@aol.com Web site: candleinn.com

Casual Corners B&B
301 N Broad St, 17543
717-626-5299
800-626-5299
Ruth & Glen Lehman
All year

65-85-B&B
4 rooms, 2 pb
Visa, MC,
C-ltd/S-no/P-no/H-no

Full breakfast
Sitting room, guest private
entrance, off-street parking

Charming turn of the century home with wrap-around porch with wicker furniture. Close to Lancaster County Amish. Casual and relaxing. E-mail: ccbb@redrose.net

LANCASTER ————————————————————————————————

Churchtown Inn B&B
2100 Main St, 17555
717-445-7794 Fax: 717-445-0962
H. & S. Smith, J. Kent
All year

69-100-B&B
9 rooms, 9 pb
Visa, MC, AmEx,
Rated, •
C-ltd/S-ltd/P-no
German

Full 5 course breakfast
Dinner with Amish family
Glass garden room, piano,
game rm., carriage house,
theme weekends

In the heart of Pennsylvania Dutch country. Historic circa 1735 stone Federal Colonial. Musical evenings & tea in parlor. Antiquing, farm markets & outlets. On National Historic Register.   E-mail: chtinn@epix.net Web site: bbinternet.com/churchtown

Clock Tower B&B
441 Chestnut St, 17512
717-684-5869
800-422-5869
Chris & Becky Will
All year

75-B&B
3 rooms, 3 pb
Visa, MC, Disc,
C-yes/S-ltd/P-no/H-no

Continental breakfast
Afternoon tea
Sitting room, library,
fireplace, cable TV,
conference facilities

Victorian home, small town setting. Original woodwork throughout, unique stained glass window and wraparound porch. Maps of covered bridges, historic/heritage sites and scenic farms. Homemade sweetbreads and granola highlight breakfast.   E-mail: info@columbiapa.com Web site: columbiapa.com/clocktower

Columbian, A B&B Inn, The
360 Chestnut St, 17512
717-684-5869
800-422-5869
Chris & Becky Will
All year

75-125-B&B
8 rooms, 8 pb
Visa, MC,
C-yes/S-no/P-no/H-no

Full breakfast
Complimentary beverages
Sitting room, A/C, TVs, 4
rooms with fireplace, 2 suites

Circa 1897 restored turn-of-the-century mansion. Includes wraparound sun porches, stained-glass window, & tiered staircase. Decorated with antiques in Victorian or Country style.   E-mail: Inn@columbianinn.com Web site: columbianinn.com

Flowers & Thyme
238 Strasburg Pike, 17602
717-393-1460 Fax: 717-399-1986
Don & Ruth Harnish
All year

80-110-B&B
3 rooms, 3 pb
Visa, MC, *Rated*
C-ltd/S-no/P-no/H-no

Full breakfast
Snacks, cold drinks
Sitting rooms, library, patio &
porch, A/C, winter & group
discounts

Newly renovated 1941 house, bordered by farmlands and only minutes from outlets. E-mail: padutchbnb@aol.com Web site: members.aol.com/padutchbnb

Frogtown Acres B&B
44 Frogtown Rd, 17562
717-768-7684
888-649-2333
Joe & Gloria
All year

75-85-B&B
4 rooms, 4 pb
Visa, MC,
C-ltd/S-ltd/P-no/H-yes
PA Dutch

Full breakfast
Sitting room, fireplace,
conference facility. Amish
farm visit.

Peaceful, romantic and unique getaway in Amish country. Our Inn is located in our beautifully remodeled carriage house. This is truly our little piece of Paradise. E-mail: glo97@juno.com Web site: frogtownacres.com

Gardens of Eden B&B
1894 Eden Rd, 17601
717-393-5179 Fax: 717-397-7722
Marilyn & Bill Ebel
All year

95-130-B&B
4 rooms, 4 pb
Visa, MC, *Rated*, •
C-ltd/S-no/P-no/H-no

Full breakfast
Amish dinners arranged
Sitting room, rowboats,
canoes, tours, tea/fruit on
arrival, private baths

Eden exists along the Conestoga River where wild flowers, herbs, and perennials bloom among the trees and lawns of this circa 1867 Iron Masters mansion. E-mail: info@gardens-of-eden.com Web site: gardens-of-eden.com

LANCASTER

Hillside Farm B&B	65-175-B&B	Full breakfast
607 Eby Chiques Rd, 17552	5 rooms, 3 pb	Afternoon & evening snacks
717-653-6697 Fax: 717-653-9775	Most CC, *Rated*, •	Sitting room, library, baby
888-249-3406	C-ltd/S-no/P-no/H-no	grand piano, A/C, barn cats,
Deb & Gary Lintner		6-person spa
All year		

1863 farmhouse in Amish Country, furnished with dairy farm antiques & milk bottles. Secluded, near creek & waterfall. River cruise package, Jul-Oct. E-mail: hillside3@juno.com *Web site:* hillsidefarmbandb.com

Historic Witmer's Tavern	65-110-B&B	Continental plus breakfast
2014 Old Phila. Pike, 17602	7 rooms, 4 pb	Popcorn poppers
717-299-5305	*Rated*, •	Antique shop, sitting room,
Brant E. Hartung	C-ltd/S-ltd/P-no/H-no	air field, honeymoon room,
All year		National Register

Lancaster's only pre-Revolutionary inn & Museum still lodging travelers. Fireplaces, antiques, quilts & fresh flowers in romantic rooms. Web site: 800padutch.com/1725histwit.html

Homestead Lodging	42-69-B&B	Continental breakfast
184 E Brook Rd (Rt 896), 17576	5 rooms, 5 pb	Microwave, refrigerator
717-393-6927	Visa, MC, *Rated*, •	A/C, sandbox, large yard,
Fax: 717-393-1424	C-yes/S-no/H-no	cable TV with stereo radio,
Bob & Lori Kepiro		Amish country tours
All year		

Clean country rooms provide a "Home away from home" atmosphere. Located adjacent to an Amish farm, where you can hear the clippety clop of Amish buggies & experience their unique culture.

Inn at Twin Linden	125-210-B&B	Full breakfast
2092 Main St, 17555	7 rooms, 7 pb	Aftn. tea, snacks, dinner/Sat
717-445-7619 Fax: 717-445-4656	Most CC, •	Jacuzzi, suites, frplcs., cable
Bob & Donna Leahy	C-ltd/S-no/P-no/H-ltd	TV, business travelers, comp.
All year		sherry/brandy

Elegant accommodations in historic estate for discriminating inn-goers. Private baths, Jacuzzis, firepalces, renowned gourmet cuisine. Web site: innattwinlinden.com

King's Cottage, A B&B Inn	100-205-B&B	Full breakfast
1049 E King St, 17602	9 rooms, 9 pb	Afternoon tea, cordials
717-397-1017 Fax: 717-397-3447	Visa, MC, *Rated*, •	Sitting room, library, water
800-747-8717	C-ltd/S-no/P-no/H-yes	garden, Dinner with Amish
Karen & Jim Owens	Spanish	family available
All year		

Enjoy National Register award-winning architecture & elegance. Near Amish farms, restaurants, antiques, outlets, quilts, historic sites. Small guest kitchen. E-mail: kingscottage@earthlink.net *Web site:* bbonline.com/pa/kingscottage/

Lincoln Haus Inn B&B	60-85-B&B	Full breakfast (rooms)
1687 Lincoln Hwy E, 17602	8 rooms, 8 pb	No alcohol on premises,
717-392-9412	*Rated*, •	honeymoon suite available,
Mary K. Zook	C-ltd/S-no/P-no/H-ltd	Amish crafts nearby
All year	German	

Unique suburban home, built in late 1800s, with rooms & apts. Natural oaks woodwork, antiques. Owner is a member of the old order Amish church. Web site: 800padutch.com/linchaus.html

LANCASTER

O'Flaherty's Dingeldein Hse
1105 E King St, 17602
717-293-1723 Fax: 717-293-1947
800-779-7765
Jack & Sue Flatley
All year

95-115-B&B
5 rooms, 4 pb
Most CC, *Rated*, •
C-yes/S-no/P-no/H-no

Full gourmet breakfast
Amish meal if reserved
Sitting room, library, Amish
farmlands nearby, farmers
mkt, mall outlet

For the business traveler, why spend another night in impersonal hotel room, greeted by lonely cup of coffee. Instead, join us for all the comforts of home in our home   E-mail: oflahb@lancnews.infi.net Web site: 800padutch.com/ofhouse.html

Olde Square Inn, The
127 E Main St, 17552
717-653-4525 Fax: 717-653-0976
800-742-3533
Fran & Dave Hand
Season Inquire

95-199-B&B
5 rooms, 5 pb
Most CC, •
S-ltd/P-no

Full breakfast
All rooms equipped with
cable color TV/VCR and
phone jacks

E-mail: oldesquare@desupernet.net *Web site:* oldesquareinn.com

Penns Valley Farm
6182 Metzler Rd, 17545
717-898-7386
Mel & Gladys Metzler
All year

50-65-B&B
2 rooms, 1 pb
Visa, MC, AmEx, •
C-yes/S-no/P-no/H-no

Full breakfast
Farmhouse, open hearth, TV,
A/C

A cozy, getaway guest house that sleeps up to seven people in beautiful Lancaster County farmland, but close to attractions. $2.50 off Dutch Wonderland tickets, 7$ off Hershey Park Tickets.

Railroad House B&B
280 W Front St, 17547
717-426-4141
Richard & Donna Chambers
All year

79-109-B&B/MAP/AP
8 rooms, 8 pb
Visa, MC,
C-yes/S-no/P-no/H-ltd
Spanish, French

Full breakfast
Lunch/dinner avail, aftn. tea
Restaurant, bar service,
suites, sitting room.

Restored historic 1820s Victorian country inn. Romantic atmosphere, gardens, patio, antiques, stenciling and dining room fireplaces. Fine dining restaurant featured in Bon Appetit and Colonial Homes magazines. Special events, packages & weddings.
Web site: lancnews.com/railroadhouse/

Rose Manor
124 S Linden St, 17545
717-664-4932 Fax: 717-664-1611
800-666-4932
Susan & Anne Jenal
All year

70-120-B&B
5 rooms, 4 pb
Visa, MC, *Rated*
C-ltd/S-no/P-no

Full breakfast
Afternoon tea, comp. sherry
Picnic baskets, sitting room,
gift shop, conservatory,
gardens

Lancaster County 1905 manor house. Comfortable Victorian decor & cooking reflect "herbal" theme. Near antiquing, PA Dutch attractions, Hershey.   E-mail: rosemanor@paonline.com
Web site: bbonline.com/pa/rosemanor/

West Ridge Guest House
1285 West Ridge Rd, 17022
717-367-7783 Fax: 717-367-8468
877-367-7783
Alice Heisey
All year

60-125-B&B
9 rooms, 9 pb
Visa, MC, AmEx,
Rated, •
C-ltd/S-no/P-no

Full breakfast
Hot tubs, TV, phones, tennis
court

Country setting. Each room decorated in a different decor. Some rooms with decks, fireplaces, and whirlpool tubs. All rooms with TV, phone, and VCR. Fishing pond.
E-mail: wridgeroad@aol.com *Web site:* westridgebandb.com

LANCASTER COUNTY

Artist's Inn & Gallery
PO Box 26, 17581
717-445-0219 Fax: 717-445-0219
888-999-4479
Jan & Bruce Garrabrandt
All year

90-140-B&B
3 rooms, 3 pb
Visa, MC, •
C-ltd/S-ltd/P-no/H-ltd

Full gourmet breakfast
Snacks, aftn. tea, wine
Bicycles, sitting room, tennis,
suites, puzzle room

Spend the night in an art gallery! Antique-filled home in small town surrounded by Amish farms; gourmet breakfasts, innkeepers artwork. Let passing horse-drawn buggies take you back in time. E-mail: info@artistinn.com Web site: artistinn.com

LANDENBERG

Cornerstone Inn
300 Buttonwood Rd, 19350
610-274-2143 Fax: 610-274-0734
Linda Chamberlin
All year

75-250-B&B
7 rooms, 7 pb
Visa, MC, AmEx,
Rated, •
C-yes/S-no/P-no/H-no

Full breakfast
Afternoon tea, snacks
Sitting room, library, tennis
court, hot tub, swimming
pool

A fine 18th century country house in the heart of the Brandywine Valley just minutes from Longwood gardens, Winterthur, and Amish country. Five new rooms with fireplaces and Jacuzzi baths. E-mail: corner3000@aol.com Web site: belmar.com/cornerstone

LEWISBURG

Inn at Olde New Berlin
321 Market St, 17855
570-966-0321 Fax: 570-966-9557
800-797-2350
John & Nancy Showers
Season Inquire

90-225-B&B
13 rooms, 5 pb
Visa, MC, *Rated*, •
C-ltd/S-no/P-no/H-no

Full breakfast
Lunch dinner available
Restaurant & bar service, sit.
rm., snacks, piano, tennis
nearby, gift shop

"A luxurious base for indulging in a clutch of quiet pleasures."—Phila. Inquirer. Fine dining and lodging amidst Victorian ambiance; tranquil setting. Have a Christopher Radko Rising Star Store for mouthblown, handpainted collectible ornaments. E-mail: john@newberlin-inn.com Web site: newberlin-inn.com

Pineapple Inn
439 Market St, 17837
570-524-6200
Charles & Deborah North
All year

55-95-B&B
6 rooms, 2 pb
Most CC, *Rated*
C-ltd/S-ltd/P-no/H-no
German

Full country breakfast
Comp. tea, snacks
A/C, tea room, pool nrby,
piano, sitt. rm., tennis,
wonderful restaurants

1857 Federal Victorian home decorated completely with 19th century antiques. Just blocks from Bucknell University. Beautiful architecture, great antiquing. Upside-Down Shoppe E-mail: pineappl@jdweb.com Web site: jdweb.com/pineappleinn/

LIGONIER

Campbell House B&B
305 E Main St, 15658
724-238-9812 Fax: 724-238-9951
888-238-9812
Patti Campbell
All year

80-120-B&B
4 rooms, 4 pb
Most CC, *Rated*, •
C-ltd/S-no/P-no/H-no

Full breakfast
Snacks, comp. wine
Sitting room, off street
parking, house phone, fax
service

Cozy cottage uniquely decorated. A peaceful retreat that is within walking distance to shops, restaurants & historic sites. Scrumptious breakfast E-mail: bnb@soupkid.com Web site: soupkid.com

MECHANICSBURG

Kanaga House B&B
6940 Carlisle Pike, 17072
717-766-8654
Dave & Mary Jane Kretzing
All year

70-95-B&B
5 rooms, 4 pb
Visa, MC, *Rated*
C-ltd/S-no/P-no/H-ltd

Full breakfast
Wine
Sitting room, fireplace, cable
TV, conference, facilities

This limestone manor dates from 1775. It is in a country setting 100 yards off Hwy. 11, just 3 miles from I-81 exit 17 and 4 miles from Penna Tpk exit 16. A secure, home-like atmosphere. E-mail: kanaga@ezonline.com

MERCER

Magoffin Inn	115-125-B&B	Full breakfast
129 S Pitt St, 16137	5 rooms, 5 pb	Dinner available
724-662-4611 Fax: 724-662-4611	Visa, MC, AmEx,	Snacks, library, tennis/pool
800-841-0824	*Rated*, •	nearby, Amish suite with two
Jacque McClelland/Gene	C-yes/S-no/P-no/H-no	baths
Slagle		
All year		

1884 Queen Anne Victorian. Affordable elegance in ideal location. Outdoor activities abound: boating, fishing, golf, cross-country skiing. Near I-79 and I-80.

MERTZTOWN

Longswamp B&B	83-88-B&B	Full breakfast
1605 State St, 19539	10 rooms, 6 pb	Complimentary wine,
610-682-6197 Fax: 610-682-4854	•	cheese, etc.
Elsa & Dean Dimich	C-yes/S-ltd/P-no/H-ltd	Picnics, sitting room, library,
All year	French	piano, bicycles, horseshoes,
		bocce court

Historic country farmhouse near Amish country and skiing. Tempting delicacies prepared by area chef. Book and music collection for guests' use.   E-mail: rafer2@msn.com
Web site: longswamp.com

MILFORD

Black Walnut Country Inn	100-150-B&B	Full breakfast
179 Firetower Rd, 18337	14 rooms, 8 pb	Restaurant, complimentary
717-296-6322 Fax: 717-296-7696	Visa, MC, AmEx,	sherry
Stewart Schneider	*Rated*, •	Pool table, lawn games,
All year	C-yes/S-ltd/P-no/H-no	piano, pond, hot tub, riding
		lessons, trails

Large secluded estate for an exclusive clientele. Tudor-style stone house with marble fireplace, charming bdrms. with antiques & brass beds. Overlooks lake. Riding stable
Web site: theblackwalnutinn.com

Cliff Park Inn & Golf Crs.	93-160-B&B/MAP/AP	Full breakfast
155 Cliff Park Rd, 18337	18 rooms, 18 pb	Restaurant, bar
570-296-6491 Fax: 570-296-3982	Most CC, *Rated*, •	Sitting room, library, 2 rooms
800-225-6535	C-yes/S-yes/P-no/H-ltd	with, fireplaces, cross-
Harry W. Buchanan	French, Spanish	country skiing
All year		

Historic country inn surrounded by long-established golf course & school on secluded 600-acre estate.   E-mail: info@cliffparkinn.com *Web site:* cliffparkinn.com

Roebling Inn on Delaware	85-140-B&B	Full breakfast
PO Box 31, 18435	6 rooms, 6 pb	Afternoon tea
570-685-7900 Fax: 570-685-1718	Visa, MC, AmEx,	Sitting room, tennis, A/C, TV,
Don & JoAnn Jahn	*Rated*, •	queen beds, some rooms
All year	C-yes/S-ltd/P-no/H-no	with fireplaces

A jewel of the upper Delaware River, amid scenery to soothe the senses. Enjoy a stroll through our beautiful region. Canoe, raft, tube, hike, ski nearby. Fish on site.
E-mail: roebling@ltis.net *Web site:* poconos.org/members/roeblinginn

MOUNT JOY

Cedar Hill Farm B&B	75-80-B&B	Continental plus breakfast
305 Longenecker Rd, 17552	5 rooms, 5 pb	Central A/C, porch, 1 room
717-653-4655	Most CC, *Rated*, •	with private balcony, 1 room
Gladys Swarr	C-ltd/S-no/P-no/H-no	with whirlpool tub
All year		

Host born in this 1817 Fieldstone farmhouse. Quiet area overlooks stream. Near Lancaster's Amish country & Hershey. Near farmers' markets & quaint villages
Web site: 800padutch.com/cedarhill.html

NEW HOPE

Aaron Burr House Inn
80 W Bridge St, 18938
215-862-2570 Fax: 215-862-2570
Nadine, Carl, Jesse Glassman
All year

90-199-B&B
6 rooms, 6 pb
AmEx, *Rated*, •
C-ltd/S-no/P-no/H-yes
French, Spanish

Continental plus breakfast
Comp. liqueur, snacks
Afternoon tea, library, 2 new
fireplace suites, white wicker
porch, pool

Discover "safe haven" in vintage village Victorian inn—Aaron Burr did after his famous pistol duel with Alexander Hamilton in 1804! All guestrooms handpainted. Innkeeping seminars E-mail: stay@new-hope-inn.com *Web site:* new-hope-inn.com/aaron

Barley Sheaf Farm B&B
5281 York Rd (Rt 202), 18928
215-794-5104 Fax: 215-794-5332
Veronica & Peter Suess
All year

110-215-B&B
12 rooms, 12 pb
Rated, •
C-ltd/S-no/P-no/H-yes
French, German

Full farm breakfast
Afternoon tea
Swimming pool, sitt. rm., one
room with Jacuzzi,
conference center

30-acre working farm—raise sheep. Rooms all furnished in antiques. Good antiquing and historic sights in area. E-mail: info@barleysheaf.com *Web site:* barleysheaf.com

Bridgeton House, The
1525 River Rd, 18972
610-982-5856
888-982-2007
Charles & Bea Briggs
All year

99-299-B&B
11 rooms, 11 pb
Visa, AmEx,
Rated, •
C-ltd/S-ltd/P-no/H-no

Full gourmet breakfast
Afternoon tea & cakes
Sitting room, river swimming,
restaurant & shops,
phones/data ports, TV/VCR

Romantic guest rooms in 1836 inn on Delaware River. French doors with river views, screened porches, flowers & fruit. Featured in New York Times *&* Woman's Day *magazine.* E-mail: bestinn1@epix.net *Web site:* bridgetonhouse.com

Centre Bridge Inn
2998 N River Rd, 18938
215-862-9139 Fax: 215-862-3244
Stephen R. DuGan
All year

85-190-B&B
10 rooms, 10 pb
Most CC, *Rated*
C-ltd/S-no/P-no/H-no

Continental breakfast
Dinner available (fee),
restaurant
Bar service, sitting room,
Directly on banks of the
Delaware river & canal

"The only thing we overlook is the Delaware River and Canal . . ." Relax in the warmth & atmosphere of centuries gone by in quaint lodgings; featuring canopy beds & riverviews. Fine rest. on premises. E-mail: centreinn@aol.com *Web site:* letsmakeplans.com/centrebridgeinn

Hollileif B&B
677 Durham Rd, 18940
215-598-3100
Ellen & Richard Butkus
All year

85-160-B&B
5 rooms, 5 pb
Most CC, *Rated*, •
C-ltd/S-no/P-no/H-no
some Spanish

Full gourmet breakfast
Complimentary wine,
refreshments
Accommodate special diet,
volleyball, croquet,
badminton, horseshoes

We pamper you in our romantic 18th-century home on 5.5 beautiful country treed acres, gardens, stream. Charming country furnishings, 2 gas fireplaces. E-mail: hollileif@aol.com *Web site:* bbhost.com/hollileif

Inn to the Woods B&B
150 Glenwood Dr, 18977
215-493-1974 Fax: 215-493-7592
800-982-7619
Carol & Chris Bolton
All year

95-250-B&B
7 rooms, 7 pb
Visa, MC, AmEx,
Rated, •
C-ltd/S-no/P-no/H-no

Full breakfast on weekends
Continental plus breakfast
weekdays
Sitting room, queen beds,
Sunken tub, fireplace rooms

Nestled on 10 wooded acres. Secluded elegance in Bucks County. Close to New York, Philadelphia, Princeton. Outdoor hot tub, color cable TV/VCR, video library. E-mail: inn2woods@aol.com *Web site:* inn-bucks.com/

NEW HOPE

Pineapple Hill B&B	94-180-B&B	Full gourmet breakfast
1324 River Rd, 18938	8 rooms, 8 pb	Afternoon tea, snacks
215-862-1790 Fax: 215-862-5273	Visa, MC, AmEx,	Sitting room, library,
Kathryn & Charles Triolo	*Rated*, •	bicycles, pool, cable TV,
All year	C-ltd/S-ltd/P-no/H-no	fireplaces, telephones

Romantic rooms and suites, all with private baths. Full gourmet breakfast daily, served at individual candlelit tables. Early breakfast available. Fireplaces, pool.
E-mail: ktriolo@pineapplehill.com   *Web site:* pineapplehill.com

Tattersall Inn	95-140-B&B	Full breakfast
PO Box 569, 18950	6 rooms, 6 pb	Apple cider, snacks
215-297-8233 Fax: 215-297-5093	Most CC, *Rated*, •	Library, sitting room, piano,
800-297-4988	C-ltd/S-ltd/P-no/H-no	veranda, meetings, walk-in
Donna & Bob Trevorrow		fireplace
All year		

Bucks County historic mansion circa early 1800s. Antique phonograph collection. River canoeing & tubing, antique shops, art galleries. Two room with gas-log fireplaces
Web site: bbhost.com:8008/tattersall_inn

Wedgwood Inn of New Hope	80-240-B&B	Continental plus breakfast
111 W Bridge St, 18938	18 rooms	Aftn. tea & refreshments
215-862-2520 Fax: 215-862-2520	Visa, MC, *Rated*, •	Victorian gazebo, parlor,
Carl & Nadine Glassman	C-ltd/S-ltd/P-ltd/H-ltd	horsedrawn carriage ride,
All year	French, Hebrew, Dutch	club w/tennis, swimming

Victorian mansion. Wedgwood china, fresh flowers, original art, & Victorian gingerbread porches. Innkeepers make stay as pleasant as surroundings. OUR 1989 INN OF THE YEAR! E-mail: stay@new-hope-inn.com   *Web site:* new-hope-inn.com

Whitehall Inn, The	140-200-B&B	Full candlelight breakfast
1370 Pineville Rd, 18938	6 rooms, 4 pb	High tea, complimentary
215-598-7945	Most CC, *Rated*, •	sherry
888-37-WHITE	C-ltd/S-no/P-no/H-no	Pool & rose garden, library,
Mike & Suella Wass		sun room, piano & pump
All year		organ

Experience our four-course candlelit breakfast using European china and crystal and heirloom sterling silver.   Web site: innbook.com/whitehal.html

NEWFOUNDLAND

Panther Inn	135-185-MAP	Full country breakfast
RR, Box 215, 18445	12 rooms, 12 pb	Lunch & dinner available
570-676-5677 Fax: 570-676-5819	Most CC,	Tea, snacks, restaurant,
888-376-5677	C-yes/S-yes/P-yes/H-ltd	sitting room, library, tennis,
Lora, Judy & Patti		suites, cable TV
All year		

Tranquil, family run country inn furnished with hand-made decor. Generous homemade country meals served in quaint dining room. 50 acres for walking, picnicking or relaxing by the pond.   E-mail: info@pantherinn.com   *Web site:* pantherinn.com

NORTH WALES

Joseph Ambler Inn	100-200-B&B	Full breakfast
1005 Horsham Rd, 19454	38 rooms, 38 pb	Restaurant
215-362-7500 Fax: 215-361-5924	Most CC, *Rated*, •	3 sitting rooms,
Steve & Terry Kratz	C-yes/S-yes/P-no/H-ltd	banquet/meeting room,
All year	French, German	special diet cooking

1735 estate house set on 13 acres and furnished with antiques, four-poster beds, walk-in fireplace. E-mail: jai@philanet.com   *Web site:* philanet.com/jai/

PARADISE ─────────────────────────────

Creekside Inn B&B, The	80-105-B&B	Full breakfast
PO Box 435, 17562	5 rooms, 5 pb	Afternoon tea, snacks
717-687-0333 Fax: 717-687-8200	Visa, MC,	Sitting room, air
Cathy & Dennis Zimmermann	C-ltd/S-no/P-no/H-no	conditioning, 2 guest rooms
All year		with fireplaces

Beautifully restored 1781 stone house on Pequea Creek in the heart of Amish country. Antique furnishings, fireplace rooms, gourmet breakfast. E-mail: cathy@thecreeksideinn.com *Web site:* thecreeksideinn.com

PHILADELPHIA ─────────────────────────

1011 Clinton B&B	135-200-B&B	Continental plus breakfast
1011 Clinton St, 19107	7 rooms, 7 pb	Snacks
215-923-8144 Fax: 215-923-5757	Visa, MC, AmEx,	Sitting room, suites, fireplace,
Judith Talbot Cills	*Rated*, •	cable TV, private kitchens,
All year	C-yes/S-no/P-ltd/H-ltd	conference

1836 Federal Townhouse, walk to Independence Hall. Seven beautiful suites, fireplaces, living rooms, kitchens, TV/VCR, telephones and computer access; on the best residential street. E-mail: 1011@concentric.net *Web site:* TenEleven.com

Alexander Inn	99-159-B&B	Continental breakfast plus
304 South 12th St, 19107	48 rooms, 48 pb	Snacks
215-923-3535 Fax: 215-923-1004	Most CC, *Rated*, •	Cable TV, accommodate
877-ALEX-INN	C-ltd/S-ltd/P-no/H-ltd	business travelers, fitness
Frank Baer	Spanish, French	center-24 hour
All year		

A hotel on the national historic registry having just opened after a two year restoration. With designer rooms and baths, having large fluffy towels, direct TV, great artwork and furnishings reflective of the great cruise ships of the 40's. E-mail: info@alexanderinn.com *Web site:* alexanderinn.com

Anam Cara	75-95-B&B	Continental plus breakfast
52 Wooddale Ave, 19118	3 rooms, 3 pb	Complimentary wine
215-242-4327	•	Sitting room, fireplaces,
Teresa Vesey & Jack Gann	C-ltd/S-no/P-no/H-no	cable TV, accommodate
All year		business travlers

At Anam Cara Bed & Breakfast a special ambiance is created by owner and hostess Teresa Vesey. Teresa is a native of Ireland who brings to her B&B true Irish hospitality. E-mail: tvesey@aol.com *Web site:* anamcarabandb.com

City Garden B&B, A	100-135-B&B	Continental plus breakfast
1103 Waverly St, 19147	2 rooms, 2 pb	Suites, cable TV, conference
215-625-2599	•	facilities, air conditioned
Virginia Trosino	C-ltd/P-no/H-no	rooms
All year		

Nestled on a small street, yet within 6 blocks of theatre district, Independence Hall, antique row, City Hall, luxury shopping, & much more. E-mail: virginia.t@worldnet.att.net *Web site:* home.att.net/~acitygarden

Gaskill House B&B	135-170-B&B	Full breakfast
312 Gaskill St, 19147	3 rooms, 3 pb	Afternoon tea
215-413-0669	•	Sitting room, library,
Guy M. Davis	C-ltd/S-no/P-ltd/H-no	Jacuzzis, fireplace, cable TV
All year		

Gaskill House is a small, European type luxury B&B in Philadelphia's historic Society Hill district. Built in 1828, Gaskill House has been totally renovated and beautifully furnished. Large well appointed guest rooms feature four poster queen size beds. E-mail: gaskillbnb@aol.com *Web site:* gaskillhouse.com

PHILADELPHIA

Mellow Manor/Overbrook Farm 6359 Woodbine Ave, 19151 215-477-3311 Fax: 215-878-0475 800-342-7042 Ted Gentner All year	125-B&B 8 rooms, 1 pb Visa, MC, *Rated* C-ltd/S-no/P-no/H-ltd	Full breakfast Lunch, dinner, tea, snacks, wine Sitting room, library, fireplace, cable TV, conferences

Unique home designed in 1896 in a planned community. In 1915 changed from twin into single. The porches & plazas offer a homey invitation for browsing the gardens. E-mail: fwgbb@aol.com Web site: travelguides.com/home/mellowmanor

Penn's View Hotel 14 N Front St, 19106 215-922-7600 Fax: 215-922-7642 800-331-7634 The Sena Family All year	108-195-B&B 38 rooms, 38 pb Most CC, *Rated*, • C-yes/S-yes/P-no/H-no Italian, Spanish	Continental plus breakfast Lunch & dinner available Restaurant, bar service, Jacuzzis, fireplaces, individual wine tasting

Charming European-style hotel. Short walk to historic attractions. 2 Meeting rooms. Web site: pennsviewhotel.com

Shippen Way Inn 418 Bainbridge St, 19147 215-627-7266 Fax: 215-627-7781 800-245-4873 Ann Foringer & Raymond Rhule All year	90-120-B&B 9 rooms, 9 pb Visa, MC, AmEx, *Rated*, • C-ltd/S-ltd/P-no/H-ltd	Continental plus breakfast Afternoon tea Comp. wine, sitting room, individual wine tasting

Friendly family owned and operated Inn with a country feel in the city. Colonial herb and rose garden. Fireplaces.

Society Hill Hotel 301 Chestnut St @ 3rd, 19106 215-925-1919 Judith Kleinman All year	85-175-B&B 12 rooms, 12 pb Most CC, *Rated*, • C-yes/S-yes/P-ltd	Continental breakfast Restaurant Piano bar, telephones, individual wine tasting

An "urban inn" located in the midst of Philadelphia's Historic Park. Fresh flowers, chocolates and brass double beds grace each room.

Spring Garden Manor 2025 Spring Garden St, 19130 215-567-2484 Fax: 215-567-2484 David Katz All year	119-139-B&B 3 rooms, 3 pb • C-yes/S-no/P-ltd/H-no Hebrew	Continental plus breakfast Sitting room, suites, fireplace in one suite, Japanese garden, deck

Unique and elegant. Most artwork & furniture made by area artists. All new. Own entrance. E-mail: Naim43@aol.com Web site: members.aol.com/naim43/springbb/spring1.htm

Thomas Bond House 129 S Second St, 19106 215-923-8523 Fax: 215-923-8504 800-845-BOND Rita Mc Guire All year	95-175-B&B 12 rooms, 12 pb Visa, MC, AmEx, *Rated*, • C-yes/S-yes/P-no/H-no	Continental plus-weekdays Full breakfast on weekends Hair dryers, TV, phone, fresh-baked cookies, whirlpool tubs, parlor

Colonial period (c.1770), listed in National Register. Individually decorated rooms. In Independence National Historical Park; next to historic shrines. Fully renovated inside and out, including new wall coverings, fabrics and paint. Web site: travelguides.com/home/thomas_bond

PITTSBURGH

Inn at Oakmont, The	130-150-B&B	Full breakfast
PO Box 103, 15147	8 rooms, 8 pb	Snacks
412-828-0410	Visa, MC, AmEx, Disc,	Sitting room, library,
Fax: 412-828-1358	*Rated*	fireplace, cable TV, whirlpool
Shelly Cammisa	C-ltd/S-no/P-no/H-yes	bath tubs
All year		

A charming and meticulously designed B&B built in 1994. Eight luxurious rooms with private bath, two with fireplace and whirlpool; full gourmet breakfast.
Web site: pittsburghbnb.com/oakmont.html

Morning Glory Inn	110-160-B&B	Full breakfast
2119 Sarah St, 15203	5 rooms, 5 pb	Wine
412-431-1707 Fax: 412-431-6106	Visa, MC, AmEx, •	Sitting room, library,
Nancy Eshelman	C-yes/S-ltd/P-ltd/H-no	bicycles, suites, fireplaces,
All year		conferences

1862 Italianate Victorian town house in Pittsburgh's historic "SouthSide." Walking distance to restaurants, jazz clubs and shops. E-mail: gloryinn@city-net.com
Web site: pittsburghbnb.com/morning.html

POCONO MOUNTAINS

La Anna Guesthouse	50-B&B	Continental plus breakfast
RR 2, Box 1051, 18326	3 rooms	Sitting room, piano, cross-
570-676-4225	C-ltd/S-yes/P-ltd/H-no	country skiing, fishing,
Fax: 570-676-4225		swimming, golf
Kay Swingle & Jill Porter		
All year		

Private Victorian home nestled in Pocono Mountain village welcomes guests. Furnished with antiques. Skating ponds, waterfalls, woodland walks. Historic sights.

POCONO'S

Bischwind B&B	150-235-B&B	Full breakfast
Box 7, 18602	9 rooms, 9 pb	Afternoon tea
570-472-3820	Most CC, •	Sitting room, library, Jacuzzi,
Barbara & Al, Billi & Ralph	C-ltd/S-no/P-no/H-no	pool, 3 suites, fireplaces,
All year		cable TV

Memborable four course breakfasts: filet mignon, steamed salmon, shrimp scampi. English Tudor mansion nominated for National Historic Register. Pool, lake, walking trails under virgin pine. Guided antiquing. Close to everything. E-mail: renglish@epix.net
Web site: bischwind.com

Merry Inn, The	80-95-B&B	Full breakfast
PO Box 757, 18325	6 rooms, 6 pb	Sitting room, Jacuzzis,
570-595-2011	Visa, MC, *Rated*, •	fireplace, cable TV
800-858-4182	C-yes/S-ltd/P-ltd/H-no	
Meridyth Huggard		
All year		

The Merry Inn is a cozy home away from home. Located in the heart of the Pocono Mountains, our B&B lets you get away from it all. E-mail: merryinn@ezaccess.net
Web site: pbcomputerconsulting.com/themerryinn

POTTSTOWN

Coventry Forge Inn	75-95-B&B	Continental breakfast
3360 Coventryville Rd, 19465	5 rooms, 5 pb	Restaurant, bar
610-469-6222	Most CC, *Rated*	Dinner available, sitting
Wallis and June Callahan	C-yes/S-yes/P-no/H-no	room, library, atmosphere
All year		for piano

Superb French restaurant in Chester County horse country. Brandywine Valley & Amish country nearby. Excellent antiquing.

RIDGWAY

Faircroft B&B
17 Montmorenci Rd, 15853
814-776-2539
Lois & John Shoemaker
All year

60-B&B
3 rooms, 3 pb
Most CC, *Rated*
C-ltd/S-no/H-no

Full breakfast
Comp. beverages, snacks
Sitting room, fireplace, hiking
trails, hunting, fishing,
swimming, golf

2 miles from Rt. 219. Warm, comfortable, 1870 farmhouse on 75 acres; all rooms have A/C. Antiques, Swedish foods. Next to Allegheny Nat'l Forest E-mail: faircroft@ncentral.com
Web site: ncentral.com/~faircroft/

SCOTTDALE

Pine Wood Acres B&B
Rt 1, Box 634, 15683
724-887-5404 Fax: 724-887-3111
Ruth A Horsch
All year

65-75-B&B
3 rooms, 2 pb
•
C-ltd/S-no/P-no/H-no

Full breakfast
Afternoon tea & snacks
Herb & perennial gardens,
porch, cater to special diets

A c. 1880 farm house in a country setting. Antiques, herbs, flowers. Near Wright's Fallingwater & Kentuck Knob, Youghiogheny River Bike Trail, hiking, rafting, ski resorts, historic sites. E-mail: jrhorsch@cvzoom.net Web site: laurelhighlands.org/pinewoodacres

Zephyr Glen B&B
205 Dexter Rd, 15683
724-887-6577 Fax: 724-887-6177
Noreen & Gil McGurl
All year

75-80-B&B
3 rooms, 3 pb
Visa, MC, Disc, •
C-ltd/S-no/P-no/H-no
Some German

Full breakfast
Afternoon tea, snacks
Sitting room, fireplace,
porch, can meet most diet
needs

1822 Federal Farmhouse, antique filled, country decor, hearty breakfast, warm hospitality, near antiques, whitewater, skiing, biking, hiking, historical sites, Fallingwater. E-mail: zephyr@cvzoom.net

SHIPPENSBURG

Field & Pine B&B
2155 Ritner Way, 17257
717-776-7179 Fax: 717-776-0076
Mary Ellen & Allan Williams
All year

75-85-B&B
3 rooms, 1 pb
Visa, MC, •
C-ltd/S-no/P-no/H-no

Full breakfast
Afternoon tea, snacks, wine
Sitting room, library,
fireplaces, antiques, fly
fishing streams

Historic limestone house c.1790 on 80 acre farm. Antiques, fireplaces, gourmet country breakfast. Come stay with us—home made cookies await you. Excellent hiking, biking and nature trails. E-mail: fieldpine@aol.com

SOMERSET

Bayberry Inn B&B
611 N Center Ave, 15501
814-445-8471
Marilyn & Bob Lohr
All year

55-65-B&B
11 rooms, 11 pb
Most CC, *Rated*, •
C-ltd/S-no/P-no/H-no

Continental plus breakfast
Snacks
Sitting room, library, TV
room with VCR/stereo,
swimming pool

One and one-half blocks from turnpike exit, near Georgian Place outlet mall. Seven Springs and Hidden Valley ski resorts, whitewater rafting, "Fallingwater."

Glades Pike Inn
2684 Glades Pike, 15501
814-443-4978 Fax: 814-443-2562
800-762-5942
Janet L. Jones
All year

50-85-B&B
5 rooms, 5 pb
Most CC, *Rated*, •
C-ltd/S-no/P-no/H-no

Full breakfast
Complimentary wine on
weekends
swimming pool

Built in 1842 as a stagecoach stop; located on a 200-acre dairy farm in the center of Laurel Highlands. Close to skiing, golf, state parks, falling water. E-mail: fwmjj@sprynet.com
Web site: gladespike.com/

STARLIGHT

Inn at Starlight Lake, The	140-165-MAP	Full breakfast
PO Box 27, 18461	27 rooms, 21 pb	Lunch, dinner, full bar
570-798-2519 Fax: 570-798-2672	Visa, MC, *Rated*, •	Sitting room, piano, tennis
800-248-2519	C-yes/S-yes/P-no/H-no	courts, boating, bicycles, ski
Jack & Judy McMahon		trails
Exc. late Mar-Apr 16		

A congenial & informal atmosphere in pastoral tranquility on a beautiful lake. Excellent food & spirits; recreation for every season. E-mail: theinn@unforgettable.com
Web site: innatstarlightlake.com

STATE COLLEGE

Chatelaine B&B, The	85-150-B&B	Full breakfast
PO Box 326, 16868	4 rooms, 2 pb	Complimentary liqueur
814-238-2028 Fax: 814-238-2028	Most CC, *Rated*, •	Sodas & hot beverages,
800-251-2028	C-ltd/S-no/P-no/H-no	sitting room, antiquing,
Mae McQuade	Some Sp. & Portuguese	honeymoons
All year		

Serene setting with handsome furnishings, exciting decor, & cosmopolitan antiques. Wine for bride & groom. Lovingly known as Chatelaine at Split-Pine Farmhouse.
Web site: virtualcities.com/pa/chatelaine.html

STRASBURG

Limestone Inn B&B	75-105-B&B	Full gourmet breakfast
33 E Main St, 17579	5 rooms, 5 pb	Sitting room, library, bicycle
717-687-8392 Fax: 717-687-8256	Most CC, •	storage, patio, quilting
800-278-8392	C-ltd/S-ltd/P-no/H-no	seminars
Denise & Richard Waller &		
kids		
All year		

The Limestone Inn B&B (circa 1786) is listed in the National Register of Historic Places; situated in the heart of Lancaster's Amish country. Resident cat. E-mail: manati@bellatlantic.net Web site: members.bellatlantic.net/~manati

TYRONS

Laurel Ridge B&B	50-90-B&B	Full breakfast
159 Laurel Court, 16877	4 rooms, 4 pb	Sitting room, cable TV,
814-632-6813 Fax: 814-632-6813	Visa, MC, Disc, *Rated*,	accommodate business
Kay & Wally Lester	•	travelers
All year	C-ltd/S-no/P-no/H-no	

Not close to anywhere, but on the way to everywhere! If you seek quiet, off the beaten path, try our new rustin home with central air, gleaming baths and firm mattresses.
E-mail: fwll@psu.edu

VALLEY FORGE

Coddington House	125-200-B&B	Full breakfast
441 S Whitehorse Rd, 19460	2 rooms, 2 pb	Snacks, complimentary bar
610-935-2454 Fax: 610-935-8422	Visa, MC, AmEx,	Sitting room, Jacuzzis, pool,
Cara Walker	C-ltd/S-ltd/P-no/H-no	fireplace, cable TV,
All year		conference facilities

1730 farmhouse, adjacent to 300 acre farm with antique furniture, fireplaces, pool, hot tub, golf, complimentary bar, toiletries, bathrobes, luxurious linens, facsimile, Internet access and 5 minutes to Valley Forge. E-mail: bigcoddy@prodigy.net

Shearer Elegance B&B	90-140-B&B	Full breakfast
1154 Main St, 19468	7 rooms, 7 pb	Sitting room, library, hot tubs
610-495-7429 Fax: 610-495-7814	Most CC, *Rated*, •	
800-861-0308	C-ltd/S-no/P-no/H-no	
Shirley and Malcolm Shearer		
All year		

22 room Victorian with 3 acres of gardens in summer and 35 decorated Christmas trees in winter; close to sights and shopping E-mail: shearerc@aol.cu..
Web site: members.aol.com/shearerc/shirley1.htm

WELLSBORO

Kaltenbach's B&B	70-150-B&B	Full breakfast
RD #6 Box 106A, 16901	10 rooms, 10 pb	Afternoon tea, snacks, wine
570-724-4954	Visa, MC, *Rated*, •	Lunch/dinner by res., sitting
800-722-4954	C-yes/S-no/P-no/H-yes	room, library, tennis court,
Lee Kaltenbach	Spanish	Jacuzzis
All year		

Famous for all-you-can-eat country-style breakfast—homemade jellies, jams, blueberry muffins, farm-raised pork, ham, bacon, sausage. Golf, skiing, hunting, fishing, hiking, biking nearby. Four rooms with Jacuzzis for two.   Web site: pavisnet.com/kaltenbach

WEST CHESTER

Bankhouse B&B	70-90-B&B	Full breakfast
875 Hillsdale Rd, 19382	2 rooms	Snacks
610-344-7388	*Rated*	Sitting room, porch, library,
Diana & Michael Bove	C-ltd/S-no/P-no/H-no	A/C, private entrances
All year		

Charming 18th-century "bankhouse" located across from a 10-acre horse farm. Convenient to Longwood Gardens, Winterthur, etc. Quiet country setting.

WILKES-BARRE

Ponda-Rowland B&B Inn	75-115-B&B	Full candlelight breakfast
RR1, Box 349, 18612	6 rooms, 6 pb	Picnics, special diets
570-639-3245	Most CC, *Rated*, •	Satellite TV, fireplaces,
Fax: 570-639-5531	C-yes/S-no/P-no	wildlife sanctuary, pond,
800-854-3286		hiking, all rooms A/C
Jeanette & Cliff Rowland		
All year		

130-acre farm in the Endless Mtns. Beautiful mountain and forest scenery. Farm includes private 30-acre wildlife refuge, canoeing, fishing, paddle boats, and swimming. E-mail: bbres1@epix.net Web site: bnbcity.com/inns/20006

YORK

Warrington Farm B&B	64-90-B&B	Full breakfast
7680 Carlisle Rd, 17365	5 rooms, 5 pb	Snacks
717-432-9053	Visa, MC, Disc, *Rated*	Sitting room, fireplace.
Fax: 717-432-4537	C-ltd/S-no/P no/H-ltd	
Brad & Megan Hakes		
All year		

1860's Gentleman's Farm with Shaker decor. Relax in beautiful country setting. Full country breakfast served on enormous back porch, dining area or by fireplace when available.   E-mail: wfarm@conewago.com Web site: conewago.com/wfarm/

Rhode Island

BLOCK ISLAND

1661 Inn & Hotel Manisses	85-335-B&B	Full buffet breakfast
PO Box I, 02807	60 rooms, 53 pb	Lunch, dinner, full bar
401-466-2421 Fax: 401-466-3162	Visa, MC, *Rated*, •	New Gazebo Room added,
800-626-4773	C-ltd/P-no/H-ltd	with glass walls, overlooking
Joan & Justin Abrams		the gardens, cable TV
May-Oct.		

Island country inn overlooking Atlantic Ocean—full buffet breakfast, wine & nibble hour, flaming coffees served on ocean view deck. E-mail: biresorts@aol.com Web site: blockisland.com/biresorts

BRISTOL

William's Grant Inn	100-110-B&B	Full breakfast
154 High St, 02809	5 rooms, 3 pb	Afternoon tea,
401-253-4222 Fax: 401-254-0987	Most CC, *Rated*, •	complimentary sherry
800-596-4222	C-ltd/S-ltd/P-no/H-ltd	Complimentary
D & W Poehler/M & J Poehler		coffee/cookies, bikes, sitting
All year		room, library, picnic lunches

On a quiet tree-lined street. Filled with family antiques and artist's fine work. Ceiling fans in all rooms. E-mail: wmgrantinn@aol.com *Web site:* members.aol.com/wmgrantinn

EAST GREENWICH

1873 House, The	75-95-B&B	Suites
162 Peirce St, 02818	1 rooms, 1 pb	
401-884-9955	C-yes/S-no/P-no/H-no	
Connie & Bud Koeniger		
All year		

An elegant Victorian private suite, located in the historic dsitrct just steps to Main Street with its many restaurants, boutiques, and shops. E-mail: the1873house@hotmail.com *Web site:* angelfire.com/biz/the1873houseBandB

Vincent House	70-95-B&B	Continental breakfast
170 Cedar Ave, 02818	2 rooms, 2 pb	Guests may use kitchen
401-885-2864	Visa, MC, •	refrigerator
Vincent Bradley	C-yes/S-no/P-no/H-no	Sitting room, cable TV, air
All year		condition, modem hook-up,
		fax, copier, computer

An up-scale delightful B&B located in historic East Greenwich, guests enjoy entire B&B with all its amenities. Your host (a retired widower executive) has an insight to what guests expect in a home-away-from-home. E-mail: vincenthouse@bigplanet.com *Web site:* vincenthouse.com

GREEN HILL, KINGSTOWN

Green Shadows B&B	75-105-B&B	Full breakfast
803 Green Hill Beach Rd,	2 rooms, 2 pb	Afternoon tea, snacks
02879	C-ltd/S-no/P-no/H-ltd	Sitting room, cable TV, guest
401-783-9752		refrigerator.
Don & Mercedes Kratz		
All year		

A Cape Cod style home designed with a guest's point of view; built in 1995 as a bed and breakfast. Set on a wooded and landscaped acre with a view of Green Hill Pond from the screened porch where breakfast is served, the home is a short walk to the ocean E-mail: dckratz@home.com *Web site:* virtualcities.com/ons/ri/w/riw7701.htm

LITTLE COMPTON

Stone House Club	58-125-B&B	Continental plus breakfast
122 Sakonnet Point Rd, 02809	13 rooms, 9 pb	Restaurant, bar service
401-635-2222	Visa, MC,	Beach, nature trails, yacht
Margaret & Peter Tirpaeck	C-yes/S-ltd/P-no/H-ltd	club closeby, sitting room,
All year		library

Private ocean view Victorian Inn, Early American tavern and restaurant, banquet facility and executive retreat. Inquire about our membership and monthly newsletter. Web site: stonehouseclub.com

NARRAGANSETT

1900 House	45-95-B&B	3 course gourmet breakfast
59 Kingstown Rd, 02882	3 rooms, 1 pb	Winter cider, summer tea
401-789-7971	C-ltd/S-no/H-no	Book Swap, antique
William A. Panzeri		postcards, porch, homemade
All year		quilts

Walk to the beach, browse the shops, or tour the Mansions & return to reflections of the past in our Victorian home. Enjoy sea breezes on the porch or inside. Deep fishing nearby. New room: Frederick Victorian with private bath.

1900 House, Narragansett, RI

NARRAGANSETT

Richards, The	85-175-B&B	Full gourmet breakfast
144 Gibson Ave, 02882	4 rooms, 3 pb	Complimentary sherry in
401-789-7746 Fax: 401-789-7168	•	room
Nancy Richards	C-ltd/S-no/P-no/H-no	Library with fireplace, tennis
All year		courts nearby, fireplaces in
		bedrooms

Gracious accommodations in a English country setting. Awaken to the smell of gourmet coffee and freshly baked goods.

Sea Gull Guest House	45-95-EP	Tennis courts nearby, near
50 Narragansett Ave, 02882	7 rooms, 4 pb	gambling casino, ocean
401-783-4636	Visa, MC, *Rated*	beach 1 block
Kimber Wheelock	C-ltd/S-no/P-no/H-no	
Memorial Day-Labor Day		

Large rooms cooled by ocean breezes. Close to everything. Swim, sun, sail & fish. 2 efficiency apts., 1 cottage available.   E-mail: kimberw@etal.uri.edu

NEWPORT

1 Murray House B&B	85-175-B&B	Continental plus breakfast
1 Murray Place, 02840	5 rooms, 3 pb	Snacks, complimentary wine
401-846-3337 Fax: 401-846-3337	*Rated*, •	Sitting room, swimming pool,
Noreen O'Neil	C-ltd/S-ltd/P-yes/H-no	tennis, fishing, tennis nearby
Closed winter		

Charming, attractive, and spotless. Short walk to beach, famous turn of the century mansions. Quiet, Southern tip of the island.   E-mail: bikinicat@aol.com *Web site:* murrayhouse.com

Admiral Benbow Inn	75-185-B&B	Continental plus breakfast
8 Fair St, 02840	15 rooms, 15 pb	Complimentary wine—
401-848-8000 Fax: 401-848-8006	Visa, MC, AmEx,	special occ.
800-343-2863	*Rated*, •	Breakfast/conf. room, air
Pam Royality	C-ltd/S-no/P-yes/H-no	conditioning, telephone
February-Dec.		service, Fax

Brass beds, antiques and atmosphere, deck and spectacular view of Narragansett Bay. A treasure on our island.   E-mail: 5star@admiralsinn.com *Web site:* admiralsinn.com/page2.html

NEWPORT ─────────────────────────────────

Beech Tree Inn	125-275-B&B	Full breakfast
34 Rhode Island Ave, 02840	8 rooms	Snacks, complimentary wine
401-847-9794 Fax: 401-847-6824	Most CC, *Rated*, •	Sitting room, library,
Katherine D Wudyka	C-ltd/S-ltd/P-no/H-no	Jacuzzis, suites, fireplaces,
All year		cable TV

The Beech Tree Inn is a charming Victorian home built in 1887. It has been newly renovated, enlarged and offers spacious rooms with private baths, television, and air conditioning. Many of the rooms have fireplaces, Jacuzzi bathrooms and sun decks.
Web site: beechtreeinn.com

Black Duck Inn	89-190-B&B	Continental plus breakfast
29 Pelham Street, 02840	8 rooms, 6 pb	Sitting room, cable, Jacuzzis,
401-841-5548 Fax: 401-846-4873	Visa, MC, AmEx, •	fireplaces, A/C
800-206-5212	C-yes/S-no/P-no/H-no	
Mary A. Rolando		
All year		

A charming inn located in the waterfront area. Shops, restaurants, historic mansions and sailing in walking distance. Central air, off street parking. A non-smoking inn.
E-mail: MaryA401@aol.com *Web site:* blackduckinn.com/

Brinley Victorian Inn, The	115-199-B&B	Continental plus breakfast
23 Brinley St, 02840	17 rooms, 12 pb	Wine & lobster dinner
401-849-7645 Fax: 401-845-9634	*Rated*, •	Sitting room, Jacuzzi tubs,
800-999-8523	C-ltd/S-yes/P-no/H-no	landscaped courtyard, A/C,
John & Jennifer Sweetman		gardens
All year		

Romantic Victorian uniquely decorated with antiques, period wallpapers. Brick courtyard planted with flowers. *E-mail:* thesweetmans@brinleyvictorian.com *Web site:* brinleyvictorian.com

Captain Preston House	150-200-B&B	Continental plus breakfast
378 Spring St, 02840	•	Sitting room, air
401-867-7077 Fax: 401-867-1093		conditioning, cable TV,
Paul M. Preston		breakfast patio
Season Inquire		

This delightful B&B is located in a large 1861 Victorian house, authentically restored to its original beauty. Situated in the heart of historic Newport's Yachting Village it's within easy walking distance of the harbor, mansions, cliff walk, and more.
E-mail: Paul@captainpreston.com *Web site:* captainpreston.com

Castle Hill Inn & Resort	155-495-B&B	Full gourmet breakfast
590 Ocean Ave, 02840	35 rooms, 35 pb	Restaurant, bar service
401-849-3800 Fax: 401-849-3838	Most CC, *Rated*	Sitting room, whirlpool
888-466-1355	C-ltd/S-no/P-no/H-no	baths, private beach, trails,
Paul O'Reilly		fireplaces, ocean view
All year		

Experience Victorian splendor-private waterfront retreat on Newport's picturesque Ocean Drive. Tastefully appointed rooms & suites, superb NE regional cuisine.
E-mail: castlehill@edgenet.net *Web site:* castlehillinn.com

Cliff View Guest House	75-85-B&B	Continental plus breakfast
4 Cliff Terrace, 02840	4 rooms, 2 pb	Sitting room, piano, 2 rooms
401-846-0885	Visa, MC,	with A/C
Pauline Shea	C-ltd/S-ltd/P-no/H-no	
May 1-Nov. 1		

Two-story Victorian c.1870. East side has view of Atlantic Ocean. Two porches, open sun deck. Walk to beach or Cliff Walk.

NEWPORT ─────────────────────────────

Cliffside Inn	195-480-B&B	Full gourmet breakfast
2 Seaview Ave, 02840	16 rooms, 16 pb	Victorian tea, complimentary
401-847-1811 Fax: 401-848-5850	Visa, MC, AmEx,	Coffee/tea in rooms,
800-845-1811	*Rated*, •	fireplaces, whirlpool tubs
Stephan Nicolas	C-ltd/S-no/P-no/H-no	
All year		

Gracious Victorian home near beach & Cliff Walk. Each room individually & tastefully decorated with antiques. E-mail: cliff@wsii.com *Web site:* cliffsideinn.com

Hydrangea House Inn	145-280-B&B	Full breakfast buffet
16 Bellevue Ave, 02840	6 rooms, 6 pb	Sitting room, parlor
401-846-4435 Fax: 401-846-6602	Visa, MC, *Rated*, •	w/fireplace, A/C, private
800-945-4667	S-no/P-no/H-no	parking
Dennis Blair, Grant		
Edmondson		
All year		

*Within Newport's "Walking District." A gratifying hot breakfast buffet served in our contemporary art gallery. Fireplace suite with 2 person whirlpool & king bed.
E-mail:* hydrangeahouse@home.com *Web site:* hydrangeahouse.com

Inn at Shadow Lawn, The	85-185-B&B	Full breakfast
120 Miantonomi Ave, 02842	8 rooms, 8 pb	Complimentary wine
401-847-0902 Fax: 401-848-6529	Most CC, *Rated*, •	Sitting room, library, Tiffany
800-352-3750	C-yes/S-no/P-no/H-no	lighting, cable TV, wicker
Selma & Randy Fabricant		
All year		

Step back in time & take a leisurely stroll around the beautiful rolling lawns, at our 1853 Victorian mansion. E-mail: randy@shadowlawn.com *Web site:* shadowlawn.com

Inn on Bellevue	125-150-B&B	Full breakfast
30 Bellevue Ave, 02840	12 rooms, 10 pb	Afternoon tea
401-848-6242 Fax: 401-848-2221	Visa, MC, AmEx, •	
800-718-1446	C-yes/S-no/P-ltd/H-no	
Wayne Lloyd & Gino Difante		
All year		

Located in the heart of Newport, close to all, beaches, mansions, fine dining, and Tennis Hall of Fame. E-mail: wlawsw8432@aol.com *Web site:* innonbellevue.com

InnTowne Inn	100-224-B&B	Continental plus breakfast
6 Mary St, 02840	26 rooms, 26 pb	Afternoon tea
401-846-9200 Fax: 401-846-1534	Visa, MC, AmEx,	Sitting room, library,
800-457-7803	C-ltd/S-yes/P-no/H-no	swimming pool, health, club
Carmella L. Gardner		facilities, sundeck
All year		

Elegant traditional Inn situated in the heart of Newport. Sun deck, four poster beds, use of health club/pool nearby. Close to Mansions, shopping, beaches & fine restaurants. Small conference room.

Jailhouse Inn	55-250-B&B	Continental plus breakfast
13 Marlborough St, 02840	23 rooms, 23 pb	Afternoon tea
401-847-4638 Fax: 401-849-0605	Visa, MC, AmEx,	Cable TV, conference
800-427-9444	C-yes/S-no/P-no/H-yes	facilities, gardens
Susan Mauro		
All year		

A 1770s former colonial jailhouse inn with modern rooms & a jailhouse theme. Walk to harbor, shops & restaurants. All rooms are spacious & have cable TV, small refrig., phones

NEWPORT

Marshall Slocum Guest Hse
29 Kay St, 02840
401-841-5120 Fax: 401-846-3787
800-372-5120
Joan & Julie Wilson
All year

85-165-B&B
5 rooms, 5 pb
Visa, MC, AmEx, •
C-ltd/S-no/P-no/H-no

Full breakfast
Lunch & dinner available
Afternoon tea, comp. wine,
sitting room, library, front
porch w/rockers

Charming Victorian private home with rooms for guests. Serving an extraordinary break-
fast each morning. Located a scant block from town in a residential neighborhood
E-mail: marshallslocuminn@edgenet.net *Web site:* marshallslocuminn.com

---

Mount Vernon Inn
24 Mount Vernon St, 02840
401-846-6314 Fax: 401-846-0530
888-688-3766
Marcia Smith
All year

100-160-B&B
5 rooms, 4 pb
Most CC,
C-yes/S-no/P-no/H-no

Full breakfast
Afternoon tea, snacks, comp.
wine
Sitting room, cable TV, fax
machine, ironing boards,
A/C, guest fridge

Charming 1850 Victorian on quiet, residential street 6 minute walk from harbor shopping
& restaurants. Furnished comfortably in antiques, wicker, etc. Delicious full breakfast
served in formal dining room each day. *E-mail:* marcia@mountvernoninn.com
Web site: mountvernoninn.com

Old Beach Inn
19 Old Beach Rd, 02840
401-849-3479 Fax: 401-847-1236
888-303-5033
Cyndi & Luke Murray
All year

135-250-B&B
7 rooms, 7 pb
Most CC, *Rated*
C-ltd/S-no/P-no/H-no

Continental plus breakfast
Full breakfast Sundays
Gazebo, fish pond, patio,
Sitting room, fireplaces,
garden, some A/C & TVs

Elegant Victorian B&B filled with romance, history and charm. Ideal location, lovely
gardens, comfortable guestrooms. Special occasion champagne
E-mail: info@oldbeachinn.com *Web site:* oldbeachinn.com

Pilgrim House Inn
123 Spring St, 02840
401-846-0040 Fax: 401-848-0357
800-525-8373
Pam Bayur
Closed Jan.

75-200-B&B
10 rooms, 8 pb
Visa, MC, *Rated*, •
C-ltd/S-no/P-no/H-no

Continental plus breakfast
Complimentary sherry,
shortbread
Deck with view of harbor,
living room with fireplace,
close to attractions

Elegant Victorian inn, two blocks from the harbor in Newports historic district.
E-mail: innkeeper@pilgrimhouseinn.com *Web site:* pilgrimhouseinn.com

---

Rhode Island House
77 Rhode Island Ave, 02840
401-848-7787 Fax: 401-849-3104
Michael B. Dupre
All year

175-250-B&B
5 rooms, 5 pb
Visa, MC, AmEx,
Rated, •
C-ltd/S-no/P-no/H-no
French

Full breakfast
Afternoon tea, snacks
Sitting room, library, close to
attractions

A gracious 1881 Victorian with lots of light, awarded "Best Breakfast" by Travel and
Leisure. A genuine feel of Newport. *E-mail:* rih77@aol.com *Web site:* rhodeislandhouse.com

---

Savanas Inn
41 Pelham St, 02840
401-847-3801 Fax: 401-841-0994
888-880-FROG
Andrea & Philip Savana
All year

100-275-B&B
4 rooms, 4 pb
Most CC, •
S-ltd/P-no/H-no

Full breakfast
Cheese/cracker/fruit on
arrival
Sitting room, library, suites,
fireplaces, cable TV, hot tub,
VCRs, A/C

1865 second empire restored to its original splendor, nestled in the heart of Historic Hill.
Pampering best describes your stay, from a gourmet breakfast to complimentary cordials in
the evening. Robes, turn down, Victorian porch. *E-mail:* info@savanasinn.com
Web site: savanasinn.com

NEWPORT

Spring Street Inn
353 Spring St, 02840
401-847-4767
Patricia Golder & Jack Lang
Closed January

89-269-B&B
7 rooms, 5 pb
Visa, MC, *Rated*, •
C-yes/S-no/P-no/H-no

Full gourmet breakfast
Afternoon tea
Sitting room, parking, bus
loop, two blocks from
harbour

Charming restored Empire Victorian house, c.1858. Harbour-view suite with private deck & living room. Short walk to Newport's historic sights, mansions, shops & restaurants.
E-mail: springstinn@aol.com Web site: springstreetinn.com

Stella Maris Inn
91 Washington St, 02840
401-849-2862
Dorothy & Ed Madden
All year

85-225-B&B
8 rooms, 8 pb
Rated, •
C-ltd/S-no/P-no/H-no
Minimal French

Continental plus breakfast
Afternoon tea,
complimentary wine
Sitting room, library, small
meetings possible

1861 Victorian mansion. Newly renovated, water view rooms, fireplaces, spacious porch and gardens, antique decor, homemade muffins, walk to town. Elegant & romantic.
Web site: stellamarisinn.com

Villa Liberte
22 Liberty St, 02840
401-846-7444 Fax: 401-849-6429
800-392-3717
Leigh Anne Mosco
April 1-Nov. 15

99-325-B&B
15 rooms, 15 pb
Visa, MC, AmEx,
C-ltd/S-ltd/P-no/H-no

Continental plus breakfast
Afternoon tea
Sitting room, 4 star
restaurant nearby, small
conference room

Elegance with the intimacy of a guest house. Master suites, queen rooms & apartment suites in a 1910 "House of the Evening." Located off historic Bellevue Ave. in the heart of Newport. E-mail: innkeeper@villaliberte.com Web site: villaliberte.com

---

Wayside Guest House
406 Bellevue Ave, 02840
401-847-0302 Fax: 401-848-9374
800-653-7678
Al, Dorothy & son Don Post
All year

·150-B&B
8 rooms, 8 pb
C-yes/S-yes/P-no/H-no

Continental plus breakfast
BBQ facilities
Sitting room, flower beds,
outdoor swimming pool

Large, attractive, comfortable Georgian-style island home. Ideally located within short walk of mansions, cliff walk, & harborfront activities E-mail: wayside406.aol.com

---

Willows Romantic Inn
8 Willow St, 02840
401-846-5486 Fax: 401-849-8215
Patricia "Pattie" Murphy
All year

128-325-B&B
7 rooms, 7 pb
Rated, •
C-ltd/S-no/P-no/H-no

Continental plus breakfast
Snacks, bar service
Sitting room, award winning
Newports "Secret Garden"

Elegant breakfast in bed—cut flowers, mints on your pillow. Private parking and private bath, air conditioning. Web site: newportri.com/users/willows

PROVIDENCE

C.C. Ledbetter B&B
326 Benefit St, 02903
401-351-4699 Fax: 401-351-4699
CC Ledbetter
All year

85-130-B&B
5 rooms, 2 pb
Most CC,
C-ltd/S-ltd/P-ltd/H-no
French, some Italian

Continental plus breakfast
Afternoon tea, snacks
Sitting room 3 ultra wedding
rooms

On historic Benefit Street, close to Brown University, Rhode Island School of Design, Johnson & Wales, and Providence College.

Cady House, The
127 Power Street, 02906
401-273-5398 Fax: 401-273-5398
Anna and Bill Colaiace
All year

85-B&B
3 rooms, 3 pb
Most CC, •
C-yes/S-no/P-ltd/H-no
Heb., Fr., Ger., Sp.

Continental plus breakfast
Afternoon tea
Library, fireplaces, suites,
cable TV, 3 ultra wedding
rooms

A 1839 Victorian, centered in the historic district, near all major Universities and best restaurants. Rooms are decorated with antiques and misc. artifacts. Secluded garden patio in back. Web site: cadyhouse.com

PROVIDENCE

Edgewood Manor	110-225-B&B	Full breakfast
232 Norwood Ave, 02905	7 rooms, 7 pb	Wine
401-781-0099	Visa, MC, AmEx,	Sitting room, Jacuzzis, suites,
800-882-3285	C-ltd/S-ltd/P-no/H-no	fireplace, cable TV
Andrew Lombardi	French	
All year		

Greek Revival mansion & architectural jewel, adorned with leaded & stained glass, fine art & period antiques. Guestrooms & suites luxuriously decorated in Victorian & Empire style Web site: travelguides.com/home/edgewoodmanor/

Historic Jacob Hill Farm	110-250-B&B	Full gourmet breakfast
PO Box 41326, 02940	6 rooms, 6 pb	Snacks, complimentary
508-336-9165 Fax: 508-336-0951	Most CC, *Rated*, •	wine, tea
888-336-9165	C-ltd/S-ltd/P-no/H-ltd	Sitting room, fireplaces, A/C,
Bill & Eleonora Rezek	Polish	tennis, pool, gazebo,
All year		Jacuzzis, canopy beds

Highest elevation in Seekonk, Massachusetts. 10 min from Brown University. Central to Newport, Boston, Cape Cod. E-mail: jacob-hill-farm@juno.com Web site: Inn-Providence-RI.net

Old Court B&B, The	100-150-B&B	Full breakfast
144 Benefit St, 02903	10 rooms, 10 pb	Complimentary tea, assorted
401-751-2002 Fax: 401-272-4830	Most CC, *Rated*, •	bread
David "Dolby" Dolbashian	C-ltd/S-yes/P-no/H-no	Antiques, common TV room,
All year	French	wet bars in some rooms

Built in 1863, Italianate in design and in ornate details; combines tradition with contemporary standards of luxury. E-mail: reserve@oldcourt.com Web site: oldcourt.com

State House Inn B&B	99-149-B&B	Full breakfast
43 Jewett St, 02908	10 rooms, 10 pb	Snacks
401-351-6111 Fax: 401-351-4261	Visa, MC, AmEx,	Sitting room, Shaker art &
Monica Hopton, Frank Hopton	*Rated*, •	furniture, wet bars in some
All year	C-yes/S-no/P-no/H-no	rooms

Charming country B&B decorated with Shaker and colonial furnishings with all the privacy and amenities frequent travelers desire. King and queen rooms. Web site: providence-inn.com

SOUTH KINGSTOWN

Admiral Dewey Inn	90-140-B&B	Continental breakfast plus
668 Matunuck Beach Rd,	10 rooms, 8 pb	Snacks
02879	Visa, MC, *Rated*, •	Sitting room, bicycles, cable
401-783-2090	C-ltd/S-ltd/P-no/H-no	TV
800-457-2090	Polish	
Joan D. LeBel		
All year		

Web site: admiraldeweyinn.com

Kings' Rose, The	90-150-B&B	Full breakfast
1747 Mooresfield Rd, 02879	5 rooms, 4 pb	Dinner, afternoon tea, snacks
401-783-5222 Fax: 401-783-9984	*Rated*	Complimentary wine, bar
888-230-ROSE	C-ltd/S-no/P-yes/H-no	service, sitting room, library,
B. Larsen-Viles & Perry Viles	French	tennis court, suites
All year		

Country mini-estate, gardens; private entrance to gracious public rooms; bountiful breakfast al fresco or by firelight; nearby pristine beaches, wildlife refuges, bike paths; fine seacoast dining (American and Italian cuisine). E-mail: kingsrose@efortress.com

WAKEFIELD ——————————————————————————————

Larchwood Inn	50-150-EP	Restaurant, cocktail lounge
521 Main St, 02879	19 rooms	Sitting room, conference
401-783-5454	Most CC, *Rated*, •	facilities
Fax: 401-783-1800	C-yes/S-yes/P-yes/H-no	
800-275-5450	Spanish, French	
Francis & Diann Browning		
All year		

Intimate country inn in New England townhouse style circa 1831. Conveniently located near Newport, Mystic Seaport, Block Island and University of Rhode Island.
E-mail: larchwoodinn@xpos.com *Web site:* xpos.com/larchwoodinn.html

WESTERLY ——————————————————————————————

Shelter Harbor Inn	126-166-B&B	Full breakfast
10 Wagner Rd, 02891	24 rooms, 24 pb	Lunch, dinner, bar
401-322-8883	Most CC, *Rated*, •	Library, paddle tennis, hot
Fax: 401-322-7907	C-yes/S-yes/P-no/H-no	tub, croquet court, private
800-468-8883		beach, gardens
Jim Dey		
All year		

A charming coTuntry inn where the emphasis is on relaxation, superlative food, and a warm, friendly atmosphere.

Villa, The	130-245-B&B	Continental plus breakfast
190 Shore Rd, 02891	6 rooms, 6 pb	Hot tubs, swimming pool, 2
401-596-1054 Fax: 401-596-6268	*Rated*, •	frplc./4 Jacuzzi stes., 1.5
800-722-9240	C-ltd/S-no/P-no	acres of lawn/garden
Angela Craig & Peter Gagnon	Italian	
All year		

Escape to our Mediterranean villa. We set the stage for your romantic get-away. You'll fall in love and want to return. Outdoor pool and hot tub. Adjacent to golf course. Private & romantic. E-mail: villa@riconnect.com *Web site:* thevillaatwesterly.com

Woody Hill B&B	75-130-B&B	Full country breakfast
149 S Woody Hill Rd, 02891	4 rooms, 4 pb	Porch with swing, pool,
401-322-0452	•	winter hearth cooking
Ellen L. Madison	C-yes/S-no/P-no/H-ltd	
All year		

Near beaches and Mystic Seaport, secluded country atmosphere. 40' in-ground pool.
E-mail: woodyhill@riconnect.com *Web site:* visitri.com/south/buspages/woodyhill

South Carolina

ABBEVILLE ——————————————————————————————

Latimer Inn	39-129-B&B	Full/continental breakfast
PO Box 295, 29628	17 rooms, 14 pb	Dinner available
864-391-2747 Fax: 864-391-2747	Visa, MC, •	Fishing & water sports,
Harrison & Anne Sawyer	C-yes/S-yes/P-yes/H-no	hiking, horseshoes,
All year		swimming pool

A fisherman's paradise located near historic Abbeville with its rich Civil War heritage. Three luxury rooms with Jacuzzis and fireplaces recently added.

The Sandhurst Estate, Aiken, SC

AIKEN

Historic Holley House Hotel
235 Richland Ave W, 29801
803-648-4265 Fax: 803-649-6910
Richard Friedman
All year

70-90-B&B
48 rooms, 48 pb
Most CC, •
C-yes/S-ltd/P-ltd/H-yes

Continental breakfast
Afternoon tea,
complimentary wine
Restaurant, bar service,
tennis nearby, pool, golf at
private club

B&B Inn also elegant small guesthouse motel. 48 beautiful rooms, center of beautiful, historic city, walking distance of excellent restaurants, shops. E-mail: holleyinfo@holleyhousehotel.com *Web site:* holleyhousehotel.com

Sandhurst Estate, The
215 Dupree Pl, 29801
803-642-9259 Fax: 803-642-8677
Sandra Croy
All year

90-200-B&B
10 rooms, 9 pb
Visa, MC, *Rated*, •
C-ltd/S-ltd/P-no/H-ltd

Full breakfast
Lunch, dinner, snacks, comp.
wine
Bar service, sitting room,
library, bicycles, Jacuzzis,
suites, fireplaces

The newly-restored, 1883 mansion sits on estate in historic district. Large bedrooms are elegantly furnished with fine antiques and private marble baths. Enjoy gardens, carriage horses and miniature horses. Web site: bbonline.com/sc/sandhurst

BEAUFORT

Cuthbert House Inn, The
1203 Bay St, 29902
843-521-1315 Fax: 843-521-1314
800-327-9275
Gary & Sharon Groves
All year

145-225-B&B
7 rooms, 7 pb
Most CC, *Rated*, •
C-ltd/S-no/P-no/H-ltd

Full breakfast
Afternoon tea, snacks, wine
Sitting room, cable TV,
library, turndown service,
public tennis courts

Largest historic mansion on Beaufort's downtown waterfront. Circa 1790. Bay view rooms, verandahs, antiques. Southern breakfast & gracious hospitality. The only Antebellum inn on the waterfront in historic downtown Beaufort. E-mail: cuthbert@hargray.com *Web site:* cuthberthouseinn.com

Old Point Inn
212 New St, 29902
843-524-3177 Fax: 843-525-6544
Joan and Joe Carpentiere
All year

75-125-B&B
4 rooms, 4 pb
Visa, MC, AmEx,
C-ltd/S-ltd/P-no/H-no

Full breakfast
Complimentary wine
Library, piano, tennis,
garden, fax, beach, carriage
rides, golf

1898 Queen Anne, heart of historic district near shops, restaurants, park. Relax on verandahs, nap in our hammock; enjoy low-country hospitality. Web site: oldpointinn.com

BEAUFORT

TwoSuns Inn B&B
1705 Bay St, 29902
843-522-1122 Fax: 843-522-1122
800-532-4244
Carrol and Ron Kay
All year

128-151-B&B
6 rooms, 6 pb
Visa, MC, AmEx,
Rated, •
C-ltd/S-no/P-no/H-yes

Full breakfast
Afternoon tea,
complimentary wine
Sitting room, bicycles, public
tennis courts, computer, Fax,
cable TV

1917 Certified Historic Building with finest bayview. Breakfast fare, modern amenities. Resident owner hospitality in Beaufort. Handwoven creations by Carrol. E-mail: twosuns@islc.net *Web site:* twosunsinn.com

CAMDEN

Candlelight Inn
1904 Broad St, 29020
803-424-1057
Jo Ann & George Celani
All year

80-125-B&B
3 rooms, 3 pb
Most CC, *Rated*, •
C-ltd/S-no/P-no/H-no

Full breakfast
Snacks, complimentary wine
Sitting room, library, suites,
fireplaces, cable TV

Candlelight, comfort, camellias, charm, cookies, conversations & cooking all add up to Candlelight Inn.

CHARLESTON

27 State Street B&B
27 State St, 29401
843-722-4243 Fax: 843-722-6030
Paul & Joye Craven
All year

155-180-B&B
5 rooms, 5 pb
Rated
C-yes/S-no/P-no/H-no

Continental plus breakfast
In room snacks
Sitting room, cable TV,
newspapers, fresh flowers,
bicycles, library

Enjoy Southern hospitality in the midst of "ages past." Walk in any direction for wonderful adventures in shopping, touring, dining, entertainment. Web site: charleston-bb.com

36 Meeting Street B&B
36 Meeting St, 29401
843-722-1034 Fax: 843-723-0068
Vic & Anne Brandt
All year

95-160-B&B
3 rooms, 3 pb
Visa, MC, Disc, *Rated*
C-yes/S-ltd/P-no

Sitting room, suites, fireplace,
cable TV, conferences

E-mail: abrandt@awod.com *Web site:* 36meetingstreet.com

Ann Harper's B&B
56 Smith St, 29401
843-723-3947
Ann D. Harper
All year

85-95-B&B
2 rooms, 1 pb
Rated
C-ltd/S-ltd/P-no/H-no

Full breakfast
Small garden, cable TV, off-
street parking,
golf/swimming nearby

Charming circa 1870 home located in Charleston's historic district. The owner, a retired medical technologist, enjoys serving a full Southern breakfast each morning. Walled garden, newspaper daily. Web site: ego.net/us/sc/chs/annharpers/index.htm

Ashley Inn B&B
201 Ashley Ave, 29403
843-723-1848 Fax: 843-579-9080
800-581-6658
S. & B. Allen, L. Bartosh
All year

79-190-B&B
7 rooms, 7 pb
Visa, MC, *Rated*, •
C-ltd/S-ltd/P-no/H-no

Full breakfast
Afternoon tea, sandwiches &
cookies
Complimentary wine, sitting
room, fireplace, PB, bicycles

Sleep until the fragrance of southern cooking lures you to garden breakfast. Featured in Gail Greco's Nationally Televised "Country Inn Cooking." Complimentary afternoon sherry and tea. E-mail: ashley@cchat.com *Web site:* charleston-sc-inns.com/ashley/index.htm

Battery Carriage House Inn
20 S Battery, 29401
843-727-3100 Fax: 843-727-3130
800-775-5575
Howard M. Vroon
All year

99-250-B&B
11 rooms, 11 pb
Most CC, *Rated*
C-ltd/S-ltd/P-no/H-no

Continental breakfast
Complimentary wine
3 whirlpool baths, 4 steam
showers, bicycles

Very romantic, elegant. Located in garden of historic mansion on the Battery; silver tray breakfast, friendly and professional staff. Web site: charleston_inns.com

BEAUFORT

Belvedere B&B
40 Rutledge Ave, 29401
843-722-0973
David Spell & Rick Zender
All year

150-175-B&B
3 rooms, 3 pb
Rated
C-ltd/S-no/P-no/H-no

Continental plus breakfast
Sherry
Sitting room, newspaper, TV,
A/C, porch with view of lake

We offer hospitable accommodations in our gracious mansion overlooking beautiful Colonial Lake. Sherry and other extras.   Web site: belvedereinn.com

Cannonboro Inn B&B
184 Ashley Ave, 29403
843-723-8572 Fax: 843-723-8007
800-235-8039
S. & B. Allen, L. Bartosh
All year

79-190-B&B
6 rooms, 6 pb
Visa, MC, *Rated*, •
C-ltd/S-no/P-no/H-no

Full breakfast
Afternoon tea, sandwiches,
goodies
Sitting room, library, garden,
tennis courts, comp. touring
bikes

*Antebellum home c.1850 in Charleston's historic district. Breakfast served on a piazza overlooking a country garden. Fireplaces in rooms. 1994 "Fodor's Choice" for SC.
E-mail:* cannon@cchat.com *Web site:* charleston-sc-inns.com/cannonboro/index.htm

Country Victorian B&B
105 Tradd St, 29401
843-577-0682
Diane Deardurff Weed
All year

95-160-B&B
2 rooms, 2 pb
Rated
C-ltd/S-no/P-no/H-no

Continental plus breakfast
Afternoon tea, snacks
Parking, bicycles, TV,
restaurants nearby, piazzas

Private entrances, antique iron and brass beds, old quilts, antique oak and wicker furniture. Situated in the historic district. Walk to everything. Many extras.

Fantasia B&B
11 George St, 29401
843-853-0201 Fax: 843-853-1441
800-852-4466
Catherine & Martin Riccio
All year

115-195-B&B
5 rooms, 5 pb
Visa, MC, AmEx, *Rated*
C-yes/S-no/P-no/H-no

Continental breakfast
Snacks, complimentary wine
Whirlpool bath in master
suite, bicycles, Jacuzzi

*Classic Charleston single house in historic district near all peninsula attractions.
E-mail:* mail@fantasiabb.com *Web site:* fantasiabb.com

Fulton Lane Inn
212½ King St, 29401
843-720-2600 Fax: 843-720-2940
800-720-2688
Beth Babcock
All year

140-285-B&B
27 rooms, 27 pb
Most CC, *Rated*, •
C-yes/S-no/P-no/H-yes

Continental plus breakfast
Bar service, complimentary
wine
Sitting room, suites available,
babysitters, hot tubs, conf.
facility

Victorian inn built in 1870 by Confederate blockade runner John Rugheimer, on quiet pedestrian lane. Furnished with antiques & historically accurate reproductions. $5/day parking. E-mail: fli@charminginns.com *Web site:* charminginns.com/fultonlane.html

Governor's House Inn
117 Broad St, 29401
843-720-2070
800-720-9812
Karen & Rob Shaw
Closed Christmas Day

165-330-B&B
9 rooms, 9 pb
Rated
C-ltd/S-ltd/P-no/H-no

Continental plus breakfast
Afternoon tea
Wet bars, private verandah,
personal concierge

The inspiring 18th century national landmark mansion in Charleston's historic district became an inn in 1998, reflecting the elegance and grandeur of its sister, Two Meeting Street, one of the South's most admired inns.   E-mail: innkeeper@govhouse.com
Web site: governorshouse.com

BEAUFORT

John Rutledge House Inn
212½ King St, 29401
843-723-7999 Fax: 843-720-2615
800-476-9741
Linda Bishop
All year

185-360-B&B
19 rooms, 19 pb
Visa, MC, AmEx,
Rated, •
C-yes/S-ltd/P-no/H-yes

Continental plus breakfast
Complimentary
wine/brandy/sherry
Bar, sitting room, concierge,
turndown service,
babysitters, hot tubs

John Rutledge, a signer of US Constitution, built this elegant home in 1763. Visit and re-live history. Downtown location near shopping & historic sites. Enjoy afternoon tea. AAA 4 diamond.   E-mail: jrh@charminginns.com *Web site:* charminginns.com/johnrutledge.html

King George IV Inn
32 George St, 29401
898-723-1667 Fax: 843-723-7749
888-723-9339
Debbie, Terry & Debra
Flowers   All year

89-165-B&B
10 rooms, 8 pb
Visa, MC, *Rated*, •
C-yes/S-no/P-no/H-ltd

Continental plus breakfast
Complimentary coffees &
teas
Three levels of porches,
parking, refrigerators, sitting
room

This was originally the 1790's home of a Charleston writer. A four story Federal style home furnished in antiques. All rooms have fireplaces, hardwood floors, high ceilings with moldings. Walk to all historic sights, shopping & restaurants.
Web site: bbonline.com/sc/kinggeorge/

Kings Courtyard Inn
198 King St, 29401
843-723-7000 Fax: 843-720-2608
800-845-6119
Michelle Woodhull
All year

110-260-B&B
41 rooms, 41 pb
Most CC, *Rated*, •
C-yes/S-yes/P-no/H-yes

Continental plus breakfast
Complimentary
wine/sherry/brandy
Sitting room, parking, hot
tub, bicycles,
conference/party room

1853 historic inn, rooms with period furnishings, canopied beds, fireplaces, overlook two inner courtyards. Concierge service, evening turndown with brandy and chocolate.
E-mail: kci@charminginns.com *Web site:* charminginns.com/kingscourtyard.html

Palmer Home, The
5 East Battery, 29401
843-853-1574 Fax: 843-723-7983
888-723-1574
Mr. & Mrs. Hogan   All year

95-B&B
3 rooms, 3 pb
•
C-yes/S-no/P-no/H-no

Continental breakfast
Sitting room, piazzas, historic
district, bikes, swimming
pool, parking

Enjoy a room with a view. One of the fifty famous homes in the city; furnished in period antiques; piazzas overlook harbor and Fort Sumter where Civil War began.
E-mail: palmerbnb@aol.com *Web site:* travelguides.com/home/palmerhome/

Planters Inn
112 N Market St, 29401
843-722-2345 Fax: 843-577-2125
800-845-7082
Larry Spelts
All year

150-500-EP
Most CC, *Rated*, •
C-yes/S-yes/P-no/H-yes

Breakfast available (fee)
Complimentary hors
d'oeuvres
Wine by Chef Nuetzi, valet
parking, full turndown
service

Beautifully restored and furnished 1840s building at the center of Charleston's historic district. High ceilinged rooms all individually decorated. AAA 4 diamond rating. Breakfast available in room or in dining room.   E-mail: plantersinn@charleston.net
Web site: plantersinn.com

**Thomas Lamboll House
B&B**
19 King St, 29401
843-723-3212 Fax: 843-723-5222
888-874-0793
Marie & Emerson Read
All year

115-165-B&B
2 rooms, 2 pb
Visa, MC, *Rated*
C-yes/S-no/P-no/H-no

Continental breakfast
Swimming, tennis, golf,
harbor views, parking, near
golf

Built in 1735 in the historic district. Bedrooms have queen size beds, private baths and French doors leading to piazza.   E-mail: lamboll@aol.com
Web site: Lambollhouse.com/home.htm

BEAUFORT ————————————————————————————————————

Victoria House Inn	150-255-B&B	Continental plus breakfast
208 King St, 29401	18 rooms, 18 pb	Bar service
843-720-2944 Fax: 843-720-2930	Visa, MC, Disc, *Rated*,	Conference facilities, some
800-933-5464	•	hot tubs, babysitter available
Beth Babcock	C-yes/S-ltd/P-no/H-ltd	
All year		

Victorian inn built in 1889. Document wallpapers and paint colors. Furnished with antiques and historically accurate reproductions.   E-mail: vhi@charminginns.com
Web site: aesir.com/charminginns/victoriahouse.html

Villa de La Fontaine	125-150-B&B	Full breakfast
138 Wentworth St, 29401	6 rooms, 6 pb	Garden, terraces, tennis,
843-577-7709	Visa, MC, *Rated*	Canopy beds, off-street
A. Hancock, W. Fontaine	C-ltd	parking
All year		

Southern colonial mansion, circa 1838, in historic district; half-acre garden; fountain and terraces.   Web site: charleston.cityinformation.com/villa/

Wentworth Mansion	245-695-B&B	Continental plus buffet
149 Wentworth St, 29401	21 rooms, 21 pb	breakfast
843-853-1886 Fax: 843-720-5290	Most CC, *Rated*, •	Afternoon tea,
888-INN-1886	C-yes/S-ltd/P-no/H-yes	complimentary wine
Reg Smith		Bar service, sitting room,
All year		library, suites, cable,
		fireplaces, conference

World-class hotel furnished with antiques. Built in 1886, has original fireplaces, parquet floors, crystal chandeliers, & plaster ceilings.   Web site: wentworthmansion.com

Woodlands Resort & Inn	295-350-EP	Lunch, Dinner available, p.m.
125 Parsons Rd, 29483	19 rooms, 19 pb	tea
843-875-2600 Fax: 843-875-2603	Most CC, *Rated*, •	Restaurant, bar service,
800-744-9999	C-ltd/S-no/P-ltd/H-yes	sitting room, bikes, tennis
Marty Wall & Cathy Schefstad	German, French,	courts, swimming pool
All year	Spanish	

South Carolina's only AAA, Five Diamond exclusive resort and dining room. Meticulously restored 1906 Classic Revival mansion rests on 42 acres.   E-mail: reservations@
woodlandsinn.com *Web site:* woodlandsinn.com

FLORENCE ————————————————————————————————————

Abingdon Manor	105-140-B&B	Full breakfast
307 Church St, 29565	5 rooms, 5 pb	Snacks, complimentary wine
843-752-5090 Fax: 843-752-6034	Most CC, *Rated*, •	Sitting room, library, bikes,
888-752-5080	C-ltd/S-ltd/P-no/H-no	suites, hot tub, turn down
Michael & Patty Griffey		service, cable TV
All year		

Only luxury inn (AAA-4 diamond) with such close proximity to I-95 in North or South Carolina (5 miles east). Halfway between NYC and Miami. Historic, elegant, comfortable. E-mail: abingdon@southtech.net *Web site:* bbonline.com/sc/abingdon

GEORGETOWN ————————————————————————————————

1790 House-B&B Inn	95-135-B&B	Full breakfast
630 Highmarket St, 29440	6 rooms, 6 pb	Afternoon tea, snacks
843-546-4821	Most CC, *Rated*, •	Sitting room, gardens, bikes,
800-890-7432	C-yes/S-ltd/P-no/H-yes	central air/heat, cottage with
John & Patricia Wiley		Jacuzzi
All year		

200-year-old plantation-style inn with spacious rooms. Walk to shops, restaurants, tours. Near Myrtle Beach & Charleston.   E-mail: jwiley5211@aol.com *Web site:* 1790house.com

GEORGETOWN

DuPre House B&B	75-115-B&B	Full breakfast
PO Box 1487, 29442	5 rooms, 5 pb	Aftn. tea, snacks, comp. wine
843-546-0298 Fax: 843-520-0298	Visa, MC, AmEx,	Sitt. rm., lib., tennis, pool,
800-921-3877	*Rated*, •	frplcs., CATV, accommodate
Marshall G. Wile	C-ltd/S-no/P-no/H-no	business travelers
All year		

No agenda is necessary while experiencing this c. 1740 pre-Revolutionary home in National Register Historic District. Step from the DuPre House are the waterfront boardwalk, shopping, dining and marina. E-mail: dupre@sccoast.net *Web site:* duprehouse.com

King's Inn at Georgetown	89-139-B&B	Full breakfast
230 Broad St, 29440	7 rooms, 7 pb	Afternoon tea, snacks, comp.
843-527-6937 Fax: 843-527-6937	Visa, MC, AmEx,	wine
800-251-8805	*Rated*, •	Sitt. room, library, bicycles,
Marilyn & Jerry Burkhardt	C-yes/S-no/P-no/H-no	hot tubs, swimming pool, in-
All year		room phone/modems

Gracious hospitality, exquisite federal mansion, screened verandah, pool. A 1995 Country Inns "Top Twelve Inn." Between Myrtle Beach and Charleston. In-room phones E-mail: kingsinres@aol.com *Web site:* bbonline.com/sc/kingsinn

Mansfield Plantation B&B	95-115-B&B	Full breakfast
1776 Mansfield Rd, 29440	8 rooms, 8 pb	Dinner by reservation
843-546-6961 Fax: 843-546-5235	•	Sitting room, library, suites,
800-355-3223	C-yes/S-ltd/P-yes/H-no	fireplaces, boat dock, pets
Sally & Jim Cahalan	German	welcome
All year		

Historic Antebellum plantation house & guesthouses nestled amid moss-laden oaks, marshes and 900 private acres. Enjoy antique furnishings, paintings, collectibles; hammocks, swings, birdwatching. E-mail: mansfield_plantation@prodigy.net *Web site:* bbonline.com/sc/mansfield/

Shaw House, The	60-75-B&B	Full breakfast
613 Cyprus Ct, 29440	3 rooms, 3 pb	Complimentary wine, tea,
843-546-9663	*Rated*, •	coffee
Mary & Joe Shaw	C-yes/S-yes/P-no/H-ltd	Sitting room, piano, bicycles,
All year		bird watching

A spacious two-story home in serene natural setting, with beautiful view overlooking miles of marshland formed by four rivers which converge and flow into the Intracoastal Waterway. Perfect for bird watchers; also within walking distance to downtown.

GREENVILLE

Walnut Lane B&B	75-100-B&B	Full breakfast
110 Ridge Rd, 29365	7 rooms, 7 pb	Snacks, complimentary wine
864-949-7230 Fax: 864-949-1633	Most CC, *Rated*, •	Sitting room, library, suites,
Marie & Park Urquhart	C-ltd/S-no/P-no/H-ltd	cable TV, conferences,
All year		weddings

HIGHLANDS

Mountain High	55-210-B&B	Continental plus breakfast
306 Bush Dr, 29579	55 rooms, 55 pb	Snacks
828-526-2790 Fax: 828-526-2750	Visa, MC, AmEx,	Sitting room, Jacuzzis, suites,
800-445-7293	*Rated*, •	fireplaces, cable TV
Jesse Hites	C-yes/S-yes/P-ltd/H-yes	
All year		

Ideal for a honeymoon, romantic getaway or family vacation. You will delight in our king rooms with a gas or wood fireplace; Jacuzzi and standard double rooms, some designated "pet friendly." E-mail: mtnhi@gte.net *Web site:* mountainhighinn.com

LANDRUM

Red Horse Inn, The
310 N Campbell Rd, 29356
864-895-4968 Fax: 864-895-4968
Mary & Roger Wolters
All year

95-145-B&B
5 rooms, 5 pb
Rated, •
C-yes/S-ltd/P-ltd/H-no

Continental breakfast
Each cottage has kitchen
Dining area, living room,
fireplace, bedroom, bath,
sitting area, TV, A/C

Situated on 190 rolling acres in the midst of horse country with extraordinary mountain views. The Red Horse Inn offers charming Victorian cottages, exquisitely decorated
Web site: theredhorseinn.com

MARION

Montgomery's Grove
408 Harlee St, 29571
843-423-5220
877-646-7721
Coreen & Rick Roberts
All year

80-100-B&B
5 rooms, 4 pb
•
C-ltd/S-ltd/P-no

Full breakfast
Afternoon tea, snacks
Lunch, dinner (fee), sitting
room, library, bikes, hot tub

1893 Victorian manor in historic village between I-95 and Myrtle Beach. Dramatic architecture, stunning rms. 5 acres to explore, restful porches. Candlelight din. pkgs
Web site: bbonline.com/sc/montgomery/

MCCLELLANVILLE

Laurel Hill Plantation
PO Box 190, 29458
843-887-3708
888-887-3708
Jackie & Lee Morrison
All year

95-115-B&B
4 rooms, 4 pb
Most CC, *Rated*, •
C-ltd/S-ltd/P-no/H-no

Full breakfast
Afternoon refreshments
Sitting room bikes, hot tub

Located with a fantastic waterfront view of Cape Romain and the Atlantic Ocean, this 1850s plantation home is furnished with country antiques.
Web site: bbonline.com/sc/laurelhill/

MYRTLE BEACH

Brustman House B&B
400 25th Ave S, 29577
843-448-7699 Fax: 843-626-2478
800-448-7699
Dr. Wendell Brustman
All year

65-115-B&B
5 rooms, 5 pb
Visa, MC, AmEx,
Rated, •
C-ltd/S-ltd/P-no/H-no

Full breakfast
Afternoon tea,
complimentary wine
Bikes, phones, TVs, A/C,
whirlpool tubs for two, golf &
tennis nearby

Estate property; 300 yards to beach; rose/herb gardens; honeymoon suites with private whirlpool tubs; family suite with kitchen. Free airport pickup. Family suite for 3-5 persons. E-mail: wcbrustman@worldnet.att.net *Web site:* brustmanhouse.com

Highlands Suite Hotel
306 Bush Drive, 29579
828-526-4502 Fax: 828-526-4840
800-221-5078
Jesse Hites
All year

55-210-B&B
28 rooms, 28 pb
Visa, MC, AmEx, *Rated*
C-yes/S-yes/P-no/H-yes

Continental breakfast
Snacks, complimentary wine
Sitting room, Jacuzzis, suites,
fireplaces, cable TV

Highlands "the South's most exclusive mountain top" features fine dining, golf, shopping & fishing. Our suites are perfect for a romantic getaway or family vacation! E-mail: mtnhi@ gte.net *Web site:* highlandssuitehotel.com

PAWLEYS ISLAND

Litchfield Plantation
PO Box 290, 29585
843-237-9121 Fax: 843-237-1041
800-869-1410
Karl W. Friedrich
All year

186-540-B&B
38 rooms, 38 pb
Most CC, *Rated*, •
C-ltd/S-ltd/P-no/H-ltd
German

Continental breakfast
Dinner (fee), restaurant
Tennis courts, pool, golf,
concierge service,
oceanfront beachhouse

Escape down our avenue of live oaks to the Plantation House c.1750 or other well appointed rooms. Premier amenities, fine dining. Romance packages. Member of Small Luxury Hotels of the World. E-mail: vacation@litchfieldplantation.com *Web site:* litchfieldplantation.com

ROCK HILL

Harmony House B&B
3485 Harmony Rd, 29704
803-329-5886
888-737-0016
Winky & Cecil Stanton
All year

65-75-B&B
3 rooms, 3 pb
Rated
C-yes/S-no/P-no/H-no

Continental plus breakfast
Snacks
Sitting room, library,
TV/VCR, video library,
Amenities galore!

Tucked away on a 36 acre countryside tract. Victorian farmhouse beautifully decorated with antiques & family treasures. Relaxing atmosphere with wraparound porch, swings, gold fish pond, & garden.   Web site: bbonline.com/sc/harmony/

SPARTANBURG

Nicholls-Crook Plantation
120 Plantation Dr, 29388
864-476-8820 Fax: 864-476-8820
Suzanne & Jim Brown
All year

85-95-B&B
3 rooms, 2 pb
AmEx, *Rated*
C-ltd/S-ltd/P-ltd/H-no
Spanish, French

Full breakfast
Complimentary beverages
Sitting room, gardens,
newspaper, fax, A/C

Enjoy the restful, semi-rural setting of our beautifully restored 1793 up-country plantation home. Period antiques provide a warm, inviting atmosphere, enhanced by extensive gardens. Other meals available with prior arrangement.   Web site: bbonline.com/sc/nicholls/

SUMTER

Magnolia House
230 Church St, 29150
803-775-6694
888-666-0296
Carol & Buck Rogers
All year

80-135-B&B
5 rooms, 5 pb
Visa, MC, AmEx,
Rated, •
C-yes/S-ltd/P-ltd/H-no

Full breakfast
Sitting room, suites, cable TV,
accommodate business
travelers.

Brick Revival Mansion featuring English walled garden with fountains, flowering plants and statuary. All rooms decorated in antiques, full southern breakfast. Domestic pets in home.   E-mail: magnoliahouse@sumter.net

UNION

Inn at Merridun, The
100 Merrridun Pl, 29379
864-427-7052 Fax: 864-429-0373
888-892-6020
Jim & Peggy Waller & JD (cat)
All year

89-135-B&B
5 rooms, 5 pb
Rated, •
C-ltd/S-ltd/P-no/H-yes

Full breakfast
Meals by prior arrangement
Evening dessert, sitting
room, library, 1 room with
whirlpool bath

City close, country quiet. 1855 Antebellum mansion with many interesting architectural details. Gourmet food, Southern hospitality at its best!   E-mail: merridun@carol.net
Web site: bbonline.com/sc/merridun/

South Dakota

CANOVA

Skoglund Farm
Route 1 Box 45, 57321
605-247-3445
Alden & Delores Skoglund
All year

30-MAP
6 rooms
•
C-yes/S-ltd/P-yes/H-no
Swedish

Full breakfast
Dinner included
Sitting room, piano, bicycles,
newspaper, fax, A/C

Enjoy overnight on the South Dakota prairie. Return to your childhood—animals, country walking, home-cooked meals

Black Hills Hideaway, Deadwood, SD

CUSTER

Custer Mansion B&B
35 Centennial Dr, 57730
605-673-3333 Fax: 605-673-3033
Bob & Pat Meakim
All year

70-120-B&B
4 rooms, 4 pb
Rated, •
C-yes/S-no/P-no/H-no
Spanish

Full breakfast
Afternoon tea
Sitt. rm., bikes, tennis, hiking
& golf nearby, honeymoon &
family stes.

Historic 1891 Victorian on 1 acre in heart of beautiful Black Hills. Western hospitality & delicious, home-baked food.   E-mail: cusmanbb@gwtc.net
Web site: gwtc.net/~cusmanbb/custer.html

Strutton Inn B&B
RR 1, Box 55 S, 57730
605-673-4808 Fax: 605-673-2395
800-266-2611
Cary & Denice Strutton
All year

70-125-B&B
9 rooms, 9 pb
Visa, MC, *Rated*, •
C-yes/S-no/P-no/H-ltd

Full breakfast
Afternoon tea, snacks
Sitting room, Jacuzzis,
fireplace, satellite dish

Elegant, romantic hideaway country Victorian on four acres with veranda, gazebo, antiques. Nine rooms, each with private baths, whirlpool tubs, king beds.   E-mail: strutton@gwtc.net *Web site:* gwtc.net/users/strutton

CUSTER STATE PARK

Hermosa Hills B&B
HCR 89, Box 62, 57744
605-255-4278
800-247-4404
Lois Odien & Frank Page
May-October

69-89-B&B
4 rooms, 2 pb
Visa, MC, *Rated*
C-yes/S-ltd/P-yes/H-ltd

Full breakfast
Comp. wine
honeymoon/anniversaries
Sitting room, Jacuzzis, cable
TV, exercise room, A/C,
screened deck

Panoramic view of the Black Hills, including Mt. Rushmore. Relaxed country-western setting.   Web site: bbonline.com/sd/bbisd/hermosa.html

DEADWOOD

Black Hills Hideaway B&B
HCR 73- Box 1129, 57732
605-578-3054 Fax: 605-578-2028
Kathy & Ned Bode
All year

99-179-B&B
9 rooms, 9 pb
Visa, MC, *Rated*, •
C-ltd/S-ltd/P-no/H-ltd

Full breakfast
Lun./din.(fee), snacks
Comp. wine, sitt. rooms,
bikes, Jacuzzis, frplcs.,
decks, hot tubs, conf.

Mtn. inn with cathedral ceiling & wood interior, tucked in Nat'l Forest. You'll be pampered on 67 wooded acres with fresh mtn. air, the aroma & whispering of pines, peace, and solitude   E-mail: hideaway@enetis.net *Web site:* enetis.net/~hideaway

HILL CITY

Pine Rest Cabins
PO Box 377, 57745
605-574-2416
800-333-5306
Jan & Steve Johnson
All year

80-125-EP
12 rooms, 12 pb
Visa, MC, Disc,
C-yes/S-ltd/P-ltd/H-ltd

Equipped kitchens
Restaurant nearby, tennis
nearby, bikes, outdoor hot
tub, hiking

New in 1999, knotty pine cabins with fireplaces (12 cabins total all with private bath), cable TV, hot tub.   Web site: travelguides.com/bb/pinerest

LEAD

Deer Mountain B&B
HC 37 - Box 1214, 57754
605-584-2473 Fax: 605-584-3045
Vonnie, Bob & Carrie
Ackerman
All year

65-85-B&B
4 rooms, 2 pb
Visa, MC, *Rated*, •
C-ltd/S-ltd/P-yes/H-no

Full breakfast
Dinner with advanced notice
Snacks, pool table, box lunch
available, sitting room, hot
tubs

Unique log home. Skiing & snowmobiling minutes away. Near historic Deadwood gambling town. Mt. Rushmore, hunting, fishing all close by   E-mail: vonackerman@dtgnet.com Web site: bbonline.com/sd/deermtn/

RAPID CITY

Abend Haus & Audrie's
23029 Thunderhead Falls,
57702
605-342-7788
Hank & Audry Kuhnhauser
All year

95-145-B&B
10 rooms, 10 pb
Rated
S-no/P-no/H-no

Full breakfast
Complimentary snacks
Restaurant nearby, trout
fishing, hiking, bicycles, hot
tubs

The ultimate in charm and old world hospitality. Our spacious suites and cottages are furnished in comfortable European antiques. All feature a private entrance, private bath, patio, hot tub and full Black Hill's style breakfast.   Web site: audriesbb.com

Carriage House
721 West Blvd, 57701
605-343-6415
888-343-6415
Janice & Jay Hrachovec
All year

89-149-B&B
5 rooms, 5 pb
Visa, MC, AmEx, •
C-ltd/S-ltd/P-no/H-no

Full breakfast
Dinner (fee), snacks, tea
Library, sitting room, piano,
suites, video & music
libraries

Step back in time in our 1900 Carriage House. Escape to your suite and a 2 person whirlpool tub. Enjoy refreshments on your private deck. Awake to the tantalizing aroma of a hearty breakfast.   E-mail: info@carriagehouse-bb.com Web site: carriagehouse-bb.com

Coyote Blues Village B&B
PO Box 966, 57745
605-574-4477 Fax: 605-574-2101
888-253-4477
Christina/Hans-Peter Streich
All year

70-125-B&B/MAP
4 rooms, 4 pb
Visa, MC, Disc, *Rated*,
•
C-yes/S-ltd/P-ltd/H-yes
German, French

Full specialty breakfast
Dinner
Sitting room, Jacuzzis, suites,
fireplaces, cable, sun tanning
bed

Experience inter-cultural ambiance. Secluded, centrally located in pine trees near lake. E-mail: coyotebb@dtgnet.com Web site: cayotebluesvillage.com

Flying B Ranch B&B
RR 10, Box 2640, 57701
605-342-5324 Fax: 605-342-5324
Bonnie & Larry Henderson
All year

150-B&B
3 rooms, 3 pb
Visa, MC, *Rated*
C-yes/S-no/P-no/H-no

Full breakfast
Swimming pool, hot tubs,
sitting room, library,
fireplace, hot tub, TV/VCR.

Western hospitality of 3500 acre working cattle ranch. Large designer home in peaceful country setting.   E-mail: flyingb@rapidnet.com Web site: flyingbranch.com

RAPID CITY

Willow Springs Cabins B&B
11515 Sheridan Lake Rd, 57702
605-342-3665
Joyce & Russell Payton
All year

95-120-B&B
2 rooms, 2 pb
Rated, •
C-ltd/S-no/P-no/H-no

Full breakfast
Snacks
Outdoor hot tubs, hiking
trails, swimming, mountain
stream

Privacy at its best! Secluded log cabins in the beautiful Black Hills National Forest. Great views, gourmet breakfasts, private hot tubs. Hiking trails directly off of the front porch. E-mail: wilosprs@rapidnet.com *Web site:* oahelodge.com/wsprings.htm

WEBSTER

Lakeside Farm B&B
RR 2, Box 52, 57274
605-486-4430
Glenn & Joy Hagen
All year

45-B&B
2 rooms
Rated
C-yes/S-no/P-no/H-no

Full breakfast
Other meals possible
Comp. coffee, tea, snack,
sitting room, bicycles,
Museum, factory outlet

Sample country life with us. A family-owned farm. Northeastern SD lakes area. Fresh air, open spaces. Fresh milk, homemade cinnamon rolls E-mail: gjhagen@sullybuttes.net

Tennessee

BRISTOL

New Hope B&B
822 Georgia Ave, 37620
423-989-3343 Fax: 423-989-3422
888-989-3343
Tom & Tonda Fluke
All year

95-155-B&B
4 rooms, 4 pb
Visa, MC, AmEx,
Rated, •
C-ltd/S-ltd/P-no/H-no

Full breakfast
Afternoon tea, snacks
Sitting room, library,
Jacuzzis, fireplaces, cable TV

"Come Home to New Hope", that is how we want you to feel while visiting our 1892 late Victorian. Enjoy the porch, parlor and game room.   E-mail: newhope@preferred.com *Web site:* newhopebandb.com

BUTLER

Iron Mountain Inn
PO Box 30, 37640
423-768-2446
Fax: 423-768-2451
888-781-2399
Vikki Woods
All year

125-250-B&B
4 rooms, 4 pb
Most CC, *Rated*, •
C-ltd/S-no/P-ltd/H-no
Limited French

Full breakfast
Lunch/dinner available (fee)
Snacks, afternoon tea,
library, sitting room,
whirlpool baths

There's magic in the mountains. Casually elegant log home with spectacular surrounding and views. Share a gourmet breakfast with hummingbirds or a nearby mountain. E-mail: ironmtn@preferred.com *Web site:* ironmountaininn.com

CHATTANOOGA

Adams Hilborne Mansion Inn
801 Vine St, 37403
423-265-5000 Fax: 423-265-5555
888-I-INNJOY
Wendy and David Adams
All year

100-295-B&B/MAP
10 rooms, 10 pb
Visa, MC, AmEx,
Rated, •
C-ltd/S-no/P-no/H-yes

Continental breakfast
The Porch Cafe, wine
Hot tubs, library, sitting
room, TV, VCR, 1995
Decorator Showhouse

Adams Hilborne, a magnificent stone mansion built by the mayor of Chattanooga in 1889. On the National Register, it boasts innumerable beautiful features E-mail: innjoy@worldnet.att.net *Web site:* innjoy.com

DICKSON

East Hills B&B Inn
100 E Hills Terrace, 37055
615-441-9428 Fax: 615-446-2181
John & Anita Luther
All year

65-125-B&B
5 rooms, 5 pb
Most CC, *Rated*, •
C-ltd/S-ltd/P-no/H-yes

Full breakfast
Afternoon tea, snacks
Sitting room, library,
bicycles, firepalces, cable
TV, one room with kitchen

The Inn on 4½ acres provides a great getaway; beautifully decorated bedrooms and cottage; large living room and porches which provide areas for guests to relax and enjoy; a big delightful Southern breakfast; the hosts have years of hospitality service
E-mail: jaluther@dickson.net *Web site:* bbonline.com/tn/easthills

DOVER

Riverfront Plantation Inn
PO Box 349, 37058
931-232-9492 Fax: 931-232-9492
Fulton & Lynn Combs
All year

85-115-B&B
5 rooms, 5 pb
Visa, MC, Disc, *Rated*,
•
C-ltd/S-no/P-no/H-no

Full breakfast
Snacks, restaurant
Lunch, dinner available,
sitting room, fireplaces, cable
TV, priv. porches

The Southern hospitality of this splendidly restored Civil War era home is a relaxing experience. The historic waterfront estate borders Ft. Donelson with views of the Cumberland River & countryside. *E-mail:* flcombs@ibm.net *Web site:* bbonline.com/tn/riverfront/

DUCKTOWN

White House B&B, The
PO Box 668, 37326
423-496-4166 Fax: 423-496-9778
800-775-4166
Mardee & Dan Kauffman
All year

65-75-B&B
3 rooms, 1 pb
Visa, MC, *Rated*, •
C-ltd/S-ltd/P-no/H-no

Full breakfast
Afternoon tea, snacks
Evening dessert buffet, wraparound porches, rocking
chairs, TV

Beautiful mountain area, close to whitewater rafting, 4 TVA lakes 1 hour away, trout fishing, golf. Lovely porch with rocking chairs. Full country breakfast. Library den with TV/VCR, fireplace. *E-mail:* mardan@mail.tds.net *Web site:* bbonline.com/tn/whitehouse/

FAYETTEVILLE

Old Cowan Plantation
126 Old Boonshill Rd, 37334
931-433-0225
Paul & Betty Johnson
All year

55-B&B
2 rooms, 2 pb
C-yes/S-no/P-no/H-no

Continental breakfast
Sitting room, fireplaces,
cable TV

1886 Colonial home on 15 acres, peaceful countryside, deer, wild turkey, bird watchers delight. 2 miles from square, convenient to shopping, antiques, gift shops.

FRANKEWING

Hollow Pond Farm B&B
PO Box 775, 38459
931-424-8535 Fax: 931-424-9918
800-463-0154
J. Ann Brown
All year

85-B&B
4 rooms, 4 pb
Visa, MC, *Rated*, •
C-yes/S-no/P-yes/H-no

Full breakfast
Afternoon tea, snacks, comp.
wine
Sitting room, library, pool,
fireplaces, accommodate
business travelers

Best of country! 2 miles off I-65, plush rooms with private connecting baths. Member Tennessee Bed & Breakfast Association. Overnight stabling.
Web site: bbonline.com/tn/hollowpond/

FRANKLIN

Namaste Country Ranch Inn
5436 Leipers Creek Rd, 37064
615-791-0333 Fax: 615-591-0665
Lisa and Bill Winters
All year

80-90-B&B
4 rooms, 4 pb
Most CC, *Rated*, •
S-ltd/P-no/H-no

Full country breakfast
In-room coffee, fridge
Hot tub, phone, pool,
TV/VCR, hiking, horseback
riding trails

Quiet valley setting, poolside deck and hot tub plus hiking. Horseback trails with guided rides on the original Natchez Trace. Inn offers 4 theme suites, each with fireplace. Private baths and entrance. *E-mail:* namastebb@aol.com

GATLINBURG

Buckhorn Inn	115-150-B&B	Full breakfast
2140 Tudor Mtn Rd, 37738	11 rooms, 11 pb	Dinner available
423-436-4668 Fax: 423-436-5009	Visa, MC, *Rated*	Sitting room, fireplace, self-
Lee Mellor	C-ltd/S-ltd/P-no/H-yes	guided nature trail, small
All year		conference center

Sits on 25 acres of meadows, woodlands, & breathtaking views of highest peaks in Smokies. *E-mail:* buckhorninn@msn.com *Web site:* buckhorninn.com

Christopher Place Resort	150-300-B&B	Full breakfast
1500 Pinnacles Way, 37821	8 rooms, 8 pb	Snacks, restaurant
423-623-6555 Fax: 423-613-4771	Most CC, *Rated*, •	Sitting room, library, tennis
800-595-9441	C-ltd/S-ltd/H-yes	court, pool, hot tubs, sauna
Drew Ogle		
All year		

Nestled in the Smoky Mountains, surrounded by expansive views. We're easy to find, but hard to forget. Located near Gatlinburg, Pigeon Forge, AAA 4-diamond. *E-mail:* thebestinn@aol.com *Web site:* christopherplace.com

Colonel's Lady Inn, The	86-169-B&B	Full gourmet breakfast
1120 Tanrac Trail, 37738	8 rooms, 8 pb	Snacks
423-436-5432 Fax: 423-430-2434	Most CC, *Rated*, •	Sitting room, view of the
800-515-5432	C-ltd/S-no/P-no/H-no	Great Smokies, hot tubs,
Mary Quadrozzi-Wells		private Jacuzis, gardens
All year		

Award winning nationally acclaimed Inn of the Great Smoky Mountains. Gourmet food. Ultimate privacy. Ideal for intimate celebrations   *E-mail:* colonel@colonelsladyinn.com *Web site:* colonelsladyinn.com

Eight Gables Inn	79-179-B&B	Full breakfast
219 N Mtn Trail, 37738	12 rooms, 12 pb	Sitting room, TV lounge, 2
423-430-3344 Fax: 423-430-3344	Visa, MC, AmEx,	rooms with whirlpools, hot
800-279-5716	*Rated*, •	tubs
Don & Kim Cason	C-ltd/S-ltd/P-no/H-no	
All year		

Eight Gables Inn is a luxurious four diamond rated bed and breakfast nested at the foot of the Great Smoky Mountains. Conveniently located to all area attractions. *E-mail:* 8gables@eightgables.com *Web site:* eightgables.com

Moon Mountain Lodge	89-109-B&B	Continental plus breakfast
PO Box 606, 37738	7 rooms, 7 pb	Aftn. tea, snacks
423-436-0009 Fax: 423-436-4446	Visa, MC, •	Sitt. rm., Jacuzzis, stes.,
800-280-0622	S-ltd/P-no/H-no	frplc., cable TV,
Brian Sullivan		accommodate business
All year		travelers

The Lodge sits atop the most spectacular mountains in the Smokies & looks over the romantic night lights of Gatlinburg.   *E-mail:* drkern@vic.com *Web site:* moonmountainlodge.com

Tennessee Ridge Inn B&B	85-149-B&B	Full gourmet breakfast
507 Campbell Lead, 37738	7 rooms, 7 pb	Afternoon tea, snacks
423-436-4068	Most CC, *Rated*, •	Sitting room, library,
800-737-7369	S-ltd/P-no/H-yes	fireplaces, balconies,
Dar Hullander		Jacuzzi, honeymoon stes.
All year		

View the Smokies by day & the city lights of Gatlinburg by night. Jacuzzis, fireplaces, private balconies, king beds, swimming pool.   *E-mail:* innkeeper@tn-ridge.com *Web site:* tn-ridge.com

GREAT SMOKY MOUNTAINS

Bonny Brook B&B	120-B&B	Full breakfast
2301 Wears Valley Rd, 37862	2 rooms, 2 pb	Afternoon tea
423-908-4745 Fax: 423-908-4745	Visa, MC,	Sitting room, suites, cable TV,
Coleen Thomason	C-ltd/S-no/P-no/H-no	stone fireplace, Celtic music,
All year		tartan robes

Log structure with a Scottish decorative influence. Deck near large stream, large shady porches, surrounded by woods. Scots-Irish items for sale. We'll recommend our favorite restaurants and other places to visit. E-mail: bonnybrookbb@msn.com
Web site: bonnybrook.net

GREENEVILLE

Big Spring Inn	86-B&B	Full breakfast
315 N Main St, 37745	6 rooms, 6 pb	Dinner (in advance),
423-638-2917	Visa, MC, AmEx,	afternoon tea
Marshall & Nancy Ricker	*Rated*, •	Snacks, 2 rooms with
All year	C-ltd/S-no/P-no/H-no	fireplaces, sitting room, pool

Beautiful Greek Revival home in historic district: large porches, swimming pool, close to Cherokee National Forest & Jonesboro. Gardens expanded, Carriage House. Expanded garden includes shade garden, perenial borders, and English roses.

Hilltop House B&B Inn	75-80-B&B/MAP	Full breakfast
6 Sanford Circle, 37743	3 rooms, 3 pb	Dinner available, afternoon
423-639-8202	Most CC, *Rated*, •	tea
Denise M. Ashworth	C-ltd/S-no/P-no/H-no	Sitting room, library, hiking
All year		trails, rafting, trout fishing,
		gardens

Comfortable country home with panoramic mountain views and English antiques. Visit historic towns, hike mountain trails with local hiking club. Gourmet meals.

Nolichuckey Bluffs	75-95-B&B	Full breakfast
400 Kinser Park Ln, 37743	7 rooms, 7 pb	Afternoon tea, snacks
423-787-7947 Fax: 423-787-9247	Visa, MC, Disc, *Rated*,	Sitting room, library,
800-842-4690	•	bicycles, Jacuzzis, fireplaces
Patricia Sadler	C-yes/S-no/P-ltd/H-ltd	
All year		

Quiet luxury in country setting. Gazebos, trails, rose gardens and spectacular views. Full breakfast, teas, exercise room, laundry and much more. E-mail: cabins@usit.net

JEFFERSON CITY

HearthStone B&B	89-B&B	Full breakfast
2308 Northridge Dr, 37760	3 rooms, 3 pb	Sitting room, bikes, fireplace,
423-475-6992 Fax: 423-475-5209	Visa, MC,	located on Lake Cherokee
Allan & Ginny Schwegler	S-no/P-no/H-no	
All year	Spanish	

HearthStone, a place to stay for vacation, fun and relaxation. A remodeled log cabin located on Cherokee Lake where you can swim, boat, bike, hike or just enjoy nature E-mail: ashrkid@aol.com *Web site:* bbonline.com/tn/hearthstone/

JOHNSON CITY

Hart House B&B	70-B&B	Full breakfast
207 East Holston Ave, 37604	3 rooms, 3 pb	Afternoon tea, snacks
423-926-3147	Visa, MC, *Rated*	Sitting room, library,
Vanessa Johnson	C-yes/S-no/P-no/H-no	basketball ct, weight room,
All year		tapes/toys for children

1910 Dutch Colonial home lovingly restored to its original grandeur. Relax on the front porch or spend an evening by the fireplace. Each room has individual thermostat. E-mail: harthouseinn@worldnet.att.net

KNOXVILLE ─────────────────────────────────

Maplehurst Inn	85-195-B&B	Full breakfast
800 West Hill Ave, 37705	11 rooms, 11 pb	Snacks
423-523-7773 Fax: 423-523-7773	Visa, MC, AmEx, •	Sitting room, library, suites,
800-451-1562	C-yes/S-ltd/P-ltd/H-no	conference, facilities,
Sonny & Becky Harben		Penthouse
All year		

European style B&B in downtown Knoxville. Walk to U.T., Neyland Stadium and World's Fair Park. 11 Rooms with private baths, several Jacuzzi tubs, penthouse suite.
E-mail: mhurstinn@aol.com *Web site:* maplehurstinn.com

Masters Manor Inn	100-200-B&B	Full breakfast
1909 Cedar Lane, 37918	6 rooms, 6 pb	Snacks, evening dessert
423-219-9888 Fax: 423-219-9811	Visa, MC, AmEx,	Sitting room, library,
877-866-2667	*Rated*, •	fireplace, cable TV
Dana Hallet	C-yes/S-ltd/P-ltd/H-yes	
All year	Spanish	

Historic Victorian mansion built in 1897. Period antiques, wrap-around porch, 50 foot Southern magnolia tree. Private phones, cable TV, modem ports, and luxury amenities. The Inn place for great retreats. Let us customize yours. *E-mail:* rbhallet@nxs.net
Web site: mastersmanor.com

LYNCHBURG ─────────────────────────────────

Goose Branch Farm B&B	65-B&B	Continental plus breakfast
901 Goose Branch Rd, 37352	2 rooms, 2 pb	Dinner available
931-759-5919	Visa, MC,	
Sharon & Les Blinco	C-ltd/S-no/P-no/H-no	
All year		

Although this c. 1899 farmhouse is 3 miles from the Lynchburg Square and Jack Daniel's Distillery, it seems like a different world. Surrounded by hills and trees...the only sounds being those of nature. Private baths and entrances. *E-mail:* gbfarmbb@aol.com
Web site: bbonline.com/tn/gbfarmbb

Lynchburg B&B	68-78-B&B	Continental breakfast
PO Box 34, 37352	3 rooms, 3 pb	Afternoon tea
931-759-7158	Visa, MC, *Rated*	Tennis court, pool
Virginia & Mike Tipps	C-yes/S-no/P-no/H-yes	
All year		

Stay in one of the oldest homes in historic Lynchburg, home of Jack Daniel Distillery. Antique furnished. Private baths. *E-mail:* lynchburgbb@cafes.net
Web site: bbonline.com/tn/lynchburg/

McMINNVILLE ─────────────────────────────────

Historic Falcon Manor	95-120-B&B	Full breakfast
2645 Faulkner Springs, 37110	7 rooms, 7 pb	Dinner by res. on wkends
931-668-4444 Fax: 931-815-4444	*Rated*, •	Victorian gift shop, sitting
George & Charlien McGlothin	C-ltd/P-no/H-yes	room, library, rocking-chair,
All year		verandas

1896 Victorian mansion—one of the South's finest. 1st prize B&B Nat'l Trust restoration award. *E-mail:* falconmanor@falconmanor.com *Web site:* falconmanor.com

MEMPHIS ─────────────────────────────────

Bonne-Terre Country Inn	150-475-B&B	Full breakfast
4715 Church Rd W, 38651	15 rooms, 15 pb	Restaurant, dinner
662-781-5100 Fax: 662-781-5466	Visa, MC, AmEx,	Sitting room, library, Jacuzzi,
Max Bonnin	C-ltd/S-no/P-no/H-yes	swimming pool, fireplace
All year		

Bonne Terre is tucked way on 100 acres in the Mississippi Highlands.
E-mail: mbonnin@lunaweb.net *Web site:* bonneterre.com

Clardy's Guest House, Murfreesboro, TN

MEMPHIS

King's Cottage, The
89 Clark Place, 38104
901-722-8686 Fax: 901-725-0018
James Beene
All year

69-99-B&B
2 rooms, 1 pb
Most CC,
C-yes/S-ltd/P-no/H-ltd

Continental plus breakfast
Lunch/dinner available
Sitting room with piano,
satellite TV, modern
amenities, full kitchen

Newly renovated two bedroom cottage serenely decorated and extravagantly furnished. Secure, peaceful, and private hideaway in midtown's beautiful historic Evergreen District. Christian establishment is a great family retreat. E-mail: KingsCtg@aol.com

MONTEAGLE

Adams Edgeworth Inn
Monteagle Assembly, 37356
931-924-4000 Fax: 931-924-3236
1-87RELAXINN
Wendy & David Adams
All year

100-200-B&B
12 rooms, 12 pb
Visa, MC, AmEx,
Rated, •
C-ltd/S-ltd/P-no/H-ltd
French

Full gourmet breakfast
Candle-lit dinner available
Gift shop, library, Verandas,
swim, hike, completely
redecorated

Victorian village on mountain top. Canopy beds, fireplaces, antiques, prize-winning gardens, A/C, 1200-acre wilderness with trails, Sewanee U. 6 miles. Gourmet dinners available

MURFREESBORO

Clardy's Guest House
435 E Main St, 37130
615-893-6030
Barbara Deaton   All year

45-58-B&B
3 rooms, 2 pb
Rated, •
C-yes/S-yes/P-no/H-no

Continental plus breakfast
Complimentary beverages
Sitting room with cable TV,
porch, cable TV, gardens, spa

Built in 1898 during opulent & decorative times, with extraordinary historic architecture, antiques, and area. Murfreesboro is the South's antique center.
E-mail: rdeaton@bellsouth.net Web site: bbonline.com/tn/clardys/

Simply Southern B&B
211 N Tennessee Blvd, 37130
615-896-4988 Fax: 615-867-2899
888-723-1199
Carl & Georgia Buckner
All year

85-145-B&B
5 rooms, 5 pb
Visa, MC, Disc, *Rated*,
•
S-no/P-no/H-no

Full breakfast
Snacks
Sitting room, library, suites,
fireplaces, cable TV

Four story, fine old 1907 home with wraparound veranda, antiques, eclectically elegant, professionally decorated, private baths, gourmet breakfast, romantic, rec. room, in historic district, near Nashville, Music City, USA. E-mail: InnSouth@aol.com
Web site: citysearch.com/nas/simplysouthern

NASHVILLE

Flemingsburg House B&B
3052 Old Murfreesboro, 37046
615-395-0017 Fax: 615-395-4243
Karin & Ray Bogardus
All year

75-120-B&B
3 rooms, 3 pb
Visa, MC, *Rated*, •
C-yes/S-no/P-yes/H-no
German

Full breakfast
Snacks
Fireplaces, cable TV,
romantic dinners available
with 3 days notice

Elegant colonial, c.1830. Beautifully restored. Each guest room has private bath. Antiques, handcrafted fieplace mantels. Great room with 12 foot ceilings and chestnut floors. Bricked floored breakfast room. Central to Nashville, Franklin and Shelbyville
E-mail: rbogi@aol.com

OAK RIDGE, KNOXVILLE

Bushrod Hall B&B
422 Cumberland St NE, 37748
423-882-8406 Fax: 423-882-6056
888-880-8406
All year

75-110-B&B
3 rooms, 3 pb
Visa, MC, AmEx,
Rated, •
C-ltd/S-no/P-no/H-ltd
Spanish

Full breakfast
Snacks
Sitting room, library,
fireplaces, cable TV,
conference, kitchen

Historic home, furnished in period antiques, with exquisite woodwork. Represents long forgotten days of a bygone era and small town life. Victorian gardens.
E-mail: bushrodbb@aol.com *Web site:* bbonline.com/tn/bushrod

PIKEVILLE

Fall Creek Falls B&B Inn
Rt 3, Box 298B, 37367
423-881-5494 Fax: 423-881-5040
Rita & Doug Pruett
Closed 12/22-2/1

79-140-B&B
8 rooms, 8 pb
Visa, MC, *Rated*, •
C-ltd/S-no/P-no/H-no

Full breakfast
Sitt. rm., AC, phones, room
with whirlpool, custom gift
baskets

Romantic mountain getaway, one mile from nationally acclaimed Fall Creek Falls State Resort Park, featuring golfing, fishing, hiking, swimming, boating, suite with fireplace.
Web site: fallcreekfalls.com

SAVANNAH

White Elephant B&B Inn
304 Church St, 38372
901-925-6410
Sharon & Ken Hansgen
All year

90-110-B&B
3 rooms, 3 pb
Rated, •
C-ltd/S-no/P-no/H-no

Full breakfast
Afternoon tea/coffee
Sitting room, library, Guided
tours of Shiloh, National
Military Park

Stately 1901 Queen Anne Victorian in Savannah Historic District; breakfast served in elegant dining room; antique furnishings; well-stocked Civil War Library; guided Shiloh tours   Web site: bbonline.com/tn/elephant/

SEVIERVILLE

Calico Inn
757 Ranch Way, 37862
423-428-3833
800-235-1054
Lill & Jim Katzbeck
All year

89-99-B&B
3 rooms, 3 pb
Visa, MC, *Rated*, •
C-yes/S-ltd/P-no/H-no

Full delicious breakfast
Afternoon tea, snacks
Nature lovers delight, near
malls/outdoor sport,
shopping/entertainment

Log inn with magnificent mtn. views, antiques and country decor. Minutes from Dollywood, Smoky Mountain National Park. Near all live entertainment shows. $10 service charge on returned deposits 10 days prior to arrival. OUR 1998 INN OF THE YEAR!
Web site: bbonline.com/tn/calico/

Huckleberry Inn B&B
1754 Sandstone Way, 37876
423-428-2475
800-704-3278
Karan Bailey
All year

89-129-B&B
3 rooms, 3 pb
Visa, MC, AmEx, •
C-ltd/S-no/P-no/H-ltd

Full country breakfast
Snacks
4 Whirlpool Tubs, fireplaces,
3 porches,
shopping/entertainment

Enjoy the romantic country charm of this authentic log home. Priv. bath, fireplaces, beautiful views, mountain spring. It's all here for you.   E-mail: hberry@esper.com
Web site: bbonline.com/tn/huckleberry

SEVIERVILLE

Little Greenbrier Lodge	95-110-B&B	Full breakfast
3685 Lyon Springs Rd, 37862	10 rooms, 8 pb	Lunch & dinner available
423-429-2500 Fax: 423-429-4093	Visa, MC, Disc, *Rated*,	(fee)
800-277-8100	•	Snacks, sitting room,
Charles & Susan LeBon	C-ltd/S-no/P-no/H-no	shopping/entertainment
All year		

We are the oldest Lodge bordering on the Great Smokey Mountain National Park. Genuine antiques furnish the old place. Magnificent views of the mountains & valley. Hot pecan pullapart is to die for. E-mail: littlegreenbrier@worldnet.att.net *Web site:* bbonline.com/tn/lgl

River Piece Inn, The	81-125-B&B	Full country breakfast
PO Box 6872, 37864	5 rooms, 5 pb	Snacks, evening dessert
423-428-6547 Fax: 423-453-7099	Most CC, *Rated*	Jacuzzis, fireplaces,
888-265-3097	C-ltd/S-no/P-no/H-yes	shopping/entertainment
Bob & Janene Allen		
All year		

Farmhouse inn offering 5 guest rooms, private baths with whirlpools, queen beds, antiques, 7 fireplaces, gazebo, river benches, river tubing, & fishing. E-mail: rpiallen@gateway.net
Web site: riverpieceinn.com

Texas

ABILENE

BJ's Prairie House B&B	65-90-B&B	Continental breakfast
508 Mulberry St, 79601	4 rooms, 2 pb	Snacks, wine, bar
915-675-5855	Visa, MC, AmEx, Disc,	Sitting room, cable TV
Fax: 915-677-4694	*Rated*	complimentary movies,
800-673-5855	C-ltd/S-no/P-no/H-no	conferences
B.J. & Bob Fender		
All year		

Built in 1902, nestled in the heart of old Abilene, remodeled in 1920 to favor a Frank Lloyd Wright "prairie style" design. Renovated again in 1990 provides a warm homelike atmosphere. E-mail: bfender@earthlink.net *Web site:* bjsbedandbreakfast.bizonthe.net

ALPINE

Holland Hotel	40-65-B&B	Continental breakfast
PO Box 444, 79831	14 rooms, 14 pb	Sitting room,
915-837-3844 Fax: 915-837-2490	Visa, MC, AmEx,	catering/banquet rooms,
800-535-8040	C-yes/S-yes/P-yes/H-yes	complimentary movies
Carla McFarland	Spanish	
All year		

Enjoy the breathtaking Big Bend at Alpine's only downtown B&B (across from Amtrak). Concierge style service/catering for your special occasion.

AMARILLO

Parkview House B&B	65-135-B&B	Continental plus breakfast
1311 S Jefferson St, 79101	6 rooms, 4 pb	Afternoon tea, snacks, wine
806-373-9464 Fax: 806-373-3166	Visa, MC, AmEx,	Bicycles, tennis, Jacuzzis,
Carol & Nabil Dia	*Rated*, •	fireplaces, cable TV, suites,
All year	C-ltd/S-no/P-no/H-ltd	garden cottage
	Arabic	

Amarillo's first historic Parkview House offers friendly Texas hospitality in a Victorian setting, with attractions nearby. E-mail: parkviewbb@aol.com
Web site: members.aol.com/parkviewbb

ARLINGTON

Sanford House
506 N Center St, 76011
817-861-2129 Fax: 817-861-2030
877-205-4914
L. Bergstrom & P. Chaffin
All year

125-200-B&B
12 rooms, 12 pb
Visa, MC, AmEx,
C-ltd/S-no/P-no/H-yes

Full breakfast
Afternoon tea, snacks, comp.
wine
Sitting room, library,
Jacuzzis, swimming pool,
suites, fireplaces, cable TV

Tranquil french country-style home with antiques throughout; beautiful gardens; romantic cottages, each with living room, fireplace, dining room, king bed, over-sized bath with Jacuzzi tub for two. E-mail: info@thesanfordhouse.com *Web site:* thesanfordhouse.com

AUSTIN

Austin's Governors' Inn
611 W 22nd St, 78705
512-477-0711 Fax: 512-476-4769
800-871-8908
Lisa Monroe
All year

59-119-B&B
10 rooms, 10 pb
Most CC, *Rated*
C-yes/S-ltd/P-ltd/H-ltd
Spanish, French

Full breakfast
Afternoon tea, snacks
Vegetarian dining available,
sitting room, library

Grand neo-classical Victorian mansion built in 1897. Historical designation, lovely rooms with private baths, cable TV, phones, and beautiful antiques. E-mail: governorsinn@earthlink.net *Web site:* governorsinnaustin.com

Austin's Wildflower Inn
1200 W 22½ St, 78705
512-477-9639 Fax: 512-474-4188
Kay Jackson
All year

79-94-B&B
4 rooms, 2 pb
Visa, MC, AmEx, *Rated*
C-ltd/S-no/P-no/H-no

Full breakfast
Afternoon tea, snacks
Sitt. rm., deck, gardens,
nearby public tennis, hiking
& biking trails

Lovely old home with spacious porch that graces the front of the house; furnished with antiques; located on tree-shaded street; near University of Texas and State Capitol. Front verandah with ceiling fans. E-mail: kjackson@io.com *Web site:* austinswildflowerinn.com

Austin-Lake Travis B&B
4446 Eck Lane, 78734
512-266-3386
888-764-LTBB
Judy and Vic Dwyer
All year

150-225-B&B
4 rooms, 4 pb
Most CC, *Rated*, •
S-no/P-no/H-no

Full breakfast
Snacks, complimentary wine
Sitting room, library, Jacuzzi,
pool, cable TV, fireplaces,
suites

Romantic secluded getaway for adults at this waterfront retreat. Spectacular views, breakfast in bed or on your private deck. Intimate resort-pool, hot-tub, fitness deck/massage, dock, sail charters. E-mail: jdwyer1511@aol.com *Web site:* laketravisbb.com/

Carrington's Bluff
1900 David St, 78705
512-479-0638 Fax: 512-476-4769
800-871-8908
Ed & Lisa Mugford
All year

79-119-B&B
17 rooms, 15 pb
AmEx, *Rated*
C-ltd/S-no/P-no/H-no
French

Full breakfast
Complimentary coffee, soda
Afternoon tea, sitting room,
babysitting available (fee)

An English country inn located on a tree-covered acre in the heart of the city. Antique-filled rooms and fabulous breakfasts. E-mail: governorsinn@earthlink.net *Web site:* governorsinnaustin.com

Fairview, A B&B
1304 Newning Ave, 78704
512-444-4746 Fax: 512-444-3494
800-310-4746
Duke & Nancy Waggoner
All year

109-169-B&B
6 rooms, 6 pb
Most CC, *Rated*, •
C-ltd/S-ltd/P-no/H-no

Full breakfast
Complimentary
refreshments
Sitting room, library, tennis
close by, cable TV, phones in
rooms.

1910 Austin landmark. 1 acre of landscaped grounds in downtown area. Quiet, relaxing, spacious. Antique furnishings E-mail: fairview@io.com *Web site:* fairview-bnb.com

AUSTIN

Southard-House Inn
908 Blanco, 78703
512-474-4731 Fax: 512-478-5393
Jerry & Rejina Southard
All year

69-169-B&B
15 rooms, 15 pb
Most CC, *Rated*, •
C-ltd/S-yes/P-no/H-yes

Continental plus-weekdays
Full breakfast weekends
Porches, pool, clawfoot tubs,
bungalow with kitchen suite

Three beautifully restored homes located minutes from downtown. Fireplaces, private entrances, cable TV, and clawfoot tubs are a few of the amenities gracing our single rooms and suites. E-mail: sohouse@aol.com

Woodburn House B&B
4401 Ave D, 78751
512-458-4335 Fax: 512-458-4319
888-690-9763
Herb & Sandra Dickson
All year

90-135-B&B
5 rooms, 5 pb
Visa, MC, AmEx, •
C-ltd/S-no/P-no/H-no
Spanish

Full breakfast-flexible hours
Sitting room, porches on 2
levels, game table, gardens,
restaurant, fax.

1909 Austin landmark in a tranquil neighborhood close to everything. Antiques, gourmet breakfasts and peaceful neighborhood make for a pleasant stay. Ironing board & iron, use of laundry available. E-mail: woodburn@iamerica.net *Web site:* woodburnhouse.com

BRAZORIA

Roses & the River B&B
7074 CR 506, 77422
409-798-1070 Fax: 409-798-1070
800-610-1070
Dick & Mary Jo Hosack
All year

125-B&B
3 rooms, 3 pb
Most CC, *Rated*, •
C-ltd/S-ltd/P-no/H-no

Full breakfast
Snacks
Jacuzzis, fireplaces, cable
TV, VCRs in each room with
video library

Beautifully decorated Texas farmhouse on banks of San Bernard River landscaped with 250 rose bushes. "You deserve a little R&R" is our motto. Great breakfasts! E-mail: hosack@tgn.net *Web site:* travelpick.com/tx/roses

CENTER

Pine Colony Inn
500 Shelbyville St, 75935
409-598-7700
R. Wright, M. Hughes
All year

65-75-B&B
12 rooms, 6 pb
Visa, MC, •

Full breakfast
Lunch & dinner
Restaurant, sitting room,
fishing & hunting trips

Restored Old Country Hotel. Antiques throughout. Walk to many interesting shops and museums. Planned fishing, hunting and family excursions. E-mail: pinecolonyinn@hotmail.com *Web site:* members.tripod.com/PineColonyInn

COMFORT

Idlewilde B&B
115 Highway 473, 78013
830-995-3844
Connie Hank & Nicholas Engel
All year

77-110-B&B
2 rooms, 2 pb
C-yes/S-ltd/P-ltd/H-ltd

Full breakfast
Lunch/dinner available,
snacks
Complimentary wine, sitting
room, library, tennis court,
pool, pavilion

Customized service is our motto and our specialty is a large, full country breakfast complete with table linens, candlelight, fine china, and classical music. The main lodge was built in 1902, has a Texas Historical commission medallion.

CORPUS CHRISTI

Bay Breeze B&B
PO Box 6729, 78466
361-882-4123 Fax: 361-814-1938
887-882-4123
Frank & Perry Tompkins
All year

65-95-B&B
4 rooms, 4 pb
Visa, MC, *Rated*, •
C-ltd/S-no/P-no/H-no

Full breakfast
Complimentary wine
Sitting room, library,
1/2 block from Bay, park,
fishing pier

Located within view of the bay. Fine older home that radiates charm of yesteryear. E-mail: baybreeze@baybreeze.com *Web site:* baybreezebb.com

CORPUS CHRISTI —————————————————————————————

Fortuna Bay B&B	96-B&B	Continental plus breakfast
15405 Fortuna Bay Dr #12,	3 rooms, 3 pb	Snacks, restaurant
78418	•	Fishing off deck, pool,
361-949-7554	C-ltd/S-ltd/P-no/H-yes	conference center, golf,
John & Jackie Fisher All year	Limited Spanish	tennis, boat dock

Hideaway on Texas North Padre Island with white sand beaches. Country Club privileges, fishing off our deck. Condo living Caribbean style. White sand beaches 8 blocks, boat ride.   E-mail: 102113.555@compuserve.com   *Web site:* ccinternet.net/Fortuna-Bay/

Ginger Rose B&B, The	60-75-B&B	Full breakfast
7030 Dunsford Dr, 78413	2 rooms, 2 pb	Afternoon tea, snacks
361-992-0115 877-894-8109	•	Private swimming pool
Peg & Pete Braswell	C-ltd/S-no/P-no/H-no	
All year	French	

Easy access to the bayfront and beach; private swimming pool surrounded by palm trees & hibiscus; full gourmet breakfast; special restaurant, merchant and tourist discounts for our guests.   E-mail: ginrose@flash.net   *Web site:* gingerrose.com

CRYSTAL BEACH —————————————————————————————

Out By The Sea B&B	80-150-B&B	Full breakfast
PO Box 2046, 77650	2 rooms, 2 pb	Dinner available, snacks,
409-684-1555	Visa, MC, •	wine
888-522-5926	C-ltd/S-no/P-no/H-no	Cable TV, conference
Jim Winslett & Jerry Reitz	Limited German	facilities
All year		

Located one block from the beach on the Gulf of Mexico on the Boliver Penninsula (15 miles from Galveston Island). Newly constructed beach home with contemporary & antique furnishings. We serve full hot breakfasts & upscale seafood dinners by arrangment. E-mail: jerryj@outbythesea.com   *Web site:* outbythesea.com

DALLAS —————————————————————————————————

Oaklea Mansion	89-250-B&B	Full breakfast
407 S Main, 75494	12 rooms, 12 pb	Afternoon tea
903-342-5424 Fax: 903-342-5013	Most CC, *Rated*, •	Sitting room, suites,
Norma Wilkinson	C-ltd/S-no/P-no/H-yes	fireplaces, spa house with
All year	Spanish	hot tub/Jacuzzi

Accommodations in this 1903 historically marked mansion include luxurious suites and guest rooms filled with antique treasures. Four beautifully manicured acres of romantic grounds provide a peaceful setting.   E-mail: oaklea@bluebonnet.net
Web site: bluebonnet.net/oaklea

DECATUR —————————————————————————————————

Painted Valley Ranch B&B	89-129-B&B	Continental plus breakfast
1724 W Preskitt Rd, 76234	3 rooms, 3 pb	Pool, suites, fireplaces, cable
940-627-6377 Fax: 940-627-8056	Visa, MC, *Rated*, •	TV, horse motel, wedding
888-817-6377	C-ltd/S-no/P-ltd/H-ltd	chapel
Colonel/Captain Buford Ness		
September-June		

The youngest and strangest historical house in the U.S. (and maybe the world). The only known house to be hit by a flying gas tank. You'll see the historic photos and news stories. E-mail: pvrbandb@aol.com

FORT WORTH ————————————————————————————————

Bloomsbury House B&B	99-125-B&B	Full breakfast
2251 Lipscomb St, 76110	3 rooms, 3 pb	Complimentary beverages,
817-921-2383	Visa, MC, AmEx, •	dessert
888-652-7378	C-ltd/S-ltd/P-no/H-no	Sitting room, 1 room with
Karen & Ivan Taylor		Jacuzzi, porches, rocking
All year		chairs

Two-story Queen Anne Victorian home & carriage house furnished with antiques; gourmet breakfast; close to TCU & revitalized downtown. Carriage house has Jacuzzi bath. E-mail: i.taylor@tcu.edu   *Web site:* bestinns.net/usa/tx/bbhouse.html

FORT WORTH

Texas White House, The	105-125-B&B	Full breakfast
1417 8th Ave, 76104	3 rooms, 3 pb	Afternoon tea, snacks
817-923-3597 Fax: 817-923-0410	Most CC, *Rated*, •	Dinner (fee), sitting room,
800-279-6491	C-ltd/S-ltd/P-no/H-no	porches, rocking chairs
Jamie & Grover McMains		
All year		

Historically designated, award winning, country style home, centrally located; as warm and generous as old family friends; gracious and simply elegant. E-mail: txwhitehou@aol.com

FREDERICKSBURG

Alte Welt Gasthof B&B	135-150-B&B	Continental breakfast
PO Box 631, 78624	2 rooms, 2 pb	Afternoon tea, snacks, comp.
830-997-0443 Fax: 830-997-0040	Most CC, *Rated*, •	wine
888-991-6749	C-ltd/S-no/P-no/H-no	Jacuzzis, suites, cable TV,
Ron & Donna Maddux	German	accommodate business
All year		travelers

E-mail: stay@texas-bed-n-breakfast.com   *Web site:* texas-bed-n-breakfast.com

Das College Haus B&B	95-125-B&B	Home cooked breakfast
106 W College St, 78624	4 rooms, 4 pb	Snacks, comp. wine
830-997-9047 Fax: 830-997-9047	Visa, MC, *Rated*	Library porches, rocking
800-654-2802	C-ltd/S-no/P-no/H-ltd	chairs, sitting room, suites,
Myrna Dennis		fireplace, cable TV
All year		

Walk to historic Main Street. Beautifully appointed with comfortable period furnishings, antiques & original art. Delicious breakfast in old fashioned dining room.
E-mail: myrna@hctc.net   *Web site:* dascolleghaus.com

Delforge Place B&B Inn, The	95 and up-B&B	Full gourmet breakfast
710 Ettie St, 78624	4 rooms, 4 pb	Picnic baskets, snacks
830-997-6212 Fax: 830-997-7190	Most CC, *Rated*, •	Afternoon tea, porch swing,
800-997-0462	C-ltd/S-no/P-no	patio, horseshoes, croquet,
Betsy, George & Pete Delforge	French, Spanish	library, archery
All year		

1898 Victorian in town. Historical antiques, many authentic Clipper-ship period heirlooms. "World-class breakfast" (Gourmet Mag.) Warm, friendly ambiance. Guest privileges at private swim and tennis club.   *E-mail:* delplace@speakez.net   *Web site:* delforgeplace.com

Magnolia House	95-140-B&B	Full scrumptious bkfst.
101 E Hackberry, 78624	5 rooms, 5 pb	Snacks, comp. wine
830-997-0306 Fax: 830-997-0766	Most CC, *Rated*, •	Sitting room, swimming,
800-880-4374	C-ltd/S-no/P-no/H-ltd	tennis, health facility nearby
Joyce & Patrick Kennard		
All year		

1923 Texas historical home. Traditional, comfortable elegance as it was meant to be
E-mail: magnolia@hctc.net   *Web site:* magnolia-house.com

Schmidt Barn B&B	90-B&B	Continental plus breakfast
Rt 2 Box 112A3, 78624	1 rooms, 1 pb	German breakfast platter
830-997-5612 Fax: 210-997-8282	Visa, MC, Disc, *Rated*,	Deer and wildlife, rent entire
Charles & Loretta Schmidt	•	house
All year	C-yes/S-yes/P-ltd	
	German	

Old world ambience and hospitality. Located 1½ miles west of historic Fredericksburg. 1860s limestone barn turned into charming guest house with loft bedroom, living room, bath with sunken tub and kitchen. Hosts live next door.   *E-mail:* gasthaus@ktc.com
Web site: fbglodging.com/schmibn.htm

FREDERICKBURN

Comfort Common, The	65-110-B&B	Full breakfast
PO Box 539, 78013	10 rooms, 10 pb	Sitting room, fireplace, cable
830-995-3030 Fax: 830-995-3455	Most CC, *Rated*	TV, laundry, kitchen, gift and
Jim Lord & Bobby Dent	S-no/P-no/H-no	antique shop
All year		

Selected as one of The Southwest's Best B&B's by Fodor's and featured in numerous magazines, the C. 1880 limestone structure has wide verandas overlooking a courtyard and gardens. E-mail: comfortcommon@hctc.net *Web site:* comfortcommon.com

GAINESVILLE

Alexander B&B Acres	60-125-B&B	Full breakfast
3692 County Road 201, 76240	8 rooms, 5 pb	Lunch & dinner avail.,
903-564-7440 Fax: 903-564-7440	Most CC, •	snacks
800-887-8794	C-ltd/S-ltd/P-no/H-no	Sitting room, bicycles,
Jimmy & Pamela Alexander		Jacuzzis, swimming pool,
All year		suites, fireplace, hayrides

3 story country Queen Anne Inn and 2 story Guest House on 65 acres of woods, meadows and walking trails. Enjoy star gazing or help us feed the livestock. After a homemade country breakfast, enjoy the peace and quiet. E-mail: abba@texoma.net
Web site: bbhost/alexanderbbacres

GALVESTON

Queen Anne B&B, The	90-150-B&B	Full breakfast
1915 Sealy Ave, 77550	5 rooms, 4 pb	Afternoon snacks, beverages
409-763-7088	Most CC,	Screened porch, shaded
800-472-0930	C-ltd/S-no/P-no/H-no	deck, ground floor suite,
Ron & Jackie Metzger		bicycles available
All year		

Located on the Gulf Coast in one of Texas's most historical cities. A Queen Anne style Victorian home built in 1905. Featured in Southern Living's Texas Vacations Magazine. Antiques throughout. E-mail: queenanne@ev1.net *Web site:* welcome.to/queenanne

GLEN ROSE

Bussey's Something Special	80-100-B&B	Continental plus breakfast
PO Box 1425, 76043	2 rooms, 2 pb	Snacks
254-897-4843	Most CC, •	Suites, books, games, full
877-4-BNBBED	C-yes/S-no/P-no/H-no	kitchen, un-hosted, porch &
Morris & Susan Bussey		yard, jet tub
All year		

Private guest cottages, family friendly, relax with a good book, large breakfast provided, 2 blocks from downtown square, 2 blocks from the river. As about our special tours. Very relaxing. Unhosted.

GRANBURY

Arbor House Lakeside Inn	100-165-B&B	Full breakfast
530 E Pearl St, 76048	10 rooms, 10 pb	Snacks
817-573-0073 Fax: 817-579-1199	Most CC, *Rated*	Sitting room, Jacuzzis, suites,
800-641-0073	C-ltd/S-no/P-no/H-yes	cable TV, Accommodate
Keith & Angie, Aletha & Ron		business travelers
All year		

*A new Queen Anne Victorian home with the atmosphere of yesterday, the comforts of today and quality service that is timeless. Gourmet breakfast served daily.
E-mail:* arbor@itexas.net *Web site:* www2.itexas.net/~arbor

Pearl Street Inn B&B	59-119-B&B	Full breakfast
319 W Pearl St, 76048	5 rooms, 5 pb	Dinners by reservation
817-579-7465	*Rated*, •	Sitting room, snacks, hot
888-732-7578	C-ltd/S-ltd/P-no/H-no	tubs, private baths,
Danette D. Hebda All year		Enchanted evening pkg.

Centrally located historic home features antique clawfoot tubs, period furnishings, porches, king beds. Relax & reminisce "where days move gently in all seasons" E-mail: danette@
itexas.net *Web site:* www2.itexas.net/~danette

HENDERSON

Tree House B&B	80-90-B&B	Snacks
1305 Westwood Dr, 75654	2 rooms, 2 pb	Sitting room, library,
903-655-1210	Visa, MC, AmEx,	fireplace, TV, conferences,
Mary Jackson & Gizmo	C-ltd/S-ltd/P-no/H-ltd	dance-hall sized deck.
All year		

Luxurious accommodations, personal attentive service, in a charming setting. Your bountiful breakfast served on East Texas' favorite deck, part of a Certified Backyard Habitat, or in the formal dining room. E-mail: trehouse@ballistic.com *Web site:* texas-treehouse-inn.com

HILLSBORO

Windmill B&B	80-100-B&B	Full breakfast
Rt 2, Box 448, 76645	3 rooms, 3 pb	Dinner, afternoon tea,
254-582-7373 Fax: 972-871-7809	Most CC, •	snacks, wine
800-951-0033	C-ltd/S-no/P-no/H-no	Sitting room, bicycles,
Ruben & Gerry Marentes	Spanish	Jacuzzis, suites, cable TV.
All year		

Charming Victorian, nestled among pecan and oak trees on 21 acres. Enjoy the porches, beautiful gardens, horses in the pasture, nap in the hammock, or in your beautiful, romantic room. E-mail: windmillbb@aol.com

HOUSTON

Angel Arbor B&B	95-125-B&B	Full breakfast
848 Heights Blvd, 77007	5 rooms, 5 pb	Afternoon tea, snacks
713-868-4654 Fax: 713-861-3189	Most CC, *Rated*, •	Sitting room, library, upstairs
800-722-8788	C-ltd/S-no/P-no/H-no	solarium, ceiling fans in all
Marguerite Swanson		rooms
All year		

Convenient, near downtown location. Elegant but comfortable. Perfect for corporate & leisure guests. Full, memorable breakfasts. Murder mystery dinner parties. E-mail: b-bhoutx@wt.net *Web site:* angelarbor.com

Beacon Hill Guest House	69-185-B&B	Full breakfast
3705 NASA Road One, 77586	7 rooms, 7 pb	Snacks
281-326-7643 Fax: 281-326-2883	Visa, MC, AmEx, •	Private sun decks, pier, boat
Delaina J. Hanssen	C-yes/S-ltd/P-no/H-yes	dock, boat taxi, office
All year	German	services, hot tub

Private, waterfront guest houses with great views & access to the water for a romantic getaway or waterside entertaining. E-mail: hanssen@aol.com *Web site:* beaconhillbnb.com

Lovett Inn, The	75-175-B&B	Continental breakfast
501 Lovett Blvd, 77006	8 rooms, 8 pb	Library, swimming pool, hot
713-522-5224 Fax: 713-528-6708	Visa, MC, AmEx, *Rated*	tubs
800-779-5224	C-ltd/S-ltd/P-yes/H-no	
Tom Fricke	Spanish	
All year		

Charming 1920s former mayors mansion near downtown, museums, convention and medical centers and Galleria. E-mail: lovettinn@aol.com *Web site:* lovettinn.com

Patrician B&B Inn, The	95-135-B&B	Full breakfast
1200 Southmore Blvd, 77004	4 rooms, 4 pb	Comp. wine, snacks
713-523-1114 Fax: 713-523-0790	Most CC, *Rated*, •	Sitting room, near golf,
800-553-5797	C-ltd/S-no/P-no/H-no	perfect for weddings, parties
Patricia Thomas		or receptions
All year		

1919 mansion minutes to downtown Houston, Texas Medical Center, Museum of Fine Arts and Rice University. Some claw foot tubs. Telephone and TV in all rooms E-mail: southmor@swbell.net *Web site:* texasbnb.com

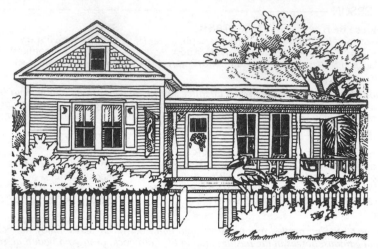

The Pelican House B&B, Houston, TX

HOUSTON

Pelican House B&B, The
1302 First St, 77586
281-474-5295 Fax: 281-474-7840
Suzanne Silver
All year

80-90-B&B
4 rooms, 4 pb
Most CC, *Rated*, •
C-ltd/S-ltd/P-no/H-no

Full breakfast
Complimentary wine
Sitting room, library, cable
TV, hot tub, champagne &
chocolate 2 nite

Whimsical country house overlooking the Back Bay. Gourmet breakfast serviced on our back deck where water-bird viewing is at its best. Located in art & antique colony.
E-mail: pelicanhouse@usa.net *Web site:* pelicanhouse.com

Sara's B&B Inn
941 Heights Blvd, 77008
713-868-1130 Fax: 713-868-3284
800-593-1130
Connie & Bob McCreight
All year

70-150-B&B
13 rooms, 11 pb
Most CC, *Rated*, •
C-ltd/S-no/P-no/H-no
Spanish

Continental plus breakfast
Cold drinks, coffee, tea
Sitting room, large deck, hot
tub, bicycles, parties or
receptions, suites

Inn in the heart of Houston just 5 minutes from downtown, furnished in antiques and collectibles. Sara's is one of the best inns in Texas.   E-mail: stay@saras.com
Web site: saras.com

JEFFERSON

Maison Bayou Waterfront B&B
300 Bayou St, 75657
903-665-7600 Fax: 903-665-7100
Jan & Pete Hochendel
All year

69-135-B&B
11 rooms, 11 pb
Visa, MC, Disc, *Rated*,
•
C-yes/S-ltd/P-no/H-ltd

Full breakfast
Experience privacy in
individual cabins, railcars,
bunkhouses

Tranquil setting on 55 wooded acres with ponds, river front and wildlife. Full breakfast served on glassed-in gallery overlooking cypress pond. Historic downtown Jefferson 1 minute away.   E-mail: cabins@maisonbayou.com *Web site:* maisonbayou.com

Pride House
409 E Broadway, 75657
903-665-2675 Fax: 903-665-3901
800-894-3526
Toby Shoemaker   All year

75-150-B&B
11 rooms, 11 pb
Visa, MC, *Rated*, •
C-ltd/S-no/P-no/H-ltd
German

Legendary full breakfast
Hot/cold drinks, snacks
Sitting room, A/C, rooms
have ceiling fans, stained
glass windows, fireplace

Breathtaking Victorian mansion in romantic Jefferson, Texas' favorite small town—where a weekend is never enough! Luscious interiors, legendary breakfast.   E-mail: jefftx@mind.net
Web site: jeffersontexas.com

LAKE TEXOMA

Terralak B&B on Lake Texoma
PO Box 630393, 75063
214-532-8062 Fax: 972-401-2715
877-Terralak
Kathy Bachand
All year

85-200-B&B
5 rooms, 4 pb
Most CC, *Rated*, •
C-yes/S-no/P-no/H-no

Full breakfast-weekends
Continental plus breakfast-weekdays
Afternoon tea, snacks, family friendly facility, fishing charters available

Your lake home away from home, located on 13 beautiful wooded acres on the #1 lake in Texas, Lake Texoma. Sailing, skiing, hiking and lots more to see and do.
E-mail: terralak@aol.com *Web site:* terralak.com

LAMPASAS

Historic Moses Hughes B&B
Rt 2 Box 31, 76550
512-556-5923
Al and Beverly Solomon
All year

75-85-B&B
3 rooms, 3 pb
Visa, MC, *Rated*, •
S-no/P-no/H-no
French, Spanish

Full breakfast
Afternoon tea, snacks
Sitting room, library, 45 acres of creek, springs, wildlife

Sparkling springs, turquoise skies, and star-filled nights set the mood for rest, recreation, and romance. Historic landmark/Texas wildscape.

LEANDER

Trails End B&B
12223 Trails End Rd #7, 78641
512-267-2901
800-850-2901
Jo Ann & Tom Patty   All year

95-185-B&B
Most CC, •
C-yes/S-no/P-no/H-no

Full breakfast
Dinner by reservation
Sitting room, library, gazebo, bikes, swimming pool, hiking

Austin-Lake Travis area. Truly unique, elegant, comfortable country B&B. Porches, decks with panoramic view of hill country. Fireplaces, hospitality. The Carriage House sleeps 4.

LONGVIEW

Longview Arms B&B
PO Box 2003, 75606
903-236-3000 Fax: 903-236-0643
888-321-4720
Julie Duke   All year

105-B&B
5 rooms, 5 pb
Visa, MC, AmEx, Disc, •
C-yes/S-no/P-no/H-no

Full breakfast
Snacks
Complimentary wine, sitting room, suites, cable TV, fax/data lines.

Restored apartment building in downtown Longview. All suite facility offering bedroom, living, kitchenette with refrigerator, microwave, coffee, breakfast nook. Fax/copy service available. Fax/data lines in suite. Unsurpassed service. E-mail: inn@longviewarms.com
Web site: longviewarms.com

NEW BRAUNFELS

Karbach Haus B&B
487 West San Antonio St, 78130
830-625-2131 Fax: 830-629-1126
800-972-5941
Kathy & Ben Jack Kinney
All year

110-200-B&B
6 rooms, 6 pb
Visa, MC, Disc, *Rated*, •
C-ltd/S-no/P-no/H-no
German

Full gourmet breakfast
Snacks, comp. beverages
Great room w/grand piano, fireplace, sun parlor, swimming pool, TVs, Jacuzzi

Historically significant mansion, downtown, romantic, luxurious, genuine antiques. Acre estate, pool, spa, all amenities of a small resort. Owner/hosts on premises. In-room TV/VCRs, VCR library, Jacuzzis.   Web site: bbhost.com/karbach

Lamb's Rest Inn
1385 Edwards Blvd, 78132
830-609-3932 Fax: 830-620-0864
888-609-3932
George & Judy Rothell
All year

95-150-B&B
5 rooms, 5 pb
Visa, MC, Disc, *Rated*
C-ltd/S-ltd/P-no/H-no

Full breakfast
Afternoon tea
Sitting room, library, bikes, Jacuzzis, pool, suites, fireplaces, cable TV

Enjoy true Texas hospitality on the Guadalupe River near the historic village of Gruene. A peaceful, romantic atmosphere awaits you in tranquil gardens. Relax on the verandah or one of the decks overlooking the pool and river.   E-mail: lambsbb@aol.com
Web site: bbhost.com/lambsrestbb

NEW BRAUNFELS

Old Hunter Rd Stagecoach	95-B&B	Full breakfast
5441 FM 1102, 78132	3 rooms, 3 pb	Sitting room, library, walking
830-620-9453 Fax: 830-620-0257	Visa, MC, AmEx,	trails
800-201-2912	*Rated*, •	
Jeff and Bettina	C-ltd/S-no/P-no/H-no	
All year		

Texas landmark constructed 150 years ago by Amish settlers. Authentically restored Fachwerk house & log cabins. Handcrafted Texas furniture & romantic gardens of herbs and roses. Corporate rates available. E-mail: stagecoach@sat.net
Web site: texasbedandbreakfast.com/stagecoachinn.com

ROCKPORT

Anthony's By the Sea	75-90-B&B	Full gourmet breakfast
732 S Pearl St, 78382	7 rooms, 4 pb	Sitting room, hot tubs,
361-729-6100 Fax: 361-729-2450	Visa, MC, *Rated*, •	swimming pool, family
800-460-2557	C-yes/S-yes/P-yes/H-no	friendly facility
Anthony & Denis		
All year		

Anthony's is casual, friendly & affordable. Pool, hot tub & covered lanai with fountains & chandeliers add to its ambiance. "Anthony's" where time is kept & memories are made.
Web site: rockport-fulton.org/ads/anthonys/anthonys.htm

Blue Heron Inn	95-105-B&B	Full breakfast
801 Patton St, 78382	4 rooms, 4 pb	Wine, snacks
361-729-7526	Visa, MC, AmEx,	Sitting room, tennis,
Jo Ann Maccurdy & Vera	*Rated*, •	fireplace, cable, conf., golf,
Archer All year	C-ltd/S-ltd/P-no/H-no	fishing, birding

Historic 100 year old home, remodeled in 1995. Spacious garden room for gourmet breakfast. Herb garden, patio & veranda for relaxing. Bird watching and rose garden.
E-mail: bluheron@pyramid3.net *Web site:* blueheronbb.com

ROUND TOP

Round Top Inn	95-125-B&B	Full breakfast
PO Box 212, 78954	5 rooms, 5 pb	Snacks, comp. wine
409-249-5294 Fax: 409-249-5506	Visa, MC, •	Sitting room, library, walking
Frank & Kathy Johnston	C-ltd/S-no/P-no/H-no	distance to town, & other
All year		historical sites

Situated amidst ancient oaks and lush gardens, 3 Texas pioneer homes have been furnished for charm & comfort. 5 historical monuments, display gardens & 2 shops for the herbal enthusiast. E-mail: frank@cvtv.net *Web site:* roundtopinn.com

Settlement at Round Top	105-200-B&B	Full breakfast
PO Box 176, 78954	10 rooms, 10 pb	Afternoon tea, snacks
409-249-5015 Fax: 409-249-5587	Most CC, *Rated*, •	Sitting room, library,
888-ROUNDTOP	S-ltd/P-no/H-no	Jacuzzis, suites, fireplaces
Karen & Larry Beevers		
All year		

An historic retreat for adults within a wonderfully restored pioneer-era complex of log cabins, German cottages, and period houses. Featured in "Country Living," "Country Home," "The Dallas Morning News." E-mail: stay@thesettlement.com
Web site: thesettlement.com

SALADO

Inn at Salado, The	70-150-B&B	Full breakfast
PO Box 320, 76571	9 rooms, 9 pb	Sitting room, fireplaces,
254-947-0027 Fax: 254-947-3144	Most CC, *Rated*	cable TV, conference,
800-724-0027	C-ltd/S-no/P-no/H-ltd	weddings and receptions
Rob & Suzann Petro		
All year		

Built in 1872, the Inn displays both a Texas Historical Marker & a Nat'l Register listing. Located walking distance to shopping & dining. E-mail: rooms@inn-at-salado.com
Web site: inn-at-salado.com

SAN ANTONIO —————————————————

A.Beckmann Inn/Carriage Hse	99-150-B&B	Full breakfast

A.Beckmann Inn/Carriage Hse
222 E Guenther St, 78204
210-229-1449 Fax: 210-229-1061
800-945-1449
Betty Jo & Don Schwartz
All year

99-150-B&B
5 rooms, 5 pb
Rated
C-ltd/S-ltd/P-no/H-ltd

Full breakfast
Welcome tea
Sitting room, historic, district, scenic river, walk, trolley, TVs

Beautiful historic district, scenic riverwalk, Alamo, trolley, gourmet breakfast with dessert, ornate antique beds featured, warm & gracious hospitality. Featured in Country Inns. Phones, refrigs., fax. E-mail: beckinn@swbell.net *Web site:* beckmanninn.com

Adams House B&B Inn
231 Adams St, 78210
210-224-4791 Fax: 210-223-5125
800-666-4810
Nora Peterson & Richard
Green   All year

99-169-B&B
4 rooms, 4 pb
Most CC, *Rated*, •
C-ltd/S-ltd/P-no/H-no

Full gourmet breakfast
Sitting room, library, copier, fax, computer, net access, carriage hse

Three story brick; King William Historic District, near Riverwalk/downtown; furnished in period antiques; spacious verandahs. E-mail: adams@san-antonio-texas.com
Web site: san-antonio-texas.com

Arbor House Inn & Suites
540 S St. Mary's St, 78205
210-472-2005 Fax: 210-472-2007
888-272-6700
D. Schuette & R Stark
All year

95-175-B&B
18 rooms, 18 pb
Visa, MC, AmEx,
Rated, •
C-yes/S-no/P-yes/H-yes

Sitting room, Jacuzzi, suites, cable TV, business travelers, phone.

Five historic buildings surround a lush garden courtyard, just one and a half blocks to Riverwalk, 2 blocks to the convention center. 11 suites & 7 rooms are furnished in the ultimate "eclecticity." E-mail: arborhous@aol.com *Web site:* harborhouse.com

B&B on the River
129 Woodward Place, 78204
210-225-6333 Fax: 210-271-3992
800-730-0019
Dr. A.D.Zucht III
All year

99-149-B&B
12 rooms, 12 pb
Most CC, *Rated*, •
C-yes/S-no/P-no/H-ltd

Full breakfast
Bicycles, Jacuzzis, fireplaces, cable TV, Accommodate business travelers.

Restored turn-of-the-century Victorian home situated on the quiet banks of the San Antonio River. The interior has period furnishings and hardwood floors. E-mail: adz@swbell.net
Web site: hotx.com/sa/bb

Bonner Garden B&B
145 E Argarita, 78212
210-733-4222 Fax: 210-733-6129
800-356-4222
Noel & Jan Stenoien
All year

85-115-B&B
5 rooms, 5 pb
Most CC, *Rated*, •
C-ltd/S-no/P-no/H-no

Full breakfast
Snacks
Sitting room, library, rooftop patio, pool, TV, VCR, phone

Award-winning (National Historic Association) Italian villa built in 1910 for Mary Bonner, the internationally known artist. Smaller bonus room at $75/night if all other rooms are booked. E-mail: noels@onr.com *Web site:* bonnergarden.com

Brackenridge House
230 Madison, 78204
210-271-3442 Fax: 210-226-3139
800-221-1412
Bennie & Sue Blansett
All year

99-300-B&B
5 rooms, 5 pb
Visa, MC, AmEx,
Rated, •
C-ltd/S-no/P-ltd/H-no

Full breakfast
Snacks, complimentary wine
Bikes, Jacuzzis, suites, cable TV, TV, VCR, phone

Native Texan owners & innkeepers will guide you through your visit from their beautiful Greek Revival home in historic King William. Served gourmet breakfasts, garden hot tub & country Victorian decor. E-mail: benniesueb@aol.com *Web site:* brackenridgehouse.com/

SAN ANTONIO

Bullis House Inn	59-99-B&B	Continental plus breakfast
PO Box 8059, 78208	7 rooms, 2 pb	Guest kitchen, snacks
210-223-9426 Fax: 210-299-1479	Most CC, *Rated*, •	Library, phones, veranda,
877-477-4100	C-yes/S-yes/P-no/H-no	movie night w/snacks,
Steven & Alma Cross	Spanish	poolside BBQs, catering
All year		

Historic 3-story, white mansion, minutes from Alamo, Riverwalk, downtown. Chandeliers, fireplaces, decorative 14-ft. ceilings, geometrically patterned floors of fine woods. Swimming pool. E-mail: hisanaton@aol.com

Christmas House B&B	75-150-B&B	Full breakfast on weekends
2307 McCullough, 78212	5 rooms, 5 pb	Continental plus breakfast
210-737-2786 Fax: 210-734-5712	Visa, MC, •	weekdays
800-268-4187	C-ltd/S-ltd/H-yes	Sitting room, library,
Penny & Grant Estes		private/semi private
All year		veranda, catering

1.5 miles from Riverwalk and Alamo. This historic 1910 home in the Monte Vista National Registered Historic District. Most unique antiques in home are for sale and it is Christmas year around! One room ADA approved. E-mail: christmashb@earthlink.net
Web site: texassleepaways.com/christmashouse

Columns on Alamo, The	89-155-B&B	Full breakfast
1037 South Alamo, 78210	11 rooms, 11 pb	Queen & king beds, in-room
210-271-3245 Fax: 210-271-3245	Most CC, *Rated*	TV & phones, off-street
800-233-3364	C-ltd/S-no/P-no	parking
Ellenor & Arthur Link	German	
All year		

1892 mansion & guesthouse—historic district, antiques, Oriental rugs, spacious common areas, verandahs. 6 Jacuzzis & 6 fireplaces. Walk to restaurants, shopping, downtown, Alamo, riverwalk! New Rockhouse: a limestone cottage with rustic, Texas decor.
Web site: bbonline.com/tx/columns

Kuebler-Waldrip Haus	95-150-B&B	Full candlelit breakfast
1620 Hueco Springs Loop,	10 rooms, 10 pb	Snacks, comp. drinks
78132	Most CC, *Rated*, •	Sitting room, library, gift
830-625-8372 Fax: 830-625-8372	C-yes/S-no/P-ltd/H-yes	shop, TV/VCR, walking trails,
800-299-8372	Spanish	pet deer.
Margaret K. Waldrip		
All year		

Relax! 43 beautiful hill country acres near rivers, Gruene, New Braunfels, San Antonio, Austin. Delicious candlelight breakfast brunch. Whirlpools, kitchenettes, porches
E-mail: kwbandb@compuvision.net Web site: cruising-america.com/kuebler-waldrip

Linden House Inn	75-B&B	Continental breakfast
315 Howard, 78212	4 rooms, 4 pb	Automatic gated parking
210-224-8902 Fax: 210-224-8902	Most CC, *Rated*, •	
888-509-8902	C-ltd/S-no/P-no/H-no	
Cathy Diaz All year	Spanish	

Built in 1902. City charm, close to everything. Walk to river center, historical "Alamo." Close to freeways, 20 minutes to sea world, Fiesta Texas. First night deposit on credit card required. Will be charged one night for failure to call and cancel.
E-mail: snippyland@aol.com

Little Flower Inn B&B	80-95-B&B	Full breakfast
225 Madison St, 78204	2 rooms, 2 pb	Afternoon tea, snacks
210-354-3116 Fax: 210-354-3116	•	Sitting room, library,
Phil & Christine Touw	C-yes/S-ltd/P-no/H-no	swimming pool, cable TV
All year	German	

Our pledge to you: a B&B that is elegant & intimate yet perfect for families, at a reasonable cost. Come experience "Pampered Privacy" at the Little Flower! E-mail: littleflower@
satexas.com Web site: members.tripod.com/~little-flower-inn

SAN ANTONIO

Monarch House B&B
128 W Mistletoe, 78212
210-733-3939 Fax: 210-734-6568
800-851-3666
Peter and Diana Sebben
All year

75-110-B&B
4 rooms, 4 pb
Visa, MC, *Rated*, •
C-ltd/S-no/P-ltd/H-no

Full breakfast
Snacks
Sitting room, library, grand
piano, TV, VCR, phone

*Elegant 3 story home built in 1914. Monarch House features high ceilings, wood floors &
fireplaces. Close to everything.   E-mail:* innkpr@flash.net *Web site:* monarchhouse.com

---

Noble Inns
102 Turner St, 78204
210-225-4045 Fax: 210-227-0877
800-221-4045
Don & Liesl Noble
All year

115-190-B&B
9 rooms, 9 pb
Most CC, *Rated*, •
C-ltd/S-no/P-no/H-yes
Spanish

Full or cont. plus bkfst
Afternoon tea, snacks
Sitting room, library, hot tub,
heated pools, kitchens,
phones, TV

*Luxurious, meticulously restored Victorian homes. King William District. Beautiful an-
tiques, fireplaces, marble baths, Jacuzzis.   E-mail:* nobleinns@aol.com *Web site:* nobleinns.com

---

O'Casey's B&B
PO Box 15308, 78212
210-738-1378 Fax: 210-733-9408
800-738-1378
John & Linda Fay Casey
All year

75-115-B&B
7 rooms, 7 pb
Most CC, •
C-yes/S-no/P-yes/H-no

Full breakfast
Sitting room, cable tv,
conference

*Friendly, comfortable, home-style B&B; full breakfast; turn-of-the-century charm; quiet
Monte Vista Historic District near downtown; we'll help you experience the best of this
great city; reasonable rates; Irish hospitality!   E-mail:* info@ocaseybnb.com
Web site: ocaseybnb.com

Oge' Inn Riverwalk
209 Washington St, 78204
210-223-2353 Fax: 210-226 5812
800-242-2770
Patrick & Sharrie Magatagan
All year

110-225-B&B
10 rooms, 10 pb
Most CC, *Rated*
C-ltd/S-ltd/P-no/H-no

Full breakfast
Sitting room, library, A/C,
cable TV, phone, set on 1/5
acres

*Elegant, romantic Antebellum mansion on 1½ acres on the Riverwalk. European antiques,
quiet comfort & luxury. Shopping, dining, and Alamo 5 blocks. Corporate rate for single
business travelers, S-Th.   E-mail:* ogeinn@swbell.net *Web site:* ogeinn.com

---

Painted Lady Inn
620 Broadway, 78215
210-220-1092 Fax: 210-299-4185
Cindy & Linda
All year

80-189-B&B
8 rooms, 8 pb
Most CC, •
C-yes/S-no/P-yes/H-yes
Spanish

Full breakfast
Bar service, snacks
2 large porches, rooftop
deck, set on 1/5 acres,
Jacuzzis, stes., fireplaces

*Hotel-style inn, intimate and private. Large suites and guestrooms with luxurious furnish-
ings. Each with private baths, phones with voice mail, stereos, refrig., coffee, microwave,
cable TV.   E-mail:* travel25a@earthlink.net *Web site:* bestinns.net/usa/tx/paintedlady.html

---

Riverwalk Inn
329 Old Guilbeau, 78204
210-212-8300
Fax: 210-229-9422
800-254-4440
Johnny Halpenny &
Tammy Hill
All year

125-175-B&B
11 rooms, 11 pb
Most CC, *Rated*, •
C-ltd/S-ltd/P-no/H-yes
Spanish

Continental plus breakfast
Fireplaces, cable TV,
conference room for max of
12 people

*Historic log homes (circa 1840) transported from Tennessee and restored along the scenic
San Antonio Riverwalk.   E-mail:* innkeeper@riverwalkinn.com *Web site:* riverwalkinn.com/

A VIictorian Lady Inn, San Antonio, TX

SAN ANTONIO

Royal Swan
236 Madison, 78204
210-223-3776 Fax: 210-271-0373
800-368-3073
Curt & Helen Skredergard
All year

85-120-B&B
5 rooms, 5 pb
Most CC, *Rated*, •
C-ltd/S-ltd/P-no/H-no

Full breakfast
Snacks, complimentary wine
Restaurant nearby, sitting
room, library, bicycles
nearby

1892 Victorian located within walking distance of the famed Alamo and worldclass dining and shopping on our beautiful Riverwalk.   E-mail: theswan@onr.com   *Web site:* royalswan.com

---

Terrell Castle B&B Inn
950 E. Grayston St, 78208
210-271-9145
Victor & Diane Smilgin
All year

70-125-B&B
10 rooms, 9 pb
Visa, MC, AmEx, Disc,
Rated, •
C-yes/S-no/P-no/H-no
Spanish, French

Full breakfast
Sitting room, library, suites,
fireplace, conferencs

Experience the charm & comfort of this 1894 Victorian castle situated on a one acre landscaped site in the downtown area. It features comfortably large rooms, private baths, library, formal dining room and antiques.   E-mail: smilgin@aol.com
Web site: geocities.com/southbeach/pier/9656

Victorian Lady Inn, A
421 Howard St, 78212
210-224-2524 Fax: 210-224-5123
800-879-7116
Kate & Joe Bowski   All year

89-135-B&B
8 rooms, 8 pb
Visa, MC, AmEx,
Rated, •
C-ltd/S-ltd/P-no/H-ltd

Full breakfast
Afternoon tea
Sitting room, library,
swimming pool, suites,
fireplaces, cable TV

1898 historic mansion just minutes from the Alamo. Experience grand guestrooms, fabulous breakfasts in the majestic dining room, pool and hot tub in a tropical setting and unsurpassed hospitality.   E-mail: vli@swbell.net *Web site:* viclady.com

---

Yellow Rose, A
229 Madison St, 78204
210-229-9903 Fax: 210-229-1691
800-950-9903
Deb & Kit Walker
All year

100-200-B&B
5 rooms, 5 pb
Visa, MC, AmEx,
Rated, •
C-ltd/S-ltd/P-no/H-no
Spanish

Full breakfast
Afternoon tea, snacks
Complimentary wine,
gardens, sitting room,
parking, 2 blocks from
Riverwalk

Elegantly restored Victorian furnished with luxurious fabrics, Persian rugs, antiques & fine art. 15 min. walk to most sights. Quietly sophisticated accommodations. Featured in Today & Holiday *magazines.   E-mail:* yellowrs@express-news.net

A Yellow Rose, San Antonio, TX

SAN MARCOS

Crystal River Inn
326 W Hopkins, 78666
512-396-3739 Fax: 512-353-3248
888-396-3739
Mike, Cathy & Sarah Dillon
All year

80-140-B&B
12 rooms, 12 pb
Visa, MC, AmEx,
Rated, •
C-ltd/S-ltd/P-no/H-yes

Full breakfast
Complimentary brandy,
chocolates
Fireplaces, courtyard, piano,
fountain, bikes, 2-room
suites, picnics

Romantic, luxurious Victorian captures matchless spirit of Texas Hill Country. Fresh flowers, homemade treats. 4-room garden cottage available: fireplace. Special packages available. Corporate apartment, fully furnished.   E-mail: cri@haysco.net
Web site: crystalriverinn.com

SMITHVILLE

Katy House, The
PO Box 803, 78957
512-237-4262 Fax: 512-237-2239
800-843-5289
Sallie Blalock   All year

65-110-B&B
4 rooms, 4 pb
Visa, MC, *Rated*, •
C-ltd/S-no/P-ltd/H-no

Full country breakfast
One suite w/kitchen
Sitting room, bicycles, queen-
size beds

Historic pecan-shaded home in beautiful central Texas. Railroad memorabilia & antique furnishings. A gracious, comfortable, charming home.   E-mail: thekatyh@onr.com
Web site: katyhouse.com

TYLER

Rosevine Inn B&B
415 S Vine, 75702
903-592-2221 Fax: 903-592-5522
Bert & Rebecca Powell
All year

85-150-B&B
7 rooms, 7 pb
Rated, •
C-ltd/S-no/P-no/H-no
French

Full breakfast
Sitting room, library, spa,
outdoor hot tub, courtyard,
gameroom

Original bed and breakfast in the rose capital of the world. Pleasant accommodations with delicious breakfast. Friendly hosts make you feel at home.   E-mail: rosevine@iamerica.net

Seasons B&B Inn, The
313 E Charnwood, 75701
903-533-0803 Fax: 903-533-8870
Jim & Myra Brown   All year

85-125-B&B
4 rooms, 3 pb
Most CC,
C-ltd/S-no/P-no/H-no

Full breakfast; Afternoon tea
Library, sitting room, TV
room, veranda sitting, family
friendly facility

Colonial home near downtown Tyler, antique shopping. Rooms decorated in 4 seasons theme; wall art/painting in each room. Original curly pine woodwork. Gourmet breakfast.   E-mail: theseasons@worldnet.att.net   Web site: theseasonsinn.com

WACO

Judge Baylor House, The
908 Speight Ave, 76706
254-756-0273 Fax: 254-756-0711
888-522-9567
Bruce Dyer
All year

73-95-B&B
4 rooms, 4 pb
Visa, MC, *Rated*, •
C-ltd/S-no/P-no/H-ltd

Full breakfast
Aftn. tea, snacks
Sitting room, library
historical landmark

Decorated with antiques & Texas Hill Country art. Quiet & comfortable bedrooms. Near Baylor University and IH-35. Easy to find.   E-mail: jbaylor@iamerica.net
Web site: judgebaylorhouse.com

WAXAHACHIE

BonnyNook Inn, The
414 W Main St, 75165
972-938-7207 Fax: 972-937-7700
800-486-5936
Vaughn & Bonnie Franks
All year

85-115-B&B
5 rooms, 5 pb
Most CC, *Rated*, •
C-yes/S-yes/P-no/H-no

Full gourmet breakfast
Dinner by reservation
Snacks, whirlpool tubs in 3
rooms, piano, antiques

1887 Victorian home, located near Square in a historic national district. Each room is a different experience. Plants & fresh flowers, country garden. Old World elegance with 20th century comforts.

Rosemary Mansion on Main
903 W Main St, 75165
972-923-1181 Fax: 972-923-1199
Judy & Dennis Cross
All year

100-250-B&B
5 rooms, 5 pb
Most CC, *Rated*
C-ltd/S-ltd/P-no/H-no

Full breakfast
Snacks, complimentary wine
Fireplaces, cable TV,
accommodate business
travelers, eve. receptions
wknds.

A tranquil acre of gardens enhance this 1916, nationally registered Georgian Revival. Luxurious antique appointments, gracious hospitality and exquisite herb-inspired cuisine await your pleasure.   E-mail: rose902WM@aol.com

WESLACO

Tropical B&B
RR 9 Box 259A, 78596
956-968-9646
Norma Roth
All year

59-79-B&B
3 rooms, 1 pb
C-ltd/S-no/P-no/H-ltd

Continental plus breakfast
Sitting room, library, TV,
garden patio

Home amidst tropical plants, flowers and citrus grove (fruit available in season), near bird sanctuaries, 25 minutes to Mexico, 1 hour to Padre Island beaches.
E-mail: tropicalb-b@juno.com Web site: homestead.juno.com/tropicalb-b.index.html

WIMBERLEY

Rancho Cama B&B
2595 Flite Acres Rd, 78676
512-847-2596 Fax: 512-847-7135
800-594-4501
Nell Cadenhead
All year

70-90-B&B
3 rooms, 1 pb
S-no/P-no/H-ltd

Full breakfast
Sitting room, library,
Jacuzzis, swimming pool,
cable TV, swings, phone

A quiet, pastoral setting, with guest houses separate from host home, invites guests to relax in the yard or porch swings.   E-mail: ranchocama@aol.com Web site: come.to/ranchocama

WINNSBORO

Hubbell House, Thee
307 W Elm St, 75494
903-342-5629 Fax: 903-342-6627
800-227-0639
Dan & Laurel Hubbell
All year

85-175-B&B
12 rooms, 12 pb
Visa, MC, AmEx,
Rated, •
C-ltd/S-ltd/P-ltd/H-ltd

Full breakfast
Continental bkfst.
Sitting room, library,
veranda, gallery, garden,
Jacuzzi, antique shoppe

1888 historic Georgian home, restored and furnished in period antiques. Massage by appointment. Plantation or continental breakfast. Centrally located to other tourist areas
Web site: bluebonnet.net/hubhouse

Utah

CEDAR CITY

Paxman Summerhouse B&B
170 North 400 W, 84720
435-586-3755
888-472-9626
Karlene Paxman
All year

65-85-B&B
3 rooms, 3 pb
MC, *Rated*, •
C-ltd/S-ltd/P-ltd/H-no

Continental plus breakfast
Sitting room, swimming pool,
tennis courts

Comfortable Victorian home, one block from Utah's Shakespearean Festival. Near Zion, Dixie and Bryce National Parks. Swimming, golf and tennis.

Willow Glen Inn
3308 N Bulldog Rd, 84720
435-586-3275
Violet & Phil Carter
All year

55-100-B&B
10 rooms, 8 pb
Visa, MC, •
C-yes/S-ltd/P-no/H-ltd

Full breakfast
Catered meals available
Sitting room, library, suites,
fireplace, conference
facilities

Country setting 1 mile from Cedar City, Utah. 3 separate buildings. Most rooms with private entrances. Gardens, tree lined paths, picnic areas, reception center. Seasonally decorated rooms. E-mail: info@willowgleninn.com Web site: willowgleninn.com

GLENDALE

Eagle's Nest B&B
PO Box 160, 84729
435-648-2200
Fax: 435-648-2221
800-293 6378
Shanoan & Dearborn Clark
All year

79-114-B&B
4 rooms, 4 pb
Visa, MC, *Rated*, •
C-yes/S-no/P-no/H-no

Full breakfast
Snacks, complimentary
wine/beer
Sitting room, library, hot
tubs, 13 acres to roam

Stay as our friends but be pampered like royalty. Enjoy our sumptuous breakfast, unique furnishings, and three spectacular National Parks. E-mail: innkeeps@eaglesnestbb.com Web site: eaglesnestbb.com

Smith Hotel B&B
PO Box 106, 84729
435-648-2156
Fax: 435-648-2156
800-528-3558
Rochelle & Bunny
April-October

42-60-B&B
7 rooms, 7 pb
Visa, MC, *Rated*, •
C-ltd/S-no/P-no/H-no

Continental plus breakfast
Sitting room, screened
porch, 13 acres to roam

Historic 1927 hotel; lovely view of nearby bluffs from the guest porch. Located in beautiful Long Valley between Zion and Bryce Canyon National Parks. New back porch with spa and coin-op laundry.

MANTI

Legacy Inn B&B
337 N 100 E, 84642
435-835-8352
Fax: 435-835-8342
Mike and Jan Crane
All year

75-95-B&B
4 rooms, 4 pb
Visa, MC, *Rated*, •
C-yes/S-no/P-ltd/H-no

Full breakfast
Snacks
Sitting room, suites,
fireplaces, cable TV, gift shop

Guests love the fantastic view of the Manti Temple from this elegant Victorian Inn. The little touches make a big difference; beautiful furnishings, a hearty breakfast, sumptious truffles, and our charming gift shop. E-mail: legacyinn@sisna.com Web site: legacyinn.com

MOAB

Sunflower Hill B&B Inn
185 N 300 E, 84532
435-259-2974 Fax: 435-259-3065
800-MOAB-SUN
Stucki family
All year

130-170-B&B
11 rooms, 11 pb
Visa, MC, *Rated*, •
C-ltd/S-no/P-no

Full breakfast
Sitting room, library, laundry
room, hot tub, gardens, patio,
BBQ

Inviting country retreat furnished with antiques, hand painting and stenciling. Serene setting with lush flower gardens. Healthy, homemade breakfast. All rooms with TV, A/C, antique beds.   E-mail: innkeeper@sunflowerhill.com *Web site:* sunflowerhill.com

MT. PLEASANT

Larsen House B&B
298 S State St # 13, 84647
435-462-9337 Fax: 435-462-2362
800-848-5263
Sally East
All year

60-110-B&B
6 rooms, 6 pb
Visa, MC, Disc, *Rated*,
•
C-ltd/S-no/P-no/H-ltd

Full breakfast
Snacks
Sitting room, library,
whirlpool tubs, pool nearby,
bicycles

Unique 100-year-old Victorian, located in the "heart of Utah"! Delicious breakfast, friendly innkeeper; you'll feel right at home. Three suites with jetted tubs.   E-mail: larsenh@juno.com

OGDEN

Jackson Fork Inn
7345 East 900 S, 84317
801-745-0051
800-255-0672
Vicki Petersen
All year

60-120-B&B
8 rooms, 8 pb
Visa, MC, AmEx, •
C-yes/S-no/P-ltd/H-no

Continental breakfast
Restaurant
Hot tubs, skiing, golf, fishing,
water sports, Jacuzzis &
VCRs in some rooms

Old dairy barn renovated into a restaurant & inn. Quiet getaway without phones. Private whirl tubs. Close to ski slopes, two lakes, hunting, fishing, golf, snowmobiles.

PARK CITY

1904 Imperial Hotel B&B
PO Box 1628, 84060
435-649-1904 Fax: 435-645-7421
800-669-8824
N. McLaughlin & K. Hart
All year

70-240-B&B
10 rooms, 10 pb
Most CC, *Rated*, •
C-yes/S-no/P-no/H-no

Full breakfast
Evening refreshments
Pub & art gallery nearby,
Jacuzzi, ski storage, TV, hot
tub, snacks, phones

Superbly restored 1904 hotel in heart of Park City. Private baths with large Roman tubs, phone, cable TV.   E-mail: stay@1904imperial.com *Web site:* 1904imperial.com

Blue Church Lodge, The
PO Box 1720, 84060
435-649-8009 Fax: 435-649-0686
800-626-5467
Nancy Schmidt
Open ski season

110-435-B&B
11 rooms, 11 pb
Visa, MC, •
C-yes/S-yes/P-ltd/H-no

Continental breakfast
Hot tubs, gameroom,
kitchens, fireplaces, ski
lockers, sitting room

Elegantly designed condos with antique country charm, 1-4 bedrooms. Listed on National Register Historic Places. Walk to Main Street and town lift.   E-mail: bcl@ditell.com
Web site: virtualcities.com/~virtual/ons/ut/k/utk3501.htm

Old Miners' Lodge, A B&B
PO Box 2639, 84060
435-645-8068 Fax: 435-645-7420
800-648-8068
Susan Wynne, Liza Simpson
All year

70-275-B&B
12 rooms, 12 pb
Most CC, *Rated*, •
C-yes/S-no/P-no/H-no

Full country breakfast
Evening refreshments
Sitting room, library,
fireplace, hot tub, games

An original miner's lodge—antique-filled rooms, down comforters, full breakfast, complimentary refreshments and fine hospitality; an unforgettable experience! In National Register of Historic Places.   E-mail: stay@oldminerslodge.com *Web site:* oldminerslodge.com

PARK CITY

Snowed Inn
3770 N Hwy 224, 84060
435-649-5713 Fax: 435-645-7672
800-545-7669
Pat Glackin?Alexandria Bullert
All year

90-415-B&B
10 rooms, 10 pb
Visa, MC, AmEx, •
C-yes/S-ltd/P-no/H-yes

Continental breakfast
Lunch & dinner (seasonal)
Complimentary sherry,
restaurant & bar, sitting
room, hot tub

All rooms have private bath, color TV, telephone, Jacuzzi on back deck. We cater for business groups, retreats, wedding receptions.

SALT LAKE CITY

Anton Boxrud B&B Inn
57 South 600 E, 84102
801-363-8035 Fax: 801-596-1316
800-524-5511
Jane & Jerome Johnson
All year

98-B&B
6 rooms, 3 pb
Visa, MC, *Rated*
C-ltd/S-no/P-no/H-no

Full breakfast
Hot tubs (winter), sitting
room, robes, down
comforters

The interior of this "Grand Old Home" is replete with beveled and stain-glass windows, burled woodwork, hardwood floors and pocked doors. Come be pampered.
E-mail: antonboxrud@inquo.net *Web site:* netoriginals.com/antonboxrud/

Haxton Manor B&B
943 E South Temple, 84102
801-363-4646 Fax: 801-363-4686
Buffi & Douglas King
All year

99-169-B&B
7 rooms, 7 pb
Visa, MC, AmEx,
Rated, •
C-ltd/S-no/P-no/H-yes
Spanish

Continental plus breakfast
Tea, snacks
Sitting room, library, Jacuzzi,
fireplace, cable TV,
conferences

English styled historic country Inn, conveniently located within walking distance of the university and downtown Salt Lake City. *E-mail:* innkeepers@haxtonmanor.com
Web site: haxtonmanor.com

Mountain Hollow B&B Inn
10209 S Dimple Dell Rd, 84092
801-942-3428 Fax: 801-733-7187
800-757-3428
Doug & Kathy Larson
All year

85-175-B&B
10 rooms, 5 pb
Visa, MC, AmEx,
Rated, •
C-ltd/S-no/P-no/H-ltd

Continental plus buffet
Snacks
Sitting room, library, Jacuzzi,
videos, hot tub, game room,
fireplace

Find the ambiance of a small European Inn with a western flavor nestled in the foothills of the Wasatch Mountains, just 15 minutes from World-class skiing, hiking, mountain biking, and bird watching. Antiques, trees, comfort. *E-mail:* sky@aros.net
Web site: mountainhollow.com

Saltair B&B
164 S 900 E, 84102
801-533-8184 Fax: 801-595-0332
800-733-8184
Jan Bartlett, Nancy Saxton
All year

79-149-B&B
7 rooms, 4 pb
Most CC, *Rated*, •
C-ltd/S-no/P-no/H-no

Full breakfast
Snacks, complimentary wine
Sitting room, A/C, hot tubs,
fresh flowers, robes, down
comforters

Historic Victorian charm complements queen brass beds & period furnishings. Near University of Utah, historic downtown, skiing & canyons. *E-mail:* saltair@saltlakebandb.com
Web site: saltlakebandb.com

Spruces B&B Inn
6151 S 900 E, 84121
801-268-8762 Fax: 801-268-6652
8SP-RUCES-BB
Richard & Amy Richardson
All year

69-99-B&B
4 rooms, 4 pb
Most CC, •
C-yes/S-no/P-no/H-no
Spanish, Japanese

Full breakfast
Snacks
Sitt. rm., Jacuzzis, stes., cable
TV, kitchenettes, priv. decks
& entrances

Our charming country inn is conveniently priced, brimming with extras and ideally located for your perfect getaway. Nestled amidst towering spruces, our historic farmhouse provides a delightful, intimate atmosphere. *E-mail:* relax@thespruces.com

SALT LAKE CITY

Wildflowers B&B
936 E 1700 S, 84105
801-466-0600 Fax: 801-466-4728
800-569-0009
Cill Sparks & Jeri Parker
All year

85-145-B&B
5 rooms, 5 pb
Visa, MC, AmEx,
Rated, •
S-no/P-no/H-no
French

Full breakfast
Restaurant nearby
Sitting room, library, reading
room, deck, stained glass
windows

National Historic 1891 Victorian offering delights of past and comforts of the present. Wildflower gardens, close to park, downtown, ski resorts.   E-mail: lark2spur@aol.com
Web site: wildflowersbb.com

ST. GEORGE

Greene Gate Village B&B
76 W Tabernacle St, 84770
435-628-6999 Fax: 435-628-0989
800-628-6999
John Greene
All year

69-129-B&B
12 rooms, 9 pb
Visa, MC, *Rated*, •
C-yes/S-no/P-yes/H-yes

Full breakfast
Lunch, Dinner
Soft drinks on arrival, sitting
room, hot tubs, tennis courts,
pool

Restored original pioneer home in a unique village close to downtown but in a quiet neighborhood. Close to Zion, Grand Canyon   E-mail: stay@greenegate.com
Web site: greenegate.com

Seven Wives Inn
217 N 100 West, 84770
435-628-3737 Fax: 435-628-5646
800-600-3737
David & Shellee Taylor
All year

70-125-B&B
13 rooms, 13 pb
Most CC, *Rated*, •
C-yes/S-no/P-no/H-ltd

Full breakfast
Lunch & tea room
Pool, conference facility,
sitting room, organ, golf &
tennis nearby

1870s pioneer home on National Register, furnished in antiques. Heart of St. George, close to national parks. Honeymoon suite with whirlpool tub room   E-mail: seven@infowest.com
Web site: sevenwivesinn.com

Vermont

ALBURG

**Thomas Mott Homestead
B&B**
63 Blue Rock Rd, 05440
802-796-3736 Fax: 802-796-3736
800-348-0843
Patrick J. Schallert, Sr.
All year

75-95-B&B
5 rooms, 5 pb
Most CC, *Rated*, •
C-ltd/S-no/P-no/H-no

Full breakfast menu
Afternoon tea, snacks
Sitting room, library, tennis
court nearby, Swim at Lake
Champlain

*75 foot private boatdock; swimming; canoeing; snorkeling; quilting decor; hand feed hundreds of quail; bike & hike; R&R; four seasons of charm.
E-mail:* tmott@together.net *Web site:* thomas-mott-bb.com

ANDOVER

Inn at Highview
753 E Hill Rd, 05143
802-875-2724 Fax: 802-875-4021
Greg Bohan & Sal Massaro
All year, exc. 2 wk. May

95-155-B&B
8 rooms, 8 pb
Visa, MC,
C-yes/S-no/P-ltd/H-no
Italian, Spanish

Full breakfast
Dinner—Sat. only
Sitting room, library, sauna,
pool, hiking

Vermont of your dreams. Secluded elegance; breathtaking views. 8 luxurious rooms with private baths, fabulous food. Tennis/golf nearby.   E-mail: hiview@aol.com
Web site: innathighview.com

ANDOVER

Rowell's Inn
1834 Simonsville Rd, 05143
802-875-3658 Fax: 802-875-3680
800-728-0842
Louise & Ski Haley
All year exc. April

110-195-MAP
5 rooms, 5 pb
Rated, •
C-ltd/S-yes/P-no/H-no

Full breakfast
Dinner included
Afternoon tea, tavern, sitting
room

1820 stagecoach hotel on National Register of Historic Places. Antique furnishings, hearty food. E-mail: inkeep@rowellsinn.com *Web site:* rowellsinn.com

ARLINGTON

Arlington Inn
PO Box 369, 05250
802-375-6532 Fax: 802-375-6534
800-443-9442
Bill & Sherrie Noonan
All year

115-265-B&B
18 rooms, 18 pb
Most CC, *Rated*, •
C-ltd/S-no
French

Full breakfast
Free dessert with dinner
Cookies and cider,
Restaurant, bar, sitting room;
tennis court

An exquisite romantic, 1848 Greek Revival mansion. 18 luxurious rooms, many with Jacuzzis and fireplaces, all with private baths. Gourmet candlelight dining, elegantly prepared by Executive Chef, Michael Hasenstaub. 1999 Yankee magazine's "Editor's Pick" E-mail: arlinn@sover.net *Web site:* arlingtoninn.com

---

Country Willows c.1850
332 E Arlington Rd, 05250
802-375-0019 Fax: 802-375-8054
800-796-2585
Anne & Ron Weber
All year

95-150-B&B
5 rooms, 5 pb
Visa, MC, AmEx, *Rated*
C-ltd/S-no/P-no/H-no

Full breakfast
Sitting room, suites, fireplace,
cable TV, conferences

Gracious Queen Anne Victorian Inn, c.1850. National Register Historic Landmark. Intimate and romantic! E-mail: cw@sover.net *Web site:* countrywillows.com

---

Hill Farm Inn
458 Hill Farm Rd, 05250
802-375-2269 Fax: 802-375-9918
800-882-2545
Kathleen & Craig Yanez
All year

80-185-B&B
15 rooms
Most CC, *Rated*
C-yes/S-no/P-no/H-no

Full country breakfast
Afternoon tea, snacks
Sitting room, cable TV,
families welcome,
accommodate business
travelers

One of Vermont's first country inns. Large farmhouse plus 4 cottages set on 50 peaceful acres. Beautiful mountain and valley views. E-mail: hillfarm@vermontel.com
Web site: hillfarminn.com

Shenandoah Farm
Battenkill Rd, 05250
802-375-6372
Woody Masterson
All year

80-B&B
5 rooms, 3 pb
Rated, •
C-yes/S-yes/P-no/H-no

Full breakfast
Comp. wine, tea
Sitting room, piano, library,
fishing/canoeing/tubing

Beautifully restored 1820 colonial furnished with antiques, overlooking Battenkill River and rolling meadows. Near skiing, golf, tennis

---

West Mountain Inn
PO Box 481, 05250
802-375-6516 Fax: 802-375-6553
The Carlson Family
All year

149-249-MAP
15 rooms, 15 pb
Visa, MC, AmEx,
Rated, •
C-yes/S-ltd/P-no/H-yes
French

Full breakfast
Dinner included, bar
Fruit, chocolate llama, piano,
dining room, flowers,
conference room

*150-acre hillside estate; hike or ski woodland trails. Fish the Battenkill. Hearthside dining, charming rooms. Relax & enjoy the llamas, goats and rabbits.
E-mail:* info@westmountaininn.com *Web site:* westmountaininn.com

BENNINGTON ───────────────

Alexandra B&B Inn	85-145-B&B	Full breakfast
RR2 Box 3617, 05201	12 rooms, 12 pb	Sitting room, library,
802-442-5619 Fax: 802-442-5592	Most CC, *Rated*, •	Jacuzzis, suites, firepalces,
888-207-9386	C-ltd/S-no/P-ltd/H-yes	cable TV, VCR
Alex Koks & Andra Erickson	French, German, Dutch	
All year		

A tasteful restored cape from 1859 with 6 deluxe rooms in main building and 6 more in recent colonial. Modern deluxe amenities. Gourmet breakfasts. E-mail: alexandr@sover.net *Web site:* alexandrainn.com

Four Chimneys Inn & Rest.	125-195-B&B	Continental plus breakfast
21 West Rd (Rte 9), 05201	11 rooms, 11 pb	Restaurant, bar
802-447-3500 Fax: 802-447-3692	Most CC, *Rated*, •	Lunch, dinner, sitting room,
800-649-3503	C-ltd/S-no/P-no/H-yes	library, golf closeby
Ron and Judith Schefkind	Spanish, Italian	
All year		

One of New England's premier inns. Classic French cuisine by master chef. Beautiful 11-acre estate, plush guest rooms with modern amenities and cocktail lounge. E-mail: innkeeper@fourchimneys.com *Web site:* fourchimneys.com/

Molly Stark Inn	70-175-B&B	Full gourmet breakfast
1067 E Main St, 05201	7 rooms, 7 pb	Champagne dinner available
802-442-9631 Fax: 802-442-9631	Most CC, *Rated*	Den with woodstove, TV,
800-356-3076	C-ltd/S-no/P-no/H-no	hardwood floors, antique,
Cammi & Reed Fendler		quilts, claw foot tubs
All year		

Charming 1860 Victorian, incl. private cottage with Jacuzzi. Decorated with country American, antiques, classical music playing. Sunporch, wood stoves, Jacuzzis. Champagne/dinner package E-mail: mollyinn@vermontel.com *Web site:* mollystarkinn.com

BETHEL ───────────────

Greenhurst Inn	50-100-B&B	Continental plus breakfast
RR2 Box 60, 05032	13 rooms, 7 pb	Sitting room, library, cable
802-234-9474	Visa, MC, •	TV, conference facilities
800-510-2553	C-yes/S-ltd/P-ltd/H-no	
Lyle & Claire Wolf	Some Spanish	
All year		

National Register of Historic Places. Library of 3000 volumes. Seven miles from the finest restaurant in the state.

BRANDON ───────────────

Churchill House Inn	95-210-MAP	Full breakfast and dinner
3128 Forest Dale Rd, 05733	9 rooms, 9 pb	Lower rate for breakfast only,
802-247-3078	Visa, MC, AmEx, [y.]	bar
877-248-7444	S-no/P-no/H-no	Swimming pool, golf, library,
Linda & Richard Daybell		piano, fishing, biking, hiking,
Closed April		skiing

Century-old farmhouse on the edge of Green Mountain Nat'l Forest. Welcoming ambiance and gourmet dining. E-mail: innkeeper@churchillhouse.com *Web site:* churchillhouseinn.com

BRATTLEBORO ───────────────

1868 Crosby House	100-140-B&B	Full breakfast
175 Western Avenue, 05301	3 rooms, 3 pb	Snacks
802-257-4914	Most CC, •	Sitting room, library, Jacuzzi,
800-528-1868	C-ltd/S-no/P-no/H-no	Suite, cable TV, fireplaces
Lynn Kuralt		
All year		

Historic home decorated with family heirlooms and collected antiques, luxurious accommodations, elegant gourmet breakfasts. Private baths, fireplaces, whirlpool, delightful amenities. Near downtown. E-mail: lynn@crosbyhouse.com *Web site:* crosbyhouse.com

BROOKFIELD

Birch Meadow Luxury B&B	95-B&B	Full breakfast
RR1 Box 294A, 05036	4 rooms, 4 pb	Cont. breakfast- cabins
802-276-3156 Fax: 802-276-3423	Visa, MC, *Rated*	Fireplaces, horseback riding,
Mary & Matt Comerford	C-yes/S-yes/P-ltd/H-ltd	pool, antique stove
All year		

"A place to get away from it all, yet close to everything." Cozy cabins for that special time together. Great for a honeymoon or family vacation. In the mtns. with spectacular views & complete privacy.   Web site: bbhost.com/birchmeadow

BURLINGTON

Heart of the Village Inn	95-195-B&B	Full breakfast
PO Box 953, 05482	9 rooms, 9 pb	Afternoon tea
802-985-2800 Fax: 802-985-2870	Visa, MC, AmEx, ●	Sitting room, Jacuzzi, cable
877-808-1834	C-yes/S-no/P-no/H-yes	TV, conferences
Bobbe, Stephanie, LouAnn		
All year		

Restored Queen Anne Victorian across from the Shelburne Museum. We serve fresh local products breakfasts.   E-mail: innkeeper@heartofthevillage.com *Web site:* heartofthevillage.com

Richmond Victorian Inn, The	70-110-B&B	Full breakfast
PO Box 652, 05477	6 rooms, 6 pb	Sitting room, television/VCR,
802-434-4410 Fax: 802-434-4411	Visa, MC, AmEx, ●	good conversation
888-242-3362	C-ltd/S-no/P-no/H-no	
Gail M. Clark	Some German	
All year		

1880's Queen Anne Victorian B&B filled with antiques; nestled in a small Vermont town minutes from Burlington. Full country breakfast served.   E-mail: gailclar@together.net *Web site:* together.net/~gailclar/frames.htm

CHELSEA

Shire Inn	105-210-B&B/MAP	Full breakfast
PO Box 37, 05038	6 rooms, 6 pb	Dinner by reservation
802-685-3031 Fax: 802-685-3871	Visa, MC, *Rated*, ●	Sitting room & porch,
800-441-6908	C-ltd/S-no/P-no/H-no	fireplaces in guestrooms,
Jay & Karen Keller		bicycles
All year		

1832 brick mansion. Large, wonderful guest room. 23 acres & river. Gracious candlelight dining. Pure romance in a vintage Vermont village!   E-mail: desk@shireinn.com *Web site:* shireinn.com

CHESTER

Fullerton Inn	99-149-MAP	Continental breakfast
PO Box 188, 05143	21 rooms, 21 pb	Dinner included, lunch
802-875-2444 Fax: 802-875-6414	Visa, MC, AmEx, ●	available
Jerry & Robin Szawerda	S-no/P-no/H-no	Restaurant, bar, sitting room,
All year		suites, fireplace, cableTV,
		conference room

Elegant yet comfortable country inn on the Village Green. Immaculate rooms, professional and courteous staff. Casual dining on our front porch, breakfast or dinner. E-mail: getaway@fullertoninn.com *Web site:* fullertoninn.com

Henry Farm Inn	66-90-B&B	Full breakfast
2206 Green Mt Turnpike, 05143	7 rooms, 7 pb	Tea, coffee, cookies
802-875-2674 Fax: 802-875-1510	*Rated*, ●	Sitting room, library, pond,
800-723-8213	C-yes/S-ltd/P-no/H-ltd	hiking
Lee and Stuart Gaw		
All year		

1750s farmhouse in charming country setting in the glorious Green Mountains. Full country breakfast each morning.   E-mail: hfinn@vermontel.net *Web site:* henryfarm.vermontel.net

CHESTER

Hugging Bear Inn & Shoppe	75-125-B&B	Full breakfast
244 Main St, 05143	6 rooms, 6 pb	Afternoon beverages, snacks
802-875-2412	Most CC, *Rated*	2 living rooms, library, den-
Fax: 802-875-3823	C-yes/S-no/P-no/H-no	games, toys, 10% shoppe
800-325-0519		discount
Georgette Thomas		
Closed Xmas/Thanksgiving		

Elegant Victorian in National Historic District, on the Village Green, thousands of Teddy Bears throughout, Extensive Teddy Bear shop. We are a family inn. FUN! Disc't. in shop for guests. E-mail: georgette@huggingbear.com *Web site:* huggingbear.com

Inn Victoria	105-175-B&B	Full breakfast
PO Box 788, 05143	7 rooms, 7 pb	Afternoon tea, wine
800-732-4288	Visa, MC, Most CC, ●	Tea Pot Shoppe on,
N Gauthier & C Hasbrouck	C-yes/S-no/P-no/H-no	premises, sitting room, hot
All year		tub

Beautiful circa-1850 home filled with antiques, soaking tubs, queen beds, bountiful breakfasts, teas & treats, piles of pillows and sumptuous sheets.   Web site: innvictoria.com

Madrigal Inn, The	95-120-B&B	Full breakfast
61 Williams River Rd, 05143	11 rooms, 11 pb	Dinner by reservation
802-463-1339 Fax: 802-463-8169	Most CC, *Rated*, ●	Afternoon tea, snacks,
800-854-2208	C-yes/S-no/P-no/H-yes	hiking, bike routes, sitting
All year		room, library

Beauty inside & out. Romantic guest rooms with baths. 60 acres mountain/meadow landscape.   E-mail: madrigal@sover.net *Web site:* sover.net/~madrigal/

Stone Hearth Inn, The	60-150-B&B	Full breakfast
698 Vt Rt 11 W, 05143	10 rooms, 10 pb	Dinner (by reserv. only)
802-875-2525	*Rated*, ●	Lunch, wine cellar, pub,
Fax: 802-875-4688	C-yes/S-ltd/P-no/H-ltd	game room, library, pianos,
Janet & Don Strohmeyer	Fr., Dutch, Flem., Ger.	whirlpool spas
All year		

Lovingly restored country inn built in 1810—beams, fireplaces, wide pine floors, attached barn. Family atmosphere.   E-mail: shinn@vermontel.com
Web site: virtualvermont.com/countryinn/shinn

CHITTENDEN

Tulip Tree Inn	150-400-MAP	Full breakfast
49 Dam Rd, 05737	9 rooms, 9 pb	Dinner included
802-483-6213	Visa, MC, *Rated*, ●	Full bar & wine cellar, sitting
Fax: 802-483-2623	C-ltd/S-no/P-no/H-no	room, library
800-707-0017	German	
Ed & Rosemary McDowell		
Exc. Apr, Nov to Thksgvg		

Small, antique-filled country inn, hidden away in the Green Mountains. Gracious dining, homemade breads and desserts, wine list. New room decor. One of Uncle Ben's 10 best. E-mail: ttinn@sover.net *Web site:* tuliptreeinn.com

CRAFTSBURY COMMON

Inn on the Common, The	240-290-B&B/MAP	Full breakfast
PO Box 75, 05827	18 rooms, 18 pb	Dinner (MAP), bar
802-586-9619 Fax: 802-586-2249	Visa, MC, *Rated*, ●	Sitting rooms, library, pool,
800-521-2233	C-ltd/S-yes/P-ltd/H-no	sauna, tennis, walking &
Joan & Michael Schmitt		biking
All year		

Superbly decorated, meticulously appointed, wonderful cuisine, complete recreation facilities. Everything an inn connoisseur could want.   E-mail: info@innonthecommon.com
Web site: innonthecommon.com/

DANBY

Quail's Nest B&B, The
PO Box 221, 05739
802-293-5099 Fax: 802-293-6300
800-599-6444
Greg & Nancy Diaz
All year

50-110-B&B
6 rooms, 6 pb
Most CC, *Rated*, •
C-ltd/S-no/P-no/H-no

Full breakfast
Complimentary tea & snacks
Sitting room with fireplace,
library, horseshoes, deck &
garden, bicycles

Nestled among the Green Mountains in a quiet Vermont village; home-baked breakfasts followed by relaxing country fun! Conference facility. Diets upon request. Special retreat packages, guided hikes.   E-mail: quailsnest@quailsnestbandb.com *Web site:* quailsnestbandb.com

Silas Griffith Inn
178 Main St, 05739
802-293-5567 Fax: 802-293-5559
800-545-1509
Paul & Lois Dansereau
All year

74-120-B&B
17 rooms, 14 pb
Visa, MC, AmEx,
Rated, •
C-yes/S-no

Full breakfast
Restaurant, bar, dinner
available
Aftn. beverages, cookies,
sitting room, library, pool,
conference 50 ppl.

Lovingly restored Victorian mansion and carriage house. Relax in antique-filled rooms; enjoy a quiet 19th-century village.   E-mail: sginn@together.net *Web site:* silasgriffith.com

DERBY LINE

Derby Village Inn
PO Box 1085, 05830
802-873-3604 Fax: 802-873-3047
C. McCormick & S. Steplar
All year

75-100-B&B
5 rooms, 5 pb
Most CC,
C-yes/S-no/P-no/H-no

Full breakfast
Snacks, complimentary wine
Sitting room, library,
fireplace, cable TV, suites,
conf. facilities

5 gracious rooms, private baths, 3 tiled fireplaces, original woodwork, library, sunporch, full breakfast, activities galore.   E-mail: dviband@together.net
Web site: homepages.together.net/~dvibandb

DORSET

Cornucopia of Dorset
PO Box 307, 05251
802-867-5751 Fax: 802-867-5753
800-566-5751
Trish & John Reddoch
Closed April & Christmas

125-255-B&B
5 rooms, 5 pb
Visa, MC, AmEx,
Rated, •
C-ltd/S-no/P-no/H-no

Full unique breakfast
Aftn. tea, snacks, wine
Sitting room, library, suites,
fireplace, cable, TV, wines for
sale

5 gracious accommodations including a cottage suite. Candlelit breakfasts, simple elegance, unmatched service and amenities.   E-mail: innkeepers@cornucopiaofdorset.com
Web site: cornucopiaofdorset.com

Marble West Inn
PO Box 847, 05251
802-867-4155 Fax: 802-867-5731
800-453-7629
Bonnie & Paul Quinn
All year

90-175-B&B/MAP
8 rooms, 8 pb
Visa, MC, AmEx,
C-ltd/S-no/P-no/H-no

Full breakfast
Dinner included with MAP
Refreshments, afternoon tea,
sitting room, library

Historic 1840 Greek Revival inn— elegant, quiet, peaceful, off busy main road, with mountain views, gardens, and ponds.   E-mail: marwest@sover.net *Web site:* marblewestinn.com

ENOSBURG FALLS

Berkson Farms
1205 W Berkshire Rd, 05450
802-933-2522
Dick & Joanne Kessler
All year

55-65-B&B
4 rooms, 1 pb
C-yes/S-no/P-yes/H-no

Full breakfast
Special menus by
arrangement
Sitting room, bicycles,
working dairy farm, farm
animals, near golf

Old restored farmhouse, full working dairy farm with large variety of animals.

Maplewood Inn, Fair Haven, VT

FAIR HAVEN

Maplewood Inn
RR 1, Box 4460, 05743
802-265-8039
Fax: 802-265-8210
800-253-7729
Cindy & Doug Baird
All year

80-145-B&B
5 rooms, 5 pb
Most CC, *Rated*, •
C-ltd/S-ltd

Continental plus breakfast
Complimentary wine, tea,
coffee
BYOB tavern, chocolates,
sitting room, toiletries,
library, TV & A/C in rms

Romantic, elegantly appointed, suites & many common areas. Turndown service, cordial bar. Fireplace, bikes, antiques. In Lakes Region close to everything.
E-mail: maplewd@sover.net *Web site:* sover.net/~maplewd

FAIRLEE

Silver Maple Lodge/Cottages
520 US Route 5 S, 05045
802-333-4852
800-666-1946
Scott/Sharon Wright   All year

56-89-B&B
17 rooms, 9 pb
Visa, MC, *Rated*, •
C-yes/S-yes/P-ltd/H-ltd

Continental breakfast
Sitting room, fireplaces,
picnic area, cottages, bicycle
& canoe rental

Quaint country inn located in scenic resort area; convenient to antique shops, fishing, golf, swimming, tennis & winter skiing. Ballooning packages available.
E-mail: scott@silvermaplelodge.com *Web site:* silvermaplelodge.com

GAYSVILLE

Laolke Lodge
PO Box 107, 05746
802-234-9205
Ms. Olive Pratt
All year

25-35-MAP
5 rooms
•
C-yes/S-yes/P-ltd/H-no

Full breakfast
Evening meal
Sitting room, piano, pool,
color TV, tennis, river
swimming, tubing

Family-style vacations in modern, rustic log cabin. Home cooking. Near skiing, horseback riding, fishing, hunting, boating, and other Vermont attractions.
E-mail: laolke@juno.com

GOSHEN

Blueberry Hill Inn
RFD 3, 05733
802-247-6735
Fax: 802-247-3983
800-448-0707
Tony Clark, Shari Brown
2/15-3/31; 6/1-10/31

130-MAP
8 rooms, 8 pb
Visa, MC, *Rated*, •
C-yes/S-ltd/P-no/H-yes
French, Spanish

Full breakfast
Dinner included, afternoon
tea
Sitting room, swimming
pond, 75km cross country
ski trails

1800 charming inn, gourmet cooking, dining by candlelight. Relax in an atmosphere of elegance and leisure. Fishing, swimming, hiking, cross-country skiing.
E-mail: tc@blueberryhillinn.com *Web site:* blueberryhillinn.com

GREENSBORO

Highland Lodge	185-245-MAP	Full breakfast
RR1, Box 1290, 05841	22 rooms, 22 pb	Lunch (fee), dinner included
802-533-2647 Fax: 802-533-7494	Visa, MC, Disc, •	Sitting rooms, library, tennis,
David & Wilhelmina Smith	C-yes/S-ltd/P-no/H-yes	beach, lawn game, golf, lake,
12/19-3/15; 5/29-10/12	Dutch	ski trails

A most comfortable, extremely clean, nicely furnished family resort with rooms & cottages. Lakeside beach & 30 miles of packed cross-country ski trails. Play program, boats, fine dining. E-mail: hlodge@connriver.net Web site: pbpub.com/vermont/hiland.htm

HANOVER

Stonecrest Farm B&B	129-144-B&B	Full breakfast
PO Box 504, 05088	6 rooms, 6 pb	Snacks, comp. wine
802-296-2425 Fax: 802-295-1135	Visa, MC, AmEx,	Sitting room, inn-to-inn canoe
800-730-2425	*Rated*, •	trips, down comforters,
Gail L. Sanderson	C-ltd/S-no/P-no/H-no	robes in room
Closed Dec 24-Jan 1	Some German, French	

Country setting 3.5 mi. from Dartmouth College. Gracious 1810 home offers antiques, terraces. All outdoor activities. 10% off 1-week stay, champagne for newlyweds, spec. group rates. Some telephones in rooms. E-mail: gail.sanderson@valley.net Web site: stonecrestfarm.com

JAMAICA

Three Mountain Inn	115-295-MAP	Full breakfast
Box 180, 05343	10 rooms, 8 pb	Dinner, bar
802-874-4140 800-532-9399	•	Sitting room, bicycles,
David, Stacy, & Baby Miles	C-ltd/S-yes/P-no/H-no	swimming pool
Exc. 4/15–5/15 & Nov		

Three Mountain Inn is all about you. Our mission is to exceed your expectations. We hope you will give us the opportunity. Our 18th century Inn evokes the period w/rich paneling & antiques, but the 21st Century is evident in our splendiferous amenities. E-mail: threemtn@sover.net Web site: threemountaininn.com/

JEFFERSONVILLE

Mannsview Inn	75-125-B&B	Full country breakfast
916 Rt 108 S, 05464	6 rooms, 2 pb	Complimentary wine
802-644-8321 Fax: 802-644-2006	Visa, MC, AmEx,	Sitting room, library,
888-937-6266	*Rated*, •	tournament billiard room,
The Manns All year	C-yes/S-no/P-no/H-no	antiques, whirlpool

Nationally recognized c.1855 colonial on Vermont's most scenic highway, 15 minutes from Stowe. On premises, canoe rentals, shuttle & 10,000 sq.ft. antique center. Closest inn to ski slopes. Fireplaces in rooms. E-mail: rsvp@mannsview.com Web site: mannsview.com

KILLINGTON

Hawk Inn & Mountain Rsrt.	260-340-B&B	Snacks, din., restaurant
HCR70 Box 64 Route 100, 05056	50 rooms, 50 pb	Bar service, sitt. rm., library,
802-672-3811 Fax: 802-672-5585	Most CC, *Rated*, •	bikes, tennis, hot tub, sauna,
800-685-HAWK	C-yes/S-ltd/P-no/H-yes	pool
J. Dinger All year		

Luxury resort Inn situated in the heart of the Green Mountains. Okomo, Killington & Woodstock nearby. Luxury private villas available. E-mail: hawkinn@vermontel.com Web site: hawkresort.com

Inn at Long Trail	68-230-B&B	Full breakfast
PO Box 267, 05751	20 rooms, 20 pb	Irish pub
802-775-7181 Fax: 802-747-7034	Visa, MC, •	Sitting room, hot tub,
800-325-2540	C-yes/S-yes/P-no/H-ltd	weekend Irish music
Murray & Patty McGrath		
Summer, fall, winter		

Rustic country inn/ski lodge high in the Vermont mountains. McGrath's Irish Pub serves pub menu daily and has live entertainment on weekends. Main dining room has candlelit dining during the fall and winter. Hot tub. E-mail: ilt@vermontel.com Web site: innatlongtrail.com

KILLINGTON

Mountain Meadows Lodge
285 Thundering Brook Rd,
05751
802-775-1010 Fax: 802-773-4459
800-370-4567
Mark and Michelle Werle
Ex. 4/15-6/1;10/15-11/21

105-300-B&B
18 rooms, 18 pb
Visa, MC, *Rated*, •
C-yes/S-ltd/P-no/H-ltd

Full breakfast
Dinner (fee), coffee, tea
Sitting room, pool, farm
animals, mountain getaway
packages

A casual, friendly family lodge in a beautiful secluded mountain and lake setting. Complete cross-country ski center. Converted 1856 farmhouse and barn. Fireplace in dining room.
E-mail: havefun@mtmeadowslodge.com *Web site:* mtmeadowslodge.com/

Salt Ash Inn
4758 Ft 100A, 05056
802-672-3748
800-SALT-ASH
Glen & Ann Stanford
All year

69-175-B&B/MAP
18 rooms, 18 pb
Visa, MC, *Rated*, •
C-ltd/S-yes/P-ltd/H-no

Continental breakfast
Dinner with MAP plan
Sitting room, piano, 10-
person California hot tub,
heated pool

Genuine old country inn with furnishings reflecting its rich past as an inn, general store, stagecoach stop, and post office. *E-mail:* innkepe@aol.com *Web site:* vermontvacation.com

Snowed Inn
Miller Brook Rd, 05751
802-422-3407 Fax: 802-422-8126
800-311-5406
Manfred & Jeanne Karlhuber
6/15-4/15

80-125-B&B
19 rooms, 19 pb
Most CC, *Rated*, •
C-yes/S-ltd/P-no/H-ltd
German

Continental plus breakfast
Sitting room, Jacuzzis, suites,
fireplaces, cable TV, exercise
room

Distinctive design and casual grace in a private setting. Contemporary country rooms/suites complemented by a fieldstone fireplace lounge, greenhouse breakfast room, outdoor hot tub overlooking brook. *E-mail:* snowdinn@sover.net *Web site:* snowedinn.com/

Vermont Inn, The
HC 34, Box 37J, 05701
802-775-0708 Fax: 802-773-2440
800-541-7795
Megan & Greg Smith
Memorial Day-April 15

50-205-B&B
18 rooms, 18 pb
Most CC, *Rated*, •
C-ltd/S-no/P-no/H-yes
French, Spanish

Full Country breakfast
MAP available, bar
Pool, sauna, whirlpool,
tennis, meeting room, A/C &
fireplace in some rooms

Award-winning cuisine; fireside dining (winter), spectacular mountain views. Screened porch, weddings. Minutes to Killington and Pico ski area. Extensive gardens.
E-mail: vtinn@aol.com *Web site:* vermontinn.com

LOWER WATERFORD

Rabbit Hill Inn
PO Box 55, 05848
802-748-5168 Fax: 802-748-8342
800-76-BUNNY
Brian & Leslie Mulcahy
All year

235-340-B&B
18 rooms, 18 pb
Visa, MC, *Rated*, •
C-ltd/S-no/P-no/H-yes
French

Full 4-course breakfast
Restaurant, bar
Afternoon tea & pastry, lawn
games, swim pond, golf, 10
fireplace bdrms

Stylish country inn established 1795. Peaceful, storybook 15-acre setting. Heartfelt service and commitment to detail, dining, decor and music. *E-mail:* info@rabbithillinn.com
Web site: rabbithillinn.com

LUDLOW

Andrie Rose Inn, The
13 Pleasant St, 05149
802-228-4846 Fax: 802-228-7910
800-223-4846
Jack & Ellen Fisher
All year

80-650-B&B/MAP
23 rooms, 23 pb
Visa, MC, AmEx, *Rated*
C-ltd/S-no/P-no/H-no

Continental plus breakfast
Tea, snacks, bar
Sitting room, library,
bicycles, jacuzzi, suites,
fireplace, cable tv

Elegant c.1829 country village. Okemo Ski Mountain.
E-mail: andrie@mail.tds.net *Web site:* andrieroseinn.com

Rabbit Hill Inn, Lower Waterford, VT

LUDLOW

Combes Family Inn, The	60-134-B&B/MAP	Full breakfast
953 E Lake Rd, 05149	11 rooms, 11 pb	Dinner available
802-228-8799	Visa, MC, AmEx,	Sitting room, piano, bicycles,
Ruth Combes	*Rated*, •	with bath & sitting room
4/15–5/15 closed	C-yes/S-ltd/P-ltd/H-yes	
	French	

The Combes Family Inn is a century-old farmhouse located on a quiet country back road. Queen size beds. E-mail: billcfi@aol.com *Web site:* combesfamilyinn.com/

Golden Stage Inn	89-110-B&B	Full breakfast
PO Box 218, 05153	10 rooms, 6 pb	Dinner, afternoon tea, snacks
802-226-7744 Fax: 802-226-7882	Visa, •	Sitting room, library,
800-253-8226	C-yes/S-no/P-ltd/H-yes	swimming pool, fireplaces,
Sandy & Peter Gregg	Swiss, German, French	cable TV, wine & beer
All year		

State coach stop in the 1790's, later an underground railroad link, this historic Colonial inn offers Vermont hospitality.

Governor's Inn, The	105-195-B&B	Full 3 course breakfast
86 Main St, 05149	9 rooms, 9 pb	Dinner available Wed-Sun
802-228-8830 Fax: 802-228-2961	Visa, MC, *Rated*, •	Picnic lunches, Culinary
800-Governor	C-ltd/S-no/P-no/H-no	Magic Cooking School, A/C,
Jim & Cathy Kubec		fireplaces in some rooms
All year		

Stylish, romantic, antique furnished, Victorian Inn c.1890. Beautiful fireplaces, generous hospitality, quiet town. E-mail: kubec@compuserve.com *Web site:* thegovernorsinn.com

LYNDONVILLE

Wildflower Inn, The	95-110-B&B	Full breakfast
Darling Hill Rd, 05851	21 rooms, 21 pb	Afternoon tea & snacks
802-626-8310 Fax: 802-626-3039	Visa, MC, *Rated*	Lib., conf. facility, pool, hot
800-627-8310	C-yes/S-no/P-no/H-ltd	tub, sauna, tennis &
Jim & Mary O'Reilly	Nepali	basketball cts.
All year		

Perched on a ridge overlooking the verdant hills and valleys of Vermont's northeast kingdom, the inn's 500 acres offer plenty of activity to keep all ages busy and happy. Near Burke Mtn. skiing. E-mail: wldflwrinn@aol.com *Web site:* wildflowerinn.com

MANCHESTER

1811 House
PO Box 39, 05254
802-362-1811 Fax: 802-362-2443
800-432-1811
Bruce & Marnie Duff
All year

120-230-B&B
14 rooms, 14 pb
Most CC, •
C-ltd/S-no/P-no/H-no

Full breakfast
Complimentary sherry
Sitting room, library, canopy
beds, fireplaces, gardens,
pond, mtn. view

Unequaled charm in a Revolutionary War-era building furnished with English & American antiques. E-mail: stay1811@vermontel.com Web site: 1811house.com

Battenkill Inn, The
PO Box 948, 05254
802-362-4213 Fax: 802-362-0975
800-441-1628
Laine and Yoshi Akiyama
Closed Christmas

100-165-B&B
11 rooms, 11 pb
Visa, MC, *Rated*
C-ltd/S-ltd/P-no/H-yes
Japanese

Full breakfast
Afternoon tea, snacks
Sitting room, library,
fireplaces, cable TV, spa
passes, meeting room

On seven acres bordered by the Battenkill River, classic 1840 Victorian farmhouse, high ceilings, fireplaces, eleven guest rooms, private baths, award winning breakfasts, minutes to Manchester. E-mail: innfo@battenkillinn.com Web site: battenkillinn.com/

Inn at Manchester, The
Route 7A, Box 41, 05254
802-362-1793 Fax: 802-362-3218
800-273-1793
Stan & Harriet Rosenberg
All year

109-179-B&B
18 rooms, 18 pb
Most CC, *Rated*, •
C-ltd/S-no/P-no/H-no

Full breakfast
Complimentary wine,
afternoon tea
Sitt. rm., lib., frplc., piano,
swimming pool, 3 lounges,
porch, A/C

Beautiful, restored Victorian mansion. On National Registry of Historic Places. Golf, tennis, shopping, antiquing nearby. E-mail: iman@vermontel.com Web site: innatmanchester.com

Inn at Ormsby Hill, The
1842 Main St, 05255
802-362-1163 Fax: 802-362-5176
800-670-2841
Ted and Chris Sprague
All year

165-325-B&B
10 rooms, 10 pb
Visa, MC, •
C-ltd/S-no/P-no/H-yes

Full breakfast
Afternoon tea
Sitting room, library, all
rooms have a fireplace and
Jacuzzi for two.

Renowned for comfort, heartfelt hospitality and profound attention to detail. Canopies, fireplaces, air-conditioning, luxurious bathrooms with Jacuzzis for two. E-mail: ormsby@vermontel.com Web site: ormsbyhill.com

Johnny Seesaw's
PO Box 68, 05152
802-824-5533 Fax: 802-824-5533
800-424-CSAW
Gary & Nancy Okun
All year exc. April–May

76-190-B&B/MAP
30 rooms, 27 pb
Visa, MC, *Rated*, •
C-yes/S-yes/P-yes/H-ltd

Full breakfast
Dinner (MAP winter)
Afternoon tea, full bar,
tennis, swimming pool,
library, sitting room

Unique country lodge, rooms with private baths, cottages with king beds & fireplaces, licensed pub, full dining room, quarter mile E. of Bromley Mtn. E-mail: gary@jseesaw.com Web site: jseesaw.com

Manchester Highlands Inn
PO Box 1754, 05255
802-362-4565 Fax: 802-362-4028
800-743-4565
Patricia & Robert Eichorn
Exc. midweek Apr & Nov

105-145-B&B
15 rooms, 15 pb
Visa, MC, AmEx,
Rated, •
C-ltd/S-yes/P-no/H-no

Full breakfast
Dinner by arrangement
Sitting rm., bar, snacks, 7
rooms with canopy beds,
carriage house remodeled

Romantic Victorian inn, charming rooms. Resident cat. Homemade country breakfast-in-bed. E-mail: relax@highlandsinn.com Web site: highlandsinn.com

MANCHESTER

Meadowbrook Inn
RR1 Box 145, 05148
802-824-6444 Fax: 802-824-4335
800-498-6445
Tony & Madeline Rundella
Closed April

85-200-B&B/MAP
8 rooms, 8 pb
Most CC, •
C-ltd/S-no/P-no/H-no

Full breakfast
Dinner, snacks, rest.
Bar service, sitting rm., 5
rooms with fireplace,
whirlpool tub

Quiet country inn nestled in the Green Mountain Nat'l Forest. Soft, antique filled rooms.
Candlelight dining with fireplaces and views   E-mail: innkeeper@meadowbinn.com
Web site: meadowbinn.com

MANCHESTER VILLAGE

Reluctant Panther Inn, The
Box 678, 05254
802-362-2568 Fax: 802-362-2586
800-822-2331
Maye & Robert Bachofen
All year

198-575-MAP
16 rooms, 16 pb
Visa, MC, AmEx,
Rated, •
C-ltd/S-no/P-no/H-ltd
French, German,
Spanish

Full breakfast
Dinner included, rest.
Bar service, aftn. tea, sitting
room, Jacuzzis, suites,
frplcs., cable

Handsome collection of exquisitely decorated 2 person Jacuzzi/2 fireplace suites; other
deluxe fireplace rooms.   E-mail: stay@reluctantpanther.com *Web site:* reluctantpanther.com

Village Country Inn
PO Box 408, 05254
802-362-1792 Fax: 802-362-7238
800-370-0300
Anne & Jay Degen
All year

160-375-MAP
33 rooms, 33 pb
Most CC, *Rated*, •
C-ltd/S-no/P-no/H-ltd

Full breakfast
Candlelight dinner included
Tavern, sitting room, pool,
fireplaces in luxury rooms,
dining room, A/C

"A Boutique Hotel" with country inn personalized service. Located in the heart of the
Green Mountains. Ask about romance packages.   E-mail: vci@vermontel.com
Web site: villagecountryinn.com

Wilburton Inn, The
PO Box 468, 05254
802-362-2500 Fax: 802-362-1107
800-648-4944
Georgette Levis
All year

125-250-B&B/MAP
35 rooms, 35 pb
Visa, MC, AmEx,
C-yes/S-ltd/P-ltd/H-ltd

Full breakfast
Afternoon tea, bar service
Swimming pool, library,
tennis court, canoeing,
bicycle touring, hiking

A twenty acre Victorian estate overlooking spectacular Battenkill Valley. Sculptures, flow-
ers, and artworks adorn the estate.   E-mail: wilbuinn@sover.net *Web site:* wilburton.com

MIDDLEBURY

Inn at Lovers Lane, The
PO Box 66, 05734
802-758-2185
Pam & John Freilich
All year

85-145-B&B
3 rooms, 3 pb
Visa, MC, AmEx,
C-ltd/S-no/P-no/H-no
Some French

Full breakfast
Snacks, wine
Sitting room, suites, fireplace,
sunroom, breakfast room
and deck

Magnificent mountain and meadow views, expansive grounds, and elegantly appointed
rooms await you at our spacious, yet intimate, c.1830 Greek Revival Inn. Middlebury and
Lake Champlain only 9 miles away.   E-mail: innlovln@together.net

Middlebury Inn, The
14 Courthouse Square, 05753
802-388-4961 Fax: 802-388-4563
800-842-4666
Frank & Jane Emanuel
All year

88-350-B&B
75 rooms
Visa, MC, *Rated*, •
C-yes/S-ltd/P-ltd/H-yes

Continental breakfast
Restaurant, bar
Afternoon tea, A/C, TV,
sitting room, library, private
bath, bath phone

Elegant 1827 historic landmark. Distinctively decorated rooms. Gracious dining. Walk to
college, unique shops, historic sites; near Shelburn Museum & VT Teddy Bear Factory.
E-mail: midinnvt@sover.net *Web site:* middleburyinn.com

MILTON

Wright's Bay 1820	85-100-B&B	Continental plus breakfast
81 Eagle Mtn Harbor Rd, 05468	7 rooms, 4 pb	Sitting room, tennis court,
802-893-6717 Fax: 802-524-0084	Visa, MC, AmEx,	cottages, private beach
Bette Wood	C-yes/S-no/P-no/H-yes	
All year		

Private guest suite in 1820 farmhouse. Cottages on Lake Champlain. Private beach, tennis, biking, in country setting.   E-mail: bette81@aol.com

MONTGOMERY

Black Lantern Inn	85-150-MAP	Full breakfast
Route 118, 05470	16 rooms, 16 pb	Dinner, restaurant, bar
802-326-4507 Fax: 802-326-4077	Most CC, •	Sitting room, bicycles,
800-255-8661	C-yes/S-ltd/P-no/H-no	Jacuzzi, suites, fireplace,
Rita & Allan Kalsmith		cable TV, conferences
All year		

Winter: Cross-country skiing from door; 15 minutes from Jay Peak Ski Area. Summer: Swimming in natural waterfalls, near long trail, country auctions.   E-mail: blantern@ together.net *Web site:* blacklantern.com

MONTGOMERY CENTER

Phineas Swann	79-145-B&B	Full breakfast
PO Box 43, 05471	6 rooms, 4 pb	Afternoon tea, snacks
802-326-4306 Fax: 802-326-4306	Visa, MC, Disc, •	Sitting room, library, tennis
G. Bartolomeo & M. Bindler	C-ltd/S-no/P-no/H-no	court, Jacuzzis, fireplaces,
All year		gardens, sun deck

E-mail: phineas@sover.net *Web site:* pbpub.com/phineasswann

MONTPELIER

Betsy's B&B	60-90-B&B	Full breakfast
74 East State St, 05602	12 rooms, 12 pb	Snacks (fruits)
802-229-0466 Fax: 802-229-5412	Most CC, *Rated*, •	Sitting room, exercise room
Betsy Anderson	C-yes/S-no/P-no/H-no	
All year	Spanish (some)	

Lavishly furnished, moderately priced Victorian B&B near great bookstores, gift shops, restaurants. Award-winning restoration & landscaping.   E-mail: betsybb@together.net *Web site:* central-vt.com/business/betsybb

Inn at Montpelier, The	99-169-B&B	Generous continental
147 Main St, 05602	19 rooms, 19 pb	breakfast
802-223-2727 Fax: 802-223-0722	Most CC, *Rated*	Full bar, dinner available,
Maureen Russell	C-yes/S-ltd/P-no/H-no	snacks
All year		Sitting room, fireplaces,
		cable TV, accommodate
		businss travelers

An elegant historic Inn in the capital city. Each room is furnished with unique antiques, art and fine reproductions.   E-mail: mail2inn@aol.com *Web site:* members.aol.com/innvt

MOUNT SNOW

Deerfield Valley Inn	69-164-B&B	Full breakfast
PO Box 1834, 05356	9 rooms, 9 pb	Afternoon tea, snacks
802-464-6333 Fax: 804-464-6336	Most CC, *Rated*, •	Sitting room, fireplace, cable
800-639-3588	C-yes/S-no/P-no/H-no	TV, conference facilities
Doreen Cooney		
All year		

Charming country inn built in 1885. All guest rooms are individually decorated, many with woodburning fireplaces, all with private bathrooms and TVs. Enjoy our full country breakfast and afternoon refreshments.   E-mail: deerinn@vermontel.com *Web site:* deerfieldvalleyinn.com

MT. SNOW VALLEY

Nutmeg Inn	89-299-B&B	Full breakfast from menu
PO Box 818, 05363	14 rooms, 14 pb	Afternoon tea
802-464-7400 Fax: 802-464-7331	Most CC, *Rated*	Sitting room, TVs, rooms &
800-277-5402	C-ltd/S-no/P-no/H-no	suites with wood buring
David & Pat Cerchio		fireplace, A/C, whirlpool
All year		

"Charming and cozy" early American farmhouse with refined country comfort. Luxurious and romantic suites. E-mail: nutmeg@sover.net Web site: nutmeginn.com

NEWFANE

Inn at South Newfane	89-130-B&B	Full breakfast
369 Dover Rd, 05351	6 rooms, 6 pb	Lunch/dinner available,
802-348-7191 Fax: 802-348-9325	Most CC, *Rated*, •	restaurant
Neville & Dawn Cullen	C-ltd/S-no/P-no/H-no	Afternoon tea, bar service,
All year		sitting room, library,
		fiesplaces, cable TV

Quiet country inn, spacious rocking chair porch overlooking spring fed pond, al fresco dining, international cuisine nightly, wedding destination. E-mail: cullinn@sover.net Web site: innatsouthnewfane.com

NORTH HERO ISLAND

Charlie's Northland Lodge	65-70-B&B	Continental breakfast
3829 US Rt 2, 05474	3 rooms, 1 pb	Complimentary wine
802-372-8822	Visa, MC, Disc, *Rated*,	Sitting room, bicycles, lake,
Dorice Clark	•	sailing, canoeing, fishing,
All year	C-ltd/S-no/P-no/H-no	kayaking

Early 1800 guest house in quiet island village on Lake Champlain. Rooms furnished with country antiques, 2 share private entrance & guest parlor. Guest cottages available.

North Hero House	89-249-B&B	Continental plus breakfast
Rt 2, PO Box 155, 05474	23 rooms, 21 pb	Restaurant, coffee, tea
802-372-4732 Fax: 802-372-3218	Most CC, *Rated*, •	Lounge, sitting room, tennis,
888-525-3644	C-yes/S-yes/P-no/H-yes	lake swimming, bicycles,
Derek Roberts	Spanish, French	sauna
June 15 October		

Lake Champlain island inn, c. 1890. Magnificent views of mountains. Crystal-clear water for marvelous swimming, boating & fishing. Common room with TV/VCR/library. E-mail: nhhlake@aol.com Web site: northherohouse.com

NORTHEAST KINGDOM

Guildhall Inn B&B	49-B&B	Full breakfast
PO Box 129, Rt 102, 05905	4 rooms	Dinner, snacks
802-676-3720	C-ltd/S-no/P-no/H-no	Sitting room, cable TV
800-987-8240		
Steve & Elenor Degnan		
All year		

Tranquil historic village inn surrounded by mountains. The inn is located along the Connecticut River within short driving distance to many nearby attractions. E-mail: elinvt@aol.com Web site: guildhallinn.com

NORTHFIELD

Northfield Inn	85-95-B&B	Full breakfast
27 Highland Ave, 05663	8 rooms, 8 pb	Lunch & dinner by
802-485-8558	Visa, MC, *Rated*, •	arrangement
Aglaia Stalb	C-ltd/S-no/P-no/H-no	Complimentary wine,
All year	Greek	snacks, new fitness room

Victorian comfort & congeniality. Antiques, brass beds & feather bedding. Hearty breakfast, beautiful porches, magnificent hillside setting.

ORWELL

Historic Brookside Farms
PO Box 36, 05760
802-948-2727 Fax: 802-948-2800
The Korda Family
All year

85-175-B&B
6 rooms, 2 pb
Rated, •
C-yes/S-yes/P-no/H-yes
French, Spanish,
German

Full country breakfast
Lunch, dinner, wine
Sitting room, library, music
room, antique shop, skating

Enjoy country elegance in our National Register Greek revival mansion, set on 300 acres and furnished in period antiques. Antique shop on premises. E-mail: hbfinbvt@aol.com
Web site: brooksideinnvt.com

PITTSFIELD

Pittsfield Inn
PO Box 685, 05762
802-746-8943
Tom and Margee Yennerell
All year

80-120-B&B/MAP
9 rooms, 9 pb
Visa, MC, *Rated*, •
C-yes/S-ltd/P-ltd/H-no

Full breakfast
Restaurant/bar service
Sitting room, cable TV,
bicycles, suites, guided, &
self guided tours

A historic stage coach inn nestled under the towering Green Mountains.
E-mail: escapert@vermontel.com *Web site:* PittsfieldInn.com

PROCTORSVILLE

Whitney Brook B&B
2423 Twenty Mile Stream,
05153
802-226-7460
Ellen & Jim Parrish
All year

55-B&B
4 rooms, 2 pb
Most CC,
C-ltd/S-no/P-no/H-no

Full breakfast
Afternoon tea
Sitting room, library, Oriental
rugs

Restored 1870 country farmhouse, private and quiet, fine dining nearby, centrally located for touring, shopping, hiking, biking, swimming or just relax near the brook.
E-mail: whitney_brook@yahoo.com

QUECHEE

Parker House Inn
1792 Quechee Main St, 05059
802-295-6077 Fax: 802-296-6696
Walt & Barbara Forrester
All year

110-140-B&B
7 rooms, 7 pb
Visa, MC, *Rated*
C-yes/S-no/P-no/H-no

Full breakfast
Restaurant, bar service
Comp. dessert w/dinner,
sitting room, library, bicycles

The Parker House Inn is a classic 19th-century Vermont inn, each room charming with Victorian furnishings. E-mail: parker_house_inn@valley.net *Web site:* theparkerhouseinn.com

RIPTON

Chipman Inn, The
PO Box 115, 05766
802-388-2310 Fax: 802-388-2390
800-890-2390
Joyce Henderson & Bill Pierce
Closed Apr. & Nov.

85-120-B&B
8 rooms, 8 pb
Visa, MC, AmEx, *Rated*
C-ltd/S-ltd/P-no/H-no
French, Arabic, Swahili

Full breakfast
Dinner available
Bar service, sitting room,
candlelit dining room

Beautiful 1828 inn in a Green Mountain village. Fine dining for guests. Skiing, country walking & sightseeing. Warm hospitality. Robert Frost lived just up the road.
E-mail: smudge@together.net

ROYALTON

Fox Stand Inn & Restaurant
5615 Rt 14, 05068
802-763-8437
Jean & Gary Curley
All year

50-85-B&B
5 rooms
Visa, MC, *Rated*
C-ltd/S-yes/P-no/H-no

Full breakfast
Lunch, dinner available
Licensed restaurant, river
swimming, tavern

Restored 1818 handsome brick building, family-owned and operated inn. Economical rates include full breakfast. E-mail: foxstand@aol.com

RUTLAND

Inn at Rutland, The	65-175-B&B	Full breakfast, weekends
70 N Main St, 05701	12 rooms, 10 pb	Cont. plus (weekdays)
802-773-0575 Fax: 802-775-3506	Most CC, *Rated*, •	TV room, library, bikes,
800-808-0575	C-yes/S-no/P-no/H-no	adjoining rms. conf. fac, 3 ski
Bob Liberman	Russian	areas nearby
All year		

Victorian city inn with views of mountains and valleys. Many great restaurants in walking distance. Close to all Vermont attractions!   E-mail: inrutlnd@vermontel.net
Web site: innatrutland.com

SPRINGFIELD

Hartness House Inn	89-150-B&B/MAP	Full country breakfast
30 Orchard St, 05156	Most CC, *Rated*, •	dinner available, dining
802-885-2115 Fax: 805-885-2207	C-yes/S-yes/P-yes/H-no	room, bar
800-732-4789	German	Sitting room, swimming pool
The Blair Family		with deck, brookside nature
All year		trails

A 1903 historic landmark built by Governor James Hartness. Nightly tours of underground museum & operating Turret Equatorial Tracking Telescope.   E-mail: innkeeper@
hartnesshouse.com *Web site:* hartnesshouse.com

ST. ALBANS

Inn at Buck Hollow Farm	63-83-B&B	Full breakfast
RR 1, Box 680, 05454	4 rooms	Beer & wine
802-849-2400 Fax: 802-849-9744	Visa, MC, *Rated*, •	Sun room, Jacuzzi, pool, hot
Brad Schwartz	C-yes/S-no/P-no/H-no	tub/spa, play area, antique
All year		shop

Our intimate inn features canopy beds, antique decor, beamed ceilings, heated pool, fireplace, Jacuzzi and 400 spectacular acres.   E-mail: inn@buckhollow.com
Web site: buckhollow.com

STOWE

Andersen Lodge-Austrian Inn	30-90-B&B	Full or continental breakfast
3430 Mountain Rd, 05672	17 rooms, 16 pb	Piano, game room, spa,
802-253-7336	Most CC, *Rated*, •	Jacuzzi, tennis court, heated
800-336-7336	C-yes/S-yes/P-ltd/H-no	pool, golf nearby
Dietmar & Getrude Helss	German, French	
Season Inquire		

Set in relaxing surroundings with lovely view of mountains. Trout fishing, horseback riding, mountain hiking. Owners and hosts of Austrian background. Austrian chef.

Brass Lantern Inn	80-225-B&B	Full country breakfast
717 Maple St, 05672	9 rooms, 9 pb	Afternoon tea, snacks
802-253-2229 Fax: 802-253-7425	Most CC, *Rated*, •	Bar, gourmet shop nearby,
800-729-2980	C-yes/S-no/P-no/H-no	sitting room with piano,
Andy Aldrich		library, fireplaces, A/C
All year		

Full award winning breakfast, afternoon tea, bar, walk to dining, fireplace, A/C, patio and mountain views.   E-mail: brasslntrn@aol.com *Web site:* brasslanterninn.com

Butternut Inn	120-160-B&B/MAP	Full country breakfast
2309 Mountain Rd, 05672	18 rooms, 18 pb	Dinner (winter)
802-253-9577 Fax: 802-253-5263	Visa, MC, *Rated*, •	Comp. sherry, aftn. tea,
800-3-BUTTER	C-ltd/S-no/P-no/H-no	sitting room, piano,
Janis & Parker Diamond		sunroom, courtyard, pool
6/15-10/20, 12/18-4/20		

Come and enjoy absolutely delightful accommodations at the Butternut—an estate setting on eight riverfront acres. Enjoy the courtyard filled with perennials—relax by the fountain— enjoy the koi fish pond. Walk along our delicately lit paths.   E-mail: innstowe2@aol.com
Web site: travelguides.com/home/butternut/

STOWE

Fitch Hill Inn	85-185-B&B	Full gourmet breakfast
258 Fitch Hill Rd, 05655	6 rooms, 6 pb	Lunch, dinner on request
802-888-3834 Fax: 802-888-7789	*Rated*, •	Complimentary wine, tea,
800-639-2903	C-ltd/S-no/P-ltd/H-no	sitting room, library, bikes
R. Pugliese & S. Corklin	Spanish, some French	
All year		

Elegant Federalist style, historic, spectacular views, fireplaces, Jacuzzis, gardens. Near Stowe. Antiques, quilts, natural wood floors. TV/VCRs. E-mail: fitchinn@aol.com
Web site: gostowe.com/saa/fitchhill

Gables Inn, The	70-210-B&B/MAP	Full breakfast
1457 Mountain Rd, 05672	19 rooms, 19 pb	Sitting room, fireplace, piano,
802-253-7730 Fax: 802-253-8989	*Rated*, •	swimming pool, hot tub,
800-GABLES-1	C-yes/S-no/P-no/H-ltd	Jacuzzi, A/C
Sol & Lynn Baumrind		
All year		

Classic country inn-antiques, wide plank floors, panoramic view. Breakfast on lawn/porch (summer). Near golf, hiking, skiing, tennis, bicycling E-mail: inngables@aol.com
Web site: gablesinn.com

Siebeness Inn, The	75-200-B&B	Full breakfast
3681 Mountain Rd, 05672	12 rooms, 12 pb	Complimentary beverages &
802-253-8942 Fax: 802-253-9232	Most CC, •	snacks
800-426-9001	S-no/P-no/H-ltd	Lounge, hot tub, biking, pool,
William Kern Ruffing		cross-country skiing, golf &
All year		tennis nearby, sitting rm.

Charming country inn, romantic rooms, antiques, quilts, A/C, some with fireplaces, Jacuzzis. Multi-course breakfast, famous recreation path from inn, pool, hot tub. Near ski slopes, hiking. Breakfasts change daily. E-mail: siebenes@together.net Web site: siebeness.com

Ski Inn	45-60-B&B/MAP	Continental breakfast
Route 108, 05672	10 rooms, 5 pb	Full breakfast (winter)
802-253-4050	*Rated*	Dinner (optional) golf &
Mrs. Larry Heyer	C-ltd/S-no/P-ltd/H-no	tennis nearby
All year	some French	

This comfortable inn, noted for good food and good conversation, is a great gathering place for interesting people. MAP available in the winter. Web site: ski-inn.com/pl

Stowe Inn at Little River	60-180-EP	Lunch, dinner, restaurant
123 Mountain Rd, 05672	46 rooms, 46 pb	Bar service, sitting room,
802-253-4836 Fax: 802-253-7308	Visa, MC, AmEx, •	Jacuzzis, swimming pool,
800-227-1108	C-yes/S-ltd/P-ltd/H-yes	suites, fireplaces
Miranda & Steve Batiste		
All year		

Beautiful 1825 Inn. Relaxation, comfort, winter hot tubs, summer pool and wonderful restaurant, deluxe and traditional rooms with king size or twin double beds, bathrooms, air conditioning and cable TV. E-mail: info@stoweinn.com Web site: stoweinn.com

Three Bears @ the Fountain	75-250-B&B	Full breakfast
1049 Pucker St, 05672	5 rooms, 5 pb	Snacks
802-253-7671 Fax: 802-253-8804	Visa, MC, AmEx,	Suites, fireplaces, cable TV
800-898-9634	*Rated*, •	
Stephen & Suzanne Vazzano	S-no/P-no/H-no	
All year		

"Where everything is just right." Enjoy homemade breakfast, relaxed atmosphere, mountain views, antiques, hot tub, large king and queen rooms with private baths and afternoon snacks in Stowe's oldest guest house. E-mail: threebears@stowevt.net
Web site: stoweinfo.com/saa/threebears

STOWE

Ye Olde England Inne
433 Mountain Rd, 05672
802-253-7558 Fax: 802-253-8944
800-477-3771
Christopher & Linda Francis
All year

125-395-B&B
23 rooms, 23 pb
Visa, MC, *Rated*, •
C-yes/S-yes/P-ltd/H-no
French, Arabic

Full gourmet breakfast
Dinner available, afternoon
tea
Library, piano, pool, pub,
banquet center, polo &
gliding packages

Classic English luxury, Laura Ashley room & cottages. 4 posters, fireplaces & Jacuzzis. Gourmet dining in Copperfield's. Mr. Pickwick's Polo Pub. Awarded chef. VT's 1997 Inn-keepers of the Year Award, specialists in romantic getaways & honeymoon packages. E-mail: englandinn@aol.com Web site: oldeenglandinne.com

VERGENNES

Strong House Inn
94 W Main St, 05491
802-877-3337 Fax: 802-877-2599
Mary & Hugh Bargiel
All year

75-250-B&B
14 rooms, 14 pb
Visa, MC, AmEx, *Rated*
C-ltd/S-no/P-no/H-yes

Full country breakfast
Lunch/dinner avail., snacks,
tea
Sitting room, suites,
fireplaces, beverage license
for beer/wine, cable TV

Atmosphere abounds at this historic inn. From the restored inn furnished in period furniture and antiques to the six acres of gardens, ponds and walking trails, the inn captures a wonderful age gone by for the enjoyment of everyone. E-mail: innkeeper@stronghouseinn.com Web site: stronghouseinn.com

WAITSFIELD

Hyde Away Inn
RR 1, Box 65, 05673
802-496-2322 Fax: 802-496-7829
800-777-4933
Bruce Hyde & Margaret
DeFour
All year

59-139-B&B
12 rooms, 4 pb
Visa, MC, AmEx, •
C-yes/S-ltd/P-ltd/H-no

Full breakfast
Rest./bar, dinner available
(fee)
Sitting room, library,
volleyball, horseshoes, near
tennis/golf/riding

Inn, restaurant & tavern with comfortable, casual "unpretentious" atmosphere. Minutes from skiing, hiking, golfing, bicycling. E-mail: hydeaway@madriver.com Web site: hideawayinn.com

Inn at Round Barn Farm
1661 East Warren Rd, 05673
802-496-2276 Fax: 802-496-8832
Anne Marie Defreest
All year

135-220-B&B
11 rooms, 11 pb
Visa, MC, AmEx,
S-no/P-no/H-ltd

Full breakfast
Afternoon tea, snacks
Sitting room, library,
Jacuzzis, swimming pool,
fireplace, cable TV

The inn that lives in your imagination that feels like home with all of the comforts and none of the demands. E-mail: roundbarn@madriver.com Web site: innattheroundbarn.com

Lareau Farm Country Inn
PO Box 563, 05673
802-496-4949 Fax: 802-496-7979
800-833-0766
Susan Easley
All year

90-145-B&B
14 rooms, 11 pb
Visa, MC, *Rated*, •
C-yes/S-ltd/P-no/H-no

Full breakfast
Apres-ski hors d'oeuvres
Dinner, wine/beer (fee),
sitting room, fireplace,
porches, picnic lunches

Picturesque Vermont farmhouse, now an inn, nestled in a picturesque meadow beside the Mad River, our 150-year-old farmhouse is minutes from skiing and shopping. Fishing, sleigh rides. E-mail: lareau@lareaufarminn.com Web site: lareaufarminn.com

Millbrook Inn
533 McCollough Hwy, 05673
802-496-2405 Fax: 802-496-9735
800-477-2809
Joan & Thom Gorman
Closed April-May & Nov.

78-140-B&B/MAP
7 rooms, 7 pb
Visa, MC, AmEx,
C-ltd/S-no/P-ltd/H-ltd

Full breakfast from menu
Full dinner from restaurant
Complimentary
refreshments, 3 sitting
rooms, vegetarian dining
menu

Charming hand-stenciled guest rooms with handmade quilts, country gourmet dining, vegetarian choices, in our small candlelit restaurant, friendly, unhurried atmosphere. E-mail: millbrkinn@aol.com Web site: millbrookinn.com

WAITSFIELD ――――

Tucker Hill Lodge	75-135-B&B/MAP	Full breakfast
RR1, Box 147, 05673	21 rooms, 16 pb	Dinner, restaurant, bar
802-496-3983 Fax: 802-496-3203	Visa, MC, AmEx, •	Sitting room, tennis, pool,
800-543-7841	C-yes/S-no/P-ltd/H-no	suites, fireplace, wedding
Susan & Giorgio Noaro	French, Italian	facilities
All year		

Classic 1940s Vermont ski lodge with wonderful Italian restaurant & cozy lounge. Entertainment every Thursday in season. Perfect for families, groups, weddings, romantic escapes.   E-mail: tuckhill@madriver.com Web site: tuckerhill.com/

Waitsfield Inn, The	79-129-B&B	Full breakfast
Box 969, Rt 100, 05673	14 rooms, 14 pb	Apres ski snacks & cider
802-496-3979 Fax: 802-496-3970	Most CC, *Rated*	Sitting room, fireplaces,
800-758-3801	C-ltd/S-no/P-no/H-no	down comforters
Pat & Jim Masson		
All year		

We offer gracious lodging in an elegant 1825 parsonage located in Vermont's beautiful Mad River Valley. Our inn is welcoming without the intrusion of TV or phones. E-mail: waitsfieldinn@madriver.com Web site: waitsfieldinn.com

WALLINGFORD ――――

I.B. Munson House B&B Inn	65-135-B&B	Full breakfast
PO Box 427, 05773	7 rooms, 7 pb	Sitting room, library, suites,
802-446-2860 Fax: 802-446-3336	Visa, MC, AmEx,	fireplaces, breakfast by fire in
888-519-3771	*Rated*, •	winter
Karen & Phil B. Pimental	C-ltd/S-no/P-no/H-no	
All year		

A charming, elegantly restored 1856 Victorian home transformed into a romantic B&B inn. Count Rumford fireplaces, feather bedding, clawfoot tubs.   E-mail: ibmunson@vermontel.com Web site: ibmunsoninn.com

WARREN ――――

Beaver Pond Farm Inn	82-118-B&B	Full breakfast
1225 Golf Course Rd, 05674	5 rooms, 5 pb	Complimentary sherry,
802-583-2861 Fax: 802-583-2860	Visa, MC, AmEx, •	brandy
Betty & Bob Hansen	C-ltd/S-yes/P-no/H-no	Sitting room, library,
Closed May	French	weddings, fishing, hiking,
		swimming, skiing

Beautifully restored Vermont farmhouse adjacent to golf course. Spectacular views from spacious deck; hearty breakfasts. King or queen beds. Summer golf/winter skiing packages. Thanksgiving package.   E-mail: beaverpond@madriver.com Web site: beaverpondfarminn.com

Sugartree Inn, The	85-175-B&B	Full country breakfast
2440 Sugarbush Access Rd, 05674	10 rooms, 10 pb	Afternoon snacks
802-583-3211 Fax: 802-583-3203	Most CC, *Rated*, •	Living room with fireplace,
800-666-8907	C-ltd/S-no/P-no/H-yes	in-room phones, brass,
Frank/Kathy Partsch All year		antique, or canopy beds

Beautifully decorated with unique country flair and antiques. Enchanting gazebo amid flower gardens. Breathtaking views of ski slopes or fall foliage.   E-mail: sugartree@ madriver.com Web site: sugartree.com

West Hill House B&B	100-155-B&B	Full breakfast
1496 West Hill Road, 05674	7 rooms, 7 pb	Afternoon tea, snacks, wine
802-496-7162 Fax: 802-496-6443	Visa, MC, AmEx,	Dinner by request, sitting
800-898-1427	*Rated*, •	room, library, guest fax, TV,
Dotty Kyle & Eric Brattstrom	C-ltd/S-no/P-no/H-ltd	fireplaces
All year		

Relax, romance, refresh. Comfortably elegant 1850s farmhouse on quiet lane. Near everything quintessentially Vermont. Ski, hike, golf, restaurants, quaint village. 6 of our 7 rooms have fireplaces some with Jacuzzis.   E-mail: westhill@madriver.com Web site: westhillhouse.com

WATERBURY

Grunberg Haus B&B &	59-145-B&B	Full breakfast
Cabins	14 rooms, 9 pb	B.Y.O.B. pub
94-LG Pine Street, 05676	Most CC, *Rated*, •	Piano, Jacuzzi, sauna,
802-244-7726	C-ltd/S-no/P-no/H-no	walking trails, flock of
800-800-7760		chickens
Chris Sellers & Mark Frohman		
All year		

We offer lodging in beautiful guestrooms, secluded cabins and a spectacular carriage house suite with many special features. Guests might enjoy our small herd of friendly rhinocerous. E-mail: grunhaus@aol.com *Web site:* waterbury.org/grunberg

Inn at Blush Hill	65-130-B&B	Full gourmet breakfast
784 Blush Hill Rd, 05676	6 rooms, 5 pb	Afternoon tea
802-244-7529 Fax: 802-244-7314	Most CC, *Rated*, •	Library, piano, lawn games,
800-736-7522	C-ltd/S-ltd/P-ltd/H-ltd	swim/boating, 1 room
Pamela Gosselin		Jacuzzi bathtub
All year		

Cozy, 1790s brick farmhouse, near 9-hole golf course, 15 min. to Sugarbush, Bolton, Stowe. Canopy queen bedroom, views, fireplaces Close to Ben & Jerry's. E-mail: innatbh@aol.com *Web site:* blushhill.com

Old Stagecoach Inn	45-150-B&B	Full breakfast
18 N Main St, 05676	11 rooms, 8 pb	Afternoon tea, bar service
802-244-5056 Fax: 802-244-6956	Most CC, *Rated*	Sitting room, library,
800-262-2206	C-yes/S-no/P-yes/H-no	bicycles, 1 room with Jacuzzi
John Barwick	German	bathtub
All year		

Village Inn on the National Register of Historic Places, located in the heart of Vermont's Green Mountains. Old world atmosphere E-mail: lodging@oldstagecoach.com *Web site:* oldstagecoach.com

Thatcher Brook Inn	89-195-B&B	Full country breakfast
PO Box 490, 05676	24 rooms, 24 pb	Dinner packages (fee)
802-244-5911 Fax: 802-244-1294	Visa, MC, AmEx,	Restaurant, pub, library,
800-292-5911	*Rated*, •	whirlpools, fireplaces,
John & Lisa Fischer	C-yes/S-ltd/P-no/H-yes	bicycles, gazebo porches
All year	French	

Beautifully restored 1899 country Victorian mansion. Centrally located between renowned resorts of Stowe and Sugarbush. Exquisite lodging & dining. E-mail: info@thatcherbrook.com *Web site:* thatcherbrook.com

WEST ARLINGTON

Four Winds Country Inn	85-115-B&B	Full breakfast
River Rd, Box 3580, 05250	5 rooms, 3 pb	Sitting room, library,
802-375-6734	*Rated*, •	surrounded by 50 acres, of
Ursula Stratmann	C-yes/S-no/P-ltd/H-no	protected land
May 1-November	German	

Former Norman Rockwell Homestead, bordering the famous Battenkill River—country retreat on back road, ideal for fishing, bicycling, canoeing.

WEST DOVER

Austin Hill Inn	100-155-B&B	Full gourmet breakfast
PO Box 859, 05356	12 rooms, 12 pb	Afternoon wine & cheese
802-464-5281 Fax: 802-464-1229	Visa, MC, AmEx,	Sitting room, game room,
800-332RELAX	*Rated*, •	pool, fireplaces, dinner for
Debbie & John Bailey	C-yes/S-no/P-no/H-no	small groups
All year		

Casual elegance, attention to detail and service. Nestled among the pines makes for a quiet romantic stay. Inquire about Murder Mystery Weekends, Summer Vacation and Winter Ski Packages. Guest refrigerator. E-mail: ahiinn@aol.com

WEST DOVER

Deerhill Inn & Restaurant	100-300-B&B/MAP	Full breakfast
PO Box 136, 05356	15 rooms, 15 pb	Dinner available, restaurant
802-464-3100 Fax: 802-464-5474	Most CC, *Rated*	Sitting room, library, suites,
800-99-DEER9	C-ltd/S-ltd/P-no/H-ltd	fireplaces, cable, conference
Michael & Linda Anelli		facilities
All year		

Romantic & relaxed hillside getaway with panoramic mountain views, fireplaces, antiques & art. Unparalleled dining & Wine Spectator Award Winning wine list. E-mail: deerhill@ sover.net *Web site:* deerhill.com

Doveberry Inn & Restaurant	90-160-B&B	Full breakfast
PO Box 1736, 05356	8 rooms, 8 pb	Afternoon tea, dinner (fee)
802-464-5652 Fax: 802-464-6229	Visa, MC, AmEx,	Restaurant, bar service,
800-722-3204	*Rated*, ●	sitting room, library, ideal for
Christine & Michael Fayette	C-ltd/S-no/P-no/H-no	family reunion
Memorial Day-Mid April		

A romantic getaway in the Green Mountains of So. Vermont. 8 guest rooms with PB, inclusive full country breakfast, fireplace, lounge, extraordinary dining. E-mail: duveberry@ aol.com *Web site:* doveberryinn.com

Mountaineer Inn	60-140-MAP	Full breakfast
PO Box 140, 05356	27 rooms, 27 pb	Dinner included
802-464-5404 Fax: 802-464-3145	Visa, MC, AmEx,	Sitting room, library, sauna,
800-682-4637	*Rated*, ●	heated pool, TV, pool table,
Royal & Ned Wilson	C-ltd/S-ltd/P-no/H-no	Ping-Pong
All year		

Charming inn; mountain setting. Year round activities and events. Newly decorated guest rooms. Spacious lounges with fireplaces. Excellent meals. E-mail: mtneer@sover.net *Web site:* mountaineerinn.com

Snow Goose Inn	95-300-B&B	Full country breakfast
PO Box 366, 05356	12 rooms, 12 pb	Complimentary wine, snacks
802-464-3984 Fax: 802-464-5322	Visa, MC, AmEx,	Sitting room, Jacuzzis, suites,
888-604-7964	*Rated*, ●	fireplace, cable TV, feather
Karen & Eric Falberg	C-yes/S-no/P-yes/H-yes	beds, decks
All year		

Comfort and charm amid 3 wooded acres, pond and country gardens, antique filled rooms, in-room fireplaces and Jacuzzis. E-mail: gooseinn@aol.com *Web site:* snowgooseinn.com

West Dover Inn	90-200-B&B	Full country breakfast
Rt 100, PO Box 1208, 05356	12 rooms, 12 pb	Gourmet dinner(fee)
802-464-5207 Fax: 802-464-2173	Most CC, *Rated*, ●	Cozy pub, fine wines, sitting
Greg Gramas & Monique	C-ltd/S-ltd/P-no/H-no	room, library,
Phelan		fireplace/Jacuzzi suites
Closed mid-April-mid-May		

Country elegant guest rooms feature antiques & hand-sewn quilts. Hearty breakfasts, memorable dinners. Ski & golf pkgs. E-mail: wdvrinn@sover.net *Web site:* westdoverinn.com

WESTON

Colonial House, The	52-100-B&B	Full breakfast
287 Route 100, 05161	15 rooms, 9 pb	Dinner available
802-824-6286 Fax: 802-824-3934	Visa, MC, *Rated*	Tea, coffee, baked goods,
800-639-5033	C-yes/S-ltd/P-ltd/H-ltd	sitting room, fireplaces,
Betty & John Nunnikhoven		soaking tubs
All year		

Your country cousins are waiting with a warm welcome, old-fashioned meals and a relaxing living room for you while you visit the attractions of southern Vermont. E-mail: innkeeper@cohoinn.com *Web site:* cohoinn.com

WESTON

Darling Family Inn, The	85-130-B&B	Full breakfast
815 Route 100, 05161	7 rooms, 7 pb	Comp. wine, refreshments
802-824-3223	C-ltd/S-yes/P-ltd/H-no	Sitting room, cottages,
Chapin & Joan Darling		swimming pool, fireplaces,
All year		soaking tubs

Restored Colonial in farmland and mountain setting with American and English country antiques. Closest inn to the famous Weston Priory.
Web site: obs-us.com/chesler/darlingfamilyinn

WILMINGTON

Inn at Quail Run, The	105-205-B&B	Full gourmet breakfast
106 Smith Rd, 05363	14 rooms, 14 pb	Afternoon refreshments
802-464-3362 Fax: 802-464-7784	Most CC, •	Sitting room, sauna, outdoor
800-34ESCAPE	C-yes/S-no/P-yes/H-no	heated pool, hiking trails
Lorin and Bob Streim		
All year		

Beautiful new outdoor heated pool with cascading waterfalls, 9 person outdoor Jacuzzi, sauna. Full gourmet breakfast. Kids and well behaved pets welcome. Cable TV with HBO in every room. *E-mail:* quailrunvt@aol.com *Web site:* bbonline.com/vt/quailrun/

Red Shutter Inn	95-210-B&B	Full breakfast
PO Box 636, 05363	9 rooms, 9 pb	Restaurant, bar service
802-464-3768 Fax: 802-464-5123	Most CC, •	Snacks, al fresco dining,
800-845-7548	C-ltd/S-no	fireplaces, guest suites,
Renee & Tad Lyon		whirlpool bath, packages
Closed mid-Apr-mid-May		

Hillside inn & renovated Carriage House at village edge with candlelight dining. Fireplace suites. *E-mail:* redshutr@sover.net *Web site:* redshutterinn.com/

Trail's End, A Country Inn	105-185-B&B	Full breakfast from menu
5 Trail's End Lane, 05363	15 rooms, 15 pb	Afternoon refreshments
802-464-2727 Fax: 802-464-2727	Most CC, *Rated*, •	Heated outdoor pool,
800-859-2585	C-ltd/S-no/P-no/H-no	fireplace/Jacuzzi suites, clay
Debby & Kevin Stephens		tennis court
All year		

"Irresistibly romantic"—Best Places to Kiss in New England. Fireplace suites with canopy beds & whirlpool tubs. *E-mail:* trailsnd@together.net *Web site:* trailsendvt.com

White House of Wilmington	118-205-B&B	Full breakfast
178 Rt 9 E, 05363	12 rooms, 12 pb	Dinner (included), bar
802-464-2135 Fax: 802-464-5222	Most CC, *Rated*, •	Sitting room, piano, hot tub,
800-541-2135	C-ltd/S-yes/P-no/H-no	sauna/whirlpool, pools,
Robert Grinold	French	weddings
All year		

"One of the most romantic inns. . ." N.Y. Times. Turn-of-the-century mansion, elegant accommodations, fireplaces. *E-mail:* whitehse@sover.net *Web site:* whitehouseinn.com

WINDSOR

Juniper Hill Inn	95-175-B&B	Full breakfast
153 Pembroke Rd, 05089	16 rooms, 16 pb	Dinner by reservation, tea,
802-674-5273 Fax: 802-674-2041	Visa, MC, Disc, *Rated*,	snacks
800-359-2541	•	Restaurant, bar, sitting room,
Robert & Susanne Pearl	C-ltd/S-no/P-no/H-ltd	library, swimming pool,
Closed 3 weeks in April		fireplace

A 1902 fully restored Colonial mansion on the National Register of Historic Places. Our guest rooms offer working wood or gas fireplaces, four poster beds, canopies and antiques. *E-mail:* Innkeeper@juniperhillinn.com *Web site:* juniperhillinn.com

WOODSTOCK

Applebutter Inn B&B	85-145-B&B	Full buffet breakfast
PO Box 24, 05073	6 rooms, 6 pb	Afternoon tea, near
802-457-4158 Fax: 802-457-4158	*Rated*	restaurant
800-486-1734	C-yes/S-no/P-ltd/H-no	Library, near tennis court,
Beverlee & Andy Cook		swimming pool and Jacuzzis,
All year		cable TV

Historic Inn with solitude and elegance filled with comfortable energy. Have greeted satisfied guests for eleven years. Innkeepers/owners hobby is hospitality. Breakfasts are prepared with natural ingredients. E-mail: aplbtrn@aol.com

Ardmore Inn	110-150-B&B	Full gourmet breakfast
23 Pleasant St, 05091	5 rooms, 5 pb	Afternoon tea
802-457-3887 Fax: 802-457-9006	Most CC, *Rated*, •	Sitting room, library,
800-497-9652	C-ltd/S-no/P-no/H-no	bicycles, tennis court,
Giorgio Ortiz	Spanish, some French	intimate gatherings
All year		

Spacious architectural detailed rooms, gracious accommodations, gourmet breakfast, silver service, great fun! Enjoy the finer things with grace and style E-mail: ardmoreinn@aol.com Web site: ardmoreinn.com

Bailey's Mills B&B	80-150-B&B	Continental plus breakfast
1347 Bailey's Mills Road, 05062	3 rooms, 3 pb	Afternoon tea, snacks
802-484-7809	•	Sitting room, library,
800-639-3437	C-ltd/S-no/P-ltd/H-no	fireplaces, pond, stream,
Barbara Thaeder		walking paths- 50 acres
All year		

History-filled country home overlooking "Spite Cemetery." Colorful breakfast in colonial dining room, solarium or front porch. Be lazy: porch swing, glides, rockers, hammock, pond float E-mail: goodfarm@vermontel.com Web site: bbonline.com/vt/baileysmills/

Canterbury House B&B, The	90-155-B&B	Full gourmet breakfast
43 Pleasant St, 05091	8 rooms, 8 pb	Tea
802-457-3077 Fax: 802-457-4630	Visa, MC, AmEx,	Sitting room, library, fishing,
800-390-3077	*Rated*, •	golf, skiing
Bob and Sue Frost	C-ltd/S-no/P-no/H-no	
All year		

Village townhouse beautifully decorated with fine antiques and comfortable reproductions. Close to fine dining, shopping, skiing, golf, hiking

Jackson House Inn, The	180-290-B&B	Full breakfast
37 Old Route 4 West, 05091	15 rooms, 15 pb	Wine & hors d'oeuvres
802-457-2065 Fax: 802-457-9290	Visa, MC, AmEx, •	Sitting room, library,
800-448-1890	C-ltd/S-no/P-no/H-yes	restaurant, cable TV, suites,
Juan Florin	Spanish, French, Italian	fireplaces, pond
All year		

Immaculate 1880 Victorian mansion in charming historic Woodstock. Period antiques, gourmet breakfast, evening champagne and snacks, 5 groomed acres, swimming pond, spa/steam room. Four star dining. E-mail: innkeepers@jacksonhouse.com Web site: jacksonhouse.com/

Kedron Valley Inn	99-230-B&B/MAP	Full country breakfast
Route 106, 05071	28 rooms, 28 pb	Contemporary American
802-457-1473 Fax: 802-457-4469	Most CC, *Rated*, •	cuisine
800-836-1193	C-yes/S-yes/P-yes/H-yes	Sitting room, swim pond,
Max & Merrily Comins	French, Spanish	piano, TVs, quilts, A/C in
All year		some rooms

Distinguished country 1822 inn. Wine list won Award of Excellence (Wine Spectator). Canopy beds, fireplaces in 15 rooms. E-mail: kedroninn@aol.com Web site: innformation.com/vt/kedron

WOODSTOCK

Lincoln Inn, The
530 Woodstock Rd, 05091
802-457-3312 Fax: 802-457-5808
Kurt & Lori Hildbrand
All year

115-160-B&B
6 rooms, 6 pb
Visa, MC, *Rated*
C-yes/S-no/P-no/H-yes
German, French

Full breakfast
Afternoon tea,
complimentary wine
Snacks, restaurant, bar
service, biking, sitting room,
library

Lovingly restored farmhouse nestled on 6 acres of lovely grounds. Office services, conference facilities, fishing, vegetarian dining. E-mail: lincon2@aol.com Web site: lincolninn.com

Quechee Inn-Marshland Farm
PO Box 747, 05059
802-295-3133
800-235-3133
Hal Lothrop
All year

80-240-MAP
24 rooms, 24 pb
Visa, MC, AmEx,
Rated, ●
C-yes/S-yes/P-no/H-ltd

Continental plus breakfast
Dinner included, bar
Wine list, sitting room, club
membership (sauna,
swimming, tennis)

The beautifully restored 18th-C. farmstead of Vermont's first lieutenant governor; nearby private Quechee Club for golf, tennis, boating, etc. E-mail: quecheeinn@pinnacle-inns.com Web site: pinnacle-inns.com

Woodstocker B&B, The
61 River St, Route 4, 05091
802-457-3896 Fax: 802-457-3897
Tom & Nancy Blackford
All year

85-155-B&B
9 rooms, 9 pb
Visa, MC, *Rated*, ●
C-yes/S-no/P-no/H-no

Full buffet breakfast
Afternoon tea, snacks
Sitting room, hot tub, sitting
room

Charming 1830s cape in the village. Walking distance to shops, restaurants & galleries. E-mail: woodstocker@valley.net Web site: scenesofvermont.com/woodstocker/index.html

Virginia

ABINGDON

Love House B&B, The
210 E Valley St, 24210
540-623-1281
Fax: 540-623-1281
800-475-5494
H. Ramos-Cano & R. Cano
All year

95-115-B&B
3 rooms, 3 pb
Most CC,
C-ltd/S-no/P-no/H-no
Spanish, Tagalog,
Japanese

Continental breakfast from
menu.
Afternoon tea, snacks, comp.
wine.
Sitting room, library,
Jacuzzis, fireplaces, fax,
computers, E-mail access.

An 1850 home built by John William Love lovingly restored to modern standards retaining the charm of wide doors, hardwood floors, hand-blown window panes, etc. E-mail: lovehouse@naxs.com Web site: abingdon-virginia.com

River Garden B&B
19080 N Fork River Rd, 24210
540-676-0335 Fax: 540-676-3039
800-952-4296
Bill Crump & Carol
Schoenherr
All year

60-70-B&B
4 rooms, 4 pb
●
C-ltd/S-no/P-ltd/H-yes

Full breakfast
Afternoon tea—request
Library, sitting room, rec.
room, covered deck, full
private baths

Located in country, private entrances for rooms, antique & period furniture, covered deck facing river, gift shop, delightful host & hostess! E-mail: wccrump@preferred.com Web site: bbonline.com/va/rivergarden

ALEXANDRIA

Alexandria B&B	70-325-B&B	Continental breakfast
PO Box 25319, 22202	2 rooms, 2 pb	Restaurant
703-549-3415 Fax: 703-549-3411	Visa, MC, AmEx, •	Sitting room, library,
888-549-3415	C-ltd/S-ltd/P-ltd/H-ltd	Jacuzzis, fireplaces, suites,
Les Garrison		cable TV
All year		

Historic, charming, authentic 1816 Townhouse in middle of Old Town Alexandria. Hospitable hostess. Delightful atmosphere. Guests keep returning. E-mail: aabbn@juno.com *Web site:* aabbn.com/#Capt

ALEXANDRIA, DC

Morrison House	175-350-EP	Continental breakfast
109 S Alfred St, 22314	45 rooms, 45 pb	Aft. tea, snacks
703-838-8000 Fax: 703-548-2489	Most CC, *Rated*, •	Restaurant, bar service,
800-367-0800	C-yes/S-ltd/P-no/H-ltd	sitting room, library, near
Wanda McKeon	Fr., It., Ger., Jap.	tennis/hot tub/pool
All year		

Small boutique, luxury hotel built in the style of 18th century manor home.
E-mail: mhresrv@morrisonhouse.com *Web site:* morrisonhouse.com

AMHERST

Dulwich Manor B&B Inn	90-125-B&B	Full sumptuous breakfast
550 Richmond Highway, 24521	6 rooms, 6 pb	Afternoon tea/request
804-946-7207 Fax: 804-946-5913	Visa, MC, *Rated*, •	Complimentary beverages,
800-571-9011	C-yes/S-ltd/P-no/H-no	study w/TV, whirlpool, A/C,
Mike & Georgie Farmer		gas fireplaces
All year		

English-style manor, Blue Ridge Mt. views, beautifully appointed. Surrounded by natural and historic beauty. Outdoor hot tub, rollaways. Fireplaces, bridal suite with Jacuzzi. A/C throughout. E-mail: mfarmer@iwinet.com *Web site:* thedulwichmanor.com

APPOMATTOX

Babcock House B&B Inn	95-120-B&B	Full breakfast
Rt 6, Box 1421, 24522	6 rooms, 6 pb	Lunch, dinner, restaurant
804-352-7532 Fax: 804-352-5532	Most CC, *Rated*, •	Sitting room, suites,
800-689-6208	C-yes/S-no/P-no/H-yes	fireplaces, cable TV, gift shop
Debbie Powell & Luella		
Coleman All year		

Located in historic Appomattox, Virginia, we are minutes from Appomattox Couthouse National Historic Park where General Robert E. Lee surrendered, thus ending the civil war. Lunch (Mon-Fri), and dinner (Wed-Sat) and monday nights by reservation.
E-mail: babcockhouse@earthlink.net *Web site:* babcockhouse.com

BASYE

Sky Chalet Mountain Lodges	34-79-B&B	Continental breakfast
PO Box 300, 22810	9 rooms, 9 pb	Delivered to your room
540-856-2147 Fax: 540-856-2436	Most CC, *Rated*, •	Restaurant, pub, next to 4
877-867-8439	C-yes/S-yes/P-yes/H-no	season resort, trail to skiing,
Ken & Mona Seay All year		views

Rustic, comfortable mountain top hideaway in the Shenandoah Valley since 1937. Property features panoramic mountain & valley views. E-mail: skychalet@skychalet.com *Web site:* skychalet.com

BERRYVILLE

Berryville B&B	95-145-B&B	Full breakfast
100 Taylor St, 22611	4 rooms, 3 pb	Snacks, complimentary wine
540-955-2200	Most CC, *Rated*	Sitting room, library,
800-826-7520	C-ltd/S-no/P-no/H-no	Jacuzzis, fireplaces, cable
Don & Jan Riviere All year		TV, suites

Comfort, elegance and convenience in a small town atmosphere. Home in the English country style furnished with antiques offers you a memorable stay. Corporate rates.
E-mail: bvillebb@shentel.net *Web site:* berryvillebb.com

BERRYVILLE

Rocks & Rills Farm
2458 Castleman Rd, 22611
540-955-1246 Fax: 540-955-4240
800-296-1246
Rolando Amador & Rita
Duncan   All year

65-100-B&B
4 rooms, 3 pb
Visa, MC, AmEx,
Rated, ●
C-yes/S-ltd/P-yes/H-ltd
Spanish, some German

Full breakfast
Afternoon tea, snacks, comp.
wine
Sitting room, library,
Jacuzzis, suites, fireplaces,
cable TV, microwave

Located in urban Winchester this lovely Dutch Colonial reproduction filled with Oriental antiques from all over the world is just seconds from I-81 and Shenandoah University; easy drive to northern entrance of Skyline Drive; outstanding cuisine.
E-mail: blurdgbb@shentel.net

BLACKSBURG

Clay Corner Inn
401 Clay St SW, 24060
540-953-2604 Fax: 540-951-0541
John Anderson   All year

74-115-B&B
12 rooms, 12 pb
Visa, MC, AmEx, *Rated*
C-ltd/S-no/P-no/H-no

Full breakfast
Heated pool, A/C, meeting
room, hot tub

Cable TV & phones in every room. Healthy breakfast served inside or out on covered deck. One block to Virginia Tech, walking trail, tennis and downtown. Inn consists of the main house and three guest houses.   E-mail: claycorner@aol.com *Web site:* claycorner.com

BOYCE

River House, The
3075 John Mosby Hwy 22620
540-837-1476 Fax: 540-837-2399
800-838-1476
Cornelia S. Niemann   All year

90-150-B&B
5 rooms, 5 pb
Visa, MC, *Rated*, ●
C-ltd/S-yes/P-yes/H-yes
French

Full brunch
Fruit, beverages/liqueur
Sitting room, library, phone
in room, Fax, modem, special
comedy weekends

1780 Fieldstone rural getaway, convenient to scenic, historical, recreational areas, superb rests. Shenandoah river fishing on property.   E-mail: rvrhouse@visuallink.com
Web site: riverhouse-virginia.com

CAPE CHARLES

Pickett's Harbor B&B
28288 Nottingham Ridge, 23310
757-331-2212 Fax: 757-331-2212
Sara & Cooke Goffigon
All year

75-125-B&B
5 rooms
●
C-ltd/S-no/P-no/H-no

Full breakfast
Afternoon refreshments
Sitting room, library, acres of
private beach, bikes

Acres of secluded, private beach on Chesapeake Bay, wildlife preserve. Queen size beds, antique filled rooms overlooking bay. Country breakfast. E-mail: pickharb@aol.com
Web site: bbonline.com/va/pickharb/

CHAMPLAIN

Linden House B&B
Plantation
PO Box 23, 22438
804-443-1170 Fax: 804-443-0107
800-622-1202
Ken Pounsberry   All year

85-135-B&B
6 rooms, 6 pb
Visa, MC, *Rated*, ●
C-ltd/S-ltd/P-no/H-yes

Full breakfast
Dinner, snacks
Bicycles, sitting room,
Jacuzzi, steam shower,
gazebo, porches

Linden House offers a beautifully decorated and properly landscaped plantation home with 204 acres. Close to winery, golf and river cruise. Dinner by reservation for groups of 10 or more. New Linden Ballroom for receptions. Farm fishing pond and trails.
Web site: bbhost.com/lindenhousebb/

CHARLOTTESVILLE

200 South Street Inn
200 South St, 22902
804-979-0200 Fax: 804-979-4403
800-964-7008
Brendan Clancy
All year

115-230-B&B
20 rooms, 20 pb
Visa, MC, AmEx,
Rated, ●
C-yes/S-yes/P-no/H-yes
French

Continental plus breakfast
Lunch M-F, dinner wkends
Restaurant, comp. wine, sitt.
rm., frplcs., lib., whirlpool
tubs, TVs

Restored residences in downtown historic district near landmarks, shops, restaurants. Room options include whirlpool tubs, fireplaces, canopy beds. E-mail: southst@cstone.net
Web site: southstreetinn.com

CHARLOTTESVILLE

Clifton— The Country Inn
1296 Clifton Inn Dr, 22911
804-971-1800 Fax: 804-971-7098
888-971-1800
Keith Halford
All year

150-315-B&B
14 rooms, 14 pb
Visa, MC, AmEx,
Rated, •
C-yes/S-no/P-no/H-yes

Full breakfast
Dinner (fee), afternoon tea
Restaurant, wine cellar,
fireplaces -all rooms,
recreational fac., weddings

18th century manor house on 40 acres. AAA 4 diamond restaurant and Wine Spectator wine list. Tennis, swimming, Jacuzzi, croquet and private lake. One of "Country Inns" 12 best inns. E-mail: reserve@cstone.net *Web site:* cliftoninn.com

Edgewood Farm B&B
1186 Middle River Rd, 22973
804-985-3782 Fax: 804-985-6275
800-985-3782
Norman & Elanor Schwartz
All year

90-120-B&B
3 rooms, 3 pb
Visa, MC, AmEx,
Rated, •
C-ltd/S-ltd/P-no/H-no

Full breakfast
Compl. cider, snacks on
arrival
Sitting room, library,
fireplaces, cable TV,
accommadate business
travelers

Beautifully restored 1760 Virginia farmhouse in the foothills of the Blue Ridge. Secluded yet accessible. Sumptuous breakfast. We'll pamper you! E-mail: edgewoodfarm@firstva.com *Web site:* firstnetva.com/edgewoodfarm

Foxfield Inn, The
2280 Garth Rd, 22901
804-923-8892 Fax: 804-923-0963
Mary Pat & John Hulburt
All year

95-160-B&B
5 rooms, 5 pb
Visa, MC, AmEx, *Rated*
C-ltd/S-no/P-no/H-yes

Full breakfast
Snacks, wine
Sitting room, Jacuzzis,
fireplace, cable TV, bay
windows

A completely restored 50 year old home with 5 individually decorated bed chambers. Renovations were designed by the hosts specially for a B&B creating a comfortable and gracious experience. E-mail: foxfieldin@aol.com *Web site:* foxfield-inn.com

High Meadows Inn
55 High Meadows Lane, 24590
804-286-2218 Fax: 804-286-2124
800-232-1832
Peter Sushka, Mary Jae Abbitt
All year

95-195-B&B/MAP
14 rooms, 12 pb
Rated, •
C-yes/S-ltd/P-ltd/H-no
French

Full breakfast
Candlelight dining
Nightly winetasting, library,
hot tub, pond, gazebo, bikes,
vineyard

Enchanting historical landmark south of Charlottesville. Large, tastefully appointed rooms; fireplaces; period antiques. Private 50 acres for walking & picnics. E-mail: peterhmi@aol.com *Web site:* highmeadows.com

Inn at Monticello, The
1188 Scottsville Rd, 22902
804-979-3593 Fax: 804-296-1344
Norm & Becky Lindway
All year exc. Chritsmas

120-140-B&B
5 rooms, 5 pb
Visa, MC, *Rated*, •
C-ltd/S-no/P-no/H-no
some French

Full gourmet breakfast
Complimentary local beer &
wine
Sitting room, hammock,
covered porch, croquet,
tennis court nearby

19th century manor, perfectly located 2 miles from Thomas Jefferson's beloved "Monticello." Antiques, canopy beds, fireplaces Golf, tennis, canoeing, wine-tasting nearby, gardens E-mail: innatmonticello@mindspring.com *Web site:* innatmonticello.com

Inn at the Crossroads
PO Box 6519, 22906
804-979-6452
John & Maureen Deis
All year

80-125-B&B
6 rooms, 6 pb
Visa, MC, *Rated*, •
C-ltd/S-no/P-no/H-no

Full breakfast
Afternoon tea, snacks
Sitting room, tennis court
nearby

Historic inn on 4 acres with panoramic mountain views only 9 miles from Charlottesville. Country breakfast served in the Keeping Room. *Web site:* crossroadsinn.com

Inn at the Crossroads, Charlottesville, VA

CHARLOTTESVILLE

Mark Addy, The
56 Rodes Farm Dr, 22958
804-361-1101 Fax: 804-361-2425
800-278-2154
John Storck Maddox
All year

90-135-B&B
9 rooms, 9 pb
Visa, MC, *Rated*, •
C-ltd/S-ltd/P-no/H-yes
German, little French

Full breakfast
Dinner available, snacks
Sitting room, library, tennis
court, Jacuzzis, pool, suites,
cable TV

Serenity and sophistication nestled at the base of Blue Ridge Mountains. Charming rooms, luxuriously appointed offer incredible views. E-mail: markaddy@symweb.com
Web site: symweb.com/rockfish/mark.html

Old Rose Tavern B&B, The
PO Box 100, 22508
540-948-5771 Fax: 540-972-3140
Jacklyn Webb
All year

125-135-B&B
3 rooms, 3 pb
Most CC,
C-ltd/S-no/P-no/H-no
German

Full breakfast
Tea, wine
Sitting room, suites
suites/fireplaces/Tavern

Historic inn located in the foothills of the Shenandoah Valley. Romantic country getaway furnished with consigned antiques and collectibles from several periods

CHATHAM

Eldon, The Inn at Chatham
1037 Chalk Level Rd, 24531
804-432-0935
Joy & Bob Lemm
All year

80-130-B&B
4 rooms, 3 pb
Visa, MC, *Rated*
C-ltd/S-ltd/P-no/H-ltd

Full breakfast
Dinner (fee), restaurant
Library, swimming pool,
croquet, bocce, winery,
nearby, antiquing

Historic 1835 plantation home. Queen canopy beds, antiques, 13 wooded acres, country setting, orchard, formal garden. Intimate gourmet restaurant
E-mail: eldoninn@gamewood.net

CHINCOTEAGUE

Cedar Gables Seaside Inn
6095 Hopkins Lane, 23336
757-336-1096 Fax: 757-336-1291
888-491-2944
Fred & Claudia Greenway
All year

135-175-B&B
4 rooms, 4 pb
Most CC, *Rated*, •
C-ltd/S-ltd/P-no/H-no
Dutch

Full breakfast
Snacks
Jacuzzis, swimming pool,
suites, fireplaces, cable TV,
canoe & kayak rental

A waterfront inn overlooking Oyster Bay and the Chincoteague Wildlife Refuge. All rooms open to waterfront decks with breathtaking views of Assateague Island. Upscale establishment with many amenities. E-mail: cdrgbl@shore.intercom.net
Web site: intercom.net/user/cdrgbl

CHINCOTEAGUE

Miss Molly's Inn	79-155-B&B	Full breakfast
4141 Main St, 23336	7 rooms, 5 pb	English afternoon tea
757-336-6686 Fax: 757-336-0600	Most CC, *Rated*, •	Vegetarian breakfast
800-221-5620	C-ltd/S-no	available, sitting room,
David & Barbara Wiedenheft	French, Dutch, German	bicycles, beach items,
March-New Years		

Charming Victorian "painted lady" overlooking the Bay. Marguerite Henry stayed here while writing her classic "Misty of Chincoteague." World-famous scones served at teatime. E-mail: msmolly@shore.intercom.net Web site: missmollys-inn.com

Watson House B&B, The	69-115-B&B	Full breakfast
PO Box 905, 23336	8 rooms, 8 pb	Afternoon tea
757-336-1564 Fax: 757-336-5776	Visa, MC, *Rated*, •	Bicycles, beach nearby,
800-336-6787	C-ltd/S-ltd/P-no/H-no	beach chairs & towels,
The Derricksons & The		wildlife, whirlpool tubs
Sneads		
March-Nov		

Beautifully restored Victorian. Furnished with antiques. View of Chincoteague Bay and beach nearby. 2 family cottages. AAA–3 diamond.   Web site: watsonhouse.com

Year of the Horse Inn	75-145-B&B	Continental breakfast
3583 Main St, 23336	5 rooms, 4 pb	Sitting room, library, cable
757-336-3221	Visa, MC,	TV, sun decks, patio, cookout
800-680-0090	C-ltd/S-no/P-no/H-no	facilities
Richard Hebert	French, spanish	
All year		

Chincotengue Island's only waterfront B&B. Three private rooms have sun decks and views of spectacular sunsets over the marshes. A two bedroom apartment with full kitchen & sun porch is also available.   E-mail: rhebert@esva.net Web site: esva.net/~rhebert

CHRISTINASBURG

River's Edge	130-155-MAP	Full breakfast
6208 Little Camp Rd, 24149	4 rooms, 4 pb	Lunch, dinner, snacks
540-381-4147 Fax: 540-381-1036	Most CC, *Rated*, •	Sitting room, library,
888-786-9254	C-ltd/S-no/P-ltd/H-yes	bicycles, fireplace,
Lee Britton	French	conference
All year		

Come restore your spirit! Beautifully restored farmhouse, private mountain valley, porches, river views from every guest room.   E-mail: lbrit@swva.net Web site: river-edge.com

COVINGTON

Milton Hall B&B Inn	95-120-B&B	Full breakfast
207 Thorny Ln, 24426	6 rooms, 6 pb	Sunday evening meals for
540-965-0196	Visa, MC, *Rated*	guests
Suzanne & Eric Stratmann	C-yes/S-ltd/P-yes/H-no	Bar service, comp. wine,
All year		afternoon tea, sitting, room,
		library, patio

English country manor c.1874 set on 44 wooded acres with gardens. This Historic Land-mark adjoins national forest, mountains, lakes, springs. Near hunting, fishing. Crib/rolla-way available. Fully redecorated with period antiques and reproductions. E-mail: milton_h@cfw.com Web site: milton-hall.com

CULPEPER

Fountain Hall B&B	95-150-B&B	Continental plus breakfast
609 S East St, 22701	6 rooms, 6 pb	Complimentary beverages
540-825-8200 Fax: 540-825-7716	Most CC, *Rated*, •	3 sitting rooms, books,
800-29-VISIT	C-yes/S-no/P-no/H-yes	fireplaces, VCR, porches, golf
Steve & Kathi Walker		nearby, bicycles
All year		

Gracious accommodations for business & leisure. Centrally located in historic Culpeper, between Washington, D.C., Charlottesville & Skyline Drive.   E-mail: visit@fountainhall.com Web site: fountainhall.com

DAMASCUS

Apple Tree B&B	50-125-B&B	Full breakfast
PO Box 878, 24236	5 rooms, 5 pb	Snacks
540-475-5261	Visa, MC,	Sitting room, library, suites,
800-231-7626	C-yes/S-no/P-no/H-yes	cable TV, accommodates
John & Beth Reese		business travelers
All year		

High comfort with a low-key, relaxed feeling. The place for outdoor activities or sit the day away on our wraparound porches. We also have a wedding chapel.
E-mail: appletree@naxs.com *Web site:* appletreebnb.com

EASTERN SHORE

Gladstone House B&B, The	65-95-B&B	Full breakfast
PO Box 296, 23350	3 rooms, 3 pb	Afternoon tea, snacks
757-442-4614 Fax: 757-442-4678	Visa, MC, AmEx,	Sitting room, bicycles, library
800-BNBGUEST	*Rated*, •	
Pat & Al Egan	S-no/P-no/H-ltd	
All year		

Step back in time in an elegant brick Georgian home. Small town atmosphere. Four-course breakfast. Vegetarian breakfast available. Coffee at your bedroom door.
E-mail: egan@gladstonehouse.com *Web site:* gladstonehouse.com

FAIRFAX

Bailiwick Inn, The	135-309-B&B	Full breakfast
4023 Chain Bridge Rd, 22030	14 rooms, 14 pb	Restaurant, afternoon tea
703-691-2266 Fax: 703-934-2112	Visa, MC, AmEx,	Sitting room, fax, phones &
800-366-7666	*Rated*, •	cable TV in all rooms
Bob & Annette Bradley	C-yes/S-no/P-no/H-yes	
All year		

Built in 1800; rooms are elegantly furnished with antiques, featuring fireplaces, Jacuzzi, full breakfast and afternoon tea. Candlelight dinners, weddings and special events. E-mail: theinn@bailiwickinn.com *Web site:* bailiwickinn.com

FREDERICKSBURG

Fredericksburg Colonial	59-89-B&B	Continental breakfast
1707 Princess Anne St, 22401	32 rooms, 32 pb	Conference room avail.,
540-371-5666 Fax: 540-371-5884	Visa, MC, *Rated*, [no]	honeymoon/anniversary,
Bonnie Echols	C-yes/S-no/P-no/H-yes	Colonial Suites
All year		

32 antique appointed rooms. Victorian/Civil War era decor. Located in the Olde Town of Fredericksburg's historic district. Wonderful restaurants, antique shops, and historic attractions within walking distance.

Hillcrest Farm Inn B&B	75-100-B&B	Full breakfast
1487 Garrisonville Rd, 22554	4 rooms, 4 pb	Afternoon tea, snacks, comp.
540-752-9341 Fax: 540-752-9341	Visa, MC, •	wine
Chip & Linda Chagnon	C-ltd/S-no/P-no/H-no	Sitting room, library,
Feb. 1-Dec. 20		Jacuzzis, swimming pool,
		cable TV, suites

Charming inn located in a country setting. Each room designed and furnished to depict a certain aspect of the American Civil War. Located 30 miles from Washington DC.
E-mail: hillcrestfarminn@erols.com

La Vista Plantation B&B	85-105-B&B	Full breakfast
4420 Guinea Station Rd, 22408	2 rooms, 2 pb	Complimentary soda and ice
540-898-8444	Visa, MC, •	Sitting room, library, A/C,
800-529-2823	C-yes/S-no/P-ltd/H-no	kitchen, TV, phones, fishing,
Michele & Edward Schiesser		gardens, radio
All year		

Lovely 1838 Classical Revival country home on 10 acres outside historic Fredericksburg. Antiques; private fireplaces; old trees; pond E-mail: lavistabb@aol.com
Web site: bbonline.com/va/lavista/

La Vista Plantation, Fredericksburg, VA

FRONT ROYAL

Killahevlin
1401 North Royal Ave, 22630
540-636-7335 Fax: 540-636-8694
800-847-6132
Susan O'Kelly Lang   All year

125-225-B&B
6 rooms, 6 pb
Visa, MC, *Rated*, •
C-ltd/S-no/P-no/H-no

Full breakfast; comp.
snacks/beer/wine
Scenic, sitting room,
Whirlpools, gazebos,
screened porch

Historic Edwardian mansion. Civil War encampment hill. Mtn. views, working fireplaces. Picturesque Koi fish pool with waterfall. Prepare to be pampered. Private Irish pub for guests E-mail: kllhvln@shentel.net *Web site:* vairish.com

GORDONSVILLE

Sleepy Hollow Farm B&B
16280 Blue Ridge Turnpk,
22942
540-832-5555 Fax: 540-832-2515
800-215-4804
Beverley & Dorsey   All year

65-150-B&B
7 rooms, 6 pb
Visa, MC, *Rated*, •
C-yes/S-yes/P-yes/H-no
Spanish, French

Full breakfast
Complimentary wine,
beverages
Sitting room, conf. room,
croquet field, gazebo, pond
fishing & swimming

Old farmhouse & cottage with whirlpool furnished in antiques, accessories. One bdrm with fireplace & Jacuzzi. In beautiful countryside, near James Madison's Montpelier.

HARRISONBURG

Inn at Keezletown Rd B&B
1224 Keezletown Rd, 24486
540-234-0644
800-465-0100
Sandy Inabinet   All year

85-105-B&B
4 rooms, 4 pb
Visa, MC, *Rated*, •
C-ltd/S-no/P-no/H-no

Full breakfast
Snacks
Sitting room

Elegant 1896 Victorian with many antiques and wonderful creature comforts. Great food and beautiful gardens, Skyline Drive, antique shops, and historic sites nearby. E-mail: keezlinn@shentel.net *Web site:* bbhsv.org/keezlinn/

IRVINGTON

Hope and Glory Inn, The
PO Box 425, 22480
804-438-6053 Fax: 804-438-5362
800-497-8228
Joyce Barber   All year

95-175-B&B
11 rooms, 11 pb
•
C-ltd/S-no/P-ltd/H-no

Full breakfast
Sitting room, messages,
bikes, tennis court, croquet
& boccee on premises

Named by Europe's Tatler/Cunard Travel Guide as one of "The 101 Best Hotels in the World," our Inn has graduated from a small school opened in 1890 into a fine little hotel. Our accommodations include 3 suites and 4 cottages. Web site: hopeandglory.com

LEESBURG

Norris House Inn, The
108 Loudoun St SW, 20175
703-777-1806 Fax: 703-771-8051
800-644-1806
Pam & Don McMurray
All year

90-145-B&B
6 rooms, 6 pb
Visa, MC, Disc, *Rated*,
●
C-ltd/S-no/P-no/H-no

Full candlelit breakfast
Complimentary wine,
afternoon tea
3 parlors, library, antique
pump organ, veranda, lovely
gardens

Noteworthy 1806 Virginia home in heart of historic district. Antique furnishings throughout. Two guest rooms with fireplaces. Stone House-British headquarters French & Indian war E-mail: inn@norrishouse.com Web site: norrishouse.com

LEXINGTON

Applewood Inn & Llama Trek
PO Box 1348, 24450
540-463-1962 Fax: 540-463-6996
800-463-1902
Linda /Chris Best   Closed Jan.

80-129-B&B
4 rooms, 4 pb
Most CC,
C-ltd/S-no/P-ltd/H-ltd
German

Full breakfast
Hot cider, beverages
Fridge, pantry, firplaces,
sitting room, porches, hot
tub, pool, hiking

Spectacular solar home on 35 acres. Mountain views. Close to historic Lexington. Adjacent 900 acre Rockbridge Hunt, llama treks. Heart healthy breakfasts. For the nature lover. 3 rooms with fireplaces, 2 with whirlpool tubs. E-mail: applewd@cfw.com Web site: applewoodbb.com/

B&B at Llewellyn Lodge, A
603 S Main St, 24450
540-463-3235 Fax: 540-464-3122
800-882-1145
John & Ellen Roberts   All year

65-110-B&B
6 rooms, 6 pb
Most CC, *Rated*, ●
C-ltd/S-yes/P-no/H-no

Full breakfast
Afternoon tea, snacks
Sitting room, cable TV,
tennis/pool/golf nearby,
hiking, fly-fishing

Charming Colonial, walkable to museums, colleges, restaurants. John invites you to test yourself on one of his hikes. Golf. Outdoor packages. E-mail: lll@rockbridge.net Web site: llodge.com

Brierley Hill
985 Borden Rd, 24450
540-464-8421 Fax: 540-464-8925
800-422-4925
Al & Jeanne Perkins
All year

95-160-B&B
5 rooms, 5 pb
Visa, MC, *Rated*, ●
C-ltd/S-ltd/P-no

Full breakfast
Afternoon tea
Hiking, canoeing, horseback
riding, packages available

English country house atmosphere. Magnificent views of Blue Ridge Mountains and Shenandoah Valley. Children over 12 welcome. Smoking permitted outside. E-mail: brierley@cfw.com Web site: brierleyhill.com

Historic Country Inns
11 N Main St, 24450
540-463-2044 Fax: 540-463-7262
877-463-2044
Merideth Family, D.
Fredenburg
All year

65-165-B&B
43 rooms, 43 pb
Most CC, *Rated*, ●
C-yes/S-ltd/P-no/H-ltd

Continental plus breakfast
Complimentary wine, dinner
avail.
Restaurant, bar service,
tennis court, Jacuzzis, suites,
fireplaces

3 lovely restored historic homes in the heart of historic district. One (Maple Hall) is a stately plantation home conveniently located at the intersection of I-81N and Rt 11N on 56 rolling acres.   Web site: innbook.com/maple.html

Hummingbird Inn
PO Box 147, 24439
540-997-9065 Fax: 540-997-0289
800-397-3214
Jeremy & Diana Robinson
All year

95-135-B&B
5 rooms, 5 pb
Most CC, *Rated*, ●
C-ltd/S-no/P-ltd

Full breakfast
Aftn. tea, snacks, dinner on
Sat.
Sitting room, library,
Jacuzzis, fireplace, cable TV

Hummingbird Inn, a unique Carpenter Gothic villa, offers accommodations in an early Victorian setting. Antique furnishings, modern bathrooms, and warm hospitality await you. E-mail: hmgbird@cfw.com Web site: hummingbirdinn.com

LEXINGTON

Lavender Hill Farm
1374 Big Spring Dr, 24450
540-464-5877
800-446-4240
Sarah & John Burleson
All year

69-79-B&B
3 rooms, 3 pb
Visa, MC, Disc, *Rated*,
•
C-yes/S-no/P-no/H-no

Full breakfast
Dinner—available to guests
Sitting room, A/C, horseback
riding, hikes, fishing, birding,
biking

English country charm and outstanding food await you. Quiet country setting on working farm located near historic Lexington in the Shenandoah Valley. E-mail: lavhill@cfw.com
Web site: lavhill.com/

Magnolia House, The
501 S Main St, 24450
540-463-2567 Fax: 540-463-4358
Tom Sakats
All year

105-140-B&B
5 rooms, 5 pb
Visa, MC, AmEx,
C-ltd/S-ltd/P-no/H-no

Full breakfast
Aftn. tea, snacks, wine
Boxed lunches & dinners
served upon request, sitting
room, library

An historic home, c. 1868, located in the heart of Lexington. Enjoy the gardens & easy access to historic downtown sites. E-mail: magnolia@rockbridge.net
Web site: magnoliahouseinn.com

Stoneridge B&B
PO Box 38, 24450
540-463-4090 Fax: 540-463-6078
800-491-2930
Norm & Barbara Rollenhagen
All year

90-160-B&B
5 rooms, 5 pb
Most CC, *Rated*, •
C-ltd/S-no/P-no/H-no

Full breakfast
Afternoon tea
Sitting room, library,
Jacuzzis, suites, fireplaces,
cable TV

Romantic 1829 Antebellum home on 36 acres. Elegant rooms have queen beds and private baths, most featuring balconies, fireplaces and double Jacuzzis. E-mail: rollo_va@cfw.com
Web site: webfeat-inc.com/stoneridge

LINCOLN

Springdale Country Inn
18348 Lincoln Rd, 20132
540-338-1832 Fax: 540-338-1839
800-388-1832
Nancy & Roger Fones
All year

125-200-B&B
10 rooms, 6 pb
Visa, MC, •
C-ltd/S-no/P-no/H-yes

Full breakfast
Lunch & dinner available
Complimentary wine, bar
service, sitting room, library,
A/C

Pristine restoration of historic Quaker boarding school, circa 1832. Babbling brook, walking bridges, wildflower meadow, terraced gardens. E-mail: springdale@vmcs.com
Web site: springdalecountryinn.com

LOVINGSTON

Harmony Hill B&B
929 Wilson Hill Rd, 22922
804-263-7750
877-263-7750
Bob & Joanne Cuoghi
All year

64-100-B&B
5 rooms, 5 pb
Visa, MC, Disc, *Rated*,
•
C-ltd/S-no/P-no/H-no

Full breakfast
Snacks
Sitting room, library, Jacuzzi,
fireplaces, accommodate
business travelers

Spacious log home surrounded by hills and farms. Enjoy coffee on the porch while aromas of a country breakfast beckon. Fruit and flowers in your room. E-mail: harmony@
nextfrontier.net *Web site:* harmony-hill.com

LURAY

Shenandoah River Inn
201 Stagecoach Ln, 22835
540-743-1144 Fax: 540-743-9100
888-666-6760
Paul Bramell
All year

135-145-B&B
3 rooms, 3 pb
Most CC, •
S-no/P-no/H-yes

Full breakfast
Afternoon tea
Sitting room, Jacuzzis,
fireplaces, cable TV, fishing
from our front yard

Historic romantic former stagecoach inn and ferryboat house directly on the river. Private baths, fireplaces in every room, king/queen beds, many porches, gourmet breakfasts, surrounded by mountains.

LURAY

Woodruff House B&B, The	135-195-MAP	Full gourmet breakfast
330 Mechanic St, 22835	6 rooms, 6 pb	Afternoon tea, snacks,
540-743-1494 Fax: 540-743-1722	Visa, MC, Disc, *Rated*,	dinner
Lucas & Deborah Woodruff	•	Candlelight dinner included,
All year	C-ltd/S-ltd/P-no/H-no	library, Jacuzzis for two

Shenandoah Valley 1882 fairytale Victorian. Chef-prepared gourmet dinners, breakfast. Morning coffee to your door. Relax in romantic garden spa. Private wine label.
Web site: woodruffinns.com

LYNCHBURG

Federal Crest Inn B&B	95-125-B&B	Full breakfast
1101 Federal St, 24504	5 rooms, 4 pb	Afternoon beverages
804-845-6155 Fax: 804-845-1445	Most CC, *Rated*, •	Snacks, sitting roomm,
800-818-6155	C-ltd/S-no/P-no/H-no	library, '50s cafe with 60" TV
Ann & Phil Ripley		
All year		

Romantic and elegant! Unique 1909 spacious mansion with BR fireplace, A/C, Jacuzzi, antiques. Theater with 60 inch TV on the 3rd floor.   E-mail: inn@federalcrest.com
Web site: federalcrest.com

Lynchburg Mansion Inn B&B	109-144-B&B	Full breakfast
405 Madison St, 24504	5 rooms, 5 pb	Library, suites, fireplaces,
804-528-5400 Fax: 804-847-2545	Most CC, *Rated*, •	cable TV, 5 person outdoor
800-352-1199	C-yes/S-ltd/P-no/H-no	spa
Bob & Mauranna Sherman		
All year		

Luxurious accommodations in historic district. 9000 square foot Spanish Georgian Mansion, deluxe suites available, king beds, 22 immense columns ring the 105 foot Spanish tiled veranda, outdoor spa.   E-mail: mansioninn@aol.com *Web site:* lynchburgmansioninn.com

MATHEWS

Ravenswood Inn	70-120-B&B	Full gourmet breakfast
PO Box 1430, 23109	5 rooms, 5 pb	Complimentary wine at
804-725-7272	Visa, MC, *Rated*	sunset
Mrs. Ricky Durham	C-ltd/S-ltd/P-no/H-no	Living room, library,
Mid-Feb-early Dec		sailboats, bicycles, hot tub

Excellent waterfront location for unwinding, bicycling and enjoying the pleasures of the Chesapeake Bay (tide water area).   E-mail: innkeeper@ravenswood-inn.com
Web site: ravenswood-inn.com

MIDDLETOWN

Wayside Inn since 1797	100-175-EP	Full breakfast (fee)
7783 Main St, 22645	22 rooms, 22 pb	Lunch, dinner appetizers
540-869-1797 Fax: 540-869-6038	Most CC, *Rated*, •	Bar serv., entertainment,
877-869-1797	C-yes/S-yes/P-no/H-yes	sitting room, piano, retreat
Margie McAllister		facilities
All year		

In Shenandoah Valley, offering Civil War history with southern cooking. Rooms are decorated in different historic styles with antiques for sale.   E-mail: waysiden@shentel.net
Web site: waysideofva.com/wayside/

MOLLUSK

Guesthouse at Greenvale	85-100-B&B	Continental breakfast
Route 354, Box 70, 22517	6 rooms, 6 pb	Kitchens
804-462-5995	C-ltd/S-ltd/P-no	Sitting room, library,
Pam Smith		veranda, pool, beach, docks,
All year		boating, bicycles

Waterfront guesthouse on 13 acres. Privacy & tranquility with pool, dock, private beach. Beautiful sunsets & birdwatcher's paradise. Fishing & crabbing.   E-mail: pegs@sylvaninfo.net

MONTEREY

Mountain Laurel Inn
PO Box 68, 24465
540-468-2055 Fax: 540-468-2183
All year

75-100-B&B
4 rooms, 4 pb
AmEx, Disc, •
C-ltd/S-no/P-no

Full breakfast
Afternoon tea
Lunch (fee), sitting room,
and golf

Perfect escape/adventure or R&R hideout. Gorgeous Victorian setting in a charming turn of the century mountain home E-mail: curryalx@cfw.com

NELLYSFORD

Meander Inn at Penny Lane
3100 Berry Hill Rd, 22958
804-361-1121 Fax: 804-361-1380
Alain & Francesca San Giorgio
All year

105-125-B&B
5 rooms, 5 pb
Most CC, *Rated*, •
C-ltd/S-ltd/P-no/H-no
French, Spanish, Italian

Full breakfast
Dinner, afternoon tea, snacks
Sitting room, library,
Jacuzzis, fireplace, cable TV,
horse boarding

Romantic getaway with a French "flair", nestled in the foothills of Virginia's Blue Ridge Mountains, The Meander Inn an 85 year old Victorian farmhouse on 40 acres of pasture and woods, skirted by hiking trails and traversed by the Rockfish River.
E-mail: meanderinn@aol.com *Web site:* bbonline.com/va/meanderinn/

Trillium House
PO Box 280, 22958
804-325-9126 Fax: 804-325-1099
800-325-9126
Betty/Ed Dinwiddie   All year

100-115-B&B
12 rooms, 12 pb
Visa, MC, *Rated*, •
C-ltd/S-ltd/P-no/H-yes

Full breakfast
Afternoon tea, bar
Dinner Fri & Sat, sitting
room, library, near tennis,
pool, golf, skiing

In a wooded setting on the 17th fairway of Wintergreen's mountaintop golf course, close to hiking, tennis, swimming and skiing. Our hospitable inn is the ideal getaway.
E-mail: trilliumln@aol.com *Web site:* trilliumhouse.com

NEW MARKET

Cross Roads Inn B&B
9222 John Sevier Rd, 22844
540-740-4157 Fax: 540-740-4255
888-740-4157
Mary-Lloyd & Roland
Freistzer   All year

55-100-B&B
6 rooms, 6 pb
Visa, MC, *Rated*
C-yes/S-no/P-no/H-ltd
German

Full breakfast
Afternoon tea, applestrudel
Sitting room, Jacuzzis,
fireplaces, cable TV, evening
beverages

Gracious country manor in garden setting with mountain views; bountiful breakfast served in sunny breakfast room; Austrian tradition of hospitality includes afternoon coffee/tea with Mary-Lloyd's famous applestrudel. E-mail: freisitz@shentel.net
Web site: crossroadsinnva.com

NORFOLK

B&B at the Page House Inn
323 Fairfax Ave, 23507
757-625-5033 Fax: 757-623-9451
800-599-7659
Stephanie & Ezio DiBelardino
All year

125-200-B&B
6 rooms, 6 pb
Visa, MC, AmEx,
Rated, •
C-ltd/S-no/P-no/H-no
Italian

Full breakfast
In-room continental
breakfast
24hr. self-serve snacks,
private in-room phones,
cable TV, suites w/refrig

Award-winning restoration. Elegantly appointed. "Year's best inn buy," Country Inns Magazine. Operated in conjunction with Bianca Boat & Breakfast. The decor at the Page House Inn is dynamic-always refreshed and refreshing! E-mail: innkeeper@pagehouseinn.com
Web site: pagehouseinn.com

ORANGE

Hidden Inn
249 Caroline St, 22960
540-672-3625 Fax: 540-672-5029
800-841-1253
Barbara & Ray Lonick
All year

79-169-B&B
10 rooms, 10 pb
Visa, MC, *Rated*, •
C-ltd/S-no/P-no/H-no

Full country breakfast
Afternoon tea
Sitting room, Jacuzzi, A/C,
fireplaces, cable TV, sitting
room

Comfortably furnished country inn tucked away in rural community. Convenient to D.C., Charlottesville, Blue Ridge Mountains. E-mail: hiddeninn@ns.gemlink.com
Web site: hiddeninn.com

PENN LAIRD

Hearth N' Holly Inn
Rd 2, Box 655, 22846
540-434-6766   800-209-1379
Dennis/Doris Brown   All year

95-B&B
3 rooms, 3 pb
Visa, MC, *Rated*,   •
S-no/P-no/H-no

Full breakfast
Afternoon tea, snacks
Sitting room, hot tubs pool,
bicycles, trails

Enjoy our hiking trails, spa, great gourmet breakfasts. An Inn where the fresh country air & tranquil surroundings are soothing to the senses   E-mail: hhinn@rioa.net
Web site: hearthnholly.com

PETERSBURG

High Street Inn, The
405 High St, 23803
804-773-0505 Fax: 804-861-2319
888-733-0505
Jim Hiller   All year

75-110-B&B
6 rooms, 4 pb
Visa, AmEx, *Rated*,   •
C-yes/S-no/P-yes/H-no

Full breakfast
Afternoon tea, snacks
Sitting room, library, suites,
cable TV

The Inn offers it's guest a unique experience: historic setting, privacy, elegance, convenience & excellent service. The six bedrooms are large and friendly. Your auto can be parked in our private facility and you can walk to restaurants.   E-mail: highst@mail.ctg.net
Web site: ctg.net/owlcat

PORTSMOUTH

Bianca Boat & Breakfast
323 Fairfax Ave, 23507
757-625-5033 Fax: 757-623-9451
800-599-7659
Stephanie & Ezio DiBelardino
All year

200-300-B&B
2 rooms, 2 pb
Visa, MC, AmEx,
Rated,   •
C-ltd/S-no/P-no/H-no
Italian, Spanish

Full breakfast
Afternoon tea, snacks
Salon, cable television,
private afternoon sailing, to
Chesapeake Bay

Romance with a capital R! Intrigued with a seafarer's lifestyle? Imagine the smell & feel of salt air! Think of falling asleep to the gentle lapping of water against the hull. Featured in "Southern Living" April, 1999.   E-mail: firstmate@boatandbreakfast.com
Web site: boatandbreakfast.com

RICHMOND

Emmanuel Hutzler House
2036 Monument Ave, 23220
804-353-6900
Lyn Benson & John
Richardson   All year

95-155-B&B
4 rooms, 4 pb
Visa, MC, *Rated*,   •
C-ltd/S-no/P-no/H-no

Full breakfast—weekends
Continental plus—wkdays
Living room, library,
fireplace in 2 of rooms,
Jacuzzi in large room

*Elegant 1914 Italian Renaissance in historic district with natural mahogany raised paneling, wainscoting, leaded glass windows and coffered ceilings with dropped beams.
E-mail:* be.our.guest@bensonhouse.com *Web site:* bensonhouse.com

ROANOKE

Inn At Burwell Place
601 W Main St, 24153
540-387-0250 Fax: 540-387-3279
800-891-0250
Mary Workman   All year

90-132-B&B
4 rooms, 4 pb
Visa, MC, AmEx, *Rated*
C-ltd/S-no/P-no/H-no

Full breakfast
Snacks, comp. wine
Sitting room, Jacuzzis, suites,
fireplaces, Cable TV,
business travelers

*AAA 3-diamond. This 7000-sq.-ft. mansion was built in 1907 with magnificent views of the Blue Ridge Mountains. Each guestroom has private vintage bathroom, plush robes, slippers, phone, CATV w/remote, A/C, down comforters, Ralph Lauren sheets, towels.
Web site:* burwellplace.com

SHENANDOAH VALLEY

Hotel Strasburg
213 Holliday St, 22657
540-465-9191 Fax: 540-465-4797
800-348-8327
Gary & Carol Rutherford
All year

75-79-B&B
29 rooms, 29 pb
Most CC, *Rated*,   •
C-yes/S-yes/P-no/H-no

Continental breakfast
Restaurant, bar service
Snacks, meeting rooms,
sitting room, near beach,
Jacuzzi in some rooms

Charming Victorian restoration, rooms with period antiques, some Jacuzzi suites. Great food & atmosphere.   E-mail: thehotel@shentel.net *Web site:* svta.org/thehotel

SHENANDOAH VALLEY

Ruby Rose Inn, The	115-145-B&B	Snacks
275 Chapel Rd, 22851	3 rooms, 3 pb	Sitting room, library, jacuzzi,
540-778-4680	Visa, MC, Disc, •	fireplace, cable TV, business
R. Mirocco & D. Magliette	C-ltd/S-no/P-no/H-no	travelers
All year		

Lovely Victorian home, c.1890, is the ideal setting for a peaceful retreat. Furnished with ecletic mix of the old and not so old. Guest awaken to a full breakfast, complete with homemade breads and fresh fruits. E-mail: rubyrz1@shentel.net *Web site:* shenandoah-RubyRoseInn.com

SMITHFIELD

Isle of Wight Inn	59-119-B&B	Full breakfast
1607 S Church St, 23430	12 rooms, 12 pb	Snacks, tea, soft drinks
757-357-3176	Visa, MC, AmEx,	Sitting room, Jacuzzi, walking
800-357-3245	*Rated*, •	tour, golf and fishing nearby
Bob Hart	C-yes/S-ltd/P-no/H-yes	
All year		

Luxurious inn & antique shop. Famous for Smithfield hams & homes dating from 1750. Saint Lukes church, 1632. Near Colonial Williamsburg & Jamestown.

Smithfield Station Inn	69-225-B&B	Continental(Mon.-Fri.)
PO Box 486, 23431	15 rooms, 15 pb	Bar/restaurant (fee)
757-357-7700	Visa, MC, AmEx, •	Riverfront boardwalk,
757-874-7700	C-ltd/S-yes/P-no/H-no	boardwalk Rawbar & Grill,
Ron & Tina Pack		rent bikes/canoes/skiffs
All year		

Romantic waterfront Inn modeled after Victorian Coast Guard Station. Full serv. Restaurant & Marina. Smithfield Historic District. 2 lighthouse suites E-mail: smfdsta@pilot.net

SOUTH BOSTON

Oak Grove Plantation B&B	55-120-B&B	Full gourmet breakfast
PO Box 45, 24535	4 rooms, 1 pb	Dinner by reservation
804-575-7137	*Rated*, •	Sitting room, library, bikes,
Pickett Craddock	C-yes/S-ltd/P-no/H-yes	wildflower walks & Reiki by
May-Sept.	Spanish	reservation

Come enjoy our Antebellum country home built by our ancestors in 1820. 400 acres with trails, creeks and wildlife. Children welcome. E-mail: oakgrove1@juno.com *Web site:* rimstarintl.com/cra00001.htm

SPERRYVILLE

Apple Hill Farm B&B	95-155-B&B	Gourmet full breakfast
117 Old Hollow Rd, 22740	4 rooms, 4 pb	Lunch baskets-ask, snacks
540-987-9454 Fax: 540-987-3139	•	Sitting room, fishing,
800-326-4583	C-ltd/S-ltd/P-no/H-no	fireplaces, fax service
Wayne & Dot Waller		
All year		

Peaceful setting, over 20 acres of woods, pastures, river frontage, secluded. Balconies with views, hiking, horseback riding, wineries, antiquing E-mail: dotsway@aol.com *Web site:* bnb-n-va.com/applehil.htm

Conyers House Inn & Stable	150-300-B&B	Hearty gourmet breakfast
3131 Slate Mills Rd, 22740	8 rooms, 8 pb	Comp. afternoon
540-987-8025 Fax: 540-987-8709	*Rated*, •	refreshments
Sandra & Norman	C-ltd/S-ltd/P-ltd/H-no	Candlelight dinners, all
All year	Fr., Ger., It., Arabic	rooms w/fireplaces, 2 pianos,
		9 porches

18th-century former country store graciously furnished with antiques. Hiking, foxhunting & trail rides. 6 course candlelit dinner by reservation. ABC license. Instruction included in trail rides. E-mail: conyers@mnsinc.com *Web site:* conyershouse.com

STAUNTON

Ashton Country House
1205 Middlebrook Ave, 24401
540-885-7819 Fax: 540-885-6029
800-296-7819
Vince & Dorie DiStefano
All year

70-125-B&B
4 rooms, 4 pb
Rated, ●
S-no/P-ltd/H-no

Full breakfast
Afternoon tea, snacks
Sitting room, A/C, live piano
music weekends
accompanies tea

1860's Greek Revival on 20 acres. One mile from town. Professional musician and professional chef entertain and care for you. Delicious! Delightful.
Web site: bbhost.com/ashtonbnb

Frederick House
28 N New St, 24401
540-885-4220 Fax: 540-885-5180
800-334-5575
Joe & Evy Harman
All year

85-200-B&B
23 rooms, 23 pb
Most CC, *Rated*, ●
C-yes/S-no/P-no/H-no

Full breakfast
Vegetarian breakfast
available
Sitting room, library,
conference facilities,
Nationall Register listing

The oldest city west of the Blue Ridge Mountains of Virginia, historic Staunton is Woodrow Wilson's birthplace. Shops and restaurants. *E-mail:* ejharman@frederickhouse.com
Web site: frederickhouse.com

Sampson Eagon Inn, The
238 East Beverley St, 24401
540-886-8200
800-597-9722
Frank & Laura Mattingly
All year

95-125-B&B
5 rooms, 5 pb
Visa, MC, AmEx, *Rated*
S-ltd/P-no/H-ltd

Full breakfast
Complimentary
snacks/beverages
Sitting area with TV/VCR,
video library, phones, porch
with swing, cable TV

Affordable luxury accommodations in a preservation award winning antebellum manor, where comfort and hospitality are key. In-town convenience, minutes away from the history, beauty and recreational activities of the Shenandoah Valley. *E-mail:* eagoninn@ rica.net *Web site:* eagoninn.com

---

Thornrose House-Gypsy Hill
531 Thornrose Ave, 24401
540-885-7026 Fax: 540-885-6458
800-861-4338
Suzy & Otis Huston
All year

70-90-B&B
5 rooms, 5 pb
Rated
C-ltd/S-ltd/P-no/H-no

Full breakfast
Afternoon tea
Sitting room, tennis, golf &
pool, across street

Stately Georgian residence with A/C and private baths in all guestrooms. In historic Victorian town. Adjacent 300 acre park offers golf, tennis, swimming.
Web site: bbhsv.org/thornrose

STEELES TAVERN

Steeles Tavern Manor
Box 39, 24476
540-377-6444 Fax: 540-377-5937
800-743-8666
Eillen & William Hoernlein
All year

135-170-B&B
Visa, MC, Disc, *Rated*

Full breakfast
Afternoon
refreshments/tea/sherry
Plush robes, extra pillows,
blankets & towels, movie
library

All rooms have TV/VCR's with a movie library, double Jacuzzis with a private bath, central A/C, fireplaces and ceiling fans. *E-mail:* hoernlei@cfw.com *Web site:* steelestavern.com

---

Sugar Tree Inn
Highway 56, 24476
540-377-2197 Fax: 540-377-6776
800-377-2197
Sarah & Hal Davis
April 1-Dec 1

100-150-B&B
11 rooms, 11 pb
Most CC, *Rated*, ●
C-ltd/S-ltd/P-no/H-yes

Full breakfast
Dinner by res., pub
Sitting room, biking, library,
porches, rocker, creek,
waterfall, conf.

Mountain inn nestled in a forest off Blue Ridge Parkway. Fireplaces in every room; 3 whirlpools, VCRs. Premium suites have A/C. *Web site:* sugartreeinn.com

STEPHENS CITY

Inn at Vaucluse Spring, The
140 Vaucluse Spring Ln, 22655
540-869-0200 Fax: 540-869-9544
800-869-0525
K & M Caplanis, N & B Myers
All year

135-250-B&B
12 rooms, 12 pb
Visa, MC, *Rated*, •
C-ltd/S-no/P-no/H-ltd

Full gourmet breakfast
Dinner available, snacks
Sitting room, library,
Jacuzzis, pool, suites,
fireplaces, conference

Twelve beautifully decorated rooms in 4 historic buildings on 100 scenic acres in Virginia's Northern Shenandoah Valley. Large limestone spring, mountain views, Saturday night dinner. E-mail: mail@vauclusespring.com *Web site:* vauclusespring.com

WARM SPRINGS

Anderson Cottage B&B
Box 176, 24484
540-839-2975
Jean Randolph Bruns
Mar-Nov

60-125-B&B
5 rooms, 4 pb
Rated, •
C-ltd/S-no/P-ltd/H-no

Full breakfast
Sitting room, library, parlors,
porches, yard, croquet,
badminton

Rambling old home in village. Walk to Warm Springs pools. Near Garth Newel Chamber Music Center. Restaurants nearby. Kitchen cottage available year-round.

Inn at Gristmill Square
PO Box 359, 24484
540-839-2231 Fax: 540-839-5770
The McWilliams Family
All year

80-140-B&B
17 rooms, 17 pb
Visa, MC, Disc, *Rated*,
•
C-yes/S-yes/P-no/H-ltd

Continental breakfast
Dinner, bar
Sauna, swimming pool,
tennis courts

Casual country hideaway, historic original mill site dating from 1800s. Each room individually decorated. Fine dining and distinguished wine cellar E-mail: grist@va.tds.net *Web site:* vainns.com/grist.htm

Meadow Lane Lodge
Route 1, Box 110, 24484
540-839-5959 Fax: 540-839-2135
Carter & Michelle Ancona
All year

115-250-B&B
14 rooms, 14 pb
Visa, MC, Disc,
C-yes/S-ltd/P-no/H-no

Full breakfast
Lunch and dinner
Tennis courts, sitting room,
library, bicycle, swimming
pool, suites

Country Inn on 1600 acres nestled in the Allegheny Mountains along the Jackson River. Fly fishing, biking/hiking trails, swimming, tennis court, canoeing, wildlife and full breakfasts await our guests. E-mail: meadowln@va.tds.net *Web site:* meadowlanelodge.com

Three Hills Inn
PO Box 9, 24484
540-839-5381 Fax: 540-839-5199
888-23-HILLS
Doug & Charlene Fike
All year

59-189-B&B
12 rooms, 12 pb
Visa, MC, Disc, *Rated*,
•
C-yes/S-no/P-yes/H-ltd
Spanish

Full breakfast
Snacks, lunch & dinner
available
Restaurant, sitting room,
suites, fireplaces, cable TV,
conference fac.

The manor house is decorated with antiques and period furnishings. Two charming dining rooms, with fireplaces and magnificent mountain views, afford a delightful setting for a relaxed dining experience. E-mail: inn@3hills.com *Web site:* 3hills.com

WARRENTON

Black Horse Inn, The
8393 Meetze Rd, 20187
540-349-4020 Fax: 540-349-4242
Lynn A. Pirozzoli
All year

125-295-B&B
7 rooms, 7 pb
Visa, MC, AmEx,
Rated, •
C-ltd/S-ltd/P-no/H-yes

Full breakfast
Afternoon tea, snacks
Comp. wine, bar service, sitt.
room, lib., fishing, bikes,
rooms w/Jacuzzis

Historic estate in the heart of hunt country, 45 minutes from Washington D.C. Horseback riding, rafting. Elegant rooms, scenic views, fireplaces, Jacuzzis, bountiful breakfasts and teas E-mail: blackhrs@citizen.infi.net *Web site:* blackhorseinn.com

WASHINGTON

Bleu Rock Inn, The	125-195-B&B	Hearty French breakfast
12567 Lee Hwy, 22747	5 rooms, 5 pb	Restaurant, bar service
540-987-3190 Fax: 540-987-3193	Most CC,	Dinner (fee), wine from,
800-537-3652	C-ltd/S-ltd/P-ltd/H-ltd	vineyards, Sunday brunch,
Bernard & Jean Campagne	French	sitting room
All year		

World class cuisine, mountain views, lake, fireplaces, rose gardens and terrace, fountains, and swans all contribute to our Inn's charm. Flagstone terrace with mountain view. E-mail: therock@mns.com

Caledonia Farm— 1812	80-140-B&B	Full breakfast from menu
47 Dearing Rd, 22627	4 rooms, 2 pb	Afternoom tea, snacks, wine
540-675-3693 Fax: 540-675-3693	Most CC, *Rated*, •	Sitting room, library, bikes,
800-BNB-1812	C-ltd/S-ltd/P-no/H-no	hot tub, piano, porch views,
Phil Irwin	German, Danish	lawn games
All year		

National Register stone home/cattle farm adjacent to Shenandoah National Park mountains. Skyline Drive views, history, recreation, hospitality, fireplaces, spa, hayride. Web site: bnb-n-va.com/cale1812.htm

Fairlea Farm B&B	85-135-B&B	Hearty country breakfast
PO Box 124, 22747	4 rooms, 4 pb	Complimentary drinks
540-675-3679 Fax: 540-675-1064	*Rated*, •	Sitting room with fireplace,
Walter and Susan Longyear	C-ltd/S-ltd/P-no/H-no	hiking, horses, shops, near
All year	French	Civil War battlflds

Spectacular mountain views, a 5-min. stroll to The Inn at Little Washington. Warm hospitality & sumptuous breakfast in fieldstone manor house, cattle & sheep. E-mail: longyear@shentel.net *Web site:* inngetaways.com/va/fairlea.html

Gay Street Inn	95-135-B&B	Full breakfast
PO Box 237, 22747	4 rooms, 4 pb	Picnic lunch, afternoon tea
540-675-3288	Visa, MC, AmEx,	Sitting room w/TV, lib., suite
Robin and Donna Kevis	*Rated*, •	w/kitchen, garden,
All year	C-yes/S-ltd/P-yes/H-yes	observatory with views
	German	

In Blue Ridge Mtns., historic country town. 1850s farmhouse with friendly, relaxing atmosphere. Furnished with period New England furniture. Bedroom with fireplace. E-mail: gaystinn@shentel.net

WAYNESBORO

Iris Inn B&B, The	80-140-B&B	Full breakfast
191 Chinquapin Dr, 22980	9 rooms, 9 pb	Snack
540-943-1991 Fax: 540-942-2093	Visa, MC, *Rated*	Sitting room, library, hot
Iris Karl	C-ltd/S-no/P-no/H-yes	tubs, walk to restaurant
All year		

Spacious, comfortable architect-designed inn (1991). Suites added 1996. Some whirlpools, fireplaces. Open year-around. Central location for Shenandoah Valley, BlueRidge, Charlottesville.   E-mail: irisinn@cfw.com *Web site:* irisinn.com

WHITE POST

L'Auberge Provencale	150-295-B&B	Full gourmet breakfast
PO Box 190, 22663	11 rooms, 11 pb	Dinner, bar service
540-837-1375 Fax: 540-837-2004	Most CC, *Rated*, •	Refreshments, flowers,
800-638-1702	C-ltd/S-yes/P-no/H-no	library, sitting room,
Alain & Celeste Borel	French	bicycles, gardens
Exc. Jan-mid-Feb		

Master chef from France presents nationally acclaimed cuisine. Extensive wine list. Elegant accommodations with fireplaces, private entrances. Weddings a specialty, new suite. New sister inn—Villa La Campagnette.   E-mail: cborel@shentel.net *Web site:* laubergeprovencale.com

WILLIAMSBURG

Annemarie's B&B	85-110-B&B	Full breakfast
610 Capitol Landing Rd, 23185	2 rooms, 2 pb	Sitting room, fireplaces,
757-564-0225	Visa, MC,	cable TV, bicycles, gardens
Marie Supplee & Anne Perry	C-ltd/S-no/P-no/H-no	
All year		

Rooms are tastefully furnished with heirlooms, and feather beds covered with fine linens await your slumber. Guests rave of exceptional breakfasts and hospitality. Memories are made at Annemarie's.

Applewood Colonial B&B	75-150-B&B	Full breakfast
605 Richmond Rd, 23185	4 rooms, 4 pb	Afternoon tea, snacks
757-229-0205 Fax: 757-229-9405	Visa, MC, *Rated*, •	Sitting room, suites,
800-899-2753	C-ltd/S-no/P-no/H-no	fireplaces, cable TV, perfect
Jan Pepper		location
All year		

A perfect location to enjoy all the historic sites or just relax and enjoy the hand-crafted architectural details throughout the house. We'll help you plan the perfect getaway. E-mail: applewood@tni.net *Web site:* applewoodbnb.com

Cedars B&B, The	95-180-B&B	Full gourmet breakfast
616 Jamestown Rd, 23185	9 rooms, 9 pb	Afternoon tea
757-229-3591 Fax: 757-229-0756	Visa, MC, *Rated*, •	Fireplaces in parlor and,
800-296-3591	C-yes/S-no/P-no/H-no	cottage, off st. parking, A/C,
Carol, Jim & Brona Malecha		cottage w/2 suites
All year		

Brick Georgian colonial house across the street from William & Mary; 10 min. walk to colonial Williamsburg. Antiques and canopy beds E-mail: cedars@widomaker.com
Web site: cedarsofwilliamsburg.com

Colonial Capital B&B	104-170-B&B	Full gourmet breakfast
501 Richmond Rd, 23185	5 rooms, 5 pb	Afternoon tea & wine
757-776-0570 Fax: 757-253-7667	Most CC, *Rated*, •	Parlor, books, solarium,
800-776-0570	C-ltd/S-ltd/P-no/H-no	games, videos, bicycles, free
Barbara & Phil Craig		on premise parking
All year		

Antique-furnished Colonial Revival-c.1926-3 blocks from Historic Area. Canopied beds & remote control ceiling fans. Garden. Business fac. avail., in-room phones. Honeymoon & other packages. E-mail: ccbb@widomaker.com *Web site:* ccbb.com

Colonial Gardens B&B	115-145-B&B	Full breakfast
1109 Jamestown Rd, 23185	4 rooms, 4 pb	AM coffee, afternoon snacks
757-220-8087 Fax: 757-253-1495	Visa, MC, *Rated*, •	Sitting room, sunroom,
800-886-9715	S-no/P-no/H-no	TV/VCR & phones in rooms,
Scottie & Wilmot Phillips		attention to detail
All year		

Quiet, romantic garden setting, in-town location. Magnificent antiques, original art, warm hospitality. Spacious suites and rooms. "Early riser" coffee. Herbal bath grains, plush monogramed robes, fresh flowers. AAA 3 diamond. E-mail: colgdns@widomaker.com
Web site: colonial-gardens.com

Edgewood Plantation B&B	128-198-B&B	Full breakfast
4800 John Tyler Hwy, 23030	8 rooms, 8 pb	Complimentary
804-829-2962 Fax: 804-829-2962	Visa, MC, *Rated*, •	refreshments
800-296-3343	C-ltd/S-yes	Tea room, shops, fireplaces,
Juilian & Dot Boulware		formal gardens, gazebos,
All year		pool, fishing, TV/VCR

1849 historical 7,000 sq. foot 4 story mansion. Double spiral staircase. Incredible furnishings & antiques-well appointed. Web site: williamsburg-virginia.com/edgewood

Colonial Gardens B&B, Williamsburg, VA

WILLIAMSBURG

For Cant Hill B&B	85-B&B	Continental plus breakfast
4 Canterbury Ln, 23185	2 rooms, 2 pb	Restaurant
757-229-6623 Fax: 757-229-1863	Visa, MC, •	Candy in rooms, bikes,
Martha & Hugh Easler	C-ltd/S-no/P-no/H-no	tennis court, furnished in
All year	Spanish, some German	antiques

City hideaway overlooking lake. Bountiful continental breakfast Short distance to historic Williamsburg & college. Visitor assistance offered Web site: bestofwilliamsburg.com/forcant

Fox & Grape	90-110-B&B	Full breakfast
701 Monumental Ave, 23185	4 rooms, 4 pb	Sitting room, rooms have,
757-229-6914	Most CC, *Rated*	antiques, counted cross
800-292-3699	S-no/P-no/H-no	stitch quilts, folk art
Pat & Bob Orendorff		
All year		

Genteel Accommodations 5 blocks north of Virgina's restored Colonial Capital. This lovely 2-story Colonial with spacious wraparound porch is a perfect place to enjoy your morning coffee, plan you day's activities or relax with your favorite book.
E-mail: info@foxandgrapebb.com

Indian Springs B&B	95-135-B&B	Full breakfast
330 Indian Springs Rd, 23185	4 rooms, 4 pb	Afternoon tea, snacks
757-220-0726 Fax: 757-220-8924	Visa, MC, *Rated*, •	Restaurant nearby, sitting
800-262-9165	C-yes/S-no/P-no/H-yes	room, library, game room,
Kelly & Paul Supplee		veranda
All year		

Short walk to historic district, William & Mary College. Family-operated restaurant nearby. Seasonal snack served in Carriage House. E-mail: indianspgs@tni.net
Web site: indian-springs.com/home.shtml

Inn at 802, The	125-155-B&B	Full breakfast
802 Jamestown Rd, 23185	4 rooms, 4 pb	Snacks, complimentary wine
757-564-0845 Fax: 757-564-7018	Most CC, •	Library, sitting room,
800-672-4086	C-yes/S-no/P-ltd/H-no	fireplaces, cable TV, fitness
Don & Janet McGarva	French	center
All year		

Great location-Colonial Williamsburg 12 minute walk away. Decorated in period style. Common areas include extensive library, large living room, & dining room.
E-mail: don@innat802.com *Web site:* innat802.com

WILLIAMSBURG

Jasmine Plantation B&B Inn	80-125-B&B	Full breakfast
4500 N Courthouse Rd, 23140	6 rooms, 5 pb	Snacks
804-966-9836 Fax: 804-966-5679	Visa, MC, AmEx,	Sitting room, common, areas,
800-NEW-KENT	*Rated*, •	bird watching, walking trails
Joyce & Howard Vogt	C-ltd/S-no/P-no/H-no	
All year		

Country at its best! Full "skip-lunch" country breakfast. Antique filled 1750s home on 47 acres. Convenient I-64 Williamsburg James River Plantations

Legacy of Williamsburg	125-165-B&B	Full breakfast
B&B	4 rooms, 4 pb	Billiards, phones, TV, Six
930 Jamestown Rd, 23185	Visa, MC, *Rated*	fireplaces, library, 18th
757-220-0524 Fax: 757-220-2211	C-ltd/S-no	Century antiques
800-962-4722		
MaryAnn Gist		
All year		

Voted best 18th Century B&B-style inn in Williamsburg. Romantic, quaint canopy beds. It will be the highlight of your vacation. The legacy. Highest ratings, AAA. OUR 1997 INN OF THE YEAR!   Web site: legacyofwilliamsburgbb.com

Liberty Rose B&B Inn	145-225-B&B	Full breakfast
1022 Jamestown Rd, 23185	4 rooms, 4 pb	Complimentary beverages,
757-253-1260	Visa, MC, *Rated*	chocolates
800-545-1825	S-no/P-no/H-no	Sitting room, gift shop, Suite
Brad & Sandra Hirz		with many amenities,
All year		TV/VCRs, movies in rooms

"Williamsburg's most romantic B&B." Charming home renovated in perfect detail. Court-yards, gardens, an acre of magnificent trees. First choice for honeymooners. AAA four diamond rating for 6 years. America's Ten Most Romantic B&Bs for 1999 (AHI). Web site: libertyrose.com

Newport House B&B	130-150-B&B	Full breakfast
710 South Henry St, 23185	2 rooms, 2 pb	Sitting room, Library,
757-229-1775 Fax: 757-229-6408	*Rated*, •	harpsichord, Ballroom for
John & Cathy Millar	C-yes/S-no/P-no/H-no	receptions
All year	French	

Designed in 1756. Completely furnished in period. 5-minute walk from historic area. Colonial dancing every Tuesday evening. Historic colonial recipes for breakfast. VA B&B Assoc. and ABBA member.

Piney Grove at Southall	130-170-B&B	Full plantation breakfast
PO Box 1359, 23187	5 rooms, 5 pb	Snacks, complimentary wine
804-829-2480 Fax: 804-829-6888	AmEx, Disc, *Rated*, •	Sitting room, library,
The Gordineer Family	C-yes/S-no/P-no/H-no	swimming pool, Ballroom for
All year	Some German	receptions

National Register landmark, built 1790, among James River Plantations. Romantic retreat with antiques, pool, fireplaces, mint juleps, gardens and served-breakfast. E-mail: pineygrove@erols.com *Web site:* pineygrove.com

Primrose Cottage, A	100-125-B&B	Full breakfast
706 Richmond Rd, 23185	4 rooms, 4 pb	Sitting room, garden, all
757-229-6421 Fax: 757-259-0717	Visa, MC, *Rated*, •	rooms w/TV's, private bath,
800-522-1901	C-ltd/S-no/P-no/H-no	2 rooms with Jacuzzis
Inge Curtis	German	
All year		

Cozy Cape Cod style home decorated with antiques and family treasures. Short walk to colonial Williamsburg. Award-winning garden. Elegant breakfast. Web site: primrose-cottage.com

WILLIAMSBURG

Williamsburg Sampler B&B	100-150-B&B	"Skip-lunch(R)" breakfast
922 Jamestown Rd, 23185	4 rooms, 4 pb	wet bar/refrig in suites
757-253-0398 Fax: 757-253-2669	*Rated*, •	18th Cty. carriage house,
800-722-1169	C-ltd/S-no/P-no/H-no	Antiques/pewter/samplers,
Helen & Ike Sisane		suites/fireplaces/Tavern
All year		

Williamsburg's finest plantation style colonial home. Richly furnished. Guests have included descendants of John Quincy Adams, Capt. John Smith, Charles Dickens.
E-mail: wbgsampler@aol.com *Web site:* WilliamsburgSampler.com

WOODSTOCK

Inn at Narrow Passage	95-145-B&B	Full breakfast
PO Box 608, 22664	12 rooms, 12 pb	Sitting room, conference
540-459-8000 Fax: 540-459-8001	Visa, MC, *Rated*, •	facility, fireplace, swimming,
800-459-8002	C-ltd/S-ltd/P-no/H-yes	fishing, rafting
Ellen & Ed Markel		
All year		

Historic 1740 log inn on the Shenandoah River. Fireplaces, colonial charm, close to vineyards. *E-mail:* innkeeper@innatnarrowpassage.com *Web site:* innatnarrowpassage.com/

WOOLWINE

Mountain Rose B&B	79-99-B&b	Full breakfast
1787 Charity Highway, 24185		Swimming pool
703-930-1057		
Reeves & Melodie Pogue		
All year		

Nestled along the banks of the Rock Castle Creek, the Mountain Rose Inn offers historical country elegance within the shadows of the Blue Ridge Mountains
E-mail: mtrosein@swva.net *Web site:* swva.net.mtroseinn

YORKTOWN

Marl Inn B&B	85-120-B&B	Continental plus breakfast
PO Box 572, 23690	4 rooms, 4 pb	Sitting room, library, bikes
757-898-3859 Fax: 757-898-3587	Visa, MC, *Rated*, •	for guest use to, tour colonial
800-799-6207	C-ltd/S-no/P-ltd/H-no	village
Eugene C. Marlin		
All year		

Marl Inn is located in the historic district of the restored town. Bicycles with helmets are offered guests to visit battleground, museums, and Revolutionary reception centers.
E-mail: eugenem918@aol.com *Web site:* bedandbreakfastnetwork.com/marlinn/

Washington

ABERDEEN

Cooney Mansion B&B Inn	70-165-B&B	Full breakfast
1705 Fifth St, 98537	8 rooms, 5 pb	Afternoon tea
360-533-0602	Most CC, •	Sitting room, library, tennis
Judi & Jim Lohr	C-ltd/S-no/P-no/H-no	court, Jacuzzi, sauna, golf
All year		

Historic Regis. Arts & Crafts style lumber baron's retreat (orig. furniture) exudes warmth & relaxation. Enjoy rose garden & Mill Creek Park E-mail: cooney@techline.com
Web site: techline.com/~cooney/

ANACORTES ─────────────

Albatross B&B	70-95-B&B	Full breakfast
5708 Kingsway, 98221	4 rooms, 4 pb	Restaurant 1 block away
360-293-0677	Visa, MC, AmEx,	King & queen beds, library,
800-622-8864	*Rated*, •	travel videos, antiques
All year	C-yes/S-ltd/P-ltd/H-no	

Cape Cod-style house near marina, Washington Park & Sunset Beach. Large deck with view. Charter boats, fine fishing, crabbing. E-mail: albatros@cnw.com
Web site: cnw.com/~albatros

Burrow's Bay B&B, A	110-135-B&B	Continental plus breakfast
4911 MacBeth Dr, 98221	1 rooms, 1 pb	Snacks
360-293-4792 Fax: 360-588-9068	Visa, MC, *Rated*	Library, fireplace, cable TV,
Beverly & Winfred Stocker	C-yes/S-ltd/P-no/H-ltd	conference facilities,
All year		microwave & fridge

Fantastic water & island view from your own deck. 1200 sq. ft. suite has a private entry, large sitting room, fireplace, TV, wetbar, and private bath/shower and bedroom with king size bed. E-mail: wdstocker@ssisp.com *Web site:* homestead.com/burbay/home.html

Nantucket Inn	75-125-B&B	Full breakfast
3402 Commercial Ave, 98221	7 rooms, 5 pb	Afternoon tea
360-293-6007 Fax: 360-299-4339	Most CC, *Rated*, •	Spa antiques
888-293-6007	C-ltd/S-no/P-no/H-no	
Lynda & Doug Bransford		
All year		

This eastern Colonial was built in 1925. Lovely gardens, hot tub and small pavilion on grounds for weddings, etc. Seven large airy rooms filled with art & antiques. Full breakfast. E-mail: nantucketinn@halcyon.com *Web site:* whidbey.com/nantucket/

ASHFORD ─────────────

Mountain Meadows Inn	85-135-B&B	Full breakfast for most rooms
B&B	6 rooms, 6 pb	Tea, coffee, s'mores
PO Box 291, 98304	Visa, MC, *Rated*, •	Natural history library,
360-569-2788	C-ltd/S-ltd/P-no/H-ltd	rooms with kitchens,
Harry & Michelle Latimer		outdoor spa
All year		

11 acres with cedar groves, hiking trails, meadows. Native American basketry exhibits. Birdwatching. Nearby Mt. Rainier National Park. E-mail: mtmeadow@mashell.com
Web site: mtn-meadows-mt-rainier.com

BAINBRIDGE ISLAND ─────────────

Buchanan Inn, The	99-159-B&B	Full breakfast
8494 NE Oddfellows Rd, 98110	4 rooms, 4 pb	Wine
206-780-9258 Fax: 206-842-9458	Most CC, *Rated*, •	Sitting room, library, Jacuzzi,
Ron & Judy Gibbs	C-ltd/S-ltd/P-no/H-no	suites, frplc., conference
All year	Some Spanish	facilities

*Located just 35 minutes from Seattle by Washington State ferry, features spacious rooms with all the amenities of a four-star hotel. Private hot tub. Walk to beach
E-mail:* jgibbs@buchananinn.com *Web site:* buchananinn.com

BELLEVUE ─────────────

Cascade View B&B, A	95-120-B&B	Full breakfast
13425 NE 27th St, 98005	2 rooms, 2 pb	Afternoon tea
425-883-7078 Fax: 425-702-9326	Visa, MC, AmEx, *Rated*	Sitting room, library,
888-883-7078	C-yes/S-ltd/P-no/H-no	fireplaces, cable TV,
Marianne & Bill Bundren		accommodate business
All year		travelers

Cozy comfort with panoramic mountain views, gorgeous rose filled garden, convenience of in-city location with natural surroundings. E-mail: innkeepers@acascadeview.com
Web site: acascadeview.com

BELLINGHAM

Schnauzer Crossing B&B Inn	125-200-B&B	Full breakfast
4421 Lakeway Dr, 98226	3 rooms, 3 pb	Sitting room, library, 1/2 acre
360-733-0055 Fax: 360-734-2808	Visa, MC, *Rated*	of gardens, new cottage
800-562-2808	C-yes/S-no/P-ltd	added 1991
Vermont & Donna McAllister	Some Fr., Sp., German	
All year		

A luxury b&b set amidst tall evergreens overlooking Lake Whatcom. Master suite with Jacuzzi. Cottage has fireplace, VCR, private deck, Jacuzzi, skylights. E-mail: schnauzerx@aol.com Web site: schnauzercrossing.com

Stratford Manor	125-175-B&B	Full breakfast
4566 Anderson Way, 98226	4 rooms, 4 pb	Snacks, complimentary wine
360-715-8441 Fax: 360-671-0840	Visa, MC,	Jacuzzis, fireplaces, fresh
Leslie & Jim Lohse	C-ltd/S-no/P-no/H-no	flowers, robes, outdoor spa,
All year		VCRs

Comfortably luxurious English Tudor home on 30 acres. Parklike grounds including perennial gardens and large pond. Wake up coffee delivered to your room followed by a delectable breakfast in the dining room. E-mail: llohse@aol.com Web site: stratfordmanor.com

CAMANO ISLAND

Camano Island Inn	100-160-B&B	Full breakfast
1054 S W Camano Dr, 98292	6 rooms, 6 pb	Lunch & dinner available
360-387-0783 Fax: 360-387-4173	Visa, MC, •	Tea, snacks, wine, sitting
888-718-0783	S-ltd/P-no/H-yes	room, Jacuzzis, suites,
Jon & Kari Soth		fireplaces
All year		

Small, luxurious, waterfront hotel. Rooms have private waterfront decks. Full breakfast and use of kayaks are included, massage also available. E-mail: reservations@ camanoislandinn.com Web site: camanoislandinn.com/

Inn at Barnum Point	99-185-B&B	Full breakfast brunch
464 S Barnum Rd, 98292	3 rooms, 3 pb	Complimentary beverages
360-387-2256 Fax: 360-387-2256	Most CC, *Rated*, •	Sitting room, library,
800-910-2256	C-yes/S-no/P-no/H-no	sidewalks, landscaping,
Carolin Barnum Dilorenzo		lighting (outside)
All year		

On the beach, spectacular sea and mountain view. Spacious rooms with private bath, fireplaces. Near golf, State Park, migrating birds. 900 square feet added for shorebird room. E-mail: barnum@camano.net Web site: whidbey.com/inn/

COUPEVILLE

Captain Whidbey Inn, The	95-225-B&B	Full breakfast
2072 W Capt. Whidbey, 98239	32 rooms, 20 pb	All meals available, bar
360-678-4097 Fax: 360-678-4110	Most CC, *Rated*, •	Sitting room, bicycles,
800-366-4097	C-ltd/S-ltd/P-ltd/H-no	library, sailboats & rowboats
Capt. John Colby Stone	French, German,	
All year	Spanish	

Historic log inn, est. 1907. On the shores of Penn Cove. Antique furnished. Fine restaurant and quaint bar. Sailboats, rowboats & bikes. E-mail: info@captainwhidbey.com Web site: captainwhidbey.com

DEER HARBOR

Palmer's Chart House	60-80-B&B	Full breakfast
PO Box 51, 98243	2 rooms, 2 pb	Library, private deck, flower
360-376-4231	•	beds, gardens, fireplaces,
Don & Majean Palmer	C-ltd/S-ltd/P-no/H-no	cable TV
All year	Spanish	

Quiet, intimate and informal atmosphere. Your hosts know how to pamper you. Fishing, hiking, golf, biking nearby. Day sails on racing-cruising sloop. Sailing on private yacht "Amante."

EVERETT

Gaylord House
3301 Grand Ave, 98201
425-339-9153 Fax: 425-303-9713
888-507-7177
Gaylord, ShirleyAnne &
Theresa
All year

85-175-B&B
5 rooms, 5 pb
Most CC, *Rated*, •
C-ltd/S-ltd/P-no/H-no
Some Italian

Full gourmet breakfast
Lunch, dinner, high tea,
snacks
Sitting room, library, Jacuzzi,
fireplace, cable TV, business
travelers

Our turn-of-the-century home has five theme rooms w/private bath, TV/VCR, data port and private phone line. ShirlyAnne's gourmet breakfasts, afternoon teas and gourmet dinners are wonderful! E-mail: gaylord-house@msn.com Web site: gaylordhouse.com

FREELAND

Cliff House & Cottage
727 Windmill Rd, 98249
360-331-1566
Peggy Moore   All year

165-410-B&B
4 rooms, 4 pb
S-no/P-no/H-no

Continental plus breakfast
Complimentary wine
Hot tub, fireplace, sitting
room, VHS, piano, stereo

A stunningly beautiful house, for one couple. Complete privacy in this forested hideaway with miles of beach. Award-winning Sea Cliff Cottage with French country decor. Web site: cliffhouse.net

FRIDAY HARBOR

Hillside House B&B
365 Carter Ave, 98250
360-378-4730 Fax: 360-378-4715
800-232-4730
Cathy & Dick Robinson
All year

65-195-B&B
7 rooms, 7 pb
Visa, MC, AmEx,
Rated, •
C-ltd/S-ltd/P-no/H-no

Full breakfast
Famous banana-choc. chip
cookies

Contemporary B&B in Friday Harbor, 3/4 of a mile from the ferry landing, overlooking harbor and Mt. Baker. Window seats enhance your view of the marina or our wooded grounds. Courtesy airport & waterfront pick-up. E-mail: info@hillsidehouse.com Web site: hillsidehouse.com

Tucker House B&B &
Cottages
260 "B" St, 98250
360-378-2783 Fax: 360-378-6437
800-965-0123
Skip & Annette Metzger
All year

75-225-B&B
5 rooms, 3 pb
Most CC, *Rated*, •
C-ltd/S-no/P-ltd/H-ltd
Dan./Swed./Nor./Ger./Fr.

Full breakfast
Kitchens
Hot tub, spa on deck,
children welcome in, cottage,
park nearby, robes

A Victorian home and cottages surrounded by flowers & picket fence in a small Washington port with marinas, gift shops, and gourmet restaurants. E-mail: tucker@rockisland.com Web site: san-juan.net/tucker

GIG HARBOR

Island Escape B&B
210 Island Blvd, 98333
206-549-2044 Fax: 253-549-7700
877-549-2044
Paula Pascoe   All year

125-B&B
1 rooms, 1 pb
Visa, MC, AmEx,
Rated, •
C-ltd/S-no/P-no/H-no

Full breakfast
Snacks
Sitting room, Jacuzzi tubs,
satellite TV, VCR, fireplaces

Relax in your own first floor executive suite in a contemporary waterfront home overlooking Puget Sound. Your bedroom is decorated with a beautifully carved German hutch, dresser and king bed, complete with downy feather comforters. E-mail: paula@island-escape.com Web site: island-escape.com

Peacock Hill Guest House
9520 Peacock Hill Ave, 98332
800-863-2318
Steven & Suzanne Savnov
All year

90-125-B&B
2 rooms, 2 pb
Rated, •
C-ltd/S-no/P-no/H-no
Spanish

Full breakfast
Snacks
Sitting room, suites, Jacuzzis,
fireplaces, cable TV

Nestled among evergreens. Sitting on a hilltop overlooking the harbor and beyond. Sit back and enjoy all the comforts of home in the Salish Suite or Sedona Room. Stroll down to the harbor and shop. E-mail: sedonasue@aol.com Web site: virtualcities.com/wa/peacock.htm

Island Escape B&B, Gig Harbor, WA

GREENBANK

Guest House Log Cottages
24371 S.R. 525, 98253
360-678-3115 Fax: 360-678-3115
Mary Jane & Don Creger
All year

145-295-B&B
6 rooms, 6 pb
Most CC, *Rated*
S-no/P-no/H-ltd

Full breakfast
Exercise room, pool, spa,
retreat & honeymoon spot,
rated 4 diamond by ΛΛΛ

Luxury log mansion for 2 ($295/night). Private cottages w/personal Jacuzzis, fireplace, kitchens, TV/VCR. Picnic area-forest/wildlife/pond. Midwk. rates Nov 1-March 15   E-mail: guesthse@whidbey.net *Web site:* whidbey.net/logcottages

KIRKLAND

Shumway Mansion
11410 99th Place NE, 98033
425-823-2303 Fax: 425-823-0421
J. Blakemore, S. & R. Harris
All year

70-95-B&B
8 rooms, 8 pb
Visa, MC, *Rated^, •
C-ltd/S-no/P-no/H-ltd

Full breakfast buffet
Evening snack, drinks
Sitting room, piano, athletic
club privileges, weddings,
receptions

Four-story mansion circa 1910. Views of lake and bay. Delicious breakfasts and afternoon goodies. Walk to beach, shops, galleries. Conferences up to 60 people with catering, weddings.

LA CONNER

Benson Farmstead B&B
10113 Avon Allen Rd, 98232
360-757-0578
800-441-9814
Jerry & Sharon Benson
All year

80-90-B&B
4 rooms, 4 pb
Visa, MC, •
C-yes/S-no/P-no/H-no
Some Norw., Fren.,
Germ.

Full breakfast
After dinner dessert &
coffee/tea
Sitting room, Jacuzzis,
accommodate business
travelers

A lovely restored 1914 farmhouse surrounded by gardens and filled with antiques, hand-made quilts and the smells of fresh baked breads and evening desserts.
Web site: bbhost.com/Beansonbnb

Katy's Inn
PO Box 869, 98257
360-466-3366
800-914-7767
Bruce & Kathie Hubbard
All year

72-120-B&B
5 rooms, 3 pb
Most CC, *Rated*, •
C-ltd/S-ltd/P-no/H-no

Full breakfast
Evening dessert
Hot tub, rocking chairs on
porch, near boating, fishing

We'll pamper you at this charming Victorian on the hillside two blocks above quaint LaConner. E-mail: katysinn@juno.com *Web site:* home.ncia.com/katysinn/

White Swan Guest House, La Conner, WA

LA CONNER

White Swan Guest House	75-150-B&B	Continental plus breakfast
15872 Moore Rd, 98273	3 rooms	Cookies
360-445-6805	*Rated*, ●	Sitting room, library, outdoor
Peter Goldfarb	C-ltd/S-no/P-no/H-no	patio, garden cottage sleeps 4
All year		

A "storybook" Victorian farmhouse 6 miles from historic waterfront village La Conner. 1 hour north of Seattle. English gardens. A perfect romantic getaway. Chocolate chip cookies. Web site: cnw.com/~wswan/

LANGLEY

Country Cottage of Langley	129-179-B&B	Continental plus breakfast
215 6th St, 98260	4 rooms, 4 pb	Scenic dining room, view
360-221-8709	Visa, MC, ●	deck, gazebo, near boating,
Bob & Mary DeCelles	C-ltd/S-no/P-no/H-no	fishing
All year		

Restored 1920s farmhouse and separate guest cottage on 2 acres of gardens. Views of village, mountains and sea. Breakfast, private baths. E-mail: bygonera@whidbeyisland.com *Web site:* acountrycottage.com

Eagles Nest Inn	105-235-B&B	Full gourmet breakfast
4680 Saratoga Rd, 98260	5 rooms, 5 pb	Complimentary bar, tea,
360-221-5331 Fax: 360-221-5331	Visa, MC, Disc, *Rated*,	coffee
Joanne & Jerry Lechner	●	Library, sitting room, TV,
All year	C-ltd/S-no	fireplace, woodstove, video
		library, hot tub

Casual elegance with native art, in country setting on Whidbey Island 2 miles to seaside village of Langley. View of Saratoga Passage. E-mail: eaglnest@whidbey.com *Web site:* eaglesnestinn.com

Island Tyme B&B	95-140-B&B	Full breakfast
4940 S Bayview Rd, 98236	5 rooms, 5 pb	Snacks
360-221-5078	Visa, MC, AmEx,	Jacuzzis, pets in 1 room,
800-898-8963	*Rated*, ●	fireplaces,
Cliff & Carol Wisman	C-ltd/S-no/P-ltd/H-yes	
All year		

Light a fire, soak in your Jacuzzi, savor your gourmet breakfast at our Victorian B&B, close to Langley, Whidbey Island. Awards: AAA-3 Diamonds; Best Places to Kiss; NW Best Places. E-mail: islandty@whidbey.com

LANGLEY

Log Castle B&B	95-120-B&B	Full breakfast
4693 E Saratoga Rd, 98260	4 rooms, 4 pb	Cider, homemade cookies
360-221-5483 Fax: 360-221-6249	Visa, MC, *Rated*, •	Sitting room, guest, canoe &
P& K Holdsworth, J & N	C-ltd/S-no/P-no/H-no	rowboat, beach, fishing,
Metcalf		hiking, birding
All year		

Unique waterfront log lodge on Whidbey Island. Turret bedrooms, secluded beach, fantastic view of mountains, 50 miles north of Seattle. E-mail: innkeepr@thelogcastle.com
Web site: thelogcastle.com

Villa Isola B&B Inn	95-160-B&B	Gourmet Continental Plus
5489 S. Coles Rd, 98260	5 rooms, 5 pb	Espresso bar/wine/snacks
360-221-5052 Fax: 360-221-5823	Visa, MC, *Rated*, •	Charm of Italian villa,
800-246-7323	S-no/P-no/H-no	Professional Bocce Court,
Gary & Gwen Galeotti		gardens, mtn. biking
All year		

Italian hospitality & Mediterranean charm, contemporary furnishing located on 3.5 beautifully landscaped acres. Full gourmet breakfast; espresso bar E-mail: villa@villaisola.com
Web site: villaisola.com

LEAVENWORTH

All Seasons River Inn B&B	95-155-B&B	Full breakfast
PO Box 788, 98826	6 rooms, 6 pb	Snacks
509-548-1425	Visa, MC, *Rated*	Sitting room, library,
800-254-0555	S-no/P-no	bicycles, Jacuzzis, suites,
Jeff & Kathy Falconer		fireplaces
All year		

Nestled in the Cascade Mountains, sleep lulled by the river in a spectacular Jacuzzi suite. Awaken to a gourmet breakfast overlooking the river. E-mail: allriver@rightathome.com
Web site: allseasonsriverinn.com

Autumn Pond B&B	89-99-B&B	Full breakfast
10388 Titus Rd, 98826	5 rooms, 5 pb	Sitting room, Jacuzzis
509-548-4482	Visa, MC, *Rated*, •	
John & Jennifer Lorenz	C-ltd/S-no/P-no/H-no	
All year		

Autumn Pond rests on three quiet country acres, surrounded by panoramic views of the majestic Cascades. The location is perfect for a brisk walk to downtown or a quiet evening stroll to the Ski Hill area where wild flowers will delight your senses. E-mail: info@autumnpond.com *Web site:* autumnpond.com

Mrs. Andersons Lodging	39-65-B&B	Buffet breakfast
Hou	9 rooms, 7 pb	Coffee & tea 24 hours/day
917 Commercial St, 98826	Visa, MC, Disc,	Central heating & A/C, cable
509-548-6173 Fax: 509-548-9113	C-yes/S-no/P-no	TV, massages, views,
800-253-8990		sundeck, garden, parking
Dee & Al Howie		
All year		

Built in 1895, renovated in 1989. Decorated with turn-of-the-century antiques, quilts and vintage clothing. The decor changes 5 times a year with the seasons. E-mail: info@quiltersheaven.com *Web site:* quiltersheaven.com

Run of the River	100-155-B&B	Full breakfast
PO Box 285, 98826	6 rooms, 6 pb	Afternoon tea, snacks
509-548-7171 Fax: 509-548-7547	Most CC, *Rated*, •	Sitting room, library, hot tub,
800-288-6491	S-no/P-no/H-yes	complimentary use of
Monty & Karen Turner	Spanish	mountain bicycles
All year		

The quintessential Northwest Log B&B Inn. From your log porch swing, view the Icicle River, surrounding bird refuge & The Cascade Peaks, known as The Enchantments. E-mail: rofther@runoftheriver.com *Web site:* runoftheriver.com

LONG BEACH

Boreas B&B Inn	120-135-B&B	Full gourmet breakfast
PO Box 1344, 98631	5 rooms, 5 pb	Afternoon tea, snacks
360-642-8069 Fax: 360-642-5353	Most CC, *Rated*, •	Sitting room, library, hot
888-642-8069	C-yes/S-no/P-no/H-no	tubs, gazebo, decks,
Susie Goldsmith & Bill Verner		reunions/weddings
All year		

Artistically remodeled 1920s beach home. Oceanview bedrooms, spacious living rooms with fireplace. New Dunes Suite added with jetted tub. E-mail: boreas@boreasinn.com
Web site: boreasinn.com

LONGVIEW

Misty Mountain Llamas B&B	85-90-B&B	Full breakfast
1033 Stella Rd, 98632	2 rooms	Dinner upon request, snacks
360-577-4772	•	Sitting room, library, llamas
Doug & Barbara Joy	C-ltd/S-no/P-no/H-no	to walk, 50" TV, with VCR
All year		

Welcome to our little piece of heaven, a 5 acre llama ranch. Beautiful, new custom home offers you 2 bedrooms. Covered patio with view of the Columbia River through the wonderful trees E-mail: bljoy@kalama.com

LOPEZ ISLAND

MacKaye Harbor Inn	89-169-B&B	Full breakfast
949 MacKaye Harbor Rd,	5 rooms, 3 pb	Afternoon aperitif
98261	Most CC, *Rated*, •	Bicycles & kayaks, exercise
360-468-2253 Fax: 360-468-2393	S-no/P-no/H-no	studio with sauna
Mike & Robin Bergstrom		
All year		

Romantic country hideaway on a protected sandy beach. Beautiful sunset views. Personal service, antiques, nostalgia and tranquillity. E-mail: mckay@pacificrim.net Web site: san-juan.net/mackayeharbor

MAZAMA

Mazama Country Inn	80-190-EP/AP	Full breakfast winter
HCR 74 Box B-9, 98833	14 rooms, 14 pb	EP/summer, AP/winter
509-996-2681 Fax: 509-996-2646	Visa, MC, •	Restaurant, sitting room,
800-843-7951	C-ltd/S-no/P-no/H-no	outdoor hot tub & sauna,
George Turner		cross-country ski rentals,
All year		bikes

Secluded year-round country inn with huge stone fireplace in dining room. Hiking, mountain-biking, horseback riding, cross-country ski trails abound. E-mail: mazamacountryinn@methow.com Web site: mazamacountryinn.com

OCEAN PARK

Whalebone House, The	95-105-B&B	Full breakfast
2101 Bay Ave, 98640	4 rooms, 4 pb	Snacks, complimentary wine
360-665-5371	Visa, MC, *Rated*, •	Sitting room, library,
888-298-3330	C-ltd/S-no/P-no/H-ltd	bicycles, accommodate
Jim & Jayne Nash All year		business travelers

Restored 1889 Victorian farmhouse, on the state historic register, in the heart of Washington's Long Beach peninsula. Close to the Pacific Ocean & the pristine estuary of the Wallapa Bay, fresh oysters & 2 lighthouses. E-mail: whalebone@wallapabay.org
Web site: willapabay.org/~whalebone

OLYMPIA

Puget View Guest House	99-119-B&B	Continental plus breakfast
7924 61st Ave NE, 98516	2 rooms, 1 pb	BBQ
360-413-9474	Visa, MC, *Rated*, •	Private dining area/deck,
Dick & Barbara Yunker	C-yes/S-yes/P-ltd/H-no	books, games, canoe, 100-
All year		acre park next door

Charming waterfront guest cottage suite next to host's log home. Breakfast to your cottage. Peaceful. Picturesque. A "NW Best Places" since 1984. Puget Sound 5 min. off I-5.

Kangaroo House B&B, Orcas island, WA

OLYMPIA

Swantown Inn
1431 11th Ave SE, 98501
360-753-9123
Lillian & Ed Peeples
Season Inquire

65-115-B&B
4 rooms, 4 pb
Visa, MC, *Rated*, •
C-ltd/S-ltd/P-no

Full breakfast
Complimentary afternoon
tea

Listed on both the city & state historical registers, this grand 1893 Queen Anne/Eastlake Victorian mansion can be your headquarters for exploring Puget Sound, or your refuge for a quiet retreat. E-mail: swantown@olywa.net *Web site:* olywa.net/swantown/

ORCAS ISLAND

Kangaroo House B&B
PO Box 334, 98245
360-376-2175 Fax: 360-376-3604
888-371-2175
Peter & Helen Allen
All year

80 130-B&B
5 rooms
Most CC, *Rated*, •
C-yes/S-no/P-no/H-no

Full breakfast
Complimentary beverages &
snacks
Special diets on request,
fireplace, sitting room, hot
tub in garden

Small country inn; stone fireplace in sitting room; gourmet breakfast in sunny dining room. Furnished in antiques. Close to town and beach. E-mail: innkeeper@KangarooHouse.com
Web site: KangarooHouse.com

Turtleback Farm Inn
1981 Crow Valley Rd, 98245
360-376-4914 Fax: 360-376-5329
800-376-4914
William & Susan C. Fletcher
All year

80-210-B&B
11 rooms, 11 pb
Visa, MC, *Rated*, •
C-ltd/S-no/P-no/H-yes

Full breakfast
Complimentary tea & coffee
Bar, complimentary sherry,
games, living room, fireplace

Romantic country inn renowned for excellent food, stunning decor, caring hospitality and serene location. New four room Orchard House includes king beds, claw-footed tubs. 80 acre farm with sheep, ducks, geese, chickens.   Web site: turtlebackinn.com

PORT ANGELES

Angeles Inn B&B
PO Box 87, 98362
360-417-0260 Fax: 360-457-4269
888-552-4263
All year

65-105-B&B
4 rooms, 2 pb
Visa, MC, *Rated*, •
C-ltd/S-no/P-no/H-no

Full breakfast
Restaurant
Sitting room, cable TV music
Saturday, Sunday

"Better Homes and Gardens" featured, award winning, contemporary dwelling.
E-mail: james@olypen.com *Web site:* northolympic.com/klahhane/

PORT ANGELES

BJ's Garden Gate	115-180-B&B	Full breakfast
397 Monterra Dr, 98362	5 rooms, 5 pb	Snacks, evening desserts
360-452-2322 Fax: 360-417-5098	Most CC, •	Sitting room, library,
800-880-1332	C-ltd/S-no/P-no/H-ltd	Jacuzzis, suites, fireplaces,
BJ & Frank Paton		cable TV
All year		

Quiet elegance in a new waterfront Victorian garden estate. Romantic European antique suites with fireplace, double Jacuzzi, luxurious bath and stunning garden & water views. E-mail: bjgarden@olypen.com *Web site:* bjgarden.com

Colette's B&B	155-195-B&B	Full breakfast
339 Finn Hall Road, 98362	2 rooms, 2 pb	Snacks
360-457-9197 Fax: 360-452-0711	Visa, MC, *Rated*	Library, Jacuzzis, suites,
Peter and Lynda Clark	C-ltd/S-no/P-no/H-no	fireplaces, cable TV/VCR, CD
All year		library, stereos

Escape to our secluded waterfront estate nestled between the majestic Olympic Range and the Strait of Juan de Fuca. Relax in our luxuriously appointed suites while enjoying the breathtaking panorama. E-mail: colettes@olypen.com *Web site:* colettes.com

Domaine Madeleine B&B	157-179-B&B	Full breakfast
146 Wildflower Ln, 98362	5 rooms, 5 pb	Afternoon tea, snacks
360-457-4174 Fax: 360-457-3037	Visa, MC, *Rated*	Sitting room, library, Jacuzzi,
888-811-8376	C-ltd/S-no/P-no/H-no	lawn games, fireplaces, cable
Madeleine & John Chambers	Fr., Sp., Farsi, Ger.	TV
All year		

Serene waterfront estate with panoramic views—Monet garden replica, unique European/Asian antiques, fireplaces, Jacuzzi, whales and eagles. E-mail: romance@ domainemadeleine.com *Web site:* domainemadeleine.com

SeaSuns B&B Inn, The	89-135-B&B	Full breakfast
1006 S Lincoln St, 98362	5 rooms, 5 pb	Lunch (fee), snacks
360-452-8248 Fax: 360-417-0465	Visa, MC, *Rated*, •	Sitting room, Carriage house
800-708-0777	C-ltd/S-no/P-no/H-no	suite can accommodate four
Bob & Jan Harbick		
All year		

Peaceful gardens with towering evergreens surrounding an elegant 1926 Dutch Colonial home. Antique furnishings, water and mountain views. Pacific Northwest breakfast specialties. Monthly specials. E-mail: seasuns@olypen.com *Web site:* seasuns.com

PORT TOWNSEND

Ann Starrett Mansion B&B	98-225-B&B	Full breakfast
744 Clay St, 98368	11 rooms, 11 pb	Complimentary sherry, tea
360-385-3205 Fax: 360-385-2976	Visa, MC, *Rated*, •	Sitting room, weddings,
800-321-0644	C-ltd/S-no/P-no/H-ltd	honeymoon cottage,
Edel Sokol		Jacuzzi/hot tub, massage.
All year		

Award winning, full-service, Victorian inn. Internationally renowned for classic Victorian architecture, frescoed ceilings & three-tiered spiral staircase. Only 1½ hours from Seattle. E-mail: starrett@olympus.net *Web site:* starrettmansion.com

Bishop Victorian Suites	79-160-B&B	Continental plus breakfast
714 Washington St, 98368	12 rooms, 12 pb	Coffee, tea
360-385-6122	Visa, MC, AmEx,	Sitting rm., parking lot,
800-824-4738	*Rated*, •	conference facilities, small
Joe & Cindy Finnie	C-yes/S-no/P-ltd/H-no	kitchens-each room
All year		

Downtown, Victorian-era hotel; beautifully restored. Gracious suites. Mountain and water views. Walk to Port Townsend, Washington's historic Victorian seaport. Seven rooms with fireplace. E-mail: swan@waypt.com *Web site:* waypt.com/bishop/bishop.html

PORT TOWNSEND

Ecologic Place	70-100-EP	Full kitchen in each cabin
10 Beach Dr, 98358	8 rooms, 8 pb	3 miles undeveloped beach,
360-385-3077 Fax: 360-385-1181	Visa, MC,	mountains, wildlife, no one
800-871-3077	C-yes/S-no/P-no/H-ltd	around.
Allison & Steve Willing	German	
All year		

1930s Puget Sound beach hideaway, upgraded to modern basics. Island living, island pace of life (bridge to island). Dark at night to see the stars, fabulous beach for all ages to learn marine biology, great bird watching. Web site: ecologicplace.com

James House, The	80-185-B&B	Full breakfast
1238 Washington St, 98368	13 rooms, 11 pb	Complimentary sherry &
360-385-1238 Fax: 360-379-5551	Visa, MC, *Rated*, •	cookies
800-385-1238	C-ltd/S-no/P-no/H-ltd	Sitting parlors, player piano,
Carol McGough		fireplaces, porch with swing,
All year		garden

1889 Queen Anne Victorian mansion featuring unsurpassed water and mountain views, period antiques. First B&B in the Northwest, still the finest. E-mail: innkeeper@ jameshouse.com *Web site:* jameshouse.com

Old Consulate Inn	96-220-B&B	Full breakfast–banquet
313 Walker @ Washington,	8 rooms, 8 pb	Afternoon tea, snacks
98368	Visa, MC, AmEx,	Comp. wine, sitting room,
360-385-6753 Fax: 360-385-2097	*Rated*, •	library, tennis, hot tub,
800-300-6753	C-ltd/S-no/P-no/H-no	billiard and game room
Rob & Joanna Jackson		
All year		

Award winning Founding Family Mansion-on-the-Bluff. Romantic retreat offering warm hospitality, comfortable elegance, eve. cordials! E-mail: joanna@oldconsulateinn.com *Web site:* oldconsulateinn.com

Palace Hotel	59-159-B&B	Continental breakfast
1004 Water St, 98368	15 rooms, 12 pb	Restaurant
360-385-0773 Fax: 360-385-0780	Most CC, *Rated*, •	Breakfast delivered to room,
800-962-0741	H-no	conference facilities, board
Phoebe L. Mason		games
All year		

Beautifully restored hotel in the heart of downtown Port Townsend. Complimentary continental breakfast & off-street parking. E-mail: palace@olympus.net *Web site:* olympus.net/palace

Swan Hotel	79-250-EP	Small meeting facilities
714 Washington, 98368	9 rooms, 9 pb	
360-385-1718	Visa, MC, AmEx,	
800-776-1718	*Rated*, •	
Joe and Cindy Finnie	C-yes/S-no/P-no/H-yes	
All year		

A waterfront hotel which includes 4—1 bedroom suites, 2 story penthouse and 4 charming cottages. All are equipped with TVs & kitchen facilities. Close to everything. E-mail: swan@waypt.com *Web site:* waypt.com/bishop/swan.htm

REDMOND

Cottage Creek Inn B&B, A	89-125-B&B	Full breakfast
12525 Avondale Rd NE, 98052	4 rooms, 4 pb	Afternoon tea
425-881-5606 Fax: 425-881-5606	Most CC, *Rated*	Sitting room, Jacuzzis, suites,
Steve & Jeanette Wynecoop	C-ltd/S-ltd/P-no/H-no	hot tub, pond, creek,
All year	Very little German	conference facilities

Romantic English Tudor in beautiful, tranquil garden setting. Enjoy refreshing massage in hydrotherapy hot tub, relaxing afternoon in gazebo by wildlife pond or walk the nature trail. Near Microsoft, wineries, Seattle. E-mail: cotcreek@brigadoon.com *Web site:* cottagecreekinn.com

ROSLYN

Hummingbird Inn	60-75-B&B	Full breakfast
PO Box 984, 98941	3 rooms, 2 pb	Snacks
509-649-2758	Visa, MC, Disc, *Rated*	Sitting room, library,
Roberta L. Spinazola	C-ltd/S-no/P-ltd/H-no	bicycles, fireplace, cross-
All year	Minimal Spanish	country skiing, snowshoes

Circa 1890s country Victorian, formerly mine boss's home. Antiques, fireplace, music & library, lovely gardens. Web site: blueplanet-group.com/hummingbirdinn/

SAN JUAN ISLANDS

Highland Inn	175-250-B&B	Full breakfast
PO Box 135, 98250	2 rooms, 2 pb	Afternoon tea
360-378-9450 Fax: 360-378-1693	Visa, MC, AmEx,	Sitt. rm., Jacuzzis, stes.,
888-400-9850	*Rated*, •	frplcs., cable, accommodates
Helen King	S-no/P-no/H-no	business travelers
All year	Limited Spanish	

Nestled in wooded West side with ocean view to Olympics, Victoria B.C., Orca Whales, sunsets, stars from 88 foot veranda. E-mail: helen@highlandinn.com Web site: highlandinn.com

SEABECK

Willcox House Country Inn	129-199-B&B	Full breakfast
2390 Tekiu Rd NW, 98380	5 rooms, 5 pb	Lunch, dinner (fee)
360-830-4492 Fax: 360-830-0506	Visa, MC, *Rated*, •	Comp. wine and cheese,
800-725-9477	C-ltd/S-no/P-no/H-no	library, game room, with
Cecilia & Phillip Hughes		pool table
All year		

Secluded 1930s estate on Hood Canal; quiet relaxation in an elegant, historic mansion with landscaped grounds, private pier and beach. Vegetarian dining available with advance notice. Web site: willcoxhouse.com

SEATTLE

Angels of the Sea B&B	75-125-B&B	Full breakfast
26431 99th Ave SW, 98070	3 rooms, 1 pb	Afternoon tea
206-463-6980 Fax: 206-463-2205	Visa, MC, *Rated*, •	Sitting room, bikes, pool,
800-798-9249	C-yes/S-no/P-yes/H-no	tennis, summer sailing,
Marnie Jones		country club pool/golf
All year		

1917 converted country church in lush woods and meadow on island near Seattle/Tacoma. Live harp with breakfast in sanctuary. $10/room fee for one night stays. The Dolphin Room can be made into a king size bed. E-mail: angelssea@aol.com Web site: angelsofthesea.com

Artist's Studio Loft B&B	85-150-B&B	Continental plus breakfast
16529 91st Ave SW, 98070	3 rooms, 3 pb	Bicycles, Jacuzzis, suites,
206-463-2583 Fax: 206-463-3881	Most CC, *Rated*	fireplace, conference
Jacqueline Clayton	C-ltd/S-ltd/P-no/H-no	facilities
All year		

Enchanting and romantic getaway nestled in a flower garden and meadow setting on five acres on beautiful Vashon Island. Healing, quiet, serence atmosphere, private entrances/baths. Relaxing hottub spa in Gazebo. E-mail: medowart@asl-bnb.com Web site: asl-bnb.com

Bacon Mansion	79-154-B&B	Continental plus breakfast
959 Broadway E, 98102	11 rooms, 9 pb	Sitt. rm., lib., conference rm.,
206-329-1864 Fax: 206-860-9025	Most CC, *Rated*	TV, hair dryer, private
800-240-1864	C-ltd/S-no/P-no/H-no	voicemail/dataport
Daryl King		
All year		

One of Capitol Hill's gracious mansions c. 1909. Luxury antique-filled rooms, hand-carved woodwork. E-mail: baconbandb@aol.com Web site: baconmansion.com

SEATTLE

Chelsea Station on the Park
4915 Linden Ave N, 98103
206-547-6077 Fax: 206-632-5107
800-400-6077
Karen Carbonneau/John
Griffin
All year

95-175-B&B
9 rooms, 9 pb
Most CC, *Rated*
C-ltd/S-no/P-no/H-no

Full hearty breakfast
Bottomless cookie jar
Walk to restaurants, next to
zoo & rose gdns., spacious
view rooms

One of Seattle's finest neighborhood inns, circa 1929. Comfortable ambiance, antiques throughout. Minutes north of downtown. Come, refresh your spirit
E-mail: info@bandbseattle.com *Web site:* bandbseattle.com

Green Gables
1503 Second Ave West, 98119
206-282-6863
Reonn Rabon
89-159

E-mail: greengab@wolfenet.com *Web site:* greengablesseattle.com

Mildred's B&B Inn
1202 15th Ave E, 98112
206-325-6072 Fax: 206-860-5907
Mildred & Melodee Sarver
All year

105-135-B&B
3 rooms, 3 pb
Rated
C-yes/S-ltd/P-no/H-no

Full breakfast
Afternoon tea or coffee
Sitting room, fireplace,
library, veranda, grand
piano, queen beds

1890 Victorian. Wraparound verandah, lace curtains, red carpets. City location near bus, electric trolley, park, art museum, flower conservatory. Play area across the street.   E-mail: mildredsbb@foxinternet.net *Web site:* mildredsbnb.com

Palisades B&B at Dash Pt
5162 SW 311th Place, 98023
253-838-4376 Fax: 253-838-1480
888-838-4376
Dennis & Peggy LaPorte
All year

220-235-B&B
1 rooms, 1 pb
Most CC, *Rated*, •
S-no/P-no/H-no

Full breakfast
Afternoon appetizers,
snacks, wine
Sitting room, bicycles,
Jacuzzis, suites, fireplaces,
cable TV

Secluded, private, extremely elegant, waterfront suite; overlooks Puget Sound and breathtaking sunsets beyond Olympic Mt. Range. Featherbed in luxurious linens, fresh flowers from the garden; marbled Jacuzzi spa and delectable breakfast.   E-mail: laporte2@ix.netcom.com *Web site:* palisadesbb.com

Pioneer Square Hotel
77 Yesler Way, 98104
206-340-1234 Fax: 206-467-0707
800-800-5514
Jo Thompson
All year

99-199-B&B
75 rooms, 75 pb
Most CC, *Rated*, •
C-yes/S-ltd/P-no/H-yes
Spanish, French

Continental plus breakfast
Lunch/dinner available
Snacks, bar service,
restaurant, sitting room,
library

Small luxury boutique accommodation in downtown Seattle's waterfront Pioneer Square Historic District. Near ferry terminals, nightlife, shopping.   E-mail: info@pioneersquare.com *Web site:* pioneersquare.com

Prince of Wales B&B
133 13th Ave E, 98102
206-325-9692 Fax: 206-322-6402
800-327-9692
Faith Addicott
All year

99-125-B&B
4 rooms, 4 pb
Most CC,
C-ltd/S-no/P-no/H-no

Full breakfast
Morning coffee to room
Sitting room, fireplaces,
garden, attic suite, priv. deck

Downtown 1.5 miles away; on bus line; walk to convention center; turn-of-the-century ambiance; panoramic views of city skyline, sound and mountains.
E-mail: addicott2@waonline.com *Web site:* pricebedandbreakfast.com

510   Washington

SEATTLE

Salisbury House
750 16th Ave E, 98112
206-328-8682 Fax: 206-720-1019
Cathryn & Mary Wiese
All year

78-149-B&B
5 rooms, 5 pb
Most CC, *Rated*
C-ltd/S-no/P-no/H-no

Full vegy breakfast
Complimentary tea/coffee 24
hours
Sitting room, porch, down
comforters, phones with
voice mail in each room

Elegant Capitol Hill Inn. Ideal location for business or pleasure. Take advantage of Seattle's excellent transit system. E-mail: sleep@salisburyhouse.com Web site: salisburyhouse.com

---

Swallow's Nest Cottages
6030 SW 248th St, 98070
206-463-2646 Fax: 206-463-2646
800-ANY-NEST
Bob Keller
All year

65-170-EP
6 rooms, 6 pb
Most CC, *Rated*, •
C-yes/S-no/P-ltd/H-ltd

Cottages with kitchens
Coffee, tea, cocoa, some hot
tubs/fireplaces, golf, boating
nearby

Comfortable country cottage on bluffs overlooking Puget Sound & Mt. Rainier, 3 locations, fishing & kayaking available. Country club privileges. Extended stay discounts. Massage, tennis. E-mail: anynest@vashonislandcottages.com Web site: vashonislandcottages.com

---

Tugboat Challenger
1001 Fairview Av N 1600, 98109
206-340-1201 Fax: 206-621-9208
Rick Anderson
All year

80-170-B&B
14 rooms, 4 pb
Rated, •
C-ltd/S-no/P-no/H-no

Continental plus breakfast
Soft drinks
Sitting room, library,
bicycles, fireplace, boat
rentals nearby

On board a fully functional, exceptionally clean, restored 102' tugboat. Located in the heart of the Seattle area. Closed circuit TV. Carpeted throughout. Nautical antiques. Nearby restaurants. E-mail: mvchallenger@bigfoot.com

---

Villa Heidelberg
4845 45th Ave SW, 98116
206-938-3658 Fax: 206-935-7077
800-671-2942
John & Barb Thompson
All year

80-140-B&B
6 rooms, 2 pb
Visa, MC, AmEx, *Rated*
C-ltd/S-ltd/P-no/H-no

Full breakfast
Sitting room, New king suite
w/views, and private bath

1909 Craftsman country home just minutes from the airport and downtown Seattle. Two blocks to shops, bus and restaurants. Sweeping views of Puget Sound & Olympic Mountains. E-mail: info@villaheidelberg.com Web site: villaheidelberg.com

SEAVIEW

Shelburne Inn
PO Box 250, 98644
360-642-2442 Fax: 360-642-8904
L. Anderson, D. Campiche
All year

109-229-B&B
16 rooms, 13 pb
Visa, MC, *Rated*, •
C-ltd/S-yes/P-no/H-yes
French, German, Port.

Full country breakfast
Restaurant, pub
Lobby with fireplace, organ,
2 suites

The oldest surviving Victorian hotel in Washington state, with the time-honored tradition of superb service, decor and distinguished cuisine. Can accommodate small meetings of up to 30. E-mail: innkeeper@theshelburneinn.com Web site: theshelburneinn.com

SEQUIM

Greywolf Inn
395 Keeler Rd, 98382
360-683-5889 Fax: 360-683-1487
800-914-WOLF
Peggy & Melang
All year

70-150-B&B
5 rooms, 5 pb
Most CC, *Rated*, •
C-ltd/S-ltd/P-no/H-no

Full breakfast, 4-course
Complimentary champagne
Fireplace, patio, decks,
Japanese hot tub, gazebo,
gardens & woodswalk

Enjoy fine food & good cheer in this splendid little inn. The perfect starting point for light adventure on the Olympic Peninsula or sailing to Victoria, BC E-mail: info@grywolfinnf.com Web site: greywolfinn.com

Marianna Stoltz House B&B, Spokane, WA

SPOKANE

Marianna Stoltz House B&B
427 E Indiana Ave, 99207
509-483-4316 Fax: 509-483-6773
800-978-6587
Phyllis Maguire
All year

65-99-B&B
4 rooms, 2 pb
Most CC, *Rated*, •
C-ltd/S-no/P-no/H-no

Full breakfast
Veranda, cable TV, guest
refrigerators, bathrobes in
rooms

Antique quilts, lace curtains, oriental rugs. Delicious breakfasts. Friendly hosts await you in our centrally located 1908 historic B&B. Close to Gonzaga University.
E-mail: mstoltz@aimcomm.com *Web site:* aimcomm.com/stoltzhouse

SUNNYSIDE

Sunnyside Inn
804 E Edison Ave, 98944
509-839-5557 Fax: 509-839-3520
800-221-4195
Karen & Donavon Vlieger
All year

59-99-B&B
8 rooms, 8 pb
Visa, MC, AmEx, *Rated*
C-yes/S-no/P-no/H-no

Full breakfast
Snacks, hot tubs
Sitting room, Jacuzzi, near
tennis, golf, and, over 20
wineries

Eight luxurious rooms, all with private baths, 7 with private Jacuzzi tubs. In the heart of Washington wine country. E-mail: suninn@bentonrea.com *Web site:* bbhost.com/sunnysideinn

TACOMA

Commencement Bay B&B
3312 N Union Ave, 98407
253-752-8175 Fax: 253-759-4025
Sharon & Bill Kaufmann
All year

80-125-B&B
3 rooms, 3 pb
Most CC, *Rated*, •
C-ltd/S-ltd/P-no/H-no
Some Spanish

Full breakfast
Afternoon tea, snacks
Exercise room, game room,
bikes, hot tubs, cable
TV/VCR, massuse available

Elegantly decorated colonial home overlooking scenic Tacoma. 6 blocks to waterfront parks & historic "proctor" shopping district. Bay & mountain views from all rooms.
E-mail: greatviews@aol.com *Web site:* great-views.com

TACOMA ───────────────────────

Inn at Burg's Landing, The
8808 Villa Beach Rd, 98303
253-884-9185   800-431-5622
Ken & Annie Burg   All year

75-125-B&B
3 rooms, 3 pb
Most CC, *Rated*, •
C-yes/S-no/P-no/H-no

Full breakfast
Lunch, dinner with notice
Outdoor gazebo, golf nearby,
deck & hot tub

Magnificent log home loaded with country charm, on the beach with a spectacular view of Mt. Ranier and Puget Sound.   E-mail: innatburgslanding@mailexcite.com

---

Villa, The
705 N 5th St, 98403
253-572-1157 Fax: 253-572-1805
800-572-1157
Becky Anglemyer   All year

95-160-B&B
6 rooms, 6 pb
Visa, MC, AmEx,
Rated, •
C-ltd/S-no/P-no/H-yes

Full breakfast
Snacks, complimentary wine
Sitting room, library,
Jacuzzis, suites, fireplaces,
cable TV, exercise room

Only B&B in the Seattle/Tacoma area to be accepted into "Unique New Inns", based on the beauty, cleanliness, and amenities offered. Truly one of a kind.   E-mail: villabb@aol.com
Web site: villabb.com

WHITE SALMON ───────────────────────

Inn of the White Salmon
PO Box 1549, 98672
509-493-2335   800-972-5226
Janet & Roger Holen
All year

99-129-B&B
16 rooms, 16 pb
Most CC, •
C-yes/S-ltd/P-yes/H-no

Full breakfast
Beer & wine available
Sitting room, suites, outdoor
hot tub

Furnished with antiques, this Inn has the ambiance of a B&B and the privacy of a hotel. The breakfast is "to die for." Across the Columbia from Hood River, Oregon.   E-mail: innkeeper@gorge.net *Web site:* gorge.net/lodging/iws

WINTHROP ───────────────────────

Chewuch Inn
223 White Ave, 98862
509-996-3107 Fax: 509-996-3107
800-747-3107
Dan Kuperberb   All year

70-200-B&B
12 rooms, 12 pb
Visa, MC, AmEx,
Rated, •
C-yes/S-no/P-no/H-ltd

Continental plus breakfast
Afternoon tea, snacks
Sitting room, library,
bicycles, Jacuzzi, fireplaces,
cable TV

A craftsman style country inn, located within walking distance of an authentic western theme town. High in the North Cascade mountains, wildlife and recreation abound. Let us plan your day!   E-mail: chewuch@methow.com *Web site:* chewuchinn.com

---

Sun Mountain Lodge
PO Box 1000, 98862
509-996-2211 Fax: 509-996-3133
800-572-0493
Brian Charlton
All year

110-310-EP
112 rooms, 112 pb
Visa, MC, AmEx,
Rated, •
C-yes/S-ltd/P-no/H-yes
German

Full breakfast (fee)
Restaurant, bar service,
snacks
Sitt. room, library, bikes,
tennis court, jacuzzi, pool,
suites, fireplaces

Spectacular mountain top location, luxury log and stone lodge, gourmet dining and wine, 3,000 acres of outdoor fun.   E-mail: smtnsale@methow.com *Web site:* sunmountainlodge.com

West Virginia

AURORA ───────────────────────

Brookside Inn
Rt 1 Box 217B, 26705
304-735-6344 Fax: 304-735-3563
800-588-6344
Bill Reeves & Michele Moure
All year

85-145-MAP
4 rooms, 1 pb
Visa, MC, *Rated*, •
C-yes/S-no/P-no/H-no

Full breakfast
Dinner, snacks, wine
Sitting room, library

Historic mountain lodge overlooking Cathedral State Park, a virgin forest of hemlock, rhododendron and mountain streams. Cool summers, fall days of unsurpassed beauty and abundance of snow in the winter.   E-mail: mmoure@access.mountain.net

BUCKHANNON

Governor's Inn, A	69-99-B&B/MAP	Full breakfast
76 E Main St, 26201	7 rooms, 4 pb	Afternoon tea, snacks
304-472-2516 Fax: 304-472-1613	Visa, MC, AmEx,	Dinner by reservation, sitting
800-CALL-WVA	*Rated*, •	room w/fireplace,
Jerry & Bruce Henderson	C-yes/S-no/P-no/H-no	Bridal/Celebration suites
All year		

Buckhannon's own historic Victorian B&B. Gourmet breakfast (specialty-bread pudding with amaretto sauce). Close to WVWC and Main St. Down home charm, gift shop. Restaurants nearby. A/C in rooms. Two room suite available. E-mail: henderso@msys.net
Web site: bbonline.com/wv/governors

Post Mansion Inn B&B	50-80-B&B	Full breakfast
8 Island Ave, 26201	3 rooms, 1 pb	Snacks
304-472-8959	C-ltd/S-ltd/P-no/H-no	Sitting room, accommodate
800-301-9309		business travelers
Larry & Suzanne Reger		
All year		

Stately three story hand-cut stone mansion. On 6½ acres, originally built in 1860. Spacious air-conditioned rooms beautifully furnished in period antiques. Large relaxing porches. Two blocks from downtown. Historic register 1993.

CHARLES TOWN

Gilbert House of Middleway	80-140-B&B	Full gourmet breakfast
PO Box 1104, 25414	3 rooms, 3 pb	Complimentary tea, wine,
304-725-0637	Most CC, *Rated*, •	snacks
Bernie Heiler	C-ltd/S-ltd/P-no/H-ltd	Sitting room, library, piano,
All year	German, Spanish	fireplaces, A/C, bridal suite

Near Harper's Ferry. HABS listed, 18th-century stone house on original settlers' trail into Shenandoah Valley. Antiques, art treasures, village ghost E-mail: gilberthouse@hotmail.com

Hillbrook Inn	160-290-MAP	Full breakfast
Route 2, Box 152, 25414	11 rooms, 11 pb	7-course dinner/wine, aftn.
304-725-4223 Fax: 304-725-4455	Visa, MC, *Rated*, •	tea
800-304-4223	C-ltd/S-ltd/P-no/H-no	Restaurant, sitting room,
Gretchen Carroll	French	library, antiques, art
Closed 12/24-12/25		collection

Award winning country inn in the European style. Intimate dining room serves 7-course dinner. Dining terrace with fountain. Sweeping lawns, gardens, woodlands, streams & ponds. E-mail: reservations@hillbrookinn.com *Web site:* hillbrookinn.com

Washington House Inn	75-125-B&B	Full breakfast
216 S George St, 25414	6 rooms, 6 pb	Afternoon tea, snacks, wine
304-725-7923 Fax: 304-728-5150	Most CC, *Rated*, •	Bar, sitting room, library,
800-297-6957	C-ltd/S-ltd/P-no/H-no	bikes, suites, health club
Nina & Mel Vogel		access
All year		

Relax in the ambience & serenity of this 1899 Victorian built by descendants of Pres. Washington. Period antiques. "The best of everything"- Victorian Decorating & Lifestyle Magazine E-mail: mnvogel@intrepid.net *Web site:* washingtonhouseinnwv.com

CHARLESTON

Brass Pineapple B&B	59-109-B&B	Full or cont. plus breakfast
1611 Virginia St, E, 25311	6 rooms, 6 pb	Afternoon tea, snacks
304-344-0748 Fax: 304-344-0748	Most CC, *Rated*, •	Sitting room, bikes, TV/VCR,
800-CALLWVA	C-ltd/S-no/P-no/H-no	phones, voice mail, A/C
B. & S. Pepper, B. Morris		
Close Thansgiving, X-mas		

Cozy but elegant, antique filled beauty located ½ block from the Capitol Complex in the historic district. Great food, Southern hospitality. E-mail: pineapp104@aol.com
Web site: wvweb.com/brasspineapplebandb

ELKINS

Post House, The	65-B&B	Continental plus breakfast
306 Robert E. Lee Ave, 26241	5 rooms, 3 pb	Afternoon tea
304-636-1792	Visa, *Rated*	AMTA-certified massage,
All year	C-yes/S-no/P-no/H-no	near 5 ski resorts, bikes

Surrounded by mountain and park recreation, yet in town. Park-like backyard with children's playhouse. Handmade quilts for sale, and certified massage on premises.
E-mail: joanbarlow@aol.com

Tunnel Mountain B&B	60-80-B&B	Full breakfast
Route 1, Box 59-1, 26241	3 rooms, 3 pb	Restaurant nearby
304-636-1684	*Rated*	Sitting room w/fireplace,
888-211-9123	C-ltd/S-ltd/P-no/H-no	patio, wooded paths, A/C,
Anne & Paul Beardslee		scenic views, cable TV
All year		

Romantic country fieldstone B&B nestled in the scenic West Virginia. Mountains next to National Forest and recreational areas. *Web site:* wvonline.com/shareourbeds/tunnelmtn/

HARPERS FERRY

Harpers Ferry Guest House	65-95-B&B	Full breakfast
PO Box 1079, 25425	3 rooms, 3 pb	Snacks, wine
304-535-6955 Fax: 304-535-6955	*Rated*	Sitting room, cable TV,
Al & Alison Alsdorf	C-ltd/S-no/P-no/H-ltd	conference, off street parking
All year		

A wonderfully friendly B&B located right in Historic Harpers Ferry WV. Walk to shops, restaurants, and Harpers Ferry National Park. *E-mail:* alsdorf@harpersferry-wv.com
Web site: harpersferry-wv.com

HEDGESVILLE

Farmhouse on Tomahawk	75-125-B&B	Full breakfast
Run	5 rooms, 5 pb	Afternoon tea
1 Tomahawk Run Place, 25427	Most CC, *Rated*	Sitting room, Jacuzzis, suites,
304-754-7350 Fax: 304-754-7350	C-ltd/S-no/P-no/H-no	fireplaces, cable TV, private
888-266-9516		balconies
Judy & Hugh Erskine		
All year		

Charming Civil War-era farmhouse by historic spring on 280 acres of hills and meadows. Enjoy many varieties of birds and other country sights and sounds with breakfast on the wraparound porch. *E-mail:* tomahawk@intrepid.net *Web site:* innformation.com/wv/farmhouse

LEWISBURG

Lillian's Antique Shop B&B	90-135-B&B	Full breakfast
204 W Main St, 24986	4 rooms, 4 pb	Library, suites, cable TV,
304-536-1048 Fax: 304-536-9101	Visa, MC, AmEx,	Allegany Outfitters for
887-536-1048	C-ltd/S-no/P-no/H-no	outdoor activities
Linda D. Kothe and son Kris		
All year		

A colinial revival Queen Anne style cottage built in 1905. A unique combination b&b and antique shop. Tastefully decorated with antiques and collectibles you can purchase.
E-mail: lillians@brier.net *Web site:* wvonline.net/lillians

MILTON

Cedar House, The	65-75-B&B	Full breakfast
92 Trenol Heights, 25541	3 rooms, 3 pb	Snacks
304-743-5516	Most CC, *Rated*	Sitting room, library,
888-743-5516	S-no/P-no/H-ltd	fireplaces, cable TV,
Carole A Vickers		conference rooms
All year		

Hilltop, tri-level ranch style house on 5½ acres with panoramic view of surrounding hills, quiet and private, convenience of contemporary with old-fashioned hospitality, hand dipped chocolates. *E-mail:* vickersc@marshall.edu *Web site:* bbonline.com/wv/cedarhouse/

Farmhouse on Tomahawk Run, Hedgesville, WV

MORGANTOWN

Fieldcrest Manor B&B
30 Kingston Dr, 26505
304-599-2686 Fax: 304-599-3796
800-765-0569
Sarah Lough   All year

90-B&B
5 rooms, 5 pb
Visa, MC, AmEx, *Rated*
C-ltd/S-no/P-no/H-no

Full breakfast
Dinner, bar service
Sitting room, fireplaces,
cable TV, special events
room for meetings/parties

Wtih its beautifully manicured lawns and romantic natural landscapes, Fieldcrest is the perfect backdrop for relaxation, romance or to reconnect with friends and family.
E-mail: innkeeper@fieldcrestmanor.com *Web site:* fieldcrestmanor.com

PETERSBURG

North Fork Mountain Inn
PO Box 114, 26855
304-257-1108 Fax: 304-257-2008
Art & Joan Ricker
All year

85-120-B&B
8 rooms, 8 pb
Visa, MC,
C-ltd/S-no/P-no/H-no

Full breakfast
Dinner (fee), snacks
Sitting room, library,
Jacuzzis, fireplaces, cable
TV, hot tub

An Outpost of Luxury in the Wilderness, secluded non-resort getaway, located at 2600' on the North Fork Mt. within National Forest. E-mail: nfi@access.mountain.net
Web site: wvweb.com/www/north_fork_inn

PIPESTEM

Walnut Grove Inn
PO Box 6, 25979
304-466-6119 Fax: 304-466-6826
Connie Wiley
All year

75-B&B
5 rooms, 5 pb
Visa, MC,
S-no/P-no/H-yes

Full breakfast
Afternoon tea, snacks
Sitting room, swimming pool,
fireplaces, cable TV,
cosmetic consultant

Country Inn on 21 acres near historic Hinton, WV. 5 miles from Pipestem State Park, Bluestone Park and Dam. Winter place for skiing. Fishing, boating on the Bluestone River—quiet and beautiful.

ROMNEY

Hampshire House 1884
165 N Grafton St, 26757
304-822-7171 Fax: 304-822-7582
800-225-5982
Jane/Scott Simmons   All year

65-100-B&B/MAP/AP
7 rooms, 6 pb
Most CC, *Rated*, •
C-ltd/S-no/P-no/H-yes

Full breakfast
Lunch, dinner
Comp. wine, snacks, sitting
room, library, bikes, near
tennis, pool

Completely renovated 1884 home. Period furniture, lamps, fireplaces. Gourmet dining. Quiet. Therapeutic massage avail. Vegy dining with advance notice.
Web site: wbweb.com/www/hampshire_chamber/hampshirehouse.html

WHEELING —————————————————————————————————

Bonnie Dwaine B&B
505 Wheeling Ave, 26038
304-845-7250 Fax: 304-845-7256
888-507-4569
Bonnie & Sid Grisell
All year

79-125-B&B
5 rooms, 5 pb
Most CC, *Rated*, •
C-ltd/S-ltd/P-no/H-no

Full gourmet breakfast
Continental plus breakfast
Snacks, complimentary
wine, sitting room, library,
bicycles, fireplaces, A/C

Victorian warmth style and elegance w/the convenience of modern amenities. This beautiful home displays many antiques. 5 guest rooms feature fireplace & private adjoining bath w/whirlpool tub/shower.   E-mail: grisell@hgo.net *Web site:* Bonnie-Dwaine.com

Wisconsin

BAILEYS HARBOR —————————————————————————

Blacksmith Inn
PO Box 220, 54202
920-839-9222 Fax: 920-839-9356
800-769-8619
Joan Holliday & Bryan Nelson
All year

145-175-B&B
7 rooms, 7 pb
Most CC, *Rated*
C-ltd/S-no/P-no/H-no

Continental plus breakfast
Sitting room, bikes, Jacuzzis,
fireplace, kayaks, snowshoes

Our 1912 stovewood & half-timber waterfront inn in Door County, WI is filled with country primitive antiques. Sand beach, whirlpools, fireplaces and extraordinary views of the harbor from every room.   E-mail: relax@theblacksmithinn.com *Web site:* theblacksmithinn.com

BARABOO —————————————————————————————

Pinehaven B&B
E 13083 Hwy 33, 53913
608-356-3489 Fax: 608-256-0818
Lyle & Marge Getschman
All year

65-135-B&B
4 rooms, 4 pb
Visa, MC, *Rated*
C-ltd/S-no/P-no/H-no

Full breakfast
Fishing, rowing, cottage with
whirlpool, gazebo, sitting
room

*Beautiful view of bluffs small private lake. Tranquil setting. Take a stroll, fish, admire the Belgian draft horses. Relax. Acres to roam. Farm tours, country walks.
Web site:* dells.com/pinehaven

CEDARBURG —————————————————————————————

Stagecoach Inn
W61 N520 Washington Ave,
53012
262-375-0208 Fax: 262-375-6170
888-375-0208
Brook & Liz Brown
All year

75-140-B&B
12 rooms, 12 pb
Visa, MC, AmEx,
Rated, •
C-ltd/S-no/P-no/H-no

Continental plus breakfast
Aftn. wine, restored pub
Lib., sitt. rm, antiques,
whirlpools, phone jacks, Fax
outlet, coffee maker

Restored 1853 stone inn furnished with antiques & Laura Ashley comforters. Historic pub & chocolate shop on 1st floor. Fireplaces in 2 whirlpool stes. Gardens for guests   E-mail: info@ stagecoach-inn-wi.com *Web site:* stagecoach-inn-wi.com

Washington House Inn
W62 N573 Westlawn, 53012
414-375-3550 Fax: 414-375-9422
800-554-4717
Wendy Porterfield
All year

75-205-B&B
34 rooms, 34 pb
Rated, •
C-yes/S-yes/P-no/H-yes

Continental plus breakfast
Afternoon social
Sitting room, fireplaces,
whirlpool baths, sauna, wet
bars, bicycles

*Country inn in center of historical district. Breakfast in charming gathering room. Shopping, golf, winter sports. Gift certificates & golf packages available.
E-mail:* whinn@execpc.com *Web site:* washingtonhouseinn.com

Blacksmith Inn, Baileys Harbor, WI

DE PERE

James Street Inn
201 James St, 54115
920-337-0111 Fax: 920-337-6135
800-897-8483
Kevin C. Flatley
All year

69-149-B&B
30 rooms, 30 pb
Rated, ●
C-yes/S-ltd/P-no/H-yes

Continental plus breakfast
Afternoon tea, snacks
Comp. wine, bar service,
sitting room, fireplaces,
private decks, whirlpool

A country inn hidden just outside of Green Bay. Built on the foundation of a c.1858 mill, the river literally flows beneath it. Gorgeous views! E-mail: jamesst@netnet.net
Web site: jamesstreetinn.com

EGG HARBOR

Bay Point Inn
7933 Hwy 42, 54209
920-868-3297
800-709-6660
Myles Dannhausen
All year

155-225-B&B
10 rooms, 10 pb
Most CC, *Rated*, ●
C-yes/S-ltd/P-no/H-yes

Continental plus breakfast
Jacuzzis, swimming pool,
suites, fireplaces, waterview

Bay Point overlooks the Green Bay shoreline at Egg Harbor. Each suite offers romantic sunset views, award winning hospitality & gardens. E-mail: stay@baypointinn.com
Web site: baypointinn.com

EPHRAIM

Eagle Harbor Inn
PO Box 588, 54211
920-854-2121 Fax: 920-854-2121
800-324-5427
Nedd & Natalie Neddersen
All year

89-169-B&B
21 rooms, 21 pb
Visa, MC, *Rated*
C-ltd/P-no/H-yes

Full gourmet breakfast
Continental plus breakfast
Nov-Apr
Pool with current, bakery,
cottages have TV & grill, 200
yds to sandy beach

An intimate New England-styled country inn. Antique-filled, period wallpapers. Close to boating, beaches, golf course, parks. 12 private cottages. Queen-size or double beds.
E-mail: nnedd@eagleharbor.com Web site: eagleharbor.com

Hillside Hotel of Ephraim
PO Box 17, 54211
920-854-2417 Fax: 920-854-4240
800-423-7023
David & Karen McNeil
May-Oct., Jan-Feb

89-94-B&B/MAP
12 rooms
Visa, MC, Disc, *Rated*
C-ltd/S-no/P-no/H-no

Full specialty breakfast
6-course gourmet dinner
Full rest., aftn. tea,
featherbeds, ceiling fan,
private beach, mooring

Country-Victorian hotel in resort with harbor view, original furnishings, spectacular views; near galleries, shops. Deluxe cottages with whirlpool baths. Web site: hillsidehotel.com

Thorp House Inn & Cottage, Fish Creek, WI

FISH CREEK

Thorp House Inn & Cottages
PO Box 490, 54212
920-868-2444
C. & S. Falck-Pedersen
All year

85-175-B&B
10 rooms, 10 pb
Rated
C-ltd/S-no
Norwegian

Continental plus breakfast
Restaurants nearby
Sitting room with fireplace,
bikes, library, cross country
skiing

Antique-filled historic home backed by wooded bluff, overlooking bay. Kids O.K. in cottages, 5 with fireplace, 4 with whirlpool. On National Register.   E-mail: innkeeper@thorphouseinn.com *Web site:* thorphouseinn.com

GILLS ROCK

Harbor House Inn
12666 Hwy 42, 54210
920-854-5196 Fax: 920-854-9717
David and Else Weborg
May-Oct

59-159-B&B
15 rooms, 15 pb
Visa, MC, AmEx, *Rated*
C-yes/S-ltd/P-ltd/H-ltd
Danish

Continental plus breakfast
Sitting room, bikes, Jacuzzis,
suites, fireplace, sauna,
beach

1904 Victorian with a new Scandinavian country wing, 1998 lighthouse & 2 cottages situated across from quaint fishing harbor w/view of bay,m bluff, & sunsets.
Web site: door-county-inn.com

GREEN BAY

Astor House, The
637 S Monroe Ave, 54301
920-432-3585 Fax: 920-436-3145
888-303-6370
Doug Landwehr
All year

109-149-B&B
5 rooms, 5 pb
Most CC, *Rated*, •
C-ltd/S-no/P-no/H-no

Continental plus breakfast
Complimentary wine
Hot tubs, sitting room, gas
fireplaces, phone, cable TV,
stereo, VCR

Welcome to Green Bay's historic Astor Neighborhood. Five decorative motifs & in-room amenities indulge our guests, including whirlpool and fireplaces.   E-mail: astor@execpc.com
Web site: astorhouse.com

HARTLAND

Monches Mill House
W301 N9430 Hwy E, 53029
414-966-7546
Elaine Taylor
May-Dec.

50-75-B&B
4 rooms, 2 pb
C-yes/S-yes/P-yes/H-yes
French

Continental plus breakfast
Sitting room, hot tub, bikes,
tennis, canoeing, hiking

House built in 1842, located on the bank of the mill pond, furnished in antiques, choice of patio, porch or gallery for breakfast enjoyment.

HAYWARD

New Mountain B&B	65-85-B&B	Full breakfast
16199 W Musky Point Dr, 54876	5 rooms, 4 pb	Snacks
715-865-2486 Fax: 715-865-3022	Visa, MC, *Rated*, •	Sitting room, library, sauna,
800-NEW-MTBB	C-yes/S-ltd/P-no/H-ltd	dock, hiking/ski trail,
Jim & Elaine Nyberg		wildlife/nature
All year		

Enjoy Scandinavian lodging in our hilltop home overlooking Big Sissabagama Lake. Class A Musky Lake offering excellent fishing opportunities. E-mail: newmtbb@cheqnet.net
Web site: win.bright.net/~newmt/index.html

HUDSON

Jefferson-Day House	99-179-B&B	Four course breakfast
1109 - 3rd St, 54016	5 rooms, 5 pb	Snacks
715-386-7111	*Rated*	Special diets avail., sitting
Tom and Sue Tyler	C-yes/H-yes	room, library, 3 room suite
All year	Spanish	sleeps 5

1857 home blocks away from beautiful St. Croix River. All rms. with dbl. whirlpools, fireplace, A/C. Skiing nearby. 15 min. from St. Paul/Minneapolis.
E-mail: jeffersn@pressenter.com *Web site:* jeffersondayhouse.com

LAKE GENEVA

11 Gables on Lake Geneva	109-275-B&B	Full breakfast, weekends
493 Wrigley Dr, 53147	12 rooms, 12 pb	Continental plus-midweek
414-248-8393	Most CC, *Rated*, •	Private pier, swim, fish,
A. F. Milliette	C-ltd/S-ltd/P-no/H-ltd	hiking, bike rental, courtesy
All year		phone, Fax

Lakeside historic inn. Romantic bedrooms, bridal chamber, family "country cottages." Fireplaces, down quilts, wet bars, TVs, balconies. Prime location.
E-mail: egi@lkgeneva.com *Web site:* lkgeneva.com

Geneva Inn, The	150-350-B&B	Continental plus breakfast
N-2009 State Rd 120, 53147	37 rooms, 37 pb	Restaurant, lunch/dinner
414-248-5680 Fax: 414-248-5685	Most CC,	Turndown cognac & choc.,
800-441-5881	C-yes/S-yes/P-no/H-yes	whirlpools, fitness room,
Richard B. Treptow	German, French,	atrium, lake swimming
All year	Spanish	

A relaxing retreat on the shores of Lake Geneva. Deluxe accommodations touched with English charm. Restaurant & lounge. Banquet/meeting facilities; marina
E-mail: luxury@genevainn.com *Web site:* genevainn.com

Lazy Cloud Lodge	120-215-B&B	Continental plus breakfast
N2025 N Lake Shore Dr, 53125	9 rooms, 9 pb	Comp. wine, snacks, din.
414-275-3322 Fax: 414-275-8340	Most CC,	Sitting room, library, Jacuzzi,
Carol and Keith Tiffany	C-ltd/S-ltd/P-no/H-yes	suites, fireplaces
All year		

Romantic hideaway with luxury suites. All rooms include double whirlpool with a view of fireplace. Each room is decorated around a different theme-log cabin, Victorian, garden, rustic, country, etc. E-mail: lzcloud@genevaonline.com *Web site:* lazycloud.com

T.C. Smith Historic Inn B&B	125-375-B&B	Full breakfast
865 Main St, 53147	8 rooms, 8 pb	Afternoon tea, snacks
414-248-1097 Fax: 414-248-1672	Most CC, *Rated*, •	Sitting room, library,
800-423-0233	C-yes/S-yes/P-yes/H-no	fireplaces, whirlpools, A/C,
Marks Family		TV, fireplaces
All year		

Relax by fireplaces to experience romance & warmth of Grand Victorian era in downtown lakeview mansion of 1845. Honeymoon suite with lighted whirlpool. On National Register. Web site: tcsmithinn.com

LODI

Victorian Treasure Inn	95-190-B&B	Full breakfast
115 Prairie St, 53555	8 rooms, 8 pb	Aftn. tea, snacks, wine
608-592-5199 Fax: 608-592-7147	Visa, MC, *Rated*, •	Whirlpools, fireplaces,
800-859-5199	C-yes/S-no/P-no/H-no	Canopy beds, library,
Todd & Kimberly Seidl		porches, parlors
All year		

Luxurious, romantic Victorian accommodations between Madison & Dells. Meticulous rooms, thoughtful amenities, fussy innkeepers. 4 miles off of I90/94.   E-mail: innkeeper@victoriantreasure.com *Web site:* victoriantreasure.com

MADISON

Annie's B&B	143-189-B&B	Full breakfast
2117 Sheridan Dr, 53704	1 rooms, 2 pb	Library, fireplace, A/C,
608-244-2224 Fax: 608-244-2224	Visa, MC, AmEx, *Rated*	tennis, nature trails,
Anne & Lawrence Stuart	C-ltd/S-no/P-no/H-no	swimming
All year		

Beautiful country garden setting in the city, with romantic gazebo. Full recreational options. Six minutes to downtown/campus. Woodland Whirlpool Room. Web site: bbinternet.com/annies

Arbor House	85-205-B&B	Full breakfast on weekends
Environmental	8 rooms, 8 pb	Continental breakfast
3402 Monroe St, 53711	Visa, MC, AmEx, *Rated*	weekdays
608-238-2981 Fax: 608-238-1175	C-yes/S-no/P-no/H-yes	Cable, massage available,
John & Cathie Imes		cross-country skiing, 5
All year		fireplaces.

Historic landmark across from UW Arboretum has an environmental emphasis. Minutes from the Capitol & UW campus. Comp. canoeing & Gehl's iced cappuccino. Corporate rates. Natiopnal award winning   Web site: arbor-house.com

Cameo Rose Victorian Inn	95-145-B&B	Full breakfast
1090 Severson Road, 53508	5 rooms, 5 pb	Sitting room, suites, fireplace
608-424-6340	Visa, MC,	
Dawn & Gary Bahr	C-ltd/S-no/P-no/H-no	
All year		

Rated prettiest Victorian B&B in the country. 120 acres of hills and woods. Peaceful, romantic, elegant; best beds, breakfast and hospitality. Located between Madison and New Glarus (America's Little Switzerland).   E-mail: innkeeper@cameorose.com *Web site:* cameorose.com

Collins House, The	95-160-B&B	Full breakfast
704 E Gorham St, 53703	5 rooms, 5 pb	Complimentary chocolate
608-255-4230 Fax: 608-255-0830	Visa, MC, *Rated*	truffles
Barb Pratzel	C-yes/S-ltd/P-yes/H-no	Sitting room w/fireplace,
All year		library, movie videos,
		whirlpools, fireplace, deck

Restored prairie school style. Overlooks Lake Mendota, near university and State Capitol. Elegant rooms, wonderful gourmet breakfasts and pastries. Meeting room available. E-mail: inncollins@aol.com *Web site:* collinshouse.com

Livingston Inn, The	139-269-B&B	Continental plus breakfast
752 E Gorham St, 53703	4 rooms, 4 pb	Complimentary wine &
608-257-1200 Fax: 608-257-1145	Visa, MC, AmEx,	appetizers
Bill & Kim Giesecke	C-ltd/S-no/P-no/H-no	Sitting room, suites,
All year		fireplaces, cable TV, fax,
		laundry, local reservations

An 1857 Gothic Revival mansion on Lake Mendota. Elegant and gracious with 9 fireplaces, antiques, English Conservatory, garden path to the lake, walking distance to downtown Madison, breakfast & wine.   E-mail: reservations@thelivingston.com *Web site:* thelivingston.com

MADISON

Mansion Hill Inn
424 N Pinckney St, 53703
608-255-3999 Fax: 608-255-2217
800-795-9070
Janna Wojtal
All year

140-320-B&B
11 rooms, 11 pb
Visa, MC, AmEx,
Rated, •
C-ltd/S-yes/P-no/H-no

Continental plus breakfast
Afternoon tea, snacks, comp.
wine
Bar service, sitting room, hot
tubs, sauna, steam showers

Victorian elegance abounds in our antique-filled guest rooms. Fireplaces, private baths with whirlpools, valet service. We await your pleasure. Web site: mansionhillinn.com

MILWAUKEE

Crane House B&B, The
346 E Wilson St, 53207
414-483-1512 Fax: 414-486-1613
P Tirrito & S Skavroneck
All year

65-91-B&B
4 rooms
Visa, MC,
C-yes/S-ltd/P-no/H-no

Full breakfast
Snacks
Sitting room, library,
accommodate business
travelers

Friendly, eclectic atmosphere. Sumptuous, 3 course breakfast served in our dining room or garden. Bedtime treats served by warm, gracious hosts. Close to downtown and airport. E-mail: cranehousesp@msn.com Web site: cranehouse.com

OCONOMOWOC

Inn at Pine Terrace
351 E Lisbon Rd, 53066
262-567-7463
Richard Borb
All year

80-145-B&B
13 rooms, 13 pb
Most CC, *Rated*
C-yes/S-yes/P-no/H-ltd

Continental Plus
Snacks, complimentary wine
Sitting room, Jacuzzis,
swimming pool, cable TV,
accommodate business
travel

Elegantly restored Victorian mansion for a discerning traveler. In the tradition of a small European hotel and on the list of National Historic Places.
E-mail: innkeeper@pineterrace.com Web site: innatpineterrace.com

PLATTEVILLE

Walnut Ridge B&B
2238 Hwy A, 53818
608-348-9359 Fax: 608-348-3898
Jill & Chuck Staab
All year

140-B&B
1 rooms, 1 pb
Visa, MC, *Rated*
C-ltd/S-no/P-no/H-no

Continental breakfast plus
Snacks, complimentary wine
Sitting room, fireplaces,
double whirlpool, robes,
handmade soaps, CD player

Private, luxury log cottage. Perfect for romantic getaway with wood burning fireplace, double whirlpool in bedroom. Kitchenette, loft sitting room. Historic country furnishings and setting. Attention to detail is evident throughout E-mail: wlntrdge@mhtc.net

PLYMOUTH

Timberlake Inn B&B
PO Box 367, 53011
920-528-8481 Fax: 920-528-8585
888-528-8481
Juanita & Rick Levandowski
Open all year

75-100-B&B
6 rooms, 6 pb
Visa, MC, Disc, •
C-ltd/S-ltd/P-ltd/H-no
German

Full breakfast
Afternoon tea
Guest kitchen & BBQ,
Bicycles, Accommodate
business travelers

Rustic, small-town relaxation just 40 minutes N. of downtown Milwaukee. Distinctly unique rooms & fantastic breakfasts along with hometown hospitality at reasonable rates. Midweek & group discounts negotiable. E-mail: tmbrlkin@timberlakeinn.com
Web site: timberlakeinn.com

PRESCOTT

Arbor Inn, The
434 North Court St, 54021
715-262-4522 Fax: 715-262-5644
888-262-1090
Marv & Linda Kangas
All year

125-159-B&B
4 rooms, 4 pb
Visa, MC, AmEx, *Rated*
C-ltd/S-no/P-no/H-no

Full breakfast
Afternoon tea, snacks, wine
Sitting room, bikes, Jazuzzis,
fireplace, cable TV

Located in the scenic St. Croix River Valley, this 1902 inn is reminiscent of an English country cottage. Vines, porches, and 4 antique filled rooms set the scene for relaxation or romance year round. E-mail: arborinn@pressenter.com Web site: thearborinn.com

Lamb's Inn B&B, Spring Green, WI

REEDSBURG

Parkview B&B
211 N Park St, 53959
608-524-4333
Fax: 608-524-1172
Tom & Donna Hofmann
All year

70-90-B&B
4 rooms, 2 pb
Visa, MC, AmEx,
Rated, •
C-ltd/S-no/P-no/H-no

Full breakfast
Snacks, wake-up coffee
Sitting room, playhouse on
property, park across the
street

1895 Victorian home with comfortable antiques, across from City Park. Wisconsin Dells, Baraboo, Spring Green, bike trails, state park nearby. E-mail: parkview@jvlnet.com Web site: parkviewbb.com

SPARTA

Franklin Victorian, The
220 E Franklin St, 54656
608-269-3894
800-845-8767
Lloyd & Jane Larson
All year

75-95-B&B
4 rooms, 2 pb
Rated
C-ltd/S-no/P-no/H-no

Full 3-course breakfast
Afternoon tea, snacks
Sitting room, library, canoe
rental

Relax in quiet, gracious comfort—spacious rooms, fine woods. Delectable breakfasts. Surrounding area abounds with beauty. E-mail: fvbb@centuryinter.net Web site: spartan.org/fvbb

SPRING GREEN

Lamb's Inn B&B
23761 Misslich Dr, 53581
608-585-4301
Dick & Donna Messerschmidt
All year

80-130-B&B
6 rooms, 6 pb
Visa, MC, Disc, *Rated*
C-ltd/S-no/P-no/H-ltd

Full breakfast—B&B
Continental plus breakfast-
cottage
Library, Suites, Fireplaces,
snacks

180 acre farm located in a beautiful valley. King or queen beds with private baths, full breakfast. Also cottage with 2 levels. Lower level has a gas fireplace, upper level has deck with a grill. E-mail: lambsinn@mwt.net Web site: lambs-inn.com

STEVENS POINT

Dreams of Yesteryear B&B
1100 Brawley St, 54481
715-341-4525
Fax: 715-344-3047
Bonnie & Bill Maher
All year

55-142-B&B
6 rooms, 4 pb
Visa, MC, *Rated*, •
C-ltd/S-no/P-no/H-no

Full breakfast
Afternoon tea, snacks
Sitting room, library, tennis
court, hot tub, bike, pool, 2 3-
room suites

Victorian restoration featured in Victorian Homes Magazine. It's truly the kind of place Victorian Dreams are made of. House is A/C. E-mail: bonnie@dreamsofyesteryear.com Web site: dreamsofyesteryear.com

Reynolds House B&B, Sturgeon Bay, WI

STEVENS POINT

Victorian Swan on Water, A
1716 Water St, 54481
715-345-0595
Fax: 713-345-0569
Joan Ouellette
All year

60-140-B&B
4 rooms, 4 pb
Most CC, *Rated*, •
C-ltd/S-no/P-no/H-no

Full breakfast
Snacks, complimentary wine
Sitting room, library, log
cabin available

Enjoy award winning breakfast, beautiful gardens, a secret room and whirlpool in this 1889 Victorian home. Central Wisconsin location. Part of 2 bicycle tour packages.
E-mail: victorian@g2a.net *Web site:* bbinternet.com/victorian-swan

STURGEON BAY

Hearthside Farm B&B Inn
2136 Taube Rd, 54235
920-746-2136
Don & Lu Klussendorf
All year

60-75-B&B
4 rooms, 4 pb
Rated
C-yes/S-no/P-no/H-ltd

Full breakfast
Sitting room, walking trails,
gardens

Country decor with four-poster bed and private baths. E-mail: hearthside@itol.com
Web site: hearthside-farm-bb.com

Inn at Cedar Crossing
336 Louisiana St, 54235
920-743-4200 Fax: 920-743-4422
Terry Smith
All year

99-169-B&B
9 rooms, 9 pb
Most CC, *Rated*
C-ltd/S-no/P-no/H-no

Continental plus breakfast
Complimentary beverages,
cookies
Restaurant, bar, sitting room,
whirlpool in some rooms,
fireplaces in rooms

Elegant 1884 inn situated in historic district near shops, restaurants, museum, beaches. Elegant romantic antique decor, fireplaces, whirlpools. 6 rooms have fireplaces Rated "Top 25 Restaurants." E-mail: innkeeper@innatcedarcrossing.com *Web site:* innatcedarcrossing.com

Reynolds House B&B
111 S 7th Ave, 54235
920-746-9771 Fax: 920-746-9441
All year

90-155-B&B
4 rooms, 4 pb
Visa, MC,
S-no/P-no/H-no

Full breakfast
Afternoon tea, snacks
Sitting room, library,
Jacuzzis, suites, fireplaces,
cable TV

The architecturally significant Queen Anne Home built in 1900 is located within walking distance of downtown Sturgeon Bay. Fine oak woodwork, hardwood floors, period antiques. E-mail: jsekula@reynoldshousebandb.com *Web site:* reynoldshousebandb.com

White Lace Inn, Sturgeon Bay, WI

STURGEON BAY

White Lace Inn
16 N 5th Ave, 54235
920-743-1105 Fax: 920-743-8180
Dennis & Bonnie Statz
All year

58-209-B&B
18 rooms, 18 pb
Visa, MC, *Rated*
C-ltd/S-no/P-no/H-ltd

Full breakfast
Complimentary cookies,
beverages
Sitting room, gazebo,
gardens, tandem bicycles,
fireplaces, whirlpools

The White Lace Inn's four historic homes are nestled in a friendly old neighborhood, bordered by a white picket fence and surrounded by gardens. E-mail: romance@ whitelaceinn.com *Web site:* whitelaceinn.com

Whitefish Bay Farm B&B
3831 Clark Lake Rd, 54235
920-743-1560
Dick & Gretchen Regnery
All year

65-90-B&B
4 rooms, 4 pb
Visa, MC, Disc, *Rated*
S-no/P-no/H-no
Danish

Full breakfast
Sitting room, ceiling fans,
abundant homemade
breakfast, bed turndown
serv.

Quiet country B&B on 80 acre farm raising sheep. Comfortable rooms, private baths. Abundant homemade breakfast. Eclectic decor with Scandinavian influence, original artwork and handweavings throughout. E-mail: dregnery@mail.wiscnet.net
Web site: whitefishbayfarm.com

WASHBURN

Pilgrim's Rest B&B
27705 S Maple Hill Rd, 54891
715-373-2964
Kent & Mary Beth Seldal
All year

B&B
2 rooms, 2 pb
Rated
C-ltd/S-no/P-no/H-no

Full breakfast
Dinner, snacks
Sitting room, suites, cable TV,
hot springs spa, movies &
popcorn

Country retreat with view of oldest mountains in North America. Furnished with antiques & lodge decor. Four course breakfast, trails & wildlife all around. Quiet, private gardens & woods. E-mail: pilgrimr@ncis.net *Web site:* ncis.net/pilgrimr

WHITE LAKE

Jesse's Wolf River Lodge
W2119 Taylor Rd, 54491
715-882-2182
Joan Jesse   All year

80-160-B&B
10 rooms, 10 pb
Most CC, •
C-yes/S-ltd/P-yes/H-no

Full breakfast
Restaurant, bar
Sitting room, hot tubs, 2
bedroom guesthouse

Comfortable north woods rustic log building overlooking the whitewater Wolf River. Handmade quilts, braided rugs, antique-filled rooms. Huge stone fireplace. All rooms have air-conditioning. E-mail: wlfrvrldg@aol.com *Web site:* wolfriverlodge.com

WISCONSIN DELLS

Thunder Valley	65-95-B&B	Full breakfast
W 15344 Waubeek Rd, 53965	6 rooms	Snacks, summer restaurant
608-254-4145 Fax: 608-254-2645	Visa, MC,	Sitting room, bikes, farm
Anita, Kari, & Sigrid Nelson	C-yes/S-no/P-ltd/H-yes	pets, hiking, campfire.
All year		

Scandinavian hospitality in country setting. Homemade breads, jams will delight you. Real old fashioned comfort. Stroll the farmstead, pet the animals or relax with a good book, cider or Norwegian coffee. Summer "threshing suppers." E-mail: neldell@midplains.net

Wyoming

CHEYENNE

A. Drummond's Ranch B&B	65-175-B&B	Full breakfast
399 Happy Jack Rd, 82007	4 rooms, 2 pb	Afternoon tea, snacks
307-634-6042 Fax: 307-634-6042	Visa, MC, *Rated*, ●	Lunch, dinner (fee), sitting
Taydie Drummond	C-ltd/S-no/P-yes/H-ltd	room, library, bikes, hot tub,
All year	French	sauna

Quiet gracious retreat on 120 acres. Pristine mountain views; glorious night sky; private outdoor Jacuzzis; sauna; fine dining. Complimentary snacks. E-mail:adrummond@juno.com
Web site: cruising-america.com/drummond.html

Nagle Warren Mansion B&B	98-115-B&B	Full breakfast
222 E 17th St, 82001	12 rooms, 12 pb	Aftn. tea, restaurant
307-637-3333 Fax: 307-638-6835	Visa, MC, AmEx, ●	Jacuzzis, suites, fireplaces,
800-811-2610	C-ltd/S-no/P-ltd/H-yes	cable TV, conference
Jim Osterfoss	Spanish, German	facilities
All year		

This is a newly restored 1888 Victorian mansion with all of today's comforts. Luxuriate in the elegance while you explore the original west. Our staff and ourselves strive to make your stay special. E-mail: josterfoss@aol.com

CODY

Lockhart B&B Inn	85-99-B&B	All-you-can-eat breakfast
109 W Yellowstone Ave, 82414	7 rooms, 7 pb	Complimentary brandy,
307-587-6074 Fax: 307-587-8644	Most CC, *Rated*, ●	coffee
800-377-7255	C-yes/S-ltd/P-no/H-no	"Elegant Tea" lunch(fee),
Don & Cindy Baldwin Kramer		sitting room, phones, cable
All year		TV

Historic home of famous western author Caroline Lockhart—featuring antiques, old-style comfort & hearty breakfast. Western hospitality E-mail: dckramer@nemontel.net
Web site: nemontel.net/~dckramer/index.htm

JACKSON

Huff House Inn B&B, The	119-198-B&B	Full breakfast
Box 1189, 83001	9 rooms, 9 pb	Family friendly facility, sitting
307-733-4164 Fax: 307-739-9091	Most CC, *Rated*, ●	room, library, hot tubs
Jackie & Weldon Richardson	C-yes/S-no/P-no/H-no	
All year		

Historic house one and one-half blocks east of the town square, on the quiet side of town. Furnished with antiques and original art. E-mail: huffhousebnb@blissnet.com
Web site: jacksonwyomingbnb.com

JACKSON HOLE

Painted Porch, The
PO Box 6955, 83002
307-733-1981
Martha & Matt MacEachern
All year

115-235-B&B
4 rooms, 4 pb
Visa, MC,
C-ltd/S-no/P-no/H-no
Spanish

Full breakfast
Sitting room, library,
porches, decks, beautiful
setting

Country elegance abounds at our 1901 farmhouse nestled in 3 and a half acres of Aspen and Pine trees at the base of the Tetons where wide open hospitality reins
E-mail: thepaintedporch@wyoming.com *Web site:* jacksonholenet.com/paintedporch/

Parkway Inn, The
PO Box 494, 83001
307-733-3143 Fax: 307-733-0955
800-247-8390
Carmen & Tom Robbins
Closed November

89-195-B&B
49 rooms, 49 pb
Most CC, *Rated*, •
C-ltd/S-ltd/P-no
Spanish, German

Continental breakfast
Afternoon tea
Sitting room, Jacuzzis, pool,
suites, cable TV, excercise
gym with saunas

The style of the inn is reminiscent of turn of the century architecture with white spindle rails and a cupola.   *E-mail:* info@parkwayinn.com *Web site:* parkwayinn.com

Wildflower Inn, The
PO Box 11000, 83002
307-733-4710 Fax: 307-739-0914
Ken & Sherrie Jern
All year

150-270-B&B
5 rooms, 5 pb
Visa, MC, *Rated*, •
C-yes/S-no/P-no/H-no

Full breakfast
Complimentary wine, tea,
coffee
Sitting room, deck, library,
hot tubs, pond, solarium,
wild ducks

Lovely log home on 3 acres of aspens, cottonwoods, &, of course, wildflowers. 5 sunny guest rooms, some with private decks. 2 rm. suite with fireplace, Jacuzzi, deck. Near racquet club, golf club, ski area.   E-mail: wildflowerinn@compuserve.com
Web site: jacksonholenet.com/wildflower/

PINEDALE

Lozier's Box "R" Ranch
Box 100-TG, 82925
307-367-4868 Fax: 307-367-6260
800-822-8466
Irv, Robin, Levi, Donna Lozier
May 28-Oct 1

995-1295-AP
10 rooms, 10 pb
Visa, MC, Disc, *Rated*,
•
C-ltd/S-ltd/P-no/H-no

Full breakfast
Lunch & dinner included
Snacks, sitting room, library,
fireplaces, pool table,
horseshoes, games

Live that life long dream of being a cowboy/cowgirl for a week! True working cattle/horse guest ranch, private horse & tack, riding freedoms, cattle drives, and weekly ranch vacations.   E-mail: info@boxr.com *Web site:* boxr.com

Window on the Winds B&B
PO Box 996, 82941
307-367-2600 Fax: 307-367-2395
888-367-1345
Leanne McClain & Family
All year

75-115-B&B
4 rooms
Most CC, *Rated*, •
C-yes/S-no/P-yes/H-no

Full gourmet breakfast
Snacks
Guest living room with
mountian views, sunroom
with hot tub

Beautiful log home decorated in Western and Plains Indian decor, lodgepole pine queen beds, with breathtaking mountain views, and the hosts are archaeologists.
E-mail: lmcclain@wyoming.com *Web site:* cruising-america.com/windowonwinds

SARATOGA

Wolf Hotel
PO Box 1298, 82331
307-326-5525
Doug & Kathleen Campbell
All year

37-79-EP
9 rooms, 9 pb
Most CC, *Rated*
C-yes/S-ltd/P-no/H-no

Breakfast, lunch, dinner
Luxury suite, Restaurant, TV
in 5 rooms, bar, blue ribbon
trout stream

Hotel built in 1893 as a stage stop. Listed in National Register. Blue Ribbon fishing, golf, hot springs nearby. Dining room (AAA approved) & lounge redone in Victorian style.

Puerto Rico

CEIBA

Ceiba Country Inn
PO Box 1067, 00735
787-885-0471
Fax: 787-885-0471
877-885-1002
Sue Newbauer & Dick Bray
All year

70-B&B
9 rooms, 9 pb
Most CC, *Rated*, •
C-yes/S-yes/P-no/H-yes

Continental plus breakfast
Bar service, library, family
friendly facility

Pastoral setting with a view of the sea. Centrally located for trips to the rain forest, beaches, outer islands, and San Juan. The surroundings are lush and green, with exotic flowers in abundance. E-mail: prinn@juno.com

ISLA VERDE

Hotel La Playa
Calle Amapola #6, 00979
787-791-1115
Fax: 787-791-4650
800-791-9626
B. & D. Yourch, M. Godinez
All year

75-105-B&B
15 rooms, 15 pb
Most CC, •
C-yes/S-yes/P-no/H-yes
Spanish

Continental breakfast
Lunch & dinner available
(fee)
Restaurant, bar service,
open air deck located on
beach

Small family oriented hotel, relaxing casual atmosphere located on the beach, family owned business for over 35 years in a residential area. E-mail: manager@hotellaplaya.com Web site: hotellaplaya.com

PATILLAS

Caribe Playa Beach Resort
HC 764 Box 8490, 00723
787-839-6339 Fax: 787-839-1817
800-221-4483
George Engel
All year

104-EP
32 rooms, 32 pb
Visa, MC, AmEx, •
C-yes/S-yes/P-yes/H-yes
Spanish

Restaurant, bar service,
sitting room, library, beach
swimming, snorkel

Modern studios on private picturesque coconut beach on the Caribbean Sea; swimming, snorkeling, fishing, pool, Sundeck, bar, scuba diving, music room, beach barbecues, TV. E-mail: geobeach@coqui.net Web site: caribeplaya.com

SAN GERMAN

Hotel y Parador Oasis
PO Box 144, 00753
787-892-1175
All year

61-63-B&B
Visa, MC, AmEx, •
C-yes/S-no/P-yes/H-no
Spanish, English, French

Full breakfast
AP & MAP available
Afternoon tea, snacks, wine,
restaurant, bar, swimming
pool, Jacuzzi

Relax in the friendly atmosphere of this 200-year-old Spanish mansion. Close to beaches, historical sites, and the world famous Phosphorescent Bay.

SAN JUAN

El Canario by the Sea
4 Avenida Condado, 00907
787-722-8640 Fax: 787-725-4921
Christine Nash
All year

65-140-B&B
25 rooms, 25 pb
Most CC, *Rated*, •
C-yes/S-yes/P-no/H-no
Spanish, French

Continental breakfast
Cable TV, phones, wicker

El Canario By The Sea is ideally located on the beach in the heart of Condado. It is in the midst of casinos, restaurants, etc. Hotle was renovated in 1999. We are a clean, well located, well priced inn on San Juan. Helpful staff. E-mail: canariopr@aol.com Web site: canariohotels.com

SAN JUAN —————————————————————————————

El Canario Inn
1317 Ashford Ave, 00907
787-722-3861 Fax: 787-722-0391
800-533-2649
Marcos Santana
All year

75-114-B&B
25 rooms, 25 pb
Visa, MC, AmEx,
Rated, •
C-yes/S-yes/P-no/H-no
Spanish

Continental plus breakfast
Jacuzzi, patios, rooms with
A/C, cable TV, phones,
wicker

In heart of Condado, near beach, casinos, boutiques and fine restaurants. Jacuzzi in patio area, tropical patio and sun deck for sun, fun, and relaxation. E-mail: canariopr@aol.com
Web site: canariohotels.com

Embassy Guesthouse-
Condado
PO Box 16876, 00907
787-725-8284 Fax: 787-725-2400
Jacuqes & Thierry
All year

45-145-EP
20 rooms, 20 pb
Most CC, *Rated*, •
C-yes/S-yes/P-no/H-ltd
Spanish, French

Jacuzzis, pool, cable TV, bar
service

Located in the center of Condado, only steps to the beaches in San Juan. New fresh water swimming pool and Jacuzzi. E-mail: embassyguesthouse@worldnet.att.net
Web site: home.att.net/~embassyguesthouse/

Tres Palmas Inn
2212 Park Blvd, 00913
787-727-4617 Fax: 787-727-5434
888-290-2076
Manuael & Eileen Peredo
All year

59-160-B&B
15 rooms, 15 pb
Visa, MC, AmEx,
Rated, •
C-yes/S-ltd/P-no/H-yes
Spanish

Continental plus breakfast
Sitting room, Jacuzzis,
swimming pool, suites, cable
TV, phone with dataport

This quaint 15 room beachfront Inn recently renovated is a refreshing alternative to traditional high priced and crowded hotels. Our top priority is the personal attention & service that we provide to our guests. We like to call our guests our friends. E-mail: trespalm@coqui.net Web site: trespalmasinn.com

VIEQUES —————————————————————————————

Hacienda Tamarindo
PO Box 1569, 00765
787-741-8525 Fax: 787-741-3215
Burr and Linda Vail
All year

135-190-B&B
15 rooms, 15 pb
Visa, MC, AmEx,
Rated, •
C-ltd/S-yes/P-no/H-yes
Spanish

Full breakfast
Bar service
Sitting room, library, tennis
court, swimming pool

Perched on windswept hilltop overlooking the turquoise Caribbean. Charming. Uniquely designed and decorated with an accumulation of art and antiques E-mail: hactam@aol.com
Web site: enchanted-isle.com/tamarindo

Virgin Islands

CRUZ BAY —————————————————————————————

Estate Lindholm
PO Box 1360, 00831
340-776-6121 Fax: 340-776-6141
800-322-6335
Brion & Lauren Morrisette
All year

325-B&B
11 rooms, 11 pb
Visa, MC, AmEx, •
C-yes/S-ltd/P-no/H-ltd
Spanish

Continental breakfast
Tea, snacks, wine,
restaurant, bar
Sitting room, swimming pool,
cable TV, conferences, A/C,
phones, wet bar

An intimate bed and breakfast inn located within the Virgin Islands National Park on St. John's scenic Northshore. Enjoy continental breakfast each morning overlooking pictur-esque harbor of Cruz Bay. E-mail: lindholm@viaccess.com Web site: estatelindholm.com

ST. CROIX

Breakfast Club, The	60-B&B	Full gourmet breakfast
18 Queen Cross St, 00820	9 rooms, 9 pb	Bar service
340-773-7383 Fax: 340-773-8642	Visa, MC,	Sitting room, library, hot
Toby & Barb Chapin	C-yes/S-yes/P-no/H-no	tubs, tour colonial village
All year		

Six blocks from downtown Christiansted. Private kitchens, baths. Harbor island views from deck, rooms. Tax included. Groups inquire about villa.   E-mail: tchapin@virginislands.net

Tamarind Reef Hotel	145-180-B&B	Continental breakfast
5001 Tamarind Reef, 00820	46 rooms, 46 pb	Restaurant
340-773-4455 Fax: 340-773-3989	Most CC, *Rated*, •	Bar service, sitting room,
800-619-0014	C-yes/P-no/H-yes	tennis court, pool, family
Dick & Marcy Pelton		friendly facility
All year		

Small hotel with intimate atmosphere & personalized service. Off the beaten track, yet 5 minutes to Christiansted. Beachfront elegance, all watersports, adjacent to marina. Conference center, gift shop.   E-mail: tamarind@usvi.net Web site: usvi.net/hotel/tamarind

ST. THOMAS

Danish Chalet Inn	64-99-B&B	Continental breakfast
PO Box 4319, 00803	15 rooms, 6 pb	Bar service ($1 drinks)
340-774-5764 Fax: 340-777-4886	Visa, MC, *Rated*, •	Sitting room, spa, Jacuzzi,
800-635-1531	S-yes/P-ltd/H-yes	sun deck, beach towels,
Frank & Mary Davis	English	games
All year		

Family inn overlooking Charlotte Amalie harbor, 5 min. to town, duty-free shops, restaurants. Cool breezes, honor bar, sun deck, Jacuzzi. Beach-15 min. Lovely 3 room apartment added.   E-mail: fhd4319@aol.com Web site: winninn.com

Galleon House Hotel	59-119-B&B	Continental plus breakfast
PO Box 6577, 00804	14 rooms, 13 pb	A/C in rooms, pool, snorkel
340-774-6952 Fax: 340-774-6952	*Rated*, •	gear, veranda, beach towels
800-524-2052	C-yes/S-yes/P-no/H-no	
Dolena Paul		
Dec.-April		

Visit historical Danish town. Superb view of harbor with city charm close to everything. Duty-free shopping, beach activities in 85-degree weather.

Island View Guest House	65-100-B&B	Continental breakfast
PO Box 1903, 00803	15 rooms, 13 pb	Full breakfast available
340-774-4270 Fax: 340-774-6167	*Rated*, •	Hors d'oeuvres (Friday),
800-524-2023	C-ltd/S-yes/P-no/H-no	sandwiches, bar, gallery,
Barbara Cooper		swimming pool
All year		

Overlooking St. Thomas harbor, honor bar and freshwater pool. Spectacular harbor view from all rooms. Convenient to town and airport   E-mail: islandview@worldnet.att.net Web site: st-thomas.com/islandviewguesthouse/

Mafolie Hotel	75-135-B&B	Continental breakfast
7091 Estate Mafolie #4, 00802	23 rooms, 23 pb	Lunch & dinner available
340-774-2790 Fax: 340-774-4091	Visa, MC, AmEx, •	Restaurant, bar service,
800-225-7035	C-yes/S-yes/P-no/H-no	snacks, swimming pool, A/C,
Tony & Lyn Eden	Spanish	Cable TV, Fax serv.
All year		

800 feet above town & harbor, world-famous view. 10 mins. from everything. Family owned & operated. Recent total renovation.   Web site: St-thomas.com/mafolie/

ST. THOMAS ───────────────────────

Miller Manor	55-65-B&B/EP	Continental plus breakfast
PO Box 1570, 00804	24 rooms, 24 pb	Restaurant
340-774-1535 Fax: 340-774-5988	Most CC, ●	Swimming pool, cable TV,
888-229-0762	H-ltd	A/C, Cable TV, Fax service
Aida & Leo	Spanish	
All year		

Family oriented, family run, 5 minute walk to town, view of town and harbor, A/C, refrigerator, microwave, toaster, coffee maker, private bath in each room, centrally located, taxi service available.   E-mail: millermanor-aida-leo@worldnet.att.net
Web site: travelguides.com/home/millermanor/

Alberta

BANFF ─────────────────────────────

Banff Squirrel's Nest	67 and up-B&B	Continental plus breakfast
PO Box 1141, T0L 0C0	2 rooms, 2 pb	Tea
403-762-4432 Fax: 403-762-5167	Visa, ●	Sitting room, family friendly
Calvin & Paula Shakotko	C-yes/S-no/P-no/H-no	facility, downtown location,
All year		library, cable TV

Newly renovated, five minutes from downtown. 5 minute walk to bus and train station. Private baths, common sitting guest room, non-smoking, clean, year round. E-mail: paulas@telusplanet.net *Web site:* canadianrockies.net/squirrelsnest

Cougar Canyon B&B	50-80-B&B	Full breakfast
3 Canyon Rd, T1W 1G3	2 rooms, 2 pb	Afternoon tea
403-678-6636 Fax: 403-678-6636	Visa, MC, *Rated*	Sitting room, library,
800-289-9731	C-ltd/S-no/P-no/H-no	fireplace, cable TV,
Fred & Andrea Gailus	German	conference facilities, patios
All year		

Hospitality is our "gift." Charming home with quiet elegance. Backs onto creek and hiking trails. Guide books and help with activity planning. Resident cat. Full breakfasts. Fresh squeezed orange juice.   E-mail: gailusaf@telusplanet.net
Web site: canadianrockies.net/cougarcanyon

Enjoy Living B&B	49-70-B&B	Full breakfast
149 Cougar Point Rd, T1W 1A1	2 rooms, 2 pb	Snacks
403-678-3026 Fax: 403-678-3042	*Rated*	Sitting room, library,
800-922-8274	C-yes/S-no/P-no/H-no	Jacuzzis, cable TV,
Garry & Nancy Thoen		accommodate business
All year		travelers

Modern B&B with mountain views in all directions, within walking distance to cafes, specialty shops, art galleries & fine dining. Home ocoked breakfast served in sunny eating area. Outdoor hot-tub.   E-mail: enjoy@telusplanet.net *Web site:* canadianrockies.net/enjoyliving

BRAGG CREEK ───────────────────────

Morningside Inn	65-95-B&B	Full breakfast
Box 974, T0L 0K0	3 rooms, 1 pb	Afternoon tea
403-949-3244 Fax: 403-949-3244	Visa, ●	Sitting room, library,
D. Vanderveer	C-yes/S-no/P-no/H-ltd	fireplace, conference
All year		facilities

Valley setting close to mountains. Within walking distance to restaurants, shopping and the hamlet centre. Close to golf, skiing, hiking, mountain climbing and caving. Come and join us.   E-mail: deadonv@aol.com *Web site:* bbalberta.com/bbpages.asp?inn=418

Big Springs B&B, Calgary, AB

BRAGG CREEK

Sierra Manor B&B
PO Box 238, T0L 0K0
403-949-2390
Pamela & James Johnston
Feb.-Nov.

75-85-B&B
4 rooms
Visa, MC, *Rated*
S-no/P-no/H-no

Full or Continental breakfast
Afternoon tea, snacks, wine
Sitting room, library,
fireplaces, garden deck, hot
tub

Country estate, horse farm, mountain view, gourmet breakfasts served on deck, luxury rooms with antique furnishings, gorgeous setting close to golf, hiking, restaurants.
E-mail: sierrabb@telusplanet.net *Web site:* bbcanada.com/1796.html

CALGARY

Big Springs B&B
RR 1, T4B 2A3
403-948-5264 Fax: 403-948-5851
Carol & Earle Whittaker
All year

100-125-B&B
4 rooms, 4 pb
Visa, MC, *Rated*, •
C-yes/S-no/P-no/H-no

Full gourmet breakfast
Afternoon tea, snacks
English Garden sitt. rm.,
bridal suite with thermo,
masseur tub

Luxury accommodation. Country secluded valley setting. 20 min. from Calgary, 1 hour from Rocky Mountains. Elegant rooms. English Garden sitting room. Evening "goodies." Romantic packages. Extra personalized touches. *E-mail:* bigsprings@bigsprings-bb.com
Web site: bigsprings-bb.com

Calgary Westways House
216 25th Ave SW, T2S 0L1
403-229-1758 Fax: 403-229-1758
Jonathan Lloyd
All year

50-100-B&B
6 rooms, 6 pb
Visa, MC, AmEx,
Rated, •
C-ltd/S-no/P-yes/H-no
French

Full breakfast
Sitting room, Jacuzzis,
fireplaces, cable TV, heated
kennels

1912 Central Heritage Home furnished with antiques & curios from all over the world. Located in historic "Mission District" with many restaurants & craft shops. Pets welcome
E-mail: calgary@westways.ab.ca *Web site:* westways.ab.ca

EDMONTON

Catchick's B&B
8836 187 St NW, T5T 1R9
780-481-2710 Fax: 780-486-3211
800-477-6065
Anthony & Lilani Catchick
All year

45-60-B&B
3 rooms, 2 pb
Visa, MC, *Rated*, •
C-yes/S-no/P-no/H-no

Full breakfast
Afternoon tea,
complimentary coffee
Sitting room, library, suites,
fireplaces, cable TV

Located in Edmonton's quiet West End. Enjoy this luxurious B&B whether in town for business or vacation. Grandiose shopping center that takes up to 24 city blocks. The world's largest mall and entertainment complex. *E-mail:* catchickbb@compusmart.ab.ca
Web site: compusmart.ab.ca/catchickbb

HINTON

Black Cat Guest Ranch
PO Box 6267, T7V 1X6
780-865-3084 Fax: 780-865-1924
800-859-6840
Amber and Perry Hayward
All year

130-178-AP
16 rooms, 16 pb
Visa, MC, •
C-yes/S-no/P-no/H-no

Full breakfast
All meals included in rate
Sitting room, piano, adult
oriented, trails, patio,
outdoor hot tub

A year-round lodge facing the front range of the Rockies, featuring trail rides and hiking in summer, cross-country skiing in winter. E-mail: bcranch@telusplanet.net
Web site: telusplanet.net/public/bcranch

Overlander Mountain Lodge
Box 6118, T7V 1X5
780-866-2330 Fax: 780-866-2332
Garth & Kathy Griffiths
All year

54-118-B&B
Rated, •
C-ltd/S-ltd/P-no/H-no
French, German

Continental breakfast
Dinner, afternoon tea,
restaurant
Bar service, sitting rm.,
library, fireplaces,
conference facilities

Beautiful lodge and rustic cabins overlooking Jasper National Park. Exquisite fine dining, intimate lounge along with true western hospitality. E-mail: overland@telusplanet.net
Web site: overlander-mtn-lodge.com

WATERTON LAKES NATL PARK

Kilmorey Lodge
Box 100, T0K 2M0
403-859-2334 Fax: 403-859-2342
Leslie and Gerry Muza
All year

89-176-EP
23 rooms, 23 pb
Most CC, *Rated*, •
C-yes/S-ltd/P-no/H-yes
French, German,
Spanish

Lunch, dinner, tea, snacks
Restaurant, bar, sitting room,
library, suites, fireplace

This Log Style Country Inn with fine dining restaurant and lounge, true elgance on the lake shore, wtih an atmosphere of antique furnishings and cozy down comforters on every bed. E-mail: travel@watertoninfo.ab.ca *Web site:* watertoninfo.ab.ca/kilmorey.html

British Columbia

CAMPBELL RIVER

Petersons April Point Lodge
PO Box 1, V9W 4Z9
250-285-3177 Fax: 250-285-2411
888-334-3474
The Peterson Family
April 15–October 15

150-200-EP
36 rooms, 36 pb
Most CC, *Rated*, •
C-yes/S-yes/P-ltd/H-ltd
Fr., Rus., Ger., Jap.

Full breakfast
Restaurant, bar
Sitting room, piano,
entertainment (summer),
saltwater pool, fishing

Personal service is our pride. More than one staff member per guest. Saltwater pool, many languages spoken. From one to five bedroom deluxe guest houses.
E-mail: stay@aprilpoint.com *Web site:* petersonsataprilpoint.com

COURTENAY

Forbidden Plateau B&B
RR 4, S 473, C31, V9N 7J3
250-703-9622 Fax: 250-703-9624
888-288-2144
Mary & Bruce Jaffary
All year

45-55-B&B
3 rooms, 3 pb
Visa, MC, *Rated*, •
C-yes/S-ltd/P-yes/H-no

Full breakfast
Afternoon tea
Sitting room, library, cable
TV, garden hot tub, patios
and sundecks

A quiet country home only eight minutes from Courtenay at the base of forbidden Plateau Mountain. 2 rooms in our house plus a cottage, all with separate entrances and ensuites.
E-mail: jaffary@island.net *Web site:* island.net/~jaffaray

CUMBERLAND

Wellington House B&B
PO Box 689, V0R 1S0
250-336-8809 Fax: 250-336-2321
All year

50-74-B&B
4 rooms, 3 pb
Visa, *Rated*
C-ltd/S-ltd/P-no/H-no

Full breakfast
Complimentary coffee/tea
Aftn. tea, sitting room, cable
TV, suites, parking lot

Unique, modern home, suites overlooking multi-level park-like garden, nestled in the foothills of the Beaufort Mountains, original coal mining weigh scale on property.
E-mail: CMA_CHIN@island.net *Web site:* vquest.com/wellington/

GIBSONS

Bonniebrook Lodge B&B
RR 4, S-10, C-34, V0N 1V0
604-886-2887 Fax: 604-886-8853
877-290-9916
Karen & Philippe Lacoste
February-Dec.

60-100-B&B
7 rooms, 4 pb
Most CC, *Rated*, •
C-yes/S-no/P-no/H-ltd
French

Full Canada Select breakfast
Dinner, restaurant
Jacuzzis, suites, fireplaces,
cable TV, tennis courts

A romantic oceanside Inn. Anne Garber of the Vancouver Province sums up Bonniebrook, "Beyond a doubt the best accommodation and restaurant on the Sunshine Coast. Perfect for an intimate getaway." *E-mail:* info@bonniebrook.com *Web site:* bonniebrook.com

KELOWNA

Bluebird Beach House B&B
3980 Bluebird Rd, V1W 1X6
250-764-8992 Fax: 250-764-8992
B. Breit & B. Voigt-Breitkreuz
May-Oct.

70-110-B&B
5 rooms, 5 pb
Visa, *Rated*
C-ltd/S-no/P-no/H-no
German

Full breakfast
Beach cabana with full
kitchen & BBQ for guests,
hot tub, fishing guide

"Simply the best mini-resort right on private sandy beach." Relax on a beach chair & enjoy the ambience. Sip a glass of local wine on the dock & sleep with soothing sounds of the waves.

KIMBERLEY

Wasa Lakeside B&B
Box 122, V0B 2K0
250-422-3688 Fax: 250-422-3551
888-422-3636
James & Mary Swansburg
April 1-October 30

90-B&B
3 rooms, 3 pb
Visa, MC, *Rated*, •
C-yes/S-no/P-no/H-ltd

Full breakfast
Sitting room, library, bikes,
tennis, Jacuzzis, suites, water
sports

Your lake oasis hidden in the Rocky Mountains, south of Banff and Lake Louise near Kimberley. Private, sandy beach, lush green lawns and tall shade trees.
E-mail: info@wasalakeresort.com *Web site:* wasalakeresort.com

LANGLEY

Heart and Home B&B
20886 Yeomans Crescent, V1M
2P8
604-888-4480 Fax: 604-888-5197
888-588-4222
Rachel/David Wiens All year

60-70-B&B
2 rooms, 2 pb
C-yes/S-no/P-no/H-ltd

Full breakfast
Evening dessert
Sitting room, fireplace, cable
TV, conference facility, hot
tub

Elegantly cozy new home in countryside of Vancouver just 45 minutes from city centre, ferries, airport. Minutes from golf, skiing, fishing, boating, shopping, antiques.
E-mail: hearthomebb@home.com *Web site:* hearthomebb.com

MAYNE ISLAND

Blue Vista Cottages
Box C19, Charter Rd, V0N 2J0
250-539-2463
877-535-2424
John & Val Walters
Mid Feb.-Mid Jan.

35-50-EP
11 rooms, 11 pb
Visa, MC, *Rated*, •
C-yes/S-ltd/P-ltd/H-no

Library, bicycles, suites,
fireplaces, accommodate
business travelers

Close to restaurants our cozy 1 & 2 bedroom cottages are in a park-like setting with decks, some fireplaces, barbeques, adult bicycles as well as freestyle bocce, croquet, and badminton.

MAYNE ISLAND ————————————————————————

Oceanwood Country Inn	78-213-B&B	Full breakfast
630 Dinner Bay Rd, V0N 2J0	12 rooms, 12 pb	Dinner (fee), aftn. tea
250-539-5074 Fax: 250-539-3002	Visa, MC, *Rated*, •	Bar service, library, sitting
Marilyn & Jonathan Chilvers	C-ltd/S-ltd/P-no/H-ltd	room, bikes, hot tubs, sauna,
March 1 - Nov 30	French	tennis

Waterfront island retreat; English country house atmosphere; award-winning cuisine; luxurious rooms with fireplace, whirlpool, private deck; ferry from Vancouver or Victoria.
E-mail: oceanwood@gulfislands.com *Web site:* oceanwood.com

POWELL RIVER ————————————————————————

Beacon B&B	60-90-B&B	Full breakfast
3750 Marine Ave, V8A 2H8	3 rooms, 3 pb	Packed lunch available
604-485-5563 Fax: 604-485-9450	MC, *Rated*, •	Comp. coffee/cold drinks,
877-485-5563	C-ltd/S-ltd/P-no/H-ltd	sitting room, library, hot tub,
Shirley & Roger Randall		TV, massage
All year		

Panoramic ocean view & spectacular sunsets. BC is a paradise for canoeing, kayaking, mt. treking. Fish, golf, hike. "Our specialty is relaxation." Rejuvenating bodywork available.
E-mail: beacon@aisl.bc.ca *Web site:* vancouver-bc.com/beaconbb/

QUALICUM BEACH ————————————————————————

Bahari B&B	60-125-B&B	Full breakfast
5101 Island Hwy W, V9K 1Z1	4 rooms, 4 pb	Complimentary wine, snacks
250-752-9278 Fax: 250-752-9038	Visa, MC, *Rated*, •	Sitting room, library, tennis
877-752-9278	C-ltd/S-no/P-no/H-no	court, hot tubs, families
Yvonne & Len Hooper		welcome in apt.
Feb. 1-Nov. 30		

Tranquilly elegant waterfront, panoramic views from decks & "Rotenburo" (outdoor hot tub), spacious rooms, fireplaces. Golfers', artists' & soft adventurers' paradise.
E-mail: ihooper@macn.bc.ca *Web site:* baharibandb.com

REVELSTOKE ————————————————————————

MacPherson Lodge B&B	45-60-B&B	Full breakfast
PO Box 2615, V0E 2S0	3 rooms, 1 pb	Wine
250-837-7041 Fax: 250-837-7077	Visa, MC, *Rated*, •	Sitting room, library, suites,
888-875-4924	C-yes/S-ltd/P-yes/H-no	fireplace, cable TV,
Lisa Longinotto All year	French	conference facilities

7 km from Revelstoke on Hwy 23 S, rustic log home furnished in antiques on 20 acres natural wilderness, view rooms, balcony(s), king beds, loft sitting room, private baths, satellite TV, family oriented, pets on approval, full breakfast & taxes included.
E-mail: bookrev@junction.net *Web site:* bbcanada.com/1957.html

Mulvehill Creek Wilderness	85-195-B&B	Full breakfast
PO Box 1220, V0E 2S0	8 rooms, 8 pb	Dinner, tea, snacks, wine
250-837-8649 Fax: 250-837-8649	Visa, MC, *Rated*, •	Sitting room, library,
877-837-8649	C-yes/S-ltd/P-ltd/H-no	bicycles, Jacuzzi, swimming
Cornelia Hueppi All year	German, Italian, Spanish	pool, fireplace, cable TV

Quiet country setting, wooded peninsula, waterfall, first class queen/twin/king rooms, family suite, honeymoon suite, all with ensuite bath; all summer and winter sports on property or nearby. E-mail: mulvehil@junction.net *Web site:* mulvehillcreek.com

SALT SPRING ISLAND ————————————————————————

Anne's Oceanfront	125-152-B&B	Full breakfast
Hideaway	4 rooms, 4 pb	Snacks
168 Simson Rd, V8K 1E2	Visa, MC, *Rated*, •	Sitting room, library, bikes,
250-537-0851 Fax: 250-537-0861	S-no/P-no/H-yes	hot tubs, adult oriented,
888-474-2663		sunsets
Rick & Ruth-Anne Broad		
All year		

Come share the beauty & tranquility. . .luxurious 1995 home, 7000 square feet, verandahs, hydromassage tubs, showers, private entrance, some balconies, panoramic ocean views.
E-mail: annes@saltspring.com

SALT SPRING ISLAND

Old Farm House B&B, The	119-B&B	Full breakfast
1077 North End Rd., V8K 1L9	5 rooms	Tea, wine
250-537-4113 Fax: 250-537-4969	Visa, MC, *Rated*, ●	Sitting room, library,
Karl & Gerti Fuss	C-ltd/S-no/P-no/H-ltd	conference, Ferry and Plane
Feb. 1- Sept. 30	German	pickup

Exclusive European Country retreat, newly restored 105 year old Farmhouse in park-like setting. Walking distance to tennis court and golf course. E-mail: farmhouse@saltspring.com *Web site:* bbcanada.com/oldfarmhouse

Perfect Perch B&B, A	92-120-B&B	Full breakfast
225 Armand Way, V8K 2B6	3 rooms, 3 pb	½ bottle Sherry
250-653-2030 Fax: 250-653-2045	Visa, MC, *Rated*, ●	Sitting room, library, Jacuzzi,
888-663-2030	S-no/P-no/H-no	2 headed shower, soaker tub
Libby Jutras	French	on sun deck
All year		

Gulf Island, 1000 ft. above sea level, 5 wooded acres, spectacular views, exquisite cuisine, immaculate comfort, private entrances & balconies E-mail: ljutras@saltspring.com *Web site:* saltspring.com/perfectperch

SATURNA ISLAND

Saturna Lodge & Restaurant	90-112-B&B	Full breakfast
130 Payne Rd, V0N 2Y0	7 rooms, 5 pb	Restaurant, bar service
250-539-2254 Fax: 250-539-3091	Visa, MC, *Rated*, ●	lunch & dinner (fee), Sitting
888-539-8800	C-yes/S-no/P-yes/H-no	room, bicycles, hot tubs,
Rebecca & Steve Corine		large sun deck
All year		

Luxurious Pacific Northwest island country inn overlooking beautiful ocean cove. Romantic and relaxing with fully licensed, gourmet restaurant. E-mail: rpage@pro.net *Web site:* saturna-island.bc.ca

SECHELT

Davis Brook Retreat	65-80 B&B	Continental breakfast plus
RR 3 Sandy Hook Sit C-17, V0N	2 rooms, 2 pb	Snacks
3A0	Visa, MC, *Rated*	Jacuzzis, swimming pool,
604-885-9866	C-ltd/S-ltd/P-no/H-no	suites, fireplaces, cable TV,
John and April Mackenzie-Moore	Spanish	steam sauna
All year		

Beautiful country rain forest acreage with ponds and gardens. Breakfast served to your suite with homemade breads, muffins and jams. A peaceful, refreshing retreat any time of the year. Web site: pixsell.bc.ca/bb/228.html

SHAWNIGAN LAKE

Marifield Manor	75-150-B&B	Full breakfast
2039 Merifield Lane, V0R 2W0	6 rooms, 5 pb	Afternoon tea
250-743-9930 Fax: 250-743-1667	●	Sitting room, library, bikes,
Cathy Basskin	C-ltd/S-no/P-no/H-no	suites, fireplaces, sauna
All year	Some French	

From a gentler time, this grand Edwardian mansion overlooks the lake and oversees the valley. Marifield continues to warmly welcome guests from throughout the Empire and the world. E-mail: mariman@pccinternet.com *Web site:* vancouverisland-bc.com/marifieldmanor

SOOKE

Eliza Point B&B by the Sea	73-83-B&B	Full breakfast
6514 Thornett Rd, V0S 1N0	2 rooms, 2 pb	Snacks, bar fridge
250-642-2705 Fax: 250-642-2704	●	Coffee, hot chocolate,
Cheryl and Doug Read	C-ltd/S-no/P-no/H-no	fireplaces, cable TV, Tennis
All year		court, Jacuzzi

Situated in Canada's South Pacific. Casually elegant home, west facing waterfront on scenic Sooke Harbour. Free transport to East Sooke trails. E-mail: eliza@tnet.net *Web site:* vvv.com/~eliza

SOOKE

Ocean Wilderness Inn & Spa
109 West Coast Rd, V0S 1N0
250-646-2116 Fax: 250-646-2317
800-323-2116
Marion Rolston
All year

60-140-B&B
9 rooms, 9 pb
Visa, MC, *Rated*, •
C-yes/S-no/P-yes/H-yes

Full breakfast
Will make dinner
reservations
Snacks, refrigerator, sitting
room, hot tubs

5 wooded acres with beach; whales, seals; hot tubs in romantic rooms with canopied beds.
Honeymoon? Birthday? Plant a Douglas Fir "Memory Tree" E-mail: ocean@sookenet.com
Web site: sookenet.com/ocean/

Seascape Inn B&B
6435 Sooke Rd, V0S 1N0
250-642-7677 Fax: 250-642-7677
888-516-8811
Sandy Bohn
All year

65-135-B&B
3 rooms, 3 pb
Most CC, •
C-ltd/S-ltd/P-ltd/H-no
German

Full breakfast
Suites, fireplaces, cable TV,
hot tubs, large stone
fireplace

Waterfront property overlooking Sooke Harbour. Unique "cabin," cottage and in house
suite. Exceptional views. "Eggs Beni" our specialty. E-mail: seascape@islandnet.com
Web site: sookenet.com/seascape

Snuggery by the Sea, The
5921 Sooke Rd, V0S 1N0
250-642-6423 Fax: 250-642-3771
David & Carol Mallett
All year

75-85-B&B
2 rooms, 2 pb
Visa, MC, *Rated*, •
C-ltd/S-no/P-ltd/H-no
French, German

Full breakfast
Snacks
Sitting room, library, cable
TV, VCR, large stone
fireplace

Elegant, architecturally designed B&B home located on the Sooke Basin; new but old world
charm. Gourmet breakfasts, peaceful & private garden walks amongst cedars & rhododen-
drons E-mail: dmallett@castnet.com *Web site:* coastnet.com/~dmallett

---

Sooke Harbour House
1528 Whiffen Spit Rd, V0S 1N0
250-642-3421 Fax: 250-642-6988
800-889-9688
Sinclair & Frederique Philip
All year

175-465-B&B
28 rooms, 26 pb
Most CC, *Rated*, •
C-yes/S-no/P-ltd/H-yes
French and English

Full or cont. breakfast
Set lunch incl., dinner
Wet bar, entertainment,
sitting room, piano, Jacuzzi,
bikes, hot tubs

Romantic, relaxing, magical, memorable. Gourmet restaurant serves local sea & land
bounty. Golf nearby. Romance packages & midweek, off-season rates.
E-mail: shh@islandnet.com *Web site:* sookeharbourhouse.com

TOFINO

Cable Cove Inn
PO Box 339, V0R 2Z0
250-725-4236 Fax: 250-725-2857
800-663-6449
P. and J. Van Bourgowdien
All year

88-150-B&B
6 rooms, 6 pb
Visa, MC, AmEx, *Rated*
S-no/P-no/H-ltd

Continental plus breakfast
Sitting room, hot tubs, adult
oriented, bicycles, airport
trans

Cable Cove Inn offers you 6 beautifully decorated romantic rooms with fireplaces, private
waterfront decks and marble Jacuzzi tubs. E-mail: cablecin@island.net
Web site: victoriabc.com/accom/cablecov.htm

Silver Cloud B&B
Box 188, V0R 2Z0
250-725-3998 Fax: 250-725-3908
888-611-1988
Olivia A. Mae
All year

60-140-B&B
3 rooms, 3 pb
Visa, MC, *Rated*
C-ltd/S-no/P-no/H-no
Danish

Full breakfast
Sitting room, library, cable
TV, waterside deck & gazebo

Secluded walk-on waterfront; magnificent gardens midst old growth forest. Romantic
guestwings all with private ensuite baths, one with private hot tub. Elegant breakfasts
overlooking the sea. BC Toursim inspected and approved. E-mail: silvercloud@mail.tofino-
bc.com *Web site:* tofino.cc/silvercloud

TOFINO

Tide's Inn B&B, The
PO Box 325, V0R 2Z0
250-725-3765 Fax: 250-725-3325
Valerie & James Sloman
Closed Christmas

68-75-B&B
3 rooms, 3 pb
Rated
C-ltd/S-no/P-no/H-no

Full breakfast
Coffee bar with teas, hot
chocolate
Sitting room, hot tub, mini
refrigerators, bicycles,
airport trans

Waterfront with lovely sea, mountain and forest views. Seaside decks, hot tub, full delicious breakfasts, private entrances and baths. Jacuzzi in one room.
E-mail: tidesinn@island.net   *Web site:* island.net/~tidesinn

---

West Wind
PO Box 436, V0R 2Z0
250-725-2224 Fax: 250-725-2212
Dale or James
All year

65-175-EP
3 rooms
Visa, MC, AmEx, *Rated*
C-ltd/S-ltd/P-no/H-no

Coffee and teas
Library, Jacuzzis, suites,
fireplace, cable TV,
bathrobes, hairdryers

Casually elegant accommodations on two acres just 5 minute walk to beach. Designed with privacy in mind, rooms feature high quality mattresses and linens, some with kitchen.
E-mail: westwind@island.net   *Web site:* island.net/~westwind

---

**Wilp Gybuu (Wolf House)
B&B**
Box 396, V0R 2Z0
250-725-2330 Fax: 250-725-1205
Wendy & Ralph Burgess
All year

70-75-B&B
3 rooms, 3 pb
Visa, MC, *Rated*
C-ltd/S-no/P-no/H-no

Full breakfast
Complimentary beverages &
cookies
Sitting room, library, cable
television, piano, fireplaces,
fridge

First Nations artist's contemporary cedar home. Watch passing boats while enjoying breakfast in dining rm. Walk to restaurants, tour offices, beach.   E-mail: wilpgybu@island.net
Web site: island.net/~wilpgybu

UCLUELET

Amphitrite Inn, The
920 Amphitrite Place, V0R 3A0
250-726-4224 Fax: 250-726-4234
Elke Loof-Koehler
All year

110-B&B
3 rooms, 3 pb
Visa, MC, •
C-ltd/S-ltd/P-ltd/H-no
German

Continental breakfast
Fireplaces

Sheltered bay on Pacific Ocean, ocean views, private, close to lighthouse on Amphitrite Point. Hiking trails at doorstep, short drive to Long Beach, stormwatching, whalewatching.   E-mail: memorylane@pacificcoast.net   *Web site:* ucluelet.com/amphitriteinn

---

Snug Harbour Inn, A
PO Box 367, V0R 3A0
250-726-2686 Fax: 250-726-2685
888-936-5222
Denise and Skip Rowland
All year

135-195-B&B
4 rooms, 4 pb
Visa, MC, *Rated*, •
C-ltd/S-no/P-no/H-no
Thai

Full breakfast
Snacks
Sitting room, hot tubs, frplcs.,
private beach &, decks,
incredible views

One of Canada's finest Inns. Exceptional privacy, romance, & incredible cliffside ocean front setting. Honeymoon packages and winter storm watching. "God took his time here"-David Connor. Featured on TVs "Best Places to Kiss."   E-mail: asnughbr@island.net
Web site: asnugharbourinn.com

VANCOUVER

"A" Place at Penny's
2564 Charles St, V5L 3A3
604-254-2229 Fax: 604-255-3708
All year

60-95-B&B
4 rooms, 4 pb
Visa,
C-yes/S-no/P-ltd/H-yes

Continental breakfast
Full kitchens
Sitting room, suites,
accommodates business
travelers, free parking

Penny's offers antique decorated suites with full kitchens in a 700 sq. ft. area.
E-mail: stay@pennysplacevancouver.com   *Web site:* pennysplacevancouver.com

VANCOUVER

"O Canada" House B&B	89-148-B&B	Full breakfast
1114 Barclay St, V6E 1H1	6 rooms, 6 pb	Afternoon tea, snacks
604-688-0555 Fax: 604-488-0556	Visa, MC, *Rated*, •	Complimentary wine, sitting
Jim Britten	C-ltd/S-ltd/P-no/H-no	room, library
All year		

Historic beautifully restored Victorian house in quiet downtown location just steps to everything. Gourmet breakfast, complimentary pantry, parking, concierge service
Web site: vancouver-bc.com/ocanadahouse/

Albion Guest House	75-120-B&B	Full gourmet breakfast
592 West 19th Ave, V5Z 1W6	3 rooms, 1 pb	Snacks, comp. wine, tea
604-873-2287 Fax: 604-879-5682	Visa, MC, AmEx,	Sitt. rm., Jacuzzis, picnic
Lise & Richard	*Rated*, •	lunch serv., diets by request,
All year	C-ltd/S-no/P-no/H-no	bikes.
	French	

Turn-of-the-century home, antiques & contemporary furnishings on a quiet residential street in one of Vancouver's finest neighborhoods. Beautiful gardens; comp. aperitif. Cable TV. Gay friendly guest house. Ample free parking.   E-mail: albion@direct.ca

Barclay House	89-150-B&B	Full breakfast
1351 Barclay, V6E 1H6	5 rooms, 5 pb	Snacks, evening sherry
604-605-1351 Fax: 604-605-1382	Visa, MC, •	Sitting room, suites, cable TV
Patrik Burr & Bruce Warner	C-ltd/S-no/H-no	
All year		

Notably, one of the most elegantly crafted late Victorian heritage homes in Vancouver's extraordinary residential district— The West End. Minutes on foot to Stanley Park, beaches, Robson Street shopping and Cruise Ship Terminals.   Web site: barclayhouse.com

Capilano B&B	55-105-B&B	Full breakfast
1374 Plateau Dr, V7P 2J6	5 rooms, 3 pb	Afternoon tea
604-990-8889 Fax: 604-990-5177	Visa, MC, *Rated*, •	Sitting room, suites, fireplace,
877-990-8889	C-yes/S-no/P-no/H-no	cable TV
Soledad Lu	Chinese, Dutch	
All year		

Warm hospitality awaits in this new executive style modern house ranging from a double room to one or two bedrooms with full kitchen, private entrance. 8 minutes from Stanley Park, downtown Vancouver.   E-mail: capilano@direct.ca *Web site:* vancouver-bc.com/CapilanoBB

Chelsea Cottage B&B	130-B&B	Full breakfast
2143 West 46 Ave, V6M 2L2	4 rooms, 2 pb	Coffee/tea, beverages
604-266-2681 Fax: 604-266-7540	Visa, MC, *Rated*, •	Sitting room, library, cable
Kim & Bob Jess	C-ltd/S-no/P-no/H-no	TV, robes, hairdryers
All year		

1925 home in prestigious neighborhood only 10 minutes from downtown, airport, major attractions. Relax in guest lounge after your busy day & in morning enjoy the full gourmet breakfast E-mail: chelsea@bc.sympatico.ca *Web site:* vancouver-inn.com

Chickadee Tree B&B	85-105-B&B	Full breakfast
1395 3rd St, V7S 1H8	3 rooms, 3 pb	In-suite coffee makers
604-925-1989 Fax: 604-925-1989	C-ltd/S-ltd/P-no/H-ltd	Hot tubs, sauna, swimming
Herb & Lois Walker		pool, Jacuzzi, fireplace,
All year		kitchen

Secluded, woodsy, award winning! Two suites/cozy cottage, private entrances/baths/balconies/gazebo. Close to Stanley Park/downtown/beaches/ferries/restaurants/shops.
E-mail: lowalker@direct.ca *Web site:* loiswalker.com/bandb/index.html

VANCOUVER

Collingwood Manor B&B
1631 Collingwood St, V6R 3K1
604-731-1107 Fax: 604-731-9443
888-699-1631
Stefanie & Howie Todd
All year

60-120-B&B
3 rooms, 1 pb
Visa, MC, •
S-no/P-no/H-no

Full breakfast
Afternoon tea,
complimentary wine
Sitting room, fireplaces,
robes, hairdryers

Beautifully restored 1912 heritage home. 1 block from ocean and 3 blocks to Jericho Park. Stunning ocean, mountain, & city views. Hardwood floors, vaulted ceiling and fireplace add to serene scenery. E-mail: info@collingwoodmanor.com Web site: collingwoodmanor.com

Columbia Cottage
205 W 14th Ave, V5Y 1X2
604-874-5327 Fax: 604-879-4547
Paul & Lynne Jacobs
All year

50-150-B&B
Visa, MC, *Rated*
C-ltd/S-no/P-no/H-no

Full gourmet breakfast
Afternoon tea, sherry
Chocolates, cookies, sitting
room, robes & slippers

A 1929 Art Deco cottage fully renovated in 1999. Queen-size rooms with private bathrooms and one suite. Lush gardens. E-mail: info@columbiacottage.com Web site: columbiacottage.com

Cornish House B&B
3190 St. George's Ave, V7N 1V2
604-802-5410 Fax: 604-988-1447
888-730-5410
Bev & Joe Arduini
All year

55-70-B&B
3 rooms
Visa, MC, •
C-ltd/S-ltd/P-no/H-no

Continental plus breakfast
Afternoon tea, wine
Sitting room, library,
fireplace, bathrobes & beach
towels

Tastefully restored 1911 heritage home, in quiet residential neighborhood, views of Vancouver. Near tourist attractions, public transportation. E-mail: info@cornishhouse.com Web site: cornishhouse.com

Crescent Green B&B
3467 141st St, V4P 1L7
604-538-2935 Fax: 604-538-2987
888-972-9333
Louisa & Keith Surges
All year

60-85-B&B
4 rooms, 4 pb
Visa, MC, AmEx,
Rated, •
C-yes/S-no/P-ltd/H-ltd
French, Cantonese

Full breakfast
Complimentary wine
Sitting room, library,
bicycles, Jacuzzis, swimming
pool, fireplaces, cable

Single level country home on quiet forested acreage with award-winning garden; near greater Vancouver attractions. Spacious, private entrance and patio, ensuite rooms. Spa, sauna, library, lounge. E-mail: surges@direct.ca Web site: pixsell.bc.ca/bcbbd/2/2000044.htm

Gazebo In the Garden B&B, A
310 St James Rd East, V7N 1L2
604-983-3331 Fax: 604-980-3215
Monika & Jack Rogers
All year

50-115-B&B
4 rooms, 2 pb
Visa, MC, *Rated*, •
C-ltd/S-no/P-no/H-no
Swedish

Continental plus breakfast
Afternoon tea
Sitting room, suites, cable TV,
gazebo, garden

1910 Frank Lloyd Wright Prairie style heritage home. Antique furnishings and old wicker. Resident Master Gardener. 15 minutes to Seabus, downtown Vancouver and Horseshoe Bay Ferries. E-mail: mrogers@direct.ca Web site: vancouver-bc.com/gazebo

Graeme's House
2735 Waterloo St, V6R 3J1
604-732-1488
Ms. Graeme Webster
All year

50-80
4 rooms, 2 pb
C-ltd/S-no/P-no/H-no

Continental plus breakfast
Afternoon tea, snacks
Sitting room, sundeck, roof
garden, near English Bay

Charmingly decorated, renovated 1920's cottage on a quiet street very close to shops, restaurants, and buses. Lovely garden. Beach 1 km. away. E-mail: graeweb@bc.sympatico.ca Web site: GraemeWebster.com

VANCOUVER

Henley House B&B
1025 8th Ave, V3M 2R5
604-526-3919 Fax: 604-526-3913
Anne O'Shaughnessy/Ross Hood
All year

45-55-B&B
3 rooms, 1 pb
Visa, MC, •
C-ltd/S-ltd/P-no/H-no

Full breakfast
Guest lounge, library,
Jacuzzi, robes, fireplace,
cable TV, air-conditioning

Handsome character home furnished with antiques & warm hospitality. Scrumptious gourmet breakfast served. Beautiful garden setting. E-mail: henley@istar.ca
Web site: home.istar.ca/~henley

Johnson Heritage House B&B
2278 W 34th Ave, V6M 1G6
604-266-4175 Fax: 604-266-4175
Sandy & Ron Johnson
April-October 31

80-120-B&B
3 rooms, 3 pb
Rated, •
C-ltd/S-no/P-no/H-no
Some French

Full hearty breakfast
Fireplaces, robes, TVs, guest
parlor, room phones &
laptop jacks

A classic 1920 Craftman home, romantic view rooms, fireplaces, full of antiques, carousel horses, gardens, quiet tree-lined avenue, safe, central, lovely area. E-mail: fun@johnsons-inn-vancouver.com *Web site:* johnsons-inn-vancouver.com

Kenya Court Ocean Front
2230 Cornwall Ave, V6K 1B5
604-738-7085
Dr. & Mrs. H. Williams
All year

85-105-B&B
5 rooms, 5 pb
C-ltd/S-no/P-no/H-no
Italian, French, German

Full breakfast
Complimentary tea/coffee
Sitting room, library, tennis
courts, solarium, salt water
swimming pool

Ocean-front heritage guesthouse overlooking Kitsilano Beach, mountains, English Bay. Gourmet breakfast served in solarium with panoramic view. Minutes to downtown Vancouver, Granville Island. Private ocean suites. E-mail: h&dwilliams@bc.sympatico.ca

Lighthouse Retreat B&B
4875 Water Lane, V7W 1K4
604-926-5959 Fax: 604-926-5755
Hanna & Ron Pankow
All year

70-95-B&B
2 rooms, 2 pb
Rated, •
S-no/P-no/H-no
German

Full vegy breakfast
Afternoon tea, sherry
In-suite coffee makers,
private sitting rooms with
cable TV, phone

2 private romantic suites each with its own living room, bedroom, bathroom & entrance. Close to ocean, mountains, ferries & downtown Vancouver. Nature trails at our doorstep. Guest refrigerator. Romantic courtyards. 2 night minimum stay May-September.
E-mail: innkeeper@lighthouseretreat.com *Web site:* lighthouseretreat.com

Manor Guest House, The
345 W 13th Ave, V5Y 1W2
604-876-8494 Fax: 604-876-5763
Brenda Yablon
All year

55-120-B&B
12 rooms, 8 pb
Visa, *Rated*, •
C-ltd/S-ltd/P-no/H-no
French, German

Full gourmet vegetarian
breakfast
Galley kitchen use
Conference facilities for up to
25, parlor/music room,
English garden, decks

An Edwardian heritage manor. Convenient to everything. Spacious rooms, fine breakfasts & helpful hosts make your stay memorable. Top-floor suite sleeps six.
E-mail: manorguesthouse@bc.sympatico.ca *Web site:* manorguesthouse.com/

Maple House B&B
1533 Maple Street, V6J 3S2
604-739-5833 Fax: 604-739-5877
Fumi and Brian Pendleton
All year

54-90-B&B
3 rooms, 2 pb
•
C-ltd/S-no/P-no/H-no
Japanese

Full breakfast
English garden, decks

Restored 1900 Heritage Home. Best Location. One block to Kitsilano beach. Walking distance to downtown. Restaurants, cafes, and shops nearby. E-mail: info@maplehouse.com
Web site: maplehouse.com

Nelson House, Vancouver, BC

VANCOUVER

Massary B&B
3625 St. Andrews Ave, V7N
2A4
604-729-5724
Fax: 604-986-3254
604-986-3254
Gerardo
All year

70-B&B
2 rooms, 2 pb
•
S-no/P-no/H-no
Spanish & French

Full breakfast
Private eating area
Microwave, bar, fridge, coffee
maker, tea maker, sauna

Best location in the Historic District of North Vancouver. In one of the best residential areas and quiet settings. Close to the most interesting tourism areas.   E-mail: B8B8Com@aol.com

Murrayville B&B
22054 Old Yale Rd, V2Z 1B3
604-534-5014
888-534-8225
John & Susan Howard
All year

50-75-B&B
4 rooms, 1 pb
•
C-ltd/S-no/P-ltd/H-no

Full gourmet breakfast
Snacks, afternoon tea
Cable TV, free coffee on
arrival, hot tub, sauna, tennis

Elegant new home furnished with antiques & original artwork. Gourmet, five course breakfast. Bridge nights on short notice. Advise on local fishing-antique sources. Convenient for Vancouver PGA.   E-mail: mvillebb@wave.home.com

Nelson House
977 Broughton St, V6G 2A4
604-684-9793
David Ritchie
Except 12/24–25,31 & 1/1

B&B
6 rooms, 4 pb
Visa, MC,
C-ltd/S-ltd/P-no/H-no
French

Full breakfast
Sitting room, library,
Jacuzzis, suites, fireplaces,
cable TV

We are an adult-oriented B&B with six guestrooms, one shared and four private baths. E-mail: bestinvan@lightspeed.bc.ca *Web site:* bbcanada.com/nelsonhousebnb

Norgate Parkhouse B&B
1226 Silverwood Cres, V7P 1J3
604-986-5069
Fax: 604-986-8810
Vicki Tyndall
All year

60-95-B&B
3 rooms
Visa, MC, *Rated*, •
C-ltd/S-no/P-no/H-no

Full breakfast
Sitting room, TV, fireplace, in-
room phones

Relax in this quiet ranch-style home. Guests enjoy lush garden, sitting room with TV, travel treasures, and stimulating conversation.   E-mail: relax@oldenglishbandb.bc.ca
Web site: bandbinn.com/homes/9/

542 British Columbia

Penny Farthing Inn
2855 W 6th Ave, V6K 1X2
604-739-9002 Fax: 604-739-9004
Lyn Hainstock
All year

68-121-B&B
4 rooms, 4 pb
•
C-ltd/S-ltd/P-no/H-no
Some French

Full breakfast
Complimentary sherry,
snacks
Videos, CDs, Books,
Fireplaces, Cable TV, Sitting
room, business travelers

The Inn is a 1912 heritage house with wood floors, stained glass windows and wood panelling. Situated 5-10 minutes from downtown in a safe, vibrant Kitsilano district of Vancouver. We are close to the beach, cafes, restaurants, shops and university.
E-mail: farthing@uniserve.com *Web site:* pennyfarthinginn.com

Shaughnessy Village B&B
1125 West 12th Ave, V6H 3Z3
604-736-5511 Fax: 604-737-1321
604-736-5512
Jan Floody
All year

49-109-B&B/MAP/AP
15 rooms, 15 pb
Visa, MC, •
C-ltd/S-yes/P-no/H-yes
Fr., Ger., Jap., Chinese

Full breakfast
Lunch/dinner available, bar
service
Gym, billiards, library, crazy
putt golf, sauna, swimming,
tennis nearby

Our resort-style residence accommodates "B&B" visitors in a friendly & beautiful nautical atmosphere in theme rooms, "like cruise ship cabins" *E-mail:* info@shaughnessyvillage.com
Web site: shaughnessyvillage.com

Southlands House
1160 Boundary Bay Rd, V4L
2P6
604-943-1846 Fax: 604-943-2481
Lyla-Jo & Bruce Troniak
All year

90-180-B&B
6 rooms, 6 pb
Visa, MC, AmEx,
Rated, •
C-ltd/S-no/P-ltd/H-ltd

Full breakfast
Sherry at 5:30 pm
Sitt. rm., lib., frplcs., bikes,
Jacuzzis, suites, cable TV,
conf. fac.

A romantic retreat on the shores of Boundary Bay. Guest rooms feature feather beds, PB, fireplaces, TV. *E-mail:* btron@bc.sympatico.ca *Web site:* vancouver-bc.com/SouthlandsHouseBB/

Sue's Victorian GuestHouse
152 E 3rd, V7L 1E6
604-985-1523 Fax: 604-985-1523
800-776-1811
Jen Lowe & Sue Chalmers
All year

50-75-EP
5 rooms, 3 pb
•
S-no/P-no/H-no

Guests have a refrigerator
Color TV/video in rooms,
ceiling fan, local phone,
kitchen/laundry access

Restored 1904 home, four blocks from harbour, centrally located for transportation, shopping, restaurants and tourist attractions. Fully equipped kitchen available 4 pm-10 am

Sunflower B&B
1110 Hamilton St, V3M 2M9
604-522-4186 Fax: 604-522-4176
Rosina & Francis David
All year

51-B&B
4 rooms
Visa, MC, *Rated*, •
C-yes/S-no/P-no/H-no
French, Italian

Afternoon tea
Sitting room, fireplace,
library, cable TV, fax,
newspaper, magazines

You will appreciate the comfort and tranquility of a heritage house, located just minutes away from downtown Vancouver. *E-mail:* yourhosts@sunflower-bnb.com *Web site:* sunflower-bnb.com

Tall Cedars B&B
720 Robinson St, V3J 4G1
604-936-6016 Fax: 604-936-6016
Dwyla & Ed Beglaw
All year

50-60-B&B
3 rooms
Rated, •
C-ltd/S-ltd/P-no/H-no

Continental plus breakfast
Restaurants nearby, sitting
room, garden, TV, videos

Comfortable "home away from home" inspected and approved by B.C. Ministry of Tourism. Comfy beds, flower garden, balcony. Stanley Park, lakes, mountains and parks. Great dining. *E-mail:* tallcedars_bnb@bc.sympatico.ca *Web site:* bbcanada.com/2490.html

VANCOUVER

Treehouse B&B, A
2490 49th Ave West, V6M 2V3
604-266-2962 Fax: 604-266-2960
Barb & Bob Selvage
All year

85-118-B&B
3 rooms, 3 pb
Visa, MC, AmEx,
Rated, •
C-ltd/S-ltd/P-no/H-no

Full gourmet breakfast
Snacks
Sitting room, adult oriented,
TV, videos, on street parking,
private decks.

Sophisticated metropolitan home featuring contemporary art, on bus line and near most major attractions, prestigious Kerrisdale residential neighborhood, gourmet breakfasts. Champagne for honeymoon, anniversary, birthday... celebrations.
E-mail: bb@treehousebb.com *Web site:* treehousebb.com/

Walnut House B&B
1350 Walnut St, V6J 3R3
604-739-6941 Fax: 604-739-6941
Liz Harris & Mike Graham
All year

80-95-B&B
3 rooms, 3 pb
Visa, MC, *Rated*, •
C-ltd/S-no/P-no/H-no

Full breakfast
Afternoon tea, snacks
Sitting room, library,
fireplaces, cable TV, videos

Romantic, friendly, peaceful & convenient, adjacent to downtown. Restored 1912 Edwardian home, 2 blocks from sandy beaches and next to Granville Island public market. Walk to downtown & Stanley Park. *E-mail:* info@walnuthousebb.com *Web site:* walnuthousebb.com

VANCOUVER, BURNABY

Patterson Guest House
7106 18th Ave, V3N 1H1
604-524-0110 Fax: 604-524-0110
Dave Myles & Luci Baja
All year

30-45-B&B
3 rooms
•
C-yes/S-ltd/P-yes/H-no
French & Spanish

Continental breakfast
Lunch, dinner, tea, snacks
Sitting room, bicycles,
fireplaces, cable TV,
aromatherapy from Luci Baja

Lovely Edwardian Heritage Home, average accommodations *E-mail:* myles@bc.sympatico.ca

VERNON

Melford Creek Country Inn
7810 Melford Rd, V1B 3N5
250-558-7910 Fax: 250-542-0886
Karin & Steve Shantz
All year

70-120-B&B
3 rooms, 3 pb
Visa, MC, *Rated*
C-ltd/S-no/P-ltd/H-no
German

Full breakfast
Jacuzzis, swimming pool,
fireplaces, sauna,
accommodate business
travelers

"French Country" hideaway, in the foothills on the way to Silver Star; gourmet breakfast served in cathedral dining room. Romantic rooms with balconies/fireplaces & unbelievable pool with roman hot tub. *E-mail:* melford@melfordinn.com *Web site:* melfordinn.com

VICTORIA

Abbeyrose B&B
3960 Cedar Hill Cross Rd, V8P
2N7
250-479-7155 Fax: 250-479-5422
800-307-7561
Joanne and Arnie Davis
All year

70-90-B&B
2 rooms, 2 pb
Visa, *Rated*, •
C-yes/S-no/P-no/H-no
French

Full breakfast
Afternoon refreshments
Sitting room, family friendly
facility, views of city, ocean

Country home setting. Central to all Victoria highlights, Butchart Gardens, golf, beaches, harbour, UVIC, island highways, & ferries. Cozy rooms, delicious breakfasts.
E-mail: abbeyrose@pacificcoast.net *Web site:* victoriabc.com/accom/abbeyrose.html

Abigail's Hotel
906 McClure St, V8V 3E7
250-388-5363 Fax: 250-388-7787
800-561-6565
Daniel & Frauke Behune
All year

79-219-B&B
22 rooms, 22 pb
Visa, MC, AmEx,
Rated, •
C-ltd/S-no/P-no/H-no

Full gourmet breakfast
Afternoon refreshments
Social hour, library, sitting
room, Jacuzzi in some rooms

Luxuriously updated 1930 classic Tudor building. Private Jacuzzi tubs, firepalces, goose-down comforters. *E-mail:* innkeeper@abigailshotel.com *Web site:* abigailshotel.com/

Abigail's Hotel, Victoria, BC

VICTORIA

At Hemingways "Finca" B&B
1028 Bewdley Ave, V9A 6S9
250-384-0862 Fax: 250-384-8113
877-384-0862
Ricky & Hona Pomplun
All year

68-125-B&B
6 rooms, 4 pb
Visa, MC, *Rated*, ●
C-yes/S-ltd/P-no/H-ltd
German

Full breakfast
Aftn. tea, snacks, wine
Sitting room, Jacuzzis, suites,
frplcs., cable, TV, conf. fac.,
garden

A lovely Tudor-style mansion located in a quiet residential area in old historic Esquimalt.
E-mail: hemingways@webtv.net *Web site:* accommodationsbc.com/hemingways.html

B&B at Swallow Hill Farm, A
4910 William Head Rd, V9C 3Y8
250-474-4042 Fax: 250-474-4042
Gini & Peter Walsh
All year

60-90-B&B
2 rooms, 2 pb
Visa, MC, AmEx,
Rated, ●
C-ltd/S-no/P-no/H-no

Full farm breakfast
Complimentary tea/coffee
Sitting room, bikes, hiking,
books & games, picnics,
working farm, sauna

Apple Farm with spectacular ocean & mountain sunrise view. 2 separate suites, priv. baths,
Q/T beds, Inspected & approved home. CP 5 days. Come help us celebrate the B&B's 10th
anniversary in 2000! E-mail: info@swallowhillfarm.com *Web site:* swallowhillfarm.com

B&B at Witty's Lagoon, A
3888F Duke Rd, V9C 4A5
250-474-7497 Fax: 250-474-7397
Barbara McDougall
All year

56-63-B&B
3 rooms, 2 pb
Visa, MC, *Rated*, ●
C-ltd/S-no/P-no/H-no
Basic Spanish

Full breakfast
Sitting room, library,
Jacuzzis, suites, fireplace,
outside deck & veranda

Grand country home located next to spectacular Witty's Lagoon Park & bird sanctuary with
its beach, rainforest walking trails. E-mail: bmcdougall@coastnet.com
Web site: discovervictoria.com/wittys

Beaconsfield Inn
998 Humboldt St, V8V 2Z8
250-384-4044 Fax: 250-384-4052
Con & Judi Sollid
All year

135-295-B&B
9 rooms, 9 pb
Visa, MC, *Rated*, ●
S-no/P-no/H-no

Full gourmet breakfast
Complimentary sherry,
afteroon tea
Sun room, library, 7 rooms
with Jacuzzis, 11 with
fireplaces

Award-winning restoration of an English mansion. 4 blocks to downtown & oceanfront.
Antiques—rich textures, warm woods. Ralph Lauren linens & florals. E-mail: beaconsfield@
islandnet.com *Web site:* islandnet.com/beaconsfield/

VICTORIA

Bethany's B&B	45-75-B&B	breakfast
614 Craigflower, V9A 2W2	3 rooms, 3 pb	Afternoon tea, snacks
250-381-5471	*Rated*	Accommodate business
Lisa Berndt	C-yes/P-no	travelers
All year	German	

Walking distance from downtown

Birds of a Feather Ocean	55-85-B&B	Full breakfast
206 Portsmouth Dr, V9C 1R9	5 rooms, 5 pb	Afternoon tea, snacks
250-391-8889 Fax: 250-391-8883	Visa, *Rated*, ●	Sitting room, library,
Annette & Dieter	C-yes/S-no/P-ltd/H-no	bicycles, hot tubs, courtesy
All year	German	canoes

First class hospitality on the shores of a Pacific Ocean migratory bird sanctuary. Whale-watching, beach-combing, fishing, hiking, golfing, bicycles, canoes.   E-mail: frontdesk@victorialodging.com *Web site:* victoria.to/

Boathouse B&B, The	110-B&B	Continental plus breakfast
746 Sea Dr, RR 1, V8M 1B1	1 rooms, 1 pb	9-ft. rowing dinghy
250-652-9370	Visa, MC,	
Jean & Harvey Merritt	C-ltd/S-no/P-no/H-no	
March 1-mid-October	German	

A unique ocean-front cottage offering seclusion, privacy and the luxury of quiet time for two non-smoking adults.   E-mail: boathouse@home.com *Web site:* members.home.net/boathouse

---

Cadboro Bay B&B	46-B&B	Full gourmet breakfast
3844 Hobbs St, V8N 4C4	3 rooms, 1 pb	Afternoon tea on arrival
250-477-6558 Fax: 250-477-4727	Visa, *Rated*, ●	Sitting room, tennis court,
877-741-2440	C-yes/S-no/P-no/H-no	family park nearby
Rene Barr		
All year except X-mas		

Quiet secluded location; full gourmet breakfast; vegetarian cuisine available; enjoy sitting in an English country garden; separate one room cottage; near University, beach, restaurants, village, pub; 15 minutes from downtown.   E-mail: rene_barr@bc.sympatico.ca
Web site: www3.bc.sympatico.ca/cadborobay

Eagle's Nest B&B	85-125-B&B	Full breakfast
4769 Cordova Bay Rd, V8Y 2J7	2 rooms, 2 pb	Sitting room, Jacuzzis, suites,
250-658-2002 Fax: 250-658-0135	Visa, MC, AmEx,	cable TV, accommodate
800-658-2002	*Rated*, ●	business travelers
Pat & Kathy McGuire	C-yes/S-no/P-no/H-no	
All year		

*Eagle's Nest is a Government Approved and Inspected "Canada Select" 4 star accommodation, offering luxury, modern accommodations at an affordable price.
E-mail:* eagle@islandnet.com *Web site:* victoriabc.com/accom/eagles.htm

---

Gatsby Mansion, The	83-253-B&B	Full breakfast from menu
309 Belleville St, V8V 1X2	19 rooms, 19 pb	Restaurant on property
250-388-9191 Fax: 250-920-5651	Visa, MC, AmEx,	Suites with harbour views,
800-563-9656	*Rated*, ●	martini lounge, ice cream
Michel Loiseleux	C-yes/S-no/P-no/H-no	parlour, aromatherapy
All year		

*Unique accommodations overlooking harbor in Heritage Mansion. 5-minute walk to City Center. Old-world charm, modern service. TVs and in-room movie. Currency exchange, martini lounge, restaurant on premises. Boutiques, Artisians Lane.
E-mail:* huntingdon@bctravel.com *Web site:* bctravel.com/gatsby.html

VICTORIA

Gus's In Town B&B
430 Government St, V8V 2L5
250-383-7938 Fax: 250-383-7938
Gus's In Town B&B
All year

58-B&B
3 rooms, 3 pb
S-no/P-no/H-ltd
German, Russian, Polish

Full breakfast
Cable TV

11-year-old house 3 blocks away from Bus Station Museum. Only 20 miles from Victoria airport. Transportation supplied by shuttle (fee).

Haterleigh Heritage Inn, A
243 Kingston St, V8V 1V5
250-384-9995 Fax: 250-384-1935
Paul & Elizabeth Kelly
All year

135-195-B&B
6 rooms, 6 pb
Visa, MC, *Rated*, •
S-no/P-no/H-no

Full breakfast
Private Jacuzzis, sitting
room, library, hot tubs

5 star rated by Tourism BC. 1901 heritage mansion lovingly restored. Full of stained glass and antiques. Only two blocks to centre. Gourmet breakfasts. E-mail: paulk@haterleigh.com
Web site: haterleigh.com

Henderson House, The
522 Quadra St, V8V 3S3
250-384-3428
Cliff Whitehead
Spring/summer/fall

60-100-B&B
4 rooms, 4 pb
Visa, MC, •
C-ltd/S-no/P-no/H-no

Full breakfast
Afternoon tea
Sitting room, bikes, Jacuzzis,
cable TV

Historic house, very beautiful, two blocks from the Victoria Inner Harbor. Well established as a traditional bed and breakfast guest house. E-mail: henderson@coastnet.com
Web site: coastnet.com/~henderson

Iris Garden Country Manor
5360 W. Saanich Rd, V9E 1J8
250-744-2253 Fax: 250-744-5690
877-744-2253
Sharon & Dave Layzell
All year

75-115-B&B
4 rooms, 4 pb
Visa, MC, •
C-no/S-no/P-no/H-no

Full breakfast
Sitting room, library, pool,
fireplaces, conference
facilities, jacuzzi

An unforgettable retreat with casual elegance among tranquil meadows and wooded hillsides. Theme rooms with bold colours and sumptuous linens. E-mail: irisgarden@
pacificcoast.net *Web site:* irisgardenvictoria.com

Mandeville, Tudor Cottage
1064 Landsend Rd, V8L 5L3
250-655-1587
Averil & Maurice Clegg
All year

75-B&B
2 rooms, 2 pb
•
C-yes/S-ltd/P-ltd/H-no
Some French

Full breakfast
Sitting room, suites,
fireplaces, cable TV,
accommodate business
travelers

Mandeville, at the northend of the Saanich Peninsula on Vancouver Island, is a picturesque Tudor Cottage set in one acre of forest, with lawns and gardens leading to the beach. Enjoy breath-taking views acrooss the Satellite Channel to Salt Spring Island
Web site: pixsell.bc.ca/bb/164.htm

Markham House B&B
1853 Connie Rd, V9C 4C2
250-642-7542 Fax: 250-642-7538
888-256-6888
Lyall & Sally Markham
All year

74-123-B&B
4 rooms, 4 pb
Most CC, *Rated*, •
C-ltd/S-no/P-no/H-no
French

Full breakfast
Afternoon tea, snacks
Comp. wine, sitting room,
library, bikes, hot tubs,
private cottage w/frplc.

10 acre country hideaway, Tudor style home, antiques- 30 minutes to Victoria, near beaches and hiking trails. Peace and tranquility. Garden suite with luxurious amenities
E-mail: mail@markhamhouse.com *Web site:* sookenet.com/markham

VICTORIA ─────────────────────

Oak Bay Guest House	45-115-B&B	Full breakfast
1052 Newport Ave, V8S 5E3	11 rooms, 11 pb	Complimentary tea & coffee
250-598-3812 Fax: 250-598-0369	Visa, MC, AmEx,	Sitting room, library, beach
800-575-3812	*Rated*, •	walks, bike riding
Karl & Jackie Morris	S-no/P-no/H-no	
All year	French	

Charming, peaceful historic home furnished with antiques, beautiful gardens, elegant neighborhood, scenic walks, beaches, golf, minutes drive to Inner Harbor.
E-mail: oakbay@beds-breakfasts.com *Web site:* beds-breakfasts.com

Ocean View B&B, An	60-80-B&B	Full buffet breakfast
715 Suffolk St, V9A 3J5	4 rooms, 4 pb	Garden patios, TV, hot tub,
250-386-7330 Fax: 250-389-0280	Visa, MC, *Rated*	king/queen beds, frplcs.,
800-342-9986	C-ltd/S-no/P-no/H-no	refrigerators
Yvette & Ralf	German, French	
All year		

Modern "holiday home" overlooks outer harbour, ocean & snow-capped Olympic Mountains. Walk to town on scenic ocean walkway. Privacy. Private ensuite bathrooms.   E-mail: 74561.3556@compuserve.com *Web site:* travelguides.com/home/oceanview/

Oceanside Inn	99-200-B&B	Full breakfast
Box 50, V0N 2M0	4 rooms, 4 pb	Afternoon tea, dinner
250-629-6691	Visa, •	available
Geoff Clydesdale	S-ltd/P-yes/H-no	Sitting room, library,
March-November		Jacuzzis, suites, firepalces,
		cable TV

Oceanside Inn, offering affordable tranquility, is nestled on 3 acres of secluded oceanfront on beautiful Pender Island, in the heart of the Canadian Gulf Islands. The perfect hide-a-way for a romantic interlude.   E-mail: oceanside@penderisland.com *Web site:* penderisland.com

Old Farm B&B	50-80-B&B	Full breakfast
2075 Cowichan Bay Rd, V0R	3 rooms, 3 pb	Sitting room, Jacuzzis, suites,
1N0	Visa, MC, *Rated*, •	cable TV, garden spa
250-748-6410 Fax: 250-748-6410	C-ltd/S-no/P-no/H-no	
888-240-1482	Little French	
Barbara & George MacFarlane		
All year		

Historic 3-story house on two acres overlooking tidal estuary. Gardens, fruit trees. Rural but convenient to urban conveniences. Gazebo, badminton, horseshoes on property. Gourmet breakfasts. Each room has a full bathroom.   E-mail: oldfarm@seaside.net
Web site: cvnet.net/cowb&b/oldfarm

Palace On Dallas B&B, A	45-80-B&B	Full breakfast
1482 Dallas Rd, V8S 1A2	5 rooms	Snacks
250-361-9551 Fax: 250-385-1725	Visa, AmEx, •	Sitting room, bicycles, cable
Jodi & Tim Baker	C-ltd/S-no/P-no/H-no	TV, accommodate business
May-September		travelers

Oceanfront 1908 character B&B where you're treated like royalty!   E-mail: palacebb@brookenet.com *Web site:* brookeline.com/palace

Scholefield House	100-150-B&B	5 course champagne
731 Vancouver St, V8V 3V4	3 rooms, 3 pb	breakfast
250-385-2025 Fax: 250-383-3036	Visa, MC, *Rated*, •	Complimentary sherry,
800-661-1623	S-no/P-no/H-no	tea/coffee
Tana Dineen		Private guest library, English
All year		flower garden, 3 blocks to
		The Empress

Do Victoria the Victorian way! Gracious hospitality, authentically restored 1892 historical house, short stroll to heart of downtown.   E-mail: mail@scholefieldhouse.com
Web site: scholefieldhouse.com

Top O' Triangle Mountain B&B, Victoria, BC

VICTORIA

Seabird House
1 Midwood Rd, V9B 1L4
250-479-2930 Fax: 250-744-2998
Ilima Szabo
March-Dec.

40-60-B&B
2 rooms
•
C-yes/S-no/P-yes/H-no
German

Full breakfast
Sitting room, cable TV, 3
blocks to The Empress

On the edge of scenic tidal Portage Inlet, a bird sanctuary. Beautiful garden with palm trees. Serenity, no traffic, & only 10 mins. from downtown. Families get privacy of whole upper level.   Web site: bbcanada.com.1854.html

Shady Shores Beach Resort
Box 18 Site 118 Bowser, V0R
1G0
250-757-8595
Fax: 250-757-9507
888-863-4455
Carolyn Graeme
All year

55-125-EP
7 rooms, 7 pb
Visa, MC, *Rated*, •
C-yes/S-ltd/P-no/H-ltd

Jacuzzis, suites, fireplaces,
cable TV, gazebo hot tub.

*Centrally located on secluded beachfront, enjoy beachcombing, bonfires, clam oyster picking & salmon fishing. View an abundance of marine life from one of our seven fully-equipped suites. A golfers mecca!   E-mail: pat@bctravel.com
Web site: bctravel.com/ci/shadyshores.html*

Shipsview Place B&B
255 Shipsview Place, V9C 1S3
250-474-5303
Fax: 250-474-5307
Janet & Bill Bassal
All year

56-85-B&B
3 rooms, 3 pb
Visa, MC, *Rated*, •
S-no/P-ltd/H-yes
French

Full breakfast
Afternoon tea
Sitting room, library,
bicycles, suites, fireplace,
cable TV

*Unique contemporary home close to ocean beaches and lagoon. Beautiful, spacious suites. Enjoy a gourmet breakfast served on the deck or in the dining room.
E-mail: Bassal@inetex.com Web site: shipsview.com*

Top O' Triangle Mtn. B&B
3442 Karger Terrace, V9C 3K5
250-478-7853
Fax: 250-478-2245
800-870-2255
Henry & Pat Hansen
All year

50-70-B&B
3 rooms, 3 pb
Visa, MC, *Rated*, •
C-yes/S-ltd/P-no/H-ltd
Danish

Full breakfast
Kettle, hot/cold drinks
Sitting room, great views,
near parks, golf, city

*Best known for our panoramic view of city, sea and mountains. Also great food and sincere hospitality. Clean, comfortable accommodations.   E-mail: pat@hospitalityvictoria.com
Web site: hospitalityvictoria.com*

VICTORIA ────────────────────────────────────

Tree Tops' Views B&B, A	60-75-B&B	Full gourmet breakfast
3444 Karger Terrace, V9C 3K5	2 rooms, 2 pb	Snacks
250-474-5505 Fax: 250-474-5957	Visa, MC, •	Accommodate business
888-82-VIEWS	C-ltd/S-ltd/P-no/H-no	travelers, spectacular views
DSpence	French	from suites, gardens
All year		

Romantic and intimate; beautifully decorated suites with panoramic views of Victoria, Pacific Ocean and snow-capped mountains. Relax in our lovely gardens surrounded by wonderful views. Unforgettable gourmet breakfast—an elegant escape!
E-mail: treetops@treetopsviews.com *Web site:* treetopsviews.com

Wayward Navigator B&B, The	65-B&B	Full breakfast
337 Damon Dr, V9B 5G5	2 rooms, 2 pb	Dinner, snacks, wine
250-478-6836 Fax: 250-478-6850	Visa, MC, •	Sitting room, library,
884-478-6808	C-ltd/S-ltd/P-ltd/H-no	Jacuzzis, fireplace, cable TV,
Nancy Fry		conferences
All year		

Classic passenger ship opulence with modern conveniences. Our first class state rooms and guest lounges are spacious and well appointed with elegant Victorian furnishings. Cedar decks, gazebos and hot tub. *E-mail:* nancy@wayward.com *Web site:* wayward.com

Wooded Acres B&B	75-B&B	Full country breakfast
4907 Rocky Point Rd, V9C 4G2	2 rooms, 2 pb	Complimentary champagne,
250-478-8172	•	tea
Elva & Skip Kennedy	S-no/P-no/H-no	Coffee, hot tubs, sitting room,
All year		library, beaches, trails,
		fishing

Acreage in the countryside of Victoria. Cozy log home is decorated with antiques. Perfect for honeymoon & special occasions. Relax in your own private hot tub. Adult oriented.
E-mail: cabin@lodgingvictoria.com *Web site:* LodgingVictoria.com/countryside

WEST VANCOUVER ──────────────────────────

Ambleside-by-the-Sea	60-B&B	Full breakfast
763 17th St, V7V 3T4	5 rooms	Sitting room, bicycles, cable
604-922-4873	*Rated*	TV, off-street parking
Kenneth Walters	C-ltd/S-no/P-no/H-no	
Feb.-Nov. inclusive	French	

A three-story traditional house in a quiet residental area, two blocks from shops, parks, a seawall walkway and restaurants with West Coast & international cuisine. Solarium and TV room. On Business route, 15 minutes from downtown Vancouver.
E-mail: 6048310952@msg.clearnet.com

Creekside B&B	80-100-B&B	Full gourmet breakfast
1515 Palmerston Ave, V7V 4S9	2 rooms, 2 pb	Complimentary wine/snack
604-926-1861 Fax: 604-926-7545	Visa, MC, •	Color TV, fireplace, 2 person
604-328-9400	C-ltd/S-no/P-no/H-no	Jacuzzi tubs, stocked
John Boden & Donna	Ukrainian	refrigerator in rooms
Hawrelko All year		

Private, woodsy creekside hideaway. Close to parks, skiing, beaches & ocean. Honeymoon suite available. 2 day minimum. *E-mail:* donnajohnboden@bc.sympatico.ca

WHISTLER ────────────────────────────────────

Alta Vista Chalet B&B Inn	70-150-B&B	Full breakfast
3229 Archibald Way, V0N 1B3	8 rooms, 6 pb	Dinner (fee), afternoon tea
604-932-4900 Fax: 604-932-4933	Most CC, *Rated*	Sitting room, library, hot
888-768-2970	C-yes/S-no/P-no/H-no	tubs, sauna, daily maid
Tim & Yvonne Manville	French	service
All year		

Alpine chalet, 2 kms south of the village ski slopes overlooking Alta Lake and valley trail. Quiet and comfortable. AAA & Tourism B.C. approved. *E-mail:* avcb-b@direct.ca
Web site: whistlerinns.com/altavista/

WHISTLER ——

Golden Dreams B&B	55-90-B&B	Full breakfast
6412 Easy St, V0N 1B6	3 rooms, 1 pb	Full guest kitchen
604-932-2667 Fax: 604-932-7055	Visa, MC, •	Complimentary Sherry,
800-668-7055	C-yes/S-ltd/P-no/H-no	snacks, fireside lounge,
Ann & Terry Spence All year		TV/VCR, outdoor hot tub

1 mile to skiing/sightseeing! Large garden deck with BBQ. Unique "theme rooms." Bike rental on-site, ski/lift rental disc'ts.   E-mail: goldendreams@whistlerweb.net
Web site: cantravel.ab.ca/goldendr.html

New Brunswick

CHANCE HARBOUR ——————————————————————————————————————

Mariner's Inn	65-90-AP	Continental breakfast plus
32 Mawhinney Cove Rd, E5J	11 rooms, 11 pb	Lunch, dinner, restaurant
2B8	Visa, MC, *Rated*, •	Bar service, sitting room,
506-659-2619 Fax: 506-659-1890	C-ltd/S-no/P-no/H-ltd	library, suites, fireplaces
888-783-2455	French, German, Dutch	
Susan & Bill Postma		
All year		

Enjoy awe-inspiring ocean scenery of the world's highest tides, in a secluded romantic setting on the Bay of Fundy.   E-mail: posma@nbnet.nb.ca   *Web site:* bayoffundy.com/mariner

SHEDIAC ——

Auberge Belcourt Inn	60-95-B&B	Full breakfast
PO Box 631, E0A 3G0	7 rooms, 5 pb	Dinner (off season)
506-532-6098 Fax: 506-533-9398	Visa, MC, AmEx,	Sitting room, library,
Pauline & Christopher Pike	*Rated*, •	fireplaces, cable TV
February-Novemeber	C-ltd/S-ltd/P-no/H-no	
	French, Cantonese	

A spacious and elegantly restored Victorian home handsomely furnished with antiques. Breakfast is served in an oval dining room on fine antique china.
E-mail: belcourt@nbnet.nb.ca   *Web site:* sn2000.nb.ca/comp/auberge-belcourt

ST. ANDREWS ——

Windsor House of St	150-225-B&B	Lunch, dinner, restaurant,
Andrews	6 rooms, 6 pb	bar
132 Water St, E5B 1A8	Visa, MC, AmEx, •	Fireplace, cable TV,
506-529-3330 Fax: 506-529-4063	C-no/S-ltd/P-no/H-ltd	conferences, pool table,
888-890-9463	French	garden courtyard
Jay Remer & Greg Cohane		
All year		

Historic restoration of a 1798 Georgian sea captain's house with the most comfortable rooms filled with period antiques & the finest dining available in Eastern Canada.
E-mail: greg@nbnet.nb.ca   *Web site:* townsearch.com/windsorhouse

ST. ANDREWS BY THE SEA ——————————————————————————————————

Pansy Patch	110-175-B&B	Full gourmet breakfast
59 Carleton St, E5B 1M8	9 rooms, 9 pb	Fine dining aftn., eve.
506-529-3834 Fax: 506-529-9042	Visa, MC, *Rated*, •	Tennis court, hot tubs,
888-726-7972	C-yes/S-no/P-no/H-no	sauna, pool, library, kites,
Jeannie Foster		bikes, antiques
May to October		

Most photographed home in New Brunswick, St. Croix Courier; featured in New York Times, Brides, Canadian Homes & Gardens. *A fantasy   E-mail:* pansypatch@nb.aibn.com
Web site: pansypatch.com

Newfoundland

L'ANSE AUX MEADOWS

Viking Nest B&B	38-45-B&B	Full breakfast
Box 127, A0K 2X0	4 rooms, 1 pb	Dinner avail., comp. snack
709-623-2238 Fax: 709-623-2238	Visa, MC, *Rated*, •	Sitting room, cable TV,
877-858-2238	C-yes/S-no/P-ltd/H-no	accommodate business
Thelma Hedderson All year		travelers, suites

Viking Nest B&B serves a full breakfast every day. Complimentary evening snack also available and we will recommend our favorite restaurants.   E-mail: thedders@avint.net
Web site: bbcanada.com/2671.html

ST. JOHN'S

Gower Street House B&B, A	30-B&B	Continental plus breakfast
180 Gower St, A1C 1P9	8 rooms, 7 pb	Afternoon tea, snacks
709-754-0047	Visa, MC, AmEx,	Sitting room, library, bikes,
800-563-3959	*Rated*, •	suites, fireplace, cable TV
Neil & Irene	C-ltd/S-ltd/P-ltd/H-ltd	
All year	Russian	

Comfortable rooms & suites with all the amenities. Parking, center of downtown St. John's historic properties. Halfway between Hotels Newfoundland and Delta. 5 minute walk to all tourist attractions. Whale, iceberg, seabird watching.   E-mail: abba@roadrunner.nf.net
Web site: bbonline.com/can/nf/gower/index.html

McCoubrey Manor	53-100-B&B	Continental plus breakfast
6-8 Ordnance St., A1C 3K7	7 rooms, 7 pb	Tea, snacks, evening wine &
709-722-7577 Fax: 709-579-7577	Most CC, *Rated*, •	cheese
888-753-7577	C-ltd/S-no/P-no/H-no	Sitting room, Jacuzzis, suites,
Jill & Roy Knoechel All year		fireplace, cable TV, phone

Downtown Queen-Anne heritage home retains its spacious rooms, wood trim, fireplaces, & decorative plaster mouldings. 3 deluxe suites w/queen-size bed, double Jacuzzi, fireplace, Housekeeping apartments for families/longer stays. Cd player.   E-mail: mccmanor@nfld.com
Web site: wordplay.com/mccoubrey

Nova Scotia

CHESTER

Haddon Hall	99-286-B&B	Continental plus breakfast
PO Box 640, B0J 1J0	10 rooms, 10 pb	Dinner, restaurant
902-275-3577	Visa, MC, *Rated*, •	Sitting room, bar service,
Cynthia O'Connell	C-ltd/S-ltd/P-no/H-ltd	bicycles, fireplaces, cable
April 1-Oct. 31		TV, swimming pool

Haddon Hall is Nova Scotia's only four diamond AAA resort inn. Built in 1905 this 120 acre estate offers a spectacular panoramic ocean view.   E-mail: haddon@tallships.ca
Web site: innbook.com/haddonhall.html

HALIFAX

Halliburton House Inn	90-B&B/MAP	Continental breakfast
5184 Morris St, B3J 1B3	28 rooms, 28 pb	Dinner available, tea
902-420-0658 Fax: 902-423-2324	Visa, MC, AmEx,	Restaurant, bar, suites,
Robert B. Pretty	*Rated*, •	fireplace, cable, TV, garden
All year	C-yes/S-no/P-no/H-no	courtyard

Located on a quiet street in Historic Halifax, Halliburton House Inn offers the charm and elegance of a four-star country inn with the convenience of a central downtown location. E-mail: innkeeper@halliburton.ns.ca *Web site:* halliburton.ns.ca

552 Nova Scotia

MIDDLETON

Fairfield Farm Inn
PO Box 1287, B0S 1P0
902-825-6989
800-237-9896
Richard Griffith   All year

45-70-B&B
5 rooms, 5 pb
Most CC, *Rated*, •
C-ltd/S-no/P-no/H-no

Full choice breakfast
Afternoon tea
Sitting room, library, video
library, game room,
kitchen/laundry, A/C

Fully restored 1886 Victorian Country Inn furnished in period antiques to enhance its original charm. The 110 acre Inn property has birding and walking trails and the Annapolis River.   E-mail: griffith@glinx.com *Web site:* valleyweb.com/fairfieldfarminn

PEGGY'S COVE

Peggy's Cove B&B
19 Church Rd, B0J 2N0
902-823-2265 Fax: 902-852-4493
888-726-8322
Audrey O'Leary   May 1-Oct 31

70-80-B&B
5 rooms, 3 pb
Visa, MC, AmEx, •
C-ltd/S-ltd/P-ltd/H-no

Full breakfast
Sitting room, Jacuzzis,
satellite TV—VCR in lounge,
TV—VCR in some rooms

Overlooking beautiful Peggy's Cove, an artist's and photographer's paradise, our B&B with its five bright, spacious rooms offers a perfect vantage point from which to experience life ·in this world-famous little fishing village.   E-mail: peggyscovebandb@ns.sympatico.ca
Web site: www3.ns.sympatico.ca/peggyscovebandb

PROSPECT VILLAGE

Prospect B&B
1758 Prospect Bay Rd, B3T 2B3
902-852-4493 Fax: 902-852-4493
800-SALT-SEA
H. Prsala & S. O'Leary
All year

85-115-B&B/MAP
5 rooms, 5 pb
Visa, MC, AmEx,
Rated, •
C-yes/S-no/P-no/H-no
Czech, German, French

Continental plus breakfast
Dinner available
Sitting room, library, Family
friendly facility,
kitchen/laundry, A/C

Restored oceanfront Convent located in quaint fishing village near Peggy's Cove offering coastal hiking, eco adventure packages, complimentary canoeing. All rooms with private ensuite baths, queen beds.   E-mail: dynamic.realty@ns.sympatico.ca
Web site: destination-ns.com/lighthouse/prospectbnb/

WOLFVILLE

Farmhouse Inn, The
PO Box 38, B0P 1H0
902-582-7900 Fax: 902-582-7900
800-928-4346
Doug & Ellen Bray   All year

37-80-B&B
5 rooms, 5 pb
Visa, MC, *Rated*, •
C-yes/S-no/P-no/H-ltd

Full breakfast
Afternoon tea
Sitting room, library,
Jacuzzis, suites, fireplaces,
cable TV

Cozy 1840s renovated farmhouse in centre of a quaint village. Elegant country charm, antiques, quiet parlours with wood-burning fireplaces, lovely dining room with original pine floor   E-mail: farmhous@ns.sympatico.ca *Web site:* valleyweb.com/farmhouseinn

---

Inn the Vineyard B&B
Box 106, B0P 1M0
902-542-9554 Fax: 902-542-1248
800-565-0000
John Halbrook & Carl Jordan
June 1-October 16

37-65-B&B
4 rooms, 4 pb
Visa, MC, *Rated*, •
C-yes/S-no/P-yes/H-no
French

Full breakfast
Afternoon tea
Sitting room, fireplaces, in
the family since 1779.

Heritage property, family owned since 1779. Nova Scotia art and antiques. Lovely breakfasts. Pastoral, historic village, heritage conservation district. Orchards and seaviews. Excellent restaurants.   E-mail: jhalbrook@bigfoot.com *Web site:* bestinns.net/canada/ns/vineyard.html

YARMOUTH, HALIFAX

Blandford Inn B&B
RR 1, B0J 1T0
902-228-2016 Fax: 902-228-2016
888-228-2016
Maureen Zinck   All year

49-B&B
4 rooms, 4 pb
Visa, MC,
C-yes/S-ltd/P-no/H-yes

Full breakfast
Evening meals order in
advance
Ocean ambiance

A charming century old house with a new addition can accommodate small groups. Breakfast is served overlooking the harbor. A good place to relax, unwind, relieve strees and restore your mind and body.   E-mail: blandford.inn@ns.sympatico.ca
Web site: www3.ns.sympatico.ca/blandford.inn.com

Ontario

1000 ISLANDS

Trinity House Inn
90 Stone St S, K7G 1Z8
613-382-8383 Fax: 613-382-1599
800-265-4871
Jacques O'Shea & Brad
Garside
Closed January

62-131-B&B, MAP
8 rooms, 8 pb
Visa, MC, *Rated*
C-ltd/S-ltd/P-no/H-ltd

Continental breakfast plus
Dinner, restaurant, bar
service
Sitting room, suites, cable TV,
waterfall gardens

Trinity House Inn is for those who appreciate Old-World charm and hosptitality, together with the genuine beauty of surroundings and the quality of comfort it brings.
E-mail: trinity@kingston.net   *Web site:* trinityinn.com

BARRIE

Cozy Corner
2 Morton Cresent, L4N 7T3
705-739-0157 Fax: 705-739-1946
Charita & Harry Kirby
All year

43-73-B&B
4 rooms, 2 pb
Visa, *Rated*, •
C-ltd/S-no/P-no/H-no
German, Spanish

Full or continental breakfast
Sitting room, Jacuzzi, A/C,
TVs, we'll pick you up at the
airport

Enjoy elegant retreat surrounded by Muskoka Lakes, Georgian Bay. Quality bedding, A/C. European theme gourmet breakfasts, vegetarian dining. Different country food daily. Award winning B&B.   E-mail: cozycorner@cois.on.ca *Web site:* cois.on.ca/~cozycorner

Nicholyn Farms and B&B
RR 2, L0L 2K0
705-737-4498 Fax: 705-737-4498
888-203-8313
Lynda & Nicholas Van
Casteren
All year

43-55-B&B
4 rooms, 4 pb
Visa, MC, *Rated*
C-yes/S-no/P-no/H-no
Dutch

Full breakfast
Afternoon tea, dinner, snacks
Sitting room, bicycles,
fireplaces, accommodate
business travelers

Quaint country setting, farm fresh food, lovely clean spacious rooms. Minutes to endless summer and winter activities. Guest lounge with wood burning fireplace. Central air. Quality linens and duvets. Separate area for families. 10 minutes N of Barrie.
E-mail: nicholyn@simcoe.net *Web site:* nicholyn.com

BRIGHTON

Butler Creek B&B
202—City Road 30, RR#7, K0K
1H0
613-475-1248 Fax: 613-475-5267
877-477-5827
Burke & Ken
All year

50-B&B
5 rooms, 1 pb
Visa, MC, *Rated*, •
C-yes/S-no/P-no/H-no
German, French

Full breakfast
Sitting room, fireplaces, large
country property with
meadows and stream

Enjoy the rare combination of Victorian elegance, convenient location and peaceful setting. We can also reserve other B&Bs in Ontario for you.   E-mail: obbrs@reach.net
Web site: bbcanada.com/425.html

COLLINGWOOD

Pretty River Valley Inn
RR 1, L0M 1P0
705-445-7598 Fax: 705-445-7598
Steve & Diane Szelestowski
All year

60-87-B&B
8 rooms, 8 pb
Visa, MC, *Rated*, •
C-ltd/S-no/P-no/H-ltd

Full breakfast
Jacuzzis, suites, fireplaces,
accommodate business
travelers

Country Inn nestled in scenic Blue Mountains. Pine furnished studios and suites with in-room whirlpool baths, private bathrooms, woodburning fireplaces & spa. Close to shops, skiing, beaches, golf and hiking trails.   Web site: travelinx.com/prettyrivercountryinn

GANANOQUE

Manse Lane B&B
465 Stone St S, K7G 2A7
613-382-8642
888-565-6379
Jocelyn & George Bounds
All year

37-70-B&B
4 rooms, 2 pb
Visa, MC, AmEx,
Rated, •
C-ltd/S-no/P-no/H-no
French

Full breakfast
Afternoon tea
Sitting room, swimming pool,
AC, indoor bike storage

Clean, comfortable, tastefully appointed surroundings. Relaxing atmosphere, warm, friendly hospitality. Century brick home. Cruise/theatre packages. Off street parking.
Web site: bbcanada.com/942.html/

Victoria Rose Inn, The
279 King St West, K7G 2G7
613-382-3368
888-246-2893
Liz & Ric Austin   All year

65-125-B&B
8 rooms, 8 pb
Visa, MC, AmEx, *Rated*
C-ltd/S-no/P-no/H-no
Italian

Full breakfast
Wine for honeymooners
Bicycles, Jacuzzi, A/C,
gardens, tea room, parlour,
ballroom

Stately mansion built in 1872 elegantly appointed with Canadian antiques. Veranda overlooks 2 acres of estate grounds. Fine dining and antique shops.
E-mail: vv@victoriaroseinn.com *Web site:* victoriaroseinn.com

GRIMSBY

**Denwycke House at
Grimsby**
203 Main St E, L3M 1P5
905-945-2149 Fax: 905-945-6272
Patricia & John Hunter
All year

80-90-B&B
2 rooms, 2 pb
Visa, MC, AmEx,
C-ltd/S-no/P-no/H-no
French

Full or continental plus
breakfast
Fridge, coffee maker
Sitting room, suites,
fireplaces, cable TV, data
ports

Luxurious suites in a gracious 1846 heritage home on the Niagara Wine Route. English and Canadian antiques-one acre English garden-gourmet breakfasts-cable TV, private phones-central A/C. E-mail: johnhunter@compuserve.com
Web site: town.grimsby.on.ca/denwycke/denwycke.html

HAMILTON

Inchbury Street B&B
87 Inchbury St, L8R 3B7
905-522-3520 Fax: 905-522-5216
800-792-8765
Sharon Lehnert
All year

35-45-B&B
2 rooms
Visa, MC, •
C-yes/S-ltd/P-no/H-no
German, French

Full breakfast
Snacks, complimentary cold
drinks
Sitting room, TV/VCR,
phones, bikes, data ports

Quiet enclave next to Dundurn Castle. Walk to downtown. Turn-of-the-century house is also an art gallery. E-mail access and fax receiving for business travelers.
E-mail: inchbury@lara.on.ca *Web site:* fobba.com/1159.html

KINGSTON

Painted Lady Inn
181 William St, K7L 2E1
613-545-0422
Carol Franks
All year

90-150-B&B
7 rooms, 7 pb
Visa, MC, AmEx, *Rated*
C-ltd/S-no/P-no/H-no

Full breakfast
Snacks
Sitting room, Jacuzzis, suites,
fireplaces, cableTV, balcony,
parking

1872 Victorian manse offers seven elegant rooms with ensuite baths, antiques, queen beds and central air. Gourmet breakfast. Close to all attractions, restaurants and shopping. Fireplace/Jacuzzi suites.   Web site: aracnet.net/~paintedldy/

Secret Garden B&B Inn
73 Sydenham St., K7L 3H3
613-531-9884 Fax: 613-531-9502
John & Maryanne Baker
All year

67-95-B&B
5 rooms, 5 pb
Visa, MC, AmEx, Most
CC,
C-ltd/S-ltd/P-no/H-no

Full breakfast
Tea, wine
Sitting room, library,
Jacuzzis, fireplace,
conference, central A/C

Historical 1888 Victorian, downtown Kingston. Victorian courtyard, gourmet breakfast served in formal dining room or courtyard. King & Queen poster beds, antiques, stained glass windows, & antique fireplaces.   E-mail: baker@the-secret-garden.com
Web site: the-secret-garden.com

KITCHENER

Aram's Roots & Wings B&B
11 Sunbridge Crescent, N2K
1T4
519-743-4557 Fax: 519-743-4166
877-763-4557
Fay Teal-Aram   All year

45-65-B&B
5 rooms, 3 pb
Visa, MC, AmEx, *Rated*
C-yes/S-ltd/P-yes/H-ltd

Full breakfast
Sitting room, Jacuzzis,
swimming pool, suites,
fireplaces, cable TV, trails

Country living right in the city. Warm hospitality and a hearty breakfast awaits you. Heated pool, Jacuzzi and comfortable large rooms with king/queen beds, TV/VCR and ensuite bathrooms.   E-mail: ia660@worldchat.com *Web site:* bbcanada.com/1039.html

---

Roses and Blessings
112 High Acres Crescent, N2N
2Z9
519-742-1280 Fax: 519-742-8428
Marg & Norm Warren
All year

45-B&B
2 rooms, 2 pb
Visa, MC, *Rated*
C-ltd/S-no/P-no/H-no
Basic French

Full breakfast
Snacks
Sitting rm., library, fireplace,
CATV, A/C, indoor hot tub &
exercise equip.

Be pampered! Renowned, sumptous candle-lit breakfasts including fresh baked goods, fruits and entrees. Double/queen, sunroom and flower gardens. Daily newspaper, memento given, excursion planning & reservation assistance.   E-mail: nmwarren@golden.net
Web site: bbcanada.com/2077.html

MERRICKVILLE

Rideau Bank B&B
PO Box 609, K0G 1N0
613-269-3864   800-461-3695
Aline & Lorne Caldwell
All year

45-B&B
2 rooms
Visa, MC,
C-yes/S-no/P-no/H-no
French

Full breakfast

Turn of the century large brick home on spacious grounds located on Rideau Canal in historic village, judged Canada's prettiest village. Walking distance to fine dining, shopping, & leisure activities.   E-mail: rideau_bank_bb@hotmail.com

NIAGARA FALLS

Danner House B&B
12549 Niagara River Pky, L2E
6S6
905-295-5166 Fax: 905-295-0202
Pierre & Rolland
All year

75-B&B
3 rooms, 3 pb
Visa, MC, AmEx, •
S-no/P-no/H-no
French

Full breakfast
Snacks
Sitting room, bikes, fireplaces

*Stately historic stone home with rooms overlooking the Niagara River in quiet country setting. 10 minutes drive to the Falls and all its attractions. 15 minutes to Buffalo.
E-mail:* comniag@vaxxine.com *Web site:* vaxxine.com/danner

**Eastwood Tourist Lodge,
The**
5359 River Rd, L2E 3G9
905-354-8686 Fax: 905-371-1292
Joanne
All year

54-103-B&B
4 rooms, 4 pb
Most CC,
C-ltd/S-no/P-no/H-no
Spanish, German

Full breakfast
Sitting room, library, tennis,
cable TV, balconies with
view of Gorge

Ideally located minutes by foot from Falls. Situated on hill providing clear view of Niagara Gorge. Charming, spacious rooms with balconies and in room refrigerators. Beautiful rock garden. Home cooked full breakfast. 38 years in business.   E-mail: vacation@eastwood.com
Web site: eastwood.com

Kiely House Inn, The
PO Box 1642, L0S 1J0
905-468-4588
Ray & Heather Pettit
All year

50-120-B&B
12 rooms, 12 pb
Visa, MC, AmEx,
Rated, •
C-ltd/S-yes/P-no/H-no

Continental plus breakfast
Afternoon tea, snacks
Full-service dining room,
sitting room, bicycles,
verandas, garden

Elegant early Victorian inn on one-acre garden. Cool verandas, screened porches, many fireplaces. Walking distance to theaters, stores, restaurants   E-mail: kielyinn@on.aibn.com
Web site: oncomdis.on.ca/kiely_inn/

NIAGARA FALLS

Post House, Circa 1835	91-203-B&B	Full varied breakfast
PO Box 8000, Suite 381, L0S 1J0	3 rooms, 3 pb	Special "healthy table"
905-468-9991 Fax: 905-468-9584	Visa, MC, AmEx, •	Library, bikes, Jacuzzis,
888-472-9991	C-ltd/S-ltd/P-no/H-no	heated pool, suites, fireplace,
Barbara & Dr. Charles Ganim		CATV, conservatory
All year		

*Historic, 1835 property within a short stroll to Shaw theaters. Our home has been complete-
ly restored with ensuites and offers a lavish breakfast in the conservatory. Tennis available.   E-mail:* posthsebb@aol.com   *Web site:* shawfest.sympatico.ca

Tintern Vacations	40-55-B&B	Full breakfast
2869 Tintern Rd, RR #1, L0R	5 rooms, 3 pb	Lunch/dinner available,
2C0	Visa, MC, AmEx,	snacks
905-563-4000 Fax: 905-563-3446	C-yes/S-no/P-yes/H-no	Sitting room, bicycles,
888-298-7291	Dutch, French	swimming pool, suites,
Jane & Andre Tieman		fireplace.
All year		

*Country home offering canoeing on our backyard river. Walk our llamas, visit over a
dozen wineries, golf, hike, swim, see Niagara Falls. Go antiquing or take a day trip to
Toronto.   E-mail:* tintern.vacations@sympatico.ca   *Web site:* tourismniagara.com/tintern

NIAGARA ON THE LAKE

Acute B&B Inn	95-165-B&B	Full breakfast
PO Box 447, L0S 1J0	5 rooms, 5 pb	Snacks
905-468-1328 Fax: 905-468-4386	Visa, MC, •	Sitting room, library,
888-208-2340	C-ltd/S-no/P-no/H-ltd	bicycles, suites, fireplace,
Edwinna & Peter Syta	Polish	cable TV
All year		

*Historic 1843 Inn with original hardwood floors surrounded by cedar hedges tastfully
furnished.   E-mail:* acute@vaxxine.com   *Web site:* acutebedandbreakfast.com

NORTH BAY

Hotel Miwapanee Lodge	45-75-B&B	Breakfast available (fee)
1100 Miwapanee Rd, J0Z 2H0	6 rooms, 6 pb	Lunch and dinner available
819-627-3773 Fax: 819-627-1838	MC, AmEx, *Rated*	(fee)
800-461-9076	C-yes/S-ltd/P-no/H-no	Restaurant, bar service,
Suzanne & James Mullin		sitting room, suites,
All year		fireplaces, hot tub, lake

*Hotel Miwapanee Lodge awaits you on the shores of beautiful Lake Kipawa, Quebec. From
its sandy beaches to the serenity of its forest setting, Miwapanee offers the adventure of a
rugged outpost with all the comforts of home.   E-mail:* miw@efni.com   *Web site:* efni.com/~miw

Hummingbird Hill B&B	50-65-B&B	Full breakfast
254 Edmond Rd, P0H 1B0	3 rooms, 2 pb	Lunch, diner, tea, snacks,
705-752-4547 Fax: 705-752-5150	Visa,	wine
800-661-4976	C-ltd/S-ltd/P-no/H-ltd	Sitting room, library,
Marianne & Gary Persia		bicycles, tennis, jacuzzi,
All year		fireplace, cable TV, spa

*Unique geodesic domes, country setting, surrounded by English country gardens. Screened
cedar gazebo for summer dining, outdoor hot tub, sauna, spa services-complete pamper
packages.   E-mail:* mabb@vianet.on.ca   *Web site:* northbay-online.com/hummingbirdhill

OTTAWA

Albert House Inn	85-140-B&B	Full English breakfast
478 Albert St, K1R 5B5	17 rooms, 17 pb	Tea, coffee, juices
613-236-4479 Fax: 613-237-9078	Visa, MC, AmEx,	Sitting room, color cable TV
800-267-1982	*Rated*, •	in rooms, telephones
John & Catherine Delroy	C-ltd/S-yes/P-no/H-no	
All year	French, English	

*Fine restored Victorian residence designed by Thomas Seaton Scott in post-Confederate
period. Complimentary breakfast, parking.   E-mail:* 73354.3271@compuserve.com
Web site: alberthouseinn.on.ca

OTTAWA

Auberge McGEE'S Inn
185 Daly Ave, K1N 6E8
613-237-6089 Fax: 613-237-6201
800-2MCGEES
Anne Schutte & Mary Unger
All year

60-120-B&B
14 rooms, 14 pb
Visa, MC, AmEx, *Rated*
C-ltd/S-no/P-no/H-no
French, Spanish

Full breakfast
Phone, 2 ensuite Jacuzzis,
cable TV, fireplaces, voice
mail & dataport.

Downtown 1886 historic inn, central to Congress Centre, University of Ottawa. Breakfast is served in the 12 foot ceiling art gallery dining room. Romantic Jacuzzi suites with fireplace. Recipient of the Ottawa Hospitality Award.   Web site: coatesb.demon.co.uk/McGees/

Blue Spruces B&B
187 Glebe Ave, K1S 2C6
613-236-8521 Fax: 613-231-3730
888-828-8801
John and Phyllis Kennedy
All year

60-B&B
3 rooms, 3 pb
Visa, MC, *Rated*
C-ltd/S-no/P-no/H-no
French, English

Full breakfast
Afternoon tea
Sitting room, central air-
conditioning, vegetarian
dining

Elegant Edwardian home with antiques in Glebe, Ottawa's downtown village. Close to all major tourist attractions. Lavish breakfast served in gracious dining room. E-mail: kennedyp@cyberus.ca Web site: bbcanada.com/926.html

Gasthaus Switzerland Inn
89 Daly Ave, K1N 6E6
613-237-0335 Fax: 613-594-3327
888-663-0000
Sauter Sabina
All year

88-188-B&B
22 rooms, 22 pb
Visa, MC, *Rated*
C-ltd/S-no/P-no/H-no
German, Serb., French

Full Swiss breakfast
Sitting room, TV room, air-
conditioned, barbecue,
garden

Warm Swiss atmosphere in Canada's beautiful capital. Clean, cozy rooms; close to tourist attractions; free parking.   E-mail: switzinn@magi.com Web site: infoweb.magi.com/~switzinn/

Paterson House B&B
500 Wilbrod St, K1N 6N2
613-565-8996
Fax: 613-565-6546
Renee C. Bates
All year

95-137-B&B
4 rooms, 4 pb
Most CC, *Rated*, •
S-no/P-no/H-no
French

Continental plus breakfast
Noah's restaurant
Sitting room, library,
executive, deluxe B&B, very
elegant & luxurious

Elegant & luxurious in quiet area of city. 15 minute walk to market, shops, attractions & theatre. Unique ayurvedic health centre for luxurious massage & steam baths. E-mail: paterson@cyberus.ca Web site: welcome.to/paterson_house

Pension Wunderbar Hotel
PO Box 272, J0X 3G0
819-459-2471
Margaret Kuen
All year

40-60-EP
6 rooms, 6 pb
Visa, MC, AmEx, •
C-yes/S-yes/P-no/H-no
French, Dutch, German

Bar, Fully equipped kitchens
Suites, fireplaces, VCR & TV

Authentic Austrian inn nestled in Gatineau Hills, near skiing and oterh sports, 32 km from Ottawa. Romantic apartments with kitchens, wood-burning fireplaces, and in-suite movies on VCR.

PORT HOPE

Butternut Inn B&B
36 North St, L1A 1T8
905-885-4318
Fax: 905-885-5464
Bob & Bonnie Harrison
All year

63-70-B&B
4 rooms, 4 pb
Visa, MC, *Rated*, •
C-ltd/S-no/P-no/H-no

Full gourmet breakfast
Aftn. tea, soft drinks
Sitting room, solarium, large
private garden, landscaped
grounds

Luxuriously appointed 1850s town home in the heart of antique, cycling & fishing country. Gourmet cooking packages our specialty E-mail: info@butternutinn.com Web site: butternutinn.com

PORT PERRY

Landfall Farm	45-B&B	Full breakfast
3120 Hwy 7A, RR1, L0B 1B0	3 rooms, 1 pb	Afternoon tea
905-986-5588	C-yes/S-ltd/P-ltd/H-no	Sitting room, swimming pool,
Merle Heintzman	French	fireplaces, TV, antique shop,
All year		natural pond

1868 Victorian stone farmhouse with original gingerbread trim, pine floors, etc., extensive grounds, lighted/heated pool with cabana, antique shop, natural pond, country comfortable "at-home" atmosphere, welcoming guests for over 20 years.

PORT ROWAN

Bayview B&B	B&B	Full breakfast
PO Box 9, N0E 1M0	3 rooms, 1 pb	Sitting room, suites, cable TV,
519-586-3413	*Rated*	accommodate business
800-646-0668	C-ltd/S-ltd/P-no/H-no	travelers
Laura-Jane Carlton/Ron		
Duncan		
All year		

Welcoming home catering to your needs. Victorian-style, modern facilities, sundecks, very comfortable. Guests quotes—"great food, peaceful, excellent visit, right at home, tranquil & relaxing, great hospitality." E-mail: bayview@nornet.on.ca *Web site:* bbcanada.com/2220.html

SAULT STE. MARIE

Knight Home B&B	35-45-B&B	Full breakfast
61 Lansdowne Ave, P6B 1K5	3 rooms, 0 pb	Sitting room, cable TV,
705-949-3241	*Rated*	accommodate business
877-949-4874	C-yes/S-no/P-ltd/H-no	travelers
Jim & Joyce Duncan		
All year		

Modernized cozy, older family home centrally located in quiet residential area overlooking city; large private backyard deck, front porch enclosure; near tourist attractions, shopping, restaurants; great hospitality, food; comfortable king/twin beds E-mail: knighth@soonet.ca *Web site:* staycanada.com/knight-home/

STRATFORD, KITCHENER

Waterlot Restaurant & Inn	50-80-B&B	Continental breakfast
PO Box 1077, N0B 2G0	3 rooms, 1 pb	Lunch & dinner available,
519-662-2020 Fax: 519-662-2114	Visa, MC, AmEx,	bar
Gordon & Leslie Elkeer	S-no/P-no/H-no	Gourmet shop sitting room
All year		

Just the place for a romantic gourmet. Quiet riverside escape. One of Ontario's finest dining establishments.   E-mail: waterlot@sympatico.ca *Web site:* www3.sympatico.ca/waterlot

THORNBURY

Carriages Country Inn	55-90-B&B	Full breakfast
PO Box 370, N0H 2P0	4 rooms, 4 pb	Lunch, dinner, rest.
519-599-2217 Fax: 519-599-3135	Visa, MC, AmEx, •	Aftn. tea, snacks, bar, sitting
Rob & Ann Wildeman	C-yes/S-no/P-no/H-no	room, Jacuzzi tubs in suites
All year		

Beautifully restored Victorian manor home in the heart of picturesque Thornbury. Luxurious guest suites, elegant dining, friendly pub & patio and glorious gardens. E-mail: carriages@georgian.net

THUNDER BAY

Pinebrook B&B	30-50-B&B	Full breakfast
RR #16, P7B 6B3	4 rooms, 1 pb	Lunch, dinner available,
807-683-6114 Fax: 807-683-6114	Visa, MC, AmEx, •	snacks
Armin Weber & Sar Jeffrey	C-yes/S-no/P-yes/H-ltd	Sitting room, library,
All year	German	mountain bikes, Jacuzzi,
		fireplace, beach, canoe

Unique, friendly and tranquil—close to city. Sauna, Jacuzzi, whirlpool, situated by the river in meadows and pine forest, very quiet. Perfect in summer or for skiers. One room has a Jacuzzi bath ensuite. E-mail: pinebrok@baynet.net *Web site:* bbcanaada.com/1184.html/

TORONTO

Aberdeen Guest House	61-65-B&B	Full breakfast-weekends
52 Aberdeen Ave, M4X 1A2	3 rooms	Continental plus (weekdays)
416-922-8697 Fax: 416-922-5011	Visa, MC, AmEx,	All rms. have queen beds,
Gary Stothers	C-ltd/S-no/P-no/H-no	A/C, ceiling fans, TV &
All year	French, Jap., English	private locks

A fountain welcomes you to this peaceful, gracious home on a quiet "mews" street in the historic Cabbage Town neighborhood. E-mail: aberinn@interlog.com
Web site: interlog.com/~aberinn

Alcina's B&B	55-65-B&B	Continental plus breakfast
16 Alcina Ave, M6G 2E8	3 rooms, 3 pb	Sitting room, quiet English
416-656-6400	C-ltd/S-ltd/P-no/H-no	garden, parking
Jennie Coxe		
All year		

Central, gracious, old Victorian house with "good bones." Enjoy the casual elegance of old oak stained glass, soft furnishings, and a quiet, English garden. E-mail: alcinas@idirect.com
Web site: bbcanada.com/1104.html

Amazing Space B&B	65-110-B&B	Full breakfast
34 Monteith St, M4Y 1K7	10 rooms, 2 pb	Fireplaces, cable TV
416-968-2323 Fax: 416-968-7194	Visa,	
Roger Johnson	S-no/P-ltd/H-no	
All year		

Central downtown location. Walking distance to shopping, gay village, theatre, parks, museums. 2 sun decks. Clean, quiet, affordable rooms in the centre of the city. We cater to mainly gay/lesbian clientele. E-mail: mhughes@istar.ca

Lucy's B&B	40-60-B&B	Full breakfast
5465 Middleport Cres, L4Z 3V2	4 rooms, 3 pb	Afternoon tea,
905-507-2364 Fax: 905-507-4219	Visa, MC, •	Complimentary wine
Lucy Jones & Robert Jones	C-yes/S-no/P-no	TV in each room, overhead
All year	Italian	fan in each room,
		accommodate business
		travelers

Located on Highlands Golf Course in Central Mississauga. Beautiful home with large wooded lot, close to major highways and shopping centers in secluded, quiet neighborhood. E-mail: bed@lucysbedandbreakfast.com Web site: lucysbedandbreakfast.com

Mayfair B&B	55-70-B&B	Full breakfast
78 Indian Grove, M6R 2Y4	4 rooms, 4 pb	Sitting room, cable TV, free
416-769-1558 Fax: 416-769-9655	Visa,	parking
Karen & Ken Snelson	C-ltd/P-no/H-no	
All year		

Our 1911 Edwardian home's highlights include antiques, Oriental carpets, original oak paneling and stained glass. Your suite includes a sitting area and a four piece bathroom. E-mail: ksnelson@compuserve.com

Palmerston Inn B&B	75-133-B&B	Full breakfast
322 Palmerston Blvd, M6G 2N6	8 rooms, 3 pb	Afternoon sherry & goodies
416-920-7842 Fax: 416-960-9529	Visa, MC, *Rated*	Deck, garden, park, TV
Judy Carr	S-no/P-no/H-no	lounge, phones, ceiling fans
All year		in all rooms

In charming downtown residential area. Nearby public transportation to downtown. Some rooms have fireplaces. All rooms have hair dryers and complimentary mineral water. Computer hookups available. Web site: bbcanada.com/241.htm

TORONTO

Red Door B&B, The	60-70-B&B	Full breakfast
301 Indian Rd, M6R 2X7	3 rooms, 2 pb	Sitting room, library, suites,
416-604-0544	Visa,	fireplaces, cable TV
Jean and Paul Pedersen	C-ltd/S-no/P-no/H-no	
All year		

Spacious luxury accommodation on a quiet, tree-lined residential street close to High Park and minutes from downtown Toronto by Subway. E-mail: reddoor@idirect.com
Web site: webhome.idirect.com/~reddoor/

Robin's Nest B&B	125-175-B&B	Full breakfast
13 Binscarth Rd, M4W 1Y2	2 rooms, 2 pb	Afternoon tea,
416-926-9464 Fax: 416-926-3730	Visa, *Rated*, •	complimentary wine
Robin Wilson	S-no/P-no/H-no	Sitting room, library, bikes,
All year		Jacuzzis, suites, fireplaces,
		breakfast trays

Located in an exclusive downtown neighborhood, this romantic century home includes just 2 intimate suites which combines the elegance of a 5 star hotel with the charm of an English country inn. E-mail: nest@pathcom.com *Web site:* toronto.com/robinsnest

WINDSOR

Kingswood Inn	65-192-B&B	Full breakfast
101 Mill St W, N9Y 1W4	5 rooms, 5 pb	Continental plus breakfast
519-733-3248 Fax: 519-733-8734	Visa, MC, •	Snacks, sitting room, library,
H & J Koop, B & B Dick	C-ltd/S-no/P-no/H-no	bicycles, Jacuzzi, pool,
Closed X-mas-New Year's	Some german	fireplaces, cable TV

Luxury 1859 octagonal manor; elegant air-conditioned guest rooms feature fine linens, robes, canopy beds; breakfast served on fine china; 3 acres of landscaped grounds with mature trees; romantic getaway. E-mail: kingswd@mnsi.net *Web site:* lsol.com/kingswood

Prince Edward Island

MURRAY RIVER

Bayberry Cliff Inn	95-135-B&B	Full breakfast
RR 4, C0A 1W0	4 rooms, 4 pb	Dinner by reservation
902-962-3395 Fax: 902-962-3395	Visa, MC, *Rated*, •	Library, craft shop, sitting
Nancy & Don Perkins	C-ltd	room, breezeway, cliff to
May 15-Sept.	Spanish	shore

Two remodeled post & beam barns; antiques, marine paintings. 8 minutes to WI's ferry. Perfect for honeymooners. VIP treatment for celebrants. Web site: bbcanada.com/528.html

SOUTH RUSTICO

Barachois Inn	84-98-B&B	Full breakfast
PO Box 1022, C1A 7M4	6 rooms, 6 pb	Complimentary tea or coffee
902-963-2194	*Rated*	Sitting room, pump organ,
Judy & Gary MacDonald	C-ltd/S-no/P-no/H-no	library, bicycles
May-October	English, French	

Victorian house offers lovely views of bay, river and countryside. Antique furnishings and modern comforts. Walk to seashore. $25 (Canadian) for extra person in room. E-mail: barachoisinn@pei.sympatico.ca *Web site:* metamedia.pe.ca/barachois/

Province of Quebec

CAP A L'AIGLE ─────────────────

La Pinsonniere
124 St-Raphael, G0T 1B0
418-665-4431 Fax: 418-665-7156
800-387-4431
Authier Family
Closed Oct 31-Dec 17

140-450-MAP
26 rooms, 26 pb
Visa, MC, AmEx,
Rated, •
C-yes/S-yes/P-no/H-no
French

Lunch & dinner only
Aftn. tea, snacks, restaurant,
bar
Sitting room, library, sauna,
pool, tennis, 3-bedroom apt.,
fireplace

Saint Lawrence River. Beach, golf, ski, tennis, horseback riding. Wine cellar, gourmet food, beautiful view, fresh air. Conference rooms and rooms with Jacuzzi and fireplaces. Cable TV. Massage therapy, wine tasting sessions. E-mail: pinsonniere@relaischateaux.fr
Web site: lapinsonniere.com

GEORGEVILLE ─────────────────

Auberge Georgeville 1889
71, Chemin Channel, J0B 1T0
819-843-8683 Fax: 819-843-5045
888-843-8686
Steven Beyrouty & Megan
Seline
All year

130-190-MAP
13 rooms, 8 pb
Visa, MC, AmEx,
Rated, •
C-ltd/S-ltd/P-no/H-no
French

Full gourmet breakfast
Dinner, afternoon tea
Restaurant, bar service,
sitting room, library, bikes,
walk to lake

Quebec's oldest historic inn with Laura Ashley & Waverly elegance on Lake Memphrema-gog. Multiple award-winning dining, wine cellar, bikes, golf, skiing & more. 20 min. north of I-91. Luxurious suite. E-mail: aubgeorg@abacom.com *Web site:* fortune1000.ca/georgeville

LACHUTE ─────────────────

Auberge Pluscarden Inn
182 Dunany Rd, J8H 3W8
450-562-4781 Fax: 450-562-3757
Bill & Careen MacKimmie
All year

60-100-B&B
3 rooms, 1 pb
Visa, MC,
C-ltd/S-no/P-no/H-ltd
French

Full breakfast
Bar service
Sitting room, bikes, pool,
suites, canoeing.

Nestled amongst the apple trees of a 14 acre riverfront property in the lower Laurentians. Tour the country roads of Argenteuil Country and take time to enjoy some of your favorite activities. E-mail: pluscardbb@aol.com *Web site:* bbcananda.com/2163.html

LADYSMITH ─────────────────

Cushing Nature Retreat
197 Ch. Fierobin, J0X 2A0
819-647-3226 Fax: 819-647-6645
Geoffrey and Joellen Cushing
All year

120-MAP
5 rooms, 5 pb
Visa, •
C-yes/S-no/P-no/H-no
French

Full breakfast
Dinner included
Sitting room, Jacuzzi,
fireplaces, private lake

Nature retreat/bed and breakfast encompassing over 500 acres, private lake, 20km of hiking trails through wilderness sanctuary, wildlife, birds of prey centre, native-led healing circle workshops. E-mail: info@cushing-nature.com *Web site:* cushing-nature.com

LAURENTIANS ─────────────────

Le Provincialat
2292 Rue Sacre-Coeur, J0W
1R0
819-278-4928 Fax: 819-278-4928
877-278-4928
Pierre Seers/Guillaume Petit
All year

25-30-B&B
5 rooms, 3 pb
Visa, MC, *Rated*, •
C-ltd/S-no/P-ltd/H-no
French

Full breakfast
Lunch/dinner available,
snacks
Afternoon tea,
complimentary wine,
restaurant, sitting room,
fireplaces

Historical country inn amidst the well protected laurentians woodlands, home-made cook-ing direct from the property's garden. Lac Nominigue, 2 hours north of Montreal's center is your gateway to relaxing adventure. E-mail: atl@laurentides.com
Web site: laurentides.com/membres/002a.html

MONTREAL

Armor Manoir Sherbrooke
157 Sherbrooke E, H2X 1C7
514-285-0895 Fax: 514-284-1126
800-203-5485
Annick Morvan
All year

39-73-B&B
15 rooms, 7 pb
•
C-yes/S-yes/P-no/H-no
French

Continental breakfast
Complimentary coffee
3 rooms with whirlpool,
Jacuzzis, lake swimming,
bicycles

Once a fine Victorian townhouse in downtown Montreal. Fine woodwork in foyer and some guest rooms Web site: travelguides.com/home/armormanoir/

Auberge De La Fontaine B&B
1301 Rachel East Street, H2J 2K1
514-597-0166 Fax: 514-597-0496
800-597-0597
Celine Boudreau
All year

78-147-B&B
21 rooms, 21 pb
Visa, MC, AmEx,
Rated, •
C-yes/S-yes/P-no/H-yes
French

Continental plus buffet
Afternoon tea
Some whirlpools; suite with
view of park; private, terrace
with whirlpool

Facing Parc La Fontaine (84 acres), located near downtown. A charming inn where you are welcomed as friends. Public transportation nearby. Access to kitchen for snacks. Many rooms recently renovated in warm coors with nice fabrics. Non-smoking floors.
E-mail: info@aubergedelafontaine.com Web site: aubergedelafontaine.com

---

Gite Maison Jacques
4444 Paiement St, H9H 2S7
514-696-2450 Fax: 514-696-2564
Micheline & Fernand Jacques
All year

38-40-B&B
3 rooms, 3 pb
Rated, •
C-yes/S-no/P-no/H-no
French

Full breakfast
Complimentary tea, coffee,
juice
Sitting room, piano, fireplace,
public transit nearby, parking
on grounds

Come and experience a warm and delightful stay in Quebec & live with a real Canadian lively couple. Offers old world charm with 20th century comforts. Just minutes from downtown attractions. E-mail: gite.maison.jacques@sympatico.ca Web site: maisonjacques.qc.ca

---

Manoir Ambrose
3422 Stanley St, H3A 1R8
514-288-6922 Fax: 514-288-5757
Lucie Gagnon
All year

55-95-B&B
22 rooms, 17 pb
Visa, MC, *Rated*, •
C-yes/S-yes/P-no/H-no
Eng., Fr., Sp., Ger.

Continental breakfast
Phone in each room, cable
TV, sitting room, air
conditioning

Perfect location of this Victorian-style lodge close to McGill Univ., musee, restaurants, shopping. Quiet surroundings & friendly home atmosphere. E-mail: webmaster@ manoirambrose.com Web site: manoirambrose.com

---

Montreal Oasis, A
3000 de Breslay, H3Y 2G7
514-935-2312 Fax: 514-935-3154
Lena Blondel
All year

45-110-B&B
3 rooms, 1 pb
C-ltd/S-ltd/P-no/H-no
Swed., Fr., Ger., Sp.

Full gourmet breakfast
Sitting room, lake swimming,
bicycles

Spacious, downtown house with garden. Close to the Fine Arts Museum and Crescent Street. Gourmet 3-course breakfast, world-traveled hostess, Swedish, African, and Asia art. Siamese cat. E-mail: bb@aei.ca Web site: bestinns.net/canada/qu/mo.html

PIKE RIVER

Auberge—Inn La Suisse
119, Route 133, J0J 1P0
450-244-5870 Fax: 450-244-5181
Roger Baertschi
Closed 2 weeks in Jan.

50-60-B&B
4 rooms, 4 pb
Most CC, *Rated*, [No]
C-ltd/S-no/P-no/H-no
French, Swiss, German

Continental Plus
Lunch & Dinner available
Sitting room, a/c, nature
path, TV

Small country inn, 45 minutes south of Montreal. We are a Swiss family who have been here over 30 years. E-mail: aubergelasuisse@hotmail.com Web site: bbcanada.com/1899.html

POINTE AU PIC

Auberge Donohue	53-133-B&B	Continental plus breakfast
51 Chemin du Havre, G0T 1M0	19 rooms, 19 pb	Afternoon tea, piano
418-665-4377 Fax: 418-665-3634	*Rated*, •	Sitting room, pool, fireplaces,
Monique & Orval Aumont	C-ltd/S-yes/P-no/H-no	garden, whirlpool/fireplace
All year	French	available

Cozy house situated right by the St. Lawrence River. Very large living room with fireplace. Every room has private bath; most rooms have view of the river.   E-mail: aub.donohue@ sympatico.ca   *Web site:* cite.net/dona

QUEBEC

Battlefield B&B	60-B&B	Full breakfast
820 Eymard Ave, G1S 4A1	3 rooms	Restaurant
418-681-6804 Fax: 418-681-7093	*Rated*	Sitting room, pool, bikes,
Dolores Dumais, Yvon	C-no/S-no/P-no/H-no	tennis courts, Internet
Turcotte	French, Spanish	facilities
All year		

Residential area between Laval U. & historic Quebec City. Accommodations in a "haut-de-gamme" house with a warm atmosphere & furniture dating back to the Victorian era. E-mail: dodoy@videotron.ca   *Web site:* travelguides.com/home/battlefield

Hotel Marie-Rollet	45-95-EP	Fireplaces, A/C, rooftop
81, Rue Ste-Anne, G1R 3X4	10 rooms, 10 pb	terrace with garden view
418-694-9271	Visa, MC, *Rated*, •	
800-275-0338	C-yes/S-yes/P-no/H-no	
G. Giroux & D. Chouinard	French	
All year		

The tradition of small European hotels. In the heart of old Quebec. A heaven of peace, warm hospitality. Splendid & charming Victorian House, warm wood work, functional fireplaces.

Le Chateau Blanc	50-65-B&B	Full breakfast
311 de la Seine, G7A 2P8	5 rooms	Sitting room, private living
418-831-9119 Fax: 418-831-8800	Visa, •	room with the suite.
Monique Boucher	C-ltd/S-no/P-no/H-no	
All year	French	

E-mail: bed@chateau-quebec.qc.ca   *Web site:* chateau-quebec.qc.ca

ST. EUGENE L'ISLET

Auberge des Glacis	110-170-B&B/MAP	Full breakfast
46 Rt Tortue, G0R 1X0	10 rooms, 10 pb	Lunch, dinner, restaurant
418-247-7486 Fax: 418-247-7182	Visa, MC, AmEx,	Bar service, sitting room,
Micheline & Pierre Watters	*Rated*, •	bicycles, suites, swimming,
All year	C-yes/S-ltd/H-yes	massotherapy
	French	

This onetime flour mill will seduce you through it's sheer charm, warm ambience, country decor and gourmet food.   Web site: microtec.net/~avocat/augerge

STE. AGATHE DES MONTS

Auberge du Lac des Sables	56-88-B&B	Full breakfast
230 St—Venant, J8C 2Z7	24 rooms, 24 pb	Dinner, snacks, bar service
819-326-3994 Fax: 819-326-9159	Visa, MC, AmEx,	Sitting room, bicycles,
800-567-8329	*Rated*, •	Jacuzzis, fireplaces, cable
Dominique Lessard/ Luc	C-ltd/S-ltd/P-no/H-no	TV, conference
Menard	French	
All year		

Most of the conveniences of a bigger resort plus the warm welcome, the charm & the cozy atmosphere of an authentic country inn in an exceptional scenic site on the lake. 1 hour north of Montreal.   E-mail: info@aubergedulac.com   *Web site:* aubergedulac.com

ST. PETRONILLE ──────────────────────────────

Auberge La Goeliche
22 Chemin du Quai, G0A 4C0
418-828-2248 Fax: 418-828-2745
Andree Marchand
All year

77-140-B&B
18 rooms, 16 pb
Visa, MC, AmEx, •
C-yes/S-yes/P-no/H-yes
French, Spanish

Continental plus breakfast
French cuisine
Sitting room, art shop,
outdoor swimming pool, bar
service

Overhanging the St. Lawrence River, this castle-like inn offers a breathtaking view of Quebec City, a 15-minute drive away. It is also close to famous Mt. Ste. Anne ski center.
E-mail: aubergelagoeliche@oricom.ca   *Web site:* oricom.ca/aubergelagoeliche

Yukon Territory

WHITEHORSE ──────────────────────────────

Hawkins House B&B
303 Hawkins St, Y1A 1X5
867-668-7638 Fax: 867-668-7632
Carla Pitzel
All year

70-119-B&B
4 rooms, 4 pb
Most CC, *Rated*
C-ltd/S-no/P-no/H-no
French, German

Full breakfast
Sitting room, library, jacuzzi,
cable TV, accommodates
business travelers.

Lavish, spacious and bright best describes our new Victorian home in downtown White-horse. Experience one of our four Yukon theme rooms in our 5-star B&B.
E-mail: cpitzel@internorth.com   *Web site:* hawkinshouse.yk.ca

Africa
South Africa

CAPE TOWN──────────────────────────────

Hilltop Guest House
30 Forest Rd. Oranjezicht 8001
0027-21-461-3093
Fax: 0027-21-461-4069
Linda Lapping
Open all year

500-799 SA$-B&B
7 rooms, 7 pb
Visa, Mastercard,
American Express, •
C-yes/S-yes/P-no/H-no
English

Full breakfast
Afternoon tea, bar service
Sitting room, swimming pool,
verandahs for private
breakfast, Walk to all
amenities

Set on the slopes of Table Mountain, Hilltop House offers spectacular views of Table Bay as well as stylish suites and excellent hospitality.   E-mail: hilltophouse@iafrica.com
Web site: hilltophouse.co.za

DURBAN──────────────────────────────

Baton Rouge On Sea
P.O. Box 85, Kwazulu Natal,
Eingindhlovu 3800
035-337-1540
Fax: 035-337-1510
Di Talmage
All year, closed Dec. 24–Jan. 4

60 US$-B&B
3 rooms, 2 pb
C-ltd/S-yes/P-no/H-yes
English

Full breakfast
Dinner by request, bar
service
Sitting room, tennis,
swimming pool, cable TV.

Country hideaway overlooking the Indian Ocean. Full English breakfast served in court-yard with swimming pool. Dinner on request. Three golf courses nearby. 2 hours visit to Umfolozi/Hluhluwe game reserves   E-mail: talmage@intekom.co.za

SOMERSET————————————————————————————

Villa Louise	500-700 SA$-B&B	Full breakfast
43 Firmount & Goedehoop St,	5 rooms, 4 pb	Dinner, afternoon tea,
The Cape 7130	Visa, Mastercard,	snacks, lunch
021-852-1630	American Express	Bar service, sitting room,
Fax: 021-852-1648	C-yes/S-yes/P-yes/H-yes	library, bicycles, pool,
Christian-Edmee Voarick	Eng., Ger., It., Fr., Dutch,	swimming pool,
Open all year	Afrikaan	complimentary wine

Very personal and delightfully civilised guesthouse, charming and individual with a mixture of Mediterranean and African style. Full amenities, delicious breakfast, full assistance and airport pick-up.   E-mail: villalou@iafrica.com *Web site:* villalouise.com

Asia

Indonesia

BALI————————————————————————————————

Poppies Bali	85 US$-20 rooms, 20 pb	Full breakfast (fee)
Gang Poppies I/19, Jl.	Visa, Mastercard,	Lunch, Dinner (fee)
Legian, Kuta 80033	American Express,	Afternoon tea, snacks,
62-361-751059	Diners, •	restaurant, bar, laundry,
Fax: 62-361-752346	C-yes/S-yes/P-no/H-no	sitting room, bicycles, AC,
Ms. Melati	English, Indonesian	swimming pool, hot water,
Open all year		IDD, Tours

After 26 years Poppies continues to surprise and delight the world's most discerning travellers and those wishing to escape the glitz and glamour of grandiose hotels. Internet facilities, tours, Videos.   E-mail: info@bali.poppies.net *Web site:* poppies.net/

Australia-S. Pacific

Australia

HENLEY BEACH————————————————————————————

Meleden Villa	65-85 Australian$-B&B	Continental breakfast
268 Seaview Rd 5022	5 rooms, 3 pb	Tea & coffee facilities in all
61-08-8235-0577	Visa, Mastercard,	rooms
Mel & Lee Dennett	*Rated*, •	Swimming pool,
Open all year	C-yes/S-no/P-no/H-ltd	refrigerators, TV. Tennis and
	English	golf nearby.

Charming Federation Villa offering comfortable modern amenities in heritage style near beach, safe swimming, short stroll to cosmopolitan restaurants on the square. Quiet, friendly area. "The charming alternative".   E-mail: meleden@senet.com.au

STRAHAN————————————————————————————————

Franklin Manor	130-208 Australian$-B&B	Full breakfast
Box 67, The Esplanade,	18 rooms, 18 pb	Dinner, restaurant, afternoon
Tasmania 7468	Most CC, •	tea, bar
61-3-64-71-7311	C-yes/S-no/P-yes/H-no	Sitting room, library
Fax: 61-3-64-71-7267	English	
Tony Wurf All year		

Franklin Manor—an award winning boutique hotel offering fine food, wine, premium accommodation and friendly service. Perfectly positioned to enjoy the many activities located in this World Heritage Wilderness area.   E-mail: Franklin.Manor@tassie.net.au
Web site: franklinmanor.com.au

SYDNEY————————————————————————————————

Victoria Court	99 Australian$-B&B	Continental breakfast
122 Victoria St 2011	25 rooms, 25 pb	Ask about food service
61-2-9357-3200	Most CC, •	Sitting room, library, with
Fax: 61-293-57-7606	P-no/H-no	fountains, bikes, library, pool
Michele & Bill Lawrence	English, French,	
Open all year	German, Spanish	

1880's Boutique Hotel in elegant Victorian terrace house. Central, quiet location. Within minutes of Opera House and Harbour. Affordable rates from Australian $99.00 and up. E-mail: info@VictoriaCourt.com.au *Web site:* VictoriaCourt.com.au

New Zealand

AUCKLAND————————————————————————————————

Amersham House	200-380 NZ$-B&B	Full breakfast
1 Canterbury Place	4 rooms, 3 pb	Dinner (fee), afternoon tea
+64-9-3030-321	Visa, Mastercard, •	Hot tub, sauna, jacuzzy, fruit
Fax: +64-9-3030-621	C-ltd/S-no/P-no/H-no	basket, heated pool, bikes;
Jill & Rob Stirling	English	closed by: restaurant, library,
Open all year		tennis.

In historic Parnell, luxurious, central with sweeping harbour views, parking, easy walk to major tourist and sporting attractions. Free bottle of wine.   E-mail: stirling@xtra.co.nz

Bavaria B&B Hotel	80-120 NZ$-B&B	Delightful breakfast buffet
83 Valley Rd, Mt. Eden	11 rooms, 11 pb	Afternoon tea, cookies and
0064-9-638-9641	Visa, Mastercard,	coffee
Fax: 0064-9-638-9665	American Express,	Sitting room, all rooms have
Rudi Schmidt & Ulrike	Most CC, •	private baths, telephones,
Stephan	C-yes/S-no/P-no/H-no	pool, fruit basket, sundeck,
Open all year	English, German, French	garden, TV lounge, off street
		parking

Generous, airy rooms all with private facilities in immaculately restored villa. First class service and very welcoming.   E-mail: bavaria@xtra.co.nz
Web site: nz.com/webnz/bbnz/bavaria.htm

Chalet Chevron B&B Hotel	108-150 NZ$-B&B	Full breakfast
14 Brighton Rd, Parnell 1001	12 rooms, 12 pb	Afternoon tea, coffee (self
64-9-309-0290	Most CC, C-yes/S-ltd/P-	help), snack
Fax: 64-9-373-5754	no/H-yes	Sitting room, shopping,
Brett & Jennie Boyce	English	beaches and islands.
Open all year		

Chalet Chevron, an old-world hotel with extensive sea views in Central Auckland. Close to Parnell Village, Newmarket and an exciting selection of restaurants. A great location for buses and walks.   E-mail: chaletchevron@xtra.co.nz *Web site:* nz.com/webnz/bbnz/chevron.htm

Gulf Haven	85-165 NZ$-B&B	Continental plus breakfast
49 Great Barrier Road,	4 rooms, 2 pb	Dinner, wine (fee)
Encl. Bay	Visa, Mastercard, •	Sitting room, library, rock
09-372-6629	C-no/S-no/P-no/H-no	pools, bicycles, dramatic
Fax: 09-372-8558	English	views, scenery, compliment
Alan Ramsbottom, Lois		wine, bowling
Baucke		
Open all year		

2 acre garden setting overlooking ocean with own seashore. Breakfast on the deck. Relaxed island life. Only 35 minutes from downtown Auckland. 2 guestrooms, 2 studios (extra). Free courtesy car from most ferries. Web site: nz.com/webnz/bbnz/haven.htm/

AUCKLAND

Kodesh Christian Community
31 c Cradock St, Avondale
09-828-5672
Fax: 09-828-5684
Gayle or Sue Thirkettle
Open all year

45 NZ$-B&B
3 rooms
Rated
C-yes/S-no/P-no/H-no
English

Continental plus breakfast
Sitting room, library,
dramatic views, scenery,
compliment wine, bowling.

Kodesh is a residential ecumenical christian community. Modern facilities in a quiet location. 8 minutes by car from downtown Auckland. E-mail: kodesh@xtra.co.nz

---

Peace & Plenty Inn
6 Flagstaff Terr, Devonport
064-944-52925
Fax: 064-944-52901
Graham & Carol Ward
Open all year

200-230 NZ$-B&B
5 rooms, 5 pb
Most CC, •
C-ltd/S-ltd/P-no/H-no
English

Full breakfast
Complimentary wine
Sitting room, beach across
the road, fireplaces, garden,
water skiing, golf

Romantic luxury; historic waterfront home. Restaurants, shopping, ferry to city, steps away. Antiques, flowers, elegance, comfort, gourmet breakfasts; personal service.
E-mail: peaceandplenty@extra.co.nz Web site: peaceandplenty.co.nz

---

Sedgwick-Kent Lodge
65 Lucerne Rd, Remuera
64-9-524-5219
Fax: 649-520-4825
Wout & Helma van der Lans
Open all year

170 NZ$-B&B
5 rooms, 5 pb
Visa, Mastercard,
American Express,
Rated, •
C-ltd/S-ltd/P-ltd/H-ltd
English, French,
German, Dutch

Breakfast included
Complimentary wine, dinner
TV, 1 with kitchen Coffee &
Tea maker, Massage, Beach
front, Horseback

Sited in the premium suburb of Remuera, Sedgwick Kent Lodge is a restored 1910 farmsread. It features native timbers, stained glass windows and is complimented by antique furniture. Persian rugs and original paintings. All rooms with private bathsroom.
E-mail: sklodge@ibm.net Web site: sedgwick.co.nz

BAY ISLANDS

Villa Casablanca
18 Goffe Dr., Haruru Falls,
Paihia
649-402-6980
Fax: 649-402-6980
Derek & Barbara Robertson
All year

80 US$-B&B
6 rooms, 5 pb
Visa, Mastercard,
American Express, •
C-ltd/S-ltd/P-no/H-no
English, French, German

Full breakfast
Dinner, wine
Sitting room, library,
bicycles, jacuzzis, suites,
fireplace, conferences.

Villa Casablanca is a private hilltop guesthouse enjoying spectacular views of historic Waitangi and the Bay Islands. A secluded retreat amidst gardens of flowering shrubs and native bush. E-mail: sales@bestprice.co.nz Web site: bestprice.co.nz/casablanca

CHRISTCHURCH

Kleynbos B&B Homestay
59 Ngaio St
64-3332-2896
Fax: 64-3332-2896
64-252234144
G. De Kleyne, Hans Van den
Bos
Open all year

50-80 NZ$-B&B
3 rooms, 2 pb
Rated, •
C-yes/S-ltd/P-ltd/H-ltd
English, Dutch, some
German

Continental plus breakfast
Free coffee, tea
Off street parking, sitting
room, garden, restaurants
nearby, bush walks, fishing

Exclusive character home, charming wooden decors, tranquil street. New Zealand artwork, good beds, large en suite room on request, excellent value for money.
E-mail: lucien.dol@xtra.co.nz

CHRISTCHURCH

Windsor B&B Hotel
52 Armagh St 8001
64-3-366-1503
Fax: 64-3-3669796
Carol Healy & Don Evans
All year

From 66 to 136 NZ$-B&B
40 rooms
Most CC, •
C-yes/S-ltd
English

Full breakfast
Complementary tea and
coffee
Sitting room, parking,
laundry facilities, smoking
area provided in main foyer.

Family owned and operated an inner city residence of "traditional style", providing comfortable and friendly accommodation, ample shared bathroom facilities, bathrobes available on request. The Windsor vintage car ever popular with guests. E-mail: reservations@ windsorhotel.co.nz *Web site:* windsorhotel.co.nz

DEVONPORT

Devonport Villa Inn
46 Tainui Rd
09-445-8397
Fax: 09-445-9766
Yvonne Lambert
Open all year

175-245 NZ$-B&B
5 rooms, 5 pb
Visa, Mastercard,
American Express,
Rated
C-yes/S-no/P-no/H-ltd
English

Full breakfast
Tea and coffee all day
Sitting room, library, beach 2
minute walk, golf near,
swimming pool, pool, fruit
basket

Historic Edwardian timber guest house restored to the highest standard. Romantic rooms with queen-size beds, handmade quilts, and colonial furniture. Tourism Award winner. E-mail: dvilla@ihug.co.nz *Web site:* devonportvillainn.co.nz

Superior Inns Of NZ
PO Box 32-130
64-9-445-8397
Fax: 64-9-445-9766
Philip Brown
All year

Rates: Inquire-23 rooms,
23 pb
C-ltd/S-no/P-ltd/H-ltd
English

All inns that we offer have private facilities, delicious breakfasts, attention to detail & range from historic city houses to tranquil farm & country stays. Please call/E-mail/fax for brochure. Meet the real NZ people and share in their local knowledge. E-mail: pbb@pop.ihug.co.nz *Web site:* superiorinns.co.nz

NELSON

The Cathedral Inn
369 Trafalgar St South 7001
64-03-548-7369
Fax: 64-03-548-6369
0800-883-377
Suzie & Jim Tohill
All year

150-190 NZ$-B&B
7 rooms, 7 pb
Most CC, •
C-yes/S-ltd/P-no/H-no
English

Full breakfast
Afternoon tea,
complimentary wine, snack
Sitting room, library, bar
service, laundry service,
luggage hoist, off-street
parking, TV, phones, fax,
computers

Circa 1870s manor in tranquil setting, 3 minutes stroll from city, offering spacious comfort, elegance and charm. Beautifully appointed sunny bedrooms include TVs, phones. Open fire, verandah and complimentary refreshements. Quiet, sunny, warm & welcomin E-mail: cathedral.inn@clear.net.nz *Web site:* nz.com/webnz/bbnz/cathdral.htm

PICTON

Ribbonwood
Moenui Bay, Queen Charlotte
Dr, RD1
64-035-742-217
Audrie & David
All year

110 NZ$-B&B
1 rooms, 1 pb
•
C-ltd/S-no/P-no/H-ltd
English

Continental plus breakfast
Afternoon tea, dinner, snacks
Sitting room, library, hot tub,
large bathroom with tub and
separate shower. Separate
toilet with hand basin.

This is a resting place, bush sheltered. Cross the Queen's chain to swim at the beach. Fishing rods available. An ideal base for tripping about the Marlborough Sounds. My home is available for the whole year.

WANAKA

Te Wanaka Lodge
23 Brownston St, Otago
03-443-9224
Fax: 03-443-9246
Rowland & Nora Hastings
Open all year

115-155 NZ$-B&B
13 rooms, 13 pb
Visa, Mastercard,
American Express, •
C-ltd/S-no/P-no/H-yes
English, French, Tagalog

Continental plus breakfast
Snacks
Sitting room, hot tubs tea and
coffee available 24 hours
FOC.

Located in the heart of Wanaka within easy walking distance of shops, restaurants, the beach and golf courses. Te Wanaka Lodge is cozy yet contemporary in design. Trout fishing and golf packages a speciality.   E-mail: tewanakalodge@xtra.co.nz *Web site:* tewanaka.co.nz

WELLINGTON

Tinakori Lodge B&B
182 Tinakori Rd
04-473-3478
Fax: 044-725-554
Mel & John Ainsworth
Open all year

95 NZ$-B&B
9 rooms, 5 pb
Most CC, •
C-ltd/S-no/P-no/H-no
English

Full breakfast
complimentary tea and
coffee

Situated in historic Thorndon. Comfortable furnished 1870s house. Short walk to the Goverment Center and city which features a selection of fine restaurants. TV and phone in rooms.   E-mail: 100035.3214@compuserve.com

WESTLAND

The Breakers Seaside Lodge
Nine Mile Creek—Rapahoe,
South Island 7821
0064-3-762-7743
Fax: 0064 3 762-7733
800-350-590
Frank & Barbara Ash
Closed in June

125-165 NZ$-B&B
3 rooms, 3 pb
Visa, Mastercard,
Rated, •
C-no/S-no/P-no/H-no
English

Full breakfast
Dinner (fee), complimentary
wine
Sitting room, library,
walking, touring, beach and
bush walks, fishing

Stunning views of the coast line, private access to beach. Fall sleep to the sound of waves crashing on the beach below. Dinner by prior arrangement, family owned and operated E-mail: breakers@minidata.co.nz *Web site:* minidata.co.nz/breakers

Caribbean

Caribbean

ANTIGUA

Admiral'S Inn
Nelson's Dockyard,
English Harbour
268-460-1027/1153
Fax: 268-460-1530
Miss Ethelyn Philip
October 16 to
    November 29

84-150 US$-EP
14 rooms, 14 pb
Visa, Mastercard,
American Express, •
C-yes/S-yes/P-no/H-no
English

Full breakfast (fee)
Restaurant, bar, snacks
Sitting room, transportation
to beaches, beachfront
apartments with kitchens
available.

Cozy Inn, lovely historic Georgian brick building, in Nelson's Dockyard, a yachting center. Terrace restaurant overlooking the water. Free welcome cocktail. Flowers in room. E-mail: admirals@candw.ag *Web site:* gray.maine.com/people/admiralsinn

570   Caribbean

BAHAMAS

Romora Bay Club
Colebrooke St,
Harbor Island, Eleuthera
242-333-2325
Fax: 242-333-2500
800-688-0425
Lionel Rotcage
Open all year

200-320 US$-MAP
31 rooms, 31 pb
Visa, Mastercard,
American Express,
Rated, •
C-yes/S-yes/P-no/H-yes
English, French, Italian

Continental plus breakfast
Restaurant under world class
chef
Bar, sitting room, library,
tennis, pool, snorkeling,
scuba diving, deep sea
fishing, horseback riding.

4-star facility on 9 acres of lush gardens; bay side of Harbour Island. Oceanfront protected swimming and sunbathing area with floating docks; water sports available to guests. Original decor with art pieces in rooms and public areas. E-mail: info@romorabay.com
Web site: romorabay.com

BARBADOS

Edgewater Inn
Bathsheba Beach
246-433-9900
Fax: 246-433-9902
The Ross Family
All year

49-149 US$-B&B
20 rooms, 20 pb
Most CC, •
C-yes/S-yes/P-no/H-yes
English, Spanish,
German, French

Continental breakfast
included in rate
Afternoon tea, full menu
available
Bar, room service, oceanside
pool

Romantic and historic old world charm. Modestly furnished. Surrounded by spectacular scenery: ocean, 9 miles of pristine beach, river, rain forest, casual full service dining. A nature lover's and photographer's paradise! E-mail: reservations@edgewaterinn.com
Web site: edgewaterinn.com

BEQUIA

Frangipani Hotel
PO Box 1 St Vincent, The
Grenadines
784-458-3255
Fax: 784-458-3824
M. Kingston & L. Keane
Closed September

40-150 US$-EP
15 rooms, 10 pb
Most CC, •
C-yes/S-yes/P-no/H-no
English, French

Ask about breakfast
Restaurant open
continuously from 7:30am
Bar, laundry, tennis court,
own yacht for trips to other
islands, bikes can be rented.
Dive shop next door

*Charming Caribbean inn coverted from former home of a Bequia Sea Captain with addition of stone built units in hillside garden. Relaxed and friendly with good food and personal service. Restaurant serves breakfast, lunch, snacks, dinner.
E-mail:* frangi@caribsurf.com *Web site:* frangipani.net

BERMUDA

Cambridge Beaches
30 Kings Point,
Sandys Parish MA 02
441-234-0331
Fax: 441-234-3352
800-468-7300
Michael J. Winfield
Open all year

400-650 US$-MAP
81 rooms, 81 pb
•
C-no/S-yes/P-no/H-yes
English, German, Italian,
French

Full breakfast
Lunch, dinner, snacks,
restaurant
Afternoon tea, bar service,
library, bicycles, sauna,
steam, tennis court, 2
swimming pools, bowling,
massage & wellness center.

25 acre peninsula surrounded by beaches. Unique resort environment, cottage style accommodations with a wealth of activities. Romantic, private, special! E-mail: cambeach@ibl.bm
Web site: cambridgebeaches.com

Newstead
PO Box PG BX 196,
Paget PG BX
441-236-6060 Fax: 441-236-7454
800-468-4111
General Manager

Rates: Inquire
52 rooms, 52 pb
Visa, Mastercard,
American Express,
English

Restaurant, Bar
Baby-sitting, pool, dock,
putting green, 2 tennis
courts, putting green,
exercise room, Beach front,
Horseback

BERMUDA

Surf Side Beach Club
90 South Shore,
Warwick WK BX
441-236-7100
Fax: 441-236-9765
800-553-9990
Brynony B. Harvey
All year

125-250 US$-EP
37 rooms, 37 pb
Visa, Mastercard,
American Express, •
C-yes/S-yes/P-yes/H-yes
English

Full breakfast (fee)
Restaurant, snacks, lunch,
dinner
Meeting rooms, business
services, pool, fitness centre,
sauna, cable TV, near center
of Hamilton, Beach front,
Horseback riding

You can have your own cottage set on a terrace above the ocean. The rooms are large, airy and bright with all the touches made for comfort and they have porches as well. Outstanding cuisine, fine wines E-mail: surf@ibl.bm *Web site:* surfside.bm

CAYMAN ISLANDS

Pirates Point Resort
Preston Bay, Box43, Little
Cayman
345-948-1010
Fax: 345-948-1011
Gladys Howard
Ask about time of operation

250 US$-Meals: Inquire
10 rooms, 10 pb
Visa, Mastercard
C-ltd/S-ltd/P-no/H-no
English

All meals included
Excellent Gourmet cuisine
Full dive facilities, 45'
Newton dive boat, dive
classes, scuva rental, nature
walk, birdwatch

You'll be glad the meals are included once you have your first fabulous meal here. The owner is a well trained chef, lucky you! The rooms are in stone and wood cottages set on the beach. Web site: travelguides.com/home/piratespoint/

DOMINICA

Anchorage Hotel
Castle Comfort
767-448-2638
Fax: 767-448-5680
Janice & Carl Armour
All year

100-135 US$-EP
33 rooms, 33 pb
Visa, Mastercard,
American Express, •
C-yes/P-no/H-no
English

Restaurant, lunch, dinner,
afternoon tea
Sitting room, bar service,
snacks, swimming pool,
squash court, dive centre,
whalewatching, tour desk

Anchorage is an informal, elegant hotel. The lounge pool terrace and restaurant open out to a wide expance of Caribbean Sea and brilliant sunsets. The staff are attentive and friendly natives. Anchorage is a home away from home. E-mail: anchorage@mail.com
Web site: anchoragehotel.dm

Portsmouth Beach Hotel
P.O. Box 34, Roseau
767-445-5142
Fax: 767-445-5599
Janice A. Armour
All year

50-60 US$-EP
40 rooms, 40 pb
Visa, Mastercard,
American Express, •
C-yes/P-no
English

Lunch, dinner, afternoon tea,
snacks
Sitting room. bar service,
swimming pool

An informal and relaxing place to enjoy the sea, sand and sun, yet within minutes from the extravaganza of nature found in Dominica—waterfalls, parrot preserve, historic Fort Shirley, rowing up Indian River, flora and fauna.... E-mail: pbh@cwdom.dm
Web site: anchoragehotel.dm

JAMAICA

Charela Inn
Norman Manley Blvd, Negril
809-957-4648/49
Fax: 809-957-4414
Daniel Grizzle
Open all year

108-210 US$-MAP (fee)
49 rooms, 49 pb
Visa, Mastercard,
Rated, •
C-yes/S-yes/P-no/H-yes
French, German, English

Full breakfast (fee)
Lunch, dinner, restaurant
Bar service, sitting room,
library, swimming pool, free
garage 1st. night, garage

A quiet, intimate hideaway on Negril beach, for singles, couples, and families. Set amidst lush tropical gardens, gourmet Jamaican/French cuisine is served.
E-mail: charela@cwjamaica.com *Web site:* negril.com/cimain.htm/

JAMAICA

Native Son Villas
Manley Blvd,
Seaward Side, Negril
908-598-1158
Fax: 908/598-1151
Wesley & Sarah Burton
Open all year

130-275 US$-B&B
4 rooms, 4 pb
Visa, Mastercard,
American Express,
C-yes/S-yes/P-no/H-ltd
English, Jamaican Patois

Full breakfast
Sitting room, library,
welcome beverages, free
garage 1st. night, garage. Four
houses available.

Exclusive beachfront complex of four elegant houses in lush tropical gardens on private beach. Spacious rooms. Personal housekeeper/cook. A unique beach experience.
E-mail: sarahburt@aol.com *Web site:* travelguides.com/bb/native_son/

ROATAN

Georphy'S Hideaway
West Bay, Honduras
504-445-1794
508-856-0854
Rudy
Open all year

30-75 US $-EP
10 rooms, 10 pb
Visa, Mastercard,
American Express
C-yes/S-yes/P-no/H-yes
Spanish, English

Best breakfast in town
cooked by Rudy
Restaurant, Bar, lunch,
snacks
AC, Cabins for one or five,
conference room, gym,
ceiling fans, phones

Exquisite lodgins next to the beach. Superb food cook by locals. The best deal on the beach. Snorkeling trips arranged for you. Can arrange to pick up and return to airport.
E-mail: georphi@webtv.net

Sunset Inn
West End Village,
West End, Honduras
504-445-1925
Fax: 504-445-1925
Philip Stevens & Loretta Miles
Open all year

30-50 US$-MAP
15 rooms, 15 pb
Visa, Mastercard,
American Express, •
C-yes/S-yes/P-yes/H-yes
Spanish, English

Full breakfast
Lunch, dinner (fee)
Afternoon tea & snacks (fee),
restaurant, bar service,
swimming pool, dive shop,
snorkel, kayak, car rental

Sunset Inn, a beachfront resort, centrally located in West End Village, offers professional personal, attentive services through our own dive operation Ocean Divers. A recognised center of excellence by PADI, BSAC, NAVI and TDI.   E-mail: oceandivers@globalnet.hn
Web site: roatanet.com/sunset_inn

ST. LUCIA

Sea Horse Inn
P.O. Box 1825, Castries,
Marigot Bay
758-451-4436
Fax: 758-451-4872
Erica & Jim Kany
All year

100-120 US$-B&B
8 rooms, 6 pb
Visa, Mastercard,
American Express, •
C-ltd/S-ltd/P-no/H-no
English, German

Full breakfast
Restaurants, soups,
sandwiches
Sitting room, library,
swimming pool, welcome
drinks, Monteverde Forest

A small and intimate hideaway set on a tropical hillside overlooking Marigot Bay. Highly personalised service, unique Caribbean/European ambiance. Pool on premises, restaurants, beach, shops withing walking distance. Tours, water-sports arranged.
E-mail: seahorse@candw.lc *Web site:* seahorse-inn.com

TRINIDAD TOBAGO

Laguna Mar Resort
65.5 Marker, Paria Rd,
Blanchisseuse
868-628-3731
Fax: 868-628-3737
G. (Fred) & Barbara Zollna
Open all year

50-75 TT$-EP
16 rooms, 16 pb
Visa, Mastercard,
Rated, •
C-yes/S-yes/P-no/H-no
English, German

Full breakfast (fee)
Restaurant-all meals,
afternoon tea
Peaceful co-existence of,
humans with nature,
oceanfront property, in-
house sauna, canoes, bar
service, library

A unique blend of safe ocean front and river bathing as well as rain forest waterfalls. Hiking trails, excellent birding, fish with our local fishermen, great ethnic and seafood cooked by locals.   E-mail: info@lagunamar.com *Web site:* lagunamar.com/

TRINIDAD TOBAGO────────────

Mount Marie Resort	45 US$-MAP	Full breakfast
Mt. Marie, PO Box 404,	11 rooms, 11 pb	Lunch, dinner, restaurant
Scarborough	Most CC, *Rated*, •	Bar service, sitting room,
868-639-2014-2056	C-yes/S-yes/P-no/H-yes	bicycles, tennis court, hotel
Fax: 868-639-1607	English	shuttle to airport.
Mrs. Jeni Stanisclaus		
Open all year		

Features and service include: bar and lounge, restaurant, ocean-view terrace, car rental, direct-dialing telephone. All rooms are fully carpeted and air-conditioned. Masseur, taxi service.   E-mail: options@trinidad.net

TURKS/CAICOS────────────

The Windmills Plantation	595-995 US$-AP	Full breakfast
N. Beach Road, Salt Cay	8 rooms, 8 pb	Restaurant, complimentary
649-946-6962	Visa, Mastercard,	wine, snacks
Fax: 649-946-6930	American Express, •	Sitting room, library,
800-822-7715	C-no/S-no/P-no/H-no	bicycles, swimming pool, bar
Pat & Guy Lovelace	English	service, lunch and dinner at
Nov. 1 to May 31		our restaurant

Island hideaway, population 60, on historic salt island. All inclusive; meals beverages, wines and island tours. Meals feature a culinary tour of the Caribbean.   E-mail: plantation@tciway.tc *Web site:* saltcaysite.com

Central-S. America

Belize

SAN IGNACIO────────────

Duplooy'S	80-175 Belize$-EP, MAP,	Afternoon tea, snacks,
P.O. Box 180, Cayo	AP	Restaurant, lunch
501-0-92-3101	20 rooms, 11 pb	Bar service, Library, Lunch
Fax: 501-0-92-3301	Visa, Mastercard,	and Dinner for a fee,
Judy duPlooy	American Express, •	Receptions, room service,
All year	C-yes/S-no/P-no/H-no	concierge, complimentary
	English, Spanish	coffee in A.M.

Remote nature lover's eco-lodge. Known for beautiful location, friendly staff, good food. Birding, swimming, horses, canoes, trails, botanic garden, tours   E-mail: duplooys@btl.net *Web site:* duplooys.com

Costa Rica

SANTA BARBARA DE HEREDIA────────────

Finca Rosa Blanca	145 US$-B&B	Full breakfast
SJO 1201	9 rooms, 9 pb	Restaurant, bar (fee)
011-506-269-9392	Visa, American Express,	Waterfall pool, horses,
Fax: 011-506-269-9555	*Rated*, •	recreation room, library,
Glenn & Teri Jampol	C-yes/S-no/P-no/H-no	barbeque, country quiet,
Open all year	Eng., Spanish, French,	Tractor Museum
	Dan., Grm., Dutch	

Famous country hideaway, extraordinary architecture. Six suites, two villas filled with original art. Waterfall pool, horseback riding. 15 minutes from International Airport. Other innkeepers receive 20% disc't.   E-mail: info@finca-rblanca.co.cr *Web site:* finca-rblanca.co.cr

Guatemala

ANTIGUA ─────────────────────────────────

Posada Del Angel
4a Avenida Sur #24 "A"
011-502-8-320-260
Fax: 011-502-8-320-260
800 934-0065
Mary Sue Morris
Open all year

110 US$-B&B
5 rooms, 5 pb
Visa, Mastercard,
American Express,
Rated, •
C-ltd/S-ltd/P-no/H-no
English, Spanish

Full breakfast
Ask about food service
Golf, horseback riding,
mountain bikes, tennis,
heated pool, exploring,
hiking, crafts markets, Sauna,
solarium.

*Romantic, elegant, comfortable Spanish Colonial Inn. Fireplaces & cable TV in each room.
Our concierge will help you plan the perfect trip. 10% discount per month.   E-mail: elangel@
ibm.net Web site: travellog.com/guatemala/antigua/posadangel/welcome.html*

Mexico

ACAPULCO ───────────────────────────────

Mision Hotel
Felipe Valle 12 39300
74-82-3643
Fax: 74-82-2076
Maria Elena S. Alcerreca
Open all year

200-400 Mexican$-EP
28 rooms, 28 pb
C-yes/S-yes/P-yes/H-yes
Spanish, English, Greek

Continental breakfast
Full breakfast available
Shaddy and peacefull, patio
with mango trees,
Refrigerators, electric
blankets.

*Built in the 1700s and remodeled on 1966. Next to downtown and all services. Unique
colonial design. It is an Oasis! Free continental breakfast.   E-mail: mision@usa.net*

GUANAJUATO ─────────────────────────────

**La Casa De Espiritus
Alegres**
La Ex-Hacienda La Trinidad
#1, Marfil 36250
011-52-473-31013
Fax: 011-52-473-31013
Betsy McNair
Open all year

95-150 US$-B&B
8 rooms, 8 pb
Visa, Mastercard,
American Express,
Rated
C-no/S-no/P-no/H-yes
Spanish, English

Full sumptuos breakfast
Dinner by request, Bar in the
garden
A skeleton in every closet,
US phone: 408-423-0181,
sitting room, library,
Snorkeling, diving

*The House of Good Spirits is located in a former silver mining hacienda dating back to the
1700's. California artists, Joan & Carol Summers, bought the house in 1979, restored,
remodeled, & filled it with folk art from all over Mexico.   E-mail: casaspirit@aol.com*

PATZCUARO ──────────────────────────────

Hotel Mansion Iturbe
Portal Morelos 50, Michoacan
61600
434-2-03-68
Fax: 43-13-45-93
Margarita Arriaga & Sons
All year

70-90 US$-B&B
14 rooms, 14 pb
Visa, Mastercard,
American Express, •
C-yes/S-no/P-no/H-no
Spanish, French,
German, English

Full breakfast
Restaurant, afternoon tea,
comp. wine
Sitting room, bar service,
snacks, library, bicycles,
Spanish, French and cooking
courses available.

*A historical mansion of the XVII century with 14 rooms, individually decorated. Enjoy the
secrets of the Michoacan cuisine in our Dona Paca Restaurant. Exclusive tours can be
arranged. Bicycles available.   E-mail: pazcuaro@mail.giga.com
Web site: mexonline.com/iturbe.htm*

SAN MIGUEL DE ALLENDE————————————————————

Casa De Liza En El Parque	105-225 US$-B&B	Full breakfast
Bajada del Chorro #7 37700	5 rooms, 5 pb	Complimentary wine, lunch
011 52 415 2 0352	Visa, •	(fee)
Fax: 011 52 415 2 6144	C-yes/S-no/P-no	Library, jacuzzi
Liza Kisber & Charlotte Levine	Spanish, English	
All year		

On the paradise-like grounds of an in-town colonial estate. Romantic and elegant accommodations designed like walk-in paintings. Beautiful gardens and fountains, antiques, fireplace, fine art.   E-mail: casaliza@unisono.net.mx *Web site:* infosma.com/casadeliza

Casa Luna B&B	90 US$-B&B	Full breakfast
Pila Seca #11,	8 rooms, 8 pb	Snacks, bar service
Guanajuato 37700	Visa, Mastercard,	Sitting room, library, suites,
52-415-2-1117	Most CC, *Rated*, •	fireplace, tours available, can
Fax: 51-415-2-1117	C-ltd/S-ltd/P-no/H-no	rent entire property to one
Dianne Kushner	English, some Spanish	party with special services.
Open all year		

Casa Luna is a restored, 300-year-old villa in the historic center of the city, which embodies the romance of Mexico with patios, fountains, colorfully decorated with rooms with fireplaces and plant-filled courtyards.   E-mail: casaluna@unisono.net.mx *Web site:* casaluna.com

Hacienda De Las Flores	46-117 US$-B&B	Full breakfast
Hospicio 16 37700	16 rooms, 14 pb	Restaurant & catering on
415-2-1808/1859	Visa, Mastercard,	request
Fax: 415-2-8383	*Rated*, •	Bar, pool, boutique,
A. Franyuti, C. Finkelstein	C-yes/S-yes/P-yes/H-ltd	bathroom amenities, small
Open all year	English, French	conference room, tennis, golf
		nearby.

Located only 2 blocks from downtown. Colonial style with TV, electric blankets, beautiful gardens & a pool. Connections to golf, tennis, horseback riding. Great cultural city. Fresh flowers, basket of fruits. Some rooms rent for long term.   E-mail: hhflores@unisono.net.mx *Web site:* bapqro-mex.com/hhflores/

Hotel Villa Jacaranda	130-190 US$-EP, B&B	Breakfast by arrangement
Aldama 53 37700	16 rooms, 16 pb	Restaurant, bar
011-52-415-21015	Visa, Mastercard,	Tennis courts, golf,
Fax: 011-52-415-20883	American Express,	salon/theater, 10 person
Don & Gloria Fenton	Most CC, *Rated*, •	jacuzzi, Sauna, solarium.
Open all year	C-yes/S-yes/P-yes/H-ltd	
	Spanish, English	

Two cobblestoned streets from Mexico's loveliest colonial square. The worlds best year-round climate. Free use of golf course, tennis courts. Free "Gourmet Magazine Margarita".   E-mail: jacaranda@mpsnet.com.mx *Web site:* villajacaranda.com

Mi Casa B&B	75-85 US$-B&B	Full breakfast
Canal 58, Apartado 496 37700	4 rooms, 4 pb	Morning coffee sent to room
001-52-415-2-2492	*Rated*C-yes/S-ltd/P-	in a.m.
Fax: 001-52-415-2-0121	yes/H-no	Sitting room, laundry,
Carmen McDaniel	Spanish, English	bicycles, interesting sites
Open all year		nearby. Bar service

Mi Casa, a National Historical Monument, serves a hearty (and attractive) home-cooked breakfast. Rooms in flower filled roof-top patio. Morning coffee or cocktails watching pink sunsets of San Miguel. Free Margaritas & guacamole dip   E-mail: tism@mpsnet.com.mx *Web site:* travelguides.com/bb/micasa

ZIHUATANEJO————————————

Puerto Mio	225-750 US$-B&B	Full breakfast
Paseo del Morro, #5 40880	30 rooms, 30 pb	Lunch, dinner, afternoon tea,
011-52-755-43344	Visa, Mastercard,	restaurant
Fax: 011-52-755-43535	American Express, •	Snacks, bar service, library,
888-633-3295	C-no/S-yes/P-no/H-no	swimming pool, private
Jaime Cantarell	Spanish, English, French	beach, diving, fishing, sailing,
Open all year		antique markets

Situated on 25 lush tropical acres, Puerto Mio offers a truly unique get-away. All rooms have magnificent views of the bay and the Pacific Ocean. Live life on a private estate with a staff of 70 ready to please you. E-mail: puertomio@puertomio.com.mx
Web site: puertomio.com.mx

Panama

BOCAS ISLAND————————————

Hotel Las Brisas	12-35 US$-EP	Lunch, Dinner (fee)
PO Box #1	37 rooms, 37 pb	Sitting room, library,
507-757-9248	Visa, Mastercard,	bicycles, kayaks, boats for
Fax: 507-757-9247	American Express, •	rent, fish from the bedroom
Harry Bendiburg	C-yes/S-yes/P-no/H-yes	
Open all year	Spanish, English, Indian	

Boats come to our hotel to pick-up our guests and take them for tours to surrounding islands and indian villages. Our hotel sits on the tranquil waters of the Caribbean sea. E-mail: bendi69@yahoo.com

Peru

IQUITOS————————————

Explorama Lodges	768-1223 US$-AP	Full breakfast
Ave La Marina #340, Box 446,	142 rooms, 118 pb	All meals included
Amazon	Visa, Mastercard,	Restaurant, bar, sitting room,
51-94-25-2530	American Express,	library, virgin rainforest
Fax: 51-94-25-2533	Most CC, •	trails, canoeing, medicinal
Peter S. Jenson	C-yes/S-yes/P-no/H-no	plant garden, horseback
Open all year	Sp., Eng., Ger., Port.,	riding.
	French, Italian	

35 years as foremost Amazon lodge operator. Owner/operator of four jungle lodges. Visits can include the world's longest canopy walkway-160 km. on the Amazon and Napo rivers. E-mail: amazon@explorama.com *Web site:* explorama.com/

Europe

Austria

DURNSTEIN

Hotel Scholss Durnstein
A-3601
+43-2711-212
Fax: +43-2711-212-30
Hans & Rosemarie Thiery
April - October

2200-2800 Austrian$-
B&B, MAP
38 rooms, 38 pb
Most CC, *Rated*C-
yes/S-yes/P-ltd/H-yes
English, French, Italian

Full breakfast
Restaurant (fee)
Bar service, sitting room,
library, bicycles, sauna,
swimming pool.

Built in 1630, Renaissance castle converted into a hotel of great style. Magnificent position in the most picturesque section of the Danube. 10% discount on room rates.
E-mail: schlosshotel@duernstein.at *Web site:* duernstein.at/schlosshotel/

REITH IM ALPBACHTAL

Schloss Matzen
Reith im Alpbachtal, Tyrol A-
6230
707-937-0618
Fax: 707-937-0618
888-837-0618
Margaret Fox Kump
May–October;
mid Dec –end of Feb.

140-250 US$-B&B
10 rooms, 10 pb
Visa, Mastercard, •
C-yes/S-no/H-no
English, German, French

Full breakfast
Complimentary wine, snacks
Sitting room, swimming pool.

Tyrolean country castle with modern comforts. American-run, near Innsbruck. Convenient for day trips into Italy & Germany. Year-round sports. All bookings from U.S. may use 888-837-0618 to make reservations. E-mail: info@schlossmatzen.com *Web site:* schlossmatzen.com

SALZBURG

Schloss Haunsperg
Hammerstr. 32 A-5411
6245-80-662
Fax: 6245-85680
Fam. Von Gernerth
Open all year

1900 Austrian$-B&B
8 rooms, 8 pb
Most CC, •
C-yes/S-yes/P-yes/H-no
Enlgish, Italian, German

Full breakfast
Snacks, complimentary wine
Sitting room, library,
bicycles, tennis court, Free
golf fees if available

Our gracious 14 century country manor house offers 8 superbly appointed double rooms and suites with period furniture for 2-5 people. 3rd night 50% off.
E-mail: office@schloshotels.co.at *Web site:* schloshotels.co.at/schloshotels

VIENNA

Hotel Kugel
Siebensterngasse 43 A-1070
43-1-523-3355
Fax: 43-1-523-3355-5
Johannes Roller
February 4 - January 7

600-990 Austrian$-B&B
38 rooms, 18 pb
•
C-yes/S-yes/P-yes/H-yes
Ger., Eng., Polish, Fr.,
Ital., Russian

Continental plus breakfast
Bar service
Library, sport center, bicycle
renting, gyms, Fitness center
1 minute.

Historic building, family operated in the 4th generation. Ideally situated amidst restaurants, shopping facilities & art galleries. Excellent access to all parts of Vienna by public transport. 4th night 25% off. 5 minutes to European swim-sports hall.
Web site: travelguides.com/home/hotelkugel/

Belgium

BRUGES

The Egmond Hotel
Minnewater I5, Brugge, W.
Vlaanderen B-8000
32-50-341445
Fax: 32-50-342940
Kris Van Laere
February 15 - January 5

3,600-4,250 Belgium$-
B&B
8 rooms, 8 pb
Rated, •
C-yes/S-yes/P-no/H-no
English, German,
French, Dutch

Full breakfast buffet
Afternoon tea, honesty bar
Sitting room, bicycles–all
rooms have garden, park
view, fitness massage

This charming manor house kept the romantic interior. 18th century fireplaces. Rooms are ensuite & individually decorated. Setting next to "The Lake of Love". Private parking, lounge with coffee and tea facilities. Family-run property.   E-mail: info@egmond.be *Web site:* egmond.be

BRUGGE

Alegria B&B
St.Jakobsstraat 34b, W.
Flanders B-8000
+32-50-330937
Fax: +32-50-437686
Veronique De Muynck
All year

2,000-2,500 Belgian$-B&B
3 rooms, 3 pb
Visa, Mastercard, •
C-yes/S-yes/P-yes/H-no
Italian, French, Dutch,
German

Full breakfast
Gilde der Brugse
Gastenkamers, beauty shop,
solarium, private garage

Alegria B&B is situated in the heart of Bruges near the market place. Our personalised formula: daily cleaned newly decorated rooms with personal bathrooms, and breakfast in bed. Beauty treatments available.   E-mail: alegriabb@skynet.be *Web site:* users.skynet.be/alegriabb/

BRUSSELS

Welcome Hotel
5 Rue de Peuplier B-1000
32-02-219-9546
Fax: 32-02-217-1887
Michael & Sophie Smeesters
All year

Rates: Inquire-EP
6 rooms, 6 pb
Visa, Mastercard, Diners,
C-yes/S-yes/P-yes/H-yes
Flemish, English

Full breakfast (fee)
1 small restaurant, seats 18
people
Meeting rooms, limousine for
airport transfer, nice bar

A charming small hotel where the bed are large and comfortable. A popular spot, so book well ahead. Totally renovated in 98. Very close to the green Plaza—4 blocks. E-mail: info@hotelwelcome.com *Web site:* hotelwelcome.com/

Czech Republic

PRAGUE

Hotel U Krale Karia
Nerudova-Uvoz 4 CZ-11800
+4202-5753-1211
Fax: +4202-5388-11
+4202-5753-2869
Ing. Karel Klubal
All year

4,400-6,700 Czk$-B&B
19 rooms, 19 pb
Visa, Mastercard,
American Express,
Diners, •
C-yes/S-yes/P-yes/H-no
Czech, English, German

Full breakfast
Restaurant, lunch, dinner,
afternoon tea
Sitting room, bar service,
snacks, solarium, hair
dryers, TV/Satellite,
fireplaces

Our hotel is significant with family atmosphere and we take that same care of our clients. Originally a gothic building—a part of Benedictine Order—was rebuilt in 1639 into a baroque house.   E-mail: ukrale@tnet.cz *Web site:* romantichotels.cz/mainhkk.htm

England, U.K.

AMBLESIDE

Rothay Manor Hotel
Rothay Bridge, Cumbria LA22
0EH
015-394-33605
Fax: 015-394-33607
Nigel and Stephen Nixon
Closed January

122 English$-B&B
18 rooms, 18 pb
Visa, Mastercard,
American Express,
Rated, •
C-yes/S-yes/P-no/H-yes
English

Full breakfast
Lunch, dinner, restaurant
Bar service, sitting room,
free use of leisure club
nearby, cross-country ski,
mountain bike, self
contained apartment.

Situated in the heart of the Lake District, this Regency country-house hotel has an international reputation for cuisine, comfort, and relaxed atmosphere.
E-mail: hotel@rothaymanor.co.uk *Web site:* rothaymanor.co.uk

BATH

Bailbrook Lodge Hotel
35/37 London Rd W, Avon BA1
7HZ
01225-859090
Fax: 01225-852299
Mrs. K.M. Addison
Open all year

58-70 English$-MAP
12 rooms, 12 pb
Visa, Mastercard,
American Express,
Rated, •
C-yes/S-yes/P-no/H-ltd
English

Full breakfast
Bar, Restaurant (fee)
Historic houses and, famous
villages nearby, cross-
country ski, mountain bike,
self contained apartment.

Splendid Georgian hotel close to world heritage City Bath. Beautiful countryside. Traditional decorations, rooms with all facilities; some four-poster beds.   E-mail: hotel@
bailbrooklodge.demon.co.uk *Web site:* bailbrooklodge.demon.co.uk

Marlborough House
1 Marlborough Lane, Avon
BA1 2NQ
011-440-1225-318-175
Fax: 011-440-1225-466-127
Laura & Charley Dunlap
All year

60-85 English$-B&B
7 rooms, 7 pb
Visa, Mastercard,
American Express,
Diners, •
C-yes/S-no/P-yes/H-no
English

Full breakfast
Lunch, Dinner, tea, snacks,
restaurant
Good conversation, bar
service, sitting room

Enchanting small hotel in the heart of Georgian Bath, specializing in organic foods, world cuisine & good conversation. Elegantly furnished with antiques including four-poster beds, but operated in a friendly & informal style.   E-mail: mars@manque.dircon.co.uk
Web site: s-h-systems.co.uk/hotels/marlbor1.html

Oakleigh House
19 Upper Oldfield Park, Avon,
Somerset BA2 3JX
01225-315698
Fax: 01225-448223
Jenny King
All year

60-68 English$-B&B
4 rooms, 4 pb
Visa, Mastercard,
American Express, •
C-no/S-no/P-no/H-no
English, French, German

Full breakfast
Sitting room

Secret guesthouse welcoming visitors from all over the world for over 16 years. Exquisitely situated, quiet yet a pleasant walk from town centre. This is how all guesthouses should be. Private car park.   E-mail: oakleigh@which.net *Web site:* oakleigh-house.co.uk

Paradise House
86-88 Holloway, Avon,
Somerset BA2 4PX
01225-3-17723
Fax: 01225-4-82005
David & Annie Lanz
Open all year

65 English$-B&B
8 rooms, 8 pb
Visa, Mastercard,
American Express,
Most CC, *Rated*
C-yes/S-ltd/P-no/H-ltd
English, German, French

Full breakfast
Sitting room, English
Croquet, French Boules
(when the weather permits),
color TV with remote.

Elegant Georgian house on a quiet street, only 5 minutes walk from Bath centre. Lovely garden with panoramic city views. 3 nights or more 10% reduction.   E-mail: paradise@
apleyhouse.easynet.co.uk *Web site:* gratton.co.uk/paradise

BATH

Wentworth House
106 Bloomfield Rd, NE
Somerset BA2 2AP
01225-339193
Fax: 01225-310460
Geoff & Avril Kitching
Open all year

60-95 English$-B&B
15 rooms, 15 pb
Visa, Mastercard,
American Express,
Most CC, *Rated*, •
C-ltd/S-ltd/P-no/H-no
English

Full breakfast
Bar service
Sitting room, library, color
TV with remote. Car park,
outdoor swimming pool
open in the summer months,
direct dial phones.

Victorian Mansion set in grounds in quiet part of city, large free car park & views. Golf and walks closeby. Most rooms have antique beds. Being fully licenced, you could also enjoy the pleasure of a quiet drink in the resident's lounge.   E-mail: wentworthhouse@dial.pipex.com *Web site:* dspace.dial.pipex.com/wentworthhouse/

BATTLE

Little Hemingfold
Hastings Rd. Telham,
East Sussex TN33 0TT
004-41424-774338
Fax: 004-41424-775351
Paul Slater
February 11 - January 3rd.

76-88 English$-B&B
12 rooms, 12 pb
Visa, Mastercard,
American Express, •
C-yes/S-yes/P-yes/H-no
English, French

Full breakfast
Dinner, afternoon tea,
restaurant, bar
Sitting room, tennis court,
swimming pool, 2 acre trout
lake, 40 acre farmland, self
contained apartment.

Part 17th century hotel set in 40 acres farm and woodland with 2 acre trout lake and grass tennis court. 12 individual bedrooms, 6 on ground floor in adjoinning courtyard. Renownned cuisine in relaxed informal atmosphere.

BELFORD

Waren House Hotel
Waren Mill,
Northumberland NE70 7EE
016-682-14581
Fax: 016-682-14484
Anita & Peter Laverack
Open all year

115 English$-B&B
10 rooms, 10 pb
Visa, Mastercard,
American Express,
Most CC, *Rated*, •
C-no/S-no/P-yes/H-no
English

Full breakfast
Dinner, restaurant
Bar service, sitting room,
library, hot tubs, seven acres
of land, self contained
apartment.

Traditional country house hotel, rural setting. On coast overlooking Holy Island, excellent food, superb accommodations. 250 plus bin wine list. Special discount available.   E-mail: enquiries@warrenhousehotel.co.uk *Web site:* warrenhousehotel.co.uk

HAMPSHIRE, LONDON

Squirrels Leap
Queen Mary Close,
Fleet GU13 8QR
0-1252-616746
Fax: 0-1252-627473
Judith Cooper
Open all year

45-60 English$-B&B
3 rooms, 3 pb
C-yes/S-no/P-no/H-ltd
English

Continental plus breakfast
Bicycles, suites, conference
room, TV, 2 ground floor
suites have VCRs,
refrigeratorts & kitchenettes.
Washing machine available.

Squirrels Leap is an old English coach house in a beautiful wooded garden setting, but close to all amenities. An ideal base for exploring London(45 minutes) and Southern England.   E-mail: sldetails@aol.com *Web site:* members.aol.com/SLdetails

HOLT

Morston Hall Hotel
Morston, Norfolk NR25 7AA
012-637-41041
Fax: 012-637-40419
Galton & Tracy Blackiston
February - January

180 English$-MAP
6 rooms, 6 pb
Visa, American Express,
Rated
C-yes/S-ltd/P-yes/H-yes
English

Full breakfast Sundays
Lunch, dinner (included),
restaurant
Sitting room, afternoon tea,
three acre garden,
Conservatory, self contained
apartment.

On the Norfolk coast, large spacious luxurious bedrooms, overlooking beautiful gardens with unobtrusive service. Food being of the highest standard. Rated by AA, Tourist Board and Michelin. STAR   E-mail: reception@morstonhall.demon.co.uk *Web site:* morstonhall.demon.co.uk/

LONDON————————————————————————————————

22 Jermyn Street	200 English$-Meals:	Continental or full breakfast
22 Jermyn St,	Inquire	(fee)
St. James's SW1Y 6HL	18 rooms, 18 pb	Lunch, dinner (fee)
44-171-734-2353	Most CC, *Rated*, •	Complimentary champagne,
Fax: 44-171-734-0750	C-yes/S-yes/P-yes/H-yes	CD Rom library, bicycles,
800-682-7808	English, French, Italian,	near health and sports club,
Henry Togna, Laurie Smith	Sp., Arabic	Sauna, solarium
Open all year		

Luxurious award winning townhouse in the heart of London, ideal for theatre. Let Henry and Laurie take care of you! Complimentary wine & snacks. 13 of the rooms are suites.
E-mail: office@22jermyn.com *Web site:* 22jermyn.com/

Viarage Private Hotel	68-95 English$-B&B	Full breakfast
10 Vicarage Gate, Kensington	18 rooms, 2 pb	
W8 4AG	C-yes/S-yes/P-no/H-no	
0171-229-4030	English, Spanish	
Fax: 0171-792-5989		
Eileen & Martin Diviney		
All year		

The Vicarage is a family-run hotel, taking pride in offering its guests a relaxing and charming "home away from home" in London with many guests returning on a regular basis. E-mail: reception@londonvicaragehotel.com *Web site:* londonvicaragehotel.com

MAIDSTONE————————————————————————————————

Willington Court	48-65 English$-B&B	Full breakfast
Willington St.,	10 rooms, 10 pb	Lunch, dinner, snacks,
Kent ME15 8JW	Visa, Mastercard,	restaurant
44-0-1622-738885	American Express, •	Bar, beautifull en suite
Fax: 44-0-1622-631790	C-ltd/S-ltd/P-no/H-ltd	bathroom, sitting room,
Sylvette & Martin	Fr., It., Germ., Spa.,	library, cable TV, conference
All year	Arab., Jap., Rus.	facility, antiques, Leeds
		Castle, London

Magnificent house with a large famous collection of modern paintings acquired over 50 years and huge wine cellars. Perfect for newely weds and romantic couples. Free wine for 3rd. night E-mail: willington@maidstone.prestel.co.uk *Web site:* bbchannel.com/bbc/p604332.asp

PAR————————————————————————————————

Nanscawen House	76 English$-B&B	Full English breakfast
Prideaux Rd, St. Blazey,	3 rooms, 3 pb	Bar service
Cornwall PL24 2SR	Visa, Mastercard,	Sitting room, hot tubs,
017-2681-4488	*Rated*	swimming pool, self
Fax: 017-2681-4488	C-ltd/S-no/P-no/H-no	contained apartment.
Keith & Fiona Martin	English	
Closed Christmas		

Granite-built Georgian house beautifully set in Luxulyan Valley. Luxurious rooms, each with spa bath. South facing garden of five acres. E-mail: keithmartin@tesco.net
Web site: homepages.tesco.net/~keithmartin

RYE————————————————————————————————

Little Orchard House	64 English$-B&B	Full breakfast
West Street,	3 rooms, 3 pb	Complimentary wine
East Sussex TN31 7ES	Visa, Mastercard,	Sitting room, library, garden
017-972-23831	C-no/S-yes/P-no/H-no	for guest use, Winter
Fax: 017-972-23831	English	houseparties.
Sara Brinkhurst		
Open all year		

Elegant Georgian townhouse in medieval Rye. Antique furnishings, quiet central location, generous country breakfasts. Relaxed country house. Atmosphere is excellent.

ST. AUSTELL————————————————————

Boscundle Manor	110-130 English$-B&B	Full breakfast
Tregrehan, Cornwall PL25 3RL	10 rooms, 10 pb	Dinner, restaurant
017-268-13557	Visa, Mastercard,	Bar service, sitting room,
Fax: 017-268-14997	American Express,	swimming pool, croquet,
Andrew & Mary Flint	*Rated*, •	library, golf, table tennis,
April - October	C-yes/S-yes/P-yes/H-no	gymnasium, snooker
	English	

Lovely 18th century house set in wooded grounds. Run like luxurious private house with many antiques. Beautifully prepared fresh food, outstanding wine list.

STRATFORD-UPON-AVON————————————

Victoria Spa Lodge	60 English$-B&B	Full breakfast
Bishopton Lane,	7 rooms, 7 pb	Restaurant, lunch, dinner,
Warwickshire CV37 9QY	Visa, Mastercard,	afternoon tea
01789-267985	*Rated*	Country setting by canal.
Fax: 01789-204728	C-yes/S-no/P-no/H-no	Tennis, bicycles, pool, sauna,
Paul and Dreen Tozer	English	hot tub, library, bar service,
Open all year		sitting room, snacks,
		complimentary wine.

Attractive and very comfortable home. Walks along tow-paths to Stratford and other villages. Once home to Sir Barry Jackson (founder of B'ham Rep:) and cartoonist Bruce Bairnsfather.   E-mail: ptozer@victoriaspalodge.demon.co.uk *Web site:* stratford-upon-avon.co.uk/victoriaspa.htm

SWAFFHAM————————————————————

Strattons	90-150 English$-B&B	Full breakfast
4 Ash Close, Norfolk PE37 7NH	7 rooms, 7 pb	Dinner, restaurant, bar
01760-723845	Most CC	service.
Fax: 01760-720458	C-yes/S-no/P-yes/H-no	Afternoon tea, snacks, sitting
Les & Vanessa Scott	English	room, hot tubs, swimming
Open all year		pool, having Royal Coat of
		Arms, self contained
		apartment.

Emma Hamilton stayed in this beautiful Palladian Villa "on a trip to the theatre in 1806",- continues to impress the diletante and virtuosos with it's artistry, antiques and award winning cooking.

TOTNES————————————————————

The Old Forge At Totnes	52-72 English$-B&B	Full breakfast
Seymour Place,	10 rooms, 10 pb	Snacks, restaurant, bar
Devon TQ9 5AY	Visa, Mastercard,	service, tea
0044-1803-862-174	Most CC, •	Afternoon tea, bar service,
Fax: 0044-1803-865-385	C-yes/S-no/P-no/H-yes	sitting room, bicycles, hot
Jeannie Allnutt	English, French, German	tubs, conservatory lounge,
Open all year		whirlpool spa, hands-on
		courses

Delightful creeper-clad 600-year-old stone building. Walled garden, coacharch, working smithy-pottery. Cottage suite suitable most disable/families. Huge choice breakfast: traditional, vegetarian, continental, special diet Web site: co.uk/oldforgetotnes

WHITBY————————————————————

Dunsley Hall Hotel	104.50 English$-B&B	Full breakfast
Dunsley, Yorkshire YO21 3TL	18 rooms, 18 pb	Lunch, dinner, afternoon tea,
01947-893437	Visa, American Express,	restaurant
Fax: 01947-893505	•	Bar service, snacks, sitting
Ian & Rosalie Buckle	C-yes/S-yes/P-no/H-yes	room, tennis court, sauna,
All year	English, Spanish	swimming pool, fitness room

Country house hotel set in four acres of landscaped gardens. Countryside and coastal views. Peacefull, relaxing setting. Mini suites and four poster beds.

WINDERMERE————————————————————————————————

Linthwaite House Hotel	75-189 English$-26	Lunch, dinner, restaurant,
Crook Rd, Cumbria,	rooms, 26 pb	tea, snacks
The Lakes LA23 3JA	Visa, Mastercard,	Bar service, sitting room,
0044-15394-88600	American Express,	swimming pool; sauna; hot
Fax: 0044-15394-88601	*Rated*, ●	tubs; tennis courts; off-site.
Mike Bevans	C-no/S-yes/P-no/H-yes	Tarn stocked with trout for
Open all year	English, French	fishing.

"Unstuffy" country house in 14 acres of hilltop gardens with stunning views of Lake Windermere. Excellent modern British cuisine using local produce, extensive worldwide wine list and attentive staff. E-mail: admin@linthwaite.com *Web site:* linthwaite.com

The Archway	54-60 English$-B&B	Full breakfast
13 College Road,	4 rooms, 4 pb	Dinner by arrangement
Cumbria LA23 1BU	Visa, Mastercard, Delta,	Sitting room, color TV in all
015-394-45613	*Rated*C-no/S-no/P-	rooms, tea and coffee making
Fax: 015-394-45328	no/H-no	facilities and biscuits in each
Vanessa Price	English	room.
Open all year		

Impeccable Victorian home, beautifully furnished throughout with breakfast well worth getting up for. Good food and comfort the priority. Superb mountain views, easy access to lakes and Wordsworth country. E-mail: archway@btinternet.com
Web site: communiken.com/aechway

YORK————————————————————————————————————

Holmwood House Hotel	55-85 English$-B&B	Full breakfast
114 Holgate Rd,	14 rooms, 14 pb	Drinks available
N. Yorkshire YO2 4BB	Visa, Mastercard	Sitting room, walking
+44-1904-626183	C-yes/S-no/P-no/H-no	
Fax: +44-1904-620899	English, French	
Rosie Blanksby & Bill Pitts		
Open all year		

Victorian terrace hotel, elegantly converted, with stylish decor, antiques, all en-suite bathrooms. Most beds king or queen size, some fourposters. Feast on our breakfast to classical music. Let us cherish you! E-mail: holmwood.house@dial.pipex.com
Web site: homewoodhousehotel.co.uk/holmwood.house/

France

ALOXE-CORTON————————————————————————————————

Villa Louise	650-950 French$-B&B	Full breakfast
Burgundy F-21420	10 rooms, 10 pb	Afternoon tea,
33-03-80-26-4670	Visa, Mastercard,	complimentary wine
Fax: 33-03-80-26-4716	American Express,	Bar service, sitting room,
Christian Voarick	*Rated*	library, bicycles, walking,
Open all year	C-yes/S-yes/P-yes/H-yes	baby-sitting
	English, German, Dutch,	
	French, Italian	

17th century mansion in a 1930 minimalist style with exposed timberwork and beamed ceilings. Situated on the edge of grandeur vineyards of Corton. Delicious breakfast served under the trees in the Summer and by the fireplace in the Winter. E-mail: villalou@
iafrica.com *Web site:* villalouise.com

AUXERRE

Le Parc Des Marechaux
6 avenue Foch,
Bourgogne F-89000
03-86-51-4377
Fax: 03-86-51-3172
Esperance Herve
All year

380-515 French$-B&b
25 rooms, 25 pb
Visa, Mastercard,
American Express,
Master,   •
C-yes/S-yes/P-yes/H-yes
French, English, Spanish

Full breakfast buffet
Afternoon tea, snacks, comp.
wine
Bar service, sitting room,

Inside old cathedral city, a residence of Napoleon III period, fully restored with a two acre park; 25 cozy bedrooms; plush bar and louges, breakfast in rooms and gardens; restaurants nearby.

AVOINE

Chateau De La Poiteviniere
Huismes F-37420
33-247-95-5840
Fax: 33-247-95-4343
Marie-Christine Pesquet
April - November

180 US$-B&B
5 rooms, 5 pb
C-yes/S-no/P-ltd/H-no
English, French

Buffet breakfast
Restaurant
Library, salons, hairdryers,
antiques, new restaurant Le
Dauphin, tennis, sauna, pool

The Chateau is situated on 12 acres of beautifully maintained parks parks and gardens. There is a spring-fed pond with ducks and swans. Furnished with French antiques.
E-mail: pesquet@chateauloire.com *Web site:* chateauloire.com

CARSAC-AILLAC

Le Relais Du Touron
Le Touron, Dordgogne F-24200
33-5-53-28-16-70
Fax: 33-5-53-28-52-51
Claudine Carlier
April - Mid November

295-375 French$-B&B
12 rooms, 12 pb
Visa, Mastercard
C-yes/S-no/P-yes/H-ltd
English, Italian, Arabic

Breakfast (fee 38 FF)
Dinner, restaurant,
complimentary wine
Afternoon tea, pool, TV
lounge, fishing, miniature
golf, fishing, tennis, sauna,
pool, sitting room, library

Le Relais du Touron offers a friendly atmosphere, plus good regional and traditional cooking. Set in a large park. Near castles & golf. Free bottle of wine.

CAUNES-MINERVOIS

L'Ancienne Boulangerie
Rue St. Genes F-11160
33-4-68-78-0132
Terry & Lois Link
February to December

225-325 French$-B&B
5 rooms, 3 pb
C-yes/S-yes/P-yes/H-no
French, English

Continental plus breakfast
Sitting room, library, bicycles

Comfortable, renovated bakery with pleasant terrace more than three centuries old in the heart of a medieval village with a 1,200-year-old abbey; surrounded by vineyards and communal forest.   E-mail: ancienneboulangerie@compuserve.com

CHAMONIX-MONT-BLANC

Le Hameau Albert 1Er
119 Impasse du Montenvers F-74402
0033-0-4505-30509
Fax: 0033-0-4505-59548
Martine Carrier
Closed in November

760-3,500 French$-EP
42 rooms, 42 pb
Visa, Mastercard,
American Express, JCV,
•
C-yes/S-yes/P-yes/H-yes
English, German,
Spanish, French

Full breakfast (fee)
Bar service, two restaurants
Sitting room, library, sauna,
mini golf, swimming pool,
skiing, tennis, sauna, pool,
bicycles

A small family hotel which combines Alpine charm and modern comfort, with 2 famous restaurants. Four generations of hotel-keepers Mont-Blanc or Chamonix Aiguilles view.
E-mail: info@hameaualbert.fr *Web site:* hameaualbert.fr

COCURES

La Lozerette Hotel
Florac F-48400
04-66-45-06-04
Fax: 04-66-45-12-93
The Agulhon Family
Easter to 2nd. November

290-410 French$-B&B
21 rooms
Visa, Mastercard,
American Express
C-yes/S-yes/P-yes/H-yes
French, English, Spanish

Continental breakfast
Full breakfast 40 Francs,
restaurant
Afternoon tea,
complimentary wine, sitting
room, library, bicycles, bar
service, lunch & dinner
available

Located along the path taken by Robert Louis Stevenson. Web site: amatable.fr

CONDOM

Hotel Des Trois Lys
38 rue Gambetta F-32100
33-05-62-28-3333
Fax: 33-05-62-28-4185
Jeannette Manet
Closed February

470 French$-EP
10 rooms, 10 pb
Visa, Mastercard,
American Express, •
C-yes/S-yes/P-yes/H-yes
English, Spanish, Italian

Full breakfast (fee)
Lunch, dinner (fee)
Bar service, sitting room,
tennis courts, pool,
restaurant Le Dauphin,
tennis, sauna, pool.
Climatisation daus les
chambres.

The Hotel is a marvellous mixture of tradition and modernization. It is the perfect balance between the architectural style of the 18th century, and the comfort of the 20th.
E-mail: hoteltroislys@minitel.net *Web site:* gascogne.com/Htroislys/

FONTVIEILLE

Auberge La Regalido
Rue Frederic Mistral,
Provence F-13990
33-490-54-6022
Fax: 33-490-54-6429
Michel Family
Mid Feb. to End of Dec.

1,040-1,640 French$-B&B
15 rooms, 12 pb
Most CC, •
C-yes/S-yes/P-yes/H-yes
French, English, German

Full breakfast
Lunch, dinner, afternoon tea,
restaurant
Sitting room, bar service,
private garden. Mini bar,
safe, TV. AC, Private locked
car-park.

An old olive oil mill transformed into a hotel. 15 individual guest rooms some with private terraces overlooking village rooftops. Enjoy dinner on the terrace amidst the flowery garden. Just the place you're looking for. *E-mail:* regalido@relaischateaux.fr
Web site: relaischateaux.fr/regalido

LE THOR

La Bastide Rose
99 Chemin des Croupieres,
Avignon F-84250
011-33-4-90-02-1433
Fax: 011-33-4-90-02-1938
Poppy Salinger/France Allfrey
Spring, Summer, Autumn

125-225 US$-B&B
7 rooms, 7 pb
Visa, •
C-ltd/S-ltd/P-ltd/H-yes
French, Spanish,
Portuguese

Continental breakfast
Tea, dinner (24hr notice),
snacks, wine
Sitting room, cable TV,
swimming pool, suites,
Festival D'Avignon, Opera
festival, antique markets.
Bicycles, cable TV, suites.

Traditional XVIII century provencal house nestling between the Luberon and Les Alpilles, on the River Sorgues ideal for antiques lovers—5 minutes from the biggest antique market of the south L'Isle Sur La Sorgue. *E-mail:* poppynicol@aol.com *Web site:* bastiderose.com

MEGEVE

Hotel Les Fermes De Marie
Chemin de Riante
Colline F-74120
33-04-50-93-0310
Fax: 33-04-50-93-0984
Jocelyne et Jean-Louis Sibuet
Winter and Summer

890-2200 French$ per
person-69 rooms, 69 pb
Most CC, •
C-yes/S-no/P-no/H-yes
French, English, Italian,
German

A festival of delights to be
savoured
Sitting room, library,
bicycles, hot tub, sauna,
pool, beauty farm, body
treatments, ski-shop, garden,
mountain chalet

Little old Savoyard hamlet reconstructed in a two hectare park. At the hotel, the Beauty Farm awaits you; face and body care. Cozy atmosphere and exceptional location.
E-mail: contact@Fermesdemarie.com *Web site:* skifrance.fr/~fermesdemarie

MEURSAULT

Hotel Les Magnolias	420-800 French$-Meals:	Continental breakfast (fee)
8 Rue Pierre Joigneaux F-21190	Inquire	Afternoon tea
03-80-21-23-23	12 rooms, 12 pb	Bar service, sitting room,
Fax: 03-80-21-29-10	Most CC, *Rated*, •	library, fireplaces, garden,
Monsieur Antonio Delarue	C-yes/S-ltd/P-no/H-yes	water skiing, golf.
March - November	English, German, French	

Hotel Les Magnolias is situated in a peaceful wine growing village in the heart of Burgundy. It dates from the 18th century. Each room has its own style and character.
Web site: travelguides.com/bb/magnolias/

ORNAISONS

Le Relais Du Val D'Orbieu	500 French$-B&B	Continental breakfast (fee)
Route Departementale 24,	20 rooms, 20 pb	Restaurant (fee) lunch
Languedoc F-11200	Visa, Mastercard,	Bar service, sitting room,
33-468-27-10-27	American Express,	library, bicycles, pool, tennis,
Fax: 33-468-27-52-44	Most CC, *Rated*, •	tennis, sauna, pool
Agnes & Jean-Pierre	C-yes/S-yes/P-yes/H-ltd	
Gonzalvez	English, Spanish, French	
Open all year		

Facing the picturesque Montagne Noire, Le Relais sits in an atmosphere of calm. Delicious breakfasts are served, filled with fresh fruit & pasteries. 3rd night 50% off.
Web site: travelguides.com/home/lerealaisduvaldorbieu/

PARIS

Hotel Britannique	870-995 French$-EP	Breakfast "buffet" 60 French
20 Ave Victoria F-75001	40 rooms, 40 pb	Francs
01-42-33-7459	Most CC, •	Afternoon tea
Fax: 01-42-33-8265	C-yes/S-yes/P-yes/H-no	Bar service, Sitting room,
J.F. Danjou	English, Spanish, French	massage
Open all year		

A charming hotel in the historic heart of Paris. Special discount according to the season, on request. Delicious, generously-served breakfast. Extra bed 130 French$. Single bredroom 725 French$. All taxes included (even city tax).   E-mail: mailbox@hotel-britannique.fr
Web site: hotel-britannique.fr

Hotel Des Tuileries	790-1,200 French$-B&B	Continental plus breakfast
10, Rue Saint-Hyacinthe F-75001	26 rooms, 26 pb	Afternoon tea
33-1-42-61-0417	Visa, Mastercard,	Sitting room, room service,
Fax: 33-1-49-27-9156	American Express,	air-conditioned rooms,
Poulle-Vidal Family	Most CC, •	fireplaces, garden, water
Open all year	C-yes/S-yes/P-yes/H-no	skiing, golf
	English, Spanish, Italian, Dutch	

Eighteenth century residence. Privileged location next to the Tuileries, Louvre, Orsay Museums, and Place Vendome. Complimentary bottle of champagne.
E-mail: htuileri@aol.com *Web site:* members.aol.com/htuilerang/

Hotel Le Clos Medicis	900 French$-B&B	Buffet breakfast
56 Rue Monsieur le Prince F-75006	38 rooms, 38 pb	Afternoon tea
01-43-29-10-80	Visa, Mastercard,	Bar service, sitting room,
Fax: 01-43-54-26-90	American Express,	fireplaces, garden, water
Pascal Beherec	Most CC, *Rated*, •	skiing, golf
Open all year	C-yes/S-yes/P-yes/H-yes	
	English, Italian, Spanish, French	

Formerly private residence dating to 1860. Magnificent provencal style house. Attractive garden & lounge with open fire. Elegant surroundings. 3rd night 50% or free breakfast.
E-mail: clos_medicis@compuserve.com *Web site:* planetpsyche.com/medicis_e.htm

PEPIEUX

Carrefour B&B	350 French$-B&B	Continental breakfast
1 Rue de L'Etang, Languedoc,	4 rooms, 3 pb	Dinner (100 FF fee) with
Carcassonne F-11700	Most CC, ●	notice
33-46-89-16-929	C-ltd/S-no/P-no/H-no	Complimentary wine with
Fax: 33-46-89-16-929	French, English	dinner, sitting room, library,
Sally Worthington		cable TV. We can also colect
All year		guest from planes.

Rambling village house, XVII, very comfortable, with English/American/French melange of furniture. Area attractions include: wine tasting, swimming, sightseeing, hiking, riding, churches, mountains, sea and golf. E-mail: sally.worthington@wanadoo.fr Web site: le.guide.com/carrefour/index.html

SAINT-CIRQ LAPOPIE

Hotel De La Pelissaria	400-700 French$-MAP	Continental breakfast
F-46330	10 rooms, 10 pb	Restaurant, bar service
5-65-31-25-14	Visa, Mastercard, ●	Complimentary wine, tea,
Fax: 5-65-30-25-52	C-yes/S-yes/P-yes/H-ltd	sitting room, swimming pool,
Marie-Francoise MatUchet	English, French Italian	Folk Museum, St. Marks
April 1 - November 3		Church, Tractor Museum.

13th century house in a medieval village ("The first village of France"–say the "Beaux-Arts") with the river Lot just beyond. Web site: quercy.net/

STRASBOURG

Hotel Du Dragon	565 French$-B&B	Continental breakfast
2 rue de l'Ecarlate,	32 rooms, 32 pb	Afternoon tea
Alsace F-67000	Most CC, *Rated*, ●	Bar service, sitting room,
+33-388-35-7980	C-yes/S-ltd/P-ltd/H-yes	court yard in front, new
Fax: +33-388-25-7895	English, Spanish, Italian,	improved rooms, Golf, fitness
Jean Zimmer	German	center.
Open all year		

Down a quiet street of the old part of town, a 17th century house converted into a very modern, cool, contemporary decorated hotel. Special holiday rates available. E-mail: hotel.dragon@wanadoo.fr Web site: dragon.fr

VENTABRE

Le Mistral	600-850 French$-B&B	Continental breakfast
8 Rue Frederic Mistral F-13122	4 rooms, 4 pb	Lunch & dinner (fee)
00-33-442-288-727	●	Restaurant service, bar,
Fax: 00-33-442-288-737	C-yes/S-ltd/P-yes/H-no	sitting room, library, guests
Lynn McDonald	English, French, Spanish	have own kitchen.
Open all year		

22 years in Provence gives you the "best typed tours" of the musts of Provence as known by the owner. We have our own restaurant next door, the very "in" La Table de Ventabren. Aix en Provence, 10k. E-mail: lynnmcd@aix.pacwan.net Web site: lemistral.com

VERVINS

La Tour Du Roy	500-700 French$-B&B	Full breakfast
45 rue de General Leclerc,	23 rooms, 23 pb	Lunch, dinner, snacks,
Picardie F-02140	Visa, Mastercard,	restaurant
33-03-23-98-00-11	American Express,	Bar service, sitting room,
Fax: 33-03-23-98-00-72	Most CC, ●	complimentary bottle of
Annie Desvignes	C-yes/S-ltd/P-yes/H-yes	wine, Golf, fitness center,
Open all year	English, French	tennis court

A Manor house where Henry IV's ascension to the throne was announced. Stained-glass windows, rooms overlooking terraces, park or landscaped square. Free glass of champagne. Elegant cuisine by Annie. Perfect stopover on the way to Belgium, or the Ardennes Web site: pageszoom.com/la-tou-du-roy

Germany

OFFENBURG————————————————————————————————————

Hotel Sonne
Hauptstrasse 94 D-77652
0781-71039
Fax: 0781-71033
Gabriele Schimpf-Schoppner
Open all year

98-190 German$-Meals:
Inquire
34 rooms, 27 pb
Visa, Mastercard
C-yes/S-yes/P-yes/H-no
English, French, German

Full breakfast
Restaurant (fee)
Starting point for Baden-
Baden outings Hot tubs,
sauna, swimming pool,
excursions arranged.

One of the oldest hotels in Germany. Rooms are furnished with antique furnitures of the 19th century. Center of Offenburg next to baroque townhall.

PFRONTEN————————————————————————————————————

Berghotel Schlossanger Alp
Am Schlossanger 1, Bayers D-
87459
083-631-381-914550
Fax: 083-631-91455555
Schlachter & Ebert Family
Ask about time of operation

160 German$-B&B
30 rooms, 30 pb
Visa, Mastercard,
American Express, •
C-yes/S-yes/P-ltd/H-no
English, French, German

Full breakfast
Restaurant (fee), lunch
Sitting room, sauna,
swimming pool, toiletries,
excursions arranged.

The chalet is built amid open fields, full of wooden beams & local folk ornaments. A comfortable room & excellent breakfast awaits you. 6th night free. The restaurant is mentioned in the important restaurant guides of Europe. E-mail: ebert@online-service.de Web site: online-service.de/schlossanger/home.html/

Hungary

BUDAPEST————————————————————————————————————

Hotel Victoria
11 Bem RKP H-1011
36-1-457-8080
Fax: 36-1-457-8088
Zoltan Palmai Jr
Open all year

144-199 German$-B&B
27 rooms, 27 pb
Most CC, •
C-yes/S-yes/P-yes/H-no
Hungarian, German,
English

Full breakfast
Snacks, bar service
Sauna, A/C, mini bar,
Satellite TV, room-safe,
phones with modems, room
service.

Small 4-star hotel with familiar atmosphere. Each room has a splendid roundview of the city. Central location with reasonable prices. E-mail: victoria@victoria.hu Web site: victoria.hu/

Ireland

BALLYMOTE————————————————————————————————————

Temple House
Slogo
353-71-83329
Fax: 353-71-83808
Deb & Sandy Perceval
April 1 - November 30

80 Irish$-B&B, MAP
5 rooms, 5 pb
Visa, Mastercard,
American Express,
Rated, •
C-yes/S-no/P-no/H-no
French, English

Full breakfast
Dinner, afternoon tea
Sitting room, hot tubs, lake,
boats, fishing, archeology,
castle, gardens, woods,
access to the Internet and
fax.

Family owned Georgian mansion on 1000 acres overlooking 13th century castle. Sheep farm, boats, garden walks, golf, riding nearby, canopied beds. Featured in Bon Appetit. No perfumes or aftershaves please. E-mail: guest@templehouse.ie Web site: templehouse.ie/

CARLOW TOWN

Barrowville Town House
Kilkenny Rd., Carlow
0503-43224
Fax: 0503-41953
General Manager
All year

45-50 Irish$-B&B
7 rooms, 7 pb
Visa, Mastercard,
American Express, •
S-no/P-no/H-no
English, German, some
French

Full breakfast
Sitting room, car park, use of
gardens

A premier guesthouse of quality. 3 star Georgian listed house. Antique furnishings, traditional or buffett breakfast in conservatory overlooking gardens. As recommended by most good guide books including "Best 100 B&Bs".

CONNEMARA

Ballynahinch Castle
Recess, Connemara,
Galway
+353-095-31006
Fax: +353-095-31085
Patrick O'Flaherty
Closed Christmas week &
February

114.40-209.00 Irish$-B&B
40 rooms, 40 pb
Most CC, •
C-yes/S-yes/P-no/H-no
English, Spanish,
German, French/Russian

Restaurant, lunch, dinner,
afternoon tea
Tennis court, bicycles, horse
riding, open log fires, library,
sitting room, bar service

18th.C. manor castle, now a 4 star hotel in 350 acre private estate overlooking own wild salmon fishery. Luxurious rooms with four-poster beds, superb restaurant service, fresh fish and local produce. Fisherman's pub & open log fires. 7 miles from the se E-mail: bhinch@ iol.ie *Web site:* commerce.ie/ballynahinch/

Lough Inagh Lodge
Recess, Co. Galway
095-347-06
Fax: 095-347-08
888-60-MANOR
Maire O'Connor
Mid March-Mid December

110-136 Irish$-B&B
12 rooms, 12 pb
Visa, Mastercard,
American Express,
Diners, •
C-ltd/S-yes/P-yes/H-no
Irish, English, French,
German

Full Irish breakfast
Restaurant, lunch, diner,
afternoon tea
Tennis, bicycles, horse
riding, open log fires, river
and lake fishing, walking, bar
service, snacks, library, hill
climbing.

Lough Inagh Lodge is situated in a deep valley on the shores of Lough Inagh. We have 12 charming bedrooms with loving view of our gardens and lake. E-mail: inagh@iol.ie

DINGLE

Doyle'S Townhouse
John Street, Kerry
+35-066-91-51174
Fax: +35-066-91-51816
Sean Cluskey
Mid Feb. to Dec.

25-45 Irish$-B&B
8 rooms, 8 pb
Visa, Mastercard, •
C-no/P-no/H-yes
English, French, Irish,
Flemish

Full breakfast
Dinner, restaurant, bar
service
Sitting room

E-mail: cdoyles@iol.ie *Web site:* iol.ie/~cdoyles/index.html

DUBLIN

Ariel House
52 Lansdowne Rd.
Ballsbridge 4
01-668-5512
Fax: 01-668-5845
Michael O'Brien
Mid Jan. - Mid Dec.

50-169 Irish$-EP
28 rooms, 28 pb
Visa, Mastercard, •
C-no/S-no/P-no/H-yes
English, French, Spanish

Full Irish breakfast (fee)
Restaurant, bar
Sitting room, bedrooms hung
with original oil paintings
and watercolors. Central
heating, color TV, direct dial
phone, hair dryers, full tub
baths, real Irish linen.

Ariel House (built in 1850 for a whealthy merchant) is a historic listed Victorian mansion which has recently been restored to its former splendour. We offer an air of quiet luxury and elegant decor which befits a building of its period.

DUBLIN

The Fitzwilliam Park
No. 5 Fitzwilliam Square 2
0++353-1-662-8200
Fax: ++353-1-662-8281
Mary Madden
Closed 23-29 December

98-110 Irish$-B&B
20 rooms, 20 pb
Visa, Mastercard,
American Express, •
C-yes/S-yes/P-no/H-yes
English, French

Full Irish breakfast
Lunch, Dinner (fee)
Restaurant, Full business
facilities, parking, phone, fax,
limousine & taxi service

Possibly one of the best preserved examples of early 19th century grandeur, built in 1816 by Peter La Touche on land leased from Richard, 5th Viscount Fitxwilliam. Excellent cuisine. E-mail: info@fitzpark.ie *Web site:* fitzpark.ie

ENNISCORTHY

Ballinkeele House
Ballymurn, c/o Wexford
053-38105
Fax: 053-38468
John & Margaret Maher
March 1 - November 6

70-90 Irish$-B&B, MAP
5 rooms, 5 pb
Visa, Mastercard,
American Express,
Most CC, *Rated*, •
C-ltd/S-ltd/P-no/H-no
English

Full breakfast
Dinner available (fee) L25
Book dinner before noon,
adult oriented, drawing
room, Snorkeling, diving

Work off hostess home-cooked breakfasts (and dinners-by arrangement). Wellingtons for walking, large drawing room. 10% off on 3-plus nights.   E-mail: balnkeel@indigo.ie *Web site:* Ballinkeele.com

KILLALOE

Rathmore House
Ballina, Clare
00-353-061-379296
Fax: 00-353-061-376431
Patricia Byrnes
April-October

32-38 Irish$-B&B
6 rooms, 4 pb
Visa, Mastercard, •
C-yes/S-no/P-no/H-yes
English

Full breakfast
Afternoon tea, snacks
Sitting room

Country home of Patricia and Christopher close to heritage town of Killaloe. Private luxury guest lounge and breakfast served in our high pine-ceilinged breakfast room looking onto our lawns and the hills of Birdhill.   E-mail: rathmorebb@oceanfree.net

LIMAVADY

Streeve Hill
25 Downland Road,
Londonderry BT49 0HP
44-0-15047-66563
Fax: 44-0-15047-68285
June & Peter Welsh
Closed New Year & Christmas

90 Irish$-B&B
3 rooms, 3 pb
Visa, Mastercard,
American Express, •
C-yes/S-yes/P-no/H-no
English, Spanish

Full Irish breakfast
Gourmet Dinner, bar service
Sitting room, excellent local
golf courses, riding, fishing,
walking.

Elegant early Georgian country house furnished with fine antiques and lovingly restored. Views over parkland to distant Sperrin Mountains. Irresistible Irish breakfast and gourmet dinners. Your host love entertaining and are keen gardeners

MOUNTRATH

Roundwood House
Laois
353-0-502-32120
Fax: 353-0-502-32120
Frank & Rosemarie Kennan
Open all year

41 Irish$-B&B
10 rooms, 10 pb
Visa, Mastercard,
American Express,
Most CC, *Rated*, •
C-yes/S-yes/P-yes/H-no
English, Spanish, French

Full breakfast
Dinner available
Bar service, sitting room,
library, hot tubs, fitness
massage.

Beautiful Palladian villa surrounded by its own woods. A piece of warm and welcoming history.   E-mail: roundwood@tinet.ie *Web site:* hidden-ireland.com/roundwood

NEWMARKET-ON-FERGUS

Thomond House	130-170 Irish$-B&B	Full breakfast
Dromoland Estate	6 rooms, 6 pb	Dinner by arrangement
353-061-368-304	Visa, Mastercard,	Golf, Fishing, Tennis, Riding,
Fax: 353-061-368-285	American Express,	Clay shooting, deer stalking,
Helen Inchiquin	*Rated*, •	4X4 course, open log fires
Open all year, except	C-yes/S-yes/H-yes	
Christmas	English, basic French	

Luxurious and Charming. We offer superb hospitality, delicious food. 10 minutes from Shannon Airport. Golf 5 minutes; tennis, swimming, shooting and magnificent walks.

SCHULL

Corthna Lodge House	20-25 Irish$-B&B	Full breakfast
Cork	6 rooms	Afternoon tea, snacks
028-28517	•	Sitting room, library,
Fax: 028-28032	C-yes/S-no/P-yes/H-yes	bicycles, swimming in the
Loretta Davitt	English	Atlantic Ocean, beautiful
All year		beaches, walking

Corthna Lodge Country House is situated 1 km. from the beautiful fishing village of Schull. It lies amidst the mountains and looks to the sea and friends. It is peaceful and inviting for a relaxing stay.

TYRRELLSPASS

The Village Hotel	50-60 Irish$-B&B	Full breakfast
Westmeath	10 rooms, 10 pb	Restaurant, lunch & dinner,
044-231-71	C-yes/S-yes/P-ltd/H-yes	snacks, tea
Fax: 044-234-91	English, some French	Sitting room, bar service,
Gerard Clery & Sandra Dane		fishing & golf nearby
All year		

Hotel is part of an elegant Georgian crescent of houses built around the village green by Jane, Countess of Belvedere in the early 1800s. The family takes great pride in retaining the charm and atmosphere of an earlier time.

WATERFORD

Brown'S Townhouse	90 US$, 60 Irish$-B&B	Full breakfast
29 South Parade	6 rooms, 6 pb	Sitting room, suites,
051-870-594	Visa, Mastercard, •	fireplaces, cable TV, tour
Fax: 051-871-923	C-ltd/S-ltd/P-no/H-no	south east of Ireland, Visit
Ms Leslie Brown	English	Waterford crystal
Open all year, closed		showrooms, Walk to all
Christmas		amenities

City centre Victorian townhouse tastefully refurbished to include all modern comforts. All rooms are individually decorated and an extensive breakfast menu is available. 6 nights or more claim 1 free night. E-mail: info@brownstownhouse.com *Web site:* brownstownhouse.com

Italy

ANAGNI

Villa La Floridiana	160-250,000 Italian$-B&B	Continental breakfast
Via Casilina, km. 63700 I-03012	9 rooms, 9 pb	Lunch, Dinner, Restaurant
0039-775-769960-1	Visa, Mastercard,	Bar service, train to Rome or,
Fax: 0039-775-769960-1	American Express	car rentals available,
Sigra. Camerini	C-yes/S-yes/P-ltd/H-no	massages, tours.
All year	French, English	

A classic red-coloured relai, is an enterily restored 19th century villa with a wide 19th century park around. Special weekends, Christmas and Easter packages. We invite you to come to our delicious relais gourmet to visit Ciociaria.

CANNERO RIVIERA

Hotel Cannero	200-240,000 Italian$-B&B	Full breakfast
Via Lungo Lago 2,	50 rooms, 50 pb	Lunch, dinner, restaurant,
Verbania I-28821	Most CC	snacks
0323-788-046	C-yes/S-yes/P-yes/H-yes	Library, bicycles, tennis,
Fax: 0323-788-048	English, French,	swimming pool, Nature and
M.C. Gallinotto	German, Italian	Cannero castles tours, ping
March - November		pong, Solarium

A pretty courtyard and an ancient well serve as vestiges of the 17th century monastery that once stood on this site. Characteristic old world charm and attentive service ensure our guest relax and well looked after.   E-mail: hcannero@tin.it *Web site:* cannero.com

CASTELFRANCO EMILIA

Villa Gaidello Club	150-330,000 Italian$-B&B	Continental plus breakfast
Via Gaidello 18/20,	6 rooms, 6 pb	Restaurant, lunch, dinner
Modena I-41013	Visa, Mastercard,	3 acres of lovely grounds,
059-92-6806	American Express,	swimming pool nearby,
Fax: 059-92-6620	Diners	tennis court nearby, lake
Paola Giovanna Bini	C-yes/S-ltd/P-no/H-no	with swans, bicycles, pond
Closed August	Italian, French, English	with tanning area

250 year-old farmhouse located in the beautiful Po Valley. A vast agricultural estate, once the summer retreat of the Bini family. "Gaidello is a forgotten angle that will help you forget the chaos of everyday life."
E-mail: gaidello@tin.it *Web site:* members.aol.com/gaidello

CERENENTE

Castello Dell' Oscano	220-380,000 Italian$-	Breakfast buffet (fee)
Strada della Forcella 37,	Meals: Inquire	Dinner (fee), afternoon tea,
Perugia I-06134	30 rooms, 30 pb	snacks
++75-690-125-6	Visa, Mastercard,	Minibar, Parking, swimming
Fax: ++75-690-666	American Express, •	pool, sitting room, bicycles,
Michelle Ravano	C-yes/S-yes/P-yes/H-yes	centuries old trees park of
Open all year	Italian, English, French	250 hectars.

Our castle and villa Ada (at 10 meters) are only 8 km. from the town center, but on a top of a hill with wonderful views in the middle of a luxury park of many species of trees.
E-mail: oscano@krenet.it *Web site:* oscano-castle.com

CHIAVERANO D'IVREA

Castello San Giuseppe	175-270.000 Italian$-B&B,	Complimentary breakfast
Locality Castello San	MAP	Restaurant (fee)
Giuseppe, Torino I-10010	16 rooms, 16 pb	Bar service, conference
_39-0125-42-4370	Visa, Mastercard,	facility for 20 to 40 people,
Fax: +39-0125-64-1278	American Express,	color TV, direct phone line.
L. Naghiero & Renata	Most CC, •	
Banchieri	C-yes/S-yes/P-ltd/H-ltd	
Open all year	English, French,	
	German, Spanish	

A Convent in 1600, a Castle under Emperor "Napoleon" in 1800. Recently restructured and converted   into   a   charming   hotel   with   all   the   comforts.
Web site: ntn.it/canavese/hotel/sangiuseppe

CORTINA D'AMPEZZO

Hotel Menardi	250,000 Italian$-B&B	Continental plus breakfast
Via Majon No. 110 I-32043	55 rooms, 55 pb	Lunch, Dinner (fee)
0436-2400	Visa, Mastercard,	Afternoon tea, bar,
Fax: 0436-862183	American Express, •	restaurant, complimentary
The Menardi Family	C-yes/S-yes/P-no/H-no	wine, sitting room, library,
Summer and Winter	English, German,	bicycles, large garden.
	French, Italian	

From the turn of the century: an ancient house, a family. Today: the same house & family. Relaxed atmosphere, rich vegetation, comfortable, modern. Beauty of the Dolomites. Garage free for 1 night. Stable and a barn.   E-mail: hmenardi@sunrise.it
Web site: sunrise.it/cortina/alberghi/menardi/

FLORENCE

Hotel Morandi Alla Crocetta	220-280.000 Italian$-EP	Full breakfast (fee)
Via Laura 50 I-50121	10 rooms, 10 pb	Afternoon tea
055-234-4747	Visa, Mastercard,	Bar service, sitting room,
Fax: 055-248-0954	American Express,	library, sitting room, library,
Antuono Family	Most CC, *Rated*, •	bicycles, large garden, garage
Open all year	C-yes/S-yes/P-yes/H-no	
	English, French, Italian,	
	German	

A restored old Italian home that once was the monastery of the Crocetta. Furnished with original antiques, it provides plenty of charm and atmosphere.   E-mail: welcome@ hotelmorandi.it *Web site:* hotelmorandi.it

ISOLA DEL GIGLIO

Pardini's Hermitage	90-135 Euro$-AP	Full breakfast
Cala degli Alberi,	13 rooms, 13 pb	Lunch and Dinner included
Giglio Porto I-58013	Visa, •	in rate
0039-0564-80-9034	C-yes/S-yes/P-yes/H-no	Private beach, bar, sitting
Fax: 0039-0564-80-9177	Italian, German, English,	room, library,
Federigo Pardini	French	complimentary wine,
Open all year		bowling.

Right on the sea-front, far away from any built-up area. Reachable from Giglio Porto only by boat or on foot -about 1 hour's walk- and can't accommodate more than 25 guests at a time. Pottery workroom, open air gymnasium. .   E-mail: hermit@ats.it *Web site:* finalserv.it/heritage/

LEVANTO

Hotel Nazionale	190,000 Italian$-AP	Full breakfast
Via Jacopo Da Levanto 20 I-	32 rooms, 32 pb	Restaurant (all meals)
19015	Visa, Mastercard,	Bar service, afternoon tea,
39-0187-808102	American Express,	snacks, sitting room, parking,
Fax: 39-0187-800901	Most CC, *Rated*C-	suites, foot path, overlooks
Angela Lagomarsino	yes/S-yes/P-ltd/H-ltd	mediterranean style garden,
March - November	English, German, French	bicycles, large garden

Friendly family-run hotel, conveniently situated for town, beach, train, boats & "Cinque Terre". Delightful restaurant offering regional cooking. Secluded garden for dining and breakfast "al fresco". Private roof terrace and car park.   E-mail: hotel@nazionale.it *Web site:* nazionale.it

LUCCA

Villa Alessandra	160-190,000 Italian$-B&B	Full breakfast
Via Arsina 1100/B,	6 rooms, 6 pb	Afternoon tea, snacks, Bar
Toscana I-55100	Visa, Mastercard,	service
39-0583-39-5171	American Express	Sitting room, library,
Fax: 39-0583-39-5828	C-yes/S-yes/P-yes/H-no	swimming pool, shops, art,
Enrica Bottini Tosca	Italian, English, French	sports, Beach front,
All year		Horseback.

Elegant villa of the XVIII century, situated on the hills of Lucca surrounded by olive-groves and vineyard. Fully restored, furnished in genuine antiques. Gardens. Beaches of Viareggio and Forte dei Marmi.   E-mail: villa.ale@mailcity.com *Web site:* mailcity.lycos.com/villa.alelucca

Villa la Principessa	300-550,000 Italian$-EP	Breakfast (fee)
Via nuova per Pisa, 1616 I-	42 rooms, 42 pb	Dinner, restaurant, afternoon
55050	Visa, Mastercard,	tea, snack
+39-0583-370037	American Express,	Swimming pool, formal park,
Fax: +39-0583-379136	Diners, •	bar service, sitting room
Family Mugnani	C-yes/S-yes/P-yes	
Open all year	Italian, English, French,	
	German	

Ancient country villa furnished in antiques. Enjoy the formal park (20,000 meters) with its plantings and great trees, the open air meals and the swimming pool.   E-mail: principessa@ lunet.it *Web site:* lunet.it/aziende/villaprincipessa

MARATEA————————————————————————————————

Villa Cheta Elite
Loc. Acquafredda,
Potenza I-85046
0973-878134
Fax: 0973-878135
Lamberto Aquadro
Open all year

195-210,000 Italian$-
Meals: Inquire
17 rooms, 17 pb
Most CC, *Rated*, •
C-yes/S-yes/P-yes/H-no
German, English, Italian

Full breakfast
Restaurant
Bar service, sitting room,
tennis court in the vicinity,
massages, tours.

Splendid Liberty-style villa views the sea, beach close. Refined, efficient hospitality. Restaurant features local products. History, art, culture. Free bottle of wine.
E-mail: shlogos@labnet.it *Web site:* costadimaratea.com/villacheta

MERANO————————————————————————————————

Castle Fragsburg
Via Fragsburg 3 I-39012
++39-0473-24-4071
Fax: ++39-0473-24-4493
Alexander Ortner Family
April - November

130-190.000 Italian$-B&B
20 rooms, 20 pb
•
C-yes/S-yes/P-yes/H-yes
Italian, German, Engl.,
Spanish, French

Full breakfast
Restaurant, lunch, dinner
sitting room, library,
bicycles, sauna, swimming
pool, bicycles, large garden

Old small hunting-Castle built by the Count of Memmingen. Superb position with splendid views to the valley below. 10,000 meters private park, heated swimming pool, exclusives suites with panoramic-balcony. Excellent cuisine. E-mail: info@fragsburg.com
Web site: fragsburg.com

MILANO————————————————————————————————

Hotel London
Via Rovello 3 I-20121
02-720-20166
Fax: 02-805-7037
Gambino Francesco
Open all year

230,000 Italian$-B&B
29 rooms, 24 pb
Visa, Mastercard
C-yes/S-yes/P-no/H-no
Italian, English, Spanish,
French

Continental breakfast
Bar service, afternoon tea
Sitting room, complimentary
wine, Cable TV, phones,
Leeds Castle, London

Located in the historical centre, near theatre La Scala, Duomo and Sforzesco Castle. Satellite connected colot TV, air conditioned and direct telephone line in each room. E-mail: hotel.london@traveleurope.it *Web site:* traveleurope.it/hotellondon.htm

MONTECATINI————————————————————————————

Il Frassinello
Via Della Miniera 22, Pisa I-
56040
0038-0588-30080
Fax: 0038-0588-30080
Elga Schlubach-Giudici
Easter - end of October

150.000 Italian$-B&B
7 rooms, 5 pb
Most CC, *Rated*
C-yes/S-yes/P-yes/H-no
French, Italian, English,
German

Continental plus breakfast
Snacks, complimentary wine
Sitting room, library, Evening
meals (fee), deer farm.

Located in the countryside with beautiful views; seaside 35 kms away. Little chapel and Christian meditation room available. 3rd nite 25% off and free bottle of wine. E-mail: frassinello@sirt.pisa.it

MONTEFALCO————————————————————————————

Hotel Villa Pambuffetti
Via della Vittoria, 20, Perugia I-
06036
0742-379417
Fax: 0742-379245
Alessandra Angelucci
Open all year

135,000 Italian$-B&B
15 rooms, 15 pb
Most CC, *Rated*, •
C-yes/S-yes/P-no/H-yes
English, French, German

Buffet breakfast
Dinner available
Minibar, Safe, Parking,
swimming pool, solarium
grotta

Family country house in the hilltop town of Montefalco. Famous for its 13th century Frescoes, centuries-old park with a swimming pool. Cumbrian cuisine and wines. E-mail: villabianca@interbusiness.it *Web site:* assind.perugia.it/hotel/pambuffetti/

ORTA SAN GIULIO

San Rocco Hotel	260-380,000 Italian$-B&B	Restaurant (fee)
Via Gippini 11 I-28016	74 rooms, 74 pb	Lunch, dinner, bar
039-0322-911977	Visa, Mastercard,	Sitting room, sauna,
Fax: 039-0322-911964	American Express,	swimming pool, bicycles,
Pier Giorgio Barone	Most CC, •	large garden
Open all year	C-yes/S-yes/P-no/H-no	
	French, English, German	

A converted convent located on the romantic Lake Orta and facing the island of San Giulio. Absolute tranquility, refined restaurant. Local and international cuisine.
E-mail: sanrocco@intercom.it *Web site:* hotelsanrocco.it

OSTUNI

Il Frantoio	110.000 Italian$-B&B	Continental plus breakfast
S.S. 16-Kilom. 874, Brandisi I-	8 rooms, 8 pb	Dinner (fee), Afternoon tea,
72017	•	snacks
39-831-330-276	C-yes/S-no/P-yes/H-no	Complimentary wine, bar,
Fax: 39-831-330-276	English, French, Italian	sitting room, library, bikes,
Rosalba Ciannamea		riding, private beach, organic
Ask about time of operation		produce cuisine, bicycles

Romantic, peaceful country hacienda: historic bedrooms & antiques, exquisite Mediterranean cooking and hosp., ancient olive oil mill, fragrant groves. Free bottle of estate-bottled extra-virgin olive oil.

PARMA

Hotel Torino	110-165,000 Italian$-EP	Full breakfast (fee)
Borgo Angelo Mazza, 7 I-43100	33 rooms, 33 pb	Bar service
0521-281046/7	Visa, Mastercard,	Sitting room, bicycles,
Fax: 0521-230725	American Express,	private garage, bicycles,
Chiri Giulia Maria	Most CC	large garden.
Open all year	C-yes/S-yes/P-yes/H-ltd	
	Italian, English, French,	
	German	

B and B hotel located right in the "centro storico" of a city of great cultural tradition, a few steps from the 12th Century Duomo & Baptistery. Offers a very pleasat stay at affordable rates.

PAVONE CANAVESE

Castello Di Pavone Hotel	145-200,000 Italian$-AP	Continental plus breakfast
Via Ricetti, #1	13 rooms, 13 pb	Full breakfast on request,
39-125-672111	Visa, Mastercard,	comp. wine
Fax: 39-125-642114	American Express,	Bar service, restaurant,
Familia Giodice-Laner	Diners, •	jogging paths on hills with
All year	C-yes/S-yes/P-ltd/H-yes	indicators.
	Italian, English, French,	
	German	

A charming hotel inside a fabulous medieval castle, overlooking the old village of Pavone Canavese among hills & mountains. Furnished in style with all the best conveniences. Gourmet restaurant with the best selection of Italian dishes & upscale wines.
E-mail: castello.pavone@flasnet.it

PENANGO

Locanda Del Sant'Uffizio	300.000 Italian$-B&B	Full breakfast
Frazione Cioccaro, Asti I-14030	43 rooms, 43 pb	Lunch, dinner, restaurant
0141-916292	Visa, Mastercard,	Bar service, sitting room,
Fax: 014-1916068	Most CC, *Rated*	bicycles, tennis, pool,
Beppe and Carla Firato	C-yes/S-yes/P-yes/H-ltd	gymmasium, park, fitness
Closed from the 10th - 20th	English, Italian	massage
August		

Countryside XVIth century Benedictine convent furnished in genuine antiques, surrounded by wineyards. Gourmet dinner & buffet with homemade jams & typical salami & cheeses.

PETTENASCO

Giardinetto Hotel
Via Provinciale 1 I-28028
0323-89118
Fax: 0323-89219
General Manager
Jan. 4 to Oct. 25

120-150,000 Italian$-B&B
54 rooms
Visa, Mastercard,
American Express,   •
C-yes/S-yes/P-yes/H-no
Italian, English, Deutch,
French

Continental breakfast
Lunch, dinner, afternoon tea,
restaurant
Sitting room, bicycles,
swimming pool, bar service,
private beach. Comfortable
halls, coffee shop, fully
equipped congress hall.

Beautifuly located directly on the lakefront, the Terrace Restaurant offers excellent meals inside or outside by candlelight. Swimming pool, private beach boat from hotel for the island, very interesting excursion point.   E-mail: giardinetto@micanel.it

POMPONESCO

Il Leone
Piazza IV Martiri 2,
Mantua I-46030
0375-86077/86145
Fax: 0375-86770
Antonio & Anna Mori
Closed January & 1 week in
August

160,000 Italian$-B&B
8 rooms, 8 pb
Visa, Mastercard,
American Express,   •
C-yes/S-yes/P-yes/H-no
English, French

Continental plus breakfast
Restaurant, lunch, dinner
Bar service, sitting room,
swimming pool, very good
cellar, bicycles, large garden

A Renaissance Palace with painted ceiling and frescoes in the main hall. Breakfast served next to the pool, traditional cuisine of the Po Valley with a complete wine list. Ancient furniture and paintings.

ROME

Hotel Locarno
Via della Penna, 22 I-00186
06-361-0841
Fax: 06-321-5249
Mrs. Maria Teresa Celli
Open all year

200 US$-B&B
48 rooms, 48 pb
Most CC, *Rated*
C-yes/S-yes/P-no/H-ltd
English, Spanish, Italian

Continental breakfast
Afternoon tea, snacks
Bar service, library, sitting
room, bicycles, cable TV,
roof garden, massages, tours.

Located in the very heart of Rome. Near the splendid Piazza del Popolo. Hotel of the artist (area crowded with art galleries). Federico Fellini used to have coffee at the bar. All rooms are refurbished with antiques and marble bathrooms.   E-mail: info@hotellocarno.com
Web site: hotellocarno.com

La Posta Vecchia Hotel
Loc. Palo Laziale, Ladispoli I-
00055
39-06-9949501
Fax: 39-06-9949507
Harry C.N. Scio
April - November

Rates: Inquire-B&B
17 rooms, 13 pb
Most CC, *Rated*,   •
C-yes/S-ltd/P-no/H-no
English, German,
French, Italian

Continental breakfast
Restaurant (fee)
Sitting room, library,
bicycles, swimming pool,
ocean, garden, park view,
bicycles, large garden

Villa XVII century. Furnished in genuine antiques. Private Roman Museum. Small private beach. Special: upgrade room when possible.   E-mail: postavec@caerenet.it
Web site: lapostavecchia.com/

Residenza Antica Roma
Via del Tritone 82 I-00187
0335-533-1341
Fax: 0335-688-3500
Sig. Bellia
All year

250-300,000 Italian$-B&B
6 rooms, 6 pb
Visa, Mastercard,
American Express,   •
C-yes/S-yes/P-no/H-yes
Italian, English, French,
Deutch

Continental breakfast
Sitting room

The six rooms of Antica Roma are all fitted with private facilities, minibar, frigo, TV set, direct phone, climatization and room safe. It's located in the best area of Roma, between Pzza Barberini - Pzza di Spagna and Fontana di Trvi. Closed to subway.

SAN MAMETE──────────────────────────────

Hotel Stella D'Italia
Piazza Roma 1, Como.
Valsolda I-22010
+39-0344-68139
Fax: +39-0344-68729
Ortelli Franco
March 30 – September 30

195,000 Italian$-B&B
35 rooms, 35 pb
Visa, Mastercard,
American Express, •
C-yes/S-yes/P-yes/H-no
Italian, English, French,
German

Full breakfast buffet
Lunch, dinner, open air
restaurant
Afternoon tea, bar service,
library, snacks, swimming
pool at Lido, bicycles, large
garden.

Directly on lake Lugano. Garden restaurant, private Lido. Located in a quiet area.   E-mail: stelladitalia@mclink.it

SPOLETO──────────────────────────────

Palazzo Dragoni
Via del Duomo, 13 I-06049
743-22-2220
Fax: 743-22-2225
Erminia Diotallevi
Open all year

200-300.000 Italian$-B&B
15 rooms, 15 pb
Most CC, •
C-yes/S-yes/P-yes/H-ltd
Italian, Francese,
Tedesco

Continental plus breakfast
Afternoon tea
Bar service, sitting room,
library, solarium grotta

In the historical centre of Spoleto next to the Cathedral. Built in XIV century and considered a "Historic Residence". Furnished in original style, available for conferences.
E-mail: rodiota@tin.it

TAORMINA──────────────────────────────

Hotel Villa Ducale
Via Leonardo da Vinci, 60,
Sicily I-98039
+39-0942-28153
Fax: +39-0942-28710
Andrea & Rosy Quartucci
Closed January 15 –
February 21

250-420,000 Italian$-B&B
15 rooms, 15 pb
Most CC, •
C-yes/S-yes/P-yes/H-ltd
English, French,
German.

Buffet continental plus
breakfast
Afternoon tea, snacks
Bar service, library, sitting
room, hot tubs, solarium
grotta.

Rooms individually decorated antique style, hand-painted furniture, modern comfort. Unique view of Mediterranean & volcano. Ten minute walk to famous Greek-Roman Medieval old town.   E-mail: villaducale@tao.it *Web site:* italyhotel.com/sicilia/taormina/villaducale

TRENTO──────────────────────────────

Albergo Accademia Di
Fambri Camillo
SPA Vicolo Colico, 4/6 I-38100
0461-23-36-00
Fax: 0461-23-01-74
General Manager

Rates: Inquire-43 rooms
Italian

VALLE D'AOSTA──────────────────────────────

Les Neiges D'Antan
11027 Fraz Perreres, Cervinia,
Breuil I-11021
0166-948775
Fax: 0166-948852
Maurizio Bich
Open all year

210.000 Italian$-AP, MAP
28 rooms, 28 pb
Visa, Mastercard,
Rated
C-yes/S-yes/P-yes/H-ltd
Italian, English, French,
German

Continental plus breakfast
Restaurant (fee)
Sitting room, library, cross
country ski track, boules,
fireplace, solarium, grotta.

Chalet in tranquil mountain valley. Warm family atmosphere, excellent cuisine and wine cellar. 1996 Best Italian Breakfast Award, skiing and mountaineering.   E-mail:
hotel.neigesantan@cervina.alpcom.it *Web site:* breuil-cervinia.com/hotels/neigesdantan.htm

VARENNA

Hotel Du Lac
Via del Prestino 4, Como I-
22050
0341-83-0238
Fax: 0341-83-1081
Dend Ileana   March – Dec.

180.000 Italian$-MAP
19 rooms, 18 pb
Most CC, •
C-yes/S-yes/P-yes/H-yes
English, French, German

Continental breakfast
Lunch, dinner, restaurant
Bar service, sitting room,
people may swim in lake,
free garage 1st. night, garage

Ancient villa with a deeply romantic atmosphere. Meals are served on the terrace over-looking the lake, far from traffic. Free place in the garage 1st night.
Web site: italioabc.com

VENICE

Albergo Quattro Fontane
Via delle Quattro Fontane, 16 I-
30126
041-526-0227   Fax: 041-526-0726
Family Bevilacqua
April 4th to Nov. 15th.

400-555,000 Italian$-B&B
59 rooms
Most CC, •
C-yes/S-yes/P-yes/H-no
Italian, French, English,
German

Continental breakfast
Restaurant, afternoon tea,
snacks
Bar service, sitting room,
library, bicycles, tennis
court, hot tubs

Country house in a garden, near the beach, 15 minutes from San Marco Square - all rooms and public spaces are furnished with antiques.   E-mail: quafonve@tin.it
Web site: space.tin.it/turismo/benteb

Ill Fae
Via Fae #3, San Pietro di
Feletto I-31020
+390438-787117
Fax: +390438-787818
Sabina & Salvatore Valerio
All year

74 US$-B&B
6 rooms, 6 pb
Visa, •
C-yes/S-ltd/P-ltd
Italian, French

Continental breakfast
Tea, snacks, wine
Sitting room, library,
bicycles, jacuzzi, pool, suites,
fireplace, cable TV,
conference room

Beautifull hills & vineyards surround the Fae B&B. Home made breakfast served in the garden. Beautifull panorama, quiet life, quite place. Historical area, car and bike rental available. Other facilities on request.   E-mail: mail@ilfae.com *Web site:* ilfae.com

---

La Fenice Et Des Artistes
San Marco 1936 I-30124
041-52-03-2333
Fax: 041-52-03-721
Roberta, Chistian & Romina
All year

280-380,000 Italian$-B&B
68 rooms, 65 pb
Most CC, •
C-yes/S-yes/P-no/H-no
Italian, English, French,
German

Full breakfast
Afternoon tea, snacks,
restaurant
Sitting room, bar service,

Charming Venetian style hotel close to the famous Opera House La Fenice, 300 meters from San Marco Square. Prefered by artist and business-men for the quite and intimate atmosphere. Small garden, breakfast room, small apartment for family.
E-mail: fenice@fenicehotels.it

Netherlands

AMSTERDAM

Canal House Hotel
Keizersgracht 148 NL-1015 CX
020-622-5182
Fax: 020-624-1317
Brian & Mary Bennett
Open all year

225-345 Netherlands$-
B&B
26 rooms, 26 pb
Visa, Mastercard,
American Express,
Rated, •
C-ltd/S-yes/P-no/H-no
English, Dutch

Full Dutch breakfast
Boiled eggs
Bar service, period antiques,
park view, fitness massage.

On quiet residential canal in Centrum. Five minutes to Anne Frank and Dam. Antique decor, no TV, illuminated garden, telephones and fax, very nice. We like our guests to carry the feeling that they have found "A home away from home".   E-mail: canalhousehotel@compuserve.com *Web site:* canalhouse.nl

AMSTERDAM ────────────────

Toro Hotel
Koningslaan 64 NL-1075 AG
31-20-673-7223
Fax: 31-20-675-0031
J. Plooy and M.G. Plooy-Cok
Open all year

260 Netherlands$-B&B
22 rooms, 22 pb
Most CC, *Rated*, •
C-yes/S-ltd/P-no/H-ltd
Dutch, English, German,
French, Spanish

Full breakfast
Ask about food availabilty
Bar service, sitting room, and
terrace, park view, fitness
massage

A small hotel with a great personality. Peaceful location, completely rebuilt mansion, near the center & museum, own garden borders canal of park. Furnished in genuine antiques. Paid parking in front of hotel.   Web site: travelguides.com/bb/toro_hotel/

Portugal

LISBON ────────────────

Quinta Da Capela
Estrada Velha de Monserate,
Sintra P-2710
351-1-929-0170
Fax: 351-1-929-3425
Arturo D. Pereira
Open all year

24,000 Portugese$-B&B
10 rooms, 10 pb
Most CC, *Rated*, •
C-yes/S-yes/P-yes/H-yes
English, German, French

Buffet breakfast
Dinner, tea, snacks, wine
Bar service, library, sitting
room, sauna, swimming
pool, Massage therapist.
Garden suite big bathroom,
lounge with fireplace, 2
private terrasses.

30 minutes from Lisbon, surrounded by Sintra hills. Spectacular views, botannical gardens, lush vegetation, ancient castles, historical monuments. Beaches 10 minutes away.

Scotland, U.K.

CARDROSS ────────────────

Kirkton House
Darleith Rd, Dunbarton G82
5EZ
44-0-1389-841-951
Fax: 44-0-1389-841-868
Stewart & Gillian Macdonald
February-November

52.50 English$-B&B
6 rooms, 6 pb
Most CC, *Rated*, •
C-yes/S-yes/P-yes/H-ltd
English, French, Dutch

Full breakfast
Dinner, snacks
Sitting room, library, resid.
drinks licence, easy drive to
Glasgow, Massage therapist

Converted 18/19th century farm in tranquil rural position, commanding panoramic views of the River Clyde. Informal and relaxing ambience. Wine and dine by oil lamplight. Informal relaxed ambience, friendly & unobtrusive, personal service of your host. E-mail: info@kirktonhouse.com Web site: kirktonhouse.co.uk

DUNOON ────────────────

Abbot'S Brae Hotel
West Bay, Argyll PA23 7QJ
440-1369-705021
Fax: 440-1369-701191
Helen & Gavin
All year

50-62 English$-B&B
77 rooms, 7 pb
Visa, Mastercard, JCB,
•
C-yes/S-yes/P-yes/H-no
English

Full breakfast
Restaurant,dinner, snacks,
bar
Sitting room

Victorian country house hotel set in wooded seclusion with breathtaking views of seas and hills. Spacious rooms with many extras, quality dinners. Excellent base to explore the west highlands of Scotland.   E-mail: enquiries@abbotsbrae.ndirect.co.uk Web site: abbotsbrae.co.uk

ISLE OF SKYE————————————————————————

Kinloch Lodge	80-170 English$-B&B	Full breakfast
Sleat, Highland IV 43 8QY	10 rooms, 10 pb	Restaurant (fee), tea
1471-833214	Most CC, *Rated*, •	Sitting room, library,
Fax: 1471-833277	C-yes/S-yes/P-yes/H-no	fireplace, phone.
Lord & Lady MacDonald	English	
March - November		

Home of Lord and Lady MacDonald, Kinloch has achieved an enviable reputation for everything excellent over the past 25 years. E-mail: kinloch@dial.pipex.com
Web site: kinloch-lodge.co.uk

South Wales, U.K.

CRICKHOWELL————————————————————————

Gliffaes Country House	60-70 English$-B&B	Full breakfast
Gliffaes Road, Powys NP8 1RH	22 rooms, 22 pb	Lunch, dinner, restaurant
01874-730-371	Visa, Mastercard,	Bar service, sitting room,
Fax: 01874-730-463	American Express,	tennis, croquet, fishing,
N & P Brabner, J & S Suter	Most CC, *Rated*	putting, golf practice,
Open all year	C-yes/S-ltd/P-ltd/H-no	washing machine, iron
	Spanish, French, English	

This 1885 Italian gem set in stunning surroundings has delicious food, spacious sitting rooms and sun room and a warm welcome. Walking, birdwatching, fishing on private 2.5 miles stretch of river. E-mail: calls@gliffaeshotel.com *Web site:* gliffaeshotel.com/

Spain

ALHAURIN EL GRANDE————————————————————

Finca La Mota	7-10,000 Spanish$-B&B	Full breakfast
Carretera de Mijas,	15 rooms, 10 pb	Lunch, dinner, restaurant
Malaga E-29120	Visa, Mastercard,	Bar service, sitting room
95-2490901	American Express,	pool, tennis, golf 1 Km., mini
Fax: 95-2594120	Most CC, *Rated*, •	golf, Beach 15 Km, Horse-
Arun and Jean Narang	C-yes/S-yes/P-yes/H-yes	riding at inn, swimming pool
Open all year	English, Spanish, French	

Three-hundred year old Andalucian farmhouse inn, decorated in rustic style and surrounded by agricultural land. Informal, family atmosphere. Children very welcome.
E-mail: lamota@maptel.es *Web site:* flamota.com

ARCOS DE LA FRONTERA————————————————————

Hacienda El Santiscal	12,000 Spanish$-Meals:	Continental full Andalucian
Avenida del Santiscal No. 129	Inquire	breakfast
E-11638	12 rooms, 12 pb	Restaurant (fee)
0034-956-708313	Most CC, *Rated*, •	Sitting room, garden,
Fax: 0034-956-708268	C-ltd/S-yes/P-ltd/H-no	swimming pool, nautical,
Paqui Gallardo Carrasco	English, French, Arabic,	sports, cultural visits, tennis,
Open all year	German, Spanish	sauna, pool

Splendid hotel & rest. in a restored 15th century Andalusian manor house. Lovely & quiet surroundings next to lake of Arcos, capital of the White Villages.
F-mail: santiscal@gadesino.com *Web site:* estauciases.com

ASTURIAS

La Tahona De Besnes
Besnes, Alles E-33578
98-541-5749
Fax: 98-541-5749
Lorenzo & Sarah Nilsson
Open all year

8,000 Spanish$-EP, B&B
13 rooms, 13 pb
Visa, Mastercard,
American Express,
Most CC, *Rated*
C-yes/S-yes/P-no/H-ltd
Spanish, English

Restaurant (fee)
Lunch, dinner, snacks
Bar service, bicycles, sitting
room, swimming pool

Charmingly restored stone bakery offering rustic hideaway. Outdoor activities all year. Cozy restaurant specializing in local cuisine. Free bottle of wine with dinner.
E-mail: latahona@ctv.es

BINISSALEM

Scott'S Hotel
Plaza de la Iglesia, #12,
Mallorca E-07350
34-971-87-0100
Fax: 34-971-87-0267
George Scott
All year

165-225 US$-B&B
17 rooms, 17 pb
Visa, Mastercard, •
C-ltd/S-ltd/P-no/H-ltd
Spanish, German,
Russian, Catalan, Czech

Continental plus breakfast
Afternoon tea, snacks, bar
Sitting room, library,
jacuzzis, swimming pool,
suites, fireplace, cable TV,
conference facilities.

Scott's has been reviewed as "One of the most elegant and comfortable small B&B hotels in the Mediterranean." Located in the wine capital of Mallorca, Spain, Europe's number one holiday destination.   E-mail: scotts@bitel.es *Web site:* scottshotel.net

BOLVIR

Torre Del Remei
Cami Reial s/n, Girona E-17539
34-972-140-182
Fax: 34-972-140-449
Josep M. & Loles Boix
Open all year

28-45,000 Spanish$-EP
11 rooms, 11 pb
Visa, Mastercard,
American Express, •
C-yes/S-yes/P-yes/H-no
Spanish, English, French,
Italian

Full breakfast (fee)
Lunch, dinner, restaurant,
bar service
Jacuzzi, snacks,
complimentary wine, sitting
room, bicycles, swimming
pool, golf 1 Km. away,
horseback riding, hot air
balloning.

A beautiful summer palace, with 11 rooms. Here you can almost feel as though this is your very own palace nestled in the Pyrenees, amidst an 8 acre forest near the Cadi National Park transformed into an elegant luxury hotel.   E-mail: t.remei@gro.servicom.es
Web site: relaischateaux.fr/torreremei/

CUENCA

Posada De San Jose
Julian Romero 4 E-16001
969-21-1300
Fax: 969-23-0365
Antonio & Jennifer Cortinas
Open all year

4,100-9,100 Spanish$-
Meals: Inquire
30 rooms, 21 pb
Most CC, *Rated*, •
C-yes/S-yes/P-no/H-no
English, French, Spanish

Continental breakfast
Afternoon tea, snacks
Bar service, sitting room,
terrace and garden.

The Posada de San Jose is situated in the heart of the old historic quarter of Cuenca, in a 17th century building. Its old portal tempts you to admire the views.
E-mail: psanjose@arrakis.es *Web site:* arrakis.es/~psanjose/

MERANGES

Hotel Can Borrell
Retorn #3, Girona E-17539
972-880-033
Fax: 972-880-144
Antonio Forn Alonso
Ask about time of operation

12,000 Spanish$-EP
8 rooms, 8 pb
Visa, Mastercard,
Eurocard, •
C-yes/S-yes/P-no/H-no
Spanish, English, French,
German, Ital.

Full breakfast (fee)
Lunch, dinner, afternoon tea,
snacks
Complimentary wine,
restaurant, bar, sitting room,
cross-country ski, mountain
bike, self contained
apartment

A 200-year-old farmhouse country hydeaway, furnished in absolute keeping with the nature of the building. Its restaurant is well known in Spain for Catalan country-style cooking. Wonderful walking areas & views.   E-mail: info@canborrell.com *Web site:* canborrell.com/

PALMA DE MALLORCA————————————————————————

Palacio Ca Sa Galesa	30-250 Spanish$-B&B	Continental plus breakfast
Carrer de Miramar, 8 E-07001	12 rooms, 12 pb	Restaurant, afternoon tea,
971-71-5400	Most CC, •	comp. wine
Fax: 971-72-1579	C-yes/S-yes/P-no/H-no	Sitting room, bar service,
Pere Crespi	Spanish, English,	library, sauna, indoor
All year	German, French, Ital.	swimming pool, fitness
		facilities.

Mallorcas Palace from the 15th century. Situated in the heart of the old part of Palma, with all the 20th century facilities. Inside pool, outside terrace, solarium and sauna.
E-mail: reserves@fehm.es

Switzerland

GSTAAD————————————————————————————

Hotel Le Grand Chalet	340 Swiss$-B&B	Full breakfast
Neueretstrasse, Berne CH-3780	23 rooms, 23 pb	Lunch, dinner, restaurant
033-748-7676	Most CC, *Rated*, •	Bar service, sitting room,
Fax: 033-748-7677	C-yes/S-yes/P-yes/H-yes	library, sauna, pool, golf
Franz Rosskogler	English, German,	corner. .
Closed Nov, May, April	French, Italian, Dutch	

Cozy hotel, very quiet, with the most beautiful view in Gstaad. Highly rated restaurant - high standard of service. Golf nearby. E-mail: hotel@granchalet.ch
Web site: forum.ch/chalet_gstaad

LUGANO————————————————————————————

Villa Principe Leopoldo	290-700 Swiss$-B&B	Buffet breakfast
Via Montalbano 5 CH-6900	75 rooms, 75 pb	Restaurant, lunch, dinner,
+41-91-985-8855	Visa, Mastercard,	afternoon tea
Fax: +41-91-985-8825	American Express, •	Fitness room,
Maurie R.L. Urech	C-yes/S-yes/P-yes/H-no	Indoor/outdoor pool,
All year	GB., DL., FR., SP., PORT.,	Solarium, Whirlpool, Tennis,
	ITA.	TV, AC, Minibar, Balconies,
		Indoor golf, Sauna.

Superb hydeaway mansion dominating Lugano and the arch which starts in Paradiso to reach Castagnola and shape one of the most inland-lake golf's in Europe. Weather permitting lunches and dinners al fresco in our gourmet restaurant. E-mail: info@leopoldo.ch
Web site: leopoldo.ch

REGENSBERG————————————————————————————

Rote Rose	250-300 Swiss$-B&B	Continental plus breakfast
CH-8158	5 rooms, 5 pb	Afternoon tea, snacks
011-41-1-853-1013	•	Kitchens and sitting rooms,
Fax: 011-41-1-853-1559	C-ltd/S-no/P-no/H-yes	in suites, rose gardens, art
Christa Schaefer	English, German,	gallery, pond with tanning
March - December	French, Italian	area

Elegant country inn. Spacious antique-filled suites. Unspoiled Medieval village. Rose gardens, spectacular views. Near Zurich airport, but worlds away! Free assortment of local wines. E-mail: karen@karenbrown.com *Web site:* travelguides.com/home/roterose/

ZERMATT

Hotel Antares
Schluhmatte CH-3920
+41-027-967-3664
Fax: +41-027-967-5236
Schnidrig-Holenstein Family
Open all year

130 Swiss$-B&B
36 rooms, 36 pb
Most CC, *Rated*, •
C-yes/S-yes/P-yes/H-ltd
English, French,
German, Italian

Buffet breakfast
Lunch, gourmet dinner,
restaurant
Bar service, sitting room,
sauna, steam bath,
complimentary wine after 3
nights.

Attractive hotel in a peaceful location with lovely views of the Matterhorn; gourmet meals served in the restaurant or on the sunny terrace. E-mail: hotel.antares@zermatt.ch
Web site: zermatt.ch/antares/

ZURICH

Top Hotel Tiefenau
Steinwiesstrasse 8-10 CH-8032
41-1-267-87-87
Fax: 41-1-251-2476
Beat R. Blumer
Open all year

330-580 Swiss Francs$-EP
30 rooms, 30 pb
Visa, Mastercard,
American Express,
Diners, *Rated*, •
C-yes/S-yes/P-yes/H-no
Eng., French, German,
Spanish, Chinese

Full champagne-breakfast
buffet (fee)
Snacks, coffee, luncheon, ice
cream
Sitting room, own parking,
famous Swiss pastries and
cakes. Business Corner,
direct internet & E-mail
access, modem hook up in
every room, flowery garden.

Situated right in the City Center yet in a very quiet position. A complimentary welcome Swiss mineral awaits you in your room. Member of the Swiss Hotel Association and TOP International Hotels. Welcome cocktail in restaurant with your meal.
E-mail: info@tiefenau.ch *Web site:* tiefenau.ch/

Wales, U.K.

CARDIFF

Egerton Grey Country House
Porthkerry, Rhoose, Cardiff,
Glamoran CF62 3BZ
0044-1446-711666
Fax: 0044-1446-711690
Anthony J. Pitkin
Open all year

92-120 English$-B&B
10 rooms, 10 pb
Most CC, *Rated*, •
C-yes/S-yes/P-yes/H-no
French, German, Welsh

Full breakfast
Lunch, dinner, restaurant
Bar service, sitting room,
library, tennis, hot tubs,
travel agency "Turisbus",
washing machine, iron.

Beautiful old rectory on 7 acres of lush gardens. Outstanding views of coast. "The definitive country house hotel for South Wales." Winner of many awards cuisine and comfort.
E-mail: info@egertongrey.co.uk *Web site:* egertongrey.co.uk

Sant-Y-Nyll House
St. Brides-Super-Ely,
Glamoran CF5 6EZ
014-46-760209
Fax: 014-46-760897
Paul & Monica Renwick
Open all year

25 English$-B&B
6 rooms, 1 pb
American Express,
Rated, •
C-yes/S-yes/P-yes/H-no
French, Danish, Swedish

Ask about breakfast
Dinner, afternoon tea, snacks
Bar service, sitting room
swimming pool, washing
machine, iron

Georgian country house set in vale of Glamorgan, spectacular views, 6 acre garden, 15 mins. from Cardiff city centre. Beautifully furnished rooms. 3rd night 20% off.
E-mail: sant-y-nyll@msn.com

CONWY————————————————————————

Old Rectory Country House
Llanrwst Road, Colwyn Bay,
Llansaffraid LL28 5LF
01492-580-611
Fax: 01492-584-555
Michael & Wendy Vaughan
February - December

90-139 English$-
MAP/B&B
6 rooms, 6 pb
Visa, Mastercard,
Most CC, *Rated*, •
C-ltd/S-no/H-no
English, Welsh

Full breakfast
Dinner, tea/coffee in room
Bar service, sitting room,
library, private garden,
bathrobes, iron in room,

Idyllicaly set in glorious gardens. Uninterupted vistas of Snowdonia, and historic Conwy. Relaxing country house atmosphere where antiques and paintings abound. Wendy's a master chef, Michael helps plan your routes.
E-mail: oldrect@aol.com *Web site:* wales.com/oldrectory

LLANABER————————————————————————

Llwyndu Farmhouse
Llwyndu, Gwynedd LL42 1RR
0341-280144
Fax: 01341-281236
Paula & Peter Thompson
All year

32-70 English$-MAP
7 rooms, 7 pb
Visa, Mastercard, Access
C-yes/S-no/P-yes/H-no
English

Full breakfast
Restaurant, bar service,
dinner
Sitting room

Llwyndu Farmhouse was built around 1,600 for a local lawyer, now restored, it has a wealth of immense character. E-mail: petethompson@btinternet.com

TREFRIW————————————————————————

Hafod Country Lodge
Village Trefriw,
Conwy LL27 ORQ
01492-640029
Fax: 01492-61351
Rosina & Chris Nichols
Early Feb. to Early Jan.

60-103 English$-B&B
7 rooms, 7 pb
Visa, Mastercard,
American Express, •
C-no/S-no/P-yes
English

Full breakfast
Lunch, dinner, restaurant
Garden, private car park.

Converted 17th. Century farmhouse furnished with antiques. Outstanding food, prepared entirely on the premises. Open fire, oak panelled bar. Quiet village location yet ideal base for exploring North Wales.

Middle East

Israel

JERUSALEM————————————————————————

Mount Of Olives Hotel
53 Mount of Olives Rd 91190
+972-2-628-4877
Fax: +972-2-626-4427
800-762-9295
Ibrahim Dawud
Open all year

48-78 US$-Meals: Inquire
61 rooms, 61 pb
Visa, Mastercard,
American Express,
Rated, •
C-yes/S-yes/P-no/H-no
English, French, Arabic,
Hebrew

Restaurant (fee)
Lunch, dinner, snacks
Bar service, sitting room,
best view of Jerusalem, leave
the crowds behind.., tennis,
sauna, pool.

A family hotel situated at the summit of the Mount of Olives, next to the Chapel of Ascension. Ideal for Pilgrims. Stay six nights, seventh night free.
E-mail: info@mtolives.com *Web site:* mtolives.com

More Bed & Breakfast Inns

Alabama

Albertville	Twin House B&B, 705 Baltimore Ave, 35950 256-878-7499
Alexander City	Mistletoe Bough, 497 Hillabee St, 35010 205-329-3717
Aliceville	Myrtlewood, 602 Broad St, 35442 205-373-2121
Aliceville	WillowBrooke, 501 Broad St, 35442 205-373-6133
Auburn	Crenshaw Guest House, 371 N College St, 36830 334-821-1131
Boaz	Boaz B&B, 200 Thomas Ave, 35957
Cherokee	Easterwood House B&B Inn, 200 Easterwood St, 35616 205-359-4688
Citronelle	Citronella B&B Inn, 19055 S. Main St, 36522 205-866-2849
Collinsville	Madaperca B&B, 7802 Al Hwy 68, 35961 205-634-4792
Daleville	Gingerbread House, 204 Carroll Dr, 36322 334-598-4366
Decatur	Hearts and Treasures, 911 Seventh Ave,SE, 35601 256-353-9562
Elba	Aunt B's B&B, 717 W. Davis St, 36323 334-897-6918
Eufaula	Kendal Manor, 534 W. Broad St, 36027 334-687-8847
Eufaula	St. Mary's B&B, 206 Rivers Ave, 36027 205-687-7195
Eufaula	The John Dill House, PO Box 909, 36072
Eutaw	Kirkwood Plantation, 111 Kirkwood Dr, 35462 205-372-9009
Fairhope	Away At The Bay, 557 North Mobile St, 36532 205-928-9725
Fairhope	Barons on the Bay Inn, 701 S. Mobile Ave, 36532 334-928-8000
Fairhope	Bay Breeze Guest House, PO Box 526, 36533 334-928-8976
Fairhope	Church Street Inn, 51 S. Church St, 36532 334-928-5144
Fairhope	Doc & Dawn's Garden B&B, 314 De La Mare Ave, 36532 205-928-0253
Fairhope	Marcella's Tea Room & Inn, 114 Fairhope Ave, 36532 334-990-8520
Fairhope	Mershon Court B&B Inn, 203 Fairhope Ave, 36532 205-928-7398
Fairhope	The Guest House, 63 S Church St, 36532 334-928-6226
Fayette	Rose House Inn, 325 - 2nd Ave NW, 35555 205-932-7673
Foley	Katy's Gourmet B&B, 603 S McKenzie St, 36535 334-970-1529
Ft. Payne	Knotty Pine Resort, 1492 County Rd 618, 35967 256-845-5293
Geneva	Live Oaks, 307 S Academy St, 36340 334-684-2489
Greensboro	Blue Shadows B&B, Box 432, 36744 334-624-3637
Greenville	The Martin House B&B, 212 E Commerce St, 36307 334-382-2011
Gulf Shores	Beach House, 9218 Dacus Ln, 36542 334-540-7039
Gulf Shores	Square Flower B&B, 7013 Sea Shell Dr, 36542 334-540-7279
Guntersville	Lake Guntersville, 2204 Scott St, 35976 205-505-0133
Huntsville	Nestled Amongst the Trees, 4117 Darby Court, 35442 256-554-2577
Jemison	The Jemison Inn, 212 Hwy. 191, 35085 205-688-2055
Loxley	Europa Inn, 26221 Hwy 59, 36551 334-964-4000
Magnolia	Magnolia Springs B&B, PO Box 329, 36555 334-965-7321
Marion	Myrtle Hill, 303 W. Lafayette St, 36756 334-683-9095
Mentone	Mentone Springs Hotel, 6114 Hwy 117, 35984 256-634-4040
Mentone	Raven Haven, 651 Country Rd 644, 35984 205-634-4310
Mentone	Valhalla, 672 Country Rd 626, 35984 205-634-4006
Montgomery	The Lattice Inn, 1414 So. Hull St, 36104 334-264-0075
Montrose	The Green House, PO Box 352, 36559 800-763-5672
Mount Meigs	Colonel's Rest, 11091 Atlanta Hwy, 36117 334-215-0380
Munford	Cedars Plantation, 590 Cheaha Rd, 36268 205-761-9090
Northport	China Grove Plantation, 15526 Kevin Cv, 35475
Oneonta	Capps Cove B&B, 4126 County Hiway 27, 35121 256-625-3039
Opelika	Heritage House, 714 Second Ave, 36701 334-705-0485
Orange Beach	Acadian Inn, 4633 Wilson Blvd, 36561 334-981-6710
Pisgah	Lodge on Gorham's Bluff, 101 Gorham Dr, 35765 205-451-3435
Prattville	The Plantation House, 752 Loder St, 36067 334-361-0442
Sylacauga	Towassa, A B&B, 301 S Broadway Ave, 35150 256-249-3450
Talladega	Historic Oakwood B&B, 715 E. North St, 35160 205-362-0662
Talladega	Orangevale, 1400 Whiting Rd, 35160 205-362-3052
Talladega	Somerset House, 701 North St E, 35160 205-761-9251
Talladega	The Governor's House, 500 Meadowlake Lane, 35160 205-763-2186
Talladega	Veranda, 416 Cherry St, 35160 205-362-0548
Toney	The Church House B&B, 2017 Grimwood Rd, 35773 256-828-5192
Troy	The House of Dunn's, 204 S. Brundidge St, 36081 205-566-9414
Valley Head	Winston Place, 353 Railroad St, 35989 256-635-6381

Alaska

Anchor Point	Herrick's Haven B&B, PO Box 87, 99556 907-235-8322
Anchorage	42nd Avenue Annex, 410 W. 42nd Ave, 99503 907-561-8895
Anchorage	A Cousin Of Mine In Alaska, 4406 Forest Rd., 99517 907-248-3462
Anchorage	Airport B&B, 2904 Aspen Dr, 99517 907-243-6050
Anchorage	Alaska Holidays, 605 W 2nd Ave, 99501 907-276-1917
Anchorage	Alaska Sunset Inn B&B, 340 East 2nd Court, 99501 907-272-1321
Anchorage	Alaska's Bayshore View B&B, 3861 Chiniak Bay Dr, 99515 907-349-4446

Anchorage	Alaska's Morovia House B&B, 3800 Delwood Pl, 99504 907-337-3400
Anchorage	Alaskan B&B Tess's Place, 1836 Scenic Way, 99501
Anchorage	All The Comforts of Home, 12531 Turk's Turn St, 99516 907-345-4279
Anchorage	Alpine Woods B&B, 6200 Downey Finch Dr, 99516 907-345-5551
Anchorage	Anchorage Downtown B&B, 1401 W 13th Ave, 99501
Anchorage	Anna's B&B, 830 Jay Circle, 99504 907-338-5331
Anchorage	Arctic B&B, 2607 Artic Blvd., 99503 907-272-1853
Anchorage	Arctic Circle Adventures, 200 W 34th Ave., #903, 99503 907-276-0976
Anchorage	Arctic Fox Inn B&B, 326 E Second Court, 99501
Anchorage	At Schenll's B&B, 6608 Chevigny St., 99502 907-243-2074
Anchorage	Aurora Winds B&B Resort, 7501 Upper Omalley Rd, 99516 907-346-2533
Anchorage	B&B on the Park, 602 W 10th Ave, 99501 907-277-0878
Anchorage	Big Bear B&B, 3401 Richmond Ave., 99508 907-277-8189
Anchorage	Blackberry B&B, 6060 Blackberry Rd, 99502 907-243-0265
Anchorage	Caribou B&B Inn, 501 L St, 99501
Anchorage	Chateau on the Bluff, 6050 W. Dimond Blvd, 99502 907-245-6224
Anchorage	Cheney Lake B&B, 6333 Colgate Dr, 99504 907-337-4391
Anchorage	Chickadee B&B, 961 Coral Ln, 99515
Anchorage	Claddaugh Cottage, 2800 White Birch Ln, 99517 907-248-7104
Anchorage	Cloudcroft B&B, 6720 Cloudcroft, 99516
Anchorage	Coastal Trail B&B, 3100 Lliamna Dr, 99517 907-243-5809
Anchorage	Colonial Inn B&B, 1713 Northwestern Ave, 99508 907-277-6978
Anchorage	Copper Whale Inn, 440 L Street, 99501
Anchorage	Deals B&B, 2910 W 35th Ave, 99517
Anchorage	Earth B&B, 1001 W. 12th Ave, 99511 907-279-9907
Anchorage	Elderberry B&B, 8340 Elderberry, 99502 907-243-6968
Anchorage	English Country B&B, 2911 Rocky Bay Circle, 99515 907-344-0646
Anchorage	Fancy Moose B&B, 3331 W 32nd Ave, 99517 907-243-7596
Anchorage	First Lady B&B Inn, 2700 Arlington Dr, 99516 907-272-3131
Anchorage	Fran's Place, 3909 Turnagain Blvd, 99517 907-243-4009
Anchorage	Garden Beds B&B, 3105 W 29th Ave., 99517 907-243-8880
Anchorage	Glacier Way B&B, 2051 Glacier St, 99508 907-337-5201
Anchorage	Gourmet Fleurs B&B, 10000 Hillside Dr, 99516 907-346-1759
Anchorage	Greens' Garden B&B, PO Box 142288, 99514 907-333-7268
Anchorage	Hans Meyer's Homestead B&B, 1901 Otter St, 99504
Anchorage	Heidi's B&B, 3904 Lois Dr, 99517 907-563-8517
Anchorage	Hillside Hosts, 7745 Port Orford Dr, 99516 907-346-3096
Anchorage	Hospitality Plus B&B, 7722 Anne Circle, 99504 907-333-8504
Anchorage	Internet Lodgings, 7600 E 17th St, 99504
Anchorage	Ivy Inn, 13570 Westwind Dr, 99516 907-345-4024
Anchorage	Kenai Magic Lodge, 2440 E Tudor Rd #205, 99507
Anchorage	Kennicott Glacier Lodge, PO Box 103940, 99510 907-258-2350
Anchorage	Leopold David House B&B In, 605 W. 2nd Ave, 99501 907-279-1917
Anchorage	Moosewood Manor, PO Box 113188, 99511 907-345-8788
Anchorage	North Country Castle B&B, PO Box 111876, 99511 907-345-7296
Anchorage	Rox Run B&B, 5601 Naknek Lane, 99516
Anchorage	Salmon Run Guest House, 2411 W 69th Court, 99502 907-243-7022
Anchorage	Sixth & B B&B, 1134 L St, 99501 907-279-5293
Anchorage	Slim Walstons B&B, 611 M St, 99501 907-277-8215
Anchorage	Snowline B&B, 11101 Snowline Dr, 99516 907-346-1631
Anchorage	Snowshoe Inn, 826 K Street, 99501
Anchorage	Swan House B&B, 6840 Crooked Tree Dr, 99516 907-346-3033
Anchorage	Swiss Chalet B&B, 1761 Eastridge Dr, 99501 907-224-3939
Anchorage	The Aerie, 17920 Steamboat Dr., 99516 907-345-9837
Anchorage	The Mangy Moose B&B, 5560 E 112th Ave, 99516 907-346-8052
Anchorage	The Teddy Bear House, 500 Dailey Ave, 99515 907-344-3111
Anchorage	Tree House B&B, 13000 Admiralty Pl., 99515 907-345-5421
Anchorage	Two Morrow's Place B&B, 3213 Minnesota Dr #B, 99503 907-277-9939
Anchorage	Wesleyan House, 3412 Wesleyan Dr, 99508 907-337-7383
Anchorage	Your Home Away From Home, 1801 Stanton Ave, 99508
Angoon	Favorite Bay Inn, PO Box 101, 99820 907-788-3123
Auke Bay	Adlersheim Lodge, PO Box 210447, 99821 907-723-4447
Auke Bay	Grandview B&B, PO Box 210705, 99821 907-790-2648
Bethel	Bentley's Porterhouse B&B, 62 First Ave Box 529, 99559
Bethel	Pacifica Guest House, PO Box 1208, 99559 907-543-4305
Big Lake	Dollar Lake Lodging B&B, PO Box 521433, 99652 907-892-7620
Big Lake	Jeanie's on Big Lake, Box 520598, 99652
Chickaloon	Chickaloon B&B, Box 1166, 99674 907-745-1155
Chugiak	Peters Creek Inn B&B, PO Box 671487, 99567 907-688-2776
Cooper Center	Nugget B&B, HC60, Box 157, 99573 907-822-5388
Cooper Landing	Red Salmon Guest House, Mi 48.2 Sterling Hwy #D, 99572
Cordova	Midnight Sun Lodging, PO Box 1183, 99574 907-424-3492
Cordova	Northern Nights Inn, PO Box 1564, 99574 907-424-5356
Cordova	Queens Chair B&B, PO Box 1475, 99574 907-424-3000
Delta Junction	Peggy's Alaskan Cabbage Pt, 5052 Arctic Grayling, 99737 907-895-4200
Denali	North Face Lodge, Denali National Park, 99755
Dillingham	Beaver Creek B&B, PO Box 563, 99576
Douglas	Windsock Inn B&B, PO Box 240223, 99824

Eagle River	3-B's, 12607 Iris Way, 99577 907-694-4041
Eagle River	Alaska Chalet B&B, 11031 Gulkana Circle, 99577
Eagle River	Andy's Eagle Park B&B, 9907 Wren Ln, 99577 907-694-2833
Eagle River	Bandy's B&B, 17215 Baranoff Ave, 99577 907-696-2344
Eagle River	Cranberry Cliffs B&B, 18735 Monastery Dr, 99577 907-696-3326
Eagle River	Log House B&B, 10925 Corrie Way, 99547 907-694-9231
Eagle River	Terrace Hills B&B, 11317 Terrace Hills Dr, 99577 907-694-3722
Fairbanks	AAA Care B&B, 557 Fairbanks St, 99709 907-479-2447
Fairbanks	Ah, Rose Marie Downtown, 302 Cowles St, 99701
Fairbanks	Alaska Heritage Inn, PO Box 74877, 99707
Fairbanks	Bell House B&B, 909 6th Ave, 99701 907-452-3278
Fairbanks	Birch Grove Inn B&B, Box 81387, 99708 907-479-5781
Fairbanks	Birch Haven Inn B&B, PO Box 82856, 99708 907-457-2451
Fairbanks	Bonnie's Abode, 12 Blanche Ave, 99701 907-452-7386
Fairbanks	By The River B&B, 229 Iditarod Ave, 99701 907-456-5063
Fairbanks	Chena River B&B, 1001 Dolly Varden Lane, 99709 907-479-2532
Fairbanks	Chokecherry Inn, 946 Coppet St, 99709
Fairbanks	Country Comforts, 174 Crest Dr, 99712 907-457-6867
Fairbanks	Cranberry Ridge B&B, 795 Cranberry Ridge Dr, 99712 907-457-4424
Fairbanks	Eleanor's Northern Lights, 360 State St, 99701 907-452-2598
Fairbanks	Fairbanks Downtown B&B, 1461 Gillam Way, 99701 907-452-7700
Fairbanks	Fireweed Hideaway, PO Box 82057, 99708 907-457-2579
Fairbanks	Forget-Me-Not-Lodge, PO Box 80128, 99708
Fairbanks	Frog Pond B&B, 131 Frog Pond Circle, 99712 907-457-4006
Fairbanks	Jan's B&B, 1605 Marika Rd, 99709 907-456-5431
Fairbanks	Lizzie's Nest B&B, 1012 Goldmine Trail, 99712 907-457-1957
Fairbanks	Marilyn's B&B, 651 9th Ave, 99701 907-456-1959
Fairbanks	Minnie Street B&B, 345 Minnie St, 99701 907-456-1802
Glennallen	Cranberry Hill B&B, PO Box 329, 99588 907-822-3302
Glennallen	McCarthy Lodge, PO Box MXY, 99588 907-554-4402
Gustavus	Annie Mae Lodge, PO Box 80, 99826 800-478-2346
Gustavus	Bear Track Inn, 255 Rink Creek Rd, 99826 907-697-3017
Gustavus	Glacier Bay Country Inn, PO Box 5, 99826 907-697-2288
Gustavus	Good River B&B, PO Box 37, 99826
Gustavus	Puffin's B&B Lodge, PO Box 3, 99826 907-697-2260
Gustavus	TRI B&B, PO Box 214, 99826
Gustavus	Whalesong Lodge, PO Box 389, 99826 907-697-2742
Haines	Bear Creek Camp, PO Box 908, 99827 907-766-2259
Haines	Chilkat Eagle B&B, 67 Soapsuds Alley, 99827 907-766-2763
Haines	Chilkat Valley Inn, PO Box 861, 99827 907-766-3331
Haines	Officers Inn B&B, PO Box 1589, 99827 907-766-2000
Haines	Sheltered Harbor B&B, PO Box 806, 99827 907-766-2741
Haines	Summer Inn B&B, PO Box 1198, 99669 907-766-2970
Healy	Alaskan Chateau B&B, PO Box 187, 99743 907-683-1377
Healy	At Timberline B&B, Box 13, 99743
Healy	Denali Dome B&B, PO Box 262, 99743 907-683-1239
Healy	Dry Creek B&B, PO Box 371, 99743 907-683-2386
Healy	Healy Heights Fam. Cabins, PO Box 277, 99743 907-683-2639
Healy	Rock Creek Country Inn, HCI Box 3450, 99743 907-683-2676
Healy	Rustic Ridge B&B, PO Box 46, 99743
Healy	Valley Vista B&B, PO Box 395, 99743
Homer	Alaska's Pioneer Inn, PO Box 1430, 99603 907-235-5670
Homer	Almost Home Accommodations, 1269 Upland Ct, 99603 907-235-2553
Homer	Bear Creek B&B, 41855 Bear Creek Dr, 99603 907-235-8522
Homer	Beeson B&B, 1393 Bay Ave, 99603 907-235-3757
Homer	Chocolate Drop B&B, PO Box 70, 99603 907-235-3668
Homer	Cloudy Mountain Inn B&B, PO Box 3801, 99603
Homer	Crestwood Manor, PO Box 412, 99603 907-235-6282
Homer	Driftwood Inn, 135 W. Bunnell Ave, 99603 907-235-8019
Homer	Forest Light Cottage, PO Box 2613, 99603
Homer	Halcyon Heights B&B, PO Box 3552, 99603 907-235-2148
Homer	Holland Days B&B Cabins, PO Box 2449, 99603 907-235-7604
Homer	Kachemak Kiana B&B, PO Box 855, 99603 907-235-8824
Homer	Lily Pad B&B, 3954 Bartlett St, 99603 907-235-6630
Homer	Magic Canyon Ranch, 40015 Waterman Rd, 99603 907-235-6077
Homer	Morning Glory B&B Charter, 1015 Larkspur Ct, 99603 907-235-8084
Homer	Old Town B&B, 106 W. Bunnell Ave,St D, 99603 907-235-7558
Homer	Sadie Cove Wilderness Ldge, Box 2265-VP, 99603 907-235-7766
Homer	Seaside Farm, HCR 58335 East End Rd, 99603
Homer	Shorebird Guest House, PO Box 204, 99603 907-235-2107
Homer	Spruce Acres B&B Cabins, 910 Sterling Hwy., 99603 907-235-8388
Homer	The Sea Lion Cove, PO Box 2095, 99603
Homer	Tutka Bay Wilderness Lodge, PO Box 960, 99603 907-235-3905
Homer	Victorian Heights B&B, PO Box 2363, 99603 907-235-6357
Homer	Wandering Star B&B, PO Box 1934, 99603 907-235-6788
Hoonah	Hubbard's B&B, PO Box 205, 99829 907-945-3414
Juneau	Alaska Discovery Inn, 5449 Shaune Dr., #4, 99801
Juneau	Alaska House B&B, PO Box 21321, 99802

Juneau	Alaska Wolf House B&B, PO Box 21321, 99801 907-586-2422
Juneau	Alaskan Hotel, 167 S. Franklin, 99801 800-327-9347
Juneau	Blueberry Lodge on Tide., 9436 N. Douglas Hwy, 99801
Juneau	Cashen Quarters B&B, 315 Gold St, 99801 907-586-9863
Juneau	Channel View With A Room, 1775 Diamond Dr, 99801
Juneau	Cozy Log B&B, 8668 Dudley St, 99801 907-789-2582
Juneau	Crondahls B&B, 626 5th St, 99801
Juneau	Dawson's B&B, 1941 Glacier Hwy, 99801 907-586-9708
Juneau	Eagle's Nest B&B, PO Box 20537, 99802
Juneau	Entrance Pt. Homestead, 11260 N Douglas, 99801 907-463-2684
Juneau	Gould's Alaskan View B&B, 3044 Nowell Ave, 99801 907-463-1546
Juneau	Inn At The Waterfront, 455 S Franklin St, 99801 907-586-2050
Juneau	Jan's View B&B, PO Box 32254, 99803
Juneau	Lucia's Retreat, 6680 N. Douglas Rd, 99801
Juneau	Pot Belly B&B, 5115 N. Douglas Rd, 99801
Juneau	Sepel Hallow B&B, 10901 Mendenhall Loop, 99801
Juneau	Silverbow Inn & Restaurant, 120 - 2nd St, 99801 907-586-4146
Juneau	The Evergreen B&B, 300 W 11th St #3, 99801
Juneau	The Lost Chord, 2200 Fritz Cove Rd, 99801
Juneau	Water View B&B, c/o 1018 Capital Ave, 99801 907-586-3163
Kasilof	Deals Den B&B, HC2, Box 525A, 99610
Kasilof	Raven Mt. Farm B&B, PO Box 344, 99610
Kenai	Aksala Bunk and Breakfast, PO Box 3522, 99611
Kenai	Log Cabin B&B, PO Box 2886, 99611 907-283-3653
Ketchikan	Alaskan Home Fishing B&B, 11380 Alderwood St N, 99901
Ketchikan	Blueberry Hill B&B, 500 Front St, 99901 907-247-2583
Ketchikan	Captain's Quarters B&B, 325 Lund St, 99901 907-225-4912
Ketchikan	Eagle's Roost, PO Box 9187, 99901 907-247-9187
Ketchikan	Hillberry's B&B Inn, PO Box 9578, 99901 907-789-0604
Ketchikan	House of Stewart B&B, 3725 S. Tongass Hwy, 99901 907-247-3725
Ketchikan	Lundberg's South Shore Inn, 7446 S Tongass Hwy, 99901 907-225-0909
Ketchikan	Mink Bay Lodge, PO Box 6440, 99901
Ketchikan	Nestling Cove B&B, 3930 S Tongass Hwy, 99901 907-225-9782
Ketchikan	The Narrows Inn, PO Box 8296, 99901 907-247-2600
Ketchikan	Velda's Victorian B&B, 609 Pine St, 99901 907-225-4940
Ketchikan	Waterfall Resort, 320 Dock St, 99901 907-225-9461
Ketchikan	Yes Bay Lodge, PO Box 6440, 99901 907-225-7906
Kodiak	Berry Patch B&B Inn, 1616 Selief Lane, 99615 907-486-6593
Kodiak	Country B&B, 1415 Zentner Ave, 99615 907-486-5162
Kodiak	Otter Crest B&B, 1814 E. Rezanof, 99615
Lake Louise	Evergreen Lodge, HC 1 Box 1709 GennAllen, 99588 907-822-3250
Moose Pass	Alaska Nellie's Inn, PO Box 88, 99631 907-288-3124
Moose Pass	Spruce Moose, Mile 30 1 Seward Hwy, 99631 907-288-3667
Nenana	Finnish Alaskan B&B, PO Box 274, 99760 907-832-5628
Nenana	Welcome Home B&B, HCR 66 Box 28800, 99760 907-582-2234
Ninilchik	Bluff House B&B, PO Box 39327, 99639 907-567-3605
Ninilchik	Creekside Inn B&B, PO Box 236, 99639 907-567-7333
Ninilchik	Deep Creek B&B, PO Box 39544, 99639 907-567-5367
Ninilchik	Drift Inn B&B, PO Box 39068, 99639 907-567-3448
Ninilchik	Kennedy's Lookout B&B, HC 67, Box 2100, 99639 907-567-3482
Nome	June's B&B, PO Box 489, 99762 907-443-5984
Nome	Ocean View Manor B&B, PO Box 65, 99762 907-443-2133
North Pole	Alaskan's Lazy Daze B&B, 1819 Endicot Ave, 99705 907-488-7044
North Pole	Birch Tree B&B, 3104 Dyke Rd., 99705 907-488-4667
Palmer	Alaskan Spinning Wheel B&B, PO Box 4457, 99645 907-746-6858
Palmer	Colony Inn, 606 S Alaska St, 99645
Palmer	Country Inn @ Teddy Bear, PO Box 1151, 99645 907-745-4156
Palmer	Hatcher Pass B&B, HC 5, Box 6797-D, 99645 907-745-6788
Palmer	Knoll Haus B&B, PO Box 2155, 99645
Palmer	Lazy Acres B&B, PO Box 4013, 99645 907-745-6340
Palmer	Moose Creek B&B, PO Box 3011, 99645 907-745-1146
Palmer	Piccolo B&B, HCO5 Box 6937-Q, 99645 907-745-4838
Palmer	Timberlings B&B, Mile 57.3 Glenn Hwy, 99645 907-745-4445
Palmer	Tundra Rose B&B, HC03 Box 8484, 99645 907-745-5865
Pelican	Otter Cove B&B, PO Box 618, 99832
Petersburg	Harbor Day B&B, 404 Noseeum St., 99833 907-772-3971
Petersburg	Scandia House, PO Box 689, 99833 907-772-4281
Petersburg	Water's Edge B&B, PO Box 1201, 99833 907-772-3736
Port Graham	Fedora's B&B, PO Box 5516, 99603 907-284-2239
Seldovia	Dancing Eagles B&B & Cabin, PO Box 264, 99663 907-234-7624
Seward	Alaska's Point Of View, PO Box 312, 99664 907-224-5695
Seward	Alaska's Silver Lining B&B, PO Box 1654, 99664 907-224-2244
Seward	Alaska's Treehouse B&B, Box 861, 99664 907-224-3867
Seward	Benson B&B, PO Box 3506, 99664 907-224-5290
Seward	Berry Patch B&B, PO Box 2536, 99664
Seward	Farm B&B, Box 305, 99664 907-224-5691
Seward	Harborview B&B, PO Box 1305, 99664 907-224-3217
Seward	Moby Dick Lodging, PO Box 624, 99664 907-224-7072

Seward	Northern Nights, PO Box 491, 99664 907-224-5688
Seward	Riningers, PO Box 548, 99664 907-224-5918
Seward	Seward Waterfront Lodging, PO Box 618, 99664 907-224-5563
Seward	Six Mile B&B, PO Box 112, 99664 907-224-3848
Seward	Stoney Creek Inn B&B, PO Box 1352, 99664 907-224-3940
Sitka	Abner's B&B, 200 Seward St, 99835 907-747-8779
Sitka	Biorka B&B, 611 Biorka St, 99835 907-747-3111
Sitka	Cresent Harbor Hideaway, 709 Lincoln St., 99835 907-747-4900
Sitka	Finn Alley Inn, 711 Lincoln St, 99835 907-747-5007
Sitka	Forget-Me-Not B&B, 702 Pherson St, 99835 907-747-6813
Sitka	Helga's B&B, Box 1885, 99835
Sitka	Jamestown Bay Inn B&B, 1903 Sawmill Creek Rd, 99835 907-747-7100
Sitka	Karras B&B, 230 Kogwanton St, 99835 907-747-3978
Sitka	Mountain View B&B, PO Box 119, 99835 907-747-8966
Sitka	The Dacha, 500 Lincoln #M15, 99835 907-747-4872
Skagway	Cindy's Place, 1/4 Mile Dyea Rd, 99840 907-983-2674
Soldotna	Alaska Kenai River Raven, PO Box 1670, 99669 907-262-5818
Soldotna	Alaskan Paradise B&B, PO Box 152, 99669 907-262-3214
Soldotna	Casa Norte B&B, PO Box 2468, 99669 907-262-1257
Soldotna	Denise Lake Lodge B&B, PO Box 1050, 99669 907-262-1789
Soldotna	Holly House B&B, 220 Small Circle St, 99669 907-262-4762
Soldotna	Knight Manor B&B, 36420 Northern Lights, 99669 907-262-2438
Soldotna	Krog's Kamp, PO Box 3913, 99669 907-262-2671
Soldotna	Longmere Lake B&B, HC 1 Box 157H, 99669 907-262-5665
Soldotna	Loon Lake Resort, 43645 Sports Lake Rd, 99669 907-262-8435
Soldotna	Lotties Place B&B, PO Box 3458, 99669
Soldotna	Marlow's Kenai River B&B, PO Box 2465, 99669
Soldotna	Moose Hollow B&B, PO Box 2996, 99669
Soldotna	Ron Fay's Moose Creek B&B, PO Box 2247, 99667 907-260-3380
Soldotna	Soldotna B&B Inn, 399 Lover's Ln, 99669 907-262-4779
Soldotna	Spruce Ave. B&B, 35985 Pioneer Dr, 99669 907-262-9833
St. Paul Island	Lillian Capener's B&B, PO Box 105, 99660 907-546-2334
Sterling	Angler's Lodge & Fish Camp, PO Box 508, 99672
Talkeetna	Bays B&B, PO Box 527, 99676 907-733-1342
Talkeetna	Denali View B&B, HC 89, Box 8360, 99676 907-733-2778
Talkeetna	Eye of Denali Inn, PO Box 296, 99676 907-733-2655
Talkeetna	River Beauty B&B, PO Box 525, 99676 907-733-2741
Talkeetna	Talkeetna & Beyond, Box 236, 99676 907-733-3050
Talkeetna	Trapper John's B&B, PO Box 243, 99676
Tok	Cleft of the Rock, Sundog Trail Box 122, 99780
Tok	Lois' B&B, PO Box 527, 99780 907-883-5647
Tok	The Stage Stop B&B, PO Box 69, 99780 907-883-5338
Tok	Winter Cabin B&B, PO Box 61, 99780 907-883-5655
Trapper Creek	McKinley Foothills B&B Inn, PO Box 13089, 99683 907-733-1454
Trapper Creek	North Country B&B, PO Box 13377, 99683
Unalakleet	Unalakleet River Lodge, 99684 414-248-1978
Valdez	Alaska Forget-Me-Not B&B, PO Box 1153, 99686 907-835-2717
Valdez	Angie's Downhome B&B, PO Box 1394, 99686 907-835-2832
Valdez	Best Of All B&B, PO Box 1578, 99686 907-835-4524
Valdez	Boathouse, PO Box 1815, 99686 907-835-4407
Valdez	Cooper's Cottage B&B, 324PO Box 563, 99686 907-835-4810
Valdez	Easy Living B&B, PO Box 2435, 99686 907-835-4208
Valdez	Head Hunters Inn, 328 Egan Dr., 99686 907-835-2900
Valdez	Johnson House, Box 364, 99686
Valdez	Raven's Nest B&B, PO Box 2480, 99686 907-835-2482
Valdez	Think Pink B&B, PO Box 788, 99686 907-835-4367
Valdez	Wendy's B&B, PO Box 629, 99686 907-835-4770
Wasilla	Agate B&B Inn, 4725 Begich Circle, 99654 907-373-2290
Wasilla	Agate Inn B&B, 4525 Begich Circle, 99654 907-373-2290
Wasilla	Alaskan Sampler B&B, PO Box 876054, 99654 907-745-7829
Wasilla	Alpaca Inn, HC31 Box 5249P, 99654 907-357-2223
Wasilla	Bridge Stone Cottage B&B, 200 Bridge Stone Dr, 99654 907-376-6262
Wasilla	Country Lakes B&B, PO Box 876694, 99687 907-373-5868
Wasilla	Gate House B&B, PO Box 870563, 99687 907-376-5960
Wasilla	Town & Country Inn, 801 Hermon Rd, 99654 907-373-6695
Wasilla	Wasilla Lake B&B, 961 N. Shore Dr., 99654 907-376-5985
Willow	Alaskan Host B&B, PO Box 38, 99688 907-495-6448
Willow	Gigglewood Lakeside Inn, HC89 Box 1601, 99688 907-495-1014
Willow	Ruth Lake Lodge, PO Box 87, 99688 907-495-9000
Willow	Susitna Wilderness B&B, Box 74, 99688
Willow	Willow Trading Post, PO Box 49, 99688
Willow	Willow Winter Park B&B, PO Box 251, 99688 907-495-7547
Wrangell	Harbor House Lodge, PO Box 2027, 99929 907-874-3084
Wrangell	Rooney's Roose, 206 McKinnon, 99929 907-874-2026
Yakutat	Johnny's East River Lodge, Glacier Bay National Pk, 99689 907-780-5158
Yakutat	Shirley's B&B, 99689 907-784-3652
Yakutat	The Blue Heron, PO Box 254, 99689 907-784-3287
Yakutat	The Mooring Lodge, 720 Ocean Cape Dr., 99689 888-551-2836

Arizona

Ajo	Guest House Inn, 700 Guest House Rd, 85321 520-387-6133
Ajo	Mine Managers House B&B, 601 Greenway Rd, 85321 602-387-6505
Amado	Amado Territory Inn, PO Box 81, 85645 520-398-8684
Amado	Rex Ranch, PO Box 636, 85640
Apache Junction	Meanwhile Back @ the Ranch, 6300 E Pioneer St, 85219 602-982-2112
Benson	Redington Land & Cattle Co, PO Box 116, 85602 520-212-5555
Bisbee	Calumet & Arizona Guest Hs, 608 Powell St, 85603 520-432-4815
Bisbee	Inn at Castle Rock, PO Box 1161, 85603 520-432-4449
Bisbee	Main Street Inn, PO Box 454, 85603 520-432-5237
Bisbee	School House Inn B&B, PO Box 32, 85603 520-432-2996
Bisbee	The Clawson House, PO Box 454, 85603
Bisbee	The Curry House, 608 Powell, 85603
Bisbee	The Greenway House, 401 Cole Ave, 85603 520-432-7170
Bisbee	The Oliver House, PO Box 1897, 85603 520-432-4286
Carefree	Desert Farren Private Hac., PO Box 5550, 85377
Cave Creek	Andora Crossing, 6434 Military Rd, 85327 602-488-3747
Cave Creek	Gotland's Inn Cave Creek, PO Box 4948, 85331 602-488-9636
Cave Creek	Lazy H Ranch B&B, 41848 N Fleming Springs, 85331 602-488-0264
Chandler	Cone's Tourist Home, 2105 E Galveston St, 85225 602-839-0369
Chandler	La Casa Sevilla, 2545 W. Barrow Dr, 85224 602-775-0815
Choride	Shep's B&B, PO Box 527, 86431 602-565-3643
Clarkdale	Flying Eagle B&B, 2700 Windmill Ln, 86324 520-634-0211
Cottonwood	Dixon Farm, 2117 E Aspen, 86326 520-634-5915
Douglas	Family Crest, PO Box 1016, 85607
Eagar	Paisley Corners B&B, 287 N Main St, 85925
Flagstaff	Arizona Mountain Inn, 4200 Lake Mary Rd, 86001 520-774-8959
Flagstaff	Aspen Inn B&B, 218 N Elden, 86601 520-773-0295
Flagstaff	Cedar B&B, 425 W. Cedar, 86001 602-774-1636
Flagstaff	Dierker House B&B, 423 W. Cherry, 86001 602-774-3249
Flagstaff	East Cherry Inn B&B, 427 E Cherry Ave, 86001 520-744-1153
Flagstaff	Lynn's Inn B&B, 614 W Santa Fe Ave, 86001 520-226-1488
Flagstaff	Starlit Farm B&B, 2521 Eva Loop, 86004 602-526-1173
Flagstaff	The Tree House, 615 W Cherry Ave, 86001 520-774-7598
Florence	Rancho Sonora Inn & RV Pk, 9198 N Hwy 79, 85232
Fountain Hills	Fountain Hills B&B, 16240 E Kingstree Blvd, 85268
Fountain Hills	The Eagle House B&B, 10621 N Eagle Lane, 85268
Greer	Greer Lodge, PO Box 244, 85927 520-735-7216
Greer	White Mountain Lodge B&B, PO Box 143, 85927
Hereford	Casa de San Pedro B&B, 8933 S. Yell Ln, 85615 520-366-1300
Jerome	Inn at Jerome, PO Box 901, 86321 520-634-5094
Jerome	Surgeon's House, Hill Street District, 86321 520-639-1452
Jerome	The Rose Garden B&B, PO Box 313, 86331 520-634-3270
Lake Powell	Hummers Rest, PO Box 3532, 86040 520-645-2558
Lakeside	Aspen's Edge on Rainbow Lk, 779 S Lake Rd, Rt 2, 85929 520-368-4305
Mayer	Serenity House B&B, PO Box 1254, 86333 520-632-4430
Mesa	Casa Del Sol, 6951 E. Hobart, 85207 602-985-5956
Mesa	Elmhurst B&B, 13020 N Bush Hwy, 85215
Mesa	Hearthside B&B Inn, 5539 E Evergreen St, 85205
Mohave Valley	Old Trails Inn, 1805 South Dr, 86440
Mount Lemmon	Aspen Trail B&B, 11120 E Miami, 85619
Page	Hibberts Homestay, PO Box 2526, 86040 520-645-9690
Patagonia	Circle Z Ranch, PO Box 194, 85624 520-394-2525
Patagonia	The Little House, PO Box 461, 85624 602-394-2493
Pearce	Grapevine Canyon Ranch, PO Box 302, 85625 520-826-3185
Pearce	Sunglow Guest Ranch, HCI Box 385, 85625 520-824-3334
Phoenix	Camelback Mountain Guest, 5319 E Valle Vista Rd, 85018 602-837-4284
Phoenix	El Rancho Camposieno GH, 43 W Southgate Ave, 85040 602-268-6763
Phoenix	Nana's Room, 3223 W. Vogel Ave, 85051 602-943-0782
Phoenix	Posthouse B&B, 2241 W S Mountain Ave, 65041
Phoenix	The Harmony House B&B Inn, 7202 N 7th Ave, 85021 602-331-9554
Phoenix	Windsor Cottage, 62 W Windsor, 85003 602-264-6309
Pinetop	Gretchen's B&B, HC 66, Box 67310, 85935 520-367-0867
Pinetop	Meadows Inn On Woodland, PO Box 1110, 85935 520-367-8200
Pinetop	Sierra Springs Ranch, HC 62 Box 32100, 85935 520-369-3900
Prescott	Briar Wreath Inn, 232 S. Arizona Ave., 86303 520-778-6048
Prescott	Hotel Vendome, 230 S Cortez St, 86303 520-776-0900
Prescott	Juniper Well Ranch, PO Box 11083, 86304 520-442-3415
Prescott	Prescott Country Inn, 503 S. Montezuma St, 86303 520-445-7991
Prescott	Prescott Riviera B&B, 614 Robinson Dr, 86303 520-717-2696
Prescott	Rocamadour B&B, 3386 N Hwy 89, 86301 520-771-1933
Prescott	The Marks House Inn, 203 E. Union, 86303 602-778-4632
Prescott	The Pleasant Street Inn, 142 S Pleasant St, 86303
Prescott	Victorian Inn of Prescott, 246 S Cortez St, 86303
Sababe	Rancho de la Osa, One La Osa Ranch Rd, 85633 520-823-4257
Safford	Olney House B&B, 1104 Central Ave, 85546 602-428-5118
Sahuarita	Mi Gatita B&B, HCR 70, Box 3401, 85629 520-648-6129

Scottsdale	Endeavour Park Guest Ranch, 9840 N 110th St, 85259 602-661-5225
Scottsdale	Hideout at RedBuck Ranch, 30212 N 154th St, 85262 602-837-4284
Scottsdale	Inn at the Citadel, 8700 E. Pinnacle Pk 108, 85255 602-585-6133
Scottsdale	Jaste's Place, 11259 E Via Linda, 85259 520-391-9164
Scottsdale	La Paz in Desert Springs, 6309 E Ludlow Dr, 85254 602-922-5379
Scottsdale	Redwood Suites, 12002 N 68th St, 85254 602-368-8852
Sedona	Adobe Hacienda, 10 Rojo Dr, 86351 520-284-2020
Sedona	B&B @ Saddle Rock Ranch, 255 Rock Ridge Dr, 86336 520-282-7640
Sedona	Cathedral Rock Lodge, 61 Los Amigos Ln, 86336 520-282-7608
Sedona	Country Gardens B&B, PO Box 2603, 86339 520-282-1343
Sedona	Garland's Oak Creek Lodge, PO Box 152, 86339 520-282-3343
Sedona	Greyfire Farm B&B, 1240 Jacks Canyon Rd, 86352 520-284-2340
Sedona	Kennedy House, 2075 Red Rock Loop Rd, 86336 602-282-1624
Sedona	Lantern Light Inn B&B, 3085 W. Hwy 89A, 86336 602-282-3419
Sedona	Moestly Wood B&B, 2085 Red Rock Loop Rd, 86336 602-204-1461
Sedona	Red Rock Cottage, 656 Jordan Rd., 86336 520-282-5328
Sedona	Slide Rock Lodge, 6401 N Hwy 89A, 86336 602-282-3531
Sedona	Stoneflower B&B, 90 Chavez Ranch Rd, 86336 520-282-2977
Show Low	High Country B&B, 1291-B E Woolford, 85901 520-532-0567
Sierra Vista	San Pedro B&B, PO Box 885, 85636 520-458-6412
Skull Valley	Oasis Ranch, PO Box 256, 86338 520-442-9559
Sonoita	The Vineyard B&B, PO Box 1227, 85637 520-455-4749
Springerville	Paisley Corner, PO Box 458, 85938 602-333-4665
Springerville	X Diamond Ranch, PO Box 791, 85938 502-333-2286
Star Valley	Opal Ranch Inn, 2160 Moonlight Dr, 85541 520-472-6193
Tempe	Mi Casa-Su Casa B&B, PO Box 950, 85280 602-990-0682
Tempe	Tempe Mission Palms, 60 E 5th St, 85281 602-894-1400
Tombstone	Pricilla's B&B, PO Box 700, 85638 520-457-3844
Tombstone	Tombstone Boarding House, PO Box 906, 85638 602-457-3716
Tonto Basin	Whipple Tree Inn & Farm, PO Box 7, 85553
Tubac	Tubac Country Inn, Box 1540, 85646 520-398-3178
Tubac	Valle Verde Ranch, PO Box 157, 85640 520-398-2246
Tucson	Adobe Rose Inn B&B, 940 N Olsen Ave, 85719 520-318-4644
Tucson	Arizona Inn, 2200 E. Elm St, 85718 520-325-1541
Tucson	Car-Mar's Southwest B&B, 6766 W Oklahoma St, 85735 520-578-1730
Tucson	Casa Tierra, 11155 West Calle Pima, 85743 520-578-3058
Tucson	Casita de la Tortuga, 1641 E Waverly, 85719 520-322-5829
Tucson	Congenial Quail, 4267 N. Fourth Ave., 85705 520-887-9487
Tucson	Coyote Crossing B&B, 6985 N Camino Verde, 85743 520-744-3285
Tucson	Desert Dove B&B, 11707 E Old Spanish Tr, 85730 520-722-6879
Tucson	Desert Trails B&B, 12851 E Speedway, 85748 520-885-7295
Tucson	Double K Ranch B&B, 3930 N Smokey Topaz Ln, 85749 520-749-5345
Tucson	Elysian Grove Market, 400 W Simpson, 85701 520-628-1522
Tucson	Ford's B&B, 1202 N Avenida Marlene, 85715 520-885-1202
Tucson	Hacienda Del Rey, 7320 N Cortaro Rd, 85743 520-579-0425
Tucson	Hacienda del Sol Ranch, 5601 N Hacienda del Sol, 85718 520-299-1501
Tucson	Hideaway B&B, 4344 E. Poe St, 85711 520-323-8067
Tucson	Katy's Hacienda, 5841 E. 9th St, 85711 520-745-5695
Tucson	Kelly's Whistlestop B&B, 5525 E Hawthorne St, 85711 520-586-7515
Tucson	La Posada del Valle, 1640 N Campbell Ave, 85719 520-795-3840
Tucson	Llama Lee Ranch, 15415 N Lago De Oro Pky, 85739 520-825-0422
Tucson	Melissa's Desert Classic, 7400 W Juniper Rd., 85741 520-044-1669
Tucson	Mesquite Retreat, 3770 N. Melpomene Way, 85749 520-749-4884
Tucson	Milagras B&B, 11185 W. Calle Pima, 85743 520-578-8577
Tucson	Natural B&B, 3150 E. Presidio Rd, 85716 520-881-4582
Tucson	Ranch House B&B, 3053 N Camino de Oeste, 85746 520-743-9749
Tucson	Redbud House B&B, 7002 E. Redbud Rd, 85715 520-721-0218
Tucson	Rocking M Ranch, 6265 N Camino Verde, 85743 520-744-2457
Tucson	SunCatcher, 105 N Avenida Javalina, 85748 520-885-0883
Tucson	Tanque Verde Ranch, 14301 E. Speedway, 85748 520-296-6275
Tucson	The Mesquite Tree, 860 W Ina Rd, 85704 520-297-9670
Tucson	White Stallion Ranch, 9251 W Twin Peaks Rd, 85743 520-297-0252
Tucson	Zion Ponderosa, 1032 S Desert Senna, 85748 800-293-5444
Wickenburg	Chez Rina B&B, 701 S Saguaro Dr, 85390 520-684-0776
Wickenburg	Historic Sombrero Ranch, 31910 W Bralliar Rd, 85390 520-684-0222
Wickenburg	J Bar J Ranch B&B, PO Box 524, 85358
Wickenburg	Kay El Bar Ranch, Box 2480, 85358 602-684-7593
Williams	Route 66 Inn, 128 E Rt 66, 86046 520-635-4791
Williams	The Johnstonian B&B, 321 W. Sheridan Ave, 86046 520-635-2178
Williams	The Sheridan House Inn, 460 E Sheridan Avenue, 86046 520-635-9441
Yuma	Casa de Osgood, 13762 E Fortuna Palms, 85367 520-342-0471

Arkansas ———————————————————————

Arkadelphia	Buckelew's B&B, 921 Walnut St, 71923
Arkadelphia	Iron Mountain Lodge, 1 Marina Dr, 71923 501-246-4310
Bismarck	Bar Fifty Ranch B&B, PO Box 309, 71929 501-865-4757
Brinkley	Great Southern Hotel, 127 W. Cedar, 72021 501-734-4955

Caddo Gap	River's Edge B&B Inn, HC 65, Box 5, 71935 870-356-4864
Calico Rock	Arkansas and Ozarks B&B, HC 61, Box 72, 72519 501-297-8221
Calico Rock	Forest Home Lodge, HC 61 Box 72, 72519
Calico Rock	Happy Lonesome Log Cabins, HC 61, Box 72, 72519 870-297-8764
Calico Rock	River View Hotel B&B, Box 631, 72519 501-297-8208
Calico Rock	The Cedars B&B, HC 79 Box 330, 72519
Cherokee	Pelton Place Inn & Rest, Two Chickasha Dr, 72529 501-257-2000
Chester	Chester House B&B, 72934
Compton	Misty Mountain B&B, HC33 Box 100-B, 72624 870-420-3731
Conway	Olde Towne B&B, 567 Locust, 72032 501-329-6989
Conway	The Bruce House, 1379 Bruce St, 72032 501-327-2947
Conway	The Cottage Guest House, 1221 Watkins St, 72032 501-329-7703
Crossett	The Trieschmann House, 707 Cedar, 71635 501-364-7592
Des Arc	The 5-D's, PO Box 364, 72040 501-256-4789
Devall's Bluff	Palaver Place B&B, Rt 1 Box 29A, 72401 501-998-7206
Elkins	Maguiretown B&B, Hwy 74 N, 72727
Eureka Springs	1876 Inn & Restaurant, Rt 6, Box 247, 72632 501-253-7183
Eureka Springs	Angel at Rose Hall, 56 Hillside, 72632 501-253-5405
Eureka Springs	Apple Annie's B&B, PO Box 160, 72632
Eureka Springs	Beaver Lake B&B, Rt 2 Box 318, 72632 501-253-9210
Eureka Springs	Bell Spring Cottage, Roiute 1, Box 981, 72632 501-253-8581
Eureka Springs	Benton Place Inn, 32 Benston, 72632 501-253-7602
Eureka Springs	Bridgeford House B&B, 263 Spring St, 72632 501-253-7853
Eureka Springs	Cedarberry Cottage, 3 Kings Highway, 72632 501-253-6115
Eureka Springs	Crescent Moon, PO Box 429, 72632 501-253-9463
Eureka Springs	Dr. R. G. Floyd House, 246 Spring St, 72632 501-253-7525
Eureka Springs	Edelweiss Inn, Rt 1, Box 279, 72632 501-253-7316
Eureka Springs	Edgewood Manor, 27 Paxos St, 72632 501-253-6555
Eureka Springs	Ellis House at Trails End, One Wheeler St, 72632 800-243-8218
Eureka Springs	Elmwood House, 110 Spring St, 72632 501-253-5486
Eureka Springs	Evening Shade Inn, RR 1 Box 446, 72632 501-253-6264
Eureka Springs	Fairwinds Mtn. Cottages, 637 CR 111, 72632 501-253-9465
Eureka Springs	Four Winds B&B, 3 Echols St, 72632 501-253-9169
Eureka Springs	Fuller Cottage, 229 Spring St, 72632 501-751-7766
Eureka Springs	Garden of Dreams, 3969 Mudell Rd, 72631
Eureka Springs	Gardener's Cottage, 11 Singleton, 72632 501-253-9111
Eureka Springs	Gaslight Inn, 19 Judah St, 72632 501-253-8887
Eureka Springs	Harvest House B&B, 104 Wall St, 72632 501-253-9363
Eureka Springs	Hidden Springs B&B, 23 Hillside Ave, 72632 501-253-8688
Eureka Springs	Inn at Rose Hall, 56 Hillside, 72632 501-253-5405
Eureka Springs	Jordan Drive Hideaway B&B, RR 4 Box 102, 72632 800-245-5931
Eureka Springs	Land-O-Nod Victorian Inn, Rt 6, Box 9, 72632 501-253-6262
Eureka Springs	Lazee Daze, Route 1, Box 196, 72632 501-253-7026
Eureka Springs	Lookout Cottage, 12 Lookout Circle, 72632 501-253-9545
Eureka Springs	Maple Leaf Inn, 6 Kingshighway, 72632 501-253-6876
Eureka Springs	Mariposa Inn, 3 Echols St, 72632 501-253-9169
Eureka Springs	Miss Priscilla's, PO Box 171, 72632 501-253-7617
Eureka Springs	Morningstar Retreat, 370 Star Lane, 72632 501-253-5995
Eureka Springs	Peabody House, 7 Armstrong, 72632 800-506-0060
Eureka Springs	Pointe West Resort, 11882 Hwy 187, 72631 501-253-9050
Eureka Springs	Primrose Place, 9 Steele St, 72632 501-253-9818
Eureka Springs	Red Bud Manor, 7 Kingshighway, 72632 501-253-9649
Eureka Springs	Ridgeway House, 28 Ridgeway St, 72632 501-253-6618
Eureka Springs	Roadrunner Inn, Rt 2, Box 158, 72632
Eureka Springs	Rock Cottage Gardens, 10 Eugenia St, 72632 501-253-8659
Eureka Springs	Rogue's Manor at Sweet Spg, 124 Spring St, 72632 501-253-4911
Eureka Springs	Rosalie House, 282 Spring St, 72632
Eureka Springs	Rosewood Guest Cottage, One Kings Highway, 72632 501-253-7674
Eureka Springs	Scandia B&B Inn, 33 Avo, Hwy. 62 W, 72632 501-253-8922
Eureka Springs	Sunnyside Inn, 28 Ridgeway, 74105 501-253-6638
Eureka Springs	Sweet Dreams, 76 Center St, 72632 501-253-5885
Eureka Springs	Sweet Seasons Cottages, PO Box 642, 72632 501-253-7603
Eureka Springs	Swiss Village Inn, Rt 6, Box 5, 72632 501-253-9541
Eureka Springs	Taylor-Page Inn, 33 Benton St., 92632 501-253-7501
Eureka Springs	The Border House, 2 Armstrong St, 72632 501-253-7676
Eureka Springs	The Brownstone Inn, 75 Hillside Ave, 72632 501-253-7505
Eureka Springs	The Carriage House, 75 Lookout Lane, 72632 501-253-5259
Eureka Springs	The Carriage Inn, 20856 Hwy 62 W, 72631 501-253-8828
Eureka Springs	The Kansas House, 2 Singleton, 72632 501-253-5558
Eureka Springs	The Old Homestead, 82 Armstrong, 72632 501-253-7501
Eureka Springs	Tweedy House B&B, 16 Washington St, 72632 501-253-5435
Eureka Springs	Wellspring, Inn at More Mt, RR 4, Box 432, 72632 501-253-6026
Eureka Springs	White Dove Manor, 8 Washington St, 72632 501-253-6151
Eureka Springs	Willow Ridge, 85 Kingshighway, 72632 800-467-1737
Eureka Springs	Wisteria Lane Lodging, RR 7 Box 575, 72632 501-253-7544
Fairfield Bay	Serenity Guest House, 116 Racquet Rd., 72088 501-884-3899
Fayetteville	Colonial House B&B, 5855 Tackett Dr, 72701 501-582-1677
Fayetteville	Hill Avenue B&B, 131 Hill Ave, 72701 501-444-0865

Fayetteville	Johnson House B&B, PO Box 431, 72741 501-756-1095
Fayetteville	The North Forty, 40 N. Crossover Rd, 72101 501-521-3739
Flippin	Fair Haven Lodge, HC 62, Box 88B, 72634 501-453-2371
Flippin	Riverbelle B&B, HC 62 Box 102B, 72634 870-453-8735
Fordyce	Wynne Phillips House, 412 W. Fourth St, 71742 501-352-7202
Fort Smith	Thomas Quinn Guest House, 815 N B St, 72901
Garfield	Shawnee Mountain Lakeside, 20462 Tacker Rd, 72732 501-359-3514
Gilbert	Riverside Kitchen & Ctgs, PO Box 42, 72636 501-439-2288
Glenwood	Riverwood Inn, 363 Hwy 70 E, 71943 870-356-4567
Greers Ferry	Puddin' Ridge Farm B&B, 3050 Browsville Rd, 72067 501-825-6544
Harrison	Edgewood Inn B&B, Edgewood Estate, 72601 501-741-4166
Harrison	Hathaway House B&B, 322 West Ridge, 72601 501-741-3321
Harrison	Merry Otter B&B, 103 W South Ave, 72601 501-743-2355
Harrison	Peaches N Cream B&B, RR 1, Box 96FF, 72601
Heber Springs	Little Red River Cottage, PO Box 1242, 72543 501-206-1242
Heber Springs	Oak Tree Inn, 1802 W Main St, 72543 501-362-7731
Helena	Edwardian Inn, 317 Biscoe, 72342 501-338-9155
Helena	Magnolia Hill, 608 Perry, 72342 501-338-6874
Hot Springs	Ann Cogburn's Inn, 222 Klein Shore Rd, 71901 501-767-5208
Hot Springs	Dogwood Manor, 906 Malvern Ave, 71901 501-624-0896
Hot Springs	Heavenly Homes Homestay, 7 Monte Circle, 71909 501-922-1527
Hot Springs	Stillmeadow Farm, Route 1, Box 434-D, 71913 501-525-9994
Hot Springs	The Gables Inn, 318 Quapaw Ave, 71901 501-623-7576
Hot Springs	The Park Hotel, 211 Fountain St, 71901 501-624-5323
Hot Springs	The Stitt House, 824 Park Ave, 71901
Hot Springs	Vintage Comfort B&B Inn, 303 Quapaw Ave, 71901 501-623-3258
Hot Springs	Wildwood 1884 B&B, 808 Park Ave, 71901 501-624-4267
Hot Springs	Woodbine Place B&B, 213 Woodbine, 71901 501-624-3646
Huntington	Country Cottage B&B, 115 US 71 South, 72940 501-928-4622
Jasper	Brambly Hedge Cottage B&B, HCR 31 Box 39, 72641 501-446-5849
Jessieville	Mountain Thyme B&B Inn, 10860 Scenic Byway 7 N, 71949 501-984-5428
Johnson	Inn at the Mill, PO Box 409, 72741 501-443-1800
Johnson	Johnson House 1882, PO Box 431, 72741 501-756-1095
Kingston	Fools Cove Ranch B&B, HCR 30, Box 198, 72742 501-665-2986
Langley	Country School Inn, Ark Hwys 84 & 369, 71952 501-356-3091
Little Rock	Dr. Witt's Quapaw Inn, 1868 S Gaines, 72206 501-376-6873
Little Rock	Hotze House, PO Box 164087, 72216 501-376-6563
Little Rock	Pinnacle Vista Lodge, 7510 Ark. 300, 72212 501-868-8905
Little Rock	Quapaw B&B Inn, 1868 S Gaines St, 72206 501-376-6873
Little Rock	The Carriage House, 1700 Louisiana, 72206 501-374-7032
Little Rock	The Josolyn House B&B, 501 N Palm St, 72205 510-666-5995
Magnolia	Magnolia Place, 420 E Main, 71753 501-234-6122
Malvern	Gatewood House, 1117 N Park Dr, 72104 501-337-4681
Mammoth Spring	The Roseland Inn, 570 Bethel St, 72554 501-625-3378
Marianna	Mulberry Inn, 116 Mulberry St, 72360 501-295-4200
McGehee	Evans House, PO Box 258, 71654 501-222-6425
McGehee	The Magnolia House, 1010 N Second St, 71654 501-222-6425
Monticello	Country Manor B&B, 2221 Hwy 35 W, 71655 870-367-1198
Monticello	Miss Rosalind's B&B, 800 N Main, 71655 501-367-2703
Monticello	The Trotter House B&B, 404 N Main St, 71655 870-367-0200
Mountain Home	Grandma's House, The B&B, 1636 CR 635, 72653 870-425-1445
Mountain View	Country Charm B&B, PO Box 1361, 72560 870-269-2177
Mountain View	Country Oaks B&B, HC 70, Box 63, Hwy 9, 72560 800-455-2704
Mountain View	The Lowe House B&B, PO Box 1746, 72560 501-269-2191
Mountain View	Wildflower On The Square, PO Box 72, 72560 870-269-4383
Norfolk	Schroder Haus B&B, 57 River Ridge Rd, 72658 870-499-7775
Omaha	Aunt Shirley's Sleeping Lf, 7250 Shirley Lane N, 72662 870-426-5408
Omaha	Ozark Country Inn, An, 23765 Stonigton Rd, 72662 870-426-6942
Ozark	1887 Inn B&B, 100 E Commercial, 72949 501-667-1121
Ozark	The Bunkhouse, Mulberry Ranch, 72852 501-292-3725
Ozark	The Lamplighter B&B, 905 W River St, 72949 501-667-3889
Parthenon	Thomas Creek B&B, HCR 72, Box 89, 72666 501-861-5555
Pine Bluff	Margland B&B, PO Box 8594, 71611 501-536-6000
Russellville	The Summit House, PO Box 2483, 72811 501-229-1000
Salem	Lespedeza B&B, PO Box 251, 72576 870-895-3061
Salem	Off the Beaten Path B&B, 109 Mill ST, 72576 501-895-3867
Springdale	Faubus House on Governor's, PO Box 1442, 72765 501-751-2005
Springdale	Magnolia Gardens Inn, 500 N Main, 72764 501-756-5744
Van Buren	O'Malley's B&B, 600 Main St, 72956
Van Buren	Old Van Buren Inn, 633 Main, 72956 501-474-4202
Warren	B&B of Warren Burnett Hse, 273 Bradley, 71671 870-226-5305
Warren	Colvin House B&B Inn, 415 E Cedar, 71671 501-226-7757
Washington	Old Washington Jail B&B, Old WA Hist. State Park, 71862 870-983-2461
West Helena	Coolidge-Peterson House, 345 N 9th St, 72390 501-338-7237
Winslow	Sky-Vue Lodge B&B, 22822 N Hwy 71, 72959 501-634-2003
Yellville	Buffalo River Lodge, PO Box 9, 72687 870-439-2373
Yellville	Eagle's Nest Lodge, 72687 870-449-5050
Yellville	Red Raven Inn, PO Box 1217, 72687 501-449-5168

California

Acton	Thousand Trails-Soledad Cy, 4700 Crown Valley Rd, 93510 805-269-1740
Ahwahnee	Apple Blossom Inn B&B, 44606 Silver Spur Tr., 93601 209-642-2001
Ahwahnee	The Homestead, 41110 Road 600, 93601 209-683-0495
Ahwahnee	Yosemite's Apple Blossom, 44606 Silver Spur Trail, 93601 209-642-2001
Albion	Fensalden Inn, PO Box 99, 95410 707-937-4042
Albion	Huckleberry House, 29381 Albion Ridge Rd, 95410 707-937-2374
Albion	The Wool Loft, 32751 Navarro Ridge Rd, 95410 707-937-0377
Alta	Crystal Springs Inn, PO Box 753, 95701 916-389-2355
Amador City	Mine House Inn, PO Box 245, 95601 209-267-5900
Anaheim	Granada Inn, 2375 W Lincoln Ave, 92801 714-774-7370
Anaheim	Sojourner Christian B&B, 1819 W La Palma Ave, 92801 714-535-2994
Angels Camp	Cooper House B&B Inn, PO Box 1388, 95222 209-736-2145
Angels Camp	Utica Mansion Inn, 1090 Utica Lane, 95222 209-736-4209
Angelus Oaks	The Lodge at Angelus Oaks, PO Box 366, 92305 909-794-9523
Angwin	Forest Manor, 415 Cold Springs Rd, 94508 707-965-3538
Arcata	Cat's Cradle B&B, 815 Park Pl., 95521 707-882-2237
Arnold	Lodge at Manuel Mill, PO Box 998, 95223 209-795-2622
Arroyo Grande	Crystal Rose Inn, 789 Valley Rd, 93420 805-481-1854
Arroyo Grande	Grieb Farmhouse Inn B&B, 851 Todd Ln, 93420 805-481-8540
Arroyo Grande	House of Another Tyme B&B, 227 Le Point St, 93420 805-489-6313
Atascadero	Lakeview B&B, 9065 Lakeview Dr, 93422 805-466-5665
Auburn	Tin Roof B&B, 550 Landis Cir, 95603
Avalon	Catalina Is. Seacrest Inn, PO 128, 90704 310-510-0800
Avalon	Seacrest Inn, PO Box 128, 90704 310-510-0800
Avalon	The Old Turner Inn, 232 Catalina Ave., 90704
Avalon	Zane Grey Pueblo Hotel, PO Box 216, 90704 310-510-0966
Bakersfield	Helen K Inn, 2105 - 19th St, 93301 805-325-5451
Balboa Pen.	Balboa Inn, 105 Main St, 92663 949-675-3412
Ballard	The Ballard Inn, 2436 Baseline Ave, 93463 805-688-7770
Bass Lake	Ducey's on the Lake, PO Box 109, 93604 800-350-7463
Bear Valley	Tamarack Pines, PO Box 5039, 95223 209-753-2080
Benicia	Captain Walsh House, 235 East L St, 94510 707-747-5653
Benicia	The Painted Lady B&B, 141 East F St, 94510 707-746-1646
Benicia	Union Hotel & Gardens, 401 First St, 94510 707-746-0100
Berkeley	B&B Accomm. in Berkeley, 2235 Carleton St, 94704 510-548-7556
Berkeley	Bancroft Club Hotel, 2680 Bancroft Way, 94704 510-549-1000
Berkeley	Bonita Studio B&B, 1420-A Bonita Ave, 94709
Berkeley	Elmwood House B&B, 2609 College Ave, 94704 510-540-5123
Berkeley	Gramma's Rose Garden Inn, 2740 Telegraph Ave, 94705 510-549-2145
Berkeley	Mary Joes Guest House, 801 Channing Way, 94710 510-622-8391
Berkeley	Oxford Place, 1151 Oxford St., 94707 510-559-0089
Berry Creek	Lake Oroville B&B, 240 Sunday Drive, 95916 916-589-0700
Big Bear Lake	Apples, PO Box 7172, 92315 909-866-0903
Big Bear Lake	Eagle's Nest B&B, PO Box 1003, 92315 909-866-6465
Big Bear Lake	Truffles, A Special Place, PO Box 1377, 92315 909-585-2772
Big Sur	Deetjen's Big Sur Inn, Hwy 1, 93920 408-667-2377
Big Sur	Post Ranch Inn, PO Box 219, 93920
Big Sur	Ventana Inn, Hwy 1, 93920 408-667-2331
Blairsden	Gray Eagle Lodge, PO Box 38, 96103 916-836-2511
Bodega Bay	Compass Rose Gardens, PO Box 1060, 94923 707-875-2343
Bodega Bay	Holiday Inn - Bodega Bay, PO Box 55, 94923 707-875-2217
Bolinas	Blue Heron Inn, PO Box 309, 94924 415-868-1102
Bolinas	Elfriede's Haus, PO Box 57, 94924 415-868-9778
Bolinas	One Fifty-Five Pine B&B, Box 62, 94924 415-868-0263
Boonville	Anderson Creek Inn, PO Box 217, 95415 707-895-3091
Boonville	Indian Creek Inn, PO Box 603, 95415 707-895-3861
Boonville	Toll House Restaurant/Inn, PO Box 268, 95415 707-895-3630
Borrego Springs	Borrego Valley Inn, PO Box 2524, 92004 619-767-4356
Borrego Springs	Palms at Indianhead B&B, 2220 Hoberg Rd, 92004 800-519-2624
Bridgeport	Hunewill Guest Ranch, PO Box 368 AW, 93517 760-932-7710
Brownsville	Mountain Seasons Inn, 9067 La Porte Rd., 95919 916-675-2180
Burnt Ranch	Madrone Lane B&B, HCR #34, 95527 916-629-3642
Calistoga	Aurora Park Inn, 1807 Foothill Blvd, 94515 877-942-7700
Calistoga	Bear Flag Inn, 2653 Foothill Blvd, 94515 707-942-5534
Calistoga	Brannan's Loft, PO Box 561, 94515 707-963-2181
Calistoga	Calistoga Inn, 1250 Lincoln Av., 94515 707-942-4101
Calistoga	Calistoga Wayside Inn, 1523 Foothill Blvd, 94515 707-942-0645
Calistoga	Carlin Country Cottages, 1623 Lake St, 94515 707-942-9102
Calistoga	Chateau de Vie B&B, 3250 Hwy 128, 94515 707-942-6446
Calistoga	Christopher's Inn, 1010 Foothill Blvd, 94515 707-942-5755
Calistoga	Comfort Inn, 1865 Lincoln Ave, 94515 707-942-9400
Calistoga	Cottage Grove Inn, 1711 Lincoln Ave, 94515 707-942-8400
Calistoga	Culver's, A Country Inn, 1805 Foothill Blvd, 94515 707-942-4535
Calistoga	Falcon's Nest, 471 Kortum Canyon Rd, 94515 707-942-0758
Calistoga	Fanny's, 1206 Spring, 94515 707-942-9491
Calistoga	Golden Haven Hot Springs, 1713 Lake St, 94515 707-942-6793

Calistoga	Indian Springs Resort/Spa, 1712 Lincoln Ave., 94515 707-942-4913
Calistoga	La Chaumiere, 1301 Cedar St, 94515 707-942-5139
Calistoga	Meadowlark Country House, 601 Petrified Forest Rd, 94515 707-942-5651
Calistoga	Pine Street Inn, 1202 Pine St, 94515 707-942-6829
Calistoga	Scott Courtyard, 1443 2nd St, 94515 707-942-0948
Calistoga	Silver Rose Inn, 351 Rosedale Rd, 94515 707-942-9581
Calistoga	The Pink Mansion, 1415 Foothill Blvd, 94515 707-942-0558
Calistoga	Village Inn & Spa, 1880 Lincoln Ave, 94515 707-942-0991
Calistoga	Wine Way Inn, 1019 Foothill Blvd, 94515 707-942-0680
Calistoga	Wisteria Garden B&B, 1508 Fairway, 94515 707-942-5358
Cambria	Beachside Inn, 233 Weymouth St., 93428 805-927-8723
Cambria	Captain's Cove, 6454 Moonstone Beach Dr, 93428 805-927-8581
Cambria	Pinestone, 221 Weymouth St, 93428 805-927-2494
Cambria	Sand Pebbles Inn, 6252 Moan Stone Beach, 93428 805-927-5600
Cambria	Sylvia's Rigdon Hall Inn, 4022 Burton Dr, 93428 805-927-5125
Cambria	The Beach House B&B, 6360 Moonstone Beach Dr, 93428 805-927-3136
Campbell	Tom Sawyer Inn, 1645 Curtner Glen Ct, 95008 408-559-3636
Capistrano	Capistrano Seaside Inn, 34862 Pacific Coast Hwy, 92624 949-496-1399
Capitola	Monarch Grove, 623 Gilroy St., 95010
Cardiff	Cardiff-by-the-Sea Lodge, 142 Chesterfield, 92007 760-944-6474
Carlsbad	Pelican Cove B&B Inn, 320 Walnut Ave, 92008 760-434-5995
Carmel	Adobe Inn, PO Box 4115, 93921 831-624-3933
Carmel	Blue Sky Lodge, 10 Flight Rd., Box 233, 93924 831-659-2256
Carmel	Briarwood Inn, PO Box 5245, 93921 800-999-8788
Carmel	Candle Light Inn, PO Box 1900, 93921 831-624-6451
Carmel	Carmel Fireplace Inn, PO Box 4082, 93921 831-626-1981
Carmel	Carmel Garden Court Inn, PO Box 6226, 93921 831-624-6926
Carmel	Carmel Wayfarer Inn, PO Box 1896, 93921 831-624-2711
Carmel	Coachman's Inn, PO Box C-1, 93921
Carmel	Cobblestone Inn, PO Box 3185, 93921 831-625-5222
Carmel	Colonial Terrace Inn, PO Box 1375, 93921 831-624-2741
Carmel	Crystal Terrace Inn B&B, PO Box 2623, 93921 831-624-6400
Carmel	Dolphin Inn, PO Box 1900, 93921 831-624-5356
Carmel	Forest Lodge, PO Box 1316, 93921 831-624-7023
Carmel	Green Lantern Inn, PO Box 2619, 93921 831-624-4392
Carmel	Gulls Nest, 81 Corona Rd, 93923
Carmel	Hidden Valley Inn, 102 W Carmel Valley Rd, 93924 800-367-3336
Carmel	Holiday House, PO Box 782, 93921 831-624-6267
Carmel	Lincoln Green Inn, PO Box 2747, 93921 831-624-1880
Carmel	Mission Ranch, 26270 Dolores, 93923 831-624-6436
Carmel	Monte Verde Inn, PO Box 394, 93921 831-624-8046
Carmel	San Antonio House, PO Box 97, 93921 831-624-4334
Carmel	Sundial Lodge, PO Box J, 93921 831-624-8578
Carmel	Sunset House, PO Box 1925, 93921 831-624-4884
Carmel	Svends Gaards Inn, PO Box 1900, 93921 831-624-1511
Carmel	Tickle Pink Inn, 155 Highland Dr., 93923 831-624-1244
Carmel	Wayside Inn, PO Box 1900, 93921 831-624-5336
Carmel Valley	Robles del Rio Lodge, 200 Punta Del Monte, 93924 831-659-3705
Castro Valley	Lore's Haus, 22051 Betlen Way, 94546 510-881-1533
Cayucos	The Saltbox, PO Box 668, 93430 888-SALTBOX
Cazadero	Cazanoma Lodge, PO Box 37, 95421 707-632-5255
Cedarville	J.K. Metzker House, PO Box 630, 96104 530-279-2650
Chester	Cinnamon Teal B&B, PO Box 1517, 96020 916-258-3993
Chico	Johnson's Country Inn, 3935 Morehead Ave, 95928 530-345-STAY
Chico	L'abri B&B, 14350 Hwy 99, 95973 530-893-0824
Chico	Miller Mansion, 2185 Esplanade, 95926 916-343-1692
Chico	Music Express Inn, 1091 El Monte Ave, 95928 530-345-8376
Chico	The Esplanade B&B, 620 The Esplanade, 95926 530-345-8084
Clearlake	Inn Oz, PO Box 1046, 95424 707-995-0853
Clearlake	Muktip Manor, 12540 Lakeshore Dr, 95422 707-994-9571
Cloverdale	Abrams House Inn, 314 N Main St, 95425 714-894-2412
Cloverdale	The Shelford House, 29955 River Rd, 95425 707-894-5956
Cloverdale	Ye Olde' Shelford House B&, 29955 River Rd., 95425 707-894-5956
Clovis	Cowboy's Palace, 446 Woodworth Ave, 93612 209-322-9024
Coloma	Golden Lotus B&B Inn, PO Box 491, 95613 530-621-4562
Coloma	Sierra Nevada House, PO Box 496, 95613 530-621-1649
Corona	Morgan Zahuranec, 11557 Chadwick Rd., 91720
Corona del Mar	Cliffside Cottage, 239 Carnation Ave, 92625 714-548-6646
Coronado	Coronado Victorian House, 1000 Eighth St, 92118 619-435-2200
Coronado	Coronado Village Inn, 1017 Park Pl., 92118 619-435-9318
Costa Mesa	Country Side Inn, 325 Bristol, 92626 949-549-0300
Cottonwood	Smithey's Heritage Oaks, 19145 Country View Dr, 96022 530-347-4223
Coulterville	Historic Hotel Jeffery, Box 440, 95311 209-878-3471
Coulterville	Sherlock Homes B&B Inn, PO Box 7, 95311 209-878-3915
Covina	Hendrick Inn, 2124 E. Merced Ave, 91791 626-919-2125
Crescent City	Fernbrook Inn, 4650 N. Bank Rd, 95531 707-458-3202
Crescent City	Historic Requa Inn, 155 King St, 95531 707-482-8205
Crescent City	Lighthouse Cove B&B, 215 S "A" St, 95534 707-465-6565

Cromberg	20 Mile House, Box 30001, 96103
Dana Point	The Blue Lantern Inn, 34343 Blue Lantern St, 92629 949-661-1304
Davenport	New Davenport, 31 Davenport Avenue, 95017 408-426-4122
Del Mar	Del Mar Inn, 720 Camino Del Mar, 92014 619-755-9765
Del Mar	The Blue Door, 13707 Durango Dr, 92014 619-755-3819
Dillon Beach	Windmist Cottage, PO Box 291, 94929 707-878-2465
Dillsboro	Mountain Creek Cottages, PO Box 356, 28725 704-586-6042
Dinuba	Country Living B&B, 40068 Rd 88, 93618 209-591-6617
Dorrington	Dorrington Hotel, PO Box 4307, 95223 209-795-5800
Downieville	Saundra Dyer's Resort B&B, 9 River St., 95936 916-289-3308
Downieville	Slate Castle Ranch, 100 Slate Castle Rd., 95936 916-289-3185
Duarte	White Horse Estate B&B Inn, 330 Las Lomas Rd., 91010 626-358-0798
Duncans Mills	Superintendent's House, 24951 Highway 116, 95430 707-865-1572
Dunsmuir	Shasta Alpine Inn, 4221 Siskiyou Ave., 96025
Durham	Durham White House, 9447 Dillon Ct., 95938
El Cajon	At Your Leisure B&B, 525 S 3rd St, 92019 619-444-3124
Elk	Greenwood Pier Inn, PO Box 336, 95432 707-877-9997
Elkcreek	Stony Creek Retreat B&B, PO Box 205, 95939 916-968-5178
Emigrant Gap	Tancho Sierra Inn, PO Box 130, 95715 916-389-8572
Escondido	Zosa Ranch, 9381 W Lilac Rd., 92026
Eureka	Campton House B&B, 305 M St, 95501 707-443-1601
Eureka	Eagle House Victorian Inn, 139 Second St, Old Town, 95501 707-444-3344
Eureka	Hollander House, 2436 E. St, 95501 707-443-2419
Eureka	Old Town B&B Inn, 1521 Third St, 95501 707-445-3951
Eureka	Upstairs At the Waterfront, 102 F St, 95501 707-443-9190
Fair Play	Fitzpatrick Winery & Lodge, 7740 Fairplay Rd, 95684 916-620-3248
Fairfax	Fairfax Inn, 15 Broadway, 94930 415-455-8702
Fallbrook	La Estacia Inn, 3135 S. Hwy 395, 92028
Fawnskin	Windy Point Inn, PO Box 375, 92333 714-866-2746
Felton	The Inn at Felton Crest, 780 El Solyo Heights Dr, 95018 831-335-4011
Ferndale	Grandmother's House, PO Box 1004, 95536 707-786-9704
Ferndale	Shaw House B&B, PO Box 1125, 95536 707-786-9958
Fish Camp	Apple Tree Inn, PO Box 41, 93623 209-683-5111
Fish Camp	Narrow Gauge Inn, 48571 Hwy 41, 93623 209-683-7720
Fish Camp	Owl's Nest Lodging, PO Box 33, 93623 209-683-3484
Fish Camp	Yosemite Fish Camp Inn B&B, PO Box 25, 93623 209-683-7426
Folsom	Bradley House, 606 Figueroa St., 95630 530-355-1962
Folsom	Plum Tree Inn, 307 Leidesdorff St, 95630 530-351-1541
Fort Bidwell	Fort Bidwell Hotel, Main & Garrison, 96112 916-279-2050
Fort Bragg	Anchor Lodge, PO Box 1429, 95437 707-964-4283
Fort Bragg	Annie's Jughandle Beach BB, 32980 Gibney Ln, 95437 707-964-1415
Fort Bragg	Colonial Inn, PO Box 565, 95437 707-964-9979
Fort Bragg	Country Inn B&B, 632 N Main St, 95437 707-964-3737
Fort Bragg	Ebb Tide Lodge, 250 S Main St, 95437 707-964-5321
Fort Bragg	Glass Beach B&B, 726 N Main St, 95437 707-964-6774
Fort Bragg	Harbor Lite Lodge, 120 N Harbor Dr, 95437 707-964-0221
Fort Bragg	Ocean Breeze Lodge, 212 S Main St, 95437 707-961-1177
Fort Bragg	Old Stewart House Inn, 511 Stewart St., 95437 707-961-0775
Fort Bragg	Pudding Creek Inn, 700 N Main, 95437 707-964-9529
Fort Bragg	Rendezvous Inn & Restauran, 647 N. Main St., 95437
Fort Bragg	Seabird Lodge, 191 South St, 95437 707-964-4731
Fort Bragg	Shoreline Cottages, 18725 N Hwy One, 95437 707-964-2977
Fort Bragg	Surf and Sand Lodge, 1131 N Main St, 95437 707-964-9383
Fort Bragg	The Lodge at Noyo River, 500 Casa del Noyo Dr, 95437 707-964-8045
Fort Bragg	Todd Farm House, 100 Hwy 20, 95437 707-964-6575
Fort Bragg	Wishing Well Cottages, 31430 Hwy 20, 95437 707-961-5450
Fort Jones	Wild Goose Country Victori, PO Box 546, 96032 916-468-2735
Freestone	Green Apple Inn, 520 Bohemian Hwy, 95472 707-874-2526
French Gulch	French Gulch Hotel B&B, PO Box 249, 96033 916-359-2112
Fresno	Casa Laguna Inn, 3110 N Blackstone, 93703 800-233-0449
Fresno	Country Victorian B&B, 1003 S Orange Ave, 93702 209-233-1988
Garden Grove	Armstrong Manor, PO Box 4567, 92842
Garden Valley	Mountainside B&B, 5821 Spanish Flat Rd, 95633 916-626-1119
Georgetown	American River Inn, PO Box 43, 95634 916-333-4499
Geyserville	Hope-Merrill/Hope-Bosworth, PO Box 42, 95441 707-857-3356
Geyserville	Isis Oasis Lodge, 20889 Geyserville Ave, 95441 707-857-3524
Glen Ellen	Above the Clouds, 3250 Trinity Rd., 95442 707-996-7371
Glen Ellen	Cottage Grove, PO Box 459, 95442 707-938-3859
Glen Ellen	Glenelly Inn, 5131 Warm Springs Rd, 95442 707-996-6720
Glen Ellen	Jack London Lodge, PO Box 300, 95442 707-938-8510
Glen Ellen	Tanglewood House, 250 Bonnie Way, 95442 707-996-5021
Goodyears Bar	Helmes St. Charles Inn, PO Box 49, 95944
Graeagle	Feather River Inn, PO Box 67, 96103 916-836-2623
Grass Valley	Elam Biggs B&B Inn, 220 Colfax Ave., 95945 530-477-0906
Grass Valley	Peacock, 439 S Auburn St, 95945 530-477-2179
Grass Valley	Swan-Levine House, 328 S. Church St, 95945 530-272-1873
Gridley	McCracken's B&B Inn, 1835 Sycamore Ln., 95948 916-846-2108
Groveland	Berkshire Inn, PO Box 207, 95321 209-962-6744

Groveland	Hotel Charlotte, Box 787, 95321 209-962-6455
Gualala	Gualala Hotel, PO Box 675, 95445 707-884-3441
Gualala	Inn at Getchell Cove, PO Box 1086, 95445
Gualala	Saint Orres, PO Box 523, 95445 707-884-3303
Gualala	Wagner's Windhaven, 35281 S Hwy 1, 95445
Gualala	Whale Watch Inn by the Sea, 35100 Hwy 1, 95445 707-884-3667
Guerneville	Santa Nella House, 12130 Hwy. 116, 95446 707-869-9488
Guerneville	The Willows, 15905 River Rd, 95446 707-869-2824
Half Moon Bay	Emard Manor, 483 Winged Foot Rd, 94019
Half Moon Bay	Harbor House B&B, 346 Princeton Ave, 94019 650-728-1572
Half Moon Bay	Plum Tree Court, PO Box 10, 94019 650-712-0104
Half Moon Bay	Pumpkin Cottages Inn, PO Box 69, 94019 415-726-6644
Half Moon Bay	San Benito House, 356 Main St, 94019 650-726-3425
Half Moon Bay	Zaballa House, 324 Main St, 94019 650-726-9123
Hanford	The Irwin Street Inn, 522 N. Irwin St, 93230 209-583-8000
Healdsburg	Belle de Jour Inn, 16276 Healdsburg Ave, 95448 707-433-7892
Healdsburg	Frampton House B&B, 489 Powell Ave, 95448 707-433-5084
Healdsburg	Holcomb House, 401 Piper St, 95448 707-433-9228
Healdsburg	Madrona Manor, PO Box 818, 95448 707-433-4231
Healdsburg	Villa Messina, 316 Burgundy Rd, 95448
Helena	Trinity Canyon Lodge, HCR 1 Box 51, 96048 916-623-6318
Hollister	H&H Ranch Enterprises, 280 Mansfield Rd., 95023 831-637-8510
Hollywood	La Maida House, 11147 La Maida St, 91601 818-769-3857
Hollywood	Le Montrose Suite Hotel, 900 Hammond St, 90069 310-855-1115
Homeland	Rancho Kaeru, 24180 Juniper Flats Rd, 92548
Homewood	Tahoma Medows B&B, PO Box 810, 96141 916-525-1553
Hopland	Hopland House, PO Box 310, 95449 707-744-1404
Idyllwild	Cedar Street Inn, PO Box 627, 92549 909-659-4789
Idyllwild	Fern Valley Inn, PO Box 116, 92549 714-659-2205
Independence	Winnedumah Hotel, PO Box 147, 93526 619-878-2040
Indio	Palm Shadow Inn, 80-761 Hwy. 111, 92201 619-347-3476
Inverness	Blackthorne Inn, PO Box 712, 94937 415-663-8621
Inverness	Dancing Coyote Beach, PO Box 98, 94937 415-669-7200
Inverness	Hickman House, PO Box 235, 94937 415-669-7428
Inverness	Inverness Lodge, PO Box 1110, 94937 415-669-1034
Inverness	Inverness Valley Inn, PO Box 429, 94970 415-669-725-
Inverness	MacLean House, PO Box 651, 94937 415-669-7392
Inverness	Sandy Cove Inn, PO Box 869, 94937 415-669-2683
Inverness	The Ark, PO Box 273, 94937 415-663-9338
Inverness	The Patterson House, PO Box 13, 94937
Ione	The Heirloom B&B, PO Box 322, 95640 209-274-4468
Isleton	Delta Daze Inn, 179 Oxbow Marina Dr, 95641 916-777-4667
Jackson	Gate House Inn, 1330 Jackson Gate Rd, 95642 209-223-3500
Jackson	The Wedgewood Inn, 11941 Narcissus Rd, 95642 209-296-4300
Jamestown	Palm Hotel B&B, 10382 Willow St, 95327 209-984-3429
Joshua Tree	Joshua Tree Inn, PO Box 340, 92252 619-366-1188
Julian	Artists' Loft, PO Box 2408, 92036 760-765-0765
Julian	Homestead B&B, PO Box 1208, 92036 760-765-1536
Julian	Julian Lodge, PO Box 1930, 92036 760-765-1420
Julian	Julian White House, PO Box 824, 92036 760-765-1764
Julian	Orchard Hill Country Inn, PO Box 425, 92036 760-765-1700
Julian	Pine Hills Lodge, PO Box 701, 92036 760-765-1100
Julian	Random Oaks Ranch, PO Box 454, 92036 760-765-1094
Julian	Shadow Mountain Ranch, PO Box 791, 92036
Kenwood	Kenwood Inn, 10400 Sonoma Hwy, 95452 707-833-1293
Klamath	The Rhodes' End B&B, 115 Trobitz Rd, 95548 707-482-1654
La Grange	Vredesrust House, 10035 Alamo Dr., 95329 209-852-9538
La Habra	Fran's Around a Corner B&B, 1584 N. Cypress St, 90631 310-690-6422
La Jolla	Buena Vista Home B&B, 5446 Candlelight Dr, 92037 858-454-9646
La Jolla	JC Resorts - Scripps Inn, 555 Coast Blvd S, 92037 858-454-3391
La Quinta	Two Angels Inn, 78-120 Caleo Bay Dr., 92253 619-546-7332
Lafayette	Donner Country Inn, 9 Green Valley Dr., 94549 925-587-5574
Laguna Beach	Eiler's Inn, 2891 Chateau Way, 92651 949-494-3004
Laguna Beach	Inn at Laguna Beach, 211 N. Coast Hwy., 92651 949-497-9722
Laguna Beach	La Casa Del Camino, 1289 S Coast Hwy, 92651 949-249-7875
Laguna Beach	The Carriage House B&B, 1322 Catalina St, 92651 949-494-8945
Lake Almanor	Lake Almanor Inn, 3965 Hwy. A-13, 96137 916-596-3910
Lake Arrowhead	Bracken Fern Manor, 815 Arrowhead Villas Rd, 92352 909-337-8557
Lake Arrowhead	Chateau Du Lac, PO Box 1098, 92352 909-337-6488
Lake Arrowhead	Prophet's Paradise B&B Inn, PO Box 2116, 92352 909-336-1969
Lake Arrowhead	Romantique Lakeview Lodge, PO Box 128, 92352 909-337-6633
Lake Arrowhead	Saddleback Inn, 300 S. State Hwy 173, 92352 909-336-3571
Lake Arrowhead	The Carriage House B&B, PO Box 982, 92352 909-336-1400
Lake Hughes	Lake Hughes Rock Inn, PO Box 404, 93532 805-724-1855
Lake Tahoe	Angel's Haven, An, 3773 Pioneer Trail #4, 96158 916-544-9297
Lake Tahoe	Richardson's Resort, PO Box 9028, 96158 800-544-1801
Lake Tahoe	The Tamarack Creek B&B, PO Box 8841, 96158 916-659-0325
Lakeport	Arbor House, 150 Clearlake Ave, 95453

Lakeport	Wooden Bridge B&B, 1441 Oakwood Ct, 95453 707-263-9125
Lee Vining	Tioga Lodge, 54411 Hwy 395, 93541 760-647-6423
Leggett	Madcreek Inn, 58974 Hwy 101, 95585 707-984-6206
Lemon Cove	Lemon Cove B&B, 33038 Sierra Hwy, 93244 209-597-2555
Lewiston	Lewiston B&B, PO Box 688, 96052 916-778-3385
Little River	Blanchard House B&B, PO Box 521, 95456 707-937-1627
Little River	Glendeven Inn & Gallery, 8221 N Hwy, 95456 707-937-0083
Little River	Heritage House, 5200 N. Highway 1, 95456 707-937-5885
Little River	Little River Inn, 7751 N Hwy One Drawer B, 95456 707-937-5942
Livermore	Purple Orchid Inn Resort, 4549 Cross Rd., 94550 925-606-8855
Loleta	Southport Landing, PO Box 172, 95554 707-733-5915
Long Beach	Crane's Nest, 319 W. 12th St, 90813 562-435-4084
Long Beach	Gemini Sisters Inn, 814 Cedar Ave, 90813 562-432-8881
Loomis	Emma's B&B, 3137 Taylor Rd, 95650 916-652-1392
Loomis	Old Flower Farm Inn, 4150 Auburn-Folsom Rd., 95650 916-652-5040
Los Alamos	Depot Hotel, PO Box 25, 93440 805-344-1006
Los Alamos	Union Hotel, PO Box 616, 93440 805-344-2744
Los Altos	Pedigrift House, PO Box 1754, 94023 503-482-1888
Los Angeles	Carlyle Inn, 1119 S. Robertson Blvd, 90035 310-275-4445
Los Angeles	Casablanca Villa, 449 N. Detroit St, 90036 213-938-4794
Los Angeles	Le Auberge Maison Magnolia, 1007 W 24th, 90007 213-746-1314
Los Angeles	Rainbow's End B&B, 1618 Mountcrest Ave, 90069 213-650-2345
Los Angeles	Terrace Manor, 1353 Alvarado Terrace, 90006 213-381-1478
Los Angeles	The Inn at 657, 657 W. 23rd St, 90007 800-347-7512
Los Angeles	The Secret Garden B&B, 8039 Selma Ave, 90046
Los Osos	Pacific Breeze B&B Suites, 2710 Pecho Valley Rd, 93402 805-528-0132
Lower Lake	Big Canyon Inn, PO Box 1311, 95457 707-928-5631
Loyalton	Clover Valley Mill House, PO Box 928, 96118 916-993-2442
Lucerne	Kristalberg B&B, PO Box 1629, 95458 707-274-8009
Magalia	J & J's B&B, PO Box 1059, 95954 916-873-4782
Malibu	Casa Malibu, 22752 Pacific Coast Hwy, 90265 310-456-2219
Malibu	Malibu Beach Inn, 22878 Pacific Coast Hwy, 90265 213-456-6444
Malibu	Malibu Country Inn, 6506 Westward Beach Rd, 90265 213-457-9622
Mammoth Lakes	Tamarack Lodge Resort, PO Box 69, 93546 760-934-2442
Mammoth Lakes	White Horse Inn, PO Box 2326, 93546 760-924-3656
Mariposa	5th Street Inn, PO Box 1917, 95338 209-966-6048
Mariposa	Boulder Creek, 4572 Ben Hur Rd, 95338 209-742-7729
Mariposa	Finch Haven B&B, 4605 Triangle Rd, 95338 209-966-4738
Mariposa	Granny's Garden B&B, 7333 Hwy 49 N, 95338 209-377-8342
Mariposa	Ken and Flo's B&B, PO Box 2141, 95338 209-966-7677
Mariposa	Little Valley Inn, 3483 Brooks Rd, 95338 209-742-6204
Mariposa	Mariposa Hotel Inn, PO Box 745, 95338 209-966-4676
Mariposa	Meadow Creek Ranch B&B Inn, 2669 Triangle & Hwy 49S, 95338 209-966-3843
Mariposa	Poppy Hill B&B, 5218 Crystal Aire Dr, 95338 209-742-6273
Mariposa	Rock & Rill, PO Box 1036, 95338 209-742-4494
Mariposa	Rockwood Gardens, 5155 Tip Top Rd, 95338 209-742-6817
Mariposa	Shangri-La, 6316 Jerseydale, 95338 209-966-2653
Mariposa	Shiloh, 3265 Triangle Park Rd, 95338 209-742-7200
Mariposa	Shirl's B&B, PO Box 1293, 95338 209-966-2514
Mariposa	Sierra House, 4981 Indian Peak Rd, 95338 209-966-3515
Mariposa	Sky View Village, PO Box 1482, 95338 209-966-6972
Mariposa	The Chubb's, PO Box 1060, 95338 209-966-5085
Mariposa	The Guest House, 4962 Triangle Rd, 95338 209-742-6869
Mariposa	The Pelennor B&B, 3871 Hwy 49 S, 95338 209-966-2832
Mariposa	The Verandah B&B, 5086 Tip Top Rd., 95338 209-742-6493
Mariposa	Twelve Oaks Carriage House, 4877 Wildwood, 95338 209-966-3231
Mariposa	Villa Monti, PO Box 1888, 95338 209-966-2439
Mariposa	Yosemite Gardens, PO Box 2105, 95338
Mariposa	Yosemite-Mariposa Townhse, PO Box 1947, 95338
Marshall	Inn at Tomales Bay, 22555 Highway 1, 94940 415-663-9002
McCloud	Hogan House, PO Box 550, 96057 916-964-2882
McCloud	Joanie's B&B, PO Box 924, 96057 916-964-3106
McCloud	McCloud Hotel B&B, PO Box 730, 96057 530-964-2822
McCloud	McCloud River Inn B&B, PO Box 1560, 96057 530-964-2130
McCloud	Stoney Brook Inn, PO Box 1860, 96057 916-964-2300
McCloud	The McCloud Guest House, PO Box 1510, 96057 916-964-3160
Mendocino	1021 Main St. Guest House, PO Box 803, 95460 707-937-5150
Mendocino	Annie's Jughandle Beach, PO Box 228, 95460 707-964-1415
Mendocino	Blackberry Inn, 44951 Larkin Rd, 95460 707-937-5281
Mendocino	Blair House, PO Box 1608, 95460
Mendocino	Blue Heron Inn B&B, PO Box 1142, 95460 707-937-4323
Mendocino	Brewery Gulch Inn, 9350 Coast Highway 1, 95460 707-937-4752
Mendocino	Captain's Cove Inn, PO Box 803, 95460 707-937-5150
Mendocino	Glendeven Inn & Gallery, 8221 N. Hwy 1, 95456 707-937-0083
Mendocino	Hill House Inn, PO Box 625, 95410 707-937-0554
Mendocino	McElroy's Inn, PO Box 1881, 95460 707-937-1734
Mendocino	Mendocino Farmhouse, PO Box 247, 95460 707-937-0241
Mendocino	Mendocino Village Inn, PO Box 626, 95460 707-937-0246

Mendocino	Nicholson House, PO Box 707, 95460 707-937-4478
Mendocino	Rachel's Inn, Box 134, 95460 707-937-0088
Mendocino	Reed Manor, PO Box 127, 95460 707-937-5446
Mendocino	Sallie & Eileen's Place, Box 409, 95460 707-937-2028
Mendocino	Sea Gull Inn, PO Box 317, 95460 707-937-5204
Mendocino	Seafoam Lodge, PO Box 68, 95460 707-937-1827
Mendocino	Stevenswood Lodge, PO Box 170, 95460 707-937-2810
Mendocino	Sweetwater Spa & Inn, PO Box 337, 95460 707-937-4076
Mendocino	The Headlands Inn, PO Box 132, 95460 707-937-4431
Mi Wuk Village	Mi-Wuk Lodge, PO Box 70, 95346 209-586-3031
Middletown	Harbin Hot Springs Retreat, PO Box 782, 95461 707-987-2477
Midpines	Pimentel's B&B, PO Box 207, 95345 209-966-6847
Midpines	Ponderosa B&B Guest House, PO Box 104, 95345
Mill Valley	Le Petite Bijou, 11 Lomita Dr., 94941
Mill Valley	Michael's House, 100 Sarah Ave., 94941 415-389-6017
Mill Valley	Mill Valley Inn, 165 Throckmorton Ave, 94941 415-389-6608
Mill Valley	Singing Trees, 425 Wellesley Ave, 94941 415-381-4147
Mill Valley	Tree Tops B&B, 215 Marlin Avenue, 94941 415-383-3169
Modesto	Touch of Mexico, 400 Cottonwood Dr, 95356
Modesto	Vineyard View B&B, 2837 Michigan Ave., 95351 209-523-9009
Mono Hot Springs	Mono Hot Springs Resort, General Delivery, 93642 209-325-1710
Montara	Farallone Inn B&B, PO Box 371325, 94037 650-728-8200
Montara	Montara B&B, PO Box 493, 94037 650-728-3946
Monte Rio	Highland Dell Inn, PO Box 370, 95462
Monterey	Charlaine's Bay View B&B, 44 Sierra Vista Dr, 93940 831-655-0177
Monterey	Del Monte Beach Inn, 600 Martin St, 93940 831-649-4410
Monterey	Merritt House, 386 Pacific St, 93940 831-646-9686
Monterey	The Spindrift Inn, 652 Cannery Row, 93940
Monterey	Victorian Inn, 487 Foam St., 93940
Morro Bay	Marina Street B&B, 305 Marina St, 93442 805-772-4016
Moss Beach	Seal Cove Inn, 221 Cypress Ave, 94038 415-728-4114
Mount Shasta	Dream Inn B&B, 326 Chestnut St., 96067
Mount Shasta	Strawberry Valley Inn, 1142 S Mt Shasta Blvd, 96067 916-926-2052
Mount Shasta	Ward's "Big Foot" Ranch, PO Box 585, 96067 916-926-5170
Mt Baldy	Snow Crest Lodge, PO Box 307, 91759 909-931-1402
Murphys	Trade Carriage House, 230 Big Trees Rd, 95247
Myers Flat	Myers Inn, PO Box 173, 95554 707-943-3259
Napa	Churchill Manor, 485 Brown St, 94559 707-253-7733
Napa	Country Garden Inn, 1815 Silverado Trail, 94558 707-255-1197
Napa	Hillview Country Inn, 1205 Hillview Ln, 94558 707-224-5004
Napa	Inn At Sunrise Point, 1713 Partrick Rd, 94558 707-255-2211
Napa	Inn on Randolph, 411 Randolph St, 94559 707-257-2886
Napa	McClelland-Priest B&B Inn, 569 Randolph St, 94559 707-224-6875
Napa	Sybron House, 7400 St Helena Hwy, 94558 707-944-2785
Napa	The Napa Inn, 1137 Warren St, 94559 707-257-1444
Napa Valley	Stahlecker House B&B Inn, 1042 Easum Dr, 94558 707-257-1588
Nevada City	Downey House B&B Inn, 517 W Broad St, 95959 530-265-2815
Nevada City	Emma Nevada House, 528 E. Broad St, 95959 530-265-4415
Nevada City	Flume's End B&B Inn, 317 S Pine St, 95959 530-265-9665
Nevada City	Marsh House B&B Inn, 254 Boulder, 95959 530-265-5709
Nevada City	National Hotel, 211 Broad St, 95959 530-265-4551
Nevada City	Outside Inn, 575 E Broad St, 95959 530-265-2233
Nevada City	Parsonage B&B, 427 Broad St., 95959 530-265-9478
Nevada City	Piety Hill Inn, 523 Sacramento St, 95959 530-265-2245
Nevada City	The Deer Creek Inn, 116 Nevada St, 95959 530-265-0363
Nevada City	The Kendall House, 534 Spring St, 95959 530-265-0405
Nevada City	The Red Castle Inn, 109 Prospect St, 95959 530-265-5135
Nevada City	U.S. Hotel B&B, 233-B Broad St, 95959 530-265-7999
Newport Beach	Doryman's Inn, 2102 W. Oceanfront, 92663 949-675-7300
Newport Beach	Island Cottage B&B, 1305 Park Ave, 92662 949-723-1125
Newport Beach	Newport Channel Inn, 6030 W. Coast Hwy, 92663 949-642-3030
Newport Beach	Newport Classic Inn, 2300 W. Coast Hwy, 92663
Newport Beach	Portofino Beach Hotel, 2306 W Oceanfront, 92663 949-673-7030
Nipton	Hotel Nipton, HC1 Box 357, 92364 760-856-2335
North Fork	Ye Olde South Fork Inn, PO Box 731, 93643 209-877-7025
Oak Glen	St. Anley Inn, 39796 Pine Bench Rd., 92399
Oakhurst	China Creek, 49522 Road 426, 93644 209-642-6248
Oakhurst	Estate by the Elderberries, PO Box 577, 93644 209-683-6860
Oakland	Washington Inn, 495 10th St, 94607 510-452-1776
Occidental	The Inn at Occidental, PO Box 857, 95465 707-874-1047
Ojai	Canyon Creek Home, 2125 McNell Rd, 93023 805-646-6933
Ojai	Casa de La Luna, 710 S La Luna, 93023 805-646-4528
Ojai	Ojai B&B, 921 Patricia Ct, 93023 805-646-8337
Ojai	Ojai B&B, 901 Saddle Lane, 93023
Ojai	Ojai Manor Hotel, PO Box 608, 93024 805-646-0961
Olema	Bear Valley Inn, PO Box 33, 94950 415-663-1777
Olema	Olema Inn, PO Box 37, 94950 415-663-9559
Olema	Pt. Reyes Seashore Lodge, PO Box 39, 94950 415-663-9000

Orland	Inn at Shallow Creek Farm, 4712 Road DD, 95963 916-865-4093
Oroville	Montgomery Inn, 1400 Montgomery St, 95965 916-532-1400
Oxnard	Mama Bear's Orchard B&B, 4810 Del Oro Pl, 93033 209-528-3614
Pacific Grove	Gosby House Inn, 643 Lighthouse Ave, 93950 831-375-1287
Pacific Grove	Green Gables Inn, 104 Fifth St, 93950 831-375-2095
Pacific Grove	Lighthouse Lodge Suites, 1249 Lighthouse Ave, 93950 831-655-2111
Pacific Grove	Pacific Grove Inn, 581 Pine Ave., 93950 831-375-2825
Pacific Palisades	Olinda Country Inn, 15237 Sunset Blvd #301, 90272 310-459-6900
Palm Desert	Desert Patch Inn, 73758 Shadow Mountain, 92260 619-346-9161
Palm Springs	Estrella Inn, 415 S Belardo, 92262 619-320-4117
Palm Springs	Monte Vista, 414 N. Palm Canyon Dr, 92262 619-325-5641
Palm Springs	Morningside Inn, 888 N Indian Canyon, 92262 760-325-2668
Palm Springs	Orchid Tree Inn, 261 S. Belardo Rd, 92262 619-325-2791
Palm Springs	Sakura Japanese B&B, PO Box 9403, 92263
Palm Springs	The Terra Cotta Inn, 2388 E Racquet Club Rd, 92262 760-322-6059
Palm Springs	Villa Rosa Inn, 1577 S Indian Trail, 92264 760-327-5915
Palm Springs	Windermere Manor, PO Box 9568, 92263 909-336-3292
Palo Alto	Hotel California, 2431 Ash St., 94306 650-321-7358
Parkfield	Parkfield Inn, Parkfield Rt Box 3560, 93451 805-463-2300
Pasadena	Pasadena Hotel, 76 N Fairoaks Ave, 91103 626-568-8172
Paso Robles	Just Inn, 11680 Chimney Rock Rd, 93446
Paso Robles	The Arbor Inn, PO Box 3260, 93447 805-227-4673
Pescadero	Ocean View Farms B&B, PO Box 538, 94060 650-879-0698
Pescadero	Old Saw Mill Lodge, PO Box 96, 94060 650-879-0111
Petaluma	Flower Garden B&B, 517 Petaluma Blvd S, 94952 707-622-7837
Philo	Anderson Valley Inn, 8480 Hwy 128, 95466 707-895-3325
Philo	Pinoli Ranch Country Inn, 3280 Clark Rd., 95466
Pine Grove	Druid House, 13887 Druid Ln, 95665 209-296-4156
Placerville	Combellack-Blair House, 3059 Cedar Ravine, 95667 530-622-3764
Placerville	James Blair House, 2985 Clay St, 95667 530-626-6136
Placerville	The Seasons B&B, 2934 Bedford Ave, 95667 530-626-4420
Placerville	The Shafsky House, 2942 Coloma St, 95667 530-642-2776
Pleasanton	Evergreen, 9104 Longview Dr, 94588 925-426-0901
Plymouth	Amador Harvest Inn, 12455 Steiner Rd, 95664 209-245-5512
Plymouth	Indian Creek B&B, 21950 Hwy 49, 95669 209-245-4648
Pocket Canyon	The Estate, 13555 Hwy 116, 95446 707-869-9093
Point Arena	Point Arena B&B, PO Box 1076, 95468 707-882-3455
Point Arena	Pt Arena B&B, PO Box 1076, 95468 707-882-2320
Point Reyes	Carriage House, PO Box 1239, 94956
Point Reyes	Casa Mexicana, PO Box 365, 94956 415-663-8313
Point Reyes	Cottages on the Beach, PO Box 501, 94956 415-663-9696
Point Reyes	Holly Tree Inn/Cottages, PO Box 642, 94956 415-663-1554
Point Reyes	Horseshoe Farm Cottage, PO Box 332, 94956 415-663-9401
Point Reyes	Jasmine Cottage & Retreat, PO Box 56, 94956 415-663-1166
Point Reyes	Knob Hill, PO Box 1108, 94956 415-663-1784
Point Reyes	Point Reyes Station Inn, PO Box 824, 94956 415-663-9372
Point Reyes	Point Reyes Vineyard Inn, 12700 Highway #1, 94956 415-663-1011
Point Reyes	Pt. Reyes Country Inn, PO Box 501, 94956 415-663-9696
Point Reyes	Pt. Reyes Station Inn, PO Box 824, 94956 415-663-9372
Point Reyes	Roundstone Farm, PO Box 217, 94950 415-663-1020
Point Reyes	Sea Star Cottage, Box 642, 94956 415-663-1554
Point Reyes	Seven Gray Foxes, PO Box 459, 94956 415-663-1089
Point Reyes	The Cherry Tree Cottage, PO Box 1082, 94956 415-663-1689
Point Reyes	The Country House, PO Box 98, 94956 415-663-1627
Point Reyes	Tradewinds B&B, PO Box 1117, 94956 415-663-9326
Point Reyes	Windsong Cottage, PO Box 84, 94956 415-663-9695
Portola	Pullman House, 256 Commercial St, 96122 916-832-0107
Posey	Road's End at Paso Creek, RR #1, Box 450, 93260 805-536-8668
Quincy	Bucks' Lake Hideaway, 16860 Bucks Lake Rd, 95971 916-283-4577
Quincy	New England Ranch, 2571 Quincy Junction Rd, 95971
Ramona	Lake Sutherland B&B, 24901 Dam Oaks Dr, 92065 800-789-6483
Rancho Cucamonga	Christmas House B&B Inn, 9240 Archibald Ave, 91730 714-980-6450
Rancho Mirage	Leanne's House, 44 Santo Domingo Dr., 92270
Randsburg	The Cottage Hotel B&B, PO Box D, 93554 760-374-2285
Ravendale	Spanish Springs Ranch, PO Box 70, 96123
Red Bluff	Beresford House B&B & Barn, PO Box 154, 96080 530-527-0515
Red Bluff	Jarvis Mansion, 1313 Jackson St., 96080 530-527-6901
Red Bluff	Jeter Victorian Inn, 1107 Jefferson St, 96080 530-527-7574
Redondo Beach	Ocean Breeze Inn, 122 S. Juanita Ave, 90277 310-316-5123
Redondo Beach	Sea Breeze B&B, 122 S. Juanita, 90277 310-316-5123
Reedley	Fairweather Inn, 259 South Reed, 93654 209-638-1918
Reedley	Hotel Burgess, 1076 N. Kady, 93654 209-638-6315
Reedley	Reedley Country Inn B&B, 43137 Rd 52, 93654 209-638-2585
Ridgecrest	Bev Len Haus, 809 N Sanders St, 93555 760-375-1988
Rio del Mar	Marvista B&B, 212 Martin Dr, 95003 408-684-9311
Running Springs	Spring Oaks B&B, PO Box 2918, 92382 909-867-7797
Rutherford	Auberge du Soleil, 180 Rutherford Hill Rd, 94573 707-963-1211
Rutherford	Rancho Caymus, PO Box 78, 94573 707-963-1777

S. San Francisco	Oyster Point Marina Inn, 425 Marina Blvd., 94080 650-737-7633
Sacramento	Abigail's B&B, 2120 "G" St, 95816 916-441-5007
Sacramento	Driver Mansion Inn, 2019 21st St., 95818 916-455-5243
Sacramento	Moon River Inn, 8201 Freeport Blvd, 95832 916-665-6550
Sacramento	Savoyard, 3322 H St, 95816 916-442-6709
Sacramento	Scandia House, 903 28th St, 95816 206-725-7825
Sacramento	Vizcaya B&B, 2019 21st St, 95818 916-455-5243
Samoa	Samoa Airport B&B, 900 New Navy Base Rd, 95564 707-445-0765
San Andreas	The Robin's Nest, 247 W St Charles St, 95249 209-754-1076
San Anselmo	San Anselmo Inn, 339 San Anselmo Ave, 94960 415-455-5366
San Clemente	Casa de Flores B&B, 184 Ave La Cuesta, 92672 949-498-1344
San Diego	Balboa Park Inn, 3402 Park Blvd, 92103 619-298-0823
San Diego	Bay Breeze B&B, 3032 Serbian Place, 92117 619-275-3995
San Diego	Beach Hut, PO Box 90334, 92169 619-272-6131
San Diego	Bears at the Beach, 3616 Yosemite St, 16042
San Diego	Buena Vista B&B, 5446 Candlelight Dr, 92037 619-454-9646
San Diego	Crones Cobblestone Cottage, 1302 Washington Place, 92103 619-295-4765
San Diego	Keating House Inn, 2331 Second Ave, 92101 619-239-8585
San Diego	Monets Garden, 7039 Casa Ln, 91945 619-464-8296
San Diego	Quince St. Trolley B&B, PO Box 7654, 92167 619-226-8454
San Diego	San Diego Yacht & Breakfas, 1880 Harbor Island Dr, 92101 619-297-9484
San Diego	The Blom House B&B, 1372 Minden Dr, 92111 619-467-0890
San Diego	Vera's Cozy Corner, 2404 Loring St, 92109 619-296-1938
San Diego	Yacht & Breakfast, 1450 Harbor Island, 92101 619-297-4862
San Francisco	Albion House Inn, 135 Gough St, 94102 415-621-0896
San Francisco	Andora Inn, 2434 Mission St, 94110
San Francisco	Anna's Three Bears, 114 Divisadero St, 94117 415-255-3167
San Francisco	Ansonia-Cambridge Hotel, 711 Post St, 94109 415-673-2670
San Francisco	Art Center Wamsley B&B, 1902 Filbert at Laguna, 94123 415-567-1526
San Francisco	Bella Vista Inn, 114 Divisadero St, 94117 415-255-3167
San Francisco	Brady Acres, 649 Jones Street, 94102 415-929-8033
San Francisco	Casita Blanca, 330 Edgehill Way, 94127 415-564-9339
San Francisco	Dockside Boat & Bed, Pier 39, 94133 510-444-5858
San Francisco	Edward II Inn & Suites, 3155 Scott St, 94123 415-922-3000
San Francisco	Glenwood Hotel, 717 Sutter St, 94109 415-673-0700
San Francisco	Haus Kleebauer a B&B, 225 Clipper St, 94114 415-821-3866
San Francisco	Hill Point B&B, 15 Hill Point Ave., 94117 415-753-0393
San Francisco	Hotel Boheme, 444 Columbus Ave, 94133 415-433-9111
San Francisco	Hotel David B&B, 480 Geary St, 94102 415-771-1600
San Francisco	Inn at the Opera, 333 Fulton, 94102 415-863-8400
San Francisco	Inn on Castro, 321 Castro St, 94114 415-861-0321
San Francisco	Jackson Court, 2198 Jackson St, 94115 415-929-7670
San Francisco	Marina Inn, 3110 Octavia St, 94123 415-928-1000
San Francisco	Morgan Hill Vineyards B&B, 2591 26th Ave, 94116
San Francisco	No Name Victorian B&B, PO Box 420009, 94142 415-479-1913
San Francisco	Nob Hill Lambourne, 725 Pine St., 94108 415-433-2287
San Francisco	Obrero Hotel, 1208 Stockton St., 94133 415-989-3960
San Francisco	Parsonage, 198 Haight St, 94102 415-863-3699
San Francisco	Pension San Francisco, 1668 Market St, 94102 415-864-1271
San Francisco	Petite Auberge, 863 Bush St, 94108 415-928-6000
San Francisco	Red Victorian Peace Center, 1665 Haight St, 94117 415-864-1978
San Francisco	Seal Rock Inn, 545 Point Lobos Ave, 94121 415-752-8000
San Francisco	Shannon-Kavanaugh House, 722 Steiner St., 94117 415-563-2727
San Francisco	Sherman House, 2160 Green St, 94123 800-424-5777
San Francisco	Spencer House, 1080 Haight St, 94117 415-626-9205
San Francisco	The Bed & Breakfast Inn, 4 Charlton Court, 94123 415-921-9784
San Francisco	The Herb'n Inn, PO Box 170106, 94117 415-543-8542
San Francisco	The Langtry, 993 Haight St., 94117 415-668-0410
San Francisco	The Mansions Hotel, 2220 Sacramento St, 94115 415-929-9444
San Francisco	The Queen Anne Hotel, 1590 Sutter St, 94109 415-441-2828
San Francisco	The Washington Square Inn, 1660 Stockton St, 94133 415-981-4220
San Francisco	Union Street Inn, 2229 Union St, 94123 415-346-0424
San Francisco	Victorian Garden B&B, 4046 26th St., 94131 415-206-1999
San Francisco	Villa, 379 Collingwood, 94114
San Francisco	White Swan Inn, 845 Bush St, 94108 415-775-1755
San Francisco	Willows B&B Inn, 710 - 14th St, 94114 415-431-4770
San Juan Bautista	Arboleda, PO Box 138, 95045 831-623-2066
San Juan Bautista	B&B San Juan, PO Box 613, 95045 831-623-4101
San Luis Obispo	Garden Street Inn B&B, 1212 Garden St, 93401 805-545-9802
San Mateo	Coxhead House, 37 E Santa Inez Ave, 94401 650-685-1500
San Mateo	Twin Gates B&B, 27 El Cerrito Ave, 94402
San Miguel	Ranch B&B, 71840 Cholame Rd, 93451
San Miguel	Victorian Manor B&B, PO Box 8, 93451 805-467-3306
San Pedro	Grand Cottages, 325 W Seventh St, 90731 213-548-1240
San Rafael	425 Mission, 425 Mission, 94901 415-453-1365
San Rafael	Casa Soldavini, 531 "C" St, 94901 415-454-3140
Santa Barbara	Bath Street Inn, 1720 Bath St, 93101 805-682-9680
Santa Barbara	Bayberry Inn, 111 W Valerio St, 93101 805-682-3199

Santa Barbara	Blue Dolphine Inn, 420 W. Montecito St, 93101 805-965-2333
Santa Barbara	Blue Quail Inn & Cottage, 1908 Bath St., 93101 805-687-2300
Santa Barbara	Coast Village Inn, 1188 Coast Village Rd, 93108 805-969-3266
Santa Barbara	Harbor House Inn, 104 Bath St, 93101 805-962-9745
Santa Barbara	Ivanhoe Inn, 1406 Castillo St, 93103 805-963-8832
Santa Barbara	Laguna Garden Inn, PO Box 272, 93101 805-962-1165
Santa Barbara	Montecito Inn, 1295 Coast Village Rd, 93108 805-969-7854
Santa Barbara	The Eagle Inn, 232 Natoma Ave, 93101 805-965-3586
Santa Barbara	The Goodfriend Inn, 1734 Bath St, 93101 805-898-9336
Santa Barbara	The Mary May Inn, 111 W Valerio St, 93101 805-569-3398
Santa Barbara	Villa d'Italia, 780 Mission Canyon Rd, 93105 805-687-6933
Santa Barbara	Villa Rosa, 15 Chapala St, 93101 805-966-0851
Santa Cruz	Black Pearl Cottage, 104 Second Ave, 95062 408-429-5377
Santa Cruz	Cliff Crest B&B Inn, 407 Cliff St, 95060 831-427-2609
Santa Cruz	Harbor Boat B&B, 210 Benito Ave, 95062 831-353-8710
Santa Cruz	Inn Laguna Creek, 2727 Smith Grade, 95060 831-425-0692
Santa Monica	Shutters On The Beach, 1 Pico Blvd., 90405 800-334-9000
Santa Paula	The Fern Oaks Inn, 1025 Ojai Rd, 93060 805-525-7747
Santa Paula	The White Gables Inn, 545 6th Street, 93060 805-933-3041
Santa Rosa	Cooper's Grove Ranch, 5763 Sonoma Mountain Rd, 95404 707-571-1928
Santa Rosa	Melitta Station Inn, 5850 Melita Rd, 95409 707-538-7712
Santa Rosa	Pygmalion House B&B Inn, 331 Orange St, 95401 707-526-3407
Santa Rosa	Ray's Resort, 701 Monroe St., 95404 707-542-3137
Saratoga	Trinity Center Inn, PO Box 2358, 95070 408-266-3223
Sausalito	Butterfly Tree, PO Box 790, 94966 415-383-8447
Sausalito	Casa Madrona Hotel, 801 Bridgeway, 94965 415-332-0502
Sausalito	The Inn Above Tide, 30 El Portal, 94965 415-332-9535
Sebastopol	Creekwood, 546 Sparkes Rd, 95472 707-963-3590
Sebastopol	Gravenstein Inn, 3160 Hicks Rd, 95472 707-829-0493
Shelter Cove	Shelter Cove B&B, 148 Dolphin, 95589 707-986-7161
Sherman Oaks	El Camino Real B&B, PO Box 5598, 91403 818-785-8351
Shingletown	Weston House, PO Box 276, 96088 916-474-3738
Sierra City	Holly House, PO Box 350, 96125
Skyforest	Greystone & Cottage, PO Box 300, 92385 909-337-0278
Skyforest	Sky Forest B&B Inn, PO Box 482, 92385 909-337-4680
Smith River	Casa Rubio, 17285 Crissey Rd., 95567 707-487-4313
Smith River	White Rose Inn, 149 S Fred Haight Dr, 95567 707-487-9260
Solvang	Chimney Sweep Inn, 1554 Copenhagen Dr., 93463 805-688-211
Solvang	Danish Country Inn, 1455 Mission Dr, 93463 805-688-2018
Solvang	Story Book Inn, 409 First St, 93463 805-688-1703
Somerset	Seven Up Bar Guest Ranch, 8060 Fairplay Rd, 95684 916-620-5450
Sonoma	Big Dog Inn, PO Box 1512, 95476 707-996-4319
Sonoma	Country Cottage, 291 1st St E, 95476 707-938-2479
Sonoma	El Dorado Inn, 405 First St W, 95476 707-996-3030
Sonoma	Hidden Oak, 214 E. Napa St, 95476 707-996-9863
Sonoma	Holly Hock House, PO Box 845, 95476 707-939-1809
Sonoma	Morningsong Country Lodgin, 21725 Hyde Rd., 95476 707-936-8616
Sonoma	Sonoma Chalet B&B, 18935 Fifth St W, 95476 707-938-3129
Sonoma	Sonoma Hotel, 110 W Spain St, 95476 707-996-2996
Sonoma	Sparrows Nest Inn, 424 Denmark St., 95476 707-996-3750
Sonoma	Starwae, 21490 Broadway, 95476
Sonoma	Stone Grove, 240 Second St. E, 95476
Sonoma	The Cottage Inn, 302 First St E, 95476 707-996-0719
Sonora	Barretta Gardens B&B Inn, 700 S Barretta St, 95370 209-532-6039
Sonora	Eller House B&B, PO Box 4056, 95370 209-532-0420
Sonora	Hammons House Inn B&B, 22963 Robertson Ranch, 95370 209-532-7921
Sonora	Laurel Ridge Cottage Inn, 22890 Comstock Ranch Rd, 95370 415-633-1286
Sonora	Ryan House, 1855, 153 S. Shepherd St, 95370 209-533-3445
Sonora	Serenity - A B&B Inn, 15305 Bear Cub Dr, 95370 209-533-1441
Sonora	Tudor Oaks, PO Box 4395, 95370 209-533-1619
Sonora	Wy's Acres, 8773 Fraguero Rd, 95370 209-536-9004
Soulsbyville	Benjamin Soulsby, PO Box 159, 95372 209-536-9349
St. Helena	Asplund Country Inn, 726 Rossi Rd, 94574 707-963-4614
St. Helena	Auberge Brisebois, 271 Via Monte, 94574 707-963-4658
St. Helena	Barro Station, 1112 Lodi Lane, 94574 707-963-5169
St. Helena	Chestelson House B&B, 1417 Kearney St, 94574 707-963-2238
St. Helena	Creekside Inn, 945 Main St, 94574 707-963-7244
St. Helena	Elsie's Conn Valley Inn B&, 726 Rossi Rd, 94574 707-963-4614
St. Helena	Farmhouse, 300 Taplin Rd., 94574 707-963-3431
St. Helena	Glass Mountain Inn, 3100 Silverado Trail, 94574 707-963-3512
St. Helena	Harvest Inn, One Main St, 94574 707-963-9463
St. Helena	Hotel St. Helena, 1309 Main St, 94574 707-963-4388
St. Helena	Inn at Southbridge, 1020 Main St., 94574 707-967-9400
St. Helena	Oliver House Country Inn, 2970 Silverado Tr, 94574 707-963-4089
St. Helena	Prager Winery B&B, 1281 Lewelling Ln, 94574 707-963-3720
St. Helena	Rose Garden Inn, 1277 St. Helena Hwy S, 94574 707-963-4417
St. Helena	Rustridge Ranch, 2910 Lower Chiles Valle, 94574
St. Helena	Vigne del Uomo Felice, 1871 Cabernet Lane, 94574 707-963-2376

St. Helena	Villa St. Helena, 2727 Sulphur Springs Av, 94574 707-963-2514
St. Helena	Vineyard Country Inn, 201 Main St, 94574 707-963-1000
Stinson Beach	The Redwoods Haus B&B, PO Box 404, 94970 415-868-1034
Stirling City	Stirling City Hotel, PO Box 130, 95978 916-873-0858
Strawberry	Strawberry Inn, PO Box 61, 95375 209-965-3662
Sunset Beach	Harbour Inn, PO Box 1439, 90742 310-592-4470
Sunset Beach	Sunset B&B Inn, PO Box 1202, 90742 213-592-1666
Susanville	Red Ranch House @ Willow C, 490-800 Horse Lake Rd, 96130 916-257-5712
Sutter Creek	Foxes in Sutter Creek, PO Box 159, 95685 800-987-3344
Sutter Creek	Grey Gables B&B Inn, PO Box 1687, 95685
Sutter Creek	Picturerock Inn, PO Box 395, 95685
Sutter Creek	The Gold Quartz Inn, PO Box 55, 95685 209-267-9155
Sutter Creek	The Hanford House B&B Inn, PO Box 1450, 95685 209-267-0747
Tahoe City	Chateau Place, PO Box 5254, 96145 800-773-0313
Tahoe City	Cottage Inn at Lake Tahoe, PO Box 66, 95730 530-581-4073
Tahoe City	River Ranch Lodge, PO Box 197, 96145 530-583-4264
Tahoe City	Sunnyside Resort, PO Box 5969, 96145 530-683-7200
Tahoma	Chateau Arbre Country B&B, PO Box 262, 96142 800-726-1308
Tahoma	Norfolk Woods Inn, PO Box 262, 96142 916-525-5000
Tahoma	Sugar Pines, Box 153, 96142 916-525-1259
Tahoma	Tahoma Meadows B&B, 6821 Westlake Blvd, 96142 800-355-1596
Tahoma	The Captain's Alpenhaus, PO Box 262, 96142
Templeton	Country House Inn, 91 Main St, 93465 805-434-1598
Three Rivers	Cort Cottage, PO Box 245, 93271 209-561-4671
Three Rivers	Organic Gardens B&B, 44095 Dinely Dr, 93271 209-561-0916
Three Rivers	Sequoia Village Inn, PO Box 1014, 93271 209-561-3652
Tomales	U.S. Hotel, 36985 Hwy 1, 94971 707-878-2742
Torrance	The White's House, 17122 Faysmith Ave, 90504 310-324-6164
Trinidad	Trinidad Bay B&B, PO Box 849, 95570 707-677-0840
Trinidad	Turtle Rocks Inn, 3392 Patrick's Point Dr, 95570 707-677-3707
Tustin	Royal Hotel, 1100 Irvine Blvd #54, 92680 714-835-8787
Twain Harte	Twain Harte's B&B, PO Box 1718, 95383 209-586-3311
Twenty Nine Palms	29 Palms Inn, 78950 Inn Ave, 92277 760-363-3305
Twenty Nine Palms	Homestead Inn B&B, 74153 Two Mile Rd., 92277 760-367-0030
Ukiah	Oak Knoll B&B, 1270 Homewood Dr, 95482 707-468-5646
Ukiah	Sanford House, 306 S. Pine, 95482 707-462-1653
Valley Ford	Inn at Valley Ford, PO Box 439, 94972 707-876-3182
Valley Ford	Llamas Loft B&B Cottage, PO Box 448, 94972 707-795-5726
Valley Ford	Valley Ford Hotel, PO Box 573, 94972
Venice	Mansion Inn, 327 Washington Blvd, 90291 310-821-2557
Venice	Venice Beach House, 15 30th Ave, 90291 310-823-1966
Ventura	Bella Maggiore Inn, 67 S California St, 93001 805-652-0277
Ventura	Pierpont Inn by the Sea, 550 Sanjon Rd, 93001 805-643-6144
Walnut Creek	Diablo Mountain Inn, 2079 Mount Diablo Blvd, 94596 925-937-5050
Walnut Creek	Swedish House, 1201 Ptarmigan Dr, 94595
Warner Springs	Warner Springs Ranch, Box 10, 92086 619-782-4219
Watsonville	Dunmovin' B&B, 1006 Hecker Pass Rd, 95076 408-728-4154
Weaverville	Weaverville Hotel, PO Box 537, 96093
Westport	Bowen's Pelican Lodge, PO Box 35, 95488 707-964-5588
Whittier	Coleen's California Casa, PO Box 9302, 90608 310-699-8427
Williams	Wilbur Hot Springs, Star Route, 95987 916-473-2306
Willits	Doll House, 118 School St, 95490 707-459-4055
Willits	Little Creek Mansion, 22400 Tomiki Rd, 95490
Windsor	Country Meadow Inn, 11360 Old Redwood Hwy, 95492 707-431-1276
Woodlake	Wicky-Up Ranch B&B, 22702 Ave 344, 93286 559-564-8898
Wrightwood	Wrightwood Whistle Inn, PO Box 1256, 92397
Yosemite	Chateau du Sureau, PO Box 577, 93644 209-683-6860
Yosemite	Yosemite Peregrine B&B, 7509 Henness Circle, 95389 209-372-8517
Yosemite	Yosemite West High Sierra, 7460 Henness Ridge Rd, 95389 209-372-4808
Yountville	Maison Fleurie, 6529 Yount St, 94599 707-944-2056
Yountville	Vintage Inn, 6541 Washington St., 94599
Yuba City	Harkey House B&B, 212 C St, 95991 530-674-1942
Yuba City	Moore Mansion Inn, 560 Cooper Ave, 95991 530-674-8559

Colorado

Allenspark	Allenspark Lodge, PO Box 247, 80510 303-747-2552
Arvada	On Golden Pond B&B, 7831 Eldridge, 80005 303-424-2296
Arvada	The Tree House, 6650 Simms, 80004 303-431-6352
Aspen	Crestahaus Lodge, 1301 E. Cooper Ave, 81611 970-925-7081
Aspen	Hearthstone House, 134 E. Hyman St, 81611 970-925-7632
Aspen	Little Red Ski Haus, 118 E. Cooper Ave, 81611 970-925-3333
Aspen	McKay Cottages, PO Box 11238, 81612
Aspen	Ullr Lodge, 520 W. Main St, 81611 303-925-7696
Aurora	Dave & Lynn's Breckenridge, 4255 S Buckley Rd, 80013 303-680-8881
Basalt	Altamira Ranch B&B, PO Box 875, 81621 970-927-3309
Bellvue	Gypsy Terrace B&B, 4167 Poudre Canyon Hwy, 80512 970-224-9389
Bellvue	Raindrop B&B, 6901 McMurry Ranch Rd, 80512 303-493-0799

Bethoud	Berthoud B&B, 444 1st St, 80513 970-532-4566
Beulah	Red Gable Ranch B&B, 8741 Central Ave, 81023 719-485-3198
Boulder	Coburn Hotel, 2040 16th St, 80302 303-545-5200
Boulder	Earl House Historic Inn, 2429 Broadway, 80304 303-938-1400
Boulder	Gunbarrel Inn, 6901 Lookout Rd, 80301 303-530-1513
Boulder	The Boulder Victoria, 1305 Pine St, 80302 303-938-1300
Breckenridge	Fireside Inn, PO Box 2252, 80424 970-453-6456
Breckenridge	Little Mountain Lodge, PO Box 2479, 80424 970-453-1969
Breckenridge	Morningstar House, Box 603, 80424 970-453-6732
Breckenridge	Muggins Gulch Inn, 4023 Tiger Rd., 80424 970-453-7414
Breckenridge	Ridge Street Inn, PO Box 2854, 80424 970-453-4680
Breckenridge	The Swiss Inn, PO Box 556, 80424 970-453-6489
Breckenridge	The Walker House, PO Box 5107, 80424 970-453-2426
Brighton	Country Gardens, 1619 E. 136th Ave, 80601 303-451-1724
Buena Vista	Potter's House B&B, PO Box 1842, 81211 719-395-6458
Buena Vista	Streamside B&B, 18820 CR 162, 81236 719-395-2553
Buena Vista	Trout City Inn, Box 431, 81211 719-495-0348
Burlington	Twelfth Street Station, 250 12th St, 80807 719-346-7180
Canon City	DeWeese Lodge, 1226 Elm Street, 81212 719-269-1881
Carbondale	Ambiance Inn B&B, 66 N. 2nd Street, 81623 970-963-3597
Carbondale	Christmas Inn, PO Box 627, 81623 970-925-3822
Carbondale	Roaring Fork B&B, 16613 Hwy 82, 81623 970-963-8853
Carbondale	Stoneacres Farm, 3023 Country Rd 112, 81623 970-945-2430
Carbondale	Van Horn House-Lions Ridge, 0318 Lions Ridge Rd, 81623 303-963-3605
Cascade	Black Bear Inn, 5250 Pikes Peak Hwy, 80809 719-684-0151
Cedaredge	Timberline B&B, 2457 U50 Rd, 81413 303-856-7379
Central City	Winfield Scott GuestQrtrs., PO Box 369, 80427 303-582-3433
Chipita Park	Chipita Lodge B&B Inn, 9090 Chipita Park Rd., 80809 719-684-8454
Clark	Home Ranch, Box 822, 80428 303-879-1780
Clark	Inn at Hahn's Peak, Box 867, 80486
Clifton	Mt. Garfield B&B, 3355 F Road, 81520 970-434-8120
Colorado Springs	Alpine Chalet Country Inn, 11685 Howells Rd, 80908 719-495-9266
Colorado Springs	Awarenest Victorian B&B, 1218 W Pikes Peak Ave, 80904 719-630-8241
Colorado Springs	Chalice House B&B, 1116 N Wahsatch Ave, 80903 719-475-7505
Colorado Springs	Hearthstone Inn, 506 N Cascade, 80903 719-473-4413
Colorado Springs	Hughes Hacienda, 12060 Calle Corvo, 80926 719-576-2060
Colorado Springs	Keith House, 1815 Alamo Ave., 80907 719-630-3949
Colorado Springs	Silver Wood B&B at Divide, 463 Country Rd 512, 80814 719-687-6784
Colorado Springs	Spurs and Lace Inn, 2829 W Pikes Peak Ave, 80904 719-227-7662
Colorado Springs	Twilight Canyon Inn, 2275 Twilight Canyon, 80866 719-576-7707
Colorado Springs	Wedgewood Cottage B&B, 1111 W Pikes Peak Ave, 80904 719-636-1829
Cortez	B&B on Maple, PO Box 327, 81321 970-565-3906
Cortez	Kelly Place B&B, 14663 Road G, 81321 970-565-3125
Cortez	The Manor B&B, 406 N Ash St, 81321 970-325-4574
Crawford	Becker Ranch B&B, 3798 Highway 92, 81415 970-921-6877
Crawford	Van Engen House B&B, 345 Cedar St., 81415 970-921-6177
Creede	Blessings Inn, PO Box 124, 81130 719-658-0215
Crested Butte	Alpine Lace Inc. B&B, PO Box 2183, 81224 970-349-9857
Crested Butte	Crested Butte Club, 512 Second, Drawer 309, 81224 970-349-6655
Crested Butte	Crystal Inn B&B, PO Box 125, 81224 970-349-1338
Crested Butte	Gothic Inn B&B, PO Box 1488, 81224 970-349-7215
Crested Butte	Purple Mountain Lodge, PO Box 547, 81224 970-349-5888
Crested Butte	The Inn at Crested Butte, PO Box 2619, 81224
Crested Butte	The Last Resort, PO Box 722, 81224
Crestone	Rendevous Cottage Inn, PO Box 297, 81131 719-256-4821
Cripple Creek	Imperial Casino Hotel, PO Box 869, 80813 719-689-7777
Cripple Creek	Iron Gate Inn, 204 N 2nd, 80813 800-315-3384
Del Norte	La Garita Creek Ranch, 38145 County Rd E-39, 81132 719-754-2533
Delta	La Casita, 2115 H Rd., 81416 970-874-3244
Denver	Franklin House B&B, 1620 Franklin St, 80218 303-331-9106
Denver	The Gregory Inn, LoDo, 2500 Arapahoe St, 80205 800-925-6570
Denver	The Lumber Baron Inn, 2555 West 37th Ave, 80211 303-477-8205
Denver	Twin Maples B&B, 1401 Madison St, 80206 303-393-1832
Dillon	Lodge at Caorlina in Pines, PO Box 1047, 80435 970-262-7500
Dillon	Piney Acres Inn, PO Box 4016, 80435 970-468-6206
Dillon	Snowberryhill B&B, 236 Snowberry Way, 80435 970-468-8010
Dillon	Swan Mountain Inn, PO Box 2900, 80435 970-453-7903
Divide	Silver Wood B&B at Divide, 463 County Rd 512, 80814 719-687-6784
Dolores	Historic Rio Grand Souther, PO Box 516, 81323 970-882-7527
Dolores	Lebanon Schoolhouse B&B, 24925 County Rd T, 81323 970-882-4461
Dolores	Lost Canyon Lodge, PO Box 1396, 81323 800-992-1098
Dolores	Mountain View B&B, 28050 County Road P, 81323 970-882-7861
Drake	Dripping Springs B&B, 2551 US Hwy 34, 80515 970-586-3406
Durango	Edgemont Ranch, 281 Silver Queen, 81301 970-247-2713
Durango	General Palmer Hotel, 567 Main Ave., 81301 970-247-4747
Durango	Logwood B&B and Lodge, 35060 Hwy 550N, 81301 970-259-4396
Durango	River House B&B, 495 Animas View Dr, 81301 970-247-4775
Durango	Scrubby Oaks B&B Inn, PO Box 1047, 81302 303-247-2176

Durango	Southwest-A-Retreat, 31380 US Hwy 550 N, 81301 970-247-4356
Durango	The Gable House, 805 E. Fifth Ave, 81301 970-247-4982
Durango	Vagabond Inn B&B, PO Box 2141, 81302 303-259-5901
Durango	Waterfall B&B, 4138 Country Rd 203, 81301
Eaton	Victorian Veranda, 515 Cheyenne Ave., 80615 970-454-3890
Eldora	Goldminer Hotel, 601 Klondyke Ave., 80466 303-258-7770
Empire	Mad Creek B&B, PO Box 404, 80438 303-569-2003
Englewood	Crystle's B&B, 3770 S Clarkson St, 80110
Estes Park	Aspen Lodge at Estes Park, 6120 Hwy. 7, 80517 970-586-8133
Estes Park	Baldpate Inn, PO Box 4445, 80517 303-586-6151
Estes Park	Big Horn Guest House, 341 Big Horn Dr, 80517 970-586-4175
Estes Park	Cottonwood House, PO Box 1208, 80517 303-586-5104
Estes Park	Glenn's Mtn. Vista Acre, PO Box 5219, 80517 970-586-3547
Estes Park	Henderson House B&B, PO Box 3134, 80517 970-586-4639
Fairplay	Bear's Den B&B, PO Box 1326, 80440 719-836-0921
Fairplay	Fairplay Hotel, 500 Main St, 80440 719-836-2565
Fort Collins	Edwards House Historic B&B, 402 W. Mountain Ave, 80521 970-493-9191
Fort Collins	Elizabeth St Guest House, 202 E Elizabeth St, 80524 970-493-2337
Fort Collins	Helmshire Inn, 1204 S. College, 80524 303-493-4683
Fort Collins	Mariposa on Spring Creek, 706 E Stuart St, 80525 970-495-0789
Fort Collins	Sky Watch Farm B&B, 11562 N County Rd 17, 80524 970-568-7114
Fort Collins	Spring Creek House Inn, 706 E Stuart St., 80525 970-495-9604
Fort Collins	The Edwards House B&B, 402 W Mountain Ave, 80521 970-493-9191
Fort Collins	West Mulberry Street B&B, 616 W. Mulberry St, 80521 970-221-1917
Fraser	Nordic B&B, PO Box 758, 80442 970-726-8459
Fraser	The Anna Leah a B&B, PO Box 305, 80442 970-726-4414
Frederick	Hoffman's Hide-Away B&B, PO Box 623, 80530 303-833-0444
Frisco	Frisco Lodge, PO Box 1325, 80443 303-668-0195
Frisco	Mar Dei's B&B, PO Box 1767, 80443 970-668-5337
Frisco	Twilight Inn, PO Box 397, 80443 970-668-5009
Fruita	Grapeland B&B, 1763 K 6/10 Rd, 81521 970-858-0741
Fruita	Stonehaven B&B, 798 North Mesa St, 81521
Georgetown	Hardy House B&B Inn, PO Box 156, 80444 303-569-3388
Georgetown	Hillside House, 1034 Main St, 80444 303-569-0912
Georgetown	Kip on the Creek Inn, PO Box 754, 80444
Glenwood	Adducci's Inn & Restaurant, 1023 Grand Ave., 81601 970-945-9341
Glenwood	Back in Time, 927 Cooper, 81601
Glenwood	Sunlight Bavarian, 10252 County Rd 117, 81601 970-945-5225
Glenwood	The Kaiser House, 928 Cooper Ave, 81601 970-945-8827
Golden	Antique Rose B&B, 1422 Washingtin Ave, 80401 303-277-1893
Golden	Ashley House B&B, 30500 US Hwy 40, 80401 303-526-2411
Golden	Royal Scot B&B, 30500 US Hwy 40, 80401 303-526-2411
Granby	Circle H Lodge, 6732 US Highway 34, 80446 970-887-3955
Granby	Trail Mountain B&B, 4850 County Rd 41, 80446 970-887-3044
Grand Junction	House On Ouray B&B, 760 Ouray Ave., 81501 970-245-8452
Grand Junction	Junction Country Inn, 861 Grand Ave, 81501 303-241-2817
Grand Junction	Los Altos B&B, 375 Hillview Dr, 81503 970-256-0964
Grand Lake	Columbine Creek Ranch, PO Box 1675, 80447 970-627-2429
Grand Lake	Spirit Mountain Ranch, PO Box 942, 80447 970-887-3551
Greeley	Sod Buster Inn B&B, 1221 Ninth Ave., 80631 970-392-1221
Green Mountain	Lakeview Terrace Hotel, Box 115, 80819 719-684-9119
Grover	Plover Inn, 223 Chatoga, 80729 970-895-2275
Grover	West Pawnee Ranch B&B, 29451 WCR 130, 80729 970-895-2482
Gunnison	Mountain Meadow, 237 Country Rd #48, 81230 970-641-9501
Hayden	Granny's B&B, PO Box 1203, 81639
Hesperus	La Plata Vista Ranch B&B, 13400 Country Rd 120, 81326 970-247-9062
Hesperus	Sunflower B&B, 10829 Country Rd 141, 81326
Highlands Ranch	Benson's B&B, 5375 E. Wangaratta Way, 80126 719-264-9225
Hot Sulphur Springs	Stagecoach Country Inn, PO Box 71, 80451 970-725-3910
Howard	Whit's End B&B, 9100 US Hwy 50, 81233 719-942-4176
Idaho Springs	Lodge at Idaho Springs, 1601 Colorado Blvd, 80452
Idaho Springs	St. Mary's Glacier B&B, 336 Crest Dr, 80452
Idaho Springs	White Horse Inn, PO Box 1169, 80452 303-567-2566
Ignacio	Kelsall's Ute Creek Ranch, 2192 County Rd 334, 81137 303-563-4464
Keystone	Keystone Resort, 1580 Oak Hills Dr, 80013 719-548-0663
Keystone	Ski Tip Lodge, Box 38, 80435 303-468-4202
La Junta	Jane Ellen Inn, 722 Colorado Ave, 81050 719-384-8445
La Junta	My Wife's Inn B&B, 12 E 8th St, 81050 719-384-7911
La Veta	La Veta Inn, PO Box 129, 81055 719-742-3700
Lake City	Alpine Loop B&B, PO Box 955, 81235
Lake City	Moncrief Mountain Ranch, Slumgullion Pass, 81235 970-944-2796
Lake City	Old Carson Inn, PO Box 144, 81235 970-944-2511
Lake City	Ryan's Roost, PO Box 218, 81235 970-944-2339
Lake George	Stuart House, 120 Broken Arrow Path, 80929
Lake George	Ute Trail River Ranch, 21446 CR 77, 80827 719-748-3015
Lakewood	The Gourmet B&B, 2020 Brentwood, 80215 303-237-8395
Leadville	Peri & Ed's Mountain Hidew, 201 W. 8th St., 80461 719-486-0716
Leadville	Wood Haven Manor B&B, PO Box 1991, 80461 719-486-0109

Longmont	Ellen's B&B, 700 Kimbark St., 80501 303-776-1676
Longmont	The Ranch at Thunder Road, 100 Thunder Rd, 80503 303-823-5567
Loveland	Derby Hill Inn B&B, 2502 Courtney Dr, 80537 970-667-3193
Lyons	Benam B&B, PO Box 577, 80540
Lyons	Peaceful Valley Lodge, 475 Peaceful Valley Rd, 80540 800-95-LODGE
Mancos	Alice Ann's B&B, PO Box 775, 81328 970-533-1083
Mancos	Bauer House B&B, PO Box 1049, 81328 970-533-9707
Mancos	East Valley Accommodations, 30031 Rd L, 81328 800-889-7180
Mancos	Ryter House B&B, 40580 County Rd H, 81328 970-533-7661
Mancos	The Gingerbread Inn, 41478 Highway 184, 81328 970-533-7892
Mancos	Willowtail Springs, PO Box 89, 81328 970-533-7592
Manitou Springs	Frontier's Rest, 341 Ruxton Ave, 80829 719-685-0588
Manitou Springs	Gray's Avenue Hotel, 711 Manitou Ave, 80829 719-685-1277
Manitou Springs	On a Ledge, 336 El Paso Blvd, 80829 719-685-4265
Manitou Springs	Red Eagle Mountain B&B, 616 Ruxton Ave, 80829 719-685-4541
Manitou Springs	Spring Cottage, 13 Pawnee Ave, 80827
Manitou Springs	Victoria's Keep B&B, 202 Ruxton Ave, 80829 719-685-5354
Marble	Ute Meadows Inn B&B, 2880 County Rd 3, 81623 970-963-7088
Meredith	Double Diamond Ranch B&B, PO Box 2, 81642 303-927-3404
Minturn	Eagle River Inn, 145 N Main St, 81645 970-827-5761
Minturn	The Minturn Inn, PO Box 186, 81645 970-827-9647
Moffat	Willow Spring B&B, PO Box 500, 81143 719-256-4116
Monte Vista	Windmill B&B, 4340 W US Hwy 160, 81144 719-852-0438
Montrose	Annie's Orchard Hist. B&B, 14963 63.00 Rd, 81401 970-249-0298
Montrose	The Uncompahgre B&B, 21049 Uncompahgre Rd, 81401 970-240-4000
Morrison	Cliff House Lodge B&B, 121 Stone St, 80465 303-697-9732
Mosca	Blue House B&B, PO Box 97, 81146 719-873-9890
Mosca	Inn at Zapata Ranch, 5303 Highway 150, 81146 719-378-2356
Nathrop	Claveau's Streamside B&B, 18820 C.R. 162, 81236 719-395-2553
Ouray	Box Canyon Lodge, PO Box 439, 81427 303-325-4981
Ouray	Main Street B&B, PO Box 641, 81427 970-325-4871
Ouray	Ouray Hotel, PO Box 1862, 81427 970-325-0500
Pagosa Springs	Davidson's Country Inn B&B, Box 87, 81147 303-264-5863
Pagosa Springs	TLC's, A B&B, PO Box 3337, 81147
Palisade	Garden House B&B, 3587 G Road, 81526 970-464-4686
Paonia	Bross Hotel B&B, PO Box 85, 81428 970-527-6776
Parker	Damn Yankee Country Inn, 6311 N Lakepoint Pl, 80134 970-325-4219
Pine	Meadow Creek B&B Inn, 13438 US Hwy 285, 80470 303-838-4167
Pitkin	Gingerbread House B&B, PO Box 160, 81241 970-641-5120
Red Cliff	The Pilgrim's Inn, PO Box 151, 81649 303-827-5333
Redstone	Cleveholm Manor, 0058 Redstone Blvd, 81623 303-963-3463
Redstone	Crystal Dreams B&B, 0475 Redstone Blvd, 81623
Redstone	Redstone Castle, 0058 Redstone Blvd, 81623 970-963-3463
Salida	Beddin' Down B&B, 10401 County Rd 160, 81201 719-539-1815
Salida	Pinon & Sage B&B, 803 F St, 81201
Salida	The Century House B&B, 401 E. 1st St, 81201 719-539-7064
Salida	Thomas House B&B, 307 East 1st St, 81201
Salida	Yellow House B&B, 16665 W US Hwy 50, 81201 719-539-7531
Silver Plume	Brewery Inn B&B, PO Box 473, 80476 303-674-5565
Silverton	Alma House Hotel, PO Box 359, 81433 970-387-5336
Silverton	Christopher House B&B, 821 Empire St, Box 241, 81433 303-387-5857
Silverton	Teller House Hotel, PO Box 2, 81433 970-387-5423
Silverton	Villa Dalla Vale His. Inn, 1257 Notorious Blair, 81433 970-387-5555
Silverton	Wyman Hotel & Inn, PO Box 780, 81433 970-387-5372
Snowmass	Starry Pines B&B, 2262 Snowmass Creek Rd, 81654 970-927-4202
Springfield	Plum Bear Ranch, PO Box 241, 81073 719-523-4344
Steamboat Springs	Caroline's B&B, PO Box 880013, 80488 970-870-1696
Steamboat Springs	Inn at Steamboat B&B, PO Box 775084, 80477 970-879-2600
Steamboat Springs	Log Cabin B&B, 47890 Country Road 129, 80487 970-879-5837
Steamboat Springs	Mariposa B&B, PO Box 772302, 80477 303-879-1467
Steamboat Springs	Moving Mountains Chalet, PO Box 881728, 80488 610-678-1387
Steamboat Springs	Oak St. B&B, PO Box 772434, 80477
Steamboat Springs	Steamboat B&B, Box 775888, 80477 970-879-5724
Steamboat Springs	The Alpine Rose B&B Inn, PO Box 775602, 80477 970-879-1528
Stoneham	Elk Echo Ranch Country B&B, 47490 WCR 155, 80754 970-735-2426
Stratton	Claremont Inn, PO Box 3, 80836 719-348-5125
Telluride	Manitou Lodge B&B, 666 W Colorado Ave, 81435 970-728-4011
Telluride	New Sheridan Hotel, PO Box 980, 81435 970-728-4351
Telluride	Pennington's Mountain Inn, PO Box 2428, 81435 800-543-1437
Trinidad	Chicosa Canyon B&B, 32391 County Rd 40, 81082 719-846-6199
Twin Lakes	Twin Lakes Mtn. Retreat, PO Box 175, 81251 719-486-2593
Victor	Victor Hotel, 397 Victor Ave, 80860 719-689-3553
Walsenburg	La Plaza de los Leones Inn, 118 West Sixth, 81089 719-738-5700
Westcliffe	Purnell's Rainbow Inn, PO Box 578, 81252
Westcliffe	Rainbow Inn, PO Box 578, 81252 719-783-2313
Westminister	The Victorian Lady, 4199 W. 76th Ave, 80030 303-428-9829
Wheat Ridge	Inn At Soda Creek, 3834 Union Ct, 80033 303-670-3798
Winter Park	Beau West B&B, PO Box 587, 80482 970-726-5145

Winter Park	Brother Moose B&B, PO Box 3264, 80482 970-726-8255
Winter Park	Byers Peak B&B Inn, PO Box 3029, 80482
Winter Park	Engelmann Pines, PO Box 1305, 80482 970-726-4632
Winter Park	Outpost B&B Country Inn, PO Box 41, 80482 970-726-5346
Winter Park	Something Special, PO Box 800, 80482 970-726-5346
Winter Park	The Bear Paw Inn, PO Box 334, 80482 970-887-1351
Woodland Park	Woodland Inn B&B, 159 Trull Rd, 80863 719-687-8209
Yellowjacket	Wilson's Pinto Bean Farm, House No. 21434 Rd 16, 81335

Connecticut

Berlin	Hawthorne Inn, 2387 Wilbur Cross, 06037 860-828-1634
Bethel	Tailoring Inn, 40 Durant Ave., 06801 203-778-8740
Bethlehem	The Dutch Moccasin, 51 Still Hill Rd, 06751 203-266-7364
Bolton	Jared Cone House, 25 Hebron Rd, 06043 203-643-8538
Bozrah	Blueberry Inn, PO Box 146, 06334 860-889-3618
Bozrah	Bozrah House B&B, 347 Salem Turnpike R82, 06334 860-823-1551
Bozrah	Fitch Claremont House, 83 Fitchville Rd, 06334 860-889-0260
Brookfield	Twin Tree Inn, 1030 Federal Rd, 06804 207-775-0220
Brooklyn	Friendship Valley B&B Inn, PO Box 845, 06234 860-779-9696
Canterbury	Woodchuck Hill, 256 Cemetery Rd., 06331 860-546-1278
Colchester	Hayward House Inn, 35 Hayward Ave, 06415 203-537-5772
Cornwall Bridge	The Cornwall Inn, 270 Kent Rd, 06754 860-672-6884
Cornwell	College Hill Farm, College St, 06759 203-672-6762
Coventry	Birdin House, 2011 Main St, 06238 203-742-0032
Coventry	Special Joys B&B, 41 N. River Rd, 06238 860-742-6359
East Windsor	The Stephen Potwine House, 84 Scantic Rd, 06088 203-623-8722
Fairfield	Mountain Trails B&B, 1143 Sasco Hill Rd, 06430 413-528-2928
Fairfield	Seagrape Inn, 1160 Reef Road, 06430 203-255-6808
Farmington	Centennial Inn Suites, 5 Spring Lane, 06032
Farmington	The Barney House, 11 Mountain Spring Rd, 06032 860-674-2796
Goshen	Twelve Maples, PO Box 23, 06756 203-491-9316
Greenwich	Homestead Inn, 420 Field Point Rd, 06830 203-869-7500
Greenwich	Stanton House Inn, 76 Maple Ave, 06830 203-869-2110
Groton	Bluff Point B&B, 26 Fort Hill Rd, Rt 1, 06340 860-445-1314
Groton	Shore Inne, 54 E. Shore Rd, 06340 203-536-1180
Guilford	B&B At B, 279 Boston St., 06437 203-453-6490
Hartford	1895 House B&B, 97 Girard Ave, 06105
Kent	Chaucer House, 88 North Main St, 06757 203-927-4858
Kent	Constitution Oak Farm, 36 Beardsley Rd, 06757 203-354-6495
Kent	Number 81, 81 N Main St, 06757
Lakeville	Alices B&B, PO Box 46, 06039
Lakeville	Iron Masters Motor Inne, 229 Main St., 06039 203-435-9844
Lakeville	Wake Robin Inn, PO Box 660, 06039 203 435 2515
Ledyard	Abbey's Lantern Hill Inn, 780 Lantern Hill Rd, 06339 860-572-0483
Ledyard	Stonecroft, 515 Pumpkin Hill Rd., 06339 860-572-0771
Litchfield	The Litchfield Inn, PO Box 798, 06759 203-567-4503
Litchfield	Tollgate Hill Inn & Rest., PO Box 1339, 06759 860-567-4545
Madison	Honeysuckle Hill B&B, 116 Yankee Peddler Path, 06443 203-245-4574
Madison	Madison Beach Hotel, PO Box 546, 06443 203-245-1404
Moodus	Fowler House, PO Box 340, 06469 203-873-8906
Mystic	Brigadoon B&B, 180 Cow Hill Rd., 06355 860-536-3033
Mystic	House of 1833 B&B, 72 North Stonington Rd, 06355 860-536-6325
Mystic	Inn at Mystic, PO Box 216, 06355 860-536-9604
N. Stonington	John York House, 1 Clark's Falls Rd., 06359 860-599-3075
New Canaan	Maples Inn, 179 Oenoke Rd, 06840 203-966-2927
New Canaan	Roger Sherman Inn, 195 Oenoke Ridge Rt#12, 06840 203-966-4541
New Haven	Three Chimneys Inn @ Yale, 1201 Chapel St, 06511 203-789-1201
New London	Lighthouse Inn, 6 Guthrie Pl, 06320
New London	The Queen Anne Inn, 265 Williams St, 06320 860-447-2600
New Preston	Altha House B&B, PO Box 2015, 06777 203-355-7387
New Preston	Mavis, 143 N Shore Rd, 06777
New Preston	The Inn on Lake Waramaug, PO Box 2248, 06777 860-868-0563
Noank	The Palmer Inn, 25 Church St, 06340 860-572-9000
Norfolk	Angel Hill B&B, PO Box 504, 06058 860-542-5920
Norfolk	Covered Bridge B&B, PO Box 447A, 06058 203-542-5944
Norfolk	Mountain View Inn, PO Box 467, 06058 860-542-6991
Norwich	Norwich Inn & Spa, 607 West Thames St, 06360 860-886-2401
Old Lyme	Indian Ledge B&B, 411 Hamburg Rd, 06371
Old Saybrook	Saybrook Point Inn & Spa, Two Bridge St, 06475 860-395-2000
Pomfret	Clark Cottage, Wintergreen, Box 94, Rt. 44 & 169, 06259 860-928-5741
Pomfret Center	Quail Run, 1 Town House Dr, 06259
Poquetanuck	Captain Grant's, 1754, 109 Route 2A, 06365 860-887-7589
Portland	The Croft B&B, 7 Penny Corner Rd, 06480 203-342-1856
Preston	Hideaway Inn, 87 Cooktown Rd., 06365 860-887-5059
Preston	Roseledge Farm B&B, Rt 164, #418, 06365 860-892-4739
Preston	The Inn at Willowbrook, 81 Cooktown Rd., 06365 860-885-1336
Putnam	The Felshaw Tavern, Five Mile River Rd, 06260 203-928-3467

Quinebaug	Cpt.Parker's Inn/Quinebaug, 32 Walker Rd, 06262 800-707-7303
Ridgefield	Stonehenge Inn, PO Box 667, 06877 203-438-6511
Salem	Woodbridge Farm, 30 Woodbridge Rd., 06420 860-859-1169
Salisbury	The White Hart, PO Box 385, 06068 203-435-0030
Salisbury	Under Mountain Inn, 482 Under Mountain Rd, 06068 203-435-0242
Sandy Hook	The Barrymore, 11 Glen Rd, 06482 203-270-8688
Sharon	1890 Colonial B&B, PO Box 25, 06069 203-364-0436
Simsbury	Merrywood, 100 Hartford Rd, 06070 860-651-1785
Somers	Victorian Sentiment, 87 Main St., 06071 203-763-2762
Somersville	The Old Mill Inn B&B, PO Box E, 06072 860-763-1473
Southbury	Cornucopia at Oldfield, 782 Main Street North, 06488 203-267-6707
Thompson	Hickory Ridge, 1084 Quaddick Tn.Fm.Rd, 06277 203-928-9530
Thompson	Samuel Watson House, PO Box 86, 06277 203-923-2491
Tolland	Old Babcock Tavern B&B, 484 Mile Hill Rd, 06084 203-875-1239
Torrington	Yankee Pedlar Inn, 93 Main St, 06790 860-489-9226
Union	Staughton Brook Farm, 510 Buckley Hwy, Rt 190, 06076
Wallingford	High Meadow B&B, 1290 Whirlwind Hill Rd., 06492 203-269-2351
Watertown	The Clarks, 97 Scott Ave, 06795 860-274-4866
Watertown	The Graham House, 1002 Middlebury Rd, 06795 203-274-2647
West Cornwall	Hilltop Haven, 175 Dibble Hill Rd, 06796 860-672-6871
West Cornwall	Trinity Inn & Conf. Center, PO Box 59, 06796 203-672-1000
Westbrook	Captain Stannard House, 138 S. Main St, 06498 203-399-4634
Westbrook	Welcome Inn B&B, 433 Essex Rd., 06498 860-399-2500
Westport	The Inn at National Hall, Two Post Rd W, 06880 203-221-1351
Wethersfield	Chester Bulkley House B&B, 184 Main St, 06109 860-563-4236
Windsor	Charles Hart House, 1046 Windsor Ave, 06095 860-688-5555
Windsor	Cumon Inn, 130 Buckland Rd, 06074 860-644-8486
Winsted	B&B by the Lake, 19 Dillon Beach Rd, 06098 203-738-0230
Woodbury	Curtis House, Inc., 506 Main St S, 06798 203-263-2101
Woodbury	Hummingbird Hill, 891 Main St S, 06798 203-263-3733
Woodbury	Merryvale B&B, 1204 Main St S, 06798 203-266-0800
Woodbury	The Everview Inn, PO Box 557, 06798 203-266-4262
Woodstock	English Neighborhood B&B, 595 English Neighborhoo, 06281 203-928-6959
Woodstock	Inn at Woodstock Hill, PO Box 98, 06267 203-928-0528

Delaware

Bethany Beach	Addy Sea, PO Box 275, 19930 302-539-3707
Bridgeville	Teddy Bear B&B, 303 Market St, 19933
Bridgeville	The Rawleigh House, 109 N Main St, 19933
Dagsboro	Becky's Country Inn, 401 Main St, 19939 302-732-3953
Dewey Beach	Barry's Gull Cottage B&B, 116 Chesapeak St, 19971 302-227-7000
Dover	Inn At Meeting House Sq, 305 S Governors Ave, 19901 302-734-7583
Frankford	Chandler Inn, 13 Main St, 19945 302-732-3481
Greenwood	Eli's Country Inn, PO Box 779, 19950 302-349-4265
Laurel	Spring Garden B&B Inn, RD 5, Box 283A, 19956 302-875-7015
Lewes	Blue Water House, 407 E Market St., 19958 302-645-7832
Lewes	Kings Inn, 151 Kings Hwy, 19958 302-645-6438
Lewes	New Devon Inn, 142 - 2nd St., 19958 302-645-6466
Lewes	Savannah Inn, 330 Savannah Rd, 19958 302-645-5592
Lewes	The Bay Moon B&B, 128 Kings Hwy, 19958 800-917-2307
Milford	Causey Mansion B&B, 2 Causey Ave., 19963 302-422-0979
Milford	Inns on the Mispillion, 112 NW Front St., 19963 302-422-5708
Milford	The Towers B&B Inn, 101 NW Front St, 19963 302-422-3814
Milton	Captain William Russell Hs, 320 Union Street, 19968 302-684-2504
Montchanin	Inn at Montchanin Village, Rt 100 & Kirk Rd., 19710 302-888-2133
New Castle	The Jefferson House B&B, 5 The Strand at Wharf, 19720 302-325-1025
New Castle	The Terry House B&B, 130 Delaware St., 19720 302-322-2505
Odessa	Cantwell House B&B, 107 High St, 19730 302-378-4179
Rehoboth Beach	Chesapeake Landing B&B, 101 Chesapeake St., 19971 302-227-2973
Rehoboth Beach	Lighthouse Inn, 20 Delaware, 19971 302-226-0407
Rehoboth Beach	Pleasant Inn Lodge, 31 Olive Ave @ 1st St, 19971 302-227-7311
Rehoboth Beach	Sand In My Shoes, 6th & Canal St., 19971 302-226-2006
Rehoboth Beach	Sea Voice Inn, 14 Delaware Ave., 19971 302-226-9435
Rehoboth Beach	Sea Witch Manor B&B, 71 Lake Ave., 19971 302-226-9482
Rehoboth Beach	The Corner Cupboard Inn, 50 Park Ave, 19971 302-227-8553
Rehoboth Beach	The Delaware Inn, 55 Delaware Ave, 19971 302-227-6031
Rehoboth Beach	The Mallard Guest House, 60 Baltimore Ave., 19971 302-226-3448

District of Columbia

Washington	1836 California, 1836 California St. NW, 20009 202-462-6502
Washington	Adams Inn, 1744 Lanier Pl NW, 20009 202-745-3600
Washington	Aiko's B&B, 1411 Hipkins St. NW, 20036 202-293-3039
Washington	Capitol Hill Guest House, 101 Fifth St NE, 20002 202-547-1050
Washington	Capitol Place, 134 12th St SE, 20003 202-543-1020
Washington	Columbia Guest House, 2005 Columbia Rd NW, 20009 202-265-4006

Washington	Connecticut-Woodley House, 2647 Woodley Rd NW, 20008 202-667-0218
Washington	Hereford House, 604 S. Carolina Ave, SE, 20003 202-543-0102
Washington	Intl House of United Tel, 1110 6th St NW, 20001 202-289-4411
Washington	Little White House B&B, 2909 Pennsylvania Av SE, 20020 202-583-4074
Washington	Molly's B&B, PO Box 9490, 20016 202-363-7767
Washington	Mrs. Jay's B&B, 2951 Upton St. NW, 20008 202-364-0228
Washington	Normandy Inn, 2118 Wyoming Ave, 20037 202-483-1350
Washington	Tabard Inn, 1739 N Street, NW, 20036 202-785-1277
Washington	Taft Bridge Inn, 2007 Wyoming Ave NW, 20009 202-387-2007
Washington	The Inn at Canal Square, 3201 New Mexico Ave 258, 20016
Washington	The Madison House, PO Box 9490, 20016 202-363-7767

Florida

Amelia Island	1735 House B&B, 584 S Fletcher Ave, 32034 904-261-4148
Amelia Island	Hoyt House B&B, 804 Atlantic Ave, 32034 904-277-4300
Apalachicola	The Gibson Inn, PO Box 215, 32329 904-653-2191
Apollo Beach	B&B of Apollo Beach, 6350 Cocoa Lane, 33572 813-645-2471
Arcadia	Arcadia's Magnolia House, 500 W Oak St, 34266 941-494-4299
Arcadia	Historic Parker House, 427 W Hickory St, 33821
Auburndale	Juliana Lakeside B&B, 585 State Rd 559, 33823 941-984-8352
Bartow	The Stanford Inn, 555 E. Stanford St, 33830 941-533-2393
Bell	Quinta's Funny Farm B&B, 9419 NW 15th Ave., 32008 904-935-3320
Beverly Hills	Pine Breeze Inn, PO Box 640180, 34464
Big Pine Key	B&B-on-the-Ocean Casa, PO Box 378, 33043 305-872-2878
Big Pine Key	Canal Cottage B&B, PO Box 430266, 33043 305-872-3881
Boca Grande	Barrier Island Marine B&B, PO Box 175, 33921 813-964-2626
Bonita Springs	Shangri-La Historic Inn, PO Box 367269, 34136 800-279-3811
Bradenton	Betts House, 1523 1st Ave W, 34205 941-747-3607
Bradenton	Point Pleasant B&B, 1717 1st Ave W, 34205 941-351-1807
Brandon	Behind the Fence B&B, 1400 Viola Dr, 33511
Brandord	The Smokahouse Ranch, Rt 1, Box 518, 32008 904-935-2662
Bushnell	Cypress House B&B, 5175 SW 90th Blvd., 33513 904-568-0909
Cedar Key	Island Hotel, PO Box 460, 32625 352-543-5111
Clearwater	Harbour Lights, 205 Brightwater Dr., 34630 813-441-1393
Clearwater	Lanning's Green Gables B&B, 1040 Sunset Point Rd., 34615 813-443-3675
Clewiston	The Clewiston Inn, 108 Royal Palm Ave, 33440 947-983-8151
Cocoa Beach	Indian River House, 3113 Indian River Dr., 32922 407-631-5660
Cocoa Beach	Sea Esta Villas, 686 S Atlantic Avenue, 32931 407-783-1739
Coconut Grove	Cherokee Rose Lodge, 3734 Main Hwy, 33133 305-858-4884
Coconut Grove	Coconut Grove B&B, PO Box 331891, 33233 305-665-3724
Coleman	The Son's Shady Brook B&B, PO Box 551, 33521
Coral Gables	Hotel Place St. Michel, 162 Alcazar Ave, 33134 305-444-1666
Crescent City	Sprague House Inn, 125 Central Ave, 32112 904-698-2430
Davie	Mt. Kenya Lodge, 4201 SW 95 Ave, 33328 305-940-5046
Daytona Beach	Live Oak Inn/Restaurant, 444-448 South Beach St, 32114 904-252-4667
Daytona Beach	The Coquina Inn B&B, 544 S. Palmetto Ave, 32114 904-254-4969
Daytona Beach	The Villa B&B, 801 N Peninsula Dr, 32118 904-248-2020
DeFuniak Springs	Hotel DeFuniak, 400 E Nelson Ave, 32433 850-892-4383
Deland	The 1888 House, 124 N Clara Ave, 32720 904-822-4647
Dunedin	JO Douglas House B&B, 209 Scotland St., 34698 813-735-9006
Edgewater	The Colonial House, 110 E. Yelkca Terr, 32132 904-427-4570
Englewood	Manasota Beach Club, 7660 Manasota Key Rd, 34223 813-474-2614
Eustis	Dreamspinner, Moses Home, 117 Diedrich St, 32726 352-589-8082
Eustis	The Oaks, 1390 E Lakeview Ave, 32726
Everglades City	The Ivey House, PO Box 5038, 33929 941-695-3299
Fernandina Beach	Amelia House B&B & Sail, 222 N 5th Ave, 32034 904-321-1717
Fernandina Beach	Amelia Island Plantation, PO Box 3000, 32034 904-261-6161
Fernandina Beach	Greyfield Inn, PO Box 900, 32034 904-261-6408
Fernandina Beach	Posada San Carlos, 212 Estrada St., 32034 904-277-8744
Fernandina Beach	The 1735 House, 584 So Fletcher Ave, 32034 904-261-4148
Fernandina Beach	The Tabor House, PO Box 734, 32035
Flagler Beach	Shire House B&B, 3398 N Oceanshore Blvd., 32136 904-445-8877
Flagler Beach	The White Orchid, 1104 S Oceanshore Blvd, 32136 904-439-4944
Fort Lauderdale	La Casa Del Mar B&B, 3003 Granada St, 33304 954-467-2037
Fort Lauderdale	Myralynns' B&B, 1705 SW 4th St, 33312 954-522-3234
Fort Myers	Embe's Hobby House, 5570-4 Woodrose Ct, 33907 813-936-6378
Fort Myers	Island Rover Sailing, 11470 S. Cleveland Ave, 33907 941-936-9300
Fort Pierce	Villa Nina Island Inn, 3851 North A 1 A, 34949 561-467-8673
Grayton Beach	Hibiscus Coffee Guest Hous, 85 Defuniak St., 32459 904-231-2733
Haines City	Holly Garden Inn, 106 First St S, 33844 813-421-9867
Havana	Graver's B&B, 301 E. 6th Ave, 32333 904-539-5611
Havana	Historic Havana House B&B, 301 E Sixth Ave, 32333 850-539-5611
High Springs	Grady House B&B, PO Box 205, 32655 904-454-2206
High Springs	Rustic Inn, 3105 S Main St, 32643 904-454-1223
Hobe Sound	Tembo B&B, PO Box 2294, 33475
Hollywood	Maison Harrison House, 1504 Harrison St, 33020 604-922-7319
Homestead	Redland Herb Farm, 18470 SW 296 St, 33030 305-246-5825

Hudson	Phyllis's B&B, 13822 Eagles Rock Ct, 34667
Hutchinson Island	Villa Nina Island Inn, 3851 N A-1-A, 34949 561-467-8673
Indian Shores	Meeks B&B on the Gulf, 19418 Gulf Blvd #407, 34635 813-596-5424
Inverness	Crown Hotel, 109 N. Seminole Ave, 32650 352-344-5555
Inverness	Magnolia Glen B&B, 7702 E Allen Dr, 34450 352-726-1832
Inverness	Running Deer Lodge, 3405 E Stagecoach Trail, 34452 352-860-1791
Islamorada	B&B of Islamorada, 81175 Old Highway, 33036
Jacksonville	The San Marco Point House, 1709 River Rd, 32207 904-396-1448
Jensen Beach	Hutchinson Inn, 9750 S Ocean Dr, 34957 407-229-2000
Key Biscayne	Hibiscus House, 345 W. Endid Dr, 33149 305-361-2456
Key Largo	Jules' Undersea Lodge, 51 Shoreland Dr, 33037 305-451-2353
Key Largo	Kona Kai Bayfront Resort, 97802 Overseas Hwy, 33037 305-852-7200
Key West	Abaco Inn, 415 Julia St., 33040 305-296-2212
Key West	Ambrosia House, 615 Fleming St, 33040 305-296-9838
Key West	Banana's Foster, 537 Caroline St, 33040 305-294-9061
Key West	Banyan Resort, 323 Whitehead St, 33040 305-296-2786
Key West	Cade House, 1501 Truman Ave, 33040 305-296-4724
Key West	Casa Buena Honeymoon Cott., 317 Whitehead St, 33040
Key West	Casablanca Hotel, 900 Duval St., 33040 305-296-0815
Key West	Chelsea House, 707 Truman Ave, 33040 305-296-2211
Key West	Coconut Beach Resort, 1500 Alberta, 33040
Key West	Colours Key West The Guest, 410 Fleming St, 33040
Key West	Coral Tree Inn, 822 Fleming St, 33040
Key West	Courtney's Place, 720 Whitmarsh Ln, 33040 305-294-3480
Key West	Cuban Club Suites, 422 Ameila St, 33040 305-296-0465
Key West	Curry House, 806 Fleming St, 33040
Key West	Denoit's Cottage, 512 Angela St, 33040 305-294-6324
Key West	Duval Suites, 524 Eaton St #150, 33040 305-293-6600
Key West	Eaton Lodge, 511 Eaton St, 33040 305-292-2170
Key West	Eaton Manor, 1024 Eaton St, 33040
Key West	Eaton Square, PO Box 1836, 33041
Key West	Fleming Street Inn, 618 Fleming St, 33040 305-294-5181
Key West	Frances Street Bottle Inn, 535 Frances St, 33040
Key West	Island City House Hotel, 411 William St, 33040 305-294-5702
Key West	L'Habitation, 408 Eaton St, 33040
Key West	La Casa de Luces, 422 Amelia St, 33040 305-296-3993
Key West	Lightbourn Inn, 907 Truman Ave., 33040 305-296-5152
Key West	Mangrove House, 3312 Northside Dr #501, 33040
Key West	Marquesa Hotel & Cafe, 600 Fleming St, 33040 305-292-1919
Key West	Merlinn Inn, 811 Simonton St, 33040 305-296-3336
Key West	Newton Street Station, 1414 Newton St, 33040
Key West	Old Customs House Inn, 124 Duval St, 33040
Key West	Papa's Hideaway Guesthouse, 309 Louisa St, 33040 305-294-7709
Key West	Pier House Caribbean Spa, 1 Duval St., 33040 305-296-4600
Key West	Red Rooster Inn, 709 Truman Ave, 33040 305-296-6558
Key West	Simonton Court Inn, 320 Simonton St, 33040 305-294-6386
Key West	Southernmost Point, 1327 Duval St, 33040 305-294-0715
Key West	Speakeasy Inn, 1117 Duval St, 33040
Key West	The Gardens, 526 Angela St., 34741 305-294-2661
Key West	The Grand, 1116 Grinnell St., 33040 305-294-0590
Key West	The Palms Hotel, 820 White St, 33040 305-294-3146
Key West	The Potters Cottage, 1011 Whitehead St, 33040
Key West	The Watson House, 525 Simonton St, 33040 305-294-6712
Key West	The William House, 1317 Duval St, 33040 305-294-8233
Key West	Tradewind Guesthouse, 415 Julia St, 33040 305-296-2212
Key West	Travelers Palm, 815 Catherine St, 33040
Key West	Treetop Inn Historic B&B, 806 Truman Ave, 33040 305-293-0712
Key West	Tropical Inn, 812 Duval St, 33040 305-294-9977
Key West	Washington Street Inn, 807 Washington St, 33040 305-296-0550
Key West	Westwinds, 914 Eaton St, 33040 305-296-4440
Key West	Wicker Guesthouse, 913 Duval St, 33040 305-296-4275
Kissimmee	Unicorn Inn, English B&B, 8 S. Orlando Ave, 34741 407-846-1200
Lake Wales	Noah's Ark, 312 Ridge Manor Dr, 33853 941-676-1613
Lake Worth	Hummingbird Hotel B&B Inn, 631 Lucerne Ave, 33460 561-582-3224
Lauderdale	Breakaway Guest House, 4457 Poinciana, 33308 305-771-6600
Lighthouse Point	Country House Inn, 2001 NE 31st Ct., 33064 608-527-5399
Maderia Beach	Lighthouse B&B, 13355 2nd St E, 33708 813-391-0015
Madison	Manor House, 111 N Range St., 32340 904-973-6508
Marathon	Seascape, 1075 75th St., 33050 305-743-6455
Marianna	Hinson House B&B, 4338 Lafayette St., 32446 850-526-1500
Mayo	Jim Hollis Inn Rendevous, Route 2, Box 90, 32066 904-294-2510
Mayo	Le Chateau de Lafayette, PO Box 566, 32066 904-294-2332
Melbourne	Old Pineapple Inn, 1736 Pineapple Ave., 32935 407-253-0808
Merritt Island	Rainbow Inn B&B, 1898 Sykes Creek Dr, 32953
Miami	Greenview, 1671 Washington Ave., 33119 305-531-6588
Miami	Miami River Inn, 118 SW South River Dr, 33130 305-325-0045
Miami	Roberts Ranch, 6400 SW 120 Ave, 33183 305-598-3257
Miami Beach	Lafayette Hotel, 944 Collins Ave., 33139 305-673-2262

Miami Beach	Penguin Hotel, 1418 Ocean Dr, 33139 305-534-9334
Miami Beach	Sunshine Inn, 800 West Ave, 33139 305-672-9297
Micanopy	The Shady Oak, PO Box 327, 32667 352-466-3476
Milton	Wolfecreek Schoolhouse Inn, Rt 6, Box 283, 32570 850-623-6197
Mims	Dickens Inn, 2398 N Singleton Ave, 32754 407-269-4595
Monticello	Palmer Place B&B, PO Box 507, 32345 850-997-5519
Mount Dora	Amapola, Ville of Poppies, 347 E. Third Ave., 32757 904-735-3800
Mount Dora	Christopher's, 539 Liberty Ave, 32757 904-383-2244
Mount Dora	Farnsworth House, 1029 E 5th Ave, 32757 352-735-1894
Mount Dora	Lakeside Inn, 100 N Alexander St., 32757 352-383-4101
Mount Dora	Magnolia Inn, 347 E 3rd Ave, 32757 352-735-3800
Mount Dora	Raintree House, 616 Chautauqua Dr, 32757
Mount Dora	Simpson's B&B, 441 N Donnelly St, 32757 352-383-2087
Mount Dora	The Emerald Hill Inn, 27751 Lake Jem Rd, 32757 352-383-2777
Naples	Inn by the Sea, 287 - 11th Ave S, 34102 941-649-4124
Naples	Old Naples Trianon, 955 Seventh Ave S, 34102 941-435-9600
Naples	The Olde Naples Inn, 801 Third St S, 33940 941-262-5194
New Smyrna Beach	Honey Bear Hideaway Farm, 2650 Sunset Dr, 32168
New Smyrna Beach	Indian River Inn, 1210 S Riverside Dr., 32168 904-428-2491
New Smyrna Beach	Little River Inn, 532 N Riverside Dr., 32168 904-424-0100
New Smyrna Beach	Riverview Hotel, 103 Flagler Ave, 32169
Nokomis	Bayshore B&B, 210 Castle Dr, 34275
North Palm Beach	Orchard Terrace, PO Box 13017, 33408
Ocala	Heritage Country Inn, 14343 W Hwy 40, 34481 352-489-0023
Ocala	Neva's B&B, 520 Southeast 17th Pl, 32671 904-732-4607
Ocala	Seven Sisters Inn, 820 SE Fort King St, 34471 352-867-1170
Ocklawaha	Lake Weir Inn, Rt. 2,, 32179 904-288-3723
Oklawaha	Wits End Farm, PO Box 964, 32179 352-288-4294
Orlando	Courtyard at Lake Lucerne, 211 N. Lucerne Cr E, 32801 407-648-5188
Orlando	The Rio Pinar House, 532 Pinar Dr, 32825
Palatka	The Azalea House B&B, 220 Madison St, 32177
Palm Beach	Bardley House Apts., 280 Sunset Ave., 33480 561-832-7050
Palm Beach	Heron Cay, 15106 Palmwood Rd, 33410 407-744-6315
Palm Beach	Palm Beach Historic Inn, 365 S. Country Rd, 33480 407-832-4009
Palm Harbor	B&B of Tampa Bay, 126 Old Oak Circle, 34683 813-785-2342
Palm Harbor	B&B Suncoast Accommodation, 816 11th St, 34683
Pensacola	Buena Vista B&B, PO Box 30572, 32503
Pensacola	Gulf Beach Inn, 10655 Gulf Beach Hwy, 32507 850-492-4501
Pensacola	Hospitality Inn B&B, 6900 Pensacola Blvd, 32505
Pensacola	New World Inn, 600 S Palafox St., 32501 850-432-4111
Pensacola	Noble Manor, 110 W Strong St, 32501 850-434-9544
Pensacola	Pensacola Victorian B&B, 203 W. Gregory St, 32501 850-434-2818
Plant City	Rysdon House B&B, 702 W. Reynolds St., 33566 813-752-8717
Port Charlotte	Noreen's Nest, 18477 Lake Worth Blvd, 33948
Port St Joe	Turtle Beach Inn, 140 Painted Pony Rd, 32456 850-229-9366
Punta Gorda	Gilchrist B&B Inn, 115 Gilchrist St., 33950 941-575-4129
Ramrod Key	Florida Keys House, 27441 W. Indies Dr, 33042 800-833-9857
Ramrod Key	Knightswood, Box 151, 33042
Riverview	The Doll House Inn, 9506 Glenpointe Dr, 33569
San Mateo	Ferncourt B&B, PO Box 758, 32187 904-329-9755
Sanibel Island	Sanibel's Seaside Inn, 541 E Gulf Dr, 33957 941-472-1400
Sanibel Island	Song of the Sea/European, 863 E. Gulf Dr, 33957 941-472-2220
Santa Rosa	Highlands House, PO Box 1189, 32459 850-267-0110
Sarasota	Breeze Lodge, 1301 Dixie Lee Ln, 34231 941-924-6409
Sarasota	Cypress - A B&B Inn, 621 Gulfstream Ave. S, 34236 941-955-4683
Sarasota	Villa at Raintree Gardens, 1758 Vamo Dr, 34231 941-966-6596
Seagrove Beach	Sugar Beach Inn B&B, 3501 E Scenic 30-A, 32459 904-231-1577
Seaside	Dolphin Inn at Seaside, PO Box 4732, 32459 904-231-5477
Seaside	Josephine's French Inn, PO Box 4767, 32459 904-231-1940
Sebastian	The Davis House Inn, 607 Davis St., 32958 407-589-4114
Sebring	The Idly Our Inn, 747 SE Lakeview Dr, 33870 941-385-8101
St. Augustine	Casa de Solana, B&B Inn, 21 Aviles St, 32084 904-824-3555
St. Augustine	Casa de Suenos B&B, 20 Cordova St., 32084 904-824-0887
St. Augustine	Casablanca Inn on the Bay, 24 Avenida Menendez, 32084 904-829-0928
St. Augustine	Coquina Gables Oceanfront, 1 F Street, 32084 904-461-8727
St. Augustine	Old City House Inn & Rest., 115 Cordova St, 32084 904-826-0113
St. Augustine	Old Mansion Inn, 14 Joyner St., 32084 904-824-1975
St. Augustine	Our House of St. Augustine, 7 Cincinnati Ave, 32084
St. Augustine	The Old Powder House Inn, 38 Cordova St, 32084 904-824-4149
St. Augustine	The Secret Garden Inn, 56-1/2 Charlotte St, 32084 904-829-3678
St. Augustine	Victorian House B&B, 11 Cadiz St, 32084 904-824-5214
St. Augustine	Westcott House, PO Box 3793, 32085 904-824-4301
St. George Island	St. George Inn, 135 Franklin Blvd, 32328
St. Pete Beach	Inn on the Beach, 1401 Gulfway, 33706 813-360-8844
St. Pete Beach	Island's End Resort, 1 Pass-A-Grill Way, 33706 813-360-5023
St. Pete Beach	Sunset Bay Inn, 635 Bay St, NE, 33701 813-570-9506
St. Pete Beach	Swan House, 8690 Gulf Blvd., 33706 813-360-1753
St. Petersburg	Bayboro House B&B, 1719 Beach Dr SE, 33701 813-823-4955

St. Petersburg	Bayboro Inn & Hunt Room, 357 3rd Street South, 33701 727-823-0498
St. Petersburg	Orleans Bishop B&B, 256 1st Ave, N, 33701 727-894-4312
Stuart	The Homeplace B&B, 501 Akron Ave, 34994 561-220-9148
Summerland Key	Andrew's Inn, PO Box 420381, 33042 305-294-7740
Summerland Key	Knightswood, PO Box 151, 33042 305-872-2246
Suwannee	Pelican's Roost, PO Box 177, 32692 352-542-9712
Tallahassee	Calhoun Street Inn, 525 N Calhoun St., 32301 850-425-5095
Tallahassee	The Riedel House B&B, 1412 Fairway Dr, 32301 904-222-8569
Tampa	Guava House B&B, 1923 E 6th Ave, 33605 813-247-4422
Tampa	Hyde Park Inn, 404 W Kennedy, 33606 813-254-5834
Tarpon Springs	B&B on the Bayou, 976 Bayshore Dr, 34689 727-942-4468
Tarpon Springs	East Lake B&B, 421 Old East Lake Rd, 34689 727-937-5487
Tarpon Springs	Fiorito's B&B, 421 Old E. Lake Rd. 34689 727-937-5487
Tarpon Springs	Heartsease, 272 Old E. Lake Rd, 34689 727-934-0994
Tarpon Springs	Inn on the Bayou, PO Box 1545, 34688 727-942-4468
Tavares	Fleur Du Lac, 426 Lake Dora Dr, 32778
Tavernier	Historic Tavernier Hotel, 91865 Overseas Hwy, 33070 305-852-4131
Venice	Inn at the Beach Resort, 101 The Esplanade, 34285 941-484-8471
Vero Beach	Seafarer Inn, 1776 Cypress Ln, 32963
Wakulla Springs	Wakulla Springs Lodge, #1 Springs Dr, 32305 904-224-5950
West Palm Beach	Hibiscus House B&B, 501 30th St, 33407 561-863-5633
West Palm Beach	Tropical Gardens B&B, 419 32nd St, 33407 561-848-4064
Winter Garden	Casa Adobe, PO Box 770707, 34777 407-876-5432
Winter Haven	J.D.'s Southern Oaks, 3800 Country Club Rd, 33881
Winter Haven	The Forget Me Not, 1006 Medinah Dr, 33884

Georgia

Americus	Wise Olde Pine Plantation, 590 Three Bridges Rd., 31709 912-846-5491
Andersonville	Place Away B&B, 110 Oglethorpe St, 31711 912-924-2558
Athens	Magnolia Terrace Guest Hou, 277 Hill St, 30605 706-548-3860
Athens	Nicholson House, 6295 Jefferson Rd., 30607 706-353-2200
Athens	Oakwood B&B, 4959 Barnett Shoals Rd, 30605 706-546-7886
Atlanta	Bentley's B&B, 6860 Peachtree-Dunwoody, 30328 770-396-1742
Atlanta	Brookridge B&B, 758 Brookridge Dr., 30306 404-872-7980
Atlanta	Buckhead B&B Inn, 70 Lenox Pointe, NE, 30324 404-261-8284
Atlanta	Cornell Cottage, 1537 Emory Rd., 30306 404-371-9552
Atlanta	Deborah & Mark's Atlanta, 1746 Flagler Ave., 30309 404-875-3071
Atlanta	Georgia B&B, 2472 Lauderdale Dr, 30345
Atlanta	Greycourt B&B, 47 Delta Place, 30307 404-523-4239
Atlanta	Heartfield Manor, 182 Elizabeth St NE, 30307 404-523-8633
Atlanta	Linden Manor, 810 Flat Shoals Ave, 30316 404-627-9701
Atlanta	Mason Transplant Guest Hse, c/o Emory U,1762 Clifton, 30322 404-727-7611
Atlanta	Oakwood House B&B, 951 Edge Wood Ave NE, 30307 404-521-9320
Atlanta	Seymour B&B, 67 Avery Dr NE, 30390 404-872-4657
Atlanta	Shellmont B&B Lodge, 821 Piedmont Ave NE, 30308 404-872-9290
Atlanta	The 1223 at Emory, 1223 Clifton Rd, NE, 30307 404-377-4987
Atlanta	The Wise House, 945 Niskey Lake Circle, 30331 404-691-9473
Atlanta	The Woodruff B&B Inn, 223 Ponce de Leon Ave, 30308 404-875-9449
Atlanta	University Inn At Emory, 1767 N Decatur Rd., 30307 404-634-7327
Atlanta	Virginia Highland B&B, 630 Orme Circle, NE, 30306 404-892-2735
Augusta	Augusta Budget Inn, 441 Broad St., 30901 706-722-0212
Augusta	Azalea Inn, 312 Greene St, 30901 706-724-3454
Augusta	Perrin Guest Hotel, 208 Lafayette Dr, 30909
Bainbridge	The White House B&B, 320 Washington St, 31717 912-248-1703
Barnesville	The Rose Inn, 643 Greenwood St, 30204 770-358-6969
Blackshear	Pond View Inn, 421 Acosta St, 31516 912-449-3697
Blairsville	7 Creeks Housekeeping Cabi, 5109 Horseshoe Cove Rd., 30512 706-745-4753
Blairsville	Misty Mountain Inn, PO Box 2237, 30512 706-745-4786
Blairsville	Nottley Damn Guest House, 2266 Nottely Dam Rd, 30512
Blairsville	Souther Country Inn, 2592 Collins Lane, 30512 706-379-1603
Blue Ridge	Harry & June's B&B, Box 1247, 30513 404-632-8846
Brunswick	Rose Manor Guest House, 1108 Richmond St, 31520 912-267-6369
Buena Vista	Morgan Towne House, PO Box 522, 31803
Calhoun	Stoneleigh B&B, 316 Fain St, 30701 706-629-2093
Chatsworth	Hearthstone Hall B&B, 2755 Hwy 282, 30705 706-695-6515
Clarkesville	The Charm House, PO Box 392, 30523 706-754-9347
Clayton	Beechwood Inn, PO Box 120, 30525
Clayton	Old Clayton Inn, S Main St, 30525 706-782-7722
Colquitt	Tarrier Inn, 155 S Cuthbert St., 31737 912-758-2888
Columbus	Woodruff House B&B, The, 1414 Second Ave, 31901 706-320-9300
Concord	Inn Scarlett's Footsteps, 40 Old Flat Shoals Rd, 30206 770-884-9012
Conyers	Haynes Ridge Inn, PO Box 81127, 30208 770-922-9151
Conyers	Lakeside Inn B&B, 3051 N Tower Way, 30207 770-922-7269
Dahlonega	Another Place in Time B&B, 168 Main St W, 30533 706-864-7002
Dahlonega	B&B Inn & Gardens, 78 Meanders St N, 30533 706-864-6114
Dahlonega	Cavender Castle Winery, 121 Cavender Castle Dr, 30533 706-864-4759
Dahlonega	Laurel Ridge, PO Box 338, 30533 404-864-7817

Dahlonega	Royal Guard Inn, 65 Park St S, 30533 706-864-1713
Dahlonega	Stanton Storehouse, 78 N Meaders St, 30533
Dahlonega	The Smith House, 84 S Chestatee St, 30533 706-867-7000
Dahlonega	Worley Homestead Inn, 410 W. Main St, 30533 404-864-7002
Decatur	Sycamore House B&B, 624 Sycamore St., 30030 404-378-0685
Eastanollee	Apple Orchard Country Inn, RT 2, PO Box 353, 30538 706-779-7292
Eastman	The Dodge Hill Inn, 105 Ninth Ave, 31023 912-374-2644
Eatonton	Rosewood, 301 N Madison Ave, 31024
Eatonton	The Crockett House, 671 Madison Rd, 31024 706-485-2248
Ellijay	Elderberry Inn B&B Home, 75 Dalton St, 30540 404-635-2218
Eton	Ivy Inn, PO Box 406, 30724 706-517-0526
Fernandina Beach	Greyfield Inn, PO Box 900, 32035 904-261-6408
Fitzgerald	Dorminy-Massee House B&B, 516 W Central Ave, 31750 912-423-3123
Forsyth	Forsyth Square B&B Inn, 22 W Main St, 31029 912-994-0204
Fort Oglethorpe	Captain's Quarters B&B Inn, 13 Barnhardt Circle, 30742 706-858-0624
Fort Valley	The Evans-Cantrell House, 300 College St, 31030 912-825-0611
Grantville	Bonnie Castle B&B, PO Box 359, 30220 770-583-3090
Greensboro	Higdon House B&B, 301 W Greene St, 30642
Greenville	Samples B&B, PO Box 735, 30222 706-672-4765
Greenville	The Georgian Inn, PO Box 1000, 30222 706-672-1600
Griffin	Hill Street B&B Inn, 525 S Hill St, 39224 770-412-9483
Hamilton	Magnolia Hall, PO Box 326, 31811 706-628-4566
Hawkinsville	Black Swan Inn, 411 Progress Ave, 31036 912-783-4466
Hiawassee	Henson Cove Place B&B, 3840 Car Miles Rd, 30546 706-896-5252
Hiawassee	Mountain Memories, 385 Chancey Dr, 30546 706-896-VIEW
Hiawassee	Swan Lake B&B, 2500 Hickorynut Cove, 30546 706-896-1582
Hogansville	Fair Oaks Inn at Plantatio, 633 Ralls Rd, 30230 706-637-8828
Homerville	The Helmstead, PO Box 61, 31634 912-487-2222
Jackson	The Carmichael House, 149 McDonough Rd., 30233 770-775-0578
Jekyll Island	Jekyll Island Club Hotel, 371 Riverview Dr, 31527 912-635-2600
Jesup	Trowell House B&B, 256 E. Cherry St, 31545 912-530-6611
Kennesaw	Magnolia Hill Inn, 3515 Brandywide Rd NW, 30144
Lakemont	The Inn at Lofty Branch, Rt 1 Box 2907, 30552 706-782-3863
Lawrenceville	Touch of Home B&B, 489 Hearth Pl, 30043 770-277-3579
Lindale	Bay View B&B, 3787 Cedartown Hwy, 30147 616-526-7782
Lyons	Robert Toombs Inn, 101 South State St, 30436 912-526-4489
Macon	1842 Inn, 353 College St, 31201 912-741-1842
Macon	Tarrer Inn, 355 First St., 31201 912-741-7996
Madison	Brady Inn, 250 N 2nd St., 30650 706-342-4400
Madison	Burnett Place, 317 Old Post Road, 30650 706-342-4034
Madison	Farmhouse Inn @ 100 Acre F, 1051 Meadow Ln, 30650 706-342-7933
Marietta	Blue & Grey B&B, 2511 Kingswood Dr., 30066 770-425-0392
Marietta	Sixty Polk Street B&B, 60 Polk St., 30064 800-497-2075
Marietta	The Whitlock Inn, 57 Whitlock Ave, 30064 770-428-1495
Midway	Melon Bluff, 2999 Islands Hwy, 31320 912-884-5779
Milledgeville	Hinson House, 1311 N Columbia, 31061 912-453-3993
Milledgeville	Maras Tara, 330 W Greene St, 31061
Mountain City	The York House, PO Box 126, 30562 706-746-2068
Newnan	Parrott-Camp-Soucy Home, 155 Greenville St, 30263 404-253-4846
Newnan	The Old Garden Inn, 51 Temple Ave, 30263 770-304-0594
Oakman	Sugar Valley Cottage B&B, PO Box 37, 30732
Oxford	Hopkins House B&B, 1111 Wesley St., 30054 770-784-1010
Palmetto	Boxwood Heights B&B, 511 Toombs St, 30268 770-463-9966
Palmetto	Serenbe B&B, 10950 Hutcheson Ferry, 30268 770-463-2610
Perry	Swift Street Inn, 1204 Swift St, 31069 912-988-4477
Pine Mountain	The Storms House, PO Box 1011, 31822 706-663-9100
Plains	The Plains B&B Inn, PO Box 217, 31780 912-824-7252
Quitman	Malloy Manor, 401 W Screven St, 31643
Rome	Claremont House, 906 E Second Ave, 30161 706-291-0900
Rome	Royale's Stone House, 2979 Big Texas Valley, 30161 706-232-0740
Roswell	Ten-Fifty Canton St B&B, 1050 Canton St., 30075 404-998-1050
Sautee	Nacoochee Valley House, Box 249, 30571 404-878-3830
Sautee	The Lumsden Homeplace, Guy Palmer Rd, 30571 404-878-2813
Savannah	17 Hundred 90 Inn, 307 E. President St, 31401 912-236-7122
Savannah	Ballastone Inn, 14 E Oglethorpe Ave, 31401 912-236-1484
Savannah	Bed & Breakfast Inn, 117 W Gordon St, 31401 912-238-0518
Savannah	Broughton Street B&B, 511 E Broughton St, 31401 912-232-6633
Savannah	Catherine Ward House Inn, 118 E Waldburg St, 31401 912-234-8564
Savannah	Claudia's Manor, 101 E 35th St, 31401 912-233-2379
Savannah	Gaston Gallery B&B, 211 E. Gaston St, 31401 912-238-3294
Savannah	Habersham at York Inn, 130 Habersham St, 31401 912-234-2499
Savannah	Hospitality House, 409 E Charlton St, 31401 912-236-6448
Savannah	McMillan Inn, 304 E Huntingdon St, 31401 912-233-1447
Savannah	Park Avenue Manor, 107-109 West Park Ave, 31401 912-233-0352
Savannah	Remshart-Brooks House, 106 W Jones St, 31401 912-234-6928
Savannah	River Street Inn, 115 E. River St, 31499 912-234-6400
Savannah	Savannah's B&B Inn, 117 W Gordon St, 31401 912-238-0518
Savannah	The Gastonian, 220 E Gaston St, 31401 912-232-2869

Savannah	The Grande Toots Inn, 212 W Hall St @ Tattnal, 31401 800-835-6831
Savannah	The Manor House, 201 West Liberty St, 31401 912-233-9597
Savannah	The Midnight Inn B&B, 11 W Gordon St, 31401 912-231-9814
Senoia	The Veranda, PO Box 177, 30276 770-599-3905
St. Marys	Riverview Hotel, 105 Osborne St, 31558 912-882-3242
St. Marys	Spencer House Inn B&B, 101 E Bryant St., 31558 912-882-1872
Statesboro	Statesboro Inn, Restaurant, 106 S. Main St, 30458 912-489-8628
Swainsboro	Edenfield House Inn, 426 W Church St, 30401 912-237-3007
Sylvania	Willowbend Plantation, 307 N Main, 30467 912-564-7275
Tate	Tate House Resort, PO Box 33, 30177 404-735-3122
Thomasville	1884 Paxton House, 445 Remington Ave., 31792 912-226-5197
Thomasville	Deer Creek B&B, 1304 S. Broad St, 31792 913-226-7294
Thomasville	Moss Oaks B&B, PO Box 2011, 31799 912-377-6280
Thomasville	Our Cottage on the Park, 801 S Hansell St, 31792
Thomasville	Susina Plantation Inn, Route 3 Box 1010, 31792 912-377-9644
Thomson	Four Chimneys B&B, 2316 Wire Rd, SE, 30824 706-597-0220
Tiger	Mountain Oaks B&B, PO Box 368, 30576 706-782-4625
Toccoa	Habersham Manor House, 326 W. Doyle St, 30577 404-886-6496
Tybee Island	Fort Screven Inn, 24 Van Horn, 31328 912-786-9255
Tybee Island	Hunter House B&B, 1701 Butler Ave, 31328 912-786-7515
Villa Rica	Ahava Plantation B&B, 2236 S. Van Wert Rd, 30180 770-459-2836
Villa Rica	Twin Oaks B&B Cottages, 9565 E. Liberty Rd, 30180 404-459-4374
Warm Springs	Hotel Warm Springs B&B, PO Box 351, 31830 706-655-2114
Watkinsville	Rivendell B&B, 3581 S. Barnett Shoals, 30677 706-769-4522
Waverly Hall	Raintree Farms of Waverly, 8060 Georgia Highway, 31831 706-582-3227
West Point	The Nesting Place, 408 E 7th St, 31833 706-643-8164
Young Harris	Brasstown Valley Resort, 6321 U.S. Highway 76, 30582 706-379-9900

Hawaii —————————————————————————————————

Captain Cook	Artist Retreat, PO Box 60, 96704 808-328-8766
Captain Cook	Cedar House B&B, PO Box 823, 96704 808-328-8829
Captain Cook	Doc Boones Capt. Cook B&B, 82-6296 Manini Beach Rd, 96704 808-323-3231
Captain Cook	Fragrant Tree Farm, PO Box 1051, 96704 808-328-9595
Captain Cook	R & R Nut Farm, 82-1130 Kinue Rd., 96704 808-323-3423
Hilo	Arnott's Lodge, 98 Apapane Rd, 96720 808-969-7097
Hilo	Hale Kai Bjornen, 111 Honolii Pali, 96720 808-935-6330
Hilo	Hilo Seaside Retreat B&B, PO Box 10960, 96721 808-934-9462
Hilo	Holmes' Sweet Home, 107 Koula St, 96720 808-961-9089
Hilo	Oceanfront B&B, 1923 Kalanianaole St, 96720 808-961-5754
Hilo	Pineapple Park, PO Box 5844, 96720
Hilo	Wild Ginger Inn, 100 Puueo St., 96720 808-935-5556
Holualoa	A'Hui' Hou Coffee Plantati, PO Box 349, 96725 808-324-0510
Holualoa	Rosy's Rest, 76-1012 Mamalahoa Hwy, 96725 808-324-1713
Honaunau	Affordable Accommodations, PO Box 236, 96750 808-937-0621
Honaunau	Da Third House, PO Box 321, 96726 808-328-8410
Honaunau	Horizon Guest House, PO Box 268, 96726 808-328-2540
Honaunau	Lions Gate B&B, PO Box 761, 96726 808-328-2335
Honaunau	The Dragonfly Ranch, PO Box 675, 96726 808-328-2159
Honokaa	Kalopa Homestead Guest Hse, PO Box 1614, 96727 808-775-7167
Honokaa	Kalopa Orchard Hale B&B, PO Box 1463, 96727 808-775-0568
Honokaa	Luana Ola B&B Cottages, PO Box 430, 96727 808-775-7727
Honokaa	Mauka B&B, PO Box 767, 96727 808-775-9983
Honokaa	Mountain Meadow Ranch, PO Box 1697, 96727 808-775-9376
Honokaa	Waipio Treehouse, PO Box 5086, 96727 808-775-7160
Honokaa	Waipio Wayside B&B Inn, PO Box 840, 96727 808-775-0275
Honomu	Akaka Falls Inn, 28-1676 Government Rd, 96728 808-963-5468
Kailua Kona	Adrienne's Casa Del Sol, PO Box 5445, 96740 800-328-9726
Kailua Kona	Annie's Three Bears B&B, 72-1001 Puukala St., 96740 808-325-7563
Kailua Kona	Hale Pueo B&B, 73-1339 Loio St, 96740 808-325-1056
Kailua Kona	Kiwi Gardens, 74-4920 Kiwi St, 96740 808-326-1559
Kailua Kona	Manu Mele B&B, 153 Kailuana Pl, 96734 808-262-0016
Kailua Kona	Pu' Ukala Lodge, PO Box 2867, 96745 808-325-1729
Kailua Kona	Puanani B&B, 74-4958 Kiwi St, 96740 808-329-8644
Kailua Kona	Secret Gardens B&B, PO Box 366, 96745 808-328-8394
Kailua Kona	Silver Oaks Ranch B&B, 75-1027 Henry St #310, 96740 808-325-2000
Kailua Kona	Sleepy Hollow, 73-1530 Apela Place, 96740 808-325-5043
Kailua Kona	Starfire Retreat B&B, 78-6737 Walua Rd., 96740 808-322-3187
Kailua-Kona	Hale Kipa 'O Pele, PO Box 5252, 96745 808-329-8676
Kamuela	Belle Vue Cottage & Suites, PO Box 1295, 96743 808-885-7732
Kamuela	Kamuela Inn, PO Box 1994, 96743 808-885-4243
Kamuela	Kamuela's Mauna Kea View, PO Box 6375, 96743 808-885-8425
Kamuela	Waimea Gardens, PO Box 563, 96743 808-885-4550
Kaneohe	Alii Bluffs Winward B&B, 46-251 Ikiiki St, 96744 808-235-1124
Kapaau	Big Sky Ranch, Kohala G.C., PO Box 1468, 96755 808-889-0564
Kauai, Anahola	Mahina Kai, PO Box 699, 96703 808-822-9451
Kauai, Hanalei	Ainalani Tropical Farms, PO Box 835, 96714 808-826-9400
Kauai, Hanalei	Kauai Getaway Vacation Stu, PO Box 1212, 96714 808-826-4468

Kauai, Hanalei	Tassa Hanalei, PO Box 856, 96714	
Kauai, Hanalei	The Historic B&B, PO Box 1662, 96714 808-826-4622	
Kauai, Kalaheo	Aloha Vacation Rentals, 5155 Kikala Rd., 96741 808-332-7080	
Kauai, Kalaheo	Classic Vacation Cottages, PO Box 901, 96741	
Kauai, Kalaheo	Sea View Suite B&B, 3913 Ulualii St, 96741	
Kauai, Kalaheo	South Shore Vista, 4400 Kai Ikena Dr, 96741 808-332-9339	
Kauai, Kapaa	Alohilani B&B, 1470 Wanaao Rd., 96746 808-823-0128	
Kauai, Kapaa	Candy's Cabin, 5940 Ohe St., 96746 808-822-5451	
Kauai, Kapaa	Hale O'Wailele, 7084 Kahuna Rd, 96795 808-822-7911	
Kauai, Kapaa	Hotel Coral Reef, 1516 Lijop Jwu, 96746 808-822-4481	
Kauai, Kapaa	Hotel of Leaping Waterfall, 7084 Kahuna Rd., 96746 808-822-7911	
Kauai, Kapaa	House of Aleva B&B, 5509 Kuamoo Rd., 96746	
Kauai, Kapaa	Ikena Nani Loa B&B, 139 Royal Dr., 96746 808-822-4010	
Kauai, Kapaa	Kakalina's B&B, 6781 Kawaihau Rd., 96746	
Kauai, Kapaa	Kaua'i Kualapa Cottage, 1471 Kualapa Place, 96746 808-822-1626	
Kauai, Kapaa	Lampy's B&B, 6078 Kolopua St, 96746 808-822-0478	
Kauai, Kapaa	Mohala Ke Ola, 5663 Ohelo Rd. #A, 96746 808-823-6398	
Kauai, Kapaa	Momi's Halekipa B&B, 44 Loloa St, 96746 808-823-0149	
Kauai, Kapaa	Opaekaa Falls Hale, 120 Lihau St., 96746 808-822-9956	
Kauai, Kapaa	Rosewood, 872 Kamalu Rd., 96746	
Kauai, Kapaa	Suzie's Retreat, 6820 Kawaihau Rd., 96746 808-822-1018	
Kauai, Kapaa	Wailua Country B&B, 505 Kamalu Rd., 96746	
Kauai, Kapaa	Winters Mac Nut Farm & Inn, 6470 Makana Rd., 96746 808-822-3470	
Kauai, Kilauea	Hale Ho'o Maha, PO Box 422, 96754 808-828-1341	
Kauai, Koloa	Gloria's Spouting Horn B&B, 4464 Lawai Beach Rd, 96756 808-742-6995	
Kauai, Koloa	Island Home, 1707 Kelaukia St, 96756 808-742-2839	
Kauai, Koloa	Mango's B&B, 4333 Naulu Place, 96756 808-742-1216	
Kauai, Koloa	Maukalani, 2381 Kipuka St., 96756 808-742-1700	
Kauai, Koloa	Poipu Plantation, 1792 Pee Rd., 96756 808-742-6757	
Kauai, Lawai	Marjorie's Kauai Inn, 3307-D Hailima Rd., 96765 808-332-8838	
Kauai, Lawai	Victoria Place B&B, PO Box 930, 96765 808-332-9300	
Kauai, Poipu	Brenneke's B&B, 2255 Nalo Rd., 96756 808-742-1116	
Kauai, Poipu Beach	Poipu B&B Inn/Vac. Rentals, 2720 Hoonani Rd, 96756 808-742-1146	
Keaau	Blue Buddha B&B, HCR 2 Box 13008, 96749 808-982-7210	
Keaau	Ohio Cottage, HCR 2 Box 9591, 96749	
Keaau	Rainforest Retreat, HCR 1 Box 5655, 96749 808-982-9601	
Kealakekua	Kealakekua Bay B&B, PO Box 1412, 96750 808-328-8150	
Kealakekua	Reggie's Tropical Hideaway, PO Box 1107, 96750 808-322-8888	
Kealakekua	The Bird of Paradise, PO Box 2613, 96750 808-323-2433	
Kurtistown	B&B Mt. View, PO Box 963, 96760 808-968-6868	
Lanai, Lanai City	Hotel Lanai, PO Box A-119, 96763 800 321-4666	
Maui, Haiku	Hale Kokomo, 2719 Kokomo Rd, 96708 808-572-5270	
Maui, Haiku	Halfway to Hana House, PO Box 675, 96708 808-572-1176	
Maui, Haiku	Pilialoha B&B Cottage, 2512 Kaupakalua Rd, 96708 808-572-1440	
Maui, Hana	Hana Plantation Houses, PO 249, 96713 808-248-7867	
Maui, Hana	Hana's Tradewind Cottages, PO Box 385, 96713 800-327-8097	
Maui, Hana	Hotel Hana-Maui, PO Box 8, 96713 808-248-8211	
Maui, Kihei	Aloha Eva Villa B&B, PO Box 365, 96753 808-874-6407	
Maui, Kihei	Aloha Kai's Maui B&B, 80 Welakahao Rd, 96753 808-874-6431	
Maui, Kihei	Ann/Bob's Vacation Rental, 3371 Keha Dr, 96753 808-874-1166	
Maui, Kihei	Anuhea B&B Health Retreat, 3164 Mapu Place, 96753 808-874-1490	
Maui, Kihei	Babson's B&B, 3371 Keha Dr, 96753 808-874-1166	
Maui, Kihei	By the Sea B&B, 20 Wailana Place, 96753 808-879-2700	
Maui, Kihei	Hideaway N'Paradize, 3416 Kehala Dr, 96753 808-875-0356	
Maui, Kihei	Jasmine House, 883 Kupulau Dr, 96753 808-875-0400	
Maui, Kihei	Sea Escape, 3088 Manu Hope Pl, 96753 808-874-5077	
Maui, Kihei	Sunnyside of Maui B&B, 2840 Umalu Pl, 96753 808-874-8687	
Maui, Kihei	Three Leis Inn, 723 Kupulau Dr., 96753 808-874-8645	
Maui, Kula	Country Garden Cottage B&B, RR2 Box 224-A, 96790 808-878-2858	
Maui, Kula	Hunter Farms Hideaway, 263 Kula Hwy, 96790 808-878-3539	
Maui, Kula	Kula Lodge, RR 1 Box 475, 96790 808-878-2517	
Maui, Kula	Silver Cloud Ranch, RR 2, Box 201, 96790 808-878-6101	
Maui, Lahaina	Aloha Lani Inn, 13 Kauaula Rd, 96761 808-661-8040	
Maui, Lahaina	Bambula B&B Inn, 518 Ilikaha St, 96761 808-667-6753	
Maui, Lahaina	Belladonna B&B, 418 Front St, 96761 808-661-0358	
Maui, Lahaina	House of Fountains Inn, 1579 Lokia St, 96761 808-667-2121	
Maui, Lahaina	Lahaina Inn, 127 Lahainaluna Rd, 96761 808-661-0577	
Maui, Lahaina	The Guesthouse, 1620 Ainakea Rd., 96761	
Maui, Lahaina	The Plantation Inn, 174 Lahainaluna Rd, 96761 808-667-9225	
Maui, Makawao	Hale Ho'okipa Inn Makawao, 32 Pakani Placae, 96768 808-572-6698	
Maui, Makawao	Heavenly Gate B&B, 276 Hiwalani Loop, 96768 808-572-0321	
Maui, Makawao	Olinda Country Cottage Inn, 536 Olinda Rd, 96768	
Maui, Napili	Coconut Inn, 181 Hui Rd "F", 96761 808-669-5712	
Maui, Pa'ia	Huelo Point Lookout, 96779 808-573-0914	
Maui, Wailuku	Old Wailuku Inn @ Ulupono, 2199 Kahookele St, 96793 808-244-5897	
Molokai, Kaunakakai	A'ahi Place B&B, PO Box 528, 96748 808-553-5860	
Molokai, Kaunakakai	Kamalo Plantation, PO Box 28, 96748 808-558-8236	
Molokai, Kaunakakai	Potts House B&B, PO Box 528, 96748 808-553-5860	

Molokai, Kawela	Ka Hale Mala, PO Box 1582, 96748 808-553-9009
Mtn. View	Hale Nui B&B, PO Box 127, 96771 808-968-6577
Naalehu	Becky's B&B, PO Box 673, 96772 808-929-9690
Naalehu	Hobbit House B&B, PO Box 269, 96772 808-929-9755
Oahu, Honolulu	B&B Manoa, 2651 Terrace Dr, 96822 808-988-6333
Oahu, Honolulu	Bev & Monty's B&B, 4571 Ukali St, 96818 808-422-9873
Oahu, Honolulu	John Guild Inn, 2001 Vancouver Dr, 96822 808-947-6019
Oahu, Honolulu	Manoa Valley Inn, 2001 Vancouver Dr, 96822 808-947-6019
Oahu, Kailua	Akamai B&B, 172 Kuumele Pl, 96734 808-261-2227
Oahu, Kailua	Ali'i B&B, 237 Awakea Rd, 96734 800-262-9545
Oahu, Kailua	Hailer House, 57 Pilipu Place, 96734 808-262-9530
Oahu, Kailua	Ingrid's Place, 571 Pauku St., 96734 808-261-3584
Oahu, Kailua	Lanikai B&B, 1277 Mokulua Dr., 96734 808-261-7895
Oahu, Kailua	Papaya Paradise B&B, 395 Auwinala Rd, 96734 808-261-0316
Oahu, Kailua	Paradise Palms B&B, 804 Mokapu Rd., 96734 808-254-4234
Oahu, Kailua	Pillows in Paradise, 336 Awakea Rd, 96734 808-262-8540
Oahu, Kailua	Sheffield House, 131 Kuulei Rd, 96734 808-262-0721
Oahu, Waimanalo	Kom A'Ona, A Hawaiian B&B, 41-926 Laumilo St., 96795 808-259-8180
Paauilo	Suds Acres B&B, PO Box 277, 96776 808-776-1611
Pahala	Auntie Jessie's Wood Vly, PO Box 37, 96777 808-928-8212
Pahala	Wood Valley B&B, PO Box 37, 96777
Pahoa	Al's Volcano Ranch, 13-3775 Kalapana Hwy, 96778 808-965-8800
Pahoa	Aloha B&B, 13-3591 Luana St, 96778 808-965-7434
Pahoa	Huliaulea B&B, PO Box 1030, 96778 808-965-9175
Pahoa	Kalani Oceanside Resort, RR2, Box 4500, 96778 808-965-7828
Pahoa	Pamalu-Peaceful Enclosure, RR 2, Box 4023, 96778
Pahoa	Pearl's Shell B&B, 23-3432 Kupono St, 96778
Pahoa	Puna B&B, PO Box 1199, 96778 808-965-8784
Pahoa	Village Inn, PO Box 1987, 96778 808-965-6444
Papaikou	Hale Lamalani, 27-703A Kaieie Homestead, 96781 808-964-5401
Pukalani	Sea Q Maui, 249 Kaualani Dr, 96768 808-572-7914
Volcano	Carson's Volcano Cottage, PO Box 503, 96785 808-967-7683
Volcano	Hale Kilauea, PO Box 28, 96785 808-967-7591
Volcano	Kilauea Volcano Kabins, PO Box 963, 96785 808-967-7773
Volcano	Lokahi Lodge, PO Box 7, 96785 808-985-8647
Volcano	My Island B&B, PO Box 100, 96785 808-967-7110
Volcano	The Lodge at Volcano, PO Box 998, 96785 808-967-7244
Volcano	Volcano B&B, PO Box 998, 96785 808-967-7779
Volcano	Volcano Country Cottages, PO Box 545, 96785 800-967-7960
Volcano	Volcano Rainforest Retreat, PO Box 957, 96785 800-550-8696

Idaho

Ahsahka	Mule Shoe II Lodge, 4244 Old Ahsahka Grade, 83520 208-476-9980
Albion	Mountain Manor B&B, PO Box 128, 83311 208-673-6642
Almo	Old Homestead, PO Box 186, 83312 208-824-5521
Athol	Bear Creek Inn, 13645 E Twete Rd., 83801 208-683-3861
Boise	Idaho Heritage Inn, 109 W. Idaho, 83702 208-342-8066
Boise	J.J. Shaw House B&B Inn, 1411 W Franklin St, 83702 208-344-8899
Boise	Robin's Nest B&B, 2389 W. Boise, 83706 208-336-9551
Bruneau	Pleasant Hill Country Inn, HC 85, Box 179A, 83604 208-845-2018
Cambridge	Cambridge House B&B, PO Box 313, 83610 208-257-3325
Coeur d'Alene	Amor's Highwood House, 1206 Highwood Ln., 83814 208-667-4735
Coeur d'Alene	Ann & Mel's Log House, 4850 E Long Shadowy Ln, 83814 208-667-8015
Coeur d'Alene	Baragar House B&B, 316 Military Dr, 83814 208-664-9125
Coeur d'Alene	Country Ranch B&B, 1495 S. Green Ferry Rd, 83814 208-664-1189
Coeur d'Alene	Cricket on the Hearth, 1521 Lakeside Ave, 83814 208-664-6926
Coeur d'Alene	Highwood House B&B, 1206 Highwood Ln, 83814 208-667-4735
Coeur d'Alene	Katie's Wild Rose Inn, E. 5150 Lake Dr, 83814 208-765-9474
Coeur d'Alene	Roosevelt Inn B&B, 105 Wallace Ave, 83814 208-765-5200
Coeur d'Alene	Silver Beach House B&B, 1457 Silver Beach Loop, 83814 208-667-5406
Coeur d'Alene	Someday House B&B, 790 Kidd Island Rd, 83814 208-664-6666
Coeur d'Alene	Summer House by the Lake, 1535 Silver Beach Rd, 83814 208-664-9395
Coeur d'Alene	Warwick Inn B&B, 303 Military Dr, 83814 208-765-6565
Coeur d'Alene	Wolf Lodge Creek B&B, 715 N Wolf Lodge Creek, 83814 208-667-5902
Council	Old Heartland Inn B&B, PO Box 0, 83612 208-253-6423
Dixie	Lodgepole Pine Inn, PO Box 71, 83525 208-842-2343
Downey	Downata Hot Springs, PO Box 185, 83234 208-897-5736
Driggs	Teton Creek B&B, 41 S. Baseline Rd, 83422 208-354-2584
Driggs	Three Peaks Inn B&B, 53 S Hwy 33, 83422 208-354-8912
Driggs	Willowpine B&B Guest House, PO Box 105, 83422 208-354-2735
Fish Haven	Bear Lake B&B, 500 Loveland Lane, 83287 208-945-2688
Fruitland	Elm Hollow B&B, 4900 Hwy 95, 83619 208-452-6491
Garden Valley	Warm Springs Creek B&B, HC 76, Box 2540, 83622 208-462-3516
Hagerman	The Cary House, 17985 U.S. 30 North, 83332 208-837-4848
Hailey	Povey Pensione, 128 W Bullion, 83333 208-788-4682
Hayden Lake	Clark House on Hayden Lake, E. 4550 S. Hayden Lake, 83835 208-772-3470
Hayden Lake	Hayden Hideaway B&B, 5735 English Point Rd., 83835 208-772-1667

Hayden Lake	Hitching Post Manor B&B, 1155 Lancaster Rd., 83835 208-762-3126
Idaho City	Idaho City Hotel, PO Box 70, 83631 208-392-4290
Idaho City	One Step Away B&B, PO Box 55, 83631 208-392-4938
Island Park	Henry's Fork Lodge, Rt 20, 83429 208-558-7953
Kellogg	Inn at Silver Mountain, 305 S. Division, 83837 208-786-2311
Kellogg	Patrick's Inn, PO Box 11, 83837 208-786-2311
Kellogg	Scott's Inn, 126 E. Mullan Ave, 83837 208-786-8581
Ketchum	Busterback Ranch, HC 64 Box 9385, 83340 208-774-2217
Ketchum	Knob Hill Inn, PO Box 800, 83353 208-726-8010
Kingston	Kingston 5 Ranch B&B, PO Box 130, 83839 208-682-4862
Kooskia	Bear Hollow B&B, HC 75, Box 16, 83539 208-926-7146
Kooskia	Three Rivers Resort, HC 75, Box 61, 83539 208-926-4430
Laclede	River Birch Farm B&B, PO Box 280, 83841 208-263-3705
Lava Hot Springs	Lava Hot Springs Inn, PO Box 420, 83246 208-776-5830
Lava Hot Springs	Riverside Inn & Hot Spring, PO Box 127, 83246 208-776-5504
Lewiston	Carriage House B&B, 611 - 5th St, 83501 208-746-4506
Mackay	Martini's Mountainside B&B, PO Box 456, 83251 208-588-2940
Malad City	Chantilly B&B, 63 South Main, 83252
McCall	1920 House B&B, PO Box 1716, 83638 208-634-4661
McCall	Hotel McCall, PO Box 1778, 83638 208-634-8105
McCall	Northwest Passage B&B, PO Box 4208, 83638 208-634-5349
Moscow	Pardise Ridge B&B, 3377 Blaine Rd, 83843 208-882-5292
Mountain Home	Rose Stone Inn, 325 s 5th E, 83647 208-587-8866
Nampa	The Pink Tudor B&B, 1315 12th Ave S, 83651 208-465-3615
New Meadows	Bear Creek Lodge, PO Box 8, 83654 208-634-3551
Nordman	Huckleberry Heaven B&B, 83848 208-443-3011
North Fork	100 Acre Wood B&B-Resort, Box 202, 83466 208-865-2165
North Fork	Indian Creek Guest Ranch, HC 64 Box 105, 83466 208-394-2126
Oakley	Poulton's B&B, 200 E. Main St, 83346 208-682-3649
Old Town	All Aboard B&B, Rt 2 Box 453, 83822 208-437-2593
Pierce	Cedar Inn, PO Box 494, 83546 208-464-2704
Pocatello	Back O' Beyond Victorian, 404 S Garfield Ave, 83204 208-232-3825
Pocatello	Dan Schroeder, 1741 Satterfield, 83201
Pocatello	Hales Half Acre B&B, Rt 2, Box 26, 83202 208-237-7130
Pocatello	Z B&B, 620 S 8th, 83201 888-235-1095
Post Falls	River Cove, PO Box 1862, 83854 208-773-9190
Priest Lake	Whispering Waters B&B, HRC 5, Box 125B, 83856 208-443-3229
Rexburg	Porter House B&B, 4232 W 1000 N, 83440 208-356-6632
Ririe	Granite Creek Guest Ranch, 392 N 4500 E, 83443 208-538-7140
Sagle	Pinewoods B&B, 1065 Lignite Rd., 83860 208-263-5851
Salmon	Country Cottage Inn, 401 S Saint Charles St, 83467 208-756-8114
Salmon	Heritage Inn, 510 Lena St, 83467 208-756-3174
Salmon	Syringa Lodge, 2000 Syringa Dr, 83467 208-756-4424
Sandpoint	Coit House B&B, 502 N. Fourth St, 83864 208-265-4035
Sandpoint	Green Gables Lodge, 10000 Schweitzer Mnt., 83864 208-263-0257
Sandpoint	Page House, 506 N. 2nd, 83864 208-263-6584
Sandpoint	Schweitzer Mountain B&B, 110 Crystal Ct, 83864 208-265-8080
Sandpoint	Serendipity Country Inn, 305 W Dearborn St, 83864 208-265-9049
Sandpoint	Whitaker House, 410 Railroad Ave. #10, 83864 208-263-0816
Shoshone	Governor's Manion, PO Box 326, 83352 208-886-2858
Shoup	Smith House B&B, 49 Salmon River Rd, 83469 208-394-2121
Spirit Lake	Fireside Lodge, PO Box 445, 83869 208-623-2871
St. Anthony	Riverview B&B, 155 E. 3rd S, 83445 208-624-4323
St. Maries	Fort Hemenway Manor, 1101 W Jefferson Ave, 83861
Stanley	Redfish Lake Lodge, PO Box 9, 83278 208-774-3536
Sun Valley	High Country Motel, PO Box 197, 83313 208-788-2050
Sun Valley	Idaho Country Inn, PO Box 2355, 83353 208-726-1019
Swan Valley	Swan Valley B&B, PO Box 115, 83449 208-483-4663
Tensed	Seven Springs Farm B&B, HCR 1, Box 310, 83870 208-274-2470
Tetonia	Teton Sunrise Inn, 313 N 200 W, 83452 208-456-2777
Wallace	Beale House B&B, 107 Cedar St, 83873

Illinois

Aledo	The Great Escape, 309 S College Ave., 61231 309-582-3001
Algonquin	Victorian Rose Garden, 314 Washington St., 60102 847-854-9667
Alton	Jackson House, 1821 Seminary St, 62002 618-462-1426
Anna	The Goddard Place, 1585 Campground Road, 62906 618-833-6256
Antioch	Serendipity B&B, 18863 W Stateline Rd., 60002 847-838-5212
Arcola	Curley's Corner B&B, 425 E. Country Rd 200 N, 61910 217-268-3352
Arcola	The Flower Patch, 225 East Jefferson, 61910 217-268-4876
Arthur	The Village Inn B&B, 525 S Pine St., 61911 217-543-3605
Athens	Bailey House, PO Box 206, 62613 217-636-7695
Atwood	At the Woods B&B & Antique, 250 N 1500 E, 61913 217-578-3784
Atwood	Harshbarger Homestead, PO Box 110, 61913 217-578-2265
Batavia	Villa Batavia, 1430 S Batavia Ave, 60510 630-406-8182
Beardstown	Nostalgia Corner, 115 W. 7th, 62618 217-323-5382
Belknap	Bridges B&B, 425 Bridges Lane, 62908 618-777-2946

Belle Rive	Enchanted Crest, PO Box 216, 62810 618-736-2647
Bishop Hill	The Colony Hospital B&B, 110 N Olson, 61419 309-927-3506
Breese	Timmerman House B&B, 6130 Old Hwy 50, 62230 618-228-7068
Brighton	God's Whispering, RR 1, Box 27B, 62012 618-372-0147
Buncombe	Valley View Cabin B&B, 7025 Lick Creek Rd, 62912 618-833-6356
Cairo	Windham, 2606 Washington Ave, 62914 618-734-3247
Carlinville	Victoria Tyme Inn, 511 E. First South St, 62626 217-854-8689
Carlyle	Country Haus B&B Inn, 1191 Franklin, 62231 618-594-8313
Champaign	Burke's Country Inn B&B, 2804 Pine Valley Dr, 61821 217-359-3332
Champaign	Grandma Joan's B&B, 2204 Brett Dr, 61820 217-356-5828
Champaign	Norma's Hideaway, 1714 Scottsdale Dr, 61821 217-359-5876
Champaign	The Glads B&B, RR 3, Box 69, 61821 217-586-4345
Charleston	Lincolnland B&B, PO Box 422, 61920 217-345-2711
Chicago	B&B Lincoln Park/Sheffield, 2022 N Sheffield, 60614 773-327-6546
Chicago	Flemish House of Chicago, 68 E Cedar St, 60611 312-664-9981
Chicago	Gregory House, W Gregory St, 60640 773-878-3019
Chicago	Lake Shore Drive B&B, PO Box 148643, 60614 773-404-5500
Chicago	Old Town B&B, 1442 N North Park Ave, 60610 312-440-9268
Chicago	The Heritage B&B, 75 E Wacker Dr,St 3600, 60601 312-857-0800
Chicago	The Inn on Early B&B, 1241 W Early Ave, 60660 773-334-4666
Chillicothe	Homolka House, 721 Fifth St, 61523 309-274-5925
Cobden	Shawnee Hill B&B, 290 Water Valley Rd, 62920 618-893-2211
Collinsville	Happy Wanderer Inn, 309 Collinsville Ave., 62234 618-344-0477
Collinsville	Maggie's Bed & Breakfast, 2102 North Keebler Rd, 62234 618-344-8283
Dahinda	The Barn B&B, Box 92, 61428 309-639-4408
Dallas City	1850's Guest House, PO Box 267, 62330 217-852-3652
Danforth	Fannie's House B&B, PO Box 194, 60930 815-269-2145
Danville	The Bookwalter House, 1701 N. Logan Ave, 68132 217-443-5511
Decatur	Younker House B&B, 500 W Main, 62522
Dundee	Ironhedge Inn B&B, 305 Oregon Ave, 60118 708-426-7777
East Peoria	Ami's E. Inn B&B, 137 Spring St, 61611 309-699-8646
East Peoria	Red Barn B&B, 1451 Highview Rd., 61611 309-694-6079
East St Louis	Parker Garden B&B, 2310 State St, 62205 888-298-3834
Effingham	Garnet Hall B&B, 1007 S 4th, 62401 217-342-5584
Eldred	Bluffdale Vacation Farm, Rt. 1, Box 145, 62027 217-983-2854
Elizabeth	Brookside B&B, 1298 E Menzemer Rd, 61028
Elizabeth	Forget-Me-Not B&B, 1467 N. Elizabeth Scale, 61028 815-858-3744
Elsah	Corner Nest B&B, PO Box 220, 62028 618-374-1892
Elsah	Green Tree Inn, PO Box 96, 62028 618-374-2821
Fairfield	Glass Door Inn, R.R. 3, Box 101, 62837 618-847-4512
Freeburg	The Westerfield House, 8059 Jefferson Rd, 62243 618-539-5643
Galena	Aldrich Guest House, 900 Third St, 61036 815-777-3323
Galena	Avery Guest House B&B, 606 S. Prospect St, 61036 815-777-3883
Galena	Belle Aire Mansion, 11410 Route 20 W, 61036 815-777-0893
Galena	Brierwreath Manor, 216 N. Beach St, 61036 815-777-0608
Galena	Cloran Mansion B&B, 1237 Franklin St., 61036 815-777-0583
Galena	Craig Cottage, 505 Dewey Ave., 61036 815-777-1461
Galena	Early American Settlement, PO Box 250, 61036 815-777-4200
Galena	Farster's Executive Inn, 305 N. Main St, 61036 815-777-9125
Galena	Felt Manor Guest House, 125 N. Prospect St, 61036 800-383-2830
Galena	Grandview Guest Home, 113 S. Prospect St, 61036 815-777-1387
Galena	Hellman Guest House, 318 Hill St, 61036 815-777-3638
Galena	John Henry B&B Guest House, 812 S Beach St, 61036 815-777-3595
Galena	Main St. Inn, 404 S. Main St, 61036 815-777-3454
Galena	Mars Avenue Guest House, 515 Mars Ave, 61036 815-777-2808
Galena	Meadows House, 1004 Park Ave, 61036
Galena	Spring Street Guest House, 414 Spring St, 61036 815-777-0354
Galena	The Goldmoor, 9001 Sand Hill Rd, 61036 815-777-3925
Galena	The Inn at Irish Hollow, 2800 S Irish Hollow Rd, 61036
Galena	Wild Turkey B&B, 1048 N. Clark Ln, 61036 815-858-3649
Galesburg	Fahnestock House, 591 N Prairie St, 61401 309-344-0270
Galesburg	Seacord House, 624 N. Cherry St, 61401 309-342-4107
Galesburg	The Great House, 501 E. Losey St, 61401 309-342-8683
Geneva	Oscar Swan Country Inn, 1800 W. State St, 60134 630-232-0173
Geneva	The Herrington Inn, 17 No. First St, 60134
Golcanda	Mansion of Golconda, PO Box 339, 62938 618-683-4400
Grafton	Tara Point Inn, PO Box 640, 62037
Grafton	Wildflower Inn B&B, PO Box 31, 62037 618-465-3719
Grand Detour	The Colonial Rose Inn, 8230 S. Green St, 61021 815-652-4422
Grant Park	Bennett Curtis House, 302 W. Taylor, 60940 815-465-6025
Greenville	Prairie House Country Inn, RR 4, PO Box 47AA, 62246 618-664-3003
Greenville	The Rench House, 316 W Main St, 62246 618-664-9698
Gurnee	Sweet Basil Hill Farm, 15937 W. Washington St, 60031 708-244-3333
Harrisburg	House of Nahum, 90 Sally Holler Ln, 62946 618-252-1414
Harrisburg	White Lace Inn, 204 W. Poplar St, 62946 618-252-7599
Havana	McNutt Guest House, 409 W. Main St, 62644 309-543-3295
Highland	Phyllis's B&B, 801 9th St., 62249 618-654-4619
Highland	Tibbetts House B&B, 801 9th St, 62249 618-654-4619

Hillsboro	Breakfast in the Country, 1750 E. St Rt #133, 61930 217-346-2739
Hillsboro	Red Rooster Inn, 123 E. Seward St, 62049 217-532-6332
Jerseyville	The Homeridge B&B, 1470 N. State St, 62052 618-498-3442
Jonesboro	Trail of Tears Lodge, 1575 Fair City Rd, 62952 618-833-8697
Junction	The Thomas House, 12680 Hwy 1, 62954 618-272-7046
Kankakee	Norma's B&B, 429 So. Fourth Ave, 60901
Kansas	Cottonwood, RR 1 Box 229, 61933
Knoxville	Knox Station Bed & Rails, 976 Mine Rd, 61448 309-289-4047
Knoxville	Walnut Tree House, 112 W Main St., 61448 309-289-6933
Lanark	Victorian Lace, 326 E Prairie, 61046 815-493-2546
Lena	Sugar Maple Inn, 607 Maple, 61048 815-369-2786
Lincoln	Prairie Fields Inn B&B, R.R. 3, Hwy 121, 62656 217-732-7696
Lombard	The Whitney House, 741 W Sunset Ave, 60148 815-456-2526
Macomb	The Brockway House, 331 E. Carroll, 61455 309-837-2375
Macomb	The Pineapple Inn, 204 W. Jefferson, 61455 309-837-1914
Maeystown	Corner George Inn, PO Box 103, 62256 618-458-6660
Mendota	Elizabeth's B&B, 1100 5th St, 61342 815-539-5555
Mendota	Lord Stocking's, 803 3rd Ave, 61342 815-539-7905
Minonk	Victorian Oaks B&B, 435 Locust, 61760 309-432-2771
Moline	River Drive Guest House, 4326 River Dr, 61625
Monticello	Linda's Country Loft B&B, 1199 Sandra Lane, 61856 217-762-7316
Mossville	Old Church House Inn, 1416 E. Mossvill Rd, 61552 309-579-2300
Mount Carmel	Living Legacy Homestead BB, Box 146A, 62863 618-298-2476
Mt. Carroll	Country Palmer House, 17035 Elizabeth Rd, 61053 815-244-2343
Mt. Carroll	Prairie Path Guest House, 1002 N. Lowden Rd, 61053 815-244-3462
Mt. Carroll	The Farm, 8239 Mill Rd, 61053 815-244-9885
Mt. Morris	Kable House, Sunset Hill, 61054 815-734-7297
Mundelein	Round-Robin B&B, 231 East Maple Ave, 60060 847-566-7664
Naperville	Harrison House B&B, 26 N. Eagle St, 60540 708-420-1117
Nashville	Mill Creek Inn, 560 N. Mill, 62263 618-327-8424
Nauvoo	Mississippi Memories B&B, Box 291, 62354 217-453-2771
Nauvoo	The Ancient Pines B&B, 2015 Parkley St, 62354 217-453-2767
Nebo	Harpole's Heartland Lodge, Rt 1 Box 8A, 62355 217-222-0899
Oak Park	Cheney House, 520 N.E Ave, 60302 708-524-2067
Oak Park	Toad Hall, 301 N. Scoville Ave, 60302 708-386-8623
Oak Park	Under The Ginkgo Tree, 300 N Kenilworth Ave, 60302 708-524-2327
Oakland	Inn-on-the-Square, 3 Montgomery St, 61943 217-346-2289
Oakland	Johnson's Country Home B&B, 109 E. Main St, 61943 217-346-3274
Oglesby	Brightwood Inn, 2407 N 11 Rt. 178, 61354 815-667-4600
Olney	Rich's Inn, PO Box 581, 62450 618-392-3821
Onarga	Dairy on the Prairie, R.R. 2, Box 185, 60955 815-683-2774
Oregon	Pinehill B&B, 400 Mix St, 61061 815-732-2061
Oswego	Gilbert Gaylord House B&B, 1542 Plainfield Rd, 60543
Ottawa	Marcia's B&B, 3003 N. Rt. 71, 61350 815-434-5217
Ottawa	Prairie Rivers B&B, 121 E Prospect Ave., 61350 815-434-3226
Paris	The Madison, 300 W Madison St, 61944
Paris	Tiara Manor, 302 W Crawford St, 61944 800-531-1865
Paxton	Westlawn Manor, 139 Elm, 60957 217-379-2594
Pekin	Herget House, 420 Washington, 61554 309-353-4025
Peoria	Ruth's B&B, 10205 Eva Ln, 61615 309-243-5977
Peoria	Wildlife Prairie Park B&B, 3826 N Taylor Rd, 61600
Petersburg	Bit of Country B&B, 122 W. Sheridan, 61615 217-632-3771
Petersburg	Robert Frackelton House, 207 S. 12th, 62675 217-632-4496
Petersburg	The Oaks B&B, 510 W. Sheridan Rd, 61615 217-632-4480
Pinckneyville	Oxbow B&B, PO Box 47, 62274 618-357-9839
Plymouth	Plymouth Rock Resort, 201 W. Summer, 62367 309-458-6444
Port Byron	The Olde Brick House, 502 No. High St, 61275 309-523-3236
Prairie Du Rocher	La Maison du Rocher Inn, 2 Duclos & Main, 62277 618-284-3463
Princeton	The Phoenix Inn, 1930 S Main St, 61356
Princeton	Yesterday's Memories, 303 East Peru St, 61359 815-872-7753
Quincy	The Kaufmann House, 1641 Hampshire, 62301 217-223-5202
Red Bud	Magnolia Place, 317 S. Main, 62278 618-282-4141
Richmond	Gazebo House B&B, 10314 East St., 60071 815-678-2505
Robinson	The Heath Inn, PO Box 322, 62454 618-544-3410
Rock Island	The Potter House, 1906 - 7th Ave, 61201 309-788-1906
Rock Island	Top O' The Morning B&B Inn, 1505 - 19th Ave, 61201 309-786-3513
Rockford	The Barn of Rockford, 6786 Guilford Rd, 61107
Rossville	The Farmhouse B&B, 11786 E. 3550 N. Rd, 60963 217-748-6505
Rushville	Bottenberg B&B, 505 N Liberty St., 62681 217-322-6100
Salem	Badollet House, 401 N Jefferson, 62881 618-548-0982
Salem	Salem Creamery Company B&B, 401 N. Jefferson, 62881 618-548-0982
Savanna	Granny O'Neil's River Inn, 31 3rd St, 61074 815-273-4726
Savoy	Shurts House Inn, 1001 N Dunlap, 61874 217-398-4444
Scales Mound	The Franklin House B&B, 701 N Franklin St., 61075 815-845-2304
Sesser	The Hill House, 503 S. Locust, 62884 618-625-6064
St. Charles	Charleston Guest House, 612 W Mian St, 60174 708-377-1277
St. Charles	Cornfields "Grotto", 3N698 Bittersweet Rd, 60175 630-584-3376
Sullivan	Little House OnThe Prairie, PO Box 525, 61951 217-728-4727

Sycamore	Country Charm Inn, 15165 Quigley Rd, 60178 815-895-5386
Sycamore	Stratford Inn, 355 W. State St, 60178 815-895-6789
Taylorville	Market Street Inn, 220 East Market Street, 62568 217-824-7220
Toulon	Rockwell Victorian B&B, 404 N. Washington, 61483 309-286-5201
Tuscola	Quiet Crossing, RR 2 Box 257, 61953 217-253-5637
Tuscola	Sutter's B&B, 400 S. Main St, 61953 217-253-5270
Urbana	Shurts House In Urbana, 710 W. Oregon St, 61810 217-367-8793
Villa Grove	Four Oaks Inn, 73 Willow Ln, 61956 217-832-9313
Warrenville	The Silver Key B&B, 3S674 Melcher Ave, 60555
Waterloo	Senator Rickert Residence, 216 E. Third St, 62298 618-939-8242
Waterloo	The Painted Lady, 116 S Market, 62236 618-939-5545
Watseka	The Razzano House, 210 S 5th, 60970 815-432-4240
Wenona	Hart of Wenona, 303 North Walnut, 61377 815-853-4778
West Dundee	Ironhedge Inn B&B, 305 Oregon, 60118 708-426-7777
West Salem	Thelma's Bed & Breakfast, 201 South Broadway, 62476 618-456-8401
Wheaton	The Wheaton Inn, 301 W Roosevelt Rd, 60187 630-690-2600
Williamsville	Bed & Breakfast at Edie's, PO Box 351, 62693 217-566-2538
Windsor	Deerfield B&B, R.R. 1, Box 99A, 61957 217-459-2750
Winnebago	The Victorian Veranda B&B, 8430 W. State Rd, 61088 815-963-1337
Yorkville	The Fox and Hounds B&B, 201 E Jackson St., 60560 630-553-1369

Indiana

Alexandria	Country Gazebo Inn, RR 1, Box 323, 46001 317-754-8783
Alexandria	Inter Urban Inn, 503 S. Harrison, 46001 317-724-2001
Anderson	Plum Retreat, 926 Historic W 8th St, 46016
Angola	Chef's Nest B&B, 417 E Maumee, 46703 219-665-9080
Angola	Potawatomi Inn, 6 Lane 100 A Lake James, 46703 219-833-1077
Angola	Sycamore Hill, 1245 S. Golden Lake Rd, 46703 219-665-2690
Angola	Tulip Tree Inn B&B, 411 N Wayne St, 46703 219-668-7000
Atlanta	Asher Walton House, 100 E Main St., 46031 765-292-2422
Attica	Apple Inn Museum B&B, PO Box 145, 47918 317-762-6574
Auburn	Hill Top Country Inn, 921 Golden Hawk Dr, 46706 219-281-2529
Auburn	Yawn to Dawn B&B, 211 W 5th St, 46706 219-925-2583
Austin	Carousel Inn B&B, 190 N High St, 47102 812-794-2360
Austin	Morgan's Farm, 730 West St Rd 256, 47102 812-794-2536
Bainbridge	Sycamore Island Get Away, Rt 1 Box 178C, 46105
Batesville	The Sherman House, PO Box 67, 47006 812-934-2407
Berne	Hans Haus of Berne, PO Box 182, 46711 219-589-3793
Bethlehem	Inn at Bethlehem, 101 Walnut St, 47104 812-293-3975
Bloomington	Scholars Inn, 801 N. Gollege, 47404 800-765-3466
Bluffton	Washington Street Inn, 220 Washington St, 46714 219-824-9070
Bluffton	Wisteria Manor, 1140 W 300 N, 46714 219-824-4619
Brookville	Duck Creek Farm B&B, 12246 SR 1, 47012 317-647-4575
Brookville	Sulina Farm, 10052 U.S. 52, 47012 317-647-2955
Cannelton	Castlebury Inn, 615 Washinston, 47520 812-547-4714
Centerville	Historic Lantz House Inn, 214 National Rd W, 47330 317-855-2936
Columbus	Country Chalet, 624 N Hickory Hills Dr, 47201 812-342-7806
Columbus	Ruddick-Nugent House, 1210 16th St, 47201 812-379-1354
Columbus	The Columbus Inn B&B, 445 5th St, 47201 812-378-4289
Connersville	Maple Leaf Inn B&B, 831 N Grand Ave, 47331 765-825-7099
Corydon	Kinter House Inn, PO Box 95, 47112 812-738-2020
Crawfordsville	Davis House, 1010 W. Wabash Ave, 47933 317-364-0461
Crawfordsville	Sugar Creek's Queen Anne, PO Box 726, 47933 800-392-6293
Danville	Fairhavens, 320 W. Main St, 46122 317-745-0417
Danville	Marigold Manor, 368 W. Main St, 46122 317-745-2347
Decatur	Cragwood Inn B&B, 303 N Second St, 46733 219-728-2000
Evansville	Brigadoon B&B Inn, 1240 SE 2nd St, 47713 812-422-9635
Evansville	The River's Inn, 414 SE Riverside Dr., 47713 812-428-7777
Fishers	The Frederick-Talbott Inn, 13805 Allisonville Rd, 46038 317-578-3600
Fort Wayne	At The Herb Lady's Garden, 8214 Maysville Rd, 46815
Fort Wayne	Carole Lombard House, 704 Rockhill St, 46802 219-426-9896
Goshen	B&B on the Farm, 26620 C.R. 40, 46526 219-862-4600
Goshen	Front Porch Inn, 320 S Fifth St., 46528 219-533-4258
Goshen	Garbers Guesthouse B&B, 24641 CR 142, 46526 219-875-6606
Goshen	Indian Creek B&B, 20300 Cr. 18, 46526 219-875-6606
Goshen	Ol' Barn B&B, 63469 C.R. 33, 46526 219-642-3222
Goshen	Royer's, 22781 C.R. 38, 46526 219-533-1821
Goshen	Spring View B&B, 63189 C.R. 31, 46526 219-642-3997
Goshen	The Checkerberry Inn, 62644 CR 37, 46526 219-642-4445
Goshen	Waterford B&B, 3004 S. Main St, 46526 219-533-6044
Goshen	Whippoorwill Valley Inn, 63763 CR 11, 46526 219-875-5746
Goshen	White Birch B&B, 17200 Institutional Dr, 46526 219-533-3763
Goshen	Woody Acres, 64588 CR 15, 46526 219-875-8294
Greencastle	Walden Inn of Greencastle, PO Box 490, 46135 317-653-2761
Greenville	Stone Rest B&B Inn, 8757 Rufing Rd., 47124 219-923-8242
Greenwood	Candlestick Inn, 402 Euclid Ave, 46142 317-888-3905
Greenwood	Persimmon Tree B&B, 1 N Madison Ave., 46132 317-889-0849

Hagerstown	The Teetor House, 498 S Washington St, 47346 317-489-4422
Hartford City	Stitch in Time Country Inn, 201 Westwood Dr., 47348 765-348-2548
Howe	Lasata B&B, PO Box 131, 46746 219-562-3655
Huntington	Purviance House B&B, 326 S. Jefferson, 46750 219-356-4218
Indianapolis	Boone Docks on the River, 7159 Edgewater Pl, 46240 317-257-3671
Indianapolis	Harney House Inn, 345 N. East St, 46202 317-636-7527
Indianapolis	Old Northside B&B Inn, 1340 N Alabama St, 46202 317-635-9123
Indianapolis	Stonegate B&B, 8955 A Stonegate Rd, 46227 317-887-9614
Indianapolis	The Frederick-Talbott Inn, 13805 Allisonville Rd, 46038 317-578-3600
Indianapolis	The Hoffman House, 545 E 11th St, 46202 317-635-1701
Indianapolis	The Nuthatch B&B, 1241 River Heights Rd, 46240 317-257-2660
Jamestown	Oakwood B&B, 9530 W. US Hwy 136, 46147 317-676-5114
Jeffersonville	1877 House Country Inn, 1408 Utica-Sellersburg, 47130
Kendallville	McCray Mansion Inn, 703 E Mitchell St., 46755 219-347-3647
Koontz Lake	Koontz House B&B, 7514 N. Hwy 23, 46574 219-586-7090
La Grange	Atwater Century Farm, 4240 W. US 20, 46761 219-463-2743
La Grange	M & N B&B, 215 N. Detroit, 46761 219-463-2699
Ladoga	Vintage Reflections, 125 W. Main St, 47954 317-942-1002
Lafayette	Harmony Farm B&B, 3930 S 950 E, 47905 765-474-1293
Lafayette	Historic Loeb House Inn, 708 Cincinnati St., 47901 765-420-7737
Laotto	Tea Rose B&B, 7711 E. 500 S, 46763 219-693-2884
Lapel	Kati-Scarlett B&B, PO Box 756, 46051 317-534-4937
Laurel	Ferris Inn, PO Box 197, 47024 317-698-2259
Lawrenceburg	Aurora Inn, 19330 Alpine Dr, 47025 812-926-4412
Lawrenceburg	Folke Family Farm, PO Box 66, 47025 812-537-7025
Leesburg	Prairie House B&B, 495 E. 900 N, 46538 219-658-9211
Leo	Pathfinder Country Inn, 8727 Gerig Rd, 46765 219-636-2888
Ligonier	Minuette, 210 S. Main St, 46767 219-894-4494
Loogootee	Stone Ridge Manor B&B, 612 Kentucky Ave, 47553 812-295-3382
Madison	Carriage House B&B, 308 W 2nd St, 47250 812-265-6892
Madison	Cliff House B&B, 122 Fairmount Dr, 47250 812-265-5272
Madison	Main Street B&B, 302 Elm St, 47250 812-265-3539
Marion	Golden Oak B&B, 809 W 4th St, 46952
Marshall	Turkey Run Inn, R.R. 1 Box 444, 47859 317-597-2211
Metamora	Gingerbread House, PO Box 28, 47030 317-647-5518
Metamora	Grapevine Inn, PO Box 207, 47030 317-647-3738
Metamora	Publick House, PO Box 202, 47030 317-647-6729
Metamora	Thorpe House Country Inn, PO Box 36, 47030 317-647-5425
Michigan City	Bennett's Motel B&B, 10303 NE US Hwy 12, 46360 219-872-0212
Michigan City	Creekwood Inn, Rt 20/35 at I-94, 46360 219-872-8357
Middlebury	Auer House, 11584 C R 14, 46540 219-825-5366
Middlebury	Bittersweet Hill, PO Box 1147, 46540 219-852-5953
Middlebury	Bontreger Guest Rooms, 10766 C.R. 16, 46540 219-825-2647
Middlebury	Empty Nest B&B, 13347 C R 12, 46540 219-825-1042
Middlebury	Lookout B&B, 14544 CR 12, 46540 219-825-9809
Middlebury	Mill Street B&B, PO Box 91, 46540 219-825-5359
Middlebury	That Pretty Place B&B Inn, 212 US Hwy 20, 46540 219-725-3021
Middlebury	The Country Victorian B&B, 435 South Main St, 46540 219-825-2568
Middlebury	The Tayler House, PO Box 1131, 46540 219-825-7296
Middlebury	Theora's B&B, PO Box 2040, 46540 219-825-2242
Middlebury	Varns Guest House, PO Box 93, 46540 219-825-9666
Middlebury	Windmill Hideaway B&B, 11380 W. SR 120, 46540 219-825-2939
Middlebury	Yoder's Zimmer, PO Box 1396, 46540 219-825-2378
Middletown	Country Rode B&B, 5098 N.Mechanicsburg Rd, 47356 317-779-4501
Middletown	Maple Hill B&B, 9909 N.C.R. 600W, 47356 317-354-2580
Millersburg	Big House in Little Woods, 4245 S. 1000 W, 46543 219-593-9076
Mishawaka	Beiger Mansion Inn, 317 Lincoln Way E, 46544 219-256-0365
Mishawaka	Kamm House, 617 Lincolnway W, 46544 800-664-5790
Mitchell	Spring Mill Inn, PO Box 68, 47446 812-849-4081
Monon	Bestemor's House B&B, 201 Market Box 205, 47959 219-253-8351
Monticello	1887 Black Dog Inn, 2830 Untalulti, 47960 219-583-8297
Monticello	The Victoria B&B, 206 S. Bluff St, 47960 219-583-3440
Monticello	Zimmer Frei Haus, 409 N Main St, 47960 219-583-4061
Morgantown	Rock House Country Inn, PO Box 10, 46160 812-597-5100
Muncie	Ole Ball Inn B&B, 1000 W. Wayne St, 47304 317-281-0466
Nappanee	Homespun Country Inn, PO Box 369, 46550 219-773-2034
Nappanee	Market Street Guest House, 253 E. Market St, 46550 219-773-2261
Nappanee	Olde Buffalo Inn, 1061 Parkwood Dr, 46550 800-272-2135
Nappanee	Victorian Guest House, 302 E. Market, 46550 219-773-4383
Nashville	Abe Martin Lodge, PO Box 547, 47448 812-988-4418
Nashville	Always Inn B&B, 8026 E State Rd 46, 47448 812-988-2233
Nashville	Artists Colony Inn, PO Box 1099, 47448 812-988-0600
Nashville	Aspen Leaf Inn, 2785 Clay Lick Rd., 47448 812-988-0073
Nashville	Cornerstone Inn, PO Box 275, 47448 812-988-0300
Nashville	Fifth Generation Farm, 4564 N. Bear Wallow Rd, 47448 812-988-7553
Nashville	Orchard Hill Inn, 1958 N State Rd 135, 47448 812-988-4455
New Albany	Honeymoon Mansion B&B, 1014 E. Main St, 47150 812-945-0312
New Castle	Country Haven Inn, 395 N.C.R. 300 W, 47362 317-533-6611

New Harmony	Raintree Inn B&B, PO Box 566, 47631 812-682-5625
North Webster	Backwater Bend B&B, 9266 E. Backwater Rd., 46555 219-834-2118
North Webster	Sunset House B&B, 7463 E. Sunset Trail, 46555 219-834-1621
Osgood	Victorian Garden B&B, 243 N Walnut St, 47037 812-689-4469
Paoli	Big Locust Farms, 3295 W.C.R 25 S, 47454 812-723-4856
Paoli	Braxtan House Inn B&B, 210 N. Gospel St, 47454 812-723-4677
Pendleton	Snoozy Goose B&B, 311 S Broadway, 46064 765-778-4546
Peru	Rosewood Mansion Inn, 54 North Hood St, 46970 765-472-7151
Plymouth	Driftwood, PO Box 16, 46563 219-546-2274
Porter	Spring House Inn, 303 N Mineral Springs, 46304 219-929-4600
Richmond	Norwich Lodge, 920 Earlham Dr, 47374 317-983-1575
Richmond	Philip W. Smith B&B, 2039 E Main St, 47374 765-966-8972
Rising Sun	Mulberry Inn & Gardens B&B, 118 S Mulberry St., 47040 812-438-2206
Rockport	Rockport Inn, 130 S. Third St, 47635 812-649-2664
Rockport	Trail's End B&B, 47635 502-771-5590
Salem	Lanning House, 206 E. Poplar St, 47167 812-883-3484
San Pierre	Lomax Station B&B Cabins, 3153 S 900 W, 46374 800-535-6629
Schererville	Sunset Pines B&B, 862 Sunset Dr., 46375 219-322-3322
Shipshewana	Green Meadow Ranch, 7905 W. 450 N, 46565 219-768-4221
Shipshewana	Morton Street B&B, PO Box 775, 46565 219-768-4391
Shipshewana	Old Carrriage Inn, 140 Farver St., 46565 219-768-7217
Shipshewana	Shipshewana Amish Log Cabi, 5970 N ST 5, 46565 219-768-7770
Shipshewana	Tyler's Place, 2540 N 900 W, 46565 219-848-7145
Shipshewana	Weaver's Country Oals, PO Box 632 0310 US 20, 46565 219-768-7191
South Bend	Home B&B, 21166 Clover Hill Ct, 46614 219-291-0535
South Bend	Home Based B&B, 18401 Gardenia Dr., 46637 219-271-0989
South Bend	Irish Country B&B, PO Box 8291, 46660 219-243-2981
South Bend	Jamison Inn, 1404 N. Ivy Rd, 46637 219-277-9682
South Bend	Queen Anne Inn, 420 W Washington St, 46601 219-234-5959
Spencer	Canyon Inn, PO Box 71, 47460 812-829-4881
Syracuse	Anchor Inn, 11007 N State Rd 13, 46567 219-457-4714
Syracuse	Victoria Bay B&B, 300 E Main St, 46567 219-457-5374
Tippecanoe	Bessinger's Hillfarm B&B, 4588 SR 110, 46570 219-223-3288
Topeka	Four Woods B&B, 4800 South SR 5, 46571 219-593-2021
Unionville	Possum Trot B&B, 8310 N. Possum Trot Rd, 47468 812-988-2694
Unionville	Slippery Elm Shoot Inn, 5365 Tailhook Lane, 47468 812-988-2377
Vincennes	The Harrison Inn, 902 Buntin St, 47591 812-882-3243
W. College Corner	The Doctor's Inn, PO Box 663, 47003 765-732-3772
Wabash	Around Window Inn, 313 W. Hill St, 46992 219-563-6901
Wabash	Lamp-Post Inn, 261 W. Hill St, 46992 219-563-3094
Wakarusa	Farmwood B&B, 27473 County Rd 42, 46573
Walkerton	Hesters Cabin B&B, 71880 S.R. 23, 46574 219-568-2105
Walkerton	Koontz House B&B, R.R. 3 Box 592, 46574 219-586-7090
Warsaw	Candlelight Inn, 503 E. Fort Wayne St, 46580 219-267-2906
Warsaw	Ramada White Hill Manor BB, 2513 E Center St, 46580 219-269-6933
West Baden	E. B. Rhodes B&B, PO Box 7, 47469 812-936-7378
West Lafayette	Commandant's Home B&B, 3848 State Rd 43 N, 47906 765-463-5980
Westfield	Camel Lot, 4512 W. 131st St, 46074 317-873-4370
Westfield	Country Roads Guesthouse, 2731 West 146th St, 46074 317-846-2376
Whiteland	Oak Haven, 4187 E 575 N, 46184 317-535-9491

Iowa

Adel	The Clarke House B&B, 207 N 15 St, 50003 515-993-2199
Adel	The Grey Goose B&B, 1740-290th, 50003 515-833-2338
Akron	Wildflower Log Cabin B&B, Box 1, RR 3, 51001 712-568-2206
Albia	Arvine White House B&B, 309 N Main St, 52531 515-932-3329
Alta	Addie's Place B&B, 121 Cherokee St, 51002 712-284-2509
Ames	Green Belt B&B, RR 2, 50010 515-232-1960
Ames	Iowa House, 138 Gray Ave., 50014 515-292-8870
Aurora	Maxine's B&B, 13 Union St, 50607 319-634-3713
Battle Creek	The Inn at Battle Creek, 201 Maple St, 51006 712-365-4949
Bellevue	Mont Rest Inn, 300 Spring St, 52031 319-872-4220
Bellevue	Spring Side Inn, PO Box 41, 52031 319-872-5452
Bettendorf	The Abbey Hotel, 1401 Central Ave, 52722
Boone	Barkley House B&B, 326 Boone St, 50036 515-432-7885
Brayton	The Hallock House B&B, PO Box 9, 50042 712-549-2449
Buckingham	The ABC Country Inn, 2637 Hwy. D-65, 50612 319-478-2321
Calmar	Calmar Guesthouse B&B, 103 North St, 52132 319-562-3851
Carlisle	Tutte House B&B, 286 Hwy 65/69, 50047 515-287-5162
Carroll	Shari's Garden Home B&B, 827 N Adams St, 51401 712-792-1638
Cedar Falls	Carriage House Inn B&B, 3030 Grand Blvd, 50613 319-277-6724
Cedar Falls	Melody Acres Country B&B, 3609 Knoll Ridge Dr, 50613 319-277-8206
Cedar Rapids	Gwendolyn's B&B, 1809 Second Ave SE, 52403 319-363-9731
Cedar Rapids	Snoozie's B&B, 1570 Hwy. 30 E, 52403 319-364-2134
Centerville	One of a Kind, 314 W. State, 52544 515-437-4540
Charles City	Sherman House B&B, PO Box 457, 50616 515-228-6831
Cherokee	Prairie Path Cabins, 5148 South Ave, 51012

Clarinda	Colonial White House B&B, 400 N. 16th-Glen Miller, 51632 712-542-5006
Clarinda	Paiges of Thyme, 222 W. Washington, 51632 712-542-5796
Clarinda	Westcott House, 510 W. Main, 51632 712-542-5323
Clear Lake	Larch Pine Inn, 401 N. 3rd St, 50428 515-357-7854
Clear Lake	Norsk Hus By-The-Shore, 3611 N. Shore Dr, 50428 515-357-8368
Clear Lake	North Shore House, PO Box 345, 50428 515-357-4443
Clermont	Mill St. B&B, PO Box 34, 52135 319-423-5531
Clermont	The Miller House, 302 Larrabee St., 52135 319-422-5338
Colo	Martha's Vineyard, Box 247, 50056 515-377-2586
Columbus Junction	The Wren's Nest, 711 Second St., 52738 319-728-7145
Conrad	Conrad Grove Guesthouse, PO Box 696, 50621 515-366-2371
Conrad	Makarios Mansion, 31121 Hawk Ave, 50621 515-366-2484
Council Bluffs	Lions Den, 136 S 7th St., 51501 712-322-7162
Council Bluffs	Robin's Nest, 327 9th Ave, 51503 712-323-1649
Council Bluffs	Terra Jane Country Inn, 24814 Greenview Rd, 51503 712-322-4200
Cresco	Corner Inn B&B, 129 6th Ave E, 52136
Davenport	Bishop's House Inn, 1527 Brady St, 52803 319-322-8303
Davenport	Fulton's Landing, 1206 E. River Dr, 52803 319-322-4069
Delmar	Lee Ar's Victorian Retreat, 401 Market, 52037 319-674-4157
Denison	Conner's Corner B&B, 104 S. 15th St, 51442 712-263-8826
Denison	Queen Belle Country Inn, 1430 3rd Ave S, 51442 712-263-6777
Des Moines	Carter House, 640 Twentieth St, 50314 515-288-7850
Des Moines	Jardin Suite, 6653 NW Timberline Dr, 50313 515-289-2280
Dubuque	FitzGerald's Inn B&B, 2988 W 32nd St, 52001 319-538-4872
Dubuque	Juniper Hill Farm B&B, 15325 Budd Rd, 52002 319-582-4405
Dubuque	Lore House-Valleyview, 15937 Lore Mound Rd, 52002
Dubuque	The Redstone Inn, 504 Bluff St, 52001 319-582-1894
Dunlap	The Get-Away, PO Box 109, 51529 712-643-5584
Durango	Another World/Paradise Inn, 16338 Paradise Vly Rd, 52039 319-552-1034
Elk Horn	Joy's Morning Glory B&B, 4308 Main St, 51531 712-764-5631
Elkader	Elkader B&B, PO Box 887, 52043
Emmetsburg	Queen Marie Victorian B&B, 707 Harrison St, 50536 712-852-4700
Fairfield	Polly's B&B, 201 E. Burlington Ave, 52556 515-472-2517
Forest City	1897 Victorian House, 306 S. Clark St, 50436 515-582-3613
Fort Madison	Coffe House, 1020 Avenue D, 52627 319-372-1656
Fort Madison	Kountry Klassics, 2002 295th Ave, 52627 319-372-5484
Galva	Pioneer Farm B&B, RR1 Box 96, 51020
Garner	Mrs. B's B&B, 920 Division St, 50438 515-923-2390
Greenfield	The Brass Lantern, 2446 State Hwy 92, 50849 515-743-2031
Greenfield	The Wilson House, 2446 Hwy 92, 50849 515-743-2031
Grinnell	Clayton Farms, 621 Newburg Rd. 50112 515-236-3011
Guttenberg	Old Brewery B&B, PO Box 217, 52052 319-252-2094
Guttensberg	Candlelight Mountain Inn, 28958 Kale Ave, 52052
Hampton	Country Touch B&B, RR 2, 1034 Hwy 3, 50441 515-456-4585
Hampton	Spring Valley B&B, RR 4, PO Box 47, 50441 515-456-4437
Hartley	Heartland B&B, 120 N Central, 51346 712-728-3494
Hartley	Time Out B&B, 250 W. Maple Dr, 51346 712-728-2213
Homestead	Die Heimat Country Inn, Main St, Amana Colonies, 52236 319-622-3937
Independence	Riverside B&B, 506 2nd Ave SW, 50644 319-334-4100
Indianola	Summerset Inn, 1507 Fairfax, 50125 515-961-3545
Iowa City	Bella Vista Place, 2 Bella Vista Pl, 52245 319-338-4129
Iowa City	Haverkamp Linn St Homestay, 619 N. Linn St, 52245 319-337-4363
Iowa City	Sugar Woods B&B, 14848 Sand Rd SE, 52240
Iowa City	The Brown Street Inn, 430 Brown Street, 52245 319-338-0435
Iowa City	The Golden Haug, 517 E. Washington, 52245 319-338-6452
Keokuk	The Grand Anne B&B, 816 Grand Ave, 52632 319-524-6310
Keosauqua	Hotel Manning, 100 Van Buren St., 52565 319-293-3232
Keosauqua	Mansion Inn, 500 Henry, 52565 319-293-2511
Keosauqua	Mason House/Bentonsport, RR 2, Box 237, 52565 319-592-3133
Keota	Elmhurst, Rt. 1 Box 3, 52248
Knoxville	Strawtown Inn & Lodge, 126 Skyline Dr, 50138
Lake View	Armstrong Inn, 306 5th St, 51450
Lake View	Marie's B&B, PO Box 817, 51450 712-657-2486
Lambs Grove	Aerie Glen B&B, 2364-1st Ave W, 50208 515-792-9032
Lansing	Lansing House, 291 Front St, 52151 319-538-4263
LaPorte City	Brandt's Orchard Inn, 1279 53rd St, 50651 319-342-2912
LeClaire	Country Inn, 22755 282 Ave, 52753
LeClaire	Mississippi Sunrise B&B, 18950 Great River Rd, 52753 319-332-9203
Lucas	Ralph & Norma's Inn, RR 1 Box 28, 50151 515-766-6770
Malcom	Pleasant Country B&B, R.R. #2, Box 23, 50157 515-528-4925
Manilla	B&D's Memory Lane, 3016 Hwy 141, 51454 712-654-4382
Maquoketa	Decker Hotel, 128 N Main St, 52060
Marengo	Loy's B&B, 2077 KK Ave, 52301 319-642-7787
Maynard	Boedeker's Bungalow West, 125 7th St N, 50655 319-637-2711
McGregor	River's Edge B&B, 112 Main St, 52157 319-873-3501
Middle	Dusk to Dawn B&B, Box 124, 52307
Missouri Valley	Apple Orchard Inn, RR 3 Box 129, 51555 712-642-2418
Missouri Valley	Hilltop B&B, 2368 290th St., 51555 712-642-3695

Missouri Valley	White House B&B, 2495 Liberty Ave. #3, 51555 712-642-2827
Mitchellville	Whitaker Farms, 11045 NE 82nd Ave, 50169 515-967-3184
Montpelier	Varner's Caboose, PO Box 10, 52759 319-381-3652
Nevada	Queen Anne B&B, 1110 9th St, 50201 515-382-6444
New London	Old Brick B&B, 2759 Old Hwy 34, 52645 319-367-5403
Nora Springs	Cupola Inn B&B, 20664 Claybanks Dr., 50458 515-422-9272
Oskaloosa	Logan House B&B, 416 B Ave. E, 52577 515-673-6684
Ottumwa	The Guest House B&B, 645 North Court, 52501 515-684-8893
Paullina	White House Inn, PO Box 82, 51046
Pella	Sunset View B&B, PO Box 65, 50219
Postville	Old Shepherd House, 256 W.Tilden, Box 251, 52162 319-864-3452
Prairie City	Country Connection B&B,The, 9737 W 93rd St. S, 50228 515-994-2023
Princeton	The Woodlands Inn B&B, PO Box 127, 52768 319-289-4661
Red Oak	Heritage Hil B&B, 1020 Boundary, 51566
Rockwell City	Pine Grove B&B, 2361 270th St, 50579 712-297-7494
Sabula	The Castle B&B, 616 River St, 52070 319-687-2714
Sac City	Brick Bungalow B&B, 1012 Early St, 50583 800-848-7656
Sac City	Drewry Homestead, 3225 210th St, 50583 712-662-4416
Scotch Grove	Sweet Memories B&B, RR 160th St, 52331 319-465-4112
Scotch Grove	The Grove, 16468 110 Ave., 52331 319-465-3858
Sheldon	Touch of Murray, 802 4th Ave, 51201 712-324-3292
Sioux City	English Mansion B&B, 1525 Douglas, 51105 712-277-1386
Sioux Rapids	Hansen House B&B Inn, PO Box 448, 50585 712-283-2179
South Amana	Babi's B&B, Route 1, Box 66, 52334 319-662-4381
South Amana	Baeckerei, 507 Q St, 52334 319-622-3597
Spencer	Hannah Marie Country Inn, RR 1, 51301 712-262-1286
Spillville	Taylor Made B&B, PO Box 255, 52168 319-562-3958
Spillville	The Old World Inn, PO Box 158, 52168 319-562-3739
Spirit Lake	Francis Hospitality Manor, 608 Lake St, 51360 712-336-4345
St. Ansgar	Blue Belle Inn, PO Box 205, 50472 515-736-2225
Stratford	Hook's Point Farmstead B&B, PO Box 222, 50249 515-838-2781
Stratford	The Valkommen House, PO Box 175, 50249 515-838-2440
Tama	Hoskins House, 1603 Siegel St, 52339
Thurman	Plum Creek Inn, PO Box 91, 51654 712-628-2191
Turin	The Country Homestead B&B, RR 1, Box 53, 51059 712-353-6772
Walnut	Antique City Inn, 400 Antique City Dr, 51577
Walnut	Clark's Country Inn B&B, 701 Walnut St., 51577 712-784-3010
Washington	Quiet Sleeping Room, 125 Green Meadow Dr, 52353
Waterloo	The Daisy Wilton Inn, 418 Walnut St, 50703 319-232-0801
Waterloo	Wellington B&B, 800 West Fourth St, 50702 319-234-2993
Waverly	Villa Fairfield B&B, 523 4th St NW, 50677 319-352-0739
Webster City	Centennial Farm B&B, 1091-220th St, 50595 515-832-3050
West Branch	Inn Nearby the Wapsinonoc, PO Box 209, 52358 319-643-7484
West Des Moines	Ellendale B&B, 5340 Ashworth Rd, 50265 515-225-2219
West Union	Butler House B&B, 214 W Maple Street, 52175 319-422-5944
Whiting	Lighthouse Marina Inn, PO Box 72, 51063 712-458-2066
Whittemore	Prairie Oasis, 5720 430th St, 50598 515-887-4953
Williamsburg	Lucille's Bett Und Brkfast, 2835 225th St, 52361 319-668-1185

Kansas

Abilene	Balfours' House B&B, Rt 2, Box 143 D, 67410 913-263-4262
Abilene	Spruce House, 604 N. Spruce, 67410 913-263-3900
Abilene	Victorian Reflections, 820 NW Third, 67410 913-263-7774
Ashland	Rolling Hills B&B, 204 E. 4th Ave, 67831 316-635-2859
Ashland	The Slaton House, 319 W. 7th, 67831 316-635-2290
Ashland	Wallingford Inn B&B, Box 799, 67831 316-635-2129
Atchison	The Williams House, 526 N. 5th, 66002 913-367-1757
Atwood	Country Corner, PO Box 88, 67730 913-626-9516
Auburn	Lippincott's Fyshe House, 8720 W. 85th St, 66402
Baldwin	Three Sisters Inn, 1035 Ames, 66006
Baldwin City	Grove House, Box 212, 66006
Barnes	Gloria's B&B, PO Box 84, 66933 913-763-4569
Basehor	Bedknobs & Biscuits B&B, 15202 Parallel, 66007 913-724-1540
Brookville	Castle Rock Ranch, 1086 29th Rd., 67425 913-225-6865
Cawker City	Oak Creek Lodge, R.R. 2, 67430
Chapman	Windmill Inn, 1787 Rain Rd, 67431 913-263-8755
Columbus	Maple Common Guesthouse, 120 E Maple, 66725 316-429-3130
Columbus	Meriwether House B&B, 322 W. Pine, 66725 316-429-2812
Cottonwood Falls	The 1874 Stonehouse, RR1 Box 67A, 66845 316-273-8481
Council Grove	Flint Hills B&B, 613 W. Main, 66846 316-767-6655
Dodge City	Boot Hill B&B & Guest Hse, 603 W Spruce, 67801 316-225-7600
Dorrance	Dorrance-The Country Inn, HC 01, Box 59, 67634 913-666-4468
Dorrance	The Country Inn, HC 01, Box 59, 67634 913-666-4468
Dover	Sage Inn, PO Box 24, 66420
Elk Falls	The Sherman House, PO Box 15, 67345
Elkhart	The Cimarron, PO Box 741, 67950 405-696-4672
Ellis	Grape Vine Boarding House, 101 E. 12th, 67637

Elmdale	Clover Cliff Ranch B&B, Rt. 1 Box 30-1, 66850
Emporia	Plumb House B&B, 628 Exchange, 66801 316-342-6881
Emporia	The White Rose Inn B&B, 901 Merchant, 66801 316-343-6336
Enterprise	Ehrsam Place B&B, 103 S Grant, 67441 785-263-8747
Fort Scott	Bennington House, 123 Crescent Dr, 66701 316-223-1837
Fort Scott	Lyon's Victorian Mansion, 742 South National, 66701 800-78-Guest
Fort Scott	The Chenault Mansion, 820 S. National Ave, 66701 316-223-6800
Fort Scott	The Courtland B&B Inn, 121 East First, 66701 316-223-0098
Fowler	Creek Side Farm B&B, Rt. 1, Box 19, 67844 316-646-5586
Girard	La Forge's B&B, 505 N Summit, 66743 316-724-4767
Glasco	Rustic Rememberances B&B, Rt. 1, Box 68, 67445 913-546-2552
Gorham	Runnin S Ranch B&B, 2652 Emmeram Rd, 67640 785-735-2808
Halstead	Nee Murray Way, 220 W. 3rd, 67056 316-835-2027
Hays	Aurora Hill B&B, 898 W. Hwy 40, 67601
Hiawatha	Pleasant Corner, R.R. 5, Box 222, 66434 913-742-7877
Highland	Meadowlark B&B & Tea Room, 207 S. Ives, 66035
Hill City	Pheasant Run B&B, 609 N 4th Ave, 67642 913-674-2955
Hillsboro	Carousel B&B, 312 E A St, 67063 913-989-3537
Hillsboro	Nostalgic B&B Place, 310 South Main, 67063 316-947-3519
Holton	Country Reflections, 20975 "R" Rd, 66436
Hutchinson	Hedrick's B&B Inn & Farm, 7910 N Roy L Smith Rd, 67561 888-489-8039
Independence	Rose Wood B&B, 417 W. Myrtle, 67301 316-331-2221
Lakin	Windy Heights, PO Box 347, 67860 316-355-7699
Leavenworth	Salt Creek Valley B&B, 16425 Fort Riley Rd, 66048 913-651-2277
Lenora	Barbeau House B&B, 210 E. Washington Ave, 67645
Liberal	The Bluebird Inn, 221 W 6th St, 67901
Lindsborg	Morning Mist B&B, 618 N Chestnut St, 67456 785-227-3801
Lindsborg	Smoky Valley B&B, 130 North 2nd Street, 67456 913-227-4460
Lindsborg	Swedish Country Inn, 112 W. Lincoln, 67456 913-227-2985
Louisburg	Red Maple Inn, 201 S. 11th St, 66053
Manhattan	Barbara's B&B, 2132 Blue Hills Rd, 66502 913-776-9738
Manhattan	Colt House Inn, 617 Houston St, 66502 785-776-7500
Manhattan	Guest Hause B&B, 1724 Sheffield Cir, 66503 785-776-6543
Manhattan	Kimble Cliff B&B, 6782 Anderson Ave, 66502 785-539-3816
Marienthal	Krause House, Route 1, Box 42, 67863 316-379-4627
Marion	Country Dreams, Rt. 3, Box 82, 66861 316-382-2250
Marquette	Rustic Remembrances, Box 458, 67464
McPherson	Carnberry House, 1021 N Maple St, 67460 316-241-3331
Melvern	School House Inn, 106 E. Beck, 66510 913-549-3473
Meriden	Village Inn, RR 2, Box 226D, 66512 913-876-2835
Moran	Hedge Apple Acres B&B, 4430 US 54, 66755 316-237-4646
Moundridge	Underhil Farms, 187 21st Ave, 67107
Oberlin	LandMark Inn, 189 S Penn, 67749 785-475-2340
Olathe	Martin Van Buren Parker Hs, 631 W Park, 66061 913-780-4587
Osage City	Rosemary Inn B&B, 210 Market, 66523 913-528-4498
Overbrook	The Pinemoore Inn, R.R. 1, Box 44, 66524 913-453-2304
Overland Park	Heritage House B&B, 12701 Wedd St, 66213
Paola	The Victorian Lady B&B, 402 South Pearl, 66071
Parsons	Bricktoria B&B, 1520 Broadway, 67357 316-423-3000
Pawnee Rock	Ark-River-Inn, RR 1 Box 83A, 67576 316-348-2041
Pleasanton	Cedar Crest, PO Box 387, 66075 913-352-6706
Pratt	Pratt Guest House, PO Box 326, 67124 316-672-1200
Randolph	Shadow Springs Farm, 13170 Tuttle Creek Blvd, 66554
Rose Hill	Queen Anne's Lace B&B, 15335 Queen Anne's Lace, 67133 316-733-4075
Salina	Happy Trail B&B, 507 Montclair Dr, 67401
Scott City	Lady Di's Court B&B, 1520 Court St., 67871 316-872-3348
Sedan	Wild World Inn, 150 E Main, 67361 316-725-5633
Seneca	The Stein House B&B, 314 N. 7th St, 66538
Shawnee Mission	Lebanon's Queen Anne, 8153 Monrovia St, 66215
Tecumseh	Holly House B&B, 4240 McMahan Court, 66542 785-379-5053
Tonganoxie	Almeda's B&B Inn, 220 S Main Box 103, 66086 913-845-2295
Topeka	Brickyard Barn Inn, 4020 NW 25th St, 66618 785-235-0057
Topeka	Heritage House, 3535 SW Sixth Ave, 66606 785-233-3800
Topeka	The Elderberry B&B, 1035 S.W. Fillmore St, 66604 785-235-6309
Topeka	The Senate Luxury Suites, 900 SW Tyler, 66612 785-233-5050
Topeka	The Sunflower B&B, 915 SW Munsion Ave, 66604 785-357-7509
Topeka	The Woodward, 1272 Fillmore, 66604 785-354-7111
Ulysses	Fort's Cedar View, RR 3, Box 120B, 67880 316-356-2570
Valley Falls	The Barn B&B Inn, 14910 Bludemound Rd, 66088 913-945-3225
WaKeeney	Thistle Hill B&B, Rt 1, Box 93, 67672 785-743-2644
Wakefield	Wakefield Country B&B, 197 Sunflower Rd, 67487 913-461-5533
Wamego	Eagle View Inn, 728 Lincoln, 66547 785-456-9053
Wells	Traders Lodge, 1392 210th Rd, 67488 785-488-3930
Wichita	Holiday House-Res. B&B, 8406 W. Maple, 67209 316-721-1968
Wichita	Inn at the Park, 3751 E Douglas, 67218 316-686-2290
Wichita	The Inn at Willowbend, 3939 Comotara, 67226 316-636-4032
Wichita	Vermilion Rose B&B, 1204 N Topeka Ave, 67214 316-267-7636
Winfield	The Iron Gate Inn, 1203 East 9th, 67156

Kentucky

Allensville	Pepper Place, PO Box 95, 42204 502-265-9859
Auburn	David Williams Guest House, 421 West Main St, 42206 502-542-6019
Auburn	Federal Grove B&B, 11115 Bowling Green Rd, 42206 502-542-6106
Augusta	Augusta White House Inn BB, 307 Main St, 41002 606-756-2004
Augusta	Lamplighter Inn, 103 W. 2nd St, 41002 606-756-2603
Augusta	White Rose B&B, 210 Riverside Dr., 41002 606-756-2787
Bardstown	Amber LeAnn B&B, 209 E Stephen Foster, 40004 502-349-0014
Bardstown	Bruntwood Inn, 714 N. 3rd. St, 40004 502-348-8218
Bardstown	Coffee Tree Cabin, 980 McCubbin's Lane, 40004 502-348-1151
Bardstown	Kenmore Farms B&B, 1050 Bloomfield Rd, 40004 502-348-8023
Bardstown	Old Talbott Tavern, 107 W Stephen Foster Av, 40004 502-348-3494
Bardstown	Talbott Tavern, 107 W Stephen Foster, 40004
Bardstown	Victorian Lighthouse B&B, 112 S Third St, 40004 502-348-8087
Bellevue	Mary's Belle View Inn, 444 Van Voast Ave, 41073 606-581-8337
Bellevue	Weller Haus, 319 Poplar St, 41073 606-431-6829
Berea	The Doctor's Inn of Berea, 617 Chestnut St, 40403 606-986-3042
Berea	The Morning Glory B&B, 140 N Broadway St, 40403 606-986-8661
Blaine	The Gambill Mansion, PO Box 98, 41124 606-652-3120
Bloomfield	The Vintage Rose, PO Box 38, 40008 502-252-5042
Boston	The Inn at Tara-Dawn Farm, 14600 Boston Rd, 40107 502-833-4553
Bowling Green	1869 Homestead, 212 Mizpah Rd, 42101 502-842-0510
Bowling Green	Alpine Lodge, 5310 Morgantown Rd, 42101 502-843-4846
Bowling Green	Bowling Green B&B, 3313 Savannah Dr, 42104 502-781-3861
Brandenburg	Doe Run Inn, 500 Doe Run Hotel Rd, 40108 502-422-2982
Brandenburg	East Hill Inn, 205 LaFayette St, 40108 502-422-3047
Bronston	Raintree Inn B&B, 3314 Old Highway 90, 42518 606-561-5225
Burkesville	Cumberland House, PO Box 7069, 42717 502-433-5434
Burlington	Burlington's Willis Graves, 5825 Jefferson St, 41005 606-689-5096
Burlington	Willis Graves B&B Inn, 5825 Jefferson St, 41005 606-689-5096
Cadiz	Round Oak Inn, PO Box 1331, 42211 502-924-5850
Cadiz	Whispering Winds Inn, 43 Channel Ct, 42211 888-207-3065
Calvert City	Wildflowers Farm B&B, 348 New Hope Rd, 42029 502-527-5449
Campbellsville	The Yellow Cottage, 400 N. Central, 42718 502-789-2669
Campton	Torrent Falls B&B, 1435 N KY 11, 41301 606-668-6441
Carrollton	Highland House, 1705 Highland Ave, 41008 502-732-5559
Carrollton	The P.J. Baker House B&B, 406 Highland Ave, 41008 502-732-4210
Catlettsburg	Levi Hampton House, 2206 Walnut St, 41129 606-739-8118
Cave City	Rose Manor B&B, 204 Duke St, 42127 888-806-7673
Cave City	The Wayfarer B&B, 1240 Old Mammoth Cave, 42127 502-773-3366
Covington	Amos Shinkle Townhouse B&B, 215 Garrard St, 41011 606-431-2118
Covington	Christopher's B&B, 604 Poplar St, 41073 606-491-9354
Covington	Licking Riverside Historic, 516 Garrard St, 41011 606-291-0191
Covington	Sandford House B&B, 1026 Russell St, 41011 606-291-9133
Covington	The Carneal House Inn, 405 E. 2nd St, 41011 606-431-6130
Covington	The Summer House, 613 E 18th St, 41014 606-431-3121
Cynthiana	Seldon Renaker Inn, 24 S. Walnut St, 41031 606-234-3752
Cynthiana	Side Saddle Inn, PO Box 564, 41031 606-234-8600
Danville	Morning Glory Manor & Ctg, 244 E Lexington Ave., 40422 606-236-1888
Danville	Randolph House, 463 W. Lexington, 40422 606-236-9594
Danville	Twin Hollies Retreat, 406 Maple Ave, 40422 606-236-8954
Dawson Springs	Ridley House, 108 W Walnut St, 42408 502-797-2165
E. Bardstown	Kenmore Farms, 1050 Bloomfield Rd, 40004 502-348-8023
Eubank	The I.E. Payne House B&B, 185 Ellison Pulaski Rd, 42567 606-379-2014
Falls of Rough	Ole' Porter Place B&B, 8233 Yeaman Rd, 40119 502-879-4095
Falmouth	The Frontier Farm B&B, Blanket Creek,Rt2 B 275, 41040 606-654-2212
Falmouth	The Red Brick House B&B, 201 Chapel St, 41040 606-654-4834
Farmers	Brownwood B&B & Cabins, PO Box 210, 40319 606-784-8799
Frankfort	Cedar Rock Farm B&B, 3569 Mink Run Rd, 40601
Frankfort	Taylor-Compton House, 419 Lewis St, 40601 502-227-4368
Franklin	College Street Inn, 223 South College, 42134 502-586-9352
Franklin	Park Place, 406 E Ceder St, 42134 502-586-8178
Georgetown	Blackridge Hall B&B, 4055 Paris Pike, 40324 800-768-9308
Georgetown	Bourbon House Farm B&B, 584 Shropshire Ln, 40324 606-987-8669
Georgetown	Log Cabin B&B, 350 N. Broadway, 40324 502-863-3514
Ghent	The Poet's House B&B, PO Box 500, 41045 502-347-0161
Glasgow	B&B Country Cottage, 1609 Winn School Rd, 42141 502-646-2940
Glasgow	Four Seasons Country Inn, 4107 Scottsville Rd, 42141 502-678-1000
Glasgow	Hall Place, 313 S. Green, 42141 502-651-3176
Glendale	Petticoat Junction, PO Box 36, 42740 502-369-8604
Harned	Kentucky Holler House B&B, Rt 1 Box 51BB, 40144 502-547-4507
Harrodsburg	Bauer Haus B&B, 362 N College St, 40330 606-734-6289
Harrodsburg	Baxter House, 1677 Lexington Rd., 40330 606-734-5700
Harrodsburg	Beaumont Inn, PO Box 158, 40330 606-734-3381
Harrodsburg	Canaan Land Farm B&B, 4355 Lexington Rd, 40330 606-734-3984
Harrodsburg	Shakers Landing B&B, 171 Shakers Landing Rd., 40330 606-734-6985
Hartford	Historic Hillside B&B, 403 E Union St, 42347 502-298-4BED

Hartford	Ranney Porch B&B, 3810 Hwy 231 North, 42347 502-298-7972
Hazel	Outback B&B, Box 4, 42049 502-436-5858
Henderson	L&N B&B, Ltd., 327 N Main St, 42420 502-831-1100
Hindman	Quilt Maker Inn, PO Box 973, 41822 606-785-5622
Hodgenville	Cabin Fever #2, 3030 Old Elizabethtown, 42748 502-358-4415
Hopkinsville	Oakland Manor, 9210 Newstead Rd, 42240 502-885-6400
Kuttawa	The Davis House B&B, Rt 2, Box 21A1, 42055 502-388-4468
Lancaster	Perkins Place Farm, PO Box 553, 40444 800-762-4145
Lawrenceburg	Kavanaugh House, 241 E Woodford St, 40342 502-839-9880
Lebanon	Myrtledene, 370 N Spalding Ave, 40033 502-692-2223
Lebanon	Shreve Manor, 145 Shreve Ln, 40033 502-692-3489
Lexington	B&B at Silver Springs Farm, 3710 Leestown Pike, 40511 606-255-1784
Lexington	Brand House at Rose Hill, 461 N Limestone St., 40508 606-226-9464
Lexington	Cherry Knoll Farm B&B, 3975 Lemons Mill Rd, 40511 606-253-9800
Lexington	Gratz Park Inn, 120 W 2nd St, 40507 606-231-1777
Lexington	Swann's Nest-Cyqnet Farm, 3463 Rosalie Ln, 40510 606-226-0095
Lexington	True Inn B&B, 467 W Second St, 40507 606-252-6166
Liberty	Liberty Greystone Manor, PO Box 1329, 42539 606-787-5444
Louisa	Lake View Hideaway B&B, Rt 3 Box 4125, 41230 606-686-1155
Louisville	Angelmelli Inn, 1342 S. 6th St, 40208 800-245-9262
Louisville	Ashton's Victorian Secret, 1132 South First St, 40203 502-581-1914
Louisville	Central Park B&B, 1353 S 4th St, 40208 502-638-1505
Louisville	Gallery House B&B, 1386 S Sixth St, 40208 502-635-2550
Louisville	Inn off the Alley, 1325 Bardstown Rd, 40204 502-451-0121
Louisville	Isaac Stone Farm B&B, 3916 Handley Ave, 40218
Louisville	Samuel Clubertson Mansion, 1432 S Third St, 40208 502-634-3100
Louisville	St. James Court, 1436 St. James Court, 40208 502-636-1742
Louisville	The Columbine B&B, 1707 S. Third St, 40208 502-635-5000
Louisville	The Rocking Horse Manor, 1022 S. Third St, 40203 502-583-0408
Louisville	The Victorian Secret B&B, 1132 S First St, 40203
Louisville	Towne House B&B, 1460 St James Ct, 40208 502-636-5673
Louisville	Woodhaven B&B, 401 S Hubbards Ln, 40207 502-895-1011
Mammoth Cave	The Mello Inn, 2856 Nolin Dam Rd, 42259
Manchester	Blair's Country Living, RR #3, Box 865-B, 40962 606-598-2854
Marion	LaFayette Club House, 173 LaFayette Hights, 42064 502-965-3889
Marion	Myers' B&B, 124 E Depot St, 42064
Mayfield	Magnolia Manor B&B, 52 State Rt 2205, 42066 502-247-4108
Maysville	Kleier Haus, 912 U.S. 62, 41056 606-759-7663
Middlesborough	The RidgeRunner B&B, 208 Arthur Heights, 40965 606-248-4299
Mill Springs	Mill Springs B&B, Hwy 1275, General Del, 42632 606-348-0780
Morgantown	Helm House, 309 S. Tyler, 42261 800-441-4786
Mount Sterling	Trimble House, 321 N. Maysville, 40353 606-498-6561
Mount Vernon	Singing Hills Inn, Rt 3 Box 33C, 40456 606-256-2474
New Haven	Sherwood Inn, PO Box 86, 40051 502-549-3386
Newport	Ash-Ley House B&B, 310 E Third St, 41071 606-291-1114
Newport	Getaway B&B, 326 E. 6th St, 41071 606-581-6447
Newport	Mansion Hill Manor, 315 E 3rd St, 41071 606-291-1700
Newport	Taylor Spinks House, 702 Overton, 41071 606-291-0092
Nicholasville	Cedar Haven Farm, 2380 Bethel Rd, 40356 606-858-3849
Oak Grove	Tuckaway Farms Inn, 14400 Fort Campbell Bl., 42262 502-439-6255
Old Kuttawa	Silver Cliff Inn, 1980 Lake Barkley Dr, 42055 502-388-5858
Olive Hill	The Spanish Manor Inn, US Rt 60 E, 41164 606-286-8593
Owensboro	The Helton House, 103 E 23rd St, 42303 502-926-7117
Owensboro	Trail's End B&B, 5931 Key 56W, 42301 502-771-5590
Owensboro	WeatherBerry B&B, 2731 W. Second St, 42301 502-684-8760
Paducah	1868 B&B, 914 Jefferson St, 42001 502-444-6801
Paducah	Ehrhardts B&B, 285 Springwell Dr, 42001 502-554-0644
Paducah	Farley Place, 166 Farley Pl., 42003 502-442-2488
Paducah	Fisher Mansion B&B, 901 Jefferson St, 42001 502-443-0716
Paducah	Paducah Harbor Plaza B&B, 201 Broadway, 42001 502-442-2698
Paducah	Rosewood Inn, 2740 S Friendship Rd, 42003 502-554-6632
Paducah	Trinity Hills Home, 10455 Old Lovelaceville, 42001 502-488-3999
Paris	Rosedale B&B, 1917 Cypress St, 40361 800-644-1862
Perryville	Elmwood Inn, 205 East Fourth, 40468 606-332-2400
Pikesville	Huffman's Landmark Inn, Bypass Rd., 41501 606-432-2545
Richmond	Barnes Mill B&B, 1268 Barnes Mill Rd, 40475 606-623-5509
Richmond	Riverhill B&B, 661 River Hill Dr, 40475 606-624-3222
Rogers	Cliffview Resort, PO Box 65, 41365 606-668-6558
Russell Springs	White Pillars B&B, 100 Thrasher Ct., 42642 502-866-4132
Russellville	`Log House, 2139 Franklin Rd, 42276 502-726-8483
Sandy Hook	Charlene's Country Inn B&B, HC 75, Box 265, 41171 606-738-5712
Shelbyville	Marcardin Inn, 115 Old Mt Eden Rd, 40065 502-633-7759
Shelbyville	Wallace House, 613 Washington St, 40065 502-633-4272
Simpsonville	Old Stone Inn, 6905 Shelbyville Rd., 40067 502-722-8882
Smiths Grove	Cave Spring Farm, PO Box 365, 42171 502-563-6941
Smiths Grove	Victorian House, PO Box 104, 42171 502-563-9403
Somerset	Osborne's of Cabin Hollow, 111 Fietz Orchard Rd, 42501 606-382-5495
South Union	Shaker Tavern, PO Box 181, 42283 502-542-6801

Springfield	Glenmar Plantation B&B, 2444 Valley Hill Rd, 40069 606-284-7791
Springfield	Maple Hill Manor B&B, 2941 Perryville Rd, 40069 606-366-3075
Sterns	Marcum-Porter House, PO Box 369, 42647 606-376-2242
Taylorsville	Bowling's Villa, 1090 Stumps Ln, 40071 502-477-2636
Trenton	Rockspring Farm B&B, 5802 Clarksville Hwy, 42286 615-552-3111
Versailles	Bluegrass B&B, 2964 McCracken Pike, 40383 606-873-3208
Versailles	Inn at Morgan, 135 Morgan St, 40383 606-873-1183
Versailles	Rabbit Creek B&B, 1010 Steele Pike, 40383 606-873-1711
Versailles	Tyrone Pike B&B, 3820 Tyrone Pike, 40383 606-873-2408
Versailles	Victorian Rose, 160 S Main St, 40383 606-873-5252
Versailles	Western Fields B&B, 5108 Ford's Mill Rd, 40383 606-873-8143
Whitesburg	The Salyers House B&B, PO Box 768, 41858 606-633-2532
Wilmore	Scott Station Inn, 305 E. Main, 40390 606-858-0121
Winchester	Guerrant Mountain Mission, 21 Valentine Ct, 40391 606-745-1284
Winchester	Windswept Farm B&B, 5952 Old Boonesboro Rd, 40391 608-745-1245
Zachariah	Inn The Woods Country Ctg, PO Box 215, 41301 606-668-9999

Louisiana ───────────────────────────────

Abita Springs	Trail's End B&B, 71648 Maple St, 70808 504-748-5886
Amite	Blythewood Plantation, 400 Daniel St, 70422 504-748-5886
Amite	Dr. Stewart's Cottage B&B, 116 E. Chestnut St., 70422 504-748-3700
Amite	Elliott House, 801 North Duncan Ave, 70422 504-748-8553
Arnaudville	Vin-O-Lyn's, 1160 Joe Kidder Rd, 70512 318-754-8153
Bastrop	Johnson House, 409 S. Washington, 71220 318-283-2200
Bossier City	Beauvais House B&B, 1289 Delhi, 71111 318-221-3735
Bourg	Julia's Cajun Country B&B, 4021 Benton Dr., 70343 504-851-3540
Breaux Bridge	Bayou Cabins, 100 Mills Ave, 70517 308-332-6158
Breaux Bridge	Cafe des Amis, 140 E Bridge St, 70517 318-332-5773
Breaux Bridge	Country Oaks B&B, 1138A Lawless Tauzin Rd, 70517 318-332-3093
Breaux Bridge	Maison Des Amis, 140 E Bridge St, 70517 318-332-5273
Broussard	La Grande Maison, 302 E Main St, 70518 318-837-4428
Broussard	Maison d'Andre' Billeaud, 2023 East Main St, 70518 318-837-3455
Calloway Corners	Calloway Corners, PO Box 85, 71073 800-851-1088
Carencro	Bechet Homestay B&B, 313 N Church St, 70520 318-896-3213
Carencro	The Country House, 825 Kidder Rd, 70520 318-896-6529
Covington	Mill Bank Farms, 75654 River Rd, 70435 504-892-1606
Covington	Riverside Hills Farm, 96 Gardenia Dr, 70433
Cut Off	Hassell House B&B, 500 E 74th St, 70345 504-632-8088
Cut Off	The Cheremie's Loft B&B, 152 W 117th St, 70345 504-632-6824
Darrow	Tezcuco Plantation Village, 3138 Hwy. 44, 70725 225-562-3929
Eunice	La Petite Maison, 530 S 7th, 70535 318-457-7136
Eunice	Potier's Prairie Cajun Inn, 110 West Park Ave, 70535 318-457-0440
Franklinton	ShaTims B&B Inn, 43106 Hwy 38, 70438 504-839-5962
Gibson	Wildlife Gardens, 5306 N Bayou Black Dr, 70356 504-575-3676
Hayes	La Retraite Lorrain, 7727 Lorraine Rd, 70646 318-622-3412
Houma	Crochet House B&B, 301 Midland Dr, 70360 504-879-3033
Houma	Grand Manor, 217 Lynwood Dr, 70360 504-876-5493
Houma	Le Jardin Sur Le Bayou, 256 Lower Country Dr, 70343 504-594-2722
Husser	Grand Estate Mansion, 55314 Highway 445, 70442 888-792-2915
Jeanerette	Alice Plantation B&B, 9217 Old Jeanerette Rd, 70544 318-276-3187
Krotz Springs	Country Store B&B Inn, 204 Main St, 70750 318-566-2331
Lafayette	Acadien B&B, 127 Vincent Rd, 70508 318-856-5260
Lafayette	Alida's B&B, 2631 SE Evangeline Tway, 70508 318-264-1191
Lafayette	Bois de Chenes Inn, 338 N. Sterling St, 70501 318-233-7816
Lafayette	Cajun Country Home B&B, 1601 LaNeuville Rd, 70508 318-856-5271
Lafayette	Jane Fleniken's B&B, 616 General Mouton, 70501 318-234-2866
Lafayette	l'Auberge Creole, 204 Madison St, 70501 318-232-1248
Lafayette	T'Frer's House, 1905 Verot School Rd, 70508 318-984-9347
Lake Charles	Adelaide's, 321 Peake St, 70601 318-439-5200
Lake Charles	Ramsay-Curtis Mansion B&B, 626 Broad St, 70601 318-439-3859
Lake Charles	The Eddy House B&B, 722 Pujo St, 70601 318-436-3980
Lecompte	Hardy House B&B, PO Box 368, 71346 318-776-5876
Leesville	Huckleberry Inn, 702 Alexandria Hwy, 71446
Mansura	Victorian House, PO Box 387, 71350
Metairie	Angel Haven, 1817 Abadie Ave, 70003
Montegut	Amanda-Magenta Plantation, PO Box 529, 70377 504-594-8298
Natchitoches	Beau Fort Plantation B&B, PO Box 2300, 71457 318-352-9580
Natchitoches	Breazeal House B&B, 926 Washington St., 71457 318-352-5630
Natchitoches	Cane River House B&B, 910 Washington St., 71457 318-352-5912
Natchitoches	Cloutier Townhouse, 416 Jefferson St, 71457 318-352-5242
Natchitoches	Dogwood Inn, 222 Adelaide St, 71457 318-352-9812
Natchitoches	Fleur de Lis B&B, 336 Second St, 71457 800-489-6621
Natchitoches	Jefferson House B&B, 229 Jefferson St, 71458 318-352-3957
Natchitoches	Judge Porter House B&B, 321 Second St., 71457 800-441-8343
Natchitoches	River Oaks B&B, 112 South Williams, 71457 318-352-2776
Natchitoches	Starlight Plantation B&B, 2228 Hwy 494, 71457 318-352-3775
Natchitoches	The Levy-East House, 358 Jefferson St, 71457 318-352-0662

New Iberia	Cook's Cottage, 5505 Rip Van Winkle Rd, 70560 318-365-3332
New Iberia	La Maison Du Teche, 417 East Main St, 70560 800-667-9456
New Iberia	Pourtos House, 4018 Old Jeanerette Rd., 70560 318-367-7045
New Orleans	Acadian House, 2234 Napoleon Ave., 70115 504-891-4024
New Orleans	B&B As You Like It, 3500 Upperline St., 70125 504-821-7716
New Orleans	B&W Courtyards B&B, 2425 Chartres St., 70117 504-945-9418
New Orleans	Bayou St John B&B, 1318 Moss St, 70119 504-482-6677
New Orleans	Beau Sejour, 1930 Napoleon Ave, 70115 504-897-3746
New Orleans	Benachi House, 2257 Bayou Rd, 70119 504-525-7040
New Orleans	Bonne Chance B&B, 621 Opelousas Ave, 70114 504-367-0798
New Orleans	Casa Conchita, 2121 Dauphine St., 70116 504-528-9330
New Orleans	Chartres Street House, 2517 Chartres St., 70117 504-945-2339
New Orleans	Chimes Cottages, 1360 Moss St, 70152 504-525-4640
New Orleans	Columns Hotel, 3811 St. Charles Ave, 70115 504-899-9308
New Orleans	Cotton Broker's House, 610 Poydras St, Ste 318, 70130 504-525-7040
New Orleans	Crescent City Guest House, 612 Marigny St, 70117 504-944-8722
New Orleans	Degas House, 2302 Esplanade Ave, 70119 504-821-5009
New Orleans	Dive Inn, 4417 Dryades St, 70115 504-895-6555
New Orleans	Dufour-Baldwin House, 1707 Esplanade Ave, 70116 504-945-1503
New Orleans	French Quarter B&B, 1132 Ursulines, 70116 504-522-7333
New Orleans	French Quarter Lanaux Hous, Esplanade at Chartres, 70152 504-488-4640
New Orleans	Garden District B&B, 2418 Magazine St, 70130
New Orleans	Grenoble House Inn, 329 Dauphine St, 70112 504-522-1331
New Orleans	Historic Inns/New Orleans, 911 Burgundy St, 70116 504-524-4401
New Orleans	Hotel Maison de Ville, 727 Toulouse St, 70130 504-561-5858
New Orleans	Hotel Provincial, 1024 Chartres St., 70116 504-581-4995
New Orleans	Hotel St. Marie French Qtr, 827 Toulouse St, 70112 800-366-2743
New Orleans	Hotel St. Pierre, 911 Burgundy St, 70116 504-524-4401
New Orleans	Hotel Ste. Helene, 508 Rue Chartres, 70130 504-522-5014
New Orleans	Jude Travel Park, 7400 Chef Menteur Hwy, 70126 504-241-0632
New Orleans	La Maison Guest House, 608 Kerlerec, 70116 504-271-0228
New Orleans	La Maison Marigny, Box 52257, 70152 504-488-4640
New Orleans	Lagniappe B&B, 1925 Peniston St, 70115 504-899-2120
New Orleans	Marigny Guest House, 621 Esplanade Ave, 70116 504-944-9700
New Orleans	Marquette House, 2253 Carondelet St, 70130 504-523-3014
New Orleans	Mazant Guest House, 906 Mazant St, 70117
New Orleans	McKendrick-Breaux House, 1474 Magazine St, 70130 504-586-1700
New Orleans	Mechling's Guest House, 2023 Esplande Ave, 70116 504-943-4131
New Orleans	Mentone B&B, 1437 Pauger St, 70116 504-943-3019
New Orleans	Nefertiti's Guest House, 70115 609-494-0491
New Orleans	New Orleans Guest House, 1118 Ursulines Ave, 70116 504-566-1177
New Orleans	Olivier Estate B&B, 1425 N Prieur, 70116 504-949-9600
New Orleans	Parkview Guest House, 7004 St. Charles, 70118 504-861-7564
New Orleans	Place d'Armes French Qtr, 625 St Ann St, 70116 800-366-2743
New Orleans	Prince Conti French Qtr, 830 Conti St, 70112 800-366-2743
New Orleans	Private Garden, 1718 Philip St, 70113 504-523-1776
New Orleans	Rampart Cottage, 1422 N. Rampart St., 70116 504-947-4475
New Orleans	Rathbone Inn, 1227 Esplanade Ave, 70116 504-947-2100
New Orleans	Reid House, 3313 Prytania St, 70115 504-269-0692
New Orleans	Rose Manor B&B, 7214 Pontchartrain Blvd, 70124 504-282-8200
New Orleans	Rose Walk House, 320 Verret St, 70114 504-368-1500
New Orleans	Royal Street Courtyard, 2446 Royal St, 70117 504-943-6818
New Orleans	Royal Street Inn & Bar, 1431 Royal St, 70116 504-948-7499
New Orleans	Rue Royal Inn, 1006 Royal Street, 70116 504-524-3900
New Orleans	Streetcar B&B, 100 Industrial Ave, 70118 800-341-4665
New Orleans	Sun & Moon B&B, 1037 N Rampart St, 70116 504-529-4652
New Orleans	Sun Oak Museum, Guesthouse, 2020 Burgundy St, 70116 504-945-0322
New Orleans	Terrell House, 1441 Magazine St, 70130 504-524-9859
New Orleans	The Duvigneaud House, 2857 Grand Route, 70119
New Orleans	The Levee View, 39 Hennesey Ct, 70123 504-737-5471
New Orleans	The Robert Gordy House, 2630 Bell St, 70119 504-486-9424
New Orleans	The Soniat House Hotel, 1133 Chartres St, 70116 504-522-0570
New Orleans	The Tessier House, 1617 Peniston St., 70115 504-895-9487
New Orleans	Whitney Inn, 1509 St Charles Ave, 70130 504-521-8000
New Roads	Jubilee B&B, 11704 Pointe Coupee Rd, 70760 225-638-8333
New Roads	Mon Reve B&B, 9825 False River Rd., 70760 225-638-7848
New Roads	Pointe Coupee B&B, 405 Richey St, 70760 225-638-6254
New Roads	River Blossom Inn, 300 N. Carolina Ave, 70760 225-638-8650
New Roads	Sunrise on the River, 1825 False River Dr, 70760 225-638-3642
Nitchitoches	Tante Huppe Inn, 424 Jefferson St, 71457
Opelousas	Maison de Saizan, 412 S Court St, 70570 318-942-1311
Patterson	Rest on the River, PO Box 1216, 70392 504-395-2527
Plaquemine	Old Turnerville B&B, 23230 Nadler St, 70764 225-687-5337
Ponchatoula	Bella Rose Mansion, 255 N Eighth St, 70454
Ponchatoula	Grand Magnolia Villa, 255 W Hickory St, 70454 504-386-6406
Ponchatoula	The Guest House, 248 W Hickory St, 70454 504-386-6275
Rayne	Maison D'Memoire, 8450 Roberts Cove Blvd, 70578 318-334-2477
Rayne	Maison Daboval, 305 E Louisiana Ave, 70578 318-334-3489

Ruston	Melody Hills Ranch, 804 N Trenton, 71270 318-255-7127
Scott	Sunny Meade B&B, 230 Topeka Rd, 70583 318-873-3100
Shreveport	Slattery House B&B, 2401 Fairfield Ave, 71104 318-222-6577
Slidell	Dixie Queen B&B, PO Box 2082, 70459 504-649-1255
St. Francisville	Cottage Plantation, 10528 Cottage Lane, 70775 225-635-3674
St. Francisville	Hemingbough, PO Box 1640, 70775 225-635-6617
St. Francisville	Lake Rosemound Inn, 10473 Lindsey Ln., 70775 225-635-3176
St. Francisville	Myrtles Plantation, PO Box 1100, 70775 225-635-6277
St. Francisville	Propinquity, PO Box 516, 70775 225-635-4116
St. Francisville	Rosedown Plantation B&B, 12501 Hwy. 10, 70775 225-635-3332
St. Francisville	St. Francisville Inn/Rest., PO Box 1369, 70775 225-635-6502
St. Francisville	Stillwater Farm B&B, 8996 Hwy 61, 70775 225-635-0007
St. Martinville	La Maison Louie B&B, 517 E Bridge St, 70582 318-394-1872
St. Martinville	Maison Bleue B&B, 417 N Main St, 70582 318-394-1215
St. Martinville	The Old Castillo Hotel, 220 Evangeline Blvd, 70582 318-394-4010
Sunset	Chretien Point Plantation, 665 Chretien Point Rd, 70584 318-662-5876
Sunset	La Caboose B&B, PO Box E, 70584 318-662-5401
Vacherie	Bay Tree Plantation, 3785 Hwy 18, 70090 504-265-2109
Vacherie	Oak Alley Plantation, 3645 Highway 18, 70090 800-442-5539
Ville Platte	Maison Deville, 513 W Jackson St, 70586 318-363-1262
West Monroe	Rose Lee Inn, 318 Trenton St, 71291

Maine

Addison	Pleasant Bay B&B, Box 222, 04606 207-483-4490
Andover	Andover Arms B&B, PO Box 387, 04216
Ashville	Green Hill Farm, RR 1, Box 328, 04607 207-422-3273
Bailey Island	The Lady and the Loon, PO Box 98, 04003
Bangor	Breakwater, 29 Heritage Ln, 04401 800-238-6309
Bar Harbor	B&B at Atlantic Oakes, Rt 3, 04609 207-288-5801
Bar Harbor	Bar Harbor Inn, Box 7, 04609
Bar Harbor	Bayview Inn, 111 Eden St (Route 3), 04609 207-288-5861
Bar Harbor	Cove Farm Inn, RFD 1, Box 420, 04609 207-288-5355
Bar Harbor	Ivy Manor Inn, 194 Main St, 04609 207-288-2138
Bar Harbor	Quimby House Inn, 109 Cottage St, 04609
Bar Harbor	Seacroft Inn, 18 Albert Meadow, 04609
Bar Harbor	Shady Maples, RFD #1, Box 360, 04609 207-288-3793
Bar Harbor	Skiff House of Poets Inn, 65 Cottage St, 04609 207-288-3023
Bar Harbor	Stratford House Inn, 45 Mt. Desert St, 04609 207-288-5189
Bar Harbor	The Kedge Historic B&B, 112 West Street, 04609 207-288-5180
Bar Harbor	The Ridgeway Inn, 11 High St, 04609 207-288-9682
Bar Harbor	Twin Gables Inn, PO Box 282, 04609 207-288-3064
Bar Harbor	Wayside Inn B&B, 11 Atlantic Ave., 04609 207-288-5703
Bath	Elizabeth's B&B, 360 Front St, 04530 207-443-1146
Bath	Emma Patten House, 1024 Washington St., 04530 207-443-5202
Bath	Garden Street B&B, HC 63 Box 195, 04530 207-443-6791
Belfast	Belhaven Inn B&B, 14 John St, 04915 207-338-5435
Belfast	Londonderry Inn B&B, SR 80 Box 3, 04915 207-338-3988
Belfast	The Alden House B&B, 63 Church St, 04915 207-338-2151
Belfast	White House @ No 1 Church, 1 Church St, 04915 207-338-1901
Belgrade	Whisperwood Lodge, Taylor Woods RD, 04917 800-355-7170
Belgrade Lakes	Wings Hill B&B, PO Box 386, 04918 207-495-2400
Bethel	Briar Lea Inn & Restaurant, 150 Mayville Rd, 04217 207-824-4717
Bethel	Douglass Place, 162 Mayville Rd, 04217 207-824-2229
Bethel	L'Auberge Country Inn, PO Box 21, 04217 207-824-2774
Bethel	The Hammons House, PO Box 16, 04217 207-824-3170
Bingham	Mrs. G's B&B, PO Box 389, 04920 207-672-4034
Blue Hill	Arcady Down East, RR 1, Box 358, 04614 207-374-5576
Blue Hill	Auberge Tenney Hill, PO Box 1027, 04614 207-374-2169
Blue Hill	Blue Hill Farm Country Inn, Route 15, Box 437, 04614 207-374-5126
Blue Hill	John Peters Inn, PO Box 916, 04614 207-374-2116
Blue Hill	The Blue Hill Inn, PO Box 403, 04614 207-374-2844
Boothbay	Hodgdon Island Inn, PO Box 492, 04571 207-633-7474
Boothbay Harbor	Captain Sawyer's Place, 87 Commercial St, 04538 207-633-2290
Boothbay Harbor	Greenleaf Inn, 91 Commercial St, 04538 207-633-7346
Boothbay Harbor	Howard House Lodge B&B, 347 Townsend Ave, 04538 207-633-3933
Boothbay Harbor	Jonathan's B&B, 15 Eastern Ave., 04538 207-633-3588
Boothbay Harbor	Kenniston Hill Inn, PO Box 125, 04537 207-633-2159
Boothbay Harbor	Seafarer Inn, 38 Union Ct., 04538 207-633-2116
Boothbay Harbor	Spruce Point Inn, Atlantic Ave, Box 237, 04538 207-633-4152
Boothbay Harbor	Waters Edge B&B, 8 Eames Rd, 04538
Brewster	Tide Watch Inn, PO Box 2135, 02631 207-832-4987
Bridgton	Pleasant Mountain Inn, PO Box 246, 04009 207-647-4505
Bridgton	Tarry-a-While B&B Resort, RR 3, Box 1067, 04009 207-647-2522
Brooksville	Breezemere Farm Inn, RR1, Box 290, 04617 207-326-8628
Brooksville	Eggemoggin Reach B&B, RR 1 Box 33A Herrick Rd, 04617 207-359-5073
Brunswick	Bethel Point B&B, Bethel Point Rd 2387, 04011 207-725-1115
Brunswick	Harriet Beecher Stowe Hse, 63 Federal St, 04011 207-725-5543

Brunswick	Seven Hearth Inn @ Oak Hil, 481 Woodside Rd, 04011
Brunswick	The Dove B&B, 16 Douglas St, 04011 207-729-6827
Bucksport	Island View Inn, PO Box 628, 04416 207-422-3031
Bucksport	Jed Prouty Inn, PO Box 826, 04416 207-469-7972
Bucksport	L'ermitage, PO Box 418, 04416 207-469-3361
Bucksport	Old Parsonage Inn, PO Box 1577, 04416 207-469-6477
Camden	Black Horse Inn, PO Box 1093, 04843
Camden	Blue Harbor House, 67 Elm St, 04843 207-236-3196
Camden	Camden Harbour Inn, 83 Bayview St, 04843 207-236-4200
Camden	Camden Main Stay, 22 High St, 04843 207-236-9636
Camden	Captain Swift Inn, 72 Elm St, 04843 207-236-8113
Camden	Hosmer House B&B, 4 Pleasant St, 04843 207-236-4012
Camden	Inn at Sunrise Point, PO Box 1344, 04843 207-236-7716
Camden	Little Dream, 66 High St, 04843 207-236-8742
Camden	Norumbega Inn, 61 High St, Route 1, 04843 207-236-4646
Camden	Owl & Turtle Harbor View, PO Box 1265, 04843 207-236-9014
Camden	The Bean House, One Mountain St., 04843 207-236-2345
Camden	The Belmont, 6 Belmont Ave., 04843 207-236-8053
Camden	The Nathaniel Hosmer Inn, 4 Pleasant St, 04843 207-236-4012
Camden	Victorian B&B by the Sea, PO Box 1385, 04849 207-236-3785
Camden	Whitehall Inn, PO Box 558, 04843 207-236-3391
Capé Elizabeth	Inn by the Sea, 40 Bowery Beach Rd, 04107 207-799-3134
Cape Neddick	Wooden Goose Inn, PO Box 195, 03902 207-363-5673
Cape Newagen	Newagen Seaside Inn, Box H, 04552 207-633-5242
Caribou	Old Iron Inn B&B, 155 High St, 04736
Casco	Maplewood Inn, RR 1 Box 627, 04015 207-655-7586
Casco	Pleasant Lake House, RR 1, Box 293, 04015 207-627-6975
Castine	Castine Inn, PO Box 41, 04421 207-326-4365
Castine	The Manor, Box 276, 04421 207-326-4861
Castine	The Pentagoet Inn, PO Box 4, 04421 207-326-8616
Center Lovell	Center Lovell Inn, Rt 5, 04016
Chebeague Island	Chebeague Island Inn, RR Box 492, 04017 207-846-5155
Cranberry Isles	Red House, PO Box 164, 04625 207-244-5297
Damariscotta	Barnswallow B&B, HC 61 - Box 135, 04543 207-563-8568
Damariscotta	Inn At Damariscotta, Bristol Rd HC 61 Box 61, 04545 207-563-5332
Damariscotta	Oak Gables B&B, PO Box 276, 04543 207-563-1476
Deer Isle	Pilgrim's Inn, PO Box 69, 04627 207-348-6615
Dexter	Brewster Inn, 37 Zion's Hill Rd., 04930 207-924-3130
Dixfield	Von Simm's Victorian Inn, PO Box 645, Rt 2, 04224
East Boothbay	Sailmaker's Inn, PO Box 377, 04544
East Machias	Riverside B&B, Rt 1, 04630 207-255-4134
Eastport	The Inn at Eastport, 13 Washington St, 04631
Eastport	Weston House B&B, 26 Boynton St, 04631 207-853-2907
Edgecomb	Edgecomb Inn, US Route One, Box 51, 04556 207-882-6343
Eliot	Farmstead B&B, Rt 236, 03903
Eliot	Moses Paul Inn B&B, 270 Goodwin Rd, 03903
Ellsworth	Capt'n N Eve's Eden B&B, Rt 184, 04605 207-667-3109
Farmington	Blackberry Farm B&B, RR3 Box 7048, 04938 207-778-2035
Freeport	181 Main Street B&B, 181 Main St, 04032 207-865-1226
Freeport	Anita's Cottage Street Inn, 13 Cottage St., 04032 207-865-0932
Freeport	Captaim Josiah Mitchell, 188 Main St., 04032 207-865-3289
Freeport	Cottage Street Inn B&B, 13 Cottage St, 04032
Freeport	Country at Heart B&B, 37 Bow St, 04032 207-865-0512
Freeport	Freeport Inn & Cafe, US Route One, Box 335, 04032 207-865-6364
Freeport	Holbrook Inn, 7 Holbrook St, 04032 207-865-6693
Freeport	Kendall Tavern B&B, 213 Main St, 04032 207-865-1338
Freeport	Merrymen Inn, 1 Summer St, 04032 207-865-0991
Freeport	Porter's Landing B&B, 70 South St, 04032 207-865-4488
Freeport	The Isaac Randall House, 5 Independence Dr, 04032 207-865-9295
Freeport	The James Place Inn, 11 Holbrook St., 04032 207-865-4486
Friendship	Friendship By-The-Sea, Shipyard Lane, 04547 207-832-4386
Friendship	Harbor Hill B&B, PO Box 35, 04547 207-832-6646
Friendship	Outsiders' Inn B&B, Box 521A, 04547 207-832-5197
Gardiner	Harbor View House of 1807, PO Box 1202, 04345
Greenville	Devlin House B&B, PO Box 1102, 04441 207-695-2229
Greenville	Manitou Cottage, PO Box 1208, 04441
Greenville	Northern Pride Lodge, HC 76 Box 588, 04441
Greenville	Sawyer House B&B, Lakeview St., 04441 207-695-2369
Greenville	The Whitman House, PO Box 524, 04441 207-695-3543
Guilford	The Trebor Inn, PO Box 299, 04443 207-876-4070
Hancock	Crocker House Country Inn, HC 77 Box 171, 04640 207-422-6806
Hancock	Le Domaine Restaurant/Inn, PO Box 496, 04640 207-422-3395
Harpswell	Bellevue By the Sea B&B, 144 Lookout Point Rd., 04079 207-784-5691
Harpswell	Harpswell Inn, RR1 Box 141, 04079 207-833-5509
Harpswell	The Vicarage by the Sea, RR 1, Box 368B, 04079 207-833-5480
Harrington	Harrington House - An Inn, Main St, 04643 207-483-4044
Harrison	Harrison House B&B, RR 2 Box 2035, 04040
Holden	Tether's End B&B, 50 Church Rd, 04429 207-989-7886

Jefferson	Blueberry Hill B&B, 101 Old Madden Rd., 04348 207-549-7448
Jefferson	Jefferson House B&B, PO Box 985, 04348 207-549-5768
Kennebunk	Ellenberger's, 154 Port Rd., 04043 207-967-3824
Kennebunk	English Meadows Inn, 141 Port Rd, 04043 207-967-5766
Kennebunk	Waldo Emerson Inn, 108 Summer St, 04043 207-985-4250
Kennebunkport	1802 House B&B Inn, PO Box 646-A, 04046 207-967-5632
Kennebunkport	Breakwater Inn, Ocean Ave, 04046 207-967-3118
Kennebunkport	Bufflehead Cove, PO Box 499, 04046 207-967-3879
Kennebunkport	Captains Hideaway, PO Box 2746, 04046 207-967-5711
Kennebunkport	Cove House, 11 S Main St, 04046 207-967-3704
Kennebunkport	Harbor Inn, PO Box 538A, 04046 207-967-2074
Kennebunkport	Kylemere House 1818, PO Box 1333, 04046 207-967-2780
Kennebunkport	MacNichol's on the River, 68 Ocean Ave., 04046 207-967-3970
Kennebunkport	Maude's Courtyard, PO Box 182, 04046 207-967-7433
Kennebunkport	Schooners Inn & Restaurant, PO Box 1121, 04046
Kennebunkport	Seaside Inn & Cottages, Gooch's Beach/Beach Sts, 04046 207-967-4461
Kennebunkport	The Dock Square Inn, Temple St, 04046 207-967-5773
Kennebunkport	The Green Heron Inn, PO Box 2578, 04046 201-967-3315
Kennebunkport	The Inn on South Street, PO Box 478A, 04046 207-967-5151
Kennebunkport	The Tides Inn By-The-Sea, 252 Kings Highway, 04046 207-967-3757
Kents Hill	Home-Nest Farm, RR 3, Box 2350, 04349 207-897-4125
Kingfield	River Port Inn, RR 1 Box 1270, 04947 207-265-2552
Kingfield	The Herbert Country Inn, PO Box 67, 04947 207-265-2000
Kingfield	Winter's Inn, RR1, Box 1272, 04947 207-265-5421
Kittery	Melfair Farm B&B, 11 Wilson Rd, 03904 207-439-0320
Lamoine	Lamoine House, Rt. 184, Box 180, 04605 207-667-7711
Lee	Dunloggin B&B, PO Box 306, 04455 207-738-5014
Lincolnville	Mount'n Sea Motel & B&B, 185 Atlantic Hwy, 04849 207-338-5707
Lincolnville	The Spouter Inn B&B, PO Box 270, 04849 207-789-5171
Lincolnville	The Youngtown Inn, Rt 52 & Youngtown Rd, 04849 207-763-4290
Lincolnville	Victorian B&B, PO Box 258, 04849 207-236-3785
Lincolnville	Youngtown Inn & Restaurant, RR 1, Box 4246, 04849 207-763-4290
Lubec	Breakers By The Bay, 37 Washington St, 04652
Lubec	Home Port Inn, 45 Main St, 04652 207-733-2077
Lubec	Peacock House, 27 Summer St, 04652
Lucerne	The Lucerne Inn, Rt 1A, RR 3, 04429 207-843-5123
Machias	Clark Perry House, 59 Court St, 04654 207-255-8458
Madison	The Colony House Inn B&B, PO Box 251, 04950 207-474-6599
Matinicus Island	Tuckanuck Lodge, PO Box 217, 04851 207-366-3830
Medomak	Roaring Brook B&B, RR 32 Box 130, 04551 207-529-5467
Milbridge	Moonraker B&B, Main St, Route 1, 04658 207-546-2191
Milford	Little Bit Country B&B, 294 Main Rd, 04461 207-827-3036
Millinocket	Kataahdin Area B&B, 94-96 Oxford St., 04462 207-723-5220
Millinocket	Sweet Lillian, 88 Pine St., 04462 207-723-4894
Milo	Down Home B&B, RFD 1, Box 11A, 04463
Mt. Desert	B&B Year 'Round-MacDonalds, PO Box 52, 04660 207-244-3316
Mt. Desert	Long Pond Inn, Box 120, 04660 207-244-5854
N. Haven Island	Pulpit Harbor Inn, RR 1, 04853 207-867-2219
N. New Portland	Gilman Stream B&B, HCR 68, Box 706, 04961 207-628-6257
Naples	Lamb's Mill Inn, RR1, Box 676/PO Box 547, 04055 207-693-6253
New Harbor	Pemaquid Beach House B&B, PO Box 200, 04554 207-677-3361
New Harbor	The Bradley Inn, HC 61, Box 361, 04554 207-677-2105
Newcastle	Flying Cloud B&B, PO Box 549, 04553 207-563-2484
Newcastle	The Captain's House B&B, PO Box 242, 04553 207-563-1482
Nobleboro	Glendon Inn, 63 US Highway 1, 04555
Nobleboro	Holidae House A Country In, PO Box 851, 04555 207-824-3400
Nobleboro	Mill Pond Inn, Rt. 215, 04555 207-563-8014
North Anson	The Olde Carrabassett Inn, Union St, 04958 207-635-2900
North Berwick	Old Morrell Farm B&B, 182 Morrell's Mill Rd, 03906 207-676-7600
North Brooklin	The Lookout, HC 64, Box 4025, 04461 207-359-2188
Northeast Harbor	Asticou Inn, PO Box 406, 04662 207-276-3344
Northeast Harbor	Grey Rock Inn, 04662 217-276-9360
Ogunquit	Admiral's Inn, PO Box 2241, 03907 207-646-7093
Ogunquit	Beauport Inn, PO Box 1793, 03907 207-646-8680
Ogunquit	Chestnut Tree Inn, PO Box 2201, 03907 207-646-4529
Ogunquit	Cliff House, PO Box 2274, 03907 207-361-1000
Ogunquit	Inn At Tall Chimneys, PO Box 2286, 03907 207-646-8974
Ogunquit	Juniper Hill Inn, 196 US Rte 1, Box 2190, 03907 207-646-4501
Ogunquit	Leisure Inn B&B, PO Box 2113, 03907 207-646-2737
Ogunquit	Moon Over Maine, PO Box 1478, 03907
Ogunquit	Nellie Littlefield House, PO Box 1599, 03907 207-646-1692
Ogunquit	Sparhawk Resort, 36 Shore Rd, Box 936, 03907 207-633-7138
Ogunquit	The Beachmere Inn, PO Box 2340, 03907 207-646-2021
Ogunquit	The Gazebo, PO Box 668, 03907 207-646-3733
Ogunquit	The Milestone, PO Box 2010, 03907 207-646-4562
Ogunquit	The Morning Dove B&B, PO Box 1940, 03907 207-646-3891
Ogunquit	The West Highland Inn, PO Box 1667, 03907 207-646-2181
Orchard Beach	Aquarius Motel, 5 Brown St, 04064

Orchard Beach	Atlantic Birches Inn, 20 Portland Ave., 04064 207-934-5295
Orchard Beach	Beachwood Motel, 29 W Grand Ave, 04064 207-934-2291
Orchard Beach	White Lamb Cottages, 3 Odessa Ave, 04064 207-934-2231
Orient	Chiputneticook Sporting Lg, PO Box 171, 04471
Orland	Alamoosook Lodge, PO Box 6, 04472
Orland	Sign of the Amiable Pig, PO Box 232, 04472 207-469-2561
Orono	High Lawn B&B, 193 Main St, 04473 207-866-2272
Otisfield	Claibern's B&B, PO Box B, 04270 207-539-2352
Pemaquid Point	Bradley Inn @ Pemaquid Pt., H.C.61, Box 361, 04554 207-677-2105
Phippsburg	Captain Drummond House B&B, Parker Head Rd, 04562 207-389-1394
Phippsburg	The 1774 Inn B&B, 44 Parker Head Rd, 04562 207-389-1774
Portland	Andrews Lodging B&B, 417 Auburn St, 04103 207-797-9157
Portland	Danforth, 163 Danforth St., 04102 207-879-8755
Portland	Inn at Parkspring, 135 Spring St, 04101 207-774-1059
Portland	Pomegranate Inn, 49 Neal St, 04102 207-772-1066
Rangeley	Farmhouse Inn, PO Box 165, 04970 207-864-5805
Rangeley	Northwoods B&B, PO Box 79, 04970 207-864-2440
Raymond	Crescent Lake Cottages, 7 Cottage Lane, 04071 207-655-3393
Readfield	Echo Lake Lodge & Cottages, Box 528, 04355 207-685-9550
Rockland	Beech Street Guest House, 41 Beech St, 04841 207-596-7280
Rockland	Captain Lindsey House Inn, 5 Lindsey St., 04841 207-596-7950
Rockland	Lathrop House, 16 Pleasant St, 04841
Rockland	Lime Rock Inn, 96 Lime Rock St., 04841 207-594-2257
Rockport	Sign of the Unicorn House, PO Box 99, 04856 207-236-8789
Round Pond	Briar Rose B&B, PO Box 27, 04564
S. Brooksville	Buck's Harbor Inn, PO Box 268, 04617 207-326-8660
Saco	Hobson House Celtic Inn, 398 Main St, 04072 207-284-4113
Scarborough	Higgins Beach Inn, 34 Ocean Ave, 04074 207-883-6684
Searsport	Capt. Butman Homestead,The, PO Box 306, 04974
Searsport	Capt. Green Pendleton B&B, 428 E Main St, 04974 207-548-6523
Searsport	Captain A.V. Neckels Inn, 127 E Main St, 04974
Searsport	Carriage House Inn, PO Box 238, 04974 207-548-2289
Searsport	Flowering Plum, PO Box 259, 04974
Searsport	Old Glory Inn, PO Box 461, 04974
Searsport	Sea Captain's Inn, PO Box 518, 04974
Searsport	The Victorian Inn, PO Box 807, 04974 207-548-0044
Searsport	Thurston House B&B Inn, PO Box 686, 04974 207-548-2213
Searsport	William & Mary Inn, PO Box 813, 04974 207-548-2190
Sebasco Estates	Sebasco Harbor Resort, Box LP, 04565 207-389-1161
Sebasco Estates	Small Point B&B, Rt 216 HC 32 Box 250, 04565 207-389-1716
Small Point	Edgewater Farm B&B, HC 216, Box 464, 04565 207-389-1322
South Berwick	Academy Street Inn, 15 Academy St, 03908 207-384-5633
South Freeport	Atlantic Seal B&B, PO Box 146, 04078 207-865-6112
South Thomaston	Blue Lupin B&B, 372 Waterman Beach Rd, 04858
South Waldoboro	The Barn B&B, 2987 Friendship Rd, 04572 207-832-5781
Southwest Harbor	Claremont, Box 137, 04679 207-244-5036
Southwest Harbor	Harbour Woods Lodging, PO Box 1214, 04679 207-244-5388
Southwest Harbor	Island Watch B&B, PO Box 1359, 04679 207-244-7229
Southwest Harbor	Lindenwood Inn, PO Box 1328, 04679 207-244-5335
Southwest Harbor	The Chickadee's Nest, 458 Main St, 04679 207-244-3167
Southwest Harbor	The Inn at Southwest, PO Box 593, 04679 207-244-3835
Southwest Harbor	The Moorings Inn, Shore Rd, 04679 207-244-5523
Stockton Springs	The Hichborn Inn, Church Street, 04981 207-567-4183
Stockton Springs	Whistlestop B&B, RFD 1, Box 639, 04981
Stonington	Burnt Cove B&B, RFD 1, Box 2905, 04681 207-367-2392
Stonington	Inn on the Harbor, Main St, 04681
Stratton	Putts Place B&B, PO Box 126, 04982
Stratton	Tranquillity B&B Inn, PO Box 9, 04982 207-246-4280
Stratton	Widow's Walk, Box 150, 04982 207-246-6901
Sullivan Harbor	Sullivan Harbor Farm, Box 96, 04664 207-422-3735
Sunset	Goose Cove Lodge/Deer Isle, PO Box 40, 04683 207-348-2508
Surry	Surry Inn, PO Box 25, 04684 207-667-5091
Tenants Harbor	Harbor View Guest House, PO Box 268, 04860
Tenants Harbor	Passed Times, Rte 131, Box 509, 04860 207-372-6125
The Forks	Crab Apple Acres Inn, Route 201, 04985 207-663-2218
The Forks	Northern Outdoors, Russell Walters, Rt 201, 04985 207-663-4466
Thomaston	Alpine Inn B&B, 6 Wadsworth St, 04861
Thomaston	Cap'n Frost's B&B, 241 W. Main St, 04861 207-354-8217
Thomaston	Doorway Inn, 145 Main St, 04861 888-300-4907
Thomaston	Serenity on the Oyster, Box 5915, 04861 800-737-3631
Topsham	Black Lantern B&B, 6 Pleasant St, 04086 207-725-4165
Van Buren	Farrell-Michaud House, 231 Main St., 04785 207-868-5209
Vassalboro	Loons Call Inn, RR 3 Box 6890M, 04989 207-968-2025
Vinalhaven	Libby House B&B, PO Box 273, 04863 207-863-4696
Waldoboro	Le Va Tout, 218 Kalers Corner, 04572 207-832-4969
Waldoboro	The Roaring Lion B&B, 995 Main St, 04572 207-832-4038
Waterford	Kedarburn Inn, Route 35, Box 61, 04088 207-583-6182
Waterford	Lake House, PO Box 82, 04088 800-223-4182

Waterford	The Waterford Inne, PO Box 149, 04088 207-583-4037
Weld	Kawanhee Inn Lakeside, Mt. Blue, Box 119, 04285 207-585-2000
Weld	Lake Webb House B&B, PO Box 127, 04285 207-585-2479
Weld	The Weld Inn, PO Box 8, 04285 207-585-2429
Wells	Hilltop Lodging, 20 Roe St, 04090
Wells	Purple Sandpiper, RR 3 Box 226B, 04090
Wells	Tatnic B&B, 62 Tufts Rd, 04090 207-676-2209
Wells	Village by the Sea, Route 1, Box 1107, 04090 207-646-1100
West Falmouth	Quaker Tavern B&B, 377 Gray Rd., 04150 207-797-5540
West Levant	Terra Field B&B, Box 1950, 04456 207-884-8805
Windham	Lincoln House Country Inn, 26 Main St, 04062 207-726-3953
Winter Harbor	Main Stay Inn, PO Box 459, 04693 207-963-2601
Wiscasset	Snow Squall B&B, PO Box 730, 04578 207-882-6892
Wiscasset	The Stacked Arms B&B, 80 Birch St Rd, 04578 207-882-5436
York Beach	Golden Pineapple Inn, 12 Long Beach Ave., 03910 207-363-7837
York Beach	Homestead Inn B&B, PO Box 15, 03910 207-363-8952
York Beach	Katahdin Inn, PO Box 193, 03910
York Beach	Red Shutters B&B, 7 Cross St, 03910 207-363-6292
York Beach	The Candleshop Inn, PO Box 1216, 03910
York Beach	The Tide Watch, 46 Shore Rd, 03910 207-363-4713
York Beach	Willow B&B, Box 794, 03910 207-363-9900
York Harbor	Bell Buoy B&B, PO Box 445, 03911
York Harbor	Canterbury House, Box 881, 03911 207-363-3505
York Harbor	Edwards Harborside Inn, PO Box 866, 03911 207-363-3037
York Harbor	Riverbank on the Harbor, PO Box 1102, 03911
York Harbor	Rivermere B&B, 45 Verrell Lane, 03911 207-363-5470
York Harbor	Stage Neck Inn, PO Box 97, 03911 207-363-3850

Maryland

Allen	Allendale Cottage, PO Box 54, 21810 410-860-2800
Annapolis	55 East B&B, 55 East St, 21401 410-295-0202
Annapolis	American Heritage B&B, 108 Charles, 21404 410-280-1620
Annapolis	Annapolis B&B, 235 Prince George Sr, 21401 301-269-0669
Annapolis	Ark & Dove B&B, 149 Prince George St, 21401 410-268-6277
Annapolis	Coggeshall House, 198 King George St, 21404 410-263-5068
Annapolis	College House Suites, One College Ave., 21401 410-263-6124
Annapolis	Corner Cupboard Inn, 30 Randall St, 21404 410-263-4970
Annapolis	Flag House Inn, 26 Randall St, 21404 410-280-2721
Annapolis	Gatehouse B&B, 249 Hanover St, 21401
Annapolis	Georgian House B&B, 170 Duke of Gloucester, 21401 410-263-5618
Annapolis	Gibson's Lodgings, 110 Prince George St, 21401 410-268-5555
Annapolis	Hunter House B&B, 154 Prince George St, 21401 410-626-1268
Annapolis	Magnolia House, 220 King George St, 21404 410-268-3477
Annapolis	Prince George Inn, 232 Prince George St, 21401 410-263-6418
Annapolis	Rachel's B&B, HC 77, Box 237, 63620 410-598-4656
Annapolis	Schooner Woodwind, PO Box 3254, 21403
Baltimore	Admiral Fell Inn, 888 S Broadway, 21231 410-522-7377
Baltimore	Bauernschmidt Manon B&B, 22316 Bauernschmidt Dr, 21221
Baltimore	Colonnade Inn, 4 W University Pkwy, 21218 410-235-5400
Baltimore	Cross Keys Inn, 5110 Falls Rd., 21210 410-532-6900
Baltimore	Hargrove House, 2901 Hargrove St., 21218 410-366-3480
Baltimore	Inn at Government House, 1125 North Calvert St, 21202 410-539-0566
Baltimore	Society Hill–Hopkins, 3404 St. Paul St, 21218 410-235-8600
Baltimore	Tair ar Ddeg, 13 Elmwood Rd., 21210 410-323-5279
Baltimore	The Biltmore Suites Hotel, 205 W. Madison St, 21201 410-728-6550
Baltimore	The Inn At Fells Point, 1718 Thames St., 21231 410-276-8252
Barnesville	Haven Spring, PO Box 423, 20838 301-349-3943
Berlin	Atlantic Hotel, 2 N Main St, 21811 410-641-3589
Berlin	Holland House B&B, 5 Bay St., 21811 410-641-1956
Brookeville	Longwood Manor B&B, 2900 DuBarry Lane, 20833 301-774-1002
Bryantown	Shady Oaks of Serenity, PO Box 842, 20617 800-597-0924
Buckeystown	Catoctin Inn & Conf Center, PO Box 243, 21717 301-874-5555
Buckeystown	The Inn at Buckeystown, 3521 Buckeystown Pike, 21717 301-874-5755
Burtonsville	The Taylors' B&B, PO Box 238, 20866 301-236-4318
Cabin John	Winslow House, 8217 Caraway St, 20818 301-229-4654
Cambridge	Commodore's Cottage B&B, 215 Glenburn Ave, 21613 800-228-6938
Cambridge	Glasgow B&B Inn, 1500 Hambrooks Blvd, 21613 410-228-0575
Cascade	Bluebird on the Mountain, 14700 Eyler Ave, 21719 391-241-4161
Cecilton	The Anchorage, 5667 Augustine Herman, 21913 410-275-1972
Chesapeake City	Bohemia House, 1236 Town Point Rd, 21915 410-885-3024
Chesapeake City	Chesapeake City B&B, PO Box 128, 21915
Chestertown	April Inn, 407 Campus Ave., 21620 410-778-5540
Chestertown	Chesapeake Hunt Club, PO Box 609, 21620
Chestertown	Imperial House, 208 High St, 21620 410-778-5000
Chestertown	Inn at Mitchell House, 8796 Maryland Pkwy, 21620
Chestertown	Lauretum Inn B&B, 954 High St, 21620 410-778-3236
Chestertown	Widow's Walk Inn, 402 High St, 21620 410-778-6455

Church Creek	Loblolly Landings & Lodge, 2142 Liners Rd, 21622 410-397-3033
Church Creek	The Sportman's Retreat, 2142 Liners Rd, 21622 410-397-3033
Clear Spring	Breeze Hill Farm B&B, 12140 St. Paul Rd., 21722 301-842-2608
Clear Spring	Harbine House B&B, PO Box 27, 21722 301-842-2553
Clear Spring	Wilson House B&B, 14923 Rufus Wilson Rd, 21722 301-582-4320
Columbia	Peralynna Manor Guesthouse, 10605 Route 108, 21044 410-715-4602
Crisfield	My Fair Lady B&B Inn, 38 W. Main St., 21817 410-968-3514
Crownsville	The Good Sheperd Inn, 1077 Omar Dr, 21032
Cumberland	Red Lamp Post B&B, 849 Braddock Rd, 21502 301-777-3262
Deale	Makai Pierside B&B, 5960 Vacation, Box 439, 20751 301-261-9580
Derwood	Reynolds of Deerwood B&B, 16620 Bethayres Rd, 20855 301-963-2216
Easton	Ashby 1663, PO Box 45, 21601
Easton	Chaffinch House B&B, 132 S Harrison St., 21601 410-822-5074
Easton	Gross' Coate Plant. 1658, 11300 Gross Coate Rd, 21601
Easton	John S. McDaniel House, 14 N Aurora St, 21601
Easton	McDaniel House, 14 N Aurora St., 21601 410-822-3704
Elkton	Garden Cottage Sinking Spr, 234 Blair Shore Rd, 21921 410-398-5566
Ellicott City	The Wayside Inn, 4344 Columbia Rd, 21042 410-461-4636
Ellicott City	The White Duck B&B, 3920 College Ave, 21043 410-992-8994
Emmitsburg	Stonehurst Inn, 9436 Waynesboro Rd., 21727 301-447-2880
Fairplay	Candlelight Inn, 8620 Sharpsburg Pike, 21733 301-582-4852
Frederick	Morningside Inn, 7477 McKaig Rd., 21701 301-898-3920
Frederick	National Pike Inn, 150 Lauren Ct, 21703
Frederick	The Tyler Spite House, 112 W. Church St, 21701 301-831-4455
Frederick	Turning Point Inn, 3406 Urbana Pike, 21701 301-874-2421
Gaithersburg	Gaithersbury Hospitality, 18908 Chimney Place, 20879 301-977-7377
Galena	Rosehill Farm, 13842 Gregg Neck Rd., 21635 410-648-5538
Hagerstown	Lewrene Farm B&B, 9738 Downsville Pike, 21740 301-582-1735
Hagerstown	Sunday's B&B, 39 Broadway, 21740 301-797-4331
Hagerstown	Sword Fireplace Country, 12238 Walnut Pt. Rd, 21740 301-582-4702
Hagerstown	The Wingrove Manor, 635 Oak Hill Ave, 21740 301-733-6328
Havre de Grace	Currier House B&B, 800 S Market St, 21078 410-939-7886
Havre de Grace	Spencer Silver Mansion, 200 S Union Ave, 21078 410-939-1097
Highland	Inn at Paternal Gift Farms, 13555 Rte 108, 20777 301-854-3353
Huntington	Ches' Bayvu, 4720 Paul Hance Rd, 20639
Huntington	Serenity Acres B&B, 4270 Hardesty Rd., 20639 410-535-3744
Little Orleans	Town Hill B&B, Exlt 68, Interstate 68, 21766 301-478-2794
McHenry	Lake Pointe Inn B&B, 174 Lake Pointe Dr, 21541 301-387-0111
McHenry	Savage River Inn, PO Box 147, 21541 401-245-4440
Middleburg	Bowling Brook Country Inn, 6000 Middleburg Rd., 21757 410-848-0353
New Market	The Strawberry Inn, PO Box 237, 21774 301-865-3318
North Beach	Angels in the Attic, PO Box 70, 20714 410-257-1069
North East	North Bay B&B, 9 Sunset Dr, 21901
North East	The Mill House, 102 Mill Ln., 21901 301-287-3532
Oakland	Harley Farm B&B, 16766 Garrett Hwy, 21550 301-387-9050
Oakland	Red Run Inn, 175 Red Run Rd, 21550 301-387-6606
Oakland	The Oak & Apple B&B, 208 N Second St, 21550 301-334-9265
Ocean City	The Lighthouse Club Hotel, 201 60th St, 21842 410-524-5400
Olney	Thoroughbred B&B, 16410 Batchellor Forest, 20832 301-774-7649
Oxford	1876 House, PO Box 658, 21654 301-226-5496
Oxford	Combsberry, 4837 Evergreen Rd., 21654 410-226-5353
Poolesville	Rocker Inn, 17924 Elgin Rd, 20837 301-972-8543
Princess Anne	Hayman House B&B, 30491 Prince William St, 21853 410-651-1107
Queenstown	The House of Burgess' B&B, PO Box 2012, 21658 410-827-3396
Rock Hall	Huntingfield Manor B&B, 4928 Eastern Neck Rd, 21661 410-639-7779
Rock Hall	Moonlight Bay Marina & Inn, 6002 Lawton Ave, 21661 410-639-2660
Rock Hall	The Inn at Osprey Point, 20786 Rock Hall Ave, 21661 410-639-2194
Royal Oak	Part of Retreat Farm, PO Box 305, 21662
Royal Oak	Pasadena Inn, PO Box 187, 21662 410-745-5053
Saint Michaels	Harris Cove Cottages, 8080 Bozman Neavitt Rd, 21663
Scotland	St. Michael's Manor B&B, 50200 St Michaels Manor, 20687 301-872-4025
Sharpsburg	Ground Squirrel Haller, 6736 Sharpsburg Pike, 21782 301-432-8288
Sharpsburg	Jacob Rohrback Inn, PO Box 706, 21782 301-432-5079
Sharpsburg	Piper House B&B Inn, PO Box 100, 21782 301-797-1862
Silver Spring	Park Crest House, 8101 Park Crest Dr, 20910 301-588-2845
Smith Island	Inn of Silent Music, Tylerton, 21866 410-425-3541
Snow Hill	Chanceford Hall, 209 W Federal St, 21863 410-632-2231
Snow Hill	Snow Hill Inn, 104 E. Market St, 21863 301-632-2102
Solomons	Back Creek Inn B&B, PO Box 520, 20688 410-326-2022
Solomons	By-The-Bay B&B, PO Box 504, 20688 410-326-3428
Solomons	Webster House, PO Box 1607, 20688 410-326-0454
St. George Island	Camp Merryelande Vacation, Camp Merryelande Rd., 20674 301-862-3301
St. Michaels	Brick House, 202 N Talbot St., 21663 410-745-6146
St. Michaels	Dr. Dodson House B&B, PO Box 956, 21663 410-745-3691
St. Michaels	Inn at Perry Cabin, 308 Watkins Lane, 21663 410-745-2200
St. Michaels	Rigby Valliant House, PO Box 88, 21663
St. Michaels	Victoriana Inn, 205 Cherry St, Box 449, 21663 410-745-3368
St. Michaels	Wades Point Inn On The Bay, PO Box 7, 21663 410-745-2500

Stevenson	Gramercy Mansion, 1400 Greenspring Valley, 21153 410-486-2405
Stevenson	Mesana Inn, 1718 Greenspring Valley, 21153
Takoma Park	Annie's B&B, 7414 Birch Ave, 20912
Tall Timbers	Potomac View Farm B&B, PO Box 315, 20690 301-994-2311
Taneytown	Antrim 1844, 30 Trevanion Rd, 21787 410-756-2744
Thurmont	Cozy Country Inn, 103 Frederick Rd, 21788 301-271-4301
Tilghman Island	Lazyjack Inn, PO Box 248, 21671 410-886-2215
Tilghman Island	Sinclair House B&B, Box 145, 21671 410-886-2147
Tilghman Island	Tilghman Island Inn, PO Box B, 21671 410-886-2141
Timonium	Union Square House B&B, 103 E Aylesbury Rd, 21093 410-233-9064
Vienna	Governor's Ordinary, PO Box 156, 21869 301-376-3530
Vienna	Nanticoke Manor House, PO Box 248, 21869 301-376-3530
Westminster	Winchester Country Inn, 430 S. Bishop St, 21157 301-876-7373
Wingate	Wingate Manor B&B, 2335 Wingate-Bishop's, 21675 410-397-8717

Massachusetts ————————————————————————

Amherst	Amity House, 194 Amity St., 01002 413-549-6446
Amherst	Black Walnut B&B, 1184 N Pleasant St, 01002 413-549-5649
Amherst	Ivy House B&B, 1 Sunset Ct., 01002 413-549-7554
Andover	Andover Inn, Chapel Avenue, 01002 508-475-5903
Andover	Tage Inn, 131 River Rd., 01810 508-685-6200
Attleboro	The Col. Blackinton Inn, 203 N Main St, 02703 508-222-6022
Barnstable	Charles Hinkley House, PO Box 723, 02630 508-362-9924
Barnstable	Crocker Tavern B&B, 3095 Main St, 02630 508-362-5115
Barnstable	Henry Crocker House, 3026 Main St, Rt 6A, 02630 508-362-6348
Barnstable	Thomas Huckins House, PO Box 515, 02630 508-362-6379
Barre	The Jenkins Inn, PO Box 779, 01005 508-255-6444
Bass River	Belvedere B&B Inn, 167 Main St, 02664 508-398-6674
Becket	The Long House, High St, Box 271, 01223 413-623-8360
Bedford	Timothy Jones House, 231 Concord Road, 01730 781-275-8579
Beverly	Beverly Farm B&B, 28 Hart St, 01915 978-922-6074
Beverly	Bunnys B&B, 17 Kernwood Heights, 01915 978-922-2392
Boston	463 Beacon Street GH, 463 Beacon St., 02115 617-536-1302
Boston	Abercrombie's Farrington, 23 Farrington Ave, 02134
Boston	Amsterdammertje: Euro-Amer, PO Box 1731, 02205 617-471-8454
Boston	Appleton St. Herbst Haus, Appleton St, 02116 617-266-5537
Boston	B&B at 64 Chandler St.,The, 64 Chandler St., 02116 617-451-3882
Boston	Baileys Copley B&B House, 2 Lawrence St., 02116 617-262-4543
Boston	Boston (Brookline) #36, PO Box 1142, 02146 617-277-5430
Boston	Buckminster, 645 Beacon St., 02215 617-236-7050
Boston	Chandler Inn, 26 Chandler St., 02116 617-482-3450
Boston	Clarendon Square B&B, 81 Warren Ave, 02116
Boston	Howard Johnson Hotel, 1271 Boylston St, 02215 617-267-8300
Boston	John Jeffries House, 14 Embankment Rd., 02114 617-367-1866
Boston	Rudy's B&B, 46 Tremlett St, 02124 617-282-5671
Boston	The Coach House B&B, 16 Lime St, 02108 617-227-5013
Bourne	Cape Cop Canalside B&B, 7 Coastal Way, 02532 508-759-6564
Brewster	Bramble Inn & Restaurant, PO Box 807, 02631 508-896-7644
Brewster	Brewster Farmhouse Inn, 716 Main St, 02631 508-896-3910
Brewster	High Brewster, 964 Satucket Rd, 02631 508-896-3636
Brewster	Isaiah Clark House, PO Box 169, 02631 508-896-2223
Brewster	Ocean Edge Resort & Golf, 2907 Main St, 02631 508-896-9000
Brewster	Ocean Gold B&B, 74 Locust Ln, 02631 508-255-7045
Brewster	Pepper House Inn, PO Box 2085, 02631 508-896-4389
Brewster	Ruddy Turnstone B&B, 463 Main St, 02631 508-385-9871
Brewster	The Inn at the Egg, PO Box 453, 02631 508-896-3123
Buckland	1797 House, Charlemont Rd, 01338 413-625-2697
Buzzards Bay	Fox Run B&B, 171 Puritan Rd., 02532 508-759-1458
Cambridge	Cambridge Bed & Muffin, 267 Putnam Ave., 02139 617-576-3166
Cambridge	Carolyn's B&B, 102 Holworthy st., 02138 617-864-7042
Cambridge	Hamilton House, 335 Pearl St., 02139 617-491-0274
Cambridge	Margaret's B&B, 75 Wendell St., 02138 617-876-3450
Cambridge	Missing Bell B&B, 16 Sacramento St, 02138 617-876-0987
Cataumet	Wood Duck Inn, 1050 County Rd., 02534 508-564-6404
Centerville	Copper Beech Inn, 497 Main St, 02632 508-771-5488
Centerville	Trade Winds, PO Box 477, 02632
Chatham	Azubah Atwood Inn, 177 Cross Street, 02633 508-945-1030
Chatham	Carriage House Inn, 407 Old Harbor Rd, 02633 508-945-4688
Chatham	Chatham Bars Inn, Shore Road, 02633 508-945-0096
Chatham	Cranberry Inn at Chatham, 359 Main St, 02633 508-945-9232
Chatham	Dolphin of Chatham, 352 Main St, 02633 508-945-0070
Chatham	Inn Among Friends, 207 Main St., 02633 508-945-0792
Chatham	Pleasant Bay Village Resrt, PO Box 772, 02633 508-945-1133
Chatham	Queen Anne Inn, 70 Queen Anne Rd, 02633 508-945-0394
Chester	Frog Hollow Farm, Holcomb Rd, off Skyline, 01011 413-354-9678
Chilmark	Captain R. Flanders House, North Rd., 02535 508-645-3123
Chilmark	Inn at Blueberry Hill, North Rd., 02535 508-645-3322

Cohasset	Saltmarsh Farm B&B, 116 S Main St., 02025 617-383-6205
Colrain	Maple Shade Farm B&B, 34 Nelson Rd, 01340
Concord	Anderson-Wheekler Homestea, 154 Fitchburg Tpke, 01742
Concord	North Bridge Inn, 21 Monument St., 01742 978-371-0014
Concord	The Colonial Inn, 48 Monument Square, 01742 978-369-9200
Cotuit	Salty Dog Inn, 451 Main St, 02635 508-428-5228
Cummaquid	Fox Glen Manor B&B, 4001 Main St., 02637 508-362-4657
Cummington	Swift River Inn, 151 South St, 01026 413-634-5751
Dennis	The Four Chimneys Inn, 946 Main St, Rte 6A, 02638 508-385-6317
Devens	Devens Inn & Conference Ct, 100 Sherman Ave, 01432 978-772-4300
East Dennis	Mermaid Cottage B&B, 58 Hillside Dr, 02641 617-351-2360
East Falmouth	B&B of Waquoit Bay, PO Box 3638, 02536 508-457-0084
East Falmouth	Bayberry Inn, 226 Trotting Park, 02536 508-540-2962
East Falmouth	Cape Babs Cottage B&B, 23 Blueberry Lane, 02536 888-811-2280
East Falmouth	The Coppage Inn, 224 Waquoit Hwy, 02536 508-548-3228
East Orleans	The Parsonage Inn, PO Box 1501, 02643 508-255-8217
East Sandwich	Azariah Snow House, 529 Rt 6A, 02537
East Sandwich	Spring Garden Motel, 578 Rte. 6A, Box 867, 02537 508-888-0710
Eastham	Anchorage on the Cove, 450 St Hwy, Rt 6, 02642 508-255-1442
Eastham	Eastham Windmill B&B, 55 Samoset Rd., 02642 508-255-8366
Edgartown	Ashley Inn, 129 Main St, 02539 508-627-9655
Edgartown	Daggett House, PO Box 1333, 02539 508-627-4600
Edgartown	Daniele Paul & Carolyn GH, 81 Herring Creek Rd., 02539 508-627-6033
Edgartown	Edgartown Heritage Hotel, 227 Upper Main St, 02539 617-627-5161
Edgartown	Point Way Inn, PO Box 5255, 02539 508-627-8633
Edgartown	Summer House, PO Box 727, 02539 508-627-4857
Edgartown	The Edgartown Inn, PO Box 1211, 02539 508-627-4794
Edgartown	The Shiretown Inn, 44 N Water St, 02539 508-627-3353
Edgartown	The Victorian Inn, PO Box 947, 02539 508-627-4784
Essex	George Fuller House, 148 Main St (Rt 133), 01929 978-768-7766
Falmouth	Beach House at Falmouth Ht, 10 Worcester Ct., 02540 508-457-0310
Falmouth	Gaslight Inn, 9 Fairmont Ave., 02540 508-457-1647
Falmouth	Gladstone Inn, 219 Grand Ave S, 02540 508-548-9851
Falmouth	Hawthorne Lodge, 211 Grand Ave., 02540 508-548-0389
Falmouth	Red Horse Inn, 28 Falmouth Neights Rd, 02540 508-548-0053
Falmouth	Scalloped Shell Inn, 16 Massachusetts Ave, 02540
Falmouth	Sea Gull Inn, 335 Grand Ave, 02540
Falmouth	The Palmer House Inn, 81 Palmer Ave, 02540 508-548-1230
Falmouth	The Seawinds, PO Box 393, 02541 508-548-3459
Florence	Lupine House B&B, PO Box 60483, 01062 413-586-9766
Gardner	Colonial B&B Resort, Betty Spring Rd, 01440
Gay Head	Duck Inn, RR 1 Box 160, 02535 508-645-9018
Gay Head	The Outermost Inn, RR 1, Box 171, 02535 508-645-3511
Gloucester	Julietta House, 84 Prospect St, 01930 978-281-2300
Gloucester	Ocean View Inn, 171 Atlantic Rd, 01930 978-283-6200
Gloucester	Williams Guest House, 136 Bass Ave, 01930 617-283-4931
Great Barrington	Bread & Roses, Star Rt 65, Box 50, 01230 413-528-1099
Great Barrington	Greenmeadows, 117 Division St., 01230 413-528-3897
Great Barrington	Round Hill Farm Nonsmokers, 17 Round Hill Rd, 01230 413-528-6969
Great Barrington	Seekonk Pines Inn, 142 Seekonk Cross Rd, 01230 413-528-4192
Great Barrington	The Turning Point Inn, 3 Lake Buel Rd, 01230 413-528-4777
Great Barrington	The Uttermost Barn, 17 Round Hill Rd, 01230 413-528-3366
Great Barrington	Wainwright Inn, 518 S Main St Rt 7, 01230
Hadley	Clark Tavern Inn B&B, 98 Bay Rd, 01075 413-586-1900
Hancock	Mill House Inn, PO Box 1079, 01237 413-738-5348
Harwich	Victorian Inn at Harwich, PO Box 340, 02645 508-432-8335
Harwich	Wishing Well Motel, PO Box 685, 02671 508-432-2150
Harwich Port	Captain's Quarters B&B Inn, 85 Bank St, 02646 508-432-1991
Harwich Port	Country Inn, 86 Sisson Rd (Rte 39), 02646 508-432-2769
Harwich Port	Harbor Breeze of Cape Cod, 326 Lower County Rd, 02646 508-432-0337
Harwich Port	Inn on Bank Street, 88 Bank St, 02646 508-432-3206
Harwich Port	No. 10 Bed & Breakfast, 10 Cross St, 02646 508-432-9313
Harwich Port	Sea Heather Inn, 28 Sea St, 02646
Harwich Port	The Beach House Inn, 4 Braddock Ln., 02646 508-432-4444
Harwich Port	The Coach House, 74 Sisson Rd, 02646 508-432-9452
Harwich Port	Wedgewood House B&B, 115 Sisson Rd., 02645 508-432-1378
Haydenville	Shingle Hill B&B, PO Box 212, 01039 413-268-8320
Holyoke	Yankee Pedlar Inn, PO Box 6206, 01041 413-532-9494
Housatonic	Christine B&B, Rt 41, 01236 413-274-6149
Hull	The Allerton House B&B, 15 Tierney Ave., 02045 617-925-4569
Huntington	Carmelwood, 8 Montgomery Rd, 01050 413-667-5786
Hyannis	Captain Sylvester Baxter, 156 Main St, 02601 508-775-5611
Hyannis	Mansfield House, 70 Gosnold St., 02601 508-771-9455
Hyannis	Ocean Manor, 543 Ocean St., 02601 508-771-2186
Hyannis	Salt Winds Guest House, 319 Sea St, 02601 508-775-2038
Hyannis	Sea Beach Inn, 388 Sea St., 02601 508-775-4612
Lee	Applegate B&B, 01238 413-243-4451
Lee	Haus Andreas, 85 Stockbridge Rd., 01238 413-243-3298

Lee	Morgan House Inn, 33 Main St., 01238 413-243-0181
Lee	Parsonage On The Green, 20 Park Pl, 01238 413-243-4364
Lee	Sunset Farm B&B, 74 Tryingham Rd, 01238
Lenox	Apple Tree Inn, 224 West St, 01240 413-637-1477
Lenox	Blantyre, PO Box 995, 01240 413-637-3556
Lenox	Brook Farm Inn, 15 Hawthorne St, 01240 413-637-3013
Lenox	Candlelight Inn, 53 Walker St, 01240 413-637-1555
Lenox	Cliffwood Inn, 25 Cliffwood St, 01240 413-637-3330
Lenox	Forty-Four St. Ann's Ave., PO Box 718, 01240 413-637-3381
Lenox	Seven Hills Country Inn, 40 Plunkett St, 01240 413-637-0060
Lenox	Strawberry Hill, PO Box 718, 01240 413-637-3381
Lenox	Whistler's Inn, 5 Greenwood St, 01240 413-637-0975
Leverett	The Hannah Dudley House, 114 Dudleyville Rd, 01054 413-367-2323
Lexington	Desiderata B&B, 189 Wood St, 02173
Lexington	Flanesford Cottage, 54 Woburn St., 02173 617-860-0984
Lexington	Halewood House, 2 Larchmont Ln, 02173 617-862-5404
Manchester	Old Corner Inn, 2 Harbor St, 01944 508-526-4996
Manchester	Sixty-One Forest, 61 Forest St., 01944 508-526-7089
Marblehead	Brimblecomb Hill B&B, 33 Mechanic St, 01945
Marblehead	Guesthouse @ Lowender Gate, One Summer St., 01945 781-631-3243
Marblehead	Spray Cliff "On the Ocean", 25 Spray Ave, 01945 781-631-6789
Marblehead	Stillpoint, 27 Gregory St, 01945 781-631-1667
Marblehead	The Blue Door B&B, 15 Village St, 01945 781-631-0893
Marblehead	The Nesting Place B&B, 16 Village St., 01945 781-631-6655
Marblehead	Victorian Rose B&B, 72 Prospect St., 01945 781-631-4306
Marion	Pineywood Farm B&B, PO Box 322, 02738 508-748-3925
Marshfield Hill	Linden Tree Farm, 758 Summer St., 02051 617-837-4116
Martha's Vineyard	1720 House, PO Box 1193, 02568 508-693-6407
Martha's Vineyard	Hanover House, 28 Edgartown Rd, 02568 508-693-1066
Martha's Vineyard	Hob Knob Inn, PO Box 239, 02539 508-627-9510
Martha's Vineyard	Kelley House, PO Box 37, 02539 508-627-7900
Mashpee	Island in the Sun B&B, 33 Russell Rd, 02649 508-539-3935
Menemsha	Beach Plum Inn, Beach Plum Lane, 02552 508-645-9454
Menemsha	Menemsha Inn & Cottages, Box 38, 02552 508-645-2521
Middleborough	On Cranberry Pond B&B, 43 Fuller St, 02346
Middleton	The Blue Door, 20 East St, 01949 508-777-4829
Nantucket	Brass Lantern, 11 N. Water St, 02554 508-228-4064
Nantucket	Carlisle House Inn, 26 N. Water St, 02554 508-228-0720
Nantucket	Centerboard Guest House, PO Box 456, 02554 508-228-9696
Nantucket	Centre Street Inn, 78 Centre St, 02554 508-228-0199
Nantucket	Cobblestone Inn, 5 Ash St., 02554 508-228-1987
Nantucket	Corner House, PO Box 1828, 02554 508-228-1530
Nantucket	Easton House, Box 1033, 02554 617-228-2759
Nantucket	Eighteen Gardner St. Inn, 18 Gardner St, 02554 508-228-1155
Nantucket	Fair Winds, 29 Cliff Rd, 02554
Nantucket	Folger Hotel & Cottages, PO Box 628, 02554 508-228-0313
Nantucket	Jared Coffin House, PO Box 1580, 02554 508-228-2400
Nantucket	Lynda Watts B&B, 30 Vestal St, Box 478, 02554 508-228-3828
Nantucket	Maiden Lane House, 6 E York St, 02554 508-228-4362
Nantucket	Paul West House, 5 Liberty St, 02554 508-228-2495
Nantucket	Safe Harbor Guest House, 2 Harbor View Way, 02554 508-228-3222
Nantucket	Seven Sea Street Inn, 7 Sea St, 02554 508-228-3577
Nantucket	Sherburne Inn, 10 Gay St, 02554 508-228-4425
Nantucket	Ten Lyon Street Inn, 10 Lyon St., 02554 508-228-5040
Nantucket	The Ships Inn, 13 Fair St, 02554 508-228-0040
Nantucket	The White House, 48 Centre St, 02554
Nantucket	Union Street Inn, 7 Union Street, 02554 508-228-9222
Nantucket Island	Brant Point Inn, 6 N. Beach St, 02554 508-228-5442
Nantucket Island	Quaker House Inn & Rest., 5 Chestnut St, 02554 508-228-0400
Nantucket Island	The Ivy Lodge, 2 Chester St, 02554 508-228-7755
Needham	Brock's B&B, 60 Stevens Rd, 02192 781-444-6573
Needham	Thistle, 31 Fairfield St, 02192 617-444-5724
New Bedford	Cynthia & Steven's, 36 Seventh St, 02740 508-997-6433
New Bedford	The Melville House, 100 Madison St, 02740 508-990-1566
New Marlborough	Red Bird Inn, PO Box 592, 01230 413-229-2433
Newburyport	Clark Currier Inn, 45 Green St, 01950
Newburyport	Essex Street Inn, 5 Essex St, 01950 508-465-3148
Newburyport	Garrison Inn, 11 Brown Square, 01950
Newburyport	Morrill Place Inn, 209 High St, 01950 508-462-2808
Newton Centre	New England B&B, PO Box 9100, Suite 176, 02159 617-244-2112
Newtonville	Sage and Thyme B&B, 65 Kirkstall Rd, 02160 617-964-4077
North Adams	Blackinton Manor B&B, 1391 Massachusetts Ave, 01247
North Carver	Bittersweet B&B, PO Box 279, 02355 508-866-2104
North Eastham	Jane Higgins House, Box 5, Massasoit Rd, 02651 508-255-6290
North Falmouth	Captains Inn, PO Box 1448, 02556 508-564-6424
Northfield	Centennial House, 94 Main St, 01360 413-498-5921
Northfield	Northfield Country House, 181 School St, 01360 413-498-2692
Oak Bluffs	Admiral Benbow Inn, 81 New York Ave, 02557 508-693-6825

Oak Bluffs	Four Gables Inn, PO Box 1441, 02557 508-696-8384
Oak Bluffs	The Beach House B&B, PO Box 417, 02557 508-693-3955
Oak Bluffs	The Inn At Dockside, Box 1206, 02557
Oak Bluffs	The Tucker Inn, PO Box 2680, 02557 508-693-1045
Oak Bluffs	The Wesley House, PO Box 2370, 02557
Oak Bluffs	Tivoli Inn, PO Box 1033, 02557 508-693-7928
Onset	Onset Pointe Inn, PO Box 1450, 02558 508-295-8442
Onset	Reynolds House, Box 420, 02558
Orleans	Orleans Inn, PO Box 188, 02653 508-255-2222
Orleans	Seashore Park Inn, PO Box 175, 02653 508-255-2500
Orleans	The Cove, Route 28, Box 279, 02653 508-255-1203
Otis	Joyous Garde Inn, PO Box 132, 01253 413-269-6852
Paxton	Pine Hill Farm B&B, 11 Pond St, 01612 508-791-1762
Peru	The Stall, 108 East Windsor Rd, 01235 413-655-8008
Plymouth	Colonial House Inn, 207 Sandwich St, 02360 617-746-2087
Plymouth	Hall's B&B, 3 Sagamore St., 02360 508-746-2835
Plymouth	Hawthorne Hill B&B, 3 Wood St, 02360 508-746-5244
Plymouth	John Carver Inn, 25 Summer St, 02360 508-746-7100
Plymouth	Morton Park Place, 1 Morton Park Rd, 02360 508-747-1730
Plymouth	Sea Cliff Cottage B&B, 45 Black Pond Rd, 02360 508-224-3517
Plymouth	Steeple View B&B, 69 Cliff Street, 02360 508-747-0823
Plymouth	White Swan B&B, PO Box 190, 02381 508-224-3759
Pocasset	Somewhere Among My Flowers, 927 County Rd, 02559 508-563-5028
Princeton	Fernside B&B, 162 Mountain Rd, 01541 508-464-2741
Princeton	The Harrington Farm, 178 Westminster Rd, 01541 508-464-5600 ·
Provincetown	1807 House, 54 Commercial St, 02657
Provincetown	Ampersand Guest House, PO Box 832, 02657
Provincetown	Bayberry Accommodations, 16 Winthrop St., 02657 508-487-4605
Provincetown	Beaconlight Guest House, 12 Winthrop, 02657 508-487-9603
Provincetown	Benchmark Inn, 6-8 Dyer St., 02657 508-487-7440
Provincetown	Black Pearl, 11 Pearl St., 02657 508-487-6405
Provincetown	Bradford Gardens Inn, 178 Bradford St, 02657 508-487-1616
Provincetown	Captain Lysander Inn, 96 Commercial St, 02657 508-487-2253
Provincetown	Carpe Diem Guesthouse, 12 Johnson St, 02657 508-487-4242
Provincetown	Ireland House, 18 Pearl St., 02657 508-487-7132
Provincetown	Lady Jane's Inn, 7 Central St, 02657 508-487-3387
Provincetown	Lamplighter Inn, 26 Bradford St, 02657 508-487-2529
Provincetown	Rose and Crown Guest House, 158 Commercial St, 02657 508-487-3332
Provincetown	Sandpiper Beach House Htl, 165 Commercial St, 02657
Provincetown	Six Webster Place, 6 Webster Place, 02657 508-487-2266
Provincetown	Somerset House, 378 Commercial St, 02657 508-487-0383
Provincetown	The Fairbanks Inn, 90 Bradford St, 02657 508-487-0386
Provincetown	The Sunset Inn, 142 Bradford St., 02657 508-487-9810
Provincetown	Three Peaks, Victorian B&B, 210 Bradford St., 02657 508-487-1717
Provincetown	Tucker Inn @ Twelve Center, 12 Center St, 02657
Provincetown	Valentine Guest House, 88 Commercial St., 02657 508-487-0839
Provincetown	Watership Inn, 7 Winthrop St, 02657
Provincetown	White Wind Inn, PO Box 1307, 02657 508-487-1526
Provincetown	Windamar House, 568 Commercial St, 02657 508-487-0599
Rehoboth	Five Bridge Inn, PO Box 462, 02769 508-252-3190
Richmond	Peirson Place, 1238 State Rd., 01254 413-698-2750
Richmond	The Inn at Richmond, 802 State Rd. (SR 41), 01254 413-698-2566
Rockport	Addison Choate Inn, B&B, 49 Broadway, 01966 978-546-7543
Rockport	Beach Knoll Inn, 30 Beach St, 01966 508-546-6939
Rockport	Old Farm Inn, 291 Granite St, Rt 127, 01966 508-546-3237
Rockport	Peg Leg Inn & Restaurant, 2 King St, 01966 800-346-2352
Rockport	Pleasant Street Inn, 17 Pleasant St, 01966 508-546-3915
Rockport	Pratt John F., 37 Mount Pleasant, 01966
Rockport	Seaward Inn & Cottages, 62 Marmion Way, 01966 800-648-7733
Rockport	Yankee Clipper Inn, PO Box 2399, 01966 978-546-3407
Rowe	Maple House B&B, 51 Middletown Hill Rd, 01367
Rowley	Country Garden, 101 Main St., 01969 508-948-7773
Sagamore Beach	Sea Cliff, 2 Indian Trail, Box One, 02562 508-888-0609
Sagamore Beach	Widow's Walk B&B, Box 605, 02562 508-888-0762
Salem	Hawthorne Hotel, On the Common, 01970 978-744-4080
Salem	Inn at Seven Winter St., 7 Winter St, 01970 978-745-9520
Salem	Morning Glory B&B, 22 Hardy St, 01970 978-741-1703
Salem	The Red Maple B&B, 51 Washington Sq N, 01970
Sandwich	Barclay Inn, 40 Grove St, 02563 508-888-5738
Sandwich	Captain Otis House, 60 Gully Ln, 02563 508-362-9277
Sandwich	Dan'l Webster Inn, 149 Main St, 02563 508-888-3622
Sandwich	Dillingham House, 71 Main St, 02563 508-833-0065
Sandwich	Hawthorn Hill, PO Box 777, 02563 508-888-3333
Sandwich	Marshall House, 83 Famersville Rd, 02563
Sandwich	Seth Pope House 1699 B&B, 110 Tupper Rd, 02563 508-888-5916
Sandwich	Shady Nook Inn & Motel, PO Box 402, 02563 508-888-0409
Sandwich	The Dunbar House, 1 Water St, Rt 130, 02563 508-883-2485
Seekonk	Johnson & Wales Inn, 213 Taunton Ave, 02771 508-336-8700

Sharon	Sharon Inn, 7775 Providence Highway, 02067 617-784-5800
Sheffield	Centuryhurst Antiques B&B, PO Box 486, 01257 413-229-8131
Sheffield	Ivanhoe Country House, 254 S. Umdermountain Rd, 01257 413-229-2143
Sheffield	Orchard Shade B&B, PO Box 669, 01257 413-229-8463
Sheffield	Race Brook Lodge, 864 S. Undermountain Rd, 01257 413-229-2916
Sheffield	Staveleigh House, PO Box 608, 01257 413-229-2129
Shelburne Falls	Inn at Weston, PO Box 222, 01370 802-824-5804
Shelburne Falls	Parson Hubbard House, Old Village Rd, 01370 413-625-9730
South Chatham	Ye Olde Nantucket House, PO Box 468, 02659 508-432-5641
South Dartmouth	The Little Red House, 631 Elm St, 02748 508-996-4554
South Hadley	Grandmarys, 11 Hadley St, 01075
South Sudbury	Wayside Inn, Wayside Inn Road, 01776 617-443-8846
South Yarmouth	Four Winds, 345 High Bank Rd, 02664 508-394-4182
Southborough	Apple Tree B&B, 51 Sears Rd., 01772 508-460-0960
Sterling	Chocksett Inn, 59 Laurelwood Rd., 01564 508-422-3355
Stockbridge	Berkshire Thistle B&B, PO Box 1227, Rt 7, 01262 413-298-3188
Stockbridge	Broad Meadows, PO Box 485, 01262
Stockbridge	Olde Lamplighter B&B, 8 Church St., 01262 413-298-3053
Stockbridge	Roeder House B&B, PO Box 525, 01262 413-298-4015
Stockbridge	Seekees B&B, Mahkeenac Rd, 01262 413-298-0204
Stockbridge	Taggart House, Rt 102, 01262 413-298-4303
Stockbridge	The Red Lion Inn, Main St, 01262 413-298-5545
Stockbridge	Tom Carey's B&B, 3 Sergeant St, 01262
Stow	Amerscot House B&B, PO Box 351, 01775 508-897-0666
Sturbridge	Bethany B&B, 5 McGregory Rd., 01566 508-347-5993
Sturbridge	Col. Ebenezer Crafts Inn, PO Box 187, 01566 508-347-3313
Sturbridge	Commonwealth Cottage, PO Box 368, 01566 508-347-7708
Sturbridge	Publick House, Rt 131, Box 187, 01566 508-347-3313
Sudbury	Longfellow's Wayside Inn, Boston Post Rd, 01776 508-443-1776
Swampscott	Oak Shores, 64 Fuller Ave, 01907 617-599-7677
Townsend	Wood Farm, 40 Worcester Rd, 01469 508-597-5019
Tyngsboro	Stonehedge Inn, 160 Pawtucket Blvd., 01879 508-649-4400
Tyringham	Golden Goose, PO Box 336, 01264 413-243-3008
Vineyard Haven	Adworth Manor, PO Box 4058, 02568 508-693-3203
Vineyard Haven	Crocker House Inn, PO Box 1658, 02568 508-693-1151
Vineyard Haven	Deux Noisettes, 114 Main St., 02568 508-693-0253
Vineyard Haven	Franklin Oaks, 169 Franklin St, 02568
Vineyard Haven	Lambert's Cove Country Inn, RR 1, Box 422, 02568 508-693-2298
Vineyard Haven	Nancy's Auberge, 102 Main St, Box 4433, 02568 508-693-4434
Vineyard Haven	Sea Horse Guests, RFD Box 373, 02568 508-693-0594
Vineyard Haven	The Hanover House, PO Box 2107, 02568 508-693-1066
Vineyard Haven	The Lothrop Merry House, PO Box 1939, 02568 508-693-1646
Vineyard Haven	The Post House, PO Box 717, 02568 508-693-5337
Vineyard Haven	Twin Oaks Inn, PO Box 1767, 02568 508-693-8633
Wareham	Cranberry Rose B&B, 200 Tihonet Rd, 02571
Wellesley	Wellesley Inn on the Squar, 576 Washington St., 02181 617-235-0180
Wellfleet	Blue Gateways, 252 Main St., 02667 508-349-7530
Wellfleet	Cahoon Hollow B&B, PO Box 38, 02667 508-349-6372
Wellfleet	Holden Inn, PO Box 816, 02667
Wellfleet	The Inn at Duck Creeke, PO Box 364, 02667 508-349-9333
West Falmouth	Sjoholm Inn B&B, PO Box 430, 02574 508-540-5706
West Falmouth	The Elms, 15 Widgeon Rd, 02540 508-540-7232
West Groton	Wrangling Brook Farm, PO Box 138, 01472 978-448-8253
West Harwich	Cape Winds, 28 Shore Rd, 02671
West Harwich	Lion's Head Inn, PO Box 444, 02671 508-432-7766
West Harwich	The Tern Inn, 91 Chase St, 02671 508-432-3714
West Harwich	Willow House, 23 Willow St, 02671
West Springfield	Storrowton Tavern, 1305 Memorial Avenue, 01089 413-732-4188
West Stockbridge	Card Lake Country Inn, Main St, 01266 413-232-0272
West Stockbridge	Marble Inn, 4 Stockbridge Rd., 01266 413-232-7092
West Stockbridge	Shaker Mill Inn, Box 521, 01266 413-232-8596
Westhampton	Outlook Farm, 136 Main Rd, 01027 413-527-0633
Weston	Webb-Bigelow House, 863 Boston Post Rd, 02193 617-899-2444
Williamstown	1896 House Brookside, Routes 7 & 2, 01267 413-458-8125
Williamstown	Fairfields B&B, 954 Green River Rd., 01267 413-458-3321
Williamstown	Jericho Valley Inn, Rt 43, Hancock Rd, 01267 413-458-9511
Williamstown	River Bend Farm, 643 Simmons Rd, 01267 413-458-3121
Williamstown	Williams Inn, On the Green, 02167 413-458-9371
Woods Hole	Gardeners House, 251 Woods Hole Rd, 02540
Woods Hole	The Marlborough, PO Box 238, 02543 508-548-6218
Woronoco	General Knox House, 706 General Knox Rd, 01097 413-562-6439
Worthington	Tamarack Lodge, 68 Thrasher Hill Rd, 01098 413-238-4449
Worthington	The Hill Gallery B&B, 137 E Windsor Rd, 01098 413-238-5914
Yarmouth Port	Crook's Jaw Inn, 186 Main St., 02675 508-362-6111
Yarmouth Port	Fishers' Net, 626 Main St., 02675 508-362-8264
Yarmouth Port	Old Yarmouth Inn, PO Box 353, 02675
Yarmouth Port	Strawberry Lane B&B, PO Box 311, 02675 508-362-8631
Yarmouth Port	The Inn at Cape Cod, PO Box 96, 02675 508-375-0590

Michigan

Flint	The Courtyard, G-3202 W. Court St, 48532 313-238-5510
Frankenmuth	B&B at The Pines, 327 Ardussi St, 48734 517-652-9019
Frankenmuth	Franklin Haus, 216 S. Franklin St, 48734 517-652-3383
Frankenmuth	The Hillside, 575 Cass St., 48734 517-652-6232
Frankfort	Captains Quarters B&B, PO Box 1132, 49635 616-352-6227
Frankfort	Chimney Corners Resort, 1602 Crystal Dr., 49635 616-352-7522
Frankfort	Frankfort Land Company, PO Box 267, 49635 616-352-9267
Frankfort	Haugen's Haven B&B, PO Box 913, 49635 616-352-7850
Frankfort	The Birch Haven Inn, Box 411, 49635 616-352-4008
Freeland	Stonehedge Inn B&B, 8243 Midland Rd, 48623 517-894-4342
Fremont	Gerber House B&B, 6130 W 56th St, 49412 616-924-2829
Fruitport	Village Park B&B, 60 West Park St, 49415 616-865-6289
Galesburg	Pine Arbor, 13800 E. Michigan Ave, 49053 616-746-4271
Galesburg	The Byrd House, 11483 E. G Ave, 49053 616-665-7052
Galien	The Valentine House, 19639 Jeffery Rd, 49113 616-756-2223
Gaylord	North Branch Outing Club, 6122 E County Rd 612, 49738 517-348-7951
Gladwin ·	Eggleston Schoolhouse B&B, 10539 Nolan Rd, 48624 517-426-1964
Glen Arbor	Glen Arbor B&B, PO Box 526, 49636 231-334-6789
Glen Arbor	North Oak B&B, 5760 N Oak, 49636 231-334-6445
Glenn	Culpepper Inn B&B, PO Box 22, 49416 616-227-3028
Gobles	Kal-Haven B&B, 23491 Paulson Rd, 49055
Grand Haven	Boyden House Inn B&B, 301 South 5th St, 49417 616-846-3538
Grand Haven	Harbor House Inn, 114 S Harbor Dr, 49417 616-846-0610
Grand Haven	Seascape B&B, 20009 Breton, 49456 616-842-8409
Grand Haven	The Looking Glass Inn, 1100 S Harbor, 49417 616-842-7150
Grand Ledge	Edwards' Wind Crest, 11880 Oneida Rd, 48837 517-627-2666
Grand Rapids	Fountain Hill B&B, 222 Fountain, NE, 49503 616-458-6621
Grand Rapids	Heald-Lear House, 455 College Ave, SE, 49503 616-459-9055
Grand Rapids	Peaches B&B, 29 Gay Ave SE, 49503 616-454-8000
Grand Rapids	The Brayton House, 516 College SE, 49503
Grass Lake	Coppys Inn, 13424 Phal Rd, 49240 571-522-4850
Grayling	Belknap's Hanson House, 604 Peninsular, 49738 517-348-6630
Grayling	Heritage House B&B, PO Box 766, 49738 517-732-1199
Harbor Springs	Caribou Lake B&B, PO Box 474, 49740 231-663-7489
Harbor Springs	Four Acres B&B, 684 W. Bluff Dr, 49740 231-525-6076
Harbor Springs	Harbor Springs Cottage Inn, 145 Zoll St., 49740 231-526-5431
Harbor Springs	Highland Hideaway B&B, 6767 Pleasantview Rd, 49740 231-526-8100
Harbor Springs	Windy Ridge B&B, 6281 S. Lakeshore Dr, 49740 800-409-4095
Harrison	Carriage House Inn, PO Box 757, 48625 517-539-1300
Harrisville	Red Geranium Inn, PO Box 613, 48740 517-724-6153
Harrisville	Springport Inn B&B, 659 U.S. 23 South, 48740 517-724-6308
Harrisville	Stratton's Springport Inn, 659 U.S. 23 S, 48740
Harrisville	Widow's Watch B&B, PO Box 245, 48740 517-724-5465
Hart	Rooms At "The Inn", 515 State St, 49420 616-873-2448
Hartland	Farmstead B&B, 13501 Highland Rd, 48353 313-887-6086
Hiawatha Forest	Buck Stop Sporting Lodge, PO Box 156, 49878 906-446-3360
Hillsdale	Bluebird Trails B&B, 8591 Blount Rd, 49242 517-254-4754
Holland	Bonnie's Parsonage 1908, 6 E. 24th St, 49423 616-396-1316
Holland	Centennial Inn B&B, 8 E 12th St, 49423 616-355-0998
Holland	Reka's B&B, 300 N. 152nd Ave, 49424 616-399-0409
Holland	The Thistle Inn, 300 N 152nd Ave, 49424 616-399-0409
Holly	Holly Crossing B&B, 304 S. Saginaw, 48442 810-634-7075
Houghton	Charleston House B&B, 918 College Ave, 49931 906-482-7790
Houghton Lake	Stevens White House, PO Box 605, 48629 517-366-4567
Interlochen	Between the Lakes B&B, PO Box 280, 49643 616-276-7751
Interlochen	Interlochen Aire, 4550 State Park Hwy, 49643 616-276-6941
Interlochen	Sandy Shores B&B, 4487 State Park Hwy, 49643 616-276-6941
Ithaca	Bon Accord Farm B&B, 532 E. Polk Td, 48847 517-875-3136
Jackson	Rose Trellis B&B, 603 W. Michigan Ave, 49201 517-787-2035
Jackson	Summit Place B&B, 1682 W. Kimmel Rd, 49201 517-787-0468
Jones	Sanctuary at Wildwood, 58138 M40 N, 49061 616-244-5910
Kalamazoo	Kalamazoo House, 447 W. South St, 49007 616-343-5426
Karlin	Hall Creek B&B, 7450 Hall Creek Rd, 48643 616-263-2560
Kearsarge	Belknap's Garnet House, 237 Stuart Ave, 49942 906-337-5607
Laingsburg	Seven Oaks Farm, 7891 Hollister Rd, 48848 517-651-5598
Lake City	B & B In The Pines, 1940 Schneider Park Rd, 49651 616-839-4876
Lake Leelanau	Centennial Inn, 7251 E. Alpers Rd, 49653 616-271-6460
Lake Leland	Centennial Inn, 7251 E. Alpers Rd, 49653 616-271-6460
Lake Orion	The Indianwood, 80 Cayuga Rd, 48362 810-693-2257
Lakeside	Lakeside Inn, 15281 Lakeshore Rd, 49116
Lakeside	The Pebble House, PO Box 297, 49116 616-469-1416
Lanse	Bungalow B&B, Route 1, Box 123, 49946 906-524-7595
Lansing	Ask Me House, 1027 Seymour, 48906 517-484-3127
Lansing	Maplewood, 15945 Wood Rd, 48906 517-485-1426
Laurium	Keweenaw House, 209 Pewabic St., 49913 906-337-4822
Laurium	Laurium Manor & Vict. Hall, 320 Tamarack St, 49913 906-337-2549
Lawrence	Oak Cove Resort, 58881 46th St, 49064 616-674-8228
Leland	Aspen House, PO Box 722, 49654 616-256-9724

Leland	Snowbird Inn, PO Box 1124, 49654 616-256-9773
Leland	The Highlands of Leland, PO Box 101, 49654 616-256-7632
Lewiston	Gorton House, Wolf Lake Dr, 49756 517-786-2764
Lewiston	Pine Ridge Lodge, CR 489 & Pine Haven Rd, 49756 517-786-4789
Lexington	Britannia House English, PO Box 5, 48450 313-359-5772
Lexington	Governor's Inn B&B, PO Box 471, 48450 313-359-5770
Lexington	The Powell House B&B, 5076 S. Lakeshore Rd, 48450 313-359-5533
Lowell	Alden Pines B&B, 1320 Alden Nash, 49331 616-897-5655
Ludington	B&B at Ludington, 2458 S. Beaune Rd, 49431 800-275-4616
Ludington	Doll House Inn, 709 E. Ludington Ave, 49431 213-843-2286
Ludington	Inland Sea B&B, 5393 S. Lakeshore Dr, 49431 213-845-7569
Ludington	Schoenberg House, 409 E Ludington Ave, 49431 213-843-4435
Ludington	The Lamplighter B&B, 602 E Ludington Ave, 49431 213-843-9792
Mackinac Island	Bay View at Mackinac, Box 448, 49757 906-847-3295
Mackinac Island	Cloghaun, PO Box 203, 49757 906-847-3885
Mackinac Island	Haan's 1830 Inn, PO Box 123, 49757 906-847-6244
Mackinac Island	Hotel Iroquois on Beach, Box 456, 49757
Mackinac Island	Small Point B&B, Box 427, 49757 906-847-3758
Mackinac Island	The Inn on Mackinac, PO Box 476, 49757 906-847-3361
Mackinac Island	The Island House, PO Box 1410, 49757 906-847-3347
Mancelona	Cedar Bend Farm, 1171 B Doerr Rd, 49659 616-587-5709
Manistee	1879 E.E. Douville House, 111 Pine St, 49660
Manistee	Inn Wick-A-Te-Wah, 3813 Lakeshore Dr, 49660 616-889-4396
Manistee	Lake Shore B&B, 3440 Lake Shore Rd, 49660 616-723-7644
Manistee	Manistee Country House, 1130 Lakeshore Rd, 49660 616-723-2367
Manistee	The Ivy Inn, 552 Harvard Lane, 49660 616-723-8881
Manistee	The Maples, 435 Fifth St, 49660 616-723-2904
Maple City	Country Cottage B&B, 135 E. Harbor Hwy, 49664 616-228-5328
Marine City	Heather House, 409 N. Main St, 48039 313-765-3175
Marlette	Country View B&B, 3723 S. Van Dyke, 48453 517-635-2468
Marquette	Blueberry Ridge B&B, 18 Oak Dr, 49855 906-249-9246
Marshall	National House Inn, 102 S. Parkview, 49068 616-781-7374
Mears	The Dunes B&B, PO Box 53, 49436 616-873-5128
Mecosta	Blue Lake Lodge B&B, PO Box 1, 49332 616-972-8391
Mendon	Mendon Country Inn B&B, 440 W Main St, 49072 616-496-8132
Menominee	Gehrke's Gasthaus, 320 1st St., 49858 906-863-6345
Midland	The Bramble House B&B, 4309 Bramble Ridge, 48640 517-832-5082
Monroe	Lotus B&B, 324 Washington St., 48161 734-384-9914
Mount Pleasant	The Roycroft Inn B&B, 2265 Broomfield, 48858
Munising	The Homestead B&B, 713 Prospect St, 49862
Muskegon	Blue Country B&B, 1415 Holton Rd (M-120), 49445 616-744-2555
Muskegon	Emery House B&B, 446 W. Webster, 49440 616-722-6978
Muskegon	Hackley-Holt House B&B, 523 W. Clay Ave, 49440 616-725-7303
Muskegon	Port City Victorian Inn, 1259 Lakeshore Dr, 49441 616-759-0205
New Buffalo	All Suites Inn-New Buffalo, 231 E Buffalo St, 49117 616-469-1000
New Buffalo	Bauhaus On Barton, 33 N Barton St., 49117 616-469-6419
New Buffalo	Tall Oaks Inn B&B, Box 6, 49117 616-469-0097
New Era	Okapi Inn, 4664 3rd St., Box 87, 49446 616-861-4077
Northport	Birch Brook, 310 S. Peterson Park Rd, 49670 616-386-5188
Northport	North Shore Inn, 12271 N Northport Pt Rd, 49670 616-386-7111
Northport	The Old Mill Pond Inn, 202 West Third St, 49670 616-386-7341
Northville	Atchison House, 501 W. Dunlap St, 48167 313-349-3340
Omena	Omena Shores B&B, PO Box 154, 49674 616-386-7313
Omena	Omena Sunset Lodge B&B, PO Box 242, 49674 616-386-9080
Omer	Rifle River B&B, 500 Center Ave., 48749 517-653-2543
Onaway	Stillmeadow B&B, 6658 M-33 South, 49765
Onekama	Lake Breeze House, 5089 Main St, 49675 616-889-4969
Onekama	Portage Point Inn, PO Box 596, 49675
Ontonagon	Northern Light Inn, 701 Houghton St, 49953
Oscoda	Huron House B&B, 3124 N US 23, 48750 517-739-9255
Ossineke	Fernwood B&B, 10189 Ossineke Rd., 49766 517-471-5176
Owosso	Atchers Castle, 203 E King St, 48867
Pellston	Nickerson Inn, PO Box 986, 49449 616-869-6731
Pentwater	Historic Nickerson Inn, PO Box 986, 49449 616-869-6731
Pentwater	The Hexagon House, PO Box 1030, 49449 616-869-4102
Petoskey	510 Elizabeth Inn, 510 Elizabeth St, 49770 616-348-3830
Petoskey	Benson House B&B, 618 E Lake St, 49770 616-347-1338
Petoskey	Gull's Way, 118 Boulder Lane, 49770 616-347-9891
Petoskey	Mottls Getaway, 1101 Old Tannery Creek, 49770 616-526-9682
Petoskey	Stafford's Bay View Inn, PO Box 3 G, 49770 616-347-2771
Pinckney	Bunn-Pher Hill, 11745 Spencer Lane, 48169 313-878-9236
Plymouth	932 Penniman B&B, 932 Penniman Ave, 48170 313-414-7444
Plymouth	Auburn on Sheldon B&B Inn, 448 N Sheldon Rd, 48170 734-459-3022
Port Austin	Lake Street Manor B&B, 8569 Lake St, 48467
Port Austin	Questover Inn, PO Box 574, 48467 517-738-5253
Port Austin	The Garfield Inn, 8544 Lake St, 48467 517-738-5254
Port Sanilac	Holland's Little House, 1995 N. Huron View, 48469 810-622-9739
Rapid River	The Buck Stop B&B, PO Box 156, 49878 906-446-3360

Minnesota

Albert Lea	The Victorian Rose Inn, 609 W Fountain St., 56007 507-373-7602
Alexandria	Carrington House B&B, 2203 S Le Homme Dieu Dr, 56308 612-846-7400
Alexandria	The Pillars, 1004 Elm St, 56308
Annandale	Thayer B&B Inn, PO Box 246, 55302 320-274-8222
Anoka	Bendemere On Mississippi, 1701 Bendemere, 55303 612-427-1815
Anoka	Ticknor Hill B&B, 1625 3rd Ave S, 55303 612-421-9687
Backus	Pine Mountain Inn, PO Box 144, 56435 218-947-3050
Battle Lake	Xanadu Island B&B, RR 2, Box 51, 56515 218-864-8096
Bemidji	Lakewatch B&B, 609 Lake Blvd NE, 56601 218-751-8413
Bemidji	Meadowgrove Inn B&B, 13661 Pwrdm Rd, 56601
Brainerd	Pine Haven B&B, 1625 McKay Rd, 56401 218-829-1234
Brooklyn Park	Meadows B&B, 10500 Noble Ave N, 55443 612-315-2865
Caledonia	The Inn on the Green, Route 1, Box 205, 55921 507-724-2818
Cannon Falls	Candlewick Country Inn, 300 W Mill St, 55009 651-263-0879
Cannon Falls	Country Quiet Inn, 37295 112th Ave Way, 55009 651-258-4406
Cannon Falls	Quill & Quilt, 615 W. Hoffman St, 55009 651-263-5507
Chaska	Bluff Creek Inn, 1161 Bluff Creek Dr, 55318 612-445-2735
Chatfield	Lund's Guest House, 218 Winona St SE, 55923 507-867-4003
Cook	Moosebirds on Lake Vermilo, 3068 Vermilion Dr, 55723 218-666-2627
Crosby	Nordic Inn Medieval B&B, 210 1st Ave NW, 56441 218-546-8299
Crosslake	Lo Kiandy Inn, PO Box 33, 56442 218-692-2714
Detroit Lakes	Acorn Lake B&B, 1316 Lyndale Ave, 56501
Detroit Lakes	Idlewood By the Lake, 1106 W Lake Dr., 56501 218-847-1229
Duluth	Manor On The Creek, 2215 E Second St., 55812 218-728-3494
Duluth	PJ's B&B, 5757 Berquist Rd., 55804 218-525-2508
Duluth	Spinnaker Inn B&B, 5427 N Shore Scenic Dr., 55804 218-525-2838
Duluth	The Olcott House B&B Inn, 2316 E 1st St., 55812 218-728-1339
Dundas	Martin Oaks B&B, PO Box 207, 55019 507-645-4644
Duquette	Home in the Pines B&B Inn, Box 688, 55729 218-496-5825
Ely	Blue Heron B&B, HCI 3298 County Rd 16, 55731 218-365-4720
Ely	Burntside Lodge, 2755 Burntside Lodge Rd, 55731 218-365-3894
Ely	Sandemar Lodge, PO Box 689, 55731 218-365-2769
Ely	Trezona House B&B, 315 E Washington St., 55731 218-365-5916
Embarrass	Finnish Heritage Homestead, 4776 Waisanen Rd, 55732
Excelsior	Christopher Inn, 201 Mill St, 55331 612-474-6816
Excelsior	James Clark House B&B, 371 Water St., 55331 612-474-0196
Falcon Heights	Rose B&B, 2129 Larpenteur Ave W, 55113 612-642-9417
Faribault	Cherub Hill, 105 NW 1st Ave, 55021 507-332-2024
Fergus Falls	Bergerud 'B'S, RR 5 Box 61, 56537
Finlayson	Giese B&B Inn, 770 Aitkin County Rd 23, 55735 320-233-6429
Glencoe	Glencoe Castle B&B, 831 13th St East, 55336
Glenwood	Victory Inn, 15 erd Ave SW, 56334 320-634-5070
Grand Marais	Clearwater Lodge, 355-B Gunflint Trl, 55604
Grand Marais	MacArthur House B&B, PO Box 1270, 55607 218-387-1840
Grand Marais	Naniboujou Lodge, HC 80 Box 505, 55604
Grand Marais	Pincushion Mountain B&B, 968 Gunflint Trail, 55604 218-387-1276
Grand Marais	Snuggle Inn II B&B, PO Box 915, 55607 218-387-2847
Grand Marais	The Superior Overlook B&B, PO Box 963, 55604 218-387-1571
Grand Marais	The Woods B&B, PO Box 905, 55604 218-663-7144
Grand Rapids	Judge Thwing House, 1604 Co. Rd A, 55744
Grand Rapids	Seagren's Pokegama Lodge, 931 Crystal Springs Rd, 55744 218-326-9040
Harmony	Judy's Lane Guest House, 710 Main St, 55939 507-886-4166
Harmony	Selvig House B&B, PO Box 132, 55939 507-886-2200
Hastings	Country Rose, 13452 90th St S, 55033 651-436-2237
Hastings	Hearthwood B&B, 17650 200th St East, 55033
Hastings	Rosewood Inn, 620 Ramsey St., 55033 651-437-3297
Hastings	Thorwood Historic Inns, 315 Pine St, 55033 651-437-3297
Henderson	Henderson House, 104 N 8th St, 56044 507-248-3719
Hibbing	Adams House B&B, 201 E 23rd St, 55746 218-263-9742
Hibbing	Northland B&B, 4859 1st Ave, 55746 218-263-7864
Hickley	Dakota Lodge, Rt 3, Box 178, 55037 612-384-6052
Hinckley	Down Home B&B, RR 2 Box 177A, 55037 320-384-0396
Houston	Addie's Attic, 117 S Jackson St, 55943
Houston	The Bunk House, 501 S. Jefferson, 55943 507-896-2080
Ivanhoe	Weaver's Haus B&B, 315 E George St, 56142 507-694-1637
Jackson	Moorland Country Inn, PO Box 5, 56143 507-847-4707
Jackson	Old Railroad Inn, 219 Moore St., 56143 507-847-5348
Jackson	The Burnham House B&B, 511 South St., 56143 507-847-4327
Kenyon	Grandfather's Woods, 3640 450th St, 55946
Knife River	Emily's Inn General Store, PO Box 174, 55609 218-834-5950
Lake Benton	Benton House, 211 W Benton St, 56149 507-368-9484
Lake Benton	Sweet Memories B&B, 204 Fremont St S, 56149 507-368-9244
Lake Benton	Wooden Diamond B&B, 504 Shady Shore Dr, 56149 507-368-4305
Lake City	Red Gables B&B Inn, 403 N. High St, 55041 651-345-2605
Lake Shore	Lake Shore B&B, 5210 Christy Dr., 56468 218-568-4450
Lanesboro	Birch Knoll Ranch B&B, Rt 2 Box 11, 55949 612-475-2054

Lanesboro	Cady Hayes House, 500 Calhoun Ave, 55949
Lanesboro	Cottage House, 209 Parkway N, 55949 507-467-2577
Lanesboro	Galligan House, 706 Parkway Ave S, 55949 612-926-9312
Lanesboro	Habberstad House, 706 Fillmore Ave S, 55949 507-467-3560
Litchfield	Birdwing Spa, 21398 575th Ave., 55355 320-693-6064
Little Falls	Lottie Lee's B&B, 206 SE 3rd St, 56345 320-632-8641
Long Prairie	Crabtree Corners B&B, 224 2nd Ave N, 56347 320-732-6688
Mabel	Mabel House B&B, 117 S. Main, 55954 507-493-5768
Manhattan Beach	Manhattan Beach Lodge, PO Box 719, 56442 218-692-3381
Marshall	Ashgrove Farm B&B, RR 1, 56258 507-532-2208
McGregor	Savanna Portage Inn, HCR 4, Box 96, 55760 218-426-3500
Minneapolis	Le Blanc House, 302 University Ave NE, 55413 612-379-2570
Minnetonka	Babette's Inn, 18707 Red Cherry Cir, 55345 507-247-3962
Morris	The American House, 410 E. Third St, 56267 612-589-4054
New Ulm	Deutsche Strasse B&B, 404 S German St, 56073 507-354-2005
New York Mills	Whistle Stop Inn, Rt 1 Box 85, 56567
Oak Park Heights	The Cover Park Manor, 15330 58th St N, 55082 612-430-9292
Onamia	Cour du Lac B&B, 10654-390th St, 56359 320-532-4627
Osage	Lady Slipper Inn, Rt 2 Box 75, 56570 218-573-3353
Owatonna	Northrop House, 358 East Main St, 55060
Park Rapids	Carolyn's Hideaway, HC 05 Box 534, 56470 218-732-1101
Park Rapids	Gramma's B&B, 900 N Park Ave., 56470 218-732-0987
Park Rapids	Heartland Trail B&B, Box 39, 56470 218-732-3252
Paynesville	Donna's B&B, 16093 Lake Koronis Rd., 56362 800-950-4610
Pelican Rapids	Prairie View Estates, Rt 2 Box 443, 56572
Peterson	Wenneson Historic Inn, PO Box 11, 55962 507-875-2587
Pillager	Pinecrest Cottage, Rt 1, Box 150, 56473 218-746-3936
Preston	Inn Town Lodge, 205 Franklin St, 55965 507-765-4412
Preston	Jailhouse Historic Inn, PO Box 422, 55965 507-765-2181
Princeton	Oakhurst Inn B&B, 212 S 8th Ave., 55371 612-389-3553
Princeton	Rum River Country B&B, 5002 85th Ave, 55371 612-389-2679
Ranier	Sandbay B&B @ Tara's Wharf, PO Box 333, 56668 218-286-5699
Ray	Bunt's B&B Inns, Lake Kabetogama, 56669 218-875-2691
Red Wing	St. James Hotel, 406 Main St, 55066 651-388-2846
Red Wing	The Golden Lantern Inn, 721 East Ave, 55066 651-388-3315
Rochester	Hilltop B&B, 1735 3rd Ave NW, 55901 507-282-6650
Rochester	Inn at Rocky Creek, 2115 Rocky Creek Dr NE, 55906 507-288-1019
Saint Cloud	Edelbrock House, 216 N 14th Ave., 56303 320-259-0071
Sanborn	Sod House on the Prairie, RR 2 Box 75, 56083 507-723-5138
Sauk Centre	Palmer House Hotel/Inn, 228 Original Main St, 56378 612-352-3431
Shakopee	The Nicholas House, 134 Fourth Ave East, 55379
Sherburn	Four Columns Inn, 668 140th St, 56171 507-764-8861
Side Lake	McNair's B&B, PO Box 155, 55781
Side Lake	Pine Beach Resort Inc, PO Box 5, 55781 218-254-3144
Silver Bay	Norsk Kubbe Hus, Box 131 B, 55614 218-226-4566
Sleepy Eye	W. W. Smith Inn, 1901 Linden St SW, 56805 507-794-5661
Spring Grove	Stratford-Lee Inn, Rt 1 Box 108, 55974 507-498-5707
Spring Valley	Chase's B&B, 508 N. Huron Ave, 55975 507-346-2850
St. Cloud	Riverside Guest Haus, 912 Riverside Dr SE, 56304 320-252-2134
St. Cloud	Victorian Oaks B&B, 404 9th Ave S, 56301 320-202-1404
St. Paul	McCracken House, 1153 Portland Ave, 55105 612-224-7003
St. Paul	The Garden Gate, 925 Goodrich Ave, 55105 612-227-8430
St. Peter	Engesser House B&B, 1202 S. Minnesota Ave., 56082 507-931-9594
Starbuck	311 Ivy Inn, PO Box 28, 56381 320-239-4868
Stephen	Grandma's House B&B, PO Box 199, 56757 218-478-2743
Stillwater	Harvest Restaurant & Inn, 114 Chestnut St., 55082 651-430-8111
Stillwater	Laurel Street Inn, 210 E. Laurel St, 55082 651-351-0031
Stillwater	Lowell Inn, 102 N. Second St, 55082 651-439-1100
Stillwater	The Heirloom Inn B&B, 1103 S. Third St, 55082 651-430-2289
Stillwater	The Lady Goodwood, 704 S 1st St, 55082 651-439-3771
Taylors Falls	Hudspeth House B&B, 21225 Victory Ln, 55084 612-465-5811
Taylors Falls	The Cottage B&B, 30495 Herberg Rd Box 71, 55084 612-465-3595
Tower	Pike Bay Lodge, 9422 Hearthside Dr., 55790 218-753-2430
Tracy	Valentine Inn B&B, 385 Emory St, 56175 507-629-3827
Truman	The Whittler's Lady B&B, 621 W Ciro, Box 324, 56088 507-776-8555
Two Harbors	Gowdys Inn and B&B, 1446 Hwy 61 E, 55616 218-226-4614
Two Harbors	The Bryan House, 123 Third Ave, 55616 218-834-2950
Underwood	Aloft in the Pines, PO Box 294, 56586 218-495-2862
Utica	Ellsworth B&B, 100 Hwy 14 RR 1 Box 15A, 55979 507-932-5022
Wabasha	Bridgewaters B&B, 136 Bridge Ave, 55981 651-565-4208
Wabasha	Eagles on the River B&B, PO Box 18, 55981 651-565-3509
Walker	Chase On The Lake Lodge, PO Box 206, 56484 218-547-1531
Walker	Tianna Farms, 1 Tianna Farms Rd., 56484 218-547-1306
Warroad	Hospital Bay B&B, 620 NE Lake St, 56763
Watertown	Wander Inn B&B, 2590 Vega Ave., 55360 612-955-2230
Welch	Hungry Point Inn, One Olde Deerfield Rd, 55089 651-437-3660
Welch	Red Wing Blackbird B&B, 722 W 5th St, 55066 651-388-2292
Willmar	Buchanan House B&B, 725 SW Fifth St, 56201

Mississippi

Aberdeen	Huckleberry Inn, 500 S Hickory St, 38730 601-369-7294
Aberdeen	Morgan's Country Home, 20147 Adams Rd, 39730 601-369-8151
Aberdeen	Morgan's Hill Top Inn, 20136 Adams Rd, 39730 601-369-6521
Ackerman	Candlewick Inn, 165 Cockran St, 39735 601-285-4466
Bay St. Louis	Bay Town Inn, 208 N Beach Blvd, 39520 601-466-5870
Bay St. Louis	Heritage House, 116 Ulman Ave, 39520 601-467-1649
Belzoni	Magnolia Inn, PO Box 254, 39038 601-247-4932
Biloxi	Father Ryan House Inn, 1196 Beach Blvd, 39530 228-435-1189
Biloxi	Lofty Oaks Inn, 17288 Highway 67, 39532 601-392-6722
Biloxi	River B&B of Mississippi, 12099 Doctor Lake Dr, 39532
Brookhaven	Edgewood, 412 Storm Ave, 39601 601-833-2001
Cleveland	Molly's B&B, 214 S Bolivar Ave, 38732 601-843-9913
Columbus	Amzi Love B&B, 305 S. 7th St, 39701 601-328-5413
Columbus	Backstrom's Country B&B, PO Box 2311, 39704 601-328-7213
Columbus	Fourth Avenue Cottage, 912 Fourth Ave South, 39701
Columbus	Ninth Street Suite, 403 Ninth St S, 39701 601-328-9575
Columbus	Temple Heights, 515 Ninth St. N, 39701 601-328-0599
Corinth	General Quarters, 924 Fillmore St, 38834 601-286-3325
Corinth	Madison Inn, 822 Main St, 38834 601-287-7157
Corinth	Ravenswood B&B, 1002 Douglas St., 38834 601-665-0044
Corinth	Robbins Nest B&B, 1523 Shiloh Rd., 38834 601-286-3109
Corinth	Samuel D. Bramlitt House, 1125 Cruise St., 38834 601-286-5370
Crystal Springs	Wisteria Inn, 106 W Railroad, 39059 601-892-2526
Dundee	Uncle Henry's Place & Inn, 5860 Moon Lake Rd., 38626 601-337-2757
French Camp	French Camp B&B Inn, 1 Blue Bird Ln, 39745 601-547-6835
Glen Allan	Linden-on-the-Lake, PO Box 117, 38744 601-839-2181
Gloster	The Forest Retreat, 6060 Cobb Rd., 39638 504-895-0000
Greenville	Azalea House B&B, 548 S Washington Ave., 38701 601-335-0507
Greenville	Miss Lois' Victorian Inn, 1139 Arnold Ave, 38701 601-335-6000
Greenwood	Bridgewater Inn, 501 River Rd., 38930 601-453-9265
Greenwood	The Rivers' Inn, 1109 River Rd., 38930 601-453-5432
Gulfport	No-Mistake Plantation B&B, 16400 Bob White Rd, 39503
Hattiesburg	Dunhopen Inn B&B, 3875 Veterans Memorial, 39401 601-543-0707
Hattiesburg	Tally House, 217 S 15th Ave, 39401 601-582-3467
Hernando	Faulkner Inn, 2424 Hwy 301 S, 38632 601-429-3195
Hernando	Magnolia Grove B&B, 140 E Commerce, 38632 601-429-2626
Hernando	Shadow Hill, 2310 Elm St, 38632 601-449-0800
Holly Springs	Fort-Daniel Hall B&B, 184 S Memphis, 38635 601-252-6807
Holly Springs	Somerset Cottage, 310 S Cedar Hills Rd, 38635 601-252-4513
Iuka	Eastport Inn B&B, 100 S. Pearl St, 38852 601-423-2511
Jackson	Millsaps Buie House, 628 N. State St, 39202 601-352-0221
Jackson	Old Capitol Inn, 226 N State St, 39202 601-359-9000
Jackson	Poindexter Park Inn, 803 Deer Park St, 39203 601-944-1392
Kosciusko	Lucas Hill, 213 Galloway Dr, 39090 601-289-7860
Kosciusko	The Hammond-Routt House, 109 S Natchez, 39090 601-289-4131
Lake Cormorant	Bonne Terre Country Inn, 4715 W Church Rd, 38641 601-781-5100
Laurel	The Wisteria Cottage, 556 N Sixth Ave, 39440 601-425-2561
Leakesville	Grand Avenue Inn, PO Box 803, 39451 601-394-4503
Long Beach	McCarter Lane Guest House, 5501 McCarter Ln, 39560 601-863-9942
Lorman	Canemount Plantation, Hwy 552 West, 39096 601-877-3784
Lucedale	Chisholm House, 68 Holmes St, 39452 601-947-3308
Madison	Kirkhaven, 187 Dogwood Lane, 39110 601-856-8163
Magnolia	The Coney House, 204 S Clark Ave, 39652 601-783-3000
Magnolia	The Hiatt House, 315 S Cherry St, 39652 601-783-3343
McComb	Cedar Cove On The Lake, PO Box 525, 39648 601-542-3332
Memphis	Doler B&B, 3351 Hickory Hill Rd, 38115 601-637-2695
Meridian	Camellia B&B, 2303 23rd Ave, 39303 601-482-5483
Meridian	Dogwood B&B, 3111 29th Ave, 39303 601-482-5483
Natchez	Aunt Clara's Cottage, 718 N. Union, 39120 601-442-9455
Natchez	Aunt Pitty Pat's, 306 S. Rankin, 39120 601-446-6111
Natchez	Cedar Grove Plantation, 617 Kingston Rd, 39121 601-445-0585
Natchez	Clifton Heights, 212 Linton Ave, 39120 601-446-8047
Natchez	Coyle House, 307 S. Wall St, 39120 601-445-8679
Natchez	Dorsey House, 305 N. Pearl St, 39120 601-445-4649
Natchez	Dunleith House & Gardens, 84 Homochitto, 39120 601-446-8500
Natchez	Elgin Plantation, Elgin Rd, Hwy 61 S, 39120 601-446-6100
Natchez	Glen Auburn, 300 S. Commerce St, 39120
Natchez	Governor Holmes House, 207 S. Wall St, 39120 601-442-2366
Natchez	Guest House Historic Hotel, 201 N. Pearl St, 39120 601-442-1054
Natchez	Harper House, 201 Arlington, 39120 601-445-5557
Natchez	Highpoint, 215 Linton Ave, 39120 601-442-6963
Natchez	Hope Farm, 147 Homochitto St, 39120 601-445-4848
Natchez	Lansdowne Plantation, PO Box 2045, 39121 601-446-9401
Natchez	Lisle House, 701 N. Union St, 39120 601-442-7680
Natchez	Mark Twain On Main, 320 Main, 39120 601-442-3544
Natchez	Oakland Plantation, 1124 Lower Woodville Rd, 39120 601-445-5101

Natchez	Oakwood, Upper Kingston Rd, 39120 601-445-4738
Natchez	Pleasant Hill, 310 S. Pearl St, 39120 601-442-7674
Natchez	Ravenna, S Union at Ravenna Ln, 39120 601-446-9973
Natchez	Riverside, 211 Clifton Ave, 39120 601-446-5730
Natchez	Riverview, 47 New St, 39120 601-446-6526
Natchez	T.A.S.S. House, 404 S. Commerce St, 39120 601-445-4663
Natchez	The Burn, 712 N. Union St, 39120 601-442-1344
Natchez	The Wigwam, 307 Oak St, 39120 601-442-2600
Natchez	The William Harris House, 311 Jefferson St, 39120 601-445-2003
Natchez	Wensel House, 206 Washington St, 39120 601-445-8577
Natchez	White Wings, 311 N. Wall St, 39120 601-442-2757
Nesbit	Sassafras Inn B&B, PO Box 429, 38661 601-429-5864
Oakland	Magnolia Lodge, Rt 1, Box 61, 38948 601-623-0445
Ocean Springs	Cottage Retreat, 507 E Beach, 39564 601-875-7049
Ocean Springs	Oak Shade B&B, 1017 La Fontaine, 39564 601-872-8109
Ocean Springs	Wilson House, 6312 Allen Rd., 39565 601-875-6933
Oxford	Oliver-Britt House, 512 Van Buren Av., 38655 601-234-8043
Oxford	Puddin Place, 1008 University Ave, 38655 601-234-1250
Oxford	Worthy Guest House, 1301 Buchanan, 38655 601-234-3310
Pass Christian	Harbour Oaks Inn, 126 W Scenic Dr, 39571 228-452-9399
Pass Christian	Inn at the Pass, 125 E Scenic Dr, 39571 228-452-0333
Petal	Chateau Walker B&B, PO Box 488, 39465 601-582-5855
Poplarville	Jerine's Guest Cottage, 512 S Main St, 39470 601-795-4546
Poplarville	Swallow Fork Lake, PO Box 14, 39470 601-795-8396
Port Gibson	Gibson's Landing, PO Box 195, 39150 601-437-3432
Ridgeland	Mimi's Lake House, PO Box 6, 39158 601-856-7558
Robinsonville	Cottage Inn, Rt 1 Box 40, 38664 601-363-2900
Senatobia	Spahn House, 401 College St, 38668 601-562-9853
Starkville	Carpenter Place, 120 Oakridge St, 39759 601-323-4669
Starkville	The Caragen House, 1108 Hwy 82 W, 39759 601-323-0340
Starkville	The Cedars, 2173 Oktoc Rd, 39759 601-324-7569
Tunica	Levee Plantation Guest Hse, PO Box 607, 38676 601-363-1309
Tunica	Tunica Levee Inn, 1070 Riverview Dr, 38676 601-363-2002
Tupelo	The Mockingbird Inn B&B, 305 N Gloster, 38801 601-841-0286
Union	Old McDonald Hotel, Rt 5, Box 336, 39365 601-656-1944
Vicksburg	Balfour House, PO Box 781, 39181
Vicksburg	Cherry Street Cottage, 2212 Cherry St, 39180 601-636-7086
Vicksburg	Floweree Cottage, 2309 Pearl St, 39180
Vicksburg	The Belle of the Bends, 508 Klein St, 39181
Vicksburg	The Columns, 2002 Cherry St, 39180 601-638-6108
Vicksburg	The Corners, 601 Klein St, 39180 601-636-7421
Vicksburg	The Duff Green Mansion, PO Box 75, 39180 601-636-6968
Vicksburg	The Stained Glass Manor, 2430 Drummond St, 39180 601-638-8893
Water Valley	Town Creek Inn B&B, 304 Railroad St., 38965 601-473-1010
Waynesboro	Pou Plantation, 824 Pou Dr, 39367 601-735-5250
West	The Alexander House, PO Box 187, 39192 800-350-8034
Woodville	Desert Plantation, 411 Desert Ln, 39669 601-888-6188
Woodville	Henderson House, PO Box 19, 39669 601-888-6738
Woodville	Rosemont Plantation, PO Box 814, 39669 601-888-6809

Missouri

Annapolis	Rachel's B&B, 202 Second St, 63620 573-598-4656
Arrow Rock	Borgman's B&B, 706 Van Buren, 65320 816-837-3350
Arrow Rock	Cedar Grove B&B/Antiques, Cedar Grove, 65320 816-837-3441
Arrow Rock	DownOver Inn, 602 Main St, 65320 816-837-3268
Augusta	Quarry House, 4598 S Hwy 94, 63332 314-228-4070
Boonville	Lady Goldenrod Inn B&B, 629 E Spring St., 65233 816-882-5764
Boonville	Morgan Street Repose, 611 E. Morgan St, 65233 816-882-7195
Bourbon	Meramec Farm B&B, HC 1, Box 50, 65441
Bourbon	The Wildflower Inn, Route 2, Box 101, 65441 314-468-7975
Branson	Aunt Sadie's, 163 Fountain St, 65616 417-336-6772
Branson	Barger House B&B, 621 Lakeshore Dr, 65616 800-266-2134
Branson	Free Man House, 1773 Lakeshore Dr, 65616 417-334-6262
Branson	Josie's Peaceful Getaway, HCR 1, Box 1104, 65616 417-338-2978
Branson	Journey's End B&B, Box 2306, 65737 417-338-2685
Branson	Lakeshore B&B, HC #1, Box 935, 65616 417-338-2698
Branson	Rhapsody Inn B&B, 296 Blue Meadows Rd, 65616 417-335-2442
Branson	Schroll's Lakefront B&B, 418 N. Sycamore St, 65616 417-335-6759
Branson	Thurman House B&B, 888 State Hwy F, 65616 417-334-6000
Branson	We Lamb Farm, PO Box 338, 65615 417-334-1485
Brownbranch	Brown Branch Inn B&B, 122 Campbell Ranch Rd, 65608 417-796-2452
Camdenton	Castleview B&B, RR 1, Box 183M, 65020 573-346-9818
Canton	College Inn B&B, 801 College St, 63435
Cape Fair	Fantasea Inn, PO Box 123, 65624 417-538-2742
Carthage	The Leggett House, 1106 Grand, 64836 417-358-0683
Columbia	Missouri Manor, 1121 Ashland Rd, 65201 573-499-4437
Columbia	University Ave B&B, 1315 University Ave., 65201 573-499-1920

Concordia	Fannie Lee B&B Inn, 902 Main St, 64020
Cook Station	Cook Station Cottages, 41 Cook Station Rd., 65449 573-743-6900
Defiance	Das Gast Haus Nadler, 125 Defiance Rd, 63341 314-987-2200
Eldon	My Elusive Dream Country, RR 5 Box 125aa, 65026 573-392-7055
Eminence	River's Edge B&B Resort, HCR 1, Box 11, 65466 314-226-3233
Ethel	Recess Inn, 203 E. Main, 63539 660-486-3328
Ferguson	The Gables, 404 Darst Rd., 63135 314-521-2080
Gerald	Bluebird B&B, 5734 Mill Rock Rd, 63037 573-627-2515
Hannibal	Cliffside Mansion, 8 Stillwell Pl, 63401 573-248-1461
Hannibal	Fifth Street Mansion B&B, 213 S. Fifth St, 63401 573-221-0445
Hannibal	Queen Anne's Grace, 313 N Fifth St, 63401
Hannibal	Rothacker House B&B Inn, 423 N Fourth, 63401 573-221-6335
Hermann	Alice's Wharf Street B&B, 206 Wharf St., 65041 573-486-5785
Hermann	Angels In The Attic, 108 E Second St, 65041 573-486-5037
Hermann	Aunt Flora's B&B, 127 E. 5th St, 65041 314-486-3591
Hermann	Bide-A-Wee, 104 E Second St, 65041 573-486-3961
Hermann	Birk's Goethe St. Gasthaus, PO Box 255, 65041 314-486-2911
Hermann	Captain Wohlt Inn, 123 E 3rd St., 65041 573-486-3357
Hermann	Das Rheinhaus B&B, 126 W. 2nd St, 65041 314-486-3976
Hermann	Esther's Ausblick, 236 W. 2nd St, 65041 314-486-2170
Hermann	Hammock Hollow Guest Farm, RR 1 Box 206A, 65041 573-928-3021
Hermann	Lark's Nest B&B, HCR 62, Box 102B, 65041 314-943-6305
Hermann	Market Street B&B, 210 Market St, 65041 314-486-5597
Hermann	Meyer's Hilltop Farm B&B, RR3, Box 16, 65041 314-486-5778
Hermann	Mumbrauer Gasthaus, 223 E. 2nd St, 65041 314-486-5246
Hermann	Patty Kerr B&B, 109 E Third, 65041 573-486-2510
Hermann	Pelze Nichol Haus B&B, PO Box 147, 65041 573-486-3886
Hermann	Reiff House, 306 Market St, 65041
Hermann	Schmidt Guesthouse, 300 Market, 65041 314-486-2146
Hermann	Strassner Suites, 132 E. 4th St, 65041 314-486-2682
Hermann	The Country Porch B&B, 108 E 2nd St, 65041
Hermann	Weber-Schulte Haus, 229 E 4th, 65041 573-486-8965
Hermann	White House Hotel-1868-, 232 Wharf St, 65041 314-468-3200
Hermann	William Klinger Inn, PO Box 116, 65041 314-486-5930
Hollister	Bayside Inn, 387 Dale Ave, 65672 417-337-7478
Hollister	Ye English Inn, 355 Carpenter, 65672 417-334-4142
Houston	Windstone House B&B, 539 Cleveland Rd., 65483 417-967-2008
Independence	Serendipity B&B, 116 S. Pleasant St., 64050 816-833-4719
Jackson	Trisha's B&B & Tea Room, 203 Bellevue, 63755 314-243-7427
Jamesport	Country Colonial B&B, PO Box 46, 64648 816-684-6711
Jefferson City	Jefferson Inn, 801 W High St, 65101 573-635-7196
Joplin	Visages B&B, 3546 S Pearl Ave, 64804 417-624-1397
Kansas City	Basswood Country Inn, 15880 Interurban Rd, 64079 816-858-5556
Kansas City	Dome Ridge B&B, 14360 N.W. Walker Rd, 64164 816-532-4074
Kansas City	Hotel Savoy, 219 W 9th St, 64105 816-842-3575
Kansas City	Inn the Park B&B, 3610 Gillham Rd, 64111 816-931-0797
Kansas City	La Fontaine Inn, 4320 Oak St, 64111 816-753-4434
Kansas City	Southmoreland on the Plaza, 116 E 46th St, 64112 816-531-7979
Kimberling City	Cinnamon Hill B&B, 24 Wildwood Ln, 65686 417-739-5727
Kimmswick	The Wenom-Drake House, PO Box 125, 63053 314-464-1983
Labadie	Hunter's Hollow Inn, PO Box 127, 63055 314-458-3326
Labadie	Staats Waterford Estate, 4550 Boles Rd, 63055 314-451-5560
Lampe	Grandpa's Farm, Box 476, HCR 1, 65681 417-779-5106
Lampe	Just Like Grandma's, HC1, Box 432J, 65681 417-779-5817
Lampe	Williams Mountain B&B Inn, HC 1 Box 229A, 65681 417-779-5211
Leasburg	The Sleepy Seal B&B, 1459 Steuber Rd, 65535
Liberty	James Inn, 342 N. Water, 64068 800-781-3677
Libery	WynBrick Inn, 1701 WynBrick Dr, 64068 816-781-4900
Lonedell	Peppermint Spings Farm, PO Box 240, 64067 314-629-7018
Louisiana	Louisiana Guest House B&B, 1311 Georgia St, 63353 573-754-6366
Louisiana	Meadowcrest B&B, Route 1, 63353
Louisiana	Riverview B&B, 403 N Main St, 63353
Louisiana	Serando's House, PO Box 205, 63353 314-754-4067
Macon	St. Agnes Hall B&B, 706 Jackson, 63552 660-385-2774
Marshall	Bell Street Family GH, 228 E North St, 65340 816-886-8445
Marshfield	Stevens Farm Inn B&B, 4900 Hwy 00, 65706 417-859-6525
Marshfield	The Dickey House B&B, 331 S. Clay St, 65706 417-468-3000
Marthasville	Gramma's House, 1105 Highway D, 63357 314-433-2675
Maryville	The Magnolia Inn Ltd., 733 Windsor Ave, 64468 660-562-2225
Mexico	La Paz, 811 S. Jefferson, 65265 314-581-2011
Mineral Point	Green Acres Farm Family, Rt 1 Box 575, 63660
Mound City	Hugh Montgomery Home B&B, 410 E 6th St, 64470 660-442-5634
Mountain View	Jack's Fork Country Inn, Route 1 Box 347, 65548 805-934-1000
Mountain View	Merrywood Guest House, PO Box 42, 65548 417-934-2210
Neosho	The Heaton House B&B, 355 S Wood St, 64850 417-455-0788
Nevada	Red Horse Inn, 217 S. Main St, 64772 417-667-7796
New Franklin	Rivercene B&B, 127 County Rd 463, 65274 816-848-2497
Osage Beach	Cliff House B&B, RR 1 Box 885, 65065 573-348-9726

Ozark	Barn Again, 904 W Church St, 65721 417-581-2276
Ozark	Dear's Rest B&B, 1408 Cap Hill Ranch Rd, 65721 417-581-3839
Ozark	Smokey Hollow Lake B&B, 880 Cash Spring Rd, 65721 417-485-0286
Ozark	Summer Hill Cottage, 1975 Rockhill Rd, 65721 417-581-0365
Paris	Jackson House, PO Box 125, 65275 816-327-4283
Parkville	Down to Earth Lifestyles, 12500 N. Crooked Rd, 64152 816-891-1018
Perry	Perry's Guest House, 604 E Martin St., 63462 314-565-3191
Perryville	Pecan Corner B&B, 919 Sunset Dr, 63775 314-883-7171
Plattsburg	Apple Blossom Inn, 200 W Broadway, 64477 816-930-3243
Poplar Bluff	The Stuga, 900 Nooney St, 63901 573-785-4085
Potsi	Bust Inn, 612 E High St., 63664 573-438-4457
Reeds Spring	Martindale B&B, HCR 4, Box 3570, 65737 417-338-2588
Reeds Spring	Seldom Seen Cottage B&B, HCR 3, Box 5999, 65737 417-272-3593
Roach	Prairie Hollow B&B, HCR 67, Box 1160, 65787 573-346-9881
Rocheport	Roby River Run, 201 N. Roby Farm Rd, 65279 314-698-2173
Rocheport	School House B&B Inn, PO Box 88, 65279 573-698-2022
Rocheport	Yates House B&B, 305 Second St., 65279 314-698-2129
Rolla	Miner Indulgence, PO Box 672, 65402 573-364-0680
Saginaw	Lakeside Cottages & Aviary, PO Box 99, 64864 417-781-9230
Salem	Ashley Creek Farm B&B, Rt 5 Box 310 A, 65560 573-548-2451
Sedalia	Sedalia House Country B&B, Rt 4, Box 25, 65301 816-826-6615
Shell Knob	Shore Hollow B&B, HCR 1, Box 4310, 65747 417-858-3500
Sikeston	Klein House, 427 S Kingshighway, 63801 573-471-2501
Springfield	Frying Pan River Ranch, 2500 E Kearney St, 65803
Springfield	The Mansion at Elfindale, 1701 S Fort, 65807 417-831-5400
Springfield	The Outback Inn, 3973 E Farm Road 132, 65805
St. Charles	Lady B's B&B, 631 N Benton, 63301
St. Charles	Lococo House II, 1309 N 5th St, 63301
St. Charles	Sage House B&B, 1717 Elm, 63301 314-947-4843
St. Charles	Saint Charles House B&B, 338 S. Main St, 63301 314-946-6221
St. Joseph	Harding House B&B, 219 N. 20th St, 64501 816-232-7020
St. Joseph	Shakespeare Chateau, 809 Hall St, 64501 816-232-2667
St. Louis	Doelling Haus, 4817 Towne South, 63128 314-894-6796
St. Louis	Geandaugh House B&B, 3835-37 S. Broadway, 63118 314-771-5447
St. Louis	Lehmann House B&B, #10 Benton Place, 63104 314-231-6724
St. Louis	Lemp Mansion Inn, 3322 DeMenil Pl, 63141 314-664-8024
St. Louis	Seven Gables Inn, 26 N. Meramec, 63105 314-863-8400
St. Louis	Somewhere!! A B&B Guesthse, 2049 Sidney St, 63104 314-664-4PAM
St. Louis	The Fleur-de-Lys Inn, 3500 Russell Blvd., 63104 314-773-3500
Ste. Genevieve	Creole House B&B, 339 St. Mary's Rd, 63670 800-275-6041
Ste. Genevieve	Main Street Inn B&B, PO Box 307, 63670 573-883-9199
Ste. Genevieve	Somewhere Inn Time B&B, 383 Jefferson, 63670 573-883-9397
Steelville	Frisco Street B&B, PO Box 1219, 65565 573-775-4247
Versailles	The Hilty Inn, 206 E. Jasper, 65084 314-378-2020
Vienna	Gasconade Getaway B&B Inn, 14992 Maries Rd 302, 65582 573-744-5947
Walnut Shade	Light in the Window B&B, PO Box 165, 65771 417-561-2415
Warrensburg	The Camel Crossing, 210 E Gay St, 64093 660-429-2973
Warsaw	Victorian Garden Inn, 214 E Jackson St, 65355 660-438-3005
Washington	Weirick Hoelscher B&B, 716 W Main St., 63090 314-239-4469
Waynesville	The Home Place, 302 S Benton, 65583 573-774-6637
Weston	Apple Creek B&B, 908 Washington St., 64098 816-386-5724
Weston	Benner House B&B, 645 Main St, 64098 816-386-2616
Weston	Inn at Weston Landing, PO Box 97, 64098 816-640-5788
Weston	The Hatchery, 618 Short St, 64098 816-386-5700
Wheatland	Pine Homestead Country Inn, Fourth & Sherman, 65779 417-282-6003
Zanoni	Zanoni Mill Inn, PO Box 2, 65784 417-679-4050

Montana ————————————————————————

Absarokee	The Stillwater Lodge, 28 Woodard Ave, 59001 406-328-4899
Anaconda	Davidson Inn, 205 Cherry St., 58711 406-563-2745
Babb	Wagners Guest Lodge, PO Box 218, 59411 406-338-5770
Big Sandy	Raven Crest, RR 1, Box 662, 59520 406-378-3121
Big Sandy	Sky View, Box 408, 59520 406-378-2549
Big Sky	Lone Mountain Ranch, PO Box 160069, 59716 406-995-4644
Big Sky	Rainbow Ranch Lodge, PO Box 160336, 59716 406-995-4132
Big Timber	Big Timber Inn, PO Box 328, 59011 406-932-4080
Big Timber	Lazy K Bar Ranch, Box 550, 59011 406-537-4404
Big Timber	The Grand Hotel, PO Box 1242, 59011 406-932-4459
Bigfork	Cherry Way Inn, 26400 E Shore Rte, 59911 406-837-6803
Bigfork	Gustin Orchard B&B, E. Lake Shore, 59911 406-982-3329
Bigfork	Jubilee Orchards Lake Reso, 836 Sylvan Dr, 59911 406-837-4256
Bigfork	Schwartz's B&B, 890 McCaffery Rd, 59911 406-837-5463
Bigfork	Swan Lake Inn B&B, 78401 Montana Hwy 83, 59911 406-837-3600
Bigfork	The Deck House, Box 865, 59911
Billings	Pine Hills Place B&B, 4424 Pine Hills Dr, 59101
Billings	Sanderson Inn, 2038 S 56th St W, 59106 406-656-3388
Boulder	Boulder Hot Springs B&B, PO Box 930, 59632 406-225-4339

Bozeman	B&B Western Adventure, PO Box 4308, 59772 406-259-7993
Bozeman	Bear Canyon, 3111 Bear Canyon Rd, 59715
Bozeman	Beartooth Wilderness Lodge, 8950 Chapman Rd, 59718
Bozeman	Bergfeld B&B/Llama Ranch, PO Box 3044, 59715 406-586-7778
Bozeman	Bridger Inn, 3691 Bridger Canyon Rd., 59715 406-586-6666
Bozeman	Chokecherry Guest House, 1233 Storymill Rd., 59715 406-587-2658
Bozeman	Kirk Hill B&B, 7960 S. 19th Rd, 59715 406-586-3929
Bozeman	Lindley House, 202 Lindley Pl, 59715 406-587-8403
Bozeman	Millers of Montana B&B, 1002 Zacharia Lane, 59718 406-763-4102
Bozeman	Sun House B&B, 6271 Alamosa Ln, 59718 406-587-3651
Bridger	Circle of Friends, Rt 1 Box 1250, 59014
Broadus	Oakwood Lodge, S. Pumpkin Creek Rd, 59317
Butte	Copper King Mansion, 219 W. Granite St, 59701
Butte	Scott B&B, 15 W. Copper, 59701 800-844-2952
Choteau	Country Lane B&B, Route 2, Box 232, 59422 406-466-2816
Clyde Park	Gibson Cassidy House, 105 2nd Ave N, 59018 406-686-4743
Columbia Falls	La Villa Montana, 3800 Hwy. 40, 59912 800-652-8455
Columbia Falls	Plum Creek House, 985 Vans Ave, 59912 406-892-1816
Columbia Falls	Smoky Bear B&B, 4761 Smoky Bear Lane, 59912 406-387-4249
Columbia Falls	Turn in the River Inn, 51 Penny Ln., 59912
Condon	Holland Lake Lodge, S.R. Box 2083, 59826 800-648-8859
Conner	Bunky Ranch Outfitters, PO Box 215, 59827 406-821-3312
Coram	Wild Rose B&B, PO Box 130396, 59913 406-387-4900
Corvallis	Daybreak B&B, 616 Willow Creek Rd., 59828 406-961-4530
Corvallis	Heavenly View Hideaway B&B, 472 Woodcrest Lane, 59828
Darby	Triple Creek Ranch, 5551 W. Fork Route, 59829 406-821-4664
De Borgia	Hotel Albert, PO Box 300186, 59830 406-678-4303
Deer Lodge	Coleman-Fee Mansion B&B, 500 Missouri Ave., 59722 406-846-2922
Dillon	Hildreth Livestock GR, PO Box 149, 59725 406-681-3111
Emigrant	Paradise Gateway B&B, PO Box 84, 59027 800-541-4113
Emigrant	Querencia B&B, PO Box 184, 59027 406-333-4500
Emigrant	Yellowstone Country B&B, Box 1002, 59027 406-333-4917
Ennis	9T9 Ranch B&B, PO Box 564, 59729
Essex	Izaak Walton Inn, PO Box 653, 59916 406-888-5700
Essex	Paola Creek B&B, Paola Cr Rd/Mile 172.8, 59916 406-888-5061
Eureka	Huckleberry Hannah's B&B, 3100 Sophie Lake Rd, 59917 406-889-3381
Eureka	Trail's End B&B, 57 Trail's End Rd, 59917 406-889-3486
Gallatin Gateway	Aspen Grove B&B, 9 Rabel Lane, 59730 406-763-5044
Gallatin Gateway	Gallatin Gateway Inn, PO Box 376, 59730
Gardiner	Yellowstone Suites B&B, 506 4th St (Box 277), 59030 800-948-7937
Gold Creek	Lingenfelter Hansen Ranch, I-90 Exit 166, 59733 406-288-3436
Great Falls	Old Oak Inn, 709 4th Ave N, 59401
Great Falls	The Sovekammer B&B, 325 Skyline Dr NE, 59404 406-453-6620
Hamilton	Bavarian Farmhouse B&B, 163 Bowman Rd, 59840 406-363-4063
Hamilton	Sleeping Child Creek B&B, 1580 Sleeping Child Rd, 59840 406-363-4462
Hamilton	Trout Springs, 721 Desta St, 59840
Hardin	Kendrick House Inn, 206 N Custer Ave, 59034
Helena	Apppleton Inn B&B, 1999 Euclid Ave., 59601 406-449-7492
Helena	Barrister B&B, 416 N. Ewing, 59601 800-823-1148
Helena	Montana's Mountain Meadow, 2245 Head Lane, 59602 406-443-7301
Helena	The Sanders-Helena B&B, 328 N. Ewing, 59601 406-442-3309
Helena	The St. James B&B, 114 N. Hoback, 59601 406-449-2623
Hungry Horse	Glacier B&B, 220 Beta Road, 59919 406-387-4153
Huson	Schoolhouse and Teacherage, 9 Mile, 59846 406-626-5879
Kalispell	Blaine Creek B&B, 727 Van Sant Rd, 59901
Kalispell	Bonnie's B&B, 265 Lake Blaine Rd, 59901
Kalispell	Creston Country Inn, 70 Creston Rd, 59901 406-755-7517
Kalispell	River Rock B&B, 179 Schrade Rd, 59901
Lewiston	Spring Creek B&B, HC 87 Box 5050, 59457 406-538-9548
Libby	Bobtail B&B, 4909 Bobtail Rd, 59923 406-293-3926
Libby	The Kootenai Country Inn, 264 Mack Rd, 59923 406-293-7878
Livingston	Absaroka Cabins, 431 S H St, 59047 406-222-6519
Livingston	Davis Creek, Rt. 38, Box 2179, 59047 406-333-4353
Livingston	Remember When B&B, 320 S. Yellowstone, 59047 406-222-8367
Livingston	The Island, 79 Island Dr., 59047 406-222-3788
Marion	Rocky Meadow Ranch, 400 Lower Lost Prairie, 59925
Martin City	Little Matterhorn Cabin, 167 Martin Lane, 59926 406-387-5072
Missoula	Country Gallery, 9755 Waldo Rd., 59802 406-721-3378
Missoula	Foxglove Cottage B&B, 2331 Gilbert Ave, 59802
Missoula	Goldsmith's Inn, 809 E Front St., 59802 406-721-6732
Missoula	Gracenote Garden, 1558 S. 6th St, 59801
Missoula	Greenough B&B, 631 Stephens, 59801
Nashua	Petticoat Junction, Rt Box 264, 59248
Nevada City	Nevada City Hotel, 59755 406-843-5377
Ovando	White Tail Ranch, 82 White Tail Ranch Rd, 59854 888-987-2624
Polson	Hammond's B&B, 10141 East Shore, 59860 406-887-2766
Polson	Hidden Pines, 792 Lost Quartz Rd., 59860 406-849-5612
Polson	Swan Hill B&B, 460 Kings Pt. Rd, 59860 406-883-5292

Pony	Lodge at Potosi Hot Spring, PO Box 651, 59747 406-685-3594
Red Lodge	Inn on the Beartooth, Inc., PO Box 1515, 59068 406-446-3555
Red Lodge	Pitcher Guest House, PO Box 3450, 59068 406-446-2859
Roberts	The Wolves Den B&B, Rt. 1, Box 2123, 59070 406-446-1273
Ronan	The Timbers B&B, 1184 Timberlane Rd, 59864 406-676-4373
Seeley Lake	Rich Ranch, PO Box 495A, 59868 406-677-2317
Sheridan	King's Rest B&B, 55 Tuke Ln., 59749 406-842-5185
Somers	Osprey Inn, 5557 Hwy 93 S, 59932 800-258-2042
Somers	Outlook Inn B&B, PO Box 177, 59932 406-857-2060
St. Ignatius	Stoneheart Inn B&B, PO Box 236, 59865 406-745-4999
Stevensville	Big Creek Pines B&B, 2986 Hwy. 93, 59870 406-642-6475
Stevensville	Mystical Mountain Inn, 126 Indian Prairie Loop, 59870 406-642-3464
Three Forks	Madison River Inn, 5255 Madison River Rd, 59752 406-285-3914
Townsend	Lambs Rest Guest House, 16 Carson Ln, 59644 406-266-3862
Trego	Tucker's Inn, 220 Fortine Creek Rd, 59934 406-882-4200
Troy	Bull Lake Guest Ranch, 15303 Bull Lake Rd, 59935 406-295-4228
Troy	River Bend B&B, 40800 Yaak River Rd, 59935 406-295-5493
Victor	Bear Creek Lodge, 1184 Bear Creek Trail, 59875 406-642-3750
Victor	Lazy N Ranch, 1752 Pleasant View Dr, 59875 406-642-3668
Victor	Wildlife Outfitters GR, 1765 Pleasant View Dr., 59875 406-642-3262
Virginia City	Just an Experience, Highway 287 West, 59755
Virginia City	Stonehouse Inn, 306 E Idaho, 59755
W. Yellowstone	Bar-N-Ranch, PO Box 127, 59758 406-646-7229
W. Yellowstone	Sportsman's High B&B, 750 Deer St, 59758 406-646-7865
West Glacier	Glacier-West Chalet, 125 Edgar Lane, 59936 406-888-5507
West Glacier	Mountain Timbers Lodge, Box 94, 59936 800-841-3835
Westby	Hilltop House B&B, 301 East 2nd, 59275
White Sulphur Sp.	Montana Mountain Lodge, 1780 Hwy 89, 59645 406-547-3773
Whitefish	Crenshaw House B&B, 5465 Hwy 93 S, 59937
Whitefish	Eagle's Roost B&B, 400 Wisconsin Ave, 59937
Whitefish	Garden Wall, 504 Spokane Ave, 59937 406-862-3440
Whitefish	Hidden Moose Lodge, 1735 E Lakeshore Dr, 59937 406-862-6516
Wibaux	Nunberg's N Heart Ranch B&, Box 7315, 59353
Wolf Creek	Bundalow B&B, PO Box 168, 59648
Wolf Point	Forsness Farm B&B, Box 5035, 59201 406-653-2492

Nebraska

Adams	Edna's Main House, PO Box 1241, 68301 402-988-2020
Ainsworth	Ainsworth Inn, RR1 Box 126, 69210 402-387-0408
Ainsworth	The Upper Room B&B, 409 N Wilson, 69210 402-387-0107
Bartley	Pheasant Hill Farm, HCR 68, Box 12, 69020
Berwyn	1909 Heritage House, PO Box 196, 68819 308-935-1136
Big Springs	Phelps Hotel, PO Box 473, 69122 308-889-3447
Brewster	Eliza's Cottage, HC 63, Box 34, 68821 308-547-2432
Brewster	Sandhills B&B, HC 63, Box 13, 68821 308-547-2460
Brewster	Uncle Buck's Lodge, PO Box 100, 68821 308-547-2210
Broken Bow	Pine Cone Lodge, RR 2, Box 156C, 68822 308-872-6407
Brownville	Thompson House, Route 1, 68321 402-825-6551
Callaway	The Traveler's Inn, PO Box 189, 68825 308-836-2200
Cambridge	The Cambridge B&B, 606 Parker St, 69022 308-697-3220
Cedar Rapids	River Road Inn, RR2 Box 112, 68627 308-358-0827
Chadron	Olde Main Street Inn, PO Box 406, 69337 308-432-3380
Clarkson	Annie's B&B, 310 Cherry St, 68629 402-892-3660
Crete	The Parson's House, 638 Forest Ave, 68333 402-826-2634
Crofton	Historic Argo Hotel, PO Box 460, 68730 402-388-2400
Dannebrog	Nestle Inn, 209 E. Roger Welsch Ave, 68831 308-226-8252
Dannebrog	The Heart of Dannebrog, 121 E. Elm St, 68831 308-226-2303
Dixon	The George's, 57759 874 Rd, 68732 402-548-2625
Elgin	Plantation House B&B, RR 2, Box 17, 68636 402-843-2287
Eustis	Hotel Eustis, PO Box 11, 69028 308-486-5345
Fairbury	Parker House B&B, 515 4th St, 68352 402-729-5516
Fairbury	Personett House, 615 6th St, 68352 402-729-2902
Funk	Uncle Sam's Hilltop Lodge, Box 110, 68940 308-995-5568
Geneva	Dempster Woods, 1212 M St, 68361 402-759-4171
Gering	Monument Heights B&B, 2665 Grandview Rd, 69341 308-635-0109
Gordon	Bed & Breakfast Bunkhouse, HC 91 Box 29, 69343 308-282-0679
Gordon	Horse Thief Cave Ranch, RR 1 Box 159, 69343 308-282-1017
Gordon	Spring Lake Ranch, H.C. 84, Box 103, 69343 308-282-0835
Grand Island	The Kirschke House B&B, 1124 W. 3rd, 68801 308-381-6851
Gretna	Bundy's B&B, 16906 S. 155th St, 68028 402-332-3616
Gretna	Cedar Creek Farm B&B, 19202 S Hwy 31, 68028
Harrison	Sowbelly B&B Hide-a-way, Box 292, 69346 308-668-2537
Hemingford	Hansen's Homestead, HC 60 Box 77, 69348 308-487-3805
Holdrege	The Crow's Nest, 503 Grant St, 68949 308-995-5440
Hooper	Empty Nest B&B, 1454 Country Rd K, 68031 402-664-2715
Hooper	The White House B&B, 2287 County Rd J, 68031 402-654-2185
Howells	Beran B&B, RR 2 Box 142, 68641 402-986-1358

Howells	Prairie Garden, Box 448, 68641 402-986-1251
Leigh	B&B on the Farm, RR 2 Box 38, 68643 402-487-2482
Lexington	Memories, 900 N. Washington, 68850 308-324-3290
Lincoln	Rogers House, 2145 "B" St, 68502 402-476-6961
Lincoln	Sweet Dream, 2721 P St, 68503 402-438-1416
Lincoln	Weil Mansion B&B, 1149 S 17th St, 68502 402-477-3143
Madrid	Clown 'N Country, RR Box 115, 69150 308-326-4378
Merna	The Country Nest, RR1 Box 62, 68856 308-643-2486
Merriman	Twisted Pine Ranch B&B, Box 84, 69218 308-684-3482
Minden	Home Comfort B&B, 1523 N. Brown, 68959 308-832-0533
Minden	Prairie View, Rt. 2, Box 137, 68959 308-832-0123
Murdock	The Farm House, 32617 Church Rd., 68407 402-867-2062
Nebraska City	Peppercricket Farm B&B, RR1, Box 304, 68410
Nebraska City	Whispering Pines B&B, 21st St & 6th Ave, 68410 402-873-5850
Newman Grove	Crystal Key Inn, 314 S 4th, 68758 402-447-2772
North Bend	Platte Valley Guernsey B&B, RR2, Box 28, 68649 402-652-3492
North Platte	Knoll's Country Inn, 6132 S. Range Rd, 69101 308-368-5634
Oakland	Benson B&B, 402 N. Oakland Ave, 68045 402-685-6051
Omaha	River View Garden, 9641 N 29th St, 68112 402-455-4623
Ord	The Shepherd's Inn B&B, RR 3 Box 108A, 68862 308-728-3306
Osmond	Willow Way B&B, Rt. 2, Box A20, 68765 402-748-3593
Oxford	North York B&B, RR 2 Box 22, 68967 308-337-2380
Pawnee City	My Blue Heaven, 1041 5th St, 68420 402-852-3131
Pierce	Willow Rose B&B, RR 2 Box 575, 68767 402-329-4114
Plainview	The Rose Garden Inn, PO Box 148, 68769 402-582-4708
Ravenna	Aunt Betty's B&B, 804 Grand Ave, 68869 308-452-3739
Seneca	McCawley House, HC 75 Box 17B, 69161 308-639-3300
Seward	Plum Creek Guest House, 538 E Pinewood, 68434 402-643-2573
Spalding	Esch Haus, Rt. 1, 68665 308-497-2628
Springview	Big Canyon Inn, HC 82 Box 17, 68778 402-497-3170
Springview	Larrington's Guest Cottage, HC 82 Box 2, 68778 402-497-2261
Steinauer	Convent House, 311 Hickory, 68441 402-869-2276
Stromsberg	Stromberg's vardshus, RR 1 Box 14B, 68666 402-764-8167
Stuart	Sisters' House B&B, PO Box 14, 68780 402-924-3678
Sutton	Maltby House, 409 S. Maltby, 68979 402-773-4556
Table Rock	Hill Haven Lodge, RR 1, Box 5AA, 68447 402-839-2023
Trenton	Flying A Ranch B&B, PO Box 142, 69044 308-334-5574
Trenton	The Blue Colonial Inn, HC2 Box 120, 69044 308-276-2533
Valentine	Lovejoy Ranch B&B, HC 37, Box 16, 69201 402-376-2668
Valentine	Niobrara Inn, 525 N Main St, 69101 402-376-1779
Verdigre	The Commercial Hotel, PO Box 269, 68783 402-668-2386
Waterloo	J.C. Robinson House B&B, 102 Lincoln Ave, 68069 402-779-2704
Wayne	Grandma Butch's B&B, 502 Logan, 68787 402-375-2759
Wayne	Swanson's B&B, Rt.2, 68787 402-584-2277
Weeping Water	Lauritzen's, 1002 E. Eldora Ave, 68463 402-267-3295
Wilber	Hotel Wilber, PO Box 633, 68465 402-821-2020

Nevada

Austin	Pony Express House, PO Box 28, 89310
Fallon	1906 House, 10 S Carson St., 89406 702-428-1906
Gardnerville	The Adaven Hotel B&B, 1435 Highway 395, 89410 702-782-8720
Genoa	Genoa House Inn, PO Box 141, 89411 702-782-7075
Gold Hill	Gold Hill Hotel, PO Box 710, 89440 702-847-0111
Hope Valley	Sorensen's Resort, 14255 Hwy 88, 96120 530-694-2203
Imlay	Old Pioneer Garden B&B, 2805 Unionville Rd, 89418 702-538-7585
Las Vegas	Brittany Acre, 121 E. Robindale Rd, 89123
Las Vegas	Your Inn Toquerville, 5013 Glenarden Dr, 89130 801-635-9964
Minden	Nenzel Mansion, 1685 Lantana Dr, 89423 702-782-7644
Paradise Valley	Stonehouse Country Inn, Highway 290, 89426 702-578-3716
Reno	B&B South Reno, 136 Andrew Ln, 89511 702-849-0772
Reno	Carriage House Inn, 4259 Greenhorn Ct., 89509 702-746-0598
Reno	Oakleigh, 2153 Camellia Dr, 89512
Silver Springs	Secret Garden, PO Box 1150, 89429 702-577-0837
Stateline	Castle at Summer Place B&B, PO Box 2077, 89449 702-586-8338
Virginia City	Chollar Mansion, PO Box 889, 89440
Wells	Grandma's Farm House B&B, HC 62, Box 300, 89835 702-752-3065

New Hampshire

Amherst	Bethany House B&B, 314 State Rt 101, 03031
Amherst	Fox Brook Farm, 17 Thornton's Ferry, #1, 03031 603-672-7161
Amherst	Whipple B&B, 11 Corduroy Rd, 03031
Andover	Andover Arms Guest House, Main St, 03216
Andover	Potter Place Inn, HCR 64, Box 223, 03216 603-735-5141
Andover	The English House, PO Box 162, 03216 603-735-5987
Antrim	Maplehurst Inn, PO Box 155, 03440

Ashland	Country Options, PO Box 736, 03217 603-968-7958
Ashuelot	The Crestwood Pavilion, 400 Scofield Mtn. Rd, 03441 603-239-6393
Bedford	Bedford Village Inn, 2 Village Inn Ln, 03110 603-472-2001
Bethlehem	Adair Country Inn, Old Littleton Rd, 03574 603-444-2600
Bethlehem	Gables of Park and Main, Box 190, 03574 603-869-3111
Bethlehem	Grande Victoria Cottage, PO Box 426, 03574 603-869-5755
Bethlehem	Highlands Inn, PO Box 118C, 03574 603-869-3978
Bethlehem	The Little Guest House, 1161 Prospect St, 03574
Bradford	The Rosewood Country Inn, Pleasant View Rd, 03221 603-938-5253
Bristol	Pleasant View B&B, PO Box 427, 03222
Campton	Osgood Inn B&B, PO Box 419, 03223 603-726-3543
Campton	The Campton Inn, RR 2, Box 12, 03223 603-726-4449
Canaan	The Inn on Canaan St., RR 1, Box 92, 03741 603-523-7310
Center Harbor	Kona Mansion Inn, PO Box 458, 03226 603-253-4900
Center Ossipee	Hitching Post Village Inn, Old Rt. 16 & Grant Hill, 03814 603-539-3360
Center Sandwich	Corner House Inn, PO Box 204, 03227 603-284-6219
Chichester	Hitching Post B&B, Dover Rd. #2, 03263 603-798-4951
Chocorua	Mt. Chocorua View House, PO Box 348, 03817 603-323-8350
Chocorua	Riverbend Country Inn, Box 288, 03817 603-323-7440
Chocorua	Staffords in the Field, Box 270, 03817 603-323-7766
Colebrook	Monadnock B&B, 1 Monadnock St, 03576 603-237-8216
Concord	The Centennial Inn, 96 Pleasant St, 03301 603-225-7102
Conway	Mountain Valley Manner B&B, PO Box 1649, 03818 603-447-3988
Danbury	Inn at Danbury, Route 104, 03230 603-768-3318
Danbury	Schoolhouse Corner, 61 Eastern District Rd, 03230 603-768-3467
Dover	Paynes Hill B&B, 141 Henry Law Ave, 03820 603-742-4139
Dover	The Silver Street Inn, 103 Silver St, 03820 603-743-3000
Dover	University Guest House, PO Box 5030, 03821
Dunbarton	The Inn at Arbutus Farm, 1 Tenney Hill Rd, 03045 603-744-4554
Durham	Dewey's Hannah House, 191 Packers Falls Rd, 03824 603-659-5500
Durham	Hannah House B&B, 191 Packers Falls Rd., 03824 603-659-5500
Durham	Hickory Pond Inn & Golf, 1 Stagecoach Rd., 03824 603-659-2227
Durham	Holly House B&B, 117 Madbury Rd., 03824 603-868-7345
Durham	Pines Guest House, 47 Dover Rd, 03824 603-868-3361
Eaton Center	The Inn at Crystal Lake, PO Box 12, 03832 603-447-2120
Enfield	Boulder Cottage, RR 1 Box 257, 03748
Exeter	The Inn by the Bandstand, 4 Front St, 03833 603-772-6352
Exeter	The Inn of Exeter, 90 Front St, 03833 603-772-5901
Francestown	Inn at Crotched Mountain, Mountain Rd, 03043 603-588-6840
Franconia	Bungay Jar B&B, PO Box 15, 03580 603-823-7775
Franconia	Horse and Hound Inn, 205 Wells Rd, 03580 603-823-5501
Franklin	The Atwood Inn, 71 Hill Rd, Rt#3A, 03235 603-934-3666
Franklin	The Englewood B&B, 69 Cheney St., 03235 603-934-1017
Freedom	Freedom House B&B, PO Box 456, 03836 603-539-4815
Gilford	Cartway House Inn, 83 Old Lakeshore Rd, 03246 603-528-1172
Gilford	Gunstock Country Inn, 580 Cherry Valley Rd, 03246 603-293-2021
Gilmanton	Temperance Tavern, PO Box 369, 03237 603-267-7349
Gilmanton	Temperance Tavern, PO Box 369, 03237 603-267-7349
Glen	Lodge at Linderhof, PO Box 126, 03838 603-383-4334
Glen	The Covered Bridge House, PO Box 989, 03838 603-383-9109
Goshen	Back Side Inn, 1171 Brook Road, 03752 603-863-5161
Goshen	Cutter's Loft, 686 Washington Rd., 03752 603-863-1019
Greenland	Ayres Homestead B&B, PO Box 15, 03840 603-436-5992
Greenland	Captain Folsom Inn B&B, PO Box 396, 03840
Hampton	Hampton Village Resort, 660 Lafayette Rd, 03842 603-926-6775
Hampton	Inn at Elmwood Corners, 252 Winnacunnet Rd, 03842 603-929-0443
Hampton	Lamie's Inn & Tavern, 490 Lafayette Rd, 03842
Hampton	Stone Gable Inn, 869 Lafayette Rd, 03842 603-926-6883
Hampton	Victoria Inn At Hampton, 430 High St, 03842
Hanover	Hanover Inn, Main St., 03755 603-643-4300
Hanover	The Trumbull House B&B, 49 Etna Rd., 03755 603-643-2370
Hart's Location	The Notchland Inn, Rt. 302, 03812 603-374-6131
Henniker	Henniker House, Box 191, 03242 603-428-3198
Henniker	Meeting House Inn & Rest., 35 Flanders Rd, 03242 603-428-3228
Hill	Snowbound B&B, Murray Hill Rd, 03243 603-744-9112
Hillsboro	Stonebridge Inn, 365 W Main St, 03244 603-464-3155
Hillsborough	The Inn at Maplewood Farm, PO Box 1478, 03244 603-464-4242
Holderness	The Manor on Golden Pond, PO Box T, 03245 603-968-3348
Holderness	The Mary Chase Inn, Rt 3, 03245 603-968-9454
Hopkinton	Windyledge B&B, 1264 Hatfield Rd, 03229 603-746-4054
Intervale	Riverside Inn, PO Box 33, 03845 603-356-9060
Intervale	The Forest, A Country Inn, PO Box 37, 03845 603-356-9772
Intervale	The New England Inn, PO Box 100, 03845 603-356-5541
Intervale	The Old Field House, PO Box 1, 03845 603-356-5478
Jackson	Blake House, PO Box 246, 03846 603-383-9057
Jackson	Eagle Mountain House-1879, Carter Notch Rd., 03846 603-383-9111
Jackson	Harmony House, PO Box 92, 03846 603-383-4110
Jackson	Inn at Thorn Hill, PO Box A, 03846 603-383-4242

Jackson	Lodge at Jackson Village, Box 593, 03846 603-383-0999
Jackson	Paisley and Parsley B&B, Box 572, 03846 603-383-0859
Jackson	The Village House, PO Box 359, 03846 603-383-6666
Jackson	The Wentworth, Carter Notch Rd, 03846
Jefferson	Stag Hollow Inn, Route 115, 03583 603-586-4598
Jefferson	The Jefferson Inn, RFD 1, Box 68A, 03583 603-586-7998
Kearsarge	By the Brook Inn, PO Box 303, 03847 603-356-2874
Kearsarge	Isaac Merrill House, PO Box 8, 03847 603-356-9041
Keene	Wright Mansion Inn, 695 Court St., 03431 603-355-2288
Lincoln	Pollard Brook Resort, RR#1, Box 42, 03251 603-745-9900
Lisbon	Ammonoosuc Inn, 641 Bishop Rd, 03585 603-838-6118
Littleton	Continental 93 Travellers, 516 Meadow Rd, 03561 603-444-5366
Loudon	Lovejoy Farm B&B, 268 Lovejoy Rd, 03301 603-783-4007
Lyme	Breakfast At Tiasquam, 651 River Rd, 03768
Lyme	Dowds Country Inn, PO Box 58, 03768 603-795-4712
Madison	Madison Carriage House, PO Box 35, 03849 603-367-4605
Madison	Maple Grove House, PO Box 340, 03849 603-367-8208
Manchester	Derryfield B&B, 1081 Bridge St, 03104
Manchester	Highlander Inn, 2 Highlander Way, 03103 603-625-6426
Meredith	Inn at Bay Point, Rt 25, Bay Point, 03253 603-279-7006
Meredith	Meredith Inn B&B, PO Box 115, 03253 603-279-0000
Meredith	The Nutmeg Inn, 80 Pease Road, RFD 2, 03253 603-279-8811
Milford	The Ram in the Thicket, 24 Maple St, 03055 603-654-6440
Milford	Zahn's Alpine Guest House, PO Box 75, 03055 603-673-2334
Mount Sunapee	The 1806 House, PO Box 54, 03255 603-763-4969
New Castle	Great Islander, 62 Main St., 03854 603-436-8536
New London	Colonial Farm Inn & Antiqu, PO Box 1053, 03257 603-526-6121
New London	Maple Hill Farm, 200 Newport Rd, 03257 603-526-2248
New London	New London Inn, PO Box 8, 03257 603-526-2791
Newport	Eagle Inn at Coit Mountain, HCR 63, Box 3, Route 10, 03773 603-863-3583
North Conway	1768 Country Inn, PO Box 378, 03860 603-356-3836
North Conway	Cranmore Inn, PO Box 1349, 03860 603-356-5502
North Conway	Cranmore Mountain Lodge, PO Box 1194, 03860 603-356-2044
North Conway	Eastman Inn, PO Box 882, 03860 603-356-6707
North Conway	Green Granite Inn, Rt 16 & 302, Box 3127, 03860 603-356-6901
North Conway	Merrill Farm Resort, 428 White Mountain Hwy, 03860 603-447-3866
North Conway	New England Inn, PO Box 428, 03860 603-356-5541
North Conway	Sunny Side Inn, PO Box 557, 03860 603-356-6239
North Conway	The Center Chimney–1787, PO Box 1220, 03860 603-356-6788
North Conway	The Farm "By the River", 2555 West Side Rd, 03860 603-356-2694
North Conway	The Open Door B&B, PO Box 1178, 03860 800-300-4799
North Conway	Wyatt House Country Inn, PO Box 777, 03860 603-356-7977
North Salem	George P. Johns, III, PO Box 49, 03073
Northwood	Lake Shore Farm, Jenness Pond Rd., 03261 603-942-5521
Northwood	Wild Goose Farm, RFD 1 Box 3205, 03261 603-942-5596
Orford	White Goose Inn, PO Box 17, 03777 603-353-4812
Peterborough	Apple Gate B&B, 199 Upland Farm Rd., 03458 603-924-6543
Pittsburg	The Glen, 77 The Glen Road, 03592 603 538-6500
Pittsfield	Appleview B&B, PO Box 394, 03263 603-435-7641
Plainfield	Home Hill Country Inn, 703 River Rd, 03781 603-675-6165
Plymouth	Colonel Spencer Inn, PO Box 206, 03264 603-536-3438
Plymouth	Northway House, R.F.D. 1, Box 71, 03264 603-536-2838
Portsmouth	Bow Street Inn, 121 Bow St., 03801 603-431-7760
Portsmouth	Inn at Christian Shore, 335 Maplewood Ave, 03801 603-431-6770
Portsmouth	Leighton Inn, 69 Richards Ave, 03801 603-433-2188
Portsmouth	Sise Inn, 40 Court St, 03801 603-433-1200
Portsmouth	Wren's Nest Village Inn, 3548 Lafayette Rd, 03801 603-436-2481
Rindge	Grassy Pond House, Grassy Pond House, 03461 603-899-5166
Rindge	The Cathedral House B&B, 63 Cathedral Entrance, 03461 603-899-6790
Rindge	Tokfarm Inn, Box 1124, 03461 603-899-6646
Rindge	Woodbound Inn, 62 Woodbound Rd, 03461 603-532-8341
Rochester	The Governor's Inn, 78 Wakefield St., 03867 603-332-0107
Salisbury	Horse Haven B&B, 462 Raccoon Hill Rd., 03268 603-648-2101
Sanbornton	Ferry Point House B&B, 100 Lower Bay Rd, 03269 603-524-0087
Snowville	Snowvillage Inn, Box 68, 03832 603-447-2818
South Hampton	The Inn at Kinney Hill, 96 Woodman Rd, 03827 603-394-0200
Strafford	Province Inn, PO Box 309, 03884 603-664-2457
Stratham	Maple Lodge, 68 Depot Rd., 03885 603-778-9833
Sugar Hill	Foxglove, A Country Inn, Route 117, 03585 603-823-8840
Sugar Hill	Ledgeland, RR1, Box 94, 03585 603-823-5341
Sugar Hill	Sunset Hill House, Sunset Hill Rd, 03585 603-823-5522
Sugar Hill	The Hilltop Inn, Rt. 117, 03585 603-823-5695
Sunapee	Dexter's Inn & Tennis Club, PO Box 703, 03782 603-763-5571
Sunapee	The Inn at Sunapee, PO Box 336, 03782 603-763-4444
Sutton Mills	The Village House, Box 151, 03221 603-927-4765
Tamworth	Whispering Pines B&B, Rt 113A & Hemenway Rd, 03886 603-323-7337
Temple	Birchwood Inn, Route 45, 03084 603-878-3285
Thornton	Bridge House Inn, Rt 49, 03223 603-726-9853

Tilton	Black Swan Inn, 308 W. Main St, 03276 603-286-4524
W. Chesterfield	Chesterfield Inn, PO Box 155, 03443 603-256-3211
Wakefield	Lake Ivanhoe Inn, 631 Acton Ridge Rd., 03830 603-522-8824
Wakefield	Wakefield Inn, 2723 Wakefield Rd., 03872 603-522-8272
Walpole	Josiah Bellows House, PO Box 818, 03608 800-358-6302
Warner	Jacob's Ladder B&B, 69 E Main St., 03278 603-456-3494
Warren	Black Iris B&B, PO Box 83, 03279 603-764-9366
Waterville	Silver Fox Inn, PO Box 80, 03215 603-236-8325
Waterville	Silver Squirrel Inn, Snow's Brook Rd, 03223
Waterville	Snowy Owl Inn, PO Box 407, 03215 603-236-8383
Wentworth	Hilltop Acres B&B, PO Box 32, 03282 603-764-5896
Whitefield	Maxwell Haus B&B, 700 Parker Rd., 03598 603-837-9717
Whitefield	Spalding Inn, RR 1, Box 57, 03598 603-837-2572
Whitefield	The Inn at Whitefield, Rt. 3 N, 03598
Wolfeboro	Wolfeboro Inn, PO Box 1270, 03894 603-569-3016
Woodstock	The Birches B&B, Rt. 175, 03262
Woodstock	The River's Edge B&B, Rt. 3, 03262
Woodstock	Woodstock Inn, 80 Main St, 03262 603-745-3951

New Jersey

Absecon	White Manor Inn, 739 S Second Ave, 08201 609-748-3996
Andover	Crossed Keys B&B, 289 Pequest Rd, 07821 973-786-5260
Avalon	The Sealark B&B, 3018 1st Ave., 08202 609-967-5647
Avon by the sea	Candlewick Inn, 28 Woodland Ave, 07717 732-774-2998
Avon by the sea	Ocean Mist Inn, 28 Woodland Ave, 07717 732-775-9625
Avon by the sea	The Summer House, 101 Sylvania Ave, 07717 732-775-3992
Bay Head	Bay Head Harbor Inn, 676 Main Ave, 08742 908-899-0767
Bay Head	Bay Head Sands B&B, 2 Twilight Rd, 08742 732-899-7016
Bay Head	Grenville Hotel, 345 Main Ave., 08742 908-892-3100
Bay Head	The Bentley Inn, 694 Main Ave, 08742 201-892-9589
Beach Haven	Green Gables Inn & Rest., 212 Center St, 08008 609-492-3553
Beach Haven	Pierrot-by-the-Sea B&B, 101 Centre St, 08008 609-492-4424
Beach Haven	St. Rita Hotel, 127 Engleside Ave, 08008 609-492-9192
Beach Haven	The Bayberry Barque, 117 Centre St, 08008 609-492-5216
Beach Haven	Victoria Guest House, 126 Amber St, 08008 609-492-4154
Belmar	House by the Sea, 406 Fifth Ave, 07719 732-681-8386
Belmar	The Seaflower, 110 Ninth Ave, 07719 908-681-6006
Belmar	The Shannon Inn, 200 9th Ave, 07719 908-681-1388
Belvidere	Mustard Seed B&B, 209 Hardwick-on-the-sq, 07823 908-475-4411
Bernardsville	The Bernards Inn, 27 Mine Brook Rd, 07924 908-766-0002
Bradley Beach	Sundowner Inn, 204 3rd Ave, 07720
Cape May	Abigail Adams B&B by Sea, 12 Jackson St, 08204 609-884-1371
Cape May	Columns by the Sea, 1513 Beach Dr, 08204 609-884-2228
Cape May	Doctors Inn at Kings Grant, 2 N. Main St, 08204 609-463-9330
Cape May	George Allen Estate, 720 Washington St., 08204 609-898-9694
Cape May	Henry Sawyer Inn, 722 Columbia Ave., 08204 609-884-5667
Cape May	Holly House, 20 Jackson St, 08204 609-884-7365
Cape May	Jayor's Hearth, 223 Perry St., 08204 609-898-0017
Cape May	Kelly's Celtic Inn, 24 Ocean St, 08204 609-898-1999
Cape May	Manor House, 612 Hughes St, 08204 609-884-4710
Cape May	Pharo's House, 617 Columbia Ave., 08204 609-448-1940
Cape May	Primrose Inn, 1102 Lafayette St, 08204 609-884-8288
Cape May	Saltwood House, 28 Jackson St, 08204 609-884-6754
Cape May	Sand Castle Victorian Inn, 829 Stockton Ave, 08204 609-884-5451
Cape May	Sea Holly B&B, 815 Stockton Ave, 08204 609-884-6294
Cape May	Southern Mansion, 720 Washington St, 08204 609-884-7171
Cape May	Springside, 18 Jackson St, 08204 609-884-2654
Cape May	The Brass Bed Inn, 719 Columbia Ave, 08204 609-884-8075
Cape May	The Inn of Cape May, PO Box 31, 08204 800-257-0432
Cape May	The King's Cottage, 9 Perry St, 08204 609-884-0415
Cape May	The Mission Inn, 1117 New Jersey Ave, 08204 609-884-8380
Cape May	The Moffit House, 715 Broadway, 08204
Cape May	The Prince Edward, 38 Jackson St, 08204 609-884-2131
Cape May	The Puffin, 32 Jackson St., 08204 609-884-2664
Cape May	Twin Gables, 731 Columbia Ave, 08204 609-884-7332
Cherry Hill	Tannenbaum & Milask, 614 Haddonfield Rd, 08002 215-923-2951
Cream Ridge	Earth Friendly B&B, 17 Olde Noah Hunt Rd., 08514 609-259-9744
Edgewater Park	Historic Whitebriar B&B, 1029 S Cooper St, 08010 609-871-3859
Flemington	The Cabbage Rose Inn, 162 Main St, 08822 908-788-0247
Freehold	Hepburn House, 15 Monument St, 07728 732-462-7696
Frenchtown	National Hotel, 31 Race St, 08825 201-996-4871
Frenchtown	The Hunterdon House, 12 Bridge St, 08825 908-996-3632
Haddonfield	Queen Anne Inn, 44 West End Ave, 08033 609-428-2195
Highlands	Water Witch House, 254 Navesink Ave, 07732 732-708-1900
Hope	The Inn at Millrace Pond, PO Box 359, 07844 908-459-4884
Jersey City	p&p*b&b, 290 Barrow St., 07302 201-435-0181
Lambertville	Apple Inn, 31 York St., 08530 609-397-9250

Lambertville	Bridge Street House, 75 Bridge St., 08530 609-397-2503
Lambertville	Inn @ Lambertville Station, 11 Bridge St, 08530 609-397-4400
Manahawkin	Goose N. Berry Inn, 190 N. Main St, 08050 609-597-6350
Mays Landing	Abbott House B&B, 6056 Mainhamltn Twp, 08330
Medford	Main Stay B&B, 45 S Main St, 08055
Milford	Chestnut Hill on Delaware, PO Box N, 08848 201-995-9761
Monmouth Beach	Ocean Gables, 35 Ocean Ave., 07750 732-263-9265
Montclair	The Marlboro Inn, 334 Grove St, 07042 201-783-5300
Newton	The Wooden Duck B&B, 140 Goodale Rd, Andover, 07860 201-300-0395
North Wildwood	Cameo Rose B&B, 109 E 24th Ave, 08260 609-523-8464
Ocean City	Laurel Hall, 48 Wesley Rd., 08226 609-399-0800
Ocean City	New Brighton Inn B&B, 519 Fifth St, 08226 609-399-2829
Ocean City	Plymouth Inn, 710 Atlantic Ave., 08226 609-398-8615
Ocean City	The Adelmann's, 1228 Ocean Ave, 08226 609-399-2786
Ocean City	The Charleston, 928 Ocean Ave., 08226 609-399-6049
Ocean City	The Enterprise B&B Inn, 1020 Central Ave, 08226 609-398-1698
Ocean City	The Manor B&B, 730 Moorlyn Ter., 08226 609-399-4509
Ocean City	The ParkView Inn, 23 Seaview Ave, 07756 732-775-1645
Ocean Grove	Bellevue Stratford Inn, 7 Main Ave, 07756
Ocean Grove	Carol Inn, 11 Pitman Ave, 07756
Ocean Grove	Lillagaard Inn, 5 Abbot Ave, 07756
Ocean Grove	Ocean Plaza, 18 Ocean Pathway, 07756 908-774-6552
Ocean Grove	The Amherst Inn, 14 Pitman Ave, 07756 201-988-5297
Ocean Grove	The Manchester House, 26 Webb Ave, 07756
Pemberton	Isaac Hilliard House B&B, 31 Hanover St, 08068 609-894-0756
Point Pleasant	Lake Inn, 37 Arnold Ave., 08742 732-295-4420
Princeton	B&B of Princeton, PO Box 571, 08542 609-924-3189
Princeton	Peacock Inn, 20 Bayard Ln, 08540 609-924-1707
Salem	Brown's Historic Home B&B, 41-43 Market St., 08079 609-935-8595
Sea Girt	The Beacon House B&B, 100 & 104 Beacon Blvd, 08750 908-449-5835
Sea Isle City	Colonnade Inn, 4600 Landis Ave., 08243 609-263-0460
Seaside Heights	Cranbury Inn, 201 Hiering Ave, 08751 908-793-5117
Spring Lake	Atlantic House, 201 Atlantic Ave, 07762 732-449-8500
Spring Lake	Carriage House, 208 Jersey Ave, 07762 732-449-1332
Spring Lake	Doolan's, 700 Hwy 71, 07762 732-449-3666
Spring Lake	Evergreen Inn, 206 Hwy 71, 07762 732-449-9019
Spring Lake	Hewitt Wellington, 200 Monmouth Ave, 07762 732-974-1212
Spring Lake	Hollycroft Inn, PO Box 448, 07762 732-681-2254
Spring Lake	Johnson House Inn, 25 Tuttle Ave, 07762 732-449-1860
Spring Lake	Katherine's Inn, 310 Jersey Ave, 07762 732-974-6883
Spring Lake	Tara Inn, 307 Jersey Ave, 07762 732-974-0445
Spring Lake	The Breakers, Ocean & Newark Ave, 07762 732-449-7700
Spring Lake	The Chateau, 500 Warren Ave, 07762 732-974-2000
Spring Lake	The Giraffe House, 209 First Ave, 07762 732-449-9870
Spring Lake	The Grand Victorian Hotel, 1505 Ocean Ave, 07762 732-449-5327
Spring Lake	The Kenilworth, 1505 Ocean Ave, 07762 732-449-5327
Spring Lake	The Ocean House, 102 Sussex Ave., 07762 732-449-9090
Spring Lake	The Sandpiper Inn, 7 Atlantic Ave, 07762 800-824-1779
Spring Lake	Walden on the Pond, 412 Ocean Rd, 07762 732-449-7764
Spring Lake	White Lilac Inn, 414 Central Ave, 07762 732-449-0211
Stockton	The Stockton Inn, PO Box C, 08559 609-397-1250
Ventnor	Carrisbrooke Inn, 105 S Little Rock Ave, 08406 609-822-6392
Wall	Holly Harbor Guest House, 2107 Hiddenbrook Dr, 07719 908-449-9731
West Cape May	Annabel Lee Gouest House, 116 N. Broadway, 08204 609-898-1109
West Cape May	Wilbraham Mansion, 133 Myrtle Ave, 08204 609-884-2046
West Milford	Simplicity Inn on Blueberr, 81 Otterhole Rd, 07480 973-697-0494
Westfield	Amber House Victorian Inn, 224 Cowperthwaite Pl, 07090 908-735-7881
Westfield	The Guest House, 726 Woodland Ave., 07090 908-232-7010
Whitehouse Station	Holly Thorn House, 143 Readington Rd, 08889 908-534-1616
Wildwood	Angela's Place Inc., 419 E. Magnolia Ave., 08260 609-729-2631
Wildwood	Pope Cottage B&B, 5711 Pacific Ave, 08260 609-523-9272
Wildwood	Stuart's Once Upon A Time, 2814 Atlantic Ave., 08260 609-523-1101

New Mexico

Abiquiu	Abiquiu Inn, Hwy. 84, 87510 505-685-4378
Albuquerque	Adobe and Roses B&B, 1011 Ortega NW, 87114 505-898-0654
Albuquerque	Anderson's Victorian House, 11600 Modesto Ave NE, 87122 505-856-6211
Albuquerque	Canyon Crest B&B, 5804 Canyon Crest NE, 87111 505-821-4898
Albuquerque	Casa Del Granjero, 414 C de Baca Lane NW, 87114 505-897-4144
Albuquerque	Casas de Suenos, B&B Inn, 310 Rio Grande Blvd SW, 87104 505-247-4560
Albuquerque	Depot Corner Inn, 1609 Camino Rosario NW, 87107
Albuquerque	Devonshire Adobe Inn, 4801 All Saints NW, 87120 505-898-3366
Albuquerque	Enchanted Vista B&B, 10700 Del Rey NE, 87122 505-823-1301
Albuquerque	Home Is Where the Heart Is, 4601 Taylor Ridge Rd., 87120 505-890-1195
Albuquerque	Jazz Inn B&B, 11 Walter NE, 87102 505-242-1530
Albuquerque	Maggie's Raspberry Ranch, 9817 Eldridge Rd NW, 87114 505-897-1523
Albuquerque	Rio Grande House, 3100 Rio Grande Blvd NW, 87107 505-345-0120

Albuquerque	Sarabande, 5637 Rio Grande NW, 87107 505-345-4923
Albuquerque	Silver Hill B&B, 1815 Silver SE, 87106 505-764-8464
Albuquerque	The Corner House, 9121 James Place NE, 87111
Albuquerque	The Inn at Paradise, 10035 Cntry Club Ln NW, 87114 505-898-6161
Albuquerque	The Rainbow Lodge, PO Box 26872, 87125
Albuquerque	The Ranchette, 2329 Lakeview Rd SW, 87105
Albuquerque	The W.J. Marsh House B&B, 301 Edith SE, 87102 505-247-1001
Albuquerque	Unitarian B&B, 3015 Quincy Ne, 87110 505-883-0368
Angel Fire	Monte Verde Ranch B&B, Box 173, 87710 505-377-6928
Angel Fire	Wildflower B&B, 40 Halo Pines Terrace, 87710 505-377-6869
Arroyo Hondo	New Buffalo B&B, Box 257, 87513 505-776-2015
Arroyo Seco	Casa Grande Guest Ranch, PO Box 417, 87514 888-236-1303
Caliente	The Inn at Ojo, PO Box 215, 87549 505-583-9131
Canoncito	Apache Canyon Ranch B&B, 4 Canyon Dr., 87026 505-836-7220
Cedar Crest	Elaine's A B&B, PO Box 444, 87008 505-281-2467
Chama	Enchanted Deer Haven B&B, PO Box 608, 87520 505-588-7535
Chama	Lightheart Inn, PO Box 223, 87520 505-756-2908
Chama	The Gandy Dancer B&B Inn, 299 Maple Ave, 87520
Chimayo	Hacienda Rancho de Chimayo, Box 11, 87522 505-351-2222
Chimayo	La Posada de Chimayo, PO Box 463, 87522 505-351-4605
Chimayo	Rancho Manzana, HCR 64 Box 18, 87522 505-351-2227
Cimarron	St. James Hotel, Rt 1 Box 2, 87714
Clayton	The Rose House, 10 Main St, 88415
Cloudcroft	Burro St B&B, 608 Burro St, 88317 505-682-3601
Cloudcroft	Country Quilt Cottage, PO Box 11104, 88317 505-682-3153
Cloudcroft	Lodge at Cloudcroft, PO Box 497, 88317 505-682-2566
Cloudcroft	The Crofting, 300 Swallow Pl, 88317 505-682-2288
Coolidge	Stauders Navajo Lodge B&B, HC 32 Box 1, 87312 505-862-7553
Corrales	Casa Entrada B&B, PO Box 2320, 87048 505-897-0083
Corrales	Corrales Inn B&B, PO Box 1361, 87048 505-897-4422
Corrales	The Sandhill Crane B&B, 389 Camino Hermosa, 87048 505-898-2445
Corrales	Yours Truly B&B, PO Box 2263, 87048 505-898-7027
Costilla	Costilla B&B, PO Box 186, 87524 505-586-1683
El Prado	Dobson House, PO Box 1584, 87529 505-776-5738
El Prado	Little Tree, PO Box 960, 87529 505-776-8467
El Prado	Salsa del Salto B&B Inn, PO Box 1468, 87529 505-776-2422
Espanola	Inn at the Delta, 304 Paseo de Onate, 87532 505-753-9466
Espanola	The Inn of La Mesilla, Rt 1, Box 368-A, 87532
Fairview	Rancho De San Juan, PO Box 4140, 87533
Farmington	Kokopelli's Cave B&B, 206 W. 38th St, 87401 505-325-7855
Hillsboro	Enchanted Villa B&B, PO Box 456, 88042 505-895-5686
Jemez Springs	Riverdancer Inn, 16445 Scenic Hwy 4, 87025 505-829-3262
Jemez Springs	The Dancing Bear B&B, PO Box 128, 87025 505-829-3336
Kingston	Black Range Lodge, Rt 2 Box 119, 88042 505-895-5652
Las Cruces	Lundeen Inn of the Arts, 618 S. Alameda Blvd, 88005 505-526-3327
Las Cruces	T.R.H. Smith Mansion B&B, 909 N Alameda Blvd, 88005 505-525-2525
Las Vegas	Carriage House B&B, 925 Sixth St, 87701 505-454-1784
Lincoln	Casa de Patron B&B Inn, PO Box 27, 88338 505-653-4676
Lincoln	Ellis Store & Co., PO Box 15, 88338 800-653-6460
Los Alamos	Castillo del Alba, 135 La Senda, 87544 505-672-9494
Los Alamos	North Road B&B, 2127 North Rd, 87544 505-662-3678
Los Alamos	Renata's Orange Street B&B, 3496 Orange St, 87544 505-662-2651
Los Alamos	Victorian Inn, 3312 Orange St, 87544
Los Ojos	Casa De Martinez B&B Inn, PO Box 96, 87551 505-588-7858
Mesilla	Meson de Mesilla, PO Box 1212, 88046 505-525-9212
Nogal	Monjeau Shadows Inn, Bonito Route, 88341 505-336-4191
Placitas	Hacienda de Placitas B&B, 491 Hwy 165, 87043 505-867-3775
Ramah	The Vogt Ranch B&B, Box 716, 87321 505-783-4362
Rancho de Taos	Red Cloud Ranch, PO Box 2800, 87557 505-770-0713
Rancho de Taos	The San Geronimo Lodge, PO Box 2950, 87557 505-751-3776
Ranchos de Taos	Adobe & Pines Inn, PO Box 837, 87557 800-723-8267
Raton	Red Violet Inn, 225 Parsons Ave, 87740 505-445-9778
Rinconada	Casa Rinconada del Rio, Box 10A, 87531 505-579-4466
San Juan Pueblo	Chinguague Compound, PO Box 1118, 87566 505-852-2194
Santa Fe	Ancient Crossroads Adobe, 818 Old Santa Fe Trail, 87501 505-820-2820
Santa Fe	Arius Compound, PO Box 1111, 87504 505-982-2621
Santa Fe	Camas de Santa Fe, 323 E Palace Ave, 87501 505-984-1337
Santa Fe	Casa del Toro B&B, 229 McKenzie St, 87501 505-995-9689
Santa Fe	Casita in Santa Fe GH, 511 Douglas St, 87501 505-984-2270
Santa Fe	Castillo Inn, 622 Castillo Pl, 87501 505-982-1212
Santa Fe	Chapelle St. Casitas, PO Box 9925, 87504 505-988-2883
Santa Fe	Dancing Ground of the Sun, 711 Paseo de Peralta, 87501 505-986-9797
Santa Fe	Don Gaspar Compound Inn, 623 Don Gaspar Ave, 87501 505-986-8664
Santa Fe	Inn of the Anasazi, 113 Washington Ave., 87501 505-988-3030
Santa Fe	Inn of the Animal Tracks, 707 Paseo de Peralta, 87501 505-988-1546
Santa Fe	Inn of the Victorian Bird, PO Box 3235, 87501 505-455-3375
Santa Fe	Inn on the Alameda, 303 E. Alameda, 87501 505-984-2121
Santa Fe	Inn On the Paseo, 630 Paseo De Peralta, 87501 505-984-8200

Santa Fe	Manzano House, 423 Camino Manzano, 87501 505-983-2054
Santa Fe	Open Sky, 134 Turquoise Trail, 87505 505-471-3475
Santa Fe	Polly's Adobe Guest House, 410 Camino Don Miguel, 87501 505-983-9481
Santa Fe	Rancho Jacona, Route 5, Box 250, 87501 505-455-7948
Santa Fe	Ten Thousand Waves Spa, PO Box 10200, 87504 505-982-9304
Santa Fe	Territorial Inn, 215 Washington Ave, 87501 505-989-7737
Santa Fe	The Guadalupe Inn, 604 Agua Fria, 87501 505-989-7422
Santa Fe	Water Street Inn, 427 W. Water St, 87501 505-984-1193
Silver City	Bear Mountain Guest Ranch, Cottage San Rd, 88061 505-538-2538
Silver City	The Carter House, 101 N. Cooper St, 88061 505-388-5485
Silver City	Wilderness Lodge, Rt 11 Box 85, 88061 505-536-9749
Socorro	Eaton House B&B Inn, 403 Eaton Ave, 87801 505-835-1067
Taos	Amizette Inn & Restaurant, PO Box 756, 87525 505-776-2451
Taos	Austing Haus Hotel, PO Box 8, 87525 505-776-2649
Taos	Casa Benavides B&B, 137 Kit Carson Rd, 87571 505-758-1772
Taos	Casa de las Chimeneas, 405 Cordoba, Box 5303, 87571 505-758-4777
Taos	Casa de Milagros B&B, PO Box 2983, 87571 505-758-8001
Taos	Casa Homestay, PO Box 5107 NDCBU, 87571 505-751-1861
Taos	El RincÛn B&B, 114 Kit Carson, 87571 505-758-4874
Taos	Fechin Inn, 227 Paseo Del Pueblo N, 87571 505-751-1000
Taos	Harrison's B&B, PO Box 242, 87571 505-758-2630
Taos	Hotel Edelweiss, PO Box 83, 87525 505-776-8687
Taos	Little Tree B&B, PO Drawer II, 87571 505-775-8467
Taos	Mountain Light Gallery B&B, PO Box 241, 87571
Taos	Rancho Rio Pueblo Inn, Box 2331, 87571 505-758-4900
Taos	Taos Hacienda Inn, Box 4159, 87571 800-530-3040
Taos	Taos Mountain Outfitters, 114 South Plaza, 87571 505-758-8125
Thoreau	Lodge at Bluewater Lake, 40 Perch Dr., 87323 505-862-7616
Thoreau	Zuni Mountain Lodge B&B, HC 62 Box 5114, 87323 505-862-7769
Truchas	Casa Milagro, PO Box 451, 87578 505-689-2591
Truchas	Rancho Arriba B&B, PO Box 338, 87578 505-689-2374
Vallecitos	Vallecitos Retreat, PO Box 226, 87581 505-582-4226

New York —————————————————————————

Albany	Mansion Hill Inn & Rest., 45 Park Ave, 12202 518-465-2038
Albion	Friendship Manor B&B, 349 S Main St, 14411 716-589-7973
Albion	Sweet Apple Guest House, Rt 98, 14411 716-682-3311
Alexandria Bay	Bach's Alexandria Bay Inn, 2 Church St, 13607 315-482-9697
Alpine	The Fontainebleau Inn, 2800 St Rt 228, 14805 607-594-2008
Altamont	Appel Inn, Box 18, RD#3, 12009 518-861-6557
Athens	The Stewart House, 2 N Water St., 12015 518-945-1357
Auburn	Fay's Point Beachhouse, RD 1, Box 1479, 13021
Auburn	Springside Inn, PO Box 327, 13021 315-252-7247
Averill Park	Ananas Hus B&B, Route 3, Box# 301, 12018 518-766-5035
Averill Park	Gregory House Country Inn, PO Box 401, 12018 518-674-3774
Avoca	Avoca House B&B, 37 N Main St., 14809 607-566-8589
Avon	Avon Inn, 55 E. Main St, 14414
Avon	Mulligan Farm B&B, 5403 Barber Rd, 14414 716-226-6412
Bainbridge	Berry Hill Gardens B&B, 242 Ward Loomis Rd, 13733 607-967-8745
Barneveld	Sugarbush B&B, 8451 Old Poland Rd., 13304 315-896-6860
Barryville	All Breeze Guest Farm, Haring Rd, 12719 914-557-6485
Bedford	Commodore Murray House, 622 Guard Hill Rd, 10506
Bellport	Great South Bay Inn, 160 S Country Rd., 11713 516-286-8588
Berkshire	Kinship B&B & Doll Shop, 12724 Rt 38, 13736 607-657-4455
Big Indian	Big Indian Springs B&B, PO Box 66, 12410 914-254-5905
Binghamton	Pickle Hill B&B, 795 Chenango St, 13901 607-723-0259
Binghamton	The White Pillars Inn, 76 Laurel Ave, 13905 607-467-4191
Blasdell	Morning Glory B&B, 45 Kent Ave, 14219 716-824-8989
Boiceville	Onteora, The Mountain Hse, PO Box 356, 12412 914-657-6233
Bolton Landing	Sagamore on Lake George, 110 Sagamore Rd, 12814 518-644-9400
Bouckville	Ye Olde Landmark Tavern, PO Box 5, 13310 315-893-1810
Bovina	Sunset View Farm, HC 74, 13740 607-832-4589
Bovina Center	Swallows Nest B&B, RR 65 Box 112, 13740 602-832-4547
Bovina Center	The Country House, PO Box 109, 13740 602-832-4371
Brockport	The Portico B&D, 3741 Lake Rd, 14420 716-637-0220
Brockport	The White Farm B&B, 854 White Rd, 14420 716-637-0459
Bronxville	The Villa, 90 Rockledge Rd, 10708 914-337-5595
Brookfield	Gates Hill Homestead, PO Box 96, 13314 315-899-5837
Brooklyn	Akwaaba Mansion, 347 McDonough St, 11233 718-455-5958
Brooklyn	B&B on the Park, 113 Prospect Park W, 11215 718-499-6115
Brooklyn	Garden Green B&B, 641 Carlton Ave, 11238 718-783-5717
Buffalo	Beau Fleuve B&B Inn, 242 Linwood Ave, 14209 716-882-6116
Buffalo	Betty's B&B, 398 Jersey St, 14213 716-881-0700
Buffalo	Bryant House, 236 Bryant St, 14222
Buffalo	Burrow's B&B, 624 W Ferry St, 14222
Buffalo	E.B.'s B&B, 781 Richmond Ave., 14222 716-882-1428
Burdett	Country Garden, 5116 St Rt 414, 14818 607-546-2272

Burlington	Chalet Waldheim B&B, 151 Renwick Rd, 13315 607-965-8803
Burlington	Hogs Hollow Farm B&B, RD 1, Box 165, 13315 607-965-8555
Cairo	Cedar Terrace Resort, R 2, Box 407, 12413 518-622-9313
Cairo	The Warm Hearth B&B, Rt 2 Box 626, 12413 518-622-9786
Caledonia	Roberts-Cameron House, 68 North St, 14423 716-538-6316
Caledonia	Robertson Clan B&B, 75 North St., 14423 716-538-2348
Cambridge	Battenkill B&B Barn, Rt 313, RD 1, Box 143, 12816 518-677-8868
Cambridge	Maple Ridge Inn, Rt#372, Rt#1, Box 391C, 12816 518-677-3674
Camillus	Green Gate Inn, Two Main St, 13031 315-672-9276
Campbell Hall	Point of View B&B, RR2, Box 766H, 10916 914-294-6259
Canaan	Inn at Shaker Mill Farm, Cherry Ln, 12029 518-794-9345
Canaan	Inn at Silver Maple Farm, PO Box 35, 12029 518-781-3600
Canaan	Mountain Home B&B, Box 280, 12029 518-392-5136
Canandaigua	Clawson's B&B, 3615 Lincoln Hill Rd, 14424 800-724 6379
Canandaigua	Habersham Country Inn, 6124 Routes 5 & 20, 14424 716-394-1510
Candor	Sarah's Dream Village Inn, 310 Brink Rd, 13743 607-844-4321
Caneadea	Willard's Country Place, 183 Crawford Creek Rd, 14717 716-365-8317
Cape Vincent	Sunny Morn B&B, 9452 Market St, 13618
Cape Vincent	Tymes Remembered, 9494 Point St, Box 406, 13618 315-654-4354
Cazenovia	Brae Loch Inn, 5 Albany St, 13035 315-655-3431
Cazenovia	Brewster Inn, PO Box 507, 13035 315-655-9232
Cazenovia	Lincklaen House, 79 Albany St, 13035 315-655-3461
Center Moriches	Lindenmere Estate B&B, PO Box 1252, 11934 516-874-2273
Central Valley	Gasho Inn, Route 32, Box M, 10917 914-928-2277
Central Valley	Stone Gate B&B, Rt 32, 10917 914-928-2858
Chazy	Grand-Vue B&B, 2237 Lakeshore Rd, 12921 518-846-7857
Chemung	Halcyon Place B&B, PO Box 244, 14825 607-529-3544
Cherry Valley	Old Story Tavern Antiques, 171 Main St, 13320 607-264-3354
Cincinnatus	Alice's Dowry B&B, PO Box 306, 13040 607-863-3934
Claverack	Martaindale B&B Inn, Rt 23, Box 385, 12513 518-851-5405
Clifton Park	Elm Tree Grove B&B, 1-B Greenlea Dr., 12065 518-383-1397
Clinton	The Hedges, 180 Sanford Ave, 13323 315-853-3031
Clintondale	Orchard House, PO Box 413, 12515 914-883-6136
Cold Spring	Hudson House, Country Inn, 2 Main St, 10516 914-265-9355
Cold Spring	One Market Street, One Market St, 10516 914-265-3912
Cold Spring	Pig Hill Inn B&B, Box 357, 10516 914-265-9247
Cold Spring	Swan View Manor, 45 Harbor Rd., 11724 516-367-2070
Cold Spring	The Olde Post Inn, 43 Main St, 10516 914-265-2510
Cold Spring	Village Victorian, 7 Morris Ave., 10516 914-265-9159
Conesus	Conesus Lake B&B, 5332 E Lake Rd., 14435 716-346-6526
Cooperstown	Baseball B&B, 54 Chestnut St, 13326 607-547-5943
Cooperstown	Blacksmith's Guest House, RR4, Box 74, 13326 607-547-2317
Cooperstown	Brook Willow Farm Guest Hs, Middlefield Center Rd, 13326
Cooperstown	Edward's B&B, 83 Chestnut St, 13326 607-547-8203
Cooperstown	Ellsworth House B&B, 52 Chestnut St, 13326 607-547-8369
Cooperstown	Evergreen, A B&B, RD 2, Box 74, 13326 607-547-2251
Cooperstown	Gray Goose B&B, RD 1, Box 21, 13326 607-547-2763
Cooperstown	Green Apple Inn, 81 Lake St, 13326 607-547-1080
Cooperstown	Middlefield Guesthouse, RR 4 Box 614 Rt 155, 13326 607-286-7056
Cooperstown	Moon Dreams, 137 Main St, 13326 607-547-9432
Cooperstown	Nineteen Church St. B&B, 19 Church St, 13326 607-547-8384
Cooperstown	Overlook B&B, 8 Pine Blvd., 13326 607-547-5178
Cooperstown	Strawberry Hill B&B Inn, PO Box 311, 13326 607-785-5058
Cooperstown	Sunny Slope B&B, RD 3, Box 255, 13326 607-547-8686
Cooperstown	The Bassett House Inn, 32 Fair St, 13326 607-547-7001
Cooperstown	The Otesaga, PO Box 311, 13326 607-547-9931
Cooperstown	The Phoenix on River Road, Road #4 Box 360, 13326
Cooperstown	The Plane Old House, RR 4, Box 623, 13326 607-286-3387
Cooperstown	TJ's Country Inn, 124 Main St, 13326 315-858-0129
Cooperstown	Tunnicliff Inn, 34-36 Pioneer St, 13326 607-547-9611
Cooperstown	Whisperin' Pines Chalet, RD 3, Box 248, Rt 11, 13326 607-547-5640
Corning	1865 White Birch B&B, 69 E. 1st. St, 14830 607-962-6355
Corning	Rosewood Inn, 134 E. First St, 14830 607-962-3253
Cuba	33 South, 33 South St, 14727 716-968-1387
Cuba	Rocking Duck Inn, 28 Genesse Parkway, 14727
Dandee	1819 Red Brick Inn, RD 2, Box 57A, 14837 607-243-8844
Deerfield	The Pratt Smith House B&B, 10497 Cosby Manor Rd., 13502 315-732-8483
Deposit	Chestnut Inn @ Oquaga Lake, 498 Oquaga Lake Rd, 13754 607-467-2500
Deposit	Scott's Oquaga Lake House, PO Box 47, 13754 607-467-3094
Dolgeville	Adrianna B&B, 13329 315-429-3249
Dolgeville	Gatehouse Herbs B&B, 98 Van Buren St, 13329 315-429-8366
Dover Plains	Old Drovers Inn, PO Box 675, 12522 914-832-9311
Downsville	Adams' Farmhouse B&B, PO Box 18, 13755 607-363-2757
Downsville	Juniper Hill, PO Box 368, 13755 607-363-7647
Dryden	Serendipity B&B, 15 North St, St 13/38, 13053 607-844-9589
Dundee	Glenora Tree Farm B&B, 546 S. Glenora Rd, 14837 607-243-7414
Durham	Hull-O-Farms B&B, Box 48, 12422 518-239-6950
Durham	Mulberry Bush B&B, Rt 22 Box 20, 12422

Durhamville	Towering Maples B&B, 217 Foster Corners Rd, 13054 315-363-9007
Earlton	The Nightengale Inn B&B, RR 1 Box 215, 12058 518-634-2507
East Aurora	Roycroft Inn, 40 S. Grove St, 14052 716-652-9030
East Aurora	Shepherd Hill Farm, Reiter Rd, 14052 716-652-4425
East Bloomfield	Enchanted Rose Inn B&B, 7479 Routes 5 & 20, 14443 716-657-6003
East Durham	Carriage House B&B, Box 12A, 12423
East Hampton	1770 House, 143 Main St, 11937 631-324-1770
East Hampton	B&B On Cove Hollow, PO Box 2234, 11937
East Hampton	Centennial House, 13 Woods Ln., 11937 631-324-9414
East Hampton	Maidstone Arms Inn/Rest., 207 Main St, 11937 631-324-5006
East Quogue	Carole's B&B, PO Box 1646, 11942 516-653-5152
Eastport	Victorian on the Bay B&B, 57 S Bay Ave, 11941 516-325-1000
Eaton	Eaton B&B, PO Box 4, 13334
Eden	Eden Inn B&B, 8362 N. Main St, 14057 716-992-4814
Edmeston	Pathfinder Village Inn, RR 1, Box 32 A, Rt 80, 13335 607-965-8377
Elbridge	Fox Ridge Farm B&B, 4786 Foster Rd, 13060 315-673-4881
Elizabethtown	Deer's Head Inn, Court St, 12932
Elizabethtown	The Old Mill Studio B&B, Rt 9N River St, 12932
Elka Park	The Redcoat's Return, Dale Ln, 12427 518-589-6379
Ellicottville	Ilex Inn, 6416 E Washington, 14731
Elmira	Lindenwald Haus, 1526 Grand Central Ave, 14901 607-733-8753
Elmira	Strathmont–A B&B, 740 Fassett Rd, 14905 607-733-1046
Endicott	Kings Inn, 2603 E Main St, 13760 607-754-8020
Essex	Essex Inn, 16 Main St, 12936 518-963-8821
Essex	The Stonehouse, Box 43, 12936 518-963-7713
Fair Haven	Frost Haven Resort B&B, West Bay Rd, 13064 315-947-5331
Fayetteville	Beard Morgan House B&B, 126 E. Genesee St, 13066 315-637-4234
Fayetteville	Collin House, A B&B, 7860 E. Genesee St, 13066 315-637-4671
Fayetteville	Craftsman Inn, 7300 E Gowesec St, 13066 315-637-8000
Fillmore	Just a "Plane" B&B, 11152 Rt 19A, 14735
Findley Lake	Blue Heron Inn, PO Box 588, 14736 716-769-7852
Findley Lake	Nelson's Tin Cup Inn, 2737 Shadyside Rd., 14736 716-769-7764
Fleischmanns	Highland Fling Inn, Main St., 12430 914-254-5650
Fly Creek	Blueberry Acres Farm, PO Box 210, 13337 607-547-8661
Fly Creek	Toad Hall, the B&B, RD 1, Box 120, 13337 607-547-5774
Fort Plain	The Palatine House, 141 Old Mill Rd., 13339 518-993-3539
Franklinville	Enchanted Mountain B&B, 382 Hardy Corners Rd, 14737 716-676-3276
Fredonia	The White Inn, 52 East Main St, 14063 716-672-2103
Freeville	LoPinto Farms Lodge, 355 Sheldon Rd, 13068
Fulton	Battle Island Inn, 2167 State Rt 48N, 13069 315-593-3699
Gardiner	Schaible's Serendipity B&B, 1201 Bruynswick Rd, 12525
Geneva	Belhurst Castle, PO Box 609, 14456 315-781-0201
Geneva	Geneva on the Lake, 1001 Lochland Rd, 14456 315-789-7190
Geneva	Inn at Belhurst Castle, PO Box 609, 14456 315-780-0359
Germantown	Fox Run B&B, 936 Rt 6, 12526 518-537-6945
Ghent	Wolfe's Inn, 1461 Rt 21, 12075 518-392-5218
Gorham	The Gorham House, 4752 E Swamp Rd., 14461 716-526-4402
Goshen	Dobbins Stagecoach Inn, 268 Main St, 10024 914-294-5526
Gowanda	The Teepee, 14396 Four Mile Level, 14070 716-532-2168
Grafton	Grafton Inn, PO Box 331, 12082 518-279-9489
Greenfield	Wayside Inn, 104 Wilton Rd, 12833 518-893-7249
Greenport	Watson's By The Bay, 104 Bay Ave, 11944 800-700-0426
Greenport	White Lions B&B, 433 Main St, 11944
Greenville	The Homestead, Red Mill Rd, 12083 518-966-4474
Groton	Benn Conger Inn, 206 W. Cortland St, 13073 607-898-5817
Groton	Gleasons B&B, Old Stage Rd., 13073 607-898-4676
Groton	Tinkering "A" B&B, 774 Peru Rd, 13073 607-898-3864
Groton City	Gale House B&B, 114 Williams St, 13073
Guilford	Hadley House B&B, PO Box 48, 13780 607-895-6347
Guilford	Tea & Sympathy B&B Inn, Main St., 13780 607-895-6874
Hague	Ruah B&B, RR 1, Box 34, 12836 518-543-8816
Hague	The Locust Inn, Rts 9N & 8, 12836
Hague	Trout House Village Resort, Box 510, 12836 518-543-6088
Hamilton	Colgate Inn, 1-5 Payne St, 13346 315-824-2300
Hammondsport	J.S. Hubbs B&B, PO Box 428, 14840 607-569-2440
Hammondsport	Jenny's Bed & Kitchen, Main & Shethar Sts, 14840 607-569-2402
Hammondsport	Park Inn Hotel, 37-39 Sheather St, 14840
Hampton Bays	House on the Water, PO Box 106, 11946 516-728-3560
Hartford	Brown's Tavern B&B, RD #2, Box 2049, 12885 518-632-5904
Hector	Inn at Seneca Springs, PO Box 101, 14841 607-546-4066
Henderson	The Dobson House B&B, RR 1, Box 671, 13650 315-938-5901
High Falls	Captain Schoonmaker's B&B, 913 St Rt 213, 12440 914-687-7946
Highmount	Gateway Lodge, PO Box 397, 12441 914-254-4084
Hillsdale	Inn at Green River, 9 Nobletown Rd, 12529 518-325-7248
Hillsdale	Linden Valley, PO Box 157, 12529 518-325-7100
Hoosick	Hoosick B&B, PO Box 145, 12089 518-686-5875
Hopewell	Bykenhulle House, 21 Bykenhulle Rd, 12533 914-221-4182
Houseville	The Old Church Inn, NY ST Rt 26, 13473 315-376-8423

Hudson	Inn at Blue Stores, Box 99, Star Rt, Rt#9, 12534 518-537-4277
Hudson Falls	B&B on the Green, RR 2, Box 538, 12839 518-747-2462
Hunt	Edgerley B&B, 9303 Creek Rd, 14846 716-468-2149
Huntington	Manchester Inn B&B, 13 Harbor Crest Ct, 11743
Hyde Park	Back of Tranquility, 37 Lawrence Road, 12538 914-229-7485
Hyde Park	Fala B&B, E. Market St, 12538 914-229-5937
Indian Lake	1870 B&B, 36 W Main St., 12842 518-648-5377
Ithaca	Austin Manor B&B, 210 Old Peruville Rd, 13073 607-898-5786
Ithaca	Buttermilk Falls B&B, 110 E. Buttermilk Falls, 14850 607-272-6767
Ithaca	Cudde Duck Cottage, 1031 Hanshaw Rd, 14850 607-257-2821
Ithaca	Goose Lake B&B, 400 Nelson Rd, 14850
Ithaca	Peregrine House Inn, 140 College Ave, 14850 607-272-0919
Ithaca	Rita's B&B, 1620 Hanshaw Rd., 14850 607-257-2499
Ithaca	Slice of Home, 178 N Main St., 14883 607-589-0073
Ithaca	The Federal House B&B, PO Box 4914, 14852 607-533-7362
Ithaca	The Hanshaw House B&B, 15 Sapsucker Woods Rd, 14850 607-257-1437
Ithaca	Welcome Inn B&B, 529 Warren Rd, 14850 607-257-0250
Jeffersonville	The Griffin House, 178 Maple Ave, 12748 914-482-3371
Johnstown	The Olde Knox Mansion, 104 W 2nd Ave., 12095 518-762-5669
Keene	The Bark Eater Inn, Box 139, 12942 518-576-2221
Kent	Ward's Farm House, 14846 Rte 18, 14477 716-682-3037
Kinderhook	B&B of Stuyvesant, PO Box 620, 12106
Kinderhook	Gables Manor, Rt 9, 12106 518-758-1242
Kinderhook	Kinderhook B&B, 16 Chatham St., 12106 518-758-1850
Kings Park	Villa Rosa, 121 Highland St, 11754
Kingston	Black Lion Mansion, 124 W Chestnut St, 12401 914-338-0410
Lake Clear	The Lodge at Lake Clear, Adirondack Mountains, 12945 518-891-1489
Lake George	Corner Birches B&B Guests, 86 Montcalm St, 12845 518-668-2837
Lake George	English Brook Cottages, RR 2 Box 2599, 12845
Lake George	Glenmoore Lakeside Lodge, 330 Glen Lake Rd, 12845 518-792-5261
Lake George	Still Bay Resort, Route 9N, 12845 518-668-2584
Lake Huntington	Sunshine Cottage B&B, 109 Stoney Rd., 12752 914-932-8873
Lake Placid	Adirondack Inn, 217 Main St, 12946
Lake Placid	Blackberry Inn B&B, 59 Sentinel Rd, 12946 518-523-3419
Lake Placid	Highland House Inn, 3 Highland Pl, 12946 518-523-2377
Lake Placid	Lake Placid Lodge, PO Box 550, 12946
Lake Placid	Spruce Lodge, 31 Sentinel Rd, 12946 518-523-9350
Lake Placid	Stagecoach Inn, 370 Old Military Rd, 12946 518-523-9474
Le Roy	Graham's Edson House B&B, 7856 Griswold Cir, 14482 716-768-8579
Lew Beach	Beaverkill Valley Inn, Box 136, 12753 914-439-4844
Lewiston	Village Inn of Lewiston, 65 Center St, 14092 716-754-2686
Lexington	Carpathia House B&B, PO Box 126, 12452 518-989-6622
Little Falls	The Master's House, 189 Hilts Rd, 13365 518-823-0498
Liverpool	Ancestor's Inn at Basset, 215 Sycamore St, 13088 315-461-1226
Liverpool	Lakeview B&B, 204 Brow St, 13088 315-457-5269
Livingston	Covered Bridge Country B&B, PO Box 298, 12758
Livingston	Deer Crossing, PO Box 396, 12758
Livingston Manor	R.M. Farm, PO Box 391, 12758 914-439-5511
Livonia	B&B at Stefano's Countrysi, 3915 Pennimite Rd., 14487 716-346-6338
Loon Lake	The Inn at Loon Lake, HCR 1 Box 136, 12989 518-891-6464
Lowville	Hinchings Pond B&B Inn, PO Box 426, 13367 315-376-8296
Lowville	Zehrcroft B&B, 5490 River St, 13367
Lyons	Peppermint Cottage B&B, 336 Pleasant Valley Rd, 14489 315-946-4811
Lyons	Roselawne B&B, 101 Broad St., 14489 315-946-4218
Malone	Kilburn Mannor, 59 Milwaukee St., 12953 518-483-4891
Maple Springs	Maple Springs Lakeside Inn, 4696 Chaut Ave., 14756 716-386-2500
Marathon	Duke's Coop B&B, PO Box 487, 13803 607-849-6775
Marathon	Three Bear Inn, 3 Broom St, Box 507, 13803 607-849-3258
Margaretville	Margaretville Mountain Inn, Margaretville Mtn. Rd, 12455 914-586-3933
Massena	Danforth House, 27 W Orvis St, 13662 315-769-3177
Mayville	Stuart Manor B&B, 4351 W Lake Rd, 14757 716-789-9902
Mayville	The Farmington Inn B&B, 6642 E Lake Rd, 14757 716-753-7989
Mayville	The Village Inn B&B, 111 S Erie St, 14757 716-753-3583
Meridale	The Old Stage Line Stop, PO Box 125, 13806 607-746-6856
Middleport	Canal Country Inn, 4021 Peet St, 14105 716-735-7572
Milford	1860 Spencer House B&B, RD 1, Box 65, 13807 607-286-9402
Milford	Main Street B&B, RD 1, Box 105A, 13807 607-547-9530
Milford	The Cat's Pajamas B&B, RD 1, Box 98, 13807 607-286-9431
Milford	The Country Meadow Inn, PO Box 355, 13807 607-286-9496
Millbrook	Calico Quail Inn, PO Box 748, 12545
Montauk	Shepherds Neck Inn, PO Box 639, 11954 516-668-2105
Montgomery	Toulon-Sapicourt B&B, 510 Berea Rd, 12549
Monticello	Fosterdale Heights House, 115 Haddock, 12701 914-482-3369
Morrisonville	The Marshall House, 94 Kent Falls Rd, 12962 518-566-8691
Mount Tremper	La Duchesse Anne, 1564 Wittenberg Rd., 12457 914-688-5260
Mount Tremper	Mount Tremper Inn, PO Box 51, 12457 914-688-5329
Mt. Morris	Allan's Hill B&B, 2446 Sand Hill Rd, 14510 716-658-4591
Mt. Morris	Allegiance B&B Inn, 145 Main St, 14510 716-658-2769

Naples	Naples Valley B&B, 7161 County Rd. 12, 14512 716-374-6397
Nassau	Bethlehem House, 3 Lake Ave., 12123 518-766-2038
Nelliston	The Historian, Route 5, Box 224, 13410 315-733-0040
New Lebanon	Churchill House B&B, PO Box 252, 12125 518-766-5852
New York	59th Street Bridge Apts., 351 E 60th St., 10022 212-754-9388
New York	At Home In New York, PO Box 407, 10185 212-956-3125
New York	Broadway B&B Inn, 264 W. 46th St, 10036 212-997-9200
New York	Chelsea Inn, 46 W 17th St., 10011 212-645-8989
New York	Holmes B&B, 157 W 91st St, 10024 212-769-1325
New York	Incentra Village House, 32 8th Ave, 10014 212-206-0007
New York	Inn at Irving Place, 54 Irving Place, 10003 212-533-4600
New York	Inn New York City, 266 W 71 St., 10023 212-580-1900
New York	Lowell Hotel, 28 E 63rd St., 10021 212-838-1400
New York	Roger Smith B&B Boutique, 501 Lexington Ave, 10017 212-755-1400
New York	The Bedford, 118 E 40th St., 10016 212-697-4800
New York	The Gershwin, 7 E 27th St, 10016 212-545-8000
New York	The Hospitality House B&B, 145 E 49th St, 10017 212-965-1102
New York	The Roger Williams, 131 Madison Ave, 10016 212-448-7000
New York	The San Carlos, 150 E 50th St., 10022 212-755-1800
Newark	Chapman's Blue Brick Inn, 201 Scott St, 14513 315-331-3226
Newburgh	Kelsays House of Nations, 2 Scenic Dr, 12550
Newburgh	Stockbridge Ramsdell B&B, 158 Montgomery St, 12550
Newport	What Cheer Hall, PO Box 417, 13416 315-845-8312
Niagara Falls	An's House B&B, 745 4th St., 14301 716-285-7907
Niagara Falls	Olde Niagara House, 610 4th St, 14301 716-285-9408
Niagara Falls	The Holley Rankine House, 525 Riverside Dr, 14303 716-285-4790
Niagara Falls	Victoria's Angel Rose, 699 Chilton Ave, 14301 716-284-2168
North Creek	Goose Pond Inn, PO Box 273, 12853
North Granville	Chateau, PO Box 104, 12854 518-642-1511
North Granville	The White Rose Inn, PO Box 104, 12854 518-642-1511
North River	Garnet Hill Lodge, 13th Lake Rd, 12856 518-251-2444
Ocean Beach	Four Seasons, 468 Denhoff Walk, 11770 516-583-8295
Ogdensburg	Maple Hill Country Inn, Route 2, Box 21, 13669 315-393-3961
Ogdensburg	Way Back In B&B, 247 Proctor Ave, 13669 315-393-3844
Olcott	Bayside Guest House, PO Box 34, 14126 716-778-7767
Olean	Old Library Inn B&B, 120 S Union St, 14760
Olean	The White House, 505 W. Henley St, 14760 716-373-0505
Oneida Castle	Governor's House B&B, 50 Seneca Ave, 13421 315-363-5643
Oneonta	Cathedral Farms Inn, 4158 State Hwy 23, 13820 607-432-7483
Oneonta	Kountry Living B&B, Rd 3, Rt 28, Box 387, 13820 607-432-0186
Oneonta	The Murphy House B&B, 33 Walnut St, 13820 607-432-1367
Oswego	Oswego Inn Ltd., 180 E 10th St., 13126 315-342-6200
Ovid	The Driftwood Inn B&B, 7401 Wyers Point Rd, 14521 607-532-4324
Paradox	Rolling Hills, PO Box 32, 12858 518-532-9286
Pawling	Sharadu B&B, 4 Smith St, 12564 914-855-1790
Penn Yan	Heirlooms B&B, 2756 Coates Rd, 14527 315-536-7682
Penn Yan	Merritt Hill Manor B&B, 2756 Coates Rd., 14527 315-536-7682
Penn Yan	The Fox Inn, 158 Main St, 14527 315-536-3101
Penn Yan	Tudor Hall B&B, 762 E Bluff Dr., 14527 315-536-9962
Phoenix	Merritt House, PO Box 232, 13135 315-695-5601
Piercefield	High Peaks Inn, PO Box 701, 12973 518-576-2003
Pine Bush	Netherfield B&B, 198 Frey Rd, 12566 914-733-1324
Pine Hill	Pine Hills Arms, PO 225, 12465 914-254-4012
Pine Plains	Pines - A Victorian B&B, 5 Maple St, 12567 518-398-7677
Piseco	Irondequoit Inn, Old Piseco Rd Box 54, 12139
Plattsburgh	Point Auroche Lodge B&B, 463 Point Au Roche Rd., 12901 518-563-8714
Port Jefferson	Captain Hawkins Inn, 321 Terryville Rd, 11776 516-473-8211
Port Jefferson	Compass Rose B&B, PO Box 511, 11777 516-928-8087
Port Jefferson	Holly Berry B&B, 23 Dickerson Ct., 11777 516-331-3123
Portageville	Genesee Falls Hotel, PO Box 238, 14536 716-493-2484
Preble	The Martin House B&B, 1446 Masters Rd., 13141 607-749-7137
Pulaski	1880 House, 7536 S Jefferson, 13142 315-298-3511
Pulaski	Steelhead Lodge, 8363 Rome Rd, 13142
Pultneyville	Captain Throop House B&B, 4184 Washington St, 14538 315-589-8595
Purling	Shepherd's Croft, 263 Mountain Ave, 12470 518-622-9504
Putnam Station	The Lake Champlain Inn, PO Box 105, 12861 518-547-9942
Queensbury	Crislip's B&B, 693 Ridge Road, 12804 518-793-6869
Queensbury	Sanford's Ridge B&B, 749 Ridge Rd, 12804 518-793-4923
Queensbury	The Berry Farm B&B, 623 Bay Road, 12804 518-792-0341
Red Hook	1821 House B&B, RR1 box 1, 12571 914-758-5013
Red Hook	Grand Dutchess, 50 N Broadway, 12571 914-758-5818
Red Hook	The Lombard's, RD 3 Box 79, 12571
Rexford	Llenroc Mansion, 708 Riverview Rd, 12148 518-399-3119
Rexford	Rexford Crossings B&B, 1643 Route 146, 12148 518-399-1777
Rhinebeck	Beckrick House B&B, 2258 Route 9G, 12572
Rhinebeck	Beekman Arms, 4 Mill St, 12572 914-876-7077
Rhinebeck	Sepascot Farms B&B, 301 Rt 308 A-2, 12572 914-876-5840
Rhinebeck	The Heller's, 91 Astor Dr., 12572 914-876-3468

Richfield	Aunt Martha's B&B, RR 1 Box 229, 13439 315-858-1648
Richfield Springs	Country Spread B&B, PO Box 1863, 13439 315-858-1870
Richfield Springs	Summerwood B&B, PO Box 388, 13439 315-858-2024
Roscoe	Huff House, RD 2, 12776
Round Lake	Sweet Home B&B, PO Box 282, 12151 518-899-2733
Round Lake	The Olde Stone House Inn, PO Box 451, 12151 518-899-5040
Round Top	Pickwick Lodge, 12473 518-622-3364
Sag Harbor	Ocean View Farm, 2527 Deerfield Rd, 11963
Salem	Bunker Hill Inn, PO Box 3044, 12865 518-854-9339
Salisburg Mills	Gosford House, 297 Woodcock Mt. Rd, 12577 914-497-7761
Salt Point	Mill At Bloomvale Falls, Rt. 82, 12578 914-266-4234
Saranac Lake	Fogarty's B&B, 37 Riverside Dr, 12983 518-891-3755
Saranac Lake	The Doctors Inn, RR 01, Box 375, 12983 518-891-3464
Saranac Lake	Wawbeek on Uper Saranac Lk, Panther Mountain Rd., 12986 800-953-2656
Saratoga	Schrade Guest House, 108 Nelson Ave, 12866 518-587-2132
Saratoga Springs	Batcheller Mansion Inn, 20 Circular St, 12866 518-584-7012
Saratoga Springs	Brunswick B&B, 143 Union Ave, 12866
Saratoga Springs	May West Inn, 142 Lake Ave, 12866 518-583-2990
Saratoga Springs	Saratoga B&B, 434 Church St, 12866 518-584-0920
Saratoga Springs	Smart Choice, 15 Rock St, 12866 518-584-7835
Saratoga Springs	Springwater Inn, 139 Union Ave, 12866 518-584-6440
Saratoga Springs	The Eddy House, 4 Nelson Ave Extension, 12866 518-587-2340
Saratoga Springs	Willow Walk B&B, 120 High Rock Ave, 12866 518-584-4549
Saugerties	Bed by the Stream, 9 George Sickle Rd, 12477 914-246-2979
Saugerties	Upstairs At Cafe Tamayo, 89 Partition St., 12477 914-246-9371
Schoharie	Hyland House B&B, PO Box 162, 12157 518-295-7826
Schoharie	The Maples B&B, Bridge St, 12157 518-295-7352
Schroon Lake	Schroon Lake B&B, Box 274, 12870 518-532-7042
Schroon Lake	Silver Spruce Inn, PO Box 426, 12870 518-532-7031
Schuylerville	Kings-Ransom Farm, 178 King Road, 12871 518-695-6876
Seneca Falls	The Guion House, 32 Cayuga St., 13148 315-568-8129
Setauket	Littlepage Inn, 14 Highwood Rd., 11733 516-632-7904
Severance	The Red House B&B, PO Box 125, 12872
Shandaken	Auberge Des 4 Saisons, 178 State Rt 42, 12480 914-688-2223
Shandaken	The Copperhood Inn & Spa, 7039 State Rt 28, 12480 914-688-2460
Sharon Springs	Clausen Farms B&B Inn, Box 395, 13459 518-284-2527
Shelter Island	Azalea House, PO Box 943, 11964 516-749-4252
Shelter Island	The Belle Crest House, PO Box 891, 11965 516-749-2041
Sherman	Inn Between B&B, PO Box 546, 14781
Shirley	Shirley's Birdhouse, Carmen View Dr, 11967 516-281-5918
Skaneateles	The Gray House, 47 Jordan St, 13152 315-685-5224
Sodus	Tanniquetil B&B, 6237 Snyder Rd, 14551
Sodus Point	Silver Waters Guesthouse, 8420 Bay St, 14555 315-483-8098
South Colton	Braeside B&B, PO Box 410, 13687
South Otselic	Northwest Corners B&B, 769 Country Rd 42, 13155 315-653-7776
Southampton	Caldwell's Carriage House, 519 Hill St, 11968 516-287-4720
Southampton	Evergreen On Pine B&B, 89 Pine St, 11968 516-283-0564
Southampton	Old Post House Inn, 30 Old Orchard Rd, 11968 516-283-1717
Southampton	Stevens, Margaret, 12 Beechwood Dr, 11968
Southampton	The Ivy, 244 North Main St, 11968 516-283-3233
Southold	B&B The Hedges, 5665 Route 25, 11971
Speculator	The Inn at Speculator, PO Box 163, 12164
Spencertown	Spencertown Country House, Ct Rt 9, Red Rock Rd., 12165 518-392-5292
Spring Glen	Gold Mtn. Chalet Resort, PO Box 456, 12483 914-647-4332
Springfield	Country Memories Lodge, PO Box 430, 13468 518-858-2691
Springfield	Sweet Dreams B&B, PO Box 414, 13468 315-858-1319
Springville	Gaffney's B&B, PO Box 461, 14141 716-592-0240
Staatsburg	Arbor Crest B&B, 17 Reservoir Rd., 12580 914-889-4953
Stamford	Belvedore Country Inn, 10 Academy St., 12167 607-652-6121
Staten Island	Hartshorne House, 88 Henderson Ave., 10301 718-273-8105
Stephentown	Mountain Changes Inn, RR 1, Box 124, 12168 518-733-6923
Stillwater	Cottage on the Hudson, PO Box 637, 12170 518-664-8780
Stillwater	Lee's Deer Run B&B, 411 Country Rd #71, 12170 518-584-7722
Stillwater	River's Edge B&B, 90 Wrights Loop, 12170 518-664-3276
Stone Ridge	Bakers B&B, 24 Old Kings Hwy, 12484 914-687-9795
Stone Ridge	Hasbrouck House Inn, PO Box 76, 12484
Stone Ridge	The Inn at Stone Ridge, PO Box 76, 12484 914-687-0736
Stony Brook	Three Village Inn, 150 Main St, 11790 516-751-0555
Stony Creek	1000 Acres Ranch Resort, 465 Warrensburg, 12878
Syracuse	Auntie M's B&B, 4732 Cleveland Rd, 13215
Syracuse	Giddings Garden B&B, 290 W. Seneca Turnpike, 13207 315-492-6389
Syracuse	Russell-Farrenkopf House, 209 Green St, 13203 315-472-8001
Tannersville	Leggs Diamond, Main St, 12485 518-589-5555
Tannersville	The Kennedy House, PO Box 770, 12485 518-589-6082
Thendara	Moose River House B&B, Box 184, 13472 315-369-3104
Tivoli	The Bird's Nest, 21 Clay Hill Rd, 12583 914-757-4279
Troy	Sharon Fern's B&B, 8 Ethier Dr, 12180 518-279-1966
Trumansburg	Gothic Eves B&B, PO Box 95, 14885 607-387-6033

Trumansburg	Taughannock Farms Inn, 2030 Gorge Rd (Rt#89), 14886 607-387-7711
Trumansburg	The Archway B&B, 7020 Searsburg Rd, 14886 607-387-6175
Trumansburg	Westwind B&B, 1662 Taughannock Blvd, 14886 607-387-3377
Turin	Freihof Lodge, 37 W Main St, 13473 315-348-8610
Utica	Herbs & Hospitality, 2806 Ogden Pl, 13501 315-797-0079
Valley Falls	Maggie Towne's B&B, Box 82, RD 2, 12185 518-663-8369
Vernon	Jenkins House At Woodlawn, 4 Ward St, 13476 315-829-2459
Vernon	Lavender Inn, 5950 State Rt 5, 13476 315-829-2440
Verona	Greenway B&B, 5196 Brown Rd., 13478 315-336-1433
Victor	Sugar Tree B&B, 863 Victor Egypt Rd., 14564 716-924-5546
Walden	Boulevard House B&B, 1017 Route 52, 12586 914-778-1602
Walden	Heritage Farm, 163 Berea Rd., 12586 914-778-3420
Walker Valley	The Jeronimo Resort, PO Box 155, 12588 914-733-5652
Wallkill	Audreys Farmhouse B&B Corp, 2188 Bruynswick Rd, 12589 914-895-3440
Warrensburg	House on the Hill B&B, Rt. 28, PO Box 248, 12885 518-623-9390
Warrensburg	North Country Lodge B&B, PO Box 313, 12885 518-623-3220
Warrensburg	The Merrill Magee House, Box 391, 12885 518-623-2449
Warwick	Inn at 40 Oakland, 40 Oakland Ave, 10990 914-987-8269
Warwick	MeadowLark Farm, 180 Union Corners Rd., 10990 914-651-4286
Water Mill	Halsey House B&B, 258 Halsey Lane, 11976 516-726-6527
Water Mill	Seven Ponds, PO Box 98, 11976 516-726-7618
Waterloo	Historic James R. Webster, 115 E. Main St, 13165 315-539-3032
Waterville	B&B of Waterville, 211 White St, 13480 315-841-8295
Watkins Glen	1871 Benjamin Hunt Inn, 305 6th St, 14891 607-535-9843
Watkins Glen	Hannah's 1892 House, 305 E Fourth St, 14891 607-535-7943
Watkins Glen	The Rose Window B&B, 430 S. Franklin St, 14891 607-535-4687
Watkins Glen	The Victorian B&B, 216N Madison Ave, 14891 607-535-6582
West Falls	Pipe Creek Farm B&B, 9303 Falls Rd, 14170
West Shokan	Haus Elissa B&B, PO Box 95, 12494 914-657-6277
West Tahgkanic	Taghkanic Creek B&B, 624 Old Rt 82, 12521 518-851-6934
Westfield	Candlelight Lodge, 143 E Main St, 14787 716-326-2830
Westfield	The William Seward Inn, 6645 S Portage Rd, 14787 716-326-4151
Westhampton	Inn On Main, 191 Main St., 11978 516-288-8900
Westport	The Victorian Lady, 57 S Main St, 12993 518-962-2345
Wevertown	Mountainaire Adventures, Route 28, 12886 518-251-2194
White Lake	Bradstan Country Hotel, PO Box 312, 12786 914-583-4114
Whitehall	Finch & Chubb Inn, 82 N William St, 12887 518-499-2049
Williamsville	Heritage House Country Inn, 8261 Main St., 14221 716-633-4900
Wilson	Daniel Douglas B&B, 751 Lake St., 14172 716-751-9200
Wilson	Matteson House Lakefront, 2833 W Lake RD, Rt 18, 14172
Windham	Be My Guest B&D, PO Box 1071, 12496
Windham	Danske Hus, 361 South St, 12496
Wolcott	Lake Bluff Inn B&B, 9464 Lake Bluff Rd., 14590 315-587-9386
Woodridge	Sunny Oaks Hotel & Retreat, PO Box 297, 12789 914-434-7580
Woodstock	Stanford White's Carriage, 34 Ohayo Mtn. Rd, 12498
Worcester	Wild Turkey Farm B&B, W. Hill Rd, RD 1, 121B, 12197 607-397-1805
Wyoming	Hillside Inn, Circa 1851, 890 E Bethany Rd., 14591 716-495-6800
Youngstown	Joanne's B&B, 1380 Swann Rd, 14174 716-254-7052
Youngstown	The Mill Glen Inn, 1102 Pletcher Rd., 14174 716-754-4085

North Carolina

Aberdeen	Inn at the Bryant House, 214 N. Poplar St, 28315 919-944-3300
Aberdeen	Page Manor House, 300 Page St, 28315 910-944-5970
Andrews	Rail's End B&B, 11 Railroad St, 28901 828-321-4486
Asheville	Aberdeen Inn, 64 Linden Ave, 28801 828-254-9336
Asheville	Acorn Cottage B&B, 25 St Dunstan's Circle, 28803 828-253-0609
Asheville	Break Away B&B, 90 Cumberland Ave, 28801 704-255-7919
Asheville	Cairn Brae, 217 Patton Mountain Rd, 28804 828-252-9219
Asheville	Carolina B&B, 177 Cumberland Ave, 28801 828-254-3608
Asheville	Flint Street Inns, 100 & 116 Flint St, 28801 828-253-6723
Asheville	Hill House B&B Inn, 120 Hillside St, 28801 704-232-0345
Asheville	Merrymont B&B, 208 Cumberland Ave, 28801 828-281-2572
Asheville	Mountain Springs Cabins, PO Box 6922, 28816 828-665-1004
Asheville	Reed House, 119 Dodge St, 28803 828-274-1604
Asheville	Scarlette Inn & Cottage, 315 Pearson Dr, 28801 704-253-7888
Asheville	The Arbor Rose Inn, 24 Haw Creek Cir, 28805
Asheville	WhiteGate Inn & Cottage, 173 E Chestnut St, 28801 828-253-2553
Bakersville	Laurel Oaks Farm, Rt 3, Box 111 D, 28705 828-688-2652
Banner Elk	Beech Alpen Inn, 700 Beech Mountain Pkwy, 28604 704-387-2252
Banner Elk	Rainbow Inn, 317 Old Turnpike Rd., 28604 704-898-5611
Banner Elk	The Banner Elk Inn B&B, PO Box 1953, 28604 704-898-6223
Barnardsville	Hawk & Ivy B&B Retreat, 133 N. Fork Rd., 28709 704-626-3486
Barnardsville	The DOJO at Stoneycrest, 119 Stoney Fork Rd, 28709 704-626-3782
Bat Cave	Old Mill Inn & Antiques, PO Box 252, 28710 704-625-4256
Beaufort	Captains' Quarters, 315 Ann St, 28516 252-728-7711
Beaufort	Cousins B&B, 303 Turner St, 28516 252-504-3478
Beaufort	Inlet Inn, 601 Front at Queen St, 28516 252-728-3600

Beech Mountain	Beech Mountain Inns, Two Beech Mt. Parkway, 28604 704-387-2252
Belhaven	River Forest Manor B&B Inn, 600 E Main St, 27810 252-943-2151
Belhaven	The Duck Blind B&B, 313 E Front St, 27810
Belhaven	Thistle Dew Inn, 443 Water St, 27810 252-943-6900
Belhaven	Thomasina's B&B, PO Box 575, 27810 252-943-2097
Black Mountain	Black Mountain Inn, 718 W Old Hwy 70, 28711 828-669-6528
Black Mountain	Blackberry Inn, PO Box 965, 28711 828-669-8303
Black Mountain	Monte Vista Hotel, 308 W State St, 28711
Blowing Rock	Gideon Ridge Inn, PO Box 1929, 28605 828-295-3644
Blowing Rock	Meadowbrook Inn, PO Box 2005, 28605 828-295-4300
Blowing Rock	Victorian Inn, PO Box 283, 28605 828-295-0034
Boone	Eagle's Retreat, 333 Eagle Dr., 28607 828-264-3007
Boone	The Gragg House, 210 Ridge Point Dr, 28607
Boone	The Lovill House Inn, 404 Old Bristol Rd, 28607 828-264-4204
Boone	Window Views B&B, 204 Stoneleigh Ln., 28607 828-963-8081
Brevard	Rainbow Lake Resort, Rt 1, 28712 828-862-5354
Brevard	The Inn at Brevard, 410 E. Main St, 28712 828-884-2105
Bryson City	Nantahala Village Resort, 9400 Hwy 19 W, 28713 828-488-2826
Burnsville	NuWray Inn, PO Box 156, 28714 828-682-2329
Burnsville	Terrell House B&B, 109 Robertson St., 28714 828-682-4505
Buxton	Cape Hatteras B&B, PO Box 490, 27920 252-995-4511
Buxton	The Pamlico Inn, PO Box 550, 27920 252-995-6980
Carolina Beach	Beacon House Inn B&B, 715 Carolina Beach Ave, 28428 910-458-6244
Carthage	Blacksmith Inn, PO Box 1480, 28327 910-947-1692
Cashiers	Cottage Inn, PO Box 818, 28717 704-743-3033
Cashiers	High Hampton Inn, PO Box 338, 28717 704-743-2411
Cashiers	Innisfree Victorian Inn, 7 Lakeside Knoll, 28736 704-743-2946
Cashiers	Knolltop Lodge, PO Box 818, 28717 704-743-3033
Cashiers	Laurelwood Mountain Inn, PO Box 188, 28717 704-743-9939
Cashiers	Millstone Inn, PO Box 949, 28717 704-743-2737
Chapel Hill	The Village B&B, 401 Parkside Circle, 27516 919-968-9984
Charlotte	McElhinny House, 10533 Fairway Ridge Rd, 28277 704-846-0783
Charlotte	Overcarsh House, 326 West Eighth St, 28202 704-334-8477
Charlotte	The Elizabeth, 2145 East 5th St, 28204 704-358-1368
Charlotte	The Homeplace B&B, 5901 Sardis Rd, 28270 704-365-1936
Charlotte	The Inn on Carmel, 4633 Carmel Rd, 28226 704-542-9450
Charlotte	The Inn Uptown, 129 N. Poplar St, 28202 704-342-2800
Cherokee	Whispering Winds, PO Box 1953, 28719
Clemmons	Tanglewood Manor House B&B, PO Box 1040, 27012 919-766-0591
Columbia	Heart's Delight B&B, PO Box 447, 27925 252-796-2321
Columbia	The River House B&B, PO Box 765, 27925 252-796-1855
Corolla	Inn at Corolla Lighthouse, 1066 Ocean Trail, 27927 252-453-3340
Cullowhee	Cullowhee B&B, 150 Ledbetter Rd, 28723 704-293-5447
Dillsboro	Olde Towne Inn B&B, PO Box 485, 28725 828-586-3461
Dillsboro	Squire Watkins Inn, PO Box 430, 28725 828-586-5244
Dillsboro	The Dillsboro Inn, PO Box 270, 28725 828-586-3898
Dillsboro	The Jarrett House, PO Box 219, 28725 828-586-0265
Duck	The Sanderling Inn Resort, 1461 Duck Rd, 27949 252-261-4111
Dunn	Simply Divine B&B, 309 West Divine St, 28334 910-891-1103
Durham	Arrowhead Inn, 106 Mason Rd, 27712 919-477-8430
Durham	Morehead Manor, 914 Vickers Ave, 27701 888-437-6333
Durham	Old North Durham Inn, 922 North Mangum St, 27701 919-683-1885
Edenton	Albemarle House, 204 West Queen St, 27932
Edenton	Captain's Quarters Inn, 202 W. Queen St, 27932 252-482-8945
Edenton	Granville Queen Inn, 108 S. Granville St, 27932 252-482-5296
Edenton	Mulberry Hill Plantation, RR 4 Box 271, 27932 252-828-1339
Elizabeth	Culpepper Inn, 609 W. Main St, 27090 252-335-1993
Elizabeth City	Elizabeth City B&B, 108 E. Fearing St, 27909 252-338-2177
Ellerbe	Ellerebe Springs Inn, 2537 N US 220 Hwy, 28338 910-652-5600
Fairview	The Inn at Wintersun, One Wintersun Lane, 28730 704-628-7890
Flat Rock	Flat Rock Inn, PO Box 308, 28731
Flat Rock	The Woodfield Inn, PO Box 98, 28731 704-693-6016
Fleetwood	Inn at Somerleyton Manor, 117 Eagle Nest Ln, 28626 910-877-5843
Franklin	Blaine House B&B & Cottage, 661 Harrison Ave., 28734 828-349-4230
Franklin	Snow Hill Inn, 531 Snow Hill Rd., 28734 828-369-2100
Franklin	Wayah Creek Cottages, 610 Wayah Rd., 28734 828-524-2034
Germanton	MeadowHaven B&B, PO Box 222, 27019 336-593-3996
Glendale Springs	Glendale Springs Inn, PO Box 117, 28629 910-982-2103
Glendale Springs	Mountain View Lodge, PO Box 90, 28629 919-982-2233
Graham	Victorian Rose B&B Inn, 407 Graham Rd, 27253 336-578-5112
Greensboro	Greenwood B&B, 205 N Park Dr., 27401 336-274-6350
Hatteras	Cochran's Way B&B, PO Box 724, 27943 252-986-1327
Hayesville	Broadax Inn B&B/Restaurant, RR 1 Box 289A, 28904 828-389-6987
Hayesville	Vineyard Mountain B&B, 222 Hidden Forest Lane, 28904 828-389-6409
Henderson	Burnside Plantation, 960 Burnside Rd., 27536 919-438-7688
Hendersonville	Apple Inn B&B, 1005 White Pine Dr., 28739 828-693-0107
Hendersonville	Claddagh Inn, 755 N Main St, 28792 828-697-7778
Hendersonville	Echo Mountain Inn, 2849 Laurel Park Hwy, 28739 828-693-9626

Hendersonville	Melange B&B, 1230 5th Ave West, 28739 929-697-5253
Hendersonville	Old Teneriffe Inn, 2531 Little River Rd, 28739 828-698-8178
Hendersonville	Rubin Osceola Lake, PO Box 2258, 28793
Hendersonville	The Waverly Inn, 783 N Main St, 28792 828-693-9193
Hertford	Beechtree Inn, Rt 1 Box 517, 27944
Hickory	The Hickory B&B, 464 7th St, 28602 828-324-0548
High Point	The Premier B&B, 1001 Johnson St, 27262 336-889-8349
High Point	Walton House B&B, 626 E State Ave, 27262
Highlands	Chandler Inn, PO Box 2156, 28741 828-526-5992
Highlands	Lakeside Inn, 1921 Franklin Rd, 28741
Highlands	Long House B&B, PO Box 2078, 28741 828-526-4394
Highlands	Mirror Lake Suites, PO Box 1216, 28741 828-526-9726
Highlands	Mitchell Motel & Cottages, PO Box 1717, 28741 828-526-2267
Highlands	Morning Star Inn, 480 Flat Mt Estates Rd, 28741 828-526-1009
Highlands	The Guest House, Rt 2, Box 65914, 28741 828-526-4536
Highlands	The Old Creek Lodge, 165 Hwy 106, 28741
Highlands	The Old Edwards Inn, PO Box 1030, 28741 828-526-5036
Hot Springs	Duckett House Inn & Farm, PO Box 441, 28743
Kenansville	The Murray House Inn, 201 NC Highway 24-50, 28349 910-296-1000
Kitty Hawk	Three Seasons Guest House, PO Box 1429, 27949 252-261-4791
Lake Junaluska	Brookside Lodge, PO Box 925, 28745 704-456-8897
Lake Junaluska	Lagoalinda Lodge, PO Box 925, 28745 704-456-3620
Lake Junaluska	Providence Lodge, 207 Atkins Loop, 28745 704-456-6486
Lake Junaluska	Sunset Inn, 300 N. Lakeshore Dr, 28745 704-456-6114
Lake Junaluska	The Laurels, PO Box 1354, 28745 704-456-7186
Lake Lure	The Chalet Club, 532 Washburn Rd, 28746 828-625-9315
Lake Toxaway	Earthshine Mountain Lodge, Route 1, Box 216-C, 28747 828-862-4207
Lake Toxaway	The Greystone Inn, Greystone Ln, 28747 828-966-4700
Lake Waccamaw	B&B By the Lake, PO Box 218, 28450 919-646-4744
Lake Waccamaw	Lake Shore Lodge, 2014 Lake Shore Dr, 28450 910-646-3748
Laurel Springs	Burgiss Farm B&B, Rte. 1, Box 300, 28644 919-359-2995
Laurel Springs	Doughton-Hall B&B, Rt 1 Box 1, 28644
Leicester	Spring House, PO Box 997, 28748
Lexington	Bailey House Inn, 308-A E Center St., 27292 910-249-0299
Linville	Linville Cottage B&B, Box 508, 28646 828-733-6551
Little Switzerland	Switzerland Inn, PO Box 399, 28749 704-765-2153
Littleton	Littleton's Maplewood Mano, PO Box 1165, 27850 919-586-4682
Louisburg	The Hearthside Inn, 305 N. Main St, 27549 919-496-6776
Madison	The Boxley B&B, 117 E. Hunter St, 27025 910-427-0453
Maggie Valley	Abbey Inn, 6375 Soco Gap Rd, 28751 704-926-1188
Maggie Valley	Hearth & Home Inn, Hwy 19, 28751 828-926-1845
Maggie Valley	Mount Valley Lodge, 620 Soco Rd., 28751 704-926-9244
Maggie Valley	The Ketner Inn & Farm, PO Box 1628, 28751 704-926-1511
Maggie Valley	Timberwolf Creek B&B, 391 Johnson Branch Rd, 28751 828-926-2608
Manson	Kimball Oaks A B&B, Rt 1, Box 158, 27553 919-456-2004
Manteo	The White Dove Inn, PO Box 1029, 27954 252-473-9851
Manteo	Tranquil House Inn, PO Box 2045, 27954 252-473-1404
Marshall	Gingerbread House, PO Box 907, 28753 828-649-3922
Matthews	803 Elizabeth B&B, 803 Elizabeth Ln, 28105 704-847-4637
Mebane	The Old Place B&B, 1600 Saddle Club Rd., 27302 919-563-1733
Mocksville	Boxwood Lodge, Hwy 601 at 132 Becktown, 27028 704-284-2031
Mooresville	Spring Run B&B, 172 Spring Run, 28115 704-664-6686
Morehead City	Lighthouse Inn, 2300 Bridges St, 28557 252-237-3133
Mount Airy	Carriage House B&B, 218 Cherry St, 27030 336-789-7864
Mount Airy	Merritt House B&B, 618 N. Main St, 27030 800-290-6090
Mountain Home	Mountain Home Inn B&B, 10 Courtland Blvd, 28758
Murphy	Hoover House, 306 Natural Springs Dr, 28906 828-837-8734
Murphy	Park Placae B&B, 100 Hill St, 28906 828-837-8842
Nebo	Merry Heart Cabin, 1414 Merry Heart Ln., 28761 704-584-6174
New Bern	Harvey Mansion Historic In, 221 Tryon Palace Dr., 28560 252-638-3205
New Bern	Howard House Victorian B&B, 207 Pollock St, 28560 252-514-6709
New Bern	King's Arms Colonial Inn, 212 Pollock St, 28560 252-638-4409
New Bern	Magnolia House, 2306 Wild Turkey Road, 28562 252-633-9488
New Bern	New Berne House B&B Inn, 709 Broad St, 28560 252-636-2250
New London	London Gold, PO Box 353, 28127
Ocracoke	Berkley Manor B&B, PO Box 220, 27960 252-928-5911
Ocracoke	Boyette House, Box 39, 27960 252-928-4261
Ocracoke	Lightkeepers Inn, PO Box 597, 27960
Ocracoke Island	Thurston House Inn, Box 294, 27960 919-928-6037
Oriental	The Tar Heel Inn, PO Box 176, 28571 252-249-1078
Penland	Chinquapin Inn, PO Box 145, 28765 704-765-0064
Pilot Mountain	Flippin's B&B, PO Box 1520, 27401 910-368-1183
Pilot Mountain	Pilot Knob, PO Box 1280, 27041 919-325-2502
Pilot Mountain	Scenic Overlook B&B, Scenic Overlook In., 27041 910-368-9591
Pinebluff	Pine Cone Manor B&B, 450 E Philadelphia Ave, 28373 910-281-5307
Plymouth	Four Gables, PO Box 538, 27962 252-793-6696
Raleigh	William Thomas House B&B, 530 North Blount St, 27604 919-755-9400
Reidsville	Fairview Farm B&B, 1891 Harrison Crossroad, 27320

Rich Square	Windy Orchard, Rt 1, Box 540, 27869 919-539-2370
Roaring Gap	Roaring Gap Guest House, PO Box 361, 28668 910-363-1234
Robbinsville	Mountain Hollow B&B, Rt 2 Box 176 E5, 28771 828-479-3608
Rocky Mount	Sunset Inn, 1210 Sunset Ave, 27804 252-446-9524
Rutherfordton	Carrier Houses, 423 N Main St, 28139
Salisbury	Rowan Oak House, 208 S Fulton St, 28144 704-633-2086
Saluda	The Orchard Inn, PO Box 725, 28773
Seagrove	The Duck Smith House, 465 N Broad St, Bs #220, 27341 336-873-7099
Shelby	Inn at Webbley, PO Box 1000, 28150 828-481-1403
Sherrills Ford	Lake Norman B&B, 8719 Casa del Rio, 28673 704-478-2383
Siler City	Celebrity Dairy Inn, 2106 Mt. Vernon Hickory, 27344 719-742-5176
Siloam	The Blue Fawn B&B, 3052 Siloam Rd., 27047 910-374-2064
Southern Pines	Covington House, 1855 Camp Easter Rd., 28387 910-695-0352
Southport	Lois Jane's Riverview Inn, 106 W Bay St, 28461 910-457-6701
Sparta	Harmony Hill B&B, 1740 Halsey Knob Rd, 28675 910-372-6868
Sparta	Mountain Hearth Lodge, 110 Mountain Hearth Dr., 28675 336-372-8743
Sparta	Red Roof Farm, RR 2 Box 169 D, 28675 336-372-8785
Statesville	Aunt May's B&B, 532 E. Broad St, 28677 704-873-9525
Statesville	Cedar Hill Farm B&B, 778 Elmwood Rd, 28677 704-873-4332
Stokes	Sheppard Mill Farm, 3173 Sheppard Mill Rd, 27884
Supply	Doe Creek Inn B&B, 843 Ocean Hwy W, 28462 910-754-7736
Surf City	Pinke Place of Topsail, PO Box 2771, 28445
Swansboro	Mt. Pleasant B&B, RR 3, 28584 919-326-7076
Tabor City	Four Rooster Inn, 403 Pireway Rd, Rt 904, 28463 910-653-3878
Tarboro	The Barracks Inn, 1100 Albemarle Ave, 27886 252-641-1614
Taylorsville	The Barkley House B&B, 2522 NC Hwy 16 S, 28681
Tryon	Mill Farm Inn, 200 Hammon Field Rd, 28782 828-859-6992
Tryon	Mimosa Inn, One Mimosa Inn Lane, 28782 828-859-7688
Tryon	The Melrose Inn, 211 Melrose Ave, 28782 828-859-7014
Tryon	Tryon Old South B&B, 107 Markham Rd, 28782
Union Grove	Madelyn's in the Grove, PO Box 298, 28689 704-539-4151
Valle Crucis	Baird House, 1451 Watauga River Rd, 28679 828-297-4055
Valle Crucis	Bluestone Lodge, PO Box 736, 28691 704-963-5177
Valle Crucis	Mast Farm Inn, PO Box 704, 28691 704-963-5857
Valle Crucis	Rustic Barn, 2171 Broadstone Rd, 28604 828-963-7339
Vilas	Cottages of Glowing Hearth, 171 Glowing Hearth Ln, 28692 704-963-8800
Wanchese	C.W. Pugh's B&B, PO Box 427, 27981 252-473-5466
Warsaw	Squire's Vintage Inn, Rt 2 Box 130R, 28398
Waynesville	Belle Meade Inn, 1534 S Main St, 28786 704-456-3234
Waynesville	Mountain Mist Vegetarian, 142 Country Club Dr., 28786 828-452-1550
Waynesville	Palmer House B&B, 108 Pigeon St, 28786 828-456-7521
Waynesville	Snuggery B&B, 419 N Main St., 28786 828-456-3660
Waynesville	Ten Oaks B&B, 224 Love Ln, 28786 828-452-9433
Waynesville	The Evergreens, 645 Little Mountain Rd, 28786 828-452-0848
Waynesville	Wynne's Creekside Lodge, 152 Bunny Run Ln, 28786 828-926-8300
Weaverville	Dunromin Antique Log Cabin, 64 Green Ridge Rd, 28787 828-658-3345
Weaverville	Fredom Escape Lodge, 530 Upper Flat Creek Rd, 28787 828-658-0814
Weldon	Weldon Place Inn, 500 Washington Ave, 27890 252-536-4582
Wendell	Sunset Inn, 116 North Buffalo St, 27591 919-365-0353
Williamstown	Big Mill B&B, 1607 Big Mill Rd., 27892 252-792-3036
Wilmington	Armstron B&B, 5410 Pond Dr, 28409
Wilmington	Blue Heaven B&B, 517 Orange St, 28401 910-772-9929
Wilmington	Chandler's Wharf Inn, Two Ann St, 28401 910-815-3510
Wilmington	Market Street B&B, 1704 Market St, 28403 919-763-5442
Wilmington	Russell-Farrenkopf House, 335 Trails End Rd, 28409
Wilmington	Stemmerman's Inn, 130 S Front St, 28401 910-763-7776
Wilmington	Taylor House Inn, 14 N. Seventh St, 28401 910-763-7581
Wilmington	The Holladay House, 117 S. 4th St., 28401 910-763-3548
Wilmington	The Inn on Orange, 410 Orange St., 28401 910-815-0035
Winston-Salem	Henry F. Shaffner House, 150 S. Marshall St, 27101 336-777-0052
Winston-Salem	Lady Anne's Victorian B&B, 612 Summit St, 27101 336-724-1074
Winston-Salem	Mickle House B&B, 927 W. Fifth St, 27101 336-722-9045

North Dakota

Bismark	White Lace, 807 N. 6th St, 58501 701-258-4142
Bowman	Logging Camp Ranch B&B, PO Box 27, 58623 701-279-5702
Carrington	Kirkland B&B 1886, RR 2, Box 18, 58421 701-652-2775
Dickinson	Hartfiel Inn, 509 3rd Ave W, 58601 701-225-6710
Fargo	Bohlig's B&B, 1418 3rd Ave S, 58103 701-235-7867
Fargo	La Maison des Papillons, 423 8th St S, 58103 701-232-2041
Fessenden	The Beiseker Mansion, PO Box 187, 58438 701-547-3411
Glen Ullin	Rock Roof Inn B&B, 213 S 5th St, 58631
Grand Forks	511 Reeves, 511 Reeves Dr, 58201 701-772-9663
Grand Forks	Lord Byron's B&B, 521 S. 5th St, 58201 701-775-0194
Grand Forks	Merrifield House, 1216 12th Ave NE, 58201 701-775-4250
Grand Forks	The Upstairs Inn, 1120 University Ave, 58203 701-772-3853
Jamestown	Country Charm B&B, 7717 35th St SE, 58401 701-251-1372

Lidgerwood	Kaler's B&B, 9650 Highway 18, 58053 701-538-4848
Luverne	Grandma's House Farm B&B, PO Box 12, 58056 701-845-4994
McClusky	Midstate B&B, PO Box 28, 58463 701-363-2520
Medina	Chase Lake Country Inn, 2967 56th Ave SE, 58467
Medora	Dahkotah Lodge Guest Ranch, 58645 701-623-4897
Minnewaukan	Minnewaukan B&B Inn, 230 2nd St E, 58351 701-473-5731
Minot	Broadway Inn B&B, 433 N. Broadway, 58701 701-838-6075
Minot	Dakotah Rose B&B, 510 4th Ave NW, 58701 701-838-3548
Minot	Lois & Stan's B&B, 1007 11th Ave NW, 58701 701-838-2244
Mountain	221 Melsted Place, PO Box 221, 58262 701-993-8257
Napoleon	The House of 1904, 320 Ave A W, 58561 701-754-2417
Northwood	Heritage House, 440 34th St, 58267 701-587-5251
Northwood	Twin Pine B&B, PO Box 30, 58267 701-587-6075
Oakes	Houst of 29, 215 South 7th, 58474
Page	Gramz B&B, Rt 1, Box 84, 58064 701-668-2738
Parshall	The Deepwater Bay B&B, Rt 1 Box 116, 58770 701-743-4454
Reeder	Rocking Chair B&B Inn, PO Box 236, 58649 701-853-2204
Regent	Prairie Vista, 101 Rural Ave, SW, 58650 701-563-4542
Tower City	Tower City Inn B&B, 502 Church St, 58071 701-749-2660
Valley City	Valley B&B, 3611 117 R Ave SE, 58072 701-845-5893
Velva	Hagenhus B&B Inn, 406 W. 2nd St, 58790 701-338-2714
Wahpeton	Abercrombie Country Inn, 6855 177 Ave SE, 58075 701-553-9235
Wahpeton	Adama Fairview Bonanza B&B, 17170 82nd St SE, 58075 701-274-8262
Wing	Eva's B&B, HCR's Box 10, 58494 701-943-2461

Ohio ———————————————————————————

Akron	Helen's Hospitality House, 1096 Palmetto, 44306 330-724-7151
Akron	Jenkins House B&B, 1170 West Exchange, 44313 330-867-9831
Akron	Portage House, 601 Copley Rd, ST 162, 44320 330-535-1952
Akron	The O'Neil House B&B, 1290 W. Exchange, 44313 330-867-2650
Albany	Albany House, PO Box 131, 45710 614-698-6311
Andover	Whispering Pines B&B, 6699 St Rt 85, 44003 216-293-4489
Archbold	Corner Stone Inn, 300 W Street, 43502 419-445-5340
Archbold	Sauder Heritage Inn, PO Box 235, 43502 419-445-6498
Archbold	Tudor Country Inn, 706 Jantzi Dr, 43502 419-445-2531
Ashland	Winfield B&B, 1568 St Rt 60, 44805 419-281-5587
Ashtabula	Michael Cahill B&B, 1106 Walnut Blvd, 44004
Atwater	Cassidy's Country Inn, 6374 Waterloo Rd, 44201 216-047-2500
Avon Lake	Williams House, 249 Vinewood, 44012 440-933-5089
Baltimore	Canal View B&B, 710 Canal Rd, 43105 614-862-4022
Barnesville	Georgian Pillars B&B, 128 E Walnut St, 43713
Bellevue	Britannia B&B, 445 W Main St, 44811 419-483-4597
Bellville	Frederick Fitting House, 72 Fitting Ave, 44813 419-886-2863
Berlin	Carriage House Inn-Berlin, 5453 East St, 44610 330-893-2226
Berlin	Donna's Premier Lodging, PO Box 307, 44610 330-893-3068
Bolivar	Spring House B&B, 10903 St Rt 212, 44612 330-874-4255
Bryan	The Elegant Inn B&B, 215 Walnut St, 43506 419-636-2873
Caldwell	The Harkins House Inn, 715 West St, 43724 614-732-7347
Cambridge	Misty Meadow Farm B&B, PO Box 1633, 43725 614-439-5135
Cambridge	The Colonel Taylor Inn, PO Box 1333, 43725 614-432-1123
Camden	Pleasant Valley B&B, 7343 Pleasant Valley Rd, 45311
Canal Fulton	Pleasant Hill, 451 E Cherry St, 44614 330-854-0551
Carpenter	Carpenter Inn & Conf Ctr, 39655 Carpenter-Dyesvil, 45769 740-698-2450
Centerville	Yesterday B&B, 39 S. Main St, 45458 513-433-0785
Chandlersville	Quiet Rest Meadows, 3920 N. Leedom Rd, 43727
Chardon	Bass Lake Inn, 426 South St., 44024 440-285-3100
Charm	Guggisberg Swiss Inn, PO Box 1, 44617 330-893-3600
Charm	Miller Haus B&B, PO Box 126, 44617 216-893-3602
Charm	The Charm Countryview Inn, PO Box 100, 44617 216-893-3003
Chillicothe	Blair House B&B, 58 W. 5th St., 45601 614-744-3140
Chillicothe	Chillicothe B&B, 202 S. Paint St, 45601 614-772-6848
Chillicothe	Old McDill-Anderson Place, 3656 Polk Hollow Rd, 45601 614-774-1770
Chillicothe	The Greenhouse B&B, 47 E 5th St, 45601 614-775-5313
Cincinnati	Empty Nest B&B, 2707 Ida Ave, 45212 513-631-3494
Cincinnati	Mariemont Inn, 6880 Wooster Pike, 45227 513-271-2100
Cincinnati	Prospect Hill B&B, 408 Boal St, 45210 513-421-4408
Cincinnati	Ross B&B, 88 Silverwood Cir, 45246 513-671-2645
Cincinnati	Scottwood, 5 1/2 Beech Crest Ln, 45206
Cincinnati	Symphony Hotel, 210 W 14th St, 45210 513-721-3353
Cincinnati	The Parker House B&B, 2323 Ohio Ave, 45219 513-579-8236
Cincinnati	Victoria Inn of Hyde Park, 3567 Shaw Ave., 45208 513-321-3567
Cleveland	Baricelli Inn, 2203 Cornell Rd, 44106 216-791-6500
Cleveland	Glidden House, 1901 Ford Dr, 44106 216-231-8900
Cleveland	Private Lodgings, PO Box 18590, 44118 216-321-3213
Cleveland	Tudor House, PO Box 18590, 44118 216-321-3213
Columbus	157 on the Park, 157 E Deshler Ave, 43206
Columbus	50 Lincoln, 50 E. Lincoln St, 43215 614-291-5056

Columbus	Columbus B&B, 769 S 3rd St, 43206 614-443-3680
Columbus	Harrison House, 313 W 5th Ave, 43201 614-421-2202
Columbus	Juergen's German Village, 525 S. 4th St., 43206 614-224-6858
Columbus	Lansing Street B&B, 180 Lansing St., 43206 614-444-8488
Conneaut	Bennett's Homestead B&B, 263 Daniels Ave, 44030 440-593-2237
Conneaut	Buccia Vineyard B&B, 518 Gore Rd, 44030
Conneaut	Campbell Braemar B&B, 390 State St., 44030 216-599-7362
Conneaut	Homestead B&B, 255 Daniels Ave, 44030
Coshocton	Apple Butter Inn, 455 Hill St., Roscoe Vi, 43812 614-622-1329
Danville	Red Fox Country Inn, 26367 Danville Amity Rd, 43014 740-599-7369
Dayton	Candlewick B&B, 4991 Bath Rd, 45424 513-233-9297
Dayton	Prices' Steamboat House, 3317 Southern Blvd, 45409 513-223-2444
De Graff	Rollicking Hills B&B, Two Rollicking Hills Ln, 43318
Deersville	Mulberry Lane, PO Box 61, 44693 614-922-0425
Delaware	Camelot at Heater's Run, 676 Taggart Rd, 43015
Delaware	Miracle House B&B, PO Box 1496, 43015
Dellroy	Candleglow B&B, 4247 Roswell Rd, SW, 44620 216-735-2407
Dellroy	Pleasant Journey Inn, 4247 Roswell Rd SW, 44620 216-735-2987
Dellroy	Whispering Pines B&B, PO Box 340, 44620 330-735-2824
Dover	Mowrey's Welcome Home, 4489 Dover-Zoar Rd NE, 44622 330-343-4690
East Fultonham	Hill View Acres B&B, 7320 Old Town Rd, 43735 614-849-2728
Findlay	Rose Gate Cottage B&B, 423 Western Ave., 45840 419-424-1940
Franklin	The Franklin House, 318 River St, 45005
Frazeysburg	Captain Evans Hse., PO Box 27, 43822
Fredericktown	Heartland Country Resort, 2994 Township Rd 190, 43019 809-230-7030
Fredericktown	Owl Creek Country Inn, Yankee Rd, 43019 740-694-4264
Fremont	Buckland B&B, 1213 Buckland Ave., 43420 419-332-5187
Fresno	Valley View Inn-New Bedfor, 32327 SR 643, 43824 330-897-3232
Gahanna	Shamrock B&B, 5657 Sunbury Rd, 43230 614-337-9849
Galion	The Rose of Sherron, 223 Harding Way W, 44833
Gambier	Gambier House, 107 E. Wiggin St., 43022 614-427-2668
Gambier	The Kenyon Inn, 100 W Wiggin St, 43022 740-427-2202
Garrettsville	Blueberry Hill B&B, 11085 North St., 44231 216-527-5068
Geneva	Last Resort B&B, 4373 Cold Spring Rd, 44041
Geneva	The Grapevine at Duckhill, 6790 S River Rd., 44041 216-466-7300
Geneva	Warner Concord Farms B&B, 6585 S Ridge W., Rt 84, 44041 440-428-4485
Hamilton	White Rose B&B, 116 Buckeye St, 45011 513-863-6818
Higginsport	J Dugan 1830 Ohio River Hs, 101 Brown St, 45131 937-375-4395
Hillsboro	The Victoria House, 133 E North St, 45133 513-393-2743
Hiram	Lily Ponds, PO Box 322, 44234
Jackson	The Bowman House B&B, 1 Broad St, 45640
Jackson	The Maples, 14701 State Route 93, 45640 614-286-6067
Kelleys Island	Cricket Lodge B&B, Lakeshore Dr, 43438 419-746-2263
Kelleys Island	Fly Inn B&B, PO Box 471, 43438
Kelleys Island	Inn on Kelleys Island, Box 11, 43438
Kelleys Island	Rockaway B&B, PO Box 823, 43438 419-746-2445
Kelleys Island	Sweet Valley Inn, PO Box 744, 43438
Kings Mills	Kings Manor Inn B&B, 1826 Church St., 45034 513-459-9959
Kinsman	Hidden Hollow B&B, 9340 State Route 5 NE, 44428 216-876-8686
Lakeside Marblehead	Rothenbuhler's Guest House, 310 Walnut Ave., 43440 419-798-5656
Lakeside Marblehead	Victorian Inn, 5622 E Harbor Rd., 43440 419-734-5611
Lancaster	Barbara's B&B, 3705 Crumley Rd, 43130 740-687-1689
Lancaster	Butterfly Inn B&B, 6695 Lancaster-Circlevi, 43130 740-654-7654
Lancaster	Shaw's Restaurant & Inn, 123 N. Broad St, 43130 800-654-2477
Lebanon	Hexagon House, 419 Cincinnati Ave, 45036 513-932-9655
Lebanon	The Artist's Cottage, 458 E Warren St, 45036 513-932-5938
Lebanon	The Hatfield Inn, 2563 Hatfield Rd., 45036 513-032-3193
Lebanon	White Tor, 1620 Oregonia Rd, 45036 513-932-5892
London	Winchester House, 122 N Main St, 43140 614-852-0499
Louisville	Mainstay B&B, 1320 E. Main St, 44641 330-875-1021
Lucasville	Olde Lamplighter B&B, PO Box 820, 45648
Manchester	Three Island B&B, 503 E 8th St, 45144
Marblehead	Old Stone House on Lake, 133 Cemons St, 43440 419-798-5922
Marietta	Larchmont B&B, 524 2nd St., 45750 740-376-9000
Marietta	The Buckley House B&B, 332 Front St, 45750
Marion	Olde Towne Manor, 245 St. James St., 43302 740-382-2402
Martins Ferry	Mulberry Inn, 53 N. Fourth St, 43935 740-633-6058
McConnellsville	The Outback Inn, 171 E. Union Ave, 43756 614-962-2158
Medina	The Livery Building, 254 E. Smith Rd, 44256 330-722-1332
Middlefield	Yankee Lady B&B, 15471 Georgia Rd., 44062 216-632-0341
Milan	Gastier Farm B&B, 1902 Strecker Rd, 44846 419-499-2985
Millersburg	Bigham House B&B, 151 S Washington St, 44654 800-689-6950
Millersburg	Blue Moon, 47 N. Crawford St., 44654 330-674-5119
Millersburg	Das Gasthaus B&B, 4831 Holmes City Rd 207, 44654 216-893-3089
Millersburg	Indiantree Farm B&B, 5488 St Rt 515, 44654 216-893-2497
Millersburg	Jake "N" Ivy's B&B, 5409 Twp Rd 356, 44654 330-893-3215
Millersburg	The Inn at Honey Run, 6920 Country Rd #203, 44654 216-674-0011
Millersburg	Tina's House, 6521 Circle 189, 44654 330-674-6268

Mount Vernon	Accent House B&B Inn, 405 N Main St, 43050
Mount Vernon	Mt. Vernon House, 304 Martinsburg Rd., 43050 614-397-1914
Mount Vernon	The Russell-Cooper House, 115 E. Gambier St, 43050 614-397-8638
Mt. Gilead	Holiday House, 88 E High St, SR 95, 43338 419-947-8804
Newark	The Pitzer-Cooper House, 6019 White Chapel Rd, 43056 740-323-2680
North Ridgeville	St. George House, 33941 Lorain Rd, 44039 216-327-9354
Norwalk	Boos Family Inn, 5054 State Route 601, 44857
Norwalk	Bridgeview B&B, 13 Adams St, 44857 216-593-6767
Norwood	Arlene's Stone Porch B&B, 1934 Hopkins Ave., 45212 513-531-4204
Oak Harbor	Teal Point (Sports) Lodge, 4445 N St Rt 2, 43449 419-898-5106
Oberlin	Ivy Tree Inn & Garden, 195 S Professor St, 44074 216-774-4510
Oberlin	Oberlin Inn, 7 N Main St., 44074 216-775-1111
Old Washington	Zane Trace B&B, PO Box 115, 43768 614-489-5970
Orwell	Stone House In 1900, 39 N Maple Ave., 44076 216-437-5175
Oxford	The Alexander House, PO Box 190, 45056 513-523-1200
Painesville	Riders Inn, 792 Mentor Ave, 44077 440-354-8200
Paris	Pioneer's Bride B&B, 2225 Rummel Ave., 44669 330-862-4021
Plain City	Yoder's B&B, 8144 Cemetery Pike, 43064 614-873-4489
Pomeroy	Holly Hill Inn, 114 Butternut Ave., 45769 614-992-5657
Port Clinton	Island House Hotel, 102 Madison St, 43452 419-734-2166
Port Clinton	Scenic Rockledge Inn, 2772 E Sand Rd, 43452
Portsmouth	1835 House B&B, Number Eleven Offnere, 45662
Put in bay	Fether B&B, 1539 Langram Rd, 43456 419-285-5511
Put In Bay	Maple Cottage, PO Box 577, 43456
Put In Bay	Netties B&B, 1980 Put-In-Bay Rd, 43456
Ravenna	Rocking Horse Inn, 248 E Riddle Ave, 44266
Ripley	The Baird House, 201 N. 2nd. St, 45167 513-392-4918
Ripley	The Signal House, 234 N. Front St., 45167 513-392-1640
Rockbridge	Glenlaurel Inn, 14940 Mount Olive Rd, 43149 740-385-4070
Sagamore Hills	Inn at Brandywine Falls, 8230 Brandywine Rd, 44067 216-467-1812
Sandusky	Pipe Creek B&B, 2719 Columbus Ave, 44870 419-626-2067
Sandusky	Queen Anne B&B, 714 Wayne St, 44870
Sandusky	Simpson-Flint House B&B, 234 E Washington St, 44870 419-621-8679
Sandusky	Tea Rose, 218 E Washington St, 44870 419-627-2773
Sandusky	The Red Gables, 421 Wayne St, 44870 419-625-1189
Sidney	Greatstone Castle, 429 N Ohio Ave., 45365 937-492-9164
Somerset	Somer Tea B&B, 200 S Columbus, Box 308, 43783 614-743-2909
St. Clairsville	My Father's House B&B, 173 S. Marietta St, 43950 740-695-5440
Stewart	Red Bird Ranch, SR 329, 45778
Thompson	Chamomile B&B, 6458 Ledge Rd., 44086 440-298-1629
Tiffin	Zelkova Country Manor, 2348 S County Rd #19, 44883 419-447-4043
Tipp City	Willowtree Inn, 1900 W State Rt#571, 45371 513-667-2957
Toledo	Mansion View Inn B&B, 2035 Collingwood Ave, 43620 419-244-5676
Toledo	The Cummings House B&B, 1022 N Superior St, 43604 419-244-3219
Toledo	The Geer House B&B, 2553 Glenwood Ave, 43610 419-242-7065
Troy	Allen Villa B&B, 434 S. Market St, 45373 513-335-1181
Uhrichsville	Someday Valley Health Spa, 4989 Spanson Dr SE, 44683 614-922-3192
Urbana	Barnett Hill B&B, 4321 E State Route 29, 43078 513-653-7010
Urbana	Northern Plantation B&B, 3421 E Rt 296, 43078
Valley City	Reutter's Roost, 2267 Columbia Rd., 44280 330-483-4145
Vermillion	Capt. Gilchrist Guest B&B, 5662 Huron St, 44089
Versailles	The Inn at Versailles, 21 W Main St, 45380
Warsaw	Mary Harris House, 42768 US Rt 36, 43844 614-824-4141
West Alexandria	Twin Creek Country B&B, 5353 Enterprise Rd, 45381
West Alexandria	Twin Creek Townehouse B&B, 19 E Dayton, 45381
West Liberty	Liberty House, 208 N Detroit, 43357
West Milton	Locust Lane Farm B&B, 5590 Kessler Cowlesvlle, 45383 513-698-4743
West Union	Murphin Ridge Inn, 750 Murphin Ridge Rd, 45693 513-544-2263
Westerville	Cornellia's Corner B&B, 93 West College Ave, 43081
Westerville	Priscilla's B&B, 5 South West St, 43081
Williamsburg	Lewis McKever Farmhouse, 4475 McKeever Pike Rd, 45176 513-724-7044
Williamsport	Elys 1813 Mill B&B, 8120 Sr. 138, 43164
Wilmington	Cedar Hill B&B in Woods, 4003 State Route 73W, 45177
Wilmington	Grandstead Farms Ctry B&B, 733 N Curry Rd, 45177 513-382-3548
Wilmington	The General Denver, 81 W Main St., 45177 513-382-7139
Winesburg	The Grapevine House B&B, 2140 Main St., 44690 330-359-7922
Wintersville	The Lamp Post, 372 Canton Rd., 43952 614-264-0591
Wooster	Historic Overholt House, 1473 Beall Ave, 44691 330-263-6300
Wooster	Leila Belle Inn, 846 E Bowman St, 44691 330-262-8866
Wooster	Millennium Classic B&B, PO Box 1451, 44691 330-264-6005
Worthington	The Worthington Inn, 649 High St, 43085 614-885-2600
Xenia	Allendale Inn, 38 S Allison Ave, 45385
Youngstown	The Wick-Pollock Inn, PO Box 8158, 44505 330-746-1200
Zanesville	Red Cottage, 2103 E Pike, 43701
Zoar	Cider Mill B&B, PO Box 438, 44697 330-874-3240
Zoar	Cobbler Shop B&B Inn, PO Box 650, 44697 330-874-2600
Zoar	The Assembly House, PO Box 611, 44697 330-874-2239
Zoar	The Zoar Tavern & Inn, PO Box 509, 44697 216-874-2170

Oklahoma

Aline	Heritage Manor, RR 3 Box 33, 73716 580-463-2563
Bethany	Rosewood, 7000 NW 39th St, 73008 405-787-3057
Boise City	Virginia's B&B, 117 N Freeman, 73933 580-544-2834
Broken Bow	Sojourners' B&B, Rt. 2, Box 998-1, 74728 580-584-9324
Buffalo	Buffalo Trails, PO Box 526, 73834
Cheyenne	Coyote Hills, PO Box 99, 73628
Chickasha	Campbell-Richison House, 1428 Kansas, 73018 405-222-1754
Chickasha	Jordan's River Cottage, PO Box 96, 73018 405-222-3096
Claremore	Carriage House B&B Inn, 109 E 4th, 74017 918-342-2693
Claremore	Country Inn, Route 3, Box 1925, 74017 918-342-1894
Clayton	Clayton Country Inn, Rt 1, Box 8, Hwy 271, 74536 918-569-4165
Coweta	Sandhill B&B, Route 1, 74429 918-486-1041
Davis	Cedar Green B&B, 909 S. 4th, 73030 580-369-2396
Disney	Waters Edge, PO Box 594, 74340 918-435-4880
Duncan	Lindley House B&B, 1211 N Tenth, 83533 580-255-6700
El Reno	Nelson's Homestay B&B, 315 E Wade, 73036 405-262-9142
El Reno	The Victorian House B&B, 203 S Macomb, 73036 405-262-8216
Enid	Worthington House, 1224 W Maine St, 73703 580-237-9202
Eufaula	Cedar Creek B&B, PO Box 471, 74432 918-689-3009
Fairland	J-M's Country B&B, 56900 E 210 Rd, 74343 918-676-3881
Grove	Candlewyck B&B, 59600 E 307 Lane, 74344 918-786-3636
Guthrie	Harrison House Inn, PO Box 977, 73044 405-282-1000
Guthrie	Railroad House, 316 W Vilas, 73400 405-282-1827
Guthrie	The Byrd House B&B, 315 N Maple, 73400 405-282-7211
Guthrie	Victorian Garden Inn, 324 S Broad, 73400 405-282-8211
Guthrie	Victorian Rose B&B, 415 E. Cleveland, 73044 405-282-3928
Guymon	Prairie View B&B, RR 2, Box 163 A, 73942 405-338-3760
Keyes	Cattle Country Inn, HCR 1 Box 34, 73947
Mannford	Chateau in the Woods, RR 3, Box 392, 74044
Mooreland	Three Sisters Inn B&B, PO Box 938, 73852 580-994-6003
Muskogee	Graham-Carroll House, 501 North 16th St, 74401 918-683-0100
Muskogee	Miss Addie's Tea Room B&B, 821 W Broadway, 74401 918-682-1506
Norman	The Cutting Garden B&B, 927 W. Boyd St, 73069 405-329-4522
Norman	Whispering Pines B&B, 7820 E Hwy 9, 73071 405-447-0202
Nowata	Rabbit Run B&B, 305 W Delaware, 74048 918-273-2376
Oklahoma City	Country House B&B, 10101 Oakview Rd, 73112 405-840-3157
Oklahoma City	Flora's B&B, 2312 NW 46th, 73112 405-840-3157
Oklahoma City	Newton & Joann, 23312 W.W. 46, 73112
Oklahoma City	The Grandison, 1200 N Shartel Ave, 73103 405-232-8778
Oklahoma City	Willow Way, 27 Oakwood Dr, 73112 405-427-2133
Park Hill	Lord & Taylor's B&B, At Cherokee Lndng, 74451
Pawhuska	The Inn at Woodyard Farms, Rt. 2, Box 190, 74058 918-287-2699
Pawnee	Pawnee Antique Inn, PO Box 282, 74058 918-762-3133
Perkins	Accordian House B&B, 123 NE 2nd St, 74059 405-547-5533
Perry	Oklahoma Territory 1893 In, Rt 3 Box 50, 73077 580-336-9452
Ponca City	Davarnathey Inn, 719 N 14th St, 74601 405-765-9922
Ponca City	Rose Stone Inn, 120 S 3rd, 74601 405-765-9922
Poteau	The Kerr Country Mansion, 1507 S. McKenna, 74953 918-647-8221
Ramona	Jarrett Farm Country Inn, Rt 2 Box 1480, 74061 918-371-9868
Red Rock	Homestead B&B @ GT Ranch, 5101 CR 110, 74651 580-725-3466
Salina	The Plum Tree Inn, Route 2, Box 523, 74365 918-434-6000
Sapulpa	The McManor B&B, 706 S Poplar St., 74066 918-224-4665
Shawnee	Mayne Harber Inn, 2401 Highland, 74802 405-275-4700
Spiro	Aunt Jan's Cozy Cabin, Rt 1, Box 115A, 74959 918-962-2380
Stillwater	Friend House B&B, 404 S. Knoblock, 74074 405-372-1982
Stillwater	Thomasville, 4115 N. Denver, 74075 405-372-1203
Stroud	Stroud House B&B, 110 E. Second St, 73079 800-259-2978
Tahlequah	B&B of Tahlequah, 215 W. Morgan St., 74464 918-456-1309
Tulsa	McBirney Mansion Inn, 1414 S Galveston, 74127 918-585-3234
Tulsa	Old English Inn, 6140 S Memorial Dr., 74133 918-252-2020
Tulsa	The Dream Catcher B&B, 5704 S Boston Place, 74105 918-743-6704
Tulsa	The Lantern Inn, 1348 E. 35th St, 74105 918-743-8343
Watonga	Kennedy Kottage, 1017 N. Prouty, 73772 580-623-4384
Watonga	Redbud Manor B&B, PO Box 730, 73772 580-623-8587
Wilburton	Windsong Inn B&B, 100 W Cedar, 74578 918-465-5174
Woodward	Anna Augusta Inn, 2612 Lakeview Dr, 73801 580-254-5400
Woodward	Neely's Inn At The Park, 32 Boiling Springs Esta, 73801 580-254-3830

Oregon

Adams	Bar M Ranch, 58840 Bar M Ln, 97810 541-566-3381
Albany	Brier Rose Inn B&B, 206 Seventh Ave SW, 97321 541-926-0345
Aloha	Don & Kays Beach House, 20689 SW Rosa Dr, 97007
Applegate	Applegate River Lodge, 15100 Hwy 238, 97530 541-846-6690
Ashland	Adams Cottage B&B, 737 Siskiyou Blvd., 97520 541-488-5405

Ashland	Albion Inn, 34 Union St, 97520 503-488-3905
Ashland	Anne Hathaway's Cottage, PO Box 546, 97520 541-488-1050
Ashland	Antique Rose Inn, 91 Gresham, 97520 541-482-6285
Ashland	Arden Forest Inn, 261 W. Hersey, 97520 503-488-1496
Ashland	Ashberry Inn, 527 Chestnut St, 97520 541-488-8000
Ashland	Ashland Colony Inn, 725 Terra, 97520 503-482-2668
Ashland	Ashland Patterson House, 639 N. Main St., 97520 541-488-9171
Ashland	Ashland Valley Inn, 1193 Siskiyou Blvd, 97520 503-482-2641
Ashland	Ashland's English Country, 271 Beach St, 97520 541-488-4428
Ashland	Ashland's Victory House, 271 Beach St, 97520 503-488-4828
Ashland	Asland's Knight's Inn, 2359 Hwy. 66, 97520 503-482-5111
Ashland	Bayberry Inn, 438 North Main, 97520 541-488-1252
Ashland	Best Western Bard's Inn, 132 N. Main St, 97520 503-482-0049
Ashland	Buckhorn Spring's, 2200 Buckhorn Spring's, 97520 503-488-2200
Ashland	Cedarwood Inn of Ashland, 1801 Siskiyou Blvd, 97520 503-488-2000
Ashland	Chanticleer Inn, 120 Gresham St, 97520 503-482-1919
Ashland	Clarity Cottage and Suite, 868 A St, 97520 541-488-2457
Ashland	Colonel Silsby's B&B Inn, 111 N Third St., 97520 541-488-3070
Ashland	Coolidge House, 137 N. Main St, 97520 503-482-4721
Ashland	Cowslip's Belle B&B, 159 N Main St, 97520 541-488-2901
Ashland	Daniel's Roost, 1920 E. Main St., 97520 541-482-0121
Ashland	Dome Studio B&B, 8550 Dead Indian Memori, 97520 541-482-1755
Ashland	Drovers' Inn, 298 W Hersey St., 97520 541-482-6280
Ashland	Fadden's Inn, 326 Main St, 97520 503-488-0025
Ashland	Fox House Inn, 269 "B" St, 97520 503-488-1055
Ashland	Grapevine Inn, 486 Siskiyou Blvd, 97520 541-482-7944
Ashland	Green Springs Inn, 11470 Hwy 66, 97520 541-482-0614
Ashland	Hersey House & Bungalow, 451 N. Main St, 97520 503-482-4563
Ashland	Hillside Inn, 1520 Siskiyou Blvd, 97520 503-482-2626
Ashland	Laurel Street Inn, 174 N. Main St, 97520 503-488-2222
Ashland	Lithia Springs Inn, 2165 W Jackson Rd, 97520 541-482-7128
Ashland	Little House, 321 Clay St. #7, 97520 541-482-0672
Ashland	McCall House, 153 Oak St, 97520 503-482-9296
Ashland	Morical House Garden Inn, 668 N. Main St, 97520 541-482-2254
Ashland	Mousetrap Inn, 312 Helman St, 97520 541-482-9228
Ashland	Mt. Ashland Inn, 550 Mt. Ashland Rd, 97520 541-482-8707
Ashland	Nightingail's Inn, 117 North Main, 97520 541-482-7373
Ashland	Oak Hill Country B&B, 2190 Siskiyou Blvd, 97520 541-482-1554
Ashland	Pedigrift House B&B, 407 Scemic Dr, 97520 541-482-1888
Ashland	Pinehurst Inn @ Jenny Crk, 17520 Hwy 66, 97520
Ashland	Queen Anne, 125 N. Main St, 97520 503-482-0220
Ashland	Shrew's House, 570 Siskiyou Blvd., 97520 503-482-9214
Ashland	Summer Place Inn, 534 Siskiyou Blvd., 97520 541-488-5650
Ashland	The Iris Inn, 59 Manzanita St, 97520 503-488-2286
Ashland	The Peerless Hotel, 243 Fourth St, 97520 541-488-1082
Ashland	The Studio's Inn, 550 E. Main, 97520 503-488-5882
Ashland	The Woods House B&B, 333 N. Main St, 97520 503-488-1598
Ashland	Winchester Inn, 35 S. 2nd St, 97520 503 488 1113
Astoria	Astoria Inn B&B, 3391 Irving Ave, 97103 503-325-8153
Astoria	Captain's Inn, 1546 Franklin, 97103 503-325-1387
Astoria	Columbia River Inn B&B, 1681 Franklin Ave, 97103 503-325-5044
Astoria	Destination B&B, Rt 2 Box 355, 97103 503-325-0853
Astoria	Franklin St. Station, 1140 Franklin, 97103 503-325-4314
Astoria	Inn-Chanted B&B, 707-8th St, 97103 503-325-5223
Astoria	Martin & Lilli Foard House, 690 17th St, 97103 503-325-1892
Aurora	The Inn at Aurora, 15109 NE 2nd St, 97002 503-678-1932
Baker City	Baer House B&B, 2333 Main St, 97814 541-524-1812
Baker City	Demain Until Tomorrow, 1790 4th St, 97814 541-523-2509
Baker City	Oregon Trail B&B, HCR 88 Box 27, 97814 541-523-2014
Baker City	Sagebrush Sadie's, 200 Well St, 97814
Bandon	Bandon Beach House B&B, 2866 Beach Loop, 97411 541-347-1196
Bandon	Beach Street B&B, PO Box 217, 97411 541-347-5124
Bandon	Na-So-Mah, Rte. 2 Box 2485, 97411 503-347-1922
Bandon	Pacific House B&B, 2165 Beach Loop Dr., 97411 541-347-9526
Bandon	Riverboat B&B, Rt. 2 Box 2485, 97411 503-347-1922
Bandon	Sea Star Guesthouse, 375 2nd St, 97411 541-347-9632
Bandon	The Historic River House, Rt 1, Box 890-10, 97103 541-347-1414
Beaverton	The Yankee Tinker B&B, 5480 SW 183rd Ave, 97007 503-649-0932
Bend	Bear River Valley B&B, 1750 SW Forest Ridge Ave, 97702
Bend	Gazebo B&B, 21679 Obsidian Ave, 97702 503-389-7202
Bend	Swallow Ridge B&B, 65711 Twin Bridges Rd, 97701 541-389-1913
Bend	The Sather House B&B, 7 N.W. Tumalo Ave, 97701 541-388-1065
Bend	Three Sisters B&B, 20150 Tumalo Rd, 97701
Bend	Villa Genovese B&B, 222 Urania Lane, 97702 541-318-3557
Boring	Lariat Gardens B&B, 29440 SSE Lariat Ln, 97009 503-663-1967
Bridgeport	Bruno Ranch B&B, US Hwy 245, Bruno Ranch, 97819 503-446-3468
Brightwood	Maple River B&B, PO Box 339, 97011 503-622-6273
Brookings	Casa Rubie, PO Box 397, 97415

Brookings	Chart House Lodge & Outf., PO Box 6898, 97415 541-469-3867
Brookings	Hemlock Garden Guest Haus, PO Box 7994, 97415
Brookings	Holmes Sea Cove B&B, 17350 Holmes Dr, 97415 541-469-3025
Brookings	Oceancrest House B&B, 15510 Pedrioli, 97415 541-469-9200
Brookings	Pacific View B&B, 18814 Montbretia Ln, 97415 541-469-6837
Brookings	Pacific View B&B, 18814 Montbretia Lane, 97415 541-469-6837
Brookings	Sea Dreamer Inn, 15167 Mc Vay Ln, 97415 541-469-6629
Brookings	The Castle B&B, 15902 Bay View Dr, 97415 541-469-6590
Brownsville	Kirk's Ferry B&B, 203 Washburn, 97327 503-466-3214
Burns	Sage Country Inn, PO Box 227, 97220 541-573-7243
Cannon Beach	Cannon Beach Hotel, PO Box 943, 97110 503-436-1392
Cannon Beach	Capitol Hill Mansion, PO Box 1065, 97110 303-572-0050
Cannon Beach	Stephanie Inn, PO Box 219, 97110 503-436-2221
Cascade Locks	Inn at the Locks, PO Box 39, 97104 702-374-8222
Cloverdale	Hudson House B&B Inn, 37700 Hwy 101 S, 97112 503-392-3533
Coos Bay	Coos Bay Manor, 955 South Fifth St, 97420 503-269-1224
Coos Bay	Manor B&B, 955 S. 5th St, 97420 503-269-1224
Coos Bay	The Old Tower House B&B, 476 Newmark, 97420 503-888-6058
Coos Bay	The Upper Room Chalet, 306 N. 8th St, 97420 503-269-5385
Coquille	The Barton House, 715 E. First St, 97423 541-396-5306
Corvallis	Abed & Breakfast at Sparks, 2515 SW 45th St, 97333 541-757-7321
Corvallis	B&B on the Green, 2515 SW 45th St, 97333 541-757-7321
Corvallis	Courtyard Inn, 2435 NW Harrison Blvd, 97330 541-754-7136
Corvallis	Macpherson Inn, 29081 Hwy 34, 97330 541-753-2955
Corvallis	The Mellon House, 740 SW 15th St, 97330 541-753-7725
Cottage Grove	Carousel House, 337 N 9th, 97424 541-942-0046
Cottage Grove	Deermeadow Inn B&B, 78876 Bryson Sears Rd, 97424 503-942-4878
Cottage Grove	Inn at Cottage Gove Lake, 32670 Glaisyer Hill Rd, 97424 503-942-2958
Cottage Grove	River Country Inn, 71864 London Rd, 97424
Crescent Lake	Willamette Pass Inn, PO Box 35, 97425 503-433-2211
Creswell	The Country House, 30930 Camas Swale Rd, 97426 541-895-2918
Crooked River	Crooked River Ranch B&B, PO Box 1334, 97760 503-548-4804
Dallas	Historic Henkle House, 184 SE Oak St, 97338 503-831-3716
Dayville	Fish House Inn B&B, PO Box 143, 97825 541-987-2124
Depoe Bay	Pirate's Cove B&B, PO Box 701, 97341
Depoe Bay	The Channel House Inn, PO Box 56, 97341 503-765-2140
Detroit	Repose & Repast, PO Box 587, 97342
Diamond	McCoy Creek Inn, HC 72, Box 11, 97722
Diamond	Santillies' Hotel Diamond, 10 Main St, 97722 541-493-1898
Drewsey	Blue Bucket at 3E Ranch, HC 68, Box 536, 97904 541-493-2525
Elkton	Big K Guest Ranch, 20029 Hwy 138 W, 97436
Elkton	Elkqua Lodge, 221 Main St, 97436 541-584-2151
Elkton	Equua Lodge, 221 Main St, 97400
Elmira	The Dome B&B, PO Box 464, 97437 503-935-3138
Enterprise	George Hyatt House B&B Inn, 200 E Greenwood St, 97828 541-426-0241
Enterprise	Tickled Trout B&B, 507 S River St, 97828 541-426-6039
Eugene	Camille's B&B, 3277 Onyx Place, 97405 541-344-9576
Eugene	Campus Cottage B&B Inn, 1136 E. 19th Ave, 97403 503-342-5346
Eugene	Excelsior Inn, 754 E 13th St., 97401 541-342-6963
Eugene	Getty's Emerald Garden B&B, 640 Audel Ave, 97404 503-688-6344
Eugene	Kjaer's House in the Woods, 814 Lorane Hwy, 97405 541-343-3234
Eugene	Lorane Valley B&B, 86621 Lorane Hwy, 97405 503-686-0241
Eugene	McGarry House B&B, 856 E 19th Ave, 97401 541-485-0037
Eugene	McKenzie View B&B, 39422 McKenzie View Dr., 97478 541-726-3887
Eugene	The House in the Woods, 814 Lorane Highway, 97405 503-343-3234
Eugene	The Secret Garden, 1910 University St., 97403 541-484-6755
Florence	Blue Heron Inn B&B, PO Box 1122, 97439 541-997-4091
Florence	Edwin K B&B, PO Box 2687, 97439 541-997-8360
Florence	Heceta Beach B&B, 04599 Joshua Ln, 97439 541-902-0698
Florence	Oak St Victorian B&B, PO Box 2799, 97439 541-997-4000
Fort Klamath	Horseshoe Ranch, PO Box 495, 97626 541-381-2297
Fort Klamath	Sun Pass Ranch, PO Box 499, 97626 541-381-2259
Fossil	Bridge Creek Flora B&B Inn, 828 Main St, 97830 541-763-2355
Fossil	Wild River Ranch B&B, 37948 Hwy 19-207, 97830 541-468-2900
Gardiner	Gardiner Guest House, PO Box 222, 97441 541-271-4005
Garibaldi	Hill Top House B&B, PO Box 145, 97118 503-322-3221
Garibaldi	No-How Inn B&B, 119 E. Driftwood, 97118
Garibaldi	Pelican's Perch B&B, PO Box 543, 97118 503-322-3633
Gates	Dragovich House, PO Box 261, 97346 503-897-2157
Gold Beach	Endicott Gardens, 95768 Jerry's Flat Rd, 97444 503-247-6513
Gold Beach	Heather House B&B, 190 11th St, 97444 503-247-2074
Gold Beach	Hig Seas Inn, 105 Walker St Box 3, 97441
Gold Beach	Inn At Nesika Beach, 33026 Nesika Rd., 97444 541-247-6434
Gold Beach	Tu Tu' Tun Lodge, 96550 N. Bank Rogue, 97444 503-247-6664
Gold Hill	Rouge River Guest House, 41 Rogue River Hwy, 97525 541-855-4485
Government Camp	Mt. Hood Manor, PO Box 369, 97028 503-272-3440
Grande Ronde	Granny Franny's Farm B&B, 97347 800-553-9002
Grants Pass	Chriswood Inn, 233 Rouge Rvr Hwy 1213, 97527 503-474-9733

Grants Pass	The Ahlf House Inn, 762 NW Sixth St, 97526 503-474-1374
Halfway	Birch Leaf Lodge, RR 1, Box 91, 97834 503-742-2990
Halfway	Clear Creek Farm B&B, 48212 Clear Creek Rd, 97834 541-742-2238
Hammond	Officer's Inn B&B, 540 Russell Place, 97121
Hereford	Fort Reading B&B, HC 86 Box 140, 97837 541-446-3478
Hillsboro	Pleasant View Farms B&B, 16520 SW Hillsboro Hwy, 97123 503-628-1065
Hillsboro	The Hawthorne Estate, 5611 NE Elam Young Pkwy, 97124
Hood River	Brown's B&B, 3000 Reed Rd., 97031 541-386-1545
Hood River	Columbia Gorge Hotel, 4000 Westcliff Dr, 97031 541-386-5566
Hood River	Inn At The Gorge, 1113 Eugene St., 97031 541-386-4429
Hood River	Lakecliff Estate B&B, PO Box 1220, 97031 503-386-5918
Hood River	Love's Riverview Lodge, 1505 Oak St, 97031 541-386-8719
Hood River	State Street Inn, B&B, 1005 State St, 97031 503-386-1899
Jacksonville	Colonial House B&B, PO Box 1298, 97530 503-770-2783
Jacksonville	Old Stage Inn, PO Box 579, 97530 541-899-1776
Jacksonville	Orth House B&B, PO Box 1437, 97530 541-899-8665
Jacksonville	Reames House 1868, PO Box 128, 97530
Jacksonville	The Touvelle House, PO Box 1891, 97530 503-899-8938
Jacksonville	Wells Ranch House B&B, 126 Hamilton Rd, 97530 541-899-1472
Jordan Valley	Ridgeview B&B, 1888 US Hwy 95 W, 97910 541-586-2370
Joseph	Tamarack Pines Inn, 60073 Wallowa Lake Hwy, 97846 503-432-2920
Joseph	Whitetail Farm, PO Box 1066, 97846
Klamath Falls	Boarding House Inn B&B, 1800 Esplanade Ave, 97601
Klamath Falls	Lost River B&B, 1060 Lakeshore Dr., 97601 541-885-7329
La Grande	Countryside Inn B&B, 62528 Jay Bird Dr, 97850 541-963-3329
La Grande	Pitcher Inn B&B, PO Box 817, 97850 503-963-9152
La Grande	Stang Manor Inn, 1612 Walnut Ave, 97850 541-963-2400
La Pine	Diamond Stone Guest Lodge, 16693 Sprague Lp., 97739 541-536-6263
Langlois	Floras Lake House/By Sea, 92870 Boice Cope Rd, 97450 541-348-2573
Leaburg	Marjon Bed & Breakfast Inn, 44975 Leaburg Dam Rd, 97489 503-896-3145
Lebanon	Historical Booth House, 486 Park St, 97355 503-258-2954
Lincoln City	Inlet Garden B&B, 646 NW Inlet, 97367 541-994-7932
Lincoln City	Ocean Memories, PO Box 687, 97367 541-994-8183
Lincoln City	Palmer House, 646 NW Inlet, 97363 503-994-7932
Lincoln City	Spyglass Inn B&B, 2510 S.W. Dune, 97367 503-994-2785
Lincoln City	The Enchanted Cottage, 4507 SW Coast, 97367 530-996-4101
Lincoln City	The Rustic Inn, 2313 NE Holmes Rd, 97367 503-994-5111
Manzanita	Arbors at Manzanita, PO Box 68, 97130 503-368-7566
Maupin	C & J Lodge, PO Box 130, 97037 800-395-3903
McMinnville	Baker Street B&B Inn, 129 S. Baker St, 97128 503-472-5575
McMinnville	Gahr Farm B&B Cottage, 18605 SW Masonville Rd, 97128 503-472-6960
McMinnville	Mattey House B&B, 10221 NE Mattey Ln, 97128 503-434-5058
McMinnville	Orchard View Inn, 16540 N.W. Orchard View, 97128 503-472-0165
McMinnville	Steiger Haus B&B, 360 SE Wilson St, 97128 503-472-0821
McMinnville	Williams House B&B, 809 NE Evans, 97128 503-434-9016
McMinnville	Youngberg Hill Vineyard, 10660 SW Youngberg Hill, 97128 503-472-2727
Medford	Cedar Lodge Motor Inn, 518 N. Riverside, 97501 503-773-7361
Medford	Nendels Inn, 2300 Crater Lake Hwy, 97504 503-779-3141
Merlin	Morrison's Rogue River, 8500 Galice Rd, 97532 541-476-3825
Merlin	Pine Meadow Inn B&B, 1000 Crow Rd, 97532 541-471-6277
Mill City	Ivy Creek B&B, PO Box 757, 97360 503-897-2001
Mill City	The Morrison Cottage, 418 NW Adler St, 97360
Milton	Birch Tree Manor B&B, 615 S. Main St, Hwy 11, 97862 503-938-6455
Mitchell	Historic Oregon Hotel B&B, 104 Main St, 97750 541-462-3027
Monmouth	Howell's B&B, 212 N. Knox, 97361 503-847-5523
Mosier	The Mosier House B&B, PO Box 476, 97040 541-478-3640
Mt. Hood	Mt. Hood Hamlet B&B, 6741 Hwy 35, 97041 541-352-3574
Myrtle Creek	Sonka's Sheep Station Inn, 901 NW Chadwick Ln, 97457 503-863-5168
Newberg	Avellan Inn, 1669 NE Hwy 240, 97132 503-537-9161
Newberg	Belanger's Secluded B&B, 19719 NE Williamson Rd, 97132
Newberg	Etheos B&B, 36280 NE Wilsonville Rd, 97132 503-625-1390
Newberg	Secluded B&B, 19719 NE Williamson Rd, 97132 503-538-2635
Newberg	Smith House B&B, 415 N. College St, 97132
Newberg	Springbrook Hazenut Farm, 30295 Hwy. 99W, 97132 503-538-4606
Newport	Green Gables B&B, 156 SW Coast St, 97365 541-265-9141
Newport	Sea Cliff B&B, 749 NW 3rd, 97365 503-265-6664
Newport	Sylvia Beach Hotel, 267 N.W. Cliff St, 97365 503-265-5428
North Bend	Itty Bitty Inn, 1504 Sherman Ave, 97459 503-756-6398
North Bend	Sherman House B&B, 2380 Sherman Ave, 97459 503-756-3496
Oakland	Beckley House B&B, PO Box 198, 97462 503-459-9320
Oceanside	Searose B&B, PO Box 122, 97134 503-842-6126
Oregon City	Ainsworth House B&B, 19130 Lot Whitcomb Dr., 97045 503-657-5043
Oregon City	Inn of the Oregon Trail, 416 S. McLoughlin, 97045 503-656-2089
Oregon City	Tolle House, 15921 Hunter Ave, 97045 503-655-4325
Pacific City	Eagle's View B&B, PO Box 901, 97135 503-965-7600
Pacific City	Pacific View B&B, 34930 Hillcrest Rd., 97135 503-965-6498
Parkdale	Mt. Hood B&B, 8885 Cooper Spur Rd, 97041
Parkdale	Old Parkdale Inn B&B, 4932 Baseline Rd, 97041 541-352-5551

Pendelton	Dorie's Inn B&B, 203 NW Despain Ave, 97801
Pendelton	Place Apart B&B Inn, 711 SE Byers, 97801 541-276-0573
Portland	3 B's At Market, 1704 SE 22nd Ave, 97214 503-232-4223
Portland	Abernathy's B&B, 0333 SW Flower St, 97201 503-243-7616
Portland	Clinkerbrick House, 2311 N.E. Schuyler, 97212 503-281-2533
Portland	Hampshire House B&B, 10 NE 24th Ave, 97232 503-370-7081
Portland	Hillcrest B&B, 3430 SW Gale, 97201 503-225-1109
Portland	Holladay House, 1735 NE Wasco St, 97232
Portland	Hostess House, 5758 NE Emerson St., 97218 503-282-7892
Portland	Irvington Inn, 2727 NE 21 St, 97212 503-280-2299
Portland	John Palmer House B&B Inn, 4314 N. Mississippi Ave, 97217 503-284-5893
Portland	Knott Street Inn B&B, 2331 NE Knott, 97212 503-249-1855
Portland	Pittock Acres B&B, 103 NW Pittock Ave, 97210 503-226-1163
Portland	Plum Tree B&B, 2005 NE 22nd Ave, 97212 503-280-0679
Portland	Portland's White House, 1914 NE 22nd, 97212 503-287-7131
Portland	The Lion and the Rose B&B, 1517 NE Schuyler, 97212 503-287-9245
Portland	Villa, 3032 NE Rocky Butte Rd, 97220 503-252-4492
Prairie City	B&B By the River, Rt 2 Box 790, 97869
Prairie City	Riverside School House B&B, County Rd 61, 97869 541-820-4732
Prairie City	Strawberry Mountain Inn, HCR 77 #940, 97869 800-545-6913
Prineville	Historic Elliott House, 305 W First St, 97754 541-447-7442
Prospect	Prospect Hotel-Dinner Hous, 391 Mill Creek, 97536 503-560-3664
Rockaway Beach	Ocean Locomotion Motel, 19130 Alder Ave, 97136
Rockaway Beach	Sunset Station Lodge, PO Box 119, 97136 503-355-2200
Roseburg	House of Hunter, 813 SE Kane St, 97470 541-672-2335
Roseburg	The Umpqua House, 840 Oak View Dr, 97470 541-672-4353
Salem	Hopkins House B&B, 975 D St NE, 97301 503-397-4676
Salem	Vista Park B&B, 480 Vista Ave SE, 97302 503-588-0698
Sandlake	Sandlake Country Inn, 8505 Galloway Rd, 97112 503-965-6745
Sandy	Brookside B&B, 45232 SE Paha Lp, 97055 503-668-4766
Sandy	Fernwood At Alder Creek, 54850 Hwy 26 E, 97055 503-622-3570
Scappoose	Barnstormer B&B, 53758 W Lane Rd, 97056 503-543-2740
Scapposse	Malarkey Ranch Inn, 55948 Columbia River Hy, 97056 503-543-5244
Scio	Wesley House, 38791 Hwy 226, 97374 503-394-3210
Seaside	10th Ave. Inn B&B, 125-10th Ave, 97138 503-738-0643
Seaside	Anderson's Boarding House, PO Box 573, 97138 503-738-9055
Seaside	Bailey's Bide-A-Wee B&B, 606 12th Ave., 97138 503-738-0238
Seaside	Beachwood, 671 Beach Dr, 97138 503-738-9585
Seaside	Chateau on the River, 486 Necanicum Dr., 97138 503-738-8800
Seaside	Summer House, 1221 N. Franklin, 97138 503-738-5740
Seaside	The Guest House B&B, 486 Necanicum Dr, 97138 503-717-0495
Shaniko	Historic Shaniko Hotel, PO Box 86, 97057 541-489-3441
Sheridan	Brightridge Farm B&B, 18575 Brightridge Rd., 97378 503-843-5230
Sheridan	Thre'Pence B&B, 27175 SW Frys Lane, 97378 503-843-4984
Silverton	The Magnolia Cottage B&B, 504 W Main, 97381 503-873-6712
Sisters	Squaw Creek B&B Inn, PO Box 1993, 97759 541-549-4312
Sixes	The Sixes River Hotel, PO Box 327, 97476 541-332-3900
South Beach	Salmon Harbor Belle B&B, PO Box 685, 97366 541-271-1137
Springfield	Moloney's Inn B&B, 922 "B" St, 97477 541-746-1745
Stayton	Bird & Hat Inn, 717 N 3rd Ave, 97383
Stayton	Horncroft, 42156 Kingston-Lyons Dr, 97383 503-769-6287
Stayton	Our Place in the Country, 9297 Boedigheimer Rd SE, 97383 503-769-4555
Steamboat	Steamboat Inn, 42705 N. Umpqua Hwy, 97447 541-498-2230
Summer Lake	Summer Lake Inn, 31501 Hwy 31, 97640 541-943-3983
Sumpter	Sumpter B&B, 97877 800-640-3184
The Dalles	Captain Gray's Guest House, 210 West 4th St, 97058 541-298-8222
The Dalles	The Columbia House, 525 E Seventh St, 97058 541-298-4686
Tigard	The Woven Glass Inn, 14645 Beef Bend Rd, 97224 503-590-6040
Tillamook	Blue Haven Inn, 3025 Gienger Rd, 97141 503-842-2265
Troutdale	Blackberry Inn B&B, PO Box 534, 97060 503-563-2259
Umpqua	Valley's End Farm B&B, 14438 Garden Valley Rd, 97486 541-459-5916
Vale	1900 Sears & Roebuck Home, 484 N 10th, 97918 541-473-9636
Waldport	Cape Cod Cottages, 4150 SW Pacific Coast, 97394 541-563-2106
Waldport	Colleen's Country B&B, 1806 Lucy Lane, 97394 503-563-3201
Wallowa	McCrae House, 71031 Whiskey Creek Rd, 97885 503-886-4352
Welches	Mountain Shadows B&B, PO Box 147, 97067 503-622-4746
Welches	Old Welches Inn B&B, 26401 E Welches Rd, 97067 503-622-3754
Westfir	Westfir Lodge, A B&B Inn, 47365 First St, 97492 541-782-3103
Weston	Tamarack Inn B&B, 62388 Hwy 204, 97886 541-566-9348
Yachats	Morning Star B&B, 95668 Hwy 101, 97498 541-547-4412
Yachats	New England House B&B, PO Box 411, 97498 541054704799
Yachats	Quilt Haven B&B, 95435 Hwy 101 S, 97498
Yachats	Sea Hills Cabin, 95459 Hwy 101, 97498 541-547-4482
Yachats	Sea Quest B&B, PO Box 448, 97498 541-547-3782
Yachats	Serenity B&B, 5985 Yachats River Rd, 97498 503-547-3813
Yachats	The Oregon House, 94288 Hwy 101 S, 97498 541-547-3329
Yachats	Yachats Inn, 331 S Coast Hwy 101, 97498 541-547-3456
Yoncalla	Tuckaway Farm Inn, 7179 Scotts Valley Rd, 97499 541-849-3144

Pennsylvania

Adamstown	Adamstown Inn, PO Box 938, 19501 717-484-0800
Airville	Spring House, 1264 Muddy Creek Forks, 17302 717-927-6906
Akron	Boxwood Inn, PO Box 203, 17501 717-859-3466
Annville	Maison Main, 243 E Main St, 17003 717-867-0405
Annville	Swatara Creek Inn B&B, RR 02 Box 692, 17003 717-865-3259
Atglen	Gabriel's Hill B&B, 432 Noble Rd., 19310 610-593-7308
Atglen	Glen Run Valley View Farm, Rt 1 Box 69, 19310 215-593-5656
Avella	Weatherbury Farm, 1061 Sugar Run Rd, 15312 724-587-3763
Bangor	Hurryback Riverhouse B&B, RR 2, Box 2176A, 18013 215-498-3121
Barto	Inn at Bally Spring Farm, 90 Airport Rd., 19504 610-845-8900
Bellefonte	Morning Glory B&B, 550 Spring Creek R, 16823 814-422-8567
Bellefonte	Selgate House B&B, 176 Armagast Rd., 16823 814-353-1102
Bellefonte	The Annie Natt House, 127 W Curtin St, 16823 814-353-1456
Bellefonte	The Dartt House, 251 N Allegheny St, 16823
Bellefonte	The Garrett B&B, 217 W Linn St, 16823 814-355-3093
Belleville	Harmon House, 19 W Main St, 17004
Belleville	Twin Oaks B&B, RR 1 Box 1, 17004
Benton	The Red Poppy B&B, RR 2 Box 82, 17814 717-925-5823
Benton	White House on North Mt., RR 2 Box 256B, 17814 717-925-2858
Bernville	Sunday's Mill Farm, RD 2 Box, 19506 610-488-7821
Bethlehem	Sayre Mansion Inn, 250 Wyandotte St, 18015
Bethlehem	Wydnor Hall Inn, Rd 3, 18015 215-867-6851
Bird In Hand	Bird In Hand Family Inn, Box 402, 17505
Bird In Hand	Greystone Manor B&B, PO Box 270, 17505 717-393-4233
Blairsville	Comfort Inn, RR 1 Box 22 Rt 22, 15717
Blakeslee	Blue Berry Mountain Inn, HC 1 Box 1102,Thomas Rd, 18510 717-646-6269
Blossburg	Mountain Laurel B&B, 127 Williamson Rd, 16912
Boalsburg	House On Top of the Hill, 1800 Earlystown Rd., 16827 714-466-2070
Boiling Spring	The Garmanhaus, 217 Front St, 17007
Boiling Spring	Yellow Breeches House, PO Box 221, 17007 717-258-8344
Boyertown	The Enchanted Cottage, 22 Deer Run Rd, 19512 610-845-8845
Boyertown	The Twin Turrets Inn, 11 E. Philadelphia Ave, 19512 610-367-4513
Brackney	Indian Mountain Inn B&B, Box 68, 18812 717-663-2645
Bradford	Fisher Inn, 253 E Main St, 16701 814-368-3428
Bradford	Glendorn, A Country Lodge, 1032 W Corydon St, 16701 800-843-8568
Brookville	Bluebird Hollow B&B, RR 8 Box 56, 15825 814-856-2858
Buckingham	Mill Creek Farm, 2348 Quarry Box 816, 18912
Cambridge Springs	Rider Hill Inn B&B, 225 Beach Ave., 16403 814-398-4249
Canadensis	Dreamy Acres, Rt#447, 18325 570-595-7115
Canadensis	Overlook Inn, Dutch Hill Rd., Box 680, 18325 570-595-7519
Canadensis	Pump House Inn, RR1 Box 430, 18325 570-595-7501
Carbondale	Fern Hall, Box 1095, 18407 717-222-3676
Carbondale	Heritage House on the Park, 5 Park Place, 18407 717-282-7477
Carlisle	Line Limousin Farmhouse, 2070 Ritner Hwy, 17013 717-243-1281
Cashtown	The Historic Cashtown Inn, Old Route 30, Box 103, 17310 717-334-9722
Centre Hall	Earlystown Manor, RR 1 Box 181A, 16828
Centre Hall	Mt. Nittany Inn, Rt 144, Centre Hall Mt, 16828 814-364-9363
Chadds Ford	Brandywine River Hotel, PO Box 1058, 19317 215-388-1200
Chadds Ford	Pennsbury Inn, 833 Limore Pike, 19317 610-388-1435
Chalfont	Curley Mill Manor, 776 N Limekiln Pike, 18914
Chalfont	Elk Run Lodge, 272 Sellersville Rd, 18914
Chalfont	Simon Butler Mill House, 116 E Butler Ave, 18914
Chambersburg	Falling Spring Inn, 1838 Falling Spring Rd., 17201 717-267-3654
Clarion	Clarion House B&B, 77 S 7th Ave, 16214 814-226-4996
Clark	Tara–A Country Inn, 3665 Valley View Rd, 16113 412-962-3535
Clearfield	Cedarwood Lodge, 216 S Front St, 16830
Clearfield	Victorian Loft B&B, 216 S Front St, 16830 814-765-4805
Clearville	Conifer Ridge Farm, RD 2, PO Box 202A, 15535 814-784-3342
Clinton	Country Road B&B, Moody Rd, Box 265, 15026 412-899-2528
Confluence	River's Edge Cafe/B&B, 203 Yough St, 15424 814-395-5059
Confluence	The Point Guest Rooms, 201 Jacobs St, 15424 814-395-3082
Connellsville	Newmyer House B&B, 507 S Pittsburg St, 15425 724-626-0141
Cooksburg	Cook Homestead B&B, PO Box 106, 16217 814-744-8869
Corry	Day Lily Inn B&B, 113 W Main St, 16407 814-664-9047
Cowansville	Garrott's B&B, RD 1, Box 73, 16218 412-545-2432
Cranberry	Cranberry B&B, PO Box 2005, 16066 412-776-1198
Cresco	Crescent Lodge, Paradise Valley, 18326 717-795-7486
Cross Fork	Kettle Creek Lodge Ltd., 1118 Pine Hill Rd, 17729 814-435-1019
Davidsville	StoneRidge B&B, 2825 Carpenter Park Rd, 15928 814-288-3931
Dawson	Pringle House, RR & Griiscom St, 15428
Delaware Water Gap	The Shepard House, PO Box 486, 18327
Delta	The Everything & More Inn, RR 1 Box 28K, 17314
Denver	Cocalico Creek B&B, 224 S 4th St., 17517 717-336-0271
Dillsburg	Peter Wolford House B&B, 440 Franklin Church Rd, 17019
Donegal	Mountain View B&B, 10 Mountain View Rd, 15628 412-593-6349
Dover	Detters Acres B&B, 6631 Old Carlisle Rd., 17315 717-292-3172

Lancaster	Nissly's Lancaster City In, 624 W Chestnut St, 17603 717-392-2311
Lancaster	Patchwork Inn, 2319 Old Philadelphia, 17602 717-293-9078
Lancaster	Secret Garden on Chestnut, 445 W Chestnut St, 17603 717-293-5773
Lansford	Edgemont House, 4 Edgemont Rd., 18232 717-645-4943
Laughlintown	Ligonier Country Inn, PO Box 46, 15655 412-238-3651
Laurel Highlands	Mountain View Inn, 1001 Village Dr., 15601 412-834-5300
Lebanon	Zinns Mill Homestead B&B, 243 N. Zinns Mill Rd, 17042 717-272-1513
Leetsdale	Whistlestop, 195 Broad St, 15056 412-251-0852
Lewisburg	Brookpark Farm B&B, 100 Reitz Blvd, 17837 717-524-7733
Lewisburg	Inn on Fiddler's Tract, RD 2, Box 573A, 17837 717-523-7197
Lewistown	At The Gables, 900 S. Main St, 17044 717-248-4242
Ligonier	Woolley Fox, 61 Lincoln Hwy E, 15658 412-238-3004
Lima	Hamanasset, PO Box 129, 19037 610-459-3000
Lititz	Carter Run Inn B&B, 511 E Main St, Rt#772, 17543 717-626-8807
Lititz	General Sutter Inn, 14 East Main St, 17543 717-626-2115
Lititz	Spahr's Century Farm, 192 Green Acre Rd, 17543 717-627-2185
Lititz	Swiss Woods B&B, 500 Blantz Rd, 17543 717-627-3358
Lock Haven	Victorian Inn B&B, 402 E Water St., 17745 717-748-8688
Loganton	Webb Farm B&B, RR1, Box 441, 17747 717-725-3591
Lumberville	1740 House, River Rd, 18933 215-297-5661
Lumberville	Black Bass Hotel, 3774 River Rd, Rt#32, 18933 215-297-5770
Malvern	General Warren Inne, Old Lancaster Hwy, 19355 610-296-3637
Malvern	Great Valley House, Box 110, RD 3, 19355
Manheim	Herr Farmhouse Inn, 2256 Huber Dr, 17545 717-653-9852
Manheim	The Inn at Mt. Hope, 2232 E Mt. Hope Rd, 17545 717-664-4708
Manheim	The Loft Inn, 1263 S Colebrook Rd., 17545 717-898-8955
Mansfield	Crossroads B&B, 131 S Main St, 16933 717-662-2565
Marienville	Pioneer Lodge, PO Box 447, 16239
Marietta	Morning Meadows Farm, 103 Fuhrman Rd, 17547 717-426-1425
Marietta	The Noble House, 113 West Market St, 17547 717-426-4389
Marietta	The River Inn, 258 West Front St, 17547 717-426-2290
Marietta	Vogt Farm, 1225 Colebrook Rd, 17547 717-653-4810
McClure	Mountain Dale Farm, RR 02, Box 985, 17841
McDonald	Nita's on Ninth St., 311 Fort Cherry Rd, 15057
McKnightstown	Mulberry Farm B&B, PO Box 22, 17343 717-334-5827
Meadville	Fountainside B&B, 628 Highland Ave., 16335 814-337-7447
Mechanicsburg	Ashcombe Mansion B&B, 1100 Grantam Rd, 17055 717-766-6820
Mechanicsburg	Moores Mountain Inn, 450 Moores Mountain Rd, 17055 717-766-3412
Mendenhall	Fairville Inn, PO Box 219, 19357 215-388-5900
Mercer	Fitzgerald House, 1267 Mercer/Grove City, 16137 724-748-5665
Mercer	Mehard Manor B&B, 146 N Pitt St., 16137 724-662-2489
Mercer	The Stranahan House B&B, 117 E. Market St, 16137 724-662-4516
Mercersburg	Fox Run Inn, 14873 Bain Rd., 17236 717-328-3570
Mercersburg	Maplebrow, 11771 Mercersburg Rd, 17236 717-328-3172
Mercersburg	The Mercersburg Inn, 405 S. Main St, 17236 717-328-5231
Mercersburg	The Steiger House, 33 North Main St, 17236 717-328-5757
Mifflinville	Ye Olde Hotel, 124 W. Third St, 18631
Milford	Graerock B&B, 205 Cummins Hill Rd., 18337 570-296-7273
Milford	Harford Inn, 201 East Harford St, 18337 570-296-7757
Milford	Pine Hill B&B, PO Box 1001, 18337 570-296-7395
Milford	Tom Quick Inn, 411 Broad St, 18337
Mill Rift	Bonny Bank B&B, PO Box 481, 18340
Millersburg	Victorian Manor Inn, 312 Market St, 17061 717-692-3511
Millersville	Rock-A-Bye B&B, 138 W Frederick St, 17551 717-872-5990
Millersville	Walnut Hill B&B, 113 Walnut Hill Rd, 17551 717-872-2283
Milton	Pau-lyn's Country B&B, RR 3, Box 676, 17847 717-742-4110
Milton	Teneriff Farm B&B, RD 1, Box 314, 17847 717-742-9061
Milton	Tomlinson Manor B&B, 250 Broadway, 17847 717-742-3657
Mohnton	Sanada's Retreat, Spack Rd, RD 4 Box 4542, 19540 610-856-1585
Montoursville	Carriage House @ Stonegate, RR 1, Box 11A, 17754 717-433-4536
Montrose	Ridge House, 6 Ridge St, 18801
Montrose	The Montrose House, 26 S. Main St, 18801 717-278-1124
Mount Gretna	Mount Gretna Inn, 16 Kauffman Ave, 17064 717-964-3234
Mount Joy	Green Acres Farm, 1382 Pinkerton Rd, 17552
Muncy	The Bodine House, 307 S. Main St, 17756 717-546-8949
Nazareth	Inn At Heyers' Mill, 568 Heyer Mill Rd, 18064
Needmore	Lodge on Tonoloway Bluffs, 100 Tonoloway Ridge Rd, 17238 410-636-2366
New Bloomfield	The Tressler House B&B, PO Box 38, 17068 717-582-2914
New Castle	Jacqueline House, RD 5 Box 463, 16105
New Holland	Smucker Farm Guest House, 502 Peters Rd, 17557 717-354-4374
New Hope	Inn at Phillips Mill, North River Rd, 18938 215-862-9919
New Hope	Logan Inn, 10 W. Ferry St, 18938 215-862-2300
New Hope	Mansion Inn, 9 S Main St, 18938 215-862-1231
New Hope	Porches, 20 Fisher's Alley, 18938 215-862-3277
New Hope	The Fox & Hound B&B, 246 W Bridge St, 18938 215-862-5082
New Hope	Umpleby House B&B, 111 W Bridge St, 18938 215-862-2570
New Milford	Oneida Camp & Lodge, E Lake Rd., St Rt 1012, 18834 717-465-7011
New Oxford	Adam's Apple, 3 Lincoln Way W, 17350 717-624-3488

Shippensburg	Mclean House, 80 W King St, 17257 717-530-1390
Shippensburg	Thornbury Farm B&B, 550 Springfield Rd., 17257 717-776-5617
Shrewsbury	Christof Kolter House B&B, 403 N Main St, 17327 717-235-5528
Slippery Rock	Applebutter Inn, 666 Centreville Pike, 16057 412-794-1844
Smethport	Blackberry Inn, 820 W Main St., 16749 814-887-7777
Smoketown	Smoketown Village, 2495 Old Phila. Pike, 17576 717-393-5975
Solebury	Hollyhedge English Estate, Box 213, 18963 215-862-3136
Somerset	H.B.'s Cottage, 231 W. Church St, 15501 814-443-1204
Somerset	Highland Farm Guest House, R.D. #2, Box 94A, 15501 814-445-4015
Somerset	The Inn at Georgian Place, 800 Georgian Place Dr, 15501 814-443-1043
South Sterling	The French Manor, Box 39, 18460 717-676-3244
South Sterling	The Sterling Inn, Rt 191, 18460 717-676-3311
Spartansburg	The Red Setter B&B, 251 Main St, 16434
Spring Creek	Spring Valley B&B, RD 1, Box 117, Rt 6, 16436 814-489-5415
Spring Mills	Cooke Tavern B&B, RD 2 Box 218A, 16875 814-422-8787
Spring Mills	The Lead Horse, RR 1 Box 216, 16875 814-422-8783
Springdale	Maggie West B&B, 605 Pittsburgh St, 15144
Spruce Creek	Dell's B&B at Cedar Hill, HC-01 Box 26, Rt 45, 16683 814-632-8319
St. Marys	Old Charm B&B, 444 Brussells St., 15857 814-834-9429
St. Marys	Towne House Inn, 138 Center St, 15801 814-781-1556
Starrucca	The Nethercott Inn B&B, PO Box 26, 18462 717-727-2211
State College	Accommodations, 200 Houserville Rd., 16801 814-238-5195
State College	Brewmeister B&B, 2070 Cato Ave, 16801
State College	Ginther's B&B, 104 Farmstead Lane, 16803 814-234-0772
State College	Vincent Douglas House B&B, 490 Meakley Dr, 16801
State College	Windswept Farm, 1000 Fillmore Rd, 16803 814-355-1233
Strasburg	Strasburg Village Inn, One W. Main St, 17579 717-687-0900
Strasburg	The Decoy B&B, 958 Eisenberger Rd, 17579 717-687-8585
Stroudsburg	Stroudsmoor Country Inn, PO Box 153, 18360
Susquehanna	April Valley B&B, RR 1, Box 141, 18847 717-756-2688
Tannersville	The Inn at Meadowbrook, Cherry Lane Rd, 18301 717-629-0296
Thompson	Farm House B&B, Campsite Rd, 18465
Thornton	Pace One Rest./Country Inn, PO Box 108, 19373 610-459-3702
Three Springs	Aughwick House B&B, Box 977, RD 1, 17264 814-447-3027
Tionesta	Kellygreen B&B, 131 Elm St, 16353 814-755-8808
Titusville	Knapp Farm B&B, 43778 Thompson Run Rd, 16354 814-827-1092
Troy	Golden Oak Inn B&B, 196 Canton St Rt 14 S, 16947 717-297-4315
Troy	Holcombe House, 150 W Main St, 16947 717-297-2460
Tunkhannock	Sharpe's House B&B, PO Box L, 18657 717-836-4900
Tunkhannock	The Weeping Willow Inn, RR 7 Box 254, 18657
Tyrone	Riley's B&B, 863 Washington Ave, 16686
Ulysses	Susque Hannock Lodge, RR 1 Box 120 Rt 6, 16948 814-435-2163
Union Deposit	Union Canal House Cntry Inn, 107 S Hanover St., 17033 717-566-0054
Valley Forge	Great Valley House, 110 Swedesford Rd, RD 3, 19355 610-644-6759
Valley Forge	Valley Forge Mountain B&B, Box 562, 19481
Volant	Candleford Inn B&B, PO Box 212, 16156 412-533-4497
Warfordsburg	Buck Valley Ranch, Rt 2 Box 1170, 17267 717-294-3759
Washington	Long Stretch Harbour B&B, RD 8 Rt 40 Natl Pk B277, 15301
Waynesboro	The Shepherd & Ewe B&B, 11205 Country Club Rd, 17268 717-762-8525
Wellsboro	Four Winds B&B, 58 West Ave, 16901 717-724-6141
Wellsboro	Waln Street B&B, 54 Waln St, 16901
West Chester	1810 House B&B, 1280 W Strasburg Rd, 19382 610-430-6013
West Chester	Broadlawns B&B, 629 N Church St, 19380 610-692-5477
West Chester	Faunbrook B&B, 699 W. Rosedale Ave, 19382 215-436-5788
West Chester	Lenape Springs Farm, 580 W. Creek Rd, 19382 610-793-2266
West Chester	Sadonjaree Farm, 505 Broad Run Rd., 19382 610-793-1838
West Chester	White Cloud Inn, 1125 S New St, 19382 717-676-3162
White Horse	Fassitt Mansion B&B, 6051 Philadelphia Pike, 17527 717-442-3139
Williamsport	The Reighard House, 1323 E 3rd St, 17701 717-326-3593
Willow Street	Cook's Guest House, 22 West Penn Grant Rd, 17584 717-464-3273
Witmer	Folk Craft Center B&B, 441 Mt. Sidney Rd, 17585 717-397-3609
Woodbury	Waterside Inn B&B, RD #1, Box 52, 16695 814-766-3776
Woodward	Woodward Inn, PO Box 177, 16882 814-349-8118
Wycombe	Wycombe Inn, PO Box 204, 18980 215-598-7000
York	Briarwold B&B, 5400 Lincoln Hwy, 17406 717-252-4619
York	Friendship House B&B, 728 E Philadelphia St, 17403
Zelienople	Historic Benvenue Manor, Box 21 RD 3, 16063
Zelienople	The Inn on Grandview, 310 E Grandview Ave, 16063 412-452-0469

Rhode Island

Block Island	Barrington Inn, PO Box 397, 02807 401-466-5510
Block Island	Bellevue House, PO Box 1198, 02807 401-466-2912
Block Island	Block Island Resorts, Spring St, Box 1, 02807 401-466-2421
Block Island	Captain Willis House, Corn Neck Rd, 02807 401-466-5113
Block Island	Gothic Inn, PO Box 1197, 02807 401-466-2918
Block Island	Islander, 371 High St., 02807 401-466-2897
Block Island	New Shoreham House Inn, PO Box 160, 02807 401-466-2651

Block Island	Perry Cottage, PO Box A-2, 02807 401-466-2342
Block Island	Samuel Peckham Inn, New Harbor, 02807 401-466-2439
Block Island	The Atlantic Inn, PO Box 1788, 02807 401-466-5883
Block Island	The Blue Dory Inn, Box 488, 02807 401-466-5891
Block Island	The Rose Farm Inn, Roslyn Rd, 02807 401-466-2034
Block Island	The Sheffield House, PO Box C-2, 02807 401-466-2494
Block Island	The Spring House Hotel, PO Box 902, 02807 401-466-5844
Block Island	The White House, Spring St, 02807 401-466-2653
Block Island	Willow Grove, PO Box 156, 02807 401-466-2896
Bristol	Bradford-Dimond-Norris Hou, 474 Hope St., 02809 401-253-6338
Bristol	Joseph Reynolds House, 956 Hope St, 02809 401-254-0230
Bristol	Reynolds House Inn (1698), PO Box 5, 02809 401-254-0230
Carolina	Country Acres B&B, Box 551, 02812 401-364-9134
Charlestown	Harte's-On the Pond, 65 Quail Ln, 02813 401-364-3148
Charlestown	Hathaways, Box 731, 02813 401-364-6665
Charlestown	Inn the Meadow, 1045 Shannock Rd, 02813 401-789-1473
Charlestown	One Willow by the Sea, 1 Willow Rd, 02813 401-364-4162
Charlestown	Ye Ole General Stanton Inn, PO Box 222, 02813 401-364-0100
Lincoln	Whipple-Cullen Farmstead, 99 Old River Rd., 02865 401-333-1899
Little Compton	Ballyvoreen, 561 W Main Rd, 02837 401-635-4396
Little Compton	Roost at Sakonnet Vineyard, 170 W Main Rd., 02837 401-635-8486
Middletown	Bartram's B&B, 94 Kane Ave., 02842 401-846-2259
Middletown	Flag Quarters, 11 Sherri Lane, 02842 401-849-4543
Middletown	North Fenner Lodge, 209 N Fenner Ave, 02842 401-841-0484
Middletown	Rhea's B&B, 120 W Main Rd., 02842 401-841-5560
Middletown	Sea Breeze, 36 Kane Ave., 02842 401-247-5626
Middletown	The Briar Patch, 42 Briarwood Ave, 02842 401-841-5824
Narragansett	Chestnut House, 11 Chestnut St, 02882 401-789-5335
Narragansett	Four Gables, 12 S Pier Rd., 02882 401-789-6948
Narragansett	Murphy's B&B, 43 South Pier Rd, 02882 401-789-1824
Narragansett	Ocean Road, 195 Ocean Rd, 02882 401-783-4299
Narragansett	Pleasant Cottage, 104 Robinson St, 02882
Narragansett	Regina Cottage, 125 Kingstown Rd., 02882 401-783-1875
Narragansett	Seafield Cottage, 110 Boon St., 02882 401-783-2432
Narragansett	The Canterbury, 4 Sumac Trail, 02882 401-783-0046
Narragansett	The Old Clerk House B&B, 49 Narragansett Ave., 02882 401-783-8008
Narragansett	White Rose B&B, 22 Cedar St, 02882 401-789-0181
Narragansett	Windermere B&B, 116 Central St, 02882 401-783-0187
Newport	1812 House B&B, 98 Mill St, 02840 401-847-1188
Newport	Admiral Farragut Inn, 8 Fair St, 02840 401-848-8000
Newport	Cleveland House Inn, 27 Clarke St., 02840 401-849-7397
Newport	Cliff Walk Manor, 117 Memorial Blvd, 02840 401-847-1300
Newport	Covell Guest House, 43 Farewell St, 02840 401-847-8872
Newport	Culpepper House, 7 Division St, 02840
Newport	Flower Garden Guests, 1 Kyle Terrace, 02840 401-846-3119
Newport	George Champlin Mason Hse, 31 Old Beach Rd, 02840 401-847-7081
Newport	Halidon Hill Guest House, Halidon Ave., 02840 401-847-8318
Newport	Hammett House Inn, 505 Thames St, 02840 800-548-9417
Newport	Harborside Inn, Christie's Landing, 02840 401-846-6600
Newport	Inn at Newport Beach, Memorial Blvd., 02840 401-846-0310
Newport	Inn at Washington Square, 39 Touro St, 02840 401-VIP-7319
Newport	Ivy Lodge, 12 Clay St, 02840 401-849-6865
Newport	James B. Finch House B&B, 102 Touro St., 02840 401-849-9700
Newport	Melville House, 39 Clarke St, 02840 401-847-0640
Newport	Mill Street Inn, 75 Mill St, 02840 401-849-9500
Newport	Polly's Place, 349 Valley Rd, 02842 401-847-2160
Newport	The Clarkeston, 28 Clarke St, 02840 401-524-1386
Newport	The Francis Malbone House, 392 Thames St, 02840 401-846-0392
Newport	Viewpoint, 231 Coggeshall Ave, 02840
Newport	Wander Inn, 15 Greenough Place, 02840 401-849-5208
Newport	Yankee Peddler Inn, 113 Touro St, 02840 401-846-1323
North Kingstown	Country House B&B, 10 Kent St., 02852 401-294-4688
North Kingstown	Fifty Seven B&B, 57 Thomas Street, 02852 401-294-7201
North Kingstown	Mount Maple of Wickford, 730 Annaquatucket Rd, 02852 401-295-4373
Portsmouth	Founder's Brook, 314 Boyd Lane, 02871 401-683-1244
Providence	Charles Hodges House, 19 Pratt St., 02906 401-861-7244
Prudence Island	Lighthouse B&B, 048 John Oldham Rd., 02872 401-683-4642
South Kingstown	Green Hill B&B, 803 Green Hill Beach Rd, 02840
Wakefield	Almost Heaven B&B, 49 West St, 02879 401-783-9272
Warwick	Fair Street B&B, 525 Fair Street, 02888 401-781-5158
Warwick	Pawtuxet B&B, 76 Bayside Ave, 02840
Warwick	The Enchanted Cottage, 16 Beach Ave., 02889 401-732-0439
Watch Hill	Watch Hill Inn, 38 Bay St, 02891 401-348-8912
West Kingston	The Stone Cottage B&B, 61 Old Usquepaugh Rd., 02892 401-789-0039
Westerly	Sand Dollar Inn, 171 Post Road, 02891 401-322-2000
Wickford	The Haddi Pierce House, 146 Boston Neck Rd., 02852 401-294-7674
Wickford	The Moran's B&B, 130 W. Main St, 02852 401-294-3497
Wyoming	Cookie Jar B&B, 64 Kingstown Rd, 02898 401-539-2680

South Carolina

Abbeville	Abbewood B&B, 605 N. Main St, 29620 803-459-5822
Abbeville	Belmont Inn, 104 E. Pickens St, 29620 803-459-9625
Abbeville	The Vintage Inn, 1205 N Main St, 29620 803-459-4784
Aiken	Chancellor Carroll House, 112 Gregg Ave, 29801 803-649-5396
Aiken	Pine Knoll Inn, 305 Lancaster St SW, 29801 803-649-5939
Aiken	The Briar Patch, 544 Magnolia Ln, 29801 803-649-2010
Aiken	The Brodie Residence, 422 York St, 29801 803-648-1445
Aiken	The Willcox Inn, 100 Colleton Ave, 29801 803-649-1377
Aiken	Town & Country Inn B&B, 2340 Sizemore Circle, 29803 803-642-0270
Aiken	White House Inn B&B, 240 New Berry St SW, 29801 803-649-2935
Anderson	1109 Inn, 1109 S Main St, 29624 864-225-1109
Anderson	Anderson's River Inn, 612 East River St, 29624 846-231-9847
Anderson	Centennial Plantation, 1308 Old Williamston Rd, 29621 864-225-4448
Anderson	River Inn, 612 E. River St, 29624 803-226-1431
Anderson	The Jefferson House, 2835 Old Willianston Rd, 29621 864-224-0678
Beaufort	Craven Street Inn, 1103 Craven St., 29902 843-522-1668
Beaufort	Dolly's B&B, 1103 Craven St, 29902 843-522-1668
Beaufort	The Beaufort Inn, 809 Port Republic St, 29902 843-521-9000
Beaufort	The Rhett House Inn, 1009 Craven St, 29902 843-524-9030
Beaufort	The Scheper House, 915 Port Republic St., 29902 843-770-0600
Belton	Belton Inn, 324 S. Main St, 29627 803-338-6020
Bennettsville	Breeden Inn-Carriage House, 404 East Main St, 29512 803-479-3665
Bishopville	The Foxfire B&B, 416 N. Main St, 29010 803-484-5643
Blackville	Floyd Hall Inn B&B, PO Box 486, 29817 803-284-3736
Branchville	Branchville Country Inn, 207 Dorange Rd, 29432 803-274-8894
Camden	Carolina Oaks, 127 Union St, 29020
Camden	Coach House Inn, 2012 Broad St., 29020 803-432-0986
Camden	Greenleaf Inn, 1308/10 Broad St, 29020 803-425-1806
Camden	The Carriage House, 1413 Lyttleton St, 29020 803-432-2430
Charleston	1837 B&B/Tearoom, 126 Wentworth St, 29401 843-723-7166
Charleston	Ansonborough Inn, 21 Hasell St, 29401 843-723-1655
Charleston	Beaufain Street B&B, 106 Beaufain St., 29401 843-722-7952
Charleston	Bed, No Breakfast, 16 Halsey St, 29401 843-723-4450
Charleston	Brasington House B&B, 328 E Bay St, 29401 843-722-1274
Charleston	Carriage House, 4 Greenhill St, 29401 843-577-0392
Charleston	Church St. Inn, 177 Church St, 29401 843-722-3420
Charleston	East Bay B&B, 301 E Bay St, 29401 843-722-4186
Charleston	Elliott House Inn, 78 Queen St, 29401 843-723-1855
Charleston	Hasell Street B&B, 52 Hasell St, 29401 843-722-0860
Charleston	Historic Charleston B&B, 57 Broad St, 29401 843-722-6606
Charleston	Indigo Inn, One Maiden Ln, 29401 843-577-5900
Charleston	Jasmine House, 8 Cumberland, 29401 843-577-5900
Charleston	Johnson's Six Orange St BB, 6 Orange St, 29401 843-722-6122
Charleston	King Street B&B, 19 King St, 29401 843-723-3212
Charleston	Kitchen House (c.1732), 126 Tradd St, 29401 843-577-6362
Charleston	Lodge Alley Inn, 195 E. Bay St, 29401 800-722-1611
Charleston	Loundes Grove Inn, 266 St. Margaret St, 29403 843-723-3530
Charleston	Maison Du Pre, 317 E. Bay St, 29401 843-723-8691
Charleston	Middleton Inn @ Middleton, Ashley River Rd, 29414 843-556-0500
Charleston	Rutledge Victorian Inn, 114 Rutledge Ave, 29401 843-722-7551
Charleston	The Anchorage Inn, 26 Vendue Range, 29401 843-723-8300
Charleston	The Hayne House, 30 King St., 29401 843-577-2633
Charleston	Thirty Six Meeting St. B&B, 36 Meeting St, 29401 843-722-1034
Charleston	Timothy Ford's Kitchen, 54 Meeting St, 29401 843-577-4432
Charleston	Two Meeting Street Inn, 2 Meeting St, 29407 843-723-7322
Charleston	Vendue Inn, 19 Vendue Range, 29401 843-577-7970
Charleston	Wortham House, 54 Montagu St, 29401 843-723-4668
Charleston	Zero Water Street, 31 East Battery, 29401 843-723-2841
Cheraw	314 Market Street B&B, 314 Market St., 29520 803-537-5797
Cheraw	501 Kershaw, 501 Kershaw St, 29520 803-537-7733
Cheraw	505 Market St., 505 Market St, 29520 803-537-9649
Chester	The Pinckney Inn, 110 Pinckney St, 29706 803-377-7466
Clemson	Nord-Lac, PO Box 1111, 29633 803-639-2939
Clio	Henry Bennett House B&B, 301 Red Bluff St, 29525 803-586-2701
Columbia	Chesnut Cottage B&B, 1718 Hampton St, 29201 803-256-1718
Columbia	Clarkes Place In Country, 83 Windward Way, 29212
Columbia	Claussen's Inn, 2003 Greene St, 29401 803-765-0440
Columbia	Richland Street B&B, 1425 Richland St, 29201 803-779-7001
Columbia	Rose Hall B&B, 1006 Barnwell St, 29201 803-771-2288
Conway	The Cypress Inn, PO Box 495, 29528 843-248-8199
Dale	Coosaw Plantation, PO Box 160, 29914 803-723-6516
Darlington	Croft Magnolia Inn, 306 Cashua St, 29532 803-393-1908
Dillon	Magnolia Inn, 601 E Main St, 29536 843-774-0679
Edgefield	Carnoosie Inn, 407 Columbia Rd, 29824 800-622-7124
Edgefield	Cedar Grove Plantation, Rt 1 Box 1806, 29824 803-637-3056
Edgefield	Pleasant Lane Acres, Rt 2 Box 221, 29824

Edgefield	The Plantation House, Ct. House Square, 29824 803-637-3789
Edgemoor	Country House @ Rose Haven, 1778 Curry Rd, 29712
Edisto Island	Cassina Point Plantation, PO Box 535, 29438 843-869-2535
Edisto Island	Seaside Plantation B&B, PO Box 359, 29438 843-869-0971
Ehrhardt	Broxton Bridge Plantation, Box 97, 29081 803-267-3882
Ehrhardt	Ehrhardt Hall, 400 South Broadway, 29081 803-267-2020
Fort Mill	Pleasant Valley, PO Box 446, 29715 803-547-7551
Gaffney	Jolly Place B&B Inn, 405 College Dr, 29340 864-489-4638
Georgetown	Alexandra's Inn B&B, 620 Prince St., 29440 843-527-0233
Georgetown	Ashfield Manor, 3030 S. Island Rd, 29440 843-546-5111
Georgetown	Dozier Guest Houses, 220 Queen St, 29440 843-527-1350
Georgetown	Winyah Bay B&B, 403 Hellena St, 29440 843-546-9051
Greenville	Blu Veranda B&B, 409 Wilton St, 29609 864-271-5047
Greenville	Creekside Plantation B&B, 3118 S Hwy 14, 29615 864-297-3293
Greenville	Pettigru Place B&B, 302 Pettigru St, 29601 864-242-4529
Greenwood	Grace Place B&B, 115 Grace St, 29646 803-229-0053
Greenwood	Inn on the Square, 104 Court St, 29646 803-223-4488
Greer	Arlington House, 104 W Arlington Ave, 29653 864-877-3201
Hartsville	Missouri Inn B&B, 314 E. Home Ave, 29550 803-383-9553
Hilton Head Island	Fripp House Inn, 275 Moss Creek Rd, 29926 843-757-2139
Honea Path	Sugerfoot Castle, 211 S. Main St, 29654 803-369-6565
Johns Island	Capers Motte House, 2586 Seabrook Island Rd, 29455
Johnston	Cox House Inn, PO Box 486, 29832 803-275-4552
McClellanville	Village B&B, 333 Mercantile Rd, 29458 843-887-3266
Moncks Corner	Rice Hope Plantation Inn, 206 Rice Hope Dr, 29461 843-761-4832
Mt. Pleasant	Guilds Inn, 101 Pitt St, 29464 803-881-0510
Mt. Pleasant	Sunny Meadows, 1459 Venning Rd, 29464 803-884-7062
Myrtle Beach	Cain House B&B, 206 29th Ave S, 29577 843-448-3063
Myrtle Beach	Serendipity Inn, 407 N 71st Ave, 29572 843-449-5268
Newberry	Barklin House, 1710 College St., 29108 803-321-9155
Newberry	College St. Tourist B&B, 1710 College St, 29108 803-321-9155
North Augusta	Bloom Hill, 772 Pine Log Rd, 29841 803-593-2573
North Augusta	Rosemary Hall, 804 Carolina Ave, 29841 803-278-6222
Pawleys Island	Sea View Inn, PO Box 210, 29858 843-237-4253
Pawleys Island	The Magnolia House B&B, 984 Hawthorn, 29585
Pendleton	195 E. Main, 195 E Main, 29670
Pendleton	235 East Queen, A B&B, 235 E. Queen St., 29670 864-646-8259
Pendleton	Liberty Hall Inn, 621 S. Mechanic St, 29670 803-646-7500
Pickens	The Schell Haus, 117 Hiawatha Trail, 29671 803-878-0078
Ridge Spring	Southwood Manor, PO Box 434, 29129 803-685-5100
Rock Hill	East Main Guest House, 600 E. Main St, 29730 803-366-1161
Rock Hill	Park Avenue Inn, 347 Park Ave, 29730 803-325-1764
Rock Hill	The Book & The Spindle, 626 Oakland Ave, 29730 803-328-1913
Salem	Sunrise Farm B&B Inn, 325 Sunrise Dr, 29676 864-944-0121
Simpsonville	Hunter House B&B, 201 E. College St, 29681 803-967-2827
Spartanburg	St. Francis Inn, 355 Cedar Springs Rd., 29302 904-824-6068
Starr	The Gray House, 111 Stones Throw Ave, 29684 803-352-6778
Sullivan's Island	Palmettos, PO Box 706, 29482 803-883-3389
Summerville	B&B Of Summerville, 304 S. Hampton St, 29483 803-871-5275
Summerville	Camellia Walk, 116 South Oak St, 29483 803-871-3553
Summerville	Flowertown B&B, 710 S Main St, 29483 843-851-1058
Summerville	Linwood, 200 S Palmetto, 29483 803-871-2620
Summerville	Simply Carolina B&B, 114 Ridge Rd, 29485 803-875-1222
Summerville	The Magnolia Inn, 103 S Magnolia St, 29483 803-873-8134
Sumter	Calhoun Street B&B, 302 West Calhoun St, 29150 803-775-7035
Sumter	The B&B of Sumter, 6 Park Ave, 29150 803-773-2903
Sunset	Laurel Springs Country Inn, 1137 Moorefield Hwy, 29685 803-878-2252
Union	Juxa Plantation, 117 Wilson Rd, 29379 864-427-8688
Union	The Inn of Fairforest, 2403 Cross Keys Hwy, 29379 864-429-3950
Walhalla	Liberty Lodge B&B, 105 Liberty Ln., 29691 864-638-0940
Walhalla	Walhalla Liberty Lodge B&B, 105 Liberty Lane, 29691 8646380940
Walterboro	Bonnie Doone Plantation, 5878 Bonnie Doone Rd, 29488 843-893-3396
Walterboro	Old Academy B&B, 904 Hampton St., 29488 803-549-3232
Winnsboro	Brakefield B&B, 214 High St, 29180 803-635-4242
Winnsboro	Songbird Manor, 116 N Zion St, 29180 803-635-6963

South Dakota

Arlington	Lakeside Country Manor, RR 3, Box 87, 57212 605-983-5073
Batesland	Wakpanni B&B, HC 64 Box 43, 57716 605-288-1800
Belle Fourche	Candlelight, 819-5th Ave, 57717 605-892-4568
Belle Fourche	Patti's B&B, 920 Sixth Ave., 57717 605-892-4228
Belvidere	Fortune Ranch Adventures, HC 76 Box 24, 57521 605-344-2200
Britton	Hartman's B&B, 908 8th St., 57430 605-448-2103
Brookings	Cottonwood House, PO Box 227, 57006 605-693-4361
Buffalo	Real Ranch, HC 66, Box 112, 57720
Canistota	Gossel Rooms & Cottage, PO Box 235, 57012 605-296-3420
Canistota	West Side Cabins, 610 W Pine St, 57012 605-296-3589

Chamberlain	Riverview Ridge B&B, HC 69, Box 82A, 57325 605-734-6084
Crooks	Janet's Country Homestead, RR 11, Box 339, 57020 605-543-5232
Custer	Black Hills Balloons B&B, PO Box 210, 57730 605-673-2520
Custer	French Creek Guest Ranch, PO Box 588, 57730 605-673-4790
Custer	Hartman Haven B&B, RR 1, Box 108A, 57730 605-673-2714
Custer	Raspberry and Lace B&B, 12175 White Horse Rd., 57730 605-574-4920
Custer	The Cabin B&B, PO Box 210, 57730 605-673-2520
Custer	The Rose Garden, Hwy 385, 57730 605-673-2714
Custer	West View Estates, HCR 83, 57730 605-673-3637
Dallas	Bolton Guest Ranch, RR2 Box 80, 57529 605-835-8960
De Smet	The Prairie House Manor, RR2 Box 61A, 57231 605-854-9131
Deadwood	Adam's House, 22 Van Buren, 57732 605-578-3877
Deadwood	Phatty Thompson's B&B, 15 Washington, 57732 605-578-3257
Deadwood	Strawberry, HCR 73 Box 264, 57732 605-578-2149
Deadwood	Vicky's B&B, 786 Main St., 57732 605-578-2278
Doland	Hofer's B&B, HC 68, Box 2, 57436 605-635-6176
Freeman	Farmers Inn, 28193 US Hwy 81, 57029 605-925-7580
Freeman	Golden Robin Nest, 1210 E 4th St., 57029 605-925-4410
Gary	Pleasant Valley Lodge, RR 1 Box 256, 57237
Geddes	The Barn, RR1 Box 111, 57342 605-337-2483
Gettysburg	Harer Lodge & B&B, Route 1, Box 87A, 57442 605-765-2167
Gregory	Gray House Inn, RR 2, Box 29E, Hwy 18, 57533 605-835-8479
Hermosa	Behrens' Ranch B&B, 15070 Spring Creek Rd, 57744 605-342-1441
Hermosa	Bunkhouse B&B, 14630 Lower Spr Crk Rd, 57744 605-342-5462
Hermosa	Rosemary for Remembrance, PO Box 291, 57744 605-394-5431
Hermosa	Spring Creek B&B, HC 89, Box 250, 57744 605-342-1441
Hill City	Alpine Inn, PO Box 211, 57745 605-574-2749
Hill City	Black Hills Llarna Lodge, PO Box 109, 57745 605-574-2455
Hill City	Cornelison Country, PO Box 408, 57745 605-574-2602
Hill City	Country Manor, PO Box 410, 57745 605-574-2196
Hill City	Creekside Cottage, HC 87 Box 52-A, 57745 605-574-4609
Hill City	Emerald Pines Refuge B&B, 23836 Emerald Pines Dr, 57745 605-574-4462
Hill City	High Country Ranch B&B, 12172 Deerfield Rd, 57745 605-574-9003
Hot Springs	Cascade Ranch B&B, PO Box 461, 57747 605-745-3397
Hot Springs	Rocking G, RR1, Box 101 D, 57747 605-745-3698
Hot Springs	Villa Theresa Guest House, PO Box 790, 57747 605-745-4633
Huron	Marie's, 870 Dakota S, 57350 605-352-2934
Interior	Badlands Ranch Resort, HCR 53 Box 3, 57750 605-433-5599
Interior	Grandma's Bunkhouse, PO Box 125, 57750 605-433-5486
Interior	Prairie's Edge B&B, PO Box 11, 57750 605-433-5441
Keystone	Anchorage B&B, 24110 Leaky Valley Rd, 57751 605-574-4740
Keystone	Bed & Breakfast Inn, PO Box 662, 57751 605-666-4490
Keystone	Mountain Suites, PO Box 648, 57751 605-666-4686
Kimball	Red Barn Inn, RR 2 Box 102, 57355 605-778-6332
Lead	Cheyenne Crossing B&B, Box 1220, HC-37, 57754 605-584-3510
Lead	Collins House, 515 Fox Street, 57754 605-584-1736
Lead	The Mars Inn, HC 37 Box 900, 57754 605-584-3074
Lemmon	The 49'er, HCHR 63, Box 305, 57638 701-376-3280
Lennox	Steever House B&B, 46850 276th St, 57039 605-647-5055
Madison	Katharine's Mysterious Hse, 518 N Egan Ave, 57042 605-256-4118
Madison	Lakeside B&B, RR 3 Box 109, 57042 605-256-3676
Madison	The Cline House, 615 N Egan, 57042 605-256-2190
Madison	The Farm House, RR 1 Box 91, 57042
Miller	Guest House B&B, 215 W. 2nd Ave, 57362 605-853-2863
Mitchell	The 3 B's, Bliss B&B, 516 E 4th Ave, 57301 605-996-4234
Mound City	Calico's B&B, PO Box 85, 57646 605-955-3535
Nemo	Nemo Guest Ranch, PO Box 77, 57759 605-578-2708
Newell	Castle Rock, HC 66 Box 60, 57760 605-866-4604
Newell	Moore's Rooms, 113 3rd St., 57760 605-456-2211
Oelrichs	Dakota Prairie Ranch, PO Box 123, 57763 605-535-2001
Okaton	Roghair Herefords B&B, HCR 74 Box 16, 57562 605-669-2529
Owanka	Reeves B&B Prairie Inn, 57767 605-798-5405
Philip	Thorson's Homestead, HCR 2 Box 100, 57567 605-859-2120
Philip	Triangle Ranch, HCR 1 Box 62, 57567 605-859-2122
Piedmont	Valley View, HC 80, Box 613, 57769 605-787-4425
Pierre	River Place Inn, 109 River Pl, 57501 605-224-8589
Plankinton	The Nobleman, PO Box 402, 57368 605-942-7587
Platte	Grandma's House B&B, RR 1 Box 54, 57369 605-337-3589
Presho	Sweeney's B&B, 132 Main Ave, 57568 605-895-2586
Rapid City	Abibail's Garden, 13137 Thunderhead Falls, 57702 605-343-6530
Rapid City	Anemarie's Country B&B, 10430 Big Piney Rd, 57702 605-343-9234
Rapid City	Annie Lee's, 820 South St., 57701 605-399-0926
Rapid City	Apple Annie's Guest House, 13131 Thunderhead Falls, 57702 605-343-6035
Rapid City	Black Forest Inn, 23191 Hwy. 385, 57702 605-574-2000
Rapid City	Canyon Lake B&B, 2928 Palls Dr., 57702 605-348-9702
Rapid City	Cliff Creek B&B, 4510 Buckhorn Dr, 57702 605-399-9970
Rapid City	First Thunder Ranch, PO Box 9008, 57709 605-341-7080
Rapid City	H-Bar-D Lodge, 23101 Triangle Trail-Hi, 57702

Rapid City	Hayloft B&B, 9356 Neck Yoke Rd, 57701 605-343-5351
Rapid City	J-D Guest Ranch, 4256 Penrose Pl, 57702 605-255-4700
Rapid City	Madison Ranch B&B, Rt. 1, Box 1490, 57702 605-342-6997
Rapid City	Pine Bloom Suites, PO Box 9283, 57709 605-787-6303
Rapid City	The Gingerbread House, 1602 Mt. Rushmore Rd., 57701 605-348-6299
Rapid City	The Rimrock, 13145 Big Bend Rd, 57702
Rochford	Pinetop B&B, PO Box 14, 57778 605-584-3021
Rochford	Silver Creek B&B, 22425 Silver Creek Rd, 57778 605-584-1596
Salem	Jacobson Farm, RR 2, Box 428, 57058 605-247-3247
Scenic	Jobgen Ranch Homestead B&B, 24800 Sage Creek Rd, 57780 605-993-6201
Seneca	Rainbow Lodge, 16388 337th Ave., 57473 605-436-6795
Sioux Falls	The Emery House, 305 E 26th St, 57105
Sisseton	Sisseton B&B, 716 W Pine, 57262 605-698-7224
Spearfish	Christensen's Country Home, 432 Hillsview, 57783 605-642-2859
Spearfish	Hitson Post, 345 Main, 57783 605-642-2853
St. Charles	Dakota Hunting & Guest Rch, RR 2 Box 58, 57571 605-654-2260
Sturgis	Bear Butte, Box 366, 57785 605-347-2137
Sturgis	Old Stone House, 1513 Jackson St, 57785 605-347-3007
Sturgis	Poker Alice House, 1802 S. Junction, 57785 605-347-5675
Vale	Dakota Shepherd, RR3, Box 25C, 57788 605-456-2836
Vermillion	Goebel House, 102 Franklin St, 57069
Vermillion	Talk of the Town B&B, 855 Eastgate Dr, 57069 605-997-5170
Vivian	Rafter L Ranch B&B, PO Box 67, 57576 605-895-2202
Wall	Western Dakota Ranch, 19102 Creighton, 57790 605-279-2198
Waubay	M's, RR 1 Enemy Swim Lake, 57273 605-947-4955
Wessington Sp.	Winegar Farms, 37292 231st St, 57382 605-539-1594
White	Sunny Crest Quarter Horse, RR 2 Box 61, 57276 605-693-4043
Woonsocket	Sand Creek B&B, RR 1 Box 545, 57385 605-796-4036
Yankton	Gavins Point B&B, RR 1, Box 148, 57078 605-668-0691
Yankton	Mulberry Inn, 512 Mulberry St, 57078 605-665-7116

Tennessee

Allardt	School House B&B, PO Box 115, 38504 615-879-8517
Altamont	The Manor, PO Box 156, 37301 615-692-3153
Altamont	Woodlee House, PO Box 310, 37301 615-692-2368
Arrington	Xanadu Farm, 8155 Horton Hwy, 37014 615-395-4771
Athens	Forrest Ridge B&B, 207 Forrest Ave, 37303 615-744-9918
Athens	Majestic Mansion B&B, 202 E Washington Ave, 37303 423-746-9041
Athens	Woodlawn B&B, 110 Keith lane, 37303 800-745-8213
Baxter	Li'l Bit of Heaven, 289 Dunn Ridge Rd, 38544 931-858-6388
Bell Buckle	Spindle House B&B, 201 Hinkle Hill, 37020 615-389-6766
Belvidere	Falls Mill Log Cabin, Rt. 1 Box 44, 37306 615-469-7161
Blountville	Woodland Place B&B, 937 Childress Ferry Rd, 37617 615-323-2848
Brentwood	English Manor B&B, 6304 Murray Lane, 37027 615-373-4627
Buffalo Valley	Happy Hollow B&B, 5428 Medley Amonette Rd, 38548 931-858-3528
Chattanooga	Alford House, Alford Hill Dr Rt 4, 37419 423-821-7625
Chattanooga	Bluff View Inn, 412 E. Second St, 37403 615-265-5033
Chattanooga	Lookout Lake B&B, 3408 Elder Mtn. Rd, 37419 423-821-8088
Chattanooga	McElhattan's Owl Hill B&B, 617 Scenic Hwy, 37409 423-821-2040
Clarksville	Hachland Hill Inn, 1601 Madison St, 37042 615-647-4084
Clarksville	South Sycamore B&B, 2700 Seven Miles Ferry, 37040 615-645-4328
Cleveland	Chadwick House, 2766 Michigan Ave Rd NE, 37312 615-339-2407
Cleveland	Rose Hill Inn B&B, 367 Horton Rd, 37323 423-614-0700
Clinton	Brick House B&B, 200 Howard St, 37716 423-463-8254
College Grove	Peacock Hill, 6994 Giles Hill Rd, 37046 800-327-6663
Columbia	Locust Hill B&B, 1185 Mooresville Pike, 38401 615-388-8531
Columbia	Oak Springs Inn & Gallery, 1512 Williamsport Pike, 38401 615-388-7539
Conasauga	Chestnut Inn, Box 124, 37316 423-338-7873
Cordova	Bridgewater House B&B, 7015 Raleigh LaGrange, 38018 901-394-0080
Cornersville	Lairdland Farm B&B, 3174 Blackburn Hallow, 37047 615-363-9080
Covington	Havenhall Farm, 183 Houston Gordon Rd, 38019 901-476-7226
Crossville	Homestead B&B, 1165 Hwy 68, 38555 931-456-6355
Culleoka	Sweetwaer Inn, 2346 Campbells Station, 38451 615-987-3077
Dandridge	Milldale Farm, 140 Mill Dale Rd., 37725 423-397-3470
Dandridge	Mountain Harbor, 1199 Highway 139, 37725 615-397-3345
Dandridge	Sugar Fork B&B, 743 Garrett Rd, 37725 615-397-7327
Dayton	Bailey House B&B Inn, 1598 Market St, 37321 423-570-1925
Decatur	Cross Creek Farm B&B, PO Box 1235, 37322 423-334-9172
Dickson	Deerfield Country Inn, 170 Woodycrest Close, 37055 615-446-3325
Dickson	The Inn on Main Street, 112 S. Main St, 37055 615-441-6879
Ducktown	The Company House B&B Inn, PO Box 154, 37326 423-496-5634
Elizabethton	Old Main Manor, 708 N. Main St, 37643 615-543-6945
Fairview	Sweet Annie's B&B Barn, 7201 Crow Cut Rd SW, 37062 615-799-8833
Fayetteville	Bagley House B&B, 1801 Winchester Hwy, 37334 931-433-3799
Flat Creek	Bottle Hollow Lodge, PO Box 92, 37160 615-695-5253
Franklin	Blueberry Hill B&B, 4591 Peytonsville Rd, 37064 615-791-9947
Franklin	Carothers House B&B, 4301 S. Carothers Rd, 37064 615-794-4437

Franklin	Inn at Walking Horse Farm, 1490 Lewisburg Pike, 37064 615-790-2022
Franklin	Magnolia House B&B, 1317 Columbia Ave, 37064 615-794-8178
Franklin	The Old Marshall House, 1030 John William Rd, 37067 615-591-4121
Gallatin	The Hancock House, 2144 Nashville Pike, 37066 615-452-8431
Gatlinburg	7th Heaven Log Inn, 3944 Castle Rd, 37738 423-430-5000
Gatlinburg	Butcher House-Mountains, 1520 Garrett Ln, 37738 423-436-9457
Gatlinburg	Castle on the Green, 3950 Castle Rd, 37738 615-675-2462
Gatlinburg	Cornerstone Inn B&B, PO Box 1600, 37738 615-430-5064
Gatlinburg	Fountainview Inn, 104 Fred's Way, 37738
Gatlinburg	Laurel Springs B&B, 204 Hill St, 37738 423-430-7219
Gatlinburg	Olde English Tudor Inn B&B, 135 W. Holly Ridge Rd, 37738 423-436-7760
Gatlinburg	The Brevard Inn, PO Box 326, 37738 615-436-7233
Goodlettsville	Crocker Springs B&B, 2382 Crocker Springs Rd, 37072 615-876-8502
Goodlettsville	Terrawinn B&B, 304 Highland Heights Dr, 37072
Greenbrier	Triple Springs B&B, 2120 Hwy 41 S, 37073 800-816-3114
Greeneville	Oak Hill Farm B&B, 3035 Lonesome Pine Trl, 37743 423-639-5253
Hampshire	Ridgetop B&B, PO Box 193, 38461 615-285-2777
Hartsville	Miss Alice's B&B, 8325 Hwy 141 S, 37074 615-374-3015
Hendersonville	Morning Star B&B, 460 Jones Ln, 37075 615-264-2614
Hendersonville	Music City Respite, 111 Wonder Valley Rd, 37075
Hendersonville	Spring Haven B&B, 545 E Main St, 37075 615-826-1825
Hillsboro	Lord's Landing B&B, 375 Lord's Landing Ln, 37342 931-467-3830
Jackson	Highland Place B&B, 519 N. Highland Ave, 38301 901-427-1472
Jamestown	Wildwood Lodge, HC 61 Box 160, Rock Crk, 38556 615-879-9454
Johnson City	Ashley Ryan Guest House, 3908 Marable Ln, 37601 423-283-4677
Jonesborough	Aiken-Brow House, 104 3rd Ave S, 37659 615-753-9440
Jonesborough	Bowling Green Inn B&B, 901 W College St, 37659 615-753-6356
Jonesborough	Bugaboo B&B, 211 Semore Dr, 37659 615-753-9345
Jonesborough	Hawley House B&B, 114 E Woodrow Ave, 37659 423-753-8869
Jonesborough	Jonesborough B&B, PO Box 722, 37659 615-753-9223
Kingsport	C J's Place B&B, 634 Arch St, 37660
Kingsport	Shadowilde Manor, 252 Olis Bowers Hill Rd, 37664 615-323-3939
Kingston	Whitestone Country Inn, 1200 Paint Rock Road, 37763 423-376-0113
Knoxville	Magnolia Manor B&B, 1909 Cedar Lane, 37918 423-688-8999
Knoxville	Maple Grove Inn, 8800 Westland Dr, 37923 423-690-9565
Kodak	Grandma's House B&B, PO Box 445, 37764 615-933-3512
LaFollette	Blue Moon B&B, Rt 2, Box 236G3, 37766 800-340-8832
LaFollette	Dogwood Acres B&B Inn, Rt. 4, Box 628, 37766 615-566-1207
LaFollette	Mountain-Ayer, PO Box 1467, 37766 615-562-4941
Lebanon	Watermelon Moon, 10575 Trousdale Ferry, 37090 615-444-2356
Lenoir City	The Captain's Retreat, 3534 Lakeside Dr, 37772 423-986-4229
Linden	Avaleen Springs, Rt 3, Box 161, Hwy 412, 37096 931-589-5287
Livingston	Cornucopia B&B, 303 Mofield St, 38570 931-823-7522
Loudon	The Mason Place B&B, 600 Commerce St, 37774 423-458-3921
Lynchburg	Cedar Lane B&B, Rt 3, Box 155E, 37352 615-759-6891
Madisonville	Hillside Heaven B&B, 2920 Highway 68, 37354 615-337-2714
Memphis	Talbot Heirs Guesthouse, 99 S Second St., 38103 901-527-9772
Monteagle	North Gate Inn, PO Box 858, 37356 615-924-2799
Monterey	The Garden Inn, 1400 Bee Rock Rd, 38574 615-839-1400
Morresburg	The Home Place, 132 Church Lane, 37811 423-921-8424
Morristown	Victoria Rose B&B, 307 E. Second North St, 37814 423-581-9687
Mountain City	Butler House B&B, 309 Church St, 37683 423-727-4119
Mt. Juliet	Natureview Inn, 3354 Old Lebanon Dirt R, 37122 615-758-4439
Mt. Pleasant	Academy Place B&B, 301 Goodloe St, 38474 615-379-3198
Mulberry	Dream Fields Country Inn, 9 Back St, 37359 615-438-8875
Mulberry	Mulberry House, 8 Old Lynchburg Hwy, 37359 931-433-8461
Murfreesboro	Carriage Lane Inn, 411 N Maney Avenue, 37130 615-890-3630
Murfreesboro	Quilts and Croissants, 2231 Riley Rd, 37130 615-893-2933
Nashville	Apple Brook B&B, 9127 Hwy 100, 37221 615-646-5082
Nashville	Carole's Yellow Cottage, 801 Fatherland St, 37212 615-226-2952
Nashville	Commodore Inn & Guest Hse, 1614 19th Ave S, 37212 615-269-3850
Nashville	Hillsboro House, 1933 20th Avenue S, 37212 615-292-5501
Nashville	Lyric Springs Country Inn, PO Box 120428, 37212 615-329-3091
Nashville	Rose Garden, 6213 Harding Rd, 37205 615-356-8003
Nashville	The Savage House, 165 8th Ave North, 37203
New Market	Barrington Inn Rest. & B&B, 1174 McGuire Rd, 37820 423-397-3368
Normandy	Parish Patch Farm & Inn, 625 Cortner Rd, 37360 615-857-3017
Orlinda	Aurora Inn–B&B, 8253 Hwy. 52, 37141 615-654-4266
Paris	Sunset View Inn, 1330 Shady Grove Rd, 38242 901-642-4778
Pegram	Chigger Ridge B&B, 1060 Hwy 70 W, Box 349, 37143 615-952-4354
Pigeon Forge	Day Dreams Country Inn, 2720 Colonial Dr, 37863 423-428-0370
Pigeon Forge	Evergreen Cottage Inn, PO Box 1168, 37868 423-453-4000
Pigeon Forge	Hilton's Bluff B&B Inn, 2654 Valley Heights Dr, 37863 423-428-9765
Red Boiling Spring	Armour's Red Boiling Sprng, 321 E. Main St, 37150 615-699-2180
Red Boiling Spring	The Thomas House, PO Box 408, 37150
Rockford	Porter-Brakebill House, 803 Martin Mill Pike, 37853 423-982-0200
Rockford	Wayside Manor B&B, 4009 Old Knoxville Hwy, 37853 615-970-4823
Rogersville	Lee Valley Farm, 142 Drinnon Lane, 37857 615-272-4068

Rogersville	Silver Lace B&B, 615 E Main St, 37857 423-272-4650
Rugby	Clear Fork Farm, 328 Shirley Ford Rd, 37852 615-628-2967
Rugby	Newbury House Inn, PO Box 8, 37733 423-628-2441
Rugby	Ted & Barbara's B&B, Shirley Ford Rd, 37733 615-628-2967
Savannah	Ross House, PO Box 398, 38372 901-925-3974
Sevierville	Blue Mountain Mist Country, 1811 Pullen Rd, 37862 423-428-2335
Sevierville	Camelot B&B, 2659 Boyd's Creek Hwy, 37876 423-429-2070
Sevierville	Persephone's Retreat, 2279 Hodges Ferry Rd, 37862 423-428-3904
Sevierville	Place of the Blue Smoke, 3760 Cove Mountain Rd, 37862 800-453-4216
Sevierville	Von Bryan Mountaintop Inn, 2402 Hatcher Mtn Rd, 37862 423-453-9832
Seymour	The Country Inn, 701 Chris-Haven Dr, 37865 615-577-8172
Shelbyville	Cinnamon Ridge B&B, 799 Whitthorne St, 37160 615-685-9200
Shelbyville	Taylor House B&B, 300 E Lane St, 37160 931-684-3894
Shelbyville	The Old Gore House, 410 Belmont, 37160 931-685-0636
Signal Mountain	Bluff View Inn, 8034 Mill Creek Rd., 37377 423-886-5919
Signal Mt.	The Charlet House, 111 River Pt. Rd, 37377 615-886-4880
Smithville	Evins Mill Retreat, PO Box 606, 37166 615-597-2088
South Carthage	Gibbs Landing, 136 Gibbs Landing, 37030 615-735-2006
Talbott	Arrowhill, 6622 W. Andrew Johnson, 37877 423-585-5777
Townsend	Abode & Beyond B&B, 275 Little Mountain Way, 37882 423-448-9097
Townsend	Richmont Inn, 220 Winterberry Ln, 37882 615-448-6751
Townsend	Tuckaleechee Inn, PO Box 89, 37882 615-448-6442
Walland	Mill House & Restaurant, 4537 Old Walland Hwy, 37886 423-982-5726
Walland	The Inn @ Blackberry Farm, West Millers Cove Rd, 37886 615-984-8166
Walland	Twin Valley B&B Horse Rch, 2848 Old Chilhowee Rd, 37886 423-984-0980
Wartrace	Ledford Mill B&B, RT 2 Box 152B, 37183 931-455-2546
Wartrace	Log Cabin B&B, 171 Loop Rd, 37183 931-389-6713
Watertown	Watertown B&B, 116 Depot St, 37184 615-237-9999
Waverly	Nolan House Inn, 375 Highway 13 N, 37185 615-296-2511
Waynesboro	Waynesboro Inn, 406 S Main St, 38485 615-722-7321
Williston	Pleasant Retreat B&B, 420 Hotel St, 38076 901-465-4599
Winchester	The Antebellum Inn, 974 Lynchburg Rd, 37398 615-967-5550

Texas

Albany	Ann's B&B, 318 N Walnut, 76430 915-762-3200
Albany	The Foreman's Cottage B&B, Box 1477, 76430 915-762-3576
Allen	Blee Cottage, 103 W Belmont Dr., 75013 214-390-1884
Alpine	The Corner House, 801 E Avenue E, 79830 915-837-7161
Alpine	White House Inn, 2003 Fort Davis Hwy, 79830 915-837-1401
Alto	Lincrest Lodge, PO Box 799, 75925
Amarillo	Galbraith House, 1710 South Polk, 79102 806-374-0237
Amarillo	Gatlin Guesthouse, 4003 Clearwel, 79109
Amarillo	The Harrison House B&B, 1710 Harrison, 79102 806-374-1710
Archer City	Spur Hotel, PO Box 1047, 76351
Argyle	Argyle Country Mansion, PO Box 50, 76226 940-455-2575
Athens	Oak Meadow Farm B&B, 2781 FM 2495, 75751 903-675-3407
Austin	Aunt Dolly's Attic B&B, 12023 Rotherham Dr, 78753 512-837-5320
Austin	Gardens on Duval St, 3210 Duval St, 78705 512-477-9200
Austin	Inn at Pearl St., PO Box 201494, 78701 512-477-2233
Austin	Palmhouse, 902 Challenger St, 78734
Austin	Rive Oaks Farm B&B, 2105 Scenic Dr, 78703 512-474-2288
Austin	The Brook House B&B, 609 W 33rd St, 78705 512-459-0534
Austin	The Chequered Shade B&B, 2530 Pearce Rd, 78730 512-346-8318
Austin	The McCallum House, 613 W 32nd, 78705 512-451-6744
Austin	The Strickland Arms B&B, 604 E 47th St, 78751 512-454-4426
Austin	Triple Creek Ranch, Inc., 16301 Fitzhugh Rd., 78736 512-264-1371
Austin	Vintage Villas, 4209 Eck Ln, 78734 512-266-9333
Ballinger	Miz Virginia's B&B, Olde Park Hotel, 76821
Bandera	Bandera Creek B&B, PO Box 964, 78003
Bandera	Cool Water Acres, Rt 1 Box 785, 78003 210-796-4866
Bandera	Diamond H Ranch B&B, HC-02 Box 39C, 78003
Bandera	Flying L Guest Ranch, Hwy 173 & Whartons Dock, 78003
Bandera	Running-R Ranch, Rt 1, Box 590, 78003 830-796-3984
Bay City	Bailey House, 1704 Third St, 77414 409-245-5613
Baytown	Tygger's Lair, 3411 Garth Rd. Ste. 207, 77521 281-839-0102
Beaumont	Grand Duerr Manor, 2298 McFaddin, 77701 409-833-9600
Beeville	Nueces Inn, PO Box 29, 78104 713-362-0868
Belton	Belle of Belton B&B Inn, 1019 N. Main St., 76513 817-939-6478
Big Sandy	Annie's B&B Country Inn, PO Box 928, 75755 903-636-4355
Bluffdale	Hideaway Country Cabins, Rt 2 Box 148, 76433 254-823-6606
Bluffdale	Pleasant Valley, Rt 2 Box 12A, 76433
Boerne	Boerne Lake Lodge B&B, 47 Dodge Rd, 78006
Boerne	Borgman's Sunday House B&B, 911 S Main, 78006 830-249-9563
Boerne	Guadalupe River Ranch, 605 F.M. 474, 78006 830-537-4837
Boerne	The Meyer, 128 W Blanco, 78006 800-364-2218
Boerne	The Orchard Inn, 128 W Blanco Rd, 78006 830-995-2304
Boerne	Ye Kendall Inn, 128 W. Blanco, 78006 830-249-2138

Boerne	Yellow House, 128 W Blanco, 78006 830-249-2138
Bowie	Old Tucker Homeplace B&B, Rt 2 Box 355, 76230 940-872-2484
Bowie	The Gazebo B&B, 906 Sessions St, 76230 940-872-4852
Brady	Brady House B&B, 704 S Bridge, 76825 915-597-5265
Brazoria	River House, Rt 7-303 Lazy Oak Ranch, 77422 713-493-0754
Brenham	Ant Street, 107 W Commerce, 77833 409-836-7393
Brenham	Far View, 1804 S Park St, 77833 409-836-1672
Brenham	Mariposa Ranch B&B, 8904 Mariposa Ln, 77833 409-836-4737
Brenham	Mill House, 3000 Pecan Mill Lane, 77833
Brenham	Mockingbird Hill Farm, 6503 Baranowski Rd, 77833
Broaddus	Sam Rayburn B&B Cole House, Rt 1 Box 258, 75929 409-872-3666
Bryan	Angelsgate B&B, 615 E 29th St, 77803 409-779-1231
Bryan	Reveille Inn, 4400 Old College Road, 77801 409-846-0858
Bryan	The Vintner's Loft, 4545 Old Reliance Rd., 77802 409-778-1616
Buchanan Dam	Mystic Cove B&B, RR 1, Box 309B, 78609 512-793-6642
Burnet	Airy Mount Historic Inn, PO Box 351, 78611 512-756-4149
Burton	Cedar Tops Cottage, PO Box 179-AA, 77835 281-496-4724
Burton	Knittel Homestead Inn, PO Box 132, 77835 409-289-5102
Burton	Long Point Inn, Rt 1 Box 86-A, 77835 409-289-3171
Calvert	Pink House Gourmet B&B, PO Box 328, 77837 409-364-2868
Canton	B&B Country Style, PO Box 1011, 75103
Canton	Saline Creek Farm, Rt 2 Box 152, 75140 903-829-2709
Canyon	Country Home B&B, Rt 1 Box 447, 79015 806-655-7636
Canyon	Hudspeth House B&B, 1905 4th Ave, 79015 806-655-9800
Canyon Lake	Holiday Lodge, 537 Skyline Dr., 78133 210-964-3693
Carmine	Sugar Hill Retreat, PO Box 9, 78932 409-278-3039
Castroville	The Landmark Inn, 402 Florence St., 78009 210-931-2133
Center	John C. Rogers House, 416 Shebyville, 75935 409-598-3971
Chappell Hill	Browning Plantation, Rt. 1, Box 8, 77426 409-836-6144
Chappell Hill	Mulberry House, PO Box 5, 77426
Chappell Hill	Stagecoach Inn-Chappell Hl, Texas, Main at Chestnut, 77426 409-836-9515
Cleburne	1896 Railroad House, 421 E. Henderson St, 76031 817-517-5529
Cleburne	Anglin Queen Anne, 723 N. Anglin, 76031 817-645-5555
Clifton	Joann's Courtney House B&B, 1514 W 5th St., 76634 817-675-3061
Clifton	The River's Bend B&B, PO Box 228, 76634 817-675-4936
College Station	Twin Oaks, 3909 F & B Rd., 77845 409-260-9059
Columbus	Magnolia Oaks, 634 Spring St, 78934 409-732-2726
Comfort	Brinkman House B&B, PO Box 400, 78013 210-995-3141
Comfort	Carrington House B&B, 13 Hwy 87, 78013 830-995-2220
Comfort	Haven River Inn, PO Box 899, 78013 210-995-3834
Comfort	Kleina Himmul, RR 1 Box 127, 78013 210-995-2003
Conroe	Heather's Glen...A B&B, 200 E. Phillips, 77301 409-441-6611
Corpus Christi	Ocean House, 3275 Ocean Dr, 78404 512-882-9500
Crockett	Log Cabin, PO Box 707, 75835 409-636-2002
Crockett	Warfield House B&B, 712 E Houston Ave, 75835 409-544-4037
Crosbyton	Smith House, 306 W. Aspen, 79322 806-675-2178
Crystal Beach	Cottage By the Sea, PO Box 1227, 77650 409-684-3451
Dallas	B & G, 15869 Nedra Way, 75248 214 386 4323
Dallas	Courtyard on the Trail, 8045 Forest Trail, 75238 214-553-9700
Dallas	Good Neighbors, 5725 Penrose Ave., 75206 214-827-6390
Dallas	Hotel St. Germain, 2516 Maple Ave, 75201 214-871-2516
Dayton	Audubon Lodge B&B, PO Box 1439, 77535 409-258-9141
Del Rio	La Mansion Del Rio, 123 Hudson Dr., 78840 800-995-1887
Del Rio	The 1890 House B&B Inn, 609 Griner St, 78840 800-282-1360
Denison	Ivy Blue B&B, 1100 W Sears St, 75020 903-463-2479
Denison	The Molly Cherry, 200 W Prospect St., 75020 903-465-0575
Denton	Country Place at Cross Rds, 400 Historic Lane, 76227 940-365-9788
Denton	The Redbud Inn B&B, 815 N Locust, 76201 817-565-6414
Dickinson	Desel House - 1895, 5303 Desel Dr, 77539
Doss	Hill Top Cafe & Guesthouse, 10661 N U.S. Hwy 87, 78618 512-997-8922
Doss	Quiet Hill Ranch, 110 Quiet Hill Ranch Rd, 78618 830-669-2253
Draingerfield	Edge of the Canyon B&B, RR1 Box 152-R, 75638
Dripping Springs	Short Mama's B&B, PO Box 541, 78620 512-858-5684
Dripping Springs	The Cabin on Barton Creek, PO Box 414, 78620 512-858-4407
Dumas	The Serendipity House, PO Box 1132, 79029 806-935-0339
Eastland	Eastland, The B&B Hotel, 112 North Lamar, 76448 817-629-8397
Edgewood	Crooked Creek Farm, Rt 1 Box 180, 75117
El Paso	Bergmann Inn, 10009 Trinidad Dr, 79925 915-599-1398
El Paso	Chisholm Trail Ranch, 4770 Vista Del Monte, 79922
El Paso	Sunset Heights B&B Inn, 717 W. Yandell Ave, 79902 915-544-1743
Elgin	Ragtime Ranch Inn, Ragtime Ranch Rd, CR 98, 78621 512-285-9599
Eliasville	Andrews House, HC 75 Box 775, 76481 940-362-4243
Emory	Sweet Seasons, 630 Honeysuckle Ln, 75440 903-473-3706
Fischer	Stage Stop Ranch, 1100 Old Mail Route Rd, 78623 830-935-4455
Floydada	Lamplighter Inn, 102 S. 5th, 79235 806-983-3035
Fort Davis	The Hotel Limpia, Box 1341, 79734 915-426-3237
Fort Davis	The Webster Guest House, PO Box 288, 79734 409-899-1079
Fort Davis	Veranda Country Inn B&B, PO Box 1238, 79734 915-426-2233

Fort Davis	Wayside Inn B&B, PO Box 2088, 79734 915-426-3535
Fort Worth	Azalea Plantation B&B, 1400 Robinwood Dr., 76111 817-838-5882
Fort Worth	B&B at the Ranch, 8275 Wagley Roberson Rd, 76131 817-232-5522
Fort Worth	Miss Molly's Hotel B&B, 109-1/2 W. Exchange Ave, 76106 817-626-1522
Fort Worth	The Coloney, 2611 Glendale Ave, 76106 817-624-1981
Franklin	Dream Catcher Guest Ranch, RR 2 Box 115, 77856
Fredericksburg	Allegani Sunday Haus, 418 W Creek St, 78624 830-997-7448
Fredericksburg	Allegani's Little Horse In, 307 South Creek, 78624 830-997-7448
Fredericksburg	Barons Creek Cottage, 507 W Ufer St, 78624 830-997-6578
Fredericksburg	Bell Cottage, 503 E Morse, 78624 830-997-5612
Fredericksburg	Blumenthal Farms B&B, 9400 E US Hyway 290, 78624 830-997-6327
Fredericksburg	Creekside Inn, 304 S Washington, 78624 830-997-6316
Fredericksburg	Das Garten Haus, 604 S Washington, 78624 830-990-8408
Fredericksburg	Fredericksburg Bed & Brew, 243 E Main St, 78624
Fredericksburg	Granary & Alfred's @ Giles, 110 N Bowie, 78624 830-990-8400
Fredericksburg	Herb Haus @ Fredericksburg, 402 Whitney, 78624 830-997-8615
Fredericksburg	Historic Queen Isabell, 231 W Main, 78624 830-997-5612
Fredericksburg	Immel Haus B&B, 404 E Centre, 78624 830-997-5612
Fredericksburg	J Bar K Ranch B&B, 272 V-K Road, 78624 830-669-2471
Fredericksburg	Longhorn Corral & Western, 207 S Bowie, 78624 830-997-3049
Fredericksburg	Metzger Sunday House, 231 W Main, 78624 830-997-5612
Fredericksburg	Patsy's Place B&B, 703 W Austin, 78624 830-493-5101
Fredericksburg	Town Creek B&B, 304 N Edison, 78624 830-997-6848
Fredericksburg	Trails End, 222 W Centre St., 78624 830-990-8191
Fredericksburg	Watkins Hill, 608 E Creek St., 78624 830-997-6739
Fredericksburg	Way of the Wolf Ranch B&B, HC 12 Box 92-H, 78624 830-997-0711
Freeport	Anchor B&B, 342 Anchor Dr, 77541 409-239-3543
Gainesville	Rose House B&B, 321 S Dixon, 76240 940-665-1010
Galveston	Inn at 1816 Postoffice, 1816 Postoffice, 77550 409-765-9444
Galveston	Inn on the Strand, 2021 Strand St., 77550 409-762-4444
Galveston	The 1887 Coppersmith Inn, 1914 Avenue M, 77550 409-763-7004
Galveston	The Gilded Thistle, 1805 Broadway, 77550 409-763-0194
Galveston	Victorian Inn, 511 - 17th St, 77550 409-762-3235
Georgetown	Claiborne House, 912 Forest St, 78626 512-930-3934
Georgetown	Harper-Chessher Hist. Inn, 13300 E Hwy 29, 78626 512-863-4057
Georgetown	Heron Hill Farm B&B, 1350 County Rd. 143, 78626 512-863-0461
Georgetown	Historic Page House, 1000 Leander Rd, 78628 512-863-8979
Gilmer	Corner Cottage, 219 Butler St., 75644 903-843-2466
Gladewater	Boyce House, 117 W Quitman, 75647 903-845-3233
Gladewater	Honeycomb Suites, 111 N Main St., 75647 903-845-4430
Glen Rose	Hummingbird Lodge, PO Box 128, 76043 817-897-2787
Glen Rose	Inn on the River, PO Box 1417, 76043 254-897-2929
Glen Rose	Nature Escapes, Fossil Ring Wildlife Ct, 76043 817-289-7493
Glen Rose	Popejoy Haus B&B, PO Box 2023, 76043
Glen Rose	The Lodge at Fossil Rim, PO Box 2189, 76043 817-897-7452
Gonzales	St. James Inn, 723 St. James, 78629 210-672-7066
Gonzales	The Houston House B&B, 621 E St. George St., 78629 830-672-6940
Granbury	Alfonso's Loft, 137 E Pearl, 76048 817-573-3308
Granbury	Apple Gate B&B, 221 W Pearl St, 76048 817-573-2811
Granbury	Dabney House, 106 S. Jones, 76048 817-579-1260
Granbury	Derrick-Hoffman Farm, PO Box 298, 76048 817-573-9952
Granbury	Elizabeth Crockett B&B, 201 W. Pearl, 76048 817-573-7208
Granbury	Nutt House Hotel & Dining, 121 E. Bridge St, 76048 817-573-5612
Granbury	Plantation Inn, 1451 E Pearl St, 76049
Granbury	The Captain's House, 123 W Doyle St, 76048 817-579-6664
Granbury	The Doyle House, 205 W. Doyle, 76048 817-573-6492
Granbury	The Iron Horse Inn, 616 Thorp Spring Rd, 76048 817-579-5535
Granbury	The Victorian Rose, 404 W Bridge St, 76048 817-279-0879
Grand Saline	Lil'l Fannies, RR 2 Box 47, 75140 903-962-3737
Granite Shoals	Island View B&B, 1710 Lakecrest Dr., 78654 512-244-7126
Hallettsville	Enchanted Oaks Lodge B&B, 2184 US Hwy 77 N, 77964 512-798-4410
Hamilton	Hamilton Guest Hotel, 109 North Rice, 76531 800-876-2502
Harlingen	The Ross Haus, PO Box 2566, 78551 956-425-1717
Henrietta	Henrietta Township B&B, 604 E Gilbert St, 76365 817-538-6968
Hico	Indian Mountain Ranch B&B, RR 1 Box 162, 76457 817-796-4060
Hillsboro	Hillsboro House B&B Inn, 301 E Franklin St., 76645 817-582-0211
Hillsboro	Tarlton House, 211 N. Pleasant St, 76645 817-582-7216
Houston	Barbara's B&B, 1122 Banks St, 77006
Houston	Country Cottage Inn, 10302 Sugar Hill Dr, 77042 210-997-8549
Houston	Country Cottage Inn, 10302 Sugar Hill Rd, 77042
Houston	Durham House, 921 Heights Blvd, 77008 713-868-4654
Houston	Hidden Oaks B&B, 7808 Dixie Dr, 77087 713-640-2457
Houston	Montrose Inn, 408 Avondale, 77006 713-520-0206
Houston	The Oaks Cottage B&B, 1118 So. Shepherd Dr, 77019
Houston	Webber House B&B, 1011 Heights Blvd, 77008
Hubbard	Bell House B&B, 200 3rd St, 76648 817-576-2107
Hughes Springs	Mary and the Butler, PO Box 219, 75656 903-639-2244
Hunstville	Blue Bonnet B&B, 1704 Avenue O, 77340 409-295-2072

Hunt	Roddy Tree Ranch, PO Box 394, 78024 830-367-2871
Hunt	Waldemar B&B Resort, FM 1340, 78024 210-238-4821
Huntsville	The Whistler B&B, 906 Avenue M, 77340 409-295-2834
Ingram	River Oaks Lodge, HCR 78 Box 231-A, 78025
Iraan	Parker Ranch, PO Box 1320, 79744 915-639-2850
Itasca	Park House of 1908 B&B Inn, 206 N. Wesley, 76055 817-687-2515
Jacksonville	English Manor, 540 El Paso St., 75766 903-586-9821
Jefferson	Busy B Ranch, Rt 2 Box 87, 75657 903-665-7448
Jefferson	Chapelridge B&B, Rt 1, Box 2695, 75657
Jefferson	Cottonwood Inn B&B, 901 S Line St, 75657
Jefferson	Falling Leaves B&B, 304 Jefferson St, 75657 903-665-8803
Jefferson	Hale House, 702 S Line St., 75657 504-456-2648
Jefferson	McKay House B&B Inn, 306 E. Delta St, 75657 800-468-2627
Jefferson	Old Mulberry Inn, 209 Jefferson St, 75657 903-665-1945
Jefferson	The Terry McKinnon House, 109 W Henderson, 75657 903-665-1933
Jefferson	White Oak Manor B&B, 502 Benners, 75657 903-665-1271
Johnson City	Dream Catchers B&B, RR 1 Box 345, 78636 210-868-4875
Johnson City	Smith's Tin House on Squar, PO Box 334, 78636 210-868-4870
Katy	Log Cabin B&B, 1407 Breezy Bend Dr, 77494
Keerville	River Run B&B, 120 Francisco Lemos St., 78028 830-896-8353
Kemah	1874 Kipp House, 701 Bay Ave, 77565 713-334-4141
Kemah	Captain's Quarters, 701 Bay Ave, 77565 281-334-4141
Kingsland	The Antlers, Rt 2 Box 430, 78639 800-383-0007
Kingsville	B Bar B Ranch Inn, 325 E Country Rd 2215, 78363 512-296-3331
Knox City	Inn of the Blue Goose, PO Box 96, 79529 817-658-5329
Kyle	The Inn Above Onion Creek, 4444 FM 150 West, 78640 800-579-7686
La Granbe	The Y Knot B&B, 2819 Frank Rd., 78945 409-247-4529
Lacoste	Swan & Railway Country Inn, PO Box 429, 78039 210-762-3742
Lakehills	Wandering Aengus Cottage, RR 4 Box 4725, 78063 210-751-3345
Leakey	Whiskey Mountain Inn, HCR 1 Box 555, 78873 210-232-6797
Ledbetter	Ledbetter B&B, PO Box 212, 78946 409-249-3066
Llano	Dabbs Railroad Hotel, 112 E Burnet St, 78643
Llano	Ford Street Inn, 1119 Ford St., 78643 915-247-1127
Llano	Fraser House Inn, 207 E. Main, 78643 915-247-5183
Llano	Pecan Creek Cottage & Lodg, PO Box 488, 78643 915-247-4074
Lockhart	Albion B&B, 604 W San Antonio, 78644 512-376-6775
Lubbock	Broadway Manor B&B, 1811 Broadway, 79401 806-749-4707
Lubbock	Continental B&B, 2224 Broadway St, 79401
Lubbock	Woodrow House B&B, 2629 19th St, 79410 806-793-3330
Luckenback	The Luckenbach Inn, Old Luckenback Rd., 78624 830-997-2205
Mabank	Birdhouse B&B, 103 E Kaufman St, 75147 903-887 1242
Mabank	Birdhouse B&B, 103 E Kaufman St., 75147 903-887-1242
Mabank	Heavenly Acres, Rt 3 Box 470, 75147
Madisonville	The Log Cabin, PO Box 1031, 77864 409-348-5490
Manor	The Victorian Manor B&B, 14000 Old Why 20, 78653 512-278-0627
Marathon	Captain Shepard's Inn, Corner Ave D & 2nd St, 79842 800-884-4243
Marathon	The Gage Hotel, 102 W Highway 90, 79842 800-884-4243
Marble Falls	Liberty Hall Historic GH, 119 Avenue G, #103, 78654 800-232-4469
Marfa	The Arcon Inn, 215 N Austin, 79843 915-729-4826
Marlin	Highlands Mansion B&B, 1413 McClanahan Rd., 76661 254-803-2813
Marshall	Heart's Hill B&B, 512 E Austin St, 75670 903-935-6628
Marshall	Three Oaks B&B, 609 N Washington, 75670 903-935-6777
Martindale	Country Garden Inn B&B, PO Box 249, 78655 830-629-3296
Martindale	Countryside Inn, PO Box 178, 78655 512-357-2550
Martindale	Forget-Me-Not River Inn, PO Box 396, 78643 512-357-6385
Mason	Hasse House, PO Box 779, 76856 915-347-6463
Mason	Mason Square B&B, PO Box 298, 76856 915-347-6398
Mason	The Bridges House, PO Box 280, 76856
Mason	Willow Creek Ranch, PO Box 1599, 76856 915-347-6781
McGregor	Lighthouse B&B, 421 S Harrison St., 76657 254-840-2683
McKinney	Bingham House, 800 S Chestnut, 75069 972-529-1883
Meridian	Rose Hill Terrace, 318 E Morgan St, 76665 817-435-6257
Mineola	Munzesheimer Manor, 202 N. Newsom, 75773 903-569-6634
Mineola	Noble Manor, 411 E Kilpatrick St, 75773 903-569-5720
Mineral Wells	Silk Stocking Row, 415 NW 4th St, 76067 940-325-4101
Montgomery	B&B of Montgomery, PO Box 1408, 77356 409-597-3900
Nacogdoches	Anderson Point, 29 East Lake Estates, 75964 409-569-7445
Nacogdoches	Haden Edwards Inn, 106 N. Lanana, 75961 409-564-9999
Nacogdoches	Hardeman Guest House, 316 N Church St., 75961 409-569-1947
Nacogdoches	Llano Grande Plantation, Route 4, Box 9400, 75964 409-569-1249
Nacogdoches	Moundstreet B&B, 408 N. Mound, 75961 409-569-2211
Nacogdoches	Pine Creek Lodge, Rt 3 Box 1238, 75964 409-560-6282
Navasota	The Castle Inn, 1403 E Washington, 77868
New Braunfels	Antik Haus B&B, 118 S Union Ave, 78130 830-625-6666
New Braunfels	Bretzke Lane B&B, 1924 Bretzke Ln, 78132 512-606-1049
New Braunfels	Gruene Country Homestead, 832 Gruene Rd., 78130 830-606-0216
New Braunfels	Gruene Mansion Inn, 1275 Gruene Rd, 78130 210-629-2641
New Braunfels	Hotel Faust, 240 S. Seguin, 78130 512-625-7791

New Braunfels	Oak Hill Estate, 1355 River Rd., 78132 830-625-3170
New Braunfels	Prince Solms Inn, 295 E San Antonio St, 78130 210-625-9169
New Braunfels	River Haus B&B, 817 E. Zipp Rd, 78130 210-625-6411
New Braunfels	Riverside Haven B&B, 1491 Edwards Blvd, 78132
New Braunfels	Texas SunCatchers Inn, 1316 W Coll St, 78130 830-609-1062
New Braunfels	The White House, 217 Mittman Cr., 78130 210-629-9354
Newton	Butterfly House, 606 Main St., 75966 409-379-3638
Odessa	K-Bar Ranch Lodge, 15448-A S Jasper Ave, 79763
Odessa	Mellie's Historic Inn B&B, 903 N Sam Houston St., 79761 915-337-3000
Paige	Cedar Lodge, Rt 1 Box 22A, 78659
Palacios	Moonlight Bay B&B, 506 S. Bay Blvd., 77465 512-972-3408
Palestine	Bailey Bunkhouse, Rt 7 Box 7618, 75801 903-549-2028
Palestine	Spirit Bed N' Breakfasts', 109 E Pine, 75801 903-723-9565
Palestine	Wiffletree Inn B&B, 1001 N Sycamore St, 75801 903-723-6793
Paris	Old Magnolia House B&B, 731 Clarksville St., 75460 903-785-5593
Pettus	Victorian Manor, PO Box 17, 78146
Pittsburg	Carson House Inn & Grill, 302 Mt. Pleasant St, 75686 903-856-2468
Plainview	Harman-Y House B&B, 815 Columbia St, 79072
Plano	Carpenter House, 1211 E. 16th St., 75074 214-424-1889
Port Isabel	Queen Isabel Inn, 300 Garcia St, 78578
Port Isabel	Yacht Club Hotel, PO Box 4114, 78578 210-943-1301
Post	Hotel Garza B&B, 302 E. Main, 79356 806-495-3962
Pottsboro	Yacht-O-Fun, PO Box 1480, 75076 903-786-8188
Queen City	Antique Rose, 205 Miller St, 75572 903-796-5980
Raymondville	The Inn at El Canelo, PO Box 487, 78580
Rio Grande	La Borde House, 601 E. Main St, 78582 512-487-5101
Rio Medina	The Haby Settlement Inn, 2240 CR271, 78066 512-538-2441
Round Rock	St. Charles B&B, 8 Chisholm Trail, 78681 512-244-6850
Round Top	Briarfield B&B, 219 FM 954, 78954 409-249-3973
Round Top	Broomfields B&B, 419 N. Nassau Rd, 78954
Round Top	Ginzel Haus, PO Box 187, 78954 409-249-3060
Round Top	Heart of My Heart Ranch, PO Box 106, 78954 409-249-3171
Round Top	Outpost at Cedar Creek, Rt 1, Box 73, 78954 409-836-4975
Round Top	Tricklecreek Farms B&B, PO Box 187, 78954 409-249-3060
Roxton	The Drogheda B&B, c/o Old Magnolia House, 75460 903-785-5593
Rusk	Beans Creek Ranch, RR 4 Box 411, 75785 903-683-6235
S. Padre Island	Brown Pelican Inn, PO Box 2667, 78597 956-761-2722
S. Padre Island	The Moonraker, 107 E Marisol, 78597 210-761-2206
Salado	Inn on the Creek, PO Box 858, 76571 817-947-5554
Salado	The Rose Mansion, PO Box 613, 76571 817-947-8200
San Antonio	Academy House, Monte Vista, 2317 North Main, 78212 210-731-8393
San Antonio	Beauregard House B&B, 215 Beauregard, 78204 210-222-1198
San Antonio	Belle Of Monte Vista, 505 Belknap Pl, 78212 210-732-4006
San Antonio	Chabot Reed Carriage House, 403 Madison, 78204 210-734-4243
San Antonio	Country Cottage Inn, 1215 S. Presa St., 78210 210-534-6288
San Antonio	Joske House B&B, 241 King William, 78204 210-271-0706
San Antonio	La Mariposa, PO Box 830512, 78283 210-225-7849
San Antonio	Sheraton Gunter Hotel, 205 E. Houston St, 78204 800-222-4276
San Antonio	Summit Haus, 240 W Skyview Dr, 78228 210-736-6272
San Antonio	The Fairmount Hotel, 401 S Alamo, 78205 800-642-3363
San Antonio	The Menger Hotel, 204 Alamo Plaza, 78205 210-223-4361
San Antonio	The Ramada Emily Morgan, 705 E. Houston St, 78205 800-824-6674
San Antonio	The Scandua Suite, 236 Madison, 78204 210-223-4006
San Antonio	The Tara Inn B&B, 307 Beauregard, 78204 210-223-5875
San Augustine	Captain Downs House, 301 E. Main St, 75972 409-275-5305
San Augustine	Wade House, PO Box 695, 75972 409-275-5489
Seabrook	The Rose Mansion, 1302 First St, 77586 281-474-5295
Seadrift	Hotel Lafitte, 302 Bay Ave, 77983
Seguin	Weinert House B&B, 1207 N. Austin, 78155
Shamrock	Ye Olde Home Place B&B, 311 E 2nd St, 79079 806-256-2295
Sherman	Hart's Country Inn, 601 N Grand Ave, 75090
Spring	McLachlan Farm B&B, PO Box 538, 77383 281-350-2400
Stephenville	The Oxford House, 563 N Graham, 76401 254-965-6885
Sulphur Springs	Hope Chest Inn B&B, 121 Turtle Creek Dr, 75482
Sunrise Beach	Sandyland Resort, 212 Skyline Dr, 78643 915-388-4521
Sweetwater	Mulberry Manor, 1400 Sam Houston St, 79556
Texarkana	Main House, 3419 Main St, 75503 903-793-5027
Texarkana	Mansion on Main B&B, 802 Main St, 75501 903-792-1835
Trinity	Parker House B&B, PO Box 2373, 75862 409-594-3260
Tyler	Azalea Inn B&B, 10886 Spur 164, 75709 903-595-3610
Tyler	Charnwood Hill Inn, 223 E. Charnwood, 75701 903-587-3980
Tyler	Chilton Grand, 433 S Chilton Ave, 75702
Tyler	Mary's Attic, 417 S. College, 75702 903-592-5181
Tyler	The Woldert-Spence Manor, 611 West Woldert St, 75702 903-533-9057
Universal City	Frieda's B&B, 109 Andorra Dr, 78148
Universal City	Frieda's B&B, 109 Andorra Dr, 78148
Utopia	Bluebird Hill B&B, PO Box 206, 78884 210-966-2320
Utopia	Utopia on the River, PO Box 14, 78884

Uvalde	Casa De Leona B&B, PO Box 1829, 78802 210-278-8550
Van	Tumble on Inn, PO Box 1249, 75790 903-963-7669
Van Alstyne	Durning House Rest. & B&B, PO Box 1173, 75495 903-482-5188
Vanderpool	Texas Stagecoach Inn, Hwy 187, 78885 830-966-6272
Victoria	Forrest Place Suites, 507 W Forrest St, 77901
Victoria	Friendly Oaks B&B, 210 E Juan Linn, 77901 512-575-0000
Waco	Colcord House, 2211 Colcord, 76707 254-753-6856
Warrenton	Warrenton Inn, PO Box 182, 78961
Waxahachie	Rose of Sharon B&B Inn, 205 Bryson, 75165 214-938-8833
Waxahachie	The Chaska House B&B, 716 West Main St, 75165 972-937-3390
Waxahachie	The Harrison B&B, 717 W Main, 75165 972-938-1922
Weatherford	St. Botolph Inn, 808 S. Lamar St, 76086 817-594-1455
Weatherford	Two Pearls B&B, 804 S Alamo St, 76086 817-596-9316
Weatherford	Victorian House B&B, PO Box 1571, 76086 817-596-8295
Wichita Falls	Guest House B&B, 2209 Miramar St, 76308
Wichita Falls	Harrison House B&B, 2014 11th St, 76301
Wimberley	Blair House, 100 Spoke Hill Rd, 78676 512-847-1111
Wimberley	Heart House B&B, 12711 Ranch Rd 12, S, 78676 512-847-1414
Wimberley	Lodge At Creekside, 11 Mill Race Ln, 78676 512-842-2107
Wimberley	Lonesome Dove River Inn, 600 River Rd, 78676 512-392-2921
Wimberley	Old Oaks Ranch B&B, PO Box 912, 78676 512-847-9374
Wimberley	Singing Cypress Gardens, PO Box 824, 78676 512-847-9344
Wimberley	Southwind B&B and Cabins, 2701 FM 3237, 78676 512-847-5277
Wimberley	The Homestead, PO Box 1034, 78676 512-847-8788
Wolforth	Country Place B&B, 160th & Upland Ave, 79382 806-863-2030
Woodville	Antique Rose B&B, 612 N Nellius, 75779 409-283-8926
Yoakum	Our Guest House B&B, 406 E Hugo St, 77995 512-293-3482

Utah

Alta	Alta Lodge, 84092 801-742-3550
Alton	Color Country B&B, 51 Dead Horse Loop, 84710 435-648-2418
Beaver	Mt. Holly Inn Outfitters, PO Box 1547, 84713 435-438-2440
Blanding	Grayson Country Inn B&B, 118 E 300 South, 84511
Blanding	Rogers House B&B, 412 S Main St, 84511 435-678-3932
Blanding	The Old Hotel B&B, 118 East 300 South St, 84511 435-678-2388
Bluff	Bluff B&B, PO Box 158, 84512 801-672-2220
Bluff	Calabre B&B, PO Box 85, 84512 801-672-2252
Bluff	Desert Rose Inn & Cabins, 6th E Black Locust Ave, 84512 435-672-2303
Boulder	Boulder Mountain Lodge, PO Box 1397, 84716 800-556-3446
Brighton	Das Alpen Haus, Star Route, 84121 435-649-0565
Cedar City	Bard's Inn, 150 S 100 West, 84720 435-586-6612
Cedar City	Desert Blossom Inn B&B, 140 S 100 W, 84720 435-865-9545
Ephraim	Ephraim Homestead, 135 W. 100 N., 84627 801-283-6367
Escalante	Rainbow Country B&B, PO Box 333, 84726 801-826-4567
Garden City	Inn Of The Three Bears, 135 S. Bear Lake Blvd, 84028 801-946-8590
Glendale	The Homeplace, PO Box 41, 84729 801-648-2194
Green River	Bankurz Hatt, PO Box 33, 84525
Gunnison	Sample House, 10 E 100 S, Box 892, 84634 435-528-7519
Hatch	Calico House B&B, 98 Main St Box 552, 84735
Heber City	Mindheim's Inn, 540 N 750 E, 84032
Heber City	Snowfire Inn, 490 W 100 South, 84032 801-654-2430
Hemefer	Dearden's B&B, 202 West 100 N, 84033
Hurricane	Pah Temple Hot Springs, 825 N. 800 E. 35-4, 84737 435-635-2879
Junction	John Morrill House B&B, PO Box 81, 84740
Kanab	Nine Gables Inn, 106 W. 100 North, 84741 801-644-5079
La Sal	La Sal Mountain Guest Rch, Box 247, 84530
Loa	Road Creek Inn, PO Box 310, 84747 801-836-2485
Logan	Alta Manor Suites, 45 E 500 North, 84321 435-752-0808
Logan	Center Street B&B Inn, 169 E. Center St, 84321 435-752-3443
Logan	Jasmine Cottage, 1533 Sumao Dr, 84331
Logan	The Logan House Inn, 168 N 100 E, 85321 435-752-7727
Manti	Heritage House, 498 N 500 W, 84642 435-835-5050
Manti	Manti House Inn, 401 N. Main St, 84642 801-835-0161
Manti	Old Brigham House Inn, 123 E. Union, 84642 801-835-8381
Manti	Temple View Lodge, 260 E 400 N, 84642 435-835-6663
Manti	Yardley B&B Inn, 190 W. 200 S, 84642 801-835-1861
Marysvale	Moore's Old Pine Inn, 60 S State, 84750 801-326-4565
Mexican Hat	Valley Of The Gods, Valley of the Gods Rd, 84531 970-749-1164
Midway	Huckleberry Country Inn, 1299 Warm Springs, 84049 435-654-1400
Midway	Inn On The Creek, 375 Rainbow Ln, 84049 435-654-0892
Midway	Kastle Inn, PO Box 335, 84049 435-654-2689
Midway	The Homestead Resort, PO Box 99, 84049 435-654-1102
Moab	Canyon Country B&B, 590 North 500 W, 84532 435-259-5262
Moab	Castle Valley Inn, HC 64 Box 2602, 84532 435-259-6012
Moab	Desert Chalet, 1275 San Juan Dr, 84532
Moab	Entrada Ranch, PO Box 567, 84532 435-259-5796
Moab	Mayor's House B&B, 505 Rose Tree Ln, 84532 435-259-3019

Moab	Pack Creek Ranch, PO Box 1270, 84532 435-259-5505
Moab	Pioneer Spring B&B, 1275 S Boulder, 84532 435-259-4663
Moab	Purple Sage B&B, 1150 Duchesne, 84532
Moab	Rose Tree B&B, 505 Rose Tree Ln, 84532 435-259-6015
Moab	Slick Rock Inn, 286 South 400 E, 84532 435-259-2266
Moab	Spanish Trail Inn, 3180 Spanish Trail Rd, 84532 435-259-4377
Moab	The Blue Heron, 900 W Kane Creek Blvd, 84532 801-259-4921
Moab	Westwood Guest House, 81 E South, 84532
Monroe	Peterson's B&B, PO Box 142, 84754 801-527-4830
Monticello	The Grist Mill Inn, PO Box 156, 84535 801-587-2597
Mt. Pleasant	Fiddler's Green Inn, 3564 W Hwy 116 #7, 84647 435-462-3276
Nephi	The Whitmore Mansion B&B, PO Box 73, 84648 801-623-2047
Oakley	Graystone Lodge, PO Box 482, 84055 801-783-5744
Old La Sal	Mt. Peale Country Inn, 1415 E Hwy 46, 84530 435-686-2284
Panguitch	Mae Mae's B&B, 501 E. Center St, 84759 801-676-2388
Park City	505 Woodside, B&B Place, PO Box 2446, 84060 435-649-4841
Park City	Angel House Inn, PO Box 159, 84060 435-647-0338
Park City	Goldener Hirsch Inn, PO Box 859, 84060 435-649-7770
Park City	Imperial Hotel, PO Box 1628, 84060 435-649-1904
Park City	Old Town Guest House, PO Box 162, 84060 435-649-2642
Park City	Owl's Roost B&B, 2326 Comstock Dr., 84060 435-649-6938
Park City	Phidias Cinaglia's B&B, 75 Matterhorn Terrace, 84098 801-645-9547
Park City	Star Hotel B&B, PO Box 777, 84060 435-649-8333
Park City	The Washington School Inn, PO Box 536, 84060 435-649-3800
Parowan	Jantelynn House B&B, PO Box 331, 84761 801-477-1133
Providence	Providence Inn B&B, PO Box 99, 84332 801-752-3432
Provo	Spencer Hines, 383 W 100 S, 84601 801-374-8400
Richfield	The Old Church B&B, 180 W. 400 S, 84701 435-896-6705
Rockville	Handcart House B&B, PO Box 630146, 84763 801-772-3867
Rockville	The Blue House B&B, 125 East Main, 84763 801-772-3912
Salina	The Victorian Inn, 190 W Main St., 84654 435-529-7342
Salt Lake City	Armstrong Mansion B&B, 667 E 100 S, 84102 801-531-1333
Salt Lake City	Brick Inn, 1030 E 100 S, 84102 801-322-4917
Salt Lake City	Brigham Street Inn, 1135 E South Temple, 84103 801-364-4461
Salt Lake City	Casa Blanca, 999 S 1200 E, 84105 801-583-6824
Salt Lake City	City Creek Park B&B, 128 E. 2nd Ave, 84103 801-533-0770
Salt Lake City	Dave's Cozy Cabin Inn, 2293 East 6200 S, 84121 801-278-6136
SSandy	Alta Hills Farm, 10852 S. 20th E. Sandy, 84092 801-571-1712
Sandy	Quail Hills Guesthouse, 3744 E. N.Little Cttnwd, 84092 801-942-2858
Spanish Fork	Escalante B&B, 733 North Main St, 84660 801-798-6652
Springdale	Novel House at Zion, PO Box 188, 84767 801-772-3650
Springdale	O'Toole's Under the Eaves, PO Box 29, 84767 801-772-3457
Springdale	Red Rock Inn, PO Box 273, 84767 801-772-3139
Springdale	Zion House B&B, Box 323, 84767 801-772-3281
Springville	Kearns Hotel, 94 W 200 South, 84663
St. George	Glacier Bay Country Inn, PO Box 1003, 84771 907-697-2288
St. George	Maurice Mulberry Inn B&B, 194 S. 600 E, 84770 435-673-7383
St. George	Olde Penny Farthing Inn, An, 278 N 100 W, 84770 435-673-7755
Sterling	Cedar Crest B&B, PO Box T, 84665 801-835-6352
Summit Park	Matterhorn Summit Lodge, 75 Matterhorn Terr., 84098 435-645-9547
Sundance	Sundance, RR #3 Box A-1, 84604 801-225-4107
Taos	Bavairan, UT, PO Box 653, 87525 505-770-0450
Teasdale	Cockscomb Inn B&B, PO Box B, 84773 435-425-3511
Toquerville	Springs Creek Gardens B&B, PO Box 296, 84770 801-635-3053
Torrey	Skyridge, A B&B Inn, PO Box 750220, 84775 435-425-3222
Tropic	Bryce Point B&B, 61 North 400 West, 84776 345-679-8629
Tropic	Canyon Livery B&B, PO Box 24, 84776 801-679-8780
Tropic	Fox's Bryce Trails B&B, PO Box 87, 84776 801-679-8700
Tropic	Francisco's B&B, 1/2 Mile S of Tropic, 84776
Tropic	Half House B&B, 320 Hwy 12, 84776
Vernal	Hillhouse Bed 'n' Breakfas, 675 W 3300 North, 84078
Vernal	Landmark Inn, 288 E 100 South, 84078 888-738-1800
Virgin	Snow Family Guest Ranch, PO Box 790190, 84779 801-635-2500

Vermont ──

Alburg	Auverge Alburg, RD 1, Box 3, 05440 802-796-3169
Alburg	The Ransom Bay Inn, PO Box 57, 05440 802-796-3399
Alburg	Ye Old Graystone B&B, RFD 1, Box 76, 05440 802-796-3911
Arlington	Ira Allen House, RD 2, Box 2485, 05250 802-362-2284
Arlington	The Inn at Sunderland, RR 2, Box 2440, 05250 802-362-4213
Arlington	Willow B&B, RR 2 Box 3070, 05250 802-375-9773
Barnard	The Maple Leaf Inn, PO Box 273, 05031 802-234-5342
Barton	Anglin' B&B, PO Box 403, 05822 802-525-4548
Barton	Our Village Inn, PO Box 317, 05822 802-525-3380
Bellows Falls	Blue Haven B&B, RDI, Box 328, 05101 802-463-9008
Bellows Falls	Horsefeathers B&B, 16 Webb Terrace, 05101 802-463-9776
Bellows Falls	River Mist B&B, 7 Burt St., 05101 802-463-9023

Belmont	The Leslie Place, Box 62, 05730 802-259-2903
Bennington	South Shire Inn, 124 Elm St, 05201 802-447-3839
Bondville	Alpenrose Inn, PO Box 187, 05340 802-297-2750
Bondville	Bromley View Inn, Route 30, 05340 802-297-1459
Brandon	Brandon Inn, 20 Park Green, 05733 802-247-5766
Brandon	Dunmore Acres, Rt 53, Box 2437, 05733 802-247-3126
Brandon	Gazebo Inn, 25 Grove St, Route 7, 05733 802-247-3235
Brandon	Hivue B&B, PO Box 1023, 05733 802-247-3042
Brandon	Old Mill Inn, 79 Stone Mill Dam Rd, 05733 802-247-8002
Brandon	Rosebelle's Victorian Inn, PO Box 370, 05733 802-247-0098
Brandon	The Adams Motor Inn, RR 1 Box 1142, 05733 802-247-6644
Brandon	The Lilac Inn, 53 Park St, 05733 802-247-5463
Brandon	The Moffett House B&B, 69 Park St, 05733 802-247-3843
Brattleboro	40 Putney Road B&B, 40 Putney Rd, 05301 802-254-6268
Brattleboro	Meadowlark Inn B&B, PO Box 2048, 05303 802-257-4582
Brattleboro	The Tudor B&B, 76 Western Ave, 05301 802-257-4983
Bridgewater	October Country Inn, PO Box 66, 05035 802-672-3412
Bridgewater Corners	Corners Inn & Restaurant, PO Box 318, 05035 802-672-9968
Bristol	23 West Street A B&B, 23 West St., 05443 802-543-2236
Bristol	Crystal Palace Victorian, 48 North St, 05443 802-453-4131
Bristol	Firefly Ranch, PO Box 152, 05443 802-453-2223
Bristol	Mary's at Baldwin Creek, Rt 116 N & Rt 17, 05443 892-453-2432
Bristol	The Cliff Hanger, RD 3, Box 2027, 05443 802-453-2013
Brookfield	Green Trails Inn, By the Floating Bridge, 05036 802-276-3412
Brownsville	Mill Brook B&B & Gallery, PO Box 410, 05037 802-484-7283
Brownsville	The Pond House, PO Box 234, 05037 802-484-0011
Burlington	Tetreault House, 251 Staniford Rd., 05401 802-862-2781
Burlington	Willard Street Inn, 349 South Willard, 05401 802-651-8710
Cabot	Creamery Inn B&B, PO Box 187, 05647 802-563-2819
Cavendish	Cavendish Inn, PO Box 82, 05142 802-226-7329
Charlotte	Inn at Charlotte, 32 State Park Rd, 05445 802-425-2934
Charlotte	Look Out Farm, 121 Garden Rd, 05445 802-425-3515
Chester	Castle Inn, RR2, Box 812, 05143 802-226-7222
Chester	Chester House B&B Inn, PO Box 708, 05143 802-875-2205
Chester	Farmhouse 'Round the Bend, 215 Mountain View, 05146 802-843-2515
Chester	Greenleaf Inn, PO Box 188, 05143 802-875-3171
Chester	Night With A Native B&B, PO Box 327, 05143 802-875-2616
Chester	Rose Arbour B&B, School & Canal Sts, 05143 802-875-4767
Chester	The Old Town Farm Inn, RR#4 Box 383 B, 05143 802-875-2346
Chittenden	Mountain Top Inn, Mountain Top Rd, 05737 802-483-2311
Colchester	Poor Farm Inn, 30 Poor Farm Rd., 05446 802-872-8712
Craftsbury	Bricabode, PO Box 59, 05827
Craftsbury	Craftsbury Inn, PO Box 36, 05826 802-586-2848
Cuttingsville	Maple Crest Farm, Box 120, 05738 802-492-3367
Danville	Danville Inn, PO Box 201, 05828 802-684-3484
Derby Line	The Birchwood B&B, PO Box 550, 05830 802-873-9104
Dorset	Barrows House, Route 30, 05251 802-867-4455
Dorset	Dovetail Inn, Route 30, Main St, 05251 802-867-5747
Dorset	Inn at West View Farm, RT 30, 05251 802-867-5715
East Burke	Mountain View Creamery, Darling Hill Road, 05832 802-626-9924
East Burke	The Garrison Inn, PO Box 177, 05832 802-626-8329
East Dorset	Christmas Tree B&B, Benedict Rd, 05253 802-362-4889
East Haven	Hansel & Gretel Haus, Box 95, 05837 802-467-8884
East Middlebury	By the Way B&B, PO Box 264, 05740 802-388-6291
East Middlebury	October Pumpkin B&B, PO Box 226, 05740 802-388-9525
East Middlebury	The Annex, Rt 125, 05740 802-388-3233
Essex	The Inn at Essex, 70 Essex Way, 05452
Fair Haven	Fair Haven Inn B&B, 5 Adams Street, 05743 802-265-4907
Fairfield	Tetreault's Hillside View, South Rd, Box 1860, 05455 802-827-4480
Gaysville	Cobble House Inn, PO Box 49, 05746 802-234-5458
Glocer	Gloverview Inn B&B, W Glover Rd., 05839 802-525-3836
Goshen	High Meadow B&B, RD 3, Box 3344, 05733 802-247-3820
Goshen	Judith's Garden B&B, Goshen-Ripton Rd., 05733 802-247-4707
Grafton	Inn At Woodchuck Hill Farm, One Middletown Rd, 05146
Grafton	The Old Tavern at Grafton, Main St, 05146 802-843-2231
Grand Isle	Farmhouse on the Lake, 116 W Shore Rd., 05458 800-372-8849
Greensboro	Greensboro House, Barr Hill Rd., 05841 802-533-7155
Hancock	Sweet Onion Inn, PO Box 66, 05748 802-767-3734
Hartford	House of Seven Gables, PO Box 526, 05047 802-295-1200
Highgate Springs	Tyler Place-Lake Champlain, PO Box 45, 05460 802-868-3301
Hinesburg	By the Old Mill Stream B&B, RR 2, Box 543, 05461 802-482-3613
Hyde Park	Arcadia House, PO Box 520, 05655
Hyde Park	Ten Bends, Black Rd., 05655 802-888-2827
Isle La Motte	Ruthcliffe Lodge, PO Box 32, 05463 802-928-3200
Jay	Village Inn, Rt. 242, 05859 802-988-2643
Jeffersonville	Jefferson House, PO Box 288, 05464 802-644-2030
Jeffersonville	Sterling Ridge Inn & Cabin, RR2 Box 5780, 05464 802-644-8866
Jeffersonville	The Smuggler's Notch Inn, PO Box 280, 05464 802-644-2412

Jericho	Henry M. Field B&B, RR 2 Box 395, 05465 802-899-3984
Jericho	Homeplace B&B, PO Box 96, 05465 802-899-4694
Jericho	Milliken's, 65 VT Rte 15, 05465 802-899-3993
Jericho	Potter House B&B, 2 Plains Rd., 05465 802-899-5072
Jericho	Sinclair Inn B&B, RD 2 Box 35, 05489 802-899-2234
Killington	Cascades Lodge, RR 1 Box 2848, 05751
Killington	Cortina Inn and Resort, HC 34, Box 33, 05751 802-773-3333
Killington	Grey Bonnet Inn, RT 100N, 05751 802-775-2537
Killington	Inn of the Six Mountains, Killington Rd., 05751 802-422-4302
Killington	The Woods, RR #1, Box 2325, 05751 802-422-3244
Londonderry	Blue Gentian Lodge, Box 29 RR #1, 05148 802-824-5908
Londonderry	Swiss Inn, RR 1 Box 140, 05148 802-824-3442
Londonderry	The Highland House, RR#1 Box 107, 05148 802-824-3019
Ludlow	Echo Lake Inn, PO Box 154, 05149 802-228-8602
Ludlow	Fletcher Manor B&B, One Elm St, 05149 802-228-3548
Ludlow	Jewell Brook Inn, B&B, 82 Andover St, Rt 100, 05149 802-228-8926
Ludlow	The Okemo Inn, RFD#1, Box 133, 05149 802-228-8834
Lyndonville	Wheelock Inn B&B, RR 2, Box 160, 05851 802-626-8503
Manchester	Barnstead Innstead, Bonnet St, 05255 802-362-1619
Manchester	Brook-N-Hearth B&B, PO Box 508, 05255 802-362-3604
Manchester	Charles Orvis Inn, Historic Rt 7A, 05254 802-362-4700
Manchester	Equinox Mountain Inn, Skyline Drive, 05250 802-362-1113
Manchester	Pinnacle Sun & Ski Lodge, PO Box 2424, 05255 802-824-6608
Manchester	Purple Passion, PO Box 678, 05254 800-822-2331
McIndoe Falls	McIndoe Falls Inne, Rt 5, 05050 802-633-2240
Mendon	Red Clover Inn, RR 2, 05701 802-775-2290
Middlebury	Cornwall Orchards B&B, 1364 Rt 30, 05753 802-462-2272
Middlebury	Fairhill, E Munger, Rd 3 Box 2300, 05753 802-388-3044
Middlebury	Linens & Lace B&B, 29 Seminary St, 05753 802-388-0832
Middlebury	Middlebury B&B, Washington St Ext, 05753 802-388-4851
Middlebury	Point of View, RD 3 Box 2675, 05753 802-388-7205
Middlebury	Swift House Inn, 25 Stewart Lane, Rt#7, 05753 802-388-9925
Middletown Springs	Middletown Springs Inn, PO Box 1068, 05757
Middletown Springs	Priscilla's Victorian Inn, 52 South St, 05757
Montgomery Center	Eagle Lodge, RR 1 Box 900, 05471
Montgomery Center	Kates Suite, Rt 1 Box 620, 05471 802-326-4434
Montpelier	Montpelier B&B, 22 North St., 05602 802-229-0878
Mount Holly	Hound's Folly, Box 591, 05758 802-259-2718
New Haven	Long Run Inn, 1323 East ST, 05472 802-453-3233
New Haven	New Haven Hills B&B, Box 121, 05472 802-453-5495
Newbury	Century Past, PO Box 186, 05051 802-866-3358
Newfane	Sugarhouse Suite, PO Box 480, 05345 802-365-7762
Newfane	The Four Columns Inn, PO Box 278, 05345 802-365-7713
Newport	Top of the Hills Inn, HCR 61, Box 38, 05855 802-334-6748
North Bennington	Henry House, RR 1 Box 214, 05207 201-262-3110
North Thetford	Stone House Inn, Box 47, Route 5, 05054 802-333-9124
Norwich	The Norwich Inn, PO Box 908, 05055 802-649-1143
Orleans	Valley House Inn, 26 East St, 05860 802-754-6665
Orleans	Willough Vale Inn, RR 2, Box 403, 05860
Orwell	Buckswood B&B, 633 Rt 73, 05760 802-948-2054
Perkinsville	Gwendolyn's, PO Box 225, 05151 802-263-5248
Perkinsville	The Inn at Weathersfield, PO Box 165, 05151 802-263-9217
Peru	The Wiley Inn, PO Box 37, 05152 802-824-6600
Plainfield	Yankees' Northview B&B, RD #2, Box 1000, 05667 802-454-7191
Plymouth	Plymouth Towne Inn B&B, HCR 70 Box 8 Rt 100, 05056 802-672-3059
Poultney	Tower Hall, 2 Bentley Ave., 05764 802-287-4004
Proctorsville	Okemo Lantern Lodge, PO Box 247, 05153 802-226-7770
Proctorsville	The Castle, PO Box 207, 05153 802-226-7222
Putney	Hickory Ridge House, 53 Hickory Ridge Rd S, 05346 802-387-5709
Putney	The Putney Inn, PO Box 181, 05346 802-387-5517
Quechee	Country Garden Inn B&B, 37 Main St, Box 404, 05059 802-295-3023
Quechee	Herron House Inn, 98 Quechee-Hartland Rd, 05059 802-296-7512
Quechee	Quechee B&B, PO Box 80, 05059 802-295-1776
Quechee	Sugar Pine Farm, Rt 4, 05059 802-295-1266
Randolph	Emerson's B&B on the Terr., PO Box 177, 05060 802-728-4972
Randolph	Foggy Bottom Farm B&B, Rt. 12, 05060 802-728-9201
Randolph	Three Stallion Inn, RD #2 Stock Farm Rd, 05060 802-728-5575
Reading	Greystone B&B, Rt 106, 05062 802-484-7206
Reading	The Peeping Cow B&B, PO Box 178, 05062 802-484-5036
Richford	Troy Street B&B, 102 Troy St., 05476 802-848-3557
Richmond	Mama Bower's B&B, PO Box 222, 05477 802-434-2632
Richmond	The Black Bear Inn, PO Box 26, 05477 802-434-2126
Rochester	Liberty Hill Farm, RR1 Box 158, 05767 802-767-3926
Roxbury	Inn at Johnnycake Flats, Carrie Howe Rd, 05669
Rutland	The Phelps House, 19 North St, 05701
S. Londonderry	Londonderry Inn, Box 301-12, Rt 100, 05155 802-824-5226
Sandgate	Green River Inn, 2480 Sandgate Rd, 05250 802-375-2272
Saxtons River	Three Chimney House, Hartley Hill, 05154 802-869-2524

Shelburne	Elliot House B&B, 2176 Dorset St., 05482 802-985-1412
Shelburne	Inn at Shelburne Farms, 1611 Harbor Rd, 05482 802-985-8498
Shoreham	Cream Hill Farm B&B, PO Box 205, 05770 802-897-2101
Shoreham	Indian Trail Farm, Box 48, 05770 802-897-5292
Shoreham	Quiet Valley B&B, RD 1, Box 175 F, 05770 802-897-7787
Shoreham	Shoreham Inn/Country Store, Rt 74 West, 05770 802-897-5081
Shrewsbury	High Pastures, Cold River Rd, 05738 802-773-2087
South Burlington	Blockhouse Farm B&B, PO Box 2097, 05407
South Burlington	Willow Pond Farm B&B, 20 Cheesefactory Ln, 05403 802-985-8505
South Hero	Paradise Bay B&B, 50 Light House Rd., 05486 802-372-5393
South Pomfret	Rosewood Inn, PO Box 125, 05067 802-457-4485
Springfield	Baker Road Inn, 29 Baker Rd., 05156 802-886-2304
St. Albans	Bayview B&B, RR 3 Box 246, 05478 802-524-5609
St. Albans	Reminisce B&B, PO Box 183, 05478 802-524-3907
Starksboro	Millhouse B&B, PO Box 22, 05487
Stockbridge	The Stockbridge Inn B&B, PO Box 45, 05772 802-746-8165
Stockbridge	The Wild Berry Inn, Rt 100, HCR 65 #23, 05772 802-746-8141
Stowe	Candlelight Cottage, 1186 Pucker St, 05672
Stowe	Edson Hill Manor, 1500 Edson Hill Rd, 05672 802-253-7371
Stowe	Fiddler's Green Inn, 4859 Mountain Rd, 05672 802-253-8124
Stowe	Golden Eagle Resort, PO Box 1090, 05672 802-253-4811
Stowe	Green Mountain Inn, PO Box 60, 05672 802-253-7301
Stowe	Trapp Family Lodge, 42 Trapp Hill Rd., 05672 802-253-8511
Stowe	Walk About Creek Lodge, 199 Edson Hill Rd, 05672 802-253-7354
Stowe	Wood Chip Inn, PO Box 816, 05672 802-253-9080
Strafford	Half Penney Inn, RR 1 Box 263-A, 05072 802-295-6082
Swanton	Heron House B&B, RR 2, Box 174-2, 05488 802-868-7433
Thetford Hill	Fahrenbrae Hilltop Retreat, Box 129, 05074 802-785-4304
Townsend	Boardman House B&B, PO Box 112, 05353 802-365-4086
Townsend	Townsend Country Inn, RR 1, Box 3100, 05353 800-569-1907
Underhill Center	Mansfield View Guest House, PO Box 114, 05490 802-899-4793
Vergennes	Basin Harbor Club, 05491 802-475-2311
Vergennes	Whiteford House, RR 1 Box 1490, 05491 802-758-2704
Vergennes	Woodman Hill House, US Rt 7, RR 2 Box 2501, 05491 802-877-2720
Waitsfield	1824 House Inn, Route 100, Box 159, 05673 802-496-7555
Waitsfield	Inn @ Slide Brook Meadows, RR1, Box 125, 05673
Waitsfield	Inn at the Mad River Barn, PO Box 88, 05673 802-496-3310
Waitsfield	Knoll Farm Country Inn, RFD 1, Box 179, 05673 802-496 3039
Waitsfield	Mad River Inn, PO Box 75, 05673 802-496-7900
Waitsfield	Mountain View Inn, Route 17, RFD Box 69, 05673 802-496-2426
Waitsfield	Weathertop Lodge B&B, Rt 17 RR 1 Box 151, 05673 802-496-4909
Wallingford	The Victorian Inn, 9 N. Main St, 05773 802 446-2099
Wallingford	White Rocks Inn, RR1, Box 297, 05773 802-446-2077
Warren	Golden Lion Riverside Inn, Route 100, 05674 802-496-3084
Warren	Pitcher Inn, Main St, 05674 802-496-6350
Warren	Sugar Lodge, Sugarbush Access, 05674 802-583-3300
Waterbury Center	The Black Locust Inn, Rt 100, Box 715, 05677 802-244-7490
Wells	The Stonebridge Inn, RR 1, Box 1080, 05774 802-287-9849
West Dover	Inn at Sawmill Farm, Box 8 (#100), 05356 802-464-8131
West Dover	The Gray Ghost Inn, PO Box 938, 05356 802-464-2474
West Swanton	High Winds B&B, RD 2, Box 349, 05488 802-868-2521
West Townsend	Windham Hill Inn, RR1 Box 44, 05359 802-874-4702
Whitingham	Candlelight B&B, 3358 Vt Rte 100, 05361 802-368-7826
Whitingham	Whitingham Farm B&B, RR 1 Box 89D, 05361 800-310-2010
Whitingham	Whitingham Inn, PO Box 556, 05361 802-368-2665
Wilmington	Hermitage Inn & Brookbound, PO Box 457, 05363 802-464-3511
Wilmington	Shearer Hill Farm B&B, PO Box 1453, 05363
Wilmington	Weathervane Lodge, 20 Grand Dr, 05363 802-464-5426
Windsor	Burton Farm Lodge B&B, RFD 1 Box 558, 05089 802-484-3300
Wolcott	Golden Maple Inn, PO Box 35, 05680 802-888-6614
Woodstock	The Charleston House, 21 Pleasant St, 05091 802-458-3843
Woodstock	Village Inn of Woodstock, 41 Pleasant St, 05091 802-457-1255
Woodstock	Woodstock House B&B, PO Box 361, 05091 802-457-1758

Virginia ——————————————————————————

Abingdon	Cabin on the River, PO Box 1202, 24210
Abingdon	Inn On Town Creek, PO Box 1745, 24212 540-628-4560
Abingdon	Maplewood Farm B&B, 20004 Cleveland Rd, 24211
Abingdon	Martha Washington Inn, 150 W. Main St, 24210 800-533-1014
Abingdon	Maxwell Manor B&B, 19215 Old Jonesboro Rd, 24211 540-628-3912
Abingdon	Shepherd's Joy, 254 White's Mill Rd, 24210 540-628-3273
Abingdon	Summerfield Inn, 101 E. Valley St, 24210 703-628-5905
Abingdon	Victoria and Albert Inn, 224 Oak Hill Street, 24210 540-676-2797
Abingdon	White Birches, 268 Whites Mill Rd, 24210 540-676-2140
Alberta	Englewood, RR 1, Box 141, 23821 804-949-0111
Aldie	Little River Inn, PO Box 116, 22001 703-327-6742
Alexandria	Black Shutter Inn, 6204 Redwood Ln, 22310

Alta Vista	Castle to Country House, 1010 Main St, 24517 804-369-4911
Amelia	Benita's B&B, 16620 Amelia Ave., 23002 804-561-6321
Amherst	Crumps Mountain Cottage, 2150 Indian Creek Rd, 24521 804-277-5563
Amherst	Fairview B&B, RR 4 Box 117, 24521 804-277-8500
Amissville	Bunree, PO Box 53, 22002 703-937-4133
Arlington	Aurora House B&B, PO Box 25319, 22202 703-549-3415
Arlington	Crystal B&B, 2620 S. Fern St, 22202 703-548-7652
Arlington	Memory House, 6404 N. Washington Blvd, 22205 703-534-4607
Ashland	The Henry Clay Inn, 114 N. Railroad Ave, 23005 804-798-3100
Bedford	Otters Den B&B, Rt 2, Box 160 E, 24523 540-586-2204
Belle Haven	Bayview Waterfront, 35350 Copes Dr, 23306 757-442-6963
Bentonville	Gooney Manor, 5865 Gooney Manor Loop, 22610
Berryville	Battletown Inn, 102 W Main St, 22611 540-955-4100
Berryville	Elmington B&B, PO Box 229, 22611 540-955-1167
Blacksburg	Brush Mountain Inn B&B, 3030 Mt. Tabor Rd, 24060 540-951-7530
Blacksburg	L'Arche B&B, 301 Wall St., 24060 540-951-1808
Blacksburg	Sycamore Tree B&B, PO Box 10937, 24062 540-381-1597
Blackstone	Epes House B&B, 210 College Ave, 23824 804-292-7941
Blackstone	Grey Swann B&B, 615 S Main St., 23824 804-292-3199
Bland	Willow Bend Farm B&B, RR 1, Box 235, 24315 703-688-3719
Boston	Thistle Hill B&B Inn, 5541 Sperryville Pike, 22713 540-987-9142
Bowling Green	Mansion View B&B, PO Box 787, 22427 804-633-2202
Bridgewater	Apple Orchard Farm B&B, PO Box 54, 22812 540-828-2126
Bristol	Glencarin Manor, 224 Old Abingdon Hwy, 24201 540-466-0224
Broadnox	Sherwood Manor Inn, Box 236, 23920
Brookneal	Staunton Hill, RR 2 Box 244B, 24528 804-376-4048
Buchanan	The Berkley House, Route 2, Box 220A, 24066 703-254-2548
Bumpass	Cove Haven B&B, 23 Covenant Way, 23024 540-872-2778
Bumpass	Rockland Farm Retreat, 3609 Lewiston Rd., 23024 703-895-5098
Callao	Strangers in Good Company, PO Box 301, 22435 804-529-5132
Cape Charles	Bay Avenue's Sunset B&B, 108 Bay Ave, 23310 757-331-2424
Cape Charles	Cape Charles House, 645 Tazwell Ave, 23310 757-331-4920
Cape Charles	Chesapeake Charm B&B, 202 Madison Ave, 23310 757-331-2676
Cape Charles	Nottingham Ridge B&B, 28184 Nottingham Ridge, 23310 757-331-1010
Cape Charles	Stillmeadow Inn B&B, 318 Tazewell Ave, 23354 804-442-2431
Cape Charles	Wilson-Lee House B&B, 403 Tazewell Ave, 23310 757-331-1954
Capron	Sandy Hill Farm B&B, 11307 Rivers Mill Rd, 23829 804-658-4381
Castleton	Blue Knoll Farm B&B, 110 Gore Rd, 22716 540-937-5234
Castlewood	Greystone Manor B&B, PO Box 820, 24224
Catawba	B&B of Blackacre Estate, 6694 Blacksburg Rd, 24070 540-384-6941
Catawba	Crosstrails B&B, 5880 Blacksburg Rd, 24070 540-384-8078
Charles City	Belle Air Plantation, 11800 John Tyler Hwy, 23030 804-829-2431
Charles City	Berkeley Plantation, 12602 Harrison Landing, 23030 804-829-6018
Charles City	Colesville Plantation, 9600 John Tyler Memoria, 23030 804-829-6433
Charles City	Evelynton Plantation, 6701 John Tyler Hwy, 23030 804-829-5075
Charles City	Indian Fields Tavern, 9220 John Tyler Highway, 23030 804-829-5004
Charles City	North Bend Plantation B&B, 12200 Weyanoke Rd, 23030 804-829-5176
Charles City	Orange Hill B&B, 18401 The Glebe Lane, 23032 804-829-6453
Charles City	Red Hill, 7500 John Tyler M. Hwy, 23030 804-829-6045
Charles City	Shirley Plantation, 501 Shirley Plantation, 23030 804-829-5121
Charles City	Westover, 7000 Westover Rd, 23030 804-829-2882
Charlottesville	1817 Antique Inn, 1211 W. Main St, 22903 804-979-7353
Charlottesville	Boar's Head Inn, PO Box 5307, 22905 804-296-2181
Charlottesville	Carrsbrook, 313 Goucester Rd, 22901
Charlottesville	Inn at Sugar Hollow Farm, PO Box 5705, 22905 804-823-7086
Charlottesville	Silver Thatch Inn, 3001 Hollymead Dr, 22911 804-978-4686
Charlottesville	Slave Quarters, 611 Preston Place, 22903 804-979-7264
Charlottesville	Sunset Mountain B&B, 3722 Foster's Branch Rd, 22911 804-973-7974
Chatham	Sims-Mitchell House B&B, PO Box 429, 24531 804-432-0595
Chesterfield	Bellmont Manor B&B, 6600 Belmont Rd, 23832 804-745-0106
Chilhowie	Clarkcrest B&B, Star Route Box 60, 24319
Chincoteague	1848 Island Manor House, 4160 Main St, 23336 757-336-5436
Chincoteague	Channel Bass Inn, 6228 Church St, 23336 757-336-6148
Chincoteague	The Inn at Poplar Corner, 4248 Main St., 23336 804-336-6115
Christiansburg	Evergreen, 201 East Main Street, 24073 540-382-7372
Church View	Dragon Run Inn B&B, Rt 17 & 602, 23032 804-758-5719
Clarksville	Winston Oaks B&B, PO Box 606, 23927 804-374-0603
Clifton Forge	Longdale Inn, 6209 Longdale Furnace, 24422 703-862-0892
Colonial Beach	Vernon House, 125 Wilder Ave, 20912 804-224-9464
Columbia	Upper Byrd Farm B&B, 6452 River Rd W, 23038 804-842-2240
Culpeper	Hazel River Inn, 11227 Eggbornsville Rd, 22701 540-937-5854
Dabneys	Bare Castle Farm B&B, Box 122A, 23102
Daleville	Baileywick Farm B&B, 1250 Roanoke Rd, 24083 703-992-2022
Deltaville	River Place-at-Deltaville, PO Box 616, 23043 804-776-9153
Deltaville	Up the Creek B&B, PO Box 438, 23043 804-776-9621
Dilliwyn	Tranquility Farm B&B, Rt 3, Box 174, 23936
Drakes Branch	Brio's School House, PO Box 387, 23937 804-568-2476
Dublin	Bell's B&B, PO Box 405, 24084 800-437-0575

Edinburg	Edinburg Inn B&B Ltd, 218 S Main St, 22824 540-984-8286
Edinburg	Mary's Country Inn, 218 S Main St, 22824 703-984-8286
Elkton	Hilltop B&B, Rt 5 Box 105, 22827 540-298-8056
Elkton	Spotswood Inn, 403 E Rockingham St, 22827
Etlan	Dulaney Hollow at Old Rag, Star Rt 6,Box 215 VB231, 22719 540-923-4470
Ewing	Monte Vista B&B, Rt 2 Box 441, 24248 540-445-4141
Exmore	Martha's Inn B&B, PO Box 606, 23350 757-442-4641
Fancy Gap	The Inn at Orchard Gap, PO Box 355, 24328
Ferrum	Old Spring Farm B&B, 7629 Charity Hwy, 24088 540-930-3404
Fincastle	WoodsEdge Guest Cottage, 2800 Ridge Trail, 24090 540-473-2992
Flint Hill	The School House, PO Box 31, 22627 703-675-3030
Forest	Summer Kitchen, RR 4 Box 538, 24551 804-525-0923
Fredericksburg	Rennaisance Manor B&B, 2247 Courthouse Rd, 22554 540-720-3785
Fredericksburg	Richard Johnston Inn, 711 Caroline St, 22401 540-899-7606
Fredericksburg	Selby House B&B, 226 Princess Anne St, 22401 540-373-7037
Fredericksburg	The Kenmore Inn, 1200 Princess Anne St, 22401 703-371-7622
Front Royal	Chester House Inn, 43 Chester St, 22630 540-635-3937
Front Royal	Fairview House, Rt 2 Box 1240, 22630
Front Royal	Woodward House-Manor Grade, 413 S. Royal Ave, 22630 540-635-7010
Glen Allen	The Virginia Cliffe Inn, 2900 Mountain Rd, 23060 804-266-1661
Gloucester	Airville Plantation, 6423 T C Walker Rd, 23061 804-694-0287
Gloucester	Willows, 5344 Roanes Wharf Rd., 23061 804-693-4066
Goodview	Stone Manor B&B, RR 2 Box 268, 24095 540-297-1414
Gordonsville	Norfields Farm B&B, RR 1, Box 477, 22942 703-832-5939
Gordonsville	Rabbit Run B&B, 305 N. High St, 22942 540-832-2892
Gordonsville	Rocklands, 17439 Rocklands Dr, 22942
Hampton	Victoria House, 4501 Victoria Blvd, 23669 757-722-2658
Hardyville	Rivers Rise B&B, PO Box 18, 23070 804-776-7521
Harrisonburg	Joshua Wilton House Inn, 412 S. Main St, 22801 703-434-4464
Harrisonburg	Kingsway B&B, 3955 Singers Glen Rd, 22802 540-867-9696
Hillsville	Bray's Manor B&B Inn, PO Box 385, 24343 703-728-7901
Hot Springs	King's Victorian Inn, RR 2, Box 622, 24445 703-839-3134
Hot Springs	Vine Cottage Inn, PO Box 918, 24445 540-839-2422
Independence	River View B&B, PO Box 686, 24348 800-841-6628
Irvington	Tides Inn, Box 480, 22480 804-438-5000
Jamilton	Stonegate B&B, PO Box 100, 22068 703-338-9519
Keswick	Keswick Hall, 701 Club Dr, 22947 804-979 3440
Keswick	Oceancrest At Chatham, 3499 Devon Pnes, 22947
Lancaster	Inn at Levelfields, PO Box 216, 22503 804-435-6887
Lexington	Asherowe, 314 S. Jefferson St, 24450 703-463-4219
Lexington	Fassifern B&B, Route 5, Box 87, 24450 703-463-1013
Lexington	Inn at Union Run, Union Run Rd, 24450 540-463-9715
Lexington	Laughing Place Farm, 1538 Blue Grass Trail, 24450 540-463-3555
Lexington	Seven Hills Inn, 408 S. Main St, 24450 540-463-4715
Lexington	The Keep B&B, 116 Lee Ave, 24450 540-463-3560
Lincoln	Creek Crossing Farm, PO Box 18, 22078
Locust Dale	Crooked Run Farm, HC 5 Box 426A, 22948 540-547-3027
Locust Dale	Inn at Meander Plantation, HCR 5, Box 460A, 22948 540-672-4912
Louisa	Ginger Hill B&B, Rt. 5 Box 33E, 23093 540-967-3260
Louisa	Whistle Stop B&B, PO Box 1609, 23093 540-967-2911
Luray	Creekside A Guest Cottage, 4632 Old Forge Rd, 22835 540-743-5040
Luray	Locust Grove Inn, 1456 N Egypt Bend Rd, 22835 540-743-1804
Luray	Shenandoah Countryside, 211 Somers Rd, 22835 540-743-6434
Luray	Spring Farm B&B, 13 Wallace Ave, 22835 703-743-4701
Luray	Spruce Mountain Chalet, Rt 3 Box 455, 22835 540-743-1582
Luray	The Mayview B&B, 439 Mechanic St., 22835 540-743-7921
Lynchburg	1880's Madison House, 413 Madison St, 24504 804-528-1503
Lynchburg	Once Upon a Time B&B, 1102 Harrison St., 24504 804-845-3561
Madison	Shenandoah Springs, HC 6, Box 122, 22727 703-923-4300
Madison Heights	Winridge B&B, 116 Winridge Dr, 24572 804-384-7220
Manassas	Bennett House B&B, 9252 Bennett Dr, 20110 703-368-6121
Manassas	Sunrise Hill Farm B&B, 5590 Old Farm Lane, 22110 703-754-8309
McGaheysville	Shenandoah Valley Farm, Route 1, Box 142, 22840 703-289-5402
McLean	Evans Farm Inn, 1696 Chain Bridge Rd, 22101 703-356-8000
Middleburg	Middleburg Country Inn, PO Box 2065, 22117 703-687-6082
Middleburg	Poor House Farm B&B, PO Box 1316, 22117
Middleburg	The Longbarn, PO Box 208, 20118 540-687-4137
Middleburg	Welbourne, 22314 Welbourne Rd, 20117 540-687-3201
Midlothian	Uli Manor, 14042 Southshore Rd, 23112 804-739-9817
Millboro	Fort Lewis Lodge, HCR 3, Box 21A, 24460 540-925-2314
Mineral	Littlepage Inn, 15701 Monrovia Rd, 23117 800-248-1803
Monroe	Cabin at Somewhere Away, 613 Wilderness Creek Rd, 24574 804-299-5345
Monroe	St. Moor House, RR 1, Box 136, 24574 804-929-8228
Monterey	Highland Inn, PO Box 40, 24465 540-468-2143
Montross	Porterville B&B, 14201 King's Hwy, 22520 804-493-9394
Mount Crawford	Pumpkin House Inn, Ltd., Route 2, Box 155, 22841 703-434-6963
Mount Jackson	Widow Kip's Country Inn, 355 Orchard Dr, 22842 540-477-2400
Natural Bridge	Burger's Country Inn, RR 2, Box 564, 24578 703-291-2464

Nellysford	Acorn Inn, PO Box 431, 22958 804-361-9357
New Church	Garden & The Sea Inn, PO Box 275, 23415 804-824-0672
New Market	Red Shutter Farmhouse, RR 1, Box 376, 22844 703-740-4281
New Market	Touch of Country, 9329 Congress St, 22844 540-740-8030
Newport	Riverbend Farm B&B, RR 2 Box 561B, 24128 540-544-7849
Occoquan	Mary Josephine Ball B&B, PO Box 58, 22125
Onancock	76 Market St. B&B, 76 Market St, 23417 757-787-7600
Onancock	Colonial Manor Inn, 84 Market St, 23417 757-787-3521
Onancock	Montrose House B&B, 20494 Market St, 23417 757-787-7088
Orange	Holladay House, 155 W. Main, 22960 800-358-4422
Orange	Mayhurst Inn, 12460 Mayhurst Ln, 22960 540-672-5597
Orange	Shadows B&B Inn, Route 1, Box 535, 22960 703-672-5057
Orange	Willow Grove Inn, 9478 James Madison Hwy, 22960 800-949-1778
Paeonian Spring	Cornerstone B&B, RR 1, Box 82C, 22129 703-882-3722
Palmyra	Danscot House, PO Box 157, 22963 804-589-1977
Palmyra	Palmer Country Manor, Rt. 2, Box 1390, 22963 804-589-1300
Pamplin	Madisonville Farm Inn, HC 1 Box 35, 23958 804-248-9020
Pamplin	Sleepy Lamb B&B, HCR 1, Box 34, 23958 804-248-6289
Paris	Ashby Inn & Restaurant, 692 Federal St, 22130 540-592-3900
Pearisburg	Linda Lorraine's-Pearisburg, 1409 Cabot Dr., 24134 703-921-2069
Petersburg	Folly Castle B&B, 323 W Washington St, 23803 804-861-3558
Petersburg	La Villa Romaine B&B, 29 S Market St, 23803 804-861-2285
Petersburg	Mayfield Inn, PO Box 2265, 23804 804-861-6775
Petersburg	Snobirds Inn Route B&B, 405 High St, 23803 804-733-0505
Pilot	Ponds of Bethlehem B&B, 4033 Bethlehem Church, 24138 540-745-4116
Pocahontas	Laurel Inn B&B, 386-387 W Water St, 24635
Port Haywood	Tabb's Creek B&B, PO Box 219, 23138 804-725-5136
Portsmouth	Olde Towne Inn, 420 Middle St, 23704 757-397-5462
Pounding Mill	Bedrock Inn, PO Box 105, 24637 540-963-9412
Pounding Mill	Cuz's Cabins and Resort, US Rt 460, 24637 540-964-9014
Pratts	Colvin Hall B&B, HC 3, Box 30G, 22731 703-948-6211
Prospect	Brooklyn Plantation, RR 1 Box 341, 23960 804-574-6853
Pulaski	Count Pulaski B&B & Garden, 821 N Jefferson Ave, 24301 540-980-1163
Pungoteague	Evergreen Inn, PO Box 102, 23422 804-442-3375
Purcellville	The Log House, 13161 Harpers Ferry Rd, 20132 540-668-9003
Raphine	Oak Spring Farm & Vineyard, RR 1, Box 356, 24472 703-377-2398
Raphine	Willow Pond Farm Cntry Hse, 137 Pisgah Rd, 24472 540-348-1310
Reedville	Cedar Grove B&B Inn, 2743 Fleeton Rd, 22539 804-453-3915
Reedville	Gables Museum House B&B, PO Box 148, 22539 804-453-5209
Reedville	Magnolia Tree B&B, Rt 1, Box 26, 22539 804-453-4720
Reedville	The Morris House, 826 Main St, 22539 804-453-7016
Richmond	Abbie Hill Guest Lodging, 8106 E Greystone Circle, 23229
Richmond	Mr. Patrick Henry's Inn, 2300 E. Broad St, 23223 804-644-1322
Richmond	The William Catlin House, 2304 E. Broad St, 23223 804-780-3746
Richmond	West-Bocock House, 1107 Grove Ave, 23220 804-358-6174
Roanoke	The Mary Bladon House B&B, 381 Washington Ave SW, 24016 540-344-5361
Rockville	Woodlawn B&B, 2211 Wiltshire Rd, 23146 804-749-3759
Rocky Mount	The Claiborne House, 119 Claiborne Ave, 24151 703-483-4616
Scottsville	Chester B&B, 243 James River Rd, 24590 804-286-3960
Scottsville	Deerfield B&B, RR 3 Box 573, 24590 804-286-6306
Smith Mountain	Manor at Taylor's Store, PO Box 510, 24184 540-721-3951
Smithfield	Four Square Plantation, 13357 Four Square Rd, 23430 757-365-0749
Smithfield	Smithfield Inn, 112 Main St., 23430 757-357-1752
Sperryville	Belle Meade B&B, 353 F.T. Valley Rd, 22740
Sperryville	Sharp Rock Farm B&B, 5 Sharp Rock Rd, 22740 540-987-8020
Spotsylvania	Roxbury Mill B&B, 6908 Roxbury Mill Rd, 22553 540-582-6611
Springfield	Mischler House, 7430 Spring Tree Dr, 22153
Stafford	Country Gallery B&B, 151 Barrett Heights Rd, 22554
Stafford	Courthouse Road B&B, 2247 Courthouse Rd, 22554 540-720-3785
Stanardsville	The Lafayette Hotel, 146 Main St, 22973 804-985-6345
Stanley	Milton House, PO Box 366, 22851 540-778-2495
Stanley	Wisteria B&B, 1126 Marksville Rd, 22851 540-778-3347
Staunton	Hilltop House, 1810 Springhill Rd, 24401 540-886-0042
Staunton	Kenwood, 235 E. Beverly St, 24401 540-886-0524
Staunton	Montclair B&B, 320 N New St, 24401 540-885-8832
Strasburg	Sonner House B&B, 208 W Queen St, 22657 540-465-4712
Surrey	Seward House Inn, PO Box 352, 23883 804-294-3810
Syria	Graves' Mountain Lodge, Rte. 670, 22743 540-923-4231
Tappanannock	Little Greenway B&B, PO Box 1387, 22560 804-443-5747
Tazewell	Van Dyke's B&B, PO Box 265, 24651 540-988-4821
Trevilians	Prospect Hill Plantation, 2887 Poindexter Rd, 23093 540-967-2574
Troutdale	Fox Hill Inn, PO Box 88, 24378 703-677-3313
Upperville	1763 Inn, PO Box 400, 20185 703-592-3848
Urbanna	Atherston Hall B&B, 250 Prince George St, 23175 804-758-2809
Urbanna	Hewick Plantation, PO Box 82, 23175 804-758-4214
Urbanna	The Duck Farm Inn, PO Box 787, 23175 804-758-5685
Vesuvius	Sugar Tree Inn, PO Box 548, 24483 703-377-2197
Virginia Beach	Angie's Guest Cottage, 302 - 24th St, 23451 757-428-4690

Virginia Beach	Barclay Cottage, 400 16th St, 23451 804-422-1956
Wachapreague	Hart's Harbor House B&B, PO Box 182, 23480 804-787-4848
Warm Springs	Hidden Valley B&B, PO Box 53, 24484 540-839-3178
Washington	Heritage House B&B, PO Box 427, 22747 540-675-3207
Washington	Middleton, PO Box 254, 22747 540-675-2020
Washington	Sunset Hills Farm, 105 Christmas Tree Ln, 22747 540-987-8804
Washington	Sycamore Hill House, 1100 Menefee Mt Ln, 22747 703-675-3046
Washington	The Foster-Harris House, PO Box 333, 22747 540-675-3757
Waynesboro	Belle Hearth B&B, 320 S Wayne Ave, 22980 540-943-1910
Williamsburg	Alice Person House, 616 Richmond Rd., 23185 757-220-9263
Williamsburg	Candlewick B&B, 800 Jamestown Rd, 23185 757-253-8693
Williamsburg	Hite's B&B, 704 Monumental Ave., 23185 757-229-4814
Williamsburg	Holland's Lodge, 601 Richmond Rd, 23185 804-253-6476
Williamsburg	Magnolia Manor, 700 Richmond Rd, 23185 757-220-9600
Williamsburg	The Aldrich House B&B, 505 Capitol Ct, 23185 757-229-5422
Williamsburg	The Greenwoode Inn, 104 Woodmont Pl, 23188 804-566-8800
Williamsburg	The Homestay B&B, 517 Richmond Rd, 23185 804-229-7468
Williamsburg	War Hill Inn, 4560 Long Hill Rd, 23188 757-565-0248
Williamsburg	White House on Washington, 111 Washington St., 23185 757-229-4495
Williamsburg	Williamsburg Manor B&B, 600 Richmond Rd, 23185 757-220-8011
Willis Wharf	Ballard House B&B, 12527 Ballard Dr, 23486
Wolftown	Tax Hollow Inn, PO Box 213, 22748
Woodstock	Azalea House B&B, 551 S Main St, 22664 540-459-3500
Woodstock	Country Fare B&B, 768 Spring Pkwy, 22664 703-459-4828
Woodstock	River'd Inn, 1972 Artz Rd, 22664 540-459-5369
Wytheville	Boxwood Inn B&B, 460 E. Main St., 24382 540-228-8911
Yorktown	York River Inn B&B, 209 Ambler St, 23690 757-887-8800

Washington

Aberdeen	Aberdeen Mansion Inn B&B, 807 N M St., 98520 360-533-7079
Aberdeen	Anchor House Book & Bed, 102 W 11th St, 98520 360-532-2099
Anacortes	B&B at The Channel House, 2902 Oakes Ave, 98221
Anacortes	Blue Rose B&B, 1811 9th St, 98221
Anacortes	Dutch Treat House, 1220 31st St, 98221 206-293-8154
Anacortes	Hasty Pudding House B&B, 1312 8th St, 98221 360-293-5773
Anacortes	Islands Motel B&B, 3401 Commercial Ave., 98221 360-293-4644
Anacortes	Outlook B&B, 608 H Ave, 98221 360-293-3505
Anacortes	Town Cottages, 1219 18th St #2, 98221
Anderson Island	Anderson House at Oco Bay, 12024 Eckenstam Johnson, 98303 206-884-4088
Anderson Island	Hideaway House B&B, 11422 Leschi Circle, 98303 253-884-4179
Arlington	Mt. Higgins House, 29805 SR 530 NE, 98223 360-435-8703
Ashford	Growly Bear B&B, 37311 SR 706, 98304 360-569-2339
Ashford	The Hershey Homestead, 33514 Mt Tahema Canyon, 98304 360-569-2897
Auburn	Blomeen House B&B, 324 B Street NE, 98002 253-939-3088
Bainbridge Island	Bainbridge House B&B, 11301 Logg Rd, NF, 98110 206-842-1599
Bainbridge Island	Monarch Manor Estates, 7656 Yeomalt Point Dr, 98110 206-780-0112
Bainbridge Island	Our Country Haus B&B, 13718 Ellingsen Rd NE, 98110 206-842-8425
Bainbridge Island	Rockaway Beach Guest Home, 5032 Rockaway Beach Rd, 98110 206-780-9427
Battle Ground	Fir 'N' Fin B&B, PO Box 93, 98604 360-686-3064
Belfair	Country Garden Inn, 2790 NE Old Belfair Hwy, 98528 360-275-3683
Bellevue	Bellevue B&B, 830 - 100th Ave SE, 98004 425-453-1048
Bellevue	Bridle Trails B&B, 2750 122 Place, NE, 98005 425-861-0700
Bellevue	Petersen B&B, 10228 SE 8th St, 98004 425-454-9334
Bellingham	Big Trees B&B, 4840 Fremont St., 98226 360-647-2850
Bellingham	Loganita By the Sea, 2863 Seaview Cr, 98225 360-758-2651
Bellingham	North Garden Inn, 1014 N. Garden, 98225 360-671-7828
Benton City	Red Mountain B&B, 12911 E SR 224, 99320 509-558-1900
Bow	Alice Bay B&B, 982 Scott Rd, 98232
Bow	Samish Point by the Bay, 447 Samish Point Rd, 98232 360-766-6610
Bremerton	Illahee Manor B&B, 6680 Illahee Rd. NE, 98311 360-698-7555
Bremerton	Jigsaw Puzzle Inn, 2038 Taft Ave, 98312 360-373-3250
Burton	Back Bay Inn, 24007 Vashon Hwy SW, 98070 206-463-5355
Cashmere	Cashmere Country Inn, 5801 Pioneer Dr, 98815 509-782-4212
Cathlamet	Bradley House, PO Box 35, 98612 360-795-3030
Cathlamet	Country Keeper B&B Inn,The, 61 Main St, 98612 206-795-3030
Cathlamet	Redfern Farm, 277 Cross Dike Rd., 98612 360-849-4108
Cathlamet	The Gallery B&B, Little Cape Horn, 98612 360-425-7395
Chelan	Captain's Quarters B&B, Rt 1 Box 86F, 98816
Chelan	Highland Guest House, PO Box 2089, 98816 509-682-2892
Clarkston	Cliff House B&B, 1227 Westlake Dr., 99403 509-758-1267
Clarkston	Highland House B&B, 707 Highland Ave, 99403
Cle Elum	Hidden Valley Guest Ranch, 3942 Hidden Valley Rd, 98922 800-526-9269
Clinton	Home by the Sea, 2388 E Sunlight Beach R, 98236 206-221-2964
Clinton	Kittleson Cove B&B, PO Box 396, 98236 206-221-2734
Clinton	Room With A View, 6369 S Bayview Rd., 98236 360-321-6264
Clinton	Sweetwater Cottage, 6111 S Cultus Bay Rd., 98236 360-341-1604
Conway	South Fork Moorage Housebo, 2187 Mann Rd., 98238 360-445-4803

Cougar	Monfort's B&B, 132 Cougar Rd., 98616 360-238-5229
Coulee City	The Main Stay, 110 W. Main, 99115 509-632-5687
Coulee Dam	Four Winds Guest House B&B, 301 Lincoln Ave., 99116 509-633-3146
Coupeville	Anchorage Inn, PO Box 673, 98239 360-678-5581
Coupeville	Colonel Crockett Farm Inn, 1012 S. Fort Casey Rd, 98239 206-678-3711
Coupeville	Compass Rose, 508 S Main St., 98239 360-678-5318
Coupeville	Cottage on the Cove, PO Box 592, 98239 360-678-0600
Coupeville	Garden Isle Guest Cottages, PO Box 1305, 98239 360-678-5641
Coupeville	Old Morris Farm B&B, 105 W Morris Rd., 98239 360-678-6586
Coupeville	The Inn at Penn Cove, PO Box 85, 98239 360-678-8000
Darrington	Hemlock Hills B&B, PO Box 491, 98241 206-436-1274
Darrington	Sauk River Farm B&B, 32629 St Rt 530 NE, 98241
Dayton	The Purple House B&B, 415 E Clay St, 99328 509-382-3159
Dayton	Weinhard Hotel, 235 E Main St, 99328
Deer Park	Love's Victorian B&B, 31317 N. Cedar Rd, 99006 509-276-6939
Deming	The Guest House, 5723 Schornbush Rd., 98244 360-592-2343
Eastsound	Old Trout Inn, Rt 1 Box 45A, 98245 360-376-8282
Eastsound	Outlook Inn on Orcas Isle, Box 210, 98245 360-376-2200
Eastsound	West Sound Cottage, RR 1, Box 41G, 98245 360-376-2172
Eastsound	Whale Watch House, PO Box 729, 98245 360-376-4793
Eatonville	Mill Town Manor B&B, PO Box 1743, 98328 360-832-6506
Edmonds	Aardvark House, 7219 Lake Ballinger Way, 98026 425-778-7866
Edmonds	Driftwood Lane B&B, 724 Driftwood Ln, 98020 425-776-2686
Edmonds	Harrison House, 210 Sunset Ave, 98020 425-776-4748
Edmonds	The Maple Tree, 18313 Olympic View Dr, 98020 425-774-8420
Ellensburg	The Treehouse B&B, 1414 North Cora St, 98926 509-925-4620
Enumclaw	White Rose Inn, 1610 Griffin Ave, 98022 206-825-7194
Ephrata	Ivy Chapel Inn B&B, 164 D St SW, 98823
Federal Way	Killarney Cove B&B, 35334 28th Ave S, 98003 253-838-4595
Ferndale	Anderson House B&B, 4461 Sucia Dr, 98248 206-384-3450
Ferndale	Slater Heritage House, 1371 W Axton Rd, 98248
Forks	Huckleberry Lodge B&B, 1171 Big Pine Way, 98331 360-374-6008
Forks	Manitou Lodge, PO Box 600, 98331 206-374-6295
Fox Island	Beachside B&B, 679 Kamus Dr., 98333 253-549-2524
Freeland	Bush Point Wharf B&B, PO Box 1042, 98249 360-331-0405
Freeland	Seaside Cottage, PO Box 970, 98249 360-331-8455
Freeland	Willow Pond B&B, 2219 Lancaster Rd, 98249 360-331-4945
Friday Harbor	Arbutus Lodge, 1827 Westside Rd. N, 98250 360-378-3573
Friday Harbor	Argyle House, PO Box 2569, 98250 360-378-4084
Friday Harbor	Blair House B&B, 345 Blair Ave, 98250 206-378-5907
Friday Harbor	Duffy House B&B Inn, 760 Pear Point Rd, 98250 360-378-5604
Friday Harbor	Friday's Historical Inn, PO Box 2023, 98250 360-378-5848
Friday Harbor	Halvorsen House B&B, 1165 Halvorsen Rd, 98250 360-378-2707
Friday Harbor	Harrison House Suites, 235 C St, 98250 360-378-2270
Friday Harbor	Mariella Inn & Cottages, PO Box 2625, 98250 206-378-6868
Friday Harbor	Panacea B&B, PO Box 2983, 98250 360-378-3757
Friday Harbor	Roche Harbor Resort, PO Box 4001, 98250 206-378-2155
Friday Harbor	San Juan Inn, PO Box 776, 98250 360-378-2070
Friday Harbor	States Inn, 2039 W. Valley Rd, 98250 360-378-6240
Friday Harbor	Tower House, 1230 Little Rd, 98250 206-378-5464
Friday Harbor	Trumpeter Inn, 420 Trumpeter Inn, 98250 800-826-7926
Friday Harbor	Wharfside B&B, PO Box 1212, 98250 206-378-5661
Gig Harbor	Angel on the Lake B&B, 10602 70th Ave NW, 98332
Gig Harbor	Cottage on the Pier B&B, 7207 120th St NW, 98332 206-857-2250
Gig Harbor	No Cabbages B&B, 7712 Goodman Dr. NW, 98332 206-858-7797
Gig Harbor	Rosedale B&B, 7714 Ray Nash Dr. NW, 98332 206-851-5420
Gig Harbor	The Fountain's B&B, 926 120 St NW, 98332 253-851-6262
Gig Harbor	The Pillars, 6606 Soundview Dr, 98335
Glacier	Mt Baker B&B, 9447 Mt Baker Hwy, 98244 360-599-2299
Glenwood	Flying L Ranch Inn, 25 Flying L Ln, 98619 509-364-3488
Goose Prairie	The Hopkinson House, 8391 Bumping River Rd, 98929 509-454-9431
Graham	Country House B&B, 25421 99th Ave Court E, 98338 206-846-1889
Grandview	Cozy Rose B&B, 1220 Forsell Rd, 98930 509-882-4669
Granite Falls	Monte Cristo B&B, 32410 Mt. Loop Hwy, 98252 360-691-4851
Hoquiam	Lytle House B&B, 509 Chenault Ave, 98550
Ilwaco	Chick-a-Dee Inn, PO Box 922, 98624 360-642-8686
Ilwaco	Kola House B&B, PO Box 646, 98624
Index	Wild Lily Guest Cabins, PO Box 313, 98256 360-793-2103
Issaquah	The Country Inn, 685 NW Juniper St, 98027
Kelso	Longfellow House B&B Cott., 203 Williams Finney Rd, 98626 360-423-4545
Kent	Victorian Gardens 1888 B&B, 9621 S 200th St, 98031 253-850-1776
Kettle Falls	My Parent's Estate, 719 Hwy 295, 99141
La Conner	Hotel Planter, PO Box 702, 98257
La Conner	La Conner Country Inn, PO Box 573, 98257 360-466-3101
La Conner	Rainbow Inn B&B, PO Box 15, 98257 360-466-4578
La Conner	Ridgeway Farm B&B, PO Box 475, 98257 360-428-8068
La Conner	The Wild Iris, PO Box 696, 98257
Lakebay	Ransom's Pond Ostrich Farm, 3915 Mahnke Rd., 98351 253-884-5666

Lakewood	Thornewood Castle Inn, 8601 N Thorne Lane SW, 98498 253-589-9052
Langley	Cristy's Country Inn, 2891 E. Meinhold Rd, 98260 360-321-1815
Langley	Drake's Landing, PO Box 613, 98260 360-221-3999
Langley	Edgecliff Romantic Cottage, PO Box 758, 98260 360-221-8857
Langley	Fox Spit Farm, 3527 S Fox Spit Rd., 98260 360-730-1337
Langley	Lone Lake Cottage & Bkfst., 5206 S. Bayview Rd, 98260 360-321-5325
Langley	Maxwelton Manor, 5278 S Maxwelton Rd., 98260 360-221-5199
Langley	Primrose Path Cottage, 3191 E. Harbor Rd., 98260 360-730-3722
Langley	The Whidbey Inn, PO Box 156, 98260 360-221-7115
Langley	Twickenham House Inn, 5023 Langley Rd, 98260
Langley	Whispering Woods Farm, 5575 S Langley Rd., 98260 360-221-1007
Leavenworth	Alpenrose Inn, 500 Alpen Pl., 98826 509-548-3000
Leavenworth	Bavarian Meadows B&B, 11097 Eagle Creek Rd, 98826 509-548-4449
Leavenworth	Bosch Garten B&B, 9846 Dye Rd., 98826 509-548-6900
Leavenworth	Cougar Inn, 16840 Fir Dr., 98826 509-763-3354
Leavenworth	Featherwinds Farm B&B, 17033 River Rd, 98826
Leavenworth	Haus Lorelei B&B, 347 Division St, 98826 509-548-5726
Leavenworth	Haus Rohrbach Pension, 12882 Ranger Rd, 98826 509-548-7024
Leavenworth	Hotel Pension Anna, PO Box 127, 98826 509-548-6273
Leavenworth	Leirvangen B&B, 7586 Icicle Rd, 98826
Leavenworth	Mountain Home Lodge, PO Box 687, 98826 509-548-7077
Leavenworth	Nelson's Creekside, 15966 Chumstick Hwy, 98826 509-548-8102
Leavenworth	Phippen's B&B, 10285 Ski Hill Dr, 98826 800-666-9806
Leavenworth	Pine River Ranch, 19668 Highway 207, 98826 509-763-3959
Long Beach	Land's End B&B, PO Box 1199, 98631 360-642-8268
Long Beach	Scandinavian Gardens Inn, 1610 California Ave SW, 98631 206-642-8877
Lopez Island	Edenwild Inn, PO Box 271, 98261 206-468-3238
Lopez Island	Inn at Swifts Bay, Route 2, Box 3402, 98261 360-468-3636
Lummi Island	The Willows Inn, 2579 West Shore Dr, 98262 360-758-2620
Lummi Island	West Shore Farm B&B, 2781 W. Shore Dr, 98262 206-758-2600
Lynden	Century House B&B, 401 S. B.C. Ave, 98264 206-354-2439
Lynden	Dutch Village Inn, 655 Front St. #7, 98264 360-354-4440
Manson	Hubbard House B&B, PO Box 348, 98831 509-687-3058
Manson	Windover House B&B, 231 Division St, 98831
Maple Falls	Yodeler Inn, 7485 Mt. Baker Hwy, 98266 206-599-2156
Marysville	Equinox B&B, 13522 12th Ave. NW, 98271 360-652-1198
Mazama	Freestone Inn, 17798 Hwy 20, 98833 509-996-3906
Mazama	Lost River Bess' B&B, 98 Lost River Rd, 98833 509-996-2457
Mercer Island	Lake View B&B, 4220 Crestwood Pl, 98040 206-230-8214
Montesano	Sylvan Haus B&B, 417 Wilder Hill Ln, 98563 206-249-3453
Montesano	The Abel House B&B Inn, 117 Fleet St, S, 98563 206-249-6002
Morton	St. Helens Manorhouse, 7476 Hwy 12, 98356 206-498-5243
Mount Vernon	Fulton House B&B, 420 E Fulton St, 98273
Mount Vernon	Ridgeway Farm B&B, 14914 McLean Rd, 98273 360-428-8068
Mount Vernon	The Parsonage on Pleasant, 1754 Chilberg Rd., 98273 360-466-1754
Mount Vernon	Whispering Firs B&B, 1957 Kanako Lane, 98273
Mukilteo	McNab-Hogland House B&B, 917 Webster St., 98275 425-742-7639
Nahcotta	Our House in Nahcotta B&B, PO Box 33, 98637
North Bend	Roaring River B&B, 46715 SE 129th St, 98045 877-627-4647
North Bend	Twin Peaks B&B, 13308 409th Ave, SE, 98045 425-888-4083
Oak Harbor	Harbor Pointe B&B, 720 W Bonnie View Acres, 98277
Oak Harbor	North Island B&B, 1589 N West Beach Rd, 98277 360-675-7080
Oak Harbor	The Victorian Rose, 438 E Sea Breeze Way, 98277
Ocean Park	Caswells on the Bay, 25204 Sandridge Rd., 98640 360-665-6535
Olalla	Child's House B&B, 8331 SE Willock Rd, 98359 253-857-4252
Olga	Buck Bay Farm B&B, Star Route Box 45, 98279 360-376-2908
Olga	Sand Dollar Inn, Star Route Box 10, 98279 206-376-5696
Olympia	Britt's Place, 4301 Waldrick Rd, SE, 98501 206-264-2764
Olympia	Harbinger Inn B&B, 1136 East Bay Dr, 98506 360-754-0389
Olympia	The Cinnamon Rabbit B&B, 1304 7th Ave. W, 98502 360-357-5520
Orcas	Chestnut Hill Inn B&B, PO Box 213, 98280 360-376-5157
Orcas	Orcas Hotel, PO Box 155, 98280 206-376-4300
Orcas	WindSong B&B, PO Box 32, 98280 360-376-2500
Orcas Island	Spring Bay in Olga, PO Box 97, 98279 206-376-5531
Peshastin	Lietz B&B, PO Box 234, 98847
Peshastin	Mount Valley Vista, PO Box 476, 98847
Point Roberts	Cedar House Inn, 1534 Gulf Rd, 98281
Port Angeles	Anniken's B&B, 214 East Whidbey Ave, 98362 206-457-6177
Port Angeles	Bavarian Inn B&B, 1126 E 7th, 98362 360-457-4098
Port Angeles	Clark's Harbor View B&B, 1426 W 4th St, 98363
Port Angeles	Country Cottage, 624 Billy Smith Rd., 98362 360-452-7974
Port Angeles	Klahhane B&B, 1203 E 7th St, 98362 360-417-0260
Port Angeles	Maple Rose Inn, 112 Reservoir Rd, 98362
Port Angeles	Our House B&B, 218 Whidbey Ave, 98362 800-882-9051
Port Angeles	The Haven B&B, 1206 W 10th St, 98363 360-452-6373
Port Angeles	Tudor Inn B&B, 1108 S Oak, 98362 360-452-3138
Port Ludlow	Inn at Ludlow Bay, 1 Heron Rd., 98365 360-437-0411
Port Ludlow	Nantucket Manor, 941 Shine Rd., 98365 360-437-2676

Port Orchard	"Reflections" - A B&B Inn, 3878 Reflection Ln, E, 98366 360-871-5582
Port Orchard	Laurel Inn, 7914 Beach Dr. E, 98366 360-769-9544
Port Orchard	Northwest Interlude, 3377 Sarann Ave E, 98366 360-871-4676
Port Orchard	Reflections - A B&B Inn, 3878 Reflection Lane E, 98366 360-871-5582
Port Townsend	Annapurna Inn, 538 Adams St, 98368 360-385-2909
Port Townsend	Baker House, 905 Franklin St, 98368 360-385-6673
Port Townsend	Chanticleer Inn, 1208 Franklin St, 98368
Port Townsend	Holly Hill House B&B, 611 Polk Street, 98368 360-385-5619
Port Townsend	Lizzie's Victorian B&B, 731 Pierce, 98368 360-385-4168
Port Townsend	Manresa Castle Hotel, PO Box 564, 98368 206-385-5750
Port Townsend	Quimper Inn, 1306 Franklin St, 98368 360-385-1060
Port Townsend	The English Inn, 718 "F" St, 98368 206-385-5302
Poulsbo	Agate Pass Waterfront B&B, 16045 Hwy 305, 98370 206-842-1632
Poulsbo	Edgewater Beach B&B, 26818 Edgewater Blvd., 98370 360-779-2525
Poulsbo	Foxbridge B&B, 30680 Hwy 3 NE, 98370 360-598-5599
Poulsbo	Solliden Guest House, 17128 Lemolo Shore Dr, 98370 206-779-3969
Poulsbo	The Murphy House B&B, PO Box 1960, 98370 360-799-1600
Pullman	Ash Street House B&B, 315 NE Ash St, 99163 509-332-3638
Pullman	Country B&B, Rt 2 Box 666, 99163
Pullman	Montana Hotel B&B, 1810 NW Turner Dr, 99163
Puyallup	Tayberry Victorian Cottage, 7406 80th St East, 98371 253-848-4594
Quilcene	Quilcene Hotel, PO Box 129, 89376 360-765-3447
Raymond	Riverview Inn B&B, 544 Ballentine St, 98577 360-942-5271
Redmond	Lilac Lea Christian B&B, 21008 NE 117th St, 98053 425-861-1898
Renton	Edgewood Inn, 401 SW Langston Rd, 98055
Renton	Holly Hedge House B&B, 908 Grant Ave S, 98055 425-226-2555
Renton	Wallin's Hilltop B&B, 16545 119th Ave SE, 98058
Republic	K-Diamond-K Ranch, 404 Hwy 21, 99166
Ritzville	Surrey House, 301 W Main Ave, 99169 509-962-9853
Ritzville	The Portico Victorian B&B, 502 S. Adams St, 99169 509-659-0800
Rockford	Rockcreek Manor & Vineyard, PO Box 10, 99030 509-291-4008
Roslyn	Roslyn B&B, PO Box 736, 98005 206-453-1356
Salkum	The Shepherd's Inn B&B, 168 Autumn Heights Dr., 98582 360-985-2434
Seabeck	Summer Song B&B, 682 Seabeck Holly Rd NW, 98380 206-830-5089
Seattle	Beech Tree Manor, 1405 Queen Anne Ave N, 98109 206-281-7037
Seattle	Bellevue Place, 1111 Bellevue Place E, 98102 206-325-9253
Seattle	Birch Bay B&B, 1618 E Lynn St, 98112 206-325-3500
Seattle	Blue Willow B&B, 213 W Comstrock St., 98119 206-284-4240
Seattle	Capitol Hill Inn, 1713 Belmont Ave, 98122 206-323-1955
Seattle	Chambered Nautilus B&B Inn, 5005 22nd Ave NE, 98105 206-522-2536
Seattle	Dibble House B&B, 7301 Dibble Ave NW, 98117 206-783-0320
Seattle	Gaslight Inn, 1727 15th Ave, 98122 206-325-3654
Seattle	Hill House B&B, 1113 E. John St, 98102 206-720-7161
Seattle	La Paloma B&B, 2113 13th Ave, 98144 206-323-1283
Seattle	Pensione Nichols, 1923 First Ave, 98101 206-441-7125
Seattle	Queen Anne Hill B&B, 1835 7th West, 98119 206-284-9779
Seattle	Roberta's B&B, 1147 16 Ave E, 98112 206-329-3326
Seattle	Seattle B&B, 2442 N.W. Market #300, 98107 206-783-2169
Seattle	Seattle Guest Cottage, 2442 NW Market St #300, 98107 206-783-2169
Seattle	Soundview B&B, 17600 Sylvester Rd., 98166 206-244-5209
Seattle	Three Tree Point, 17026 33rd Ave SW, 98166 206-669-7646
Seattle	Williams House B&B, 2637 30th Ave W, 98199
Seaview	The Lions Paw Inn, PO Box 425, 98644 360-642-2481
Sedro Woolley	South Bay B&B, 4095 South Bay Dr., 98284 360-595-2086
Sequim	Alaskan Bear B&B, 1130 W Alder Ct, 98382
Sequim	Brigadoon B&B, 62 Balmoral Ct., 98382 360-683-2255
Sequim	Diamond Point Inn, 241 Sunshine Rd., 98334 360-797-7720
Sequim	Groveland Cottage, 4861 Sequim, 98382 360-683-3565
Sequim	Hidden Meadow Inn, 901 W. Sequim Bay Rd., 98382 360-681-2577
Sequim	Margie's Inn on the Bay, 120 Forrest Rd, 98382 360-683-7011
Shoreline	Ogle's B&B, 16347 Fremont Ave N, 98135 206-876-9170
Silverdale	Dennis Fulton B&B, 16609 Olympic View Rd, 98383 206-692-4648
Silverdale	Heaven's Edge B&B, 7410 NW Ioka Dr, 98383 360-613-1111
Silverdale	Seabreeze Beach Front, 16609 Olympic View Rd, 98383
Snohomish	Carleton House B&B, 416 Ave D, 98290 425-568-4211
Snohomish	Countryman's, 119 Cedar Ave, 98290 425-568-9622
Snohomish	Redmond House B&B, 317 Glen Ave, 98290
Snohomish	Snohomish Grand Hotel, 11910 Springhetti Rd, 98296 425-568-8854
Snoqualmie	Old Honey Farm Country Inn, 9050 384th Ave SE, 98065 425-888-9399
South Cle Elum	Iron Horse Inn, PO Box 629, 98943 509-674-5939
Spokane	Angelica's Mansion B&B, W. 1321 Ninth Ave, 99204 508-624-5598
Spokane	Blakely Estate B&B, E. 7710 Hodin Dr, 99212 509-926-9426
Spokane	Cobblestone Baking B&B, 620 S Washington St, 99204 509-624-9735
Spokane	Fotheringham House, 2128 W. Second Ave, 99204 509-838-1891
Spokane	Oslo's B&B, 1821 E 39th Ave., 99203 509-838-3175
Spokane	Town & Country Cottage B&B, N7620 Fox Point Dr, 99208 509-466-7559
Spokane	Waverly Place B&B, W. 709 Waverly Pl, 99205 509-328-1856
Tacoma	Austrian B&B and Suites, 723 N Cushman, 98403 206-495-4293

Tacoma	Bay Vista B&B, 4617 Darien Dr., 98407 253-759-8084
Tacoma	Chinaberry Hill, 302 Tacoma Ave N, 98403 253-272-1282
Tacoma	DeVoe Mansion, 208 E 133rd St, 98445 253-539-3991
Tacoma	Inge's Place, 6809 Lake Grove SW, 98499 253-584-4514
Tacoma	Plum Duff House B&B, 619 N K St, 98403 253-627-6916
Tacoma	Sally's Bear Tree Cottage, 6019 West 64th St, 98467 253-475-3144
Tacoma	Sha Hol Dee B&B, 1131 S 35th St, 98408
Tacoma	The Green Cape Cod B&B, 2711 N Warner, 98407 253-752-1977
Toledo	The Farm B&B, PO Box 639, 98591 360-864-4200
Tonasket	Hidden Hills Guest Resort, 144 Fish Lake Rd., 98855 509-486-1890
Tonasket	Orchard Country Inn, Box 634, 98855 509-486-1923
Trout Lake	Huckleberry Ridge B&B, 2473 Highway 141, 98650 509-395-2965
Trout Lake	The Farm, A B&B, 490 Sunnyside Rd., 98650 509-395-2488
Uniontown	The Churchyard Inn, 206 St Boniface St, 99179 509-229-3200
Usk	The Inn at Usk, 410 River Rd., 99180 509-445-1526
Vashon Island	All Seasons Waterfront Ldg, 12817 SW Bachelor Rd., 98070 206-463-3498
Vashon Island	Betty MacDonald Farm, 12000 99th Ave SW, 98070 206-567-4227
Vashon Island	Maury Garden Cottage, 22705 Deppman Rd, SW, 98070 206-463-3034
Vashon Island	Mimi's Cottage by the Sea, 7923 SW Hawthorne Ln, 98070 206-567-4383
Vashon Island	Old Tjomsland House, PO Box 913, 98070 206-463-5275
Vashon Island	Peabody's B&B, 75 S. Main Street #301, 98070 206-463-3506
Walla Walla	Green Gables Inn, 922 Bonsella, 99362 509-525-5501
Walla Walla	Stone Creek Inn, 720 Bryant Ave, 99362 509-529-8120
Waterville	Tower House B&B, PO Box 129, 98858 509-745-8320
Wenatchee	Cherub Inn, 410 N Miller, 98801
Wenatchee	Rimrock Inn B&B, 1354 Pitcher Canyon Rd, 98801 509-664-5113
Wenatchee	Warm Springs Inn, 1611 Love Lane, 98801 509-662-8365
Whidbey Island	Mutiny Bay Hideaway B&B, 5939 S Mutiny Bay Rd, 98249 360-331-4218
White Salmon	Llama Ranch B&B, 1980 Hwy 141, 98672 509-395-2786
Winthrop	Spring Creek Ranch, 491 Twin Lake Rd, 98862
Winthrop	Sunny Meadows Inn & Golf R, 280 W Chewuck Rd., 98862 509-996-3103
Woodinville	Whispering Trees Farm B&B, 19801 NE 155th Pl, 98072 425-788-2315
Woodland	Grandma's House B&B, 4551 Lewis River Rd., 98674 360-225-7002
Yakima	Birchfield Manor Cntry Inn, 2018 Birchfield Rd, 98901 509-452-1960
Yakima	Irish House B&B, 210 S. 28th Ave, 98902 509-453-5474
Yelm	Log Guest House B&B, 11249 Bald Hill Rd. SE, 98597 206-458-4385

West Virginia

Arbovale	Buffalo Run Lodge, HC 63, Box 38C, 24915 304-456-3036
Augusta	Windsong B&B, HC 78, Box 99-1, 26704 304-496-8046
Beaver	Cedarwood Cottage B&B, 150 Sally Lane, 25813 304-253-0665
Beaver	Edelweiss Inn, 1720 Grandview Rd, 25813
Beaver	House of Granview B&B Inn, 680 Old Grandview Rd, 25813 304-763-4381
Beckley	Bavarian Gasthaus, 109 Beckley Avenue, 25801 304-253-1140
Beckwith	Woodcrest B&B, Route #2, Box 520, 25840 304-574-3870
Berkeley Springs	Aarons Acre, 501 Johnson Mill Rd, 25411 304-258-4079
Berkeley Springs	Cacapon B&B, Rt 1, Box 301A, 25411 304-258-1442
Berkeley Springs	Glens Country Estate, PO Box 160, 25411 304-258-3317
Berkeley Springs	Highlawn Inn, 304 Market St, 25411 304-258-5700
Berkeley Springs	Maria's Garden & Inn, 201 Independence St, 25411 304-258-2021
Berkeley Springs	On the Banks Guesthouse, 304 Martinsburg Rd, 25411 304-258-2134
Berkeley Springs	Sleepy Creek Tree Farm B&B, Rt 2, Box 3980, 25411 304-258-4324
Berkeley Springs	Tari's,A Premiere Cafe/Inn, 123 N Washington St, 25411 304-258-1196
Berkeley Springs	The Country Inn, 207 S. Washington St, 25411 304-258-2210
Bluefield	Country Chalet B&B, Rt 1 Box 176B, 24701 304-487-2120
Bomont	Pleasant Retreat, HC 74, Box 191, 25030 304-548-6721
Bramwell	Perry House Inn, PO Box 248, 24715 304-248-8145
Buckhannon	Deer Park Inn & Lodge, PO Box 817, 26201 304-472-8400
Bunker Hill	Edgewood Manor B&B, PO Box 509, 25413 304-229-9353
Charles Town	The Carriage Inn, 417 E Washington St, 25414 304-728-8003
Charles Town	The Cottonwood Inn, Rt. 5, Box 61-S, 25414
Charleston	Historic Charleston B&B, 114 Elizabeth St, 25311 304-345-8156
Clarksburgg	Main Street B&B, 151 E Main St, 26301 304-623-1440
Cowen	The Brass Tea Pot, PO Box 527, 26206 304-226-0687
Davis	Bright Morning, Route 32, 26260 304-259-2719
Davis	Hill House B&B, 4th St, 26260 304-259-5883
Davis	Meyers House B&B, PO Box 360, 26260
Durbin	Cheat Mountain Club, PO Box 28, 26264 304-456-4627
Elkins	Graceland Inn, 100 Campus Dr, 26241 304-637-1600
Elkins	Ramblin Rose B&B, 301 Marro Dr, 26241 304-636-1790
Elkins	The Retreat, 214 Harpertown Rd, 26241 304-636-2960
Elkins	The Warfield House B&B, 318 Buffalo St, 26241 304-636-4555
Fairmont	Acacia House B&B, 158 Locust Ave, 26554 304-367-1000
Fayetteville	Cozy Cottage, PO Box 390, 25840 304-574-0134
Fayetteville	Historic Morris Harvey Hse, 201 W. Maple Ave., 25840 304-574-1179
Fayetteville	The County Seat B&B, 306 Maple Ave, 25840 304-574-0823
Fayetteville	White Horse B&B, 20 Fayette Ave, 25840 304-574-1400

Fayetteville	Wisteria House B&B, 147 South Court St, 25840 304-574-3678
Gerrardstown	Mill Creek Manor, Box 78-0, Rt. 1, 25420 304-229-1617
Gerrardstown	Prospect Hill B&B, PO Box 135, 25420 304-229-3346
Great Cacapon	River House B&B, PO Box 254, 25422 304-258-4042
Handley	Vision Inn, PO Box 43, 25102 304-442-8446
Harpers Ferry	Between the Rivers B&B, 597 E Ridge St., 25425 304-535-2768
Harpers Ferry	Briscoe House, 828 Washington St, 25425 304-535-2416
Harpers Ferry	Lee-Stonewall Inn B&B, PO Box 1063, 25425 304-535-2532
Harpers Ferry	Ranson-Armory House B&B, PO Box 280, 25425 301-535-2142
Harrisville	Heritage Inn, PO Box 220, 26362 304-643-2938
Helvetia	Grandpa John's Country Kit, HC 76 Box 194, 26224 304-924-5503
Hico	Dogwood Ridge Farms, PO Box 239, 25854 304-658-4396
Hillsboro	The Current B&B, HC 64, Box 135, 24946 304-653-4722
Hillsboro	Yew Mountain Lodge, HC 64, Box 277, 24946
Hinton	Historic Hinton Manor, PO Box 1645, 25951 304-466-3930
Huttonsville	Hutton House B&B, Rts. 219/250, Box 88, 26273 304-335-6701
Huttonsville	Linger In, PO Box 14, 26273 304-335-4434
Huttonsville	Richard's Country Inn, U.S. 219 Rt#1 Box11-A1, 26273 304-335-6659
Huttonsville	The Cardinal Inn B&B, Rte 1 -Box 1, 26273 304-335-6149
Kingwood	The Preston County Inn, 112 W Main St, 26537 304-329-2220
Lewisburg	General Lewis Inn, 301 E Washington St, 24901 304-645-2600
Lewisburg	Lynn's Inn B&B, Rt. 4 Box 40, 24901
Logan	The Manor House B&B, 575 Main St, 25601 304-752-5824
Lost Creek	Crawford's Country Corner, Box 112, 26385 304-745-3017
Lost River	Guest House, Low-Gap, 26811 304-897-5707
Lost River	The Inn at Lost River, HC 83 Box 8A2, 26810 304-897-6788
Marlinton	Carriage House Inn, HCR 82, Box 56, 24954 304-799-6706
Marlinton	Old Clark Inn, 702 3rd Ave, 24954 304-799-6377
Marlinton	Rustic Inn B&B, Rt 1 Box 116, 24954
Martinsburg	Aspen Hall Inn, 405 Boyd Ave, 25401 304-263-4385
Martinsburg	Boydsville Inn, 609 S Queen St, 25401
Martinsburg	Inn-Surance, PO Box 1106, 25401 800-825-4667
Martinsburg	The Pulpit & Palette Inn, 516 W John St, 25407 304-263-7012
Mathias	Valley View Farm, Route 1, Box 467, 26812 304-897-5229
Maxwelton	Rocky Gap B&B, PO Box 144, 24957
Middleway	The Daniel Fry House B&B, Rt 1, Box 152, 25430
Moorefield	McMechen House Inn B&B, 109 N. Main St, 26836 304-538-7173
Morgantown	Almost Heaven B&B, 391 Scott Ave, 26505
Morgantown	Appelwood B&B, Rt 5, Box 137, 26505 304-296-2607
Morgantown	Maxwell B&B, 217 Morgan Hill Rd, 26508 304-594-0786
Mt. Pleasant	Stone Manor, 12 Main St., 25550 304-675-3442
New Creek	Thorn Run Inn B&B, HC 75 Box 125, 26743 304-749-7733
Parkersburg	The Avery-Savage House, 420 13th St, 26101 304-422-9820
Pence Springs	The Pence Springs Hotel, Rt 3, 24962 304-445-2606
Petersburg	Smoke Hole Lodge, PO Box 953, 26847
Princeton	San Souci B&B, 1234 E Main St, 24740
Princeton	The Hale House B&B, 209 Hale Ave, 24740 304-487-6783
Shepherdstown	Stonebrake Cottage, PO Box 1612, 25443
Shepherdstown	Thomas Shepherd Inn, PO Box 1162, 25443 304-876-3715
Shinnston	Gillum House B&B, 35 Walnut St, 26431 304-592-0177
Sistersville	Wells Inn, 316 Charles St, 26175 304-652-3111
Slatyfork	Slatyfork Farm B&B, PO Box 7, 26291 304-572-3900
Summersville	Historic Brock House B&B, 1400 Webster Rd, 26651 304-872-4887
Valley Chapel Weston	Ingeberg Acres, PO Box 199, 26446
Valley Head	Nakiska Chalet B&B, HC 73, Box 24, 26294 304-339-6309
Vienna	Williams House B&B, 5406 Grand Central Ave, 26105
Walkersville	Stone Farm B&B, Rt 1 Box 36, 26447 304-452-8477
Webster Springs	Country Charm B&B, 205 S. Main St, 26288 304-847-5757
West Liberty	The Atkinson Guest House, PO Box 147, 26074 304-336-7557
Wheeling	Stratford Springs Inn, 355 Oglebay Dr, 26003 304-233-5100
Wheeling	The Eckhart House, 810 Main St, 26003 304-232-5439
White Sulphur	James Wylie House B&B, 208 E. Main St, 24986 304-536-9444
Winona	Garvey House B&B, PO Box 98, 25942 304-574-3235
Wolf Creek	High Meadow Farm Lodge, General Delivery, 24993

Wisconsin

Albany	Oak Hill Manor, 401 E. Main St, 53502 608-862-1400
Albany	Sugar River Inn, PO Box 39, 53502 608-862-1248
Algoma	Amberwood Inn, N7136 Hwy 42, 54201 414-487-3471
Allenton	Addison House, 6373 Hwy 175, 53002 414-629-9993
Alma	Gallery House, 215 N. Main St, Box 55, 54610 608-685-4975
Alma	Laue House, B&B Inn, PO Box 176, 54610 608-685-4923
Alma	Tritsch House B&B, 601 S 2nd St, 54601 608-685-4090
Amherst	The Amherst Inn, 303 S Main St, 54406 715-824-2326
Appleton	Franklin Street Inn, 318 E Franklin St, 54911 414-739-3702
Appleton	The Queen Anne B&B, 837 E. College Ave, 54911 414-739-7966
Appleton	The Solie Home, 914 E. Hancock St, 54911 888-739-7966

Ashland	The Residenz, 723 Chapple Ave, 54806 715-682-2425
Avoca	Prairie Rose B&B, 107 S. Second St, 53506 608-532-6878
Baileys Harbor	The Potter's Door Inn, 9528 Highway 57, 54202 414-839-2003
Baldwin	Kaleidoscope Inn, 800-11th Ave, 54002 715-684-4575
Baraboo	Baraboo's Gollmar Guest, 422 3rd St, 53913 608-356-9432
Baraboo	Frantiques Showplace, 704 Ash St, 53913 608-356-5273
Baraboo	Gollmar Mansion Inn, 422 - 3rd St, 53913 608-356-9432
Baraboo	The Clark House, 320 Walnut St, 53913 608-356-2191
Baraboo	Victorian Rose, 423 Third Ave, 53913 608-356-7828
Barnes	Sunset Resort B&B Lodge, HCR 61, Box 6325, 54873 715-795-2449
Bay View	Victorian B&B, 346 E. Wilson, 53207
Bayfield	Apple Tree Inn, Rt. 1, Box 251, 54814 715-779-5572
Bayfield	Cooper Hill House, PO Box 1288, 54814 715-779-5060
Bayfield	Greunke's Inn, 17 Rittenhouse, 54814 715-779-5480
Bayfield	Island View Placae B&B, Rt 1 Box 46, 54814 715-779-5307
Bayfield	Lakeside Lodging, Route 1 Box 2538, 54814 715-779-5545
Bayfield	Morning Glory B&B, 119 S. 6th St, 54814 715-779-5621
Bayfield	Old Rittenhouse Inn, PO Box 584, 54814 715-779-5111
Bayfield	Pinehurst Inn @ Pike's Cr., Rt. 1, Box 222, 54814 715-779-3676
Bayfield	The Artesian House, R R 1, Box 218K, 54814 715-779-3338
Bayfield	The Baywood Place B&B, 20 N. 3rd St, 54814 715-779-3690
Bayfield	Thimbleberry Inn B&B, 15021 Pageant Rd, 54814 715-779-5757
Beaver Dam	The Victorian B&B, 518 N Center St, 53916 414-885-9601
Belleville	Abendruh B&B Swisstyle, 7019 Gehin Rd, 53508 608-424-3808
Birchwood	The Cobblestone, Balsam & S Main, 54817
Birchwood	The Farm, 718 S Main St., 54817 715-354-3367
Black Creek	Old Coach Inn B&B, 405 Burdick St, 54106 414-984-3840
Boscobel	LLaughing LLama Farm, 15859 Dry Hollow Rd, 53805 608-375-4623
Boulder Junction	Evergreen Lodge, Box 560A, 54512
Brodhead	Buckskin Lodge B&B, W781 County F, 53520 608-897-2914
Browntown	Four Seasons, 8361 County M, 53522 608-966-1680
Browntown	Honeywind Farm, W8247 County P, 53522 608-325-5215
Browntown	Inn Serendipity, 7843 County P, 53522 608-329-7056
Browntown	Old School Inn B&B, 214 School St, 53522 608-966-1848
Burlington	Hillcrest B&B Inn, 540 Storle Ave, 53105 414-763-4706
Burlington	Idle Acres Inn B&B, 8221 Hoosier Creek Rd, 53105 414-539-2229
Cable	Connors B&B, Rt 1, Box 255, 54821 715-798-3661
Cambridge	Cambridge House B&B, PO Box 365, 53523 608-423-7008
Cambridge	Country Comforts B&B, 2722 Highland Drive, 53523 608-423-3097
Cambridge	The Night Heron B&B, 315 E Water St, 53523 608-423-4141
Cambridge	Whispering Pines B&B, W0442 Hwy 12, 53523
Camp Douglas	Sunnyfield Farm B&B, N6692 Batko Rd, 54618 608-427-3686
Campbellsport	Kettlebrook Farm, Inc., W. 541 Hwy SS, 53010 414-533-5387
Campbellsport	Newcastle Pines, N1499 Hwy 45, 53010 920-533-5252
Campbellsport	The Mielke-Mauk House B&B, W977 County Hwy F, 53010 414-533-8602
Cashton	Ages Past Country House B&, PO Box 252, 54619 608-654-5950
Cashton	Cannondalen, Route 1, Box 58, 54619 608-269-2886
Cassville	Geiger House, 401 Denniston, 53806 608-725-5419
Cassville	River View B&B, 117 Front St, 53806 608-725-5895
Chetek	Canoe Bay Inn & Cottages, W16065 Hogback Rd, 54728 800-568-1995
Chetek	Sweet Dreams B&B, 309 2nd St, 54728 715-924-4590
Chetek	Trails End B&B, 641 Ten Mile Lake Dr, 54728 715-924-2641
Chilton	East Shore Inn, N2577 Lake Shore Dr, 53014 414-849-4230
Chippewa Falls	McGilvray's Victorian B&B, 312 W Columbia St, 54729 715-720-1600
Chippewa Falls	Pleasant View B&B, 16649 96th Ave, 54729 715-382-4401
Columbus	By the Okeag, 446 Wisconsin St, 53925 414-623-3007
Columbus	Maple Leaf Inn B&B, 219 N. Ludington St, 53925 414-623-5166
Columbus	The Dering House, 251 W. James St, 53925 414-623-2015
Cornell	House in the Woods, 200 N. Riverside Dr, 54732 715-239-6511
Cornucopia	Fo'c'sle B&B, PO Box 116, 54827 715-742-3337
Cornucopia	The Village Inn, PO Box 127, 54827 715-742-3941
Crandon	Courthouse Square B&B, 210 E. Polk St, 54520 715-478-2549
Cross Plains	Enchanted Valley Garden, 554 Enchanted Valley Rd, 53528 608-798-4554
Cross Plains	The Past & Present Inn, 2034 Main St, 53528 608-798-4441
Cumberland	Silver Pine Lodge B&B, 1154 - 26 1/2 Ave, 54829 715-822-3123
Cumberland	The Rectory B&B, 1575 Second Ave, 54829 715-822-3151
Darlington	Thompson House, 145 W River, 53530 608-776-2998
De Pere	Birch Creek Inn, 2263 Birch Creek Rd, 54115 414-336-7575
De Pere	Bit of the Bay, 415 Randall Ave, 54115 414-866-9901
Delavan	Allyn Mansion Inn, 511 E Walworth Ave, 53115 414-728-9090
Delavan	Lakeside Manor Inn, 1809 S Shore Dr, 53115 414-728-5354
Denmark	Dansk Hus B&B, 4820 N Cherney Rd, 54208
Dodgeville	The Grandview, 4717 Miess Rd, 53533 608-935-3261
Downsville	Creamery, Box 22, 54735 715-664-8354
Duran	Ryan House B&B, W4375 US Hwy 10 E, 54736 715-672-8563
Eagle	Eagle Centre House B&B, W370, S9590 Hwy 67, 53119 414-363-4700
Eagle	Novels Country Inn, PO Box 456, 53119 414-594-3729
Eagle River	B&B At Hilltop House, PO Box 2504, 54521 715-479-2248

Eagle River	The Inn at Pinewood, PO Box 549, 54521 715-479-4114
East Troy	Greystone Farms B&B, N. 9391 Adams Rd, 53120 414-495-8485
East Troy	Mitten Farm B&B, W2454 Hwy. J, 53120 414-642-5530
East Troy	Pickwick Inn, 2966 Union St., 53120 414-642-5529
East Troy	Pine Ridge B&B, 1152 Scout Rd, 53120 414-594-3269
Eau Claire	Apple Tree Inn, PO Box 677, 54702 715-836-9599
Eau Claire	Fanny Hill, 3919 Crescent Ave, 54703 715-836-8184
Eau Claire	Otter Creek Inn, 2536 Hwy 12, 54701 715-832-2945
Eau Claire	The Atrium B&B, 5572 Prill Rd, 54701 715-833-9045
Egg Harbor	Bittersweet Gallery Inn, PO Box 34, 54209 414-487-2341
Elkhorn	Ye Olde Manor House B&B, N7622 State Rd 12, 53121 414-742-2450
Ellison Bay	Country Woods B&B, 520 Europe Lake Rd, 54210 414-854-5706
Ellison Bay	Hotel Disgarden, PO Box 191, 54210 920-854-9888
Elroy	East View B&B, 33620 County Hwy P, 53929 608-463-7564
Elroy	Stillested B&B, N3260 Overgaard Rd, 53929 608-462-5633
Elroy	Waarvik's Century Farm, N. 4621 County Rd H, 53929 608-462-8595
Endeavor	Neenah Creek Inn & Pottery, W7956 Neenah Rd, 53930 608-587-2229
Ephraim	Ephraim Inn, PO Box 247, 54211 414-854-4515
Ephraim	French Country Inn, 3052 Spruce Ln, Box 129, 54211 414-854-4001
Ephraim	Prairie Garden B&B, 2854 Shannon Ln, 54211 414-854-2555
Evansville	Holmes Victorian Inn, 443 S First St, 53536 608-882-6866
Fennimore	Gazebo B&B, 825 12th St, 53809 608-822-3928
Ferryville	Mississippi Humble Bush, PO Box 297, 54628 608-737-3022
Fish Creek	The Birchwood B&B, PO Box 827, 54212 920-868-3214
Fish Creek	The Juniper Inn, N9432 Maple Grove Rd, 54212 920-839-2629
Fish Creek	The Whistling Swan, PO Box 193, 54212 920-868-3442
Fish Creek	White Gull Inn, Box 160, 54212 920-868-3517
Florence	Lakeside B&B, Box 54, 54121 715-528-3259
Fontana	Strawberry Hill B&B, 1071 Jenkins Dr, 53125 414-275-5998
Fort Atkinson	La Grange B&B, 1050 East St, 53538 414-563-1421
Fort Atkinson	Lamp Post Inn, 408 South Main St, 53538 414-563-6561
Frederic	Seven Pines Lodge, 1098 340th Ave, 54837 715-653-2323
Frederic	The Gandy Dancer B&B, PO Box 563, 54837 715-327-8750
Galesville	The Clark House B&B, 624 W. Ridge Ave, 54630 608-582-4190
Gay Mills	Miss Molly's B&B, PO Box 254, 54631 608-735-4433
Genoa City	House on the Hill B&B, 554 Carter St, 53128 414-279-6466
Glen Haven	Parson's Inn B&B, PO Box 67, 53810 608-794-2491
Goodman	Tiger Inn, PO Box 398, 54125
Grand View	Hummingbird B&B, Rt 1, Box 230C, 54839 715-763-3214
Gratot	Richwood, 6332 Hwy 78, 53541 608-922-6402
Green Bay	Days Inn at Lambeau Field, 1978 Holmgren Way, 54304 920-498-8088
Green Lake	Carvers on the Lake, N5529 County Road A, 54941 920-294-6931
Green Lake	McConnell Inn, 497 S Lawson Dr, Box 6, 54941 414-294-6430
Green Lake	Oakwood Lodge, 365 Lake St, 54941 414-294-6580
Greenwood	Mead Lake B&B, W9083 Scout Rd., 54437 715-267-6264
Hammond	Summit Farm B&B, 1622 110th Ave, 54015 715-796-2617
Hartford	Jordan House, 81 S. Main St, 53027 414-673-5643
Hayward	Edgewater Inn B&B, Rt 1 Box 1293 Turners, 54843 715-462-9412
Hayward	Lumberman's Mansion Inn, PO Box 885, 54843 715-634-3012
Hayward	Roos' Teal Lake Lodge, Rt 7, Ross Rd, 54843 715-462-3631
Hayward	Shepherds Inn B&B, Rt 3 Box 3306A, 54843 715-764-6142
Hayward	Spider Lake Lodge, Rt. 1, Box 1335, 54843 800-653-9472
Hazel Green	Wisconsin House Stagecoach, PO Box 71, 53811 608-854-2233
Hazelhurst	Hazelhurst Inn, 6941 Hwy 51, 54531 715-356-6571
Herbster	Bark Point Inn, Bark Point Rd, 54855 715-774-3309
Hillsboro	Edgecombe Inn, PO Box 588, 54634 608-489-2915
Holcombe	The Happy Horse B&B, 24273 St Hwy 27/24469, 54745 715-239-0707
Hollandale	The Old Granary Inn, 1760 Sandy Rock Rd, 53544 608-967-2140
Honey Creek	Honey Creek Acres, N6360 Valley View Rd, 53138 414-763-7591
Hudson	Baker Brewster Victorian, 904 Vine St, 54016 715-381-2895
Hudson	Grapeville Inn B&B, 702 Vine St, 54016 715-386-1989
Hudson	Phipps Inn, 1005 3rd St, 54016 715-386-0800
Iola	Iris Inn, PO Box 194, 54945 715-445-4848
Iola	Taylor House B&B, 210 E. Iola St, 54945 715-445-2204
Irma	Swan Song B&B, N8449 Skanawan Lake Rd, 54442 715-453-1173
Iron River	Iron River Trout Haus, 205 W Drummond Rd, 54847 715-372-4219
Janesville	Antique Rose B&B, 603 East Court St, 53545 608-754-8180
Janesville	Jackson Street Inn B&B, 210 S Jackson St, 53545 608-754-7250
Jefferson	Stoppenbach House B&B, 244 E Racine St, 53549 920-674-9747
Juneau	Country Retreat, N4589 Primrose Ln, 53039 414-386-2912
Juneau	Waters On The Bay B&B, N5121 Butternut Ct, 53039 920-349-3317
Kansasville	Linen & Lace B&B, 26060 Washington Ave, 53139 414-534-4966
Kendall	Cabin at Trails End, Rt 2, Box 84-A, 54638 608-427-3877
Kendall	Dusk to Dawn, PO Box 191, 54638 608-463-7547
Kewaskum	Country Ridge Inn B&B, 4134 Ridge Rd, 53040 414-626-4853
Kewaskum	The Doctors Inn B&B, 1121 Fond du Lac Ave, 53040 414-626-2666
Kewaunee	Chelsea Rose, 908 Milwaukee St, 54216 414-388-2012
Kewaunee	Duvall House, 815 Milwaukee St, 54216 414-388-0501

Kewaunee	Historic Norman Gen Store, E 3296 Hwy G, 54216 414-388-4580
Kewaunee	The Gables, 821 Dodge St, 54216 920-388-0220
Kewaunee	The Kewaunee House, 1017 Milwaukee St, 54216 414-388-1017
Kiel	River Terrace B&B, 521 River Terrace, 53042 414-894-2032
La Crosse	Four Gables, W5648, Hwy 14-61, 54601 608-788-7958
La Crosse	The Martindale House B&B, 237 S. 10th St, 54601 608-782-4224
La Farge	Trillium, Route 2, Box 121, 54639 608-625-4492
La Pointe	Brittany B&B, PO Box 381, 54850 715-747-5023
Lac Du Flambeau	Chippewa Lodge B&B, 3525 Chippewa Lodge Trl, 54538
Lac du Flambeau	Ty-Bach, 3104 Simpson Ln, 54538 715-588-7851
Lake Delton	The Swallow's Nest B&B, PO Box 418, 53940 608-254-6900
Lake Geneva	General Boyd's B&B, W2915 Country Trunk BB, 53147 414-248-3543
Lake Geneva	Lawrence House B&B Inn, 403 S Lake Shore Dr, 53147
Lake Geneva	Pederson Victorian B&B, 1782 Highway 120 N, 53147 414-248-9110
Lake Geneva	Roses, A B&B, 429 S Lake Shore Dr, 53147 414-248-4344
Lake Geneva	The Oaks Inn, 421 Baker St, 53147 414-248-9711
Lake Geneva	Waters Edge of Lake Geneva, W4232 W End Rd, 53147 414-245-9845
Lake Mills	Fargo Mansion Inn, 406 Mulberry, 211 Main, 53551 920-648-3654
Lancaster	Maple Harris Guest House, 445 W Maple, 53813 608-723-4717
Lancaster	Martha's B&B, 7867 University Farm Rd, 53813 608-723-4711
Laona	Laona Hostel, PO Box 325, 54541 800-669-2615
Lodi	Prairie Garden B&B, W13172 Hwy. 188, 53555 608-592-5187
Loganville	Shanahan's, S. 7979 Hwy 23, 53943 608-727-2507
Lomira	The White Shutters, W265 County Trunk H., 53048 414-269-4056
Madison	Canterbury Inn, 315 W. Gorham, 53703 608-258-8899
Madison	Stadium House B&B, 810 Oakland Ave, 53711
Madison	Stoney Oaks, 4942 Raymond Rd, 53711 608-278-1646
Madison	University Heights B&B, 1812 Van Hise Ave, 53705 608-233-3340
Madison	Victorian Garden B&B, 863 N High Point Rd, 53717
Maiden Rock	Eagle Cove B&B, W4387 120th Ave, 54750 800-467-0279
Maiden Rock	Harrisburg Inn B&B, PO Box 15, 54750 715-448-4500
Manawa	Ferg Haus Inn, N8599 Ferg Rd, 54949 414-596-2946
Manawa	Gage's Gardens & Gables, 539 Depot St, 54949 414-596-3643
Manawa	Lindsay House B&B, PO Box 304, 54949 920-596-3643
Manitowish Waters	Friar's Tuckaway B&B, Hwy 51 S 122, 54545 715-543-8231
Manitowoc	Abba's Inn B&B, 1524 S 16th St, 54220 414-793-1727
Manitowoc	Arbor Manor B&B, 860 Lincoln Bvd., 54220 414-684-6095
Manitowoc	Jarvis House B&B, 635 N. 7th St, 54220 414-682-2103
Manitowoc	Mahloch's Cozy B&B, 2104 Madson Rd, 54220 414-775-4404
Manitowoc	The Holmestead, 702 Park St, 54220 414-692-0434
Manitowoc	WestPort B&B, 635 N 8th St, 54220 920-686-0465
Marinette	M&M Victorian Inn, 1393 Main St, 54143 715-732-9531
Marshfield	EverGreen Inn B&B, M226 Hwy E, 54449 715-387-1644
Mayville	Audubon Inn, 45 N Main St, 53085 920-387-5858
Mayville	J & R's Sherm Inn, 366 N Main St, 53050 414-387-4642
Mazomanie	Quiet Woods B&B, 10901 West Hudson Rd, 53560 608-795-4954
Menomonee	Bolo Country Inn, 207 Pine Ave, 54751 715-235-5596
Menomonee	Cedar Trail Guest House, E4761 County Rd C, 54751 715-664-8828
Menomonee	Dorshel's B&B Guest House, W140 N7616 Lilly Rd, 53051 414-255-7866
Menomonee Falls	Hitching Post B&B, N88 W16954, 53051 414-255-1496
Mequon	American Country Farm B&B, 12112 N. Wauwatosa Rd, 53092 414-242-0194
Mequon	Sonnenhof Inn, 13907 N Port Washington, 53092 414-375-4294
Merrill	Candlewick Inn, 700 W. Main St, 54452 715-536-7744
Middleton	Middleton Beach Inn B&B, 2303 Middlton Beach Rd, 53562 608-831-6446
Milwaukee	Lakeside Inn Cafe, 801 N Cass St, 53202 414-276-1577
Mineral Point	Brewery Creek Inn, 23 Commerce St, 53565 608-987-3298
Mineral Point	Chesterfield Inn, 10 Commerce St, 53565 608-987-3682
Mineral Point	House of the Brau-Meister, 254 Shake Rag St, 53565 608-987-2913
Mineral Point	Knudson's Guest House, 415 Ridge St, 53565 608-987-2733
Mineral Point	The Cothren House, 320 Tower St, 53565 608-987-2612
Minocqua	Kinsale B&B, 1121 Rockwood Dr, 54548 715-356-3296
Minocqua	Minocqua Inn, 8123 Northern Rd, 54548 715-358-2578
Minocqua	Tamarack Lodge B&B, 7950 Bo-di-lac Dr, 54548 715-356-7124
Minocqua	Whitehaven B&B, 1077 Hwy. F, 54548 715-356-9097
Monroe	Chenoweth House, 2004 10th St, 53566 608-325-5064
Monroe	Thompson's Inn, N4001 County Rd M, 53566 715-223-6041
Montreal	The Inn, 104 Wisconsin Ave, 54550 715-561-5180
Mountain	Winter Green, 16330 Thelen Rd, 54149 715-276-6885
Neenah	C & R B&B, 676 Vera Ave, 54956
New Auburn	Jacks Lake B&B, 30497 Chippewa Trail, 54757 715-967-2730
New Glarus	Country House Inn, 180 Hwy 69, 53574 608-527-5399
New Glarus	Jeanne-Marie's B&B, 318 10th Ave, 53574 608-527-5059
New Glarus	Linden Inn, 219 5th Ave, 53574 608-527-2675
New Glarus	Spring Valley Creek B&B, N9098 Old Madison Rd, 53574 608-527-2314
New Glarus	Zentner Haus, N. 8588 Zentner Rd, 53574 608-527-2121
New Holstein	Krupp Farm Homestead, W. 1982 Kiel Rd, 53061 414-782-5421
Norwalk	Lonesome Jake's Ranch, Route 2, Box 108A, 54648 608-823-7585
Oconomowoc	The Victorian Belle, 520 W. Wisconsin Ave, 53066 414-567-2520

Ogema	Timm's Hill B&B, N 2036 County Rd C, 54459 715-767-5288
Onalaska	Lumber Baron Inn, 421 2nd Ave N, 54650 608-781-8938
Ontario	Inn at Wildcat Mountain, PO Box 112, 54651 608-337-4352
Osceola	Pleasant Lake Inn, 2238 60th Ave, 54020 715-294-2545
Osceola	St. Croix River Inn, PO Box 356, 54020 715-294-4248
Pardeeville	Gator Gully B&B, 208 Riverview Dr, 53954 608-429-2754
Pardeeville	The Country Rose B&B, N7398 Hwy 22, 53954 608-429-2035
Pepin	Harbor Hill Inn, 310 Second St., 54759 715-442-2002
Pepin	Summer Place, 106 Main St, 54759 715-442-2132
Pepin	The Pepin House, 120 S Prairie St, 54759 612-345-4454
Phelps	Limberlost Inn, 2483 Hwy 17, 54554 715-545-2685
Phelps	The Hazen Inn, 1549 Hazen Ln, 54554 715-545-3600
Phillips	East Highland School B&B, W4342 Hwy. D, 54555 715-339-3492
Phillips	Hidden Valley Inn, W7724 Cty West, 54555
Plain	Bettinger House B&B, 855 Wachter Ave, 53577 608-546-2951
Plain	The Kraemer House B&B Inn, 1190 Spruce St, 53577 608-546-3161
Plainfield	Johnson Inn B&B, 231 W North St, 54966 715-335-4383
Platteville	Cunningham House, 110 Market St, 53818 608-348-5532
Platteville	The Gribble House B&B, 260 West Cedar St, 53818 608-348-7282
Plymouth	52 Stafford (Irish House), PO Box 217, 53073 920-893-0552
Plymouth	B. L. Nutt Inn, 632 E. Main St, 53073 920-892-8566
Plymouth	Beverly's Log Guest House, W6926 Stoney Ridge Ln, 53073 920-892-6064
Plymouth	Hillwind Farm B&B, N 4922 Hillwind Rd, 53073 920-892-2199
Plymouth	Spring Farm, N. 4502 County Rd S, 53073 920-892-2101
Plymouth	Tulip House Spring Farm, N4502 County Rd S, 53073 920-892-2101
Plymouth	Yankee Hill Inn B&B, 405 Collins Street, 53073 920-892-2222
Port Washington	Grand Inn, 832 W. Grand Ave, 53074 414-284-6719
Port Washington	Inn at Old Twelve Hundred, 806 W. Grand Ave, 53074 414-268-1200
Port Washington	Port Washington Inn, 308 W Washington St, 53074 414-284-5583
Portage	Breese Waye B&B, 816 Macfarlane Rd, 53901 608-742-5281
Portage	Country Aire B&B, N. 4452 County U, 53901 608-742-5716
Portage	Inn at Grady's Farm B&B, W10928 Hwy 33, 53901 608-742-3627
Portage	Riverbend Inn, W10928 Hwy 33, 53901 608-742-3627
Poynette	Jamieson House, 407 N. Franklin St, 53955 608-635-4100
Prairie du Chien	Neumann House B&B, 121 N. Michigan St, 53821 608-326-8104
Prairie du Sac	The Graff House B&B, N1177 Steckelberg Lane, 53578 608-643-6978
Princeton	The Gray Lion Inn, 115 Harvard, 54968 414-295-4101
Racine	Linen & Lace B&B, PO Box 085418, 53408 414-534-4966
Racine	Lochnaiar Inn, 1121 Lake Ave, 53403 414-633-3300
Racine	The Manor House, 116 10th St, 53403 414-658-0014
Racine	The Mansards on the Lake, 827 Lake Ave, 53403 414-632-1135
Reedsburg	Lavina Inn, 325 3rd St, 53959 608-524-6706
Rhinelander	Cranberry Hill Inn, 209 East Frederick St, 54501 715-369-3504
Richland Center	Littledale, Rt. 1, Box 74, Hwy ZZ, 53581 608-647-7118
River Falls	Knollwood House, N. 8257 950th St, 54022 715-425-1040
River Falls	Trillium Woods B&B, N7453 910th St, 54022 715-425-2555
Shawano	Five Keys B&B, 103 S Franklin St., 54166 715-526-5567
Shawano	The Prince Edward, 203 W 5th St, 54166 715-526-2805
Sheboygan	Brownstone Inn, 1227 N 7th St, 53081 920-451-0644
Sheboygan	English Manor B&B, 632 Michigan Ave, 53081 920-208-1952
Sheboygan	Gramma Lori's B&B, W 1681 Garton Rd., 53083 920-565-3853
Sheboygan	The Scheele House, 625 Fairway Dr, 53081 414-458-0998
Sheboygan Falls	Rochester Inn, 504 Water St, 53085 414-467-3123
Shell Lake	Maple Syrup Ranch B&B, N3534 Hwy 63N, 54871 715-468-2251
Sister Bay	Hidden Gardens B&B, 241 Fieldcrest Rd, 54234 414-854-5487
Sister Bay	Sweetbriar B&B, 102 Orchard Dr, 54234 920-854-7504
Sister Bay	The Inn On Maple, 414 Maple Dr, 54234 414-854-5107
Sister Bay	The Wooden Heart Inn, 11086 Hwy 42, 54234 414-854-9097
Sparta	Justin Trails B&B, Route 1, Box 274, 54656 608-269-4522
Sparta	Strawberry Lace Inn, 603 North Water St, 54656 608-269-7878
Spooner	Green Valley Inn, N 4781 Julie Ann Blvd, 54801 715-635-7300
Spread Eagle	The Lodge at River's Edge, HC2 Box 244-6, 54121 715-696-3406
Spring Green	Deer Acres, S11569 Hwy 23, 53588 608-588-7299
Spring Green	Hill Street B&B, 353 Hill St, 53588 608-588-7751
Spring Green	Usonian Inn, PO Box 777, 53588
Springbrook	The Stout Trout B&B, Rte.1, Box 1630, 54875 715-466-2790
St. Croix Falls	Amberwood B&B, 320 McKenney St, 54024 715-483-9355
St. Germain	St. Germain B&B, PO Box 6, 54558 715-479-8007
Stanley	Roe House B&B, 410 N Franklin St., 54768 715-644-5611
Stevens Point	Marcyanna's B&B, 440 N. Old Wausau Rd, 54481 715-341-9922
Stevens Point	The Birdhouse, 1890 Red Pine Ln, 54481 715-341-0084
Stockholm	Great River B&B, PO Box 11, 54769 715-442-5656
Stockholm	Hyggelig Hus, 171 2nd St, 54769 715-442-2086
Stockholm	Merchants' Hotel, 118 Spring, 54769 715-442-2113
Stone Lake	Lake House B&B & Art Galle, 5793 Division Ave, 54876 715-865-6803
Stone Lake	Randall's Morningside, 6138N Morningside Land, 54876 715-865-2213
Stoughton	Naeset-Roe B&B, 126 E Washington St, 53589 920-877-4150
Stoughton	Wild Rose Guest House, 1437 CTH W, 53589 608-877-9942

Sturgeon Bay	48 West Oak, 48 W Oak St, 54235
Sturgeon Bay	Chadwick Inn, 25 N 8th Ave., 54235 920-743-2771
Sturgeon Bay	Chanticleer Guest House, 4072 Cherry Rd, 54235 920-746-0334
Sturgeon Bay	Cliff Dwellers Resort, 3540 N Duluth Ave, 54235
Sturgeon Bay	Colonial Gardens B&B, 344 N Third Ave, 54235 920-746-9192
Sturgeon Bay	Cozy Quilt, 114 N 7th Ave., 54235 920-743-3020
Sturgeon Bay	Inn The Pines, 3750 Bay Shore Dr, 54235 920-743-9319
Sturgeon Bay	Nautical Inn, 234 Kentucky St, 54235 920-743-3399
Sturgeon Bay	Quiet Cottage, 4608 Glidden Dr, 54235 920-743-4526
Sturgeon Bay	The Barbican, 132 N 2nd Ave, 54235 920-743-4854
Sturgeon Bay	The Gray Goose B&B, 4258 Bay Shore Dr, 54235 920-743-9100
Sturgeon Bay	The Scofield House B&B, PO Box 761, 54235 920-743-7727
Sturgeon Bay	Van Clay Guest House, 434 N Third Ave, 54235 920-743-6611
Sturgeon Bay	White Birch Inn, 1009 S. Oxford Ave, 54235 920-743-3295
Superior	Crawford House B&B, 2016 Hughlitt Ave, 54880 715-394-5271
Tomah	Sisters B&B, 603 Superior Ave, 54660 608-372-2311
Two Rivers	Red Forest B&B, 1421 - 25th St, 54241 414-793-1794
Union Grove	Doverwood Farm B&B, 21626 Church Rd., 53182 414-878-5350
Verona	Beat Road Farm B&B, 2401 Beat Rd, 53593 608-437-6500
Viola	The Inn at Elk Run, S4125 Country Hwy SS, 54664 800-729-7313
Viroqua	Eckhart-Dyson House, 217 East Jefferson, 54665 608-637-8644
Viroqua	Viroqua Heritage Inn B&B, 220 E. Jefferson St, 54665 608-637-3306
Wabeno	Crystal Bell B&B, 4226 River St., 54566 715-473-2202
Washington Island	Findlay's Holiday Inn, PO Box 135, 54246 414-847-2526
Washington Island	Island House B&B, RR 1, Box 139, 54246 414-847-2779
Waterford	River View Inn, 202 W Racine St, 53185 414-534-5049
Waterloo	Carousel B&B, 144 E Polk St, 53594 414-478-2536
Watertown	Brandt Quirk Manor, 410 S. Fourth St, 53094 414-261-7917
Watertown	Karlshuegel Inn B&B, 749 N.Church St, Hwy 26, 53094 414-261-3980
Waukesha	Joanie's B&B, 615 E. Newhall Ave, 53186 414-542-5698
Waukesha	Mill Creek Farm B&B, S47W22099 Lawnsdale Rd, 53186 414-542-4311
Waupaca	Crystal River B&B, E1369 Rural Rd, 54980 715-258-5333
Waupaca	Green Fountain Inn, 604 South Main St, 54981 715-258-5136
Waupaca	Thomas Pipe Inn, 11032 Pipe Rd, 54981 715-824-3161
Waupaca	Walker's Barn B&B, E1268 Cleghorn Rd, 54981 715-258-5235
Waupaca	White Horse B&B, E2341 Crystal Rd, 54981 715-258-6162
Waupaca	Windmill Manor, N 2919 Hwy QQ, 54981 715-256-1770
Waupun	Rose Ivy Inn, 228 S. Watertown St, 53963 414-324-2127
Wausau	Everest Inn, 601 McIndoe St, 54403 715-848-5651
Wausau	Rosenberry Inn, 511 Franklin St, 54401 715-842-5733
Wausau	The Eliza Inn, 504 Franklin St, 54403 715-842-2722
Wauwatosa	The Little Red House B&B, 9212 Jackson Park Blvd, 53226 414-479-0646
West Bend	Mayer-Pick Haus, 710 Beech St, 53095 414-335-1524
West Salem	Wolfway Farm, Rural Route 1, Box 18, 54669 608-486-2686
Westby	Westby House, 200 W State St, 54667 608-634-4112
Westfield	Martha's Ethnic B&B, 226 2nd St, 53964 608-296-3361
Westfield	Millpond B&B, PO Box 22, 53964 608-296-1495
Whitehall	The Augustine House, W18821 North River Rd, 54773 175-538-4749
Whitewater	Greene House Country Inn, W5666 US Hwy. 12, 53190 414-495-8771
Whitewater	Hamilton House B&B, 328 West Main St, 53190 414-473-1900
Whitewater	Victoria on Main B&B, 622 West Main St, 53190 414-473-8400
Wild Rose	Birdsong B&B, PO Box 151, 54984 414-622-3770
Williams Bay	Bailey House, 372 Geneva St, 53191 414-245-9149
Wilton	Dorset Ridge Guest House, Rt. 1, Box 205, 54670 608-463-7375
Wilton	Rice's Whispering Pines, R #2, Box 225, 54670 608-435-6531
Winter	Chippewa River Inn B&B, N4836 County Road G, 54896 715-266-2662
Wisconsin Dells	Bennett House, 825 Oak St, 53965
Wisconsin Dells	Hawk's View B&B, E11344 Pocahontas Cl, 53965 608-254-2979
Wisconsin Dells	Historic Bennett House, 825 Oak St, 53965 608-254-2500
Wisconsin Dells	The White Rose B&B Inn, 910 River Rd, 53965 608-254-4724
Wisconsin Rapids	Sigrid's B&B, 340 Lincoln St, 54494 715-423-3846
Woodruff	Jo's Place North B&B, PO Box 1744, 54568 715-356-6682
Woodruff	Stonehouse B&B, 11371 Wihega Rd, 54568
Wrightstown	R & R Homestead, 444 Janet Court, 54180 920-336-8244

Wyoming

Alta	Teton Canyon B&B, Rt 1 Box 3740 Alta N Rd, 83422 307-353-2208
Banner	Blue Barn B&B, PO Box 200, 82832 307-672-2381
Big Horn	Spahn's Big Horn Mountain, PO Box 579, 82833 307-674-8150
Buffalo	Cloud Peak Inn, 590 N. Burritt Ave, 82834 307-684-5794
Buffalo	Paradise Guest Ranch, PO Box 790, 82834 307-684-7876
Buffalo	TA Guest Ranch, PO Box 313, 82834
Buffalo	Triple Three Ranch, 333 French Creek Rd., 82834 307-684-2832
Casper	Antique B&B, 939 S Wolcott St., 82601 307-265-2304
Casper	Bessemer Bend B&B, 6905 Speas Rd, 82604 307-265-6819
Cheyenne	Adventurer's Country B&B, 3803 I-80 E. Service Rd, 82009 307-632-4087
Cheyenne	Bit-O-Wyo Ranch B&B, 470 Happy Jack Rd, 82009 307-638-8340

Cheyenne	Howdy Pardner B&B, 1920 Tranquility Rd, 82009 307-634-6493
Cheyenne	Porch Swing B&B, 712 E. 20th St, 82001 307-778-7182
Cheyenne	Rainsford Inn, 219 E. 18th St, 82001 307-638-2337
Cheyenne	Storyteller Pueblo B&B, 5201 Ogden Rd, 82009 307-634-7036
Cheyenne	Windy Hills Guest House, 393 Happy Jack Rd, 82007 307-632-6423
Clearmont	Powder River Experience, PO Box 208, 82831 307-736-2402
Clearmont	R.B.L. Bison Ranch, 4355 U.S. Hwy. 14-16 E, 82835 307-758-4387
Cody	Blackwater Creek Ranch, 1516 Northfork Hwy, 82414 307-587-5201
Cody	Buffalo Bill's Cody House, 101 Robertson St, 82414 307-587-2528
Cody	Chapel House B&B, 2401 Cedar Ct, 82414 307-527-5711
Cody	Cody Guest Houses, 1525 Beck Ave, 82414 307-587-6000
Cody	Goff Creek Lodge, PO Box 155, 82414 307-587-3753
Cody	House of Burgess, 1508 Alger Ave, 82414
Cody	Hunter Peak Ranch, Box 1731, 82414
Cody	Parson's Pillow B&B, 1202 14th St, 82414 307-587-2382
Cody	Rimrock Dude Ranch, 2728 Northford Rt, 82414 307-587-3970
Cody	Trout Creek Inn, U.S. Hwy.14, 16, 20, W, 82414 307-587-6288
Cody	Wind Chimes Cottage B&B, 1501 Beck Ave, 82414 307-527-5310
Devils Tower	R-Place, Box 28, 82714 307-467-5938
Douglas	Carriage House B&B, 1031 Steinle Rd, 82633 307-358-6954
Douglas	Cheyenne River Ranch, 1031 Steinle Rd, 82633 307-358-2380
Douglas	Deer Forks Ranch, 1200 Poison Lake Rd, 82633 307-358-2033
Douglas	Two Creek Ranch, 800 Esterbrook Rd, 82633 307-358-3467
Douglas	Wagonhound Ranch, 1061 Poison Lake Rd, 82633 307-358-5439
Dubois	Jakey's Fork B&B, Box 635, 82513 307-455-2769
Dubois	Lazy L&B Ranch, 1072 E Fork Rd, 82513 800-453-9488
Dubois	Mackenzie Highland Ranch, 3945 US Hwy 26, 82513 307-455-3415
Dubois	Mountain Top B&B, PO Box 538, 82513
Dubois	Wapiti Ridge Ranch, 3915 US Hwy, 82513 307-455-2219
Encampment	Grand & Sierra B&B, Box 312, 82325 307-327-5200
Encampment	Rustic Mountain Lodge, Star Route 49, 82325 307-327-5539
Evanston	Pine Gables B&B, 1049 Center St, 82930 307-789-2069
Four Corners	Four Corners Enterprises, 24713 US Hwy 85, 82715 307-746-4776
Gillette	Deer Park, PO Box 1089, 82717 307-682-9832
Gillette	Skybow Castle Ranch, PO Box 2739, 82717 307-682-3228
Glenrock	Hotel Higgins, PO Box 741, 82637 307-436-9212
Glenrock	Opal's B&B, PO Box 94, 82637 307-436-2626
Greybull	Historic Hotel Greybull, 602 Greybull Ave., 82426 307-765-2012
Hulett	Diamond L Ranch, PO Box 70, 82720 307-467-5236
Jackson	Bedroll & Breakfast, Box 3700, 83001 307-733-5171
Jackson	Bentwood B&B, PO Box 561, 83001 307-739-1411
Jackson	Davy Jackson Inn, PO Box 20147, 83001 307-739-2294
Jackson	Don't Fence Me Inn, PO Box 25170, 83001 307-733-7979
Jackson	Inn on the Creek, 295 N Millward St, 83001 307-739-1565
Jackson	Moose Creek Ranch, PO Box 3108, 83001 800-676-0075
Jackson	Nowlin Creek Inn, PO Box 2766, 83001 307-733-0882
Jackson	Rancho Alegre, PO Box 998, 83001
Jackson	Rusty Parrot Lodge, PO Box 1657, 83001 307-733-2000
Jackson	Sundance Inn, 135 W. Broadway, 83001 307-733-3444
Jackson	The Alpine House, PO Box 20245, 83001 307-739-1570
Jackson	Twin Mountain River Ranch, Star Rt 40, 83001 307-733-1168
Jackson	Wilderness Trails B&B, PO Box 3700, 83001 307-733-5171
Jackson Hole	The Sassy Moose Inn, 3859 Miles Rd, HC 362, 83001 307-733-1277
Kaycee	Grave's B&B, 1729 Barnum Rd. #410, 82639 307-738-2319
Lander	Blue Spruce Inn, 677 S 3rd St., 82520 307-332-8253
Lander	Country Fare B&B, 550 Cliff St, 82520 307-332-9604
Lander	Edna's B&B, 53 North Fork Rd, 82520 307-332-3175
Lander	The Outlaw B&B, 2411 Squaw Creek Rd, 82520 307-332-9655
Lander	Whispering Winds B&B, 695 Canyon Rd, 82520 307-332-9735
Laramie	Inn on Ivinson, 719 Ivinson, 82070 307-745-8939
Laramie	Prairie Breeze B&B, 718 Invinson Ave., 82070 307-745-5482
Laramie	Vee Bar Guest Ranch, 2091 State Hwy 130, 82070 307-745-7036
Lovell	Schively Ranch, 1062 Road 15, 92431 307-548-6688
Lovell	The.TX Guest Ranch, Rural, 82431 307-548-6751
Lusk	Mill Iron 7 Ranch, PO Box 415, 82225 307-334-2951
Lusk	Sage & Cactus Village, SR 1, Box 158, 82225 307-663-7653
Lusk	Wyoming Whale Ranch, Box 115, 82225 307-334-3598
Manderson	Harmony Ranch Cottage, PO Box 25, 82432 307-568-2514
Moose	The Cottonwoods Ranch, PO Box 95, 83012 307-733-0945
Moran	Box K Ranch, Box 110, 83013 307-543-2407
Moran	Cowboy Village Resort, PO Box 91, 83001 800-543-2847
Moran	Diamond D Ranch-Outfitters, Buffalo Valley, Box 211, 83013 307-543-2479
Moran	Heart Six Guest Ranch, PO Box 70, 83013
Moran	The Inn at Buffalo Fork, PO Box 311, 93013 307-543-2010
Newcastle	4W Ranch Recreation, 1162 Lynch Rd, 82701 307-746-2815
Newcastle	Eva-Great Spirit Ranch B&B, 1262 Beaver Creek Rd, 82701 307-746-2537
Newcastle	Horton House B&B, 17 South Summit, 82701 307-746-4366
Parkman	Double Rafter Ranch, 521 Pass Creek Rd, 82838 307-655-9362

Pinedale	Boulder Lake Lodge, Box 1100 H, 82941 307-537-5400
Pinedale	Flying A Ranch, Rte 1, Box 7, 82941 800-678-6543
Pinedale	Pole Creek Ranch B&B, PO Box 278, 82941 307-367-4433
Powell	I Can Rest Ranch, 1041 Lane 11, Rt#3, 82435 307-754-4178
Ranchester	Historic Old Stone House, 135 Wolf Creek Rd., 82839 307-655-9239
Rawlins	Bit O' Country B&B, 221 W Spruce St, 82301 307-328-2111
Rawlins	Ferris Mansion B&B, 607 W Maple, 82301 307-324-3961
Rawlins	Lamont Inn, Lander Rt. Box 9, 82301 307-324-7602
Recluse	Cow Camp, 931 Beason Rd, 82725 307-687-1210
Rock River	Dodge Creek Ranch, 402 Tunnel Rd, 82083 307-322-2345
Saratoga	Brooksong B&B Home, Star Route Box 9L, 82331 307-326-8744
Saratoga	Far Out West B&B, 304 N 2nd St, 82331 307-326-9864
Saratoga	Hood House B&B, 214 N. 3rd. St, 82331 307-326-8901
Savery	Savery Creek Thoroughbred, Ranch, Box 24, 82332 307-383-7840
Shell	Clucas Ranch B&B, 1710 Hwy. 14, 82441 307-765-2946
Shell	Mayland Ranch Recreation, Box 215, 82441 307-765-2669
Shell	Snow Shoe Lodge, Box 215, 82441 307-765-2669
Shell	Trappers Rest B&B, PO Box 166, 82441 307-765-9239
Sheridan	Old Croff House B&B, 508 W Works, 82801 307-672-0898
Sheridan	Ponderosa Pines, 122 N Main St., 82801 307-751-4210
Sheridan	Spead-O-Wigwam Ranch, PO Box 1081, 82801 307-655-3217
Story	• Piece of Cake B&B, PO Box 111, 82842 307-332-7608
Story	Piney Creek Inn B&B, 11 Skylark Lane, 82842 307-683-2338
Story	Story Cabin, PO Box 533, 82842 307-635-2398
Sundance	Canfield Ranch, Box 952, 82729 307-283-2062
Ten Sleep	The Horned Toad B&B, Box 403, 82442 307-366-2747
Thermopolis	Broadway Inn B&B, 342 Broadway, 82443 307-864-2636
Thermopolis	Faye's B&B, 1020 Arapahoe, 82443 307-864-5166
Thermopolis	Out West B&B, 1344 Broadway, 82443 307-864-2700
Wapiti	Elephant Head Lodge, 1170 Yellowstone Pk Hwy, 82450 307-587-3980
Wapiti	Kinkade Guest Kabin, 87 Green Creek Rd, 82450 307-587-5905
Wheatland	Blackbird Inn, 1101 11th St, 82201 307-322-4540
Wheatland	Homestead B&B, 431 E Havely Rd, 82201
Wheatland	Homestead B&B, 431 E. Havely Rd., 82201 307-422-3316
Wilson	Moose Meadows B&B, 83014 307-733-9510
Wilson	Teton Tree House, PO Box 550, 83014 307-733-3233
Wilson	Teton View B&B, 2136 Coyote Loop, 83014 307-733-7954

Puerto Rico

Condado	Aloe Inn On The Beach, 1125 Cale Seaview, 00907
Condado	El Prado Inn, 1350 Luchetti St, 00907 809-728-5526
Culebra Island	Casa Llave, PO Box 60, 00775 809-742-3559
La Parguera	Parador Villa Parguera, Rt. 304, 00667 809-899-3975
Luguillo	Parador Martorell, Inc., PO Box 384, 00773 787-889-2710
Maricao	La Hacienda Juanita B&B, PO Box 777, 00606 787-838-2550
Rincon	Tamboo Resorts, H-C 01 4433, 00743
San Juan	Arcade Inn Guest House, 8 Taft St. - Condado, 00911 809-725-0668
San Juan	El Convento, PO Box 1048, 00902
San Juan	Galeria San Juan, Blvd. del Valle 204-206, 00901
San Juan	L'habitation Beach, 1957 Calle Italia, 00911 809-727-2499
San Juan	La Condesa Inn-Guest House, 2071 Cacique St, 00911 809-727-3698
San Juan	Ocean Walk Guest House, 1 Atlantic Pl ,Ocean Pk, 00911 809-728-0855
San Juan	Wind Chimes, 53 Calle Taft, 00911 809-727-4153
Santurce	Hosteria del Mar, 1 Tapia St. Ocean Park, 00911 787-727-3302
Utuado	Casa Grande, PO Box 616, 00641 787-894-3939

Virgin Islands

Christiansted	Club Comanche Hotel, 1 Strand St, 00820 809-773-0210
Cruz Bay	Frank Bay B&B, PO Box 408, 00831 809-693-8617
St. Croix	Anchor Inn, 58-A King St, 00820 340-773-4000
St. Croix	Pink Fancy Hotel, 27 Prince St, 00820 340-773-8460
St. Croix	Sprat Hall Plantation, PO Box 695, 00841 340-772-0305
St. Croix	Waves at Cane Bay, PO Box 1749, 00850 340-778-1805
St. John	Caneel Bay, PO Box 720, 00830
St. John	Estate Zootenvaal, Hurricane Hole, 00830 809-776-6321
St. John	Inn At Tamarind Court, PO Box 350, 00831
St. John	Villa Bougainvillea, PO Box 349, 00830 809-776-6420
St. Thomas	Admiral's Inn, Villa Olga, 00802
St. Thomas	Blue Beard's Castle, PO Box 7480, 00801 340-774-1600
St. Thomas	Bolongo Bay Beach & Tennis, PO Box 7337, 00801
St. Thomas	Bunkers' Hill View House, 9 Commandant Bade, 00801 340-774-8056
St. Thomas	Hotel 1829, 30 Kongens Gade, 00801 340-774-1829
St. Thomas	Inn at Mandahl, PO Box 2483, 00803 340-775-2100
St. Thomas	Villa Santana, Denmark Hill, 00802 340-776-1311

Reservation Service Organizations

These are businesses through which you can reserve a room in thousands of private homes. In many cases, rooms in homes are available where there may not be an inn. Also, guest houses are quite inexpensive. RSOs operate in different ways. Some represent a single city or state. Others cover the entire country. Some require a small membership fee. Others sell a list of their host homes. Many will attempt to match you with just the type of accommodations you're seeking and you may pay the RSO directly for your lodging.

—————————————————————U.S.A.—————————————————————

ALASKA————————————————————————————————

Alaska Private Lodgings
704 West 2nd, PO Box 200047
Anchorage 99520
E-mail: apl@alaskabandb.net
Web: alaskabandb.com

907-258-1717
Fax: 907-258-6613
$65-$150
• Deposit 1 night, or CC guarantee
Visa, Mastercard, American Express
German, French, Spanish

Brochure Free
Alaska
8am - 7pm M-S
125 Houses

Ketchikan Reservation Service
412 D-1 Loop Rd
Ketchikan 99901
E-mail: krs@ktn.net
Web: ketchikan-lodging.com

907-247-5337 800-987-5337
Fax: 907-247-5337
60-125
• Deposit required
Visa, Mastercard, American Express, Discover

Alaska
40 Houses

ARIZONA————————————————————————————————

Arizona Trails B&B Reservation
PO Box 18998
Fountain Hills 85269
E-mail: aztrails@
arizonatrails.com
Web: arizonatrails.com/

888-799-4284 480-837-4284
Fax: 480-816-4224
75-545
• Deposit required,
One night plus
Visa, Mastercard, American Express, Discover

Free brochure
158 Houses

CALIFORNIA ————————————————————————————————

B&B San Francisco
PO Box 420009
San Francisco 94142
E-mail: bbsf@linex.com
Web: bbsf.com

415-899-0060 800-899-9944
$65-$250
• Deposit 1 night,
Sample list $2
Visa, Mastercard, American Express
German, French, Spanish, Russian

Free brochure
California
9:30am-5pm M-F
100 Houses

B&B California
PO Box 2247
Saratoga 95070
E-mail: info@bbintl.com
Web: bbintl.com

408-867-9662 800-872-4500
Fax: 408-867-0907
150-175
Deposit required, Listing $2
SASE
Visa, Mastercard, American Express, Discover

Free brochure
California
9am-4pm M-F
500 Houses

Cohost, America's B&B
11715 S Circle Dr
Whittier 90601

562-695-7523
90-125
Deposit in full, Free broch.
SASE

Free broch. SASE
CA/Can/Jp/Ger/UK
7am-7pm daily
23 Houses

COLORADO

Authentic Inns Pikes Peak Region
PO Box 6807
Colorado Springs 80934
E-mail: pikespeak@
bbonline.com

719-685-2388
Fax: 888-892-2237
75-150

CONNECTICUT

Bed & Breakfast, Ltd.
PO Box 216
New Haven 06513
E-mail: bandbltd@aol.com
Web: bedandbreakfastltd.com

203-469-3260
75-179
Deposit 20%, 48 hr. cancel
Visa, Mastercard
French, Spanish, German

Free broch. SASE
CT, MA, RI
4-9:pm M-F
125 Houses

Covered Bridge
69 Maple Ave
Norfolk 06058
E-mail: tremblay@esslink.com
Web: obs-us.com/chesler/
coveredbridge

860-542-5944
Fax: 860-542-5690
100-250
• Deposit in full, Booklet $5
Visa, Mastercard, American
Express
French

Free brochure
CT, MA, NY, RI
9am-6pm 7 days
75 Houses

Nutmeg B&B Agency
PO Box 271117
West Hartford 06127
E-mail: nutmeg@home.com
Web: BnB-Link.com

860-236-6698 800-727-7592
Fax: 860-232-7680
$75-$210
• Ccard for deposit,
Booklet $5
Visa, Mastercard, American
Express

Free brochure
Connecticut
9:30am-5pm M-F
100 Houses

DISTRICT OF COLUMBIA

B&B Accommodations, Ltd.
PO Box 12011
Washington 20005
E-mail: bnbaccom@aol.com
Web: bnbaccom.com

202-328-3510
Fax: 202-332-3885
$55 and up
• Deposit $25, Balance due
2 wks
Visa, Mastercard, American
Express, Discover
French, Spanish

Free brochure
Washington, D.C.
10am-5pm M-F
85 Houses

B&B League/Sweet Dreams & Toast
PO Box 9490
Washington 20016
E-mail: bedandbreakfast-
washingtondc@erols.com
Web:
bedandbreakfastwashdc.com

202-363-7767
Fax: 202-363-8396
$75-$150
Deposit $25, Non-refundable
Visa, Mastercard, American
Express, Discover

Free brochure
Washington, D.C.
9am-5pm M-Th
72 Houses

LOUISIANA

New Orleans B&B Accommodations
671 Rosa Ave, Suite 208
Metairie 70005
E-mail: smb@
neworleansbandb.com
Web: neworleansbandb.com

504-838-0071 888-240-0070
Fax: 504-838-0140
65-300
Deposit required
Visa, Mastercard, American
Express, Discover

Free brochure
Louisiana
9am-4pm Mon-Fri
75 Houses

MARYLAND

Amanda'S B&B Reservation Service 3538 Lakeway Road Ellicott City 21042 *E-mail:* amandasrs@aol.com *Web:* amandas-bbrs.com/	443-535-0008 800-899-7533 Fax: 443-535-0009 $70 and up Deposit 1 night, Listing $5 SASE Visa, Mastercard, American Express, Discover French, German, Italian, Arab	$10 brochure Maryland, PA, DE 5:30-8:30 M-F 200 Houses

MASSACHUSETTS

A B&B Agency Of Boston 47 Commercial Wharf Boston 02110 *E-mail:* bosbnb@aol.com *Web:* boston-bnbagency.com	617-720-3540 800-248-9262 Fax: 617-523-5761 $80-$160 • Deposit 30%-50% Visa, Mastercard, American Express French, Spanish, German, Arab, Italian	Free brochure Massachusetts 9am-9pm 7 days 150 Houses
B&B Reservations PO Box 600035, Newtonville Boston/Cape Cod 02460 *E-mail:* info@bbreserve.com *Web:* bbreserve.com	617-964-1606 800-832-2632 Fax: 617-332-8572 $85-$225 Deposit required Visa, Mastercard, American Express	Brochure free Boston, Cape Cod 9am-5pm, Mon-Fri. 88 Houses

NEW JERSEY

Delaware Valley Excursions PO Box 459 Stockton 08559 *E-mail:* info@ innreservations.com *Web:* innreservations.com	609-397-9494 800-981-4667 Fax: 609-397-1928 75-300 Deposit required Visa, Mastercard, American Express	Free brochure Bucks County, PA 9am-5pm Mon-Fri. 40 Houses

NEW YORK

Elaine'S B&B Selections 4987 Kingston Rd Elbridge 13060	315-689-2082 $60-$275 Deposit 1 night Visa, Mastercard, American Express	List SASE ME, MA, NY, NH, NY, VT 10am-7pm, daily 85 Houses
Abode Bed & Breakfast, Ltd. PO Box 20022 New York 10021 *Web:* abode1.com	212-472-2000 800-835-8880 $135-$400 Deposit 25%, 2 nights minimun American Express	Free brochure NY: Manhattan 9am-5pm Mon-Fri 35 Houses
At Home In New York PO Box 407 New York 10185 *E-mail:* athomeny@erols.com *Web:* travelguides.com/bb/newyork/	212-956-3125 800-692-4262 Fax: 212-247-3294 $90-$135 • Deposit 25% Visa, Mastercard, American Express French, Spanish, German	Free brochure New York 9am-5pm Mon-Fri 300 Houses
B&B Network Of New York 134 W 32nd St, #602 New York 10001	212-645-8134 800-900-8134 100-150 • Deposit 25%	Free brochure New York 8am-6pm Mon-Fri 200 Houses

NEW YORK (*cont'd.*)

Bed & Breakfast (& Books) 35 West 92nd St New York 10025	212-865-8740 Fax: 212-865-8740 $100-$120 • Deposit 25% French, German	Free list SASE Manhattan 10am-5pm, Mon-Fri 50 Houses
Assured Accommodations, Inc 225 Lafayette St New York City 10012 *E-mail:* mail@assurednyc.com *Web:* assurednyc.com	212-431-0569 Fax: 212-421-7088 115-200 • Deposit 3 nights Visa, Mastercard, American Express	Free brochure 10am-6pm Mon-Fri
A Reasonable Alternative, Inc. 117 Spring St Port Jefferson 11777 *E-mail:* kdexter@portjeff.net	516-928-4034 516-473-7402 Fax: 516-331-7641 60-250 $50 Deposit Visa, Mastercard	Free Brochure Long Island, NY Mon-Fri, 12-5 30 Houses
American Country Collection 1353 Union St Schenectady 12308 *E-mail:* carolbnbres@msn.com *Web:* bandbreservations.com	518-370-4948 800-810-4948 Fax: 518-393-1634 $85-$200 • Deposit 50% of stay Visa, Mastercard, American Express, Discover	Free brochure Vermont 10am-5pm M-F 85 Houses

NORTH CAROLINA

Advance Accommodations 56 N0rth Main St Weaverville 28787 *E-mail:* advncaccom@aol.com *Web:* AdvanceAccommodations.com	828-645-6420 800-854-4924 Fax: 828-645-6420 89-250 • Deposit required Visa, Mastercard, Discover	Free Brochure North Carolina 9am - 6pm 100 Houses

OHIO

Columbus Bed & Breakfast 763 S 3rd St Columbus 43206	614-444-8888 $65 to $75 Deposit $25	Free brochure Columbus, OH 24 hours 10 Houses

PENNSYLVANIA

Rest & Repast B&B Service PO Box 126 Pine Grove Mills 16868 *Web:* iul.com/bnbinpa/	814-238-1484 Fax: 814-234-9890 75-135 Deposit $50	Free broch. SASE Central PA 8:30-11:30am M-F 55 Houses
Assoc. Of B&Bs In Philadelphia PO Box 562 Valley Forge 19481 *E-mail:* pa@bnbassociation.com	610-783-7838 800-344-0123 Fax: 610-783-7787 50-250 • Credit card needed, for guarantee Visa, Mastercard, American Express, Discover Spanish, French	Free brochure Pennsylvania 10am-6pm 7 days 100 Houses

SOUTH CAROLINA

Historic Charleston B&B
57 Broad St
Charleston 29401
E-mail: histchasbnb@
charleston.net
Web: charleston.net/com/
bed&breakfast

843-722-6606 800-743-3583
Fax: 843-722-9589
$135-$195
Deposit 1 night,
Reservation Fee
Visa, Mastercard

Free brochure
South Carolina
9am-5pm M-F
60 Houses

TEXAS

Sand Dollar Hospitality
3605 Mendenhall Dr.
Corpus Christi 78415
E-mail: bednbrkfst@aol.com
Web: ccinternet.net/sand-dollar

361-853-1222 800-528-7782
Fax: 361-814-1285
$75-$205
• Deposit 33%
Visa, Mastercard
French

Free brochure
Texas
7:30-9:30pm
20 Houses

B&B: The National Network
Box 764703
Dallas 75376
Web: go-lodging.com

888-866-4262 972-780-1928
Fax: 972-298-7118
50-150
• Deposit 1 night
Visa, Mastercard, American
Express, Discover

Free brochure
United States
9am-5pm Mon-Fri
3,000 Houses

**Gasthaus Schmidt Reserv.
Serv.**
231 West Main St
Fredericksburg 78624
E-mail: gasthaus@ktc.com
Web: fbglodging.com

830-997-5612
Fax: 830-997-8282
$65-$150
• Deposit required, $4
catalog
Visa, Mastercard, American
Express, Discover

Free brochure
Gillespie Country, TX
9am-8pm M-F
110 Houses

VIRGINIA

Blue Ridge B&B Rso
2458 Castleman Road
Berryville 22611
E-mail: blurdgbb@shentel.net
Web: blueridgebb.com

540-955-1246 800-296-1246
Fax: 540-955-4240
$65-$250
• Full deposit
Visa, Mastercard, American
Express
Spanish

Free broch. SASE
VA, WV, MD, PA
10:30am-3:30pm
50 Houses

Guesthouses B&B, Inc.
PO Box 5737, 300 Preston Ave
Charlottesville 22905
E-mail:
guesthouses_bnb_reservations
@compuserve.com
Web: va-guesthouses.com

804-979-7264
Fax: 804-293-7791
68-200
• Deposit 25% + Tax, 2
nights minimun
Visa, Mastercard, American
Express, Discover
French, German

List $1 with SASE
Central Virginia
Noon-5pm Mon-Fri
60 Houses

**Bensonhouse Of
Fredericksburg**
2036 Monument Ave
Richmond 23220
E-mail: be.our.guest@
bensonhouse.com
Web: bensonhouse.com

804-353-6900
95-155
• Deposit 1 night
Visa, Mastercard, American
Express

Broch. Free SASE
Virginia
11am-6pm M-F
40 Houses

WASHINGTON

A Pacific Reservation Service PO Box 46894 Seattle 98146 *E-mail:* pacificb@nwlink.com *Web:* seattlebedandbreakfast.com	206-439-7677 800-684-2832 Fax: 206-431-0932 $49-$220 Deposit $25 Visa, Mastercard, American Express	Brochure $5 Washington, OR 8:30-5:30 220 Houses
Greater Tacoma B&B Reserv. 3312 N Union Ave Tacoma 98407 *E-mail:* reservations@tacoma-inns.org *Web:* tacoma-inns.org	253-759-4088 800-406-4088 Fax: 253-759-4025 $65-$200 • Deposit 1 night, 7 day cancel req. Visa, Mastercard, American Express, Discover	Free brochure Washington 9am-9pm 7 days 26 Houses

CANADA

BRITISH COLUMBIA

Old English B&B Registry 1226 Silverwood Crescent North Vancouver V7P 1J3 *E-mail:* relax@ oldenglishbandb.bc.ca *Web:* bandbinn.com	604-986-5069 Fax: 604-986-8810 $85-$175 Canadian • Credit Card to hold, 14 CP Visa, Mastercard	Free brochure British Columbia 10am-6pm Daily 35 Houses
Town & Country B&B Reservation PO Box 74542, 2803 W4th Ave Vancouver V6K 1K2 *Web:* tcbb.bc.ca	604-731-5942 Fax: 604-731-5942 75-190 Deposit 1 night, 7 days cancel Visa, Mastercard French, German, Spanish	British Columbia 9am-4:30pm Mon-Fr 30 Houses
Garden City 660 Jones Terrace Victoria, Vancouver V8Z 2L7 *E-mail:* gardencity@bc-bed-breakfast.com *Web:* bc-bed-breakfast.com	250-479-1986 Fax: 250-479-9999 41-140 • One night deposit Visa, Mastercard, American Express French, German, Spanish, Welsch, Danish, Japanese	Free brochure British Columbia 8am-10pm daily 65 Houses

ENGLAND

Uptown Reservations 41 Paradise Walk Chelsea, London SW3 4JL *E-mail:* inquiries.uptownres.co.uk *Web:* uptownres.co.uk	+44-207-351-3445 Fax: +44-207-351-9383 90-145 English$ • Deposit required Visa, Mastercard, American Express, Eurocard	Free brochure Central London 9:30-5:30 M-F 85 Houses

B&B Inns with Special Features

Antiques

Many of the inns we list are graced by antiques. These inns have put a special emphasis on antiques and period decor.

Lavender Hill B&B
Sonora, CA

Long's Sea View B&B
Santa Barbara, CA

Thirty Nine Cypress
Point Reyes, CA

Florida House Inn
Amelia Island, FL

Jailer's Inn
Bardstown, KY

Columns on Jordan
Shreveport, LA

Chetwynd House Inn
Kennebunkport, ME

Isaac Randall House
Freeport, ME

Barn on Howard's Cove
Annapolis, MD

Gibson's Lodgings
Annapolis, MD

Century House
Nantucket, MA

Four Columns Inn
Sherburn, MN

Bluebird B&B
Gerald, MO

Bungay Jar B&B
Franconia, NH

1880 House B&B
Westhampton Beach, NY

Adrianna B&B
Dolgeville, NY

Stagecoach Inn
Lake Placid, NY

Thistlebrook B&B
Cooperstown, NY

White House Lodge
Warrensburg, NY

Folkestone Inn B&B
Bryson City, NC

Lady Anne's Victorian
Winston-Salem, NC

House of Hunter
Roseburg, OR

Pookie's B&B College
Eugene, OR

Faircroft B&B
Ridgway, PA

Huntland Farm B&B
Greensburg, PA

Pineapple Inn
Lewisburg, PA

Sunflower Hill B&B
Moab, UT

Albatross B&B
Anacortes, WA

Channel House
Anacortes, WA

Oak Bay Guest House
Victoria, BC

Scholefield House
Victoria, BC

Gardens

Ah, to while away an hour in a lovely garden. What could be more relaxing? These inns are renowned for their lush gardens.

Mangels House
Aptos, CA

Mountain Home Inn
Mill Valley, CA

Murphy's Inn
Grass Valley, CA

North Coast
Gualala, CA

Stahlecker House
Napa Valley, CA

Apple Blossom
Leadville, CO

Briar Rose B&B
Boulder, CO

Bailey House
Amelia Island, FL

Admiral Peary House
Fryeburg, ME

Island House
Southwest Harbor, ME

Thurston House
Searsport, ME

York Harbor Inn
York Harbor, ME

Solomons Victorian
Solomons, MD

Ashley Manor
Barnstable, MA

Gables Inn
Lenox, MA

Whalewalk Inn
Eastham, MA

Curtis Field
Hampton, NH

Red Maple Farm
Princeton, NJ

Scarborough Inn
Ocean City, NJ

Victoria House
Spring Lake, NJ

Blushing Rose
Hammondsport, NY

Richards
Narragansett, RI

Parker House Inn
Quechee, VT

Red Shutter Inn
Wilmington, VT

Vermont Inn
Killington, VT

1880's Madison House
Lynchburg, VA

Shaughnessy Village
Vancouver, BC

Sunnymeade House
Victoria, BC

Pansy Patch
St. Andrews By-The-Sea,
NB

Gasthaus Switzerland
Ottawa, ON

Architecture

These inns are noted for their unusual and fine architecture.

Maricopa Manor
Phoenix, AZ
Ballard Inn
Ballard, CA
La Mer B&B
Ventura, CA
Shaw House B&B
Ferndale, CA
Tres Palmas B&B
Palm Desert, CA
Trinidad Bay
Trinidad, CA
Old Lyme Inn
Old Lyme, CT
Queen Anne Inn
New London, CT
Spring Bayou
Tarpon Springs, FL
Brunswick Manor
Brunswick, GA
Richards House
Dubuque, IA
"Suits Us" B&B
Rockville, IN
1886 Inn, The
La Grange, IN
Lafitte Guest House
New Orleans, LA
Madewood Plantation
Napoleonville, LA
Brannon-Bunker
Walpole, ME
Abacrombie Badger
Baltimore, MD
Chesapeake
Tilghman Island, MD
Glenburn B&B
Taneytown, MD
Kemp House Inn
St. Michaels, MD
Mary Rob B&B
Annapolis, MD
Devonfield
Lee, MA
Foxglove Cottage
Plymouth, MA

Inn at Duck Creeke
Wellfleet, MA
Manor House
West Yarmouth, MA
Parsonage Inn
East Orleans, MA
Simmons Homestead
Hyannis Port, MA
Thorncroft Inn
Martha's Vineyard
Island, MA
Village Green
Falmouth, MA
Winterwood
Petersham, MA
Dewey Lake Manor
Brooklyn, MI
Haan's 1830 Inn
Mackinac Island, MI
Raymond House Inn
Port Sanilac, MI
Sherwood Forest
Saugatuck, MI
Washington House
Washington, MO
Benjamin Prescott
Jaffrey, NH
Glynn House Inn
Ashland, NH
Inn by the Bandstand
Exeter, NH
Bay Head Gables
Bay Head, NJ
Henry Ludlam Inn
Dennisville, NJ
American Artists
Taos, NM
Dartmouth House
Rochester, NY
Inn at the Falls
Poughkeepsie, NY
William Seward
Westfield, NY
Miss Betty's B&B
Wilson, NC

Wagner's 1844 Inn
Sandusky, OH
Historic Shaniko
Shaniko, OR
Sea Star Guesthouse
Bandon, OR
Academy Street
Hawley, PA
Cedar Hill Farm
Mount Joy, PA
Roebling Inn
Lackawaxen, PA
Village Inn
Bird-In-Hand, PA
State House Inn
Providence, RI
Litchfield
Pawleys Island, SC
Shaw House
Georgetown, SC
Custer Mansion
Custer, SD
Calico Inn
Sevierville, TN
Brackenridge House
San Antonio, TX
Governor's Inn
Ludlow, VT
Grunberg Haus
Waterbury, VT
Middlebury Inn
Middlebury, VT
Watson House B&B
Chincoteague, VA
Mazama Country Inn
Mazama, WA
11 Gables
Lake Geneva, WI
Thorp House Inn
Fish Creek, WI
Bayberry Cliff
Murray River, PE
Auberge De La Fontaine
Montreal, PQ

Comfort

Old-fashioned comfort and friendly staff are important to every lodging. These inns have these qualities in abundance.

Comfy 'n Cozy
Fairbanks, AK
Birch Tree Inn
Flagstaff, AZ
Park Place B&B
Bisbee, AZ

5 Ojo Inn B&B
Eureka Springs, AR
Pelican Cove B&B
Carlsbad, CA
Pickford House B&B
Cambria, CA

Strawberry Creek
Idyllwild, CA
Zinfandel House
Calistoga, CA
Delaware Hotel
Leadville, CO

Comfort (*cont'd.*)

Eagle Cliff B&B
Estes Park, CO

Intermountain B&B
Vail, CO

William Penn
New Castle, DE

Duncan House
Bradenton Beach, FL

Dutch Cottage
Helen, GA

Golds B&B
Champaign, IL

Allison House
Nashville, IN

Grant Street
Bloomington, IN

Patchwork Quilt
Middlebury, IN

B&B at Sills Inn
Versailles, KY

Mansion B&B
Bardstown, KY

Paducah Harbor
Paducah, KY

RidgeRunner B&B
Middlesborough, KY

Gosnold Arms
New Harbor, ME

Betsy's B&B
Baltimore, MD

Beacon Hill B&B
Boston, MA

Col. Roger Brown
Concord, MA

Mulberry B&B
Wareham, MA

Seven Sea Street
Nantucket, MA

Stepping Stone
Salem, MA

Weathervane Inn
South Egremont, MA

Widow's Walk B&B
Sagamore Beach, MA

Hall House B&B
Kalamazoo, MI

Cameron's Crag
Branson, MO

Hyde Mansion
Trenton, MO

Sacajawea Inn
Three Forks, MT

Offutt House
Omaha, NE

Bretton Arms
Bretton Woods, NH

Sea Holly B&B
Cape May, NJ

Manchester House
Niagara Falls, NY

Big Lynn Lodge
Little Switzerland, NC

Claddagh Inn
Hendersonville, NC

Dry Ridge Inn B&B
Weaverville, NC

Long House B&B
Highlands, NC

Pines Country
Pisgah Forest, NC

Richmond Inn B&B
Spruce Pine, NC

Home by the Sea
Port Orford, OR

Carriage Corner
Intercourse, PA

Hillside Farm
Mount Joy, PA

Old Court B&B
Providence, RI

Sheffield House
Block Island, RI

Brasington House
Charleston, SC

Claussen's Inn
Columbia, SC

Laurel Hill
McClellanville, SC

TwoSuns Inn B&B
Beaufort, SC

White House B&B
Ducktown, TN

Southard-House
Austin, TX

Blue Church Lodge
Park City, UT

Hugging Bear
Chester, VT

Dulwich Manor
Amherst, VA

Fox & Grape
Williamsburg, VA

Isle of Wight
Smithfield, VA

Bradley House
Cathlamet, WA

Shumway Mansion
Kirkland, WA

Inn at Cedar
Sturgeon Bay, WI

Parkview B&B
Reedsburg, WI

Conference

Small conferences can be very productive when held in the inns listed, all of which have the facilities you need and the quiet and opportunity, too, for the followship you require.

Olde Stonehouse
Hardy, AR

Andrews Hotel
San Francisco, CA

Baywood Inn
Baywood Park, CA

Camellia Inn
Healdsburg, CA

Grey Whale
Fort Bragg, CA

Sea View Inn
Carmel by the Sea, CA

Whitegate Inn
Mendocino, CA

Chimney Crest
Bristol, CT

West Lane Inn
Ridgefield, CT

Chalet Suzanne
Lake Wales, FL

Herlong Mansion
Micanopy, FL

St. Francis Inn
St. Augustine, FL

King-Keith House
Atlanta, GA

Ramada White Hill
Warsaw, IN

Butler Greenwood
St. Francisville, LA

Bagley House
Durham, ME

Inn at Long Lake
Naples, ME

Egremont Inn
South Egremont, MA

Inn at Stockbridge
Stockbridge, MA

Lothrop Merry House
Vineyard Haven, MA

Old Sea Pines Inn
Brewster, MA

Doanleigh Inn
Kansas City, MO

Ashling Cottage
Spring Lake, NJ

Windward House
Cape May, NJ

Conference (*cont'd.*)

Bartlett House Greenport, NY	**Historic Falcon** McMinnville, TN	**Fountain Hall** Culpeper, VA
Inn At The Green Poland, OH	**Llano Grande** Nacogdoches, TX	**Hidden Inn** Orange, VA
Olde World B&B Dover, OH	**Patrician B&B Inn** Houston, TX	**Inn at Narrow Passage** Woodstock, VA
Evermay Erwinna, PA	**Old Miners** Park City, UT	**Killahevlin** Front Royal, VA
Magoffin Inn Mercer, PA	**Seven Wives Inn** St. George, UT	**Shelburne Inn** Seaview, WA
Quo Vadis B&B Franklin, PA	**Arlington Inn** Arlington, VT	
Thomas Bond House Philadelphia, PA	**Inn at Rutland** Rutland, VT	

Low Price

The following lodgings are particularly noted for modest pricing. It is possible to obtain a room for $40 or less.

June's B&B Tucson, AZ	**Paulus Gasthaus** Baltimore, MD	**Rose Hill Guest House** New Rochelle, NY
Anderson House Heber Springs, AR	**Anthony's Town House** Brookline, MA	**Thousand Islands Inn** Clayton, NY
Chalfant House Bishop, CA	**Captain Isaiah's** Bass River, MA	**Anderson Guest House** Wilmington, NC
Golden Gate San Francisco, CA	**Harborside House** Marblehead, MA	**B&B at Laurel Ridge** Siler City, NC
Pelennor B&B Mariposa, CA	**Irving House** Cambridge, MA	**Grandview Lodge** Waynesville, NC
Midwest Country Inn Limon, CO	**Rose Petal B&B** Dennisport, MA	**Red House Inn B&B** Brevard, NC
Embassy Inn Washington, DC	**Ship's Knees Inn** East Orleans, MA	**Grandview B&B** Astoria, OR
Gram's Place Tampa, FL	**Tuck Inn B&B** Rockport, MA	**Portland Guest** Portland, OR
Room at the Inn Homestead, FL	**Avon House B&B** Flint, MI	**Bayberry Inn B&B** Somerset, PA
Open Gates Darien, GA	**Nan's B&B** Minneapolis, MN	**Homestead Lodging** Smoketown, PA
Pittman House Commerce, GA	**Mountain Valley** Conway, NH	**Keystone Inn B&B** Gettysburg, PA
Tranquil Cherub Indianapolis, IN	**Cordova B&B Inn** Ocean Grove, NJ	**Runnymede Farm** Quarryville, PA
Almeda's B&B Inn Tonganoxie, KS	**Springside** Cape May, NJ	**Lindsey's Guest House** Newport, RI
Diuguid House Murray, KY	**El Paradero** Santa Fe, NM	**Sea Gull Guest House** Narragansett, RI
Dusty Mansion New Orleans, LA	**Laughing Horse Inn** Taos, NM	**Brustman House B&B** Myrtle Beach, SC
Arundel Meadows Arundel, ME	**Alexander's Inn** Deposit, NY	**Lakeside Farm B&B** Webster, SD
Black Duck Corea, ME	**Another Tyme B&B** Hammondsport, NY	**Skoglund Farm** Canova, SD
Burnt Cove B&B Stonington, ME	**Country Road Lodge** Warrensburg, NY	**Hart House B&B** Johnson City, TN
Todd House Eastport, ME	**Iris Stonehouse B&B** Utica, NY	**Laolke Lodge** Gaysville, VT
Lewrene Farm B&B Hagerstown, MD	**Red House Country** Burdett, NY	**Oak Grove Plantation** Cluster Springs, VA

Low Price (*cont'd.*)

Post House
Elkins, WV
Annie Moore's
Laramie, WY
Black Cat
Hinton, AB

Battery Street
Victoria, BC
Blue Spruces
Ottawa, ON

Armor Manoir
Sherbrooke
Montreal, PQ

Gourmet

An excellent meal can add a lot to your stay. The inns listed here are particularly celebrated for their fine cuisine.

Casa Alegre B&B
Tucson, AZ
Cinnamon Bear
St. Helena, CA
Columbia City
Columbia, CA
Ridenhour Ranch
Guerneville, CA
Upham Hotel
Santa Barbara, CA
Adobe Inn
Buena Vista, CO
Cottonwood Inn
Alamosa, CO
Leland House
Durango, CO
Butternut Farm
Glastonbury, CT
Copper Beech Inn
Ivoryton, CT
Checkerberry Inn
Goshen, IN
Old Hoosier House
Knightstown, IN
A Little Dream
Camden, ME
Bass Cove Farm
Sorrento, ME
Holbrook House
Bar Harbor, ME
Welby Inn
Kennebunkport, ME

Sunday's B&B
Hagerstown, MD
Cape Cod Claddagh
Harwich West, MA
Inn at the Pass
Pass Christian, MS
Southmoreland
Kansas City, MO
Torch & Toes B&B
Bozeman, MT
Deer Run Ranch
Carson City, NV
Stillmeadow B&B
Hampstead, NH
Inn On Ocean
Cape May, NJ
Chalet Waldheim
Burlington Flats, NY
Goose Creek
Southold, NY
Saltbox B&B
Hyde Park, NY
Veranda House
Rhinebeck, NY
Blooming Garden
Durham, NC
Bouldin House
High Point, NC
Bridle Path Inn
Asheville, NC
Buttonwood Inn
Franklin, NC

Stone Hedge Inn
Tryon, NC
B&B—The Manor
Lancaster, PA
Bankhouse B&B
West Chester, PA
Creekside Inn
Paradise, PA
Beaufort Inn
Beaufort, SC
Big Spring Inn
Greeneville, TN
Hawley House B&B
Jonesborough, TN
Fairview, A B&B
Austin, TX
Seasons B&B Inn
Tyler, TX
Canterbury House
Woodstock, VT
Thornrose House
Staunton, VA
Schnauzer Crossing
Bellingham, WA
Hampshire House 1884
Romney, WV
A Montreal Oasis
Montreal, PQ

Historic

Inns situated in historic buildings or locales hold a special appeal for many people. The following is a sampling.

1881 Crescent
Eureka Springs, AR
Cornelius Daly
Eureka, CA
Grove Inn
San Francisco, CA
Palmer Inn
Mystic, CT

Darley Manor Inn
Wilmington, DE
Reeds
Washington, DC
1810 West Inn
Thomson, GA
Homestead
Evanston, IL

New Orleans First
New Orleans, LA
Nottoway Plantation
White Castle, LA
Lawnmeer Inn
West Boothbay Harbor, ME
Parsonage Inn
St. Michaels, MD

Historic (*cont'd.*)

Union Square House
Baltimore, MD

Ashley Inn
Edgartown, MA

Colonial Inn
Edgartown, MA

Cyrus Kent House
Chatham, MA

Knoll
Florence, MA

Martin House
Nantucket, MA

Perryville Inn
Rehoboth, MA

Rivertown Inn
Stillwater, MN

Oak Square Plantation
Port Gibson, MS

Cedarcroft Farm
Warrensburg, MO

Inn St. Gemme Beauvais
Ste. Genevieve, MO

Three Rivers
North Woodstock, NH

Carroll Villa
Cape May, NJ

Humphrey Hughes
Cape May, NJ

Arius Compound
Santa Fe, NM

Don Gaspar
Santa Fe, NM

Asa Ransom House
Clarence, NY

Pink House
East Hampton, NY

Cover House
Andrews, NC

Inn at Old Fort
Old Fort, NC

Campbell House
Eugene, OR

Historic Witner
Lancaster, PA

King's Cottage
Lancaster, PA

Cliff View
Newport, RI

Stone House Club
Little Compton, RI

Ann Harper's B&B
Charleston, SC

Cannonboro Inn
Charleston, SC

Wildflowers B&B
Salt Lake City, UT

Linden Hse B&B
Champlain, VA

Harbinger Inn B&B
Olympia, WA

Luxury

These establishments are famed for their luxurious appointments and special attention to creature comforts and style.

Abigail's Mansion
Eureka, CA

Chaney House
Tahoe City, CA

Chateau du Sureau
Yosemite, CA

Deer Run Inn
St. Helena, CA

B&B on Mitchell Creek
Glenwood Springs, CO

Black Dog Inn
Estes Park, CO

Ice Palace Inn B&B
Leadville, CO

Starry Pines B&B
Snowmass, CO

Greenwoods Gate
Norfolk, CT

Castle Garden B&B
St. Augustine, FL

Greenville Inn
Greenville, ME

Kingsleigh Inn 1904
Southwest Harbor, ME

Noble House
Bridgton, ME

Beaver Creek
Hagerstown, MD

Birchwood Inn
Lenox, MA

Carriage House
Nantucket, MA

Tuckernuck Inn
Nantucket, MA

Yelton Manor B&B
South Haven, MI

School House B&B
Rocheport, MO

Voss Inn B&B
Bozeman, MT

Franconia Inn
Franconia, NH

Greenfield B&B Inn
Greenfield, NH

Inn at Smith Cove
Gilford, NH

Conover's Bay Head
Bay Head, NJ

Brae Loch Inn
Cazenovia, NY

Crown Point B&B
Crown Point, NY

Hanshaw House B&B
Ithaca, NY

Troutbeck
Amenia, NY

Colonial Pines Inn
Highlands, NC

Davidson Village
Davidson, NC

Pecan Tree Inn
Beaufort, NC

Pine Meadow Inn
Merlin, OR

Harry Packer Mansion
Jim Thorpe, PA

Kaltenbach's B&B
Wellsboro, PA

Historic Jacob Hill
Providence, RI

Adams Edgeworth
Monteagle, TN

Mason Place B&B
Loudon, TN

1811 House
Manchester, VT

Fitch Hill Inn
Hyde Park, VT

Hartness House Inn
Springfield, VT

Inn at Manchester
Manchester, VT

Kedron Valley Inn
South Woodstock, VT

Snow Goose Inn
West Dover, VT

Tulip Tree Inn
Chittenden, VT

High Meadows Inn
Scottsville, VA

Bombay House B&B
Bainbridge Island, WA

Annie's B&B
Madison, WI

Kenya Court
Vancouver, BC

Markham House B&B
Victoria, BC

Nature

Nature lovers, alert! Whether your fancy is ornithology or whale watching, these inns will speak to your heart.

Canyon Wren
Sedona, AZ
Bidwell House
Chester, CA
Coloma Country Inn
Coloma, CA
Moffatt House
San Francisco, CA
Power's Mansion
Auburn, CA
Cristiana Guesthaus
Crested Butte, CO
Lightner Creek Inn
Durango, CO
Mary Lawrence Inn
Gunnison, CO
B and B and Beach
Kauai, Hanalei, HI
Old Lahaina House
Maui, Lahaina, HI
Mandolin Inn
Dubuque, IA
Acadia Oceanside
Acadia Schoodic, ME
Captain Dexter
Edgartown, MA
Mostly Hall B&B
Falmouth, MA
Burggraf's Countrylane
Bigfork, MT

Willows Inn
Red Lodge, MT
Inn at Forest Hills
Franconia, NH
Olde Orchard Inn
Moultonboro, NH
Wilderness Inn B&B
North Woodstock, NH
Apple Valley Inn
Glenwood, NJ
Galisteo Inn
Galisteo, NM
All Tucked Inn
Westport, NY
River Run B&B Inn
Fleischmanns, NY
Slide Mt. Forest
Oliverea, NY
Lodge on Lake Lure
Lake Lure, NC
Eagles Mere Inn
Eagles Mere, PA
Golden Pheasant Inn
Erwinna, PA
Longswamp B&B
Mertztown, PA
Meadow Spring Farm
Kennett Square, PA
Pine Wood Acres
Scottdale, PA

William's Grant
Bristol, RI
Old Point Inn
Beaufort, SC
Willow Springs
Rapid City, SD
Brass Lantern Inn
Stowe, VT
Inn at Weathersfield
Perkinsville, VT
Madrigal Inn
Chester, VT
Mountaineer Inn
West Dover, VT
Ski Inn
Stowe, VT
Trail's End
Wilmington, VT
Cooney Mansion B&B
Aberdeen, WA
Run of the River B&B
Leavenworth, WA
Tunnel Mountain B&B
Elkins, WV
Golden Dreams B&B
Whistler, BC
Wooded Acres B&B
Victoria, BC
Haydon House
Ottawa, ON

Romance

Ah, romance! These inns offer a hideaway, a peaceful space in which to be together and let the world go by.

Gustavus Inn
Gustavus, AK
Abigail's B&B
Sacramento, CA
Apple Farm Inn
San Luis Obispo, CA
Beach House B&B
Cambria, CA
Brookside Farm B&B
Dulzura, CA
Casa Del Mar
Stinson Beach, CA
Casa Laguna B&B
Laguna Beach, CA
Elk Cove Inn
Elk, CA
Gold Mountain Manor
Big Bear, CA
Homestead
Ahwahnee, CA

Mansion Inn
Venice, CA
Marsh Cottage B&B
Inverness, CA
Requa Inn
Klamath, CA
Johnstone Inn
Telluride, CO
Inn at Chester
Chester, CT
Riverwind Inn
Deep River, CT
Harrington House
Holmes Beach, FL
Chateau des Fleurs
Winnetka, IL
Isle of View B&B
Metropolis, IL
Wheaton Inn
Wheaton, IL

Swan House
Camden, ME
Catoctin Inn
Buckeystown, MD
Robert Morris
Oxford, MD
Honeysuckle Hill
West Barnstable, MA
Sea Breeze Inn
Hyannis, MA
Pinewood Lodge
Au Train, MI
Inn on Newfound Lake
Bridgewater, NH
Mulburn Inn
Bethlehem, NH
Cabbage Rose Inn
Flemington, NJ
Crossed Keys B&B
Andover, NJ

Romance (*cont'd.*)

T.R.H. Smith Mansion
Las Cruces, NM

Apple Tree B&B
Ballston Spa, NY

Greenville Arms 1889
Greenville, NY

House on the Water
Hampton Bays, NY

Saratoga Rose Inn
Hadley, NY

Fearrington House
Pittsboro, NC

Fryemont Inn
Bryson City, NC

Still Waters
Charlotte, NC

Sandlake Country Inn
Sandlake, OR

Chaska House B&B
Waxahachie, TX

Colonial Gardens B&B
Williamsburg, VA

Gladstone House B&B
Exmore, VA

Inn at Meander
Locust Dale, VA

Lavender Hill Farm
Lexington, VA

Ravenswood Inn
Mathews, VA

Palmer's Chart House
Deer Harbor, WA

Prince of Wales B&B
Seattle, WA

Sports

These inns have superior sports facilities or nearby sporting opportunities.

Kern River Inn
Kernville, CA

Mount Shasta Ranch
Mount Shasta, CA

Prospect Park Inn
La Jolla, CA

Allaire Timbers
Breckenridge, CO

Capitol Hill
Denver, CO

Country Sunshine
Durango, CO

Eagle River Inn
Minturn, CO

Galena St. Mountain
Frisco, CO

Shenandoah Inn
Basalt, CO

Snow Queen Victorian
Aspen, CO

Tucker Hill Inn
Middlebury, CT

Deer Run B&B
Big Pine Key, FL

Elizabeth Pointe
Amelia Island, FL

House on Cherry St
Jacksonville, FL

Inn by the Sea
Naples, FL

Mansion House B&B
St. Petersburg, FL

Dunlap House,
Gainesville, GA

Aloha Pualani
Maui, Kihei, HI

Idaho Rocky Mtn.
Stanley, ID

Dunes Shore Inn
Beverly Shores, IN

Hawthorn Inn
Camden, ME

Penury Hall
Southwest Harbor, ME

Tavern House
Vienna, MD

Harbor Walk
Harwich Port, MA

Inn on the Sound
Falmouth Heights, MA

Over Look Inn
Eastham, MA

Bayside Inn
Saugatuck, MI

Bridge Street Inn
Charlevoix, MI

Mendon Country Inn
Mendon, MI

Dream Catcher
Grand Marais, MN

Behm's Plaza
Kansas City, MO

Kelley's B'nB
Kansas City, MO

Deer Crossing
Hamilton, MT

Haus Bavaria B&B
Incline Village, NV

Cranmore Mountain
North Conway, NH

Nereledge Inn
North Conway, NH

Village House
Jackson, NH

Normandy Inn
Spring Lake, NJ

Camas de Santa Fe
Santa Fe, NM

Casa De La Cuma
Santa Fe, NM

La Hacienda Grande
Bernalillo, NM

Orinda B&B
Taos, NM

Bonnie Castle Farm
Wolcott, NY

Book & Blanket B&B
Jay, NY

Country Life B&B
Greenwich, NY

Eggery Inn
Tannersville, NY

Friends Lake Inn
Chestertown, NY

Cherokee Inn B&B
Kill Devil Hills, NC

Emerald Isle Inn
Emerald Isle, NC

Nantahala Village
Bryson City, NC

Old Stone Inn
Waynesville, NC

Falcon's Crest
Government Camp, OR

Gateway Lodge
Cooksburg, PA

La Anna Guesthouse
Cresco, PA

Fall Creek Falls
Pikeville, TN

Adams House B&B
San Antonio, TX

Delforge Place
Fredericksburg, TX

Rosevine Inn B&B
Tyler, TX

Jackson Fork Inn
Huntsville, UT

Craftsbury Inn
Craftsbury, VT

Deerhill Inn
West Dover, VT

Fox Stand Inn
South Royalton, VT

Lake St. Catherine
Poultney, VT

Sports (cont'd.)

Lareau Farm
Waitsfield, VT

Manchester Highlands
Manchester Center, VT

Millbrook Inn
Waitsfield, VT

Woodstocker B&B
Woodstock, VT

A B&B at Llewellyn
Lexington, VA

Apple Hill Farm B&B
Sperryville, VA

Sky Chalet Mountain
Basye, VA

Trillium House
Nellysford, VA

Monches Mill House
Hartland, WI

Cheat Mountain Club
Durbin, WV

Alpine House
Jackson, WY

Wildflower Inn
Jackson, WY

Danish Chalet Inn
St. Thomas, VI

Vegetarian

These inns can prepare a vegetarian diet for their guests.

Alaska Ocean View
Sitka, AK

El Presidio B&B
Tucson, AZ

Elms B&B
Calistoga, CA

Lord Mayor's B&B
Long Beach, CA

Rockwood Lodge
Homewood, CA

Anniversary Inn B&B
Estes Park, CO

Eastholme
Colorado Springs, CO

Haus Berlin
Denver, CO

Red Brook Inn
Old Mystic, CT

Lodge on St. Simons Is.
St. Simons Island, GA

1874 Stonehouse
Cottonwood Falls, KS

Old Louisville Inn
Louisville, KY

La Maison de Campagne
Carencro, LA

Cape Neddick House
Cape Neddick, ME

Five Gables Inn
East Boothbay, ME

Jeweled Turret Inn
Belfast, ME

Keeper's House
Isle Au Haut, ME

Pointy Head Inn
Bass Harbor, ME

Allen House Victorian
Amherst, MA

Diamond District B&B
Lynn, MA

Morgan's Way
Orleans, MA

One Centre Street
Yarmouth Port, MA

Penny House Inn
Eastham, MA

Windsor House
Newburyport, MA

Inn at Ludington
Ludington, MI

Bellevue B&B
Cape Girardeau, MO

Tuc'Me Inn B&B
Wolfeboro, NH

Candlelight Inn
North Wildwood, NJ

Angelholm B&B
Cooperstown, NY

Black Mountain
Black Mountain, NC

Corner Oak Manor
Asheville, NC

Harmony House Inn
New Bern, NC

Captain's Inn
Astoria, OR

Lawnridge House B&B
Grants Pass, OR

Appleford Inn
Gettysburg, PA

Candlelight Inn
Ronks, PA

Hollileif B&B
Wrightstown, PA

Lincoln Haus Inn
Lancaster, PA

Ponda-Rowland B&B
Dallas, PA

Adams Hilborne
Chattanooga, TN

Page House Inn
Norfolk, VA

Silver Thatch Inn
Charlottesville, VA

Domaine Madeleine
Port Angeles, WA

White Swan Guest
Mount Vernon, WA

Willcox House
Seabeck, WA

Arbor House
Madison, WI

Dreams of Yesteryear
Stevens Point, WI

Gilbert House
Charles Town, WV

Sooke Harbour House
Sooke, BC

VOTE

FOR YOUR CHOICE OF
INN OF THE YEAR

Did you find your stay at a Bed & Breakfast, Inn or Guesthouse listed in this Guide particularly enjoyable? Use the form below, or just drop us a note, and we'll add your vote for the "Inn of the Year." The winning entry will be featured in the next edition of **The Complete Guide to Bed & Breakfasts, Inns and Guesthouses in the U.S., Canada, and Worldwide.**

Please base your decision on:

- Helpfulness of Innkeeper   • Quality of Service
- Cleanliness   • Amenities   • Decor   • Food

Look for the winning Inn in the next Updated & Revised edition of **The Complete Guide to Bed & Breakfasts, Inns and Guesthouses in the U.S., Canada, and Worldwide.**

To the editors of **The Complete Guide to Bed & Breakfasts**:

I cast my vote for "Inn of the Year" for:

Name of Inn _____

Address _____

_____

Phone _____

Reasons _____

_____

I would also like to (please check one)

___ Recommend a new inn ___ Comment ___ Critique ___ Suggest

Name of Inn _____

Address _____

_____

Phone _____

Comment _____

_____

Please send your entries to:
The Complete Guide to Bed & Breakfast Inns
Drawer D
Petaluma, CA 94953
or E-mail: lanier@travelguides.com

Lanier Travel Guides
In Book Stores Everywhere!

Lanier Travel Guides have set the standard for the industry:

"All necessary information about facilities, prices, pets, children, amenities, credit cards and the like. Like France's Michelin . . ."
—*New York Times.*

"Provides a wealth of the kinds of information needed to make a wise choice." —*American Council on Consumer Interest.*

Golf Courses
The Complete Guide

It's about time for a definitive directory and travel guide for the nation's 30 million avid golf players, 7 million of whom make golf vacations an annual event. This comprehensive and updated guide includes over 14,000 golf courses in the United States that are open to the public. Complete details, greens fees, and information on the clubhouse facilities is augmented by a description of each of the golf courses' best features. A beautiful gift and companion to *Golf Resorts—The Complete Guide*. Introduction by Arthur Jack Snyder.

Golf Resorts International

A wish book and travel guide for the wandering golfer. This guide, written in much the same spirit as the best-selling *Elegant Small Hotels*, reviews the creme de la creme of golf resorts all over the world. Beautifully illustrated, it includes all pertinent details regarding hotel facilities and amenities. Wonderful narrative on each hotel's special charm, superb cuisine and most importantly, those fabulous golf courses. Written from a golfer's viewpoint, it looks at the challenges and pitfalls of each course. For the non-golfer, there is ample information about other activities available in the area, such as on-site health spas, nearby shopping, and more.
Introduction by John Stirling.

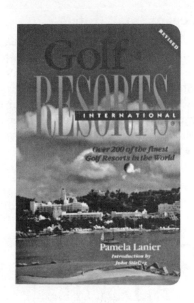

Golf Resorts
—The Complete Guide

The first ever comprehensive and recently updated guide to over 1,000 golf resorts coast to coast. Includes complete details of each resort facility and golf course particulars. "The Complete Guide to Golf Resorts is a wonderful golf destination guide."
—LPGA
Introduction by Fuzzy Zoeller.

Elegant Small Hotels
—A Connoiseur's Guide

This selective guide for discriminating travelers describes over 200 of America's finest hotels characterized by exquisite rooms, fine dining, and perfect service par excellence. Introduction by Peter Duchin. "Elegant Small Hotels makes a seductive volume for window shopping."
—*Chicago Sun Times.*

All-Suite Hotel Guide
—The Definitive Directory

The only guide to the all suite hotel industry features over 1,200 hotels nationwide and abroad. There is a special bonus list of temporary office facilities. A perfect choice for business travelers and much appreciated by families who enjoy the additional privacy provided by two rooms.

Condo Vacations
—The Complete Guide

The popularity of Condo vacations has grown exponentially. In this national guide, details are provided on over 3,000 Condo resorts in an easy to read format with valuable descriptive write-ups. The perfect vacation option for families and a great money saver!

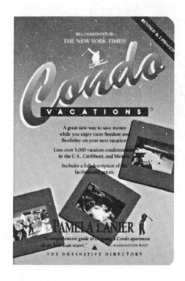

Elegant Hotels
of the Pacific Rim

Over 140 exquisite hotels and
resorts located in the burgeon-
ing Pacific Rim. Especially chosen for their inspired architecture, luxurious ambiance and
personal service *par excellence*.
A must for the globe trotter!

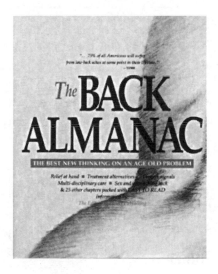

The Back Almanac
*The Best New Thinking
on an Age-Old Problem*

by Lanier Publishing

Just in the nick of time for the 4 out
of 5 Americans suffering with back
pain, a practical guide to back pain
prevention and care. Delightfully illustrated. Internationally acknowl-
edged experts offer the latest think-
ing on causes, treatment, and pain-
free life, including Danger Signals,
Sex and Back Pain, and What If
Nothing Works? Resource guide lists
back schools, pain centers and specialty items.

Revised

"The editors have amassed a wealth
of easy-to-find easy-to-read information..." —HEALTHLINE

AVAILABLE IN BOOK STORES EVERYWHERE

Travel Books from
LANIER GUIDES

ORDER FORM

QTY	TITLE	EACH	TOTAL
	Golf Courses—The Complete Guide	$19.95	
	Golf Resorts—The Complete Guide	$14.95	
	Golf Resorts International	$19.95	
	Condo Vacations—The Complete Guide	$14.95	
	Elegant Small Hotels — U.S.A.	$19.95	
	Elegant Hotels of the Pacific Rim	$14.95	
	All-Suite Hotel Guide	$14.95	
	The Complete Guide to Bed & Breakfasts	$16.95	
	Family Travel—The Complete Guide	$19.95	
	Cinnamon Mornings Cookbook	$14.95	
	The Back Almanac	$14.95	
		Sub-Total	$
		Shipping	$2.75 ea.
		TOTAL ENCLOSED	$

Send your order to:
LANIER PUBLISHING
P.O. Drawer D
Petaluma, CA 94953

We accept VISA, MasterCard, American Express

Allow 3 to 4 weeks for delivery

Please send my order to:

NAME ———————————————————————

ADDRESS ——————————————————————

CITY ————————————— STATE ——— ZIP ————